Encyclopedia of Religion in the South

Encyclopedia of Religion in the South

edited by

SAMUEL S. HILL

MERCER

ISBN 0-86554-117-5

All books published by Mercer University Press are produced
on acid-free paper that exceeds the minimum standards set by
the National Historical Publications and Records Commission.

Library of Congress Cataloging in Publication Data

Main entry under title:

Encyclopedia of religion in the South.

Includes bibliographies and index.
1. Christianity—Southern States—Dictionaries.
2. Southern States—Religion—Dictionaries.   3. Christian
biography—Southern States—Dictionaries.   I. Hill,
Samuel S.
BF535.E52   1984   277.5'003'21   84-8957
ISBN 0-86554-117-5

preface

Samuel S. Hill

Reference books exist for the sake of being useful. This *Encyclopedia* will serve its intended purpose to the degree that it enables people to learn about specific items or topics within the large and complex areas of "religion in the South." In turn, this preface is meant to assist users toward finding what they seek and even toward knowing what kinds of information are available and not available on these pages.

In order to serve readers wanting to learn about religion in the South, the *Encyclopedia of Religion in the South* must focus. The view from the range-finder is extensive; hence there are hundreds of articles here. But there might well have been hundreds of others, especially in the area of biography. As for the formulation of topics, decisions need to reflect the field being covered, in this case, religion in the American South. What is religion? What is the South? What has been and is the religion of that specific culture?

The enterprise is bold that seeks to cover a field so extensive, so difficult to delineate, and demanding of so many methods of inquiry. Yet that is what reference books seek to do. Definitive they cannot be; useful they are meant to be. What they accomplish is piecemeal, not comprehensive or interpretive. One learns about component parts of the whole—and of course there really is no such thing as the whole. Nonetheless, for those who take on the responsibility of preparing a reference book, the aim has to be to see all the parts and even a number of interrelations.

Aware of inherent limitations and unintended misrepresentations, an editor proceeds to ask several basic questions: What features and factors are present? Which ones are the most significant? How to formulate the features and factors chosen? A number of categories seemed worthy of attention, especially these nine that served to organize the assignments of articles:

(1) State histories: The career of organized religion in 16 Southern states is treated here.

(2) Denominations: What the many religious bodies stand for and something of their history in the region. They are subdivided into generic (12); large and major (14); moderate size and major (23); small (22).

...eological move-
...rincipal religious
...n currency in the South
...nents or traditions built
...hem.

...aphies: A selective but lengthy
... of significant men and women in
the region's religious life, including
literary figures.

(5) Sacred places: Communities and
sites of particular importance to the
religious people and institutions of
the region.

(6) Subject areas: Aspects and dimensions of the religious practice of the
South, such as music, architecture,
and theology.

(7) Public events and figures: Topics of
political and social significance that
have interacted with the religious
institutions and ideas.

(8) Offices, titles, and jurisdictions: The
many political forms that operate in
the organized life of the various denominations.

(9) Special features: A miscellany of aspects of the region's rich religious
life, among them funerals and cemeteries, roadside signs, bible chairs,
homecomings, and the Electronic
Church.

In the appendix one other category is
presented, the history of religion in the
South by chronological period. Two essays
appear there that examine the two least-
studied spans of time in the career of
religion in the region: the Colonial Period
(1607-1787) and the Recent Period
(1940-present).

What to include and what to exclude is
naturally a major set of decisions for any
reference volume. This issue presented
itself at the beginning with regard to
which states should be treated as Southern. In general the usual conventions were
taken seriously: included were the 13
states of the Confederacy, plus three others. But additional criteria had to be considered since religious life was the subject;
specifically, in what states do the consist-

ent religious demographic patterns prevail? On this ground Texas, Oklahoma,
and Maryland were included. Missouri
and West Virginia, especially in their
Southern tiers of counties, were judged to
be significantly Southern. Delaware was
left out because of the small number of
Baptists, as well as for the historical reason of its not being heavily identified with
the culture of the region. As far as religious patterns are concerned, the southern Indiana—southern Illinois area
should have been treated as part of the
South but, truth to tell, that cultural area
has not been thoroughly researched as an
entity and certainly not as a portion of the
South.

A number of "judgment calls" must be
made in the course of selecting topics for
treatment. In some cases these result in
departure from a standardized policy. For
example, as to the length of articles, Virginia's historic importance to the South
suggests the need for more space than
Missouri's. Martin Luther King, Jr. was
accorded fuller treatment than in most
biographies in this volume because of his
crucial role in the region's life. In some
cases, however, the length of the treatment of a topic is due to a vagary such as
the stage in the process of organizing the
Encyclopedia at which it was assigned.
Any one who has been responsible for
putting together a collection like this will
know that the editorial perception of how
much space is available and how it should
be allotted varies during the years the
operation is in progress. At the end, inevitably, there is the wish to have done some
things differently.

The omission of some subjects richly
deserving inclusion is sometimes due to
the insufficiency of completed research on
a subject. The Sunday school movement is
one such, a fact hard to believe in view of
that movement's significance in the
South. Work advances on antebellum
developments but, as far as I know, it is
sketchy at best otherwise. Similarly, and
almost as surprising, the history of black

Baptist life (see the brief article on "National Baptists") is much understudied. These and many other subjects cry out for scholarly attention.

Early a policy decision was made to omit contemporary figures from biographical treatment except in special cases, most of them leaders of advanced age whose place in history has already been secured. In other biographical instances, a few Jews were included whose careers had less to do with Judaism (the religion of the Jews) than with their public careers as Southern-born or regionally prominent persons (e.g., Bernard Baruch, Judah P. Benjamin, and Louis D. Brandeis.)

The category of Doctrines and Movements presented its own set of issues. What emerged as needful was particular treatment of doctrines and theological movements that are especially important in the South. Major classic Christian themes like the Trinity, grace, the doctrine of God, and justification by faith were, therefore, left out. By the same token, sin and salvation, atonement and incarnation, holiness and millennialism, the authority and inspiration of the Bible, revivalism and camp meetings, are included.

This *Encyclopedia* embodies several goals and hopes. Most basic and most obvious is making information about religion in the South readily accessible. It is intended as a useful resource for historians, anthropologists, sociologists, and others, professional and lay students alike. Beyond that, it is a Januslike project. It looks back to collect and organize research already completed in the myriad aspects of this broad subject. In doing so, this book stands as the first attempt at bringing together these materials. But it also looks forward by encouraging the harvesting of a field ploughed only a few decades ago and only recently bearing ripened fruits. This editor has taken the deepest satisfaction from the numerous indications that work assigned from this volume has generated new interests and heightened energies. I believe we may expect the work done here to challenge, inspire, and give direction to a great deal of research in this significant, multifaceted area. In other words, this accomplishment both utilizes what we have and impels the acquisition of more knowledge.

Speaking personally, I acknowledge the enormous benefit this task has held for me. I now know or know better scores and scores of fellow laborers in the study-of-the-South vineyard. My knowledge of my field has been enlarged in manifold ways. I have also incurred debts to many people. First, to several at Mercer University Press, in particular, Watson Mills and Joan McCord; and second, to contributors, consultants, and advisers, far and near.

Much happens during so long a span of time in the midst of so complex an undertaking. I want to mention with special gratitude and respect three colaborers who died between 1980 and 1984: Professor Solon Kimball, my colleague at Florida; Professor Guy Owen, once my colleague at Stetson and long at North Carolina State; and Professor Arnold Shankman of Winthrop, taken by cancer at much too young an age. They are chief among my fellow workers, but the list is very long, and I am grateful to and respectful of them all.

Samuel S. Hill
University of Florida

ABOLITIONISM. This movement has traditionally been identified with Northern opposition to slavery between 1831 and 1870. There were, however, abolition societies in the upper South from the 1790s into the 1820s. During the same period there were discussions of slavery within the various denominations. The QUAKERS were the most consistent opponents of slavery, although Baptists, Methodists, and Presbyterians also counted antislavery dissidents among their members. Demands for an Evangelical piety that repudiated values of the "world," that is, the inherited structures of power and prestige, and the offer of salvation to all led these dissenters to contemplate the role and fate of slaves and slaveholders. The ideology of the American Revolution added impetus to this debate as denominations tried to establish the principle that slavery was a moral evil.

Some churches even considered expelling slaveholders, but by 1820 economic interest, racial antipathy, and social policy dictated the sterilization of slavery as a moral issue in the South. In the North slavery was being abandoned by 1804. In place of the old antislavery urgency was a sentimental faith that Evangelicalism would eventually develop a moral sensitivity that would ease slavery out of existence—"no fuss, no muss, no bother." Denominational debates about slavery had proven the futility of direct confrontation. Antislavery dissidents bit their tongues, moved out of the South, or died. The moral idealism expressed in the old debates about slavery was redirected into special missions to the slaves. In this effort the Methodists were the primary force and the Reverend CHARLES COLCOCK JONES the chief publicist.

The failure of antislavery Southerners transferred the battleground from the churches of the South to the new reform movements of the North in the 1830s. As in Great Britain, a resurgence of Evangelical piety provided the cultural context within which new, voluntary associations grouped to impose moral order, encourage self-discipline, and break down institutions that deprived individuals of the chance to make the most of that self-control. Slavery attracted the most radical of these reformers as the ultimate test of Americans' commitment to Evangelical and Republican values. Those who failed to demand that slavery be abolished immediately and the freed people allowed to build new lives for themselves in the United States were condemned as untrue to American religious and political principles. Over a 40-year period, Northern Evangelical and political abolitionists agitated churches, political parties, and judicial institutions on behalf of "immediate emancipation without expatriation" and against slavery and racism.

These modern abolitionists were distinguished from their predecessors by a number of factors: their youth in 1830; their agitation of national institutions as opposed to state and local authorities alone; their ability to reach a national audience through improved means of communication; their Northern audience's growing sense that slavery was alien to the progress presumably promised by industrialization; their ability to manipulate this belief in conjunction with sectional rivalries; their demand of moral perfection; and their wholesale attack on Southern society. The resulting alienation of Southerners from national institutions forced them to secede. Abolitionists' focus on slaveholding as a sin led to the division of Evangelical churches into slaveholding and free before the Civil War and also to the belated commitment of the Federal government to abolition as a war aim. This in turn led to the Thirteenth, Fourteenth, and Fifteenth Amendments designed to guarantee the former slaves their full citizenship. In this process, white abolitionists worked with black leaders to educate and care for the free people despite opposition from Southern Evangelicals.

The response of the latter to abolitionism was to attack it as an unfortunate intrusion of the church into politics. Rejecting the naiveté and implied egalitarianism of abolitionists, white Southern Evangelicals argued that Christians were not obliged to change the way in which societies were organized. The biblical phrase that God is no respecter of persons did not mean that invidious social distinctions were contrary to God's will, but that

He loved all humanity without honoring one person over another because of social rank. All that was required of believers was to treat everyone in a Christian way no matter what their status. The result of this view among white Evangelicals was to fasten upon Southern churches an orthodoxy of silence with regard to issues of power and social responsibility.

See also article on SLAVERY.

Bibliography. Ailene Kraditor, *Means and Ends in American Abolitionism*; James M. McPherson, *Abolitionist Legacy*; *Struggle for Equality*; Donald G. Mathews, *Religion in the Old South*; *Slavery and Methodism: A Chapter in American Morality*; Russell B. Nye, *Fettered Freedom: Civil Liberties and the Slavery Controversy*; James Stewart, *Holy Warriors*; Arthur Zilversmit, *The First Emancipation*.

                            DONALD G. MATHEWS
                  UNIVERSITY OF NORTH CAROLINA
                                AT CHAPEL HILL

ACADIAN INFLUENCE: *See* CAJUN INFLUENCE.

ADAMS, THEODORE FLOYD (1898-1980), national Baptist statesman, was regarded by many as the most able minister among Southern Baptists during the middle decades of the 20th century. Adams was widely recognized as the "statesman" of his denomination. His diverse background fostered an international and ecumenical outlook in a denomination not noted for its ecumenicity.

Born in Palmyra NY, Adams was educated in various public schools in Oregon and Indiana. Following his graduation from Denison University and Colgate-Rochester Divinity School, Adams served as minister of three Baptist congregations in Cleveland and Toledo in Ohio, and Richmond VA, the last from 1936 to 1968. He was accorded emeritus status by that church, then served for 10 years as visiting professor at Southeastern Baptist Theological Seminary in Wake Forest NC.

Adams's lengthy career was marked by service in a variety of denominational posts as well as leadership in such organizations as CARE. His contribution to the

Baptist World Alliance unquestionably ranks as his most significant achievement. He served as a member of the executive committee beginning in 1934, was vice-president from 1947-1950 and president from 1955-1960. A cover story in *Time Magazine*, 5 December 1955, described Baptists as a major denominational "family" and "Ted" Adams as their most influential spokesman.

Adams was never a creative theologian; his four major works dealt with denominational and pastoral concerns. In recognition of his achievements as minister, lecturer, author, and international leader, he was awarded honorary degrees from 10 colleges and universities, North and South. The National Conference of Christians and Jews also awarded him the National Brotherhood Citation in 1964. His failure to be elected president of the Southern Baptist Convention would seem, in retrospect, more a reflection on the institution than on the man.

See also article on ECUMENISM.

Bibliography. Theodore F. Adams, *Baptists Around the World*; *Making Your Marriage Succeed.*

BERNARD H. COCHRAN
MEREDITH COLLEGE

ADGER, JOHN BAILEY (1810-1899), Presbyterian missionary, minister to slaves, and seminary professor, was a son of a Charleston merchant. After graduating from Union College in 1828, he studied at Princeton Theological Seminary. In 1834 he became a minister and a missionary of the American Board of Commissioners for Foreign Missions, providing Protestant aid and influence to Armenians in Constantinople and Smyrna.

In 1847 inheritance of slaves by Adger's wife precluded his further service with the ABCFM. He entered into ministry to slaves in Charleston, organizing the Anson Street Chapel (later Zion Presbyterian Church). After visual difficulty required him to leave that work in 1851, he operated a plantation near Pendleton SC.

In 1857 Adger became professor of ecclesiastical history and church polity at Columbia Theological Seminary and an editor of the *Southern Presbyterian Review*. After the war, faculty politics pitted him, JAMES WOODROW, and Joseph Ruggles Wilson against William S. Plumer. In 1874 Adger and Wilson resigned after the general assembly of the Presbyterian Church in the United States overturned their faction's chapel-attendance rule.

Adger returned to Pendleton, pastoring congregations until he retired in 1894. He remained an editor of the *Review* until it ceased in 1885. As an exponent of JAMES H. THORNWELL's theories of church government, Adger played a major role in drafting the PCUS *Book of Church Order* of 1879. He advocated a "high" Reformed theory of Christ's presence in the Lord's Supper and defended Woodrow in the evolution controversy of the 1880s.

Bibliography. John B. Adger, *My Life and Times*; Eugene C. Scott, *Ministerial Directory of the Presbyterian Church, U. S., 1861-1941.*

JACK P. MADDEX, JR.
UNIVERSITY OF OREGON

AFRICAN METHODIST EPISCOPAL CHURCH. The largest and strongest connectional church among black Christians in America, its origins are rooted in the late colonial period. Racial discrimination was the common practice in places of worship, a condition that became more evident and offensive to black Methodists after 1784 when their numbers became sizable in the "societies" of classes and at worship assemblies. The segregation of seating arrangements and the denial of free access to the altar for prayers or communion were regarded as humiliating and demeaning by many black Methodists.

In 1787 Richard Allen, a free member of the St. George's Methodist Episcopal Church in Philadelphia, resisted discrimination at the altar and rebelled against the institutional racism that was characteristic of the church at that time. When Allen, Absalom Jones, and William White moved forward to the prayer altar one Sunday, they were ejected. All three withdrew from St. George's and began to hold meetings in a storehouse. Allen in particular was bold to proclaim that the Bible taught inclusiveness, that heaven was open to all believers, and that freedom was intended to be a basic quality of the human spirit. Other black worshipers soon began joining them.

Later in 1787 they established the Free African Society, a ministry offering charitable services for the benefit of many in the poverty-stricken black community of Philadelphia. For the next 10 years independent prayer meetings were held in homes and at other unofficial meeting sites. A building was purchased in 1797; they gave it the name Bethel (house of God). Doing so conferred a historical identity upon this branch of the Methodist movement among people of African descent. Bethel's leaders were Allen, Jones, and White, along with Darius Jennings.

Some of the early protesters who pulled out of the St. George's Methodist Episcopal Church joined the Episcopal Church. Absalom Jones, for example, moved in that direction and, further, was ordained a deacon. In 1804 he became the first Afro-American to enter the Episcopal priesthood. However, many of these early independent-minded black Methodists did not feel the desired warmth of freedom in that denominational setting (out of which Methodism had only very recently emerged).

Richard Allen, in the beginning, was ambivalent about the relationship with the white Methodist conference leadership. On the negative side, he was concerned about his group's dependency on Bishop Francis Asbury to dedicate the Bethel congregation in 1794. Similar dissatisfaction with white leadership was widespread, especially among racially mixed Methodist congregations in Wil-

mington DE, Attleboro PA, and Salem NJ.

Finally, on 9 April 1816, after 22 years of such discontent, the African Methodist Episcopal Church was officially organized. The movement had taken on a definitive shape and life of its own. Prominent in the emergent leadership was Daniel Coker, who promoted black unity vigorously. (In 1810 Coker also wrote the first known publication by a black American, "A Dialogue between a Virginian and an African Minister.") At the organizing sessions there were representatives from four churches, the three listed above and Baltimore; lay leaders were present as well as ministers. Allen was elected chairman and Coker vice-chairman.

The African Methodist Episcopal Church, now born, developed notably. By 1818 there were 6,757 members from 16 charges (of one or more congregations each). Four years later there were 43 charges with 7,257 members. Growth was accompanied by stresses and problems, of course, as reflected in the expulsion of Daniel Coker in 1818 (he was reinstated the next year). In the Philadelphia Conference six preachers were brought into full connection with five others on trial. Three men were ordained elders, one of them MORRIS BROWN, an outstanding leader from Charleston SC who was to become the church's second bishop in 1828. One of the preachers, William Lambert, a former member of the AFRICAN METHODIST EPISCOPAL, ZION, CHURCH, was sent north into New York State where his presence precipitated a conflict between the Zion body and the AME Church. Nevertheless, new congregations were formed as far north as New Bedford MA, as far west as Pittsburgh, and as far south as Washington.

In these years of the church's infancy, two important events had taken place. First, a resolution was passed declaring the AME Church an independent organization with African-American membership that adhered to Methodist polity as outlined by the *Book of Church Discipline*. Second, although Daniel Coker was elected the first bishop, he served only eight days when a second election was called and Richard Allen was elected. (Allen had three thriving businesses in addition to the pastorate of the Bethel Church.)

About 1817, Morris Brown connected his Charleston church of 1,800 members to the Bethel AME Church in Philadelphia. However, after the aborted Denmark Vesey revolution of 1822, the church was closed under the suspicion that it was the seedbed of the Vesey plot; 35 blacks were hanged as a result. Brown escaped to Philadelphia and worked with Bishop Allen, where he became the second bishop of the AME Church (alongside Allen, who died in 1831).

While expansion in size and scope of activities was modest during the early decades, the new denomination exhibited health. Mission work in Haiti was underway by 1827. A publications department dates from 1816, for the purposes of providing a Discipline and a hymnal and for facilitating religious education. The number of members reached 19,914 in 1856, up from 7,594 in 1836.

DANIEL PAYNE was an early leader who contributed greatly to the young church, especially in the area of education. In 1829 when he was 19, he set in motion in Charleston a program of study for pastors. He undertook a similar enterprise in Philadelphia in 1842. At the General Conference of 1844 in Pittsburgh, his resolution established a formal course of study for the education of AME ministers. His greatest achievement came with the founding of Wilberforce University in central Ohio.

In the South churches were established in Louisville and in New Orleans in 1842. Both were forced to live under tight supervision by whites, however, who feared the spread of black revolutionary movements. During 1855 the Missouri

Conference of the church was organized (one for Ohio had occurred in 1840).

The AME Church regularly spoke out against slavery. In 1850, 1854, and 1856 special days of prayer for the cessation of slavery were observed by the church. It rejected the philosophy and work of the AMERICAN COLONIZATION SOCIETY.

Soon after the end of the Civil War, the church was able to move forward in the South. Bishop Payne (so ordained in 1852) sent two ministers from Baltimore and New York to South Carolina, where they started work in Port Royal, Edisto, and Beaufort. That state's conference was organized in 1865 and even included a few churches in North Carolina and Georgia. Growth was dramatic in this as in all black Protestant bodies in the South in the postwar era. One of the most prominent early Southern pastors was HENRY MCNEAL TURNER, whose contributions to Georgia in education and politics were substantial. The expanded membership brought in people from a variety of previous conditions: blacks from segregated white churches; blacks under white preachers in cities; blacks from missions to slaves; blacks seeking affinity with leadership of their own race and culture. The increase in membership in the South Carolina Conference was about 50,000 between 1865 and 1875.

During the 1870s the AME Church pressed on southward and westward into Alabama and Mississippi, and even beyond the Mississippi River into Louisiana, Texas, and Arkansas. North of the old Mason-Dixon line, the church spread into Kansas, Nebraska, and Colorado.

From difficult, circumscribed beginnings, the AME Church has emerged as a large American body in the 20th century, with an estimated membership of 1,250,000 in 1980. It carries on numerous ministries, mission work (domestic and foreign), young people's work, Sunday schools, colleges and seminaries, publications, and much more. Of particular interest is its presence in Africa, where today there are four annual conferences and in South Africa alone some 200,000 members.

See also article on BLACK RELIGION.

Bibliography. Richard Allen, *The Life, Experience and Gospel Labors of the Rt. Rev. Richard Allen*; B. W. Arnett, *Proceedings of the Quarto-centennial Conference of the African ME Church of South Carolina (1889)*; Wesley J. Gaines, *African Methodism in the South*; Daniel Payne, *Recollections of Seventy Years*; Harry V. Richardson, *Dark Salvation*; Charles S. Smith, *History of the African Methodist Episcopal Church*, 2 vols.; Charles H. Wesley, *Richard Allen, Apostle of Freedom*; R. R. Wright, *Bishops of the AME Church*; *Yearbook and Historical Guide to the African Methodist Episcopal Church*.

GEORGE O. THOMAS
INTERDENOMINATIONAL
THEOLOGICAL CENTER

AFRICAN METHODIST EPISCO-PAL ZION CHURCH. This black denomination emerged from the religious experiences of the descendants of African peoples in New York City during the latter part of the 18th century. On 6 April 1784, a charter recognized the African Methodist body called the Zion Church, in public notice among some 18 references to African petitions before the common council of New York City.

In New York City, from the time of Methodist beginnings in 1765 to 1796, black people rivaled whites in conversion to and membership in the Methodist Episcopal Church. However, African descendants, whether they were slaves or free, as members of the John Street Methodist Episcopal Church experienced segregation in seating, discrimination before the altar, and prejudice at the Lord's table. Consequently, several black leaders who were licensed local preachers refused to continue to worship under those conditions. Francis Jacobs, William Brown, and Peter Williams proceeded to secure independent meeting arrangements. Some meetings were held in local homes; others occurred in the intervals of the John Street worship schedule; and still others were held at special sites such as the African chapel in William Miller's cabinet ship. This group of independent-minded black Methodist people was will-

ing, for a time, to accept the official clergy of the New York Annual Conference and to maintain fidelity to Methodist doctrine and faith.

By 1800 the boycotting blacks pursued the course of building a rare separate place of worship. The first church constructed was named "Zion." However, in matter of ritual and polity, for the most part, the Methodist Episcopal Church through the New York Annual Conference controlled certain ministerial leadership functions. Blacks basically resented the denial of access to the elders' ordination. Nevertheless, nine black ministers were registered as officials in the incorporation of the African Methodist Episcopal Church of New York on 5 February 1801 under the signature of Peter Williams and Francis Jacobs. In this way, the legal aspect of the historical movement toward the AME Zion Church took place.

Another group of African peoples to establish a Methodist Church in New York City was the "Asbury Movement" under the leadership of William Miller, who had participated in the Zion group. These people joined with the Zion group against the political and economic injustices and formed an evangelical society, "African Methodist Episcopal Church in America," in 1813. (The name Zion, which had identified the first independent black Methodist church, was included in the name of the emerging connectional church.) At the General Conference of 1848, the Zion identity was established in the official polity and legal documents of the group. This movement parallels the emerging sister denomination in Philadelphia, called the Bethel or Allen Church Movement, and soon known as the AFRICAN METHODIST EPISCOPAL CHURCH.

Three men were ordained as elders; they in turn ordained six others as deacons in the morning and elders in the afternoon. Abraham Thompson was made president at the second Annual Conference and had the effect of unifying the Zion and Asbury Churches in the commitment to realize total and unconditional independence.

Between 1820 and 1828, some six churches held annual meetings under the active leadership of James Varick, who was first elected superintendent for the Zion Movement in 1822. Christopher Rush was elected in 1828, served for 20 years, and greatly expanded the conferences, ministry, and membership in spite of serious internal dissensions and external pressures.

Between 1830 and 1860, Zion evangelistic and missionary thrusts were made in different directions: north to upper New York State, New England, and lower Canada; south into New Jersey, Maryland, Delaware, and the District of Columbia; west across the Allegheny into western Pennsylvania, Ohio, and Indiana. These activities resulted in the formation of movements, societies, organizations, and churches, with some of the members joining Zion from white Methodism. Conferences were organized in Philadelphia in 1829, in New England in 1845; Allegheny came into being in 1849, the Genesee Conference of western New York State in 1859, and Baltimore in 1859. At this time, slavery prevented missionary outreach into the South. But the harvest of these efforts in the North and West yielded growth in membership: from 1,689 in 1831 to 4,600 in 1800; from 52 preachers in 1840 to 105 in 1860, with 85 of these ordained as elders. J. J. Moore, who later became a bishop, provides a profile of the sacrifice on the Western frontier. He walked 30 miles a day and preached in the evenings as Zion Methodism expanded.

There were inner tensions and antagonisms that led to a few schisms. Some left Zion and went into the Methodist Episcopal Church, then to the AME Church. Most came back to make peace with Zion by 1830. The name superintendent had some psychological limitations and was changed, even though bishops became coequals in the different assigned areas. George Galbreath sought unsuccessfully to rename the church as Wesleyan Methodist Episcopal. Efforts to take church property out of the denomination also failed. By 1860, a creative healing had resolved the difficulties, with all professing to lay them aside forever.

During this time, the Zion Church achieved singular success in providing and promoting leadership for the movement against slavery and oppression. Clergy and laity in the General Conference made resolutions and took practical actions to enable enslaved Africans in America to escape through the Underground Railroad. They were refreshed in homes, churches, and other community facilities in a number of Northern communities. Frederick Douglass, Harriet Tubman, and Sojourner Truth are among the known heroes and heroines of this movement. Frederick Douglass pastored in Rochester NY, New Bedford MA, and on Long Island where he was a strong abolitionist leader. Jermaine Loguen became a bishop in 1864 and was noted for his courage in the freedom struggles. He was referred to as the "Underground Railroad King." Harriet Tubman "never lost a passenger" out of over 300 people. Her motto was, "Keep Going, if you are tired, hungry, discouraged: Keep Going."

The AME Zion Church, in spite of limited financial resources, the denial of educational opportunities, and oppressive socioeconomic policies and practices, engaged the best of traditional European-American Methodism in doctrine, polity, and authentic friendship. Quite simply, it prevailed to establish the dignity of peoplehood and the capacity of institutional self-reliance through a connectional church.

The 1860s brought the Civil War. At that juncture the AME Zion Church was poised to move into the South. Bishop J. J. Clinton was elected and appointed to the Southern Conference, and came south along with five others. They carried out ministries in North Carolina, Florida, Louisiana, and Alabama. Bishop Clinton journeyed throughout the South forming conferences in North Carolina and Louisiana, and aiding in the work of the Alabama Conference, the Virginia Conference, the South Carolina Conference, and the Alabama Conference. The Kentucky Conference was organized by Sampson D. Talbot and assisted by Bishop Clinton. The Florida Conference was formed in 1869, Arkansas in 1870, and Missouri in 1890. Bishop Clinton went to California in 1868. In North Carolina, James W. Hood enabled Zion to cover the state through his work with Federal and state officials, especially in education. The greatest expansion in any state was realized in North Carolina. Colleges as well as other schools and church centers were developed: Fayetteville State, Winston-Salem State, and Livingstone Colleges. Hood Theological Seminary would later emerge and be named after him.

The Rev. Andrew Cartwright went to Bewerville, Liberia as Zion's first missionary to Africa. He organized conferences and in 1880 initiated the Women's Home and Foreign Missionary Society (now the Women's Home and Overseas Missionary Society) to support the work in Africa. The Rev. John B. Small was assigned to the West Indies and Africa by 1897. James E. Aggrey of North Carolina, known as "Aggrey of Africa," and Kobina Osam Pinanko (Frank Arthur) were two distinguished leaders whom he influenced. Bishop Alexander Walters arrived on the Gold Coast in 1909, to be followed by several other missionaries. The first resident bishop in Africa was C. C. Allene, who added the Nigeria conferences. By 1932 there were 28 churches, 11 indigenous pastors, and 2,345 members; in all of West Africa there were 18,000. Around 1900, mission work was expanded to the West Indies, South America, and South Africa. The Bahama Islands Conference was organized in 1877. Herbert Bell Shaw expanded churches in Jamaica, which became Zion's fastest-growing missions area. Work was also begun among West Indians and Africans in such English cities

as London, Birmingham, Bristol, and Manchester. The London and Birmingham conferences were formed in 1971.

The African Methodist Episcopal Zion Church, which had 4,600 members in 1856, grew to 350,000 in 1906, and by 1972 numbered 770,000.

See also articles on ABOLITIONISM; BLACK RELIGION.

Bibliography. H. H. Anderson, ed., *The Official Directory of the A.M.E. Zion Church in America*; Sarah H. Bradford, *Harriet, The Moses of Her People*; D. H. Bradley, *History of the AME Zion Church*, 2 vols.; Earl Conrad, *Harriet Tubman*; *Discipline of the AME Zion Church*; Frederick Douglass, *Narrative of the Life of Frederick Douglass, An American Slave*; J. W. Hood, *One Hundred Years of the African Methodist Episcopal Zion Church*; Jermain Loguen, *The Rev. J. W. Loguen As A Slave And As A Freeman*; Hohn J. Moore, *History of the AME Zion Church*; Harry V. Richardson, *Dark Salvation*; Christopher Rush, *A Short Account of the Rise and Progress of the African Methodist Episcopal Zion Church in America*; William Jacob Walls, *The African Methodist Episcopal Zion Church, Reality of the Black Church*.

GEORGE O. THOMAS
INTERDENOMINATIONAL
THEOLOGICAL CENTER

AFRO-AMERICAN RELIGION: *See* BLACK RELIGION.

ALABAMA. The itinerant preacher arrived about 1817 in St. Stephens to proclaim the gospel. The population of Alabama's territorial capital on the banks of the Tombigbee River was quite satisfied with conditions as they were and did not desire religious provocation. When the zealous minister persisted, ignoring the town's ban against such preaching, the people of St. Stephens set him adrift on the river. As he floated downstream, he turned back toward the town and shouted: "St. Stephens be damned. I came unto you and you received me not. I now confine this den of iniquity to the snakes, bats and owls." Within months of this curse, Cahaba was made the new capital, and St. Stephens began a decline that left no remains except tangled garden figs and crepe myrtles intertwined beneath oaks that once lined city streets.

Although St. Stephens is the only recorded incident of an Alabama town consigned to perdition for rejecting repentance, it could have been a frequent occurrence on Alabama's 19th-century frontier. Between 1800 and 1820, pioneers poured into the newly opened cotton lands of the Tennessee and Tombigbee valleys. Life was primitive, conditions squalid, the intrepid settlers often uneducated and profane. Although Alabama would later pride itself as the heart of Dixie's Bible Belt, descriptions left by the first generation of preachers were not flattering. An early Methodist leader depicted Washington County settlers as "grossly worldly and extremely wicked," who "could no more be impressed with the obligations and benefits of the Christian religion than could the beasts of the forests in which they lived." A Presbyterian report from the Tennessee Valley in the 1820s concluded that "no part of our country is more destitute of spiritual instruction, nor perhaps does any part open a wider door of usefulness."

Even nominally religious people were condemned for backsliding and moral depredations. A pioneer Presbyterian missionary believed that although there were many professing Christians (principally Methodists and Baptists, he added smugly), most had lost their first love. Their "sinful propensities" led them into fashionable amusements. Such Christians damaged the gospel even more than avowed infidels. Nor were Presbyterians immune to such temptations. The North Alabama Presbytery answered with stern advice a query concerning ministers and laymen who sent their children to dancing school: "Dancing as ordinarily practiced in society is almost invariably connected with scenes, company and indulgences of a character decidedly gay, worldly and adapted to lead to many and serious evils." The Presbytery appended to its diatribe against dancing further admonitions against theatres, circuses, jugglers' performances, and similar carnal exhibitions.

Perhaps the most enthralling entertainment that remained on that harsh and lonely frontier was religion. Although Jesuits undoubtedly had accompanied transient Spanish expeditions and had settled in the French outpost of Mobile, the Rev. LORENZO DOW is the earliest recorded Protestant to penetrate the dangerous and sparsely populated plains of the Tombigbee. Braving Indians, weather, and godless whites, Dow began preaching in the Tensaw settlements in 1803. Although he was not ordained and the Methodist Church rejected his requests for support, he was doctrinally a disciple of Wesley and considered himself a Methodist notwithstanding. An enthusiastic preacher who parted his hair in the middle and let it hang to his shoulders, Dow soon was known throughout the territory as "Crazy Dow." Driven by a fanatical zeal to spread the word of universal atonement and free salvation, he took his message to Canada, Ireland, and England, as well as to the remote wilderness of the Tombigbee. Between 1803 and 1812, Dow crisscrossed Washington County 10 times preaching salvation or damnation, depending upon mood and congregation.

Because churches were scattered and poorly organized, ministers relied upon the camp meeting as an effective device for evangelizing the godless. Methodists and Baptists in particular, and Presbyterians to a lesser extent, imported the strategy of the great CANE RIDGE KY camp meeting of 1801. Their task was to save sinners, and neither doctrinal creeds, formal education, nor denominational differences must interfere. Disagreements over methods of BAPTISM or PREDESTINATION were contained by generally good-humored toleration. One Baptist layman claimed that his Methodist wife believed in falling from grace but never fell, whereas he believed there was no fall, but fell daily.

Canaan Baptist Church in Jefferson County conducted a CAMP MEETING in October 1831. The "tents" that communicants inhabited surrounded a BRUSH ARBOR where the meetings were held. One witness described the proceedings:

> It is not unusual to have a large portion of the congregation prostrated upon the ground; and, in some instances, they appear to have lost the use of their limbs. No distinct articulation could be heard; screams, cries, groans, shouts, notes of joy, all heard at the same time, made much confusion—a sort of indescribable concert.

Whatever the physical manifestations, the meeting began a revival that resulted in three churches baptizing 500 people within 12 months' time.

Two Methodist—sponsored camp meetings in the Tennessee Valley resulted in more than 400 conversions during a six-month period of 1828. Decatur, Courtland, Tuscumbia, and Florence were "all in a flame." James W. Faris, Methodist pastor in the Franklin Circuit of the Tennessee Valley, electrified the congregations with his preaching. Oftentimes called "Faris, the eccentric," what he lacked in education he made up for in ardor. One contemporary acknowledged that Faris had no education but added that "as an orator he swept all the chords of the human soul. He touched the emotions and swayed the vast throngs of a camp meeting as absolutely as the storm sways the trees of the forest." Similarly successful Methodist camp meetings were established at Oakbowery (1837), Fredonia (1838), Bethlehem (1843), and Hillabee (1847).

Despite their predestinarian theology, Presbyterians were also active on the camp meeting circuit. Their most famous facility was at Hatchet Creek in east-central Alabama. The mountainous terrain of that area was settled by hardy Scotch-Irish Presbyterians following Indian removal in the 1820s and 1830s. Presbyterian farmers built a fence to enclose the horses, mules, and oxen that hauled inquirers to the meetings. On hills behind the church, they constructed 25 cottages, each with four rooms and a hall. As interest grew and crowds increased, they built a large pine arbor abutting the small Presbyterian church. Years passed and the soul-stirring sermons had to compete with horse-swapping, drunkenness, and other abuses that abounded in the vicinity of the camp meeting. So bad did conditions become by the end of the century that the camp meeting was abandoned in favor of an annual protracted meeting.

Frontier REVIVALISM spread rapidly, not only because of the transcendent religious hopes it offered, but because it also met basic social needs. For isolated rural people even churches that met only once monthly represented a valuable source of social intercourse. Among people who generally tended their own medical needs, where the rate of infant mortality was extremely high, where even simple fevers and maladies often took lives, and where raging epidemics occasionally wiped out entire communities, the solace of the Balm of Gilead was no small comfort. Although the evangelical sects were not limited to the sturdy yeomen or poor whites, it is true that more planters could be found in Episcopal parishes, and more common folk among Methodists and Baptists. To people with little control of their economic or political lives, the hope of ultimate vindication and the promise that every person was equally precious in God's sight was valuable for surviving the present, not an escapist theology exclusively focused on the "sweet by-and-by." On a rough disorderly frontier, institutional religion imposed order and stability by emphasizing rigid moral codes, family stability, and civic righteousness.

Even the so-called otherworldly religion of the Southern frontier maintained a tight grip on reality. Because they were farm folk dependent almost entirely upon nature for their livelihood, Alabamians looked to primary, not secondary causes.

Like the ancient Hebrews, they implored God to restrain the rains or to bring them, to stay the winds, and make fertile their lands. An impetuous Methodist layman named Billy Grizzard prayed for rain at a special meeting in the 1830s during a serious drought. Getting right to the point, Grizzard implored: "Good Lord, send us a root-soaker and a gulley-washer."

Although they were as pious as most Christian folks, Alabama's Evangelicals maintained a religious folklore that suggested that they lived out their devotion within certain practical limits. One such tale from the 19th century, containing considerable insights into the limits of religious piety, concerned a north Alabama mountain family that believed profanity was essential in the proper management of an oxen team. Attracted by the presence of a PROTRACTED MEETING in a nearby hollow, all the family except one boy attended and were saved. Afterwards, neighbors anxious for the boy's salvation pressed him for an explanation of his apparent indifference amidst such obvious movings of the spirit. The boy offered an irrefutable retort: "Dad went down there and got religion; Mom she went down there and got religion; John went down there and got religion. If I went, who'd drive the oxen?"

Even the stern Presbyterians, whose church discipline was most severe, reluctantly accepted the reality of frontier life. A. H. Slaughter of Opelika was overheard uttering profanity while highly excited. He was suspended from membership by his local church, but appealed to the East Alabama Presbytery for a new trial. That body ruled that though he was profane, because of his intense excitement, the sentence of suspension was too severe; he was admonished, then restored to membership.

Methodists and Baptists profited most from the religious excitement of the "second great awakening." Methodists had established a camp meeting as early as

1813 at Fort Easley (Wood's Bluff). Ebenezer Camp Ground near Montevallo was built about 1820, and soon nearly every circuit had its own facility. Scattered Baptist churches were not so well organized for evangelism, but their revivals and camp meetings were equally successful.

Supported by Methodist conferences in South Carolina, Tennessee, and Mississippi, that denomination made rapid progress. By the time the Alabama Conference was organized in 1832, the church contained 8,000 whites and nearly 3,000 blacks. By 1840 rapid settlement and prodigious efforts by the indefatigable circuit riders had increased membership to nearly 20,000 whites and 6,000 blacks. Five years later total membership in Alabama Methodist churches reached 40,600.

Baptists, led by a poorly educated bivocational clergy drawn from the common people, also thrived. Their first clerical witness in Alabama began in 1808, and the first Baptist church was organized in the Tennessee Valley shortly thereafter. By the time of Alabama's statehood in 1819, there were 60 Baptist ministers serving 50 small churches, and they were numerous enough in October 1823 to form the Alabama Baptist State Convention. By that date, 5,000 Baptists were organized into 125 churches. Cotton prosperity, rapid settlement, and effective evangelism raised their numbers to an estimated 65,000 black and white members of 400 churches on the eve of the Civil War.

A small band of Episcopalians was well established in the state by 1860. Appealing primarily to better educated and more affluent citizens, the church exercised political and economic influence out of proportion to its size. Congregations such as that of St. John's Church in Montgomery often furnished the state's governors and senators, and enrolled its wealthiest planters and merchants. Nonetheless, the church developed a distinctly low church orientation that allowed it to blend easily into the religious mainstream.

Other denominations were limited by geographical or ethnic factors. The Cumberland Presbyterians and Disciples of Christ established congregations mainly in the mountainous northern counties. Catholics were generally confined to the extreme south, where families of French and Spanish extraction held defiantly to the old faith. Mobile was the Catholic capital of Alabama, and Protestant work advanced slowly in that port city. Presbyterianism flourished only among Scotch-Irish in the foothills of the lower Appalachians and later among Scottish coal miners in the Birmingham district. Despite its early successes in rural camp meetings, the Presbyterian movement was quickly confined to larger towns and cities, leaving the countryside to the more democratic Methodists and Baptists.

The primary barrier inhibiting Presbyterians was a centralized church structure that maintained strict standards for licensing and ordination. For instance, the North Alabama Presbytery found unacceptable a sermon by John K. Wallace in the 1820s. Although the sermon demonstrated "considerable labour," the Presbytery did not think that there was "sufficient closeness of attention." Members also pronounced it "faulty in precision and perspicuity, and that there are too many redundant words." The South Alabama Presbytery spent two entire days examining another candidate for the ministry.

Once licensed, the Synod selected the theological seminary that the aspiring minister would attend and often paid his expenses. Upon requesting ordination, the Presbytery administered grueling examinations. During the 1850s one Alabama presbytery warned applicant R. W. Shive to be prepared to discuss the Greek New Testament, Virgil's *Aeneid* (all six volumes), the Odes of Horace, Alexander's *Evidences of Christianity*, Mosheim's church history, Kurtz's treatise on church

government, and Picket's theology. After recounting such arduous standards, a pioneer Alabama Presbyterian historian concluded: "No wonder the Baptist farmers who ploughed until Saturday, mounted their horses, then rode across the woods to their Sabbath appointments . . . found entering the ministry a simple event by comparison with a Presbyterian youth."

High intellectual standards were a premeditated policy aimed at a more cultured audience. The chairman of home missions for the Presbyterian denomination in the state commented on the changing conditions within the state in his 1859 report:

> There are numerous communities of the wealthy and intelligent throughout our bounds. The whole country is indeed highly prosperous. Learning is rapidly advancing, seminaries springing up at every step. . . .
> The religious teachers of the people have hitherto been, generally, uneducated men, following the common avocation of life, while to the best of their ability they preached the gospel. But the recent rapid developments of the human mind are beginning to throw light upon the darkest and most remote corners of all this land. It is reported to us from every quarter that there is a general longing after a different order of things.

Perhaps he overestimated the religious sophistication of Alabama's masses.

Although such accounts demonstrate that the religion of the head was by no means unknown to the Alabama frontier, they also explain the relative lack of success of the Presbyterian Church. Throughout the 19th century, Presbyterians found it impossible to staff their churches adequately. The Talladega Presbytery died for lack of ministers. In 1872 the Tuscaloosa Presbytery numbered 25 churches, 13 of them without a pastor. In 1829 only 30 Presbyterian ministers shepherded 1,713 members. In 1880 the church actually had fewer members than in 1860. After more than a half-century of activity, only 5,800 Presbyterians worshiped in 117 churches. There were numerous counties without a single Presbyterian church in 1860.

Although Alabama's Protestant churches defined their mutual tasks in similar ways, they all experienced internal factionalism and schism. The chief sources of division were familiar: race and theology.

Methodists and Baptists had been especially successful at enrolling slaves in their churches. Although white ministers usually tended these biracial blocks, black ministers were ordained and sometimes even gained renown and freedom. The Rev. Caesar Blackwell, a black minister living near Montgomery, was sought by both white and black congregations for revivals. So popular did he become that the Alabama Baptist Association (Montgomery County) purchased his freedom and provided for his old age.

As slavery became a heated issue, denominations widely stereotyped as apolitical assumed surprisingly active public roles. The Alabama Baptist Convention first defended slavery at its 1835 convention. Thomas Griffin, a prominent Methodist leader, told the 1826 Methodist General Conference that he was displeased by the opposition of some Northern Methodists to slavery: "It appears to me that some of our Northern brethren are willing to see us damned, rammed, crammed, and jammed into a 46 pounder, and touched off into eternity."

By 1844 tempers had risen to such a point that the Methodist Quarterly Conference, meeting in Tuscaloosa, passed a resolution that argued that "peaceable secession is greatly to be preferred to ceaseless denunciation, distrust, and strife." The male members of the Uniontown Methodist Church resolved in July 1844, that "a division of the M. E. Church is indispensably necessary and that under existing circumstances we cannot be satisfied without it . . . " The decision of Southern Methodists to form a regional church in 1844 and the Baptist decision to do likewise a year later met with overwhelming approval in Alabama. The Christian Church divided in 1854 and the Presbyterians in 1861. By 1861 church leaders were involved deeply in rationalizing the South's racial, political, and economic systems. In fact, they could hardly have been more deeply involved in secular politics. In January 1861, three prominent Methodist ministers addressed a Montgomery political rally and called for Alabama's immediate secession. BASIL MANLY, SR., a Baptist pastor and former president of the University of Alabama, assured the 1861 Alabama Baptist Convention that Baptists were ready to defend the state's sovereignty and independence. Throughout the Civil War, ministers served not only as chaplains and soldiers but as Dixie's apologists, bolstering morale and imploring God's blessings on the Confederacy's righteous cause.

Theological conflicts as well as political ones troubled Protestant groups. New School and Old School factions of Presbyterians waged internecine war in the Tennessee Valley. But the most divisive internal dispute occurred between missionary and antimissionary Baptists.

Many predestinarian Baptist congregations in Alabama opposed missionary, educational, benevolent, and temperance activities. Strongly anti-institutional, they even opposed the state convention and Sunday schools. Although centered in the hill counties of northern and eastern Alabama, they had some strength throughout the state. By the 1830s disagreements within churches and associations became so intense that many split. The oldest Baptist fellowship, the Flint River Association, contained a majority of antimissionary churches. In such cases, the mission advocates usually withdrew, forming new congregations and associations. More than 100 Baptist churches in the 1960s carried names such as "Liberty," "Friendship," "Fellowship," "Harmony," "Freedom," or "Union," and most dated from this divisive era.

So strong were the Primitive Baptists (as the antimission churches came to be known), that they threatened the life of the newly formed state convention. The 1837 meeting received a report that 12 of Alabama's 21 Baptist associations were divided over the missions issue, four associations had fallen to the antimissionists, and only three were clearly mission-minded.

The rapid spread of Alexander Campbell's movement into north Alabama in the 1830s also sapped Baptist energies. The Disciples of Christ established strongholds in the same general areas as the Primitive Baptists.

By the 1850s the antimission dispute subsided, to be replaced by the Landmark controversy. Containing some elements of the earlier conflict, Landmarkism was an attempt to assert traditional authority (hence the term "landmarks"), which supposedly had once characterized the church, but was now being lost. Led by JAMES R. GRAVES of Tennessee and James M. Pendleton of Kentucky, this faction opposed denominational boards and agencies, "alien baptism," open communion, or any non-Baptist minister preaching in a Baptist church. Arguing the primacy of the local congregation, they traced Baptist traditions back to the time of Christ and contended that it was the only true church. Although Southern Baptists withstood this assault also, it left deep doctrinal scars. The remaining Landmark churches finally separated from the Southern Baptist Convention (SBC) in 1905, but many Southern Baptist churches retained anti-institutional and ideological positions, refusing to contribute to denominational agencies or causes, rejecting "alien baptism" or ecumenical cooperation.

Theology constituted only one element of this struggle that also involved class structures and geography. North and east Alabama, where both Primitive and Landmark Baptists were strongest, was a land of remote hollows and mountains. Outside the fertile Tennessee Valley, there were few plantations or slaves. The counties were inhabited mainly by yeomen and poor whites who eked out a subsistence existence on small farms. They resented the political dominance of the wealthy central Alabama counties. Education was not greatly valued and was difficult to provide the scattered mountain people. Hence, they resented educated people who were sometimes haughty and arrogant.

Further to the South, Baptists and Methodists enjoyed unprecedented prosperity in the 1840s and 1850s. As the frontier receded, they began to build schools and colleges for their young. Baptist academies were established in Moulton, Greensboro, Cusseta, Six Mile, Tuskegee, Evergreen, Tuscaloosa, LaFayette, and Ruhama. They founded Judson College for women in 1839 and Howard College for men in 1842, both located in the Black Belt town of Marion. Methodists were even more active, establishing "female colleges" in Huntsville, Tuscaloosa, Tuskegee, Auburn and Athens, and Southern University at Greensboro, Wesleyan University at Florence, and the East Alabama Male College at Auburn. Because the state provided little public education, Methodists also established many academies. Such institutions produced well-educated leaders who quickly upgraded Baptist and Methodist intellectual life, and provided Alabama many of its most talented teachers, lawyers, politicians, and women.

The Civil War interrupted the prosperity and success of Alabama's churches. Theologically, it forced white Protestants to wonder why God had visited his wrath upon a cause that they considered righteous. Typical of the dilemma was an 1862 resolution proposed by a committee of the East Liberty Baptist

Association: "The present civil war which has been inaugurated by our enemies must be regarded as a providential visitation upon us on account of our sins." Following heated debate, the resolution was modified by insertion of the phrase: "Though entirely just on our part."

Reconstruction provided little time for pondering the theological implications of such weighty matters. The status of the freedmen was as vexatious an ecclesiastical problem as a political one. White Protestants were by no means of one mind regarding their black brethren. Some were delighted to see them withdraw, but others tried to preserve a biracial church dominated by whites. The 1865 Alabama Baptist Convention contended that the altered civil status of blacks did not necessitate any ecclesiastical change: "While we recognize their right to withdraw from our churches and form organizations of their own, we nevertheless believe that their highest good will be subserved by their retaining their present relation to those who know them, who love them, and who will labor for the promotion of their welfare."

One Baptist association offered to provide for the religious and educational welfare of blacks, who would be allowed to select their own pastors and teachers "from among the whites." Black Christians ignored such paternalism.

Instead, blacks organized their own schools, churches, and colleges. Some 600 blacks, who constituted two-thirds of Montgomery's First Baptist Church, withdrew under the leadership of the Rev. Nathan Ashby. In December 1868, Ashby became president of the newly organized Colored Baptist State Convention. Twelve years later, in 1880, delegates from across America met in Montgomery to organize the National Baptist Convention, which soon enrolled the majority of black Christians in the United States.

Methodists experienced similar withdrawals. The Florence District of the Methodist Church had 829 black members in 1860, but only 309 by 1865.

Despite the efforts of missionaries representing Northern white churches—Congregational, Presbyterian, Roman Catholic, Methodist, and Baptist—more than 90 percent of Alabama's black Christians enrolled in their own Methodist and Baptist churches. Outside groups made a greater contribution to the educational opportunities of blacks by sponsoring numerous colleges. From black churches and denominational schools came a generation of political, religious, educational, and business leaders.

Methodists experienced more internal divisions during Reconstruction than any religious group. Many living in north Alabama had opposed secession. In 1867 some of them organized the Alabama Conference of the Methodist Episcopal Church. The Methodist Episcopal Church, South, viewed this new group not with fraternal brotherhood, but as a meddling interloper and pawn of "Radical Reconstruction." The new church experienced trouble, especially in the Black Belt and east Alabama. The presiding elder of the Demopolis District wrote of "persecutions, sore and constant ostracism, and threats of violence . . . " The head of the East Alabama District reported that "one of my preachers . . . was assassinated by a band of ruffians and his son seriously wounded . . . " Another pastor approaching his church found a skull and crossbones posted on the door and a threatening mob outside.

In such tumultuous times, church growth slowed. After an initial increase owing to returning soldiers who had been converted in the revivals that swept the Confederate armies in 1863-1864, some denominations actually lost members because of withdrawal by blacks.

Economic change was as traumatic as racial upheaval. The "New South" crusade transformed north Alabama into one of the major industrial regions of the South.

The Birmingham district attracted not only rural dwellers to industrial jobs, but also many foreign immigrants. By 1889, 18.7 percent of the state's coal miners were foreign born, mostly from England, Ireland, and Scotland. In the years from 1890 to 1910, more immigrants came from southern and eastern Europe.

Presbyterians organized a church among Scottish miners at Pratt Mines village in 1883 and immediately encountered the problems wrought by a new industrial order; no funds could be raised because the miners were on strike. The influx of Scottish miners helped explain the rapid increase in the Presbyterian Church, from 5,800 members in 1880 to 12,000 by 1897.

The infusion of eastern and southern Europeans also brought growth to less traditional Alabama religious groups. The Catholic population of Birmingham climbed with the arrival of more than 5,000 Italian steel workers. Greek and Russian Orthodox congregations were organized in Jefferson County, formed primarily by Slavic coal miners. Jewish communities grew rapidly, especially in Birmingham and Montgomery, where peddlers established mercantile houses. Although such groups never represented more than a small fraction of Alabama's religious population, they did create a more variegated religious landscape and triggered increasing NATIVISM and anti-Catholicism.

More immediately troubling was the decline of the rural church as whites moved to the city. Ministers tended to follow them, assigning high esteem to urban pastorates and seizing the first opportunity to relocate in town. During the last 12 years of the century every name except 10 on the roster of the Presbyterian Synod changed, and one denominational historian chided the tendency of ministers "to leave a country field so soon as a city pastorate beckoned."

In the mid-1880s rural Baptist churches began criticizing the state mission board for directing too much money and attention to urban churches. They finally forced the resignation of the secretary of the mission board over this issue in 1885. Most rural Baptist churches could not afford a resident, full-time pastor and met only once a month. They had no Sunday school or educational program, or if they had one, it met only a few months a year. As late as 1898 only 744 white Baptist churches conducted a Sunday school, while 995 had none.

The Baptist dispute over mission board policy was symptomatic of a more profound division within Protestant denominations. Each of them combined several dissimilar groups. Growth occurred among more prosperous, better educated residents of bustling towns and cities. But in the country, times were hard and getting worse. As crop prices plummeted, railroad freight rates and bank interest went up, and children left the land for more promising opportunities, farmers became frustrated and angry. Denominational leaders identified more closely with the new urban business and industrial leaders. But many rural, bivocational pastors and laymen drifted into agrarian protest movements.

Samuel M. Adams, a Baptist pastor in Bibb County, served as president of the Farmers' Alliance, as head of the Populist Party, and as a state legislator. One conservative journalist heard him speak and declared that "he is so full of politics that it was a hard matter for him to keep in the road." The editor of *The Alabama Baptist*, noting divided congregations and declining contributions, warned in 1892 that Baptist pastors had "gone wild over politics."

Presbyterians attributed their financial problems in the early 1890s to the divisive gubernatorial campaign between Populist Reuben F. Kolb and Democrat Thomas G. Jones. The Church had been forced to curtail its work because of the "prevalence of great political excitement," the "heated political campaign," the "depression of the times and the political differences of our people." Despite class and theological conflicts, the 19th century was an era of spectacular growth.

Numerically, Baptists and Methodists dominated the state at the end of the century. Alabama was 97 percent Protestant: Baptists and Methodists stood at almost equal strength, 46.2 percent to 43.4 (counting whites only, the Southern Baptists numbered 17.5 percent of the total church population, the Methodist Episcopal Church, South, 15.7 percent); Presbyterians enrolled 3.8 percent of the total church population; Roman Catholics 2.4; the Disciples, 1.6; and Episcopalians 1.1. Fifteen years later, Baptists had made rapid gains to 54.9 percent, Methodists had declined sharply to 30.9, Presbyterians and Episcopalians had remained at almost exactly the same percentage of the total church population, and immigration had increased Roman Catholic membership to 5.1 percent. Although often ignored in statistical surveys, Negro Baptists outnumbered all religious groups in the 1916 census, with 30.8 percent of the total church population compared to Southern Baptists, who held second place with 20.6 percent.

The urban growth pattern was even more remarkable. In Birmingham, the state's largest city, the most numerous religious group in 1906 was Roman Catholic, which counted 28.9 percent of total church membership, followed by National Baptists (14.6 percent), and the Methodist Episcopal Church, South (14.2 percent). Southern Baptists were a distant fifth (7.5 percent).

Chaotic urban and industrial activity left in its wake grievous social and economic problems. As churches tried to cope with urban problems, they became increasingly engaged in social ministries. Alabama's Protestant churches had never been as apolitical as their critics have sometimes charged. No element of Southern life had tried harder to rationalize slavery and secession.

TEMPERANCE had required an even longer involvement in politics. The Alabama State Temperance Society had been organized in 1834 by Methodists, Presbyterians, and Baptists. Toward the end of the century, the denominations combined in a major campaign against "demon rum." The 1881 Alabama Baptist Convention announced that it was "in profound sympathy with all movements which look to the suppression of the sale and drinking of intoxicating liquors." The 1882 conference of the M. E. Church, South, adopted a report of its Committee on Temperance declaring that a "very large proportion of human misery, including poverty, disease, and crime, is induced by the use of alcohol . . ." As associations and individual churches mobilized, Protestants gained increasing skill as effective political lobbyists. Conservative Democrats resisted as best they could, but the political clout of organized Evangelicals finally swept away all opposition and instituted prohibition at both county and state levels.

PROHIBITION was a broadly conceived social movement designed to deal with poverty, crime, and disease. Having entered politics on behalf of that cause, Protestants remained to champion other reforms consistent with the Progressive impulses of the times. Most notable was their vigorous crusade against child labor.

EDGAR GARDNER MURPHY, an Episcopal priest ministering to textile workers in Montgomery, actively publicized the exploitation of children. The North Alabama Conference of the M. E. Church, South, adopted a resolution in 1901 calling for a ban on all labor of children under the age of 12. Frank W. Barnett, editor of *The Alabama Baptist*, condemned child labor as nothing less than murder, demanded that pulpits ring with denunciations, and vowed to defeat any state legislator who voted against reform. The shaken Alabama legislature passed landmark child-labor legislation in 1907.

That same year the M. E. Church, South, appointed a Commission of Social Service Movements that subsequently addressed a wide range of controversial issues. Its 1910 report denied that "social salvation" could replace individual regeneration but endorsed the social gospel as an invaluable tool against "syndicated sin." The 1911 report argued that the church should modify the entire social fabric so as to "make a kingdom of God among men . . . "

Mrs. J. B. Cumming, a leader of the Baptist Woman's Missionary Society, made her agency an instrument for reform. She believed that the root of human suffering could be found in the social and industrial order: exploitation of children for profit, poor housing for workers, excessive hours of labor, inadequate pay, and unsanitary factories and shops.

Editor Barnett of *The Alabama Baptist* chided churches that "frequently shut their eyes to the struggles of labor to get a minimum living wage; and have not heard the cry of the children who were being sacrificed in our mills; or cared when a fight was being made for shorter hours and better working conditions." The chief foe of reform was "industry and property," that sought "to rob the workmen and the tenant of life and health because it happens to be more profitable at the time."

Energized by such social visions, urban churches undertook extensive social ministries. Methodists established several settlement houses in industrial sections of Birmingham and Mobile. These provided free kindergartens, adult literacy classes, home economics classes, and free medical care. Some Baptist congregations established "institutional churches" with extensive social ministries. Presbyterians began a settlement house among Birmingham steel workers, and the city's Independent Presbyterian Church provided a "Fresh Air Farm" for poor, inner city white children, a public health nurse, and an employment service.

White Baptists, Methodists, and Presbyterians also appointed special committees to examine relations with their black brethren. The 1912 conference of the North Alabama Methodists asked for creation of a Commission on the Social Condition of the Negro to improve black housing, education, social and religious life. That same year the Woman's Auxiliary of the Presbyterian Synod of Alabama held a conference for Negro Women at Stillman College, which began a long educational ministry to that black institution. By the early 1920s, they had expanded their program to provide biracial women's Bible study.

Even attitudes toward women began to change. The small, largely rural Methodist Protestant Church led the way in its 1887 state conference voting 23 to seven that, since "in Christ there is neither male or female," "all members, whether male or female, above the age of 21 and of good standing, are alike entitled to vote in all church elections." A similar measure introduced at the 1913 North Alabama Methodist Conference was tabled. Five years later in 1918, the Alabama Conference adopted such a resolution by a vote of 136 to 20. The Alabama Baptist State Convention allowed women delegates to vote at its 1913 meetings.

Although the SOCIAL GOSPEL made significant inroads among Alabama Protestants, another of the current religious trends, liberal theology, had little influence. An occasional minister such as Alfred J. Dickinson of Birmingham's First Baptist Church, L. L. Gwaltney, editor of *The Alabama Baptist*, or Henry M. Edmonds of the city's Independent Presbyterian Church might be tainted with "higher criticism" at a northern college or theological seminary. But the result was usually ostracism or worse (Edmonds was fired for heresy by South Highlands Presbyterian Church before forming his new congregation).

Denominational moderates tended to dominate annual meetings and maintained a shaky truce during the Woodrow,

Toy, and Whitsitt controversies in the late nineteenth century. But the Fundamentalist conflict forced divisions. Only shrewd maneuvering by Baptist leaders prevented biblical tests for teachers at the denomination's Howard College. The 1914 conference of the M. E. Church, South, attacked its book concern for publishing "mere novels and unreligious literature," and expressed alarm "at the silence of our church press in the face of this relentless propaganda of higher criticism in print and in school." So outraged were delegates by 1918 that they concluded, "Let us have a book burning." The 1923 North Alabama Conference condemned "modernism," and the 1929 meeting adopted a memorial that would "prevent any man or woman from preaching or teaching in our institutions of learning, churches, training schools, or Sunday Schools, or from editing any of our connectional literature, or from holding any other place or position in our church, who does not believe in the inspiration of the Scriptures, the Virgin Birth, the death and resurrection of Jesus Christ, according to the Bible statements."

By the 1920s, theological controversies, anti-Catholicism, and excessive focus on the single issue of prohibition narrowed the range of Protestant activities. Baptists continued to grow more rapidly than other denominations, perhaps because they were less affected by theological controversy, and they remained more conservative and rural. Their bivocational ministers gave them strong identification with the common folk moving into urban areas, especially coal camps and mill towns. Between 1916 and 1926 the number of churches in Alabama increased by only 5.3 percent. Yet in only half that time, 1918-1924, Southern Baptists established 81 new churches, and increased membership by 22 percent. The Southern Baptist Convention's 75 million campaign, begun in 1919, raised 2.5 million dollars over five years for Alabama Baptist mission and benevolence causes, compared to only 825,000 dollars contrib-

uted over the previous five years. State Baptists, in fact, overexpanded and went heavily into debt, a situation not corrected until the mid-1940s.

Both Baptists and Methodists launched major drives to construct hospitals in urban areas during the 1920s, though Methodists were somewhat hampered by lagging finances. As one Methodist official put it in 1924: the problem was the "gratification of bad and useless habits at the expense of the church treasury with the result that a few hundred dollars are collected for benevolent purposes, while thousands are spent for chewing gum, dope, tobacco, movies, joyriding, and the high cost of swimming."

The 1930s were years when survival, not growth, was uppermost. Enrollments generally remained stable, while finances collapsed. In 1934 baptisms reached the lowest point in Baptist churches since 1918. Ministers accepted substantial salary cuts and were thankful to have jobs at all. The last denominational academies and high schools were closed, replaced by the expanding public school movement. The Alabama Temperance Alliance, a coalition mainly of Methodists and Baptists, succeeded in containing the legalization of alcohol to 24 counties, while keeping 43 dry.

The religious legacy of World War II was mixed. Even during the war there had been racial strife in Alabama's war industries. The return of thousands of black veterans intent on a better life posed new challenges for the church.

Consistent with their antebellum heritage, white Protestant churches rationalized segregation and provided considerable assistance to politicians who vowed to resist racial desegregation. Although the state's Southern Baptists belatedly established a Department of Work with Negro Baptists in 1951 and contributed financially to several black Baptist schools, they bitterly attacked the 1954 Brown decision and resisted integrating their churches. Leon Macon, edi-

tor of *The Alabama Baptist*, wrote that
the desegregation decision had "jarred to
the foundation a Southern institution."
John H. Buchanan, pastor of the influential Southside Baptist Church in Birmingham, concluded that the Supreme
Court "from its cloistered chambers has
overlooked the reality of the situation"
and complicated and damaged race relations. The 1954 North Alabama conference of the M. E. Church, South, resolved
that "it is our honest conviction that it is
for the good of whites and Negroes that
separate schools be maintained."

Black Christians saw the issue quite
differently. Although black churches
across Alabama finally became involved
in the CIVIL RIGHTS MOVEMENT, congregations in Montgomery pioneered many
of the strategies later adopted nationwide.
In December 1955 Montgomery black
leaders met at the Holt Street Baptist
Church and formed the Montgomery
Improvement Association. The Rev.
MARTIN LUTHER KING, JR., who had
become pastor of Dexter Avenue Baptist
Church in September 1954, was elected
president.

King's major assets were an excellent
education (Morehouse College, Crozer
Seminary, Boston University), unusual
oratorical skills, and kinship networks to
Atlanta's influential religious community.
After arriving at Dexter Avenue, King
created a Social and Political Action Committee because "the gospel of Jesus is a
social gospel . . . seeking to save the whole
man. . . ." Together with black labor leader
E. D. Nixon and fellow Baptist pastor
Ralph D. Abernathy, they organized the
Montgomery Bus Boycott. Despite provocative violence directed at them by
some whites and more widespread economic intimidation, King and his associates maintained a remarkable degree of
unity and non-violence. Drawing upon
the religious metaphor of the suffering
Savior, King articulated the most powerful idiom of the American Civil Rights
Movement in his sermon to that first

meeting at Holt Street Baptist Church just
before Christmas, 1955:

> If you will protest courageously and
> yet with dignity and Christian love,
> when the history books are written
> in future generations, the historians
> will have to pause and say, "There
> lived a great people—a black
> people—who injected new meaning
> and dignity into the veins of civiliza-
> tion." This is our challenge and our
> overwhelming responsibility.

This animus led King to crusades in
Birmingham and Selma that altered
American society in fundamental ways.
Although King soon became a national
figure, he waged his first campaign from
the black churches of Montgomery.

Racial change was not the only evidence of a new world aborning. The location of war industries and training
facilities in the South between 1940 and
1945 transformed Dixie into a relatively
prosperous region, at least for most
whites. Congregations of the M. E.
Church, South, and the Southern Baptists
became steadily more "mainstream,"
especially in the cities. Their ministers
were more likely to have formal education
and less likely to elicit emotional
responses from their congregations.

Southern Baptists proved best able to
maintain traditional evangelical zeal
while assimilating middle-class values.
The Department of Evangelism and
Enlistment, recreated in 1950, devised
ingenious programs to enlist and retain
members. Beginning in 1948 a state evangelistic conference was held annually. A
simultaneous revival conducted by all
Southern Baptist Convention churches in
1955 resulted in a record of nearly 29,000
baptisms in Alabama. In 1946 the state
convention launched a city missions program under the direction of a superintendent of missions for each city. Between
1950 and 1963, 125 new SBC churches
were begun in Alabama's six largest cities.
The increase in Baptist membership was

spectacular: Huntsville, 117 percent; Mobile, 99 percent; the Tri-Cities (Tuscumbia, Sheffield, Florence), 72 percent; Birmingham, 54 percent; Montgomery, 53 percent; Gadsden, 51 percent. Financial contributions increased a staggering 185 percent between 1944 and 1951.

The Alabama Baptist was an effective tool for promoting such causes. By 1961 its circulation was the second largest of any state journal in the Southern Baptist Convention, reaching 115,000 homes. Its readership throughout the state was second only to the secular *Birmingham News* in Alabama. Some 1,900 churches included subscriptions for all church members in their budgets.

Baptists also tackled the problem of enlisting rural whites who were moving to towns. In 1954 the state convention sponsored a "Transfer of Church Membership Week" to persuade new arrivals in industrial cities to move their church membership along with their furniture. Yet the denomination retained 1,600 churches in Alabama's open country in 1945, thus maintaining its traditional rural base.

To train the ministers necessary for its numerous congregations was a demanding task. In 1947 Howard College (now Samford University) began its Extension Division of Christian Training to take religious education to the people. A pioneer venture in adult education, it operated through church centers. Most of the teachers were local pastors or college graduates who received only actual expenses. Classes met one evening a week. Between 1947 and 1957 more than 10,000 different people enrolled in the courses, including hundreds of bi-vocational ministers for whom it was the sole opportunity for formal theological training. As late as 1980 Alabama had more bi-vocational Southern Baptist pastors than any state (1,211, or 40.3 percent of the state's total). In 1956 the extension program operated out of more than 50 centers with 2,000 students, 500 of them

pastors with little education. Academic standards were never high, and the program declined rapidly after 1958 when a college accrediting agency refused to allow the college to offer academic credit for its extension courses. Nonetheless, the extension concept provided better trained leaders during a critical period of Baptist growth, and modified versions of the Howard Extension were adopted by Baptist colleges in several other states.

By the mid-1960s Southern Baptist growth finally subsided. The 30,476 baptisms reported in 1959 was a new record, but the statistically conscious denomination had little to brag about for the next few years. Baptisms declined to 25,000 in 1965, the smallest number since 1952. Sunday school enrollments also declined.

By the 1970s, the SBC was the superpower of Alabama religion. Its sophisticated medical centers in Birmingham were among the best in the state, its computer operations modern, and its three colleges thriving. Nearly one of every three residents of Alabama was a Southern Baptist in 1971 (30.6 percent). Members of SBC churches constituted more than half the white church membership in all but six of Alabama's 67 counties. Only in Macon County did any white denomination outnumber them.

Other denominations had pockets of strength corresponding to historic patterns. Catholics numbered more than eight percent of the total church membership in six mainly urban or extreme south Alabama counties. But black and white Methodists and Baptists were the only groups with strong support statewide.

Although confined mainly to the hill counties, the most rapid post-war growth occurred among the CHURCH OF GOD (CLEVELAND TN). This mainly white, rural Pentecostal denomination was the third-largest church in 17 of Alabama's 67 counties by 1971. In many areas it was rapidly replacing Southern Baptists as the church of the plain white people.

The cycle of nearly two centuries entered a new phase. White Baptists had joined Methodists in middle class respectability but at the price of evangelical fervor. Black Baptists and Methodists often felt more in common with Pentecostal white churches than with their more sedate brethren. But the long-standing Baptist hegemony seemed as pervasive as ever, supported since 1945 by people who wielded increasing political and economic power.

See also articles on ANTIMISSION MOVEMENT; BLACK MINISTERIAL PROTEST LEADERSHIP, 1955-1970; CAMPBELLITE TRADITION; FRONTIER, INFLUENCE of; LANDMARK MOVEMENT.

Bibliography. *Alabama News of the Church of God and Alabama Kingdom Builders News;* Bureau of the Census, *Religious Bodies, 1906, 1916, 1926, 1936;* Daniel L. Cloyd, "Prelude to Reform: Political, Economic, and Social Thought of Alabama Baptists, 1877-1890," *The Alabama Review* 31 (January 1978): 48-64; Aleathea T. Cobbs, *Presbyterian Women of the Synod of Alabama;* Mark H. Elovitz, *A Century of Jewish Life in Dixie: The Birmingham Experience;* Zelia S. Evans and J. T. Alexander, ed., *Dexter Avenue Baptist Church, 1877-1977;* Walter L. Fleming, "The Churches of Alabama During the Civil War and Reconstruction," reprinted from *The Gulf States Historical Magazine,* by W. M. Rogers and Co., Montgomery AL, 1902; Wayne Flynt, "Organized Labor, Reform, and Alabama Politics, 1920," *The Alabama Review* 23 (July 1970): 163-80; "Dissent in Zion: Alabama Baptists and Social Issues, 1900-1914," *The Journal of Southern History* 35 (November 1969): 523-42; "Religion in the Urban South: The Divided Religious Mind of Birmingham, 1900-1930," *The Alabama Review* 30 (April 1977): 108-34; "Alabama White Protestantism and Labor, 1900-1914," *The Alabama Review* 25 (July 1972): 192-217; Douglas W. Johnson, et al., *Churches and Church Membership in the United States: An Enumeration by Region, State and County;* Michael Kenny, *Catholic Culture in Alabama: Centenary Story of Spring Hill College, 1830-1930;* Marion E. Lazenby, *History of Methodism in Alabama and West Florida;* James W. Marshall, *The Presbyterian Church in Alabama,* Robert Strong, ed.; Thomas M. Owen, compiler, *The Methodist Churches of Montgomery;* B. F. Riley, *A Memorial History of the Baptists of Alabama;* A. Hamilton Reid, *Baptists in Alabama: Their Organization and Witness;* George H. Watson, *History of the Christian Churches in the Alabama Area;* Anson West, *A History of Methodism in Alabama.*

WAYNE FLYNT
AUBURN UNIVERSITY

ALEXANDER, WILL W. (1884-1956), New Dealer and race-relations reformer,

was born in the Ozark farm country of southern Missouri. His family earmarked him for a Methodist ministerial career, and Alexander was ordained at the age of 17. He worked his way through nearby Scarritt-Morrisville College, and then went on to the Divinity School at Vanderbilt University, receiving a degree in 1912. Alexander remained in Nashville as the social activist pastor of the Belmont Methodist Church who believed and preached that poverty and racism were the South's greatest evils.

After the U. S. entered World War I in 1917, he left the ministry to work with the National War Work Council and YMCA. Alexander proved especially adept at dealing with the heightened racial sensitivities generated during the war, especially over the stationing of black troops at Southern military bases. During the subsequent wave of racial violence that erupted in 1919, Alexander traveled around the South forming interracial committees made up of white and black community leaders who attempted to quell rumors and avoid bloodshed.

Alexander received the private support, most notably from the Julius Rosenwald Fund, to maintain such committees on a permanent basis under the aegis of the COMMISSION ON INTERRACIAL COOPERATION, an Atlanta-based organization of which "Dr. Will"—as he became known—was the guiding spirit and director during most of its years. He became a prominent spokesman for racial justice and advocate of black education and was one of the prime movers behind the establishment of Dillard University in New Orleans.

In 1935 Alexander coauthored *The Collapse of Cotton Tenancy,* a commission-sponsored study of the desperate plight of white and black sharecroppers during the Depression. This led to his being called to Washington to work with the Resettlement Administration and its replacement, the Farm Society Administration, which Alexander headed from 1937 to 1940. As a New Dealer, Alexander was instrumental in bringing blacks into the federal government. In 1940 he left Washington to join the Chicago office of the Rosenwald Fund.

Bibliography. Wilma Dykeman and James Stokely, *Seeds of Southern Change: The Life of Will Alexander*; Morton Sosna, *In Search of the Silent South: Southern Liberals and the Race Issue.*

MORTON SOSNA
STANFORD HUMANITIES CENTER

ALIEN IMMERSION. Emerging in the late 1840s among certain Southern Baptists, the LANDMARK MOVEMENT advanced the doctrine that the only pure and true churches were Baptist churches. The Landmarkers argued that BAPTISM, to be valid, must be administered by a Baptist church. Even baptism by immersion was considered void unless authorized and executed by a local Baptist church. Alien immersion, therefore, was immersion performed by non-Baptists.

The Landmarkers held that Christ founded the first true church and that the successors to it have continued through the centuries in an unbroken chain. Such Landmark leaders as J. M. Pendleton and JAMES R. GRAVES insisted that only those churches embodying the organizational structure and doctrinal purity of the Baptist churches qualified as true successors of the original church. All others were labeled as "religious societies."

Growing out of the 19th-century CAMPBELLITE TRADITION, the CHURCHES OF CHRIST developed their own charge that alien immersion was invalid, although the phrase "alien immersion" never became popular with that fellowship. The Churches of Christ, like the Landmarkers, regarded themselves as the only true successors to Christ's original church and, therefore, the only authentic churches.

See also articles on BAPTISM; SACRAMENTS AND ORDINANCES.

Bibliography. Baptist History and Heritage (Special issue on Landmarkism) 10:1 (January 1975); A. C. Dayton, *Pedobaptist and Campbellite Immersions*; J. R. Graves, *Old Landmarkism: What Is It?*; James E. Tull, *Shapers of Baptist Thought.*

JOE E. BARNHART
NORTH TEXAS STATE UNIVERSITY

ALLIN, JOHN MAURY (1921-), presiding bishop of the Episcopal Church, was born in Helena AR. After attending the Helena public schools, he received his B.A. and B.D. degrees from the UNIVERSITY OF THE SOUTH, Sewanee TN. Later he received an honorary D.D. degree from Sewanee and a M.Ed. from Mississippi College in Clinton. He was ordained a deacon in the Episcopal Church in 1944 and a priest in 1945, and served as vicar of St. Peter's Church, Conway AR, 1945-1949.

In 1950 he moved to New Orleans where he served as the curate of St. Andrew's Church, chaplain to episcopal students at Tulane University, and as episcopal chaplain to institutions in the city. He was then rector of Grace Church, Monroe LA, for six years before becoming rector and president of All Saints Episcopal Junior College, Vicksburg MS, in 1958. In September 1961, he was elected bishop coadjutor of the Episcopal Diocese of Mississippi and consecrated in St. James' Church, Jackson, the next month.

During his five years as bishop coadjutor and eight years as diocesan bishop in Mississippi, he served as a voice of moderation in the midst of the racial turmoil of that period, and he was one of the founding members of the Committee of Concern, an ecumenical, biracial group dedicated to the rebuilding of black churches that had been burned or bombed. On the national level, he served on the Board of Directors of the Episcopal Radio-TV Foundation, as a member of the Episcopal Church's Standing Commission on Ecumenical Relations, and as a member of the Executive Council of the Episcopal Church. In addition, he served as trustee, regent, and later, chancellor of his alma mater, the University of the South.

In October 1973, Bishop Allin was elected presiding bishop of the Episcopal Church, an office that he assumed officially on 1 June 1974, and in which he is scheduled to serve through the year 1985. Presiding over the Church during a time of significant internal changes such as the adoption of a revised Book of Common Prayer and the approval of the ordination of women to the priesthood, he has reached out to all as a reconciler and healer. He has also led the Episcopal Church to a new awareness of mission throughout the world, symbolized by the Venture in Mission program so closely identified with his name.

DUNCAN M. GRAY, JR.
JACKSON, MISSISSIPPI

ALTAR CALL (INVITATION). Altar call is an invitation issued by a minister at the end of a service of worship to non-Christians or nonpracticing Christians attending a revival meeting or other worship service to come to a designated area in order to pray, to seek to encounter God, and to profess publicly faith in Christ.

Some form of invitation to personal response has existed throughout Christian history. For example, the apostle Paul wrote: "We beseech you on behalf of Christ, be reconciled to God" (2 Cor. 5:20). Also a part of the Christian faith from the beginning has been the requirement of a public confession of faith in Christ by individual disciples: "Man believes with his heart and so is justified, and he confesses with his lips and so is saved" (Rom. 10:10).

The two principal forms of initial public confession of faith traditionally have been baptism and confirmation with the recitation of the Apostles' Creed as a principal form of continuing confession. Altar calls are a relatively recent form of initial confession. They originated in REVIVALISM, when public expressions of emotion, prayer, and conversion were encouraged. The altar call gained popularity in American religion during the CAMP MEETINGS of the GREAT REVIVAL (c.

1800). In camp meetings the altar usually was an area immediately in front of the pulpit to which men and women, sometimes by name, were urged to come. It often included a "mourner's bench," which Charles G. Finney preferred to call an "anxious bench," sometimes without a back. It could include several benches, or none, and it might or might not be enclosed. Sometimes separate areas were designated for men and women. Appropriate behavior for respondents always included prayer, sometimes done while kneeling at the bench, and sometimes called "praying through," and also the expression of powerful emotions such as guilt and anxiety. Songs were sometimes sung by the people as respondents struggled to be converted or delivered from their sins, and ministers or other concerned Christians sought to assist the respondents. Both the struggle itself and, when it occurred, the peace that followed the struggle were expressed to the congregation.

When revival meetings were conducted in large tents, as by Billy Sunday, the altar call was for respondents to "walk the sawdust trail" to a designated area where individual spiritual counselors were waiting to assist respondents. In the BILLY GRAHAM crusades, the invitation is to "walk the aisle," with counselors having been instructed beforehand to lead the way themselves in order to encourage the response of others.

In the South many churches continue to follow the procedure of issuing altar calls at the close of Sunday worship services, though today this is more likely to be called "giving an invitation." What occurs in these less emotional settings is frequently a quiet confession, often privately made to the minister and then mediated through him to the people, that the respondent already has "accepted Christ." The congregation is usually asked to greet the respondent following the benediction. In many denominations, most notably Baptist and other evangelistic bodies, the altar call, rather than the observance of communion, the repetition of the Creed, or the sermon itself, is the most important and holy moment of a worship service, and the lack of respondents may be taken as implying that the service was unsuccessful in its most important effort.

The altar call has been justified in pragmatic rather than in theological terms, and its opponents often have resisted it in esthetic rather than religious terms. Its precise relation to the more ancient forms of initial public confession, baptism and confirmation, apparently has not been explored.

See also article on CONVERSION.

Bibliography. Dickson D. Bruce, *And They All Sang Hallelujah*; Charles A. Johnson, *The Frontier Camp Meeting.*

FISHER HUMPHREYS
NEW ORLEANS BAPTIST SEMINARY

AMERICAN BAPTIST ASSOCIATION.

An international fellowship of independent Baptist churches voluntarily cooperating in missionary, evangelistic, benevolent, and educational activities, its beginnings can be traced to the LANDMARK MOVEMENT of the 1850s. Led by Elders JAMES R. GRAVES and J. M. Pendleton, a significant number of Missionary Baptist churches in the South, claiming a New Testament heritage, rejected as extrascriptural the innovations, methods, and policies of the newly formed Southern Baptist Convention. They maintained that since Christ's "commission" was given to the local congregation as such, it alone could administer the ordinances and perform kingdom activities. Because they strongly advocated absolute church equality, many continued doing mission and benevolent work apart from the SBC or through their local associations.

Beginning in the 1890s, controversies over the powers of mission boards, the rise of the doctrine of "convention sovereignty," and a hotly debated dispute over the pre-Reformation origins of the church, caused a widespread disenchantment with the convention system and the

exodus of a number of churches. Many of these joined with other Landmark Baptists to form several separate statewide associations. The Baptist Missionary Association organized in Texas in 1900 was the first, followed by the State Association of Missionary Baptist Churches in Arkansas two years later. (This movement became the BAPTIST MISSIONARY ASSOCIATION OF AMERICA in 1968.) Both of these groups began foreign mission programs supporting a number of former Southern Baptist missionaries.

In order to coordinate these activities, a national association, the Baptist General Association, was organized at Texarkana TX in 1905. Although many of its churches fellowshipped in this new association, the BMAA of Texas chose to maintain a separate foreign mission work in Brazil and Portugal. The General Association supported workers in China, Lebanon, Iran, Cuba, and Italy. A missions office was opened at Texarkana in 1921.

In 1903, Ben M. Bogard, a Little Rock pastor, began the publication of Landmark Baptist Sunday school literature. This operation was purchased in 1915 by the General Association and moved to Texarkana AR. The Baptist Sunday School Committee, which was established to oversee this work, now operates two retail book stores in Texarkana, publishes thousands of pieces of religious literature annually, and has assets of over two million dollars.

In 1924, delegates from the various churches meeting at Texarkana merged the separate mission programs of the BMAA and the General Association and formed the American Baptist Association. In reality, this was not the organization of a separate Baptist denomination, but the creation of a "separate and distinct organization." Although the ABA is a strictly voluntary body, its churches are united in "faith and practice" and in their adherence to the NEW HAMPSHIRE CONFESSION OF FAITH (1833). They advocate the infallible, verbal inspiration of the entire

Bible; the virgin birth; the Genesis account of creation; salvation by grace; the bodily resurrection; the premillennial return of Christ; and a literal hell. Strong statements concerning ALIEN IMMERSION, the perpetuity of the church, and limiting the powers of cooperative bodies have also been adopted.

Since 1924, mission works have been supported in many foreign lands; in a number of cases self-supporting churches have arisen. The domestic mission effort has been even more successful, changing the ABA from a largely rural, Southern organization to one with churches in some 42 states.

In 1981, the ABA reported 1,641 U. S. churches with about 225,000 members. Sixteen institutes, seminaries, and colleges were in operation in the United States and several abroad. Eighteen newspapers and other periodicals were being published within the fellowship.

Bibliography. Conrad N. Glover and Austin T. Powers, *The American Baptist Association, 1924-1975.*

RUSSELL PIERCE BAKER
LITTLE ROCK, ARKANSAS

AMERICAN COLONIZATION SOCIETY.

The American Society for the Colonization of the Free People of Colour (by their consent) on the West Coast of Africa was founded in December 1816. It was a curious coalition of politicians, slaveholders, and antislavery reformers with a missionary vision.

Politicians with national ambitions hoped to identify themselves with the Republican antislavery tradition without surrendering Southern support. Slaveholders sought to remove free blacks as a dangerous anomaly in Southern society. Reformers, disheartened by the failure of emancipationist sentiment south of Pennsylvania, had a threefold goal: to demonstrate to skeptical whites that blacks could govern themselves, thus implying the safety of emancipation in the U. S.; to help blacks flee white racism; to establish a missionary colony from which to convert Africa to Christianity.

Blacks responded variously to the society. Bishop Richard Allen of the African Methodist Episcopal Church rallied opposition against it as a precedent for the eventual deportation of all American blacks to Africa. About 13,000 Afro-Americans, however, accepted colonization as a condition of emancipation. They and a few black nationalists seemed to agree with Paul Cuffee, a black Quaker sea captain who first popularized colonization among blacks, that they could control their destiny only in Africa. The same understanding motivated black emigrationists after emancipation failed to produce the freedom blacks wanted. Between 1865 and 1870, and in the years following 1877, blacks once again fled American racism by fleeing the U. S. Until the early twentieth century, therefore, the ACS cooperated with Afro-American leaders who had formed their own emigrant societies.

The society had a long history, enduring the angry criticism of radical abolitionists, suspicious Southerners, and practical politicians. Prior to the Civil War, the society was popular with Southern churchmen, notably Bishop WILLIAM MEADE and the Reverend Charles Wesley Andrews of Virginia, most Methodist bishops, and reforming ministers in the Baptist and Presbyterian churches; most Southern Quakers also supported it. After the war the color of its support changed, largely by the efforts of Bishop HENRY McNEAL TURNER, an eloquent and energetic black nationalist. Thus the society had been a sentimental white charity group attempting to save the few within a system that exploited the many, and it had also provided the necessary machinery to aid blacks in their search for a country of their own.

See also article on SLAVERY.

Bibliography. D. G. Mathews, *Slavery and Methodism*; Edwin S. Redkey, *Black Exodus*; P. J. Staundenraus, *The African Colonization Movements, 1816-1865.*

DONALD G. MATHEWS
UNIVERSITY OF NORTH CAROLINA
AT CHAPEL HILL

AMERICAN MISSIONARY ASSOCIATION.

Organized at Albany NY in 1846 by antislavery Christians, the AMA was intended to serve as a "pure" foreign missionary agency. It would not accept funds from slaveholding churches or give aid to slaveholding missionaries. Although the association was a secular benevolent society, its members were almost entirely Congregationalists. The AMA had no relation with the South in the early years. In 1848 the association employed its first domestic missionary, and in 1852 the secretaries of the association were instructed to promote domestic missions with increased vigor "especially at the South."

In September 1861, a missionary was sent to undertake mission work among the contraband at Fort Monroe VA and two years later, 83 missionaries and teachers labored for the association among the Freedmen. Between 1861 and 1869 the association supported 2,638 teachers in the South. The National Council of Congregational Churches, which supplied most of the funds of the association, repeatedly reminded the AMA that it was expected to establish churches; but even though most of the teachers of the AMA were Congregationalists, they concentrated more on education than on proselytization. In 1890 black Congregationalists numbered only 7,000 in the South.

In the 1870s when the state governments in the South began to establish public schools the AMA cooperated with local boards of education in operating schools with varying degrees of success. After public education was well underway, the association began to concentrate on secondary schools and colleges. With the association program operating at its fullest in 1870, the AMA was sponsoring 170 schools, but by 1878, the number had been reduced to 37 schools.

In 1895 when racially conscious blacks demanded that Negroes fill places on the faculty of denominational schools, the AMA schools added fewer black teachers than other denominational schools. They were supported by black parents and alumni who wished to maintain the high standards.

See also articles on ABOLITIONISM; ANTIMISSION MOVEMENT.

Bibliography. American Missionary Association Papers, Amistad Archives, New Orleans; Lewis Tappan, *The Life of Arthur Tappan.*

VICTOR B. HOWARD
MOREHEAD STATE UNIVERSITY

AMES, JESSIE DANIEL (1883-1972),

Southern women's activist and race-relations reformer, was born in the small east Texas town of Palestine. Her father had to struggle to make ends meet, and his own frustrations were expressed not only in a thorough dislike for religion, but in making it clear to Jessie that she was the less-favored of his two daughters. Jessie responded by joining her mother as a member of the Methodist Church and by resolving to obtain an education and achieve her own respectability.

In 1902, she graduated from Southwestern University in Georgetown TX, where her family had moved when she was 10; and in 1905 she married Roger Post Ames, an army surgeon who had worked with Walter Reed in Cuba. Their marriage was not a happy one; when Roger died in 1914, Ames found herself a 31-year-old widow with three children to support. She lived with her mother in Georgetown and helped her run a telephone business that her father had acquired shortly before his death in 1911. Ames's involvement in the business world and Methodist women's groups led her in 1915 into the women's suffrage movement in Texas, where she became a leader.

In 1920, after the passage of women's suffrage, Ames, still in Texas, became involved in the interracial meetings between white and black women's church groups now taking place with the encouragement of the recently organized COMMISSION ON INTERRACIAL

COOPERATION in Atlanta. By 1924, Ames had become the first woman executive director of a state interracial committee as well as a salaried field representative for the entire Southwest. In 1929, she moved to Atlanta to head the Interracial Commission Women's Division, and the following year, drawing upon her experience both in women's voluntary associations and with the educational and pressure tactics of the suffrage movement, she organized and directed the ASSOCIATION OF SOUTHERN WOMEN FOR THE PREVENTION OF LYNCHING. Often at odds with her male colleagues over personal matters, Ames's standing in the Southern interracial movement was jeopardized in 1938 by her open opposition to federal antilynching legislation. Nonetheless, she remained with the Interracial Commission and played an instrumental role in its transition in 1944 into the Southern Regional Council.

Bibliography. Jacquelyn Dowd Hall, *Revolt Against Chivalry: Jessie Daniel Ames and the Women's Campaign Against Lynching.*

MORTON SOSNA
STANFORD HUMANITIES CENTER

ANABAPTISM. The term Anabaptism is used to refer to the group of Christians in the 16th century who wanted to make the most radical changes in the practices of the (Roman) Catholic Church. Martin Luther's assertion that any Christian could interpret the Scriptures for himself was accepted literally by a variety of European thinkers in the years following 1517. The result was a wide variety of ideas concerning the Christian faith and the Christian church. Many of these individuals rejected the long-accepted practice of infant baptism because it did not fit the pattern of justification by faith. Consequently, they rebaptized people who had already been baptized as infants and were labelled Anabaptists; in Greek the word means "re-baptizers."

Some historians have found in Thomas Münzer an early exponent of Anabaptism, and it is true that he quarreled with

Luther on questions relating to the interpretation of Scripture and of BAPTISM. He became one of the leaders in the Peasants' Revolt of the 1520s. His leadership and his execution in 1525 as the result of the defeat at Frankenhausen have contributed to the reputation that Anabaptism has had. It is more accurate historically, however, to concentrate attention on the group of Anabaptists that was developing in Zwingli's Zurich.

Between 1523 and 1525 some of the associates of Zwingli, including Conrad Grebel, Felix Manz, Balthasar Hübmaier, and Wilhelm Reublin were discussing the nature of baptism. For example, in January 1525 Grebel, Manz, and Reublin held a conference with Zwingli and Bullinger with the town council listening, but no agreement proved possible. A few days later, George Blaurock, an ex-priest like Manz and Reublin, was baptized by Grebel, and then Blaurock baptized about 15 others who were attending a Bible study meeting. Evidently this group, called the Swiss Brethren, could no longer follow Zwingli and the town council.

Such an action could not be kept secret; the town council responded with such actions as imprisonment of Grebel, Manz, and Blaurock, banishment of Michael Sattler (formerly a monk), and torture of Hübmaier. Such actions were not sufficient to crush the nascent Anabaptist movement and execution was ordered in March 1526. One of the first to die was Manz, who was tied to a weight and thrown into the River Limmat. Persecution had begun, but the combined efforts of the Catholics, the Lutherans, and the Reformed movement of Zwingli and then of Calvin were not sufficient to destroy the Anabaptists. Altogether many thousands of people were killed by drowning—thought to be the most symbolically appropriate means—beheading, and burning.

As is frequently the case, persecution simply helped to spread the ideas of the Anabaptists. For example, Blaurock, who was not a citizen of Zurich and was consequently not executed, spent time in the Tyrol where he became an effective evangelist of Anabaptism and baptized hundreds of people before he was captured and burned in 1529. Hübmaier fled to Moravia several hundred miles eastward and for a time was the leader of Anabaptist development in the city of Prague. Eventually he got into a conflict with Hans Hut, some of whose ideas were indebted to Thomas Münzer; this controversy led to difficulty with the political authorities and in March 1528 he was burned in Vienna. His influence lived on through his writings.

The ideas of Anabaptism were also being spread by Sattler who may have been the author of the Schleitheim Confession of 1527. If he did not actually write it, its ideas are his. After being banished from Zurich, he eventually spent some time in the valley of the Neckar, where he demonstrated an evangelistic zeal and a consistent pacifism. A group of Anabaptists gathered at Schlatt in 1527 and prepared a statement of their faith, entitled "Brotherly Union of a number of Children of God concerning Seven Articles," or the Schleitheim Confession: (1) Adult baptism of believers; (2) the ban should be used against those who having once been baptized as adults then fall into sin; (3) the Lord's Supper or Eucharist is simply a memorial of Christ's suffering; (4) separation of Anabaptists from the world, including other churches; (5) pastors of Anabaptists should be men of integrity and leadership; (6) the sword is not to be used by an Anabaptist, even in self-defense; (7) oaths are prohibited. These seven articles provided an excellent summary of Anabaptist ideas and were widely circulated. For example, Zwingli incorporated the articles in a pamphlet issued in July 1527; his negative reaction to the articles served to increase the level of persecution.

The Anabaptists, being a diverse people, responded to persecution in different ways. One way was the development of fanaticism, a response best illustrated in the Münster episode. Two refugees from Dutch persecution of the Anabaptists, Jan Matthys and Jan of Leiden, fled to Münster in the early 1530s. The Anabaptists under Matthys gained control of that city and many thousands were baptized. However, the Catholic bishop recruited an army and began a siege. After Matthys's death in April 1533, Jan of Leiden took charge. By this time, there were four times as many women as men in Münster. A decision was made to permit polygamy, an action that brought Jan of Leiden and the Münster Anabaptists, as well as Anabaptism in general, into disrepute and gave their enemies additional material with which to criticize the Anabaptists. The episode ended in the summer of 1535 when the city was captured and pillaged. But the story did not end at that time, because for centuries the Münster incident caused horror in the minds of many Christians.

In contrast to these fanaticists or revolutionaries, some of the Anabaptists responded to persecution by rejecting the use of force in any way, even to the defense of one's person in the face of death. After the disaster of Münster, these quietists or pacifists were pulled together and organized by a Dutch Catholic priest named Menno Simons, who renounced his priesthood and was baptized in 1536 by Obbe Philips, the leader of a group of pacifist Anabaptists in the Netherlands. Shortly Philips departed from the area and turned over the leadership to Simons, who spent the remaining 25 years of his life as an itinerant minister, preaching and organizing Anabaptist churches in the Netherlands and northern Germany. A vigorous opponent of the Münster variety of Anabaptism, Simons arrived at the right moment to rescue the remnants of the movement.

These MENNONITES, as the followers of Menno Simons were called, preserved the finest ideas of Anabaptism as a whole.

As early as 1562, a collection of Anabaptist experiences was published in the Netherlands. This publication was expanded later by a Mennonite pastor in Amsterdam, Hans de Ries. His work became the basis of the tremendous compilation by T. J. van Braght, known in its English translation as the *Martyrs' Mirror*. He was more than a compiler, however, for he set forth the interpretation that the true Christian church has always been the church of the martyrs. This conviction has continued to be a part of the faith of the Mennonites.

A prominent Mennonite scholar of the 20th century, Harold S. Bender, has summarized the Anabaptist vision and contribution in three points: "(1) a new conception of Christianity as discipleship; (2) a new conception of the church as a brotherhood; and (3) a new ethic of love and non-resistance."

Another insight into the origins and foundations of Anabaptist ideas has been provided by Kenneth Scott Latourette: (1) The Anabaptists accepted the New Testament as their authority, and consequently they discarded all of the practices of the Catholic Church for which they could not find express commandments in the New Testament. (2) They were consciously attempting to return to the primitive Christianity of the first century. (3) They believed in a church made up only of believers rather than all of the members of the community as the state churches maintained. All such believers must have received adult baptism. (4) They did not believe in salvation by works, but they did insist that if one's salvation were genuine it would result in works. (5) They attempted consciously to live up to the ethical demands of the Sermon on the Mount. They were honest, peaceable, temperate in eating and drinking, meek, and loving.

These Anabaptist ideas have continued to make an impact on Christianity. The Mennonites are perhaps the most directly related to the Anabaptists. In the 1970s they celebrated the 450th anniversary of the activities of the Swiss Brethren in Zurich, thus claiming a direct relationship to the events of the 1520s. Other closely related groups include the Amish, named for Jacob Ammann who in the latter part of the 17th century proposed to establish a stricter discipline than the Mennonites, and the Hutterites who took their ideas from Jacob Hutter, burned at the stake in 1536. Another group that was heavily indebted to Anabaptist ideas, although its direct origin was indebted to the Pietistic Movement, was the CHURCH OF THE BRETHREN or Dunkers, which began in Germany in 1708 when eight men and women were immersed in the River Eder. And finally, across the Channel in England, the Anabaptists contributed to the origin and development of the Independents, the Baptists, and the Quakers. Perhaps it was through these English groups that Anabaptism was to have its greatest impact on modern Christianity.

See also articles on BAPTIST DENOMINATION; PROTESTANT REFORMATION; RESTORATIONISM.

Bibliography. Harold S. Bender, *The Anabaptist Vision*; William Roscoe Estep, *The Anabaptist Story*; Guy Franklin Hershberger, *The Recovery of the Anabaptist Vision*; Kenneth Scott Latourette, *A History of Christianity*; Franklin Hamlin Littell, *The Anabaptist View of the Church*; Ernest A. Payne, "The Anabaptists," in *The New Cambridge Modern History*, vol. 2; *The Reformation*, ed. G. R. Elton; James M. Stayer, *Anabaptists and the Sword*; John Christian Wenger, *Even unto Death: the Heroic Witness of the 16th Century Anabaptists*; George Huntston Williams, *The Radical Reformation*.

ROGER E. SAPPINGTON
BRIDGEWATER COLLEGE

ANCIENT ORDER: *See* RESTORATIONISM.

ANDREW, JAMES OSGOOD (1794-1871), controversial leader of antebellum Methodism, was born in Wilkes County GA, and was educated at home and in rural schools. He joined the South Carolina Conference of the Methodist Episcopal Church in 1812. So effective was his ministry in the Carolinas and Georgia that in 1832 the denomination's General Conference elected him bishop.

Andrew's marriages profoundly affected his career and his denomination. His first wife, Ann McFarlane, left him a slave; a trust bequeathed him another; and his second wife, Leonora Greenwood, was a slaveholder. Andrew legally repudiated any claim to his second wife's slaves, but Georgia law and other circumstances would not permit him to free his own. At the 1844 General Conference, antislavery sentiment among Northern delegates was so strong that they passed a resolution calling on Andrew to suspend his work until he ended his connections with slavery. He offered to resign, but Southern delegates, convinced that such action would hurt Southern Methodism spiritually and socially, would not let him. Disagreements between Southern and Northern delegates over slavery and polity led to the adoption of a Plan of Separation that blueprinted the schism Andrew dreaded.

In keeping with the plan, representatives of Southern conferences organized in 1845 the METHODIST EPISCOPAL CHURCH, SOUTH. At the new body's first General Conference in 1846, Andrew became one of its first bishops. He remained an active bishop until his retirement in 1866. His most important published works were *Family Government* (1847), and *Miscellanies* (1855).

See also articles on METHODIST CHURCH; SLAVERY.

Bibliography. George G. Smith, *Life and Letters of James Osgood Andrew.*

DANIEL LEE CLOYD
AUBURN UNIVERSITY

ANGLICAN CHURCH IN THE SOUTH.

The Church of England was established throughout the colonial South, although it enjoyed varying degrees of popular support. Southern Anglicanism evolved in Virginia in the 17th century and spread to Maryland after the Glorious Revolution. In 1704 Anglicans in South Carolina attempted to establish their religion and prevent dissenters from serving the assembly; when these measures were vetoed in England, they created a permanent state church in 1706 and administered it in a tolerant manner. North Carolina passed a series of laws in the 18th century that gave official status to the Church of England, but Quakers and Presbyterians in the colony limited its effectiveness. Fledgling Georgia also established the Church of England in 1758.

Lay control was a distinguishing characteristic of the Southern establishments. The bishop of London exercised an undefined jurisdiction over the colonies and often sent a COMMISSARY to represent his authority, but episcopal authority was weakened by the absence of a resident bishop. Acting through legislative assemblies and parish vestries, the Anglican gentry controlled their church. Virginia vestries hired parish clergymen and until the middle of the 18th century kept them on one-year contracts in order to insure good behavior. South Carolina followed Virginia's lead as did the functioning parishes of North Carolina and Georgia. Only in Maryland, where the charter gave clerical patronage to the proprietor, were Southern laymen denied a substantial amount of control over their minister.

The Anglican vestries that administered the Church of England were also important institutions of local government. Their duties varied from colony to colony and included the inspection of tobacco, the payment of bounties on wild animals, and the supervision of elections. The most widespread of these secular functions was the administration of poor relief, which involved assessing parish taxes and distributing aid among the needy. A member of the Anglican gentry who served on his parish vestry strengthened his local reputation and gained political experience at the same time he served his church. Parishioners elected vestrymen except in Virginia where vacancies were filled by co-option.

Southern Anglican clergymen have an undeserved reputation for immorality;

most of them were competent and virtuous men and some were exceptional in one respect or another. About one in 10 succumbed to alcoholism or some other moral lapse. A large number, almost all in the early years, came from England, Scotland, or the continent and were attracted by the generous salaries in the colonies. Those who survived the passage found large parishes, primitive physical conditions, hostile dissenters, and diseases to which they were particularly susceptible. Despite these hardships, they made Anglicanism the dominant cultural as well as religious force in the 18th-century South.

The teachings of the Anglican clergy were social and educational as well as religious. Through catechisms and sermons, they spread the doctrines of Christianity as they were understood by the Church of England, a basic tenet that salvation was available to those who believed in Christ and demonstrated their faith through good works. Good works meant participation in the sacraments, the practice of benevolence toward the less fortunate, and obedience to higher authority. The Anglican reverence for authority was social as well as political; social hierarchy was an institution only slightly less real than church or state. Anglican clergymen treated the colonial gentry with respect and deference. Anglican ministers were always educated men and many of them operated schools in which Southern children learned reading and writing, mathematics, and sometimes classical languages.

By nature, ANGLICANISM was a national religion, one that identified with the interests of the society that it served. In the South, Anglican clergymen gradually shifted their allegiance from the mother country to the colony that employed them. Because the colonial laity were the chief source of political and financial support for the state churches, Anglican clergymen associated with them and promoted their interest. Southern

Anglican clergymen were conservative, but that did not mean they supported imperial authority. The established authority they supported in the South was the colonial gentry and the political institutions through which it exercised its will. The movement for an American bishop that was opposed by Southern laymen had few supporters among the Southern clergy. A remarkably small number of Southern Anglican clergymen remained loyal to the mother country in 1776.

The American Revolution brought the fall of Southern Anglicanism, but it had been declining for a quarter of a century. The GREAT AWAKENING created an evangelical alternative that strengthened the Presbyterian and Baptist churches at the expense of the Church of England. Methodism provided another alternative to Anglicanism. More important was the growth of the Southern backcountry, settled after 1750 by Scots-Irish Presbyterians, Baptists from the North, and immigrants from Germany. In South Carolina the Church of England remained strong until 1776, but the backcountry by that date contained well over half the white population of the colony. The Anglican laity of Virginia quarreled with their clergymen, both groups motivated by the rising strength of dissent. In Maryland, Anglicans attacked their own establishment because of the heavy-handed and insensitive way in which it was controlled by the Calvert family. Weakened as they were, the establishments might have continued had not Southern Anglicans come to believe that political and military success required a gesture of unity with the dissenters. Many would have preferred the establishment of Christianity rather than no state support for religion, but the numerical strength of dissent and the ideology of the American Revolution led to disestablishment and denominationalism.

The influence of Southern Anglicanism lasted after the American Revolution. The theology and liturgy of the Church of

England were preserved in the Protestant Episcopal Church, whose active laity and elected bishops also testified to the influence of colonial Anglicanism. The social values of the Church of England helped to create a Southern ethic that valued class distinctions and promoted responsible behavior on the part of elites.

See also articles on COLONIAL PERIOD; DISSENTERS; ESTABLISHED RELIGION; FRONTIER, INFLUENCE OF.

Bibliography. S. Charles Bolton, *Southern Anglicanism: The Church of England in Colonial South Carolina*; George MacLaren Brydon, *Virginia's Mother Church and the Political Conditions Under Which It Grew*; John Calam, *Parsons and Pedagogues: The S. P. G. Adventure in American Education*; Joan R. Gundersen, "The Myth of the Independent Virginia Vestry," *Historical Magazine of the Protestant Episcopal Church*, 44 (1975): 133-41; "The Search for Good Men: Recruiting Ministers in Colonial Virginia," *HMPEC* 48 (1979): 453-64; Gerald E. Hartdagen, "The Anglican Vestry in Colonial Maryland: A Study in Corporate Responsibility," *HMPEC* 40 (1971): 315-35; Frederick V. Mills, Sr., *Bishops by Ballot, An Eighteenth Century Ecclesiastical Revolution*; David C. Skaggs and Gerald E. Hartdagen, "Sinners and Saints: Anglican Clerical Conduct in Colonial Maryland," *HMPEC* 48 (1978): 177-95; Alan D. Watson, "The Anglican Parish in Royal North Carolina, 1729-1775," *HMPEC* 48 (1979): 303-19.

S. CHARLES BOLTON
UNIVERSITY OF ARKANSAS
AT LITTLE ROCK

ANGLICANISM. This is the religious system of the worldwide group of autonomous national bodies representing various manifestations of the Church of England, including the EPISCOPAL CHURCH in the U. S. While jurisdictionally independent, these bodies are united by a common moral acknowledgment of the leadership of the Archbishop of Canterbury, and by association in the Lambeth Conference, the Anglican Consultative Council, and the Primates' Conference.

The Church of England may be said to have come into existence at the time of the Reformation when the church in England declared that the pope had no more authority in England than any other foreign bishop. Most Anglicans would deny that a new church came into being at that time; they would insist that the same laity continued to gather in the same church buildings for essentially the same liturgy under leadership of the same clergy. The main immediate change effected by the breach was the denial of papal jurisdiction in England.

It is customary to speak of extremes in 16th-century developments; to wit, of the work of Anabaptists and those like them as the radical Reformation and of what occurred in churches remaining loyal to the see of Rome as the Catholic or Counter-Reformation. By analogy the continental movements initiated by Luther, Calvin, and others could be called the classic reformation and what occurred in England referred to as the moderate Reformation. The English Reformation is to be distinguished from the others by its not having been shaped by the overarching vision of a single founder or group of leaders. Instead it developed through the interaction of a number of kinds of people: monarchs, statesmen, bishops, theologians, and others. At the beginning there was never any sustained sense of the direction in which the Reformation ought to go. Henry VIII (reigned 1509-1547) was essentially a religious conservative whose major interest in change was to eliminate any foreign restrictions on his sovereignty and to procure badly needed money to finance his reign through the dissolution of monasteries. He left his son, Edward VI, who was only nine at the time of his accession, under the tutelage and protection of leaders who wished to move England in the direction of the continental Reformers. However, when Edward was succeeded by "Bloody Mary" in 1553, England found itself once again under papal jurisdiction. At the end of her equally short reign, the Church of England settled down under Elizabeth I (reigned 1558-1603) into that *via media* between Roman Catholicism and continental Protestantism that has characterized its life ever since.

The popular media often give the impression that the Church of England was founded to enable a lust-crazed monarch to gain the divorce necessary to allow him to satisfy his carnal desires. This account is misleading in a number of ways. First, as noted above, it is debatable that a new church was founded. Secondly, while no one would deny Henry VIII's interest in sex, it is anachronistic to imagine that he was motivated by a passion of that sort. His sexual morals were probably no better or worse than those of most royal people of the time—or, for that matter, high ecclesiastics—but kings had mistresses to soothe such itches.

What was important for Henry was a male heir, since England at that time had had no good experience with reigning queens. His marriage to Catherine of Aragon had required a papal dispensation because she was the widow of his brother, Arthur, and Lev. 20:20 says: "If a man takes his brother's wife, it is impurity; he has uncovered his brother's nakedness, they shall be childless." After Catherine had only one child that survived infancy and that one a sickly girl, it is not surprising that the question arose whether the pope had the power to dispense with the obligation of obeying the explicit word of the Bible. The annulment of Henry's marriage would probably have been granted readily had the pope not been a virtual prisoner at the time of Charles V, the Holy Roman Emperor, who was Catherine's nephew. After all, Clement VII himself could never have become pope had not a special commission been called to discover that, all the evidence to the contrary, his father had actually married his mother. Probably more important to Henry than any woman was his unwillingness to have his sovereignty curtailed by foreign authority. This attitude won him support because England was one of the few unified nations of that time and certainly one that took pride in its independence.

It is easy to gain the erroneous impression that the English Reformation was almost exclusively the accomplishment of monarchs. There were, however, many other contributing factors and persons. These included vestiges of the Lollardism started by John Wyclif in the 14th century and Lutheran influences that had come into England as a result of trade with the continent. Renaissance humanists, whether foreigners like Erasmus or Englishmen such as John Colet and John Fisher, played their part in preparing the way. During the reign of Edward VI continental reformers such as Peter Martyr and Martin Bucer came to England as refugees. The succeeding reign of Elizabeth saw the return of many English clergy who had sought refuge at Geneva and other centers of the Reformation during the time that Mary was on the throne. Statesmen had their part to play: Thomas Cromwell under Henry, the Duke of Somerset with conviction and the Duke of Northumberland for expediency during the time of Edward, while Elizabeth had her William Cecil, Lord Burghley. None shaped the English Reformation more than the Archbishop of Canterbury, Thomas Cranmer, whom Henry had appointed. He was the editor and principal author of the first two editions of *The Book of Common Prayer* that appeared in 1549 and 1552.

The theological and religious system that emerged at the end of this process is known as the Elizabethan Settlement. Some of its main features can be discerned in the Acts of Supremacy and Uniformity, which were passed in the early months of her reign. The first of these gave her the title of "Supreme Governor" of the church, reflecting the influence of Marsiglio of Padua, the conciliarist theologian of the 14th century whose doctrine that worldly power and jurisdiction belong to the secular state rather than the church had certainly influenced Henry VIII. The authority that she claimed, of course, was administrative, not spiritual or sacramental. The changes the Act of Uniformity made in the Prayer Book of 1552 were slight but significant: a rubric was removed that said that kneeling before the sacrament does not imply worship; the words of administration for Holy Communion were altered to permit belief in the real presence; a prayer against the pope was deleted from the Litany; and the medieval vestments were permitted.

The Settlement is reflected in the *Book of Common Prayer*, the 39 Articles, the Ordinal, and the Catechism. It was given its most complete theological statement in Richard Hooker's *Laws of Ecclesiastical Polity*. The ultimate authority of the Scriptures for all doctrine was recognized, but the rightful role of tradition and reason in theology was admitted. Bible reading by the laity was encouraged. While the liturgy was to be in the language of the people, its form was provided by the Prayer Book and conducted by vested clergy. Much more regular communion was encouraged and the laity were to receive both the bread and the wine. The threefold ministry of bishops, priests, and deacons in the apostolic succession was retained. While baptism and the Eucharist were recognized as sacraments in the full sense of the word, confirmation, ordination, and holy matrimony were provided for. The church calendar was still observed, although feasts of post-biblical saints were eliminated. A number of medieval beliefs and practices were jettisoned, such as transubstantiation, purgatory, indulgences, etc. Much of the medieval organization and canon law, however, were retained.

The doctrine of justification by faith was taught and there was even a moderate statement of the reformers' doctrine of election. Much greater freedom was recognized not only for national churches but for individual laity as well, as laity were even given some authority in church government. This was the religious and theological system of the body that regarded itself as the historic Catholic church, purged of medieval errors and accretions, that was the lawful, national Church of England.

The basic shape of Anglicanism is visible in the Elizabethan Settlement, although important influences on the present-day communion were still to emerge. The Marian exiles in Geneva, for instance, were by no means satisfied with so unreformed a religious system. The Puritans and Separatists, as these groups came to be called, were further infuriated by William Laud, archbishop of Canterbury under Charles I, who strove to impose conformity on a very catholic interpretation of Anglicanism. The anger inspired by Laud was one of the major factors that led to the Civil War in which Charles I was executed and the monarchy was succeeded by a Commonwealth under the protectorate of Oliver Cromwell (d. 1658). The restoration of Charles II to the throne in 1642, however, brought with it restoration of the episcopate and the Prayer Book. Unfortunately, it also brought about the secession of the Presbyterians and Congregationalists from the Church of England and the permanent division of Christian England into conformists (Anglicans), nonconformists (others), and recusants (Roman Catholics).

Other forces were at work in the 17th century that were to have their own powerful effect on the English church. These forces include the scientific work of Isaac Newton and the philosophical activities of René Descartes, Baruch Spinoza, John Locke, and others. They produced the characteristic spirit of the 18th century, that celebration of the powers of human reason unaided by revelation known as the Enlightenment. Anticipated somewhat in the work of the Cambridge Platonists, the Enlightenment had some of its earliest manifestations in the rise of Deism in England. Defenses of Christian orthodoxy from the period, such as Joseph Butler's *Analogy of Religion* (1736) and the works of William Paley, rely heavily on arguments from fulfillment of prophecy and the existence of miracles, but themselves show the confidence in the powers of human reason characteristic of the age. Attitudes were thus being formed that would emerge fully in the controversies between religion and science in the 19th century.

During the 18th century there were intellectual currents in addition to those of the Enlightenment. Religiously, the most notable was the rise of the Evangelical movement. On the eve of the industrial revolution, at a time when the poor suffered greatly and were little cared for by the church, influences of the Pietist movement from the continent began to be felt in Great Britain. Though not the first Evangelicals, certainly the most influential ones were the founders of Methodism, John and Charles Wesley, and George Whitefield. They began preaching to coal miners in the open fields around Bristol in 1739. Their message of conversion and assurance found a great welcome. Although all three were ordained Anglican priests, their "enthusiasm" found little favor among the staid establishment of the time and they were forced to practice much of their ministry outside church buildings. Soon, though, there were many within the established church who began to preach a very similar faith within the parochial structure. Men like Henry Venn, John Newton, and Charles Simeon made the Evangelical movement the most influential group in the Church of England, a group that not only sponsored evangelism and foreign missions, but also led the way in such social reforms as factory laws and the abolition of slavery.

If the Evangelical party were to become a permanent force within Anglicanism and emphasize its heritage from the Reformation, the Oxford Movement was to occupy a similar position in reawakening the Church of England to its Catholic heritage. Beginning at the University of Oxford among a group of scholars such as John Keble, Edward Pusey, and John Henry Newman in the 1830s, this movement issued *Tracts for the Times* to advocate apostolic succession,

baptismal regeneration, Christ's real presence in the Eucharist, private confession, and other doctrines and practices that had previously been identified by many with Roman Catholicism. A number of practices that are taken for granted throughout the Anglican Communion today were restored or introduced by these early Anglo-Catholics.

As important as either of these movements was the effort made by Anglicans to come to grips with the larger universe that science was rapidly revealing. An early bout with this struggle was the debate of Bishop Wilberforce with Thomas Huxley over evolution in 1860. The acceptance of the historical-critical method of biblical interpretation was a fruit of this coming to terms with science. Liberal and Modernist parties developed within the church.

Anglicanism today continues as the *via media* of the Elizabethan and Restoration Settlements as it has been conditioned by the evangelical, catholic, and liberal movements that have grown up in the church since the 16th and 17th centuries.

See also articles on ANGLICAN CHURCH IN THE SOUTH; PROTESTANT REFORMATION; PURITANISM; ROMAN CATHOLICISM.

Bibliography: Robert Bosher, *The Making of the Restoration Settlement*; Owen Chadwick, *The Mind of the Oxford Movement*; Church of England, Book of Common Prayer 1662; A. G. Dickens, *The English Reformation*; The Doctrine Commission of the Church of England, *Believing in the Church*; O. C. Edwards, Jr., "The Word of God in Anglican (As Opposed to Lutheran) Theology," *Dialog* 13 (Summer 1974): 217; Marion J. Hatchett, *Commentary on the American Prayer Book*; William P. Haugaard, *Elizabeth and the English Reformation*; Urban T. Holmes, III, *What Is Anglicanism?*; Richard Hooker, *The Laws of Ecclesiastical Polity*; William E. Leidt, *Anglican Mosaic*; J. R. H. Moorman, *A History of the Church of England*; Paul Elmer More and Frank Leslie Gross, *Anglicanism*; Stephen Neill, *Anglicanism*; Protestant Episcopal Church, Book of Common Prayer (1979); Arthur Michael Ramsey, *The Gospel and the Catholic Church*; Stephen W. Sykes, *The Integrity of Anglicanism*; William J. Wolf, John E. Booty, and Owen C. Thomas, *The Spirit of Anglicanism*.

O. C. EDWARDS, JR.
SEABURY-WESTERN SEMINARY

ANTI-CATHOLICISM: *See* NATIVISM.

ANTILIQUOR FORCES: *See* PROHIBITION.

ANTIMISSION MOVEMENT. Antimissionism was a phenomenon among white Baptist churches in the South in the 1830s that represented resistance to social and religious innovations thought to be diluting the primitive Baptist traditions. A recent interpreter of the antimission ideology has found it rooted in areas relatively far from the increasing flow of trade and its attendant demands for cash exchanges, areas characterized by isolation from the market in sparsely settled regions throughout the South, from the Delmarva peninsula to the Ozarks. Antimissionists called themselves Old School, Predestinarian, Antimissionary, PARTICULAR, or PRIMITIVE BAPTISTS to emphasize the purity of their belief and practice when contrasted with ecclesiastical innovations of the 1820s. Their enemies thought them bigoted, ignorant, parochial, alarmist, sectarian "backwoods folks" who stood in the way of progress.

As the name suggests, Antimissionism had something to do with spreading the evangelical Christian gospel; but the issue was far more complicated than a positive or negative vote on whether or not to have missionary societies. It involved the explosion and proliferation of voluntary religious societies and the organization of Baptist state conventions in the 1820s and 1830s. During that time, young, energetic, and aggressive itinerants descended upon local churches throughout the United States to recruit members and gather donations for Bible societies, Sunday schools, female seminaries, colleges, manual labor schools, missionary societies, foreign missions, and temperance. At the same time, Baptists were whipping their state conventions into shape, creating organizations that extended the idea of Baptist cooperation beyond the local church and the more

inclusive associations into statewide networks. Primitive Baptists refused to cooperate in building these new structures that seemed to ignore the perfectly sound Baptist conviction that the Church of Christ was the local church.

Although convention Baptists, itinerant agents, and historians have left the impression that antimissionary Baptists had seceded from "fellowship with Southern Baptists," the former had really refused merely to join. The relative isolation of "primitives," from areas penetrated by agriculture linked to market exchanges suggests that ecclesiastical agencies may have been the first extralocal presence to enter the neighborhoods of the "primitives" thus accentuating their foreignness. Dunning by itinerants in order to donate scarce cash to groups beyond the locality, to address problems also alien to the neighborhood, led antimissionary partisans to label those brash young men "howling destructive wolves, the ravenous dogs, and the filthy, and their numerous whelps." In accepting the hospitality of relatively wealthy farmers, the itinerants also received a reputation for class consciousness not belied by their criticism of "ignorant" people living in "a state of moral degradation," xenophobia, and zealous commitment to the product of their ubiquitous stills. The mutual rancor of the two sides encouraged each to think the worst of the other.

The extent to which this extended controversy can be explained by the dichotomy of rural subsistence and isolation *versus* commercial farming and a relative cosmopolitan orientation is limited. Many people offended by the train of agents for benevolent societies simply refused to give money and made no issue of the matter. The "primitives," then, were people whose principles had been offended by the transformation of religious life from the bonding of the local community to a general, diffuse sense of obligations beyond the locality. Moreover, these were to be met by contributions and listening to romantic lectures on the good that would be done out there in the world beyond the horizon. There was something other than suspicion of Yankees identified with most agencies, or discomfort at an expanding market. A dissatisfaction with changes in the ideal of the church as the core of community experience ran deep in their theology. The itinerants were ministers without churches—perhaps "professionals" answering to each other and nonchurch religious agencies rather than God and His congregation. In response to changes they could not approve, they formulated their understanding of the gospel in familial, rigid terms, lapsing into a "Hyper-Calvinism," as their enemies phrased it. They repudiated all agency not substantiated by the Bible; relaxation of the predestination of their spiritual forebears; belief in human measures to achieve divine ends; and a ministry cut loose from local moorings.

Although doctrinal differences seemed to develop after divisions over the sufficiency of local churches to do the work of the Lord, a rigid Calvinist theology that nourished relative isolation from the ecumenical Evangelicalism of most Southern Protestants came to characterize antimissionists. By 1890, their relative strength in the South could be judged by their 45,000 communicants as opposed to 1.1 million people identified with convention Baptists. The "primitives" of the late twentieth century still nourish their rich tradition in both black and white churches, still express themselves in the dignity and strength of a fervent Calvinism.

Bibliography. Robert Baker, ed., *A Baptist Source Book with Particular Reference to Southern Baptists*; Keith R. Burich, "The Primitive Baptist Schism in North Carolina: A Study of the Professionalism of the Baptist Ministry," unpublished M.A. thesis, University of North Carolina, 1973; Walter B. Posey, *The Baptist Church in the Lower Mississippi Valley, 1776-1845*; Bertram Wyatt-Brown, "The Antimission Movement in the Jacksonian South: A Study in Regional Folk Culture," *Journal of Southern History* 36 (November 1970): 501-29.

DONALD G. MATHEWS
UNIVERSITY OF NORTH CAROLINA
AT CHAPEL HILL

ANTI-SALOON LEAGUE: *See* PROHIBITION.

ANTI-SEMITISM: *See* JEWS IN THE SOUTH; NATIVISM.

APPALACHIAN RELIGION. The area of the Southern highlands known as Appalachia has a diverse array of religious denominations, as well as many locally autonomous congregations. In the larger cities and towns one may find Catholic churches, mainline Protestant groups, and even Jewish synagogues. In the rural valleys and hollows one also can find the same kinds of Baptist, Methodist, Presbyterian, or even Episcopal and Lutheran churches that are found throughout the land. Also along with these are churches that would be rare elsewhere, such as PRIMITIVE BAPTISTS, Old REGULAR BAPTISTS, or United Baptists, various Holiness and Pentecostal groups, and many that have no organization beyond the individual congregations.

Appalachian people have clung to their religious ideas as they have to other traditional beliefs. This fervency has long been noted by other Christians in the country, some of whom have been troubled by mountain religion, to the extent that mainline denominations have sent great numbers of missionaries to the region, especially during the period between the Civil War and World War II. They came to preach and build churches, to establish clinics and hospitals, to build schools and provide other social services. Many mountain people joined the mission churches. Others went on worshiping as their forebears had, even though many had enjoyed the benefits of mission school education and health care.

Divisions among Appalachian Christians and between Appalachian and other American Christians date from colonial times. In the Southern colonies, but more particularly in Virginia, the Anglicans who held power persecuted other Christians and abridged their freedoms. Baptists especially were scorned. Some

Baptist groups moved as whole congregations into the mountains to gain more freedom to worship. Among these were Baptists with strong Calvinist beliefs.

The disagreements between the Calvinists and the free-will, or Arminian, groups date back to the early settlements. The Methodists brought the first ideas about human perfectibility and universal atonement. Calvinist beliefs regarding the human condition offered bleak hope in regard to improvements here on earth or sanctity in heaven. Many, therefore, eagerly listened to the Methodist gospel offering the possibility of everyone's having a chance at salvation, as well as the hope of individual and thus institutional improvement. But a great battle was shaping over the old and the new doctrines that mainly came after the GREAT REVIVAL, which started in Kentucky in 1800. Many Presbyterian and Baptist churches joined the Methodists in the revivals, thus setting themselves against their Calvinistic brothers and sisters.

Many Baptists regretted the split, and in North Carolina, Virginia, and Kentucky, they attempted to unite under the name of United Baptists. Some predestinarian Baptists scorned the revivals and the later attempts at reconciliation, seeing no sense in proselytizing those who may be predestined to be lost anyway. They were adamantly against reuniting with those who held beliefs different from their own. The two factions continued their debate over such matters as predestination, mission efforts, Sunday schools, and education for the ministry. The Old School or Primitive Baptist groups, which grew out of these debates and resultant splits, maintained that God knew his purposes and would bring into his fold all those whom he wanted; that the Bible itself is sufficient for all religious instruction and thus there is no need for Sunday school or mission tracts; that God calls preachers and imparts spiritual knowledge, and thus Sunday schools and seminaries are suspect, since they try to promote knowledge through the natural mind. The free-will side of the argument believed in the efficacy of revival preaching, of Sunday schools, missionary effort, and theological schools. There was no bringing them together, and the split was irrevocable by 1840. The Primitive Baptists represent the most radical Calvinistic stance. The United Baptists tended to move back toward Calvinism after the excitement of the Great Revival, although some joined with the Separatist strain and moved into the American Baptist and Southern Baptist conventions. Some became Regular Baptists who are now found primarily in the Appalachian region. They represent a position halfway between the Primitive and FREE-WILL BAPTISTS. They hold to some Calvinist tenets, but maintain that God never ordained that anyone would be lost and that only those who do not heed the Word of God will be lost. The services, the singing, and the sacraments are similar among the Primitive, United, and Old Regular Baptist churches. They preach in the old chanting style, by inspiration rather than prepared notes. The singing is done in the "lining" style approved by the Westminster Assembly of 1644, whereby the leader starts a hymn, then chants each line before the congregation sings it in unison. Musical accompaniment is not allowed. The sacramental service, held once a year, has the Lord's Supper, followed by the washing of feet. Only those in good standing in the church or association may participate. Church services are held only once a month, and the preachers are not paid.

There are many free-will or missionary Baptist churches in Appalachia. Most are affiliated with state conventions and the Southern Baptist Convention. A number, however, are locally autonomous. Some of the free-will churches are similar to the previously mentioned Calvinistic churches in terms of preaching style and the FOOT WASHING service. However, their music is more of the gospel variety with piano or organ accompaniment. The Southern Baptist denomination is probably the strongest among all others in the region, except in West Virginia, which is predominantly Methodist.

The 19th century gave rise to new denominations that are important in the region. The Presbyterian church was divided over some of the same issues that divided the Baptists. The "New Light" wing moved toward Arminianism. The Cumberland Presbyterian Church was formed in 1810 partially over an argument regarding the ordination of converted but uneducated ministers. In part it was a split between well-to-do Presbyterians and rural Tennessee farmers. When they were censured by the presbytery, they formed their own church. The Civil War also brought a split between Northern and Southern Presbyterians.

The Christian Church, or Restorationist Movement, grew out of the "New Light" Presbyterian movement. It was led primarily by BARTON STONE and Thomas and ALEXANDER CAMPBELL. They were bent on reforming the church and bringing it to a simple, primitive Christianity and to unity, peace, and purity. But they differed in theology from most Presbyterians and other Christians. They rejected infant baptism, but placed much greater emphasis on baptism after conversion, rejected the idea of God in three persons, and questioned the idea of substitutionary atonement. Alexander Campbell and other preachers led a new wave of evangelism on the frontiers of Kentucky, Virginia, and Tennessee which aroused antagonism among mainline Presbyterians as well as other groups. The Disciples of Christ Church was formed in 1832. Some followers of Stone and Campbell broke away from the Disciples over such issues as central government, mission programs, and musical instruments in the church and formed the Church of Christ. In this century, other Disciples churches have broken away to form independent Christian churches.

Slavery and the Civil War brought about other splits in Appalachian churches, as they did elsewhere. The Methodist, Baptist, and Presbyterian denominations all had strong antislavery factions. However, many churchmen grew wealthy, bought slaves, and became supporters of slavery. There was a strong abolitionist movement in the mountains, mainly centered at Berea KY where John G. Fee had established a church and school, and in east Tennessee where the first emancipation newspaper, *The Manumission Intelligencer*, was published by Elihu Embree at Jonesboro beginning in 1819. Many churchmen were strong supporters of the emancipation movement. Eventually, all of the principal churches split over the question of slavery. Perhaps half of the Appalachians who served in the Civil War fought on the side of the Union, and after the war, some Appalachian churchmen went against the prevailing Jim Crow tenor of the times and supported the rights of black people. Baptists of northwestern North Carolina and east Tennessee formed the body of UNION BAPTISTS to designate its members as being in sympathy with the Union cause and later the Union League, a group formed to counter the work of the KU KLUX KLAN and others who sought to deprive blacks of their rights. While most blacks in the mountains formed counterpart black churches, a few churches, notably some Old Regular Baptists, had integrated congregations or associations.

PENTECOSTALISM and the HOLINESS MOVEMENT had their beginnings in the Appalachian region, with the work of the Rev. Richard G. Spurling in Monroe County TN in 1886. He thought that the churches had become enmeshed in creeds, rituals, legalisms, and philosophy to the extent that the Bible had been displaced. He wanted to go back to Wesley's idea of holiness. With a few converts, Spurlin formed the Christian Union, which was later to become the CHURCH OF GOD. The movement spread into North Carolina where it linked with Baptists who were also concerned with the idea of perfection. A revival started on Camp Creek, Cherokee County NC, which attracted large numbers of people. The revival spread, and by 1926 some 25 Pentecostal churches were formed in the area. They were persecuted, especially in North Carolina where they were expelled from their schoolhouse meeting place; and when they built a church on donated land, it was twice destroyed. When more than a hundred persons were brought to trial in Murphy NC for tearing the church down in broad daylight, the Pentecostals pleaded for leniency. This won them some support. A new convert, an American Bible Society salesman, A. J. TOMLINSON, helped to evangelize western North Carolina, east Tennessee, and north Georgia. He moved the church headquarters to CLEVELAND TN, where its name was changed to the Church of God. Tomlinson, general overseer of the church, later fell into disagreement with his governing board, and the church split. In a legal battle over which faction was the true Church of God, the court ruled against Tomlinson and ordered that his new church be renamed. It is now the CHURCH OF GOD OF PROPHECY. The Church of God retains that name and both groups have their headquarters in Cleveland.

Other Holiness and Pentecostal churches have grown up in the region. One is the Church of God, Mountain Assembly, with headquarters in Jellico TN. The region has numerous locally autonomous churches that call themselves Holiness or Pentecostal. In addition, other well-known groups, such as the ASSEMBLY OF GOD and the CHURCH OF THE NAZARENE have local churches in Appalachia.

The earlier divisions among Christians were over CALVINISM versus ARMINIANISM. Modern misunderstandings are rooted in these older disagreements over the human condition. The conflict now is between the SOCIAL GOSPEL, a relatively recent development, and the ancient practices of preaching and worshiping. Mainline church mission workers have accused Appalachian Christians of not having a sense of community and a social conscience, of being almost solely concerned with personal salvation rather than with improving life through united effort. The Appalachian fundamentalists have countered by saying that their critics do social work rather than spiritual work. Some of the Appalachian churches have permitted only spiritual matters to be part of their church service, have deemphasized church buildings and budgets, and have discouraged any organization that did not relate directly to worship. However, as individuals and as members of nonchurch groups, many have been involved in important issues that affected them. Ollie Combs, an Old Regular Baptist, sat down in front of bulldozers trying to strip her land of coal, was carried off to jail, and later testified before the Kentucky legislature to bring about the "Widow Combs Bill," the first strong strip-mine regulation in that state. The Rev. Otis King, a Missionary Baptist preacher from Harlan County (KY), denounced absentee ownership and the rape of Kentucky's land, and lectured the Kentucky state police with equal fervor for perceived mistreatment of women on the picket lines during a bitter labor strike. A United Baptist preacher, Tom Sutton, was a leader of the Knott County (KY) Citizens for Social and Economic Justice, which fought an outside group seeking to take over the land of hundreds of people through questionable colonial charters.

There are fundamental differences between middle-class church people and the more fundamentalistic church people in the region as well as between mainline church-mission-oriented workers and many of the local church members. Appalachian people have been viewed as fundamentalistic, fatalistic, traditionalistic, and otherworldly. Many of the churches have indeed tended to stress tradition, fundamentals of the faith, rewards in heaven, and acceptance of God's will. However, these characteristics are not viewed as negative within their context, but rather as a source of strength. To a certain degree, the fundamentalistic churches are havens from, or strongholds against, a troubled world and an economic system that has often exploited mountain people.

No single description will suffice for all of the churches in Appalachia. They are varied and serve a varied people. Appalachia is not a homogeneous region, and neither are its churches.

See also articles on ANTIMISSION MOVEMENT; MUSIC, RELIGIOUS; OLD SCHOOL/NEW SCHOOL; RESTORATIONISM.

Bibliography. Robert A. Baker, *A Baptist Source Book, With Particular Reference to Southern Baptists*; Dickson D. Bruce, Jr., *And They All Sang Hallelujah*; Emory Stevens Bucke ed., *A History of American Methodism*; John C. Campbell, *The Southern Highlander and His Homeland*; Elmer T. Clark, *The Small Sects in America*; Charles W. Conn, *Like a Mighty Army Moves the Church of God*; David Edwin Harrell, Jr., *A Social History of the Disciples of Christ*; B. W. McDonnald, *History of the Cumberland Presbyterian Church*; E. A. Smith, *The Presbyterian Ministry in American Culture*; William Warren Sweet, *Methodism in American History*; *Religion on the American Frontier, The Baptists, 1783-1830*; Vinson Synan, *The Holiness-Pentecostal Movement in the United States*; U. S. Bureau of the Census, *Religious Bodies: 1936*.

LOYAL JONES
BEREA COLLEGE

ARCHITECTURE, CHURCH. Colonists brought with them a love for the homes they left behind and for the church buildings that they knew in their youth. Spanish priests settling on the Gulf coast and in Texas built chains of missions that reproduced as nearly as possible the monasteries in which they had been taught the faith. They had no cut stone, glazed tile, or stained glass. They built walls of adobe, spanned them with timber trusses, and made terra-cotta tile for floors and roofs. Spaniards took for granted the Roman separation of clergy in the chancel from laymen in the nave. When they could afford it, they built the cruciform plan, with transepts, and a dome over the crossing. This form came out of the Middle Ages; the decoration reflected Renaissance influences. The church sheltered a cloister from which opened the dormitory, refectory, and infirmary. Some mission buildings outside San Antonio are still in use today.

The English colonists who came to Jamestown in Virginia from 1607 brought with them the still-evolving results of the Protestant Reformation. They had learned from John Calvin that the church consists not of buildings, but of believing people gathered by the Holy Spirit about the Word and Sacraments. Clergymen were distinguished by training and function, not by status. They did not need the segregation of a chancel. The whole church was best accommodated in one worship room.

The oldest Protestant church still standing in the United States is St. Luke's, built in 1632 in Isle of Wight County VA. The church is a rectangular worship room. Walls are braced by heavy, brick buttresses. Round-headed windows are divided by mullions into pointed Gothic lancets. A tower forms an open vestibule below, and a belfry above. Builders who accepted the Reformation and knew something of the Renaissance had not yet let go of the Middle Ages.

In France the HUGUENOTS had faced the fact that the medieval cathedral, long, narrow, high, and echoing to the Roman Mass, was no form for the Protestant sermon. Because Protestants used the whole Bible in worship, not a lectionary, and were sure that everybody needed to understand it all, they sought for expository preaching. Everyone present must see and hear the preacher. Salomon de Brosse built the Temple of Charenton as a wide rectangle with two tiers of galleries carried around all four walls. To give the preacher eye contact with his people the pulpit was raised almost to the level of the first gallery. Charenton, built in 1623, stood until it was destroyed at the Revocation of the Edict of Nantes in 1685. During those 62 years it influenced Protestant church buildings all over Europe. In the Netherlands where war for independence from Spain had devastated church buildings, the Dutch rebuilt with many experiments. They brought their plain Protestant churches to New Amsterdam; Congregationalists brought the Plain Style to New England; Quakers to Pennsylvania; and Scots to the Shenandoah, the Carolinas, and Georgia.

The medieval Roman church had laid all stress on the Sacraments, scanting the preaching of the word. Protestant churches swung to the opposite extreme, stressing the sermon, but scanting the sacraments. Christopher Wren restored the balance. The Great Fire of London destroyed 93 Anglican church buildings in 1666. Wren rebuilt 53 of them, no two alike. Taking account of their odd-shaped sites, Wren based his plans on squares, rectangles, octagons, and in one case on a decagon. He used naves with one aisle, naves with two aisles, naves with galleries on three sides. Wren lavished this wealth of imagination to give each congregation its distinctive home. But all of his parish churches were alike in one respect. The focus of worship lay within the space occupied by the congregation. Wren employed Grinling Gibbons to carve the pulpit, table, and font. He gathered and balanced the symbols of the Word and Sacraments together. He flooded the space with light so that everyone could read his prayer book and hymnal. He made sure that lines of visibility were open, and acoustics were clear. By sheer esthetic force Wren restored to his Protestant churches the visual satisfaction that medieval churches had enjoyed.

James Gibbs learned from Wren the values of a broad, open, well-lit room for the congregation with the pulpit in the people's space. But Gibbs, a Roman Catholic, set the table apart as far as he could, in an alcove approaching an apse. His clients thought nothing of the compromise because they had not really accepted Wren's liturgical logic. Gibbs published his designs in his *Book of Architecture*, which sold widely in America. So many builders copied his designs for St. Martin's-in-the-Fields that it became the stereotype of "a church that looks like a church." To a voyager entering almost any port of the colonies it would be apparent that Gibbs's book had preceded him. In Providence the First Baptist Church adapted its building from Gibbs; so also in Boston, Newport, New Haven, New York, Philadelphia, and CHARLESTON. In the port cities wealth accumulated. Patrons could afford towers and steeples, clocks and bells, to tell the stranger where the church stood, what the time of day was, and when the service would begin.

Colonial churches in the country were much simpler. Southern colonists preferred life on their plantations to life in town. In tidewater Virginia and in the Carolina low country, owners built their churches for their convenience where roads converged, often with no hamlet or village nearby. No towers were needed, for no one lived within the sound of a bell. Clocks were not needed because worshipers gathered early and lingered late to enjoy the company of their relatives and friends.

In Virginia the tidewater church builders combined handmade brick, stone or wooden trim, slate or shingle roofs in buildings that were beautiful for their good proportions, honest expression of materials, superb craftsmanship, and human scale.

The Carolina low country also abounds in beautiful, small churches notable for their simplicity. Brick walls were often covered with stucco because their builders had come from Barbados, or because the earthquake of 1886 left the walls with scars to be repaired and concealed. If American churches must resurrect their colonial past, they should take pains not to overlook the precedent of these remarkably satisfying churches—something that is often done.

Colonists who fought for their political independence from England sought cultural independence also. THOMAS JEFFERSON knew that buildings can contribute values to life. He believed that ancient Rome had been a fountain of republican virtues. Among those virtues he counted Roman architecture. By drawing inspiration from Roman buildings, he hoped to strengthen the fragile new republic. Jefferson's originality counted for more than the classical detail he borrowed. He carefully applied a different Roman order to each of 10 pavilions at the University of Virginia. Perhaps not every student noticed. But his decision to set the professors' houses among the ranges of student rooms, all looking toward the rotunda of his library, created the academic village that he thought the university ought to be.

It was not his good Tuscan detail, but Jefferson's analysis of the style of life he wanted to lead that made Monticello so fascinating. When Jefferson took up the problem of designing a Presbyterian church, he produced an octagonal plan, entered on one side, with the pulpit set on the opposite wall, and the people gathered about the pastor in pews focused on the pulpit. His solution lay fallow for 150 years.

The young republic offered opportunity to European architects who could bring formal training to a field that had been filled by amateurs for lack of professional skills. Benjamin Latrobe came from England to Pennsylvania to claim an inheritance there. Latrobe knew how Robert Adam had lightened academic Georgian design. Latrobe had worked with Sir John Soane, who had conceived the imaginative spaces, simplified detail, and functional, natural lighting of the Bank of England. Latrobe also knew the measured drawings of Greek temples that James Stuart and Nicholas Revett had published. Jefferson saw Latrobe's potential and gave him opportunities in the new Federal city of Washington. Baltimore Cathedral, the first built in the new nation, shows Latrobe's ability to simplify with grace.

His walls are broad and simple. Arched doors and windows appear at selected points of accent. Ceilings are composed of segmental arches, pendentives, and coffered domes. Though his churches do not rise high, their interiors are broad, open, airy, and well lit. Latrobe gave character and dignity to the Federal style.

Robert Mills studied architecture at the College of Charleston in his native city, worked with James Hoban on the White House, with Jefferson on Monticello, and with Latrobe who taught him engineering as well as architectural design. From Hoban, Mills learned the classicism of the English Palladians. From Jefferson he learned the Roman revival tempered with French wit. From Latrobe he learned the simple grace of the Federal style, and the first examples of the Greek Revival. When the young Mills was commissioned by the Congregational Church in Charleston, he designed a Corinthian portico of six columns leading through a square narthex into a circular worship room 90 feet in diameter covered by a dome. A gallery ran around most of the interior.

In Richmond, Mills built the Monumental Church as a memorial to 71 people who had died in a theater fire. The portico, containing the actual monument, has such gravity that no tower was needed. Its columns were a design original to Mills. The worship room is an octagon. Robert Mills used ancient precedent, which he adapted freely, and invented where he thought appropriate. Mills defined his basic concerns for any building as three: the purpose it was to serve, the structure appropriate to that purpose, and the relation of the building to the site it was to occupy.

Not all Americans saw buildings in that light. A rage for Greek architecture swept across the country. The pattern books of Asher Benjamin and Minard Lafever showed carpenters how to build in wood what the Greeks had carved in marble. Though Greek Revival buildings are popularly called "Southern Colonial," they were never colonial; they were not even Southern. The style swept from Maine to Minnesota as freely as from Virginia to Louisiana. Churches approached through solemn Greek porticos were crammed into the rectangular box of the Greek temple cella. Windows the Greeks had never known had to be punched through the walls for light and ventilation. Therefore, ranks of columns along the side walls were sensibly omitted. On Edisto Island in South Carolina, a lovely Federal Presbyterian church was completed in 1832, featuring arched windows, and lighthearted ogee curves on the gable parapet and the cupola roof. Four years later a donor desiring "to beautify the church" added a Greek Doric portico to shelter the Roman arched doors. No one noticed the incongruity. It was the thing to do, and it was done well.

JEWS IN THE SOUTH could adapt architectural revivalism to their purposes as freely as Christians. BETH ELOHIM in Charleston was designed by C. L. Warner as a Greek Doric temple with a six-columned portico. Monumental windows in their Greek surrounds continue the scale and rhythm of the portico around the building, mastering a problem most architects never solved. The worship room is square. Segmental arches along the walls joined by pendentives carry a dome flattened as much as may be. The mahogany ark stands within Corinthian columns and entablature derived from the Choragic Monument to Lysicrates. The inventive details are superbly controlled to produce the dignity and integrity of masterly design.

Once architectural revivals were let loose by Jefferson and his generation, there were no restraints on what was to be revived. William Strickland, who had studied with Latrobe, was called to Nashville to design the Tennessee state capitol. While he was there, the First Presbyterian Church asked him to design its new building. Because the Egyptians had an interest

in life after death, and the Christian church teaches everlasting life, it seemed appropriate to the congregation to ask for an Egyptian temple. Strickland complied. Egyptian pylons, columns, and cornices made the building different from any Nashville had seen before. To the brightly painted walls of the worship room a muralist later added painted columns in receding perspective, as though the auditorium were a hypostyle hall. Architectural revivalism could take off into the realm of fantasy, a development remote from the responsibilities of the Christian faith.

Meanwhile Anglo-Catholics in England raised the question whether Christian churches could properly be housed in buildings derived from pagan prototypes. Earnestly hoping to build a bridge for unity back to the Church of Rome and supposing that Rome still lived in the Middle Ages, students and professors in Cambridge published a magazine, *The Ecclesiologist*, to propose medieval English church design because "Gothick is the only true Christian architecture." Romanticism was in the air they breathed. Augustus Welby Pugin practiced the architecture they proposed. The Lord's table was discarded. A stone altar was required, with relics if any could be found, to be set apart in a chancel as far removed from the people as possible. The pulpit stayed among the people perforce, but the baptismal font was carted back to the entry door as though entering the building could be equated with entering the Christian life. The Scots had made a careful distinction, "No place is sacred, but the Sacred does not appear apart from place." Ignoring that, the Ecclesiologists earnestly sought to sacralize the building: symbols proliferated; downspouts gushed through gargoyles; windows were crowded with saints; ceilings were stenciled with medieval script; floor tiles bore the symbols of the disciples; empty space between the gathered people and the remote altar had to be filled; robed choirs appeared as though monks had returned from exile; long vistas, rich colors, and dim religious light were thought to be essential to the faith. Wherever English was spoken, the Victorian Gothic Revival sprang up.

In Charleston, Edward Brickell White designed for the Huguenots a church embellished with details from Pugin's book, *The True Principals of Pointed or Christian Architecture*. Pugin had published in 1841; White built in 1844. His buttressed walls rose to battlements, pinnacles, and crockets; his pointed arches and vaulted ceiling made a stir in Charleston. Eight years later the Unitarians in Charleston commissioned Edward Jones and Francis Lee to renovate their classical building, keeping the square, brick walls of 1787, but adapting them "to a more pleasing structure." A Gothic tower rose at the entrance, and a chancel was extended at the rear. The architects borrowed from the Chapel of Henry VII at Westminster its fan-vaulted ceiling, though they built not of balanced stones, but of suspended lath and plaster. Unitarians in a democracy, who had no historical link with the Tudor kings of England, pleased their eyes at the expense of their reason.

Richard Upjohn began to design Trinity Church, New York, before, but completed it after, the Huguenot Church in Charleston. Trinity dominated lower Manhattan so effectively that all America came to know the building. Upjohn's office was beseiged by pleas demanding plans for small Gothic churches. In response, Upjohn published in 1852 *Upjohn's Rural Architecture*. He planned for the small town in which the local carpenter would be the builder. He designed the church of wood, its walls of board and batten, its roof of shingles. It was lit by lancet windows with splayed jambs. The altar stood in a chancel, a second room, distinguished from the nave by its lesser width and lower roof. A square tower set beside the nave contains the belfry, and carries a broach spire. Pitched roofs over

nave and chancel were supported by curved braces. If a carpenter could cut the curved window surrounds and the roof braces, he could manage the whole. Upjohn's skill shows through the clarity of conception, simplicity of construction, and good proportions. From Delafield WI to Jacksonville AL, Upjohn's small churches still serve well the purpose for which he designed them.

The Gothic craze swept the nation. Georgia built a Gothic state capitol in Milledgeville. Louisiana followed suit in Baton Rouge. Columbus MS saw classic porticos improved by Gothic tracery hung between Greek columns. James Monroe's tomb in Hollywood Cemetery, Richmond, was caged in a cast-iron Gothic screen rising to an ogee dome. The Brooklyn Bridge was swung from Gothic piers, structurally a functional design. And "The Auburn," an express locomotive of 1854, housed its engineer in a tasteful Gothic cab.

Strangely enough, no churches of that era derived from the Romanesque architecture out of which Gothic had sprung. Yet styles ran wild. Synagogues took on a Saracenic look. The First Presbyterian Church of Augusta GA, which Mills had designed in his best Federal style, was decked out with mullioned windows filled with diamond panes, and equipped with battlements to fend off attackers. A Gothic vaulted ceiling was hung within, all for show.

The Civil War halted church building in the South. Uncounted churches were defaced or destroyed. Reconstruction prolonged the halt. When the North began to build again after the war, the taste of the *nouveaux riches* brought in a swirl of succeeding styles that rose, held brief sway, to be followed by something even more surprising. Craftsmen who had bought architectural pattern books to study a single style and practice it for a lifetime were displaced by speculative builders who subscribed to the new architectural magazines whose editors sought to supply new ideas every month. High Victorian, Second Empire, the Stick Style, Queen Anne, the Shingle Style, and Chateauesque came and went. Perhaps the South should thank her poverty for what she was spared.

Out of this welter rose three men of genius in design. Henry Hobson Richardson, born and bred in New Orleans, sailed for France to study architecture at L'Ecole des Beaux Arts. The Civil War kept him there for five years. He traveled in the south of France, absorbing the power of Romanesque design. When he returned to America to open an office in Boston, Phillips Brooks saw his potential. Brooks, as rector of Trinity Church, led his congregation to build with excellence. He did not want the pretense of a cathedral. Brooks specified that the Lord's table was to be of wood. The people were to have direct access to it. The baptismal font was to stand beside the table in clear view of the congregation. Pulpit, table, font, and seats for communicants were the reason for the chancel's being. The choir would sing from a gallery over the entrance in the Protestant tradition. Richardson responded to Brooks's program with a wide, short nave enlarged by transepts and chancel also wide and short. Trinity Church became instantly famous for the power of Richardson's composition, the skill of his engineering, and the beauty of its decoration by John LaFarge, but not for the radical thinking that Phillips Brooks had invested in its chancel. That was considered a Low Church aberration. In the 20th century the congregation, which still reveres the memory of Phillips Brooks, cleared out each vestige of his thinking on faith and form. They employed Maginnis and Walsh to sacralize the chancel with marble and gold. Nevertheless, Trinity remains the most powerful preaching space of its generation. Southern-born, Richardson was never invited to build a church in his native region.

Louis Sullivan in Chicago advanced an idea that the sculptor, Horatio Greenough, had offered in his address to the first meeting of the American Institute of Architects: "Form follows function." Sullivan and his partner Adler mastered the form of the new skyscraper. Concrete foundations, steel columns, hollow tile to fireproof the steel, plate-glass windows as wide as the space between piers, and elevators for vertical transportation made a new opportunity that Sullivan captured and controlled. His rich decoration expressed the form and function, but never obscured it. Sullivan built two synagogues in Chicago, but was never invited to build a church in the South.

Frank Lloyd Wright learned from Sullivan the philosophy of architecture, which he made famous. Wright had a gift for perceiving the potential of a site, and so welding the building he designed to the ground it occupied that site and structure complemented each other. His ability to make each material express its nature keeps his buildings fresh and fascinating. And Wright was keen to analyze the lifestyle of his clients in order to design his building to enhance their lives. Wright built Unity Temple in Oak Park IL in 1906 with a balance between worship room and parish house, which we should still study today. The sanctuary dominates the group, but the church school responds so sturdily that each part of the congregation's program is offered to all who enter the courtyard as related and consistent activities. Florida Southern College in Lakeland gave Wright his only opportunity to design a religious structure in the South. Wright based his chapel on a hexagonal plan, with folded plates and skylit worship room to escape religious forms from the past, and to express aspiration toward the light.

The careers of Richardson, Sullivan, and Wright spanned a century. If Southern churches had asked for their services, they could have built original, functional, and beautiful buildings. They settled instead for men who borrowed ideas from the masters.

The 19th century saw the Sunday school spring up and flourish. What began as an afternoon class to teach illiterate children how to read the Bible soon became Christian education for all ages. In the South classes for adults meant that the church school had to meet before the worship hour. In the North school and church met at the same time. Parents saw in the school a convenient way to dispose of children during the worship service. A Methodist Sunday school superintendent in Akron OH grieved that this schedule deprived children of the experience of worship. He offered them worship by guiding them to plan and lead worship for their peers, using part of the church school hour. To save the time lost in moving from worship to learning and back again, he planned an assembly hall surrounded on three sides by two tiers of classrooms. Skylights lit the hall. Curtains closed off the cubicles. Worship was informal; no sacraments were involved. The "Akron Plan" was copied everywhere. No one asked whether children should worship without their parents, their pastor, or their choir. No one asked whether the assembly hall was a good space for worship. No one asked whether cubicles made good classrooms, nor why half the space stood empty all the time. The style of construction reflected the absence of these questions.

Revival meetings became popular at the same time. Towns were growing. Newly arrived families had no church home. Preachers and song leaders were brought in to attract sinners who ignored routine services and choirs dropped denominational divisions to sing together. Overflow crowds flocked in; more space was needed than the church would require at any other season. Some inspired planner attached the Sunday school assembly hall to one side of the sanctuary. A rolling wall could separate the two spaces through most of the year, but throw them together for the big event. The evangelist liked sloping floors and semicircular pews to bring the people near him. He liked a stage to pace across. Revival choirs left their traditional gallery over the entrance to mount the stage with the evangelist as part of the act. The people settled down in their pews as an audience settles in the theater, passively, to watch the professionals perform. Again, one part of the church's program proliferated as though it were the whole. Good architects might have solved the problems inherent in the Akron Plan school and theater-style church; but few good architects were asked to tackle them.

Chicago invited the world to its Columbian Exposition in 1893. The world came and was enchanted by a vast Court of Honor composed of white classical buildings unified by a common cornice line and varied by the changes that can be rung on classical themes. The Chicago Fair set off a new revival of classical design for every sort of building. Churches fell into line. Then all of the other architectural revivals came around for a second cycle. Architects with formal schooling were better prepared and more widely traveled. Donors riding the prosperity of the 1920s were ready to buy any design the architect proposed. Duke University commissioned a Gothic campus from Horace Trumbauer, who crowned it with a cathedral for its chapel. Rice University went Byzantine. Charles Barber built a Gothic Methodist church in Knoxville. Hobart Upjohn crowned Chapel Hill with a Federal Methodist church tower and steeple that gives distinction to the town.

World War II stopped church building, but shifted people from pillar to post. New suburbs and whole new towns sprang up. As the church school came of age, the church needed a class for every age and a room for every class. Fellowship halls were needed to facilitate congregational dinners and provide recreation for youth. Church staffs grew; they needed offices in suites for efficient cooperation. People came to church by car, necessitating parking lots on or near church property. Planned circulation from car to class to worship to fellowship and back to the car required attention and money. The church had grown from a one-room building into a small campus. Like the medieval monastery it needed a cloister on which all structures opened to unify the people who took part in the varied actions for which the structures were planned.

Denominations gathered funds to help new, small, and ethnic churches build. With the funds they offered guidance for planning. Architects who practiced across denominational lines and consultants saw that all faiths face the same problems. They set up national conferences on church architecture in which architects, artists, theologians, pastors, and members of building committees could discuss their common problems, and see exhibits of good solutions. The decisions on worship and architecture of the Second Vatican Council stirred Roman Catholics to move forward, and Protestants to revalue their heritage. Jewish architects proved to both Protestants and Catholics that religious architecture is inherently an ecumenical enterprise.

Out of such conferences came a wider understanding of the values of master planning, conceiving the whole toward which units could be built stage by stage. Master plans called for thought on goals for future growth. Choosing a goal called for studies on the quality of congregational life. It was seen that good planning requires clear definition of the church's functions; and that form follows function, but function follows faith.

Meanwhile contemporary architecture had achieved worldwide recognition. In Austria, Wagner, Loos, and Hoffman built houses with no superficial decoration. In the Netherlands, J. J. P. Oud led in functional town planning and simplified housing. Marinus Dudok turned Hilversum into a town of beautiful brick buildings so carefully massed and well composed that the structure itself was the source of beauty. In France, LeCorbusier transformed concrete into a building material capable of many finishes, with

dignity and beauty. In Germany, Walter Gropius made the Bauhaus the architectural school that gave its students daily interaction with artists in all fields, serious research into production methods, and personal experience of construction. Hitler drove the Bauhaus teachers to America.

World War II made a change. Young men and women who went all over the world saw and accepted buildings different from those with which they had grown up. They came home ready for change. During the war the architectural schools had time to clarify their philosophy. Contemporary architecture had reason for being in its openness to fresh ideas, its honest expression of structure, its use of new materials, and its economy. After the war, national conferences on church architecture consistently gave their awards to contemporary church buildings.

In the South change came slowly. Lutheran churches, black churches, and Jewish synagogues, which had no inhibiting tradition of antebellum glory, led the way. When they chose good architects, defined their faith and functions clearly, and granted control over design to the architect, they built many good contemporary buildings. Neighbors learned from their example.

A concluding unscientific postscript. Those who frequently asked God to work through pastors and doctors, can as reasonably ask him to work through building committees, artists, and architects. Church buildings will always evolve in response to changing human need. God has always defined himself in the present tense. He is everywhere and always a contemporary person. In Jesus Christ He meets us where we are. That meeting is exciting. Church buildings can report that excitement in fresh design. Such buildings are both tools for the congregation's work and symbols of its faith. They can be true symbols only if they are good tools. In the

South all faiths can now show some buildings produced by that conviction.

Bibliography. Albert Bush-Brown, *Louis Sullivan*; Alberto Busignani, *Gropius*; Andrew Landale Drummond, *The Church Architecture of Protestantism*; Wendell Garrett and Joseph C. Farber, *The Worlds of Thomas Jefferson*; Talbot Hamlin, *Greek Revival Architecture in America*; Daniel W. Hollis and Carl Julien, *Look to the Rock*; Harold Hutchison, *Sir Christopher Wren*; Harold Kalman and John de Visser, *Pioneer Churches*; Edward G. Lilly and Clifford L. Legerton, *Historic Churches of Charleston*; Calder Loth and Julius Trousdale Sadler, *The Only Proper Style*; John Fitzhugh Millar, *The Architects of the American Colonies*; Harold Wickliffe Rose, *The Colonial Houses of Worship in America*; Kenneth Severens, *Southern Architecture*; Mariana Griswold Van Rensselaer, *Henry Hobson Richardson*; Joseph Watterson, *Architecture, A Short History*; Marcus Whiffen, *American Architecture Since 1780*.

JAMES L. DOOM
DECATUR, GEORGIA

ARKANSAS. The first Christian religious service in Arkansas was conducted in 1541 near present-day Helena by Catholic priests accompanying Hernando de Soto on his journey of exploration across the South. No priest appeared again until 1673, when the French Jesuit explorer Father Marquette visited an Indian village a few miles above the mouth of the Arkansas River. In 1682 Father Membre, a Franciscan accompanying the explorer La Salle, also conducted services there.

A base for more permanent Catholic work was established when the French seigneur Henri de Tonti founded Arkansas Post, the first European settlement in the lower Mississippi Valley, in 1686 near the site of the earlier visits. De Tonti gave land to the Jesuits, and up to the end of the French period various priests held services for the few French traders, hunters, and farmers in Arkansas and did mission work among the Indians.

Few records of Catholic activity in Arkansas during the Spanish period after 1762 have survived. It is known, though, that the church at Arkansas Post was named St. Esteban's, and that priests there performed marriages and baptisms and carried out other priestly functions.

After Arkansas became part of the United States in the Louisiana Purchase of 1803, Catholic work was placed under control of Archbishop Carroll of Baltimore, who appointed Father William Dubourg administrator. Dubourg became Bishop of Louisiana and the Floridas in 1815 and entrusted Catholic work in Arkansas to the Lazarists, who remained until the arrival in 1844 of Andrew Byrne, bishop of the new Diocese of Little Rock.

In 1833 secular priests also began to work in what since 1819 had been Arkansas Territory. They founded St. Mary's Church, oldest permanent Catholic church in Arkansas, at the thriving French settlement of the same name five miles below Pine Bluff on the Arkansas River. At least 50 Catholic families lived there, with others scattered along the valley at Little Rock, Pine Bluff, New Gascony, French Town, Plum Bayou, Arkansas Post, and Napoleon. Prominent priests included Father Dupuy, Father Richard Bale, and Father P. K. Donnelley. Sisters of Loretto led by Mother Agnes Hart established a school at St. Mary's in 1838.

When he arrived in Little Rock in 1844 Bishop Byrne found only 700 Catholics in the diocese, most still in the lower valley, but a few in every county. The state (admitted in 1836) had a population of only 100,000, and Little Rock, the capital, was a small frontier village. Setting out to strengthen Catholicism in the state, Bishop Byrne solicited funds from foreign and American organizations, built the first St. Andrew's Cathedral, recruited priests from the East and abroad, and led in the founding of churches in Fort Smith, Fayetteville, Rocky Comfort, and other towns, and schools in Little Rock, Fort Smith, and Helena. Byrne attempted to arrest the relative decline of Catholicism in the state in the face of the flood of predominantly Protestant immigrants by attracting European Catholic settlers. His only success, however, was in recruiting 300 Irish Catholics to settle on 640 acres he purchased at Fort Smith. Some died of "shipboard fever" and others settled in Little Rock and St. Louis, but most went to

Fort Smith to become the nucleus of the Catholic community there. Contributing to the general failure of Bishop Byrne's project was the antiforeign, anti-Catholic Know-Nothing movement. During its height the Catholic church at Helena was burned in 1854 and an unsuccessful effort was made to invalidate purchase of the Fort Smith property.

Thus Catholicism in Arkansas was still far from thriving, with only nine priests, a few nuns, and 1,000 parishioners, when Bishop Byrne died in 1862. Rejuvenation would have to await the coming of more-welcome Catholic immigrants after the Civil War.

Protestants rapidly overtook Catholics in number in Arkansas after 1803. Particularly prominent were Methodists and Baptists, with smaller numbers of Presbyterians and Episcopalians and a few members of other denominations.

The Methodist Church was the largest denomination in the state before the Civil War. Its simplicity of doctrine and worship appealed to the frontier population, and its centralized organization made it possible to send ministers into new areas. The Methodist pioneer in Arkansas was William Stevenson of Belleview MO, who preached in 1813 in the northeast and between 1814 and 1816 along the Ouachita, Caddo, and Red rivers in the southwest. In 1816 he organized Spring River Circuit, the first in Arkansas, centered in Lawrence County in the northeast. The next year he led a colony of Methodists from Missouri to Mound Prairie in the southwest, which became an early center of Arkansas Methodism. Stevenson became presiding elder of all Methodist work in Arkansas, but moved about 1825 to Louisiana.

From its beginnings along the northeast-southwest highland line, Methodism expanded into the eastern lowlands and the western hills and mountains. The 92 members of 1815 increased to 1,634 in 1831, 5,034 in 1840, and 24,164 in 1861. By 1861 there were about 500 churches,

those in important towns such as Little Rock, Camden, Fort Smith, El Dorado, and Batesville served by full-time pastors and the remainder organized into circuits.

The structure of the Methodist Church in Arkansas became more complex as membership increased. The single district within the Missouri Conference was divided in 1832 into Arkansas District in the north and Little Rock District in the south. Arkansas Conference was created in 1836, and Ouachita (now Little Rock) Conference, covering southern Arkansas, in 1854. Overall control was in the hands of the national General Conference, which assigned bishops to Arkansas. The first was Thomas A. Morris; among others before the Civil War, all nonresident, was JAMES O. ANDREW, whose ownership of a slave precipitated the split in the Methodist Church in 1844. There would be no resident bishop until the election of H. A. Boaz in 1926.

Even before 1844 the Methodist Protestant Church had separated from the Methodist Church (1830) in protest against the power of bishops. The first church in Arkansas of this new denomination was formed at Cane Hill in the northwest, and an Arkansas Conference was organized in 1837. By 1860 there were only about 2,000 Methodist Protestants, mostly in the northwest.

Baptists began work in Arkansas only slightly later than Methodists and also in northeastern Arkansas. Although by the 20th century they would become the largest denomination in the state, they grew more slowly than Methodists in the early period. Contributing factors were the lack until 1848 of a centralized organization and disruption of some early churches by antimission, antiorganization forces, including the Campbellites, later known as the Disciples of Christ. On the positive side, Baptist churches could be formed without outside authorization or officially recognized ministers, and also had simple doctrines and forms of worship.

Salem Baptist Church, the first in Arkansas, was organized in 1818 on Fourche-a-Thomas River in present-day Randolph County by James P. Edwards, a missionary from Bethel Association in Missouri, and Benjamin Clark and Jesse James. Bethel Association helped organize several other churches in the area in the next few years. Baptist work expanded southward in 1819 with the foundation by local residents of Pecannerie Church on the Arkansas River.

The most vigorous founder of early Baptist churches was David Orr, a missionary of the American Baptist Home Mission Society. He founded at least 10 churches, including Rehobeth and Little Fork in Lawrence County and Rocky Bayou in White County, and organized Spring River Association in 1829. The first Baptist church in Little Rock was organized by Silas Toncray, a minister-jeweler, in 1824. The same year Toncray formed Little Rock Association, first in the state. After Toncray moved to Memphis in 1829 the church was taken over by Campbellites, and Baptist work would not resume in Little Rock until the present First Baptist Church was organized in 1858.

Stimulated by increased immigration after 1836, a wave of revivalism, and the organization of the Arkansas Baptist State Convention in 1848, Baptist membership grew to 372 in 1839, 2,989 in 1848, and 11,341 in 1860. The 321 churches of 1860 were mostly rural but some existed in the major towns.

Although autonomous, Baptist churches voluntarily formed associations for mutual support and concerted evangelistic effort. By 1860 there were 16 associations; they met after crops were gathered for reports of committees, worship services, and socializing among the delegates from the often-isolated churches. The need for a more comprehensive organization was filled by the Arkansas Baptist State Convention, organized in 1848 at Tulip in south-central Arkansas. Composed of delegates from churches and associations, the convention had no official ecclesiastical jurisdiction, but devoted itself primarily to promotion of missions and ministerial education. It soon affiliated with the Southern Baptist Convention, formed in 1845. Despite some tension between the state convention and churches over the question of ultimate authority, the convention operated successfully until it became inactive during the Civil War. Two other conventions arose in the 1850s, White River State Convention in northern Arkansas and the General Association of Eastern Arkansas. Neither was revived after the Civil War.

Presbyterians were the third-largest denomination in pre-Civil War Arkansas. Cumberland Presbyterians, who had split from the national Presbyterian Church in 1810, began work at Cane Hill in northwestern Arkansas in 1825 under the leadership of John P. Carnahan, and a church of the major Presbyterian group was organized in Little Rock in 1828 by James W. Moore, a missionary from Pennsylvania. Gradually Presbyterians came from the older states, some clustering in colonies around Jacksonport and Batesville on the White River and Scotland and Mt. Holly in Union County. By 1860 there were about 60 churches with about 2,500 members, plus a smaller number of Cumberland Presbyterians. Primarily rural at this time, Presbyterians later became increasingly urban.

Arkansas Presbytery, organized in 1835, and Ouachita Presbytery, formed in 1849 and covering the southern half of the state, comprised the Synod of Arkansas, constituted in 1852 with W. K. Marshall as first moderator. Previously Presbyterian work in Arkansas had been under control of the Synod of Memphis. Primary concerns of the synod were evangelism, establishment of a college, support of the work of the Presbyterian Church, especially foreign missions, and the state of religion in the churches.

Organized activities of the Episcopal Church in Arkansas began in 1838 with the election of LEONIDAS POLK, later famous as a Confederate general, as Missionary Bishop of the Southwest. The few Episcopalians in Arkansas previously were so scattered that no parishes had been formed. The number would remain small since most Episcopalians were members of the very small upper economic and social class.

Before becoming Bishop of Louisiana in 1841, Polk made two arduous missionary journeys through Arkansas and aided in organizing Christ Church, Little Rock, and St. Paul's Church, Fayetteville. Slow growth continued under the succeeding missionary bishops, JAMES H. OTEY, George W. Freeman, and Henry C. Lay, and by 1860 the 12 organized parishes had about 400 members. Most of the congregations were very small and without their own buildings and rectors.

The few Christian churches in the state not related to major denominations were mostly in the hills and mountains of the northwest. Total membership probably did not exceed a thousand.

Early religious life in Arkansas was influenced by the frontier conditions that continued until well after the Civil War. The population was small, scattered, and mostly rural, the few roads were little more than cleared tracks, and few bridges spanned the numerous streams. The state had less than 100 miles of railroad in 1860. Most houses and other buildings were built of logs or rough planks, even in the towns, the largest of which, Little Rock, had only 3,727 people in 1860.

Many churches originally held services in homes or open shelters, then typically built one-room log buildings and later frame churches. There were few brick or stone churches until much later.

Most churches had services only once or twice a month, although the two- and three-hour sermons compensated for the infrequency. Salaries of pastors were very low; in 1833 Methodist ministers received $34 per year if single and $68 if married. Consequently many preachers were also farmers or primarily made their living in other ways. The general level of ministerial education was very low, especially among Baptists and Methodists, who valued a divine "call" above education. Many early preachers suffered real personal hardship, often riding horseback hundreds of miles a year through swamps and forests to reach their remote, scattered churches.

CAMP MEETINGS were a common feature of frontier religious life. Held in the summer after the crops were "laid by," they lasted from a week to a month and often were conducted jointly by the Protestant churches of the area, with their preachers rotating in delivering the four or five sermons a day under BRUSH ARBORS or tabernacles. People came from miles around to hear the preaching and to sing, pray, testify, shout—and perhaps be converted. The accompanying social life was an almost equally important part of the camp meeting. Facilities at camp meetings usually were crude and temporary, but semi-permanent buildings were erected at some camp grounds. Some still function, and present-day assemblies such as Arkansas Baptist Assembly at Siloam Springs, Western Methodist Assembly at Fayetteville, and the Assemblies of God Ozark-Lithia Camp Ground at Hot Springs are simply more elaborate versions of the frontier camp ground.

Most of the denominations carried on mission work among the Indians who lived in sizable numbers in Arkansas until the 1830s. The best-known mission was Dwight Mission, founded in 1820 on Illinois Bayou in western Arkansas by Cephas Washburn and other Congregational missionaries but abandoned in 1829 after most Arkansas Indians were removed to Indian Territory. During the 1830s the churches often ministered to the thousands of Indians passing through on the several branches of the "Trail of Tears" leading to Indian Territory.

Jewish people began to enter Arkansas in the 1830s, but not yet in numbers large enough to organize congregations. The first were Jacob Hyman and Levy

Mitchell, who came to Little Rock from Cracow, Poland, in 1838. Edward Czarnikow arrived in Fort Smith from Posen, Poland, in 1842, and was soon followed by others from that city. The first Jew in Pine Bluff was a man named Wolf (1850) and the first in Hot Springs was Jacob Kempner (1856). Living exclusively in the towns, almost all Jews were merchants. Those in Fort Smith traded extensively with the Indians. Descendants of some of the earliest Jewish families are still prominent in Arkansas.

All of the Christian denominations in Arkansas worked among the slaves, who by 1860 comprised a quarter of the population of 435,450. Three-quarters of the slaves lived on the cotton lands of the southeastern half of the state. The motives were both spiritual and pragmatic; it was believed that white Christians were obligated to share the gospel with slaves, but also that religious slaves were more likely to remain in peaceful subjection.

Slave church members sometimes attended services with white members and sometimes separately. There were no separate official slave churches, although occasionally slave members had separate meeting places and slave preachers. Wesley Chapel was built in 1854 in Little Rock for slave members of the First Methodist Church, with the slave preacher William Wallace Andrews in charge.

Along with encouraging slaves to become members of the regular churches, all denominations also carried on mission work among them, especially in rural areas with many slaves. Methodists had at least 10 missions at various times, including one on the Red River where absentee ownership was prevalent. Baptist mission work was also extensive, if less well-organized until formation of the state convention. In its first year the convention appointed a missionary to slaves on the Red River. Associations also did mission work; Red River had as many as four at a time. Presbyterians and Episcopalians also did mission work among slaves on a smaller scale, and in small numbers slaves continued to be baptized into the Catholic church.

Despite such efforts, no more than seven percent of Arkansas slaves in 1860 were formally affiliated with the churches. But slaves also frequently held secret services unrelated to organized churches, although all secret meetings were illegal. The rapid emergence of separate black churches after emancipation demonstrated that "underground" churches were stronger and more widespread than had been popularly believed.

Only about 18 percent of the white people of Arkansas were members of slave-owning families, but many others had strong ties to slavery. By the Civil War proslavery sentiment was dominant, although a strong minority opinion existed in the north and west. Most of the churches and ministers reflected the general approval. Sermons often cited biblical justification and asserted that Christian whites had been given control of slaves for the purpose of converting them.

Ministers frequently were slave owners themselves. Baptist farmer-preachers owning a few slaves were not uncommon, and at the upper end of the scale Bishop Leonidas Polk owned 400 slaves, although not in Arkansas. In 1850 a tenth of the Methodist ministers who were members of the Arkansas Conference held slaves, including the presiding elder of the Washington District with 15. More than a fourth of the local preachers owned slaves.

A few ministers and church members spoke out against slavery, especially before the Abolitionist movement crystallized proslavery sentiment. The Methodist Jesse Haile, who became presiding elder of Arkansas District in 1825, spoke so militantly against slavery that a number of Methodists joined other denominations. As a result Haile was transferred in 1830 to Illinois.

Sentiments such as Haile's had little influence upon most Arkansas churches, which readily endorsed the divisions in their denominations over slavery. In 1845 Arkansas Methodists declared allegiance to the new Methodist Episcopal Church, South, and soon after it was organized the Arkansas Baptist State Convention affiliated with the Southern Baptist Convention. Southern Presbyterians and Episcopalians split from the national churches at the beginning of the Civil War (the latter reunited in 1865). Since there was no separate American Catholic Church, Catholics did not officially divide along sectional lines.

Division of the denominations would have profound effect upon religion in Arkansas. It would help bring on the Civil War, which in turn would lead to serious weakening of the churches for a time, emergence of separate black denominations, and, for Methodists, Baptists, and Presbyterians, continued alienation from similar denominations outside the South for decades to come.

The Civil War severely disrupted life in Arkansas. Only three states had more battles and engagements, and at least 75,000 men, including most of the white males of military age, served in the Confederate and Union armies and state troops. About a fifth were in the Union army. Others served as irregular troops as the tides of war surged across the state. Among those who served were most of the male members of the churches, and thus, in that male-dominated day, most of the leaders, lay and clerical. Women often carried on as best they could, but the churches shared in the general disruption.

Numerous ministers became chaplains, and others ministered to troops as campaigns passed their way. Among well-known chaplains were Horace Jewell, later author of a history of Arkansas Methodists, and Ebenezer Lee Compere, who left the First Baptist Church of Fort Smith to become chaplain to General

Stand Watie's Confederate Indians. Some ministers also became ordinary soldiers.

The war took its toll of church buildings, often expropriated by the armies, then damaged or destroyed. Particularly offensive to Southern Methodists was seizure of some of their churches under the Stanton-Ames joint policy of the Union army and the Northern Methodist Church. The policy provided that as an area was occupied Southern Methodist churches would be turned over to Northern bishops. In Arkansas Bishop Ames took over churches in Little Rock, Pine Bluff, Fort Smith, Fayetteville, Helena, and elsewhere and organized an Arkansas District of the Methodist Episcopal Church. But Union generals did not always cooperate or chose to use the buildings themselves, Southern Methodists in the loyal border states protested strongly, and soon after the war President Johnson returned most of the buildings to the Southern owners.

The Civil War also damaged the human spirit, leaving a legacy of bitterness, hatred, and divisiveness that would persist for a very long time.

At the end of the Civil War the first task facing the churches was reestablishment of organized religion at all levels. Along with recovery and subsequent growth, the chief developments in religion in Arkansas during the remainder of the century were the choices by the churches of continued separation or reunion with the Northern branches, the emergence and growth of separate black churches, the strengthening of the Catholic and Lutheran Churches by the coming of ethnic immigrants, the founding of schools and colleges, and the "Landmark" controversy leading to a major split within Arkansas Baptist life in 1901.

Methodists revived their conferences, appointed pastors, and sent delegates to the General Conference of the Methodist Episcopal Church, South, at New Orleans in 1866. The conference moved toward democracy by authorizing lay representation, which became policy despite adverse votes by the Arkansas conferences. Laymen steadily assumed leadership; George Thornburgh, for example, was secretary of White River Conference, formed in 1870 and dissolved in 1914, business manager of the *Arkansas Methodist*, and superintendent of the Arkansas Methodist Orphanage in Little Rock. Women would not gain full laity rights until 1918. Ladies Aid and women's missionary societies and increased emphasis upon Sunday schools also date from this period. Such innovations enabled Methodists to resume their growth.

Many Baptist churches were revived and new ones were organized, but others would never recover. Associations, which had declined from 16 in 1860 to only six, were quickly reestablished, and by 1868 there were 23. The Arkansas Baptist State Convention was revived in 1867 by a handful of delegates in Little Rock, and despite limited funds, continuing criticism from antimission elements, and the perennial Baptist struggle between centralization and decentralization, slowly regained the strength that would insure its position as the focus of Baptist work. Among those responsible for the revival and growth of the convention were W. M. Lea, prewar president reelected in 1867, J. B. Searcy, General Missionary Agent and convention secretary for many years, and James P. Eagle, Confederate soldier and officer, minister, governor of Arkansas 1888-1893, president of the convention 21 times, and president of the Southern Baptist Convention three times.

The Presbyterian Synod of Arkansas resumed meeting in 1866, but there were other interruptions during Reconstruction, and at one time a proposal was made to abolish it. But it survived and by 1877 the 60 churches of 1860 had increased to 83.

Bishop Lay provided some continuity for Episcopal work since he had been elected in 1859 and remained 10 years.

During the war he had visited the small, scattered congregations when possible, but at war's end most had to be revived.

Coordinated Catholic activity, which had almost ceased with the death of Bishop Byrne, resumed in 1867 upon arrival in Little Rock of Bishop Edward Fitzgerald, at 33 the youngest Catholic bishop in the nation. At that time there were only four functioning parishes, five priests, and schools at Little Rock and Fort Smith operated by the Sisters of Mercy. As Bishop Byrne had done, Bishop Fitzgerald encouraged Catholic immigration to Arkansas. He would eventually be highly successful, but only after the worst of the political turbulence and economic depression of Reconstruction. One of the chief monuments to Bishop Fitzgerald is the impressive present St. Andrew's Cathedral, dedicated in 1882. Very independent-minded, he cast one of only two votes against adoption of the doctrine of papal infallibility at the Vatican Council in 1870.

Additional Jews came to Little Rock during and after the war, and organized Jewish religious life began in 1866, when Congregation B'nai Israel was organized with Morris Navra as president. After meeting for several years in a single room, in 1872 the congregation built a brick temple and elected its first rabbi, Jacob Bloch. In 1873 Rabbi Bloch represented the congregation in the Cincinnati convention when it became one of the 32 charter members of the Union of Hebrew Congregations, parent organization of Reform Judaism. Meanwhile Jews moving into other towns and cities were also forming congregations.

Of the five denominations in Arkansas that had split, officially or unofficially, from their Northern brethren by the beginning of the Civil War, two reunited quickly and three remained separate. Catholics simply resumed participation in the councils of the church, and Episcopalians sent delegates to a single General Conference, where reunification was achieved easily. Neither church insisted that its Southern dioceses treat blacks as equals.

Early efforts to reunify Northern and Southern Baptists and Methodists were unsuccessful, for the animosity and suspicion most Northerners and Southerners had toward each other continued after the war. The Southern Baptist Convention resumed normal activities after the war, in 1868 officially stating that it was a permanent institution, and the Arkansas Baptist State Convention reestablished the prewar relationship.

The eventually successful effort of the Methodist Episcopal Church, South, to remain separate was accompanied by rancor and bitterness on both sides, to a great extent because of the attempts of the Northern church to "recolonize" the Southern church through the Stanton-Ames policy. Even though the policy was revoked, Southern Methodists were indignant and resentful.

Even earlier, incensed at what they considered the high-handed tactics of Northern Methodists, the Southern bishops declared in August, 1865, that the Methodist Episcopal Church, South, would not succumb to absorption. Delegates to the 1866 General Conference, including those from Arkansas, voted overwhelmingly to continue, and the Southern Methodist Church proceeded to carry on its affairs as before the war.

Any hopes of speedy reunification of Presbyterians were dashed when the Northern church announced in 1865 that the price of reunion was recantation of their errors by Southern Presbyterians, now named the Presbyterian Church in the U. S. (PCUS). Reunion became even less likely when in 1870 the PCUS charged that the Northern church, renamed that year the Presbyterian Church in the U.S.A. (PCUSA) was doctrinally unorthodox. Eventually harsh attitudes were modified somewhat, and official fraternal relations were established in 1883. But, despite such efforts as the request in 1887 by three Southern

synods, including the Synod of Arkansas, that closer relationships be sought, reunification would not come until 1983.

As Arkansas came under the control of the Union army and the slaves were freed, separate black churches began to emerge. A few people hoped that racially integrated churches could continue, but the desire of the newly freed slaves to manage their own affairs and the continuing antipathy and condescension of most Arkansas whites toward blacks determined that most blacks would soon be worshiping in black churches.

Most black Methodists found their way into one of four groups. The first was the Methodist Episcopal Church (Northern). This church had several advantages in seeking black adherents—its history of opposition to slavery, support of the Republican Reconstruction government, and a vigorous educational program through its Freedmen's Aid Society that founded numerous schools in Arkansas. Nevertheless, the church failed to attract many blacks.

The largest black Methodist group was the African Methodist Episcopal Church, founded in Philadelphia in 1787, that began to attract or organize congregations in Arkansas at the end of the war. In 1868 it organized an Arkansas conference with Bethel Church, founded in 1865 by the well-known free black Nathan Warren, as the nucleus.

The second-largest black Methodist group was a direct offshoot of the Methodist Episcopal Church, South. Soon after the war its black congregations were authorized to form quarterly conferences, and in 1870 by mutual agreement black churches in Arkansas and other states withdrew and formed the Colored Methodist Episcopal Church at Jackson TN. Blacks were given the buildings they were using, and white churches sometimes assisted them. Colored (now Christian) Methodist Episcopal members often were held in contempt by other black Methodists because of their fraternal relationship with their former masters. For many years the church operated Haygood Institute and Seminary in Arkansas.

Smallest of the black Methodist groups was the African Methodist Episcopal Zion Church, founded in New York in 1796.

Black Baptists were less fragmented, partially because Northern white Baptists, who had no true convention organization until 1907, did not attempt to organize or attract black Baptist churches. One of the first organized was the First Baptist Church of Little Rock, which traces its origin to a slave congregation in 1845. The new churches soon formed associations, the first the First Missionary Baptist Association in 1867. By the 1880s there were nine and a state convention. An Arkansas minister, E. C. Morris, was the first president of the national convention to which most black Baptist churches in Arkansas still belong, the National Baptist Convention, U.S.A., Inc., formed in 1895. Although black and white state conventions maintained fraternal relationships, prospects for organic union became increasingly dim.

A technically separate black Southern Presbyterian Church eventually was formed, but records show no Arkansas churches affiliated with it. The number of black Presbyterians in the state has always been small. No separate black Catholic and Episcopal denominations were formed, although increasingly there were separate congregations for black members.

The disruption of the Civil War followed by the instability of Reconstruction slowed immigration into Arkansas to a trickle. The state's population, which had more than doubled in the prewar decade, increased by only 11 percent to 484,000 in 1870. But after the end of Reconstruction in 1874 immigrants attracted by cheap land being opened up by new railroads again poured into the state to increase the population to 806,000 in 1880, 1,128,211 in 1890, and 1,311,564 in 1900. This near-

tripling of population in 30 years profoundly affected religion in Arkansas, accounting for great growth among well-established churches, rejuvenation of the Catholic Church, and growing prominence of other denominations. By the end of the century Arkansas had dozens of denominations in addition to the half-dozen present there prior to the war.

Most of the immigrants were Anglo-Saxon Protestants from the older South, but substantial numbers were of European Catholic and Lutheran background. The only pre-Civil War Lutheran church in the state, organized at Long Prairie south of Fort Smith in 1852 by Germans from Saxony, was inactive during the war but was revived in 1868 as the First Lutheran Church of Fort Smith. The same year the First Lutheran Church of Little Rock was organized by predominantly German people with such well-known Little Rock names as Kramer, Geyer, and Riegler. Between 1876 and 1900 churches still existing were founded, mostly by German farmers from Germany, Russia, and the American Midwest and Northeast, in widely distributed towns, some with the appropriate names of Ulm, Waldenburg, Stuttgart, and Augsburg.

Catholics established new churches at Pocahontas and Lake Village in the immediate postwar period while reviving the inactive churches, then founded no fewer than 33, most still existing, from 1875 until 1899. They generally fall into three categories. Some were founded in such non-ethnic towns as Brinkley, Forrest City, Little Rock, and Paragould. Although, sometimes for immigrants, a few were established for German railroad workers.

Five churches were formed by ethnic groups other than German. Immaculate Heart of Mary Church at Marche north of North Little Rock was organized in 1878 by Poles. The community continued to thrive until World War II, when the federal government bought much of the farmland for expansion of nearby Camp

Robinson. But the thriving church atop Jasna Gora (Blue Hill) is a familiar sight in northern Pulaski County. Bohemians founded a church near Dardanelle in 1895, but after a few years it dwindled for lack of clerical leadership. In 1898 Slovacs organized Sts. Cyril and Methodius Church at Slovac in eastern Arkansas. Two churches were formed by Italians, the first in 1895 at Sunnyside near Lake Village by immigrants brought to farm the fertile cotton lands. Malaria soon killed many of the colony of 250 families, and most of the survivors drifted away, especially to Tontitown in more climatically favorable northwestern Arkansas where under the leadership of their priest, Father Bandini, they founded a second colony and church that still thrive. The Sunnyside community and church succumbed to the boll weevil in 1912.

Almost half of the new Catholic churches were organized among German immigrant farmers, all but two, at Stuttgart in eastern Arkansas and Engelberg near Pocahontas, in the upper Arkansas River Valley. The chief motivating forces behind this movement, which greatly changed the religious composition of that section, were the Little Rock and Fort Smith (now Missouri Pacific) Railroad and Bishop Fitzgerald. The railroad widely advertised the large grants of land it had received to finance construction, and attracted thousands of mostly Catholic Germans to the largely undeveloped region. The railroad company and Bishop Fitzgerald, realizing that German-speaking priests and nuns would attract German settlers, cooperated in inviting several orders, especially the Benedictine Fathers and the Benedictine Sisters, to establish work in the valley. Benedictine Fathers from Indiana founded St. Benedict's Priory in 1878 on a square mile of land in Logan County given by the railroad. The Benedictines soon organized churches and schools in the German communities, some on land also given by the railroad. Despite early poverty and hard-

ship, the priory prospered, serving as the nucleus of Catholic work in the valley, especially by training pastors for the churches. In 1891 it became an independent abbey named New Subiaco with Swiss-born Father Ignatius Conrad as abbot. The abbey outgrew its rambling frame quarters and in 1902 moved into the massive five-story hollow-square stone structure it still occupies.

Also in 1878 German Benedictine Sisters founded St. Scholastica's Convent and School at Shoal Creek (New Blaine) on land given by the railroad twelve miles east of the abbey. Convent Maria Stein was founded at Pocahontas in 1888, but was moved to Jonesboro in 1898 and renamed Holy Angels Convent.

The ethnic communities have dissipated somewhat, especially since World War II, but as late as 1935 German-language services were still being held in some of the churches. The churches have remained strong, and have provided a greater variety in religious life than had been known previously in Arkansas.

A need for denominational schools and colleges became increasingly apparent as life in Arkansas became more settled and sophisticated in the last third of the 19th century. Public schools were inadequate, and colleges were needed for ministers and other leaders. There were not even state-operated institutions of higher education prior to the opening of the University of Arkansas at Fayetteville in 1871.

Schools of various denominations had existed before the war, but most were weak and short-lived. The closest approximation to a true college was Cane Hill College, established in 1834 by Cumberland Presbyterians. After a long lapse following the war, it was revived at Clarksville in 1891 as Arkansas Cumberland College, and later became the present College of the Ozarks, now controlled by the PCUSA. Presbyterians also operated schools before the war at Spring Hill, Mt. Holly, Lonoke, and Batesville.

Baptists sponsored schools at Mine Creek (Nashville), Arkadelphia, and Camden, while Methodist schools existed at Fayetteville, Pine Bluff, Batesville, Washington, Tulip, Arkadelphia, Centre Point, and Van Buren. Wallace Institute at Van Buren, founded in 1854 and endowed with $10,000 from the estate of Mr. and Mrs. Alfred Wallace, succumbed to the war as the other schools did. But its endowment somehow survived, and in the 1930s, grown to $25,000, went to Hendrix College.

After the war the denominations resumed their efforts to found colleges. Again the Presbyterians took the lead. In 1872 Isaac C. Long founded Arkansas College in Batesville, still operated by the Synod of Arkansas of the PCUS.

Baptist associations opened schools, some aspiring to the status of state Baptist college, in the 1870s. Best known were Judson University at Judsonia, Shiloh Institute at Springdale, Red River Academy and Arkadelphia High School at Arkadelphia, and Buckner College at Witcherville near Fort Smith. Meanwhile the state convention had resumed its strong prewar interest in ministerial education and the establishment of a college. In 1870 it authorized payment of annual subsidies of $150 to young ministers and designated Mississippi College, Clinton, as the official Arkansas Baptist college; subsequently a number of Arkansas ministers studied there and elsewhere.

But this was only an interim measure, and in 1886, after delay because of economic depression and lack of enthusiasm by many of the generally poorly-educated Arkansas Baptists, the convention opened Ouachita Baptist College in Arkadelphia. By then all of the other Baptist schools had expired except Buckner College, which came under Episcopal control from 1887 until 1890 and was transferred in 1904 to the General (Landmark) Baptist Association. Ouachita College prospered

under its first president, J. W. Conger, enrolling 476 students by the end of his administration in 1907. The strong beginning helped it to weather later economic problems and competition from other Baptist colleges to become the Ouachita Baptist University of today. Ouachita was coeducational from the first, but pressure from the women's movement of the period influenced the convention to found Central Female College at Conway in 1892. The next year White River Association opened Mountain Home College in the town of that name.

Arkansas Methodists also opened numerous short-lived schools after the Civil War, including Camden Male College, Arkansas Female College in Little Rock, and 20 district high schools throughout the state between 1871 and the 1890s. All of the latter were replaced by public high schools. But Quitman College in north-central Arkansas gave creditable college work, enrolling 3,000 students, including 30 who became Methodist ministers, from 1871 until it fell victim in 1899 to its location away from a railroad.

In 1888 an educational commission proposed that Arkansas Methodists operate only two colleges, the male Central Collegiate Institute at Altus (renamed Hendrix College in 1889), founded in 1876, and a new female college to be built at Searcy. Despite the recommendations, within two years there were four Methodist colleges. Galloway Woman's College opened at Searcy in 1889, and coeducational Arkadelphia Methodist College in 1890. The same year Hendrix was moved to Conway, where under the presidency of A. C. Millar it began to develop into one of the best small liberal arts colleges in the South.

Thus by the end of the century white Presbyterians, Baptists, and Methodists were attempting to operate many more colleges than they could support.

Three black denominational colleges still in existence were founded in Little Rock during this period. Philander Smith

College was opened in 1877 by the Methodist Episcopal Church (Northern) as Walden Seminary. Arkansas Baptist College began in 1884 as a ministerial institute related to the new black Baptist state convention. Shorter College, opened in 1886 as Bethel Institute by Bethel African Methodist Episcopal Church, later moved to Arkadelphia and then to North Little Rock.

From the beginning many Arkansas Baptists opposed centralized efforts in missions and other activities, emphasizing instead the primacy of churches and associations. In the 1850s this faction became associated with the Southern Baptist LANDMARK MOVEMENT led by JAMES R. GRAVES, editor of the *Tennessee Baptist*. Graves was very popular in Arkansas, and for a time his paper was designated as the official Arkansas Baptist paper. Landmark adherents also believed that Baptist churches were the only true churches, descended in an unbroken line from those of the New Testament. Thus they practiced closed communion and rejected ALIEN IMMERSION. They were predominantly rural and generally suspicious of an educated clergy.

As activities of the Arkansas Baptist State Convention grew after the Civil War, Landmark leaders became increasingly vocal. At the 1888 convention meeting they insisted that boards and conventions were heretical and opposed appointment of a paid corresponding secretary. The controversy came to a head at the 1901 convention meeting in Paragould over renewal of the appointment of A. J. Barton as missionary secretary. Barton was reelected, but with great difficulty. Landmark reaction to this defeat led to the organization in 1902 of the General Association of Arkansas Baptists, dominated by the Rev. Ben M. Bogard for 50 years. Although churches and associations began immediately to declare allegiance to association or convention, many vacillated, and not until the 1920s was the schism complete. Separate statistics were

not published until 1921, but in the early years the convention probably lost 60 percent of its churches, mostly small and rural, and a third of its members. By 1921, however, as a result of vigorous efforts by convention churches and of concessions to Landmark sympathizers, only 30 percent of the churches and 25 percent of the members were affiliated with the association.

In 1905 the Arkansas association joined with similar groups to form the AMERICAN BAPTIST ASSOCIATION. A schism in 1950 resulted in organization of a second Landmark group, the BAPTIST MISSIONARY ASSOCIATION. Although both are now national in scope, the core of Landmark strength is in Arkansas. In 1971 a dozen counties, more than in any other state, had more Landmark than Southern Baptist Convention members. Landmark Baptists have acquired many of the organizational characteristics against which they rebelled in 1901-1902, while many convention ministers and churches cling to elements of Landmark belief.

A general census of religious bodies in the United States in 1906 reveals the great growth of church members and denominations in Arkansas after the Civil War. Baptists had overtaken Methodists as the largest denomination, reporting 193,244 members. The 94,204 black Baptists, including 840 Primitive Baptists, outnumbered convention Baptists (about 61,000) and Landmark Baptists (about 30,000) combined. Small groups such as General, Freewill, Primitive, Seventh-Day, and Two-Seed-in-the-Spirit Baptists comprised the remaining 8,000.

Of the 142,569 Methodists, 81,699 were in the Methodist Episcopal Church, South, the largest single group in the state. There were 40,873 members of the separate black Methodist groups (AME 26,903; CME 11,506; AME Zion 2,404), 12,569 members (including some blacks) of the Methodist Episcopal Church, 6,658 Methodist Protestants, and 830 Congregational and Free Methodists.

With 32,307 members, Catholics had replaced Presbyterians as the third largest denomination. The 21,156 Presbyterians were divided as follows: Cumberland Presbyterians, soon to diminish sharply in a partial merger with the PCUSA, 11,990; PCUS, 7,357; Associate Reformed Presbyterians, 854; PCUSA, 809; and United Presbyterians, 1,461.

The CHURCHES OF CHRIST, first recognized in the 1906 census as a separate denomination, had 11,006 members, followed by the Christian Church (Disciples), from which they had split, with 10,269. The Churches of Christ had been the conservative wing of the Christian Church, and since the mid-nineteenth century had been moving toward separation based on objection to creation of missionary societies, introduction of musical instruments in services, and growth of liberal biblical scholarship. Episcopalians numbered 4,315, Lutherans 2,080, and Jews 673.

Among the remainder of the 53 individual denominations, all with small numbers, were the Seventh-Day Adventists, the Church of Christ, Scientist, the Church of the Brethren, the Amish, the Salvation Army, the Unitarian-Universalists, the Latter-Day Saints, and three still-existing denominations founded in Arkansas. The Church of the Living God was organized in 1889 at Wrightsville near Little Rock by the appropriately named ex-slave William Christian, who taught that "Freemason religion" was the only true religion. The Church of God in Christ, which now has almost a half-million members, was founded in 1895 by two Baptist ministers who believed that holiness is necessary for salvation. The Free Christian Zion Church of Christ, whose headquarters is in Nashville AR, was organized in 1905 at the equally appropriately-named town of Redemption by dissident black Methodist and Baptist ministers. There were also a few independent churches.

The 425,000 church members of 1906 comprised about 30 percent of the total population of about 1,400,000, more than twice the percentage of 1861. Almost 80 percent were Baptist or Methodist.

In the period before World War I Arkansas was still one of the most rural states in the nation. Only 12.9 percent of the 1910 population of 1,574,449 was urban, living in towns of 2,500 or more. Little Rock, by far the largest city, had a population of only 45,941, although it was an important regional center. Population growth had tapered off and would be only moderate up to 1940, when a period of decline would begin. The black population had increased from the 25.6 percent of 1860 to 28.1 percent, but thereafter would steadily decline. There was a good railroad network except in the mountains, but most roads were still unpaved. Agriculture, especially cotton growing, and lumbering dominated the economy, with manufacturing and processing increasingly important.

The churches were correspondingly rural, with at least 90 percent in the open country or small towns. Rural churches averaged little more than 50 members and town and city churches less than 200. Most rural and some town and city churches were still served by half-time or quarter-time pastors.

In this predominantly rural setting, which continued until 1970, the denominations would grow at varying rates. Of the older denominations, Baptists and Methodists would grow substantially, while Catholics, Presbyterians, Episcopalians, and Disciples would level off. Other groups showing growth were the Churches of Christ and the various Pentecostal-Holiness churches, white and black. Growing denominations tended to be more evangelistic and emotional in appeal and forms of worship.

Just before World War I a major new denomination was organized in Arkansas. In April, 1914, 300 delegates from Pentecostal churches, which had sprung up across the United States in the previous 20 years, met in HOT SPRINGS and formed the Assemblies of God. Despite insistence that it was not a new church, the group soon emerged as a distinct denomination with paid officials and a headquarters in nearby SPRINGFIELD MO. It has become the largest Pentecostal body, with Arkansas one of its strongest states.

Another development of the time resulted in further fragmentation, rather than consolidation, of churches. In 1915 a dissident faction broke away from the black National Baptist Convention, U.S.A., Inc. to form the National Baptist Convention of America. A second schism in the original group in 1961 resulted in formation of the Progressive Baptist Convention, Inc. Thus Arkansas now has three black Baptist conventions, the Consolidated Missionary Baptist Convention, the Regular Baptist Convention, and the Progressive Baptist Convention. The first, affiliated with the original national convention, is by far the largest.

Ministers and members of Arkansas churches almost universally supported World War I. A later study of attitudes of ministers in non-German, non-pacifist churches found none in Arkansas who opposed the war. But while supporting that particular war, religious organizations such as the Arkansas Baptist State Convention sometimes deplored war in general and expressed concern for the spiritual welfare of the enemy.

Support was demonstrated in various ways. Church members and ministers served as soldiers, officers, and chaplains. Civilian ministers preached, taught Bible classes, distributed tracts and Bibles, and visited the sick on military installations, especially Camp Pike near Little Rock. As the war went on, however, the War Department restricted the activities of civilian ministers on the posts, prompting the Baptist State Convention to oppose appointment of military chaplains as a violation of the principle of separation of church and state.

In the churches, though, there was little separation. Pastors preached in support of the war, sometimes using government-supplied propaganda, and promoted Liberty Loan drives, Victory gardens, and even enlistment. Members responded with equal patriotism. After the war the churches were the focal point of fund-raising drives for relief of victims of the war in Europe.

Arkansas enjoyed a measure of prosperity in the 1920s, although less than in most of the nation and fading more quickly. Least affected were farm workers, more than two-thirds of whom were tenants or sharecroppers often living little above the subsistence level. The per capita income of rural Arkansans in 1922 was only $210.

Nevertheless the churches prospered moderately, especially in the towns and cities, where some new buildings were constructed. Most rural churches still had small, one-room buildings without electricity. Financial support of churches increased; members of Baptist State Convention churches, for example, gave $468,000 in 1919, but $1,300,000 in 1924.

But the short-lived prosperity was not an unmixed blessing. Some churches had difficulty paying for new buildings, and denominations overextended themselves in building, expanding, and operating schools, colleges, hospitals, and orphans' homes. The Baptist State Convention founded an ambitious but ill-timed system of six mountain academies, closing several within a few years and the remainder during the Depression. Presbyterians had a more modest system of two mountain schools; one was closed in 1931 and the other continued to operate on a limited scale.

The full-scale arrival of the automobile age in Arkansas in the 1920s had distinct influence upon religious life. More affluent rural people could now attend church more conveniently, while urban people could more easily ignore church activities to participate in the growing variety of secular pleasures. Part-time pastors found it easier to get to their scattered churches. But the state would not have a good rural road system until after World War II.

The Great Depression of the 1930s affected everyone in Arkansas, but especially the 80 percent who were rural. The churches felt the full effect, as shown by gifts to Baptist State Convention churches. After the peak of $1,300,000 in 1924 they remained almost level until 1930, then dropped by nearly half to $685,000 in 1933. As a result of such declines salaries of some pastors of all denominations were reduced or not paid at all, denominational employees were terminated and programs curtailed, and church buildings and other facilities were not maintained properly.

Particularly hard hit were denominational institutions, especially colleges. In 1930 the Catholics closed Little Rock College, founded in 1908 by Bishop John B. Morris, successor in 1906 to Bishop Fitzgerald. Methodists transferred Henderson-Brown (formerly Arkadelphia Methodist) College to the state in 1929, then closed Galloway College in 1933. Officially, at least, the two were merged with Hendrix College. In 1934 Harding College, founded at Morrilton in 1919 by the Churches of Christ, occupied the Galloway property at Searcy.

Baptists closed Mountain Home College in 1933 and Jonesboro Baptist College, founded in 1903, in 1935. Ouachita College survived under the leadership of J. R. Grant, but only by such drastic measures as cutting faculty salaries and paying debts from endowment. Central College also weathered the Depression, but not the effects of World War II, and after shifting to North Little Rock for two years was closed in 1950. In 1948, however, the state convention had assumed control of Southern Baptist College at

Walnut Ridge, which had been founded at Pocahontas in 1941. The Landmark Association of Missionary Baptists opened a Central College on the Conway campus in 1952.

Both Presbyterian colleges survived, but remained small and financially hard-pressed. An attempt in 1951 to merge the PCUSA College of the Ozarks and the PCUS Arkansas College failed because of denominational differences and local possessiveness. The state's black denominational colleges had even greater difficulty in surviving the Depression.

In the long run religious higher education in Arkansas benefitted from the closing or divestiture of at least some small, impoverished colleges, making possible more effective use of always limited funds.

One of the most traumatic economic effects of the Depression was the near-bankruptcy of the Baptist State Convention. Its debts of the expansive 1920s grew by 1934 to the unmanageable total of $1,126,000, and when vigorous fund-raising campaigns, including collection of old gold and silver and a "God's Acre" plan, netted little, in 1936 the convention negotiated a settlement of 35 percent. By 1938 the convention was legally, at least, debt free. But it later demonstrated its moral integrity by paying the remainder of the debt between 1944 and 1952. The persistence of B. L. Bridges, executive secretary from 1931 until 1958, was largely responsible for this.

Along with hardships and setbacks there were two Depression successes, the renaissance of the Episcopal Diocese of Arkansas and the reunification of the Methodist Church. The Episcopal diocese, as a result of the Depression and years of ineffectual leadership by very elderly bishops, had become so weak and disorganized one writer described it as "the most tragic diocese in the American church." When Richard Bland Mitchell became bishop in 1938 there were only 36 parishes and missions—a third without clerical leadership, 15 priests, and 4,592 members, few more than in 1906. Contributions were small, property had been sold for operating expenses, and worship services differed little from other Protestant churches. Bishop Mitchell revived and established churches, recruited clergy, reestablished Episcopal forms of worship, and promoted giving. When he retired in 1956 churches, clergy, and contributions had increased greatly, membership had doubled, and a new pride in the diocese had emerged that would enable it to more than double again by 1980.

Arkansas Methodists were on the cutting edge of the successful 1939 reunification movement. Sentiment was generally favorable, and over the years there had been some reunification without waiting for official action. For example, in 1913 Northern and Southern churches in Eureka Springs combined into a single Southern church, and in 1920 the Rev. Claude E. Holifield of the Methodist Protestant Church joined the North Arkansas Conference of the Southern church.

Although an earlier plan of union failed in 1925 for lack of a 75 percent majority in the Southern conferences, the Arkansas conferences approved it by a three-to-one margin. Only three of 445 delegates voted against the final plan. The immediate effects of reunion were small and felt mostly by the former Methodist Episcopal and Methodist Protestant Churches, each of which had Arkansas memberships of only about 5,000. A few church buildings were closed and a few irreconcilable members withdrew; the few blacks from the Methodist Episcopal Church were placed in a separate Southwest Conference, where they remained until it was merged with the white Arkansas conferences in 1973. The serious material effects of the Depression were accompanied by some worthwhile spiritual effects. Church membership grew as people sought solace from temporal woes. Church members helped each other, unfortunates in the community, and the many destitute transients. And, as one

minister said later, the dire circumstances caused many people to be more conscious of God.

As another war loomed, some Arkansas churches expressed their opposition to militarism and its consequences. As early as 1928 the Arkansas Baptist State Convention condemned war, and in 1934 went on record against compulsory military training in denominational colleges, although Ouachita had required such training for many years. Shortly before Pearl Harbor a convention committee was expressing the hope that the world's problems could be solved without further resort to arms.

But when World War II came the churches supported it, just as they had World War I. Many more members went away to the bigger and longer war, including many ministers who served in the military chaplaincy. Since the war a number have continued to serve as career chaplains.

On the home front churches of all denominations, especially in cities located near army camps and air bases, welcomed and ministered to the many servicemen trained in the state. They also helped finance and operate social centers for the military. But the churches did not minister as enthusiastically to another large group in the state during the war—the 10,000 Japanese-Americans from the West Coast confined in War Relocation Centers at Rohwer and Jerome. Major denominations made pronouncements of welcome and concern and urged tolerance, but did little in an organized manner to minister to the spiritual and physical needs of the detainees.

The churches were affected not only by loss of members to the military, but also by sharp shifts in the population. The state's many armament plants and other defense industries at Little Rock, Pine Bluff, Bauxite, Camden, and elsewhere attracted large numbers of rural people, and from 1940 to 1950 the urban population grew by half to 33 percent of the total.

During the same period, however, people left the state, especially for California and Northern industrial states, in such numbers that the total population dropped by two percent to 1,909,511. Blacks left at a much higher rate than whites, and by 1950 had declined to 22.4 percent, less than a hundred years earlier. As a consequence rural churches, especially black churches, declined and town and city churches grew. Despite the population loss, overall church membership increased.

War prosperity raised church contributions dramatically. Income of Arkansas Baptist State Convention churches, for example, rose 258 percent to $3,314,104 during the war years. Coupled with restrictions on building this would lead to a building boom after the war.

Demographic and social trends have continued to affect religion in Arkansas since World War II. The population in 1960 was 1,786,272, down 6.5 percent from 1950. But efforts to stem outward migration, attract new people, and eradicate the image of Arkansas as backward and racist began to bear fruit, and by 1970 population was up 7.7 percent—but still lower than in 1940. The state reaped the harvest of its efforts by 1980, when the population of 2,285,513 represented a 19-percent gain, one of the highest in the South. By 1970 Arkansas had as many urban residents as rural. The trend has continued, modified by growth of population in the Ozark and Ouachita Mountains, one of the four most rapidly growing non-metropolitan regions in the United States.

By 1980 blacks comprised 16.3 percent of the population, little more than half of the peak year of 1910. The percentage decline since 1970 was contrary to Southern and national trends, but the actual number increased by 20,000. The relative decline of blacks has not been uniform, and the percentage in the central portions of larger cities, especially Little Rock, has increased.

Demographically, Arkansas in 1980 was growing and increasingly white and urban, but with blacks in some of the larger cities increasing more rapidly than whites. Thus both the number and membership of the churches are increasingly urban. From 1951 to 1978 the number of rural Baptist State Convention churches remained stable and membership increased 74 percent, while urban churches increased 222 percent in number and 207 percent in membership. Although only 28 percent of the number, urban churches had 60 percent of the membership.

The larger cities have undergone "white flight" to the sprawling suburbs. Some of the many new suburban churches merely followed their membership, while others seek to fulfill new needs. Another religious response to demographic change has been the founding by various denominations of new churches in resort and retirement communities, including Cherokee Village, Bella Vista, Horseshoe Bend, Hot Springs Village, and Fairfield Glades.

Growing affluence also has had great effect upon the churches. Although Arkansas continues to rank near the bottom nationally in per capita income, contributions to churches have increased more than ten-fold since World War II. One of the first effects of the prosperity after the war was a building boom. Few churches have not constructed new buildings or additions or renovated older facilities. Even accounting for inflation, increase in value of church property has been spectacular. In 1944 the value of all white Methodist Church buildings and parsonages was $9,000,000, but by 1974 was $93,000,000. Arkansas Baptist State Convention churches increased in value from $25,000,000 in 1951 to $281,000,000 in 1979. This was not just an urban phenomenon; open-country Baptist churches gained in value from $2,000,000 to $40,000,000 as wooden one-room buildings were replaced with modern brick and stone structures.

Many of the new churches were elaborate, containing carpeted sanctuaries, spacious educational facilities, social halls, wedding chapels, and parking lots for the almost totally-mobile generation. A few were truly grandiose, with facilities on large plots far beyond the older concept of a church—gymnasiums, jogging tracks, arts and crafts and game rooms, reducing salons, and snack bars. Much postwar church architecture is undistinguished, but a few notable buildings in traditional and modern styles have been constructed. Not all churches have shared in the general prosperity, though, and old and unkempt buildings may still be seen throughout the state.

Growth of physical facilities has been accompanied by growth in the number and variety of paid staff members. Associate pastors, ministers of education, ministers of music, and others are common in medium-sized and large churches. Similarly, programs of churches have expanded to include musical activities for all ages, activities for "senior citizens," radio and television ministries, and youth programs featuring social and recreational activities, drama, and musical productions sometimes using religious rock and folk music. The increasing attention to youth has meant that in most Protestant churches more people enter the church through Christian nurture than by the revivalistic "sawdust trail" of the past. In response to a great increase in working mothers many churches operate kindergartens and day-care centers.

The innovative church programs have to some extent counteracted a steady decline since the 1950s in participation in traditional activities such as Sunday school. Only 55 percent of the members of Baptist churches attend Sunday school now as compared to 75 percent in 1954.

The new affluence has also permitted state denominational organizations to renovate or build new facilities for their colleges, hospitals, children's homes, and assemblies, and to establish new activities such as retirement homes. A notable example is the Good Shepherd Retirement Home in Little Rock, opened in 1979 and operated by the Methodist, Episcopal, and Catholic Churches. Denominational programs have grown to include prison and industrial chaplaincies, work with Indochinese and Cuban refugees, migrant workers and Hispanics, and increased emphasis upon work with college and university students. Student organizations sponsored by Methodists, Catholics, Episcopalians, convention and association Baptists, Assemblies of God, and others are common at the state's colleges and universities. Many have their own facilities with full-time directors, while others are coordinated by local pastors.

By 1980, 60 percent of the people of Arkansas, double the percentage of 1906, were church members. Of the approximately 1,350,000 members about 750,000, or 55 percent, are Baptists, whose growth since World War II, largely due to continuing emphasis on evangelism, has been great. More than 400,000 are members of churches of the Baptist State Convention, by far the largest single group in the state, and about 150,000 of churches of the two Landmark groups, the American Baptist Association and the Baptist Missionary Association, whose growth has kept pace with that of convention Baptists.

The 150,000 black Baptists comprise only 20 percent of the total, as compared to 40 percent in 1940. Smaller groups such as Freewill, General, and Primitive Baptists account for the remainder.

Methodist growth has leveled off in recent years. All Methodists combined, including United Methodists with about 175,000 members, the three black groups, and small numbers of Free and Wesleyan Methodists, number about 230,000, or 18 percent of all church members.

The Churches of Christ, third-largest denomination in Arkansas, have grown steadily since separation from the Christian Church (Disciples) to a membership of 85,000, eight times that of 1906. Churches of Christ are found in all counties, but are most numerous in the central and northern sections of the state. The largest concentrations are in Little Rock, Searcy, Paragould, Jonesboro, Fort Smith, and Nashville. Of the 700 churches 48, almost all urban, have predominantly black memberships. The Christian Church has increased only 27 percent since 1906 to 14,000.

Catholic membership, almost level from 1906 until World War II, has since doubled to 62,000. The Assemblies of God have about 45,000 members, as do the various branches of Presbyterianism combined. There are about 17,000 Episcopalians, 10,000 Nazarenes, 12,000 Lutherans, more than 5,000 Jews, and varying numbers of many other denominations, including the United Church of Christ, the Unification, Spiritualist, and Greek Orthodox Churches, and the Black Muslims. Jehovah's Witness, the various Churches of God and other Pentecostal-Holiness groups, and the Church of Jesus Christ of Latter-Day Saints have all shown substantial growth in recent years. Northwestern Arkansas has long had some members of the Reorganized Church of Jesus Christ of Latter-Day Saints, whose headquarters is in adjacent Missouri.

Ministers and members of most Arkansas churches have tended to be theologically conservative, although there has been a small liberal minority. This is illustrated by the controversy over the teaching of evolution that has periodically appeared in the state since the 1920s.

In 1924 the Baptist State Convention passed a resolution requiring employees of the convention to sign a statement denying the theory of evolution and upholding the basic tenets of Christian Fundamentalism—plenary verbal inspiration of the Bible, virgin birth, substitutionary atonement, bodily resurrection, and literal second coming. Most convention employees signed the statement

unquestioningly, but the board of trustees of Ouachita College substituted a milder one it defended by saying that although teachers in Baptist schools should subscribe to basic Christian beliefs, "we do not sit in judgment upon the scientific views of teachers of science." But under the heat generated by the Scopes trial in Tennessee in 1925 the Ouachita board succumbed to conservative pressure and insisted that faculty members sign the convention statement. Later six refused, including the president, C. E. Dicken, who then resigned because he believed the convention had no right to require the faculty to sign when there was no evidence in the college of lack of belief in the Bible.

Meanwhile other denominations were enunciating somewhat milder positions on the issue at stake in the Scopes trial. The *Arkansas Methodist* believed that the Tennessee law forbidding the teaching of evolution would be upheld and that what is taught in the schools should be left to the state legislatures, but that Christians should not be concerned whatever the outcome, because the trial would not decide whether there is a God. The *Guardian*, the state Catholic paper, hoped that the Tennessee law would be declared unconstitutional, but as to the relationship of the Bible and science Catholics should not be disturbed since the meaning of the Bible is determined by the infallible voice of the church.

Fundamentalists in Arkansas, encouraged by the fact that although Scopes' conviction was reversed the constitutionality of the antievolution law was not ruled on, attempted to get a similar law passed. After one failed to pass in the state legislature in 1927, the Rev. Ben M. Bogard organized the American Anti-Evolution Association that succeeded in submitting the law to a public referendum in 1928. Arkansas citizens approved it by a vote of 108,000 to 63,000.

A few religious leaders opposed the law, most notably Hay Watson Smith, pastor of the Second Presbyterian Church of Little Rock, who from 1924 until 1934 successfully resisted repeated efforts to convict him of heresy for proevolution statements.

The Arkansas antievolution law was not enforced, and little was heard of it until Susan Epperson, a high school biology teacher in Little Rock, challenged its constitutionality in 1966. In 1968 the case reached the U. S. Supreme Court, which ruled the law unconstitutional on grounds that it was contrary to both the First and Fourteenth Amendments.

The *Arkansas Gazette*, which had opposed the law from the beginning, optimistically said that the Supreme Court decision marked the end of the era of antievolution laws. But a more correctly prophetic note was sounded by the Rev. M. L. Moser, pastor of the independent Central Baptist Church of Little Rock, who said that teaching the biblical account of creation along with the theory of evolution should be permitted. In 1981, with fundamentalist support, the Arkansas legislature passed a new law requiring schools that teach the theory of evolution to give equal treatment to creation science. The law was quickly challenged, and in January 1982, was ruled unconstitutional in federal district court on grounds of violation of the guarantee of separation of church and state. The Arkansas attorney general then announced that the decision would not be appealed.

Arkansas churches and their leaders also have tended to be conservative on social issues. Generally they have favored prohibition or restriction of the sale and use of alcoholic beverages and have opposed gambling, commercial activities on Sunday, liberal divorce laws, abortion, and the Equal Rights Amendment. Although women have long played active parts in church life, few have been given positions of genuine responsibility in either local churches or denominational organizations. There are relatively few ordained women ministers in the state;

most are in the various Pentecostal and Holiness churches.

Racial attitudes have moderated somewhat in recent years and blacks and whites maintain generally friendly relationships. But there has been little integration of local churches, black or white. Since the period of the controversy over integration of Little Rock Central High School in the late 1950s some churches have operated private schools that are mostly segregated in fact, if not legally. Private schools are not as common in Arkansas, though, as in the Southeastern states.

See also articles on EVOLUTION CONTROVERSY; FRENCH INFLUENCE; HAYS, BROOKS; MIGRATION, WESTWARD (1750-1900); OZARKS RELIGION.

Bibliography. The *Arkansas Baptist;* The *Arkansas Gazette;* The *Arkansas Methodist;* Kenneth K. Bailey, *Southern White Protestantism in the Twentieth Century;* John L. Ferguson and J. H. Atkinson, *Historic Arkansas;* Conrad N. Glover and Austin T. Powers, *The American Baptist Association, 1924-1974; The Guardian;* E. Glenn Hinson, *A History of Baptists in Arkansas;* Historical Commission, Diocese of Little Rock, *A History of Catholicity in Arkansas; Histories of the Arkansas Churches of the Lutheran Church-Missouri Synod;* Woodie D. Lester, *The History of the Negro and Methodism in Arkansas and Oklahoma;* Margaret S. McDonald, *A History of the Episcopal Diocese of Arkansas;* Frank S. Mead, *Handbook of Denominations in the United States; New Catholic Encyclopedia;* H. L. Paisley, ed., *Centennial History of Presbyterianism (U. S.) in Arkansas;* Ira E. Sanders and Elijah E. Palnick, *The Centennial History of Congregation B'nai Israel;* Orville W. Taylor, *Negro Slavery in Arkansas;* Ernest T. Thompson, *Presbyterians in the South,* 3 vols; Walter N. Vernon, *Methodism in Arkansas, 1816-1976;* Albert W. Wardin, Jr., *Baptist Atlas.*

ORVILLE W. TAYLOR
GEORGIA COLLEGE

ARMINIANISM. This term refers to a man and to a controversy within Protestantism that erupted around 1600 and was protracted into the 19th century. Initially, it was confined to the Reformed, or non-Lutheran, churches of the Reformation. As it seems to have been latent in the earlier reforming movement of the Netherlands, so it first surfaced there. Fermenting around the harassed figure of Jacob Arminius (1559-1609), one-time pastor of the Reformed Congregation of Amsterdam and later the learned and dedicated professor of theology of the University of Leiden (1603-1609), Arminianism emerged about the time of his death and by way of certain articles of "Remonstrance" laid before the estates of Holland in 1610. Its authors reflected doctrinal views cognate with those set forth by Arminius in his *Declaration of Sentiments* and delivered by him, on invitation of the States of Holland, 30 October 1608 at The Hague. As elsewhere, so in Holland religion and politics were two sides of the same coin.

The response to the Remonstrance was, as Jonathan Edwards was to observe in his *Doctrine of Original Sin*, precisely that of "the anti-Remonstrance." Gathering international force, it came to focus in the famed Synod of Dort (1618-1619). This was manned by learned Reformed theologians of western Europe and the British Isles. John Robinson, pastor of the English congregation of the future Pilgrims at Leiden, was in attendance. At Dort (Dordrecht) the definitive counter-Remonstrance of strict CALVINISM was formulated. In the process Arminianism was recognized and defined as the polar opposite of high Calvinism and *vice versa*. Anti-Remonstrant Calvinism was largely perpetuated by the Assembly of Divines, convoked by the English Parliament from 1643 to 1648, that issued the WESTMINSTER CONFESSION. Thereafter, the connotation of "Arminianism" broadens in scope as orthodoxy applies the term to a widening spectrum of opposition and dissent—whether Socinian, Deist, or that of moralistic rationalism—views that bore negatively upon strict Calvinism and its doctrine of human salvation; namely, the eternal decrees, double predestination, bondage of the will due to the Fall, justification by faith alone, imputed righteousness, and infallible perseverance of the saints. Among the Anglican "latitudinarians," moreover, Archbishop Tillotson's moralistic Christianity had all but retired justification by faith by the close of

the 17th century. By the mid-eighteenth century, judged by the ripe controversy among Puritan clergy of New England, the adjective "Arminian" had become interchangeable with the word "Pelagian" as attributed to Charles Chauncy and others who subscribed to the work of John Taylor of Norwich in reducing Christian salvation to morality.

In opposing the doctrine of "eternal decrees" and its corollary, "irresistible grace," the early Arminians of the "Remonstrance" had declared the opposite: grace is resistible; therefore, sin is actual *because it is possible*, and human responsibility is retained. So also they made salvation dependent upon repentance and willing acceptance of God's justifying grace. In all likelihood this same responsibility was a presupposition of the 18th-century Evangelical Revival, whether under the Wesleys or that of the Great Awakening in the American colonies and under the leadership of such Calvinists as GEORGE WHITEFIELD, William Tennent, or Edwards. While JOHN WESLEY stood in the Augustinian tradition asserting a vitiation of nature (*vitium naturae*) consequent upon original sin, he denied Calvin's *vitium natura* which, in effect, completely disempowered human nature. At the same time, he affirmed universal *prevenient grace*. These in combination retained such freedom as might correspond to saving or justifying grace and kept men and women party to their final destiny. Meanwhile, in Wesley's *Predestination Calmly Considered* (1752), he shows rather direct connection with *The Declaration of Sentiments* in its repudiation of eternal decrees as both contrary to Scripture and flatly subversive of the Christian religion. With the first issue of Wesley's *Arminian Magazine*, January 1778, the preface declared: "Each number will therefore consist of four parts: First, a defense of the grand Christian doctrine, 'God willeth all men to be saved and come to a knowledge of the truth.' " And elsewhere: "We know nothing more proper to introduce a work of this kind, than a sketch of the Life and Death of Arminius." Translated from the Latin, there followed the funeral oration (1609) by Peter Bertius and, succeeding that, Gerard Brandt's *Account of the Synod of Dort.* Since the inaugural sermon of the Revival, that *On Free Grace* at Bristol 1739, Wesley had taken the side of the Remonstrants in repudiation of the orthodoxy of Dort. Augustus Toplady, vicar of Broad-Hembury, Devon, while not untouched by the Revival and, yet, as against Wesley, wrote perhaps the last formidable "anti-Remonstrance": *The Church of England Vindicated from the Charge of Arminianism* (London, 1779).

Certainly by the middle of the 19th century in American Protestantism, and not exempting the Reformed wing, the orthodoxy of "the anti-Remonstrance" was expiring in such a silence as was unattended by last rites. Arminianism, which had begun as the particular heresy of Reformed Protestantism—the polar opposite of high Calvinism—had, by the end of the century, become something like orthodoxy, but also without notice.

See also articles on REVIVALISM; WESLEYAN TRADITION.

Bibliography. Jacobus Arminius, *Writings*, 3 vols., ed., Nichols and Bagnall, *A Declaration of Sentiments*, vol. 1; Carl Bangs, *Arminius*; Jonathan Edwards, *Treatise On Religions Affections*, ed., John E. Smith; John Wesley, *Predestination Calmly Considered.*

ROBERT E. CUSHMAN
DUKE UNIVERSITY

ARMSTRONG, ANNIE WALKER

(1850-1938), Baptist women's leader, was born in Baltimore MD. After joining the church at age 19, she was always active in religious work. Her greatest contribution was in being the driving force behind the organization of the Woman's Missionary Union (WMU) of the Southern Baptist Convention in 1888; she became its first corresponding secretary, holding that position until 1906.

Unsalaried during her entire tenure of office, she brought a deep missionary commitment and a strong leadership to the position. She was an able business woman and often when the Executive Committee of the WMU faced difficult problems it resolved, "Let Annie do it!"

Active in expanding the publishing work of the WMU, she also urged special missionary offerings. She is the major reason why the famous Lottie Moon Christmas Offering was instituted among Southern Baptists. Later her own name was honored in the creation of the annual Annie Armstrong Offering for Home Missions. In WMU circles hers was a household name among Southern Baptist women; she is still remembered each year when the offering bearing her name is collected in nearly every Southern Baptist church across the United States.

During her tenure of office she did everything from writing letters and articles to proofreading. Though tender, she also manifested an unbending quality that led at times to heartaches and frustrations for herself as well as others. Perhaps it was inevitable for this to happen with such a strong woman taking a role of leadership at a time when women were otherwise so restricted. In the long run the combination of a strong will and a sensitive spirit spelled success in the women's missionary work with which her name is significantly identified.

See also articles on MOON, CHARLOTTE D.; WOMEN IN RELIGION.

Bibliography. *Encyclopedia of Southern Baptists*, 1, 82; Alma Hunt, *History of Women's Missionary Union.*

GEORGE SHRIVER
GEORGIA SOUTHERN COLLEGE

ASBURY, FRANCIS (1745-1816), first

American Methodist bishop, was born in Handsworth Parish near Birmingham, England. Particularly close to his mother who was an intensely devout follower of the evangelical connection within the Church of England, Asbury worried over the state of his soul from a very young age. Although apprenticed to a mechanic, Asbury had begun to preach in private, and by age 16, he began a local ministry. In 1766 he became one of the traveling ministers of the Rev. John Wesley; five years later he volunteered to cross the Atlantic and become a Wesleyan missionary to the colonies.

After traveling through New York and Philadelphia, Asbury took charge of the Baltimore District in 1773. As the only Wesleyan missionary to remain during the Revolution, he became superintendent of the evangelical enterprise throughout the new nation. He attempted to maintain some discipline among the lay preachers and at the same time he implored Wesley to provide greater support and backing for the American enterprise. Finally, in 1784, Wesley sent three representatives, who met with Asbury and most of the lay ministers at the CHRISTMAS CONFERENCE in Baltimore. Although THOMAS COKE, Wesley's main representative, was putatively in charge of the meeting, the members followed Asbury's lead. After the conference created a new denomination, the Methodist Episcopal Church of the United States, Wesley's representatives ordained Asbury, made him an elder, and finally invested him with the office of superintendent, which Asbury accepted only because of the vote of his brethren. He soon began to use the term bishop rather than superintendent.

As leader of the new denomination, Asbury traveled amazing distances, mostly on horseback, occasionally in the face of great danger. He focused most of his attention upon the South and Southwest, where the greatest numbers of Methodists remained during his lifetime. Francis Asbury never received acclaim as a great preacher; he seems to have produced workmanlike but uninspired sermons. Nor was he a scholarly man, instead relying on his training under Wesley and his reading of the Bible. His great strength was a keen instinct for church politics; and he managed church expansion with intelligence and remarkable intuition, building a denomination that would become central to the meaning of

19th-century American religion. By the time of his death in 1816 a foundation had been built upon which Methodism was to grow throughout the 19th century.

See also articles on FRONTIER, INFLUENCE OF; METHODIST CHURCH.

Bibliography. Herbert Asbury, *A Methodist Saint*; Elmer Clark, ed., *The Journal and Letters of Francis Asbury*; L. C. Rudolph, *Francis Asbury*.

DAVID T. BAILEY
MICHIGAN STATE UNIVERSITY

ASSEMBLIES OF GOD. This is the most prominent of the American Pentecostal denominations historically, and few would doubt that it is also the strongest, the wealthiest, and the most visibly at ease with the values of the American heartland. In 1981 it reported a budget of $70,000,000; 9,500 churches; 1,100,000 members; and 1,700,000 regular worshipers. In addition there were 8,750,000 believers in closely affiliated sister organizations such as the Pentecostal Assemblies of Canada and *Das Assembleias de Deus Do Brasil*. The denomination's weekly magazine, the *Pentecostal Evangel*, claimed a paid circulation of 280,000, and its radio program, *Revivaltime*, was heard on 600 stations. Although AOG churches are most densely clustered in California, Oklahoma, Missouri, Texas, Arkansas, Alabama, and Florida, the constituency of the denomination is drawn from all parts of the nation, making it the least regionalized of the major Pentecostal groups.

The AOG is one of several bodies that emerged from the Pentecostal revival at the turn of the 20th century. The immediate catalyst of the revival was the preaching of Charles Fox Parham, a holiness faith healer who had opened a tiny Bible school in Topeka KS in 1900. Parham taught that the order of salvation entails three distinct experiences: CONVERSION, entire SANCTIFICATION, and BAPTISM OF THE SPIRIT. He was not the first to make this claim, but he seems to have been the first to insist that baptism in the Holy Spirit is always accompanied by speaking with other tongues (GLOSSOLALIA). In any event, Parham soon migrated to Texas, where he passed the torch to WILLIAM J. SEYMOUR, a black hotel waiter traveling to Los Angeles. In Los Angeles, Seymour's preaching sparked the legendary Azusa Street Revival of 1906.

Between 1906 and 1911 several small but thriving Wesleyan sects such as the CHURCH OF GOD IN CHRIST, the CHURCH OF GOD (CLEVELAND TN), and the PENTECOSTAL HOLINESS CHURCH were drawn into PENTECOSTALISM through the influence of travelers who had visited the Azusa Mission. The first of these groups was almost entirely black, the second fervently restorationist (like the neighboring CHURCHES OF CHRIST), and the third still closely tied to its parent, the Methodist Episcopal Church, South. All were concentrated in the South and Southeast. This is the context in which the formation of the AOG in 1914 should be framed, because the AOG, to a great extent, came into existence in order to provide an alternative to the ethnic, cultural, and theological complexion of these older Pentecostal denominations.

Five groups were involved. The most substantial was the core of Parham's followers in Texas and Arkansas known as the Apostolic Faith. Parham had been disfellowshiped in 1907 and Eudorus N. Bell had assumed the leadership of this group. Bell was a Southern Baptist minister who had graduated from the Southern Baptist Theological Seminary and had studied three years at the University of Chicago Divinity School. He was probably the best educated of the early leaders.

The second cluster was centered in Mississippi and Alabama. First calling itself the Church of God, then the Church of God in Christ, this group was led by H. G. Rodgers, an obscure figure associated with the Church of God (Cleveland TN). These Texas-Arkansas and Mississippi-Alabama bodies had struck an alliance in 1911, and thereafter maintained a loose association with the (black) Church of God in Christ, which was legally incorporated. By using the latter's name ministers in the white groups were able to obtain legal recognition and railroad clergy discounts.

The third group was rooted in Zion City (now Zion) IL. Zion City was a communitarian theocracy founded in 1900 by an Australian faith healer named John Alexander Dowie. Parham's disciples had penetrated Dowie's stronghold in 1904, and after the latter's fall from power in 1906, many of his followers converted to Pentecostalism. This faction did not have a single leader, but many who became luminaries in the AOG had once "marched to Zion."

The fourth component, based in Chicago, had coalesced around two dynamic preachers, William H. Durham at the North Avenue Mission and William H. Piper at the Stone Church. Durham had traveled to Azusa in 1907, but he and Piper probably learned about baptism in the Holy Spirit from Pentecostals in Zion City.

Finally, the fifth source consisted of persons who had withdrawn from A. B. Simpson's CHRISTIAN AND MISSIONARY ALLIANCE when Simpson became hostile to Pentecostalism around 1910. These converts were concentrated in the Old Northwest, Pennsylvania, and New Jersey. Ministers from this group were usually the best-educated men in the AOG.

These five bodies were drawn together for practical as well as theological reasons. The practical reasons stemmed from doctrinal fanaticism, emotional excess, organizational chaos, and financial fraud, because key leaders recognized that these unaffiliated believers were a target for every charlatan and religious misfit in the country. By 1912 many were persuaded that the revival would burn itself out if it were not stabilized by a formal organization.

Theological reasons grew from disenchantment with the Wesleyan emphases inherited from Parham, Seymour, and the Pentecostal denominations in the Southeast. The dissidents, drawn from Baptist, Presbyterian, and other non-Wesleyan traditions, especially disliked the Wesleyan conception of entire sanctification as a process that commences at conversion and is "perfected" in a second moment of grace. They were certain that this aspect of the Wesleyan heritage was not biblical and that it stirred up the worst kind of antinomian excesses. They wanted to return to a position more characteristic of the Reformed tradition (CALVINISM) in which sanctification is understood as a process that commences at conversion, but is never "perfected" this side of heaven's gate. This Finished-Work faction, as they were called, therefore combined conversion and entire sanctification into a single experience, followed by the second and final transformation in the order of salvation: baptism in the Holy Spirit, with the "initial physical sign of speaking with other tongues."

Beyond these practical and theological motives, regional and ethnic antagonisms may have been involved. Moreover, given the fact that two-thirds of the leaders were still in their twenties and thirties, it is reasonable to believe that a measure of self-interest was mixed into the decision to form a new organization. It offered fresh opportunities to exert leadership in the interest of one's convictions. Whatever the exact blend of motives, representatives of these five groups met in HOT SPRINGS AR, 2-12 April 1914, where they formed the General Council of the Assemblies of God. Eudorus N. Bell was elected chairman. Permanent headquarters were established four years later in SPRINGFIELD MO.

After its founding the AOG suffered two major controversies. The first was internal, while the second involved all of the larger Pentecostal denominations. The first grew from a dispute in 1914 regarding the proper baptismal formula: the trinitarian formula of Matthew 28:19 or the so-called Jesus Only formula of Acts 2:38. Soon the debate turned into a bitter confrontation over the nature of the Godhead. Advocates of the latter formula insisted that God the Father and God the Holy Spirit are simply different names for Jesus. Although one-fourth of the ministers in the AOG held the Oneness position, they were decisively ejected in 1916. (Today this faction is represented by the UNITED PENTECOSTAL CHURCH and the Pentecostal Assemblies of the World.)

The second controversy stemmed from the professionalization of FAITH HEALING. For many years faith healing had been largely confined to a small group of men and women who were specially gifted in this respect and who were esteemed as leaders with the denomination. However, in the late 1940s and 1950s, for reasons that are not wholly clear, healers in the AOG like A. A. Allen and Jack Coe skyrocketed into national prominence. Although most were soon squeezed out by leaders dismayed by the fraudulence of some of the healing claims and by persistent rumors of financial irregularity, many rank-and-file members have continued to be attracted to independent evangelists who have stressed spectacular cures and, more controversially, faith as an avenue to financial prosperity.

Like all Pentecostal groups, the AOG has always been firmly committed to the "full" or "foursquare" gospel of 1) personal salvation, 2) baptism in the Holy Spirit with the sign of tongues, 3) healing by faith, and 4) the imminent return of the Lord. To a greater extent than most Pentecostals, however, the AOG identified itself after World War I with the emerging fundamentalist movement, and after World War II with the most conservative stream of the evangelical movement. The legacy of this affiliation is evident in the denomination's literature, which continues to emphasize traditional fundamentalist concerns like the inerrancy of the Bible, the fallacy of the theory of human evolution, the restoration of Israel, and the pretribulation rapture of the saints.

Fundamentalist influence is also apparent in the denomination's rather casual attitude toward polity. In the early years its power structure was Presbyterian in form and practice. Final authority on all questions of faith and order resided in a biannual General Council of clergy and laity. Theoretically this is still the case, but since the 1940s authority has become strongly centralized. The general superintendent, executive presbyters, and general presbyters (all clergy) exercise strict supervision at the national level, while similar bodies oversee district operations. Nonetheless, the Spirit blows where it will, especially in a denomination that strongly prizes the gifts of the Spirit. Thus at the local level particular pastors have often shown astonishing independence, rooted in and legitimated by charismatic authority.

The social history of the AOG, like the social history of the Pentecostal movement in general, remains relatively unexplored. It is commonly believed, for example, that until the middle of the 20th century Pentecostal groups attracted the most economically and culturally impoverished stratum of society. On the other hand, there are persistent indications that converts were typically drawn, not from the ranks of the disinherited, but from the stable working class and sometimes the lower middle class. In any case it is impossible to doubt that growing affluence has markedly changed the face of the denomination since the 1940s. Wooden-frame tabernacles have been displaced by attractively styled suburban churches. Boisterous handclapping has given way, at least on Sunday mornings, to robed choirs and restrained (though nonliturgical) worship. Poorly equipped and fiercely sectarian Bible institutes have been transformed into a network of accredited Bible colleges, liberal arts colleges, and a two-year seminary, scattered, but with special strength in the Midwest and California. Traditional proscriptions regarding dress codes, cinema attendance, and the like have been considerably relaxed. Yet the most portentous sign of long-term upward mobility may be the fact that in recent years only a small minority of the constituency has questioned the denomination's tendency to embrace secular ideologies of economic and political conservatism, and even fewer have questioned its extensive ties with the billion-dollar industry of Television Ministries.

Even so, the AOC has retained its commitment to the distinctiveness of primitive Pentecostalism to a remarkable degree. It still devotes 50 percent of its budget to the support of overseas missions, and another 40 percent to explicitly evangelistic, soul-winning ministries at home. The denomination's Statement of Fundamental Truths has not been materially modified since it was first adopted in 1916; virtually any AOG publication reveals that the underlying world view is as starkly supernaturalistic as it was in the first blush of the pentecostal revival. There is, in short, little evidence that the "acids of modernity" have eroded the conviction that the gospel is still true. Not the old-fashioned gospel of the 19th century, but the miraculous, wonder-working Gospel of the first century.

See also articles on HOLINESS MOVEMENT; METHODIST CHURCH; RESTORATIONISM; WESLEYAN TRADITION.

Bibliography. Robert Mapes Anderson, *Vision of the Disinherited: The Making of American Pentecostalism*; Carl Brumback, *Suddenly . . . From Heaven: A History of the Assemblies of God*; Cordas C. Burnett, *Early History of . . . The Assemblies of God*; Klaude Kendrick, *The Promise Fulfilled: A History of the Modern Pentecostal Movement*; William W. Menzies, *Anointed to Serve: The Story of the Assemblies of God.*

GRANT WACKER
UNIVERSITY OF NORTH CAROLINA
AT CHAPEL HILL

ASSOCIATE REFORMED PRESBY-TERIAN CHURCH.

A rather old, quite small, and historically Southern denomination, the ARP Church is a distant cousin to other Calvinist bodies in the region.

The Southern organization of this body, which derives from the Scottish dissenters, occurred in 1822 when it took the name, the "Associate Reformed Presbyterian Church of the South." That action reflected the regional membership's decision to become independent of the Northern body. A second name change accompanied the (Northern) ARP Church's joining the United Presbyterian Church in 1858, to wit, the dropping of the phrase "of the South." Since then, this Southern communion has been the sole bearer of the original title.

This Church reported 31,518 members in 156 churches in 1981. Its area of greatest concentration is upstate South Carolina and nearby places in North Carolina. Charlotte and Greenville are also cities of some importance. Its true hub is Due West SC where Erskine College and Theological Seminary are located. Some membership is scattered through Tennessee and Florida.

The ARP Church can be termed an "ethnic" denomination in the sense that its members are typically descendants from the early American immigration of Covenanters and Seceders—groups of Scottish Presbyterians who broke away from the established Church of Scotland in the mid-eighteenth century. It has not been active in recruiting others to its fold in the United States, but it does carry on foreign missionary work, most notably in Mexico and West Pakistan.

The Church's polity accords a role to local congregations and to the General Synod, its highest governing body and court. Its doctrine is based on the traditional Calvinist standard, the Westminster Confession of Faith. A distinctive trait used to be its recognition of the biblical Psalms as the only suitable hymns; in 1946 that position was declared optional and a new hymnbook was approved. The Church has taken conservative stands on the temperance question, was moderate in its policies concerning slavery, and is rightly thought of as a standards-conscious communion.

Bibliography. Ray A. King, *A History of the Associate Reformed Presbyterian Church*; David Woodside, *The Soul of a Scottish Church.*

ASSOCIATION.

All organizations, both secular and religious, seek out like-minded bodies in their immediate vicinity, or in a state's political context, or more broadly. The name commonly used for regional groupings of congregationally governed religious bodies in the English-speaking world is "Association."

This word preserves, first of all, the idea that each local body is, finally, autonomous under God. No other body or person can prescribe for it doctrinal statements, organizational arrangements, or fiscal accountability. Specifically, church property is owned by the local congregation; its officers are elected by its own members and no one else; its life of faith is its own responsibility in materials used, orders of worship, or anything else. Such bodies freely choose to "associate" themselves for purposes of fellowship, mutual counsel, and joint missionary endeavor with others who cherish their own independence. Fellowship may be and sometimes is withdrawn from a church that has so departed from the norm as to be no longer recognizable as a member of the family. So runs a theoretical statement of congregational and associational life. However, this is greatly modified by the tendency of groups to seek to conform to an established pattern, when they can choose to do so. A remarkable degree of homogeneity in fact comes to exist in most such groups through imitation and suggestion.

In the South, Southern Baptists, the United Church of Christ, and members of the Campbellite ecclesiastical families are related to one another in associational patterns.

WILLIAM C. SMITH, JR.
GREENSBORO, NORTH CAROLINA

ASSOCIATION OF SOUTHERN WOMEN FOR THE PREVENTION OF LYNCHING.

One of the more intriguing organizations that developed during the Jim Crow era was this association, which wielded influence for a decade. Formed in 1930 under the auspices of the COMMISSION ON INTERRACIAL COOPERATION, the ASWPL represented the efforts of middle-class white church women in the South, primarily but not exclusively Methodists, to eliminate violence directed against blacks by disabusing Southerners of the notion that the protection of white Southern womanhood justified lynching. Spurred on by such inflammatory remarks as those of Cole Blease, the governor of South Carolina, who in 1930 stated that whenever the United States Constitution stood between himself and defending the virtue of white Southern womenhood, "to hell with the Constitution," the ASWPL undertook a 10-year educational and pressure campaign to remove, as the group put it, "the cross of chivalry which has been pressed like a crown of thorns on our heads."

Prior to World War I, women's church groups in the South had taken up causes of social betterment such as public-health reform, but had generally avoided confronting racial issues as conspicuous as lynching. Indeed, those that were active in the suffrage movement, which had also involved many church women, made it clear that they did not think that a constitutional amendment giving the vote to women would, or should, also give the vote to disfranchised Southern blacks. However, with the passage of the 19th Amendment and the formation of the Commission on Interracial Cooperation in 1919, Southern women found a new outlet for their feminism and religious activism. In 1920, the commission created

a women's division headed by CARRIE PARKS JOHNSON, the wife of a Georgia minister and a leader in the Women's Council of the Southern Methodist Episcopal Church. In 1929, JESSIE DANIEL AMES, a Texas suffragist who had become an effective director of the state's interracial committee, took over the leadership of the commission's women's division. She determined that women should play a more conspicuous role in the commission and that they could best do this by spearheading the organized antilynching movement in the South. It was largely at the insistence of Ames that the ASWPL was created.

Although it was financed by the Interracial Commission, Ames ran the ASWPL as a virtually autonomous organization. Its members, which numbered about 40,000 women throughout the South, did not pay dues or attend meetings. Instead, they vowed to bring whatever pressures they could to bear upon Southern police and political officials to see that no lynchings took place in the members' communities. Since many of them were the wives of influential merchants, bankers, ministers, and professionals of standing in Southern towns and cities, the pressure that they were able to exert on Southern law officers was considerable. The number of recorded lynchings did, in fact, decline measurably in the South during the 1930s from about 20 to about 5 per year. Moreover, the decline was most dramatic precisely in those Southern counties where the ASWPL had been most active. Finally, along with the carefully documented studies produced by the Interracial Commission, the ASWPL put an end, once and for all, to the argument that lynching protected the white women of the South. Even the Southern senators and congressmen who opposed federal antilynching legislation during the 1930s no longer justified and defended the practice; they now argued that the effectiveness of the ASWPL made such measures unnecessary. Ames, to the consternation of others within the Interracial Commission, took this position. This split in the Southern antilynching movement contributed to the ASWPL's demise in 1940.

See also article on WOMEN IN RELIGION.

Bibliography. Jacquelyn Dowd Hall, *Revolt Against Chivalry: Jessie Daniel Ames and the Women's Campaign Against Lynching*; John S. Reed, "An Evaluation of an Anti-Lynching Organization," *Social Problems* 16 (Fall 1968): 172-82; Morton Sosna, *In Search of the Silent South: Southern Liberals and the Race Issue.*

MORTON SOSNA
STANFORD HUMANITIES CENTER

ATONEMENT. The church has sought to express the meaning of the central mystery of the Christian faith—the self-giving of God for sinful humanity—in the doctrine of the atonement. The death of Jesus Christ on the cross posed the question, "Why did this good man die?" The answer of his followers was twofold: the cross disclosed the enormity of human SIN and the depths of divine love. In acknowledging the atonement, theologians from the earliest days of the church have struggled with several central and related questions. What was the relation of God the Father to his son Jesus, confessed by the church as Christ or Messiah of God? Was Jesus fully human; was he God? How were holy God and sinful humanity reconciled in the death of Jesus Christ? The first two questions were established for Christian orthodoxy in the early Christian councils of Nicea and Chalcedon. Unlike the doctrines of Incarnation and Trinity, however, that of atonement has never become crystallized in a credal formula of the church.

The word atonement literally means "at-one-ment." Implicitly it acknowledges the alienation of human beings, God's creation, from their Creator. It denotes the act by which those at odds have been made one. It connotes the meaning of the atonement as an act by God, the expression of unmerited love for his sinful creation. The Old Testament background of priestly sacrifice is prominent in the New Testament picture of Christ as both high priest and sacrificial victim, whose death redeemed his people and inaugurated the new covenant (see Heb. 9:1-10:18; cf. Rom. 3:24-25; 1 Cor. 11:25).

Several views of atonement have each captured an aspect of Christian faith widely shared but peculiarly shaped by its cultural ethos. The classical view of atonement, dominant for the first 1,000 years of the church, saw God as entering into battle against the powers of sin, the law, death, and Satan. The cross marked the decisive conflict in which God vanquished all the powers arraigned against humanity in a victory in which persons could participate through faith. Some statements of the atonement gave special emphasis to the sacrificial motif in the voluntary offering of Jesus' life as the suffering servant of God on behalf of sinful humanity.

In the 11th century two other influential theories of atonement were set forth, one stressing the objective character of God's action in the suffering and death of Christ, the other the subjective response on the part of human beings. Referred to as judicial, legalistic, or Latin, the view of Anselm was that human beings by their sin had incurred a debt to God that they could not pay. Only God could discharge the debt and free humanity from its sin. God did this in giving up his Son to death, thereby canceling humanity's debt of sin. The subjective theory of Abelard pictured the cross as the expression of God's love for humankind, evoking the response of gratitude, faith, and love. It took the death of Jesus to open up the human heart to receive God's forgiveness for sin.

Each of the views of atonement has roots in Biblical passages, metaphors, and imagery; each has reflected something of the time and setting in which it was formulated; and each has tapped a source of Christian experience that has kept it alive in theological discourse. While inadequacies in each of the views have kept them from receiving ecumenical endorsement by the church, together they represent the many-sided Christian response to the mystery of God's reconciling act in Jesus Christ. They testify to the faith of the church that God has done something unique, definitive, and once for all in the life, death, and resurrection of Christ to deliver humankind from the slavery of sin.

See also article on SALVATION.

Bibliography. Leonard Hodgson, *The Doctrine of the Atonement*; William Hordern, *A Layman's Guide to Protestant Theology*.

THOMAS E. MCCOLLOUGH
DUKE UNIVERSITY

AUGSBURG CONFESSION. This is a principal statement of faith of the evangelical Lutheran churches that they offered to Emperor Charles V at the Diet of Augsburg, Germany, 1530, and they included in the Lutheran Book of Concord that is still used today.

Faced with the emperor's summons to the Imperial Diet and to a further crisis regarding religious policy, Elector John of Saxony directed Martin Luther, Philip Melanchthon, and other theologians at Wittenberg to draw up a statement of the Protestant faith for presentation to the Augsburg assembly. Since the final journey to the Diet presented personal dangers to Luther, he was left behind, and the further work of drafting then rested primarily with Melanchthon. From a distance, however, Luther approved late drafts for presentation, though revisions continued to be made until the last moment.

In content, the Confession, or *Augustana* as it came to be called, strategically emphasized points in common between Catholic and Protestant beliefs and declared itself in search of the unity desired by the emperor. In this, it reflected more the attitude of Melanchthon who was on the scene than of Luther who was absent from the proceedings. For example, Article I of the Confession declares accord with the Trinitarian decree of the Council of Nicea (325) that set for the whole church the terms of equality among the persons of the God-head, Father, Son, and Holy Spirit. On such a formulation of Christ's essential divinity with the Father

God, Catholics and Protestants shared a cornerstone of unity.

Articles II and III on original sin and the Son of God likewise seek formulations of agreement on historic traditions: hereditary sin and the radical need of salvation; the coming of the divine-human person, Christ, Son of God, as propitiation for sin (using extensively the language of the Apostles' Creed). Even the language of Article IV on justification, a most sensitive issue of the time, is not so far from what would have been acceptable to many medieval theologians. St. Thomas Aquinas, for example, taught justification by faith, following the epistles of Paul, but taught that this justification was only the beginning of a process of sanctification towards salvation. The *Augustana* declares significantly, on the other hand, "that we ... become righteous before God by grace ... when we believe that for (Christ's) sake ... righteousness and eternal life are given to us." The critical word in the statement is "when," which focuses the direct personal relation of assurance between God and the believer available in the moment of faith. This is in contrast to the medieval Catholic teaching which saw assurance as implicit in a lifelong pilgrimage of faith in the church and through the sacraments.

As the Confession proceeds, issues of altercation become increasingly clear, such as the place of good works and their relation to faith, and matters of reform: the Eucharist in both kinds, priestly marriage, the Mass, fasting, and monastic vows. Catholic leadership countered later in the Diet with its *Pontifical Confutation*, and in 1531 Melanchthon replied with his *Apology*. Both the *Augustana* and the *Apology* were included in the Book of Concord (1580).

See also articles on LUTHERANISM; WESTMINSTER CONFESSION OF FAITH.

Bibliography. T. G. Tappert, trans., *The Book of Concord*; Conrad Bergendoff, *The Church of the Lutheran Reformation*.

WILLIAM MALLARD
EMORY UNIVERSITY

AUGUSTA STONE PRESBYTERI- AN CHURCH. This historic place originated in a congregation named "Triple Forks of the Shenando," founded in November 1738 by the Rev. James Anderson. The Presbyterian Synod of Philadelphia had sent Anderson to Williamsburg on behalf of "a considerable number of our brethren" planning to settle in western Virginia and asked that "their civil and religious liberties" be allowed.

Anderson lobbied in the Virginia House of Burgesses for seven weeks before the synod's request was granted, after which he returned to Pennsylvania through the Valley of Virginia and exercised his newly gained rights by establishing among Scotch-Irish already settled there the Triple Forks congregation with two meeting places, Augusta, eight miles north of present-day Staunton, and Tinkling Spring, eight miles southeast.

In September 1740 Donegal Presbytery in Pennsylvania, acting on a petition from Triple Forks, ordained JOHN CRAIG and installed him as the first settled Presbyterian minister in Virginia. This congregation remained together until Craig resigned from Tinkling Spring in 1764. He continued at Augusta until his death 10 years later.

In 1749 the Augusta group completed building a stone meetinghouse that prompted the present name and still is used as the nave of the enlarged church building today. Because of Craig's widespread missionary work, continued by his successors, the Augusta Stone Church is now the source of several other Presbyterian congregations to the north and west, including Massanutten Cross Keys, Union, Mt. Horeb, and Spring Hill.

Because a late nineteenth-century fire burned official congregational records, no comprehensive history of Augusta Stone Church has been written. The congregation has had 16 pastors, some of whom have been prominent leaders in Presbyterianism. With 271 communicants in 1980 the "Old Stone Church" is today one of 13 Presbyterian churches in Augusta, Rockingham, and Rockbridge counties that originated in John Craig's ministry.

JAMES L. MCALLISTER, JR.
MARY BALDWIN COLLEGE

BACHMAN, JOHN (1790-1874), pioneer Lutheran leader in the South, was born near Rhinebeck NY, studied with local clergy, and then completed his theological education under the Rev. P. F. Mayer in Philadelphia. Licensed in 1813, he served Gilead Parish, Centre Brunswick NY for about a year when ill health forced him to move south. He was ordained in 1814 in New York just before departing to Charleston SC, in response to a call from St. John's Lutheran Church, a parish he served from 1815 until 1870. He married Harriet Martin in 1816. His mornings were spent as a pastor, but in the afternoons he often became a naturalist. He collaborated with J. J. Audubon by collecting and describing specimens, and ultimately by writing the text for *The Viviparous Quadrupeds of North America* (1846-1854). His stature as a naturalist aided his unpopular stand against the notion of a separate origin for the black race published in the *Unity of the Human Race* (1850).

Although originally a "Union man," Bachman shared the Southern position on slavery and offered the opening prayer at the South Carolina secession convention in 1860. He encouraged able black men to study for the ministry, tutoring them himself and helping them in further education elsewhere. Bachman's ability made him a leader in the South Carolina Synod, which he served as president (1824-1833, 1839-1840, and 1844). His initiatives led, over some opposition, to the founding of a seminary in 1830, and he personally selected its first two professors. He urged the forming of an agricultural school and a church college, and served on the West Point Board of Visitors and on the board and faculty of the College of Charleston. He was elected president of the General Synod (1835-1839) and first president of the General Synod in the Confederate States of America (1863). Theologically he stood in the "American Lutheran" tradition of Schmucker, although he did not seem to favor the revivalistic practices of one wing of that group.

See also articles on LUTHERAN CHURCH; SCIENCE AND RELIGION; SOUTH CAROLINA.

Bibliography. Catherine L. Bachman, *John Bachman, D.D., L.H.D., Ph.D., the Pastor of St. John's Lutheran Church, Charleston*; Raymond M. Bost, "The Reverend John Bachman and the Development of Southern Lutheranism," unpublished Ph.D. dissertation, Yale University, 1963; Donald L. Peattie, "John Bachman," *DAB* 1:466-67.

HUGH GEORGE ANDERSON
LUTHER COLLEGE

BADIN, STEPHEN THEODORE
(1768-1853), pioneer Roman Catholic
priest and leader in the South, was born in
Orleans, France. He entered the Sulpician
Order in 1789. When the French Revolution came, Badin left for America and
finished his studies at St. Mary's College
in Maryland. He was ordained by Bishop
JOHN CARROLL on 25 May 1793, the first
Roman Catholic priest ordained in the
USA.

Within a year, Badin left for Kentucky. Although he settled near
BARDSTOWN (KY), he spent most of each
year traveling, since he was the only priest
in a dispersed Catholic population. Father
Badin preached sternly on morality and
penance. He also sought a solid financial
foundation for the Catholic Church in
Kentucky. Eventually joined by more
clergy, he guided the Catholic community
for 15 years.

In 1808, Bardstown became a diocesan
see. Badin disagreed with the first bishop,
BENEDICT FLAGET, over property claims
and in 1819, he left for France where he
acted as advocate and agent for American
Catholics.

In 1828, Father Badin returned to the
U. S. to work with Indians in Ohio and
Indiana. During this mission he acquired
the land on which the University of Notre
Dame was built. In 1837, Badin became
vicar-general of Bardstown, and in 1841
he moved to Louisville, the new see. In
1849, friction with Bishop MARTIN J.
SPALDING forced him to Cincinnati, where
he died in 1853. He is buried at Notre
Dame.

Badin also wrote apologetic and historical works on Catholicism, including a
history of Kentucky Catholicism published in Paris in 1821.

Bibliography. J. H. Schauinger, *Stephen T. Badin*; Stephen Badin, *Origine et Progresse de la Mission du
Kentucky.*

GARY W. MCDONOGH
NEW COLLEGE
UNIVERSITY OF SOUTH FLORIDA

BAPTISM. Although having some historical association with Jewish ceremonies, and the baptism of John as well,
Christian Baptism is primarily the act of
initiation, the rite by which the church
incorporates its members. It has maintained this function despite long-standing
differences in mode, meaning, and administration. Immersion and sprinkling are
baptism's major forms. Treated variously
as sacrament, symbol, or ordinance, the
act is understood as representing religious
purification and cleansing, or death to life
in sin, and resurrection to life in Christ.

Authentic Baptism requires both
water and Spirit whether offered to
infants, children, or adults; however,
infant baptism (usually done by sprinkling) occasions conflicts of opinion
respecting the gift of the Spirit. Some
bodies, contending that baptism is complete without Confirmation, assume that
prevenient grace and congregational corporate faith assure the blessing of the
Spirit upon the infant. Others insist upon
Confirmation as a means to receive the
Spirit, because they hold that the faith
necessary for receiving the Spirit and
completing the rite, if absent in the infant,
cannot be supplied by congregational sur-
rogation. Baptism of responsible and
accountable believers, usually by immersion, is considered to be complete because
the person, by virtue of one's individual
faith, is thereby enabled to receive the
Spirit. In the light of these differences,
believers' baptism is usually taken to be
more symbolic and less sacramental than
infant baptism.

Baptism's identification as Christian
initiation by a majority of churches is,
ironically, also a divisive factor within the
church. For example, many Southern
churches, rigidly committed to believers'
baptism by immersion as a result of their
sectarian and evangelistic fervor, refuse to
accept letters of transfer from pedobaptist
churches. They require instead the
immersion of these candidates, treating
them as converts for the first time, and

implying that the churches from which they come are not genuinely or wholly Christian. The problem has become less severe owing to a recent trend in sectarian circles, particularly Southern Baptists, to forgo the requirement of a second baptism.

Another noteworthy and primary Southern phenomenon is that the modern CHARISMATIC MOVEMENTS, emphasizing baptism by the Spirit apart from baptism by water, have found greater acceptance in pedobaptist circles. Perhaps this is due in part to the fact that Confirmation has become less an event of receiving the Spirit and more a catechistic exercise. As a result, those baptized as infants are left without any specific occasion on which they consciously received the Spirit. The charismatic venture may be a compensatory endeavor in this respect. Believers' baptism, with its corresponding doctrine and practice of baptism simultaneously by water and Spirit, tends to cast doubt upon the need and validity of a spiritual baptism so long delayed as to have no apparent connection with the rite of water baptism. Therefore, the charismatic experience is of diminished compensational worth and finds less encouragement among those who were baptized as believers.

See also article on SACRAMENTS AND ORDINANCES.

WARREN T. CARR
WINSTON-SALEM, NORTH CAROLINA

BAPTISM OF THE SPIRIT. The term "baptism of the Holy Spirit" does not occur in the New Testament. It is derived by implication from the announcement of John the Baptist, repeated in each of the gospels, that Jesus would "baptize with the Holy Spirit." Five episodes describing initiation experiences of the Spirit are supplied in Acts: the Jerusalem Pentecost of Acts 2; the Samaritan Pentecost, ch. 8; Damascus, ch. 9; Caesarea, ch. 10; Ephesus, ch. 19. It is largely upon these passages that various theologies of baptism of the Spirit are based. Various significant evangelical and sacramental interpretations of the term have had prominence in American Christianity.

1. The classic Reformed tradition maintains that the inauguration of the church age is that to which John the Baptist had reference. It is therefore a nonrepeatable eschatalogical episode pertaining to the church at large and is not related to personal Christian experience.

2. Some Evangelicals, from the time of A. J. Gordon in the late nineteenth century to contemporary interpreters, distinguish between the unique, nonrepeatable baptism of the Holy Spirit inaugurating the church age, and subsequent personal "fillings" of the Spirit available as personal experience. Believers participate in the unique baptism of the church by the new-birth experience. However, subsequent to this, believers may experience one or more "fillings" of the Spirit, in which any of the gifts of the Spirit might be operative. That which is incipient at new birth is actualized in personal experience.

3. A typical sacramentalist charismatic understanding is that of Donald Gelpi, a Roman Catholic. He would substitute the sacramental rite of baptism for the evangelical experience as the moment of initiation into the life of the church. This is identified as baptism of the Spirit. However, at a subsequent moment this incipient potentiality may be brought to a conscious level, that is, actualized, with the manifestation of any of the varied gifts of the Spirit.

4. Keswickian theology, expressed by R. A. Torrey, shifts the terminology of baptism of the Spirit from the eschatological church event at Pentecost to the personal experience of the believer. For him, every believer needs to seek an experience subsequent to new birth, an endowment of power for witnessing and victorious living. This experience carries no particular evidence, other than power in life and service. This theology had its origins in

Oberlin Perfectionism. In turn, this influenced the theology of the Keswick conventions, which then passed rapidly throughout much of revivalistic Evangelicalism in the United States by 1900.

5. Wesleyans in the late nineteenth century tended, likewise, to adopt the term baptism of the Holy Spirit. The classic "second blessing" of Wesleyan theology, defined as a cleansing from inbred sin, or "entire sanctification," came to be looked upon as a "Pentecostal" experience, a "baptism of the Spirit" (see Carter).

6. The Pentecostal view, held by virtually all American Pentecostalists, since the Topeka KS revival of Charles Parham in 1901, is that all believers receive the Spirit at new birth, but baptism of the Spirit is a subsequent crisis event, an enduement of power for service, accompanied by the sign of speaking in other tongues. This association of Spirit-baptism and speaking in tongues is derived from what is felt to be a normative pattern in the Book of Acts (see Horton).

See also articles on CHARISMATIC MOVEMENTS; KESWICK MOVEMENT; PENTECOSTALISM.

Bibliography. Charles W. Carter, *The Person and Ministry of the Holy Spirit, A Wesleyan Perspective*; Donald Gelpi, *Pentecostalism*; A. J. Gordon, *The Ministry of the Spirit*; Stanley Horton, *What the Bible Says About the Holy Spirit*; R. A. Torrey, *The Holy Spirit: Who He Is and What He Does.*

WILLIAM W. MENZIES
ASSEMBLIES OF GOD GRADUATE SCHOOL

BAPTIST BIBLE FELLOWSHIP. A very conservative independent body, the Baptist Bible Fellowship originated on 23 May 1950 in the midst of turmoil, trauma, and conflict. Its roots date back to 1923 and the birth of the Baptist Bible Union. This organization, headed by a triumvirate of leaders such as W. B. Riley, T. T. Shields, and J. FRANK NORRIS, was initiated (according to these leaders) because of the effects of modernism upon convention schools. This Union did rally the Fundamentalist Baptists for seven

years but finally ended with the demise of Des Moines University, which had been taken over by the Union.

After the collapse, Riley returned to his church, the First Baptist Church of Minneapolis; Shields returned to the Jarvis Street Baptist Church of Toronto, and Norris to the First Baptist Church of Fort Worth. Each church started its own schools and fellowships. Norris started the World Fundamentalist Baptist Missionary Fellowship in 1936. In turn, the Baptist Bible Seminary was founded in 1939 (it was originally known as the Fundamental Baptist Bible Institute with Louis Entzminger as its first president). In 1944 the name was changed to the Baptist Bible Seminary with Norris superseding Entzminger as president.

In 1948 Norris insisted that G. Beauchamp Vick assume the presidency of the financially unstable institution. The insolvency of the institution became the focal point of the dispute between the forces of Vick and Norris. Billy Vick Bartlett in *The History of Baptist Separatism* claims the birth of the Baptist Bible Fellowship derived from suspicions of Norris's financial integrity that caused support for the seminary to wane. When Vick took over the leadership of the seminary it was $250,000 in debt and about to go into receivership. Within a few years Vick had reduced the debt to $135,000 and restored the confidence of many pastors.

The climax came when Norris decided to recapture control of the school and the leadership of the movement. The president of the Fellowship at that time, W. E. Dowell, who normally moderated the meetings, was replaced by a Norris protégé and the turmoil that ensued ended in a meeting in the historic Texas hotel. Here the anti-Norris forces voted to establish the Baptist Bible Fellowship, the Baptist Bible College, and the Baptist Bible Tribune. Noel Smith was elected the first editor of this paper.

A missionary effort was immediately launched. The five families in the field wrote Vick and announced their intentions to align themselves with the new organization. Fred S. Donnelson became the first director and initiated the slogan "Missions is the strong right arm of the Fellowship."

The Baptist Bible College campus was located centrally in SPRINGFIELD MO, on the existing five-acre city park at Kearney and Summit. Vick, Dowell, and Rawlings spent most of each summer on the road visiting pastors and churches to align friends and find financial support. In September 1950, the first dormitory was ready for occupancy with 107 students enrolled.

The growth from these early beginnings was remarkable. Starting with approximately 120 churches at its inception, the Fellowship grew to 1,200 churches in 1961 and over one million members. George Dollar has written that it became numerically the largest Fundamentalist group in the world. This was true even though the AMERICAN BAPTIST ASSOCIATION had more churches. The 1970-1971 BBF directory listed some 2,006 churches and an estimated membership of a million and a half.

After the death of the dynamic leader, G. Beauchamp Vick in 1975, W. E. Dowell assumed the presidency of the college. In 1977, the Baptist Bible Fellowship had over 3,000 churches in 50 states and represented over one and a half million people. It also had more than 500 missionaries on 52 mission fields of the world. By that time, Baptist Bible College was enrolling over 2,500 students and graduating nearly 500 each year (Jerry Falwell a famous one of the 1950s). To its members the growth of the body was seen as resulting from its doctrinal faithfulness and its evangelistic and missionary fervor.

See also articles on FUNDAMENTALISM; MODERNIST CONTROVERSY.

Bibliography. Billy Vick Bartlett, The History of Baptist Separatism; George Dollar, A History of Fundamental-ism in America; W. E. Dowell, The Birth Pangs of the Baptist Bible Fellowship, International.

ROBERT J. TERREY
BAPTIST BIBLE COLLEGE

BAPTIST DENOMINATION. As part of the left wing of 17th-century English PURITANISM, Baptists originated as an offshoot of CONGREGATIONALISM (Separatists or Independents). In opposition to the notion of a parish church that embraced all who lived within parish boundaries, Congregationalists and Baptists insisted that churches were gathered communities of believers. The point of distinction between the two branches of Congregationalism was the Baptist rejection of infant baptism. If a church was composed only of believers, the restriction of BAPTISM to those who were sufficiently mature to be able to give a credible profession of faith seemed a logical inference to Baptists, who believed this was amply supported by biblical precept and example.

From the beginning Baptists have been a varied group with a complex history and no single theological or ecclesiastical tradition. They were divided initially into General and Particular Baptists, representing variant forms of CALVINISM. The former adhered to a "general" doctrine of atonement; the latter insisted upon a "particular" doctrine of atonement, a belief that Christ died only for the "elect."

General Baptists were the first to appear, emerging from a group of Lincolnshire Separatists (Congregationalists) who sought asylum in the Netherlands in 1608, one contingent under the leadership of John Robinson in Leyden, the other with John Smyth as their leader in Amsterdam. Smyth came to the conclusion that if the Separatist contention that "churches of the apostolic constitution consisted of saints only" was correct, then baptism was appropriate only for those who could offer convincing proof of grace. Smyth proceeded to baptize first himself and then 36 others who joined with him in forming a Baptist church. Although General Baptists experienced marked growth after the meeting of the Long Parliament in 1640, they had no long future. After 1650 General Baptists suffered large defections to the Quakers. Those remaining had their vitality sapped by the inroads of skepticism. Their churches dwindled or died or became Unitarian. The line of Baptist descent, therefore, was from the Particular Baptists.

Particular Baptists stemmed from Henry Jacob's non-Separatist Independent (Congregational) church across the Thames from London. Separatists believed the Church of England to be a false church and insisted that the break with it must be complete and uncompromising. Non-Separatist Congregationalists sought to maintain some bond of unity among Christians. Recognizing that even the purest churches are subject to mixture and error, they were unwilling to regard the Church of England as utterly corrupt and to separate themselves completely from Christians who remained within the parish churches. While they believed it necessary to separate themselves from the corruptions of the Church of England by establishing gathered churches, they regarded it as a breach of Christian charity to withhold all forms of fellowship from them.

In 1638 some members of the Jacob church withdrew under the leadership of John Spilsbury to form the first Particular Baptist church. The withdrawal was accomplished in orderly fashion by mutual consent and occasioned no ill-feeling. The Baptist group, the record states, expressed a desire "to depart and not to be censured," and permission was granted with "prayer made on their behalf." After the overthrow of episcopacy and the outbreak of civil war, the number of Particular Baptists quickly multiplied. This growth continued during the 1650s. Their theological position was made clear when they adopted a slightly altered form of the WESTMINSTER CONFESSION OF FAITH

(known in England as the London Confession and in America as the Philadelphia Confession). Indeed, as an aid to survival in the dark years of persecution after 1660, the Particular Baptists fortified themselves by moving in a hyper-Calvinist direction.

A similar leftward pilgrimage was being pursued simultaneously in America, where a Baptist church was established at Providence by Roger Williams in 1639, a year after Spilsbury formed his congregation in London. Williams's church was soon left to its own devices, for Williams shortly withdrew to await the reestablishment of the true church in a new apostolic age. A more stable Baptist center was at Newport RI, where the church founded by John Clarke adopted Baptist views between 1641 and 1646. Two other Particular Baptist churches were founded in New England at an early date, one in Swansea in 1663 composed of Welsh settlers, and the other in Boston in 1665. Meanwhile, Henry Dunster was dismissed as president of Harvard in 1653 when he adopted Baptist views. There was scattered General Baptist activity in most of the American colonies at an early date, but most of these churches were later reorganized on a Particular Baptist basis by representatives of the Philadelphia Baptist Association. The only cluster of General Baptist churches to survive was centered in Rhode Island and it numbered only a few congregations.

The important center of Baptist activity in America was in the middle colonies. William Penn arrived in Pennsylvania with his first settlers in 1682. Two years later a Baptist church was established in what was to be Bucks County. The Philadelphia Association of Baptist Churches was organized in 1707, an intercolonial body that was to link Baptist churches in Massachusetts, Connecticut, New York, New Jersey, Pennsylvania, Delaware, Maryland, and Virginia. In 1751 a sister association was formed on the Philadelphia model at Charleston SC by Oliver Hart from New Jersey. Shortly thereafter two associations subsidiary to the Philadelphia Association were established, the Warren to the east in New England and the Ketochten to the west in Virginia. During much of the 18th century, emissaries from the Philadelphia Association were organizing or reorganizing Baptist churches throughout the colonies. By 1800 Baptists had become the largest denomination in the new nation with twice as many adherents as the Congregationalists, who were the next largest religious group. They were to lose that position to the Methodist denomination by 1820, but regained it early in the 20th century. (Roman Catholic membership became the nation's largest in the 1840s.)

The great spurt of Baptist growth occurred in the years immediately preceding, during, and following the American Revolution. These new churches were products of the disruptions occasioned by the GREAT AWAKENING, which provided potential recruits susceptible to Baptist contentions. In New England former "Separate" Congregationalists united with earlier Baptist churches without lengthy negotiations. But in the South a split did occur as a result of activity by "Separates" from New England (Separate Baptists). This division was not healed until roughly 1787. Another offshoot of the Awakening had its beginning in 1779 at Durham NH under the influence of Benjamin Randall. These were FREE WILL BAPTISTS; they were Wesleyan in theology. After the turn of the century, they spread east through Maine to Nova Scotia, south to the Carolinas, and west to New York State and beyond. Similar Wesleyan churches labeling themselves GENERAL BAPTISTS were to be found along the tributaries of the lower Ohio River after 1800. In England the same Wesleyan influence produced the New Connexion General Baptists.

Another New England export that took root in the South after 1845 when JAMES R. GRAVES arrived in Tennessee was the LANDMARK MOVEMENT, which represented a "high church" point of view among Baptists. Landmarkists refused to have anything to do with other Christians, including other Baptists who did not share their exclusivist convictions.

During the first decades of the 19th century, the Calvinism of the Philadelphia Confession began to be sharply modified by the Evangelicalism represented by the New Divinity of Yale and given popular expression by Charles G. Finney. Although never formally adopted or authorized, the so-called NEW HAMPSHIRE CONFESSION OF FAITH (drafted in 1833) ultimately replaced the Philadelphia Confession in most Baptist churches both South and North. In response to this softening of doctrine, churches in isolated areas from Maine to Georgia who were less subject to new trends by 1830 were drawing back into an even more staunch Calvinism. They called themselves Old School or PRIMITIVE BAPTISTS, but were more generally known as hardshell or antimissionary Baptists. In England the influence of Evangelicalism among Particular Baptists resulted in a similar reaction by those who called themselves Strict Baptists. Neither Primitive nor Strict Baptists exhibited great vitality. While steadfastly maintaining their witness, they never became more than a small minority group.

The two major divisions among Baptists were related to the issue of slavery and the Civil War. White Baptists were split in 1845 into Northern and Southern churches, although no theological issues separated them. After the Civil War, when blacks in significant numbers were free to form their own churches, most chose to be Baptists. By 1900 the white Southern Baptists had begun to outpace sharply in number of adherents their fellow white Baptists in the North and West. In 1982 the SOUTHERN BAPTIST CONVENTION reported a membership of 13,782,644, while the (northern) American Baptist Churches reported 1,607,541 members. The membership of the three large black bodies (National Baptist Convention, Inc., National Baptist Convention of America, and Progressive National Baptist Convention) is estimated at approximately 9,000,000.

Several Baptist bodies were the product of vigorous evangelistic activity among immigrant groups in the United States and Canada, the largest being the North American Baptist General Conference (German in background) and the Baptist General Conference of North America (Swedish in background). Tension over issues of polity led to the formation of the AMERICAN BAPTIST ASSOCIATION in 1905 by churches located primarily in Oklahoma, Texas, and Arkansas. Two other groups were the product of the "fundamentalist" controversy among Northern Baptists: the General Association of Regular Baptists organized in 1932 and the Conservative Baptist Association formed in 1947. In addition to churches affiliated with organized bodies, there are numerous independent Baptist churches, frequently calling themselves Bible or Gospel or Pentecostal Baptist churches.

Beginning in England with William Carey, who sailed for India in 1792, and in the United States with Adoniram Judson, who established an outpost in Burma in 1813, the 19th century became the great period of Baptist overseas expansion. The penetration of Africa was initiated from Nova Scotia by David George, a former slave who fled Charleston SC with the departing British troops. In 1819 black Baptists of Richmond VA took leadership in this enterprise. Baptists are strongly represented on every continent and are present in almost every country. According to the Baptist World Alliance, in 1892 there were 833,000 Baptists in Central and South America; 975,970 in Africa; 1,552,692 in Asia with 97,695 in Oceania; and 1,111,693 in Continental Europe. Worldwide the total number of Baptists was 30,724,761.

See also articles on ECCLESIOLOGY; EVANGELICALISM.

Bibliography. Joseph D. Ban, "Were the Earliest English Baptists Anabaptists?", *In the Great Tradition,* J. D. Dekar and Paul R. Dekar, eds.; W. W. Barnes, *The Southern Baptist Convention, 1845-1953*; Edwin S. Gaustad, *Historical Atlas of Religion in America*; Winthrop S. Hudson, ed., *Baptist Concepts of the Church*; *Baptists in Transition: Individualism and Christian Responsibility*; William L. Lumpkin, *Baptist Confessions of Faith*; *Baptist Foundations in the South*; William G. McLoughlin, *Isaac Backus and the American Baptist Pietistic Tradition*; Robert G. Torbet, *A History of the Baptists*; A. C. Underwood, *History of English Baptists*; B. R. White, *The English Separatist Tradition.*

WINTHROP S. HUDSON
CHAPEL HILL, NORTH CAROLINA

BAPTIST MISSIONARY ASSOCIATION OF AMERICA.

A national organization of independent Baptist churches, this conservative body can trace its beginnings to a disagreement which arose within the Board of Directors of the Texas Baptist Convention in 1893. This dispute centered around the question of "convention sovereignty" and was in essence a part of the southwide revolt by Landmark Baptists against the convention system. It came to a head in 1899 when the leader of the "Reform" movement, S. A. Hayden, was ousted from the convention by the "Board" faction. This resulted in the withdrawal of a large number of Landmark churches, who met at Troupe in July of 1900 and formed the Baptist Missionary Association of Texas. Over 560 churches fellowshiped with this new body in 1904. It began a college at Jacksonville, opened an orphanage at Waxahachie, and developed an extensive foreign mission program in Brazil and Portugal.

In 1924 the BMA merged its foreign mission work with that of the Baptist General Association, which had been largely based in Arkansas. This union resulted in the formation of the AMERICAN BAPTIST ASSOCIATION. In 1936 Ben M. Bogard, a leading Arkansas pastor, brought charges of impropriety against the association's business manager. When D. N. Jackson, the son-in-law of the accused, came to his defense, a bitter newspaper controversy ensued. Jackson's main support came from the BMA of Texas, whose Jacksonville College was a leading rival of Bogard's Missionary Baptist Seminary.

As the discussion progressed, a number of theological differences began to emerge between the two groups. These focused upon the joint ownership of seminaries and colleges, the methods to be used in choosing associational missionaries, and the qualifications of delegates to the ABA. A crisis developed in 1949 when a number of pro-Bogard churches were banned from the BMA of Texas. At the 1950 session of the ABA, which was held in Lakeland FL, an attempt was made by the Jackson forces to gain control of the organization. When this move was defeated, most of the BMA churches and a number from other states withdrew and called for the formation of a new national body. This was accomplished in May of 1950 at Little Rock when the North American Baptist Association was established. Its name was changed to the Baptist Missionary Association of America in 1968. Its "Doctrinal Statement and Principles of Co-operation" are very similar to those of the ABA, though more powers are vested in the association itself.

Since its formation, the BMAA has been noted for its concentration on fostering and encouraging foreign missions. This work began in 1950 when former BMA of Texas missionaries in Brazil and Portugal associated themselves with the new group. Since that time, extensive mission projects have been developed in several foreign countries. In 1981 some $1,500,000 went to the support of 80 foreign missionaries. In 1980, 1,415 BMAA churches in some 20 states reported a U.S. membership of 224,533. A denominational headquarters is maintained at Little Rock AR.

See also article on LANDMARK MOVEMENT.

RUSSELL PIERCE BAKER
LITTLE ROCK, ARKANSAS

BAPTISTS, MISSIONARY. Not the title of a specific denomination, this term designates immersionists who use means to promote religious conversion. After Baptists divided into pro- and antimission factions early in the 19th century, this title identified a modified Calvinistic position—or, in some cases, an Arminian position—which held that Christ died for every person. In areas of the South where predestinarian Baptists are numerous, it distinguishes the Southern Baptist Convention. In other places it is used by Baptists who place extreme emphasis on the local congregation and who are sometimes called Landmark Baptists. In such cases the name separates these groups from the Southern Baptists.

Even though the Southern Baptist Convention is the largest Missionary Baptist denomination in the South, the groups covered in this entry are much smaller and are opposed to the "convention system." The oldest of them is the AMERICAN BAPTIST ASSOCIATION, organized in 1924 by the merger of the General Association of Baptist Churches and the BAPTIST MISSIONARY ASSOCIATION OF AMERICA. Its *Yearbook* for 1980 lists 1,543 churches in the United States, 82 percent of which are located in the South, the majority being in Arkansas and Texas. Its estimated statistics for 1980 are set in the *Yearbook of American and Canadian Churches* at 5,000 churches and 1,500,000 members. Churches affiliate with this denomination not formally but loosely through purchase of its literature and support of its mission program. Thus it is difficult to calculate the scope of its influence.

The association's opposition to enumerating its churches symbolizes its distinctive doctrine—"the complete sovereignty of the local churches." This principle is expressed by the equal representation given each church at the association's annual meeting and by the methods used to conduct its missionary program. The missionaries related to the group are stationed in 17 foreign countries and in most parts of the United States. The association's headquarters are housed in Texarkana TX.

The Baptist Missionary Association of America broke away from the American

Baptist Association in 1950 because the older body allowed affiliated churches to send messengers to annual meetings who did not belong to those congregations. The newer group originally designated itself the North American Baptist Association, but in 1969 adopted its present name in order to eliminate the word "north" in the title of a denomination located predominantly in the South. In 1979 this group was composed of 1,439 churches with 226,290 members, 69 percent of whom lived in Texas and Arkansas. The association maintains missionaries in 17 lands overseas and in 16 states in this country.

In the 1920s J. FRANK NORRIS founded in Texas a group called the Pre-Millennial Baptist Missionary Fellowship, which later took the name World Fundamental Missionary Baptist Fellowship. It split into two parts in 1950. After two years the original group called itself the World Baptist Fellowship. Over 850 churches and missions with 170,000 members in 40 states cooperate with this organization. Its missionaries labor in 20 countries. The younger group named itself the BAPTIST BIBLE FELLOWSHIP. Its affiliated churches total 2,600 and support missionaries in 34 foreign lands.

See also articles on ANTIMISSION MOVEMENT; LANDMARK MOVEMENT.

Bibliography. American Baptist Association, Yearbook, 1980; Baptist Missionary Association of America, Directory and Handbook, 1980-1981; Arthur Carl Piepkorn, Profiles in Belief, 2: 418-21, 427-30; James E. Tull, A Study of Baptist Landmarkism in the Light of Historical Baptist Ecclesiology.

CHESTER RAYMOND YOUNG
CUMBERLAND COLLEGE

BARDSTOWN, KENTUCKY. This small town, 40 miles south of Louisville, was settled in the late eighteenth century. Many of its founders were Presbyterians; and a minister of that denomination preached there as early as 1781. The region also hosted two of the earliest Baptist and Methodist congregations in Kentucky: Cedar Creek Baptist Church (1781) and Ferguson Chapel (Methodist) (1792). Bardstown was to become more famous, however, as an early center for Southern Catholicism.

Catholic families from Maryland settled in the Bardstown area in the 1780s. Father STEPHEN T. BADIN arrived in 1793 to serve this community and organize parishes throughout the state. Two religious orders joined him in 1805, the Dominicans at St. Rose and the Trappists. These first Trappists stayed only briefly. A second group later built the Abbey of Our Lady of Gethsemani (1848), oldest Trappist foundation in the nation and the first American abbey (1850). THOMAS MERTON belonged to this community.

In 1808, Bardstown became a diocesan see under the French-born Bishop BENEDICT FLAGET. Saint Joseph's Cathedral was completed in 1819, and a seminary and college opened. The Sisters of Loretto at the Foot of the Cross, organized near Bardstown in 1812, were the first order of American nuns without foreign affiliation. The Sisters of Charity of Nazareth, also founded nearby in 1812, moved their motherhouse to Bardstown in 1822. They also ran Nazareth College. The first foundation of Dominican nuns in the U. S. began at St. Rose in 1822.

Religious activity continued vital in the 1830s. Both Catholic and Protestant newspapers appeared. In 1832, Bardstown hosted the first meeting of the Kentucky Baptist Convention. River transport, however, began to favor Louisville over Bardstown with the result that the Catholic bishop moved to Louisville in 1841. Nonetheless, Bardstown remains a spiritual and historical center for the entire area.

See also article on ROMAN CATHOLIC CHURCH.

Bibliography. W. J. Howlett, Old St. Thomas at Poplar Neck, Bardstown, Kentucky; J. H. Schauinger, Stephen T. Badin; Sarah Smith, Historic Nelson County.

GARY W. MCDONOGH
NEW COLLEGE
UNIVERSITY OF SOUTH FLORIDA

BARUCH, BERNARD (1870-1965), Jewish statesman, was born in Camden SC, the son of Simon Baruch, a Prussian immigrant who served as a surgeon in the Confederate army, and Isobel (Belle) Wolfe Baruch, a descendant of one of the first Jewish families to settle in America. In 1881 the family moved to New York, where professional opportunities were better for Dr. Baruch than in South Carolina. Soon after Bernard Baruch graduated from the College of the City of New York in 1889 he took a job with an investment firm. By age 30 he was a millionaire. During World War I he served as chairman of the War Industries Board, and he was one of Woodrow Wilson's chief economic advisors to Versailles. In World War II he was special advisor to the Office of War Mobilization. In 1946 he presented the controversial Baruch Plan, which advocated an international authority to control and inspect all atomic projects; it was rejected by Russia. Throughout his life Baruch, called the "Park Bench Philosopher," was often sought out for advice and counsel and was widely admired for his brilliance and philanthropic activities.

Married to an Episcopalian, he was not an especially observant Jew, but he celebrated the High Holy Days. He did suffer some religious discrimination and was excluded from several social clubs. Moreover, he believed that his religion prevented him from becoming president of the United States.

In 1939 Baruch advocated the creation of a United States of Africa in the region of Uganda to be a haven for Jews and other European refugees of Nazism. He personally pledged $5,000,000 for such a venture and promised to raise funds from others, but nothing came of his proposal. Baruch did not believe that the United States of Africa or any other nation should be established on a religious basis. Therefore, he was critical of Zionism and was not especially happy with the creation of Israel as a religious nation in 1948. Though some American Jews were dis-

pleased with Baruch's views on Israel, most took great pride in his achievements.

Bibliography. Margaret Coit, *Mr. Baruch.*

ARNOLD SHANKMAN

BELIEVERS' BAPTISM: *See* BAPTISM.

BENJAMIN, JUDAH PHILIP (1811-1884), the most prominent Southerner of Jewish birth in the 19th century, he was born in St. Croix, West Indies. His parents were Orthodox Jews who soon moved to Fayetteville NC, then Charleston SC. Benjamin attended, but did not graduate from, Yale College and at 17 moved to New Orleans where he became a brilliant, successful attorney as well as a slaveowning planter at nearby Belle Chasse. He married a Catholic, Natalie St. Martin, in 1833, thereby severing his already tenuous bonds to the Jewish community. Nominated by President Pierce to the U.S. Supreme Court, Benjamin declined and instead served two terms as senator from Louisiana, eloquently championing the cause of slavery. After secession Benjamin served as attorney general of the Confederacy, was promoted to secretary of war and—having won the confidence of Jefferson Davis, if not general popularity—finally secretary of state. In 1865 he fled to England and began another spectacular legal career, eventually serving as queen's counsel in Lancaster. In 1883 he rejoined his daughter and wife from whom he had long been estranged in Le Mans, France, where he died. He was buried according to Catholic rites.

Benjamin was an enigmatic figure with a reputation for guile as well as acuity; he provided few clues into his interior life for associates or biographers. But the unimpeded career of the "brains of the Confederacy" has suggested to historians that talent could blunt anti-Semitism in the antebellum South.

See also article on JEWS IN THE SOUTH.

Bibliography. Benjamin Kaplan, "Judah Philip Benjamin," *Jews in the South*, ed. Leonard Dinnerstein and

Mary Dale Palsson; Robert D. Meade, *Judah P. Benjamin, Confederate Statesman*; Richard S. Tedlow, "Judah P. Benjamin," *Turn to the South: Essays on Southern Jewry*, ed. Nathan M. Kaganoff and Melvin I. Urofsky.

STEPHEN J. WHITFIELD
BRANDEIS UNIVERSITY

BENNETT, BELLE HARRIS (1852-1922), a leader in women's missionary work in Southern Methodism, was born near Richmond KY to a wealthy and socially prominent family. Her early life, by her own admission, was largely devoted to social activities, but in her early twenties, she experienced a religious conversion and joined the local Methodist church. There she developed a strong interest in the expanding foreign missionary work being done by the women of the Methodist Episcopal Church, South. She soon became convinced that women going to foreign fields needed better training and she was appointed by the Woman's Foreign Mission Board to raise funds for a school for that purpose. Bennett traveled throughout the South seeking contributions.

The result of her efforts was the establishment in Nashville of Scarritt Bible and Training School, dedicated in 1892 to prepare missionaries for home as well as foreign work. This marked the beginning of Bennett's leadership in mission work. She served as president of the Southern Methodist Woman's Home Mission Society from 1896 to 1910, and after the foreign- and home-mission boards were merged, of the Woman's Missionary Council from 1910 to 1922. As president, Bennett encouraged and supervised diverse social programs, including settlement houses and other city-mission work among immigrants, poor whites, and blacks. She frequently condemned racial hatred and advocated a greater and more equal role for women in society and in her denomination. In 1902 she persuaded the M. E. Church, South, to create an order of deaconesses to aid in mission work, and she led the drive to obtain "laity rights" for Southern Methodist women, which were finally granted in 1918.

See also articles on SOCIAL GOSPEL; WOMEN IN RELIGION.

Bibliography. Mrs. R. W. MacDonell, *Belle Harris Bennett*; Douglas R. Chandler, "Belle Harris Bennett," *Notable American Women: A Biographical Dictionary*, ed. Edward T. James, et al.

JOHN P. MCDOWELL
ROANOKE, VIRGINIA

BERRY, MARTHA (1866-1942), innovative educator, established in 1902 an industrial school for poor mountain boys near Rome GA. This bold act by a Georgia woman who was herself an aristocrat untrained as educator, economist, or conservationist is one of this century's greatest educational stories. At a time when the state had only five high schools, Martha Berry, second of eight children of Thomas and Frances Rhea Berry, ceded land inherited from them for a school training equally the hand, heart, and head. Believing wasted humanity the world's worst sin and the South's impoverished illiterates the nation's reservoir of strength and citizenship, she overcame, with faith as her perpetual guide, seemingly impossible odds—a rigid social canon, sexual barriers, community antagonism, wars, depressions, and resistant mountaineer pride—to uplift the dispossessed around her.

She gave her money and resources and indefatigably of her energies, and saw her school (now Berry College and Academy) succeed, though its struggle forced her into the excruciating role of fundraiser. By sharing her dream of helping humanity in the making, she attracted as benefactors the famous and the not-so-famous alike. Born just after the Civil War, she lived until 1942, receiving worldwide recognition during her own lifetime. For the miracle she wrought in delivering thousands from the bondage of ignorance, she became one of the world's most admired women. President Coolidge aptly remarked that her "achievement brings the mystery and beauty of divine guidance closer to us all." The keynote to that truly remarkable life of service is carved on her simple grave: "Not to be ministered unto but to minister."

D. DEAN CANTRELL
BERRY COLLEGE

BETH ELOHIM. Kahal Kadosh Beth Elohim (Holy Congregation House of God) of CHARLESTON SC, the recognized birthplace of Reform Judaism in the United States, was organized in 1749. Only three Jewish congregations in this country are older. By 1800 it was the largest, worshiping under the traditional Sephardic liturgy in a handsome synagogue consecrated in 1794. Members of the congregation founded the Charleston Hebrew Benevolent Society (1784) and the Charleston Hebrew Orphan Society (1801), each the oldest of its kind in the United States.

In 1824 failure of the efforts of 47 congregants to effect changes in the all-Hebrew services to make them more intelligible and decorous led them to form the "Reformed Society of Israelites," the first attempt at Reform Judaism in the United States. The society lasted for nine years.

In 1838 Beth Elohim's synagogue was destroyed by fire. When a new edifice was erected in 1840, the congregation installed an organ for regular services, a first in American Jewish history. It soon adopted other progressive reforms under the leadership of Gustavus Poznanski, thus becoming the first Reform congregation in the United States. Traditionalists seceded and formed another congregation, but they reunited with Beth Elohim in 1866.

In 1838 the congregation established the second Jewish Sunday school in the United States, the first in the South. In 1842 Beth Elohim published its own hymnal, the first by an American Jewish congregation; the hymns were composed mostly by PENINA MOISE, the first American Jewish poetess.

In 1873 Beth Elohim was one of the founding congregations of the Union of American Hebrew Congregations. It still worships in its imposing 1840 Greek Revival building (now a National Historic Landmark), which has the distinction of being the second-oldest synagogue in the United States, the oldest in continuous service, and the oldest surviving Reform synagogue in the world.

See also articles on ARCHITECTURE; JEWS IN THE SOUTH.

SOLOMON BREIBART
CHARLESTON, SOUTH CAROLINA

BETHANY, WEST VIRGINIA. A village in the northwest panhandle of West Virginia lying west of Washington PA and north of Wheeling WV on Buffalo Creek. It is identified with the ministry of ALEXANDER CAMPBELL and the founding of the DISCIPLES OF CHRIST. In response to the preaching of Thomas Campbell, the Christian Association of Washington was organized in 1809, and an independent church was later formed at Brush Run on the Buffalo. Campbell's son, Alexander, commenced preaching here in 1811, the same year in which he married Margaret Brown, whose father owned a farm at the present site of Bethany. Alexander Campbell and his bride settled on the farm, and from this home Campbell led the Disciples of Christ until his death in 1866. Known originally as Buffaloe, the area was named Bethany in 1827 when a post office was established and Campbell was appointed postmaster.

Alexander Campbell's two periodicals, *The Christian Baptist* (1823-1830) and *The Millennial Harbinger* (1830-1870), which were crucial in developing a sense of identity for the congregationally governed Disciples of Christ, were published at Bethany on the editor's presses. Here Campbell organized a church in whose present building both he and his father preached their last sermons. He established Buffalo Seminary, which had a short history, and in 1840 became the founder and first president of Bethany College.

The college survives with a main building erected after 1858 that reflects the architectural style of the University of Glasgow where Alexander Campbell had studied. The Campbell home was erected by John Brown about 1793, deeded to Alexander and Margaret Brown Campbell in 1815, and enlarged in 1818, 1836, and 1840. The home has been restored and is maintained by the college as a museum. Bethany Church, erected in 1852 or 1853, is still used for worship. The Campbell cemetery near the home and the Bethany cemetery adjacent to the church contain the remains of many prominent first-generation Disciples of Christ and individuals subsequently identified with the college and the denomination.

See also articles on CAMPBELLITE TRADITION; CHRISTIAN CHURCHES AND CHURCHES OF CHRIST; CHURCHES OF CHRIST.

SAMUEL C. PEARSON
SOUTHERN ILLINOIS UNIVERSITY
AT EDWARDSVILLE

BETHUNE, MARY MCLEOD (1875-1955), was born 10 July 1875 in the little farming community of Mayesville SC. The fifteenth of 17 children born to Patsy and Samuel McLeod, both former slaves, she was the second born free and the first to attend school. A precocious child, she was enrolled by her parents at age seven in the Mayesville Presbyterian Mission School for Negroes. She completed her course of study in 1886 and received a scholarship to attend Scotia Seminary for Negro Girls in Concord, North Carolina. She graduated as a class leader in 1894 and in the fall enrolled at Moody Bible Institute in Chicago, receiving her certificate in the spring of 1895.

Early in life Mary became inspired by the Christian teachings on love, sacrifice, and fellowship. Around age eight she had a vision of becoming a missionary to Africa; this vision remained with her throughout the years. Upon completing her training at Moody Institute, she applied to the Board of Missions of the Pres-

byterian Church, U.S.A. To her dismay, her application was rejected on the grounds that no positions were then open for black women.

She returned south and took a position with Lucy Laney at Haines Institute in Augusta GA. Impressed by the work of Laney, who had been born into slavery, Mary Bethune began to think for the first time in terms of remaining in the South to serve her people. The next year she accepted a job at Kindell Institute in Sumter SC. There she met and married Albertus Bethune, a former school teacher and aspiring entrepreneur. The couple moved to Savannah GA, and in February 1899 she gave birth to her only offspring, Albert.

Nine months later the family moved to Palatka FL, where Mary Bethune assisted the Rev. C. J. Uggams, a Presbyterian minister, in establishing a grade school; but she felt her efforts were not fully appreciated there. She tendered her resignation after three years and in the fall of 1904 she moved (with her husband and son following shortly) farther south. Settling in Daytona Beach, she began a work she felt divinely called to do, the establishment of a school for girls.

Without sponsorship of any kind, she opened the Daytona Literary and Industrial School for Negro Girls on 4 October 1904. With five young students enrolled, the school opened in the humble setting of a sparse wooden-frame building. Within 15 years, however, it was transformed into an academy valued at close to a half million dollars. In 1923 it merged with Cookman Institute, a declining co-educational Methodist school in Jacksonville, to form Bethune-Cookman Collegiate Institute. The institute became an accredited junior college in 1939 and two years later a senior college, making Mary Bethune the first black woman to have founded and headed a four-year institution of higher learning in the United States.

Originally a Presbyterian, Mary Bethune joined the Methodist Church the same year of the merger. A popular churchwoman, she was voted a delegate to the General Conference for each session from 1928 to 1944 and served on numerous boards. During the 1930s she was active in the debate over reuniting the Southern and Northern wings of Methodism. She favored the principle of reunion but opposed the Plan of Union because it called for the creation of the Central Jurisdiction for blacks while all other jurisdictions were organized according to geographical region.

A social gospeler at heart, Mary Bethune witnessed to her Christian faith by promoting throughout her career the development of black youth, black womanhood, and interracial cooperation. During the Depression years of the Roosevelt administration, she accepted an appointment as director of the Negro Division of the National Youth Administration (N.Y.A.). In 1936 she organized the National Council of Negro Women, and for many years she was a key figure in such organizations as the National Association for the Advancement of Colored People (N.A.A.C.P.) and the Southern Conference for Human Welfare (S.C.H.W.).

While her concerns were global, she took special interest in the American South. She was particularly active in encouraging black voter registration and in rallying support for the antilynching campaign. Proud of her Southern heritage, she labored constantly to bring black and white Southerners closer together. She believed that a harmonious relationship between the races was the cornerstone to building a new South.

For her contribution to racial uplift and interracial understanding, she received many honors, among them the J. E. Springarn Medal from the N.A.A.C.P. and the Thomas Jefferson Award from the S.C.H.W. Still, no honor was more meaningful personally than the Doctor of Humanities degree awarded her by Rollins College in 1949. Even her appointment as an official consultant to the Charter Conference of the United Nations in San Francisco four years earlier paled by comparison. In 1927 the board of trustees of the Winter Park, Florida school denied her the privilege of speaking on campus. To receive an honorary degree 22 years later proved to her that her commitment to the Christian faith as a force for social change and progress was not ill-founded.

CLARENCE J. NEWSOME
DUKE UNIVERSITY

BIBLE, AUTHORITY OF. Authority connotes the power to command. The term "authority" with reference to the Bible has to do with the ways in which the Hebrew and Christian Scriptures are understood to make a claim on those who hold the Scriptures to be "canonical," providing a rule or guide. Such a claim may produce specific forms of behavior, belief, life-style, ritual, etc. The greater the degree and perceived applicability of scriptural authority, the greater will be the conformity of one's life to its rule. While sources of authority other than the Bible can be found (such as ministerial authority in the lower denominations, creedal and episcopal in the higher), in the evangelical mainstream of Southern religion, the Bible is second to none and often claimed to be the *only* authority.

The basic question involved in discussions of biblical authority is this: what is it that makes the Bible authoritative, from what does the Bible derive its power to command? While there are many ways in which this question may be answered, it is possible to arrange the responses within two categories: those that refer to an intrinsic quality, and those that refer to a functional quality. While this distinction is helpful, we must recognize that in no case is the authority of the Bible determined in isolation from the ecclesiological context in which the Bible is used. The first and most obvious form of intrinsic authority must come to terms with the concept of revelation simply because revelation has been so central in the understanding of the Bible from the beginning. The most conservative formulation, shared by vast numbers of evangelical Southerners, usually refers to the Bible as "inspired." At its extreme, this view holds that the Bible is infallible and inerrant because it is the literal record of God's words as spoken to the biblical authors. This understanding of the authority of the Bible constitutes the heart of FUNDAMENTALISM. Proponents of inspiration claim that it can be supported on the basis of Scripture itself (such as 2 Tim. 3:16). Critics of inspiration argue that there is little basis for it within Scripture and that it is actually a tradition founded on subsequent interpretation.

A second formulation of the intrinsic authority of the Bible focuses on its conceptual or doctrinal content. While this view may also be held by fundamentalists, it is not limited to them, and may, in fact, be found among groups far removed from the fundamentalist camp. The proponents of conceptual authority often will point to the apparently self-evident theological profundity of major biblical themes and beliefs, such as justification by faith, incarnation, redemptive suffering, and the liberation of the oppressed. Frequently it is claimed that these biblical concepts are distinctive, if not unique, when compared to those of other religions.

Other approaches to the authority of the Bible concentrate on its function within the community of faith. In general these approaches emphasize the way in which the Bible provides access to divine revelation rather than containing that revelation, although there often may be some overlapping with the conceptual approach described above. Throughout the 1950s and 1960s the dominant approach to biblical authority centered in the concept of revelation in history. Here the Bible received its primary authority as

a witness *to* God's self-revelation in historical events, and ultimately all of history (from creation to the eschaton). This salvation history (*Heilsgeschichte*) model often went hand in hand with the critical interpretation of the biblical text that sought to penetrate behind the text in an effort to discover the historical events that led to its formulation, composition, and ongoing reinterpretation. The Bible's authority derived from its status as an indispensable resource for reconstructing the history of salvation, but divine revelation was understood to reside in the historical events themselves rather than in the text. Such an approach freed its adherents from an undue reliance on the factual accuracy of the biblical texts, but it was not without its problems, not the least of which was the discrepancy between the history (or narrative) of salvation as recorded in the text and the "actual" history as reconstructed by critical interpreters. Moreover, the concept of revelation in history, especially in terms of specific "acts of God," is fraught with considerable philosophical problems.

In recent years scholars have become increasingly interested in another approach to the functional authority of the Bible. In this case biblical authority is understood to reside in the constitutive relationship between narrative and community. In attempting to deal with some of the problems inherent in the salvation-history approach, the narrative/community understanding recognizes that the Bible contains many different kinds of stories—myths, legends, folk tales, chronicles, and others—all of which are connected to history in various ways and degrees. What they usually have in common is that they render a number of agents (God as well as the human characters) and the interaction of these agents within a narrative framework provides a paradigm for the community of faith (both ancient and modern). In fact, the community understands *its* fundamental identity to be defined by the overall biblical story—in terms of both form and content—from Adam in the garden of Eden to John on the island of Patmos. The authority of Scripture resides in this process of identity formation and subsequently is exercised by the ways in which the community must conform to its sense of identity. In other words, the biblical narrative represents a sacred world—sacred precisely because it functions as the supreme guide for the community within the everyday or profane world.

The narrative/community model could probably be applied across the spectrum from the most conservative to the most liberal religious communities. However, the connection between the biblical stories and history, as well as the truth claims of particular biblical concepts, will continue to separate these communities. The dividing line is drawn in differing understandings of theology, anthropology, and language. For some (usually of a liberal persuasion) it is enough to see biblical language as a symbolic medium that indirectly expresses truth about God through human words; for many others (usually of a conservative persuasion), the Bible's authority rests on no such ambiguity but rather in the fact that it provides immediate knowledge of God that is therefore certain, however much its meaning may be open to interpretation.

See also articles on BIBLE, INSPIRATION OF; BIBLE, INTERPRETATION OF.

Bibliography. Refer to bibliography after article, "Bible, Interpretation of."

THOMAS W. MANN
SPARTANBURG, SOUTH CAROLINA

BIBLE CHAIRS. Late in the 19th century it was thought that the separation of church and state prohibited state universities from teaching religion. The Christian Women's Board of Missions of the Christian Church (Disciples of Christ) sought to circumvent that problem by establishing Bible Chairs, the first of which was established in 1893 at the University of Michigan. The church supported a teacher of religion who gave courses as an adjunct to the regular offerings of the university.

Soon after, the Disciples developed a number of other Bible Chairs, including those at the universities of Virginia, Georgia, and Texas.

In the 1920s other religious bodies began establishing Bible Chairs until at least 10, including Roman Catholics and Jews, sponsored Chairs on various campuses. Beginning in the 1960s, state and municipal junior colleges were included. The two most vigorous groups have been the Church of Jesus Christ of Latter-Day Saints, concentrated in the West, and the Churches of Christ, the work of which has centered in the South and Southwest, especially Texas.

Occasionally denominations on a campus have cooperated in Bible Chair work, sometimes using the title "school of religion," an approach also initiated by the Disciples. Normally, however, Bible Chairs have consisted of autonomous programs of campus ministry and the academic teaching of religion, under the sponsorship of a single church or denomination.

A breakthrough occurred when the state universities began offering academic credit for the religion courses. The University of Virginia in 1905 was the first state school in the nation to grant credit for such courses. However, since the 1960s, when the law was interpreted to permit teaching religion in state schools, many state universities have opened departments of religion. Although there are still Bible Chairs, this trend has removed the Chairs' ultimate reason for existence. Therefore, eventually, they may offer only ministry to students, rather than academic instruction.

Bibliography. Ronald B. Flowers, "The Bible Chair Movement in the Disciples of Christ Tradition: Attempts to Teach Religion in State Universities," unpublished Ph.D. dissertation, University of Iowa, 1967.

RONALD B. FLOWERS
TEXAS CHRISTIAN UNIVERSITY

BIBLE COLLEGES: *See* THEOLOGICAL EDUCATION.

BIBLE, INSPIRATION OF. In its traditional sense, the inspiration of the Bible has provided a basis for an understanding of biblical authority and, as a result, has had a significant effect on biblical interpretation. Belief in the inspiration of the Bible is widespread among Southern Evangelicals, especially the more conservative within that family, and universally held to in fundamentalist circles. Except in a quite general understanding, inspiration is much less likely to be held by Presbyterians, Episcopalians, Lutherans, and others of similar ecclesiology and theology.

Biblical inspiration can be construed in both a general and a strict sense. In general, inspiration usually forms the basis for the view that the Bible is inerrant and infallible. Literally, "inspiration" means a breathing in, but in its fullest theological form it refers to the process whereby the biblical authors were filled with the Holy Spirit and, in such a state, recorded the divine truth communicated to them by God. The inspired texts that resulted are held to be without error both historically and theologically. For example, the walls of Jericho must have fallen just as reported in Joshua 6, irrespective of archaeological evidence. Similarly, that God actually ordered the mass annihilation of the Canaanites must be accepted, even if it troubles the conscience of the believer. A literalist approach, in other words, is the only one viable to the reading of Scripture if it is understood to be inspired. In the more strict sense of inspiration, historical and theological information as well as the very words and grammatical structure of the text, are inspired. For many proponents of biblical inspiration, the King James Version is the only version.

Defenders of the inspiration of Scripture usually point to numerous passages within Scripture to support their position. They appeal to literary formulae in the prophets such as "The word of the Lord came to Jeremiah," or "Thus says the Lord," and, most prominently, to 2 Tim. 3:16, which is usually translated: "All scripture is inspired by God. . . ." (RSV). On the other hand, critics of inspiration assert that there is little evidence within Scripture for the doctrine and that it is instead a tradition based on interpretation that is open to serious question.

The central issue in the debate over inspiration has to do with one's understanding of divine revelation and its human reception. For strict inspirationalists, God literally spoke to the biblical authors with an audible voice and what the authors received and recorded would not differ from a tape recording. Although some proponents would allow for deviation from the "original autograph" in subsequent copying, there is little room for any "authorial" participation. Thus the text as inspired provides an immediate knowledge of God, the veracity of which is certain. Such an epistemology offers a great deal of security to the believer.

On the other hand, critics would charge that the doctrine of inspiration fails to take seriously the fundamental ambiguity of the human condition. From this perspective, God "speaks" in the same way now as in ancient times, but it is not with an audible voice. Moreover, the biblical authors were not merely scribal puppets slavishly recording the divine voice word for word. Rather, critical interpretation of the biblical texts over many years has disclosed the ways in which the authors' writings reflect not only their own thought, but also the sociological and ideological configurations of their historical settings. Semantics is also at the heart of the issue. Critics of inspiration would argue that biblical language—like all language—is inescapably symbolic. While it may well express truth, even truth about God, it does so only indirectly. In fact, many of those who hold this more liberal position would assert that the doctrine of inspiration in its most strict sense is a form of idolatry (often referred to as bibliolatry).

The critique of the traditional doctrine of the inspiration of the Bible outlined in the preceding paragraph does not obviate any use of the concept. Indeed, some understanding of Scripture as inspired is probably a necessary component of Jewish and Christian faith. However, instead of referring to some intrinsic quality of the text, a critical understanding of inspiration would focus on the way in which the text functions within the community of faith. Here the text is not a compendium of infallible truth, but a traditional collection of various kinds of writings (with narrative being prominent) that elicit from the community a distinctive sense of identity and mission. The inspiration of Scripture would be that *process* in which the text "claims" the community, and the community confesses itself to be "the people of the book."

See also articles on BIBLE, AUTHORITY; OF; BIBLE, INTERPRETATION OF.

Bibliography. Refer to bibliography after article, "Bible, Interpretation of."

THOMAS W. MANN
SPARTANBURG, SOUTH CAROLINA

BIBLE, INTERPRETATION OF. The development of Southern culture has been significantly influenced by the ways in which people have read and understood the meaning of the Bible. That the reverse is also true—the interpretation of the Bible has been influenced by established cultural norms and changing historical circumstances—simply reflects the symbiosis of religion and culture in this region.

The interpretation of the Bible (or, more technically, biblical hermeneutics) is closely related to the issue of the AUTHORITY OF THE BIBLE. One who understands the Bible to be the literal Word of God is likely to interpret a given passage differently than one who understands the text as a symbolic story produced largely by human imagination. Similarly, the denomination in which one is nurtured may well engender a distinctive mode of interpretation: a Presbyterian is very likely to approach the text in a way that would seem puzzling and even irreverent to a Two-Seed-in-the-Spirit Predestinarian Baptist. Add to authority and denomination the factors of social class, geography, and education, and it is not difficult to imagine the great variety of interpretive styles that are possible. The so-called "Bible belt" is more like a "coat of many colors."

To those trained in the academic study of religion, the interpretation of Scripture automatically denotes a set of methodological tools that are used for critical exegesis. Over the past 150 years, the development of these critical tools has spread primarily from Germany throughout Western Europe and North America and produced a revolution in biblical hermeneutics.

Until recently, the primary goal of critical interpretation has been to uncover the background of a given biblical text and its author. For example, *literary* criticism of the Pentateuch ("higher criticism") produced the "documentary hypothesis," which holds that the first five books of the Old Testament were not written by Moses, but by a number of different "authors" at widely different times in history of ancient Israel. Similarly, *form* criticism attempts to delve behind the present written text into a stage at which the content of the text was transmitted orally. The form critic is also interested in the structure and genre of a text, its peculiar language, and its sociological provenance.

Building on both literary and form criticism, *tradition* criticism (also called redaction criticism) attempts to delineate the overall process through which a text reached its present shape: how an original "author" was used by a later redactor or editor and what alternations were made to the language, structure, and meaning of the tradition in order to speak to a new audience. In short, the critical interpretation of the Bible is concerned not only with the text itself, but also with the contexts out of which the text arose.

Such a hermeneutical stance recognizes the intrinsically "occasional" nature of Scripture; that is, one must often determine its meaning through a reconstruction of the situation in which an author addressed an audience in a particular time and place. During the period in which the methods of literary form and redaction criticism were being refined, knowledge of the ancient Near-Eastern world was also enriched by an enormous wealth of archaeological and epigraphic research. One result of this explosion of evidence was the acknowledgment by many scholars that the religion of the Bible shared a great deal with the religions of the ancient world, from the time of Abraham down to the writings of Paul, and that, however much biblical religion might be distinctive, it was not unique.

Recent developments in biblical interpretation make this era a time of ferment and transition. New approaches such as structuralism and some forms of "canonical criticism" attempt to regain an appreciation for the meaning of the text in its final form, in addition to, or even irrespective of, the process through which that form was achieved. While some approaches emphasize the meaning of the text without regard to its institutional moorings, others accentuate the relation between the text and the communities (both ancient and modern) for whom the text functions as Scripture, that is, as an authoritative rule and guide. There is also increasing interest in the way in which biblical narrative renders an agent (God, Christ) irrespective of the narrative's connection with reconstructed historical events or a critical reconstruction of how the narrative reached its present shape.

Before the impact of the critical interpretation of the Bible on Southern religion can be judged in its own right, two other developments in Southern history that preceded the reaction to critical hermeneutics must be considered. It is difficult to think of any movement within American religious history that has been more determinative for Southern religion (and the respective interpretation of Scripture) than the GREAT AWAKENING of 1747-1780 and its aftermath. This movement began in New England, but quickly spread to the South and found a comfortable and permanent home in Southern religion. The Awakening was essentially a revival of intense, personal religious experience, accompanied by an emphasis on PIETY and HOLINESS. The revivals and CAMP MEETINGS that the Awakening sparked reached their peak in the South in the GREAT REVIVAL that began at CANE RIDGE KY in 1801. From that date until the present, the revival has remained a fixed institution in many Southern churches.

More importantly, the emphasis of REVIVALISM on a powerful emotional experience of conversion, to be followed by personal sanctification, provided the central tenet for the subsequent development of Southern evangelical theology. The result was a highly subjectivist understanding of religion in general and salvation in particular. The question that this type of Evangelicals tend to have always on their lips is "Have you been saved?" The proper answer to the question for them does not point to objective grace, but to subjective experience, an experience that is both intense and perennial. Religion is not real unless it is *felt*.

The result for the interpretation of the Bible and for preaching has been significant and long-lasting. The central purpose for preaching became the conversion of souls. Exegesis and proclamation led to the revivalist's "hour of decision" and the preacher's altar call. It is inevitable that such a hermeneutical orientation will influence the interpretation of a particular biblical text, and even what kinds of texts one chooses for interpretation and preaching. When the goal for both preacher and audience is a new or renewed experience of personal salvation, a text will not be attractive if it raises the ambiguities of the life of faith, or wrestles with a difficult problem of Christology, or presents a prophet's indictment of his nation and its rulers. Such a text may easily be misinterpreted or ignored altogether.

Despite obvious exceptions and degrees of emphasis, the conversionist hermeneutic sketched in the preceding paragraph is most at home in the Southern Baptist tradition and related denominations. While conversionism began among white Evangelicals, it was quickly espoused by slaves in the South and came to constitute a major feature of the black religious experience as well, although with differences.

This brings us to the second major development in Southern religious history that has profoundly affected the interpretation of the Bible—the institution of chattel slavery. The title of chapter four of Donald G. Mathews's *Religion in the Old South* aptly captures the outcome of the debate over slavery for the interpretation of Scripture: "We who own slaves honor God's law." Itself a quotation from James Furman in 1848, the title reveals the way in which this most "peculiar institution" of Southern culture led to a peculiar hermeneutic as well. The growing controversy over slavery led not only to the split between Northern and Southern Baptists, Episcopalians (briefly), Methodists, and Presbyterians, but also to the development of a distinctive social ethic. On the one hand, attempts to defend the institution of slavery on theological and biblical grounds seized on a literalistic appropriation of proof texts that appeared to condone or even recommend slavery as a socioeconomic institution compatible with the divine will for order in society. The result was a general and entrenched inclination to legitimate social institutions that would subsequently affect not only blacks, but also women, farmers, and mill workers alike. On the other hand, the formation of a slave ethic on a biblical basis, combined with the conversionist tendencies already latent in evangelical Protestantism, produced a wariness and even hostility toward a read-

ing of Scripture that saw in it a call for conversion not only of individual souls but of social and political institutions. Jesus' demand that Nicodemus be "born again" tended to obviate Amos's demand that wealthy landowners not oppress the poor. Thus conversionism and individualism yielded an interpretation of the Bible under which one could be a good Christian and still own slaves. The fact that this tack was not followed by a significant number of black Evangelicals from the antebellum period down to the present is a subject that will be examined below.

The revivalist movement and the development of a slave ethic produced a hermeneutical perspective that was already firmly in place when the implications of biblical criticism began to be realized in the late nineteenth century. The faith of most evangelical Protestants was based on the emotions of the heart rather than the reasonings of the mind and, for the former, the technical works of biblical scholarship were of little use. In fact, as Mathews has shown, the first generation of Southern Evangelicals in particular rejected preaching based on scholarly exegesis as part of the "worldly" Anglican class structure from which the community of the newly born was freed. Although the second and third generations were willing to adopt learning in general— energetically establishing academies, colleges, and seminaries as a result—such a liberal attitude toward the interpretation of the Bible did not follow. The reason for this reluctance was not only the conversionist orientation, but also the development of the slave ethic, which found a literal interpretation to be a potent weapon in the defense of socioeconomic ideology. Thus the use of the Bible in the slavery controversy helped to ensure its status as an infallible guide that, in a very real sense, did not *need* interpretation to lend it relevance to the modern world.

The major confrontation with biblical criticism did not occur until the first two decades of the 20th century when the battle raged in conjunction with the debate over evolution. Although there were not-able exceptions, most Southern Evangeli-cals rejected both Darwin and the proponents of the new criticism, both of which were seen to call into question the literal meaning of Genesis 1-2, as well as many other texts and traditional doc-trines. Out of this debate emerged the fundamentalist movement with its view of the Bible as an infallible and inerrant rule of faith, and a compendium of doc-trines that must be believed. This move-ment has informed many Southern Evangelicals down to the present.

In general, the churches that have been least comfortable with the conver-sionist and individualist hermeneutic are the Presbyterian, Lutheran, Episcopal, and Methodist (especially in more recent times). These denominations also tend to be the most open to the use of critical exegesis. It is not coincidental that each of these denominations practices infant bap-tism, nor that their polities are more hier-archical and their liturgies often more sacramental, for such ecclesiological tradi-tions directly affect the interpretation of Scripture. Here preaching is more often aimed at the nurture and theological instruction of the community rather than toward the conversion of individuals. Southern Baptists, in part because of their "free church" polity, stand somewhere in the middle. Here the interpretation of Scripture is likely to vary much more widely than in the previously mentioned denominations, from many churches that are conversionist and fundamentalist, to others that might show no external dif-ferences from, say, Presbyterians and Methodists. On or near the fundamental-ist end of the spectrum stand the Churches of Christ, Church of God, Free Will Baptist, and the various pentecostal and millennial groups. The latter two tend to use the Bible (in preaching, at least) as a kind of catalyst for the eruption of the Holy Spirit and as a compendium of doctrinal truth that must be believed, especially the belief in an imminent apoc-alyptic RAPTURE. Finally, there is a wide-spread devotional use of the Bible that cuts across many diverse groups. Here the Bible is read as a source of comfort and support in times of personal trouble, or simply as a stimulus for daily inspiration.

As already indicated above, interpre-tation of the Bible in the black church has diverged sharply from mainline white Evangelicalism in one major respect: it has always had an instinctive attraction for what would later be called the SOCIAL GOSPEL. Recent studies of slave religion have shown that the adoption of the con-versionist orientation by blacks did not lead to a view of salvation as a purely individual and spiritual experience. Emo-tionalism and hope for a "land beyond the sky" were combined with a realization that salvation included liberation from the oppressive social and political struc-tures of this world. From the spirituals of antebellum slaves to the "freedom songs" of the CIVIL RIGHTS MOVEMENT, blacks have interpreted Scripture as providing a scenario of liberation for which the exo-dus of the Israelites from Egypt was pro-totypical. Blacks have not been alone in such an interpretation of the Bible. Pro-ponents of racial integration, communal-ism, and prison reform, and organizers of tenant farmers and labor unions such as CLARENCE JORDAN, Claude Williams, and WILL CAMPBELL, have appealed to similar biblical models. Often along the same lines, the interpretation of the Bible has played a significant role in the writing of Southern fiction. For example, WILLIAM FAULKNER and FLANNERY O'CONNOR applied their interpretations of the Bible to the themes of the ownership of land and property, slavery, and pride, all based on race and class.

The present and future state of biblical interpretation in the South is difficult to determine. It may be that the recent turn to an interest in the meaning of the canonical text among biblical critics will render traditional biblical criticism more acceptable to groups who previously found it threatening. Developments in joint educational development in some of the churches (both Northern and Southern), as well as an increasing number of people who have been exposed to the critical interpretation of the Bible in colleges and universities, may well result in a growing dissatisfaction with conservative hermeneutical perspectives. There is also evidence of a growing concern among Evangelicals of all stripes for the relevance of the Bible for political and sociological issues, although the result of such interest presently runs the gamut from the "New Right" fundamentalists to more liberal orientations continuing in the tradition of the social gospel sketched above. Whatever the outcome, the interpretation of the Bible will surely play an important part in the development of Southern culture as it has in the past.

See also articles on BIBLE, AUTHORITY OF; BIBLE, INSPIRATION OF; FUNDAMENTALISM; MODERNIST CONTROVERSY; RATIONALISM, RELIGIOUS.

Bibliography. Kenneth K. Bailey, *Southern White Protestantism in the Twentieth Century*; James Barr, *The Bible in the Modern World*; *Fundamentalism*; *Old and New in Interpretation*; "Scripture, authority of," *Interpreter's Dictionary of the Bible*, supplementary volume; James Cone, *The Spirituals and the Blues*; Hans Frei, *The Eclipse of Biblical Narrative*; Nathan O. Hatch and Mark A. Noll, eds., *The Bible in America*; Samuel S. Hill, Jr., "The Shape and Shapes of Popular Southern Piety," *Varieties of Southern Evangelicalism*, ed. David E. Harrell, Jr.; *Southern Churches in Crisis*; Clarence Jordan, *The Cotton Patch Version of Luke and Acts*; *Interpretation*, 25 (January 1971); *Katallagete*, 5:1 (Spring 1974); Leander Keck, *The Bible in the Pulpit*; David Kelsey, *The Uses of Scripture in Recent Theology*; Donald G. Mathews, *Religion in the Old South*; Albert J. Raboteau, *Slave Religion: The "Invisible Institution" in The Antebellum South*; George W. Stroup, *The Promise of Narrative Theology*; Bill Troy, "The People's Institute of Applied Religion," *Southern Exposure*, 4 (Fall 1976):46-53.

THOMAS W. MANN
SPARTANBURG, SOUTH CAROLINA

BIBLE PRESBYTERIAN CHURCH.

This hyperconservative denomination was founded in 1937 when a portion of the Presbyterian Church of America withdrew from that body, which itself had formed a year earlier. J. Gresham Machen (1881-1937) had led a reaction in the PRESBYTERIAN CHURCH OF THE UNITED STATES OF AMERICA against what was perceived by the group to be pervasive liberalism in the denomination. Carl McIntire, a pastor in the movement led by Machen, led the Bible Presbyterian Church toward formation when Machen died. In 1938 the new BPC amended portions of the Presbyterian Standards—the WESTMINSTER CONFESSION OF FAITH and catechisms—to affirm the return of Christ to earth prior to the millennium (the reign of Christ for a thousand years).

McIntire, of Collingswood NJ, became increasingly active in behalf of the causes of the Radical Right in America, naming many of the religious leaders in mainstream denominations "communists," and seeking to have international organizations such as the United Nations disbanded. He, and the Bible Presbyterian Church, helped form the American Council of Churches and the International Council of Churches. Recent divisions and realignments, together with the diminished leadership of McIntire, have meant the comparative eclipse of the BPC. Statistics on the denomination are not available through ecumenical channels, and adherents within the denomination are reluctant to speak of numbers and affiliations.

LOUIS WEEKS
LOUISVILLE PRESBYTERIAN SEMINARY

BILLY GRAHAM EVANGELISTIC ASSOCIATION.

The famed Southern Baptist evangelist Billy Graham and his closest associates established this organization in 1950 to discourage rumors of his profiting from local crusade contributions and to provide for the efficient management of his various revivalistic undertakings. George Wilson, business manager of the fundamentalistic Northwestern Schools of Minneapolis, advised these people to form a nonprofit corporation to process the inquiries and finances related to Billy Graham's ministry and to coordinate his crusades. Such an organization was established according to Minnesota laws and was located near Northwestern schools, with Graham as its president and Wilson as its secretary-treasurer.

BGEA paid the salaries of Graham and his preaching associates, together with costs of management and clerical staffs of its diverse subsidiaries. Besides arranging personal appearances by the evangelist and his team members, the corporation helped supervise related enterprises such as the radio program, "Hour of Decision" (beginning in 1950); World-Wide Motion Pictures (1951); Graham's books, commencing with *Peace With God* (1953), and *Decision* magazine (1960).

Under Wilson's efficient leadership this organization expanded its operations from the Minneapolis headquarters to various American and foreign branch offices that guided evangelistic activities. The Minneapolis facility processed letters addressed to Graham for spiritual advice, sent instructional materials to converts (who were called "inquirers"), published *Decision* magazine and promotional literature, and disbursed burgeoning contributions from donors around the world. After 1965 a branch office located in Atlanta coordinated the crusade endeavors of Graham and team members such as Cliff Barrows, music director; Leighton Ford, associate evangelist; and Walter Smyth, director of crusade organization and team activities. A few years later this agency was transferred to Minneapolis.

BGEA now works with locally-run administrative offices in coordinating crusade efforts. The central organization provides: the evangelists to do the preaching; schools of evangelism held during crusades, with seminary students and local pastors in attendance; telephone counseling; and supervision of follow-up activities. Wilson has reported: "Each crusade is run by the local crusade committee which sets up its own corporation and is involved in raising its budget. An audited statement is printed at the close of the crusade to let everyone know how funds were disbursed."

Through its membership in the Evangelical Council for Financial Accountability and its compliance with accounting principles as formulated by the American Institute of Certified Public Accountants, BGEA annually reconciles its financial records. In 1981, for example, the organization received $43,243,700 (90 percent of which came from contributions), disbursed $39,860,471, with the surplus of $3,383,229 allocated for the underwriting of ministries in early 1982.

BGEA in recent years has added two significant components to its evangelistic endeavors. The first is the Billy Graham Center at Wheaton IL, a facility that combines a museum and library on evangelism and missions with a graduate school for potential leaders in these areas of Christian outreach. The second is the World Emergency Fund, which is used to provide food, medicine, and expenses for relief ministries in Bangladesh, Ecuador, India, Nigeria, and other underdeveloped countries. Through these and related activities, BGEA is fulfilling its stated purpose "to spread the Gospel by any and all means" as it combines a concern for human need with a continuing competence in financial perspicacity.

See also articles on GRAHAM, BILLY (WILLIAM FRANKLIN); REVIVALISM.

Bibliography. Alan Bestic, *Praise the Lord and Pass the Contribution*; Billy Graham Evangelistic Association, "1981 Report to Our Partners"; Stanley High, *Billy Graham: The Personal Story of the Man, His Message, and His Mission;* William G. McLoughlin, Jr., *Billy Graham: Revivalist in a Secular Age*; John Pollock, *Billy Graham: The Authorized Biography.*

EDWARD L. MOORE
NASHVILLE, TENNESSEE

BISHOP. A word widely used by Christians from New Testament times to the present to designate a minister in a position of authority; there have been various understandings of the nature and scope of that authority. The English word is a corruption of *episcopos*, the Latin form of a Greek word, meaning "overseer," "guardian," and used five times in the New Testament.

In the Episcopal Church and the Roman Catholic Church, it is the highest order of ministry (followed by priest/ presbyter and deacon). The bishop is understood to be in apostolic succession, deriving his authority from historical continuity, through successive ordinations, with the apostles. He is the chief minister in a diocese, who has general pastoral responsibility for his congregations and visits them as often as possible. The specific pastoral responsibility for an individual congregation is delegated to a priest, who, therefore, normally baptizes, celebrates Holy Communion, and preaches; the bishop usually performs these acts only on the occasions of his visits. Only a bishop has the power to confirm, to ordain priests and deacons, and with two other bishops to consecrate bishops. In large dioceses the bishop (then also known as the diocesan or ordinary) may be assisted by one or more other bishops (coadjutor or suffragan). In the Episcopal Church, the bishop is elected by his diocese and approved by the General Convention; in the Roman Catholic Church, the bishop is appointed by the Holy See. (In the Roman Catholic Church, an archbishop is the bishop of a diocese who also has certain limited authority over the bishops of other dioceses within a defined area.)

In the United Methodist Church, the bishop is the person who presides over one or more annual conferences and whose duties include presiding at sessions of conferences, ordaining ministers, appointing pastors to churches, and with two other bishops (in some cases two elders), consecrating bishops. "Bishop" is not understood to indicate a separate order of ministry but to be a part of the order of an elder (presbyter); no claim is made to apostolic succession. Some other Methodist groups also use the title.

In the American Lutheran Church and the Lutheran Church in America, the title refers to synod presidents, who serve fixed terms of office. "Bishop" is an administrative title, used only during the term of office, not an order of ministry.

Here again, no claim is made to apostolic succession.

In those Pentecostal denominations that do not hold to a strong congregational polity, church leaders are sometimes called bishops; but the understanding of the office and the authority attached to it vary widely.

Bibliography. J. H. Barton, "Episcopacy," *The Encyclopedia of World Methodism*, vol. 1, ed. N. B. Harmon; Frederick V. Mills, *Bishops by Ballot*; William Telfer, *The Office of Bishop*.

HERBERT S. WENTZ
UNIVERSITY OF THE SOUTH

BLACK CATHOLICISM. Numbering today about one million, black Roman Catholics have historically been a minority within a minority in the United States. Of the 13 original colonies, only Maryland had a significant number of Catholics. According to JOHN CARROLL, 3,000 of the 15,800 Catholics in MARYLAND in 1785 were black slaves and they, he complained, received haphazard instruction in the faith. In LOUISIANA, Capuchin friars began missionary work among the slaves in 1722, but their efforts were hindered by distances between settlements and by chronic shortages of priests. Many Louisiana slaves were baptized; few were instructed. At the beginning of the 19th century, small groups of black Catholics could also be found in Kentucky, St. Louis, and scattered outposts of the French. The vast majority of blacks were enslaved in the Protestant South where they had little, if any, contact with Roman Catholics.

In Baltimore and New Orleans, sizable communities of black Catholics emerged, made up primarily of "free persons of color," augmented by refugees from the Haitian Revolution. In these cities two congregations of black nuns were organized, the Oblate Sisters of Providence in Baltimore in 1829 and the Holy Family Sisters in New Orleans in 1842. At the time, these two communities were the only ones open to black women with a vocation to the religious life. Black nuns were all the more important, since a black Catholic clergy was slow to develop.

While black Protestant preachers had been active since the 1780s, the first black Catholic priest was not ordained until 1854 when James Healy, born a slave in Georgia, was ordained in Paris. Healy and his two brothers, Alexander and Patrick, who also became priests, did not work among black Catholics. The first black priest to serve as a pastor to those of his race was Augustus Tolton. Tolton, who had escaped slavery in Missouri as a child, was ordained in Rome in 1886. Not until 1891, when James Cardinal Gibbons ordained Charles Uncles, was the first black priest appointed in the U.S. In 1920, a major step in the development of black priests was taken when the Society of the Divine Work opened St. Augustine's Seminary in Bay St. Louis MS, specifically to train black youths for the priesthood.

The scarcity of black priests denied black Catholics, even when separated into black parishes—an increasingly common pattern after 1870—the opportunity to be pastored by men of their own race. Organizations of black laymen partially supplied the leadership missing in black parishes. From 1889 to 1894 delegates from different areas of the country, including the South, met in five Colored Catholic Congresses to discuss religious and racial issues. In 1909, the Knights of Peter Claver, a black fraternal and benevolent society, was formed in Mobile AL. In 1924, Thomas Turner, biology professor at Howard University and Hampton Institute, founded the Federated Colored Catholics to protest discrimination within the Church.

As early as 1866, a special mission to convert blacks was discussed by the American bishops. Though urged by Rome to devise a plan, the bishops, gathered at the second Plenary Council of Baltimore, failed to develop a national strategy and left the issue up to the discretion of each bishop. Among the religious orders that answered the appeal for assistance in this mission field, the Josephites and the Blessed Sacrament Sisters were the most active among Southern blacks. In 1915,

Mother Katherine Drexel, founder of the Blessed Sacrament nuns, laid the foundation for Xavier University of New Orleans, the single black Catholic university in the U. S.

Gradually, the number of black Catholics grew as black Protestants left the rural South and came into direct contact with Catholicism in the cities. The migration of black Catholics from Louisiana also spread Catholicism to black communities nationwide. In the cities, parochial schools became a major source of black converts to Catholicism. Between 1940 and 1975, the black Catholic population grew from 296,988 to 916,854, an increase of 208 percent. Between 1968 and 1970, the Black Catholic Clergy Caucus, the National Black Sisters Conference, the Black Catholic Lay Caucus, and the National Office of Black Catholics were organized to address issues of black Catholic concern. Today there are seven black bishops, three of them serving in the South.

See also articles on BLACK RELIGION; ROMAN CATHOLIC CHURCH.

Bibliography. Albert S. Foley, S.J., *God's Men of Color: The Colored Catholic Priests of the United States, 1854-1954*; John T. Gillard, S.S.J., *Colored Catholics in the United States; The Catholic Church and the American Negro*; Marilyn Wenzke Nickels, "The Federated Colored Catholics," unpublished Ph.D. dissertation, The Catholic University of America, 1975.

ALBERT J. RABOTEAU
PRINCETON UNIVERSITY

BLACK MINISTERIAL PROTEST LEADERSHIP, 1955-1970. The lack of extensive scholarly research into the origins and early years of the modern black civil rights movement in the South has left many of the movement's most important features relatively obscure. One of the most central of these was the role that young black ministers, often new to their pastorates but with solid collegiate training, played in starting many of the local protests against segregation that sprang up across the South throughout the 1950s and early 1960s.

One basic requirement for any black citizen who sought to take a public, front-

line role in antisegregation protests in the
Deep South in those years was that he or
she have some economic independence
from local whites who otherwise could
swiftly retaliate with a job dismissal, calling a note, or terminating credit.
Although some black businessmen or professionals also had relative economic
security from local whites, black pastors
generally possessed both that independence plus the social prominence and rhetorical skill that often went with the
ministerial role. Informed observers thus
were not surprised when black ministers
appeared as the leaders and spokesmen
for notable local protest movements in
cities such as Baton Rouge (1953), Montgomery (1955-1957), Tallahassee (1956-
1957), Birmingham (1956-1963), and
Danville VA (1963).

That generalization, however, should
not be exaggerated. While young ministers like MARTIN LUTHER KING, JR. and
Ralph D. Abernathy emerged as the public spokesmen for the noted bus boycott in
Montgomery, the moving forces behind
the origin of the protest actually had been
the Women's Political Council, led by
young professors and teachers and a Pull-
man porter named E. D. Nixon. Similarly,
when an energetic mass protest movement arose in Albany GA, in 1961-1962,
the local black leadership was composed
almost totally of young leaders from other
professions—a doctor, a lawyer, an insurance and real estate agent, and a postal
worker—rather than ministers. In Albany
and in other towns such as Selma AL,
where young activists from the Student
Nonviolent Coordinating Committee
sought to establish early civil rights foot-
holds, the young workers initially had
trouble finding any pastor who would
allow civil rights meetings to be held in
his church. In many rural areas of Georgia
and Mississippi that hesitancy was well-
founded; many black churches that were
used for such rallies soon were destroyed
by arson.

In Montgomery, however, the
women's council and Nixon immediately
turned to the city's black ministers to
organize and promote their idea of a bus
boycott. While younger men such as Abernathy and the Rev. E. N. French took the
lead in implementing plans, the formal
calls to the initial protest meetings were
issued in the names of the Baptist Ministerial Alliance and the Interdenominational Ministerial Alliance whose officers
initially presided. When the decision was
made to establish a new organization to
pursue the protest, the younger, more politically conscious ministers moved to the
fore.

A similar pattern emerged in the subsequent bus protest in Tallahassee, which
was initiated by students at Florida A & M
University. The black Tallahassee Ministerial Alliance convened within 24 hours,
endorsed the protest, sent representatives
to see bus company officials, and called a
citywide mass meeting at which a new
civic organization led by activist pastors
was established to pursue the boycott.

The general youthfulness of the ministers who stepped forward to take civil
rights leadership roles also could be seen
in larger cities such as Birmingham and
Atlanta where many older, more conservative, and better-established black pastors chose not to assert themselves.
Although many of these ministers who
opposed "direct action" tactics, such as
MARTIN LUTHER KING, SR. in Atlanta and
J. L. Ware in Birmingham, could hardly be
characterized as halfhearted opponents of
segregation, leadership of actual protest
efforts was exercised by younger pastors
such as Fred L. Shuttlesworth, Edward
Gardner, and Abraham Woods in Birmingham, or by students whose leadership included young men in theology
school, such as Otis Moss and Fred C.
Bennette in Atlanta.

As civil rights activism spread across
the South during the early and mid-1960s,
young ministers who believed in a politically active and socially conscious black
church continued to emerge as leaders of
local protest organizations. Men like A. I.

Dunlap, L. W. Chase, and L. G. Campbell in Danville, and L. L. Anderson and F. D. Reese in Selma comprised the vanguard of local movements that brought substantial racial changes to their respective towns.

When civil rights activism began to move northward, and to turn its attention to economic issues in the mid-1960s, young black pastors continued in the forefront of these efforts. One of the most effective and widely used tactics in this new era of the movement was a program called "Operation Breadbasket" by its sponsoring organization, the SOUTHERN CHRISTIAN LEADERSHIP CONFERENCE, which had adopted the concept from the Rev. Leon Sullivan of Philadelphia. The "Breadbasket" program consisted of black ministers organizing themselves to examine whether large companies whose products were widely sold in the black community actually offered fair job opportunities to prospective black employees. If they did not, and if private visits and ministerial persuasion failed to alter those practices, the ministers would urge their congregations not to purchase those manufacturers' products until their employment practices were improved. Companies in the bread, dairy, and soft drink industries quickly learned the power of the black church in this program, and the ministerial groups in cities such as Atlanta and Chicago were able to announce hundreds of new jobs for black employees as a result of the "Breadbasket" efforts.

From the beginning of the civil rights movement in the bus boycotts of the mid-1950s, up through the economically aimed efforts such as "Breadbasket" in the late 1960s and early 1970s, black ministers, most often young men and with the benefits of formal college training, supplied much of the leadership for the new activism of black Southerners. It represented an invaluable contribution by the black church to the political and economic well-being of its community and a further expansion of the church's role into matters beyond the religious and spiritual.

See also articles on BLACK RELIGION; CIVIL RIGHTS MOVEMENT.

Bibliography. Paul D. Bolster, "Civil Rights Movements in Twentieth Century Georgia," unpublished Ph.D. dissertation, University of Georgia, 1972; Gordon L. Hartstein, "The Montgomery Bus Protest, 1955-1956: What Precipitated, Sustained, and Prolonged the Boycott," unpublished B.A. thesis, Princeton University, 1973; Lewis W. Jones, "Fred L. Shuttlesworth, Indigenous Leader," unpublished paper, 1961, in Race Relations Department, United Church Board for Homeland Ministries Papers, Amistad Research Center, New Orleans; Martin Luther King, Jr., *Stride Toward Freedom*; Gary Massoni, "Perspectives on Operation Breadbasket," unpublished M.Div. thesis, Chicago Theological Seminary, 1971; Aldon D. Morris, "The Rise of the Civil Rights Movement and Its Movement Black Power Structure, 1953-1963," unpublished Ph.D. dissertation, State University of New York at Stony Brook, 1980; Charles U. Smith and Lewis M. Killian, *The Tallahassee Bus Protest*; J. Mills Thornton III, "Challenge and Response in the Montgomery Bus Boycott of 1955-1956," *Alabama Review* 33 (July 1980): 163-235; Jack L. Walker, *Sit-Ins in Atlanta*; Lamont H. Yeakey, "The Montgomery, Alabama Bus Boycott, 1955-1956," unpublished Ph.D. dissertation, Columbia University, 1979.

DAVID J. GARROW
UNIVERSITY OF NORTH CAROLINA
AT CHAPEL HILL

BLACK RELIGION. Convention links the black experience in religion in America to the development of the English colonies. While this perspective is useful in the sense that it helps to explain a number of aspects of black religion, it ignores the fact that African Christianity antedates English versions in the New World by some 200 years. However, the relevance of such an observation is diminished by the more extensive and graphic autobiographical data of more recent history. In short, while the black experience of religion in the South may not be considered a significant aspect of world history, world history may very well need to be drawn upon to explain black religion in context.

Tradition has it that the black experience in America is to be reckoned from the summer of 1619 when 20 "negars" were bartered to the English settlement in JAMESTOWN by some Dutch adventurers in exchange for supplies of food and water. Extant records show that at least one of the Africans was married subsequently in the Anglican Church at Jamestown and that by 1624 at least one African was baptized there. Meager though they may be, these data suggest some initial degree of social receptivity on the part of the American Anglicans as well as a certain religious adaptability on the part of at least some of the African captives. However, the Jamestown incident predates, or perhaps initiates, the American adventure in chattel slavery; for after Jamestown the Anglo-African experience in America was to become increasingly complicated by the institutionalization of that previously undefined relationship. The social and religious rapprochement that may have marked the initial patterns of comity between these two expatriated peoples disintegrated in the face of the intensification of their disparate needs and interests brought on by the crystallization of the white master-black slave dichotomy. This disintegration was inevitably expressed in the reordering of religious values by both groups to address their respective spiritual needs in the light of the newly emergent realities of slavery. Hence, "black religion" presupposes "white religion" and is for that reason incomprehensible outside a context where "white" and "black" have not been institutionalized as symbols of superordinate value or disvalue.

It is logical to assume that the Africans (like the English) brought with them from their homeland religious forms consistent with previous cultural needs and experiences. But there were differences, and these were of critical importance. The English colonists were self-consciously involved in voluntary cultural transition that was both cause and effect to their being in America. Not least among the causes was disenchantment with certain strictures of the Church of England and the desire for new forms of political and economic experience. The evolutionary

process had already set in when the first Africans arrived at Jamestown. It was to be escalated beyond any previous imagination in the next century by the identification of slavery with the cultural and economic well-being of the South and by the eventual realization of the colonists that political freedom and political contingency are forever inconsonant. All of this was to have its effect upon the fact and form of black religion, for the Africans found themselves cast in the unenviable role of involuntary auxiliaries to the English colonists, pursuing interests not their own in search of a destiny from which they were excluded in advance.

Religion is the principal means by which humanity seeks to realize ultimate value, to be reassured that the self has intrinsic worth and that life has purpose that somehow relates the individual to the creator. Hence it must be perceived that whatever the style of the various religions the Africans brought with them, those religions had functioned effectively to ward off the principal threats of spiritual anxiety common to humankind and congeneric to their own respective home cultures. But in America the familiar gods and the ancient rituals were ridiculed and proscribed. The drums of worship and communication were silenced and any known cult of believers was dispersed to minimize the ever-present risks of insurrection and to obviate the possibility of moral or religious challenge to the ideological infrastructure that undergirded the institution of slavery. While there were notable exceptions, Christian contact was generally forbidden, discouraged, or rendered impractical by the common requirements that characterized black existence in the South.

From the Jamestown barter until 1701 when the SOCIETY FOR THE PROPAGATION OF THE GOSPEL IN FOREIGN PARTS finally won the grudging permission of the Southern planters to include the African slaves in their evangelistic outreach to the Indians, any official concern for the spiritual needs of the captive blacks was distinctively exceptional, North and South alike. Such exceptions as there were usually lay with the QUAKERS who were generally revolted by human slavery, but whose humanitarian interests were seldom matched by evangelical fervor. The SPG, which was organized by the Church of England as a missionary service to the colonists, turned its interest to blacks only after finding indifferent success among the colonial whites and after being rebuffed by the Indians. The opposition of the planters to the society's proposals to bring blacks into the Church was both protracted and pronounced. The economic investment in slaves was enormous, and until the slave owners could be convinced that the Christianization of their slaves would pose no problems for them in connection with management or ownership, their resistance was unabated. Their fears that slaves might become intractable or confused about their identity on becoming Christians were allayed finally by repeated arguments on the congeniality of selected Christian doctrines with an idealized image of the slaves' personality. In the Bible, meekness, obedience, forgiveness, long-suffering, hard work, and love in exchange for spitefulness and injury were considered virtues. Would not a slave imbued with such Christian virtues be more loyal, more dependable, and therefore more valuable than one who was simply heathen? The moral and the legal issues of whether a property right could be maintained in a Christian slave were eventually resolved by official affirmations of the Church of England, which were codified into law by the colonial legislatures. The stage was thus set to reverse the century-old tradition of exclusion of blacks from the Christian community, and for the subsequent emergence of black religion as a distinctive phenomenon of the black subculture.

In time, prevailing conventions in the South would argue that not only were Christianity and slavery compatible interests, but that they were of mutual benefit to both slave and master. Be that as it may, the decision to open the faith to black involvement required the substantial modification or reconstruction of attitudes and norms and values to accommodate this new way of dealing with the African presence. A formidable theological folklore emerged to explain the African and to differentiate that people from those who required their services. It was alleged that he and she had no soul, were morally incompetent, that their intelligence was arrested, and that they were cursed of God and punished with perpetual bondage to the white man. The Africans' degraded status required differential treatment, even in common worship, in consequence of which the church became the first segregated institution in America. Black Christians attached to the "big house" often could attend service in the white churches, but they could not sit with whites nor receive the sacraments with them. Often special segregated services were held for black members before or (sometimes) after the regular services for whites, but whatever the physical arrangements for the accommodation of blacks, the burden of the message directed to them was unvaried: It was God's will and directive that they should be faithful, loyal, and obedient to their masters, for God himself had ordained their status. They were to be hard-working and long-suffering without complaint, even if they felt themselves abused. Their blackness was a sign of their disgrace, and there would be no rescue for them in this life. But if they bore their tribulations with cheerfulness and dignity, they would see God (and their masters and mistresses) in the (segregated) world to come.

While there was but cold comfort in the practices and doctrines the church in America deigned to offer its black members, that offer was the best available, and it represented the very critical difference between being within the periphery of the divine concern, or total alienation. The African stood in dire need of a conquering paladin God who could destroy his enemies and break the bonds of his captivity. What white religion offered was a God who could relativize scarce values and provide both a rationale and the inner strength required to accept a *fait accompli* in spite of its gall. The bargain was struck, but the odds were with the Africans from the beginning. No religion can survive the true interests and convictions of its true believers, for they will either modify what they need to believe to conform with revelation, or they will modify revelation to conform with what they need to believe. The African-Americans did both. That is why black religion and white religion both confront and complement each other across a wide spectrum of values and expectations.

Religion follows human needs, so it was inevitable that black membership in the white man's church would provide the blacks with but limited satisfaction. Black needs and aspirations and white needs and aspirations were totally different in derivation and incompatible in fulfillment. And it was evident very early that the black man's salvation, as he perceived it, could hardly be realized in a church of divided interests. Convention has it that the first black church was of Baptist origin and was founded at SILVER BLUFF SC around 1773; but despite this exceptional instance, black churches were almost universally forbidden, and those that were permitted were pastored or monitored by whites. This practice contributed to the early development of a substantial underground or INVISIBLE INSTITUTION that met clandestinely in the swamps and bayous until slavery was ended by the Civil War. Of the several denominations represented in postcolonial America, black Christians were overwhelmingly attracted to the Baptist and Methodist communions. Their services were simple and uncomplicated, and beyond that both groups had taken forthright positions against slavery after the middle of the 18th century, although to little avail in the practical relief of the blacks. Nevertheless, they found the evangelical churches far more congenial to their circumstances than the Anglican, Presbyterian, or Congregationalist, and beginning with the GREAT AWAKENING in the 1740s their religious identification as Methodists or Baptists could generally be assured. By 1860 there were almost a half-million black Methodists and Baptists in the South alone.

The synthetic status of blacks in the white churches was one of the five major components that together created the cultural matrix from which black religion as a unique and definitive expression of the West African diaspora is derived. The others are: (2) the retention of bits and pieces of remembered Africana that survived the depersonalization of "seasoning" in the holding pens or barracoons, the trauma of the "middle passage," and the kinship dispersals of the auction block; (3) the gross deformation of normative human relationships that characterized the entire American social structure; (4) the "invisible church" that met in secret at great risk of severe punishment; and (5) the independent black churches that undertook the delicate task of effective spiritual leadership for blacks while under the constant and critical eye of hostile white monitors. Each of these elements was to find significance in the style, structure, and values of the emergent faith, but the limited freedom experienced in the independent churches quickly became the focus around which the black church was to project itself once the strictures of slavery were removed.

The first black denomination was organized in 1816, when representatives from a number of independent Methodist churches along the eastern seaboard met in Philadelphia to form the AFRICAN METHODIST EPISCOPAL CHURCH. Other Methodist and Baptist communions emerged in due course as black Christians sought to escape the stigma and the inconvenience of segregated white churches. When the Civil War was over, the black churches were "free" as well as independent, and the passion to belong to one of the African communions had denuded the white churches of the South of the vast majority of their black members. The black church had come into its own, but not without crisis. Contending for leadership in the shaping and meaning of black religion was the suddenly manifest "invisible Church," which was made up primarily of field hands who were the least acculturated by the black masses. Their presence and their numbers were threatening to the "big house" blacks who had known greater privileges, who were more likely to have held membership in the master's church, and who were generally more accommodated to its style, if not its message. The struggle for identity was accordingly a problem for the black church from the beginning, and though diminished in tone, the disparate interests and concerns that earlier excited these primary constituencies still find their expression in such emphasis as styles of worship, concern for civil rights, preparation of clergy, and commitment to black theology. Black religion continues to be the most powerful force in the black subculture, and the black church is recognized as "the mother of the black experience."

See also articles on BLACK CATHOLICISM; CIVIL RIGHTS MOVEMENT; COLONIAL PERIOD; ETHICS, CHRISTIAN; NATIONAL BAPTISTS; SEGREGATION; SLAVERY.

Bibliography. W. E. B. DuBois, *The Negro Church*; John Hope Franklin, *From Slavery to Freedom*; E. Franklin Frazier, *The Negro Church in America*; Eugene Genovese, *Roll, Jordan Roll: The World the Slaveholders Made*; M. J. Herskovits, *The Myths of the Negro Past*; C. Eric Lincoln, *The Black Muslims in America*; *The Black Church Since Frazier*; *The Black Experience in Religion*; Benjamin E. Mays and J. W. Nicholson, *The Negro's Church*; August Meier and Elliott Rudwick, *From Plantation to Ghetto*; Kofi Asare Opoku, *West African Traditional Religion*; Henry H. Mitchell, *Black Belief*; Harry V. Richardson, *Dark Salvation*; Albert J. Raboteau, *Slave Religion*; George Eaton Simpson, *Black Religions in the New World*; Lester B. Scherer, *Slavery and the Churches in Early America*; Frank Tannenbaum, *Slave and Citizen: The Negro in the Americas*; Joseph R. Washington, *The Politics of God*; Gayraud Wilmore, *Black Religion and Black Radicalism*; Clyde Ahmad Winters, "Afro-American Muslims from Slavery to Freedom," *Islamic Studies* 17:4 (1978); Carter G. Woodson, *The History of the Negro Church*.

C. ERIC LINCOLN
DUKE UNIVERSITY

BLAIR, JAMES (1655-1743), commissary for the bishop of London in Virginia, was the founder and first president of the COLLEGE OF WILLIAM AND MARY. Born in Scotland, he received the M.A. degree from the University of Edinburgh in 1673. Ordained in the Church of England, he served Cranston parish in the diocese of Edinburgh. Later employed in the office of Master of the Rolls in London, he became acquainted with Henry Compton, bishop of London, who persuaded him to go to Virginia. There he became rector of Varina parish in 1685, renamed Henrico in 1720. In 1689, Bishop Compton, the diocesan of the English colonies, appointed Blair commissary for Virginia. Authorized to supervise the clergy, but without power to ordain, Blair called his first clergy convention in 1690 and took the initiative in founding the College of William and Mary.

In 1691, the Virginia General Assembly sent Blair to England to present the projected college to King William and Queen Mary. Assisted by the archbishop of Canterbury, John Tillotson, and others, a charter was issued in 1693 and Blair was named president "during his natural life." Blair was made rector of the board of visitors. He resigned his post in Henrico and became rector of Jamestown Church in 1694. In 1710, he became rector of Bruton parish, Williamsburg, a post he retained until his death. The king appointed him to the colonial council in 1694, and in his role he advanced the Church of England and the college against the opposition of Governors Edmund Andros and Francis Nicholson, both of whom were recalled. From December 1740 to July 1741, Blair, as president of the council, was acting governor. Although pugnacious, Blair was successful in establishing the college and enlarging the Church of England in Virginia.

Bibliography. G. MacLaren Brydon, *Virginia Mother Church and the Political Conditions Under Which It Grew*, vols. 1 and 2; D. E. Motley, *Life of Commissary James Blair*; W. S. Perry, *Papers Relating to the History of the Church in Virginia, 1660-1776.*

FREDERICK V. MILLS, SR.
LAGRANGE COLLEGE

BLUE LAWS: *See* ETHICS, CHRISTIAN.

BORN AGAIN: *See* CARTER, JAMES EARL; EVANGELICAL PROTESTANTISM; NEW BIRTH.

BOWIE, WALTER RUSSELL (1882-1969), Episcopal clergyman, editor, educator, and author, was born in Richmond VA. He received his B.A. and M.A. from Harvard and B.D. from Protestant Episcopal Theological Seminary in Virginia. Ordained a priest in 1909, he served Emmanuel Church in Greenwood VA until 1911 when he returned to Richmond to become rector of the prestigious ST. PAUL'S CHURCH. While there he was associate editor, then editor, of *The Southern Churchman.* Bowie emerged as a prominent advocate of the SOCIAL GOSPEL and liberal theology. He boosted social reforms and, after serving as a Red Cross chaplain in World War I, strongly endorsed the League of Nations. In the 1920s he led community opposition to the KU KLUX KLAN and sharply criticized Fundamentalists.

In 1923 Bowie moved to Grace Church in New York City. In 1939 he joined the faculty of Union Theological Seminary as a professor of practical theology, and in 1945 he became Dean of Students. Thereafter he returned to his alma mater in Virginia where he served as a professor of homiletics. Author of more than a score of books, Bowie wrote for groups ranging from children to theologians. Perhaps his best-known works were *The Story of the Bible* and *Sunrise in the South*, the latter the biography of his aunt, Mary-Cooke Branch Munford, a Virginia education reformer. He was an editor and contributor of *The Interpreter's Bible* and a member of the committee that produced the Revised Standard Version of the Bible.

Bibliography. Walter Russell Bowie, *Learning to Live*; Bowie Papers, Protestant Episcopal Theological Seminary in Alexandria VA.

SAMUEL C. SHEPHERD, JR.
CENTENARY COLLEGE

BOYCE, JAMES PETIGRU (1827-1888), Baptist seminary founder, was born in Charleston SC, the son of a wealthy cotton broker. Boyce never experienced financial problems; in fact, in later years he gave liberal support to the first seminary of the Southern Baptist Convention, which he is responsible for founding. While a senior student at Brown University, he announced that he wanted to become a minister. There followed two years of study at Princeton Theological Seminary under the famous Charles Hodge. In 1851 he became pastor of a small congregation in Columbia SC. By 1855 he was a professor of theology at Furman University in Greenville. Soon thereafter he urged that a seminary be founded for Southern Baptist ministerial education.

When the Southern Baptist Theological Seminary opened its doors in Greenville in 1859, James Boyce served as chairman of the faculty (president), professor of theology, and treasurer. The school was actually located in a large home owned by Boyce. During the Civil War while the seminary was closed, Boyce served as a chaplain with the Confederate army and later as aide-de-camp to Governor Magrath, holding the rank of lieutenant colonel.

In 1865 the seminary reopened and was virtually financed by Boyce. On numerous occasions he deposited thousands of dollars to the seminary's account in order to pay salaries and buy books. He played a major role in the seminary's move to Louisville KY in 1877 and almost immediately outside support was strengthened with the result that enrollment increased. Appropriately, in 1888 this scholar who had held office from 1872 to 1879 was reelected as president of the Southern Baptist Convention.

Weakened by his never-flagging efforts for the seminary, he set sail for Europe in 1888 in search of better health. He never found it, dying in France in December. The seminary's Board of Trustees observed: "Without his sagacious counsels, his heroic exertions, and his sublime self-sacrifice, the institution could not have survived its trials. The Seminary is his monument, and a blessed memorial of him is written in the hearts of the people of God."

See also article on THEOLOGICAL EDUCATION.

Bibliography. James P. Boyce, *Abstract of Systematic Theology* (1899); *Three Changes in Theological Education*; William A. Mueller, *A History of Southern Baptist Theological Seminary.*

GEORGE SHRIVER
GEORGIA SOUTHERN COLLEGE

BRANDEIS, LOUIS DEMBITZ (1856-1941), Jewish jurist, was born in Louisville KY, the son of immigrants from Prague. He graduated from high school at 15 and attended the Annen Realschule in Dresden while his parents were visiting Europe. In 1875 he entered Harvard Law School, graduating within two years with the highest academic average ever attained there. Brandeis then practiced law in Boston, where he was considered a brilliant and progressive lawyer. Perhaps his most famous legal victory came in the case of Muller *v.* Oregon (1908), in which he presented not only legal, but also economic and sociological evidence to the U. S. Supreme Court and persuaded the justices to uphold an Oregon statute limiting women laundry workers to a 10-hour day. Woodrow Wilson was greatly impressed with Brandeis and in 1916 nominated him for a Supreme Court vacancy, the first Jew to serve on the high court.

Brandeis was quite active in the American Jewish community after 1910. In that year his interest in Judaism was sparked when he helped mediate a garment workers' strike in New York and was fascinated with the intellectual qualities of the striking Jewish laborers. In 1910 he also came into contact with Jacob De Hass, editor of the *Jewish Advocate* and a former secretary to Theodore Herzl. De Haas interested Brandeis in Zionism and he became active in the movement. To him Zionism was a means for Jews to retain their identity; it was a movement that could bring social reforms to Palestine just as the Progressive Movement brought reform to the United States. Under Brandeis's leadership membership in the American Zionist movement jumped from 12,000 to over 175,000. After some internal clashes, he resigned from all offices he held in the American Zionist movement to avoid further conflict. However, he continued to be interested in Palestine and was active in promoting business ventures there.

ARNOLD SHANKMAN

BRAY, THOMAS (1656-1730), colonial Anglican clergyman, was born in Marton, Shropshire, England. He attended Oswestry School, received a B.A. from All Souls College, Oxford, in 1678 and then in 1696 the B.D. and D.D. degrees from Magdalen College, Oxford. That same year he was chosen by the bishop of London, Henry Compton, to serve as commissary in Maryland. His zeal for the Church of England led to its establishment in Maryland. Bray recruited missionaries and developed a plan to provide the clergy with libraries. He organized the Society for Promoting Christian Knowledge (chartered 1699) and actively promoted the organization of the SOCIETY FOR THE PROPAGATION OF THE GOSPEL IN FOREIGN PARTS (chartered 1701).

In 1706, Bray became rector of St. Botoloph's Without, Aldgate, in London. He was aggressive in religious philanthropy, supported a society to suppress vice, founded libraries and charity schools, and supported hospitals. Two of his societies, merged under his will, furnished the institutional basis for the Georgia Trust. These were the Trustees of Parochial Libraries (1710-1730) and the Associates of Dr. Bray, a trust created in 1723 to administer a legacy for the conversion of Negroes and Indians. He had in mind a scheme to train artisans at missions on the American frontier.

Bray's interest in the lot of the poor led him to work in Whitechapel prison. In this he anticipated the prison investigations of JAMES OGLETHORPE. This mutual interest led Oglethorpe to join the Associates of Bray. Thomas Coram, one of Bray's parishioners, wrote that in 1729 Bray hoped before he died he would find a way to settle English unemployed and foreign Protestants in America. There is evidence Bray discussed or suggested this to Oglethorpe. In 1730, the Associates embraced this third charity and petitioned for the charter of Georgia.

See also articles on COLONIAL PERIOD; ESTABLISHED RELIGION.

Bibliography. Charles T. Laugher, Thomas Bray's Grand Design; B. C. Steiner, ed., Rev. T. Bray: His Life and Selected Works Relating to Maryland; Henry P. Thompson, Thomas Bray.

FREDERICK V. MILLS, SR.
LA GRANGE COLLEGE

BRECKINRIDGE, ROBERT JEFFERSON (1800-1871), Presbyterian minister and theologian, was a son of Kentucky statesman John Breckinridge. Graduating from Union College in 1819, he became a lawyer and politician. In 1832 he entered the ministry after a few months of theological study. Until 1845 he was pastor of Second Presbyterian Church in Baltimore.

Editing the Baltimore Literary and Religious Magazine (1835-1841) and Spirit of the XIX Century (1842-1843), Breckinridge agitated against Roman Catholicism. He initiated the Old School "Act and Testimony" (1834) and precipitated the church split of 1837. He opposed denominational "boards" and advocated a greater role for ruling elders. A manumissionist, he alternately excoriated proslavery and abolitionist adversaries.

After two years as president of Jefferson College (PA), Breckinridge became pastor of First Presbyterian Church in Lexington KY in 1847. He served as state superintendent of schools, and led the Kentucky emancipation movement of 1850. He founded Danville Theological Seminary in 1851 and became its principal professor.

After 1861 Breckinridge supported the Union cause and war measures, including suppression of dissenters. In 1864 he was temporary chairman of the Union (Republican) National Convention. In 1866 he spearheaded his church's discipline of border-state critics of Unionist civil religion, driving most of them eventually into the Presbyterian Church in the United States.

Although Breckinridge wrote a systematic theology, The Knowledge of God... (1858-1859), he seemed an unsystematic thinker. An Old School Presbyterian, he denied "immediate" imputation and accepted premillennialism. His church-government tenets, developed by James H. Thornwell, flourished mainly in the PCUS.

Bibliography. Dictionary of American Biography, vol. 3; Edgar C. Mayse, "Robert Jefferson Breckinridge: American Presbyterian Controversialist," unpublished dissertation, Union Theological Seminary in Virginia, 1974.

JACK P. MADDEX, JR.
UNIVERSITY OF OREGON

BREWER, GROVER CLEVELAND (1884-1956), Churches of Christ preacher and writer, was born in a tenant house on his grandfather's farm near Lawrenceburg TN. With six months of labor, he earned two years of schooling at Ashley S. Johnson's "School of the Evangelists" at Kimberlin Heights TN and graduated from Nashville Bible School in 1911.

His ministry included tenure with some large CHURCHES OF CHRIST in Tennessee, Texas, and California; lectures in special efforts; and protracted meetings in hundreds of churches. As a writer, Brewer served on the staff of the Gospel Advocate for 45 years, authored 12 books and numerous pamphlets, and was founder and editor (1953-1956) of the Voice of Freedom, "an anti-Catholic paper." This "chief work" of his last years is one example of the combative nature of his writing and speaking, beginning with his first debate in 1906 and including a discussion with Judge Ben B. Lindsey in Memphis TN in 1928 on companionate marriage. In discussions his spirit was always that of Wordsworth's "happy warrior."

He was the first advocate of budget finance in Churches of Christ and is remembered especially as a voice for nondenominationalism. He insisted that the church of the New Testament had no distinguishing name or title, since the Bible did not speak of a "what" church as in the question: "To what church do you belong?" When asked, "What kind of Christian as you?," he replied, "I am not a *kind of Christian*. I am just a Christian, no more, no less."

See also article on DEBATES, INTERDENOMINATIONAL.

R. L. ROBERTS
ABILENE CHRISTIAN UNIVERSITY

BROADDUS, ANDREW (1770-1848),

pioneer Baptist pastor, was born in Caroline County VA. His family was of Welsh background. His father disliked DISSENTERS intensely, but Andrew was baptized into a Baptist church, Upper King and Queen, in his home county in 1789. Two years later he was ordained there. That congregation was a member of Dover Association over which Broaddus presided as moderator between 1832 and 1841. Broaddus was something of an anomaly in that leading pulpits in New York, Philadelphia, Baltimore, and Richmond sought him, but he chose to minister in rural counties in his home state. J. B. JETER, who wrote a memoir of his life, attributed this behavior in part at least to his nervousness and shyness.

Broaddus received little formal education but cultivated his mind and had a strong intellectual bent. He supplemented his income by teaching. Popular as a preacher, he was more beloved as pastor and father of his people. His presence drew many to associational gatherings, but he was not active in larger conventions. His ministry was mainly marked by long pastorates; for example, he, his son, and grandson served Salem Church, an outgrowth of Upper King and Queen, for a total of 106 years.

Broaddus wrote sermons, circular letters, a history of the Bible, and some hymns, plus he compiled several hymnals. His publications were of limited circulation, however. He was a lifelong friend of R. B. SEMPLE, famous historian of Virginia Baptists.

Four times married, his third marriage ended in estrangement, which for a time cost him popularity. Before he died, however, his standing among Virginians had been fully restored.

Bibliography. Andrew Broaddus, *A History of the Broaddus Family*; J. B. Jeter, *The Sermons and Other Writings of the Rev. Andrew Broaddus With a Memoir of His Life*; L. M. Ritter, "Andrew Broaddus," *Encyclopedia of Southern Baptists*.

WILLIAM ALLEN POE
NORTHWESTERN STATE UNIVERSITY
OF LOUISIANA

BROADUS, JOHN ALBERT (1827-1895),

Baptist theological educator and author, was born in Culpeper County VA, the son of a minister. A solid educational background was climaxed by a degree with distinction from the University of Virginia. Converted to Christianity and the Baptist faith during his college career, he began to preach almost immediately.

Soon he became pastor of the Baptist church in Charlottesville as well as teaching some courses in ancient languages at the university. When the Southern Baptists opened their first seminary in 1859 in Greenville SC, he was a member of its small faculty, with an appointment as professor of New Testament and homiletics.

The outbreak of the Civil War resulted in closing the young seminary. Confederate to the core, Broadus often preached in the camps. During these years his livelihood came from serving several rural churches as well as acting as corresponding secretary of the Baptist Sunday School Board. After the war, Broadus and the other faculty members reopened the school under very trying circumstances; the enrollment totaled seven. That year saw Broadus preparing his lectures in homiletics so as to teach effectively one blind student. Those lectures later became his most successful published work, *The*

Preparation and Delivery of Sermons, a text still in use in some Baptist seminaries.

In 1877 the seminary moved to Louisville and Broadus continued his teaching and writing career in a much more positive context. He became well enough known as a scholar that in 1889 at Yale University he delivered the famous Lyman Beecher lectures on preaching. In that same year he became the second president of the Baptist seminary he had served so faithfully. Though he was often extended invitations to teach at other schools, Broadus chose to remain at the school where he attempted a synthesis of learning and piety for young ministers of his own denominational persuasion.

See also articles on PREACHING; THEOLOGICAL EDUCATION.

Bibliography. John A. Broadus, *A Treatise on the Preparation and Delivery of Sermons; Lectures on the History of Preaching*; A. T. Robertson, *Life and Letters of John Albert Broadus*.

GEORGE SHRIVER
GEORGIA SOUTHERN COLLEGE

BROTHER. In its traditional Catholic form, "Brother" refers to a Christian man who professes the evangelical counsels of poverty, chastity, and obedience, and lives those vows in the context of a religious community (order or congregation).

In the Roman Catholic Church the vows professed by a Brother are either simple (as a member of a congregation in which temporary or perpetual vows are taken) or solemn (as a member of an order, in which only perpetual vows are taken), these vows being recognized by the Church as such.

While all Christians, in any state or walk of life, are called to the perfection of love and the fullness of Christian life, by his special consecration the Brother bears witness in a unique and intense way to the presence of Christ in the world. In this role as teacher, laborer, social worker, missionary, he brings Christ's saving love to the student in a classroom, to the poor, the suffering, the homeless, the sinner of society.

By transcending the material goodness of this world, the Brother is a sign of all of the resurrected Christ. In sacrificing the legitimate pleasures of life, he becomes a sign of the suffering Christ. In bearing the title of "Brother," he is a sign of Christ, the "Brother of all." By living the communal life, he is a sign of that Christian love in which all are called by Christ to share, in community.

Institutionalized sanctity in its origin was a lay movement; monasticism began with the layman. In the unfolding of history, the life of people dedicated to living the evangelical counsels came to be regarded as a particular state of life ("religious") and accorded special honor by the Church.

In actuality those religious, including brothers, who are not among the clergy retain their lay identity and by their lives demonstrate that the evangelical counsels are not to be equated solely with the sacerdotal state.

In the general and noncanonical sense of the term *brother*, as used by Free Church communities as well as Roman Catholics, the term applies to all men who share fellowship in Jesus Christ. For Jesus, whoever does the will of God the Father is brother and mother and sister to him.

In recent years an emphasis on this common brotherhood has arisen in most Christian churches. The ecumenical movement has fostered a sense of brotherhood in Christ spanning even denominational lines.

See also article on PRIEST.

Bibliography. *Code of Canon Law* (revised), Canons 503-505, 534; Austin P. Flannery, ed., *Documents of Vatican II*, "Constitution on the Church," Chapters 5, 6; William Modlin, *The Brother in the Church*.

ROBERT J. BAKER
ST. VINCENT DE PAUL
REGIONAL SEMINARY

BROWN, MORRIS, (1770-1844), second bishop of the AFRICAN METHODIST EPISCOPAL CHURCH, was born to racially mixed free parents in Charleston SC. Having close blood ties to aristocratic whites exempted him and similarly situated free persons of color from the application of many of the restrictions affecting other blacks. Brown acquired a reasonably good primary education by the standards of the times and was licensed to preach in the Methodist Episcopal Church as soon as he professed religion. In 1817 he was ordained a deacon and a year later an elder. In 1818 he became a traveling minister.

Following the discovery of the DENMARK VESEY slave insurrection plot in Charleston in 1822, Brown, also a prosperous shoemaker who had assisted slaves to purchase their freedom, was virtually driven into exile. "Professors" of the faith had been implicated in the plot and local authorities, suspecting that black Methodist meetings had been organizing vehicles for the plot, drastically curtailed the religious activities of free blacks like Brown. Reaching Philadelphia in 1823, he became active in the AME Church and on 25 May 1828 was elected the second bishop in the history of that denomination. Upon the death of Richard Allen, the founding bishop of the AME Church in 1831, Brown remained the sole bishop until 1836 when Edward Waters was ordained to assist him. While traveling in Canada in 1844, Bishop Brown suffered a fatal stroke.

See also article on BLACK RELIGION.

Bibliography. *Centennial Encyclopedia of the African Methodist Episcopal Church*; Peter M. Bergman and Mort N. Bergman, *The Chronological History of the Negro in America.*

ROBERT L. HALL
UNIVERSITY OF MARYLAND
BALTIMORE COUNTY

BRUSH ARBOR. A large natural canopy formed by overhanging tree branches, constructed to shelter the main area of a religious CAMP MEETING, brush arbors were most commonly employed for such meetings on the American frontier during the first half of the 19th century. Brush arbors were constructed in the creation of camp meeting sites. Camp meetings were outdoor religious services lasting for several days and distinguished by the encampment of participants on the spot. Originating during the GREAT REVIVAL (1787-1805), camp meetings were held during the antebellum period in all regions of the American frontier, but were especially prominent in the South and Midwest.

In the process of clearing a wooded grove of most of its trees and brush in order to accommodate an encampment, a brush arbor was created by leaving several selected trees standing that ran up to a substantial height. Branches on the selected trees—if any—were stripped to a height of at least 10 or 12 feet. This left the upper branches to come together over the clearing, producing a natural canopy above the meeting's activities. The foliage offered shade and some protection from the elements, and lamps could be attached to the trunks of the trees in order to provide light for night services. Such arbors had to be large, covering up to half an acre or more, since camp meeting crowds usually numbered several hundred or even a few thousand. Beneath an arbor enough plank seats were constructed to accommodate such a crowd, with separate sections for white men and women and another section for blacks, and a preacher's stand raised several feet above the ground. Participants camped in tents pitched on the arbor's periphery.

The brush arbor, like the camp meeting itself, was initially a response to a frontier environment in which large indoor meeting places were nonexistent, and brush arbor construction was reported from as early as 1802, within two years of the first identifiable camp meeting (evidently originated by JAMES MCGREADY in 1800). Moreover, to many people, the kind of setting such arbors provided virtually symbolized the campground with its religious significance. Indeed, critics and proponents of camp meeting revivalism alike tended to describe the brush arbor as a natural "cathedral" that called the attention of those on the campground to God's grandeur in a way unmatchable by any human edifice. Thus the camp meeting's admirers in particular would see the brush arbor as itself a major ingredient in the achievement of any encampment's revival goals of winning and saving souls.

As frontier regions became more settled, however, brush arbors were replaced on many campgrounds by more permanent shelters for the camp meeting crowds, most commonly long, clapboard-covered sheds or simple, rooflike structures supported on pillars. Ultimately, in the South beginning in the 1840s, the camp meeting itself was supplanted by the indoor PROTRACTED MEETING, held in a church building, as the chief vehicle for revival activities.

See also articles on FRONTIER, INFLUENCE OF; REVIVALISM.

Bibliography. Everett Dick, *The Dixie Frontier*; B. W. Gorham, *Camp Meeting Manual*; Charles A. Johnson, *The Frontier Camp Meeting*.

DICKSON D. BRUCE, JR.
UNIVERSITY OF CALIFORNIA, IRVINE

BRYAN, ANDREW (1737-1812), pioneer black Baptist minister, was born in Goose Creek SC and grew up as a slave on a plantation near Savannah. About 1782 he was converted and baptized by GEORGE LIELE, a black pastor who preached at coastal plantations before moving to Jamaica. Bryan's subsequent exhortations to fellow slaves were rewarded when his master allowed him to erect a small barn for worship services. Local antagonistic whites persecuted and imprisoned Bryan and his brother, Sampson; yet both slaves persevered by praying for their tormentors. Finally the slaves' master obtained their release and legal authorization for them to resume services.

In 1788 Bryan was ordained to the ministry by Abraham Marshall and Jesse Peter who were, respectively, white and black pastors. Marshall, a nephew of the redoubtable SHUBAL STEARNS, represented the white evangelical tradition that

preferred authentic conversions to perfunctory creedal professions. Peter, who had served SILVER BLUFF CHURCH, which possibly was the first independent black church in America, exemplified the black religious tradition that emphasized a Christian commitment that transcended caste. Through his redemptive suffering and evangelical zeal, Bryan embodied the best of both traditions.

That endurance and fervency motivated white admirers to assist his congregation in purchasing a lot in Savannah and erecting a building upon it. By 1800 this edifice, later known as the First African Baptist Church, had a membership of 700 and sponsored numerous black Baptist churches in the state. Bryan then wrote that he enjoyed "the rights of conscience to a valuable extent" as he preached "three times every Lord's day," baptized "then to thirty at a time," and conducted worship "in the presence and with the approbation" of "many" whites. He purchased freedom for his wife, daughter, and himself, and died a prosperous man. The white Savannah Baptist Association eulogized him as a pastor who suffered "inexpressible persecutions" and brought "hundreds" to "the knowledge of the truth, as it is in Jesus."

See also article on BLACK RELIGION.

Bibliography. Walter H. Brooks, "The Priority of the Silver Bluff Church and Its Promoters," *The Journal of Negro History* 7 (April 1922): 172-96; John W. Davis, "George Liele and Andrew Bryan, Pioneer Negro Baptist Preachers," *The Journal of Negro History* 2 (April 1918) 119-27; "Letters Showing the Rise and Progress of the Early Negro Churches of Georgia and the West Indies," *The Journal of Negro History* (January 1916): 69-92; Milton C. Sernett, *Black Religion and American Evangelicalism: White Protestants, Plantation Missions, and the Flowering of Negro Christianity, 1787-1865.*

EDWARD L. MOORE
NASHVILLE, TENNESSEE

BRYAN, WILLIAM JENNINGS (1860-1925), major political and religious figure, was born in Salem IL. He was graduated from Illinois College, Jacksonville, in 1881 and then read law in Chicago. He practiced law in Jacksonville and then in

Lincoln NE before taking up a career in politics.

In 1890 Bryan ran for Congress as a Democrat and won in a normally Republican Nebraska district. However, he lost the seat in the Republican landslide of 1894. His oratorical prowess and evangelical fervor won him leadership of the free-silver Democrats, and with it the Democratic nomination for president in 1896. Bryan narrowly lost to William McKinley, despite carrying the Southern and most of the Western states. Bryan won the Democratic nomination again in 1900 and 1908, but he never again equalled his 1896 vote.

Bryan was an influential figure in Southern culture and politics from 1896 until his death in 1925. As a presidential candidate and perennial Chautauqua speaker he articulated the concerns of rural and small-town Southerners. During the last decade of his life Bryan was most closely identified with the defense of a beleaguered Southern culture. In 1921 Bryan, by then a Florida resident, took the lead in a crusade to rid the public schools of evolutionary teaching. Spurred by such writings as Bryan's tract, "The Menace of Darwinism," and the burgeoning fundamentalist movement, six Southern state legislatures adopted measures that restricted or prohibited the teaching of evolution.

Bryan's attack on evolution stemmed not only from his defense of biblical literalism, but also from his commitment to social reform. Evolutionary thought, Bryan believed, undercut the theological and moral basis of reform, and in the hands of conservative social Darwinians

had been used to deny the possibility of human betterment. Urbane modernism, epitomized by evolution, seemed to threaten the small-town culture that Bryan believed was the lifeblood of the republic.

Bryan's crusade peaked in the summer of 1925, when he was called to Dayton TN to aid in the prosecution of JOHN T. SCOPES, a high school biology teacher who had intentionally violated the Tennessee antievolution law. The trial degenerated into a verbal battle between Bryan, who portrayed it as a "duel to the death" between Christianity and evolution, and defense attorney Clarence Darrow, who ridiculed Bryan's beliefs.

Scopes was convicted and given a light fine. But the highly publicized trial heightened the national perception of the South as a benighted region. Bryan knew, as W. J. Cash wrote, that the antievolution crusade was "an authentic folk movement" supported by the great mass of the Southern people. But such folk movements were neither understood nor appreciated by the arbiters of American culture in the 1920s.

Bryan did not have long to savor the "victory" of Dayton nor to ponder its implications; he died in his sleep five days after the Scopes trial had ended.

See also articles on EVOLUTION CONTROVERSY; FUNDAMENTALISM; SCOPES TRIAL.

Bibliography. William Jennings Bryan, *The First Campaign*; Paolo E. Coletta, *William Jennings Bryan*, 3 vols.; Lawrence W. Levine, *Defender of the Faith, William Jennings Bryan: The Last Decade, 1915-1925.*

ROBERT C. MCMATH, JR.
GEORGIA INSTITUTE OF TECHNOLOGY

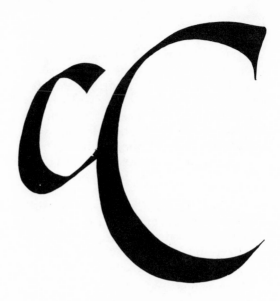

"CAJUN" INFLUENCE. The most far-reaching aspect of "Cajun" or Acadian influence on the South is perhaps the survival of a large Roman Catholic enclave in the midst of an overwhelmingly Protestant civilization. Most of the Roman Catholics living in south Louisiana and southeast Texas owe their religious heritage to Acadian immigrants who arrived between 1756 and 1778.

These settlers were the descendants of northern French colonists who had established themselves in Acadia (Nova Scotia) during the previous century. The onslaught of British military rule had uprooted many families since their loyalty to the Crown was seriously questioned. The largest group of refugees eventually found sanctuary in colonial Louisiana. Today, Roman Catholicism and many other features of Acadian, or "Cajun," culture owe their distinctiveness to several factors. Largely sealed off from the rest of the world by the Atchafalaya Swamp, a sprawling coastal marsh, and lonely expanses of piney woods, "Cajun culture" subsisted for generations on a remote edge of the rural South.

The Church became the chief institutional buttress of family life and still has a deep influence on all socioeconomic levels. The patriarchal role of the parish priest has been an influence on the male heads of families, many of whom are strongly conscious of their ultimate authority in most family matters. It is also said that the Cajun male has enjoyed dancing, drinking, gambling, and sporting without the consequent suffering of "Puritan guilt" that other Southerners may occasionally feel. On the other hand, the female spouse often wields a subtle matriarchal influence. In the past she has normally determined the religious identity of the offspring, particularly in the case of Catholic-Protestant intermarriage; her decision is often crucial in matters pertaining to the family's reputation and status within the community. Adoration of the Virgin Mary is a strong tradition among older Acadian women, and its roots go back at least to early Gallic Christianity in Europe.

In recent times, an aggressive Protestantism, ecumenism, and growing secularism have modified the religious views of younger Cajuns. Nevertheless, several traditions remain. Acadian Catholicism still exerts a strong day-to-day influence on the large majority. The Diocese of

Lafayette, covering all of southwestern Louisiana, has the second-largest percentage of Catholics nationwide. The diocese also contains the largest black population, since blacks number about 25 percent of Acadiana's total population. In the past, the birth rate among whites has approached and sometimes exceeded that of blacks in some areas, largely because of the heavier influence of Catholicism on the former. Few blacks consider themselves "Cajuns," but they have been culturally transformed by the Acadian French and have, in turn, influenced the religion and folklore of Acadiana.

Both white and black groups, for example, contain conservative lay members who still attempt to demonstrate their powers as faith healers. Some even combine religion and magic in the treatment of illness and various other problems. The practicing *traiteur* (faith healer) is usually a devout Catholic who believes that his or her powers are God-given. A more common feature among the folk-minded Cajuns is the religio-magic cure that is applied by either a practitioner or the afflicted victim himself. Recitation of certain prayers in combination with the use of holy water, blessed candles, and amulets are customs rooted in distant Europe and Africa. The remnants of Louisiana voodooism can be traced in part to the West Indies where African culture had a major encounter with French and Spanish Catholicism.

Certain holidays and church-related festivities are still observed more assiduously by Acadian Catholics than by others. Mardi Gras, the Lenten fast, Holy Week, All Saints' Day, Christmas, and New Year's Eve maintain their peculiar rituals and strict observances both in and outside of the Church. Activities may vary somewhat from one community to the next. Examples include the various harvest festivals in the different parishes (counties), including the blessing of the shrimp fleet. Likewise, there are many colorful rituals and customs that Acadians often observe in church weddings, baptisms, and funerals.

See also articles on FRENCH INFLUENCE; LOUISIANA.

Bibliography. Arthur G. Doughty, *The Acadian Exiles*; Timothy F. Reilly, "Early Acadiana Through Anglo-American Eyes," *Attakapas Gazette* (Spring and Fall 1977) (Summer 1978); Patricia Rickels, "The Folklore of Acadiana," *The Culture of Acadiana: Tradition and Change in South Louisiana*, ed. Steven L. Del Sesto and Jon L. Gibson; Lyle Saxon, ed., *Gumbo Ya-Ya: A Collection of Louisiana Folk Tales*; T. Lynn Smith and Vernon J. Perenton, "Acculturation Among the Louisiana French," *American Journal of Sociology* 44 (November 1938); Works Progress Administration, *Louisiana: A Guide to the State*.

TIMOTHY F. REILLY
UNIVERSITY OF SOUTHWEST LOUISIANA

CALDWELL, ERSKINE (1903-), a major figure in recent Southern literature, has been considered by some to be the Southern writer *par excellence*. His works fulfill a number of the expected patterns of the fiction of the region: they often depict the lives of the rural, common folk; they are populated by characters with physical abnormalities; they contain humorous, often outrageous anecdotes; and they are preoccupied with sin and its various earthly manifestations. This latter quality is indicative of Caldwell's larger fascination with religious phenomena in general, and from the publication of his first novel in 1929 until the present his works have consistently displayed the exuberant emotions associated with religion in the South.

Caldwell's interest in religion arises naturally from his background. Born in Coweta County GA in 1903, he grew up "in the shadow of the steeple." His father was an ordained minister of the ASSOCIATE REFORMED PRESBYTERIAN CHURCH whose moderately liberal views on social and doctrinal matters often put him at odds with the positions of his neighbors. "I was never able to determine the extent of my father's belief, if any, in God and traditional Protestantism," Erskine Caldwell has written, but "I knew by association and observation that he neither practised nor preached what was commonly called old-time religion." The young Erskine was educated mostly at home by his mother, a school teacher by training, and developed opinions during his youth that reflected his upbringing. Many of these ideas are, in turn, embedded in his works and his substantial corpus—over 50 volumes of fiction and nonfiction—provides a penetrating critique of Southern culture. Moreover, his works tend to represent popular Southern religion as an aberrant form of traditional Calvinism that ministers to the poor by helping them to accept their lot and by providing an outlet for their emotions.

Religion in Erskine Caldwell's fiction, then, does not offer a radically new vision of the universe; rather, it serves to maintain the status quo. Ty Ty Walden in *God's Little Acre* (1933), for example, has devoted all of his resources and energy to digging holes on his land in the obviously futile effort to discover gold. His family may be on the verge of starvation, but he does not till the earth—he only excavates it. Because Ty Ty has designated one portion of his land to be devoted to God forever and thereby to be left untouched, he figures that he is protected from the random evil of the universe. No matter that "God's little acre" is constantly being redesignated according to the needs of Ty Ty's gold prospecting and although this contrivance is his only evidence of piety, he feels at peace with God. In fact, Ty Ty does not accept any responsibility for his fate; as he reasons, "There was a mean trick played on us somewhere. God put us in the body of animals and tried to make us act like people." The task of religion is to reconcile this dichotomy.

Another equally important function of religion in Caldwell's fiction is to provide a diversion from the tedium of everyday life. The Protestant preacher is an entertainer and the community his audience. Sister Bessie in *Tobacco Road* (1932) livens up the existence of the Lester family and that of others in the surrounding community. This self-appointed

preacher prays for the substantial vices and petty sins of Jeeter Lester at the same time as she seduces his 16-year-old son Dude. Similarly, in *Journeyman* (1935), Semon Dye, the peripatetic evangelist, represents a religion that is mostly smooth talk and animated gyrations. Even though he cheats the men and sexually assaults the women in the community of Rocky Comfort, he manages to draw a large crowd to the Sunday service. His reluctant host, Clay Horey, is left destitute by Dye, but still grieves his departure: "Semon was a sort of low-down scoundrel. . . . But it does sort of leave a hollow feeling inside of men to know he aint here no longer. I feel left high and dry, like a turtle on its back that can't turn over." This reliance on religion as the primary form of entertainment is not confined to the rural poor; it is also evident in Caldwell's novel *Episode in Palmetto* (1950), where for the townspeople "going to church was the most important social event of the week."

Caldwell's rendering of religion has elicited a strong response from many of his fellow Southerners who resent his depiction of them as country bumpkins, of their culture as deprived, and of their religion as empty. Indeed, social commentary and superficial moralism, it has been charged, dominate his works. Ironically, this is the same writer whose novels were once labeled as obscene and banned from libraries in towns and cities across the country. The literary community has for the most part chosen to ignore Caldwell's works because of their alleged simplicity, vulgarity, and popularity (even though critics of no less stature than Kenneth Burke and Malcolm Cowley have found his fiction worthy of attention and comment). While Caldwell's attitude toward the South is often unsympathetic, his perspective is not that of an uninformed outsider. He consistently illustrates the predicaments, ironies, and contradictions inherent in Southern culture. Throughout his life Caldwell has been particularly concerned about the kinds of cruelty that can be performed in the name of religion and has chastised white Protestant churches for their "infectious racial hatred—a hatred germinated and cultured by perverted principles of Christian religion." In his fiction he frequently condemns Southern religion when it supports oppressive social conditions, rationalizes irresponsible behavior, and entertains rather than instructs.

See also article on LITERATURE AND RELIGION.

Bibliography. Kenneth Burke, "Caldwell: Maker of Grotesques," *New Republic* 82 (10 April 1935): 232-35; Erskine Caldwell, *Deep South*; Malcolm Cowley, "The Two Erskine Caldwells," *New Republic* 111 (6 November 1944): 599-600; Scott MacDonald, ed., *Critical Essays on Erskine Caldwell*; James J. Thompson, Jr., "Erskine Caldwell and Southern Religion," *Southern Humanities Review* 5 (Winter 1971): 33-44.

ROSEMARY M. MAGEE
EMORY UNIVERSITY

CALVERT FAMILY. A series of members of this family contributed significantly to early religious policies in the MARYLAND colony and thus to American experiments in religious freedom. George Calvert (1580-1632) rose to prominence under James I, but in 1625 he resigned his office after converting to Roman Catholicism. The king supported his former secretary of state by making him the first Baron of Baltimore, part of the Irish peerage. George attempted sporadically between 1621 and 1629 to establish a colony in Newfoundland, but it never succeeded. By 1632 further negotiations with the Crown eventually produced a grant of land north of Virginia. The new colony's charter was meant to conciliate Protestant and Catholic interests in England, avoid strife among existing American colonies, and guarantee toleration for all Christian residents by making no specific faith requirements for living there.

Cecil Calvert (1605-1675) inherited his father's title as well as vast tracts of American territory, but the second Lord Baltimore sent his brother Leonard to serve as the colony's first governor. Two

ships, the *Ark* and the *Dove*, carried over 200 persons on the first voyage, making landfall on 25 March 1634. After celebrating Mass that day, colonists soon made Saint Marys City their capital and set up a governing body. Under king and proprietor, all freemen could join the legislature without religious restrictions. This house initiated all statutes, but the governor could veto any of its proposals. In 1649 the colony enacted a notable statute, in keeping with the Calverts' long-standing sympathy for religious tolerance. "An Act Concerning Religion" promised freedom for different Christian churches to meet in peace and placed no social disadvantages on individuals who supported various creeds. Toleration did not extend to those denying belief in the Trinity, however, and penalties applied to them.

Despite such farsighted provisos, Maryland did not experience a tranquil history. Contentions between Protestant and Catholic settlers (the latter always a minority though often influential) were made worse by civil war in England and land disputes with Virginia. Troubled times abated somewhat when Charles II was restored to the throne. Charles Calvert (1637-1715) arrived as governor in 1661, although he did not succeed to the title until 1675. He perpetuated religious toleration in the traditional manner, but Protestant forces overthrew his government in 1689 while he was in England. After that, Catholics were gradually disenfranchised and placed under religious ban in the colony they had built as a refuge from religious oppression. Charles Calvert sought to regain control, but various royal administrations refused to cooperate. In 1691 the Crown withdrew Baltimore's right to govern, though it did not reduce his landholdings. In 1711 the king refused again to restore former rights because of the family's Catholicism.

Benedict Leonard Calvert (1679-1715), destined to be fourth Baron of Baltimore, converted to Anglicanism in 1713, thus removing a major obstacle to royal favor. He died only months after his father, however, and enjoyed none of the secular benefits that came from his religious change. His son Charles (1699-1751), fifth to hold the aristocratic title, saw full proprietary rights restored to the family. But he lost territory to Pennsylvania, and most Maryland affairs remained in the hands of local legislators. His son Frederick (1731-1771) was the last proprietor and proved negligent of the colony's needs. A selfish and degenerate character, he died with no legitimate heirs.

See also articles on ESTABLISHED RELIGION; ROMAN CATHOLICISM.

HENRY WARNER BOWDEN
RUTGERS UNIVERSITY

CALVINISM. Calvinism is a theological perspective based on the thought of John Calvin, further developed in the confessions and catechisms of the Reformed and Presbyterian churches, and present in other churches influenced by the particular Calvinistic emphasis on certain aspects of classical ecumenical theology (especially as it follows the Augustinian tradition) and the theology common to all the theologians of the PROTESTANT REFORMATION. It is probably fair to say that most North American denominations have been influenced by Calvinistic elements in the thought of the Puritans and the founders of the American republic. PURITANISM itself is a species of Calvinism.

There is no uniform "system" of Calvinistic theology. Calvinism has taken many forms, some of them contradictory to the original thought of Calvin himself. Underlying all these variations, however, are some common presuppositions and characteristics. Following is a summary of these, with an indication of some of the quite different conclusions that have sometimes been drawn from them.

1. *God-centered Religion.* Calvinism is recognized by its theocentric as opposed to an anthropocentric (man-centered) focus. The beginning point and center of Christian faith and life is the question of God and his promises and commands, not questions about human need, sin, and salvation, or desire for happiness and self-fulfillment. This "objective" approach has led some Calvinists to neglect the problems and insights that arise from "subjective" personal experience. It has led others to a warm evangelical concern to relate the truth of the Christian faith to personal experience.

2. *The Sovereignty of God.* All other aspects of Calvinism, including its preoccupation with the doctrines of providence and PREDESTINATION, follow from its fundamental emphasis on the sovereignty of God. Some Calvinists, following one line of thought in Calvin himself, have based their understanding of God's sovereignty on the biblical account of his covenant with Israel and the revelation of his "plan" for the world in Christ, and have consequently emphasized that God's sovereignty is loving sovereignty that enables as well as claims free human responsibility in partnership with God. Others, following another line of thought in Calvin, have developed a more abstract and speculative view of God's sovereignty that suggests that God is a capricious heavenly tyrant who determines everything that happens, arbitrarily predestines a few to salvation and most to damnation ("double predestination"), and manipulates human beings as robots. The question of the relationship between God's power and his love and between his sovereign rule and human freedom has been central for all Calvinists.

3. *Sin and Salvation.* Because of the depths of sin ("total depravity") people are totally dependent on God for salvation. This conviction led orthodox Calvinists to deny that people have the capacity to cooperate in any way in their salvation. Free will to believe, repent, accept, and follow Christ is the gift of God's enabling grace, not a natural human possession.

4. *Sanctification.* The sovereignty of God means his claim on how people live. Without forgetting that salvation is by grace and not by "good works," Calvinism emphasizes Christian "vocation" to an obedient Christian life of simplicity, discipline, and moral integrity in both the private and public spheres. This emphasis has sometimes resulted in legalistic moralism and compulsive activism. Calvinism's emphasis on frugality and hard work and its belief that God rewards these with prosperity, and the fact that Calvinism took root and has grown predominantly in the rising and established middle class, has led some scholars (despite evidence to the contrary in the life and thought of Calvin himself) to find a close connection between Calvinism, economic individualism, and modern capitalism.

5. *The Church.* According to the Calvinist position, the church is a "covenant people" composed of believers and their children (thus infant baptism) elected by God to worship and serve him. Although Calvinistic churches function by the principles of representative government, they do not understand themselves to be "voluntary associations" initiated and governed by the popular will, but as communities called together by God's initiative to be ruled by his will. The popular view of American civil religion that God has chosen (North) Americans for special blessing and responsibility is an expanded version of the Calvinist doctrine of the church rooted in the theology of American Puritanism.

6. *Civil Government.* All Calvinists have agreed that God's sovereign claim on human life extends also to the political sphere, but they have understood the implications of this claim in different ways. Some have believed that the state should enforce specific biblical-Christian laws, with the result that Calvinists have been accused of supporting a repressive "theocracy." Others, like those who supported the Puritan and American revolutions, have participated in revolutionary activity against repressive governments. Most have believed that God's will for a just society is most likely to be achieved through representative government and the democratic process, human fallibility and sinfulness making untrustworthy both pure democracy ("mobocracy") and the rule of an elite few. Some Calvinists, like those in the Southern United States who supported slavery and later racial segregation, have argued on the basis of natural law and God's ordination of "the powers that be" (Rom. 13) that any given political and social status quo is to be accepted as the will of God. In one way or another Calvinist theology is also political theology.

7. *Education and Culture.* As a Christian humanist, Calvin believed that everyone should be able to read the Bible, that human intellect is both given and claimed by God, that all truth (secular as well as religious) is from God, and that the world is God's orderly creation. Following him, Calvinism has honored scholarship, education, informed and competent preaching, scientific research, and humanistic culture in general. This aspect of Calvinism has sometimes degenerated into theological rationalism and/or a bourgeois mentality unable to relate the Christian faith to the "common man."

8. *Self-criticism and Openness to Change.* One reason for the variety of expression in Calvinism is the conviction of classical Calvinism that all theological and ethical positions, including those of Calvin himself and the confessions of the Reformed and Presbyterian churches, are to be constantly reexamined and corrected in the light of Scripture and in light of the promises and requirements of the living God for every new time, place, and situation. This conviction is expressed in the Calvinist slogan that the church is to be "always reforming."

See also article on PRESBYTERIANISM.

Bibliography. Andre Bieler, *The Social Humanism of Calvin*; John Calvin, *Institutes of the Christian Religion*; W. Fred Graham, *The Constructive Revolutionary: John Calvin and His Socio-Economic Impact*; George S.

Hendry, *The Westminster Confession for Today*; John H. Leith, *An Introduction to the Reformed Tradition*; John T. McNeill, *The History and Character of Calvinism*; Michael Walzer, *The Revolution of the Saints: A Study in the Origin of Radical Politics*.

SHIRLEY C. GUTHRIE, JR.
COLUMBIA THEOLOGICAL SEMINARY

CAMP MEETING. A religious service conducted outdoors, lasting several days, and distinguished by the encampment of participants on the meeting site, camp meetings had their greatest significance during the first half of the 19th century.

Camp meetings originated on the Southern frontier during the GREAT REVIVAL (1787-1805) in response to an environment in which population was widely scattered and church facilities were few. Because of their duration and because those in attendance could camp on the site, camp meetings drew crowds of several hundred or even a few thousand from distances that otherwise would have prevented many from attending a religious service. Although the term "camp meeting" did not come into general use until about 1802, the first identifiable camp meeting was organized by JAMES MCGREADY in July 1800 at Gasper River KY, with the most famous one taking place in August 1801 at CANE RIDGE KY (where attendance estimates ranged from 10,000 to 30,000). The earliest camp meetings were under Presbyterian auspices, or involved representatives of the Presbyterian, Baptist, and Methodist denominations. After 1805, however, camp meetings were sponsored mainly by the Methodists and, although never institutionalized by them, were an important part of Methodist practice, especially in the Midwest and South, until the 1840s.

Camp meetings were held annually in most districts, usually in the late summer. In the least settled areas, they took place under BRUSH ARBORS—large natural canopies formed by overhanging branches—around which participants camped in cloth tents. In more settled regions, services might be sheltered by a wooden shed, with cottages providing comfort for the participants. Camp meetings usually lasted four days, with services scheduled from early morning until late at night.

Camp meetings caused much controversy in antebellum religion. Camp meeting preaching came to be dominated by an Arminian theology that alienated the more Calvinistic Presbyterians and Baptists from the practice and contributed to frontier denominational warfare between them and various Arminian groups, including the Methodists. But camp meeting religion, addressed mainly to people outside the social and economic elite, produced many converts with its stress on free grace and its promise of a heavenly home where Christians would escape the frustrations of frontier life. Controversy also resulted from the emotionalism and spectacular physical exercises marking camp meeting services, as converts fell into trances, shouted, or "jerked" uncontrollably. Although camp meeting proponents defended such exercises as signs of God's power, critics questioned the validity of such emotional conversions and decried the lack of decorum in camp meeting services. Finally, critics also condemned the rowdiness accompanying many encampments, despite their sponsors' efforts to enforce fairly strict rules. Occurring yearly and drawing large crowds, camp meetings were major social as well as religious events on the frontier, and were often settings for drunkenness and disorder.

By the 1840s in the South, as many areas became more densely populated, camp meetings began to seem less necessary to sustaining religion, although some continued to be held even after the Civil War. Local churches increasingly became the centers of religious activity, as church leaders turned mainly to indoor PROTRACTED MEETINGS for their revival efforts.

See also articles on FRONTIER, INFLUENCE OF; REVIVALISM.

Bibliography. John B. Boles, *The Great Revival*; Dickson D. Bruce, Jr., *And They All Sang Hallelujah*; Charles A. Johnson, *The Frontier Camp Meeting.*

DICKSON D. BRUCE, JR.
UNIVERSITY OF CALIFORNIA, IRVINE

CAMPBELL, ALEXANDER (1788-1866),

founder of the Campbellite or "Christian" movement, was born in northern Ireland. His father, Thomas, was a minister in the Anti-Burgher Seceder Presbyterian Church. Both father and son were influenced by the evangelical movement led by such men as James and Robert Haldane, Roland Hill, and John Walker.

Disturbed by the seemingly needless divisions of the church and by the conflict between Protestants and Catholics in Ulster, the father in 1807 determined to come to America. His wife and family, led by young Alexander, came in 1809. A shipwreck that delayed their voyage gave Alexander an opportunity for study at Glasgow University.

As the family reunited in 1809 in America, both father and son had broken with the Presbyterian tradition. By 1815 the Campbells were in fellowship with the Redstone Baptist Association. While remaining separate from the Baptists in teaching and doctrine there was a 15-year period of working together. By 1830 it was obvious that the Campbells and the Baptists were not in agreement.

Campbell was giving leadership to an increasingly larger group of followers, generated in part by his debates, his publication of the *Christian Baptist* and, after 1830, *The Millennial Harbinger.*

To prepare young men for the ministry, Campbell in 1840 founded Bethany College. The college was unique in that it was the first college to teach the Bible as a subject along with other studies. By 1849 the movement had grown to such an extent that a convention was held and the American Christian Missionary Society was organized. Campbell was the first president of the convention and society, retaining the office until his death. He lived at BETHANY WV (earlier in Brook County VA). As president of the college he taught several generations of preachers and was the elder statesman of the movement he and the other leaders had founded.

Alexander Campbell was the major figure in an American religious movement to restore the unity of the church on the basis of the Scriptures. Campbell, along with BARTON W. STONE, Thomas Campbell (his father), and Walter Scott are considered the founders of the movement. Those churches today designating themselves CHURCHES OF CHRIST, CHRISTIAN CHURCHES, and CHRISTIAN CHURCH (DISCIPLES OF CHRIST) derive in great part from the leadership, writing, and publication of Campbell.

See also articles on CAMPBELLITE TRADITION; RELIGIOUS PRESS; RESTORATIONISM.

Bibliography. Lester G. McAllister, *Thomas Campbell—Man of the Book*; Robert Richardson, *Memoirs of Alexander Campbell.*

LESTER G. MCALLISTER
CHRISTIAN THEOLOGICAL SEMINARY

CAMPBELL, WILL D. (1924-),

prominent Baptist social activist and civil rights worker, is best known throughout the South as director of the COMMITTEE OF SOUTHERN CHURCHMEN. Born in Amite County in rural Mississippi, he studied at Louisiana College and Wake Forest College and received his A.B. from Wake Forest in 1948. He graduated from the Yale Divinity School in 1952 and accepted a call to the Taylor (LA) Baptist Church.

After two years he accepted a position as Director of Religious Life at the University of Mississippi. His appointment there came a few months after the famous *Brown v. Board of Education* decision of the United States Supreme Court; the impact of that decision shaped most of Campbell's ministry at the university. Campbell became one of the few white Southern ministers to support openly the crusades of MARTIN LUTHER KING, JR. in the South during the 1950s. After leaving

"Ole Miss" in 1956 he embarked on a wide-ranging ministry as a civil rights worker throughout the South. Officially he was employed by the Southern office of the National Council of Churches' Department of Racial and Cultural Relations, serving in that capacity until 1963.

Campbell played an instrumental role in the founding of the Committee of Southern Churchmen in Nashville in 1964. That committee has been a loosely organized confederation that has sponsored creative ministries for racial minorities, prisoners, farm workers, and nonunionized labor. It has also sought to interpret the Southern religious milieu to other sections of the country. It has published *Katallagete* and has provided some visible structure for Campbell's individualized mode of ministry.

In addition to his work on civil rights issues, Campbell has been known for his opposition to the death penalty, his advocacy of better living conditions in jails and prisons, his folksy style, his love of country music and folklore, and a theological stance that is anti-institutional and pessimistic about all political movements. He stresses the Christian life as doing deeds of compassion for the neighbor; his theological orientation shows many affinities with that of Jacques Ellul. He has been a frequent speaker on college and university campuses.

Campbell lives on a farm near Mt. Juliet TN. His major written work is *Brother to a Dragonfly* (New York: Seabury, 1977), which is a moving autobiographical account of his family life and his close relationship to his brother Joseph.

See also articles on ETHICS, CHRISTIAN; CIVIL RIGHTS MOVEMENT.

Bibliography. Thomas C. Connelly, *Will Campbell and the Soul of the South.*

JOHN J. CAREY
FLORIDA STATE UNIVERSITY

CAMPBELLITE TRADITION. The movement that is sometimes called the Campbellite Tradition is in reality an American religious movement that came into being on the frontier in the first decade of the 19th century. Its purpose was twofold: to restore the church to the practice and teaching of the New Testament and by this means to find a basis for reuniting all Christians. The idea was appealing to many people. If a United States of America could be formed out of diverse colonies, why not a united Church of Christ?

Similar ideas for church reformation appeared about the same time in central Kentucky and in western Pennsylvania. As a result of the famous CANE RIDGE revival meeting of 7-12 August 1801, BARTON W. STONE and several other Presbyterian ministers withdrew from the Transylvania presbytery to form the Springfield presbytery. Within two or three years it was decided that it would be more consistent with the New Testament to become simply "Christians." This resulted in the first significant document of the movement, the Last Will and Testament of Springfield Presbytery (SPRINGFIELD WILL AND TESTAMENT). It is still considered a landmark of Christian unity.

Stone and his followers were drawn to the idea of becoming undenominational Christians. They agreed to practice and to teach only what was found in the New Testament. They were organized congregationally and were evangelical in their preaching. Within a few years the movement had spread from central Kentucky into Ohio, Indiana, and Illinois, as well as northern Tennessee.

About the same time Thomas and ALEXANDER CAMPBELL, father and son, in western Pennsylvania and northwestern Virginia, were arriving at similar views. Withdrawing from the Seceder Presbyterian Church, they formed the Christian Association of Washington (PA). Thomas Campbell wrote and published in 1809 a statement of his views on Christian unity and New Testament Christianity entitled *Declaration and Address.* It became the second important statement of the movement. Depending heavily on John Locke's *Second Letter Concerning Toleration*, the document called for Christians to unite on the New Testament, in other words, on a rational basis, and to avoid making creeds tests of fellowship. By 1811 the Campbells had formed a small congregation known as Brush Run not far from Washington PA. In another four years that congregation had been taken into fellowship with the Redstone Baptist Association. For 15 years the Campbells and the Baptists lived in a relationship, but it was an uneasy one. Alexander Campbell soon became the leader, but was assisted by his father in many ways.

The younger Campbell became known far and wide through his preaching and the several debates in which he engaged, on such subjects as mode and purpose of baptism, Roman Catholicism, and socialism. Son and father and their families were immersed in June 1812. They came to believe and then to teach that immersion was for remission of sins and was into the name of Christ. It was this teaching that brought controversy with the Baptists. They also adopted the practice of observing the Lord's Supper weekly. Soon known as "Reforming" Baptists or Reformers, they promoted views that were circulated widely once the publication of the *Christian Baptist* had begun in 1823 under Alexander's impetus.

The Campbells came into contact with BARTON W. STONE and the Kentucky "Christians" as a result of a debate Alexander held in northern Kentucky in 1823. After several meetings between Barton W. Stone and Alexander Campbell it was found that they held essentially the same views. Campbell's teachings were spread in Kentucky by a former Baptist preacher, John "Raccoon" Smith. At a meeting held at Lexington in January 1832, the "Reformers" and the "Christians" agreed to unite. Two years earlier, Alexander had ceased publication of the *Christian Baptist* and had begun a new publication entitled *The Millennial Harbinger*. This publica-

tion continued for 40 years and was the main means of circulating the teachings and views of the combined Campbell-Stone movement.

Beginning in 1827 Walter Scott, an evangelist employed by the Mahoning Baptist Association of eastern Ohio, met with great success in organizing congregations and in the conversion of people to the Christian faith. He had met and talked with Alexander Campbell and came to accept many of Campbell's views. In the summer of 1830 the members of the Mahoning Association meeting at Austintown voted to disband in favor of being simply New Testament congregations. It was the evangelistic success of Scott that gave the Campbell-Stone movement its forward thrust.

Throughout the 1830s and 1840s the Campbell-Stone movement grew as the frontier moved steadily westward. Within 10 to 15 years there were large numbers of Campbell-Stone congregations in Ohio, Indiana, Illinois, Missouri, Arkansas, and Texas. Campbell's views had also moved eastward into Maryland, Virginia, North and South Carolina, and Georgia. Shortly thereafter, congregations were organized in Alabama, Mississippi, and Louisiana. By 1850 they were to be found in most of the states, including those on the West Coast.

Soon organization on a broader scale was discussed. In 1849 at Cincinnati, a general convention was held and the American Christian Missionary Society was organized with Alexander Campbell as president. He continued in this office as long as he lived. The organization of a convention and a missionary society, however, proved to be controversial. There was a question as to whether New Testament authority permitted such organizations.

As the question of slavery became a national issue, it was only a matter of time until Campbell was asked his view on it. In an editorial in *The Millennial Harbinger* he suggested that "slavery was a matter of opinion," meaning that Christians were to be in agreement on "essentials of the faith," but were to be free on subjects not considered "essential," in other words, in matters of opinion. He was echoing the 16th-century formula of Rupertus Meldinius. However, for many people this was not a satisfactory answer.

After the Civil War many leaders and churches in the Southern states felt they had been rejected, particularly as the convention and society had met during the war and voted a resolution of "loyalty" to the Union. Other matters began to surface around the question of their place in a New Testament church: the use of musical instruments in worship; salaried and located pastors; also the support of missionary societies and conventions. Well before the final separation in 1906 those who took the more conservative side in these issues were called CHURCHES OF CHRIST, their emergence constituting the first major break in the Campbell-Stone tradition.

The progressive element of the Campbell-Stone tradition continued to grow and to develop organizations as needs arose. In the second half of the 19th century there came into being additional colleges and schools, alongside Bethany founded in 1840, to provide preachers and leaders. Two foreign missionary societies were organized: one led by women (the Christian Woman's Board of Missions) and another mainly of men (the Foreign Christian Missionary Society). Soon there was a Board of Church Extension, a National Benevolent Association for orphans and widows, a Board of Ministerial Relief, and several other specialized organizations.

After Campbell's death in 1866 two publishing houses came into being with journals that continued to propagate the movement's views: the Standard Publishing Company of Cincinnati published the *Christian Standard*; and the Christian Publishing Company of St. Louis published the *Christian-Evangelist*.

At the celebration of the centennial of the *Declaration and Address* in 1909, a general feeling prevailed that consolidation of program and agencies would be desirable. By 1920 there was an International Convention of the churches (United States and Canada) formed with a Committee on Recommendations to screen business for the convention and a United Christian Missionary Society combining the work of many of the agencies into one larger organization. Resistance developed to the bigness of organization now being experienced, a condition that played on the fears of many people who were suspicious of power located in a few hands. Added to this was increasing concern arising from the newer forms of biblical interpretation that were entering the movement from Eastern universities as well as from the recently founded University of Chicago. New tensions soon developed in the movement.

Another issue soon divided the Campbell-Stone movement once again, the question of admitting into fellowship unimmersed believers. Known as "open" membership, some congregations, while still teaching believer's baptism by immersion, were admitting into membership people who had been baptized by other means. It was thought that this practice had been permitted on the mission field. Therefore, a number of congregations withdrew support from the missionary society and the convention. In 1927 the North American Christian Convention was formed as a place of fellowship for those of more conservative persuasion; this fellowship is now called the CHRISTIAN CHURCHES AND CHURCHES OF CHRIST.

The modern ecumenical movement begun in 1908 with the formation of the Federal Council of Churches of Christ and the World Missionary Conference of 1910 brought the progressive members of the movement into contact with Christians from around the world. The continuing congregations and members of the

Campbell-Stone movement were caught up in the wave of theological renewal that came over the American churches beginning in the 1930s.

After World War II the Campbell-Stone movement, now more frequently called the Christian Churches or Disciples of Christ, continued to develop churchly concepts in accord with the theological understanding of the church and its mission that was being discussed throughout the Protestant church in the United States. This branch of the movement was in full fellowship with the mainstream of American Protestantism.

By 1968, in a thoroughgoing restructuring, the semiautonomous agencies and societies that had come into being to carry on the work of the churches were restructured into the CHRISTIAN CHURCH (DISCIPLES OF CHRIST), a denomination with general, regional, and local manifestations. Its organization called for: a biennial general assembly with official delegates; regional assemblies for conducting the business of a given region, roughly following state or sectional lines; and the continuing local congregation. Recognition was accorded to the rights and responsibilities that each local manifestation of the church possessed.

There were now three major divisions in the Campbell tradition. The largest of these was the Churches of Christ, now to be found not only in the Southern states, but throughout the United States and in many overseas countries as well. These congregations continued what they conceived as the original Campbell tradition. The next-largest group of churches were those who were in fellowship through the North American Christian Convention and in process of developing other program organizations. The restructured and more liberal Christian Church (Disciples of Christ) came to realize itself as a denomination. It now seeks to achieve the goal of a united church through cooperation with other denominations in what is known as the Consultation on Christian Union. In these three groups of churches

the Campbell-Stone tradition continues today.

See also articles on BIBLE, AUTHORITY OF; DEBATES, INTERDENOMINATIONAL; RELIGIOUS PRESS; RESTORATIONISM.

Bibliography. Lester G. McAllister and William E. Tucker, *Journey in Faith: A History of the Christian Church (Disciples of Christ.)*

LESTER G. MCALLISTER
CHRISTIAN THEOLOGICAL SEMINARY

CAMPUS MINISTRY. The institutional intersection of religion and the academic community, "campus ministry" is the most common term to describe what in its 20th-century history has been also called student work, campus Christian life, and ministries in higher education. It is estimated that religious groups nationally and in individual institutions deploy over 10,000 people in professional leadership of congregational, denominational, and ecumenical ministries to and with students, faculty, and administrators of colleges and universities.

The earliest efforts to stimulate religious life on the campuses were those of the student YMCA, the Student Volunteer Movement (SVM), and those associated with the World's Student Christian Federation (WSCF) in the late 1800s. These were primarily student organizations and were to be found in both private and public institutions, from the smallest church-related college to the largest state university.

Around the turn of the century, there emerged student ministries sponsored by the major Protestant denominations. These were Wesley Foundations (Methodist), Westminster Foundations or Fellowships (Presbyterian), Canterbury Clubs (Episcopal), to be followed in later decades by Newman Centers (Roman Catholic), Hillel Foundations (Jewish), and the Baptist Student Unions.

Most historians mark 1899 as the beginning of campus ministry as it is known today at the University of Texas at Austin and at Virginia Polytechnic Institute (VPI) at Blacksburg. Other Southern campuses quickly followed the lead.

The pattern of development was not by a denominational design but by the expansion of student Bible classes, which met in churches near the campuses, and grew and thrived on the charisma of the teacher.

An increasing number of students went to state colleges and universities, and fewer, proportionately, attended the church-related colleges. As this number became a majority, churches gave support to the notion that they should follow their students to college. They aimed to provide positive influences and a strong program to preserve and nurture the faith of their young members on these secular campuses.

While not a regional phenomenon, the Southern campus took readily to the "home-away-from-home" philosophy. By the 1940s, full-time student workers took their places alongside "Y" secretaries and college or university chaplains. Soon "student centers" and "foundations" sprang up along the edges of the campus. By the late 1940s, the denomination-sponsored ministries were the dominant religious force on the major campuses of the South.

These beginnings were somewhat dormant during World War II, but the pattern was well established: Christian associations on the smaller, church-related college campuses and denominational centers on the university campuses. With the sudden postwar increase in student population, new campus student centers began to replace the temporary quarters or remodeled houses. A new generation of campus ministers, both women and men, emerged. Annual denominational gatherings of persons in higher-education ministries served this new breed of religious professionals.

These annual meetings of campus-ministry people from the early years took on the character of a family reunion. This was notable in the South where a regional consciousness added a "down-home" fla-

vor to each such gathering. The Presbyterians met at Montreat, Methodists at Lake Junaluska, and Baptists at Ridgecrest. They often included not only the professional campus ministers but faculty members, students, and college administrators. The North Carolina mountains were the Mecca that drew the faithful back for inspiration and renewal during the 1950s and 1960s.

An annual Southeast campus-ministry conference, now on an ecumenical basis, continues this long tradition in its meetings in Atlanta each spring of the year. Southwest-area, campus-ministry professionals have met regionally and by states in recent years.

Students in the 1940s and 1950s were gathered into denominational organizations, and both students and student workers attended in large numbers the quadrennial conferences of the SVM and the Interseminary Movement as well as denominationally sponsored events. *Student World*, other WSCF publications, and *Motive* magazine were widely read among student campus groups. Depth Bible study, summer work camps, and disciplined community living all became integral parts of the movement. A Faculty Christian Fellowship emerged from growing groups of faculty discovering a new vitality in faith and life issues. A healthy sense of participation in the international student Christian movement through the WSCF was manifest.

On a number of campuses, denominationally sponsored BIBLE CHAIRS were established and attached to departments of religion or philosophy. While in decline by the 1960s, the offering of elective courses for credit in both Bible and religion came to be accepted in many Southern state universities, and to an extent gained greater acceptance than in other parts of the country.

Southern universities have also perpetuated the pattern of institutionally employed chaplains or directors of religious life. Many of these are a continuation of the early YMCA-YWCA offices, although they have become interfaith in their outlook and constituency.

A more mature and prophetic character to campus ministry became evident in the 1960s. The CIVIL RIGHTS MOVEMENT gained great impetus from students on Southern campuses; and by the end of the decade, the war in Vietnam was the focus for significant student and faculty activism. The campus unrest was, in fact, the manifestation of a younger generation determined to speak its conscience and destined to be the voice of the nation. The silent generation found its niche and the issues of war and peace, nuclear power, environment, racism, and sexism became the agenda for new and succeeding generations. Campus ministry provided vital leadership to these developments.

By the 1970s, the growth in campus size and the reduction in church support brought changes. While the largest state universities continued to follow the traditional pattern of denominational centers and staff, the growth of smaller institutions and community colleges dictated a new approach. Notable among these changes were the abandonment of expensive buildings for the sake of retaining personnel, and the combining of two or more ministries under one roof. New ecumenical configurations and specialized ministries emerged.

Nowhere was this more evident than on the national level. United Ministries in Higher Education (UMHE), formed by major Protestant bodies, represented a new and important commitment of the church to higher education. Denominations continued to employ national staff, but they were deployed by the ecumenical body to form what was, effectively, a single staff for campus ministry, serving all its members. Out of this grew staff teams and programmatic emphases on ministry in medical education, career development, community colleges, and public education.

No history of campus ministry can omit the monumental Underwood study, which was published at the end of the

1960s. Authored and edited by Kenneth Underwood, under grants from the Danforth Foundation, this study focused for the religious communities, and for higher education itself, the imperative for mutual concern in the decades ahead. The four modes of campus ministry, lifted up, became its classic definition in this generation: priestly, pastoral, governance, and prophetic inquiry.

The emergence and continuation of a number of agencies and ecumenical bodies doing campus ministry indicate the support and commitment of the churches and of the participants themselves to ministries in higher education. Typical of these is the National Institute for Campus Ministries (NICM), which grew out of the older Church Society for College Work, and which has become an important support agency for both Christians and Jews in higher-education ministries. The National Campus Ministry Association and Ministry to Blacks in Higher Education incorporate this concern.

United Ministries in Education (UME) is the successor to UMHE and enters the 1980s with a broader definition of its task, viewing the total learning society as its arena for action, touching all aspects of humankind's life as the appropriate place for dialogue and faithfulness.

Along with these efforts of the major denominations and faith communities, certain Evangelicals have formed independent campus ministries. These include Inter-Varsity Christian Fellowship, Campus Crusade, and Navigators, all of whom place a high priority on personal conversion, Bible study, and missionary commitment. Many large private universities and smaller church-related colleges continue to employ chaplains who lead worship, counsel, and teach religious studies.

Together with the denominationally and ecumenically oriented ministries, these groups and persons find common cause in diverse settings in which the integrity of the faith community meets the integrity of the learning community.

Each seeks the preservation of its own life, and each sees the import of religion for the formation of social policy and cultural values. All seek resources for understanding and ministering to the human spirit.

To these worthy ends, campus ministry has emerged in the 20th century and will be present to be servant to church and higher education in the new century.

See also article on EDUCATION, CHRISTIAN HIGHER.

Bibliography. Kenneth Underwood, *The Church, The University, and Social Policy*; John H. Westerhoff, ed., *The Church's Ministry in Higher Education.*

GEORGE W. GUNN
LITTLE ROCK, ARKANSAS

CANE RIDGE, KENTUCKY. The site of the first event of the GREAT REVIVAL in 1801, it is located eight miles east of Paris in the Bluegrass section. It was given its name by Daniel Boone for a field of cane 15 miles long and nearly half as wide in what is now Bourbon County. In 1791 settlers who had migrated from North Carolina under the leadership of the Presbyterian minister, Robert Finley, built a 30-by-50-foot log meetinghouse on the site. Fifteen feet high, the building included a slave gallery. In August of 1801, Cane Ridge became the scene of a sacramental meeting, commonly known as the Cane Ridge Revival, or Cane Ridge Camp Meeting. Estimates of attendance at the week-long meeting ranged from 12,000 to 30,000. Participants camped on the grounds.

Although the meeting was organized by Presbyterian and Methodist preachers, Baptist ministers also shared in the preaching, though not in the sacrament itself. Four or five preachers frequently spoke simultaneously in different parts of the camp. Like other meetings of the Great Revival in the West (1787-1805), it was characterized by bizarre physical phenomena known as exercises. Most notable of these was the falling exercise in which persons fell as if dead, then after a time called to God for mercy, and finally

arose praising God. Other exercises reported at Cane Ridge included involuntary jerking, barking, dancing, and laughing. Because of its size and the prominence of the exercises, the Cane Ridge Camp Meeting soon became the classic symbol of the Great Revival in the West. In 1803, BARTON W. STONE, pastor of the Cane Ridge congregation, withdrew from the Presbyterian Church and helped to organize the Christian Church. In June 1804, Stone met with five other ministers at Cane Ridge to sign the *Last Will and Testament of Springfield Presbytery* (SPRINGFIELD WILL AND TESTAMENT). The building and grounds are now maintained by the Cane Ridge Preservation Project.

See also articles on CAMP MEETINGS; REVIVALISM.

D. NEWELL WILLIAMS
BRITE DIVINITY SCHOOL

CANNON, JAMES, JR. (1864-1944), Methodist bishop and prohibition crusader, was born in Salisbury MD. After graduating from Randolph-Macon College, he received a B.D. from Princeton Theological Seminary and an M.A. from Princeton. Admitted to the Virginia Annual Conference, Methodist Episcopal Church, South, in 1888, he served as president of Blackstone Female Institute from 1894 to 1918 and as editor of the *Baltimore-Richmond Christian Advocate* from 1904 to 1918. Elected bishop in 1919, Cannon thereafter directed Methodist educational and missionary projects. He was chairman of the Southern Commission on Unification of Methodism and a member of the Executive and Administrative Commission of the Federal Council of Churches. He played an important part in drafting the 1927 interdenominational "Appeal to Industrial Leaders of the South."

Cannon achieved his greatest fame as an indefatigable crusader for PROHIBITION. Between 1910 and 1919 he headed the Anti-Saloon League of Virginia and edited a prohibition daily newspaper, the *Richmond Virginian*. In 1914 after directing a campaign for a Virginia prohibition referendum, he personally supervised the writing and passage of that legislation. His vitriolic language antagonized opponents, who subsequently charged that he had made a deal with Virginia's conservative political machine. Cannon lobbied in Congress for the Nineteenth Amendment, and his political influence reached its peak in 1928 when he relentlessly campaigned against "wet" presidential candidate Al Smith. After 1929 Cannon was stigmatized by newspaper charges that he had engaged in stock-market gambling, misuse of campaign funds, and adultery. Although officially exonerated by congressional investigators and church leaders, Cannon never regained his former political stature.

Bibliography. Virginius Dabney, *Dry Messiah*; R. L. Watson, Jr., ed., *Bishop Cannon's Own Story.*

SAMUEL C. SHEPHERD, JR.
CENTENARY COLLEGE

CANON. A word used by Christians in a variety of ways, each related to the meaning of the Greek word κανών—a straight rod or bar used by artisans, sometimes as a standard of measurement.

In the Episcopal Church, canon is an ecclesiastical title given the priests who with the dean as their head form the permanent salaried staff of a cathedral and are responsible for its regular services. In the Middle Ages such men were called canons because they lived by a common rule of life. Occasionally a priest's service to the church is recognized by his being made an honorary canon of his diocesan cathedral, in which he has a special seat but no regular responsibilities. The cathedral of a diocese is the church building in which the bishop's seat or throne (Latin, *cathedra*) is located and upon which, in the early church, he sat to address his congregation.

In the Episcopal Church and the Roman Catholic Church, canon law (sometimes called "the canons") is the

body of rules that regulates the internal operation of the church.

Canon of Scripture denotes the authoritative list of uniquely inspired books that the church regards as alone composing Holy Scripture or the Bible.

The consecratory prayer in the Lord's Supper or Holy Communion, usually a standard and invariable part of the service, contains the dominical words of institution.

HERBERT S. WENTZ
UNIVERSITY OF THE SOUTH

CAPERS, WILLIAM (1790-1855), Methodist bishop and founder of Methodist MISSION TO SLAVES, was born in St. Thomas's Parish, near Charleston SC. Both his father, a rice planter, and his maternal grandfather were early converts to Methodism in the state. Educated in Georgetown and Roberts Academy in Stateburg, he entered South Carolina College in 1805. In 1808 he left college to read law in the office of Judge John S. Richardson. That same year he was converted, joined the Methodist Episcopal Church, and was admitted on trial to the South Carolina Conference. He became one of the most eloquent Southern Methodist preachers of his generation.

In 1828 he was American representative to the British Methodist Conference in London. In 1829 he led in establishing the mission to slaves in his home state and in 1833 he published a catechism for its use. As secretary of the Southern Missionary Department of the Methodist Episcopal Church, 1840-1844, he extended the mission to every Southern state. In 1844, 80 missionaries cared for over 22,000 slave members. In the General Conference of 1844 that split the church into Northern and Southern branches, Capers was a leading proponent of the Southern cause. In May 1846, he was elected one of the first bishops of the METHODIST EPISCOPAL CHURCH, SOUTH.

See also article on METHODIST CHURCH.

Bibliography. Donald G. Mathews, *Slavery and Methodism*; D. A. Reily, "William Capers: An Evaluation of His

Life and Thought," unpublished Ph.D. dissertation, Emory University, 1972; W. M. Wightman, *Life of William Capers.*

A. V. HUFF, JR.
FURMAN UNIVERSITY

CAREY, LOTT (c. 1780-1829), Baptist preacher and African emigrationist, was born a slave and only child in Charles City County VA. Lott lived in a close-knit family where he heard his grandmother prophesy that he would lead his people back to Africa. When he was 24, he moved to Richmond where he worked as a common laborer in a tobacco warehouse. A sermon on Jesus and Nicodemus helped generate Carey's conversion. He was baptized and joined the First Baptist Church in Richmond. Later, Carey went to school, began to preach, and was licensed by his church. His subsequent work with the First African Baptist Church, which he urged to support missions in Africa, led to the organization of the Richmond African Missionary Society in 1815. He became America's first black missionary to Africa when he departed 23 January 1821. The society provided $700 cash while the Baptist TRIENNIAL CONVENTION contributed cash and books totaling $300.

In the early years of the new colony of Liberia, Carey preached, taught, organized schools, and provided medical services. In 1826 he was elected vice agent. When Governor Jehudi Ashmun died in August 1828, Carey was elevated to the post of governor, which he held until his death (he was the accidental victim of a military-related explosion).

Bibliography. Miles M. Fisher, "Lott Carey, the Colonizing Missionary," *Journal of Negro History* 7 (1922): 380-418; Leroy Fitts, *Lott Carey: First Black Missionary to Africa.*

HERMAN E. THOMAS
UNIVERSITY OF NORTH CAROLINA
AT CHARLOTTE

CARIBBEAN IMMIGRATION.

Immigration from the Caribbean to the United States has been a small but constant stream from the colonial era to the present. About 1.3 million people have legally entered from that region since record keeping began in 1829, or about two percent of the total immigration into this country. The South, never a strong magnet for immigrants has, however, attracted significant numbers from the West Indies. From the British West Indies have come large numbers of slaves and in more recent times migrant laborers. From the Hispanic Caribbean have come large numbers of Cuban immigrants and refugees as well as a small number of Haitians.

The religious aspects of this immigration have been shaped almost entirely by the fact that between 1650 and 1850 the Caribbean formed the core of what has been called the South Atlantic System, an almost industrial agricultural undertaking for the production of a monocrop, usually sugar. The plantation owners in this system, unable to offer wages high enough to attract free labor from Europe, sought forced labor beyond their cultural boundaries where racial ideologies could be used to ease qualms about slavery. The economic dynamics of this system thus pulled immigrants into the Caribbean from Europe, the Americas, Africa, India, and even China. They joined with what was left of the native populations on the islands to form one of the most polyglot and culturally fragmented areas in the world.

This cultural schism between planters and labor was continued in the religious realm. The planters and their supportive bureaucracies were members of institutionalized churches the denominations of which paralleled imperial divisions. The Catholic Church dominated the Spanish and Portuguese colonies completely. Although Catholicism was also the established church in the French colonies, Protestants were tolerated even if grudgingly. The British and Dutch both established their national brand of Protestantism, Anglicanism, and Dutch Reformed (Calvinism), respectively, on their islands.

The official religions of the white planters stood over and against the often-illicit folk religions of the slaves whose derivations were largely African. Within the diversity of African religious expression certain shared belief structures are discernible. These include a polytheism that shades into pantheism, ancestor worship, and a belief in the efficacy of magic, witchcraft, and divination. These beliefs were organized around the family or the lineage rather than the congregation. In addition, many of the slaves were Muslims and some of these, frequently literate and highly educated, kept the spirit of Islam burning even while enslaved.

With time came some interpenetration of these opposing religious traditions. In the Catholic empires the slaves were absorbed into the Church through baptism at the time of enslavement. They were forced to accept, outwardly at least, alien religious beliefs, but given a place, however lowly, in the corporate social hierarchy that characterized the Hispanic Caribbean. The tension between African and European outlooks was resolved primarily through the process of syncretism whereby old religious forms are invested with new meanings. The results were neither African nor Catholic but mixtures with proportions dependent on such factors as demography. Examples range from the Cuban SANTERIA (outwardly more Catholic) to the Haitian *Vodun* or Voodoo (outwardly more African). In the Catholic Caribbean, then, the Church was corporate and inclusive and facilitated a strong sense of religious community in which one could participate with relatively little need to assimilate into the European world.

In the Protestant empires this synthetic process began much later and was never so successful in reconciling the religious dissonance between those who owned the fields and those who worked them. With the exception of the Moravian Brethren who came to Jamaica in 1754, the Christian churches were for whites only until just prior to emancipation. At that time planters began to admit missionaries and ministers from other churches such as the Baptists, Methodists,

Wesleyans, and various Mission Societies who all joined the established churches and the Jews who had been on the islands for some time. In the evangelical churches open to slaves, membership was usually through conversion, where the soul of the convert leapt across the void into the religious world of the European, leaving behind almost all remnants of Africa. Here, where participation in a religious community was not automatic and where religious life was centered on a highly personal experience, communities and even families were often split between those who had converted and those who had not. The churchgoer had entered the European world and had taken a hard first step on the path to assimilation.

As a result of these developments in the West Indies, immigrants coming to the United States have had experiences that fall into one of four broad categories. (1) The converted church member from the Protestant Caribbean finds integration into the new religious environment relatively easy. The same sects in the West Indies were active on the mainland, spawning both black and white congregations, and the assimilation implied in conversion makes adaptation easier. Very few of the immigrants to the South fall into this category, however. (2) When coming in sufficient numbers and with the determination to stay, the Catholic immigrants have also found the religious transition easy, for they have simply recreated in the United States the organic communities they left behind. This has been the experience of the many Cubans who have settled in Florida, Louisiana, Georgia, and Texas. The same factors that make their religious transition easy, however, makes cultural assimilation more difficult, for their Catholicism is not that of the host culture and their strong community frequently exists as an isolated enclave.

Those immigrants in the remaining two categories are likely to remain outsiders in both a religious and cultural sense. (3) The isolated Catholic who cannot find a transplanted community of coreligionists will often find the difference between the Catholicism of the mainland and that of his or her syncretised variant greater than that between black and white at home. (4) The nonconverts from the Protestant islands, or those who have fallen away from a Christian church, are numerically the largest group to come to the South. In this category are the slaves imported primarily by South Carolina planters from Barbados or Jamaica as well as the migrant workers who come for jobs all along the Southern seaboard, from cutting cane in Florida to picking vegetables on Maryland's Eastern Shore. Even where these immigrants can find a sizable community from their island, it is likely to be as fragmented as it was in the Caribbean. Without a shared religious experience, they are also likely to be considered strangers by American blacks as well.

The religious aspect of Caribbean immigration is thus fraught with ironies. The migrant laborers who, because of their marginal economic and cultural as well as religious status are those for whom a spiritual and institutional religious life would be of greatest value, are those least likely to find it. The Catholic Cubans face the opposite problem. The religious tradition that did much to unite their society in Cuba has, while easing some of the difficulties associated with immigration, turned into something of a liability in their efforts to integrate in their new homeland. These ironies as well as the conditions that force them to immigrate in the first place are all direct legacies of the days of sugar and slavery in the West Indies.

See also article on NATIVISM.

Bibliography. Virginia R. Dominquez, *From Neighbor to Stranger: The Dilemma of Caribbean Peoples in the United States*; Michael M. Horowitz, ed., *Peoples and Cultures of the Caribbean*; Edward Bean Underhill, *The West Indies: Their Social and Religious Condition.*

DANIEL SNYDACKER
NEWPORT, RHODE ISLAND

CARROLL, BENAJAH HARVEY

(1843-1914), Baptist pastor and educator, was born in Carroll County MS. He received the B.A. degree from Baylor University and in later years honorary doctorates from the University of Tennessee and Keatchie College in Louisiana. Following service in the Civil War, he was converted in 1865 and joined the Baptist church in Caldwell TX, being ordained the next year.

After preaching in small churches and teaching for three years, B. H. Carroll (as he is known) became pastor of the First Baptist Church in Waco where he served from 1871 until 1899. He then was elected corresponding secretary of the Texas Baptist Education Commission. In addition to his other duties, Carroll taught Bible in Waco University, later Baylor University, from 1872 to 1905. He then organized Baylor Theological Seminary in 1905 at Waco and three years later became its president. In 1908 the seminary was moved to the present campus on Seminary Hill in Fort Worth. Carroll made the move to Fort Worth and continued as president of the school until his death six years later. Carroll was an influential denominational leader serving in important offices both in Texas and in the Southern Baptist Convention. In particular, he is remembered for his administrative leadership in the field of theological education.

Carroll's published works total 33 volumes. His best-known work is a 13-volume set: *An Interpretation of the English Bible*. His books of popular sermons include *Jesus the Christ, Baptists and Their Doctrines,* and *Christ and His Church.*

Bibliography. Robert A. Baker, *The Southern Baptist Convention and Its People, 1607-1972*; W. W. Barnes, *The Southern Baptist Convention, 1845-1953.*

JOHN S. MOORE
LEXINGTON, VIRGINIA

CARROLL, JOHN (1735-1815), first Roman Catholic bishop in America, was born in Upper Marlborough MD. He entered the Society of Jesus (Jesuits) in Belgium and was ordained a priest circa 1769. Returning to the U. S. in 1774, he went on a mission to Canada for the Continental Congress. Following the Revolutionary War he spoke and wrote widely on the rights of Catholics in the new republic and on the compatibility of Catholic beliefs with free democratic institutions. In 1784 he was named superior of the American Catholic missions.

On 17 September 1789 Pope Pius VI erected Baltimore the first see in the United States and appointed Carroll its first bishop. Under his episcopal leadership a first national synod was convoked in 1791 to regulate pastoral practice and discipline among the far-flung Catholic minority. In 1808, with Carroll's encouragement, four new sees were carved out of his diocese (which became an archdiocese): Boston, New York, Philadelphia, and Bardstown KY.

Earlier Carroll had argued that bishops in the U. S. should be elected by the clergy as he had been, but he did not adhere to his own views in the appointments of the new bishops, choosing instead to recommend candidates directly to Rome. Episcopal elections would never become the practice of the church in the U. S. He encouraged foundations of religious orders of women, such as the Sisters of Charity of St. Joseph at Emmitsburg MD, whose foundress, Elizabeth Ann Seton, would become the first native-born U. S. citizen to be canonized a saint (in 1975). Similarly, he promoted the religious life for men, including aspirants to the secular clergy, for whom he established St. Mary's Seminary in Baltimore. Either under his auspices or with his participation, colleges were founded, such as Georgetown, Baltimore, and St. John's at Annapolis. Brother to Charles Carroll, a signer of the Declaration of Independence, he is perhaps most notable as a vigorous spokesman for religious liberty in the United States.

Bibliography. Thomas O'Brien Hanley, S.J., ed., *The John Carroll Papers*, 3 vols.; Annabelle M. Melville, *John Carroll of Baltimore: Founder of the American Catholic Hierarchy.*

MICHAEL V. GANNON
UNIVERSITY OF FLORIDA

CARTER, JAMES EARL (JIMMY)

(1924-), 39th president of the United States, was born in Plains GA. His forebears, all of British stock, were slaveholding planters and later businessmen with roots deep in Southern soil.

Carter joined a Baptist church as a child and was a regular churchgoer throughout his young adult life. But it was after the first defeat of his political career, when he lost his first bid to be governor of Georgia in 1966, that he experienced the religious conversion that would so deeply influence the subsequent course of his life. At this time, he would later explain during the presidential campaign of 1976, he was "born again." Although he had said even before his first race for the Georgia State Senate in 1962 that he considered a politician a "pastor" to his constituents, his rebirth confirmed his conviction that his political career carried the authority of a divine mission.

Carter was educated at the United States Naval Academy and served from 1945 to 1953 in the U.S. Navy. He resigned his commission in 1953 to return home and run the family's agribusiness enterprises. He served in the Georgia Senate from 1963 to 1967 and as governor from 1971-1975. In 1976, known only as a progressive Democrat from a Southern state and a man with sincere religious convictions, he was elected president of the United States by a coalition of minorities and independents who admired his apparent honesty and longed to end the era of Watergate.

After one term, in which the nation had peace but high inflation, in which he failed to satisfy either the liberals who wanted sweeping social reform or the conservatives who expected the Southern Baptist president to inaugurate an economic and religious millennium, Carter was soundly defeated for reelection by a public ready once more for vigorous leadership.

Bibliography. James T. Baker, *A Southern Baptist in the White House*; David Kucharsky, *The Man from Plains.*

JAMES T. BAKER
WESTERN KENTUCKY UNIVERSITY

CARVER, WILLIAM OWEN (1868-1954), Baptist educator and world statesman, was born in Wilson County TN. He was graduated from the University of Richmond with a M.A. in 1891 and the Southern Baptist Theological Seminary, Th.M. in 1895, and Th.D. in 1896. He studied in Europe and visited missions in South America and the Orient. As professor of missions and comparative religion, his thought influenced both future missionaries and mission-board executives. He was the author of 20 books, the majority of which were biblically oriented studies of the world mission.

From 1936 to 1944, Carver was a member of the executive committee of the American Association of Theological Schools, and a member of the American Theological Committee, a subsidiary of the World Conference on Faith and Order. For his ecumenical activities, Carver was more or less continuously criticized by some fellow Baptists. Some also were alarmed by certain tendencies of his theological thought, especially by his biblically determined doctrine of the church. At the same time he exercised a strong influence on the denomination, especially through the Southern Baptist Historical Society, the *Review and Expositor* of which he was managing editor and a regular columnist and contributor, and as the principal founder of the Woman's Missionary Union Training School (name later changed to Carver School of Missions and Social Work).

All his students were in awe of the range and order of his learning. Good students heard him with rich profit. His special competencies were in biblical interpretation, the theology and philosophy of history, and the nature of the Christian world mission. Among the important emphases of his teaching were: (1) the unity and catholicity of the church; (2) history as the arena in which the divine intention is realized in humanity, and this divine intention is the primary *human* fact and factor; (3) the Christian world mission continuously springs from the very nature and spirit of the Christian religion; (4) election is God's choice of individuals, groups, and institutions to carry out his purposes to others; (5) Christian truth is both fixed and changing.

See also articles on ECCLESIOLOGY; ECUMENISM; THEOLOGICAL EDUCATION.

Bibliography. Baptist History and Heritage 3 (July 1968); W. O. Carver, *The Course of Christian Missions; Out Of His Treasure.*

THERON D. PRICE
FURMAN UNIVERSITY

CASHWELL, G[ASTON] B[ARNIBUS] (1860-1916), early Pentecostal leader, was born in Sampson County NC. Beginning his ministerial career in the Methodist Episcopal Church, South, he joined the Holiness Church of North Carolina in 1903 and served for several years as a pastor in that sect. In November 1906, having heard of the Pentecostal revival then under way in Los Angeles, Cashwell traveled to that California city to seek the BAPTISM OF THE SPIRIT signified by speaking in tongues. In early December, he had a profoundly emotional religious experience that he believed to be an outpouring of the Holy Spirit. Convinced of its authenticity and anxious that others receive this new blessing, Cashwell returned to DUNN NC, and on 31 December 1906 began a Pentecostal revival there.

The Dunn revival was the first of many that Cashwell conducted in the Carolinas, Georgia, Alabama, and Tennessee during the next year. His work sparked a wave of conversions that within a matter of months brought almost the entire Southern Holiness movement into the Pentecostal camp. The PENTECOSTAL HOLINESS CHURCH, CHURCH OF GOD

(CLEVELAND TN), Pentecostal Free Will Baptist Church, and ASSEMBLIES OF GOD can trace their Pentecostal lineage at least in part to the preaching of Cashwell.

Although known as the "Pentecostal Apostle to the South," G. B. Cashwell remained a part of the movement for only a few years. By 1910 his name had been dropped from the ministerial roster of the Pentecostal Holiness Church. He apparently returned to the Methodist fold and played no further role in the burgeoning Pentecostal movement.

See also articles on HOLINESS MOVEMENT; PENTECOSTALISM.

Bibliography. Robert Mapes Anderson, *Vision of the Disinherited: The Making of American Pentecostalism*; Vinson Synan, *The Old-Time Power: A History of the Pentecostal Holiness Church.*

ROBERT F. MARTIN
UNIVERSITY OF NORTHERN IOWA

CATTS, SIDNEY JOHNSON (1863-1936), preacher, politician, and prohibitionist, was born on a Dallas County AL plantation. Although blinded in one eye, he attended Auburn University, Howard College, and Cumberland Law School. He briefly practiced law, but was converted during a Baptist PROTRACTED MEETING in 1886, and without further education immediately entered the ministry.

Catts served many small central Alabama Baptist churches. Strongly influenced by his provincial culture, he opposed drinking, dancing, expanded opportunities for blacks, and Catholicism. His volatile temper and visceral reactions kept him in trouble with his congregations.

In 1904 Catts entered politics, running unsuccessfully for Congress from Alabama's Fifth District. After a brief stint as pastor in DeFuniak Springs FL (1911-1914), he resigned because of low pay and constant controversy and began to sell insurance. His peddling won him many friends among the plain whites of Florida's panhandle, which friendships he used effectively as the Prohibitionist candidate for governor in 1916. Although a virtual

unknown without money, he parlayed warnings against Catholics and parochial schools into a stunning political upset.

As governor Catts proposed a progressive agenda including PROHIBITION, women's suffrage, and prison, educational, and labor reforms. But his inability to compromise, temperamental rages, and nepotism caused friction with the conservative legislature, which defeated most of his programs.

Catts was defeated in his race for the Senate in 1920 and narrowly lost gubernatorial contests in 1924 and 1928. In later life he became cynical, was accused of peonage and counterfeiting, and developed close political ties with south Florida gambling and liquor interests. A complex man, many of his contradictions were rooted in the religious tensions of his times.

See also articles on FLORIDA; NATIVISM.

Bibliography. Wayne Flynt, *Sidney J. Catts, Cracker Messiah.*

WAYNE FLYNT
AUBURN UNIVERSITY

CEMETERIES. Southern cemeteries have generally not been sanctified ground, but they have reflected the region's religious outlook and its cultural differences from the North. Cemeteries have shown Protestantism's pervasive influence over the Southern way of death. Southerners in cities buried their dead in the rural garden cemeteries of the mid-nineteenth century and in the lawn-park cemeteries of the modern period, but these have not been distinctively Southern nor very religious. The country graveyards have the best claim to being identifiably regional institutions containing religious elements.

In the colonial period, many Southern graveyards became disassociated from churches. Although British and New England Calvinist Protestants asserted the idea of unsanctified burial grounds, they usually maintained the location of cemeteries near churches. The diffusion of the Southern population on the frontier resulted in the emergence of private family graveyards. Frontier necessity led to acceptance of burial locations that were separate from religious institutions, yet the understanding of FUNERALS and burial was still in line with the Reformed Protestant outlook. Family burial grounds have been especially noteworthy in Dixie, dating back to the pioneer times. Many rural congregations from the 19th century onward built their churches near these small family-burial plots and then extended them into larger church graveyards.

Care of the graves resulted in a pervasive Southern rural cemetery ritual that had religious overtones. Graveyard Day, or Decoration Day, reflected the farm cycle of life, typically occurring in late July or August or else after the harvest as an autumn ritual. The goal was to clear the burial ground of unwanted vegetation and to demonstrate respect for the dead. The day was partly a solemn, sacred event, especially for those who had lost a family member during the previous year. Local ministers usually appeared to lead prayers, perhaps deliver a short message, and pitch in to help clean the graves. Even in the 20th century people who had left their small towns and rural communities would frequently return for Graveyard Day, thus reinforcing kinship and community ties.

Perhaps the most significant source of Southern cemetery distinctiveness came from grave decoration; this feature also had religious dimensions. Few commercial markers existed in rural, folk cemeteries and, in line with Protestant theology, one rarely saw Christian crosses displayed. Traditional, distinctive grave markers were either slabs of native stone, containing a minimum of information, or the more typical wooden plank found among both black and white Southern Protestants. Planks would likely be set up at the head and foot of the burial plot. They were highly individualistic, with hand-carved inscriptions and frequent biblical allusions. While overt Christian symbols were generally absent from rural

graveyards, biblical verses and language were found in abundance. Grave decorations in nonfolk cemeteries found in Southern cities and small towns included portrait statues. These representations included images of religious figures, as well as statues in the form of angels and young women personifying such spiritual qualities as grief, memory, faith, meditation, and prayer. Such elaborate monuments frequently contained religious inscriptions. Given the Protestant suspicion of graven images, the prevalence of such statuary is surprising.

Religious concepts saturated Southern culture so that in certain contexts, such as nondenominational community cemeteries, it must have seemed natural for statues and monuments to contain religious sentiments. A curious relic of the desire for sanctity in death was found in the tabernacles and small, open chapels found within those rural cemeteries not near a church. They contained benches and served as the focus for ceremonies during funerals, Graveyard Day, and Memorial Day.

Bibliography. Terry G. Jordan, " 'The Roses So Red and the Lilies So Fair': Southern Folk Cemeteries in Texas," *Southwestern Historical Quarterly* 83 (January 1980): 227-58; D. Gregory Jeane, "The Upland South Cemetery: An American Type," *Journal of Popular Culture* 11 (Spring 1978): 895-903.

CHARLES REAGAN WILSON
UNIVERSITY OF MISSISSIPPI

CHARISMATIC. A word originating from the Greek *charisma,* "free gift." When used as a nominal or adjectival form, it refers to those individuals, groups, or denominations within Christendom who have experienced a "baptism of the Holy Spirit" that usually involves the receiving of spiritual gifts, notable among these, the gift of speaking in tongues (GLOSSOLALIA). The receiving of these spiritual gifts, oftentimes as important as the conversion experience itself, usually results in a different or new style of living. Frequently the recipient of the "baptism" will enjoy a heightened public witness demonstrating a central and joyful aspect of the Christian life.

Before 1960 this phenomenon was largely associated with groups referred to as "Pentecostals." These individuals were often stereotyped by the non-Pentecostal Christians as blue-collar, uneducated, and occupying the lower rung of the socioeconomic ladder.

In the 1960s, however, there occurred a significant penetration of Pentecostalism into the mainline denominations. This phenomenon has been called "neo-Pentecostalism." It has found adherents in virtually every major denomination, including (after 1967) the Roman Catholic Church.

The neo-Pentecostal movement is often characterized as one that places a primary emphasis upon the role of the Spirit in the believer's life. Of major, but not exclusive importance, are the spiritual gifts (1 Cor. 12). Among these, the ones most frequently found in neo-Pentecostalism are the gifts of speaking in tongues and healing. Recently, however, there has been some movement toward the most traditional social ministries within some branches of the neo-Pentecostal movement.

WATSON E. MILLS
MERCER UNIVERSITY

CHARISMATIC MOVEMENTS. This kind of movement among Christians reasserts the validity of the gifts of the Pentecost, the principle of which is the capacity to "speak in unknown tongues" (GLOSSOLALIA). "Charismatic" describes those people in the mainstream denominations who have received the BAPTISM OF THE SPIRIT and have chosen to stay within their own churches or to find fellowship in nondenominational bodies rather than join the organized Pentecostal denominations. The term "charismatic" is favored over "neo-Pentecostal" to avoid association with the perceived excesses of traditional PENTECOSTALISM. The term "charismatic renewal" is favored over "charismatic

movement," especially by Roman Catholics, because it implies that the process is one of reinvigoration of the church rather than its rejection.

The charismatic movement is rooted in, but independent of, the Pentecostalism that arose in the United States at the turn of the century. Pentecostal beliefs at the time moved toward more privatistic religiosity during the 1960s when established Pentecostal bodies were among the fastest growing of religious denominations, and when many new forms, among them the charismatic movement, made their appearance.

According to a 1978 Gallup Poll, 19 percent of all adult Americans considered themselves Pentecostals or charismatic Christians. About one-third of these were members of traditional Pentecostal assemblies, but the remainder were part of the charismatic movement, scattered among more orthodox denominations. Twenty-seven percent of those identifying themselves as charismatics were Roman Catholics; 21 percent Baptist; eight percent Methodist; six percent Lutheran; and five percent were Presbyterian. Most of those polled were probably using the term "charismatic" rather loosely, to indicate simply a sense of spiritual renewal. Only 17 percent of charismatics, most of them Protestants, had actually spoken in tongues.

The original charismatics were more middle class than Pentecostals have traditionally been. But as the movement spread, the representation of socioeconomic groups evened out. Gallup found no age, education, or sex differences between charismatics and the general population. However, charismatics were likely to attend church more frequently, read the Bible more often, tithe more typically, and watch more religious television programs.

The charismatic movement has exhibited a bewildering array of organizational forms. It embraces interdenominational organizations like the Full Gospel Business Men's Fellowship International, a considerable number of prayer groups not identified with any denomination, a nondenominational "free ministry" of itinerant evangelists, local "Christian Centers," some "teaching ministries," thousands of prayer groups within the established denominations, and numerous publishing ventures. Its various "cells" are tied together, not by any central bureaucratic office, but through intersecting sets of personal relationships. The movement has grown by means of face-to-face recruitment, moving easily across class and cultural boundaries.

Charismatics believe that religious power and experience are available to ordinary people, without benefit of clergy. They are loath to admit that religious spontaneity ineluctably becomes institutionalized. Nevertheless, the movement has gradually become more structured. Beliefs and practices are standardized by means of "Life in the Spirit" seminars. These seminars function as a catechesis that each member is obliged to complete prior to full acceptance into the movement. Entrance procedures have been informally established. More and more the gift of tongues is treated as evidence of the baptism of the Holy Spirit. Indeed, speaking in tongues appears to be more important to charismatics than to traditional Pentecostals, suggesting its functional importance as an aid to commitment where organizational supports are weak.

Few charismatics regard their conversion as a dramatic change, but rather as an intensification of their former commitment, the consolidation of an identity only partially formed. They do not see themselves as schismatics. However, for centuries speaking in tongues has been condemned by the churches when it occurred spasmodically in revival movements because this and other charisms were judged to have withdrawn from other Christians. The charismatic movement thus met with considerable hostility from the established denominations. The

idea of diffused charisma was especially threatening to the power of the clergy. In time, the promise of spiritual renewal proved irresistible and a variety of attempts to keep the movement within the fold were instituted, including prayer groups and certain kinds of healing services. Ironically, the liturgical churches, furthest removed theologically and historically, were more open to the charismatic movement. Traditional Pentecostals felt that the movement undercut their rationale for an independent Pentecostalism and were antagonistic.

The charismatic movement reflects much of the restlessness and rejection of formal procedures and established institutions characteristic of the 1960s. The expressive freedom of charismatic worship was particularly liberating for those with a religious background of fixed liturgical practices and rational sermonizing. The emphasis on charisms remystified worship, engendering a new sense of wonder at the powers present in the world. However, the movement was not socially reformist; its teachings reasserted traditional gender norms, sexual morality, and family responsibilities.

Originating in the Western states and spreading rapidly through the upper Middle West to the Northern states, the charismatic movement affected those denominations that have traditionally lacked strength in the South. Denominations identified with the South, such as the Southern Baptists, were hostile to it. In the past the North has been relatively free of high-intensity, highly demonstrative forms of religion like Pentecostalism. In the South, such forms have been standard for many decades, leaving less room for variation on this theme. The South, being better provided institutionally for the kind of privative religion the charismatics sought, and being less affected by the liberalization that sparked it, remained relatively untouched by the movement.

See also article on CHARISMATIC.

Bibliography. David Edwin Harrell, Jr., *All Things are Possible: The Healing and Charismatic Revivals in Modern America*; Meredith McGuire, *Pentecostal Catholics: Power, Charisma, and Order in a Religious Movement*; Richard Quebedeaux, *The New Charismatics: The Origins, Development, and Significance of Neo-Pentecostalism.*

JOHN WILSON
DUKE UNIVERSITY

CHARLESTON, SOUTH CAROLINA.

Charleston's religious figures have been closely identified with the intellectual life of the city. The Anglican commissary Gideon Johnston assisted in placing the Church of England on a stable basis in the early eighteenth century, and his successor ALEXANDER GARDEN successfully defended the establishment from challenges posed by GEORGE WHITEFIELD in the 1740s. He also founded a school for blacks in 1743. The ministers of the Independent Church, Josiah Smith (1734-1750), William Hutson (1756-1761), and William Tennent (1772-1777), were also intellectual leaders and reflected the city's relatively unusual religious diversity. On the eve of the Revolution, Charleston was divided into two Anglican parishes, ST. PHILIP'S CHURCH and St. Michael's Church, and also housed six nonconforming churches (an Independent, Presbyterian, French, German, and two Baptist), one Quaker meetinghouse, and the second synagogue established in America, BETH ELOHIM.

In the 19th century, a strong lay population sought to increase its control in several denominations. This resulted in the Catholic Charleston Schism (1818-1820). Several figures evidence the different themes in antebellum Protestant theology. A prominent exponent of New England liberalism was SAMUEL GILMAN (1791-1858), who was minister of Charleston's Second Independent Church. Romantic liberal JAMES WARLEY MILES of Charleston (1818-1876) was rector of St. Michael's Church, where he built a substantial library of theological works in more than 30 languages. THOMAS SMYTH was a prominent spokesman for theological conservatism. He was pastor of the Second Presbyterian Church, and in 1857, the synod acquired 11,000 volumes from his personal library for the seminary in Columbia. Down to 1833, meetings of Charleston's evangelical denominations were biracial. When members of the Trinity Methodist Church expelled two mulattoes from the sanctuary where they were seated with white members of the church, they instigated a series of events that compelled pastor WILLIAM CAPERS to segregate sanctuary seating. This eventually resulted in blacks leaving the congregation entirely. The event has been construed by Donald Mathews as a symbol of a turning point in the history of Evangelical Protestantism in the South, in which whites moved from seeing blacks as coreligionists to a position of racist arrogance.

After the Civil War, the religious climate in the city tended to differ somewhat from norms across the South. Where conservative Protestantism tended to reinforce social conservatism, Charleston's newspapers, for example, objected to state-imposed Prohibition in 1916.

AMY FRIEDLANDER
MARIETTA, GEORGIA

CHESNUT, MARY BOYKIN (1823-1886),

diarist of life in the South, was born in Waxhaw SC. Her father was a lawyer, founder of the States' Rights party, state governor (1828-1830), and U. S. senator (1830-1833) until he resigned to move to Mississippi to care for his extensive plantations.

Sent to one of Charleston's finest finishing schools, Mary Boykin Miller began developing a lifelong taste for Gallic culture. She became sensitive to the social conditions and the class system of her time on a trip to Mississippi in 1836. Her writings show a continued fascination with the condition of Indians, slaves, and whites as they interrelated. Shortly after her father's death in Mississippi when she was 17, she married James Chesnut, Jr., planter and lawyer. Mary Boykin Chesnut, childless, eagerly escaped the boredom of plantation life by travel to Northern resorts and to England. When her husband was elected U. S. senator in 1859 and Confederate senator in 1861, Mrs. Chesnut was delighted to enter the social mainstream.

Mary Chesnut's *Diary* is an account of her wartime experiences in Charleston, Montgomery, and Richmond. Since a new edition, *Mary Chesnut's Civil War*, appeared in 1981, her *Diary* has received renewed interest and is now recognized as the most outstanding literary account of the Civil War. After the war, she returned to ruined plantations and overwhelming debts and her tendency to depression surfaced. She periodically "edited" her wartime *Diary*, which was finally published 19 years after her death.

Bibliography. Ben Ames Williams, ed., *A Diary from Dixie by Mary Boykin Chesnut*; Edmund Wilson, *Patriotic Gore: Studies in the Literature of the American Civil War*; C. Vann Woodward, *Mary Chesnut's Civil War*.

LOUISE PETTUS
WINTHROP COLLEGE

CHILDREN'S HOMES: *See* SOCIAL SERVICES.

CHRISTIAN ACADEMIES: *See* CHRISTIAN SCHOOLS.

CHRISTIAN AND MISSIONARY ALLIANCE. This sectarian Protestant body began in 1881 when Albert Benjamin Simpson, a Canadian-born Presbyterian minister, had a healing experience under the ministry of an Episcopal minister, Charles Cullis, who operated a summer camp at Old Orchard ME. Simpson felt a call to missionary work that "would reach the neglected fields of the world" at home and abroad.

Simpson founded a Bible school at New York City that later moved to Nyack NY, still the center of Alliance institutional life. In 1887 he formed two groups, the Christian Alliance for home missions and the International Missionary Alliance for foreign missions. In 1897 these combined to form the Christian and Missionary Alliance. The movement drew its strength from the fundamentalist movement and the HOLINESS MOVEMENT, which were both getting underway in America at that time. The early Alliance members came from varied backgrounds, ranging from the Episcopal Church to the Salvation Army.

Although the Alliance tried to remain an interdenominational mission agency, it was forced to attempt organizational and doctrinal unity as it confronted problems of the day. In 1907 the Pentecostal movement created a crisis for the Alliance as students and teachers at Nyack began speaking in tongues. A unique compromise for that time was developed by Simpson under his dictum "seek not— forbid not," which offered acceptance of GLOSSOLALIA without encouragement. Alliance leadership took a similar position in the 1960s when confronted by neo-Pentecostalism.

Twelve articles of faith were included in a statement adopted by the General Council of the Christian and Missionary Alliance in 1965. An essentially fundamentalist theology is reflected in these articles, for they are based on the view that the Bible is "inerrant as originally given." Other articles affirm the virgin birth and bodily resurrection of Christ; the substitutionary view of the atonement; the imminent premillennial Second Coming; a strong view of the Holy Trinity; and conscious punishment for unbelievers. The holiness influence is seen in their strong emphasis on sanctification as both a crisis and progressive experience in the lives of believers; prayer and anointing of the body with oil for healing; and Spirit baptism. The Lord's Supper is interpreted in memorial terms and baptism is by immersion of believers.

The "four-fold Gospel" of the Christian and Missionary Alliance was originated by Simpson and depicts Christ as Savior, Sanctifier, Healer, and Coming Lord. This four-fold Gospel is symbolized by a cross, a laver, a pitcher of oil, and a crown. The laver emphasizes God's grace, which provides "daily cleansing from the defilement of sin." Aimee Semple McPherson took these four points from Simpson and used them to organize her Church of the Foursquare Gospel.

The Alliance is congregationally organized with accent on the autonomy of the local body. The Annual Council composed of delegates of the society's members enacts all legislation, and coordinates work through 21 districts. Today there are 5,000 churches with over 350,000 members abroad, and 1,500 churches with 200,000 members in North America, about one-eighth scattered throughout the South.

See also articles on FUNDAMENTALISM; PENTECOSTALISM.

Bibliography. J. H. Hunter, *Beside All Waters: The Story of Seventy-Five Years of Worldwide Ministry by the Christian and Missionary Alliance; Manual of the Christian and Missionary Alliance.*

CARLTON T. MITCHELL
WAKE FOREST UNIVERSITY

CHRISTIAN CHURCH. The Southern Christian Church arose from the JAMES O'KELLY schism of 1792 in the early Methodist Church in North Carolina and Virginia. O'Kelly's followers, who formally organized themselves in 1794, were sometimes called O'Kellians or Republican Methodists in tribute to their leader and in reference to their utter aversion to anything that smacked of hierarchical authority in the church. O'Kelly preferred the name Christian because it suggested a fellowship of Protestant believers that transcended denominationalism.

Often confused with the Disciples of Christ, with "Campbellites," or with Christians in New England or the West, the Southern Christian Church's choice of a name was innocently—perhaps deliberately—ambiguous. During the fierce controversies between O'Kelly and the Methodists, early Southern Christians became wedded to a radically Christocentric theology and democratic church polity. Because they made adherence to the Bible the only creedal basis of fellowship

and because they insisted that every believer had direct access to the ear of the Savior, Jesus literally became "King and Head of the people" in their conception of the church, and "the all-sufficiency of a 'Bible Government'" permeated the sectarian affairs of their church. When Abner Jones left the Baptists and BARTON W. STONE the Presbyterians to affiliate with O'Kelly, they made it a remarkably nondenominational entity that was known by 1820 as the "Christian Connection." A similar group of New England Christians sought union with the O'Kellians, but insisted on baptism by immersion, which O'Kelly opposed.

From 1794 to 1810 an annual General Meeting governed Christians from Pennsylvania to Georgia, but then the nascent denomination split into two distinct conferences—Eastern Virginia and North Carolina-Virginia. The Eastern-Virginia Conference maintained close ties to New England Christians and in 1844-1846 sought again to bring about a union. However, the project collapsed in 1846 when the New England Christians issued a ringing denunciation of slavery; the *Christian Sun* of Hillsborough—which had strongly supported overtures to the North—retorted, "the Borealis of the north cannot frighten and bewilder us. . . . We have no desire to be united with you." A similar effort at the 1854 General Christian Conference in Cincinnati to persuade Northern Christians to desist from condemning slaveholding also failed amid an acrimonious debate on the Fugitive Slave Law. Accordingly, in 1856 the Eastern Virginia and North Carolina-Virginia conferences merged to form the Southern Christian Convention. In 1858 the Alabama, Mississippi, and Missouri Conferences became loosely affiliated with the convention. Over the next 40 years the denomination suffered from lack of a formally trained clergy and an inability to project a vigorous institutional image—weaknesses highlighted by a strenuous campaign for reform led by the newly elected church president, Jesse T. Whitley, in 1878. Failing to find support, Whitley simply disappeared. Finally in 1931 the Southern Christian Convention merged with the Congregationalists, and in 1957 these Congregational Christian Churches joined with the Evangelical and Reformed Churches to form the UNITED CHURCH OF CHRIST. The most enduring institutional achievements of the Southern Christians were the establishment of Elon College, near Burlington NC in 1890, and the Christian Orphanage in the town of Elon College in 1905.

Bibliography. Durward T. Stokes and William T. Scott, *A History of the Christian Church in the South.*

ROBERT M. CALHOON
UNIVERSITY OF NORTH CAROLINA
AT GREENSBORO

CHRISTIAN CHURCH (DISCIPLES OF CHRIST): *See* DISCIPLES OF CHRIST.

CHRISTIAN CHURCHES AND CHURCHES OF CHRIST. One of the three major movements within the Campbellite family of American Protestantism, and the one most recent in origin (although the Disciples' "Restructure" dates only to 1968). Its separate identity begins officially with action taken at a Christian Church convention in Cincinnati in 1927. By 1971 this body of independent congregations had sufficient particularity and cohesion in its own eyes to request a separate listing in the *Yearbook of American Churches.*

This "undenominational" fellowship stands to the right of the CHRISTIAN CHURCH (DISCIPLES OF CHRIST) and to the left of the CHURCHES OF CHRIST, the two other movements within the CAMPBELLITE TRADITION, both of which are indigenously American. "Christian Churches and Churches of Christ" is the name by which it is commonly known, but its aversion to denominational character means that no official name has been or can be designated. It is also known as the "middle group," the "Centrists," "Independent Christian Churches," or "Christian Churches," or "Christian Churches/Churches of Christ." A single

congregation is most often referred to as a "Christian Church" but sometimes as a "Church of Christ," the latter despite the clear separation between this "middle group" and the non-instrumental Campbellites regularly (but also not officially) called Churches of Christ.

Like the other two Campbellite bodies, this fellowship traces its origins to RESTORATIONISM, a theme with roots in the thinking of the Protestant Reformers. This theme took shape as the Restoration Movement in early nineteenth-century America, which was characterized by a determination to adhere rigorously to the Bible, especially in matters of congregational organization and practice. As led by Thomas and ALEXANDER CAMPBELL and BARTON W. STONE, these Christians intend (in paraphrase) to "speak where the Scriptures speak" and "to be silent where the Scriptures are silent." In practice, the focus fell less on theology than on how to organize congregational life and how to carry out public worship. The recovery and duplication of "New Testament Christianity" was its hallmark from the beginning.

The passion to restore the patterns of Primitive Christianity continues to animate these "Independent Christian Churches." Indeed, that is their stock-in-trade, their only reason for existence. As they see it, the Disciples of Christ wing has largely abandoned the Restorationist concern in favor of ecumenicity, which also was a major commitment of Campbell; however, it was to be "undenominational" rather than explicitly cooperative Christianity, especially in the earlier years of his career. On the other side, the Churches of Christ are viewed as having turned conviction into legalism, especially on the use of instrumental music in services of congregational worship. It should be noted that on the classic theme of Restoration, however, the Christian Churches and Churches of Christ fellowship hold much more in common with the Churches of Christ than with the Disciples of Christ.

Thus the Christian Churches and Churches of Christ branch of the family is more "conservative" than "liberal"; it remains committed to the words of the Bible, bent on retaining local-church independence. It stands closer to rationalism than to any other hermeneutical or epistemological method; it rejects all "man-made creeds"; it is highly self-conscious about its particular nature and mission. At the same time, it repudiates legalism and has a generally open, cooperative, and respectful attitude toward other bodies of Christians. It is as firm in its conviction that we are "Christians only" (a slogan from the first generation of the movement) as it is in its rejection of "we are the only Christians." The fellowship honors the qualities of being firm, solid, uncompromising, and earnest. This is a people who live by an acknowledged authority, who are very clear on the commission of the New Testament to Christians and on their mission to embody with purity and scrupulosity the belief and practice of the primitive church.

The Churches of Christ had become a specifiable branch of the Campbellite family in the public understanding by 1906. However, as a regional (Southern) movement having fewer and fewer fraternal ties with Northern Disciples, it was taking shape as the Civil War began and was informally recognizable as a separate body of like-minded independent churches no later than the 1880s. The Christian Churches and Churches of Christ, in somewhat similar fashion, were taking shape before the actual break in 1927. Many thousands who had maintained their connection with the Disciples "grew increasingly restive in the fellowship." The Cincinnati-based *Christian Standard* led a swelling outcry against the "liberalizing" and "modernizing" trends among Disciples, especially on the subject of biblical criticism. In a 1927 "preaching assembly" called by veteran evangelist P. H. Welshimer, these more traditional and authority-minded congregations chose to go their own way. As a result, the

North American Christian Convention was born. ("Convention," rather than "Church," is used to indicate that no corporate decisions are binding; instead congregations voluntarily convene to engage matters of common concern.)

Demographically, it is the Christian Church (Disciples of Christ) with whom the Christian Churches and Churches of Christ fellowship is closely linked. The heartland of its strength is approximately the same: from western Pennsylvania across the Midwestern states to Missouri and Iowa in the West. Sizable membership also prevails, however, in Kentucky (in both cases), the state of primary origination. Several other Southern states reflect notable growth, especially since World War II; Oklahoma, Virginia, Tennessee, Georgia, Florida, and North Carolina all have more than 150 churches and 25,000 members. Kentucky's figures are 427 and 75,000; Missouri's are 320 and 52,000. The total estimated membership nationwide was one million in 1982. Unlike sister fellowships within the Campbellite family, the Christian Churches and Churches of Christ are also strong in northern California, Oregon, and Washington.

More committed to Bible colleges than to theological seminaries, their congregations support 44 such colleges. There is one liberal arts college, Milligan, located at Johnson City TN and four graduate schools of religion, one at Johnson City and another in Cincinnati OH.

See also article on RATIONALISM (RELIGIOUS).

Bibliography. *Directory of the Ministry, 1982: A Yearbook of Christian Churches and Churches of Christ*; Robert O. Fife, David E. Harrell, and Ronald E. Osborn, *Disciples and the Church Universal*; James DeForest Murch, *Christians Only*; William J. Richardson, ed., *Christian Doctrine*; William Robinson, *Biblical Doctrine of the Church*; Dean E. Walker, *Adventuring for Christian Unity*; C. Robert Wetzel, ed., *Essays in New Testament Christianity*.

SAMUEL S. HILL
UNIVERSITY OF FLORIDA

CHRISTIAN METHODIST EPISCOPAL CHURCH. Organized in December

1870 by and for newly freed black members of the METHODIST EPISCOPAL CHURCH, SOUTH, it was originally called the Colored Methodist Episcopal Church in America. The general conference of 1954 authorized the change to its current name. In polity and theology the CME Church has belonged to the mainstream of American Methodism while incorporating folk religious patterns and, in this century, social concerns distinctive to black churches.

As a tactic of social control, a response to abolitionism, and genuine Christian concern and outreach, the program to evangelize slaves in Southern Methodism from the 1820s created a biracial membership throughout its annual conferences that sometimes licensed black local preachers to assist in missions. With the advent of freedom, more than 60 percent of the black membership dispersed to join the AFRICAN METHODIST EPISCOPAL CHURCH, the AFRICAN METHODIST EPISCOPAL, ZION CHURCH denomination, or the northern-based ME Church, all of which organized congregations and conferences in the region beginning in 1864. By 1866, only 78,742 "colored members" of 207,766 in 1860 were active in the ME Church, South.

The Southern Methodist general conference of 1866 pursued two strategies to adjust the ecclesiastical status of its black membership. It initially cooperated with the AME denomination, which sought vigorously to recruit a new constituency in the South and which claimed the property that had been used for missions to and by blacks before emancipation. The cooperative experiment failed owing to differences over political reconstruction and because white leaders refused to turn over such property to the black denomination. That result was fortuitous for the future CME denomination, whose institutional origins lay in the general conference's second strategy, which allowed a significant number of black Methodists to keep their antebellum church affiliation

unchanged. White pastors and laity aided "loyal" black members in forming racially separate congregations and annual conferences beginning in Tennessee in November 1867. The Liberty Church in Jackson, site of the conference, became known as the "Mother Church" of the CME denomination.

By 1870, seven other annual conferences were founded under Thomas Taylor, white "General Superintendent of the Colored Work," in Kentucky (1868), Georgia and Mississippi (1869), South Carolina, Alabama, Arkansas, and Texas (1870). The charter conferences of the first CME general conference convened on 16 December 1870 to structure the new denomination's future. It adopted the *Discipline* of the ME Church, South, with minor alterations, but designated the new church as a national rather than sectional organization. Its policy, made as a concession to white Southerners before title would be transferred, explicitly forbade political activity on church property. The general conference continued *The Christian Index*, under white editor Samuel Watson, as its official periodical. Finally, its delegates elected two bishops, William H. Miles of Kentucky and Richard H. Vanderhorst from South Carolina, both former slaves and ex-ministers in the postwar missions of the African Methodist denominations.

Within three years, the death of Bishop Vanderhorst and organizational problems that marked the new movement required a special general conference to elect additional bishops and to assign black editors and agents for publishing activities. Joseph A. Beebe of North Carolina, Lucius H. Holsey of Georgia, and Isaac Lane of Tennessee, all of whom were born in bondage, gave the CME church, with Miles, impressive episcopal leadership for the next two decades. The selection of Robert S. Williams of Louisiana and Elias Cottrell of Mississippi in 1894 meant that the denomination's first seven bishops had come out of slavery.

The earliest general conferences regularized denominational structures and struggled to curb factionalism. They adopted financial plans to support the bishops, a book concern, *The Christian Index*, and various educational projects. The creation of a Church Extension Society in 1890 led to divisions among denominational leaders that spilled over into competition for church offices, especially election to the episcopacy. In 1894 the office of deaconess opened new avenues for women's participation in the church. The formation of the Women's Missionary Council in 1918 consolidated female leadership, which later in the century was included in the ordained ministry.

After failures in Louisville KY and Sardis MS, the CME Church, in conjunction with the ME Church, South, founded Paine Institute (later College, 1903) in Augusta GA in 1883. It also gave support to Lane Institute (later College, 1895) in Jackson TN and, after 1894, to Texas College in Tyler. Smaller ventures like Haygood Seminary in Washington AR, the Holsey Industrial School (later Holsey-Cobb Institute) in Cordele GA, and academies in Booker City and Tuscaloosa AL met local educational needs of blacks in the first generation after freedom. In keeping with the goal of improved education, the general conference of 1910 upgraded the requirements in the course of study for ordination to the ministry.

During its first 50 years, the CME Church spread to nine new Northern and Western states. Following black migration out of the South, the pattern of extension continued between 1920 and 1945, when congregations were established in nine more states. The denomination's roots in the South, however, remained secure, with its book concern and publishing operations centered at Jackson TN, where they remained until national headquarters were moved to Memphis TN in 1970. Less than 10 percent of the church's 45 bishops were born outside the South. Its most distinguished bishop, serving in

that office for 47 years, Lucius H. Holsey, advocated racial separation, a philosophy in harmony with the ethos of Southern society during the era of legal segregation.

In the 20th century the CME Church abandoned its nonpolitical posture and gradually moved into the current of black religious support of civil rights. Its bishops joined the Triennial Council of Colored Methodist Bishops in 1908, which issued condemnations of lynching and racial segregation. The denomination also belonged to the Federal Council of Christian Churches, and later to the National Council of Churches of Christ in the USA, whose social gospel orientation harmonized with the black church's struggle for social justice. The general conference of 1978, for example, took formal positions on the ethical consequences of scientific research, housing and employment needs in American society, the Equal Rights Amendment, public education, family life, racism in South Africa, capital punishment, homosexuality, abortion, and two controversial legal cases affecting civil rights.

Likewise, the CME Church has been actively engaged in intra-Methodist organization and ecumenical discussions of church union. As early as 1873, despite being characterized by competitors as "the Rebel church" or "the old slavery church," the newest black Methodist denomination exchanged fraternal greetings with the AME and AME Zion churches. Plans for merger of the three largest black Methodist bodies were developed between 1908 and 1920 and again beginning in 1965, but none have been successful. In 1967 the CME Church joined the Consultation on Church Union. Since 1881 its representatives have contributed to Ecumenical (later World) Methodist conferences.

In 1978 the CME Church had 38 annual conferences in nine episcopal districts covering 34 states, plus conferences in Ghana and Nigeria and missions in Haiti. Its membership numbered more than 300,000 in 2,448 churches with 2,383 traveling preachers. Its bishops preside over Boards of Finance, Publication Services, Missions, Christian Education, Evangelism, Lay Activities, and Personnel Services, as well as a dozen other commissions and committees. The denomination sponsors the Collins Chapel Connectional Hospital in Memphis, which reopened in 1976. Besides Paine, Lane, and Texas colleges, Miles College in Birmingham AL, Mississippi Industrial College in Holly Springs, and Phillips Theological Seminary at the Interdenominational Theological Center in Atlanta GA receive denominational backing.

See also article on BLACK RELIGION.

Bibliography. John Brother Cade, *Holsey—the Incomparable*; Christian Methodist Episcopal Church, *Journal of the General Conference*, 1978; Thelma Jackson Dudley, "An Historical Synopsis—The Christian Methodist Episcopal Church," *Black Methodism Basic Beliefs*, ed. G. Lovelace Champion, Sr.; Ralph G. Gay, "The Christian Methodist Episcopal Church," *The Encyclopedia of World Methodism*, ed. Nolan B. Harmon; William B. Gravely, "The Social, Political and Religious Significance of the Formation of the Colored Methodist Episcopal Church," *Methodist History* 18 (October 1979): 3-25; W. P. Harrison, *The Gospel Among the Slaves*; L. H. Holsey, *Autobiography, Sermons, Addresses, and Essays*; M. F. Jamison, *Autobiography and Work of*; Othal Hawthorne Lakey, *The Rise of "Colored Methodism"*; M. C. Pettigrew, *From Miles to Johnson: One Hundred Years of Progress*, rev. ed., 1982; Charles H. Phillips, *The History of the Colored Methodist Episcopal Church in America*, 3rd ed., 1925; Horace C. Savage, *Life and Times of Bishop Isaac Lane.*

WILLIAM B. GRAVELY
UNIVERSITY OF DENVER

CHRISTIAN SCHOOLS. Since 1970, the fastest growing segment of private education in the United States has been the "Christian School Movement" (CSM). By 1980 some one million students were enrolled in about 10,000 Christian schools largely in the South and Midwest and on the West Coast. The movement was growing at the rate of three new schools a day. While not monolithic, the CSM is nevertheless primarily a phenomenon of conservative Evangelical Protestantism, particularly in its more Fundamentalist branches.

The historical roots of the CSM can be located in the work of the Christian Reformed Church, a hyperscholastic party of Dutch Calvinism that formed the National Union of Christian Schools (NUCS) in 1920. Mark Fakkema, executive director of the union, was instrumental in engaging the National Association of Evangelicals (NAE) in the movement, helping to create the National Association of Christian Schools in 1947. Still, the CSM remained relatively small until it was joined, beginning in 1970, by large numbers of independent congregations (particularly fundamentalist Baptists) and denominations of similar outlook such as the CHURCH OF GOD (CLEVELAND TN).

Extensive participation by independents rendered the NAE's National Association nearly inoperative in 1978. Now called the National Christian Education Association (NCEA), a commission of the NAE, it deals with Christian education generally, offers assistance to member churches, and refers them to other organizations within the CSM. By the early 1980s, the CSM was dominated by three major organizations. (1) The Association of Christian Schools International (ACSI), headquartered in Whittier CA, that developed in 1978 from a merger of three groups: the Western Association of Christian Schools, the Ohio Association of Christian Schools, and segments of the National Association of the NAE. The largest organization of the CSM, ASCI draws membership broadly from Evangelical Protestantism. (2) Christian Schools International (CSI), located in Grand Rapids MI, functions chiefly as the organization for the Christian Reform Church, replacing the old NUCS. (3) The American Association of Christian Schools (AACS), based in Normal IL and founded in 1972, serves primarily separatist fundamentalists, usually Baptists, maintains ties with Bob Jones University, and denies membership to charismatic Christians.

These organizations provide a wide range of services to their members. They run placement services for teachers and administrators, provide information and assistance for churches starting schools, serve as accrediting agencies and lobbying groups, offer insurance, credit unions, and testing services for member schools, provide legal advice and defense, conduct seminars and conventions on local and national levels, sponsor athletic tournaments and publish various newsletters, magazines, and pamphlets for their members.

A closely related segment of the CSM network is constituted by organizations that develop and publish curriculum materials for Christian schools. Most significant among these are A Beka Book Publications, Pensacola FL; Alpha Omega, Temple AZ; Bob Jones University; and Accelerated Christian Education (ACE), Lewisville TX. Within the CSM, ACE is widely credited with making the rapid growth of the movement possible through its pioneering efforts in developing individualized curriculum materials. The ACE curriculum, and others like it, allows churches immediately to open a school including K-12 on a "one-room-schoolhouse" basis with small enrollments and minimal staffing. Schools often begin with ACE-type materials and then switch to more traditional classroom instruction after a period of growth. Many retain the individualized approach in upper grades where enrollment is insufficient to support traditional classrooms.

Because the rapid growth of the CSM coincided with court-ordered busing to eliminate segregation, it has had to labor under the misapprehension that its schools are little more than private "segregation academies." This presumption seems to be incorrect. With few (well-publicized) exceptions, schools in the CSM do not appear to discriminate on the basis of race, sex, or national origin. That CSM schools are functionally segregated results from their association with white churches and their tuition costs, usually $800 to $1,000 per year. It is not integration that the CSM seeks to avoid,

but rather what it believes is the moral corruption of the public school system.

The CSM charges that public schools, like secular society, are dominated by an atheistic anti-Christian religion that it calls "Secular Humanism." This dominant philosophy is charged with fostering socialism and the welfare state, world government at the expense of American national interest, hostility toward Christianity, and a pervasive ethical and cultural relativism. Paralleling the dualistic cosmology of its sponsoring churches, the CSM charges that "Secular Humanism" is the root cause of most of the nation's problems—crime, violence, deviant lifestyles, economic distress, and military weakness.

To remedy this situation, the CSM stresses moral absolutism, discipline, respect for authority, "traditional values," and basic skills. The CSM describes itself as "authoritarian," understanding its task as one of molding recalcitrant and sinful children into responsible Christian citizens. Reflecting its largely fundamentalist constituency, the CSM seeks to make all subjects "Bible centered," an effort that may involve beginning world history with Genesis, or motivating the study of grammar with reflections on God's purposes in creating language. Education for the CSM is ministry, a special calling entrusted by God to parents and churches, but not to the state. Consequently, ongoing conflicts have emerged between the CSM and various branches of state governments.

While some in the CSM are willing to comply with state regulation, for many any state interference constitutes a violation of God's ordinances as well as the free exercise of religion. A small but significant number of pastors have been jailed rather than close their schools or seek accreditation. Specialized organizations such as the Christian Law Association have joined with other CSM groups in defending churches and schools against state interference.

The CSM's rapid growth parallels similar growth among conservative denominations in the United States and the "going public" of American Fundamentalism in the "Religious-Political Right" in 1980. Numerous individual leaders and some organizations of the Religious Right had begun as "movers and shakers" for the CSM. The CSM stands as a central ingredient in the resurgence of conservative American Protestantism, offering the possibility of a full-fledged "alternate society" within the nation, and serving as a training ground for leaders capable of making an increased impact upon the national culture.

See also articles on CHURCH AND STATE; FUNDAMENTALISM.

Bibliography. Alan Grover, *Ohio's Trojan Horse*; Donald Howard, *Rebirth of Our Nation*; Paul Kienel, ed., *The Philosophy of Christian Education*; David Nevin and Robert Bills, *The Schools That Fear Built*; John Whitehead, *The Separation Illusion*.

DENNIS E. OWEN
UNIVERSITY OF FLORIDA

CHRISTIAN SCIENCE. The Church of Christ, Scientist, was organized in 1879 by Mary Baker Eddy (1821-1910). An indigenous American body, it is popularly referred to as Christian Science. Most of its membership continues to be American. Great Britain and countries with cultural development similar to America have some Christian Scientists. Although the church forbids the numbering of its people, it can be safely estimated that there are about 300,000 members in the United States, mostly urban and from the upper middle class. One-sixth of all Scientists are in California, with other heavy concentrations in Massachusetts, New York, Illinois, Texas, Ohio, Michigan, and Florida. Women tend to dominate in leadership roles and it is estimated that female practitioners (the nearest equivalent to pastors) outnumber male practitioners 10 to one.

Mary Baker Eddy was in poor health as a child and never appears to have enjoyed particularly good health.

Although Christian Scientists deny it, her early relationship with the mesmerist and faith healer, Phineas P. Quimby, seems to have shaped much of her thought. After a severe fall in 1866, she read Mt. 9:1-8 (healing of the man sick of the palsy), and published *Science and Health with Key to the Scriptures* and later decreed that this book and the Bible would be pastor at all services. At Christian Science services today, two readers (one male and one female) read prescribed portions from the Bible and *Science and Health*.

Christian Scientist beliefs are difficult for others to understand. Mary Baker Eddy summarized them in four points: (1) God is All-in-All. (2) God is good. Good is Mind. (3) God, Spirit, being all, nothing is matter. (4) Life, God, omnipotent good, deny death, evil, sin, disease. —Disease, sin, evil, death, deny good, omnipotent, God, Life. (*Science and Health*, 113) Every Christian Scientist is expected to memorize the following statement, which is an indication of its significance as a creed:

> There is no life, truth, intelligence, nor substance in matter. All is infinite Mind and its infinite manifestation, for God is All-in-All. Spirit is the real and eternal; matter is the unreal and temporal. Spirit is God, and man is His image and likeness. Therefore God is not material; he is spiritual. (*Science and Health*, 468)

Christ is defined as the "Wayshower." The virgin birth, resurrection, and atoning power are seen as living demonstrations of another key Scientist concept, "the nothingness of matter." This concept does not ignore the "unreal world," but attempts to overcome through prayer and spiritual development the errors of faulty belief. The only reality of sin, sickness, or death is in the "Animal Magnetism," a term used for the hypnotic power of erroneous belief. No material elements are used in the spiritual observance of the Lord's Supper and baptism.

The latter is held to be a continuing individual spiritual "purification from all error." Heaven is "harmony." Hell is "mortal belief." Healing is not miraculous, but divinely natural. Prayer is absolute faith.

Power struggles and controversy were a part of the early Science organization until Mary Baker Eddy took absolute control herself. She worked through a self-perpetuating Board of Directors of the Mother Church in Boston, and that board became the absolute authority after her death, following another decade of struggle. Local officers must be members of the Mother Church and all other members are encouraged to belong to the Mother Church also. Within the framework of laws provided by the Manual of the Mother Church written by Eddy, there is freedom at the local level. Practitioners devote their time to healing. Teachers may have no more than 30 students in one class. The Church of Christ, Scientist, is one of the most tightly organized religious bodies in America. Scientists display a felicitous optimism, but humanitarian social concern is generally lacking and the primary goal is manifested in a this-worldly quest for health that stands in antithesis to the scientific quest for knowledge.

Bibliography. C. S. Braden, *Christian Science Today*; Mary Baker Eddy, *Science and Health with Key to the Scriptures*; Stephen Gottschalk, *The Emergence of Christian Science in American Religious Life*; Thomas Leishman, *Why I Am a Christian Scientist.*

CARLTON T. MITCHELL
WAKE FOREST UNIVERSITY

CHRISTIAN SOCIALISM. Though not unique to the era, this movement reached its zenith in the South during the Great Depression. The phenomenon, characterized by considerable theological and ideological diversity, was essentially an expression of disaffection with the region's religious and secular institutions, a disaffection stemming from their apparent failure to address the economic and social problems of the South.

The movement deemphasized the individualism and pietism of traditional Southern Protestantism, stressing instead the corporate nature of religion and the social dimension of the Christian ethic. Although committed to change, many of its adherents rejected what they regarded as the naive optimism of the SOCIAL GOSPEL. Influenced by neo-orthodox thought, especially that of Reinhold Niebuhr, they had few illusions about the potential for perfection inherent in either the individual or society. Most Christian Socialists therefore aspired not to a realization of the Kingdom of God on earth, but to an approximation of divine justice in an imperfect world.

The Christian Socialism of the depression era South rejected the materialism of classical Marxism, but readily accepted the Marxian assumption that the "collective behavior of men must be understood on the whole in the light of their economic interests." Such an economic analysis seemed to them to be wholly compatible with the Christian understanding of the sinfulness and greed of humanity. Capitalism, they believed, accentuated the individual's acquisitive nature, led to a maldistribution of wealth, precipitated domestic and international strife, and created an atmosphere in which human beings all too often were regarded as merely a means to an end, that of making a profit. Convinced that the existing economic order contained the seeds of its own destruction, they hoped to establish in its place "a genuinely social economy, democratically planned to adjust production to consumption requirements," an objective that, in their view, entailed the elimination of "the private ownership of the means of production and distribution wherever such ownership interfered with the social good."

Finding little sympathy for such views within their region's religious mainstream, the Socialist Christians frequently coalesced into such indigenous groups as the FELLOWSHIP OF SOUTHERN

CHURCHMEN, or were among the Southern members of national organizations such as the Fellowship of Reconciliation and Fellowship of Socialist Christians. Throughout the 1930s several hundred persons, among them men like James Dombrowski, Myles Horton, HOWARD KESTER, and Claude Williams, sought through labor organization, education, and racial interaction to promote economic and racial justice.

By the late 1930s and early 1940s, disillusionment, frustration, and improving economic conditions resulted in the waning of Christian Socialism in the South. Although the phenomenon has not disappeared from the periphery of regional religion, it has not in recent decades exhibited the vitality and sense of urgency that characterized the movement prior to World War II.

See also article on ETHICS, CHRISTIAN.

Bibliography. Donald B. Meyer, *The Protestant Search for Political Realism, 1919-1941*; Reinhold Niebuhr, "The Fellowship of Socialist Christians," *The World Tomorrow* 17 (14 June 1934) 298; Fellowship of Southern Churchmen Papers, Southern Historical Collection, University of North Carolina, Chapel Hill NC.

ROBERT F. MARTIN
UNIVERSITY OF NORTHERN IOWA

CHRISTMAS CONFERENCE. This gathering of 1784 in Baltimore marked the creation of a new denomination, the Methodist Episcopal Church, formalizing developments of several decades. JOHN WESLEY had sent missionaries to the colonies, who in turn recruited lay ministers. During the Revolution, all but one of Wesley's ministers returned to England, leaving the field to the lay ministers. Although Wesley's remaining representative, FRANCIS ASBURY, tried to maintain discipline, the lay ministers increasingly demanded some degree of control over American churches, a claim supported by the increasing numbers of church members they served, especially in the South.

Asbury continually pressed Wesley to provide official institutional support for the American evangelical enterprise. For complex reasons, including his evolving and often troublesome relation to the Church of England, Wesley decided to protect and encourage the enterprise in the new nation by sending three representatives, led by THOMAS COKE, across the Atlantic in 1784. Although he probably did not intend to create a separate denomination, Wesley certainly assumed authority over American Evangelicalism by giving Coke authorization to ordain the American lay preachers as superintendents over the American societies.

Asbury immediately began the business of organizing a meeting in America with Wesley's representatives. On Friday, 24 December, the first session of the "Christmas Conference" convened at the LOVELY LANE CHAPEL in Baltimore. When one of the lay ministers proposed a resolution for the creation of the Methodist Episcopal Church in the United States, a body separated from the Church of England, the resolution was adopted unanimously. During the conference, Asbury was consecrated the second superintendent of the new church. The meeting created a government, for the denomination adopted those articles of religion from the Anglican church that Wesley accepted and, perhaps most important, ordained into the Christian ministry men who had, in many instances, preached for decades as laymen.

See also article on METHODIST CHURCH.

Bibliography. Emory Burke, ed., *The History of American Methodism*, 1:213-32; Elmer T. Clark, ed., *Journal and Letters of Francis Asbury*; N. C. Hughes, "The Methodist Christmas Conference: Baltimore," *Maryland Historical Magazine* 54 (September 1959): 272-92.

DAVID T. BAILEY
MICHIGAN STATE UNIVERSITY

CHURCH AND STATE. The problem of the relationship between the church and the state is inescapable because the church is always *in the world*. Religious people are always citizens of two realms, the Kingdom of God and the civil state. Two different institutions claim the loyalty of the same people. The issue of church-state relationships, then, is the question of which of those loyalties is more important and how the two institutions relate to and affect each other.

The prevailing relationship between church and state in the Western world has been a union in which some form of Christianity was the official religion of the state. Such "official" Christianity was often intolerant of dissenters. These conditions were transported to America during the COLONIAL PERIOD: most of the colonies had an official church. In the Southern colonies it was the ANGLICAN (now called the Episcopal) CHURCH. It was in reaction to the long history of the union of church and state, with its accompanying oppression, including that in some of the colonies, which caused the framers of the United States Constitution to include guarantees for religious freedom by legally separating church and state.

The colony of Virginia took the first giant step toward making that separation possible. In 1784 the Virginia legislature considered a bill that would levy a tax to support the teaching of the Christian religion. The plan's main opponent, James Madison, wrote a brilliant statement in favor of the separation of church and state—"A Memorial and Remonstrance Against Religious Assessment." The bill was defeated and the legislature then passed Thomas Jefferson's "Bill for Establishing Religious Freedom," which disestablished religion in Virginia. These events and documents contributed significantly to the eventual construction of the religion clauses of the federal Constitution.

The original Constitution contained only one reference to religion, Article VI: ". . . no religious Test shall ever be required as a Qualification to any Office or public Trust under the United States." This was a great advance over any state church arrangement in which one could serve in public office only if one belonged to the official religion. Later the founding fathers went beyond Article VI with the First Amendment: "Congress shall make no law respecting an establishment of religion, or prohibiting the free exercise thereof. . . ." With the enactment of these principles, America launched a new era. It was the first time in history that a nation had made religious freedom a part of its legal structure and it ended over 1,400 years of oppression in the name of religion.

For approximately 150 years it was assumed that the First Amendment applied only to the federal government, but recent judicial interpretation has applied the amendment to the states through the Fourteenth Amendment, which says in part, "Nor shall any State deprive any person of life, liberty, or property, without due process of law." It is now understood that among the liberties guaranteed to American citizens by the Fourteenth Amendment are those mentioned in the First.

The establishment clause means that in matters of religion, the state must be neutral, neither aiding nor hindering religion or nonreligion. The government may not endorse or support religion, but neither may the state deny any religion the right to exist. Individuals or groups may hold any religious belief or none without threat of government interference.

The free-exercise clause means that individuals or groups may put their beliefs into action. This clause guarantees the freedom of worship and other religious activity. However, long-standing judicial interpretation has said that if religious activity takes a form that is harmful to individuals or to society, the civil authorities may stop that activity. But for the authorities to restrict religious exercise, it must be clear that the activity actually poses a serious threat to others; they may not curtail religious behavior that is regarded as merely obnoxious or absurd.

Consequently, the free exercise of religion is the rule, and restriction is the exception.

Since the 1940s the principal church-state issues that have come before the courts of our land, both federal and state, have included the place of religion in the schools. There are two primary issues here: (1) the inclusion of religious instruction and/or devotional exercises in the public schools, and (2) the provision of government funds and/or services to parochial schools.

The JEHOVAH'S WITNESSES have provided a great service to the entire society by obtaining judicial opinions on a number of church-state issues. Primary among these is the right to speak one's religious beliefs in public places, a right guaranteed by both the free-exercise and free-speech clauses of the First Amendment.

Other issues of persistent public attention are Sunday-closing laws; conscientious objection to military service on religious grounds; and, very recently, the questions of religious freedom versus the forced "reconversion" (deprogramming) of persons involved in religious cults; and various forms of taxation and tax exemption for religious groups. Church and state issues affect all the people in American society indirectly and a large portion of the society very directly.

In the South the attitude toward church-state relationships has been ambiguous. The dominant denomination in the area, the Southern Baptist Convention, has long taken a "strict separationist" approach and has led the fight for a high and impregnable wall between church and state. A Baptist institution in Texas, Baylor University, has been in the vanguard of American programs in the study of church-state relationships. Ironically, however, in the South religion has so completely permeated the culture that the separation of church and state is often breached. Many have not been able to see why there should not be prayers in the public schools, or why there should not be laws which impose the morality taught by Protestant Christianity upon the society as a whole, for its own good. The issue of church and state relationships is a highly sensitive area that will be a matter of interest and debate as long as there is a United States of America.

See also articles on DISESTABLISHMENT; ESTABLISHED RELIGION; ETHICS, CHRISTIAN.

Bibliography. Ronald B. Flowers, "The Supreme Court's Three Tests of the Establishment Clause," *Religion in Life* 45 (Spring 1976): 41; "The Supreme Court's Interpretation of the Free Exercise Clause," *Religion in Life* 49 (Fall 1980): 322; Robert T. Miller and Ronald B. Flowers, *Toward Benevolent Neutrality: Church, State, and the Supreme Court*; Leo Pfeffer, *God, Caesar, and the Constitution*; Elwyn A. Smith, *Religious Liberty in the United States*; Anson Phelps Stokes, *Church and State in the United States*, 3 vols.; "The Uneasy Boundary: Church and State," *The Annals of the American Academy of Political and Social Science* (November 1979).

RONALD B. FLOWERS
TEXAS CHRISTIAN UNIVERSITY

CHURCH, DOCTRINE OF: *See* ECCLESIOLOGY.

CHURCH OF GOD (CLEVELAND, TENNESSEE). The Church of God (Cleveland, Tennessee), one of the largest fellowships of PENTECOSTALISM, and apparently the oldest, began on 19 August 1886, when a group of Baptist and Methodist dissidents in Monroe County TN united as a "Christian Union" for the purpose of seeking revival and restoration of New Testament Christianity. Leaders of the small group of eight were Richard G. Spurling and Richard G. Spurling Jr., both Baptist ministers. The elder Spurling died shortly after the formation of the Christian Union and the son led the group alone. Ten years later, in the summer of 1896, the Tennessee congregation merged with a similar group in Cherokee County NC, led by Baptist layman W. F. Bryant.

In 1896 a revival occurred in the mountains of North Carolina, in which more than 100 persons were baptized in the Holy Spirit, with the phenomenon of

SPEAKING IN TONGUES. This extraordinary event was without precedent in the region and was identified with events of the Day of Pentecost in Acts 2:1-4. Participants in the revival were subjected to several years of intense persecution because of their spiritual experience and their doctrinal belief in the eradication of sin through sanctification as a definite work of grace.

On 15 May 1902 the growing body was reorganized in Cherokee County NC under the name of Holiness Church at Camp Creek. On 3 June 1903, A. J. TOMLINSON, a newcomer to the region, joined the group and shortly afterward other congregations were established and other ministers were ordained in the church. On 26-27 January 1906 the scattered congregations conducted a "General Assembly," which gathering would become the governing body of the church. At the Assembly of 1907 the name Church of God was unanimously adopted, and the center of operations was shifted to CLEVELAND TN. Cleveland remains the headquarters city of the church today, the center of its international operation, and the site of its major administrative offices and schools.

The early Church of God sent evangelists into all parts of the Southeast with such success that by 1910 there were congregations in Tennessee, North Carolina, Georgia, Alabama, Florida, Kentucky, and Virginia. A missions program was initiated when missionaries went to the Bahama Islands in 1910. An episcopal form of government was instituted by the church, with Tomlinson elected general overseer in 1909, and overseers appointed to the various states from 1911 onward.

The Church of God suffered a severe disappointment in 1923, when A. J. Tomlinson's strict control over the affairs of the church led to dissatisfaction and schism. Rather than step down as general overseer, he withdrew to another part of the city and organized a second group, which became the CHURCH OF GOD OF PROPHECY. F. J. Lee succeeded Tomlinson as general overseer of the Church of God; serving from 1923 until his death in 1928. An orderly administrative succession was established by the church, with 13 leaders filling the post of general overseer down to 1983.

From the period of its initial expansion the Church of God, although predominantly white, has given much attention to reaching minority groups, particularly blacks, Indians, and Latins. The first missionary effort in 1909-1910 was the joint enterprise of a black man (Edmond S. Barr) and a white man (R. M. Evans). In 1920 approximately one-tenth of Church of God congregations and pastors were black or Hispanic. This attention has resulted in making the church one of the only predominantly white Pentecostal fellowships with a sizable black constituency.

Specialized Christian ministries were also an early part of the Church of God's outreach. As early as 1910 a publishing ministry was begun with a church paper called *Church of God Evangel.* In 1918 a Bible Training School was instituted (now Lee College) and in 1920 an Orphanage and Home for Children was begun. In addition to the missions, publishing, educational, and benevolence ministries, which have been constantly expanded, further ministries and services have become prominent emphases in the Church of God. Chief among these are youth ministries (1926), Christian education (1926), women's ministries (1936), radio and television (1956), ethnic and cross-cultural ministries (1964), lay ministries (1966), general education (1968), and stewardship (1980). In addition to Lee College in Cleveland TN, numerous colleges and schools have been established through the years in diverse places: Minot ND; Fresno CA; Moose Jaw, Saskatchewan, Canada; Houston TX; Charlotte NC; Mexico; Indonesia; Germany, and many other countries. Homes for children are operated in Sevierville TN, Kannapolis NC, and Gaffney SC.

Always strongly evangelistic in purpose, the Church of God today has churches and missions in virtually every state of the USA and in 114 countries around the world. Strong national churches exist in such places as Mexico, Indonesia, South Africa, and Korea. There are presently more than one million members of the Church of God.

To further its ministries the Church of God was a founding member of several interdenominational associations in America and overseas that have kindred emphases. Among these are the National Association of Evangelicals, the Pentecostal Fellowship of North America, and the Pentecostal World Conference.

Bibliography. Charles W. Conn, *Cradle of Pentecost; Like A Mighty Army*; E. L. Simmons, *History of the Church of God.*

CHARLES W. CONN
ROANOKE, VIRGINIA

CHURCH OF GOD IN CHRIST, INC.

A black Pentecostal denomination, this body was incorporated in 1897 and until 1961 grew under the remarkable leadership of Bishop CHARLES HARRISON MASON. It regards itself as the largest Pentecostal denomination in the world today with 3,709,661 members, 10,425 clergy, 140 bishops (including 14 in 12 overseas nations), 10,211 congregations worldwide, and 2,315,299 Sunday school attendants.

It is predominantly but not exclusively a black denomination, and the only Pentecostal group considered to belong among the seven major black American Christian denominations. It is the first church to have arisen from the authentic experience of black people rather than from an existing white organization. It operates a system of Bible colleges nationwide and Saints Academy in Lexington MS. In 1970 Mason Theological Seminary was established in Atlanta, the first Pentecostal graduate school. In 1984 it plans to open All Saints University in Memphis where the first phase of "Saints Center" is in progress, a projected new 25 million dollar headquarters complex. Over 40,000

members attend the annual convocation in Memphis. The leader since 1968 has been its first elected presiding bishop, James Oglethorpe Patterson Sr., who has served several consecutive four-year terms.

Mason began in 1893 as a Missionary Baptist evangelist in Arkansas who participated fully in the late nineteenth-century emphasis upon Christian HOLINESS. In 1896 Mason joined with Charles Price Jones and other Baptist clergy to lead a revival in Jackson MS. Stress on "entire sanctification" led to their disfellowship by their Baptist organization. In 1897 an old abandoned cotton gin in Lexington MS became the site of formal organization and incorporation of the new denomination, which was soon expanded into areas of Mississippi, Arkansas, and Tennessee. Mason believed the name to have been divinely revealed to him in harmony with 1 Thes. 2:14.

A crucial turning point came in early 1907 when Mason traveled to Los Angeles to stay for five weeks with his old friend WILLIAM J. SEYMOUR, who was leading the Azusa Street Revival, the fountainhead of the 20th-century Pentecostal movement. Mason embraced the new emphasis on speaking in unknown tongues and gathering together all races and peoples in unity. When he returned to Jackson for the summer conference of his denomination in August, Charles Price Jones and others who did not share Mason's enthusiasm for speaking in unknown tongues withdrew the hand of fellowship from Mason and went on to form another denomination.

Mason called together his followers later in Memphis—some 12 other leaders and seven congregations—and there in 1907 held the first annual convocation of the organization now reconstituted as Pentecostal. From 1907 to 1914 Mason worked closely with Southern white Pentecostal leaders. Many of these sought and received ordination and ministerial credentials at his hands not only because of his denomination's well-established legal status but also because of Mason's flawless character and commanding personality. When white leaders organized their own denomination in 1914, Mason attended to give them his blessing although he had not been invited.

At the time of World War I Mason was jailed several times because of his pacifist views, although he supported obedience to the law and encouraged the Federal war-bond drives. The FBI placed him under official but secret surveillance from 1914 to 1948. In 1944 Mason Temple arose in Memphis, the largest black-owned meeting place in the United States.

Mason provided leadership to his people for over 68 years, with 64 of those since incorporation of the Church of God in Christ, a record of ecclesiastical statesmanship unequalled in American church history. After criss-crossing the country innumerable times and venturing abroad upon occasion, he saw his church reach almost a million members before his death at age 95. Although large sums of money passed through his hands, he died with one dollar in his pocket and ownership of the modest apartment building where he lived. His followers considered him to be the equal of Paul the Apostle, and when he died the denomination was stunned. Notwithstanding various administrative steps Mason had taken over the years to insure a smooth transition in leadership, the denomination entered seven years of difficult discussions and litigation to interpret constitutional principles for future leadership. In 1968 all differences were resolved with provision for their first elected presiding bishop.

The Church of God in Christ has since its inception looked for political fulfillment of Christian belief. Thus the church hosted the leadership of MARTIN LUTHER KING JR. in Memphis in 1968 for his last memorable campaign on behalf of the city sanitation workers, many of whom belonged to the Church of God in Christ.

King's final eloquent address was given from the pulpit of Mason Temple. Also amid the turbulent 1960s, following the assassination of the controversial black leader, Malcolm X, the Church of God in Christ, New York, stepped forward to sponsor his funeral arrangements amid many threats of violence and reprisal.

See also article on PENTECOSTALISM.

Bibliography. Ithiel Clemmons, *Profile of a Churchman: The Life of Otha M. Kelly in the Church of God in Christ*; Lucille J. Cornelius, *The History of the Church of God in Christ*; Leonard Lovett, *Black Holiness-Pentecostalism: Implications for Ethics and Social Transformation*, unpublished Ph.D. dissertation, Emory University, 1978; David M. Tucker, *Black Pastors and Leaders: Memphis, 1819-1972.*

DOUGLAS J. NELSON
ARLINGTON, VIRGINIA

CHURCH OF GOD OF PROPHECY.

A Pentecostal denomination of 100,000 members in the United States and 115,000 outside the U. S., this body dates its beginning from 13 June 1903. On that day A. J. TOMLINSON joined the small congregation, the "Holiness Church" at Camp Creek in North Carolina; a movement soon began from these small beginnings. For 20 years (until 1923) the Church of God of Prophecy shared a common history and existence with the CHURCH OF GOD, with headquarters in CLEVELAND TN. A division occurred in 1923 when Tomlinson formed a group made up of ministers and members loyal to himself, those who held with him that he should be general overseer for life. About 2,000 people, approximately one-third of the Church of God membership, adhered to Tomlinson. These constituted the nucleus of the Church of God of Prophecy.

The church was first called the Tomlinson Church of God (or the Church of God Over Which A. J. Tomlinson Is General Overseer). In 1952 this early name was discarded in favor of the Church of God of Prophecy. The name stems from Tomlinson's belief that that specific organization is the church referred to in

Old Testament prophecies and New Testament references. His position resulted in dividing the leadership of the denomination. Thus the new body was born. This conviction that it is the true and visible church of the Scriptures remains a fixed precept of the Church of God of Prophecy. Its tenets are basically fundamental with emphasis on the doctrine of HOLINESS and the Holy Spirit with the evidence of speaking in tongues. The group refers to itself as a "Bible Church."

The denomination established international headquarters (or a "World Capital") in Cleveland TN. A. J. Tomlinson introduced an "All Nations Flag" at the general conference of 1933; this, too, was regarded as prophetic fulfillment. In 1940 a "Church of Prophecy Marker Association" was initiated for the purpose of erecting markers at sites of special importance to the denomination. Chief of these is "Fields of the Wood," dedicated in the mountains of North Carolina on 7 September 1941.

When A. J. Tomlinson died in 1943, his son, Milton A. Tomlinson, was elected to take his place as general overseer. He has filled that post until the present. The present form of government is episcopal with a general assembly, state conventions, and local churches where all male ministers and members conduct the business. The general overseer is selected by the general assembly and he in turn appoints the overseers of states and countries.

The church has shown steady growth since 1923 and now maintains congregations in 85 countries outside the U. S. From the outset, the Church of God of Prophecy has enjoyed remarkable growth in its missionary work. The Caribbean islands have been especially prominent in recent outreach ministries. Membership and leadership in the U. S. were racially integrated long before 1954. It operates a number of schools in its missions fields and since 1965 has operated a two-year college (Tomlinson College) in Cleveland.

Among its other ministries are publications (1923), world missions (1923), radio (1957), youth (1952), and a Tomlinson Home for Children (1945). Its Annual Assemblies convene at its Assembly Auditorium in the headquarters city.

See also article on PENTECOSTALISM.

Bibliography. Charles T. Davidson, *Upon This Rock*; Harry Moore, ed., *Cyclopedic Index of Minutes and Important Business Acts*; Vinson Synan, *The Holiness-Pentecostal Movement in the United States*.

CHARLES W. CONN
ROANOKE, VIRGINIA

CHURCH OF THE BRETHREN. The Church of the Brethren began in Germany in 1708 when a group of eight Christians who had separated from the state churches decided that in order to be obedient to the New Testament commandments as they understood them, they would need to organize a different church. One major difference was that these Brethren believed that the communion service should be practiced in the evening with the washing of feet, the eating of a meal, and the sharing of the bread and wine; this service took place not more than twice a year. Another major difference was that these Brethren baptized adults by immersing them three times forward. These two rites or ordinances, as they called them, were based on their understanding of the New Testament church.

Because of their form of BAPTISM, which was described by the German word, *tunken*, they were frequently called Tunkers by others. In America, the "t" became a "d" and thus they became Dunkers or Dunkards. They called themselves "Brethren," and in the 19th century used the name German Baptist Brethren.

In 1719 and in 1729, two major movements brought most of the Brethren to Philadelphia, from which point they spread rather quickly into the interior of Pennsylvania and south into Maryland, Virginia, and the Carolinas. Their settlements were made entirely in the western mountain valleys of these colonies. Like most Germans, they established some of the finest farms in the English colonies. By 1800 they had become well established in Maryland and Virginia.

Because of their German background and because of their different religious practices, the Brethren became highly separatistic and sectarian. They were tightly organized, so much so that the Civil War did not split them. They were vigorously opposed to slavery and to war, and did not participate in the military service during the war. They had a variety of difficulties with state and national governments in both the North and South.

However, differences developing among the Brethren, including the introduction of Sunday schools, revival meetings, and employed pastors, did split them in the 1880s. The most conservative group became known as the Old German Baptist Brethren, the name it still goes by. The most progressive group became known as the Brethren Church; in the 1930s it split into two groups: one called the Brethren Church and one called the Grace Brethren. In the 1880s the largest group kept the name German Baptist Brethren, which it changed in 1908 to Church of the Brethren.

In the 20th century the latter three Brethren groups have shed their separatism, sectarianism, and conservatism, and have accepted the characteristics of the major Protestant churches. The most important area of expansion in the South has been the penetration into Florida where a number of Brethren churches have been established.

By 1980 the different Brethren groups had more than 50,000 members in the Southern states, with most of them in Maryland and Virginia, and smaller numbers in North Carolina, Tennessee, Florida, and Missouri.

See also articles on NATIVISM; PIETY; RESTORATIONISM.

Bibliography. Donald F. Durnbaugh, *European Origins of the Brethren*; *The Brethren in Colonial America*; Roger E. Sappington, *The Brethren in the New Nation*; *The Brethren in Virginia*; *The Brethren in the Carolinas*.

ROGER E. SAPPINGTON
BRIDGEWATER COLLEGE

CHURCH OF THE NAZARENE. This denomination sprang from the interdenominational HOLINESS revival of the late nineteenth century. It took shape shortly after the turn of the century through the merging of several independent holiness churches, the majority of whose members were "come-outers" from Methodist ranks. Alienated by the increasing formalism, wealth, theological innovation, and antiholiness sentiment within Methodism, many holiness folk left the parent church to organize separate associations where they were free to practice traditional revivalistic worship and to preach SANCTIFICATION as a second definite work of grace subsequent to regeneration.

These new holiness bodies, often beginning as urban missions, felt a particular call to preach and to minister among the poor. In 1895 in Los Angeles, former prominent Methodist pastor Phineas F. Bresee and his friend J. P. Whidney founded the Church of the Nazarene specifically to minister to "the neglected quarters of the cities." The new name was to represent "the toiling, lowly mission of Christ . . . the name which was used in derision of him by his enemies."

Similarly, in Nashville TN in 1898, CUMBERLAND PRESBYTERIAN CHURCH evangelist J. O. McClurkan founded the Pentecostal Mission, which grew into a network of Southern urban missions to the poor and which joined the Nazarenes in 1915. Many of the independent holiness congregations that eventually formed the Church of the Nazarene flourished in the cities, but met the spiritual, and often material, needs of a recently arrived rural constituency who desired to maintain traditional forms of worship, doctrine, and social mores. The early Nazarenes thus conserved and propagated what they perceived to be the "old-time faith," but in so doing they employed new methods such as missions, street services, rescue bands, women preachers, congregational government, and an emphasis on "liberty of the Spirit" in worship.

The Nazarenes achieved remarkable success in cooperation and eventual mergers with similar holiness groups across the country. In 1907 at Chicago, Bresee's church, then grown to 52 congregations and 3,827 members, merged with the New York-based Association of Pentecostal Churches of America with 47 churches and 2,371 members. This Northern contingent, renamed the Pentecostal Church of the Nazarene, united in 1908 at Pilot Point TX with the Holiness Church of Christ which added 92 congregations and 2,307 members. This Southern denomination was the child of the 1905 union of the New Testament Church of Christ and the Independent Holiness Church. The former had been organized by Robert Lee Harris in 1894 at Milan TN; after his death it was expanded westward by his wife, Mary Lee Harris Cagle. The latter was founded in 1901 at Van Alstyne TX by C. B. Jernigan, a promoter of rescue missions and orphanages. In 1915, after the death of J. O. McClurkan, union with the Pentecostal Mission of Nashville and its auxiliary missions in neighboring states added another strong Southern element to the denomination. A final merger within the United States was effected in 1922 with the upper-midwestern, thousand-member Laymen's Holiness Association, a fundamentalist splinter group from the Methodist Church led by J. G. Morrison. From 10,000 members in 1910, the Nazarenes burgeoned to over 100,000 by 1930 and thereafter more than doubled every 20 years. In 1980, the church claimed 484,276 members, with approximately one-third living in the South.

The distinguishing tenet of the Nazarenes remains the doctrine of sanctification as defined by the Wesleyan branch of the 19th-century HOLINESS MOVEMENT. The *Manual* states that sanctification is an "act of God, subsequent to regeneration, by which believers are made free from original sin . . . and brought into a state of entire devotement to God. Entire sanctification is provided by the blood of Jesus, is wrought instantaneously by faith, preceded by entire consecration. . . . " The evidence of sanctification is ethical love. The Nazarenes specifically reject speaking in tongues and, to eliminate misunderstanding, removed the word "Pentecostal" from their name in 1919. Broadly speaking, the church is conservative-evangelical, not fundamentalist, allowing for freedom of belief in such nonessentials as millennial theories and mode of baptism. Strictures are maintained, however, against tobacco, alcohol, gambling, pride in dress, and entertainments deemed not to glorify God, including theater and dancing. Official statements condemn divorce (except on grounds of adultery), abortion on demand, homosexuality, and support voluntary prayer in public schools. The women's rights movement is not endorsed. The church supports nine colleges and a graduate theological seminary.

Nazarene government with headquarters at Kansas City MO is representative, being a compromise between episcopacy and congregationalism. The quadrennial general assembly, "the supreme doctrine-formulating, lawmaking, and elective authority," consists of ministerial and lay delegates of equal number, elected by district assemblies. Six general superintendents elected by the general assembly supervise the worldwide program of the church, and a general board conducts business between general assemblies. Seventy-four District Assemblies, chaired by district superintendents elected by delegates from local churches, direct work in the United States. Local churches call their own pastors, but must have approval of the district superintendent.

Southern influences upon the Nazarenes have been many. The expressed antipathy of the METHODIST EPISCOPAL CHURCH, SOUTH, toward the holiness movement encouraged the formation of the regional, independent holiness groups that later united with the Nazarenes. Many Southerners have held national denominational leadership. Popular evangelists such as J. B. Chapman, C. B. Jernigan, and Bud Robinson, masters of Southern revivalist preaching rich in imagery and style, have bequeathed a unique tone to Nazarene preaching. Other Southern-born Nazarenes have served as general superintendents, editors, and educators within the church.

Women preachers achieved prominence not only in Bresee's group but also in the New Testament Church of Christ and in the Pentecostal Mission. Although the number of women Nazarene preachers today is very small, in the early years of the church, especially in the South, as much as 20 percent of the ministers were women.

Southern influence brought to the church an emphasis on healing and a strong premillennial bias that at first met opposition from the North, but during the 1920s gained dominance. Strict rules for outward conduct that were championed by the South, including prohibitions on tobacco, secret societies, wedding rings, and other adornments, conferred a lingering puritanical outlook upon much of the church. In worship, the Southern penchant for emotionalism endorsed demonstrative "freedom of the Spirit" in individuals and insured the predominance of lively gospel hymns. The Benson Company of Nashville, music publishers with a long-standing symbiotic relationship to the Nazarenes, has had nationwide effect in the popularization of gospel music. Finally, early Southern holiness groups that united with the Nazarenes possessed an uncommon zeal for overseas missions that persists in the church today.

After 1920, as the older denominations adopted increasingly liberal views, the Nazarenes turned inward to conserve and protect their traditional doctrines and ethos. With the ascendance of premillennialism and a preoccupation with institutional concerns, the once vigorous social programs of the church saw neglect, and a more sectarian spirit emerged. Renewed commitment to social involvement, however, now is evidenced by a growing minority and Nazarene youths more frequently seek education beyond denominational schools. In matters of doctrine, some Nazarenes now describe sanctification in terms of process rather than instantaneous crisis. As a result of its faithful support of foreign missions, the church at present is growing more rapidly in the Third World than in the United States.

Bibliography. John T. Benson, Jr., *History of the Pentecostal Mission, Inc.;* Church of the Nazarene, *Manual,* 1980; C. T. Corbett, *Pioneer Builders, Men Who Helped Shape the Church of the Nazarene;* Donald W. Dayton, *Discovering an Evangelical Heritage;* Constant H. Jacquet, *Yearbook of American and Canadian Churches,* 1982; C. B. Jernigan, *Pioneer Days of the Holiness Movement in the Southwest;* M. E. Redford, *The Rise of the Church of the Nazarene;* Timothy L. Smith, *Called Unto Holiness;* Mildred Bangs Wynkoop, *The Trevecca Story.*

JOHN LAWRENCE BRASHER
DURHAM, NORTH CAROLINA

CHURCHES OF CHRIST. Churches of Christ constitute a conservative and predominantly Southern wing of the Restoration Movement begun in southwestern Pennsylvania in 1809 by father and son, Thomas and ALEXANDER CAMPBELL. A similar but far more emotion-oriented movement was begun in Kentucky in 1804 by BARTON W. STONE. Ironically, however, Stone's movement—native to the South—would join ranks with the Campbell movement in 1832 and its influence would be almost completely absorbed by Alexander Campbell's more rational and cognitive leadership. Consequently, when Churches of Christ began to emerge as a separate tradition in the South following the Civil War, their theological roots reached much deeper into the thought of Alexander Campbell than into the emotional temperament of their own native son, Barton W. Stone.

The guiding principles of the Restoration Movement were stated by Thomas Campbell in the *Declaration and Address* (1809), a document heavily dependent on the presuppositions of Scottish common sense philosophy. Put succinctly, the *Declaration and Address* argued that division in Christendom is wrong, and that unity could be achieved through a restoration of the simple beliefs and practices of the primitive church, which were apparent on the pages of the New Testament to any reasonable searcher.

By 1816 Alexander Campbell had assumed the mantle of the movement's leadership. However, as the movement progressed into the 1820s, it became increasingly clear to Campbell that the theme of restoration was not adequately serving his vision of a global Christian unity. When Campbell opted for immersion of adults as Christian baptism, and when he refused to tolerate missionary societies doing the work of the church, many who favored both sprinkling and societies refused to ally with his movement.

Consequently, in 1830, as if to signify a change in his emphasis, Campbell discontinued the iconoclastic *Christian Baptist*, which he had edited since 1823, and began a new journal, the *Millennial Harbinger*. Increasingly the *Harbinger* reflected a Campbell whose position on restoring the primitive church was gradually softening and who increasingly was willing to compromise at certain points in order to achieve the fundamental goal of the movement: Christian unity. Accordingly, in the famous Lunenberg Letter of 1837, Campbell indicated that true piety was perhaps even more important than the act of immersion and, by 1849, the man who earlier had opposed missionary societies now became president of the American Christian Missionary Society. Further reflecting his pursuit of unity was his union in 1832 with the Kentucky-based movement of Barton W. Stone.

Campbell's movement toward Christian unity even at the expense of a more consistent restorationist position, however, led to tension in the movement. Some supported his increasingly ecumenical thrust, but others discovered that if they had to choose between restoration and unity, they would opt for restoration. It was among these people, who had learned their theological lessons from the *early* Alexander Campbell of the *Christian Baptist* days, that the Churches of Christ have their deepest theological roots.

Like the early Campbell, Churches of Christ have been profoundly restorationist in perspective. On the other hand, the more liberal wing of the movement, the contemporary CHRISTIAN CHURCH (DISCIPLES OF CHRIST), has largely abandoned Campbell's theme of restoration and wholeheartedly upholds instead his emphasis on Christian unity. A third major wing of the original movement, the CHRISTIAN CHURCHES AND CHURCHES OF CHRIST, thinks of itself as the middle ground between the restorationist Churches of Christ and the ecumenical Disciples, partaking of the emphases of both. Concentrated largely in the Midwest, this group began to organize separately from the Disciples in 1927 when it appeared that the Disciples were moving in an ecumenical and liberal direction at the expense of RESTORATIONISM. The process of separation from the Disciples took almost half a century and was not completed until the late 1960s.

While Churches of Christ have their theological roots in the early Alexander Campbell and his restorationist followers, the die that set them in their present mold was not cast until shortly after the Civil War. In the years between the war and 1900, the ecumenical side of the movement grew increasingly stronger in the burgeoning North where the frontier was rapidly passing, particularly in the early part of the movement from western Pennsylvania to Iowa. And during the same period, the restorationist side of the movement took root and increasingly flowered in the lingering frontier of the upper South, from Nashville west to Oklahoma and Texas. Consequently, Churches of Christ today are concentrated in Tennessee, northern Alabama, Arkansas, Oklahoma, and Texas. Another sizable concentration is in southern California, the result of migration from Oklahoma and Texas during the Dust Bowl years. Beyond this, Churches of Christ are scattered in lesser numbers throughout the United States and abroad.

Undoubtedly, the appeal of the restorationist premise, with its emphasis on the true, primitive church of the New Testament, was strong to frontier people in the postwar South who had no money, no fame, and no standing in this world: they at least could possess the Bible and true religion. But since this compensatory character of "true religion" was central to practically all Protestant groups in the South, it is fair to ask why Churches of Christ migrated only to the West and failed to gain a footing either in the Southeastern Atlantic states or in the Gulf Coast states, with the exception of Texas.

Answers emerge in the recognition that by 1830, a virtual evangelical consensus was forming in the Old South binding Methodists, Baptists, Presbyterians, and Episcopalians to the South itself as an object of religious devotion. To these Christians, there was a close and intimate connection between God, the Bible, and the Southern region, so that a Southern civic theology was in the process of forming.

But a Southern civic theology would remain foreign to the Campbell-Stone movement for two reasons. First, this religion of the Confederacy was forming in the Deep South precisely when the Campbell-Stone movement had gained significant strength only as far south as Nashville and northern Alabama. Consequently, the Campbell-Stone movement was prohibited geographically from par-

ticipating in that consensus. But even more important, the early Campbell-Stone movement, which so thoroughly influenced Church of Christ, had held to a theology that exalted the church as transcendent above national loyalties, not to mention sectional loyalties. Between 1830 and 1865, therefore, the movement in Kentucky, Tennessee, and northern Alabama was simply ill adapted to penetrate the Deep South where a religion of the Confederacy was gaining in spiritual momentum.

When the war was over, the conviction that the church transcended sectional loyalties intensified among many Southern Disciples. Some followed the lead of DAVID LIPSCOMB, prominent church leader and editor of Nashville's *Gospel Advocate*, and disavowed not only participation in carnal warfare, but also participation in civil government, including voting. Many Southern Disciples, therefore, continued to find the Deep South spiritually alien to their own purposes and perspectives. In addition, the Deep South, ravaged as it was by the war, held out no promise for economic advantage. Consequently, many members of this embryonic Church of Christ moved west, and as they did they carried their restorationist perspective with them, thereby strengthening the church in Texas, which had been slowly growing since the 1830s.

During the years between the war and 1900, tension between ecumenists and restorationists heightened, focusing particularly on the propriety of missionary societies and instrumental music. The ecumenists, typically people of some means and social standing, argued for these practices on the basis of expediency. The restorationists, often of little wealth or social standing, argued against them on the basis of Scriptural interpretation. Beginning in the 1860s and continuing through the end of the century, congregations throughout America divided over these issues. By 1906, the federal census report showed for the first time two separate churches in the restoration heritage: the Disciples of Christ, centered chiefly in the Midwestern heartland, and the Churches of Christ, centered primarily in the upper South from Tennessee to Texas with 159,658 members in 2,649 congregations.

By 1980 Churches of Christ had grown to some 1.6 million members, still centered in its original homeland from Tennessee to Texas, but also scattered over the nation and abroad. Further, while there clearly has been a mainstream, traditional Church of Christ orientation over the past 100 years, there have been significant variations within that tradition.

Traditional Churches of Christ have pursued the restorationist vision with extraordinary zeal. Indeed, the cornerstones of many Church of Christ buildings read, "Founded, A.D. 33." However, critics have claimed that the application of the restorationist perspective has been selective. The traditional focus has not been on emotional intensity or on social service, but rather on the restoration of New Testament truth, cognitively perceived, and the implementation of that truth both for church organization and worship. In this context, a peculiarly Church-of-Christ hermeneutic has evolved so that Churches of Christ traditionally have appealed to a trinity of authority: New Testament commands, examples, and necessary inferences. If this triune authority constitutes the positive hermeneutic, there also has been a negative hermeneutic: the silence of Scripture. This has been the rationale for their refusal to use instrumental music in worship.

Beyond this, the traditional focus of the restoration in the Churches of Christ has been on methods and procedures. When divisions have disrupted the church, they almost always have come over methodological disputes. How should God be worshiped: with instruments or without? How should the Gospel be preached and benevolent work be conducted: through congregations acting independently or through intracongregational cooperation? How should the Lord's Supper be observed: with individual cups for each believer or with one cup for all believers? How should biblical instruction be carried out in the congregation: through sermons alone or through Sunday schools as well?

If these issues seem insignificant to outsiders, they are meaningful to insiders who take seriously the task of restoring the form and structure of the primitive church. With the exception of the instrumental music question on which virtually all Churches of Christ are agreed, divisions in the church have taken place over each of the other questions. The traditional mainstream of the church has typically been on the liberal side of these questions, while smaller, splinter groups have formed around the conservative position.

At the heart of the traditional Church of Christ approach to Scripture is an assumption that the Bible is sufficiently plain and simple to render its message obvious to any sincere believer. Consequently, most traditional members are confident that they have properly apprehended the truths of the Bible. For this reason, Churches of Christ not only *seek* to restore the primitive church; they frequently view restoration as an accomplished fact, an assumption that fosters a certain exclusivism.

This exclusivism is apparent in the following: Church of Christ ministers typically do not belong to local ministerial alliances; evangelistic efforts traditionally have been directed toward members of other church groups; cooperation with other denominations or parachurch structures is generally frowned upon; members or clergy of other denominations generally are not allowed to preach or otherwise participate in the services of Churches of Christ.

While this exclusivism is simple and forthright, its roots are complex and may be traced to at least four different factors, two theological and two social. The first theological factor is the assumption that has traditionally been made about the Bible and the restoration theme, namely, that there is a biblical blueprint or constitution for the restored church that should be clear to any sincere and reasonable person. This factor is rooted in the church's understanding of the restoration motif. Ironically, the second factor is rooted in the ecumenical legacy of the Restoration Movement. Churches of Christ have always contended that religious division is wrong and that fellowship with a divided Christendom would be equally wrong. Churches of Christ, therefore, have gone their separate way, all the while contending for unity on the basis of their understanding of Scripture.

The sociological factors that lay behind Church of Christ exclusivism are rooted in the church's Southern experience. First, when the restoration theme drifted away from the tempering influence of Campbell's ecumenical emphasis, and then when the themes of unity and restoration finally divorced during the era following the Civil War, the natural tendency of the Southern restorationists was toward theological isolation and exclusivism. Second, this theological tendency was compounded by the reality of social isolation: these Southern Disciples, thoroughly committed to a vision of Christianity that transcended politics and sectional allegiances, felt themselves aliens and sojourners in a South that increasingly wedded Christianity and the Confederacy. For these reasons, though Churches of Christ were in the South, they were not of the South; nor did they belong to Southern Christendom.

Growing out of these experiences, traditional Churches of Christ developed a peculiar vocabulary that reflects their perception of themselves as the restored church of the New Testament. First, it is common for the terms "Christian," "church," and "New Testament church" to be used in an exclusive sense. In addition, there are terms that are preferred and terms that are shunned. Among the shunned terminology is the term "denomination." Churches of Christ do not regard themselves as a denomination, since a denomination suggests one among many rather than the one body of Christ. Further, it is commonplace among members that Churches of Christ do not belong to the historical categories, Protestant, Catholic, or Jew. They are simply Christian in the most ancient and primitive sense. Finally, Churches of Christ avoid the term "theology," preferring instead the term "doctrine": theology is what man says about the Bible; doctrine is simply what the Bible says.

It goes without saying that Churches of Christ typically are intensely evangelistic. The goal of the church is acknowledged to be the making of converts, and the measure of a successful congregation frequently is the number of conversions that are made. Consequently, both domestic and foreign missions receive heavy emphasis from the church.

Since traditional Churches of Christ strive so diligently to emulate the primitive church, they have essentially ignored developments in historic Christianity since the first century. Consequently, it is perhaps natural that they should be fundamentally heterodox at many points when compared with the mainstream of Christianity that has developed over the centuries. Their understanding of the sacraments is a case in point. Although the term "sacrament" is virtually never used in orthodox Church of Christ theology, it is nonetheless clear that there is a sacramental theology. While Catholics have seven sacraments and while orthodox Protestants have two, Churches of Christ have only one: baptism. Immersion is the one rite that puts one into the church and into the orbit of God's grace and salvation. The Lord's Supper, traditionally a sacrament for other Christians, becomes in Churches of Christ simply an "act of worship" alongside four other acts of worship that must be performed each first day of the week in obedience to God's commands: singing, preaching, praying, and giving.

There is a sense in which two other Church of Christ observances have a kind of sacramental character. Preaching is one of these observances, since it is through preaching that the saving logic of the Lord is mediated to the intellects of the hearers. Indeed, Churches of Christ are a verbal people rather than an aesthetic people, and the language typically is characterized by logical rather than by emotional or liturgical appeal. The other observance that has a kind of sacramental character for Churches of Christ is church attendance, usually three times a week. Regular church attendance typically is viewed as essential to one's spiritual well-being, especially since it is there that one attends to the proclamation of the Word, but also since attendance constitutes obedience to a biblical command (Heb. 10:25).

One of the most striking features of the Church of Christ is its relative lack of organizational structure. There is no regional, state, or national organization and no formally recognized hierarchy above the local congregation. For most of the church's history, the functional equivalent of bishops have been editors of "gospel papers," the two most influential being the *Gospel Advocate*, published since 1866 in Nashville, and the *Firm Foundation*, published since 1884 in Austin TX. Similarly, the functional equivalent of conventions or synodical meetings traditionally have been the LECTURESHIPS sponsored annually by the various Church-of-Christ-related colleges. It was there that the "issues" were fought out and the proper biblical methods and procedures ascertained.

However, within the last 20 years, power in the Churches of Christ has been greatly diffused. No single editor functions today as a bishop for the entire church or even for the church within a given state or region. Significant here is the vast array of periodicals and publications that have emerged throughout the

church's history, indicating that Churches of Christ have been devoted to the written word fully as much as to the spoken word. Many of these publications have exerted only local or regional influence, but they thereby have contributed to the diminishing of centralized power. Even more important to the diffusion of power in recent years is the emergence of members of Churches of Christ into a middle class with interests and horizons that transcend the narrowly religious. This has meant that gospel papers have had a great deal of competition from the secular press as well as from a wider religious press. Consequently, the extraordinary power once wielded by church papers and their editors has dramatically declined in recent years.

What, then, continues to hold Churches of Christ together? What continues to give their members a sense of common brotherhood? A definitive answer to this question must await further research. However, certain judgments can be made. First, there no longer is a unified brotherhood as there was between the Civil War and 1950. Second, to the extent that there continues to be a traditional, mainstream consensus, that consensus has a life of its own rooted in the traditional understanding, now several generations old, that the Church of Christ is the true, restored church. No longer is there a need for bishops to preside over and resolve controversy as did the old editor-bishops. Rather, the present need is for bishops who simply symbolize the identity of the church and reflect it back to the members. These symbolic bishops in some instances continue to be editors, but in most instances they are preachers for large, successful congregations or men who have made a reputation in past years as preachers for successful congregations.

Further, while editor-bishops once helped provide cohesion for the church by resolving debate and controversy, the symbolic bishops of today seek to downplay controversy and to build cohesion around traditional Christian values. Similarly, if the college lectureships traditionally have been forums for debate over the "issues," most college lectureships today avoid controversy altogether, focusing instead on the broad themes on which there already is consensus. Put in sociological terms, Churches of Christ today are in transition from "sect" to "denomination."

At the local level, Churches of Christ are strictly congregational and autonomous. A plurality of elders, often in conjunction with the minister, exerts power in the congregation. Deacons (no deaconesses) typically are charged with carrying out various good works under the oversight of the elders.

There are 17 colleges and universities associated with the Churches of Christ, seven of which are historically "major" institutions. Of these seven, six are in the church's geographical heartland: David Lipscomb College, Nashville; Freed-Hardeman College, Henderson TN; Harding University, Searcy AR; Oklahoma Christian College, Oklahoma City; Lubbock (TX) Christian College; and Abilene (TX) Christian University. The seventh, which is outside the geographical heartland, is Pepperdine University in Malibu CA.

See also articles on ANTIMISSION MOVEMENT; BIBLE, AUTHORITY OF; BIBLE, INTERPRETATION OF; LECTURESHIPS, CHURCHES OF CHRIST; RATIONALISM, RELIGIOUS; RELIGIOUS PRESS.

Bibliography. The American Christian Review (Cincinnati) 1856-1887; William S. Banowsky, *Mirror of a Movement*; Thomas Campbell, *The Declaration and Address*; The Christian Baptist (Brooke County VA) 1823-1830; The Christian Messenger (Georgetown KY and Jacksonville IL) 1826-1837, 1839-1845; The Evangelist (Cincinnati and Carthage OH) 1832-1844; The Firm Foundation. (Austin TX) 1884- ; The Gospel Advocate (Nashville TN) 1855-1861, 1866- ; David Edwin Harrell, Jr., *Quest for a Christian America; The Social Sources of Division in the Disciples of Christ, 1865-1900*; Lester McAllister and William Tucker, *Journey in Faith: A History of the Christian Church (Disciples of Christ)*; The Millennial Harbinger (Bethany VA) 1830-1870; Mission Journal (Abilene and Austin TX) 1967- ; James DeForest Murch, *Chris-*

tians Only; The Spiritual Sword (Memphis TN) 1970- ; The Twentieth Century Christian (Nashville TN) 1937- ; Earl Irvin West, *The Search for the Ancient Order*, 3 vols.; M. Norvel Young, *A History of Colleges Established and Controlled By Members of Churches of Christ.*

RICHARD T. HUGHES
ABILENE CHRISTIAN UNIVERSITY

CIVIL RIGHTS MOVEMENT. This significant moral-religious development in America and its Southern region can be assigned several beginning dates, even if one went back no further than World War II.

The threatened "march on Washington" of 1941, led by A. Philip Randolph, marked the first time that a forcefully articulated Negro demand elicited a concession from the federal government. The report in 1947 of the Committee on Civil Rights, the Democratic Convention of 1948, and the election of President Truman, despite defection of four states of the erstwhile solid South, confirmed the isolation of the white South from national politics until the mid-1960s. The Supreme Court's 1944 decision in *Smith vs. Allwright* began the dismantling of "white supremacy" at the ballot box. Even more important—symbolically, Constitutionally, and politically—was the 1954 and 1955 decision of *Brown vs. Board of Education* in which the Court prohibited racial segregation by state power of public school students, a decision that was logically extended in subsequent years to one form of public facility after another. *Brown* also had the effect of unleashing furious resistance by Southern politicians.

If the Civil Rights Movement could be narrowly defined as that period when the Negro struggle shifted from primary reliance on the courtroom (under the leadership of Thurgood Marshall) to popular actions, the Montgomery bus boycott that began in late 1955 might fairly be called its start. In more generalized demand, in contagious popular spread, and in willingness to practice civil disobedience, the "sit-in movement," beginning in early 1960 in Greensboro, would have a perhaps stronger claim. Finally, the so-called Freedom Rides of spring 1961 represented the nationalizing of the movement. For whereas the sit-ins until then had been almost entirely carried out by black Southerners, and their desegregating victories—which had been numerous—granted by white communities despite a hands-off policy by the federal government, now Northerners began their participation as did the federal executive.

As the above chronology suggests, the Civil Rights Movement has been a long process within United States history—in fact one of its major themes. Yet it did take on a more intense seriousness after 1954 for two main reasons. First, *Brown vs. Board of Education* settled the fundamental Constitutional question (all later race decisions were really footnotes to it) by declaring that race was not a permissible legal classification. Second, the white South—whose social, political, and even religious orders had rested on just that classification—reacted with "massive resistance" and challenge to what was now declared law; it did so by countless legal and political manuevers, by enforcing conformity of opinion and its expression (even within the churches), and by crude intimidation and violence. From 1946 on, in first one Southern state and then another (with Tennessee possibly the only exception), race had become the controlling issue in statewide and Congressional elections; but after 1954, it was as if the whole of white society was mobilized in a way it had not been since post-Reconstruction years. This time, however, Negroes had strength to promote their own cause. The federal government—first its courts, then its executive power, finally its Congress—swung to their side rather than against them as after 1876. School desegregation, the precipitating cause, would nevertheless lag in compliance and solution behind other issues.

The huge Washington rally of 1963 symbolized the determination and strength of Negro Southerners, and their impatient demand that the president do more and the Congress do something. The 1957 Civil Rights Act, the first such since Reconstruction, and its successor of 1960 had been little designed to accomplish reform. Now with the strength of a vast popular movement, a spreading moral revulsion against (and even within) the white South developed. It was helped along by a creeping realization of the economic ill-effects of continued turmoil. Congress yielded, after necessary confrontation with its Southern membership, and passed the Civil Rights Act of 1964 and the Voting Rights Act of 1965. The first effectively ended segregation in public accommodations and created machinery for combating discrimination in employment and by recipients of federal monies. The second provided effective federal protection for voting.

The price paid by the movement had been a heavy one. In the decade 1955-1965, at least 84 killings were associated with Southern civil rights drives, 30 of them in the crescendo months of 1964-1965 when the "Mississippi Summer" turned the deepest of black-belt states into a hard testing ground of wills.

Yet as deep as the anguish was at the time, the accomplishments of the Civil Rights Movement were relatively painless compared with other of history's great social upheavals, a fact principally due to the nonviolence its leaders taught and its rank-and-file practices. They had been reared for the most part in Southern Protestant churches. The black churches had taught their people what their dignity required and taught them too how to go about attaining it.

Within the white churches there was torment that occasionally escalated to turmoil. At most, they typically demonstrated a conviction that their congregations must be led as intact as possible into a new ethic, even if that might mean allowing moral leadership to come from secular sources. Many ministers who clung to the church's prophetic role were displaced. Some others were faithful to that role through work on denominational and national levels, thus perhaps encouraging the grip of conservatism on local congregations. In city after city during successive crises, "manifestos" of church leaders were issued, though until quite late they typically pled only for law and order without explicitly condemning segregation.

On the other hand, church people (especially women) were at the forefront of every reform effort within the white South—as they had been when churchwomen of an earlier generation waged their fight against lynching.

The movement featured three primary demands: personal security, such as the end of socially sanctioned terror in order to keep Negroes in their "place" and fair law enforcement; the right to vote; and the end of segregation, by order or suffrance of law. These made a modest program, and although far from fully achieved even by the early 1980s, the structure of law and bureaucracy for doing so was in place and functioning by the late 1960s. In *that* sense, the distinctively Southern regional Civil Rights Movement phased out, place by place, state by state, during the 1970s. The paradox is that even so modest a program could be realized only by the realignment of the South's social and political orders.

As a consequence, black citizens have become an integral part of the local political systems of the South, but are yet only at the edges of state and Congressional power. Their votes are assiduously solicited by white Democratic candidates, including some who but a few years earlier fought to deny civil rights. Many whites have forsaken the party of traditional allegiance and have made the Republican party its equal in regional strength; concurrently they have given powerful reinforcement to the transformation of the national Republican party into a more professedly ideological party committed to laissez-faire economics, diminished

social welfare programs, defense of parochial mores, and an enormous military force. This too must be seen as a result, at least temporarily, of the Civil Rights Movement.

Social change has been slighter, with most Southern institutions retaining their single race make-up. An exception would be the one-time white universities that now have significant (but hardly proportionate) numbers of black students, though not many black faculty members and hardly any black trustees or high administrative officers. The big law firms, banks, other businesses, churches, and newspapers are still mainly white at even the moderately high levels of prestige and income. But within all of those institutions, only the churches excepted, thousands of blacks will now be found doing clerical, technical, and junior management jobs that were closed to them before the movement.

But to say that the Civil Rights Movement is ended would needlessly invite dispute. No more than the labor movement, antiwar, or women's movements is it over. American democracy being what it is, in strengths and weaknesses, there will likely always be civil rights issues, as there are always First Amendment issues. Within the historic drive of black Americans for full citizenship and fair shares there was, however, a distinctive Southern movement that gripped the world's attention and admiration, and which for a short while made civil rights the nation's most insistent political issue. That movement essentially achieved its modest, though bitterly resisted, goals and is entitled to its acknowledged place in our history.

During its life it transcended class differences and united all blacks in the common objective of wresting full recognition of their Constitutional rights. That was achieved, along with the resultant dignity and spiritual release, for whites as well as blacks. Few reforming movements have been as successful.

The Southern movement did not travel well to Northern black communities, few of which can show improvements over the past 30 years of political, economic, educational, or social conditions. The riots and lesser civil disturbances they endured advanced them little. But if those communities have not advanced, a steady stream of people has come from them to enter the urban middle class.

Even if the movement's impact reached beyond its own specific cause, poverty remains a major problem. The bold plans and promises of the antipoverty program, begun in 1964, are unfulfilled. The "Poor Peoples March on Washington" of 1968 differed from the march of five years earlier not only in its themes, but in the absence of MARTIN LUTHER KING, JR., whose murder a few weeks before had removed from the national scene the one person who almost single-handedly was able to summon millions of blacks and whites to a moral unity. There was about the 1968 gathering a grimness and suspicion, a cynical disbelief that the American economy would provide economic "rights" to go with the hard-won political rights. No convincing cure for that disbelief has yet appeared.

See also articles on BLACK MINISTERIAL PROTEST LEADERSHIP; SEGREGATION.

LESLIE W. DUNBAR
PELHAM, NEW YORK

CIVIL WAR. The influence of the Civil War itself upon religion in the South is difficult to isolate from the broader topic of Southern religion in relation to slavery and segregation, secession, and sectionalism as the stuff of the war. From Sumter to Appomattox Catholics and Lutherans in the South were isolated from their Northern brothers and sisters. Episcopalians organized a Confederate church out of dioceses that reunited with the national denomination after 1866. Old School Presbyterians made a Southern church after Sumter that merged with the Southern New School, formed in 1857; the resulting PCUS is still extant. These

groups' influence increases in the order of their naming. The most influential denominations had divided over slavery in 1845—the founding date of the Methodist Episcopal Church, South, which reunited with the Northern church in 1939, and of the Southern Baptist Convention, which also has continued.

Complexion of membership in the main denominations changed drastically during and just after the war. Most blacks were Methodists or Baptists, and in 1860 they outnumbered whites in these denominations. All-black congregations were exceptions to the usual segregated seating or meetings of black members. Blacks deserted white churches en masse after the Confederacy fell and emancipation took hold; they formed separate Baptist and Methodist congregations and associations. For example, in 1860 more than 200,000 blacks were Southern Methodists; in 1860 fewer than 50,000 remained to be placed in a separate conference, and after just four years even they became an independent church. As blacks' chief autonomous social institutions, these churches flourished after the war.

Almost all preachers and almost all soldiers of the Confederacy were whites. Denominations assigned chaplains to military units. Revivals and conversions in the camps, the piety of high officers (and low soldiers), the service of an Episcopal bishop as a military commander, sermons assuring congregations that God favored the Confederacy, and prayers pleading for that very same favor by means of military victories—all cast the mantle of a holy crusade over the cause.

Yet these externals of religion signified profound social and cultural upheavals long antedating secession and lasting long after Reconstruction. For at least a generation, Northern Christians increasingly condemned slavery in the name of the same God invoked by Southern Christians to sanctify slavery as a blessing upon blacks and a means for whites to serve God. Against abolitionist prooftexts hallowing freedom, many Southern preachers interpreted the story of the stigma of Ham, one of Noah's sons, as God's everlasting consignment of the black race to servitude and inferiority.

The "peculiar institution" that as late as 1840 had seemed to astute observers to be on a course of ultimate extinction, rent the nation. It galvanized the South—a region of long-standing diversity as to religion, politics, class, economics, history, and custom—into unified military action, ideological conformity, and a high degree of religious (if not denominational) homogeneity. Many features dominating Southern religion after the war had been those of the evangelical denominations (Presbyterian, Methodist, Baptist) before the war: biblicism, moralism, laicism, and pietism. New features of postbellum Southern religion increased its homogeneity. In the minds of almost all preachers and believers in the South, God favored secession and slavery. Slavery ended, and with it went the shared (not to say equally shared) religious life slaves and masters had known. Secession failed, and with it went prosperity. Events saddled Southern religion, of both the free and freed groups, with a problem new for any large group of American Christians, that of theodicy, of reconciling defeat with Providence. Emancipation without liberation left black churches newly autonomous and, even more deeply than before, yearning for deliverance, particularly since the emancipator was dead. White religion renewed its commitment to white supremacy and to segregation; the separate but unequal doctrine was enacted in the churches long before the separate but equal doctrine was admitted by the Supreme Court.

In the kingdom to come, the South would rise again—so the foiled spirit of secession translated itself into religiously reinforced sectionalism. Southern Presbyterians still resist reunion with the national denomination. Southern Baptists revivalized themselves into a national denomination. Southern Methodists made their national denomination form a separate conference for blacks as the price of reunion. Southern Episcopalians trained their ministers at Southern seminaries. Taken together, they account for most Southern religion in the decades down to World War II. Their millennium lasted only a century after Appomattox, until the South rose again as part of the Sun Belt and Southern religion swept the nation as born-again Christianity.

See also articles on BLACK RELIGION; LOST CAUSE, THE; SLAVERY.

Bibliography. William A. Clebsch, *Christian Interpretations of the Civil War*; Donald G. Mathews, *Religion in the Old South*; Thomas V. Peterson, *Ham and Japheth*; Albert J. Raboteau, *Slave Religion*.

WILLIAM A. CLEBSCH
STANFORD UNIVERSITY

CLAPP, "PARSON" THEODORE

(1792-1866), liberal religious leader in New Orleans, was born in Easthampton MA. After his graduation from Yale in 1814, Clapp became a strict Calvinist. From 1822-1833, he led New Orleans' only Presbyterian congregation, but his gradual drift to universalism caused a schism with local conservatives. Clapp and his followers then formed a new "Congregational Church," which ultimately became the South's most famous "Unitarian Church." For the antebellum traveler, the chief attractions of the Crescent City reportedly were the Crescent City French Opera, the American Theater, and "Parson" Clapp's church.

The minister delivered his radical views in a manner calculated to entertain as well as to instruct. A typical congregation might include a segregated local audience of liberal-minded whites and free blacks, along with visiting planters, merchants, and professional men from different parts of the nation. Clapp's nonconformity with Southern religious orthodoxy made him famous beyond sectional borders. For instance, he denied the Calvinist doctrines of a spiritual elect and of eternal damnation to sinners. He preached that Christ was of divine origin; yet he opposed the concept of the Trinity and recognized the Holy Ghost only as a representative of a Supreme Godhead.

Although Clapp criticized the rampant materialism of New Orleans' society, he abandoned his abolitionist sympathies early in his career and became an apologist for the institution of slavery. According to Clapp, slavery's originators ". . . did not know that it was wrong." He saw the present slaveowner as a responsible guardian of the blacks "till ways and means can be revealed to transport them to the land of their ancestry." At heart, he was a colonizationist, but defended slavery as the only viable method of preserving the nation's social order as long as the black man remained. Many of Clapp's sermons were published in both Northern and Southern newspapers. One of the most famous was "Slavery: A Sermon Delivered in the First Congregational Church in New Orleans, April 15, 1838." In 1856, he moved upriver to Louisville where he spent his last 10 years.

See also article on UNITARIANS.

Bibliography. Theodore Clapp, *Autobiographical Sketches and Recollections During a Thirty-five Years' Residence in New Orleans*; Timothy F. Reilly, "Parson Clapp of New Orleans: Antebellum Social Critic, Religious Radical, and Member of the Establishment," *Louisiana History* 16 (Spring 1975) 167-92.

TIMOTHY F. REILLY
UNIVERSITY OF SOUTHWEST LOUISIANA

CLEVELAND, TENNESSEE. This small city is widely known as the headquarters for two denominations, the CHURCH OF GOD and the CHURCH OF GOD OF PROPHECY, and as the site of three colleges: Lee College, Tomlinson College, and Cleveland State Community College. County seat and principal center of Bradley County in southeast Tennessee, it began as a frontier trading post as early as 1820, and by 1836 was a modest settlement of log and frame buildings. In 1842 it was incorporated as a town by the Tennessee legislature.

Situated on the western slopes of the Appalachian Mountains, near the center of the old Cherokee Nation, Cleveland rapidly became an important town of eastern Tennessee. It experienced real growth in the 1850s when a railroad came through the town. Located 26 miles northeast of Chattanooga and 80 miles southwest of Knoxville, it was an important transportation and trading center. It quickly became as important in commerce and industry as it was colorful in situation and history. During the Civil War, Cleveland sided with the Union, though Tennessee sided with the Confederacy. President Lincoln believed that Cleveland, with its railroad, was as important as Richmond to the Union cause. An independent and conservative spirit has marked the region throughout its history.

From the beginning, Cleveland was a community of churches and schools. Methodist, Baptist, and Cumberland Presbyterian congregations were organized very early and many others have been added until the city soon became known as a religious center. The Pentecostal movement came into the town in 1904 when A. J. TOMLINSON and W. F. Bryant, early leaders of the Church of God, moved there from the mountains of eastern Tennessee and western North Carolina. Other leaders joined them and congregations were established nearby. Today, Cleveland is the headquarters city for the Church of God, a Pentecostal body with more than a million members in 114 countries, and the Church of God of Prophecy with 215,000 in 70 countries.

With a population of 27,100, Cleveland is a modern city of industry and progress, yet it retains the independence and Southern qualities that have marked it from earlier periods.

Bibliography. Charles W. Conn, *Cradle of Pentecost*; Roy G. Lillard, *Bradley County*; James L. Slay, "A History of Bradley County, Tennessee, to 1861," unpublished M.A. thesis, University of Tennessee, 1967.

CHARLES W. CONN
ROANOKE, VIRGINIA

COADJUTOR. In the Episcopal Church, this title refers to a bishop who assists the diocesan bishop in the performance of episcopal and administrative duties; unlike a suffragan bishop, he automatically succeeds the diocesan bishop at his death or resignation. A bishop coadjutor is elected by the diocese after the diocesan bishop and the General Convention have given their approval to an election. There can, of course, be but one bishop coadjutor in a diocese. Under certain conditions specified in the Constitution of the Episcopal Church, a bishop coadjutor may accept election to a position in another diocese, though it is unusual for one to do so. (In the Roman Catholic Church, the term is used infrequently and does not always indicate that the bishop has the right to succession.)

HERBERT S. WENTZ
UNIVERSITY OF THE SOUTH

COKE, THOMAS (1747-1814), early Methodist leader, was born in Brecon, Wales, the only child of affluent parents. At age 17, Coke entered Jesus College, Oxford, and following a fairly conventional path, he graduated, held minor political offices in Brecon, earned a law degree, and finally became a curate of the Church of England in Somerset in 1770.

Here Coke's career began to move away from convention. Some of the members of his congregation began to suspect him of Wesleyan (later Methodist) sympathies; by 1776 he met John Wesley, became increasingly evangelistic, and finally was dismissed from his church position. After risking a stoning by preaching outside his church's building, Coke joined Wesley and soon became one of his most trusted assistants. When Wesley decided to send support to FRANCIS ASBURY and the lay preachers in the United States, he appointed Coke superintendent to lead a delegation of three English Evangelicals who would meet with the Americans and discuss the future of the mission. Coke and his companions arrived in 1784, with Coke empowered to ordain the preachers.

Later that year in Baltimore at the CHRISTMAS CONFERENCE that brought into being the independent denomination, the Methodist Episcopal Church, he discovered that although he was putatively in charge, Asbury had effective control of the proceedings. When Coke began to ordain Asbury as superintendent, Asbury demanded that his colleagues first vote approval. Moreover, he later insisted that he and Coke should be called "bishop."

Bishop Coke viewed the new denomination as only one of his projects, along with missions to the West Indies, France and India, and, most important, the preservation of Methodism in England after Wesley's death. In nine voyages to the United States, Coke often quarreled with Asbury, who increasingly saw his fellow bishop as a meddlesome outsider. Coke made his last trip to America in 1803, and he died on his way to India.

See also article on METHODIST CHURCH.

Bibliography. Samuel Drew, *Life of the Reverend Thomas Coke*; William Sprague, *Annals of the American Pulpit*, 7: 130-42; John Vickers, *Thomas Coke: Apostle of Methodism*.

DAVID T. BAILEY
MICHIGAN STATE UNIVERSITY

COLLEGE OF WILLIAM AND MARY. The oldest institution of higher learning in the South, second oldest in America, and first Anglican college in the American colonies, the college was chartered in 1693 for Williamsburg VA by King William III and Queen Mary II. Its antecedents go back to the college begun by the Virginia Company at Henrico in 1619.

As part of the Church of England establishment of colonial Virginia, William and Mary had English bishops as chancellors and clergy as faculty. Beginning with JAMES BLAIR, several of its presidents served simultaneously as commissaries of the bishop of London and as rectors of Williamsburg's Bruton Parish. The college included an Indian School to convert and educate Virginia's Indians and a Divinity School to educate Anglican clergy.

Following the DISESTABLISHMENT (1776-1784) of Anglicanism in Virginia and the reorganization of the college by THOMAS JEFFERSON in 1779, William and Mary became a private college run by a predominantly episcopal faculty and Board of Visitors. The diocesan theological seminary established there in 1822 was short-lived.

Physically and financially ravaged by the Civil War, William and Mary closed in 1881. When episcopal attempts at revival failed, the college reopened in 1888 with aid from the commonwealth of Virginia. In 1906, the state purchased it. Coeducational since 1918, it has now grown to approximately 4,600 undergraduate and 1,500 law and graduate students. Notable faculty and alumni have included three presidents—Jefferson, James Monroe, John Tyler—and many of the early leaders of Virginia and the nation. Both Phi Beta Kappa and the Honor System originated at the college.

See also article on ANGLICAN CHURCH IN THE SOUTH.

Bibliography. Hubert Adams, *The College of William and Mary*; J. E. Morpurgo, *Their Majesties' Royall Colledge*; Lyon G. Tyler, *The College of William and Mary in Virginia.*

DAVID L. HOLMES
COLLEGE OF WILLIAM AND MARY

COLORED METHODIST EPISCOPAL CHURCH: *See* CHRISTIAN METHODIST EPISCOPAL CHURCH.

COMMISSION ON INTERRACIAL COOPERATION.

For a quarter of a century, from 1919 to 1944, this was the principal organization of white liberals in the South. Attempting to distinguish itself from both hard-line white supremacists and black and Northern critics of Southern racial practices, the commission sought a self-styled Southern liberal alternative to racial injustice in the South. More interracial in name than in fact, the commission spanned an era when Jim Crow was a virtually unchallenged reality in the South.

The commission's principal organizer and director during most of its existence was WILL W. ALEXANDER, a Methodist minister who had worked with Southern YMCA groups and the War Department to cool racial animosities and avert outbreaks of violence in the South during World War I. Alexander's efforts consisted primarily of forming committees made up of leaders from white and black Southern communities who supposedly represented the "better element" of their respective races. The racial violence that occurred throughout the nation in 1919 enabled Alexander to sell the idea of continuing these interracial committees in the South, and he received sufficient financial support from private Southern donors and Northern philanthropic associations, especially the Chicago-based Julius Rosenwald Fund, to establish a permanent organization with its headquarters in Atlanta.

From the outset, the Interracial Commission emphasized approaching the volatile Southern race issue in a manner that combined SOCIAL GOSPEL Christianity with social science analyses of the problem. An early commission declaration of principal of a few hundred words mentioned "Christ" or "Christian" 10 times, and many members of its state affiliates, such as Theodore D. Bratton of Mississippi, WILLIAM LOUIS POTEAT of North Carolina, and Robert E. Blackwell of Virginia, were either church leaders or educators at church-related schools. Its interest in social science brought the commission into contact with universities throughout the South, most notably the University of North Carolina, which in the early 1920s, under the leadership of Howard W. Odum, was establishing an Institute for Research in Social Science. With the assistance of the commission, Odum and his students produced a number of soundly researched volumes dealing with various aspects of the South's racial and economic problems. Among them was Arthur F. Raper's influential 1933 study, *The Tragedy of Lynching*, which documented that, beyond any doubt, the overwhelming majority of black lynch victims rarely met their deaths because of real or alleged attacks on white women. The commission publicized and distributed Raper's book throughout the South, which not only reduced the number of Southern lynchings, but practically eliminated the widespread and open defense of the practice that had been common up to that time.

The commission's campaign against lynching was to a great extent led by white women who, in 1930, under the leadership of JESSIE DANIEL AMES, formed the ASSOCIATION OF SOUTHERN WOMEN FOR THE PREVENTION OF LYNCHING, to denounce and campaign against the crime that was commonly justified in their name. Ames, however, opposed the NAACP-sponsored federal antilynching legislation that was introduced during the 1930s, and this put her at odds with other leaders of the Interracial Commission who by and large supported such measures. But this was about as far as the organization was willing to go in the way of challenging Southern racial mores.

The Commission on Interracial Cooperation generally avoided the issues of racial segregation and disfranchisement in the South, which by 1940 had become an increasing preoccupation among blacks and white Northern liberals. Its strengths were, in effect, its weaknesses. It kept open-minded discussions of the race issue alive in the South during an era when white supremacy was regarded as given. The commission contributed significantly to decreasing the prevalence of lynching while increasing Southern support for black education. Yet by refusing to confront segregation and disfranchisement, critics accused it of sanctioning these practices. In 1943, the commission concluded that it had outlived its usefulness, and in 1944 it disbanded so that a new and more vigorous Southern liberal organization, the Southern Regional Council, could be formed.

Bibliography. Ann Ellis, "The Commission on Interracial Cooperation, 1919-1944: Its Activities and Results," Ph.D. dissertation, Georgia State University, 1975; Gunnar Myrdal, "The Commission on Interracial Coopera-

tion," *An American Dilemma: The Negro Problem and Modern Democracy*; Morton Sosna, *In Search of the Silent South: Southern Liberals and the Race Issue*.

MORTON SOSNA
STANFORD HUMANITIES CENTER

COMMITTEE OF SOUTHERN CHURCHMEN.

Created in 1964, this Nashville-based, nondenominational Christian service organization initially represented a revival and reorganization of the larger and more ambitious FELLOWSHIP OF SOUTHERN CHURCHMEN. Funded primarily by small foundation grants, the CSC is a loose, amorphous network of friends, colleagues, and parishioners of its director, WILL D. CAMPBELL.

Throughout its history, the Committee has functioned in three ways: (a) an informal but intimate support group for its members and friends; (b) until 1983 the publisher of a sporadic but high-quality theological magazine, *Katallagete*, edited by James Y. Holloway; and (c) a "front" for the highly personalized and distinctive ministry of Will Campbell.

In its early years the CSC's program and emphases reflected its origin in the midst of both the black liberation movement and the church renewal movement, though always with a regional focus. Comprised of black and white, male and female, lay and clergy, native and transplanted Southerners, the Committee spoke directly and forcefully to the churches in the South about their calling in the racial crisis. The message was always the same: the ministry of Christian reconciliation as taught in 2 Cor. 5:15-20.

More recently the Committee, through its magazine and in the individual ministries of Campbell and others, has extended the scope of this core principle. All people are reconciled through the life, death, and resurrection of Jesus Christ, however marginal and alienated they might be: racists, monks, draft resisters, nuns, prisoners, renegade preachers, Communists. The contents of *Katallagete*, the personal ministry of Campbell to black activists and Ku Klux Klan members, and the Committee's sponsorship of Southern prison ministry all testify to this radical universalism.

As suggested by a look at *Katallagete's* contributors (e.g., William Stringfellow, THOMAS MERTON, Jacques Ellul, Vincent Harding, WALKER PERCY, the Berrigans), the Committee's theological orientation is a kind of ecumenical Christian radicalism. From its peculiar mix of Barthian, left-wing Reformation, and indigenous Southern evangelical elements, several themes may be discerned.

In the first place, Campbell and Holloway and many of their confederates are emphatically Christocentric and focused on the atonement, and somewhat less attentive to the Creator and creation and to the Holy Spirit and sanctification. Second, there is a strong doctrine of sin, especially in its collective, institutional forms (e.g., state, university, church). Third, ethics is conceived more as a mode of being rather than as a catalogue of certain things to do. The imperative, "Be reconciled!" is both necessary and sufficient for faithful, obedient Christian living.

Finally, the CSC betrays both a theological and a personal preference for the humble but assertive sects of the Southern white and black poor over the successful but worldly mainline churches of the New South's middle class, whether "conservative" or "liberal." Corresponding to this perspective is a conviction that incarnational evangelism and individual works of mercy ("a cup of cold water") are more appropriately the vocation of Christians and churches than "crusades for Christ," pietistic withdrawal, or social reform designed to fix the system or bring in the Kingdom.

See also articles on CHRISTIAN SOCIALISM; ETHICS, CHRISTIAN; SOCIAL GOSPEL.

Bibliography. Will D. Campbell and James Y. Holloway, *Up to Our Steeples in Politics*; John Egerton, *A Mind to Stay Here*; James Y. Holloway and Will D. Campbell, eds., *Callings!*; *Katallagete—Be Reconciled*, vols. 1-8 (1975-1983).

HARMON L. WRAY, JR.
NASHVILLE, TENNESSEE

COMMUNION, HOLY: *See* SACRAMENTS AND ORDINANCES.

COMMUNITARIAN MOVEMENTS: *See* UTOPIAN COMMUNITIES.

CONFERENCE. This is a group of ordained elders, persons preparing for ordination, and lay members elected by local congregations within a limited geographical area—usually a state or a part of a state—in one of the Methodist bodies. Originally conferences were bodies of ordained ministers only, but for the last century they have also had lay members. Persons entering the Methodist ministry join an annual conference and their ministry is fulfilled under the direction of, and usually within the geographical boundaries of, that conference; and it is to this body that persons are ultimately accountable for their ministry.

There are about 70 in the United Methodist Church, of which about 30 are in the South, that establish and support institutions such as colleges, homes for children and the aged, and newspapers.

They meet annually under the presidency of a bishop for inspiration, reporting on the ministry of the clergy and the churches and institutions under their care, and promotion of the ongoing ministry of the church in that area.

Conferences quadrennially elect lay and ministerial delegates to the general and jurisdictional conferences of the church. The General Conferences make the laws and develop the programs for the church and the Jurisdictional Conferences elect and assign the bishops.

JOSEPH MITCHELL
TROY STATE UNIVERSITY

CONGREGATIONALISM. Like other Protestant denominations, this English one has its roots in the 16th-century Reformation begun by Martin Luther, who protested the doctrines and practices of the Roman Catholic Church that were not prescribed by the New Testament. By study of the Bible Luther found that salvation is the free gift of a loving God to sinful humanity, attained through faith in Christ the Savior.

The Protestant movement spread across Germany, into western Europe, and extended to the Church of England as well as the Roman Church. Puritans, Separatists, and Independents differed among themselves as to whether they should withdraw from the Church of England. However, they were united in the belief that the doctrines of the church should be in strict accordance with teachings of the New Testament. Protest led to persecution and excommunication both by the Church of England and the Roman Catholic Church, and to the creation of a variety of denominations within the new Protestant movement.

Robert Browne (1550-1633) organized the first Congregational church in England, and his writings are regarded as the first expression of Congregationalism. Centrally, this new band taught that the church is a band of believers who covenant with God and with each other to obey the will of God, to live according to the teaching of the Scriptures, and to help each other to follow the Christian way of life. The local congregation is the basic unit of the church; its control lies within itself through Christ, the head of the church. Popes, priests, bishops, or state-appointed officials have no authority over the church or power to forgive sins or absolve guilt. Only God through Christ has authority or power over the congregation. Also, grace or forgiveness cannot be bought or sold. Grace is the "Free Gift of God through Christ." Creeds, the Book of Common Prayer, and set forms of worship were repudiated as requirements for the church. The mission of the church was seen as Christ's Great Commission to his disciples.

Protesting groups were persecuted and imprisoned; some were even exe-cuted. Exiled in Switzerland or Holland, they returned to England and Scotland and continued their commitment to the Christian faith and to religious freedom. The great escape for Congregationalists lay in the new land of America. The first landing of the Mayflower was in Boston Harbor in October 1620. Most of the Pilgrims were English, whether they had been Separatists, Puritans, or Independents in the Old Country. In New England most became Congregationalists. Colonies were established at many points; each colony had its church (or churches). In early colonial New England, separation of church and state was muted by the requirement that only men who were active church members were eligible for public office. Of necessity, this requirement was abandoned in time to satisfy and to include groups that were not Congregationalists.

Congregationalists still held that the local church is independent of all controls except its own: managing its own affairs, choosing its own pastors, teachers, and officers as it requires. It owns its own property, and makes its own rules and regulations for worship and other activities of the church. Though independent, Congregational churches joined in the network of associations, conferences, and a national council. These were voluntary organizations for mutual fellowship, to plan the promotion of common purposes and objectives, and to render possible enlarged strength in church extension, church building, and home and foreign missionary promotion.

From early days, Congregationalists had deep commitment to education, believing in a trained ministry and laity and committed to Sunday school and Bible teaching. Schools were established in New England and across the country as Congregationalist people moved to the Pacific. Several of these are still among the leading colleges, theological seminaries, and universities in the United States. Further, a comprehensive platform was adopted: the mission of the church of Christ was seen as proclaiming the "Gospel to all Mankind, exalting the worship of the one true God, and laboring for the progress of knowledge, the promotion of justice, the reign of peace, and the realization of human brotherhood." This mission was undertaken as Congregationalists journeyed westward from New England to the Pacific, establishing churches and schools and providing financial aid and leadership for new organizations.

Congregationalists were prominent in antislavery movements. Fugitive slaves were given food, shelter, and financial aid along secret routes into Canada. The AMERICAN MISSIONARY ASSOCIATION (AMA), organized 3 September 1846, as an interdenominational, antislavery association, was originally committed to mission and ministry to downtrodden, dispossessed people of whatever race or nationality. Gradually, the association became Congregational and formally identified with the Congregational churches of the United States.

During the Civil War, home missionaries employed by the AMA were welcomed into Union army camps to work with hundreds of slaves who had escaped, most of them destitute except for the clothing they wore. Army officers were greatly relieved by the presence and efforts of the missionaries, who provided lodging and facilities for educational, domestic, religious, and ethical training of these "contrabands of war." These missionaries followed the Union armies as they penetrated the South. When the war ended, AMA teachers and ministers were already present in the region, extending their work of educational and religious training for black people of the South. They established schools in every state of the South and at educational levels from kindergarten through college. Bible was taught in all these schools. Theological seminaries were established at colleges in Alabama, Louisiana, and Tennessee. White leaders in these institutions helped to organize black Congregational churches and to train black ministers for these churches, as well as those of other denominations.

The work of the American Missionary Association among black people and of the Congregational Home Missionary Society among underprivileged white people mostly in mountainous areas of the South marked the true beginning of Congregationalism in the region. Hundreds of schools were established, with school houses serving as meeting houses for many of the churches. Nearly all Congregational churches begun in the South in the 19th century were mission churches: that is, they received from the denomination financial support for church buildings and facilities and for pastors' salaries until they were strong enough to be self-supporting. By the close of the 19th century Congregational yearbooks carried unsegregated listings of over 500 Congregational churches in states south of the Mason-Dixon line and east of the Mississippi River.

The collapse of cotton tenancy, the outbreak of World War I, and the great migrations from the South to Northern industrial areas depleted church memberships and closed many churches, especially in small towns and rural areas. Several pastors of Southern Congregational churches followed their members and served them in the North.

Congregational churches merged with the Christian church in 1931 to become the Congregational Christian Churches; and the National Council of Congregational Churches and the General Council of the Christian Church became the General Council of Congregational Christian Churches. Adjustments in "faith and polity" were not too difficult. The autonomy of the local church became acceptable to all. Other teachings also were acceptable, among them: Christ is head of the church; Christian character is a sufficient test for church membership; the Bible is a sufficient rule for faith and practice; and the right of private judgment is one that should be exercised by and accorded to every individual member.

After the merger, custom and law in the South required racial separation in schools, churches, and conferences. Nationally, however, Congregational Christian churches moved toward an integrated community of churches without regard to race, nationality, or other divisive structures in human relations.

In 1957 the Congregational Christian Churches united with the Evangelical and Reformed Church (itself a union) to become the UNITED CHURCH OF CHRIST. The constitution of the United Church of Christ safeguards the right of the local congregation to own its own property, to control its own affairs, to choose its own minister(s) and other officers, and to decide on its own order of worship and other activities of the congregation. The local church continues as the basic unit of the United Church of Christ.

See also article on PROTESTANT REFORMATION.

Bibliography. William E. Barton, *Congregational Creeds and Covenants*; Douglas Horton, *Congregationalism, A Study in Church Polity*; J. Taylor Stanley, *A History of Black Congregational Christian Churches in the South*; Durward T. Stokes and William T. Scott, *A History of the Christian Church in the South*; Williston Walker, *A History of the Christian Church*.

J. TAYLOR STANLEY
GREENSBORO, NORTH CAROLINA

CONNER, WALTER THOMAS

(1877-1952), Baptist theological educator, was born in Cleveland County AR. Converted during a Methodist revival in Taylor County TX and baptized into a Baptist church, Conner was ordained a Baptist minister in 1899. Educated at Baylor University (B.A., 1906; M.A., 1908) and Southwestern Baptist Theological Seminary (Th.B., 1908), he was also pastor of village Baptist churches in Texas. After studying at Rochester Theological Seminary (B.D., 1910), Conner joined the faculty of the Southwestern Seminary at the time of its removal to Fort Worth in 1910 and served as professor of systematic theology for 39 years. He also studied at

the University of Chicago (1910, 1920) and at the Southern Baptist Theological Seminary (Th.D., 1916; Ph.D., 1931).

Conner combined in his theology certain aspects of the theological systems of three of his teachers, BENAJAH HARVEY CARROLL of Baylor, Augustus Hopkins Strong of Rochester, and EDGAR YOUNG MULLINS of Louisville, but he was also independent. Influenced by personalism, he stressed the moral self-consistency of the divine attributes, tended toward kenoticism in Christology, and moved from a modified penal theory of Christ's saving work to the idea of *Christus victor*. The Texas theologian explicated the doctrines of revelation and of the Holy Spirit while saying little about biblical inspiration; retained a moderate CALVINISM in respect to election and perseverance; insisted that justification is "vital" and not "declarative" and that worship, not activity, is the first duty of the church; and shifted from postmillennialism to amillennialism.

Conner wrote 15 books. His entire doctrinal system is best expressed in *Revelation and God* (1937) and *The Gospel of Redemption* (1945).

See also article on THEOLOGICAL EDUCATION.

Bibliography. Stewart A. Newman, *W. T. Conner: Theologian of the Southwest*.

JAMES LEO GARRETT, JR.
SOUTHWESTERN BAPTIST SEMINARY

CONSERVATIVE JUDAISM: *See* JUDAISM.

CONVERSION.

The Christian teaching of conversion points to the reorientation of a person's life, from being separated from God to being rightly related to God.

The Old Testament contains prophetic calls to the nation of Israel to repent, that is, to turn from idolatry and immorality to God and righteousness. The New Testament likewise records messages calling for repentance, sometimes for national repentance, and sometimes for a more individual repentance or conversion. The word "repentance" is a major term both in the Bible and throughout Christian history. However, in the New Testament the word "conversion" (*epistrophe*) and its cognates were not often used. The Latin translation (*conversio*) was rarely used by the early church, or in the medieval period, or by the reformers.

It is understandable that conversion was not a major concern in communities in which virtually everyone accepted Christian beliefs as true and Christian practices as appropriate, and in which the sacraments of baptism and confirmation were natural steps in the Christian pilgrimage. But its importance was evident in places such as the American frontier where the population increased rapidly and included many people who had not participated in the Christian life. Conversion became a dominant concept in REVIVALISM in the American South, as Donald G. Mathews has noted: "By far the most significant aspect of Evangelical ideology was its demand for a radical conversion experience to set Evangelicals off as a separate community."

Three benefits accrued to those who accepted the revivalist teaching about conversion. First, the possibility of every person's having a personal relationship with God was opened up. Intellectuals might be satisfied to know God through nature, but ordinary men and women could know him in a personal way by being converted. Second, once converted, one became a member of a separate community. In this community all the world's values were transformed. One's wealth, education, or vocation were insignificant; what counted was that one was converted. Third, the belief in conversion was a common ingredient of the three largest denominations in the South: Baptist, Methodist, and Presbyterian. Revivalism thus incorporated a kind of ecumenism, with denominational rivalries being either ignored or watered down.

The present celebrity of the idea of conversion is to be attributed to its dominant role in revivalism. In that setting, at least four practical and theological questions are raised.

First, who is the author of conversion, God or man? Early revivalists such as GEORGE WHITEFIELD were Calvinists and insisted that God alone can convert a person and that he does so without the person's assistance. Nineteenth-century revivalism sometimes spoke of a paradox, with God alone converting, yet man somehow cooperating in his repentance. Today, the common-sense view prevails in which individuals themselves must repent. If this view is accepted, the implication that a person converts himself must be guarded against.

A second issue is that if a person repents, what, if any, should be the fruits and obligations beyond one's inner life? Questions such as the nature of decision, the intensity of emotions, and the sequence and pattern of personal response become important. But are these questions in fact central to Christianity, as a revivalist understanding of conversion entails, or are they in fact peripheral to matters such as God's purposes, God's character, and God's activities?

Third, a practical concern is the role of the church in securing the conversion of sinners. What methods are appropriate? Should attempts to persuade be employed? Should emotions be aroused? Is the church authorized to offer assurance to converts?

Finally, is conversion the only possible initiation into the Christian pilgrimage? If so, what is the stance of a converted person toward someone in a nonrevivalist tradition who has had no such experience but whose faith in and love for Christ are evident? Is too much normativeness claimed for conversion? Is there no alternate pattern for receiving it?

See also article on SALVATION.

Bibliography. John B. Boles, *The Great Revival, 1787-1805*; Donald G. Mathews, *Religion in the Old South*.

FISHER HUMPHREYS
NEW ORLEANS BAPTIST SEMINARY

COOPER, THOMAS (1759-1839), scientist and religious liberal, emigrated to Pennsylvania from his native England in 1794. He made the move after incurring the wrath of Edmund Burke over his flirtation with French radicalism; he settled near his friend and fellow exile, the famous chemist, Joseph Priestley. He pursued a varied career as physician, lawyer, judge, and experimental chemist, and was both jailed for sedition and removed from the bench for arbitrary conduct.

After stints of teaching at Dickinson College and the University of Pennsylvania, his appointment to the faculty of the University of Virginia, which his friend THOMAS JEFFERSON had negotiated for him, was rejected owing to clerical opposition. Instead he became professor and then president of South Carolina College; not surprisingly he ran afoul of that state's clerical establishment because of his infidelity and his attacks upon that establishment. However, the position that he had established for himself as an extreme advocate and a theoretician of states' rights enabled him to preserve his position. While in Columbia he taught chemistry as well as political economy; his textbook, *Lectures on the Elements of Political Economy* (1826), was a pioneering venture in the field.

Philosophically, he was a utilitarian and materialist; although he was theologically a Unitarian, he never formed any formal attachments with that then nascent denomination, and was finally buried in an Episcopal cemetery. Cooper is often cited as an exemplar of religious liberalism in the antebellum South, but it is probably more accurate to see him primarily in the more negative role of anticleric and materialist. His major contribution to organized religion was to serve as a perpetual thorn in the side of the orthodox clergy who were for many years unsuccessful in dislodging him from his final academic position at Transylvania College. His major fame rests in his early advocacy of states' rights and secession, but his career also demonstrates the freedom from religious orthodoxy that could be purchased in the antebellum South by political usefulness.

See also articles on SCIENCE AND RELIGION; UNITARIANISM.

Bibliography. Dumas Malone, "Thomas Cooper," *Dictionary of American Biography* 2: 414-16; *The Public Life of Thomas Cooper 1783-1839*; I. Woodbridge Riley, *American Philosophy; The Early Schools.*

PETER W. WILLIAMS
MIAMI UNIVERSITY

COUNSELING, PASTORAL: *See* PASTORAL CARE.

CRAIG, JOHN (1709-1774), colonial Presbyterian leader, was born in Ireland and graduated from Edinburgh at age 23. Landing at New Castle DE, in 1734 he lived with the Rev. John Thompson while teaching school and studying theology. The presbytery of Donegal in Pennsylvania licensed Craig in August 1738, and sent him as supply preacher to Presbyterians in northwestern Virginia.

On 3 September 1740 Craig was ordained and installed by Donegal over the "Triple Forks of the Shenando," a congregation in the central Valley of Virginia with two preaching places that became the AUGUSTA STONE CHURCH and the Tinkling Spring Presbyterian Church. Thus Craig became the first settled Virginia Presbyterian pastor.

John Craig's parish extended over an area 20 miles wide and 39 miles long, within which today 13 Presbyterian churches trace their origins to his activity. Craig's wider missionary work spread from present-day Winchester in the north to Wythe County 240 miles to the southwest.

Associated with traditionalist Donegal Presbytery, Craig resisted itinerant New Side preachers after the 1741 Presbyterian split over revivalism. When Presbyterians reunited in 1758, Craig reluctantly joined the New Side Hanover Presbytery in Virginia. Conciliation led later to his being twice elected its moderator.

After separating from Tinkling Spring in 1764, Craig continued as pastor of Augusta Church, where he was buried. Only one printed sermon and his baptismal record remain, but Presbyterian churches all over western Virginia claim him as "Father."

JAMES L. MCALLISTER, JR.
MARY BALDWIN COLLEGE

CREEDS: *See* AUGSBURG CONFESSION; NEW HAMPSHIRE CONFESSION OF FAITH; WESTMINSTER CONFESSION OF FAITH.

CRISWELL, WALLIE AMOS (1909-), prominent Southern Baptist pastor and public figure, was born in Eldorado OK. An early volunteer for the ministry, he was educated at Baylor University in Waco TX and at the Southern Baptist Theological Seminary in Louisville where he was awarded the Doctor of Philosophy degree in 1937.

Criswell served as pastor of the First Baptist Church of Chickasha OK from 1937-1941 and First Baptist Church of Muskogee OK from 1941-1944. Since 1944 he has been pastor of the Church of Dallas. The Dallas church, perhaps the most influential Baptist church in Texas which numbers more Baptists than any state in the country, has known only one previous pastor, the famed GEORGE W. TRUETT, who was its minister for 47 years. Criswell's appointment immediately made him one of the most powerful men in the SOUTHERN BAPTIST CONVENTION.

Criswell's charismatic personality and conservative politics, which were both popular in a frontier commerical center like Dallas, built the church to a membership of nearly 20,000 with a dozen missions and an annual budget in excess of $4,000,000. Criswell himself served as a trustee for several Baptist executive agencies and colleges, including Baylor University, which he pressured to require more Bible training for all students. His fear of creeping liberalism in established denominational schools and his growing theological and political conservatism led

him in 1970 to found and serve as the first president of the Criswell Center for Biblical Studies of Dallas.

Despite his image as something of a denominational dictator and notwithstanding the radical tenor of his books, including *Did Man Just Happen?* (1957) and *Why I Preach the Bible Is Literally True* (1969), Criswell several times refused to lead movements that might divide the Southern Baptist Convention or result in a purge of moderates from its institutions. His two terms as president of the Southern Baptist Convention (1968-1970) passed without undue incidence of conflict.

See also article on BIBLE, INSPIRATION OF.

Bibliography. Billy Keith, *W. A. Criswell, The Authorized Biography.*

JAMES T. BAKER
WESTERN KENTUCKY UNIVERSITY

CRUMPLER, A[BNER] B[LACKMAN] (1864-1952), early Holiness leader, was born in Sampson County NC. He was the founder and first president of the Holiness Church of North Carolina. During the late 1880s Crumpler moved to Missouri and became a local preacher in the conference of the Methodist Episcopal Church, South. The preaching of evangelist Beverly Carradine drew Crumpler into the HOLINESS MOVEMENT in 1890. By the mid-1890s he had returned to eastern North Carolina where in 1896 he began a Holiness revival in Sampson, Wayne, and Duplin counties. Out of his preaching grew first the North Carolina Holiness Association (1897), and then the PENTECOSTAL HOLINESS CHURCH (1900).

This sect, known between 1901 and 1909 as the Holiness Church of North Carolina, grew slowly but steadily in the eastern part of the Tarheel state, but was racked by dissension following the Pentecostal revival of 1907-1908. Crumpler opposed the "tongues crowd" in his preaching and in editorials in his newspaper, the *Holiness Advocate*, but quickly found himself representing a minority view. In 1908, as a result of the debate over PENTECOSTALISM, Crumpler left the church he had founded and soon returned to the Methodist Episcopal Church, South. He spent the remainder of his days as a community leader and Methodist layman in Clinton. Although he occasionally spoke out on behalf of such causes as prohibition, he never again championed the Holiness movement.

Bibliography. Joseph E. Campbell, *The Pentecostal Holiness Church, 1898-1948;* Vinson Synan, *The Old-Time Power: A History of the Pentecostal Holiness Church.*

ROBERT F. MARTIN
UNIVERSITY OF NORTHERN IOWA

CUMBERLAND PRESBYTERIAN CHURCH.

This indigenously Southern denomination consisted of 91,000 communicants in 10 synods, 48 presbyteries, and 828 congregations in 1980. It exists in 19 states, most Southern, and such overseas countries as Colombia, Japan, and the Hong Kong/Macao (China) area.

The church began as an independent presbytery named "Cumberland" on 4 February 1810 in the log cabin home of the Rev. Samuel McAdow in Dickson County TN. Two other Presbyterian ministers, the Rev. Messrs. FINIS EWING and Samuel King, joined McAdow in the organization. These three along with a number of other ministers and licentiates had in 1805 been forbidden by the Kentucky Synod to exercise their ministry until they should comply with certain demands of the synod. The controversy between the synod and the so-called "revival party" revolved around several issues, chief of which were the questions of the ecclesiastical jurisdiction of synod over ministers and the doctrine of "fatality" that the revival party believed was taught in the WESTMINSTER CONFESSION OF FAITH under the doctrine of the Divine Decrees.

The intention of the founders was not to begin a new denomination, but rather to reorganize a former "Cumberland Presbytery" (so-called because it encompassed the "Cumberland Country") to which they had belonged and which had

been dissolved by the Kentucky Synod in 1806.

Failure at reconciliation with the synod, along with the phenomenal growth of the new presbytery, led to the organization of the Cumberland Synod in 1813. At its organizational meeting the synod adopted a doctrinal statement, part of which was a four-point dissent from the Westminster Confession, as follows:

1. That there are no eternal reprobates.
2. That Christ died not for a part only, but for all mankind.
3. That all infants dying in infancy are saved through Christ and the sanctification of the Spirit.
4. That the Spirit of God operates on the world, or as co-extensively as Christ has made atonement, in such a manner as to leave all men inexcusable.

In 1814 the synod adopted a Confession of Faith, which was a revised version of the Westminster Confession consistent with the four points of dissent listed above. The confession allegedly set forth a "medium theology," one intermediate between the extremes of CALVINISM on the one hand and those of ARMINIANISM on the other.

A General Assembly was organized in Princeton KY in 1829 with four synods and 18 presbyteries.

The church avoided a schism during the Civil War, although tension was high in both the North and the South. Until the end of the war black Cumberland Presbyterians worshiped in the churches of their masters. Historians estimate that in 1860 there were 20,000 such black Cumberland Presbyterians. After the war both white and black Cumberland Presbyterians expressed a desire for separate churches. In 1874 a General Assembly of the "Cumberland Presbyterian Church, Colored," was organized in Nashville TN with 46 ministers and 3,000 communicants. In 1960 the name was changed to SECOND

CUMBERLAND PRESBYTERIAN CHURCH. The church, which has representation in 10 states, consists of 6,494 communicants in four synods and 15 presbyteries. Its Confession of Faith is that of the Cumberland Presbyterian Church. Its chief publication is *The Cumberland Flag*, which is published at its headquarters in Huntsville AL. The General Assembly meets annually, along with the National Sunday Convention and the National Youth Work.

In 1883 the Cumberland Presbyterian Church adopted a revised Confession of Faith, the chief designs of which were to abbreviate the text, to eliminate from the original Confession the vestigial remains of strict Calvinism, and to put the Confession in the language of the people.

A union of the Cumberland Presbyterian Church with the mother church, the Presbyterian Church in the United States of America, was effected in 1906. The doctrinal basis of the union was the revised Westminster Confession adopted by the Presbyterian Church in 1903. A minority of the Cumberland Presbyterian Church rejected the union on both constitutional and doctrinal grounds and perpetuated the Cumberland Presbyterian Church.

With the union of 1906, membership (since 1884) in the World Alliance of Presbyterian and Reformed Churches went by default. In 1956 the church became a member of the World Alliance of Reformed Churches.

Several features of recent developments in the Cumberland Presbyterian Church are worth noting. It was one of the earlier Christian bodies officially to approve the ordination of women as ruling elders and ministers. The denomination has an active women's group known as Cumberland Presbyterian Women (CPW), consisting of 500 local organizations. The CPW Convention meets annually at the same time and place as the General Assembly. The Cumberland Presbyterian Youth also has an annual convention. It also participates in the international interdenominational Youth Triennium.

The denomination has two institutions of higher learning: Bethel College in McKenzie TN, and the Memphis Theological Seminary in Memphis. It also operates a Children's Home in Denton TX. The two chief publications of the church are *The Cumberland Presbyterian* and *The Missionary Messenger*. Some Christian education materials are published jointly with other churches of similar faith and order.

Cumberland Presbyterian has a ministry to the Choctaw Indians in Oklahoma. In recent years it has joined with other churches in a ministry to Hispanics in Tampa and Ruskin FL, Chicago, Fresno CA, and El Paso. Union negotiations with the independent Presbytery of Liberia, Africa, are also currently underway.

The focus of the church during the decade of the 1980s is on church growth, especially on the formation of new churches in urban areas. This interest is reflected in the current joint effort with other Presbyterian churches to organize "union churches."

In 1978 a significant joint work was begun by both Cumberland Presbyterian Churches on the revision of the Confession of Faith. The revision is designed chiefly to update both the language of the Confession and the views of both churches on current social issues. This joint effort is regarded as a major step toward the union of the two churches.

Historically, the Cumberland Presbyterian Church may best be described as evangelical and ecumenical. Its headquarters are located in Memphis.

See also articles on FRONTIER, INFLUENCE OF; REVIVALISM.

Bibliography. Ben Barrus, Milton Baughn, Thomas Campbell, *A People Called Cumberland Presbyterians*; Thomas Campbell, *Good News on the Frontier*; *Confession of Faith of the Cumberland Presbyterian Church*; E. K. Reagin, *We Believe and So We Speak.*

JOE BEN IRBY
MCKENZIE, TENNESSEE

CUMBERLAND PRESBYTERIAN CHURCH, SECOND: *See* SECOND CUMBERLAND PRESBYTERIAN CHURCH.

CURRY, JABEZ LAMAR MONROE (1825-1903), Baptist educator, was born in Lincoln County GA. In 1838 the family moved to Talladega County AL. Curry graduated from Franklin College (now University of Georgia) with a B.A. in 1843 and Dane Law School, Harvard University, B.L., 1845. He was awarded honorary degrees by Mercer University in 1867, Rochester University in 1871, and the University of Georgia in 1887.

Curry's career was multifaceted: he was a Texas ranger, a Confederate army officer, an Alabama legislator, a representative in the United States and Confederate congresses, speaker of the Confederate House, an author, a lawyer, a churchman, an educator, United States minister to Spain from 1885 to 1888, and ambassador extraordinary in 1902.

With his Confederate loyalties tempered by broad human sympathies and national concerns, Curry provided constructive leadership during the turbulent years of Reconstruction. A fluent and powerful orator, he was a popular speaker at legislative assemblies and religious gatherings. Curry was an ordained minister who served his denomination (Southern Baptist) with distinction as a trustee of its Southern Seminary in Louisville and as president of the Alabama Baptist Convention, the General Association of Virginia Baptists, and the Southern Baptist Foreign Mission Board. He effectively promoted higher education in the South through several positions: as president of Howard College for three years (1865-1868), professor at Richmond College (1868-1881), general agent for the Peabody Fund (1881-1885), and an administrator of the Slater Fund for the Education of Freedmen (1890-1903).

See also article on EDUCATION, CHRISTIAN HIGHER.

Bibliography. E. A. Alderman and A. C. Gordon, *J. L. M. Curry, A Biography*; J. P. Rice, *J. L. M. Curry, Southerner, Statesman and Educator*; G. Ryland, *The Baptists of Virginia, 1699-1926.*

DANIEL HOLCOMB
NEW ORLEANS BAPTIST SEMINARY

DABBS, JAMES MCBRIDE (1896-1970), Christian statesman, was born in Mayesville SC. He grew up on Rip Raps Plantation where his grandfather farmed 10,000 acres of cotton. After formal education at three universities—South Carolina, Clark, and Columbia—he taught English at Coker College, 1924-1942. In 1942 he left teaching for farming and writing; from then until his death, his vocation was to understand "the footprints of God" in the travail of Southern history.

He first entered into public debate with the tradition of racial segregation in 1946 when the SC legislature attempted to legalize the all-white Democratic primary. "It struck me as a case of bad manners," he said, a violation of Southern culture. Soon he was a member of the FELLOWSHIP OF SOUTHERN CHURCHMEN, president (1957-1963) of the Southern Regional Council, and—along with his wife Edith—a leader of Penn Community Services.

Dabbs published over 100 essays in national literary and religious journals. His first widely read book was *The Southern Heritage* (1958). In this and other books—*The Road Home* (1960), *Who Speaks for the South?* (1964), and *Haunted by God* (1972)—he pursued the theme, deeply rooted in his Presbyterianism, of how to interpret the sovereignty of God in relation to SLAVERY, the CIVIL WAR, industrialism, and the CIVIL RIGHTS MOVEMENT. "All Southerners are bound together by their long and tragic history," he said in Little Rock in 1960. "Though our institutions say we are two, our hearts increasingly whisper we are one." God speaks in that whisper, he claimed, and also the universal humanism of Southern culture, for suffering is the experience that makes all humans kin. By that measure, he often said, the most human of Southerners are black people, and MARTIN LUTHER KING, JR., spoke for all the South—"black and white together."

DONALD W. SHRIVER, JR.
UNION THEOLOGICAL SEMINARY

DABNEY, ROBERT LEWIS (1820-1898), influential Presbyterian theologian, was born in Louisa County VA. After education at Hampden-Sydney College and the University of Virginia, he entered Union Theological Seminary and then served as a missionary pastor with the Tinkling Spring Church in the Shenandoah Valley. He joined the faculty of his seminary alma mater in Richmond in 1853 and for 40 years offered courses in church history, polity, and theology.

His reputation and influence as a prophet of inflexible CALVINISM grew steadily and was not confined to the South. In 1860 he was offered a professorship at Princeton and called as well to the pulpit of the Fifth Avenue Presbyterian Church of New York. He considered neither invitation seriously because of his passionate identification with the South. Dabney was chaplain in the Confederate army and a major on the staff of Stonewall Jackson (about whom he published a laudatory biography). After Appomattox, feeling that the South he loved was largely destroyed and fearing Virginia could be saved only by removing it from the American nation, he endeavored for awhile to promote the emigration of Southerners to Australia or Brazil.

Seeking a healthful climate, he moved in 1883 to Texas, where he taught philosophy at the state university, and was instrumental in founding the Austin School of Theology. Though increasingly infirm and, by 1890, totally blind, he remained a powerful and moving advocate for the causes of his youth. Unreconstructed politically, socially, and theologically, he fought all Northern intervention in civic affairs, racial integration, and the reunion of Northern and Southern Presbyterians. He also resisted compromise of the Calvinist system, a classic example of this attitude being his rupture with JAMES WOODROW when his former friend found support for Christianity in the evolutionary hypothesis.

Bibliography. Thomas C. Johnson, *The Life and Letters of Robert Lewis Dabney*; David Henry Overy, *Robert Lewis Dabney, Apostle of the South.*

STUART C. HENRY
DUKE UNIVERSITY

DAGG, JOHN LEADLEY (1794-1884), Baptist clergyman, educator, and author, was born in Middleburg VA, and died in Hayneville AL. His education included limited formal schooling, between 1803

and 1810; he was awarded the honorary doctor of divinity degree by the University of Alabama in 1843.

Springing from humble rural Virginia stock, Dagg was baptized in 1812 and ordained to the ministry in 1817. He was a Virginia pastor and teacher (1817-1825) and pastor of the Fifth Baptist Church, Philadelphia PA (1825-1834). Physical infirmities finally forced him from the pulpit: he walked on crutches, was virtually blind, and lost his public-speaking voice.

Thereafter he was president and professor of theology of Haddington Literary and Theological Institute in Philadelphia (1834-1836), president of Alabama Female Athenaeum in Tuscaloosa (1836-1844), and president (1844-1854) and professor of theology (1844-1856) of Mercer University in Penfield GA.

Despite his bodily limitations, Dagg was active in the affairs of the TRIENNIAL CONVENTION, Columbian College, American Baptist Home Mission Society, Baptist General Tract Society, and American and Foreign Bible Society.

Often referred to as "the venerable Dr. Dagg," he retired in 1856, living for almost 30 years in Georgia and Alabama, and it was during this period that he made his greatest contribution to Baptist life. He prepared *Manual of Theology* (1857), *Treatise on Church Order* (1858), *Elements of Moral Science* (1859), and *Evidences of Christianity* (1869). Because of these volumes, Dagg has gained a double significance: he was the earliest Baptist theological and ethical systematizer in America, and he was the representative theological and ethical figure among antebellum Baptists in the South.

See also article on THEOLOGY.

Bibliography. John L. Dagg, *Autobiography*; R. G. Gardner, "John Leadley Dagg: Pioneer American Baptist Theologian," unpublished Ph.D. dissertation, Duke University, 1957; "John Leadley Dagg," *Review and Expositor* 54 (April 1957): 246-63.

ROBERT G. GARDNER
SHORTER COLLEGE

DAMNATION: *See* SALVATION.

DARBYITE MOVEMENT. "Darbyite" is one of the names acquired by an evangelical, antisectarian movement more properly called the "Plymouth Brethren," or more to its liking, "Christian Brethren." The Brethren movement began during the early nineteenth-century revivals in Great Britain as some Anglican and nonconforming Evangelicals attempted to shrug off sectarian and formalistic barriers to Christian unity and spiritual vitality. Their most forceful and charismatic early leaders included an Anglican priest from Ireland, John Nelson Darby; George Mueller, the widely revered orphanage master of Bristol; and Arthur N. Groves, pioneer Brethren missionary to Europe and India. Early centers of Brethren activity were Bristol, Dublin and, of course, Plymouth.

The Brethren stressed the communion of all believers and made the simple breaking of bread the center of their worship. With no ordained clergy or denominational structure, they hoped to restore the simplicity and spiritual power of the early church. Brethren have cultivated anonymity, in order to avoid imposing "self" on the gospel. Their theology has been Calvinistic, with emphases on evangelism and the imminent, premillennial second coming of Christ. Darby taught that the institutional church would become worldly and theologically heterodox as the end times drew near and called for the separation of all "true believers" from the denominations. He accused colleagues of improper Christology and lax rules of fellowship and led the "Exclusive" Brethren away from the more inclusive "Open" Brethren in 1848. Since then, the Exclusive Brethren have subdivided many times and have remained small in number, while the Open Brethren through immigration and aggressive evangelization have spread to every continent.

Brethren influence in Anglo-American evangelical circles has always outstripped their number. Their strength in biblical scholarship and foreign missions has led to a disproportionate number of evangelical leaders with Brethren backgrounds. Perhaps their greatest triumph was their shaping of the eschatological views of many American evangelical leaders during the late nineteenth century. Evangelist Dwight L. Moody became converted to Brethren premillennial eschatology, while Bible teacher Cyrus I. Scofield based the notes for his famous reference Bible on Darby's premillennial, dispensational theology. Through the Scofield Reference Bible and the "Darbyite" premillennial emphases of many Bible conferences and Bible institutes, Brethren beliefs profoundly shaped the nascent fundamentalist movement. To this day, Fundamentalists respect and avidly read Brethren Bible teachers' works. Darby's belief in the ruin of the church has fed American dispensationalists' distrust of ecclesiastical institutions and preference for independent Baptist or Bible churches. While "Plymouth Brethren" and "Darbyite" have become bywords for cranky divisiveness and exclusivity, Brethren simplicity and lay ministry are shining witnesses in a world of bureaucratization and specialization to the power of primitive Christianity.

See also article on MILLENNIALISM.

Bibliography. F. Roy Coad, *A History of the Brethren Movement*; C. Norman Kraus, *Dispensationalism in America*; Ernest R. Sandeen, *The Roots of Fundamentalism*.

JOEL A. CARPENTER
WHEATON COLLEGE

DARWINIANISM: *See* EVOLUTION CONTROVERSY; MODERNIST CONTROVERSY; SCOPES, JOHN T.; SCOPES TRIAL; WINCHELL, ALEXANDER.

DAVIES, SAMUEL (1723-1761), dominant minister in the Southern GREAT AWAKENING, was born in Delaware in 1723. He joined the Presbyterian New Light movement in his teens, attending a school run by Samuel Blair. Ordained in 1747, he visited Virginia, soon qualifying under the law as a dissenting minister. In 1748 Davies returned to Virginia permanently.

An orthodox Calvinist, he was critical of the Establishment clergy's "laxity in living and cold rationalism in theology." However, Davies had signed the Thirty-nine Articles, (of the Church of England) with minor reservations and he never questioned the right of government to test Christian loyalty. Davies's sermons reflected intense anti-Catholicism as he recruited men to fight "papists" in the French and Indian War, thus earning the accolade "best recruiting officer in the colony."

Davies was harassed by Establishment leaders who viewed him as dangerous, a fomenter of religious frenzy. Legal restrictions on dissenting meetinghouses caused Davies to charge Virginia with violating the English Act of Toleration. "We claim no liberties but what the Act of Toleration allows Protestant dissenters and those only upon our qualifying according thereto."

In 1753 Davies went to England to raise money for the College of New Jersey. War was underway with the French and Presbyterianism was growing when he returned in 1755. Later that year Hanover Presbytery was founded with Davies as moderator. By 1758 a strong presbytery and changing political conditions assured colonial application of the Toleration Act. In 1759 Davies became president of the College of New Jersey.

Owing primarily to Davies the Virginia Episcopal Establishment lost its singular control over religion in the colony. But if Davies helped break the church-state bond, its implications for the following decades were largely hidden from him. Nevertheless, Davies was a champion of toleration who laid the foundation in the emerging struggle for religious liberty and consequent DISESTABLISHMENT of the Episcopal Church.

See also articles on CHURCH AND STATE; COLONIAL PERIOD; ESTABLISHED RELIGION.

Bibliography. Robert S. Alley, "The Reverend Mr. Samuel Davies: A Study In Religion and Politics, 1747-1759," unpublished Ph.D. dissertation, Princeton University, 1962; George H. Bost, "Samuel Davies: Colonial Revivalist and Champion of Religious Toleration," unpublished Ph.D. dissertation, University of Chicago, 1959; George W. Pilcher, *Samuel Davies: Apostle of Dissent in Colonial Virginia.*

ROBERT S. ALLEY
UNIVERSITY OF RICHMOND

DAWSON, JOSEPH MARTIN (1879-1973), Baptist pastor, author, and denominational leader, was born in Ellis County TX. He was graduated from Baylor University in 1904 after having served as pastor of five Baptist churches and having edited both the campus newspaper and the campus yearbook. After brief tenures as assistant secretary, Texas Baptist Education Commission (1904-1905), pastor, First Baptist Church, Lampasas (1905-1906), and editor of *Western Evangel* and *Baptist Standard* (1906-1908), he served two more First Baptist Churches, in Hillsboro (1908-1912) and in Temple (1912-1915).

For 31 years Dawson served as pastor of First Baptist Church, Waco (1915-1946). During these years he was repeatedly the object of attacks by J. FRANK NORRIS, the Fundamentalist leader. Undaunted, Dawson was a longtime trustee of Baylor University; helped to found a Baptist hospital in Waco; was Texas publicity director for the Seventy-five Million Campaign (1922) of the SOUTHERN BAPTIST CONVENTION; then chaired its Executive Committee and its committees on worship (1941) and on world peace (1944-1946). He espoused the rights of blacks, German-Americans, and Mexican-Americans and took an antimilitarist stance.

At age 67, Dawson in 1946 became the first full-time executive director of the Baptist Joint Committee on Public Affairs, Washington DC, a position he held until 1953. In 1947 he helped organize Protestants and Other Americans United for Separation of Church and State.

Dawson's literary contribution is noteworthy. He authored 12 books, contributed to seven others, and wrote numerous book reviews and articles for religious and secular periodicals. He helped to found and was at one time president of the Texas Institute of Letters.

In 1957 Baylor University established in his honor the J. M. Dawson Studies in Church and State.

See also article on CHURCH AND STATE.

Bibliography. Joseph M. Dawson, *A Thousand Months to Remember.*

JAMES LEO GARRETT, JR.
SOUTHWESTERN BAPTIST SEMINARY

DEACON. The word "deacon" is a transliteration of the Greek word *diakonos*, which means "servant." Traditionally the institution of this office is traced to the setting apart of the seven (Acts 6:1-6) for the service of the poor and the distribution of alms. In the Pastoral Epistles, the deacons are a separate class of church officers, charged chiefly with material duties.

In episcopally ordered churches, Roman Catholic and Episcopal, the Diaconate is the lowest order of the clergy, preceding the presbyterate (priesthood), and leading to it in a manner akin to an apprenticeship. Churches in the Presbyterian and Disciples traditions recognize the diaconate (the body of deacons) as a group of lay officers concerned for the material aspects of congregational life. In Baptist and Congregational churches deacons have definite spiritual functions. They assist the pastor in caring for the congregation and also distribute the elements at Communion. The Diaconate in Southern Baptist churches consists of a board of counselors elected by the local congregation (usually in keeping with the qualifications listed in 1 Tim. 3:8-13) and ordained by a council (presbytery) to assist the pastor in serving the *ecclesia*.

WILLIAM C. SMITH, JR.
GREENSBORO, NORTH CAROLINA

DEACONESS. This is a biblical term used to designate a woman who gives herself to full-time service within the church.

In Methodism a deaconess is a woman who has had a call to ministry; has responded to that call by undergoing special preparation; has been consecrated to the office by a bishop; and then has fulfilled that call by working in various church institutions in nonsacramental ways such as teaching, nursing, counseling, and social-service work.

Deaconesses are not members of religious communities and do not take the traditional vows of obedience, chastity, and poverty. They are usually single and are known for their simplicity of dress and their willingness to live and work among the dispossessed for small salaries.

Deaconesses normally work under the supervision of boards of laypersons and clergy who follow national guidelines for such work.

Since women may now be ordained in most Methodist bodies, the office of deaconess is no longer the only one open to women who have a call to full-time Christian service, but it still attracts those women who choose to fulfill their call in nontraditional, nonpreaching kinds of ministry.

JOSEPH MITCHELL
TROY STATE UNIVERSITY

DEBATES, INTERDENOMINATIONAL. Religious controversy is itself controversial. Christians of varying opinions almost unanimously deplore doctrinal discord. Yet most American churches were born in schisms marked by violent disagreements; even the Protestant Reformation began with a religious debate.

Having broken away from Reformation communions, the sects that came to dominate the South repeatedly renewed conflicts among themselves and with others. Baptist, Methodist, Presbyterian, and "Campbellite" groups each raided the sheep of other pastures with impunity. In this cauldron of competition, public debates, both printed and oral, became for Southern sectarians a way of life that lasted well into the 20th century.

Arguments about religion were hardly an exclusive prerogative of the clergy, but traveling evangelists and local ministers were the most likely participants in formal debates. Many such contests were brief, impromptu engagements, as when the Methodist PETER CARTWRIGHT faced an "infidel" on a steamboat in 1827. Other discussions, carefully planned and elaborately staged, might carry on for months in the pages of periodicals or for a week or more on a public platform. The Presbyterian Nathan L. Rice met ALEXANDER CAMPBELL in Lexington KY for 16 days in 1843, with Henry Clay presiding. The resulting record ran to 912 closely set pages and became a frontier best-seller. For Campbell this was a climactic confrontation, his third formal debate south of the Ohio River.

TOLBERT FANNING, Campbell's most distinguished Southern ally in debate before the Civil War, confronted Presbyterians and Methodists in Tennessee, Kentucky, and Alabama. As late as 1850, Fanning engaged a Methodist preacher at Lebanon TN at the request of the local Baptist congregation. But any alliance of Baptists and Disciples, however pragmatic, was shattered by the 1851 "Cotton Grove Resolutions" in which JAMES R. GRAVES laid out the boundaries of "Landmarkism." Graves, a Vermonter who came south in 1845, became editor of the *Tennessee Baptist* in 1848, setting out to root up every plant not planted to his satisfaction. In his *Great Iron Wheel* (1856) Graves assailed Methodism; in *The Trilemma* (1860) he dissected Presbyterianism. His 1875 debate with Jacob Ditzler, a Methodist, produced a transcript of 1,184 pages in two volumes, the first concerned solely with "the mode of baptism."

Graves's work set the tone and agenda of most later debates. Carefully contrived propositions, rigorous logic, exhaustive citation of authorities, and rigid adherence to parliamentary procedure were already established practice. An appeal to paradox would have been unthinkable. The mode, design, efficacy, and administration of baptism dominated discussion; but various aspects of church order and

worship, observance of the Lord's Supper, support of missions, the person and work of the Holy Spirit, and the tenets of Calvinism were often addressed. Disputants who were nearly identical in doctrine and polity struggled fiercely over minute distinctions. "Landmark" sects and radical Disciples (later CHURCHES OF CHRIST) quarreled bitterly over the design of baptism, even as they both flayed Methodists and Presbyterians for sprinkling infants.

Inevitably, both sides in a debate would claim victory, whether measured in converts, plaudits of the press, or votes of partisans present. Often, each party both won and lost, tangibly and intangibly. J. D. TANT, a veteran of more than 200 debates by 1931, claimed that "four people will go to a debate where one will attend a meeting," and that the number of converts from debating was "500 per cent" greater than other means provided. Others were not so sure. Already success, affluence, formal education, and movement along the sect-to-denomination continuum had diminished the frequency and appeal of debates. One might doubt the validity of another's religious beliefs, but one did not wish to alienate a potential customer for goods or services. Motion pictures, radio, and finally, television cut into the enthusiastic audiences for religious controversy. In some circles, a young evangelist must still earn spurs in debate, but major clashes among sectarian groups are increasingly rare. The energy once devoted to airing of doctrinal differences is now channeled into televised assaults against social and political targets.

See also articles on LANDMARK MOVEMENT; RATIONALISM, RELIGIOUS.

DON HAYMES
MACON, GEORGIA

DECLARATION AND ADDRESS: *See* CHURCHES OF CHRIST.

DENOMINATIONALISM. The timing of the settlement of North America against the backdrop of religious developments taking place in Europe illuminates a great deal. We see this more clearly by considering such questions as: What if Jamestown or Plymouth had occurred in 1507 or 1550 or 1580? What if the settlement had been by Germans or the French or Scandinavians?

Only in England was denominationalism advanced, that is, there were several different namings of the one religion. However, that was not the case there effectively until after 1580 or even 1610, by which time there were Protestants who went by the names of Anglican, Presbyterian, Congregational, and Baptist, in addition to the Roman Catholics. There existed the "papistical" church, The Church (of England), and a few Protestant bodies. Cutting across the nation's religious life was a spirit or outlook called PURITANISM.

Perhaps denominationalism was an accomplished fact (if somewhat proleptically) as early as the 1560s. Elizabeth wanted to disturb nothing and no one, only to assure the unity and welfare of the realm; so a kind of toleration prevailed. The DISSENTERS or Nonconformists cared little about such niceties as government policy, however. Like true revolutionaries they pursued their own ends, scarcely noting other signals. Something roughly comparable was happening in Switzerland and Germany, but England was the place from which the American "denominational society" took both its origins and its propensities.

The English men and women who settled the South were Church of England (q.v., ANGLICAN CHURCH), mostly in the Puritan style. For both internal and external reasons, nevertheless, that social/religious condition bore the seeds of denominational proliferation. "Puritan style" meant a degree of subjectivism, or a claim to and reliance upon personal experience; it also meant a determination to be free to be "right." Further, it meant a somewhat relaxed attitude toward conformity. "Church of England" in a wilderness society meant that all the supports and conventions on which a society's "approved" church must rest were miss-

ing. Establishment was the law and the assumption for more than a century and a half, but the situation argued poorly for it from the beginning.

The New England story beckons our attention by its difference from the English experience. But the career of religion in the South got off to a more different start yet. And although it has veered from its own initial course, it has picked its own distinctive path ever since; so much so that the religion of the South puzzles Western people generally, not least other Americans.

During the 17th century, the Anglican denomination of Christianity (q.v., ANGLICANISM) predominated. It was the official church of Virginia, Maryland (after 1701), Carolina, and Georgia. ROMAN CATHOLICISM was the only Christian version among the few Europeans living in La Florida and was embraced by some Indians. The ROMAN CATHOLIC CHURCH was the church of the founders of Maryland and persisted as a considerable force in that colony (and later, state). Some Congregationalists (q.v., CONGREGATIONALISM) from New England brought their version of the faith with them to southeastern Virginia in the 1690s. During that same decade Baptists (q.v., BAPTIST DENOMINATION) from Maine found their way to the South Carolina coastal area. Earlier, and indeed very early in their history (q.v., QUAKERISM), QUAKERS settled in northeastern North Carolina, an area in which they were to rank first for a half century. Presbyterians from Scotland (q.v., PRESBYTERIAN DENOMINATION) turned up in the upper Cape Fear section of the same colony, but some Presbyterian work antedated their efforts on the Eastern Shore of Maryland and Virginia around 1700. Scotch-Irish Presbyterians became a formidable population in western Virginia and North Carolina and upstate South Carolina from the 1740s. German Protestant bodies gathered in the following places: the Shenandoah territory of Virginia from the 1750s—Baptists and Anabaptists (q.v.,

ANABAPTISM); the western piedmont of North Carolina about the same time—Lutherans (q.v., LUTHERANISM) and Evangelicals; various sites across South Carolina—Lutherans (q.v., LUTHERAN CHURCH). Predictably for a vast frontier territory, there were strays of almost all possible persuasions scattered here and there. (At the same time, the number of "persuasions" was not yet very large.)

Methodist influence (q.v., WESLEYAN TRADITION) was felt in the South before there was a METHODIST CHURCH. In Maryland and Virginia, evangelical doctrines and preaching succeeded in gaining hearings and winning converts; in addition, Church of England ministers found themselves less Anglican and more Methodist. In the Southern city of Baltimore, the new denomination took formal shape at the CHRISTMAS CONFERENCE, 1784. It was to be the South's most prominent—not to mention America's—for more than a half century. (It continues in second place in Dixie and as the largest communion of Christians elsewhere.) Soon it would attract black Southerners as well as whites.

As part of the same shift from established to free, from liturgical and sacramental to experiential, the Baptist people emerged. Whereas those who lived in the South earlier had been few in number and given largely to minding their own business, the Baptists who invaded the South from Connecticut in the 1750s considered the eternal destiny and spiritual condition of nearly everyone very much their business—indeed, the Lord's commission SEPARATE BAPTISTS changed the face of the upper seaboard South, about all of a South there was before independence. Together with their co-Evangelicals of the Wesleyan character, they walked and rode, preached and taught, invigorating a territory where most of the population needed even the barest introduction to the faith and to personal faith.

Thus by the 1790s white Methodists and white Baptists made up the largest religious groups. Presbyterians were a solid third, but the EPISCOPAL CHURCH (formerly Church of England) lagged poorly. Most others were small in population—whether they were black Protestants by any name, or Quakers, Lutherans, Catholics, or others—although several enjoyed localized strength in size and influence. THE GREAT REVIVAL in the years around 1800 symbolized and produced the patterns that have characterized the region ever since. The Baptist cause grew greatly; so did the Methodist. This was true among the region's whites and, as a fresh feature, also verifiable among blacks. They were joined by the DISCIPLES OF CHRIST of the CAMPBELLITE TRADITION (dedicated to the restoration of New Testament Christianity). This group was fully developed by the 1830s but with origins tracing to the years around 1800, in the supplanting of European-descended names and styles in favor of American, and even frontier American versions of Christianity. Vital piety, strong convictions, authority-based doctrines, local polity, aggressive evangelistic activities—these were the stuff of which popular regional forms were composed, in varying blends. Even some Presbyterians got into this act, including the Cumberland people of western Tennessee and Kentucky (q.v., CUMBERLAND PRESBYTERIAN CHURCH).

Catholics survived the evangelical assault on the region but enjoyed strength in limited areas of Kentucky, Missouri, Alabama, Louisiana, and Texas. Jews (q.v., JEWS IN THE SOUTH) had moved into Charleston, Norfolk, Richmond, Nashville, and New Orleans, in fact, were limited to these places by midcentury. Of them, it also can be said that they withstood the new waves, and managed to retain their historic identity.

The immigration of central Europeans, mostly Germans, into the western border states altered the character of Louisville, St. Louis, the Kentucky suburbs of Cincinnati, and a few other places. Otherwise the biggest news of the third quarter of the century was the formation of separate black organizations (q.v., BLACK RELIGION). Titles such as Baptist and Methodist remained the same in these organizations. Soon the Colored (now CHRISTIAN) METHODIST EPISCOPAL CHURCH extended the much older ministries of the AFRICAN METHODIST EPISCOPAL CHURCH and AFRICAN METHODIST EPISCOPAL ZION CHURCH. Baptist successes among the recently freed people were even more impressive. Literally within days blacks were organizing congregations, especially Baptist ones that were founded out of the sheer will to do so, given the Baptist understanding of local-church independence. Late in the century two black Baptist denominations took shape, the National Baptist Convention of America and the National Baptist Convention, United States of America, Inc. (q.v., NATIONAL BAPTISTS). The South's black population was thoroughly churched by the evangelistic efforts of the two largest white denominations before the Civil War and by its own initiatives over the following three decades.

Thus before 1900 the basic contours of Southern religious life had been mapped out. There were Baptists, white and black, all over the region; similarly, Methodists settled in the region and were represented by both races. Presbyterians (q.v., PRESBYTERIAN CHURCH IN THE UNITED STATES) continued to be quite strong in some localized areas and socially influential wherever they had congregations, mostly in towns and cities throughout the South. A comparable description applies to the Southern Episcopal presence, deployment, and strength. The Roman Catholic Church was notable wherever Catholics lived, in selected cities and towns to which immigrants were coming and that were historic Catholic locations: e.g., Maryland, Louisiana, Texas, and west-south-central Kentucky. Much the same can be said for the Southern Jewish population, although some Jews and Jewish families were moving into small towns. Congregationalists functioned largely as an ethnic community, their presence limited to a few places. The like was true for Lutherans, Mennonites, Moravians (q.v., MORAVIAN CHURCH), other German left-wing Protestant groups, Quakers, Unitarians (q.v., UNITARIAN-UNIVERSALIST ASSOCIATION), and some others.

The 15 years on either side of 1900 were to usher in quite new factors, however. The least "new" factor was the recognition in 1906 of the CHURCHES OF CHRIST as a separate member of the Campbellite family. In fact, distinctively regional versions of the RESTORATION MOVEMENT were being formed before the Civil War. These Southern "Disciples" were building their own strong tradition around non-instrumental music and opposition to missionary societies throughout the 1880s and 1890s. Then came 1906.

In addition, the Pentecostal movement (q.v., PENTECOSTALISM) and the HOLINESS MOVEMENT came into being in the 1890s for a couple of decades. Within time, these sects appeared: PENTECOSTAL-HOLINESS CHURCH; ASSEMBLIES OF GOD; CHURCH OF GOD (CLEVELAND TN); CHURCH OF GOD IN CHRIST; and others, many of them quite small and more than a few in the territories of the Appalachian and Ozarks mountains (q.v., APPALACHIAN RELIGION, OZARKS RELIGION). All of them stood in judgment on the controlled, reasonable, and low-intensity traits of the traditional denominations. Instead they practiced belief in the ready and near-total accessibility of the Holy Spirit. Directly, the Pentecostal emphasis fell on Spirit possession with speaking in unknown tongues and the Holiness on the radical sanctification of the Christian's life toward spiritual perfection. Popular among black people as well as white, these sects spread to all parts of the South.

A mapping of Dixie's religious demography in 1920 is, therefore, a bit different from what we saw for 1890.

However, to most white Southerners, the new bodies were viewed as eccentric collections of Christians not to be taken very seriously since they comprised the lower classes and such social misfits as blacks and mountaineers. All of that had changed in the 1970s and 1980s, owing partly to the spread of Pentecostal, holiness, and fundamentalist (q.v., FUNDAMENTALISM)—in general, Evangelical (q.v., EVANGELICAL PROTESTANTISM, EVANGELICALISM)—approaches to Christianity. They also made appeal to the higher classes of people, and also to the newly found social standing and political clout of sectors of the population hitherto marginal at best.

In the 1920s, the SOUTHERN BAPTIST CONVENTION took the direction it has been famous for ever since; namely, highly centralized in organization; large, aggressive, and rapidly growing; self-aware and somewhat exclusivist without being hostile toward prevailing social customs and institutions. In 1939, the METHODIST EPISCOPAL CHURCH, SOUTH, turned its back on 95 years of regional isolation from American Methodism at large. The reunion resulted in the Methodist Episcopal Church. Forty-four years later, Southern and Northern Presbyterians reached the same position after 122 years of regional separation. The new body, the Presbyterian Church, U.S.A., will be legally constituted in 1987. The Southern Baptists continue in their same status, without national ties. The Episcopal Church divided into Confederate and national bodies for four years, only practicing their sense of catholic churchmanship again in 1865. All of the large regional constituencies now participate in the National Council of Churches, including the Disciples of Christ, except the Southern Baptists, the Churches of Christ, and the numerous Pentecostal, holiness, fundamentalist, and other evangelical sects, most of which are relatively small.

True Fundamentalism exists in the South but is considered societally deviant. The Bob Jones (q.v., BOB JONES FAMILY)

orbit of influence is of moderate size and fairly widely distributed. Similar in aspect to this is the BAPTIST BIBLE FELLOWSHIP (Springfield MO). Actually, most movements of this kind flourish better in west-of-the-Mississippi soil. But all over the South independent churches have sprung up, most of them Baptist and many of them in small-to-large cities. Not denominationally affiliated, they rely on a "charismatic" pastor (often the founder) and a combination of skillful organization and congregational folksiness that smacks of traditional small-town and rural Southern ways.

In 1983, the largest religious organizations are: the Southern Baptist Convention; the United Methodist Church; the Churches of Christ; the Presbyterian Church, U. S. Black Baptists belonging to three organized bodies run into the millions. Illuminating the distinctiveness of the Southern scene is the list of groups of small-to-very-small size: Lutherans; Roman Catholics; MORMONS; Congregationalists; and Jews.

Southern denominationalism may be summarized as very strong in the evangelical Protestant column (Baptists, Methodists, and sect groups), of moderate strength in the Reformation camp (Presbyterians mostly, with some few Lutherans), of nominal strength in the Liturgical Protestantism category (Episcopalians), and weak in Liberal Protestantism, Radical Protestantism (Anabaptists), Roman Catholicism, and Judaism. Black people's versions of Christianity are strong, of course, and are related to the evangelical tradition. This deployment of groups is not really paralleled by any other society within Western civilization.

See also articles on BLACK RELIGION; HOLINESS MOVEMENT.

Bibliography. Samuel S. Hill, ed.,"A Survey of Southern Religious History," *Religion in the Southern States*; Winthrop S. Hudson, "Denominationalism as a Basis for Ecumenicity: A Seventeenth Century Conception," *Church History* 24 (January 1955): 32-50.

SAMUEL S. HILL
UNIVERSITY OF FLORIDA

DEPUTIES. In the Episcopal Church, these are the delegates chosen by each diocese to represent it in the House of Deputies, which with the House of Bishops constitutes the General Convention (the Church's highest legislative assembly). Each diocesan delegation consists of four clerical deputies (priests) and four lay deputies. Legislation must be approved by both houses of the General Convention. Often the House of Deputies gives or withholds its approval of a particular measure in a vote by orders, which requires that clerical deputies and lay deputies be polled separately and that a majority vote be obtained in each order for the House to pass the measure being considered.

HERBERT S. WENTZ
UNIVERSITY OF THE SOUTH

DEVIL, THE: *See* HELL.

DIOCESE. In the Episcopal Church and the Roman Catholic Church, this is the territorial and administrative unit served by a bishop acting in his own name and not as a delegate of another. (The unit is similar to the conference or synod in some other churches that also have the office of bishop.) The name of the diocese historically has been that of the city in which the bishop has his seat (still the Roman Catholic practice), though the Episcopal Church usually designates the diocese by the state or portion thereof with which it is coextensive.

A diocese is divided into parishes (in the Episcopal Church, also missions), each of which consists of a church building and congregation in the charge of a priest. The actual governance of the diocese and the administration of its affairs and institutions are determined by canon and are not always identical in the Episcopal Church and the Roman Catholic Church.

HERBERT S. WENTZ
UNIVERSITY OF THE SOUTH

DISCIPLES OF CHRIST. It is a body of Protestant Christians that emerged in the early years of the 19th century as an American religious movement that both reflected and shaped the ethos of that era. The movement came primarily from Presbyterian and Baptist antecedents and experienced its greatest growth and influence in Virginia, West Virginia, North Carolina, Kentucky, Tennessee, Ohio, Illinois, Missouri, Texas, and Oklahoma.

The name Disciples of Christ was first used by followers of Thomas (1763-1854) and ALEXANDER CAMPBELL (1788-1866), father and son, who emigrated from northern Ireland as Presbyterians in 1807 and 1809. Thomas Campbell was received as a minister in the Associate Synod of North America upon his arrival and assigned to Washington PA. He quickly fell into controversy over doctrine and church order with others in the presbytery and withdrew from the jurisdiction of the denomination in 1809. Campbell's simultaneous withdrawal from and expulsion by the Associate Synod led to the formation of the Christian Association of Washington. For this association, formed by Campbell and several of his former parishioners and conceived as an agency to propagate ideas of Christian cooperation, Campbell penned a *Declaration and Address*, which presented the principles of the association and subsequently of the Disciples of Christ. Central themes included the right of private judgment, the sole authority of the Bible in matters of religion, the evil of sectarianism, and the appeal for a restoration of biblical institutions and practices as a basis for Christian unity.

Just as the *Declaration* was finished, Alexander Campbell arrived in America with his own reservations about Presbyterian polity and practices and eagerly joined his father in the new program of religious reform. The Christian Association constituted itself as a church in 1811, chose Thomas Campbell as elder, and licensed the younger Campbell to preach. This new congregation celebrated communion weekly and early adopted the practice of believer's baptism by immersion. It scoffed at hireling clergy and pressed the Protestant principle of the priesthood of all believers much further than most groups. Because of similarities with Baptist churches, the Reformers or Disciples of Christ associated themselves with the Baptists in 1815. However, the relationship was never without tension and the new movement grew within but was not entirely a part of the Baptist denomination. In 1830 the relationship was dissolved.

Alexander Campbell married in 1811 and settled on his father-in-law's farm at Buffaloe in Brooke County VA, a few miles west of Washington PA. There, at a site renamed BETHANY (WV), Campbell published *The Christian Baptist* (1823-1830) and *The Millennial Harbinger* (1830-1866), periodicals that served to unite and direct an inchoate group of followers in congregationally governed churches into a coherent religious movement. Though the younger Campbell quickly emerged as the driving personality in the movement, themes enunciated by the father in the *Declaration and Address* remained normative.

The movement stressed freedom from all nonbiblical authority and Christian unity to be achieved through a restoration of the forms and practices of primitive Christianity. The New Testament, particularly the book of Acts, was regarded as the model for ecclesiology and theology. Hence all divisive names were repudiated for the name Disciple or Christian, all postbiblical ecclesiological developments were repudiated for simple congregationalism, and the ecumenical creeds were rejected as tests of orthodoxy and fellowship for biblical formulas. Membership was extended to those confessing Jesus to be the Christ and accepting his commands. Though Disciples of Christ were concerned with the moral teachings of Scripture and maintained congregational discipline, their primary interest was in those dominical commands relating to the organization and governance of the church.

They rejected Calvinism as an extrabiblical system. Like many others in the early nineteenth century, Disciples objected to Calvinism's tendency to emphasize divine sovereignty at the expense of human freedom. Disciples insisted that faith is a response to testimony and is a rational act. Faith leads to repentance and obedience and these to forgiveness and the gift of the Spirit. Thus, though they were active evangelists, there was a distinctly rationalistic character to their preaching. Disciples believed that their teachings were exclusively biblical and therefore provided a platform on which all Christians, regardless of denomination, might unite.

A second group that became part of the Disciples of Christ movement emerged from Kentucky Presbyterianism in the aftermath of the revivals of the turn of the century. The Western revivals had a profoundly unsettling effect and stimulated denominational tension as well as a heightened religious interest. Following the CANE RIDGE Camp Meeting in Bourbon County KY in August 1801, the Presbyterian clergy found itself deeply divided and charges were brought against some of the New Lights (revivalists) who had clearly deviated from Calvinist orthodoxy. The New Lights avoided synodical examination by withdrawal and formed an independent Springfield Presbytery in 1803. The anomaly of their situation was apparent, and in 1804 this group dissolved their presbytery, thereby leaving their congregations independent of one another. In a published apology, the Last Will and Testament of Springfield Presbytery (SPRINGFIELD WILL AND TESTAMENT), the New Lights repudiated presbyterial government, ecclesiastical titles, and extrabiblical authority. They advocated congregational polity, biblical study as preparation for ministry, scriptural preaching, and Christian unity on a biblical basis. The similarity of their platform to that of Thomas Campbell's *Declaration* is striking.

The group signing this *Last Will and Testament* adopted the name Christian for the new movement. Though some of the original group eventually became Shakers and others returned to the Presbyterian church, the new Christian church grew in Kentucky and spread southward and westward with migration. BARTON W. STONE, the one founder who remained in the Christian church, gave leadership to the movement; and its unity was strengthened by the *Christian Messenger*, which Stone began to publish in 1826. Stone's theological views were similar to those of the Campbells, but his rejection of Calvinism was more thorough. Even at the time of his ordination, Stone had been troubled by the doctrine of the trinity. He subsequently repudiated this doctrine along with Calvinist views of the atonement.

Thus two similar religious movements, the Disciples and the Christians, emerged in the early years of the 19th century. By 1830 when the Disciples severed their Baptist association, congregations of the two movements existed in close proximity to one another. Meetings in Georgetown and Lexington KY in 1831 and 1832 led to a gradual union of the two groups. Both were congregationally governed and the merger therefore proceeded slowly and with considerable controversy. Though Stone's enthusiasm for union was great, many of the Christian churches remained apart and formed the Christian Connexion. Nonetheless, the majority of congregations entered the union, and the resultant denomination grew to a membership of about 200,000 by the outbreak of the Civil War.

The Disciples of Christ were a people of America no less than of the Book. Their reading of Scripture reflected repudiation of the sectarianism and establishmentarianism of the old world and millennial hopes for the new. Their preaching emphasized freedom, equality, responsibility, and a hope that God's blessings would fall abundantly on a people whose lives, churches, schools, and government were founded on faith in Christ. Their quest for unity discouraged attention to such potentially divisive issues as slavery, and their congregational polity made possible considerable sectional variety in social ideas, preaching styles, and religious practices.

While the first generation of Disciples was held together by charismatic leadership and religious journals, bureaucratic structure began to emerge in the 1830s with the formation of state associations for evangelism; and in 1849 a national association, the American Christian Missionary Society, was formed to support home and foreign missions. Even though Alexander Campbell was chosen president, a national association inevitably proved fractious during a period of sectionalism that would culminate in the Civil War. While most Disciples opposed slavery on moral or economic grounds, they professed to find biblical sanctions for the institution and rarely expressed sympathy for abolitionism. Yet although most Disciples preferred unity to clarity, small groups of the high zealous and abolitionists determined to use the society as a platform on which a denominational position could be established. Though the denomination did not divide at this time, the society greatly intensified sectionalism. A resolution adopted by the society in 1863 in the absence of representatives from the South endorsed the Union cause and alienated Southern Disciples, thereby laying the foundation for a denominational schism at the end of the century. The CHURCHES OF CHRIST, first enumerated separately from Disciples of Christ in the 1906 census, objected to the use of missionary societies and of instrumental music in worship on the grounds that these practices are not commanded in Scripture. However, virtually all of the churches of the new denomination lay in the states of the Confederacy, and the roots of the division were found in the period of war and reconstruction.

Repudiation of theological study had profound effects on Disciple education. Though Alexander Campbell wrote a theology, *The Christian System*, he advocated the study of the Bible as the basis for both liberal arts and ministerial education. His own Bethany College, founded in 1840, was forbidden by charter from offering instruction in theology, even though study of the Bible was central to the curriculum. While Bethany remained the most important Disciple school until the Civil War, Lexington later emerged as a center for ministerial education. There the College of the Bible (now Lexington Theological Seminary) followed the Campbellian tradition and used the Bible as its principal textbook. Other Disciple schools of prominence in the South include Phillips, Texas Christian, and Transylvania universities.

In the late nineteenth-century transformation of America, Disciples moved with the population to the South and West and to the industrial centers of the Midwest. Some Disciples adapted to the more cosmopolitan and pluralistic character of urban American society while others held firmly to the ways of an older, simpler, more agrarian society; and many sought to live in both worlds. Disciples thus came into conflict with one another over the use of instrumental music in worship and missionary societies in the work of the church and the admission of unimmersed members by transfer from other denominations. They also struggled to assess the significance of Darwinism and biblical criticism for religious life. To many Disciples it appeared that their traditional appeal for Christian unity through the restoration of primitive Christianity was no longer viable. While a few liberal Disciples were willing to reject restoration as a platform and move forthrightly into the modern ecumenical movement and while the Churches of Christ insisted upon a platform of restorationism at the cost of alienation from other Christian churches, most Disciples sought a middle ground. Gradually liberal-

ism and ecumenism triumphed among them, but few were willing to admit their virtual repudiation of the restoration platform prior to the middle of the 20th century.

This admission was accompanied by another major division as many conservative churches withdrew from fellowship and institutional cooperation. These churches maintain a strict congregational polity but meet for consultation and fellowship in the North American Christian Convention, and they call themselves CHRISTIAN CHURCHES AND CHURCHES OF CHRIST. Though this division was gradual after 1927, it was completed in the aftermath of Disciple denominational restructure in 1968.

Disciple reluctance to grant titles and preferential status to clergy made the denomination particularly susceptible to demands for the education and ordination of women. Many Disciple colleges were coeducational from the beginning, and Bethany College admitted women in 1880. Women studied at the College of the Bible after 1895. Several women were ordained to the ministry in the late nineteenth century and most opposition ceased with the 1906 withdrawal of Churches of Christ. However, the positions available to women ministers were and are usually distinctive and subordinate.

Though there were black members of early Disciple churches, few separate black congregations were formed. In 1860 there were probably no more than 7,000 black Disciples, a figure that had grown to about 48,000 by the end of the century. Since the 1960s most urban churches have come to accept the idea of a racially inclusive fellowship, but black Disciples remain few and largely concentrated in black congregations.

The Disciples of Christ were founding members of the Federal Council of Churches in 1908 and of the National and World Councils and through these bodies have sought to witness to their traditional plea for Christian unity. Working with representatives of diverse traditions has compelled Disciples to reassess some of their own practices, and the 20th century has witnessed many changes. Disciples have developed an understanding of the role of theology in religion, and their seminaries today are ecumenically oriented and similar in curriculum to those of most Christian denominations. At their national assembly in 1968, Disciples adopted a Provisional Design for the Christian Church (Disciples of Christ), which provided a connectional polity by creating the offices of general minister, president, and moderator and establishing a biennial General Assembly of elected delegates, a general board, and an administrative committee. The character of Disciple missions has also changed in recent years with the growth of emphasis on cooperative work, on shared responsibilities, and on the development of indigenous leadership.

At the end of 1979 there were 1,217,747 Disciples in the United States and Canada (776,378 active members) organized in 3,746 congregations. An American-born religious movement, the Disciples of Christ reflect in their own development the transformation of American thought and society in the 19th and 20th centuries.

See also articles on CAMPBELLITE TRADITION; RATIONALISM, RELIGIOUS; RESTORATIONISM.

Bibliography. W. B. Blakemore, ed., *The Renewal of Church*; W. E. Garrison, *Alexander Campbell's Theology; Religion Follows the Frontier: A History of the Disciples of Christ*; Garrison and A. T. DeGroot, *The Disciples of Christ: A History*; David E. Harrell, Jr., *Quest for a Christian America*; William E. Tucker and Lester G. McAllister, *Journey in Faith: A History of the Christian Church (Disciples of Christ)*; Charles A. Young, ed., *Historical Documents Advocating Christian Union*.

SAMUEL C. PEARSON
SOUTHERN ILLINOIS UNIVERSITY
AT EDWARDSVILLE

DISESTABLISHMENT. The unique contribution of the 13 American colonies to the cause of religious freedom and separation of church and state did not occur suddenly. European countries assumed that unity of religion was essential to the unity of the state and each had its national church. This idea was evident in 9 of the 13 American colonies where established churches existed in 1775. In Massachusetts, Connecticut, and New Hampshire the Congregational Church was established. Maryland, Virginia, North Carolina, South Carolina, Georgia, New York City, and three neighboring counties had established the Church of England. With the Declaration of Independence in 1776 and the formation of new state governments, the disestablishment of state churches occurred in a number of states between 1776 and 1789, and eventually took place in all.

In America religious liberty had been won early by a number of minorities. Roger Williams in Rhode Island sought complete separation of church and state and made it a cardinal principle. Quakers and Jews who were also seeking to found communities in which people with diverse religious views could live together were received in Rhode Island. Moreover, most of the 13 colonies had been founded by proprietors, e.g., Lord Baltimore and William Penn, which meant they were able to welcome persecuted sects. These conditions necessarily produced a form of toleration even in colonies where an established church existed. The GREAT AWAKENING of the mid-eighteenth century weakened the hold of the Anglican establishments from Maryland southward as well as the Congregational establishments in New England. By the time of the War for Independence much of the population was without church affiliation and thus disposed to be hostile to the privileged position of established churches.

The fact that the American religious experience had been pluralistic contributed significantly to disestablishment while at the same time promoting religious liberty. To cite an example, in Virginia the combined efforts of liberal statesmen like THOMAS JEFFERSON and

JAMES MADISON and the Baptists secured disestablishment in 1786. Presbyterians, Lutherans, and Methodists came to support disestablishment of the Anglican Church in Virginia. Disestablishment was achieved in North Carolina and Maryland in 1776, in New York in 1777, and partially in Georgia (completed in 1789). South Carolina disestablished the Church of England in 1778 and the Christian Protestant religion in 1790. In New England, the Baptists were joined by Methodists and Episcopalians to bring about disestablishment. Aided by a growing liberal element within Congregationalism, the religious establishments were ended in Connecticut in 1818, New Hampshire in 1819, and Massachusetts in 1833.

See also articles on ANGLICAN CHURCH; CHURCH AND STATE.

Bibliography. Sydney E. Ahlstrom, *A Religious History of the American People*; Evarts B. Green, *Religion and the State*; A. P. Stokes and Leo Pfeffer, *Church and State in the United States.*

FREDERICK V. MILLS, SR.
LA GRANGE COLLEGE

DISSENTERS. These were people who refused to adhere to the Church of England after the Elizabethan religious settlement of 1559. Initially the word was applied to Roman Catholics and Puritans. The Puritans in particular were influenced by the continental Reformation and wished for a more radical reform of doctrine and ritual within the established Church. Some who became known as Separatists (later called Brownists and still later Congregationalists) were subjected to persecution; many went into exile in the Netherlands. After the Puritans failed to win King James I to their point of view in 1604, they were confronted with conforming to the Church of England or being exiled through harassment. King James was equally adamant toward Presbyterians. From among these Puritan groups emerged the Pilgrims, who left England and founded Plymouth Colony in 1620 in New England.

During the period of the Civil War and Commonwealth (1642-1660) there was a rapid growth of sectarian groups, including Quakers, who dissented from the Church of England. Because there was toleration during this period, except for Roman Catholics, dissenters were not persecuted. After the restoration of Charles Stuart as Charles II in 1660 and the reestablishment of the Church of England, those who did not accept the Thirty-nine Articles and the sacraments were called Nonconformists. Clergy who had received appointments during the Commonwealth were required to accept the Thirty-nine Articles and receive ordination in the Church of England or forfeit their positions. About 2,000 Presbyterians, Independents, and Baptists were ejected and many migrated to the New World. The Act of Religious Toleration of 1689 allowed Nonconformists places of worship and their own preachers subject to legal limitations, but Roman Catholics and Unitarians were not included.

In the English colonies in the New World, the Church of England was established by law from Maryland through Georgia. Those who did not adhere to the established Church were dissenters, and like the Nonconformists in England they were permitted places of worship and their own preachers upon securing a license from the royal governor. Nevertheless, they were required to support the established church and maintain their own meetings or conventicles by voluntary gifts. It was this system of state religion that became a major source of tension between Baptists, Presbyterians, Independents, etc., and Anglicans in the Southern colonies in the years preceding the American Revolution. During the Revolutionary War period all the Southern colonies took steps to disestablish the Church of England with Virginia completing the process in 1786. This meant that any legal distinction between churchman and dissenter was ended and that all religious bodies were equal before the law and supported solely by the contributions of their own members. In New England where the dissenters had established the

Congregational Church, the separation process for church and state was not completed until 1833.

See also articles on DISESTABLISHMENT; ESTABLISHED RELIGION.

Bibliography. D. Coomer, *English Dissent Under the Early Hanoverians*; William Haller, *Liberty and Reformation in the Puritan Revolution*; E. Routley, *English Religious Dissent.*

FREDERICK V. MILLS, SR.
LAGRANGE COLLEGE

DISTRICT. A district is the smallest geographical area into which connectional churches, like the various Methodist bodies, are divided. A district usually consists of about 50 local congregations and is administered by a superintendent, an ordained elder appointed to this office by a bishop. Most Annual Conferences in the United Methodist Church are divided into about 10 districts.

Districts have no legislative or administrative authority. Rather, they are designed as instruments for implementing the programs and policies developed by the Annual, Jurisdictional, and General Conferences. Districts normally do not have their own institutions such as colleges, hospitals, and homes for the aged, yet they may be active in establishing new congregations and in carrying out various short-term programs such as summer camping and other educational experiences.

Annual or semiannual meetings may be held for purposes of inspiration and promotion. Such meetings will be directed by the superintendent and will be attended by lay and ministerial leaders from the local congregations within the district.

Districts were originally developed in American Methodism as groups of preaching appointees to be served by the presiding elder or those local and traveling preachers under his supervision, but are now promotional units within the Annual Conference.

JOSEPH MITCHELL
TROY STATE UNIVERSITY

DIXON, A(MZI) C(LARENCE) (1854-1925), a widely traveled fundamentalist pastor-evangelist, was born in Shelby NC. He preached and served with great intensity in the South, the North, and England. He was a frequent speaker in the Bible Conference movement and in evangelistic services and took a prominent role in the early days of the fundamentalist-modernist controversy.

Graduated with highest honors in 1874 from Wake Forest College, he attended Southern Baptist Theological Seminary for one year when it was located at Greenville SC. At the age of 29 he declined an invitation to the presidency of Wake Forest College, choosing instead a career of pastoral evangelism. After early pastorates in four North Carolina communities, he served the following churches: Immanuel Baptist Church, Baltimore MD (1882-1890); Hanson Place Baptist Church, Brooklyn NY (1890-1901); Ruggles Street Baptist Church, Boston MA (1901-1906); Moody Church, Chicago (1906-1911); Metropolitan Tabernacle, London (1911-1919); and following evangelistic and Bible Conference work, University Baptist Church, Baltimore (1921-1925).

Dixon's goal was to reach the largest number of people for Christ in the most effective way. Like other Fundamentalists he rejected the SOCIAL GOSPEL, including the dispensing of charity, believing that it was easier to reach a person's body through the soul than the soul through the body. Unlike most fundamentalists, he was a pacifist; however, when World War I broke out he felt that every person should be required to serve his country in some way. His pacifism did not prevent him from being frequently engaged in religious controversy with Robert Ingersoll; sect-cult groups, especially the Christian Scientists; and theological liberals, such as William R. Harper of the University of Chicago.

Inspired by one of Dixon's sermons at a conference in Los Angeles, Lyman Stewart, a wealthy Californian, provided

Dixon with funds for the publishing of *The Fundamentals: A Testimony to the Truth.* This was a set of 12 booklets (1910-1915) by a galaxy of religious leaders from the United States, Canada, and Great Britain, setting forth the great theological issues of the day from a conservative standpoint. Some three million copies of these booklets were distributed, contributing largely to the beginning of FUNDAMENTALISM as an aggressive religious movement. As testimony to the complexity of his life and career, on the occasion of his death, the *Baltimore Sun* referred to him editorially as "a curious complex of breadth and narrowness, of pacifism and belligerency . . . [possessing] a splendid sincerity that even devils must have respected."

See also article on MODERNIST CONTROVERSY.

Bibliography. Helen A. C. Dixon, *A. C. Dixon: A Romance of Preaching*; George W. Dollar, *A History of Fundamentalism in America*; Ernest R. Sandeen, *The Roots of Fundamentalism: British and American Millenarianism, 1800-1930.*

C. ALLYN RUSSELL
BOSTON UNIVERSITY

DIXON, THOMAS, JR. (1864-1946),

literary figure and minister, was born in Cleveland County NC. On his father's side, he sprang from the pioneering Scotch-Irish who settled in the foothills of the Blue Ridge Mountains before the American Revolution and fought on the patriotic side in the battle of King's Mountain. Tom Dixon's father, Thomas Dixon Sr., was locally eminent as a Baptist minister even as a young man.

For a time after Tom's birth, the Dixons lived on a farm near Shelby. In 1865, they moved into the village, where Mr. Dixon opened a store to supplement his meager income as a minister. Like so many Southerners in those difficult years of Reconstruction, the Dixons labored strenuously for a bare subsistence. Tom worked long and hard in the fields, later declaring that he came to hate the dulling drudgery of agricultural labor.

Tom Dixon was educated at home and in the Shelby Academy. In 1879 he followed the path that his older brother, A(MZI) C(LARENCE) DIXON, had blazed to Wake Forest College. At Wake Forest, Tom distinguished himself as a scholar and orator, winning the highest honors ever attained in that eminent Baptist school. Tom's academic achievements earned him a scholarship to attend graduate school in the recently established Johns Hopkins University in Baltimore. In the fall of 1883, he enrolled in the seminar offered by Professor Herbert Baxter Adams. One of his classmates was another young Southerner, WOODROW WILSON.

In Baltimore, Tom Dixon became enamoured of the stage. Within a few months, he deserted graduate school and moved to New York, determined to become an actor. In college, Tom had established himself as a brilliant speaker, but bitter and prolonged experience finally persuaded him to abandon his ambitions in the theater. He returned to Shelby and began to read law. In 1884, before he was yet 21, he was elected to the North Carolina House of Representatives. He later claimed to have participated in the shaping of the first bill to propose pensions for Confederate veterans. After the session, he was admitted to the bar, practiced for a time in Shelby, and married Harriet Bussey, an Alabamian. Dixon soon found law practice frustrating, and after much soul-searching, he resolved to follow his father and older brother into the ministry. Ordained, he took churches in Goldsboro and Raleigh. Quickly gaining fame, he moved to Boston, and in 1889 to New York. In New York, he soon earned a reputation as an advocate of the SOCIAL GOSPEL because of his activities for political, economic, and social reform.

In 1895 Dixon left the Baptist denomination to become an independent minister. Meanwhile, he had become a very popular lecturer, junketing throughout the country, speaking night after night upon various secular subjects, earning as much as a thousand dollars for a single performance. During the late 1890s, Dixon had also established a home in Virginia. He bought Elmington Manor, a beautiful colonial estate on the banks of the lower Rappahanock. There he became a gentleman farmer and a yachtsman, while maintaining both his ministry in New York and his lecturing.

In 1901 Dixon happened to attend a performance of the long-running play *Uncle Tom's Cabin.* Incensed by what he took to be a gross libel of the South, he resolved to write an answer. For a year, he gathered material and finally took 60 days to write what became the novel, *The Leopard's Spots.* The book was a twin plea for the exclusion of blacks from American society and for a reunion of North and South. It was a tremendous success, selling more than a million copies.

Though never abandoning his title of "Reverend," thereafter Dixon was most famous as a novelist. *The Leopard's Spots* was soon followed by two other novels, both arguing dramatically for recognition of the retrogression of blacks in America and for the union of whites North and South. In 1905 he translated one of these into the play *The Clansman.* It being a great success, Dixon proceeded to write, direct, and act in others. In 1913, he agreed to allow a moving picture company headed by David W. Griffith to make the play into a film. In 1915, the production was premiered as *The Birth of a Nation,* and it too was a success, at least financially. While Dixon was writing the "trilogy" on race, he was also writing a trilogy of novels attacking socialism. These were followed by more than a score of books. The last, *The Flaming Sword,* was an attempt to alert America to the danger of Communist domination by way of the corruption of American blacks.

Thomas Dixon Jr.'s family was a most impressive one. Somehow between the stern, puritanical, and patriarchal father and the aristocratic, romantic mother, five gifted children were marked for distinction. In the year 1922, all five were included in *Who's Who.* Clarence gained international fame as a minister and evangelist in the Baptist denomination. Frank, like his father and his brothers, became a minister; in addition he was a popular figure on the lecture circuits. Delia, with financial and moral support from Thomas, became a pioneer woman physician in North Carolina. Addie Mae became a writer, a professional in public relations, and a cobiographer of Warren Gamaliel Harding.

Ever an adventurous, willful, driving person, Dixon fell upon hard times in his last years. During his life, he made at least three fortunes and lost them all. The money he made from his first books he lost on the stock and cotton exchanges in New York. His final venture in the late 1920s was a vacation resort, "Wildacres," in the mountains of western North Carolina. After spending a large amount of money on the development, the enterprise collapsed about him just as the Great Depression began. In 1937, the once affluent Dixon was appointed clerk of the federal court for the eastern district of North Carolina. His health failing and a widower, in 1939 he married the leading lady of one of his early films, Madelyn Donovan. Dixon lived in illness during his last years, the flashing intelligence still flickering through rising pain; he died at his home in Raleigh.

See also article on LITERATURE AND RELIGION.

JOEL WILLIAMSON
UNIVERSITY OF NORTH CAROLINA
AT CHAPEL HILL

DOCTOR. This is a title given to some ordained ministers either because they have finished a doctoral program of study or as an award for recognized services.

Since the end of World War II and the rise of unparalleled affluence in the United States, there has been a proliferation of ministers bearing the title of doctor in Southern churches as well as nationwide. Many of these are applied to clergy who, because of the general state of prosperity, have been able to set aside large blocks of personal time for schooling. This has also been encouraged by the establishment of many programs of academic work leading to doctoral degrees of various kinds, both in seminaries and in universities.

Seminaries have, for the most part, offered the professional Doctor of Theology degree. Lately many of them have instituted Doctor of Ministry programs, which are specifically focused on practice in the parish, hence attracting in-service ministers. Universities have established high-quality Doctor of Philosophy programs in religion and have sent graduates primarily into teaching, although some have also been parish clergy.

The honorary doctorate (usually cited as D.D. for "Doctor of Divinity") has also become increasingly common in recent years. Denominational colleges usually confer such degrees on pastors of prominent congregations in their state and often do so annually at their commencement exercises. Since many ministers now have doctorates, there is some pressure on members of the clergy to obtain them, especially if one aspires to a position of leadership in a major pulpit or within the life of his denomination.

WILLIAM C. SMITH, JR.
GREENSBORO, NORTH CAROLINA

DOW, LORENZO (1777–1834), celebrated Methodist evangelist of the frontier, was born in Coventry CT, the child of Humphrey Dean and Tabitha (Parker) Dow. He received religious training from his parents and from occasional itinerant preachers, and in 1794 began preaching himself.

From the very beginning Dow was an eccentric, if not fanatical, Methodist exhorter, so sure of his own calling that he could brook no interference from earthly authorities. In 1796 he was admitted to the Methodist circuit, but was suspended after three months, only to be readmitted in 1798. Whether an official Methodist or not, he drove himself mercilessly in preaching the Gospel. In absolute poverty, ill-clad, in weather good or bad, he walked or rode horseback hundreds of miles monthly, preaching several times a day. From late 1799 to spring 1801 he traveled across Ireland, exhorting listeners to find salvation. After arriving back in New York in May 1801, he went to Georgia for a few months, then returned to New York, then again went South on a long preaching tour, visiting Virginia, the Carolinas, Alabama (where he delivered the first Protestant sermon), and Tennessee. On 3 September 1804 he married Peggy Holcomb, his "rib," and instantly left her at home to go preach in the South once more. Later she traveled with him occasionally, including an 18-month sojourn in England beginning in November 1805 (he went again to England in 1818–1820).

During his career Dow preached constantly, covering most of the nation, and advocated everywhere the use of the CAMP MEETING. Even in an era of idiosyncratic evangelists, he stood out. He was known as "Crazy Dow," and he cultivated an image of outrageousness to help attract crowds. Recognizing the utility both of advertising and of novelty, he used both in his ministry. Dow's unbridled eccentricity led to many disputes with his Methodist elders, and his unkempt appearance put off some potential converts, but he became extremely well known across the South for his "crazy" behavior and his spirited preaching. He had the gift of self-publicity, and styling himself "Cosmopolite" went everywhere exhorting and selling the many pamphlets he wrote, including several editions of a colorful autobiography and journal, variously titled. After 1820 age succeeded in slowing him down, so he traveled less and wrote more, and argued without ceasing with everyone from hapless neighbors to Catholics to fellow Methodists.

See also articles on FRONTIER, INFLUENCE OF; GREAT REVIVAL; REVIVALISM.

Bibliography. Lorenzo Dow, History of Cosmopolite: or, the four volumes of Lorenzo's journal. Concentrated in one; containing his experience and travels, from childhood to 1814; Charles Coleman Sellers, Lorenzo Dow: The Bearer of the Word.

JOHN B. BOLES
RICE UNIVERSITY

DREHER, GODFREY (1789-1875), pioneer Lutheran leader in the South, was a native of Lexington County SC. In 1810 he was licensed to preach, baptize, and catechize in his home area by the North Carolina Synod. He was ordained two years later and led in the organization of a Special Conference for South Carolina in 1815. This body of pastors from the central part of the state met infrequently; in 1824 Dreher invited them to his church, St. Michael's, Irmo, to discuss the formation of a synod separate from the mother synod in North Carolina. In addition to the problem of distance, this separation was intended also to prevent the dissension that had erupted in North Carolina over the controversy surrounding PAUL HENKEL. Dreher himself, however, soon became the center of a division within the new synod. Elected treasurer in 1825, he served continuously in that post until 1834, when the post was designated for a layman.

Personal differences with a neighboring pastor and consequent conflicts with the synod caused him to become an independent Lutheran minister by 1837. Subsequently he brought pastors of the Henkel-dominated Tennessee Synod into the state; his congregations affiliated with that body in 1852, although he remained independent. Paralysis forced him to end his active ministry in 1854. Although apparently having no formal education, he was active in forming the Lexington Sunday School Union and served on the board of directors that founded a seminary in 1830; he led a successful campaign to locate the seminary near his congregations in Lexington. Dreher was married three times and fathered eight children.

See also article on LUTHERAN CHURCH.

Bibliography. James S. Aull, "Godfrey Dreher and The South Carolina Synod," unpublished B.D. thesis, Lutheran Theological Southern Seminary, 1960; P. McCollough, ed., A History of the Lutheran Church in South Carolina.

HUGH GEORGE ANDERSON
LUTHER COLLEGE

DRINKING: See PROHIBITION.

DUBOSE, WILLIAM PORCHER (1836-1918), prominent Episcopal theologian, was born near his father's plantation in Winnsboro SC, and educated at a Winnsboro academy, The Citadel, and the University of Virginia. Shortly after his entrance into the Episcopal diocesan seminary at Camden SC, DuBose was appointed adjutant in Holcombe's Brigade for service in the Confederate army. He saw action in Virginia near Richmond, at Second Manassas, and at Second Bull Run. Thrice wounded, he was captured and imprisoned at Fort Delaware. After a prisoner exchange, DuBose was ordained and served as chaplain with Kershaw's Brigade until the end of the war.

Following the war, DuBose served parishes at Fairfield and Abbeville in his home state. Shortly after nearly being elected bishop of the diocese, he was chosen in 1873 to serve as chaplain of moral theology at the denomination's UNIVERSITY OF THE SOUTH at Sewanee TN. Chaplain until he became dean of the university's St. Luke's School of Theology in 1893, DuBose served also as professor of moral philosophy and in his 35 years on the faculty came to embody the spirit of the university.

DuBose traced the development of his theology in a dialectical pattern from the evangelical influences of his youth through a churchly phase informed by the German theologian Isaac August Dorner and the Mercersburg theology of Philip Schaff and John Williamson Nevin to a Broad Church or Catholic phase in his mature years. At 54, he published The Soteriology of the New Testament, the first and most important of his half-dozen theological works. In dialogue with the

Lux Mundi group's Anglican modernists, especially Robert Campbell Moberly, DuBose sought to interpret the gospel in terms of modern thought. His work was more widely appreciated in England than in the United States.

See also articles on EPISCOPAL CHURCH; HIGH CHURCH/LOW CHURCH; INCARNATION; THEOLOGY.

RALPH E. LUKER
VIRGINIA POLYTECHNIC INSTITUTE
AND STATE UNIVERSITY

DUNKERS: *See* CHURCH OF THE BRETHREN.

DUNN, NORTH CAROLINA. First a center of Populist agitation, then of fiery HOLINESS preaching, this small town in central North Carolina became for a brief period the "Azusa" of PENTECOSTALISM in the Southeast. In a way, the movement had begun earlier in Falcon NC, 10 miles south of Dunn, where the Holiness Church, a tiny sect in the radical Wesleyan tradition, maintained a campground. Early in the fall of 1906 news was received of the (now) legendary Azusa Street revival in Los Angeles. Soon G(ASTON) B(ARNABUS) CASHWELL, a Holiness Church preacher who lived in Dunn, set out for Los Angeles, seeking the experience that had already become the hallmark of the Azusa meetings and of the modern Pentecostal movement: BAPTISM OF THE SPIRIT with the sign of speaking in unknown tongues (GLOSSOLALIA).

Returning to Dunn, Cashwell launched a revival in a rented tobacco warehouse 31 Dec. 1906. Tradition has it that thousands attended, but whatever the actual size of the meetings it is indisputable that news of supernatural events at the services raced across the Southeast. When the revival closed in late January

1907, it was evident that a majority of ministers in the Holiness Church, as well as a majority of ministers in a closely related sect, the FIRE BAPTIZED HOLINESS CHURCH, had converted to Pentecostalism. The revival also served as a launching pad for Cashwell who blazed across the Southern states for the next two years, drawing countless folk and several denominations into the Pentecostal fold.

The Holiness Church and the Fire Baptized Holiness Church soon proclaimed themselves officially Pentecostal in doctrine. These bodies merged in Falcon in 1911, adopting the name (which the former had used since 1909) PENTECOSTAL HOLINESS CHURCH. (The tiny octagonal meetinghouse in which the merger was consummated still stands as a historical landmark.) Falcon served as an unofficial headquarters until 1918, when more adequate facilities were secured in FRANKLIN SPRINGS GA. The Pentecostal Holiness Church is today one of the largest of the white Pentecostal denominations.

Partly as a result of the Dunn revival, three conferences of the FREE WILL BAPTIST movement, all located in eastern North Carolina, were also swept into Pentecostalism about 1910. These conferences, which merged and incorporated in 1959 as the Pentecostal Free Will Baptist Church, have maintained headquarters in Dunn since 1960, along with their school, Heritage Bible College, established in Dunn in 1972.

See also articles on HOLINESS MOVEMENT; PENTECOSTALISM; WESLEYAN TRADITION.

GRANT WACKER
UNIVERSITY OF NORTH CAROLINA
AT CHAPEL HILL

EASTERN ORTHODOXY: *See* GREEK
ORTHODOX CHURCH.

ECCLESIOLOGY (CHURCH). This
word has to do with the life of the church,
for which the Greek word is *ecclesia*. The
life of the church comes to expression in
its worship, teaching, and work in the
world. In a derived, but highly important
sense, it also appears in the organized
forms that have been developed to serve
this life: the polity of the church.

The *worship* of the church provides
for repeated experiences of renewal and
commitment. It celebrates God, seeks to
voice his word in Scripture, sermon, and
sacrament; in calls to repentance and confession; and places both itself and the
world under the judgment and promise of
the cross. Believers, both as individuals
and congregation, are engaged by this
worship. A renewal of the vision of God is
gained through worship: the disclosure of
the Real as the norm of our own duty and
possibility. This is the great business of
worship. In the light of the "vision," one
finds guideposts for life's pilgrimage, the
power to carry on in the face of obstacle or
temptation, and a sort of "grace for the
road." A principal function of worship is
the kindling of the religious imagination.

The church's *teaching* (doctrine) is
the intellective form of that truth from
which the new life of individual and community has emerged. It is both instruction
and nurture. For those beyond a circle of
its fellowship, it is the church's message of
the "good news" as both the reality and
the promise of God's favor to all. This
function of the church's life is less to
inspire the imagination than to instruct
the mind. Doctrine is a chief *intellective*
dimension of that ecclesial life whose aim
is the increase of love of God and neighbor. Doctrinal formulation must be done
with humility, since "our knowledge of
God" is never synonymous with "God."
Doctrinal formulations serve both a conservative and integrative function. They
also may serve—witness Weber's interpretation of the Protestant doctrine of
"vocation"—as agents of change.

The *work* of the church in the world
can be described in terms of vocation. In
whatever degree the church is following
after Christ, it sees, cares for, goes to the
world, and serves it at cost. The church's
very calling is to a way of looking upon the
world through the eyes of *agape*, that is, a
calling to humble sharing of the faith and
hope of the Gospel and to the loving service of others for Christ's sake. Though

the words are often misused, this is what is properly meant by the church acting in evangelism and mission. In the human and moral fruit of this vocation—undertaken with means appropriate to their ethical end—the worship and doctrine of the church find their ideal end.

Polity is the structural form of the church's life, the machinery of its organization and governance. Polity's reason for being lies outside itself. That is, polity—along with those governing powers that attend it—finds its justification only in its serving of the church's worship, teaching, and work in the world. It has no ground of its own. The structured church, whether as hierarchy, council, conference, or convention, exists to give true and effective form to the confessed faith; to provide for the authenticity and continuity of tradition; to interpret Scripture and its canonical limits; to coordinate effort and elicit support for the fulfillment of its vocation of evangelism and mission.

The *function* of the church is to serve the increase of love of God and neighbor. Since the function of the church is the clue to its nature, one could say that when the structural forms of the church are serving their true function, then these forms are "church," and the church is "Christian." In the formal more than in the substantive sense, this appears to be the *leitmotiv* recurring in such diverse themes as the "catholic" interpretation of the church as "the extension of the incarnation" (L. S. Thornton), as "event" (K. Barth), and in such words as "the church is constituted in its action" (G. Gutierrez).

In the New Testament, the church appears as a community of believers, called and gathered by God through Christ, on pilgrimage towards the full realization of God's eschatological purpose. By meeting regularly for worship, the church is commonly called an assembly.

In the United States, the unity of the church is obscured by its numerous denominational divisions. It is unfortu-

nate that denominations have been labeled "churches." The word "denomination" is the designation or name of any separately organized Christian group. But denominations are "denominations *of the church*." The word is essentially adjectival in character. When substituted for the noun, it is the source of all kinds of mischief. The noun, church, must control the adjective, denomination—not vice versa. Baptists are Baptist Christians, Methodists are Methodist Christians, Catholics are Catholic Christians, and the like. Christians, not denominations, compose the church. Denominations are "churchly" when they embody the life and do the work of the "church," but no denomination is justified by its own distinctiveness.

See also article on DENOMINATIONALISM.

Bibliography. S. E. Ahlstrom, *A Religious History of the American People;* F. J. A. Hort, *The Christian Ecclesia;* J. Moltmann, *The Church in the Power of the Spirit;* L. Newbigin, *The Household of God;* H. R. Niebuhr, *The Purpose of the Church and Its Ministry; The Social Sources of Denominationalism.*

THERON D. PRICE
FURMAN UNIVERSITY

ECUMENISM. Deriving from a Greek word meaning "household," ecumenism refers to activities involving cooperation among different bodies of Christians and efforts toward unity. The strongest impulses for ecumenism, for asserting the religious bonds that bring human beings into closer relation rather than fortifying the walls of dogma that divide, have not come from the South. Until recent times, the South has not hosted many major events or produced ecumenical leadership to give it much eminence in the chronicles of the ecumenical movement in North America. But there have been persistent, dedicated efforts that deserve to be noted.

The Sunday school and religious education movement, world and home missions, and women's religious organizations were the forces behind most interdenominational cooperation in the South up to the 20th century. A few issues, such as Sabbath observance and

TEMPERANCE, were catalysts for ecumenical action also. Slavery and the political strife of civil war tore Presbyterians, Methodists, and Baptists apart internally. Repair of family ties has been a first-order ecumenical task.

When the Federal Council of Churches was formed in 1908, the Southern Baptist, Southern Presbyterian, and Protestant Episcopal denominations did not immediately join, nor did several Lutheran bodies. To strong concern for religious education, evangelism, and home and foreign missions, the Federal Council added a forceful statement on social concerns growing out of the new industrial order. This feature was one factor in the reluctance of some bodies to participate. Southern Presbyterians did become members of the National Council of Churches of Christ in the USA and also the World Council of Churches, but the Southern Baptists remained outside and have to this day. The determination of these national or global ecumenical councils to develop a strong public voice on issues in the society runs counter to the role of religion as defined by many denominations and independent churches that are strong in the South. For example, based upon 1980 Church Membership Study figures for three regions constituting the South, eight denominations that are bulwarks of the National Council of Churches comprise roughly 12 percent of the population of those regions, while Southern Baptists comprise about 20 percent.

Despite a climate in which openness to other religious traditions is not encouraged and the ministries associated with the SOCIAL GOSPEL are not recognized as primary responsibilities of religious bodies, ecumenism has taken root in various forms throughout most of the South. Councils of churches exist at the state level and in some large cities in all but two Southern states—Mississippi and Alabama. Councils of church women have led the way in several states to the founding of ecumenical councils, and Church Women United continues to be particularly strong in the South.

While religious education, faith and order, and home mission evangelism are foundational to many ecumenical groups in the South, they have become increasingly involved in broad social issues as well. The Christian Action Council of South Carolina, which is distinctive because of the inclusion of Southern Baptists in its active membership, came into existence to oppose the repeal of the EIGHTEENTH AMENDMENT (PROHIBITION) to the U. S. Constitution, under the title "South Carolina Federated Forces for Temperance and Law Enforcement." In 1952 it extended membership to black churches; civil rights and desegregation, public affairs, Vietnam poverty, communism, and the use of communications media have since been subjects of its ecumenical conferences.

The CIVIL RIGHTS MOVEMENT invigorated and made real the ecumenical experience for many black and white Christians. North Carolina and Florida councils emphasized migrant farmworker ministries, while they and nearly all other deep South councils have become heavily involved in refugee resettlement. Hunger programs, self-development, poverty, disaster relief, and unemployment have engaged the attention of most Southern ecumenical bodies since 1970, along with some continuing attention to racism. Institutional ministries, such as chaplaincies to hospitals, prisons, and nursing homes, and ministries or legislative programs on criminal justice, aging, the disabled and handicapped, youth, alcoholism and other drugs, and public education are found in many state and local ecumenical agencies. Less common, in a review of council programs of the 1980s, are religion and the arts, Christian-Jewish dialogues, support for the Equal Rights Amendment, and peace education; but they are part of several ecumenical programs.

City ecumenical agencies sometimes also reflect a particular local undertaking, such as New Orleans' racetrack ministry, Atlanta's airport chaplaincy, and Baltimore's Seafarers' Center. The Interfaith Conference of Metropolitan Washington DC includes Jewish, Muslim, Catholic, and Protestant membership, with an emphasis upon interfaith dialogue. Roman Catholics are also participants in the Texas Conference of Churches, but their involvement is the exception rather than the rule.

Ecumenical expression is achieved through efforts other than conciliar agencies, and several of these merit mention. Wake Forest University, a Southern Baptist institution in Winston Salem NC is the home of the Ecumenical Institute, founded in 1968 for study, dialogue, and ecumenical resource development. In Boynton Beach FL the World Center for Liturgical Studies was founded in 1965 to provide continuing education opportunities for church leaders, with particular emphasis upon liturgical and pastoral areas of ministry. The Delta Ministry in Greenville MS came into existence during the turmoil of the civil rights movement and is a related movement of the National Council of Churches. Its chief activities include economic self-help programs, race relations, criminal justice, youth programs, and a program in domestic violence.

The Consultation on Church Union, constituted in 1962, continues its exploration of the formation of a united church, and its 10-communion membership has significant strength in the South, including several black bodies. The National Association of Evangelicals involves many evangelical or independent churches that do not affiliate with the more public-faith orientation of the National Council of Churches. Catholics are involved in joint dialogues with a number of confessional families, including the Southern Baptists, some of whom are carrying on their own interfamily conversations. Some ecumenically minded Southerners participate in national service agencies such as the American Bible Society, the North American Academy of Ecumenists, National Association of Ecumenical Staff, the Evangelical Press Association, and National Religious Broadcasters, or they may have outreach through academic societies such as the Society of Christian Ethics, American Society of Church History, Religious Education Association, or Association of Statisticians of American Religious Bodies.

One unique ecumenical effort stretches from northern Alabama and Georgia to New York State; namely, the Commission on Religion in Appalachia, which evolved from a regional concept of mission and planning that had roots in the Town and Country Committee of the Home Missions Council—in turn incorporated into the National Council of Churches—and in the Spiritual Life Commission of the Council of the Southern Mountains. Its purpose is to deal with religious and spiritual implications that are inherent in the Appalachian region's economic, social, and cultural conditions. Members in 1982 included 19 communions, 10 state councils of churches, the Council of the Southern Mountains, the Commission on Regional and Local Ecumenism of the NCCC, the National Catholic Rural Life Conference, the Lutheran Council in the USA, and Christian Associates of Southwest Pennsylvania.

Several Southerners have recently held key national leadership roles in the ecumenical movement, such as Claire Randall, general secretary of the National Council of Churches; Donald W. Shriver, president of Union Theological Seminary in New York City; William Bean Kennedy, secretary of the Office of Education, World Council of Churches; and LISTON POPE of the Yale Divinity School and Central Committee, World Council of Churches.

PEGGY L. SHRIVER
NEW YORK, NEW YORK

EDUCATION, CHRISTIAN HIGH-ER. In order to evaluate the role of the church-related college in the religion of the South, it is necessary to understand several contributing factors: the roots of Christian higher education in the mission of the church, the historical matrix out of which church-related higher education developed in the United States, pivotal events in the emergence of pluralism, and major current issues that are radically affecting the whole movement.

Since Tertullian raised the question as to whether the church should be involved in education, there has been a resounding affirmation that the love of God cannot be separated from the love of learning, an affirmation expressed by Origen and by Clement of Alexandria, and further strengthened by Bonaventure when he wrote *The Mind's Way to God*. Other early representative advocates of Christian education were Augustine and Anselm of Canterbury, as well as John Calvin of Geneva, all of whom were convinced that a part of the misson of the church is to capture human minds as well as hearts.

In more recent times, this idea has been reaffirmed by John Henry Newman in *The Scope and Nature of University Education*; by George H. Williams in *The Theological Idea of the University*; by Walter H. Moberly in *The Crisis in the University*; and most recently, in America, by Robert T. Sandin in *The Search for Excellence: The Christian College in an Age of Educational Competition*. Thus Christian higher education, rooted and grounded in the belief that all truth is of God, is the church's response to what it considers a divine mandate.

The early American schools were patterned exclusively on English models, particularly Cambridge. Thus the English university became the prototype for the hundreds of liberal arts colleges that later developed in the South, especially during the 19th century.

There has been a persistent myth that the early New England colleges were founded almost solely for the training of literate ministers. Recent scholarship has shown that a wider range of concerns existed. The charters of the early colleges reveal a commitment to "educating professional men in fields other than the ministry and public officials of various kinds."

As late as the middle of the 18th century, higher education in the United States was still under the aegis of the church. It should be remembered that in the charters of a number of colleges, particularly the COLLEGE OF WILLIAM AND MARY in the South, Yale, Princeton, and Brown, lasting patterns had already been established for all higher education in a great variety of issues that continue to be basic. Among them are trusteeship, governance, separation of powers between faculty and administration, pluralism in faculty selection, academic freedom, equal opportunity for students, concern for the education of women, ecumenism, transmission of values and the liberal arts tradition, and freedom from government control. These factors were later to become a positive and liberating influence for both public and private higher learning in the United States and have resulted in the development of a unique dual system of higher education.

While this dual system grew not because of, but in spite of the often militant resistance on the part of the sponsoring church bodies, nevertheless the country is indebted to individuals trained in church colleges who had the vision and saw the necessity to found public institutions. Good examples are the University of Pennsylvania in the North and the University of Georgia in the South; both were founded by people trained in church-sponsored colleges.

While several institutions that were formerly church-related colleges are now large, independent universities, they can be considered a gift from religion to private higher education; prominent among them are Vanderbilt in the South and Yale and Harvard elsewhere. They continue to make a significant contribution to religion, particularly through their theological faculties, but also through the lectures and publications of professors in other departments.

It was Alexis de Tocqueville who observed, when visiting the United States in the 1830s, that religion was its foremost and most influential institution. There can be little doubt that the denominational college was in large measure responsible for this development.

Two pivotal events in the history of education in the United States paved the way for what was to become a unique system: (1) The Dartmouth Case settled once and for all the issue of public vs. private control by giving to Dartmouth College in perpetuity the right to elect its own trustees and to manage the affairs of the institution—an action that, incidentally, was vigorously opposed by no less a light than Thomas Jefferson. From this point, there were two distinct points of view: one represented by Daniel Webster, a Dartmouth alumnus who handled and won the case for private control; and the other typified by Jefferson, who advocated strong public control. (2) The Morrill Act of 1862 and the supplementary acts of 1890 and 1907 that made possible direct financial grants to public higher education.

An awareness of these two decisions gives a background for understanding the current debates on public funds for private colleges and universities, and on what many consider to be a significant erosion of institutional autonomy through government control.

For the church-related college in the South, the period from the end of World War II to the present has been a critical era of transition. The following major factors have contributed to this change: (1) the student population shift from public to private institutions. In 1950 a little

more than 50 percent of all students enrolled in colleges throughout the nation attended private colleges. By 1982, fewer than 25 percent were enrolled in private institutions; (2) rapidly escalating costs; (3) the development of a nationwide system of state-supported community colleges with very low tuition; (4) the massive infusion of public monies into both public and private institutions; (5) the necessity for achieving academic excellence; and (6) the erosion of liberal arts programs and what many scholars feel is a general loss of purpose and distinctiveness in the church-related college.

Nevertheless, it was in the late 1960s and the 1970s that almost all church bodies conducted serious studies to reevaluate the relationship and contribution of church-related colleges to the life and work of the church. In every case the denominations concluded that the work of their colleges is valuable to the church, makes a significant contribution to the quality of American life as a whole, and consequently should be strengthened.

In a related but divergent development, there has been in recent years a rapid development of independent and interdenominational fundamentalist Christian schools at all levels of education, from kindergarten through seminary. These schools obviously do have a strong sense of purpose, and many have received full accreditation by their regional accrediting agency. While strong overtones of racism and antiestablishment fundamentalism were prevalent in many of these schools at their founding (and still exist in some), their growth indicates general public discontent emerging out of the present moral and ethical malaise, particularly in the public schools, along with the carelessness of instruction in fundamental subjects such as reading, composition, and mathematics. Motivating forces include: (1) a growing secular culture in which religious interests are no longer dominant; (2) the ever-increasing demand for narrow, technical training; (3) the rapid development of substantive educational programs by business and industry that prefer, in many instances, to train their own personnel; and (4) the decline of private wealth through the steadily increasing tax burden.

Historically, the church-related colleges in the South (like their sponsoring bodies) have tended to be more conservative than their counterparts in other sections of the country. However, any attempt to evaluate the contribution of these colleges to religion in the South requires a clear understanding of the very high degree of pluralism. In recent years, several scholarly attempts have been made to categorize the various types of Christian colleges. These include the Pattillo-Mackenzie study; more recently, C. Robert Pace's research for the Carnegie Commission, *Education and Evangelism*; and Robert Rue Parsonage's *Church-Related Higher Education*.

In the latter volume, on the Merrimon Cuninggim scale, the more liberal church-related colleges would include those sponsored by the United Church of Christ, the Episcopal Church, the Lutheran Church, the United Presbyterian Church USA, the Moravian Church in America, the Religious Society of Friends (Quaker), and the Roman Catholic Church. The more conservative would include colleges of the American Lutheran Church, the Presbyterian Church in the United States, and the Southern Baptist Convention. The most conservative would be those belonging to the Missouri Synod-Lutheran Church, the Church of the Nazarene, and the Seventh Day Adventists. (The colleges of the Pentecostal groups should also be included.)

Nevertheless, it must be noted that particularly within the major denominations such as the Roman Catholic Church, the United Methodist Church, the Southern Baptists, Lutherans, and Presbyterians, there is a wide spectrum ranging from conservative to liberal, with the largest group near the center, and with some located all along the line from one end to the other.

The principle that brings some unity into this diversity is the common belief that the church, as a part of its missionary and evangelical outreach, has an obligation to bear its witness in higher education, and that faith and learning must go hand in hand if people are to have holistic development.

Everything that has been said up to this point applies to all church-related colleges, regardless of ethnic origins; however, circumstances make it necessary to say a special word about black colleges in the South. President Prezell Robinson of Saint Augustine's College has recently pointed out that black colleges have produced a progressive religious and social leadership out of all proportion to size and enrollment, and that, generally speaking, the quality of education in these institutions has been grossly understated; this, notwithstanding the prevalence of poor facilities and understaffing. Black church-related colleges have produced such outstanding social reformers and ministers as MARTIN LUTHER KING JR., and such educators as BENJAMIN E. MAYS. Enormous strides have been made during the past two decades in improved facilities and the quality of the teaching staff and curriculum.

One of the developments that is becoming increasingly clear is that there is a growing preference on the part of black people for black institutions. This is also the opinion of observers like Freda Goldman, who says that "the major burden of responsibility for the educational implementation of the transition to integration and a good society for Negro Southerners will remain on the schools predominantly serving Negroes." Earl J. McGrath, speaking of predominantly black colleges, has pointed out that "strong psychological and social factors, as well as those of finance and geography, will cause many Negro students to gravitate toward these institutions."

Robinson stresses the fact that from the first, the primary purpose of black institutions was avowedly religious: "to raise up an educated band of missioners who would be able to reach both their American fellows and their African brethren in the nurture and admonition of the Lord." There can be no doubt that a major contribution of the black Christian college in the South has been to instill in its students the presence and power of the black church.

With this background, it is possible to list the major contributions of the church-related college. Sandin is correct when he observes that "the Chrisitan college has been one of the most effective forms in which the church has mobilized its educational ministries." Indeed, a religious phenomenon of the 20th century has been the diversification of church vocations, including ministries in the fields of religious education and church music. The same applies to a variety of specialized areas such as youth work, counseling, military, institutional, industrial chaplaincies, recreational work, and others.

The two paramount contributions of the church-related college to religion in the South are its education of these Christian vocational workers and its production of a vast body of educated lay church members, particularly professional people, with a strong commitment to Christian values and a disposition toward leadership in the work of the church. As had been the case earlier in the North, the graduates of these schools have fanned out to become leaders of their generations in all areas of American life and culture. Samuel Eliot Morison and Henry Steele Commager have observed that for the sort of training that results in ". . . faith in God, consideration for fellow men, and respect for learning, America has never had the equal of her little hill-top colleges."

To the more practical daily tasks of the churches, also, the church-related colleges, through their faculties, have made significant contributions in the following ways: writing literature for church schools and training programs; organizing workshops, seminars, and pastors' schools on such critical subjects as marriage and the family, race relations, drug abuse, alcoholism and various other social concerns, along with pastoral counseling; sponsoring adult education, both on and off campus; and furnishing interim or supply pastors, music and religious education consultants, and speakers for many occasions.

A singular contribution of the church-related college in the South has been its long struggle against anti-intellectualism. Paradoxically, the majority of church-related colleges have nearly always been in tension with their founding denomination. Church-related higher education grew and thrived, not because it had the support of a majority of the church people, but because of a determined minority, and often because of the courage of individual presidents and faculty members who were sometimes badly used. Anti-intellectualism, in the main, has taken two forms: (1) a simple suspicion coming out of a highly sectarian background that viewed all education with mistrust; and (2) a utilitarian choice that had its inception in the rapid development of state universities devoted to agriculture and mechanics. This utilitarian preference received further stimulus at the time of the launching of Sputnik in 1957 when the emphasis on technology caused further erosion of liberal arts in general education.

In a climate such as this, the contribution of church-related colleges toward preserving the tradition of liberal arts learning has been invaluable, serving as a sort of balance wheel for education in general. No less difficult, but perhaps even more significant, has been the preservation in these institutions of an emphasis on a sense of the transcendent in an ever-increasing secular culture. Moreover, the hard-line sectarianism evident in the early history of many churches has been ameliorated largely by their own church-related colleges.

Indeed, many Southern educators from these institutions have developed a practical ecumenism. This has not moved in the direction of organic unity, but as a fellowship of believers with a common sense of mission. Examples of this contribution of the church-related colleges are to be found in the fruitful participation of Southern presidents, faculty members, and educational leaders in three significant national meetings in the 1970s that eventuated in a large body of evaluative material transcending regional and denominational boundaries. The first of these meetings was the Wingspread Consultation on "Perceptions of Church-Relatedness in Higher Education," November 1977. Sponsored by the National Council of Churches, this consultation resulted in a series of papers later edited by Parsonage under the title *Church-Related Higher Education*. The second was the White House Conference on Church-Related Higher Education in December 1977, drawing together the heads of 23 denominational boards of higher education. The third and largest, the National Congress on Church-Related Colleges and Universities, met twice, once at Notre Dame in June 1979, and again in Washington in February 1980. This congress, in which 23 denominations cooperated, was heavily attended by Southern representatives and produced a set of four publications under the overall title of *Church and College: A Vital Partnership*. In listing the contributions of the church-related college, one cannot fail to note also the following important services: (1) providing a continuing theological dialectic on the great themes of the Christian faith; (2) continuing an advocacy of the evangelistic and missionary thrust of the church; (3) establishing Christian community as a context for learning, in an era when education for many is a matter of acquiring the necessary quality points and semester hours in an atmosphere devoid of supportive personal interaction; and (4) maintaining in education the pluralism so essential to a democratic society

While admittedly church-related higher education in the South, as elsewhere in the nation, no longer enjoys the enormous influence that it once had, it still exercises a stabilizing force and provides a much-needed option. Although there are those who paint a dismal picture of the future of church-related colleges in the South, more thoughtful and experienced scholars, such as McGrath, see renewed hope, particularly for those church-related colleges and universities that reaffirm their Christian purpose and maintain a close relationship with their sponsoring body. Sandin views the future work of the church-related college as a healing force in the badly fragmented pluralization of theological thought. Sandin sees "ideology without dogmatism, rational persuasion without indoctrination, orthodoxy without obscurantism." "These," he says, "are the presuppositions of a program of education which is Christian and yet free."

Bibliography. Richard Baepler and William H. K. Narum, et al., *The Quest for a Viable Saga: The Church-Related College in an Age of Pluralism*; Kenneth K. Bailey, *Southern White Protestantism in the Twentieth Century*; Kenneth Irving Brown, *Not Minds Alone: Some Frontiers of Christian Education*; John S. Brubacher and Willis Rudy, *Higher Education in Transition*; Edgar M. Carlson, *The Future of Church-Related Higher Education*; *Church and College: A Vital Partnership*, vol. 1: *Affirmation*, vol. 2: *Mission*, vol. 3: *Accountability*, vol. 4: *Exchange*, Sherman TX: National Congress on Church-Related Colleges and Universities, 1980; Merrimon Cuninggim, *The College Seeks Religion*; Harold H. Ditmanson, Howard V. Hong, and Warren A. Quanbeck, eds., *Christian Faith and the Liberal Arts*; *Endangered Service: Independent Colleges, Public Policy and the First Amendment*; Nashville TN National Commission on United Methodist Higher Education, 1976; Woodrow A. Geier, ed., *Church Colleges Today*; Richard Hofstadter, *Anti-Intellectualism in American Life*; Richard Hofstadter and Wilson Smith, *American Higher Education: A Documentary History*; Christopher Jencks and David Riesman, *The Academic Revolution*; Alexander Miller, *Faith and Learning*; Sir Walter Moberly, *The Crisis in the University*; Philip R. Moots and Edward McGlynn Gaffney, Jr., *Church and Campus: Legal Issues in Religiously Affiliated Higher Education*; Robert Rue Parsonage, ed., *Church Related Higher Education*; Manning M. Pattillo, Jr. and Donald M. Mackenzie, *Church-Sponsored Higher Education in the United States: Report of the Danforth Commission*; DeWitt C. Reddick, *Wholeness and Renewal in Education: A Learning Experience at Austin College*; Robert T. Sandin, *The Search for Excellence: The Christian College in an Age of Educational Competition*; Richard W. Solberg and Merton P. Strommen, *How Church-Related Are Church-Related Colleges?*; Erich A. Walter, ed., *Religion and the State University*.

BEN C. FISHER
MURFREESBORO, NORTH CAROLINA

EIGHTEENTH AMENDMENT. This addition to the American Constitution, effective 16 January 1920, prohibited the manufacture, sale, or transportation of intoxicating liquors in the country. It came as the climax of over a century of TEMPERANCE activity.

In the 19th century many organizations were formed to deal with drunkenness, most of which were religiously motivated. In general their effectiveness was diminished, however, because they vacillated between temperance and total abstinence. Prior to 1850 these organizations relied principally on moral persuasion to curtail the use of liquor. After that time they began to try to get antiliquor legislation passed. But about the same time Americans began to be preoccupied with the slavery issue and, at the outbreak of the Civil War, temperance was virtually forgotten. However, after the war the movement was revived, this time with the participation of Southerners. (Prior to the war, most temperance workers were also abolitionists and, partly for that reason, Southerners did not participate.)

There were two organizations that built on earlier efforts and that were principally responsible for the Eighteenth Amendment. The WOMAN'S CHRISTIAN TEMPERANCE UNION, founded in 1874, became a comprehensive reform organization, dealing with a variety of social issues under the leadership of the famous Frances Willard. Its principal emphasis was trying to end the scourge of beverage alcohol. A major contribution made by the WCTU was its alcohol education program in virtually all public schools, which helped pave the way for the Eighteenth Amendment. Overshadowing the WCTU in time was the Anti-Saloon League, founded in 1895. The league was strictly a political organization, aiming both to inform legislators and to get them to vote against the liquor traffic. Both organizations derived most of their members from churches, principally the Methodist, Baptist, Presbyterian, and Congregational denominations. Virtually no Catholics or Jews participated. At its height the league had 50 percent of the Protestant churches in the nation as affiliate members. The temperance forces fought so hard because they believed alcohol was responsible for most of the evils in America. In particular, they saw liquor as destructive to the home and family and as the reason for most prostitution, crime, and corruption. Consequently, the Eighteenth Amendment was designed to impose virtual total abstinence on the country, for its own good.

The amendment was a failure. People were determined to drink; their appetites and habits would not respond to legislation. Bootleggers, rumrunners, and speakeasies came into being to satisfy the persistent thirst. Organized crime capitalized on all this and became a potent force in American life. As a large portion of the population winked at, if not openly defied, the law, a general attitude of lawlessness enveloped the land. It became clear that PROHIBITION was causing more problems than alcohol and the saloon had ever caused, consequently Congress proposed the Twenty-first Amendment, which became law in December 1933, repealing the Eighteenth. What had been a questionable enterprise, in the context of the separation of CHURCH AND STATE, ended as a disillusionment and an embarrassment for the churches and the country was essentially no better for the effort.

Bibliography. Paul C. Conley and Andrew A. Sorensen, *The Staggering Steeple: The Story of Alcoholism and the Churches*; Andrew Sinclair, *Prohibition: The Era of Excess.*

RONALD B. FLOWERS
TEXAS CHRISTIAN UNIVERSITY

ELECTION, DOCTRINE OF: *See* PREDESTINATION.

ELECTRONIC CHURCH. This is the name given to the Christian ministries transmitted through television by denominations, congregations, individual preachers, and specifically developed networks and syndications to people watching in their homes and other places outside the church itself.

Current electronic evangels were anticipated by BILLY GRAHAM and, to a lesser degree, Norman Vincent Peale and Fulton Sheen, beginning in the 1950s. Ranging across the nation in his crusades, Graham used television as his "home" pulpit. His rise parallels the saturation of American homes with TV sets that had passed 50 percent by 1953. However, in each city crusade, many nationally televised, Graham associated himself with local denominations, aware that his early Fundamentalism needed to be tempered by traditional views in order to hold vast audiences. Two salient facts of those Graham years were established: (1) a great deal of money can be raised through television; and (2) celebrity status comes through association with the power elite.

While Graham intermittently purchased prime-time on TV, sustained religious broadcasting was confined to Sunday morning hours where, as late as the mid-1970s, viewers might encounter a half-dozen evangelists along with mainline church programming. Both were, with rare exceptions, of no more than moderate quality.

The critical year appears to be 1975. A large number of conservative Protestants sensed a mass market if their message were professionally produced and attractively packaged. As they bought time on Sunday morning they drove from the air most of the free productions from the mainline churches. Coupled with this explosion was the rapid increase in cable systems. By the close of the decade, 24-hour Christian networks were part of most cable systems. Using the latest in satellite technology, they presented both familiar and unfamiliar faces; most of the latter in time achieved fame.

It has been estimated that by 1980 the income for all religious broadcasters amounted to $400 million per year. Jeffrey Hadden suggests that these evangels put to use a technology compatible with their proselytizing theology. The computer with its highly differentiated lists is the heart of their success. Their appeals through extensive mailing have resulted in effective fund raising.

Some electronic personalities became political celebrities, interpreting the Bible as having much to say about abortion, creationism, and foreign policy. Jerry Falwell's biblicism and conservative politics catapulted him into international diplomacy and the Rose Garden, a fact beamed to the faithful as evidence of God's blessing on gifts. M. G. "Pat" Robertson devised the "700 Club," that offered daily via satellite, the Christian talk show, an interlacing of salvation, health, eschatology, culinary arts, world affairs, and much more.

Competing directly with mainline Protestant and Roman Catholic churches for pew and plate, electronic Evangelicalism began to reshape alignments in American churches. Promoting ultraconservative politics and alterations in the Bill of Rights, these Christians defined the faith as concentrating on a specified list of moral issues. While the movement is partly indigenous to the South, its impact, thus far in the social and political arenas, has been far more substantial in other parts of the nation.

Recent efforts to counter TV Evangelicals have come from "People for the American Way," founded by Norman Lear. It uses the medium to present alternative positions and has been successful in applying the FCC Fairness Doctrine to acquire air time to respond to the most obvious conservative comments on "controversial issues of public concern."

See also article on MORAL MAJORITY.

Bibliography. Robert S. Alley and Irby Brown, "The Moral Monopoly," *Emmy* 3:1 (Winter 1981) 34; Frances FitzGerald, "A Disciplined, Charging Army," *The New Yorker*, 57:13 (May 18, 1981) 53; Jeffrey Hadden and Charles Swann, *Prime Time Preachers*.

ROBERT S. ALLEY
UNIVERSITY OF RICHMOND

ELLIOTT, STEPHEN (1806-1866), was the first bishop of the Protestant Episcopal Church in Georgia, and its principal organizer and builder. His father was a scholar, and founder of the *Southern Review*. Stephen was born in Beaufort SC, and was educated at a private school, and at Harvard and South Carolina College. He read law and practiced in Charleston and Beaufort for several years.

Influenced by a traveling evangelist, Elliott sought admission to the Episcopal ministry and was ordained deacon in 1835. Very soon he was appointed chaplain of South Carolina College and professor of sacred literature there. Five years later he was called from that position to be the bishop of Georgia.

In the next 20 years his diocese increased from 6 churches to 28, and from 300 communicants to 2,000. Bishop Elliott, far more than any other person, was responsible for this growth and for the extension of the church into the newer, western parts of the state.

In the late 1850s Elliott was one of the founders of the UNIVERSITY OF THE SOUTH. He helped especially in choosing a site for the university, and in raising an endowment.

During the Civil War Elliott played a leading role in the PROTESTANT EPISCOPAL CHURCH IN THE CONFEDERATE STATES OF AMERICA. He was author of the pastoral letter issued in the name of the First General Council of the church. It professed "entire harmony" with the "doctrine, discipline and worship" of the church in the United States, and regretted that "civil strife" had necessitated a separation of the churches. It made no apology for SLAVERY, but emphasized the church's responsibility to provide "religious and moral instruction" to the slaves.

After the war, Elliott was a leader in reuniting the Confederate dioceses with the national church, which he saw accomplished a few months before his death.

See also article on CIVIL WAR.

Bibliography. Henry T. Malone, *The Episcopal Church in Georgia*; Hubert B. Owens, *Georgia's Planting Prelate*; Edgar L. Pennington, "Stephen Elliott, First Bishop of Georgia," *Historical Magazine of the Protestant Episcopal Church* 7 (September 1938): 203-63.

GEORGE R. BENTLEY
UNIVERSITY OF FLORIDA

ENGLAND, JOHN (1786-1842), a leading spokesman for the Catholic Church in the South during the early nineteenth century, was born in Cork, Ireland. Ordained a priest in 1808, he served in various clerical and educational capacities in Ireland until 1820 when he was consecrated bishop and appointed by Pope Pius VII to the newly erected see of Charleston (SC). His diocese comprised the two Carolinas and Georgia with a Catholic population of 5,000.

To answer frequent attacks made on his faith by nativist Southerners, England published, writing the majority of articles, the first Catholic newspaper in the United States. Called the *United States Catholic Miscellany*, it appeared weekly with few exceptions from 1822 to 1861. England's insistence within its pages on the compatibility of Catholic beliefs and practices with what he called U. S. "Republicanism" exerted a strong influence on Catholic thought elsewhere in the country and led to the founding of similar newspapers where the same positions frequently were taken. Not only his reputation for learning, but also his commitment to democratic principles, caused him to be invited to address both houses of Congress on 8 January 1826. In 1833 he became the first U. S. prelate chosen by the papacy to undertake a diplomatic mission to Haiti.

In his home diocese he instituted church governance reforms that gave major roles to the laity, but they did not survive his administration. In the slavery controversy he defended the institution with arguments drawn from Scripture and tradition. At the time of his death, he was the most notable public figure in the American hierarchy.

See also articles on CHURCH AND STATE; NATIVISM; ROMAN CATHOLIC CHURCH.

Bibliography. Peter Guilday, *Life and Times of John England*, 2 vols.; Ignatius A. Reynolds, ed., *The Works of the Right Rev. John England, First Bishop of Charleston*, 5 vols.

MICHAEL V. GANNON
UNIVERSITY OF FLORIDA

ENTIRE SANCTIFICATION: *See* SECOND BLESSING.

EPISCOPAL CHURCH IN THE SOUTH.

Colonial Period, 1607-1789. *Virginia.* On 20 December 1606, three small ships, *Goodspeed, Discovery,* and *Susan Constance,* with almost 105 persons sailed from the Thames, and reached the Chesapeake Bay on 6 May 1607. The expedition was under the leadership of Captain John Smith and the chaplain was Robert Hunt. On 14 May 1607 they had their first Sunday service and six weeks later they celebrated Holy Communion. Thus the Church of England took root in the American colonies with the founding of the first permanent English colony at JAMESTOWN VA.

While mercantile motives promoted this settlement, religious factors also played a part. They had a chaplain, daily morning and evening prayer, two sermons every Sunday, Holy Communion every three months, and their charter urged that they preach the Gospel to the Indians. Chaplain Hunt was replaced by the Rev. ALEXANDER WHITAKER, the "Apostle to Virginia," who promoted the colony with his *Good News from Virginia* (1613). Both Hunt and Whitaker were Puritan Anglicans.

In 1619 the first Negro indentured servants (many of whom became slaves) came to Virginia, and the first popular legislative body was formed in America. This House of Burgesses passed legislation officially establishing the Church of England in Virginia. Ministers were to conduct all services in accordance with the Anglican *Book of Common Prayer*; everyone had to attend church twice on Sundays; and ministers were to be given a "glebe" (a 100-acre plot of land) and a fixed salary usually paid in tobacco.

In 1624 King James I annulled the charter of the Virginia Company; from then until 1776 it was a royal colony governed by the king's appointees. Governor William Berkeley promoted the established Anglican church. Under him the House of Burgesses passed laws requiring that all citizens pay the tithe; that only members of the Church of England could vote; and that the church be organized with vestries. These vestries nominated their own clergy and eventually became self-perpetuating.

The bishop of London, by being on the board of the Virginia Company, had responsibility for the church in the colonies, but this was ineffective. In the same year as the Act of Toleration, 1689, Bishop (of London) Henry Compton named JAMES BLAIR the first commissary to Virginia. A commissary was the agent of the bishop who could perform all episcopal functions except confirmation and ordination. For over 50 years Blair worked to increase the number of clergy in Virginia and to improve the state of the church. His most lasting accomplishment was the founding of the COLLEGE OF WILLIAM AND MARY, of which he was the first president, 1693-1743.

South Carolina. In 1663 King Charles II gave a grant of land to the Earl of Clarendon and seven others. They named it Carolina, "of Charles." In 1669 they adopted the "Fundamental Constitution," written by John Locke and Ashley Cooper, which provided for the establishment of the Church of England, but which also gave some toleration to Dissenters. In 1680 the first Anglican clergyman arrived at CHARLESTON, the Rev. Atkin Williamson, and in 1682 the first church was established in that city, ST. PHILIP'S. In 1701 the first SOCIETY FOR THE PROPAGATION OF THE GOSPEL (SPG) missionary arrived in the colony, the Rev. Samuel Thomas. An act of 1706 continued public support of the church, and in 1707 the bishop of London named the Rev. Gideon Johnson the first commissary to South Carolina, who also served as rector of St. Philip's. He was succeeded in 1716 by the Rev. William T. Bull. The Rev. Francis Le Jau did successful missionary work among the Negroes.

North Carolina. While Carolina was a single colony, from the beginning, a distinction existed between North and South. After 1713 North and South Carolina were two distinct colonies. From the beginning North Carolina had considerable religious diversity and establishment of the Church of England came late. Several SPG missionaries worked in North Carolina, the most notable of whom was the Rev. Clement Hall. During the colonial period the Church of England was a minority body in North Carolina.

Georgia. In June 1732 King George II gave Gen. JAMES EDWARD OGLETHORPE and several other philanthropists a grant of land for a colony to be named Georgia. These philanthropists wanted to establish a refuge for imprisoned debtors. In February 1733 Oglethorpe and 130 others reached SAVANNAH. It was expected that the Church of England would be established, and an Anglican minister, the Rev. Henry Herbert, came as chaplain. He stayed only three months and was replaced by the Rev. Samuel Quincy, who stayed less than three years. Before Quincy left, John Wesley and his brother Charles arrived as SPG missionaries. Charles worked at FREDERICA on the island of St. Simon, and John worked at Savannah. In 1740 GEORGE WHITEFIELD began his tenure as rector of Christ Church, Savannah.

The Great Awakening, 1720-1770. The GREAT AWAKENING was the major religious event of the colonial period, but the Anglican church resisted it because of its enthusiasm. And this in spite of the fact that the leader of the movement was an Anglican minister, George Whitefield. Indeed, one of Whitefield's most bitter opponents was ALEXANDER GARDEN, third commissary to South Carolina. The

Anglican parish minister most active in the Great Awakening was DEVEREUX JARRATT, rector of Bath parish in Virginia. He worked closely with the Methodists, and felt betrayed when they left the Anglican church. The Great Awakening strengthened the other Protestant groups in the colonies, but it weakened the Anglican church and insured it of a minority status in America.

The Revolutionary Era, 1776-1789. The period of the Revolutionary War was most difficult for Anglicans. Because of it many of them returned to England. At the same time most of the Southern revolutionaries belonged to the Church of England, and two-thirds of the 92 clergymen in Virginia supported the Revolution. A majority of the Anglican clergy of South Carolina favored the Revolution, but most of the clergy of Georgia and North Carolina supported the king. The leading Southern Anglican opponent of the Revolution was the Rev. Jonathan Boucher who believed the success of the Revolution would be the downfall of the Anglican church in America.

The DISESTABLISHMENT of the church in the Southern colonies was also hard on the Anglicans, even though it was led by Anglican churchmen. JAMES MADISON and THOMAS JEFFERSON led the fight for disestablishment in Virginia, which was finally achieved in 1786 with the passage of "An Act for Establishing Religious Freedom." The state constitution of North Carolina (1776) guaranteed full religious freedom of conscience to all as did South Carolina's of 1790.

While disestablishment was being achieved and state constitutions, as well as the Federal Constitution, were being written, the Church of England in the colonies had to transform itself into the Protestant Episcopal Church in the United States of America. Of all the churches in the United States at this time, the Anglican was most in need of reorganization. Southern Episcopalians insisted that the reorganized church must have lay and clerical leadership. On 6-7 October 1784 representatives from eight states, including Virginia, met in New York and recommended the calling of a General Convention. Meanwhile state conventions were to elect bishops. Samuel Seabury had been elected bishop of Connecticut and was consecrated on 14 November 1784, the first American bishop. David Griffith was elected bishop of Virginia, but was never consecrated. The first General Convention met at Christ Church, Philadelphia, 27 September—7 October 1785, with representatives from seven states including Virginia and North Carolina. At the third General Convention, 1789, the first triennial convention, the Protestant Episcopal Church was fully organized.

National Period, 1789-1865. This period is characterized by missionary expansion, the organization of state churches, and the election of bishops. In 1790 JAMES MADISON was consecrated the first bishop of Virginia at Lambeth Palace; in 1795 Robert Smith was consecrated the first bishop of South Carolina; and in 1823 JOHN STARK RAVENSCROFT was consecrated the first bishop of North Carolina. With the consecration of RICHARD CHANNING MOORE as the second bishop of Virginia in 1814 and WILLIAM MEADE as coadjutor in 1839, that church took on new life with an evangelical flavor.

During this period the church moved west and new dioceses were organized and bishops elected. In 1834 JAMES HERVEY OTEY was consecrated the first bishop of Tennessee, and in 1838 the General Convention elected LEONIDAS POLK its second missionary bishop with responsibility for Alabama, Mississippi, Louisiana, and the republic of Texas. Even before Polk's election the first missionary bishop, Jackson Kemper, worked in the Southern states. As a result of Polk's work, new Southern dioceses were organized and first bishops consecrated: STEPHEN ELLIOTT of Georgia, 1841; Nicholas Hamner Cobbs of Alabama, 1844; George Washington Freeman of Arkansas, 1844; William Mercer Green of Mississippi, 1850; and Francis Huger Rutledge of Florida, 1851.

In 1851 Polk became the first bishop of Louisiana. In effect, all of these Southern bishops were missionary bishops.

During this period the Southern church organized two educational institutions. In 1823 the diocese of Virginia opened its Protestant Episcopal Theological Seminary at Alexandria, which has had a special interest in the foreign mission of the church. As early as 1832 Bishop Otey had planned for the establishment of a theological and classical seminary. In 1857 at SEWANEE TN, the formal founding of the UNIVERSITY OF THE SOUTH took place with representatives from nine Southern dioceses participating. Because of the Civil War the university did not open until September 1868. In 1835 *The Southern Churchman* began publication at Richmond; it continued until 1952 when it became *Episcopal Churchnews*.

The Oxford Movement did not have a major impact on Southern churchmen, with the exception of LEVI SILLIMAN IVES, second bishop of North Carolina, who in 1852 resigned his office and joined the Roman Catholic Church.

After the secession of the Southern states and the formation of the Confederate States of America, the Southern dioceses had to accommodate themselves to this new political reality. Bishops Polk and Elliott took the lead, and on 12-22 November 1862 the first General Council of the PROTESTANT EPISCOPAL CHURCH IN THE CONFEDERATE STATES met at Augusta. The General Convention called the roll of the missing Southern dioceses as if they were only temporarily absent. The Confederate Episcopal Church dissolved itself in November 1865.

The Modern Period, 1865-1980. From Reconstruction to World War I the Episcopal Church in the South was concerned with two primary issues: reorganizing and rebuilding after the war and continued growth with the creation of new dioceses. The Rt. Rev. CHARLES TODD QUINTARD, second bishop of Tennessee (1865-1898) is illustrative of a post-Civil

War Southern rebuilder. New dioceses were created by subdividing older dioceses: West Virginia (from Virginia) 1877, East Carolina (from North Carolina) 1883, South Florida, 1892, Southern Virginia, 1892, Western North Carolina (first called Asheville) 1895, and Atlanta, 1907.

The new theological and intellectual currents of the post-Civil War period caused little disturbance among Southern Episcopalians. The South's, if not the nation's, most creative Episcopal theologian, WILLIAM PORCHER DuBOSE (1836-1918), readily incorporated evolutionary thought into his theology. DuBose taught at the University of the South from 1870 to 1908, and served as second dean of its School of Theology, 1894-1908, which had opened in 1878. He was primarily a New Testament theologian. William Alexander Guerry, eighth bishop of South Carolina, 1908-1928, most fully incorporated SOCIAL GOSPEL teachings into his theology and pastoral addresses. FUNDAMENTALISM had little impact on the Southern church.

From 1914 to the present, most of the Southern dioceses have been organized in the Fourth Province. In 1907 the General Convention divided the dioceses and missionary districts into eight departments; these departments became provinces. The Primary Synod of the Province of Sewanee (Fourth) met in 1914 at Christ Church Cathedral, New Orleans. The provinces worked effectively in religious education and the Fourth Province conducted summer religious education conferences at Sewanee. Presently the Fourth Province includes the dioceses mentioned above except the Virginia dioceses and Arkansas, plus Kentucky (1829) and Lexington (1895), and the new dioceses created by subdivision: Upper South Carolina (1922), Central Florida (1969), Southern Florida (1969), Southwest Florida (1969), and Central Gulf Coast (1970).

In 1919 the General Convention created the National Council of the Episcopal Church; its first president was

THOMAS FRANK GAILOR, third bishop of Tennessee. Several Southern bishops have been presiding bishops of the Episcopal church: HENRY ST. GEORGE TUCKER of Virginia (1938-1946); JOHN E. HINES of Texas (1965-1974); and JOHN MAURY ALLIN of Mississippi (1974-).

See also articles on ANGLICAN CHURCH; ANGLICANISM; ESTABLISHED RELIGION; EVANGELICALISM; HIGH CHURCH/LOW CHURCH; PURITANISM.

Bibliography. Donald S. Armentrout, *The Quest for the Informed Priest: A History of the School of Theology*; G. MacLaren Brydon, *Virginia's Mother Church and the Political Conditions under which It Grew*, 2 vols.; Joseph D. Cushman, *A Goodly Heritage: The Episcopal Church in Florida, 1821-1892; The Sounds of Bells: The Episcopal Church in South Florida, 1892-1969*; Frederick Dalcho, *The Protestant Episcopal Church in South Carolina, 1670-1820*; Virgil S. Davis, "Stephen Elliott: A Southern Bishop in Peace and War," unpublished Ph.D. dissertation, University of Georgia, 1964; William A. R. Goodwin, *History of the Theological Seminary in Virginia and Its Historical Background: Centennial Edition*, 2 vols.; Francis L. Hawks, *Contributions to the Ecclesiastical History of the United States*, vol. 1: *Virginia*; David L. Holmes, "William Meade and the Church of Virginia, 1789-1829," unpublished Ph.D. dissertation, Princeton University, 1971; Henry T. Malone, *The Episcopal Church in Georgia, 1733-1957*; Margaret S. McDonald, *White Already to Harvest: The Episcopal Church in Arkansas*; Arthur H. Noll, *History of the Church in the Diocese of Tennessee*; Joseph H. Parks, *General Leonidas Polk, C.S.A.: The Fighting Bishop*; William S. Perry, ed., *Historical Collections Relating to the American Colonial Church*, vol. 1: *Virginia*; Walter B. Posey, "The Protestant Episcopal Church: An American Adaptation," *Journal of Southern History* 25 (February 1959):3-30; James B. Sill, *Historical Sketches of Churches in the Diocese of Western North Carolina: Episcopal Church*; Albert S. Thomas, *An Historical Account of the Protestant Episcopal Church in South Carolina, 1820-1957; Being a Continuation of Dalcho's Account*; Walter C. Whitaker, *History of the Protestant Episcopal Church in Alabama, 1763-1891*.

DONALD S. ARMENTROUT
UNIVERSITY OF THE SOUTH

EPISCOPALIANISM: *See* ANGLICANISM; EPISCOPAL CHURCH.

EPISCOPATE. In the early Christian community, ministry in churches that were of predominantly gentile origin was exercised by an *episkopos* (overseer), who was assisted by deacons. By the early part of the third century the *episkopoi* (bishops) emerged as the principal leaders throughout the Christian community.

The term episcopate (or episcopacy) owes its origin to these *episkopoi* of the early church and refers today to the office or ministry of a bishop, which entails the responsibility of celebrating the presence of Christ through word and sacrament, pastoring and overseeing the Christian community entrusted to his care, and insuring the truth of faith and practice of churches or groups under his direction, in unity with all other communities of the same faith.

In the Anglican, Orthodox, and Roman Catholic faiths the bishop is seen as possessing the fullness of priesthood. Only the bishop can ordain priests or take part in ordaining bishops.

A critical area of discussion among the churches centers around the relation of the episcopate to the apostleship of the Twelve chosen by Jesus. The Roman Catholic and Orthodox faiths and some scholars among the Anglican faith adhere to a strict, unbroken sacramental continuity with Christ through the apostles and the generations of their successors (the doctrine of Apostolic Succession). The office of the episcopate is held to be the agency of continuity.

In Orthodox Christianity the bishops of an area must meet periodically according to Church law; at such meetings the metropolitan or, in the case of a large territory or national church, the patriarch, presides. Bishops of the Anglican communion are not bound by a central legislation or executive authority but by "common consultation and mutual loyalty" and consequently meet together regionally (in general conventions) and internationally (at Lambeth, England) to discuss matters relating to church doctrine and pastoral practice. In the Orthodox and Anglican traditions all bishops are regarded as possessing the same authority and jurisdiction, though a patriarch or archbishop may preside over a convocation or over a particular area greater than his own diocese.

In the Roman Catholic Church the bishop of Rome is regarded as the head of the Episcopal College, Vicar of Christ, and pastor of the universal church. As such, he enjoys universal authority in the church, an authority, however, which is never detached from, but always united with the other bishops and the universal church. He exercises that particular authority either in a personal or collegial way, depending on needs and circumstances.

ROBERT J. BAKER
ST. VINCENT DE PAUL
REGIONAL SEMINARY

ESTABLISHED RELIGION. At the time of the founding of the English colonies in America, all European countries held that unity of religion was essential to the unity of the state and each had its national church. Elizabeth I (1558-1603) and her successors believed that uniformity within the Church of England was essential to the strength of the state. Royal authority was exercised in the church by the appointment of bishops who were in turn loyal to the monarch. A group within the Elizabethan church who wanted to "purify" several traditional usages became known as Puritans. In time, Puritans objected strenuously to the authority of bishops to determine matters of church government. By 1604, this issue had become a political one, and the extremists or Separatists left for Holland in 1609. Eleven years later this group provided the coterie of Pilgrims who introduced the congregational form of government in America.

The Moderates who desired reform within the Church of England found it impossible to achieve under William Laud, bishop of London (1628) and archbishop of Canterbury (1633). By 1630 many of this group migrated to Massachusetts. Although not opposed to the Church of England *per se*, their Congregational principles gave autonomy to the local congregations. Their tenets stressed the right and duty of Christian worship and the need for congregations to cooperate with one another. The Cambridge Platform of 1648 explicitly stated their position. Calvinist in doctrine, they were midway between the episcopal and Presbyterian forms of church organization. Congregational principles were influential in the founding of Harvard College in 1636 and Yale College in 1701. In Massachusetts, Connecticut, and New Hampshire the Congregational Church was established. Puritans no less than Anglicans believed that unity in religion was essential to the well-being of the state.

The Church of England was established in Virginia in 1610, and legislation was reenacted when Virginia became a royal colony. The Anglican church (the worldwide communion of the Church of England) was established in the lower counties of New York in 1693, in Maryland in 1702, South Carolina in 1706, North Carolina (nominally) in 1711, and Georgia in 1758. In 1635 the bishop of London was placed in charge of the colonial churches. Governor Edmund Andros opened King's Chapel, Boston, to Anglican services in 1689. Christ Church, Philadelphia, in 1694, and Trinity Church, New York, in 1697, received charters from King William III. The bishops of London were represented in the colonies by commissaries, among whom JAMES BLAIR (1653-1743) in Virginia and THOMAS BRAY (1656-1730) in Maryland were outstanding. Blair was responsible for founding the COLLEGE OF WILLIAM AND MARY in 1693. Thomas Bray founded the Society for the Promotion of Christian Knowledge in 1699 and was the prime mover for organizing the SOCIETY FOR THE PROPAGATION OF THE GOSPEL IN FOREIGN PARTS, chartered 1701. In 1754, King's College was founded in New York under Anglican auspices and Samuel Johnson (1696-1772) became the first president. By 1775 the Anglican communion was represented in all 13 mainland colonies and the British West Indies.

Congregationalism was the largest religious body in colonial America, but the Church of England in the 18th century grew remarkably. The increased number of S.P.G. missionaries, S.P.C.K. literature, and additional royal officials who were

Anglican were a part of this growth. In 1722, the "great defection" of Congregationalists at Yale was a major factor. Included were Timothy Cutler, president of Yale, along with Daniel Brown, Samuel Johnson, and James Wetmore. These attracted others and this group zealously promoted the Church of England in America. Through their efforts and the cooperation of the bishops of London, S.P.G., and S.P.C.K., the Church of England grew, especially in New England. This heightened tensions between Anglicans and Congregationalists, especially when Anglicans had to pay taxes to support the Congregational Church. The reverse was true in the Southern colonies where Congregationalists, Presbyterians, and others paid taxes to support the Anglican church. There were, however, numerous instances of toleration toward dissenters in both the Southern colonies and New England.

The one issue that separated the Anglican from the Congregational tradition was episcopacy. The descendants of the Puritans who left England to escape the ecclesiastical authority of Archbishop Laud were adamantly opposed to "prelacy." A proposal by Laud to place a bishop in America had been vigorously opposed. In Queen Anne's reign a planned colonial episcopate came close to fulfillment. The idea was revived by the bishop of London in the 1750s, but was suppressed by the English ministers. But in the decade following the Treaty of Paris in 1763 a major effort was made to secure a resident colonial bishop and thus complete the structure of the Church of England. Samuel Johnson, former president of King's College, was the acknowledged leader of this group. Because they believed bishops essential to the church, they were "High Church." Their efforts to secure the episcopate from England led to a major controversy in the 1760s and 1770s.

The Rev. Jonathan Mayhew and the Rev. Charles Chauncy were the foremost Congregationalist opponents to the episcopal scheme. Historical and theological differences between Anglicanism and Congregationalism were argued, but the major disagreement was over episcopacy. Congregationalists and Presbyterians viewed bishops as an extension of royal authority. In the wake of the Stamp Act of 1765, there was considerable opposition to any enlargement of England's governmental authority and many viewed the episcopal issue in this light. Many Anglicans (laity and some clergy) opposed an American episcopate for political reasons. This was especially true of Anglicans in the colonies where their church was established. These churchmen were known as "Low Church" because they viewed bishops as necessary for ordination, consecration, and confirmation, but rejected the privileged and political character of English episcopacy.

The War for Independence and the DISESTABLISHMENT of the Church of England between 1776-1789 removed the possibility that an American bishop would become a state official. The consecration of Samuel Seabury (1729-1796) by Scottish bishops in 1784 and William White (1748-1836) and Samuel Provoost (1742-1815) by English bishops in 1787 completed the structure of the Church of England, renamed the Protestant Episcopal Church.

See also articles on ANGLICAN CHURCH; COLONIAL PERIOD; PURITANISM.

Bibliography. Carl Bridenbaugh, *Mitre and Sceptre*; Arthur L. Cross, *The Anglican Episcopate and the American Colonies*; Edwin S. Gaustad, *Historical Atlas of Religion in America*; Frederick V. Mills, Sr., *Bishops By Ballot*.

FREDERICK V. MILLS, SR.
LA GRANGE COLLEGE

ETERNAL LIFE: *See* HEAVEN; HELL.

ETHICS, CHRISTIAN. The religious ethos of the South has been characterized historically by the prominence of a number of themes, which taken together have made Southern morality distinctive in comparison with that of other regions of the United States. Included among these motifs are the emphasis upon the orderly pattern of human relationships grounded in divine Providence, evangelism as the primary mission of the church, the purity of motivation and obedience to the moral law as the hallmarks of ethics, and social reform through the conversion of individuals. In the context of Southern religion, emphasis upon these ideas has frequently resulted in a spiritualistic conception of the church, a paternalistic view of society that has exalted the ideal of noblesse oblige, and a defensive morality designed to justify and preserve the dominant patterns of regional culture. Along with these generally conservative components, however, religious ethics in the South has also included elements of social protest and humanitarian appeals for social reform. Moreover, in contrast to the prevailing ethics of the white churches, the black churches have fostered an ethic of freedom and equality that has existed alongside an accommodationist morality of survival.

1. *The Pre-Civil War Period.* Throughout colonial times the great mass of the population was unchurched and, at least prior to the revivals of the 18th century, little influenced by organized religion. Two major issues were widely debated, however, by both the political and the religious leaders, namely, religious liberty and separation of the colonies from England.

Each of the colonies save Pennsylvania, Delaware, and Rhode Island had some form of state church. Congregationalism was the established religion in all of the New England colonies except Rhode Island. The Church of England was the state church in Virginia and the Carolinas throughout the colonial period, and during much of this time also in Maryland and Georgia. Although its founder was a Roman Catholic, Maryland was the first colony in America to embody the principle of religious toleration (1634). In enacting such a policy for all orthodox Christians, the proprietor—Cecil Calvert—was motivated by the need to attract non-Catholic settlers rather than by the teachings of his church. Following the English Revolution (1688), Maryland passed out of Roman Catholic control and the Church of England was established, with a resulting curtailment of religious freedom.

The Congregationalists were the leaders in support of independence in the North. In New England both Anglican clergy and laity were largely loyalists, whereas in the Southern colonies (especially in Virginia and Maryland) they were strongly patriotic. The Methodists were also divided on the issue. Under the influence of John Wesley, many supported the Tory cause; as the war progressed, however, Methodists increasingly supported the American cause. In addition to the Anglicans in Virginia and Maryland, the Presbyterians, Baptists, and Lutherans strongly supported independence in the Southern colonies. In the years following the Revolution, the Baptists and Presbyterians led the struggle for religious liberty in the South. The Methodists gradually shifted from their traditional advocacy of an established church—a position that they shared with the Anglicans—to the support of religious liberty and the separation of CHURCH AND STATE. While the Baptists were the earliest and most consistent champions of separation of church and state, the Presbyterians provided influential leadership in support of this principle.

Other issues that claimed the attention of the churches between the Revolution and the Civil War were temperance, slavery, and Sabbath observance. From colonial times through the first quarter of the 19th century drinking was almost universal. Drunkenness was widespread and often issued in quarreling, fighting, and other forms of civil disorder. In an effort to combat the evils of drink, the early reformers emphasized moderation in the use of alcoholic beverages, and they often advocated regulatory legislation to control the liquor traffic. In the latter half of the 18th century the temperance movement gained momentum in the colonies and

received increased support from the churches. For example, the General Rules of the Methodist Societies, laid down by John Wesley, forbade "drunkenness, buying or selling spirituous liquors, or drinking them (unless in cases of extreme necessity)." Following its incorporation into the *Discipline* of the Methodist Episcopal Church in this country (1789), this rule was considered advisory in its application to the lay membership, but mandatory in relation to the clergy. Prior to about 1830 the churches—like the secular temperance societies—generally called for moderation rather than abstinence, and they relied primarily upon moral suasion rather than legislation. After that time the temperance societies and the churches turned increasingly to total abstinence and legislative control of liquor sales, including Prohibition, as their goals. Thus by the end of the antebellum period Southern Presbyterians and Baptists, like the Methodists, generally supported abstinence as the Christian ideal; the Presbyterians and Methodists, in particular, also called for legislative controls.

Slavery was generally accepted in the American colonies. From 1701 onward, the Anglican Church embarked on a program of "instruction and conversion" among slaves, but it did not denounce the institution of SLAVERY itself. By the end of the Revolutionary era antislavery sentiment had become strong throughout the new nation. Churches joined in passing antislavery resolutions. In 1784 the Methodist Episcopal Church adopted legislation designed to end slaveholding among its members, but the attempt to enforce this requirement encountered such strong opposition that it was abandoned within the space of six months. During this period the Presbyterians and Baptists also supported emancipation. In 1817 the General Assembly of the Presbyterian Church strongly endorsed the aims of the AMERICAN COLONIZATION SOCIETY, which sought to solve the race problem in this country by resettling free slaves in Africa.

Although antislavery sentiment continued to grow in the North, attitudes toward the slave system began to shift in the South from about 1830 onward. Fundamentally, this change was due to the revolution that had taken place in Southern agriculture between 1790 and 1830. The invention of the cotton gin (1792) and the increased demand for cotton combined to make the region more and more dependent upon slave labor. Slavery thus came to be defended as an economic necessity; beginning in the 1830s, it was increasingly sanctioned also upon religious grounds. Among arguments that were used in its defense were the following: that it was supported by Scripture, that it was the best state for blacks, that it provided an opportunity for their conversion, and that it was part of a providential order of relationships in society. The doctrine of the sanctity of "relations" provided the fundamental basis for the justification of slavery and the hierarchical pattern of Southern culture. While it issued in an ethic that was dominantly hierarchical and paternalistic, it also on occasion provided a basis for the humanitarian appeals to justice and mutual loyalty within the system. During this period the Presbyterians began to develop a doctrine of the SPIRITUALITY OF THE CHURCH. According to this teaching, the church, a spiritual body, has no right to interfere directly with the civil relations of society; hence, slavery was no longer a question for the church but for the state to decide. In the remaining years before the Civil War, slavery became the consuming issue, attitudes in defense of that system became hardened, and the national Methodist, Baptist, and Presbyterian bodies eventually split over this issue. Opinion in the Episcopal Church was divided; however, these differences did not produce a schism because that body did not take an official stand on slavery.

2. *From the Civil War to 1900.* With the outbreak of the Civil War, the churches on both sides identified their own positions with the cause of patriotism. On both sides ministers turned the conflict into a holy war and assisted in the recruitment of troops. In the North it was a war to preserve the union; in the South "states' rights" became a sacred cause.

In the antebellum period slaves and their masters had attended the same churches, but the former had generally been seated in galleries. Following the war, the majority of free blacks withdrew from the white churches and formed separate congregations in order to escape the domination of their former masters. Most of the black members of the Methodist Episcopal Church in the South (ME Church, South, after 1885) withdrew from that body and joined the AFRICAN METHODIST EPISCOPAL CHURCH, the (Northern) Methodist Episcopal Church, and the Baptists. In 1870 most of the remaining black members of the Southern denomination, with the mutual consent of both races, organized the Colored (now CHRISTIAN) METHODIST EPISCOPAL Church. Independent Negro Baptist congregations came together to form the National Baptist Convention (q.v., NATIONAL BAPTISTS) in 1876. In the Southern Presbyterian Church (PCUS), black congregations formed separate presbyteries and eventually an independent synod (1898). While the freedmen took the initiative in withdrawing from the white churches, they did so with the encouragement of the latter. The resulting pattern of segregated churches was defended by the white religious leaders as beneficial for both races.

At the end of the war the Southern churches generally recognized their special obligations to the free blacks. Methodists, for example, acknowledged the duty to assist blacks in the formation of independent congregations, to supply their pulpits with white ministers until black preachers could be qualified, and to organize both Sabbath and day schools for their children. With the separation of Negro members and the hostilities generated by Reconstruction, the interest of the churches in the spiritual welfare of the blacks declined. Following Reconstruction, however, the sense of responsibility for the religious welfare and instruction of the blacks, including Negro ministers, was renewed. In 1876 the General Assembly of the Southern Presbyterian Church (PCUS) voted to establish the Institute for the Training of Colored Ministers at Tuscaloosa AL. Sentiment in support of educated black leadership for the uplifting of the Negro race also increased. This concern was symbolized, for example, by the assistance that the Methodist Episcopal Church, South, provided in the establishment (1882) of Paine Institute for the education not only of future ministers, but of black young people generally.

Throughout the latter part of the 19th and the first half of the 20th century, the Southern churches as a whole accepted and defended segregation not only in the churches, but also in society at large. They accepted the inferior status of blacks, but they did speak out against such extralegal injustices as lynching and for the right of blacks to a fair trial by jury. Concerned leaders also appealed to employers to aid freedmen in finding employment.

Although the TEMPERANCE movement lost support immediately after the Civil War, it gained new strength from the 1870s to the end of the century. The sale and use of intoxicating beverages became the primary social concern of the Methodists in the post-Reconstruction era. Methodists increasingly adopted the goals of total abstinence and legal Prohibition as the only effective solutions to the liquor problem. While the Baptists were relative latecomers to the temperance cause, they became strong supporters of total abstinence and Prohibition in this period, even though the latter ran counter to their traditional stand on the separation of church and state. Presbyterians generally advocated temperance and frequently supported Prohibition at the state or local levels; however, the doctrine of the spirituality of the church restrained their General Assembly from endorsing the PROHIBITION movement. The assembly relied, instead, upon regeneration and

the disciplinary powers of the church to control the evils of alcohol.

While Sabbath laws had previously been adopted in almost every state, enforcement of the former was relaxed following the war. Two major reasons for the growing secularization of the Sabbath in this period were rising urbanization and the influx of immigrants from continental Europe in the 1880s. To combat this trend the Methodist, Baptist, and Presbyterian churches admonished their members to refrain from boat and train excursions, letter writing, the reading of secular papers, social gatherings, and public entertainments, as well as all unnecessary labor on the Sabbath. When moral suasion and church discipline proved ineffective, the Protestant churches turned to legislation to effect reform in this area.

Throughout this period the churches were also engaged in efforts to combat many forms of "worldliness," including dancing, theatregoing, reading of novels, card playing, professional sports, and gambling. In the main, they relied upon personal conversion, moral suasion, and church discipline to prevent participation in such worldly evils. In addition, they also sought on occasion to control gambling, in particular, through legislation.

Although they welcomed a larger role for women in behalf of benevolent and religious causes, the Southern churches as a whole strongly opposed the feminist movement. The objectives of this movement, which became more militant in the years following the war, included the right to vote, equal rights before the law, equality in education and business, and equal rights in marriage. For Presbyterians feminism, like abolition, represented a repudiation of lawful authority. Not only was it contrary to Scripture; it threatened to undermine the entire order of human relationships. Methodists and Baptists also opposed any significant change regarding the status and role of women. Their opposition was based upon Scripture and God's providential design in creation. The two sexes, they argued, were divinely ordained to fill different (and unequal) roles in human life. In the Southern churches generally the issue that drew the loudest protest was the demand for equal suffrage.

The closing years of the 19th century saw an increased social consciousness in many of the Southern churches. In addition to temperance and antigambling crusades, by 1900 the Baptists, for example, were engaged in campaigns for the elimination of political corruption, the promotion of public morality, and care of orphans and the aged. Methodists demonstrated an awakening interest in the working class, the poor, and the downtrodden. This concern was expressed in support for a living wage and in the establishment of homes for orphans and widows as well as philanthropic agencies for the poor. Insofar as the existing social and economic order was concerned, however, the churches overwhelmingly supported the status quo. With few exceptions they made no realistic attempts to address such fundamental issues in the economy as child labor, the conditions of tenement life, the plight of new immigrants, and the exploitation of labor.

3. *The Twentieth Century, 1900-1945.* The liberal forces in the Southern churches at the turn of the century frequently made their greatest impact through secular reform movements such as the Southern Progressives and the SOUTHERN SOCIOLOGICAL CONGRESS. The latter, in particular, was influenced by the SOCIAL GOSPEL; in important respects it represented a Southern version of the latter adapted to the special ills of the South. Among the churches the Methodists were most open to the Social Gospel. In 1914 the Methodists in the South, following those in the North (1908) and the Federal Council of Churches (1908), adopted a Social Creed that dealt with a wide range of economic issues.

During the first decades of the present century race and temperance continued to be the major social concerns of the churches. The prevailing pattern of

SEGREGATION was defended on religious and secular grounds. Basically it was a hierarchical system based upon white control. The relationship of whites to blacks was paternalistic. Whites had an obligation to be just, kind, and benevolent in their dealings with blacks; the latter, in turn, were obligated to accept their inferior status with gratitude, loyalty, obedience, and diligence in their menial tasks. Within this given system, whites had a duty to work for better race relations and the removal of the severest forms of injustice, especially lynching. The churches continued to be segregated both at the congregational level and at all save their highest connectional levels.

In the South, Methodists and Baptists led the battle for national Prohibition. As individuals Presbyterians also worked for Prohibition; but, with rare exceptions, their spiritualistic doctrine of the church prevented their governing bodies from adopting resolutions on this issue. Following the enactment of the EIGHTEENTH AMENDMENT, the churches called for strict enforcement of the law. After repeal of this amendment Methodists and Baptists continued to call for total abstinence as the Christian ideal; they also continued their support for legal Prohibition at the state and local levels down to midcentury. In addition, they have broadened their approach to alcohol and other drug-related issues to include education, rehabilitation, and regulation of sales and advertising. The Episcopal Church was never officially involved in the Prohibition Movement.

While there had been some early opposition to a military conflict with Spain in 1898, the Southern churches—like those throughout the nation—generally supported the Spanish-American War once war had been declared. Shortly after the end of that conflict, many religious groups joined with secular peace societies in the denunciation of war and the advocacy of arbitration. When World War I began, the churches supported President Wilson's policy of neutrality;

but once the United States had entered the war, Methodists and Baptists quickly endorsed it as a holy war to defend the nation, democracy, and the Christian faith. Although most Southern Presbyterians also viewed the war as a crusade and strongly supported the national war effort, the assembly as well as most synods and presbyteries refrained from direct endorsement of the war. As individual citizens, however, most of their ministers also supported it as a righteous cause. Episcopalians likewise defended the war as righteous and inevitable. There were few conscientious objectors in the mainline churches, and pacifism was generally regarded as treason.

Following World War I, a peace crusade swept across the American churches. By the early 1930s pacifist sentiment was widespread among Methodists, particularly the clergy. In 1934 the Methodist Episcopal Church, South, affirmed the right of conscientious objection to war on Christian grounds and assured persons taking this stand of the support of the church. In 1944 the General Conference of The Methodist Church (UMC since 1968), which since 1939 included the ME Church, South, asserted the sinfulness of all war and declared its refusal "to endorse, support, or participate in war"; however, it pledged its full support to those who conscientiously served in the armed forces as well as conscientious objectors. When the United States entered World War II, sentiment shifted to the acceptance of the conflict as a tragic necessity. The General Conference of 1944 affirmed its support of the war along with its continued support of the right of conscientious objection. Pacifist sentiment was also strong in the Southern Presbyterian Church (PCUS) between the two world wars. In 1929 and again in 1931, the General Assembly of that body agreed that the church should never again support war or be used as an instrument of war. Faced with the threat of military conflict in Europe, the assembly declared in 1936 that America must remain neutral

in any future world conflict. With the outbreak of hostilities sentiment began to shift; after Pearl Harbor the assembly gave its support to the war as just and necessary. Unlike the Methodists and Presbyterians, the Southern Baptists were not drawn into the peace movement. Nevertheless, by the outbreak of World War II they had generally rejected the idea of war as a crusade. Following Pearl Harbor, they also endorsed the conflict as a just war. From 1943 onward the Southern churches were actively involved in planning for peace. The Crusade for a New World Order, launched by the Methodists in 1943-1944, was an effort to mobilize the total resources of the church for peace and world order. Southern Presbyterians endorsed the Federal Council of Churches' proposals for "a just and durable peace" and worked for the implementation of these principles. Southern Baptists supported the San Francisco Charter and urged its prompt ratification by the United States Senate.

Prior to the Great Depression, the Southern churches gave little attention to the injustices of economic institutions. In general they protested against child labor and defended the right of workers to organize and bargain collectively. Southern Baptists, however, strongly opposed a right to strike. On the whole, the region's churches espoused a Puritan economic ethic with an emphasis upon the duty of work and stewardship. This ethic was individualistic and conservative; it was based upon an acceptance of the existing forms of industrial and agrarian life. Following the Depression, there began to be greater criticism of capitalism and more support for economic reform, especially among Presbyterians.

The churches continued to resist the movement for women's rights. Presbyterians and Baptists were opposed to women speaking to mixed groups in churches into the 1920s. Methodists, Baptists, and Presbyterians recognized divorce only upon Scriptural grounds; prior to the mid-1950s, Methodists and Presbyterians permitted remarriage only to the innocent party.

4. *The Twentieth Century, 1945-.* The new social consciousness that had begun to emerge between 1890 and World War I suffered a setback in the 1920s, but was revived during the Depression. Since that time it has continued as a vital force in Southern religion and influenced all of the major denominations. The factors contributing to this revival were many. Departure by Southern Baptists from their traditional stand on church and state in the prohibition movement opened the way for greater involvement in other public issues. Among Presbyterians reconsideration of the doctrine of the church's spirituality from the mid-1930s onward led to a recovery of a more inclusive conception of the church's mission rooted in the Reformed tradition. Reunion of the Northern and Southern Methodist Episcopal Churches together with the Methodist Protestant Church in 1939 brought larger exposure to national religious currents and new pressures toward integration. These developments together with the inescapable impact of larger cultural events—the Depression, the failure of national Prohibition, World War II, new threats to peace and world order, and the civil rights movements—caused the Southern churches to confront the public issues that Americans generally faced at midcentury. By that time every major denomination had a full-time agency devoted to the social implications of the Gospel. Although the conservative elements still remained dominant in the churches of the region, the latter were moving increasingly into the mainstream of the religious life of the nation.

Following the war, race remained the overriding social issue in the Southern churches. The Plan of Union, which provided for Methodist reunification in 1939, included a separate (Central) jurisdiction for black churches along with five geographical jurisdictions in the united church. As a result of this plan, the segregation of black churches from the jurisdictional level down to the local congregation was complete in the South and largely so in the North. The majority of the black leadership had opposed the Plan of Union for this reason. In 1944 the General Conference began to work toward "the ultimate elimination of racial discrimination" within the reunited church. The national Methodist leadership endorsed the 1954 ruling of the U.S. Supreme Court forbidding racial segregation in the public schools. After a long struggle, the last vestiges of the Central Jurisdiction were eliminated in 1968.

From the 1930s onward the Southern Presbyterians (PCUS) also wrestled with racial discrimination in the church as well as society. The Council on Christian Relations had already prepared a report denouncing enforced segregation as contrary to Christian teachings prior to the court's ruling in May 1954. Meeting in that same month, the General Assembly adopted the report of the council and also endorsed the decision of the Supreme Court. The single all-black synod had been dissolved in 1951, and integration was completed at the presbytery level in 1968.

The Charter of Race Relations, adopted by the Southern Baptist Convention in 1947, marked the beginning of a new era in Southern Baptist teaching on race relations. The convention defended the ruling of the court on democratic and Christian grounds. Owing to its congregational polity, the denomination is forced to rely more than others upon the voluntary action of local churches in the formulation of church policy. In the postwar period, however, the Christian Life Commission (formerly, Social Service Commission) has provided effective leadership in the development of broader social consciousness among Southern Baptists.

In sum, during the three decades after 1950 the Southern churches became increasingly committed to the goals of an inclusive church and full equality in the area of social justice. Denominational seminaries, church presses, and social service agencies joined with the connectional leadership in support of civil rights in voting, education, and employment not only for blacks, but also for ethnic minorities and women. Recent studies have shown, however, that there is a significant gap between the churchwide, or connectional, leadership and local leaders, both clerical and lay, on these matters; there is an even wider gap between the connectional leadership and the membership of the churches as a whole.

Any survey of religious ethics in the South would be incomplete without some attention to the black churches. Although this subject is considered more fully elsewhere in this volume, it must be treated briefly here. Historically the black church has been the one institution in which blacks have enjoyed their greatest freedom and dignity. Both the INVISIBLE INSTITUTION of the church among the slaves and the independent black churches were expressions of freedom from white domination and control. Fear that conversion would lead to insurrection caused slaveholders to oversee the religious instruction of the slaves. Nevertheless, the yearning for freedom was kept alive by the slave preachers and through the black spirituals. In part, the latter were otherworldly songs of escape; in part, they were also songs of protest against the harsh injustices of daily life. Since the Civil War the independent black churches have been centers of community life. In them the dual pattern of quietism and prophetic protest continued from emancipation throughout the first half of the 20th century. Along with appeals for accommodation and assimilation into the prevailing white system, there was also strong criticism of the latter and support for civil rights.

The Montgomery bus boycott (1955-1956) and the Southern Christian Leadership Conference were largely products of the black church under the leadership of MARTIN LUTHER KING, JR. The call of King for nonviolent resistance to evil was rooted in a profoundly Christian understanding of human dignity and a vision of a racially inclusive community based on love and justice. While its goals and strategies have changed since the mid-1960s, the movement for black liberation has continued to be deeply influenced by the black church. Black theology—itself a product of the church—has continued to nurture and shape this movement through its emphases upon human dignity, liberation, reconciliation, and the close relationship of religion to community life.

Since the end of World War II the churches have consistently supported arms limitation and control. They were divided over Vietnam and called for fuller discussion of the issues involved in that conflict. As members of the National Council of Churches, the Methodist and Southern Presbyterian Churches increasingly reflected the influence of that body in their wrestlings with problems of war, peace, world order, economics and relationships with the Third World. Despite their traditional opposition to ecumenism, Southern Baptists more and more resemble other major Protestant denominations in their attitudes toward the foregoing issues; their conservative theology, religious individualism, and congregational government, however, continue to give their morality a distinctively individualistic and somewhat sectarian tone.

In this period the churches have also given major attention to economic issues. They have called for the fuller application of Christian principles to problems of industry and labor, poverty, world hunger, energy, and environment. The leadership of the churches has generally acknowledged the complexity of these issues and the need for realistic strategies of social change. The seminaries of most of the denominations have increasingly included economic and political issues in their curricula.

As in other sections of the nation, there has been a resurgence of conservative morality in Southern religion, symbolized by the MORAL MAJORITY, in the early 1980s. This movement has focused attention upon such issues as a constitutional amendment prohibiting abortion, prayer in the public schools, rights of homosexuals, and the proposed Equal Rights Amendment. On these issues the Moral Majority has generally opposed the positions taken by the connectional leadership of the Methodist and Presbyterian churches and by the Christian Life Commission of the Southern Baptists. The Southern Baptist Convention, in contrast, has continued to oppose ERA and rights of homosexuals. Unlike the Moral Majority, however, it has (with qualifications) supported legalized abortion. Baptists have continued to call for separation of church and state and opposed federal aid to church-related schools. Methodists and Presbyterians, on the other hand, have supported ERA, the ordination of women, and the rights of homosexuals, as well as legalized abortion. Methodists and Presbyterians have also called for the abolition of capital punishment.

See also articles on BLACK RELIGION; CHURCH AND STATE; CIVIL RIGHTS MOVEMENT; NATIVISM.

Bibliography. James Thayer Addison, *The Episcopal Church in the United States, 1789-1931*; Raymond W. Albright, *A History of the Protestant Episcopal Church*; Kenneth K. Bailey, *Southern White Protestantism in the Twentieth Century*; Erskine Clarke, *Wrestlin' Jacob: A Portrait of Religion in the Old South*; James H. Cone, *Black Theology and Black Power*; John Lee Eighmy, *Churches in Cultural Captivity: A History of the Social Attitudes of Southern Baptists*; Hunter Dickinson Farish, *The Circuit Rider Dismounts: A Social History of Southern Methodism 1865-1900*; Georgia Harkness, *The Methodist Church in Social Thought and Action*; Samuel S. Hill, Jr., *Southern Churches in Crisis*; Hill, et al., *Religion and the Solid South*; E. Brooks Holifield, *The Gentlemen Theologians: American Theology in Southern Culture, 1795-1860*; George D. Kelsey, *Social Ethics Among Southern Baptists, 1917-1969*; Martin Luther King, Jr., *Stride Toward Freedom*; C. Eric Lincoln, *The Black Church Since Frazier* (bound with E. Franklin Frazier, *The Negro Church in America*); Hart M. Nelsen, et al., eds., *The Black Church in America*; Rufus B. Spain, *At Ease in Zion: Social History of Southern Baptists, 1865-1900*; Ernest Trice Thompson, *Presbyterians in the South*, 3 vols., *The Spirituality of the Church: A Distinctive Doctrine of the Presbyterian Church in the United States*; Carter G. Woodson, *The History of the Negro Church*.

E. CLINTON GARDNER
EMORY UNIVERSITY

ETHICS, RELIGIOUS: *See* ETHICS, CHRISTIAN.

ETHICS, SOCIAL: *See* ETHICS, CHRISTIAN; SOCIAL GOSPEL.

ETHNICITY: *See* NATIVISM.

EUCHARIST: *See* SACRAMENTS AND ORDINANCES.

EVANGELICAL PROTESTANTISM. Evangelical means, quite simply, pertaining to the gospel, the good news that God redeems sinful humanity through Jesus Christ. Evangelical Protestants have stressed that people find salvation only through personal faith in Christ's atoning death and the regenerating power of the Holy Spirit. Evangelical also denotes a desire to proclaim this gospel to others by word and deed. Variations in time and place have nuanced the term's meaning and usage, and ladened it with much historic freight.

The churches of the Lutheran Reformation first put "evangelical" into common usage, using the term to describe their distinctive features: salvation by grace alone, through faith, and the Bible as the Christian's supreme authority. In time, Germanic people equated "evangelical" with Protestant, meaning especially the Lutherans.

The Reformation doctrines of *sola fides* and *sola scriptura* still inform 20th-century evangelical movements, but in the 17th century, a renewed desire for personally experienced, heartfelt, and life-transforming faith gave new content to the meaning of evangelical. The English Puritan movement stressed one's need of conversion, a personal experience of receiving God's grace, and contended that liturgy and sacraments had no inherent value. Puritans believed that conversion infused one with zeal for God's will in all of life, which prompted them to seek reform in society and government as well as the church. The Pietist movement on the Continent was a reaction against spiritual decline in the Lutheran and Reformed churches. Like Puritans, Pietists stressed the need for conversion, but they rejected rationalistic and creedal definitions of religious truth, insisting that truth be validated by experience. This "experimental" religion meant prayer, self-denial, close fellowship, Bible study, and evangelistic zeal. The MORAVIANS, a pietistic communal fellowship led by Count Zinzendorf, who was a Lutheran nobleman, sent missionary pioneers to many lands in the early eighteenth century.

Further elaborations on what it meant to be evangelical came during the revivals that swept Great Britain and her American colonies in the mid-eighteenth century. A group of Anglican priests led by Charles and John Wesley and GEORGE WHITEFIELD was convinced by the teachings of the Puritans and the Pietists that they needed to know Jesus Christ personally, and each experienced conversion. As they preached in churches, fields, and jails, the quiet witness of the Pietists and the Puritan belief that conversion usually followed a long spiritual travail were transformed. Whitefield and the Wesleys boldly urged multitudes to be "born again" that very day.

The result was a great wave of conversions, renewed religious zeal, and controversy in the mid-eighteenth century that the British called the Evangelical Revival and the Americans the GREAT AWAKENING. A strong evangelical party developed within the Church of England, which promoted a new wave of missionary endeavor and social reform. The Wesleys' ministry spawned its own cell groups, and eventually the Methodist Church, which became a major liberating force among the working classes. In America, the revival stirred all the denominations, provoking controversy, schisms, and growth. By the turn of the century, the most intensely evangelistic churches—the Baptists and Methodists— were winning scores of believers.

This new movement differed greatly from the "evangelical churches" of Luther's day. The evangelical persuasion

now included a deemphasis of the creedal and sacramental channels of faith, voluntary religious affiliation, interdenominational cooperation, aggressive evangelization, instantaneous conversions, zealous, abstemious life-styles, and revivalistic millennial expectations.

During the next half-century, American Evangelicals attempted to make America fulfill the millennial sense of destiny under which the nation had been founded. They shaped American cultural life by founding hundreds of colleges, academies, benevolent and missionary societies and, of course, congregations. Public reverence for and reference to the Bible abounded. Revival itself became an institution, the dominant paradigm for social and political change. In the North, Evangelicals embraced an ethic of progress, improvement, industry, and free choice. It fueled economic and geographic expansion as well as reforms of many kinds, most notably the antislavery movement. In the South, the evangelical movement met with sweeping success. Yet its initial power to reconcile blacks and whites and oppose slavery was compromised. Slavery became the region's social and economic foundation, and white Evangelicals who wished to be respected quietly stopped "preaching liberty to the captives" and developed biblical arguments for slavery.

These evangelically informed but radically opposed visions of a Christian America brought a confrontation that would be resolved only by civil war. Meanwhile, the slaves accepted the gospel in ever-growing numbers, but insisted on their own interpretation: that people made free in Christ would become free indeed. From that beginning a vibrant black Evangelicalism arose. It preached a gospel of liberation that propelled black communities to seek freedom and equality.

The evangelical persuasion in the 19th century flourished in a larger transatlantic context as well. British evangelical trends came to America in the early nineteenth century, notably the antislavery movement and the Disciples of Christ (Christian) movement, which was prompted by the revival-fired Scottish immigrant ALEXANDER CAMPBELL and the former Presbyterian BARTON STONE. In midcentury, American evangelists and holiness advocates Charles G. Finney and Phoebe Palmer toured the British Isles and northern Europe. Scandinavia seethed with religious ferment as Mormons, Baptists, Methodists, Adventists, the Salvation Army, and various Lutheran evangelical movements swept through those lands. A great international network was developing, with agencies such as the China Inland Mission, founded by Englishman J. Hudson Taylor; the Scandinavian Alliance Mission, founded by Swedish-American Frederik Franson; and the Salvation Army, led by the English Methodist evangelist William Booth. By 1900, evangelical Protestants were making converts around the globe through an international missionary force.

The evangelical Protestant churches in the United States in the late nineteenth century comprised an informal religious establishment that would soon change drastically. By 1925 Evangelicals would seem bizarre and antiquated to many secular-minded people. Massive immigration made the country markedly less Protestant and the new urban, industrial environment challenged the churches' effectiveness. New intellectual trends such as the critical study of the Bible, evolutionary science, and naturalistic philosophy questioned Christian claims of absolute, changeless truth and the only way of salvation.

These challenges prompted both a resurgence of revivalism and social concern as well as a striking departure from Evangelicalism. A new Wesleyan HOLINESS MOVEMENT stressed the sanctifying power of the Holy Spirit to restore Christians' zeal for holy living, evangelism, and social action. It stirred American Methodist churches in the 1870s and 1880s and eventually produced several

new holiness sects, the CHURCH OF THE NAZARENE prominent among them. Meanwhile, a "Bible school" movement centered around evangelist Dwight L. Moody of Chicago attracted people from the more "Reformed" wing of American Protestantism. It prompted renewed domestic and foreign evangelism, revitalized lay piety, and reaffirmed the power of evangelical faith. A third movement, broadly labeled as "liberal," modified evangelical doctrines of biblical authority and exclusive truth claims to accommodate the new social needs and intellectual challenges. Liberals claimed that the Bible was a noble but human record of evolving spirituality, and Christianity was the highest system of ethics and religious expression yet developed. But people would find God's will most directly in the ideals of the present age. The liberal movement rapidly gained support among distinguished Protestant spokesmen such as pulpiteer Henry Ward Beecher and became the prevailing viewpoint in the leading Northern seminaries by 1900. Responding to this search for authority, yet another movement arose, PENTECOSTALISM. Pentecostals reasserted the presence of the miraculous in the world by insisting that God answered with supernatural signs and wonders, including the gift of tongues, healings, and material provision. This movement, like the others, spread rapidly along the international evangelical network though it was opposed everywhere by liberals and Evangelicals alike.

The "Bible school" leaders became alarmed at liberal trends in the churches and led a vigorous defense of such Christian "fundamentals" as the inerrancy of the Bible, the deity of Christ, his bodily resurrection, and imminent second coming. Eventually called the Fundamentalists, they and other conservative Evangelicals clashed with liberals in several major denominations during the 1920s. Liberal and moderate forces prevailed, but the once-proud evangelical establishment was in disarray by 1930.

The liberals enjoyed nearly unchallenged leadership in the Northern denominations, but they governed a shrinking and disspirited empire, for they failed to maintain the popular commitment that had built great missionary and benevolent agencies. These old-line denominations encountered declining membership and budgets that have continued to the present day, with only a brief respite from the mid-1940s through the 1960s. The neo-orthodox movement's attempt to revive the gospel's centrality was only partially successful.

In the meantime, Evangelicals prospered in such diverse companies as fundamentalist, Wesleyan, Adventist, Pentecostal, northern European immigrant, pietistic, Anabaptist, as well as black and white Southern churches. As in the Pietist and Puritan movements, American Evangelicals became dissenters, offering attractive alternatives to the religious establishment. By 1960, they comprised half of all American Protestants and accounted for over half of the American Protestant missionaries.

By midcentury, these scattered evangelical forces showed new signs of unity. The National Association of Evangelicals was begun in 1942 by a group of moderate, irenic fundamentalists who hoped for a great national revival. They persuaded a broad spectrum of Evangelicals to unite and cooperate in this task. Even more successful was Billy Graham, an evangelist with fundamentalist roots who rose to national fame in the 1950s. Evangelicals of all kinds cast aside their differences to support Graham's massive urban campaigns. In like fashion, hundreds of interdenominational evangelical agencies sprang up, such as World Vision, which was by 1975 the nation's largest Protestant missionary and relief organization. By the late 1970s, the news media had discovered this evangelical renaissance in America; the Gallup Poll announced that perhaps one in five Americans was evangelical and one in three had had a life-changing religious experience akin to being "born again." Fundamentalists and other conservative Evangelicals mounted a political presence in the 1980 presidential election with the MORAL MAJORITY interest group, which claimed to have brought victory to Ronald Reagan. Evangelicals were discovering that their voices could be heard in a supposedly secular age.

In the midst of all this discussion, however, the term itself was taking on a new meaning. The fundamentalist-rooted leaders who initiated the NAE, launched the career of BILLY GRAHAM, and founded *Christianity Today* magazine in 1956, had appropriated the "evangelical" label for themselves. Unfortunately, their definition of what constituted "Evangelicalism" was tinged with Reformed and fundamentalist emphases and did not satisfy many Christians of obviously evangelical heritage. So we are left with the anomalous claim of contemporary black theologians that their heritage is not evangelical and the strange insistence of a Southern Baptist spokesman that "we are *not* evangelicals, that's a Yankee word. . . . We don't share their . . . fussy fundamentalism."

Still, the evangelical faith has permeated a remarkable variety of traditions and cultures. Refugees from fundamentalism have carried it into the Anglo-Catholic tradition on one hand and into the Anabaptist fold on the other while Pentecostal perspectives now live within Roman Catholic and Lutheran communions. Missionary activity and indigenous church growth have made the evangelical Protestant wing of Christianity the world's fastest-growing. Yet history shows that Evangelicalism's very flexibility and cultural adaptivity have brought its greatest shortcoming: it can be liberating and reformist as a dissenting faith, but it has yet to find out how to retain its prophetic qualities when called upon to lead a society.

See also articles on EVANGELICALISM; FUNDAMENTALISM; GREAT REVIVAL; NEW BIRTH; PIETISM; PURITANISM; REVIVALISM.

Bibliography. Robert Mapes Anderson, *Vision of the Disinherited*; Robert Bainton, *Here I Stand: The Life of Martin Luther*, ed., *World Christian Encyclopedia...A.D. 1900-2000*; Dale Brown, *Understanding Pietism*; Paul A. Carter, *The Spiritual Crisis of the Gilded Age*; Arnold Dallimore, *George Whitefield*; Frederick Hale, *Transatlantic Conservative Protestantism*; William Haller, *The Rise of Puritanism*; Robert T. Handy, *A Christian America*; Nathan O. Hatch and Mark A. Noll, eds., *The Bible in America*; William R. Hutchison, *The Modernist Impulse in American Protestantism*; Norris Magnuson, *Salvation in the Slums*; George M. Marsden, *Fundamentalism and American Culture*; Donald G. Mathews, *Religion in the Old South*; Bernard Semmel, *The Methodist Revolution*; Timothy L. Smith, *Called Unto Holiness; Revivalism and Social Reform*; Leonard I. Sweet, ed., *The Rising Tide of American Evangelicalism*; David F. Wells and John D. Woodbridge, eds., *The Evangelicals*.

JOEL A. CARPENTER
WHEATON COLLEGE

EVANGELICALISM. This is the type of Christianity with the greatest following and influence in the South. It is a religious mood, belief, and movement within the Protestant tradition that originated as a popular affirmation of radical supernaturalism in reaction against the theological naturalism of the 18th century in Great Britain and British America. In the 19th century, it became one of the determinants of Southern culture and still continues to be a major factor in defining the region's uniqueness.

The *mood* of Evangelicalism—even in the formal, institutional concreteness of its churches, schools, and leadership—is suspicious of formalism, routine, and elitism that make institutions appear to be unresponsive to ordinary, lay church members. Although the style of public discourse varies with social standing and level of education, it is always governed by the preacher's attempt to speak *for* as well as *to* the congregation, and to elicit from each believer a renewed "personal" bonding with the Divine (in Christ) and commitment to the holy life. The personal expression of this mood is shaped by a persistent sensitivity to the implications of this bonding and commitment for personal morality and, frequently, for social responsibility. The latter, however, is usually shaped by what is possible for an individual to do with regard to his or her personal life. Although the structure of social relationships can become a matter of moral discourse and sometimes has in the South (master-slave, rich-poor), the evangelical mood tends to focus more on private behavior than the social implications of public policy. This is largely the result of the historic and vivid moral dichotomy within Evangelicalism of church and world, and emphasis on an individual's choosing *either* one *or* the other. Acceptance of ambiguity, ambivalence, and complexity in human affairs is often taken as evidence of moral failure within evangelical ideology.

The evangelical *belief system* is firmly entrenched within the Protestant tradition, but there are six essential foci that characterize it. The first is belief in the Bible as the authoritative guide to faith and morals rather than such sources as historical continuity, historical experience, the episcopacy, theological analysis, or any combination of these. This Biblicism tends to burden interpretation informed by neither history, criticism, nor theology with an infallibility that suggests more the frailty of human judgment than faith in an absolute source of value and being.

The second is justification by faith, a teaching that affirms the supernatural disruption of the sinner's life and places her or him in a new relationship with God, creating in this *conversion* the basis for the personal assurance that provides psychological stamina to adopt the third focus, a way of life (sanctification) characterized by a conscious struggle to subdue the self in service to the Divine. The self-discipline and sexual repression made possible by this holy self-confidence requires the believer to be an example to others of the true life in Christ.

The internal tension created by this responsibility is released in part through the fourth, a commitment to prosyletization, that is, the mission to share one's faith with others, or evangelism. As an agent of a higher power, the convert is justified in aggressive competition with and hostility towards other ideologies, suspicion of tolerance and pluralism, and attacks on irreligion. Ultimate justification for pursuing the mission is the eventual establishment by God of the millennium (the fifth focus) as sketched out in the book of Revelation. Although Evangelicals disagree as to the means through which the direct reign of Christ will be established, and although the mood of expectancy may be expressed in various ways, insistence on the "reality" of this future state gives a meaning to the historical process similar to that of ideologies such as Marxism or other millennial religions.

The sixth focus refers to the coherence of Evangelicalism, namely, its dependence on the individual's personal experience of the truth of the Christian message. Whereas other religious moods and movements find their continuity in such objective institutions as church, pope, doctrine, sacraments, canon law, or creeds, Evangelicals focus on a continuous struggle with the self, continual engagement with the Bible, and persistent expectation of being further inspired by preaching. Each individual's conversion is the essential emblem of Christianity, the standard of religious authenticity.

Evangelical movements in the 18th century originated primarily among people at the margins and in the lowest ranks of society, a pattern that would change as the children and grandchildren of these converts came to their majority. By the early 1800s both blacks and whites had made Evangelicalism the dominant religion of the South. By then, Presbyterians were dividing into an evangelical and opposition group (OLD SCHOOL/NEW SCHOOL); SEPARATE BAPTISTS were setting the tone for what was to become the Southern Baptist Convention in 1845; and Methodists were the fastest-growing denomination in the South. Blacks were developing their own religious style— greater celebration in worship—and their own sacred history and future, emphasizing God's promise of freedom in Moses,

Daniel, and the Lord of the Apocalypse: "King Jesus rides on a milk white horse, no man can hinder Him!"

As a mood, belief system, and movement, Evangelicalism crossed the lines of time as well as race and denomination because it so easily expressed the protest and hopes of ordinary people. During the time from 1740 to 1870, white Evangelicals became part of the sociopolitical elite only to be challenged by people in the HOLINESS MOVEMENT, the LANDMARK MOVEMENT, and other "revivalists" (1880s and 1890s). As historical and critical studies seemed to move churchmen from the radical supernaturalism of the past, self-styled fundamentalists objected angrily, denounced scientific naturalism, and established their own educational and publishing institutions (1910 and after). Since the 1880s each generation in the South has experienced a resurgence of the evangelical mood. Even as religious commentators were preparing to write the epitaph of Evangelicalism in the 1970s, there was yet another affirmation through mood, belief, and action of the radical supernaturalism that had erupted first in the 18th century.

See also articles on BIBLE, AUTHORITY OF; EVANGELICAL PROTESTANTISM; FUNDAMENTALISM; PREACHING; REVIVALISM.

Bibliography. Kenneth K. Bailey, *Southern White Protestantism in the 20th Century*; Fred Bode, *Protestantism and the New South*; John B. Boles, *The Great Revival, 1787-1805: The Origins of the Southern Evangelical Mind*; John Lee Eighmy, *Churches in Cultural Captivity*; Willard Gatewood, *Preachers, Pedagogues and Politicians*; Donald G. Mathews, *Religion in the Old South*; Marshall Frady, *Billy Graham*; H. Shelton Smith, *In His Image, but . . .*; David F. Wells and John Woodbridge, *The Evangelicals*.

DONALD G. MATHEWS
UNIVERSITY OF NORTH CAROLINA
AT CHAPEL HILL

EVANGELISM: *See* EVANGELICAL PROTESTANTISM.

EVANGELIST. A title in common usage in the churches of the South, it refers to those Christians whose major calling is to convert individuals to faith in Christ. While all Christians are said to have responsibility for declaring and living the Gospel, the "Good News" (in Greek, *euaggelion*), in practice only some regard evangelism as a consuming commitment. Such men (and a few women) believe that they are evangelists by vocation. Their ministry is to preach, and also to engage in one-to-one witnessing, toward bringing about the eternal salvation of every person who has not "accepted Christ as personal Savior." This is usually understood to take place in a single, datable experience of conversion. At that moment the lost person's sins are pardoned, he or she enters into "new life in Christ," and is on the way to everlasting life with God in heaven.

Thus, in the popular EVANGELICALISM of the South, spanning denominations from the Southern Baptists to the radical sects and Fundamentalists, the work of evangelism is recognized as essential, indeed as the heart and soul of Christianity's message and ministry. Typically the title "evangelist" is applied to a "full-time evangelist," one who does "full-time evangelistic work." BILLY GRAHAM is the most famous practitioner of this calling. (He stands in a tradition running back to Charles G. Finney during the 1820s to 1850s and Dwight L. Moody during the 1870s to 1890s.) In the South SAM P. JONES and MORDECAI F. HAM have been prominent full-time evangelists. But there are scores of ministers who live by this vocation, many of them operating within a single denomination, many others functioning quite ecumenically.

At the same time, every evangelical pastor is an evangelist, particularly in the South where the standard form of Evangelicalism is preoccupied with the conversion of lost souls. In point of quantity, most Southern evangelists are settled pastors who carry on that work weekly in their own congregations and occasionally through invited visitations to other churches.

EVOLUTION CONTROVERSY.
Nothing has done more to identify the American South as a stronghold of funda-mentalist Protestantism than efforts there to curtail the teaching of Darwinian evolution. In particular, the 1925 SCOPES TRIAL at Dayton TN sensationalized the drive and the milieu that nurtured it.

Why this cause emerged as a popular issue, why it has persisted, and why its successes have been mostly in the South are significant questions. It is noteworthy, of course, that the perennial agitation against religious modernism focuses primarily on Darwinism from time to time, and that most Southern church members apparently have believed in supernatural revelation and the literal inerrancy of the Scriptures. Furthermore, it is significant that the conservative Protestant hegemony of the South probably has had no equivalent in modern Christendom. Especially in the rural South, unusual anxieties were generated by World War I and its aftermath, then later by a variety of secularistic intellectual trends, by a burgeoning technological revolution, by urbanization, and by drastic departures in common outlooks and behavior. Moreover, the expansion of public education early in this century, especially at the secondary level, was a contributing factor. With new compulsory school attendance laws, the biological sciences were presumably studied by Southern students in enlarged numbers. Nor did fundamentalists err in perceiving an irreconcilable conflict between the evolutionary theory of human origin and the Genesis account of creation as traditionally construed. Popular leaders like WILLIAM JENNINGS BRYAN pointed to these contradictions and orchestrated the reaction.

The initial drive for an antievolution statute occurred in Kentucky in 1922. As drafted and introduced in the state House of Representatives, the proposed law would have produced several results. One was the prohibition of teaching in publicly financed institutions of "Darwinism, Atheism, Agnosticism, or the Theory of Evolution in so far as it pertains to the origin of man." On a related front, offending teachers "on conviction [were to] be fined not less than Fifty ($50.00) dollars nor more than Five Thousand ($5,000) dollars or confined in the County Jail not less than ten days nor more than twelve months or both fined and imprisoned in the discretion of the jury." After fiery debate, legislators rejected the bill by margin of 42 to 41, a cliff-hanging outcome that encouraged Bryan to predict that the movement would sweep the county.

The envisaged sweep did not in fact develop in the North or West (antievolution bills introduced in Maine, New Hampshire, Delaware, West Virginia, Missouri, Minnesota, North Dakota, and California did not gain the approval of a single legislative house and were not seriously considered in most cases); but the picture was different and pronounced in the South. Antievolution bills were formally considered in every Southern legislature except that of Virginia, usually more than once, and usually with strong support. Such a measure passed one legislative house only to die in the other in South Carolina in 1922, Texas in 1923, Louisiana in 1926, Arkansas and Florida in 1927. Before the end of the decade, identical or similar measures had been adopted in Florida, Tennessee, Mississippi, Arkansas, and Oklahoma. The Oklahoma law, applying only to state-purchased textbooks through the eighth grade, was repealed two years after passage, and Florida legislators merely registered their advisory "sense." Only in Tennessee, Mississippi, and Arkansas did the statutes contain a punitive provision, apply directly to teachers, and remain a part of the legal codes for 40 or so years. The Arkansas legislation was achieved by voter initiative and referendum after the attempt in the legislature failed.

Except for the litigation of Dayton, the three laws with enforcement provisos turned out to be dead letters. Indeed, the Tennessee Supreme Court, in upholding that state's legislation, pointedly suggested that the Scopes litigation be nol-prossed. Nonprosecution in the courts did not usually signify inattentiveness or substantial retreat, however. Privately controlled religious schools in the South sometimes forbade (and sometimes today forbid) advocacy of the despised theory on their campuses. In rural public schools, community opinion and local boards of trustees generally have seen to it that the Genesis narrative was not impugned. This was noted by Howard K. Beale in 1941 when he guessed that more than one out of three teachers across the nation were "afraid to express acceptance of the theory of evolution, even if they made no effort to persuade their pupils" (and the fraction was surely larger in the South). Moreover, the sensitivity of state textbook commissions in the sphere of biology was reflected both in their adoptions and in what was submitted to them for evaluation by publishers and authors. In an unusual reaction to perceived longtime textual inadequacies, the National Science Foundation and the American Institute of Biological Sciences created a curriculum study group early in the 1960s under whose sponsorship three authorized high school biology textbooks were released. The ensuing effects upon science instruction were thought to be significant.

The dormant Tennessee law was finally repealed in 1967, and the United States Supreme Court struck down the Arkansas and Mississippi laws the following year. But the antievolution campaign continued, now not so much for an outright banning of Darwin's teachings, as before, but for a compulsory exposition of the Genesis account of creation whenever evolutionary human development was expounded. A Tennessee law of 1973 mandated that any public school textbook wherein there were formulations about humanity's evolutionary origin must specifically identify these formulations as theory rather than "scientific fact"—and that any prescribed volume containing such a passage must also present the biblical account of creation (with no disclaimer of factual certitude being required in this latter instance). Notwithstanding the invalidation of the new law by a federal appellate court, Arkansas and Louisiana adopted legislation in 1981 requiring that the biblical story of creation must be part of any public school presentation whenever the evolutionary account of human descent was introduced. These measures too were quickly struck down by federal courts.

See also articles on FUNDAMENTALISM; MODERNIST CONTROVERSY.

Bibliography. Kenneth K. Bailey, *Southern White Protestantism in the Twentieth Century*; Howard K. Beale, *A History of Freedom of Teaching in American Schools*; William E. Ellis, "Recurring Crisis: The Evolution/Creation Controversy," unpublished paper presented at convention of Organization of American Historians, Philadelphia, April 1982; Willard B. Gatewood, Jr., ed., *Controversy in the Twenties: Fundamentalism, Modernism, and Evolution.*

KENNETH K. BAILEY
UNIVERSITY OF TEXAS AT EL PASO

EWING, FINIS (1773-1841), a founder of the CUMBERLAND PRESBYTERIAN CHURCH, was its most influential early leader. Son of the clerk of the county court of Bedford County VA, Ewing married a daughter of the prominent family after whom Davidson County TN is named. In 1795 he moved to Logan County KY, where during the GREAT REVIVAL in the West (1787-1805), he was ordained to the ministry by prorevival Presbyterians. Ewing, and others ordained or licensed by prorevival ministers during the revival, had not completed a classical education and would not adopt the Confession of Faith without stating reservations concerning its teaching on predestination.

As a result of these irregular ordinations and licensings, a rupture occurred between prorevival ministers in southern Kentucky and more conservative members of the Synod of Kentucky. The major issue at stake was subscription to the Confession; the matter of educational qualifications for the ministry was clearly secondary. Though some of the prorevival ministers were reconciled to the synod on terms acceptable to its more conservative members, Ewing, wearied by unsuccessful efforts to secure reunion on other terms, united with Samuel King and Samuel McAdow to constitute an independent Cumberland Presbytery in February 1810. This body became the nucleus of the Cumberland Presbyterian Church. Ewing's theological position was deeply influenced by Enlightenment thought, which left no place for paradox. He, like John Wesley, believed the doctrine of predestination contradicted the gospel of God's love for sinners. In contrast to the Methodists, he defended the doctrine of the perseverance of the saints against the teaching that one can fall from grace. Ewing articulated his theology at length in *A Series of Lectures on the Most Important Subjects of Divinity* (1827).

See also articles on FRONTIER, INFLUENCE OF; REVIVALISM.

D. NEWELL WILLIAMS
BRITE DIVINITY SCHOOL

EXPERIENCE, RELIGIOUS: *See* PIETY.

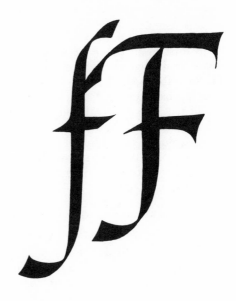

FAITH HEALING. Common among Holiness, Pentecostal, and charismatic groups, faith healing stems from a conviction that the miraculous works performed by Jesus and the disciples after Pentecost can be repeated by Christians today. Did not Jesus say that the one "who believes in me will also do the works that I do, and greater works than these will he do, because I go to the Father" (Jn. 14:12, RSV)?

Holiness associations formed in the second half of the 19th century around an interpretation of the WESLEYAN TRADITION's idea of entire sanctification or "perfect love" as a SECOND BLESSING. Some leaders began to see healing as a part of such perfection. They cited Exod. 15:26: "I am the Lord that healeth thee," and Jas. 5:14-15: "Is any sick among you? let him call for the elders of the church; and let them pray over him, anointing him with oil in the name of the Lord: And the prayer of faith shall save the sick, and the Lord shall raise him up."

Leaders such as A. B. Simpson of the CHRISTIAN AND MISSIONARY ALLIANCE preached a "Four-fold Gospel": Christ as Savior, Sanctifier, *Healer*, and Coming King. During the 1880s and 1890s the emphasis was on the "prayer of faith." Christians were exhorted to pray for the sick, laying hands on them, anointing them with oil, and believing that God would indeed heal them. Christians and the sick person were to pray and have faith; God did the healing.

Always controversial, healing became a marked tenet of the more radical groups in the HOLINESS MOVEMENT. As they increasingly emphasized the Pentecostal "enduement with power" and the signs or gifts of the Holy Spirit, they shifted to such verses as Jesus' final words in Mk. 16:17-18 (RSV): "These signs will accompany those who believe: in my name they will cast out demons; they will speak in new tongues; they will pick up serpents, and if they drink any deadly thing, it will not hurt them; they will lay their hands on the sick, and they will recover."

Specific people became known as having "the gift of healing." Charles Parham, often termed the "founder" of PENTECOSTALISM, emphasized healing in his ministry. Other early healers with influence in the South were Mary Woodworth-Etter, Aimee Semple McPherson, and Fred F. Bosworth.

Ministers in the Assemblies of God dominated what Harrell has called "The Healing Revival" of 1947-1958: Gordon Lindsay, Jack Coe, A. A. Allen, and Jimmy Swaggart. The "revival" began in 1946 with the work of Baptist William Branham among the United Pentecostal churches of Missouri and Arkansas. His popularity was soon rivaled by Oklahoman ORAL ROBERTS, a PENTECOSTAL HOLINESS CHURCH preacher who became a United Methodist in 1968. Independent healers included Morris Cerullo and Kathryn Kuhlman.

Among neo-Pentecostals or charismatics of the 1980s, two of the best-known practitioners of faith healing have been Methodist Tommy Tyson and Harvard-educated Dominican priest Francis MacNutt. They draw much of their theoretical inspiration from Episcopalian Agnes Sanford, who emphasizes prayer and faith.

See also article on CHARISMATIC MOVEMENTS.

Bibliography. Robert Mapes Anderson, *Vision of the Disinherited: The Making of American Pentecostalism*; David Edwin Harrell, Jr., *All Things Are Possible: The Healing and Charismatic Revivals in Modern America*; Richard Quebedeaux, *The New Charismatics*.

NANCY A. HARDESTY
ATLANTA, GEORGIA

FANNING, TOLBERT (1810-1874), pioneer Campbellite leader, was born in Cannon County TN. Baptized at age 17 by Stoneite preachers in Alabama, he moved to Nashville where he preached for the Disciples of Christ throughout Middle Tennessee. He entered the University of Nashville in 1831 and graduated in 1835. He gained much of his strict biblicism from his travels with ALEXANDER CAMPBELL during 1835 and 1836. Throughout his career he was opposed to the "pastor" system. Among Disciples in Tennessee, he was one of the first who advocated nonparticipation of Christians in war and government.

Fanning was known for several areas of interest. He and his wife operated a number of schools, Franklin College (1844-1865) in Nashville being the most important. There he attempted to develop a manual labor concept along with his interests in scientific agriculture. He helped form an agricultural society in Tennessee and was an editor of the *Agriculturalist* (1840-1845). His *Naturalist* (1846) was concerned with scientific matters. He founded and edited the *Christian Review* (1844-1848) and the *Gospel Advocate* (1855-). He was considered to be the outstanding evangelist among Disciples in the South prior to the Civil War.

During the 1850s, Fanning began opposing the missionary society movement among Disciples. He recognized liberal tendencies among Disciples in this movement and in what he considered a changing interpretation of the Bible. He must be considered as a leader in the development of the conservatism among Disciples that led to the CHURCHES OF CHRIST.

See also articles on ANTIMISSION MOVEMENT; CAMPBELLITE TRADITION; RELIGIOUS PRESS.

Bibliography. James R. Wilburn, *The Hazard of the Die.*

ROBERT E. HOOPER
DAVID LIPSCOMB COLLEGE

FAULKNER, WILLIAM (1897-1962), foremost Southern novelist, was born in New Albany MS. He spent most of his life in Oxford, Lafayette County, which became the site of his Yoknapatawpha County and the breeding ground for his tortured Compson family and the comic, conniving Snopes clan. While he spent a brief period in Hollywood as a script writer out of financial necessity and several years as writer-in-residence at the University of Virginia, Faulkner found his literary voice "in this little postage stamp of native soil" where his characters struggled with racial guilt, the contradictions of sex and death, and the inherited dreams and flaws of intricate family histories.

Faulkner's most creative work was in the novels of the early 1930s: *The Sound and the Fury* (1929), *As I Lay Dying* (1930), *Light in August* (1932), and *Absalom, Absalom* (1936). He invested great energy in *The Fable*, a retelling of the Passion story set in World War I, a work generally regarded as a critical failure. In 1950 Faulkner was awarded the Nobel Prize for literature and voiced his stubborn hope for humankind in his acceptance speech: "I believe that man will not merely endure: he will prevail. He is immortal."

Many critics have taken "endurance" as the central theme of Faulkner's work and the critical key to understanding him as a neo-Stoic. Honor, heroism, and duty are prime virtues in the fiction of Faulkner. And yet the endurance of Faulkner's Dilsey in *The Sound and the Fury* owes more to the naive faith of the black spirituals than to the stoicism of Marcus Aurelius.

Others have portrayed Faulkner as a hopeless nihilist or amoral cynic. His dark view of the palpable burden of human conflict seems closed to any hint of redemption. This reading would emerge from the implications of the title of *The Sound and the Fury*, borrowed from Shakespeare, and equate the viewpoint of the author with that of Quentin Compson's grandfather in the same novel: "No battle is ever won . . . victory is an illusion of philosophers and fools."

On the other hand, while it is difficult to picture Faulkner as an unambiguous witness to the Christian message, it is impossible to sunder both his life and his work from the fabric of the Christian drama of the Fall and Redemption.

He was born into a Christian home, baptized into the Methodist Church, buried a member of St. Peter's Episcopal Church in Oxford. He preached a funeral sermon for his servant woman; he was known to pray regularly at his table; he relished the Old Testament over the New ("not so many ideas"); he read Jeremy Taylor's *Holy Living, Holy Dying* during a hospitalization period; he shared his faith in life beyond the grave with his rector at St. Peter's—and his tombstone bears the inscription from *The Fable*: "Beloved, Go with God." For his own part, Faulkner stated on several occasions that he believed himself to be "a good Christian" and identified himself with the Christian memory and hope. And he is on record for scolding both Camus and Sartre for abandoning belief in God.

His literature evidences a constant preoccupation with biblical themes: preachers—the Rev. Mr. Whitfield in *As I Lay Dying*, the Rev. Mr. Shegog in *The Sound and the Fury*, the Presbyterian Rev. Mr. Hightower in *Light in August*, the Rev. Mr. Mahon, the Episcopal priest in *Soldier's Pay*, and the Rev. Mr. Tobe Sutterfield in *The Fable*; sallies at Southern Baptist obscurantism, Puritan moralism (especially in *Light in August*), and innumerable other explicit connections with Christian imagery. (For example, the two novels, *Sanctuary* and *Requiem for a Nun*, with a central character named "Temple," led Albert Camus to confess a fascination with Faulkner's "strange religion . . . a religion less strange in its substance than in the symbols he proposes for it.")

For a person who never graduated from college and who kept his distance from the religious establishment, Faulkner reveals an astonishing sensitivity to the subtle nuances of religion in the South. He moves the Snopeses through the various strata of the social hierarchy; he discerns the repressive, death-dealing power of Calvinism in *Light in August*, as well as the intricate, sure ways in which the sins of the fathers are visited down the generations in *Absalom, Absalom*. In a short story ("Golden Land"), he notes "the old strong harsh Campbellite blood" that flowed in veins and shaped character as blessing and curse.

Faulkner moves beyond stoic and romantic tendencies as his literature asks more than the upholding of honor and the exhortation to endure. He goes beyond an acceptance of fate to struggle with guilt and he invokes a call to compassion and social solidarity, virtues closer to the Christian message than to the stoic.

See also article on LITERATURE AND RELIGION.

Bibliography. Cleanth Brooks, *The Yoknapatawpha Country*; J. Robert Barth, S.J., ed., *Religious Perspectives in Faulkner's Fiction*; John W. Hunt, *William Faulkner: Art in Theological Tension*; Robert L. Johnson, "William Faulkner, Calvinism and the Presbyterians," *Journal of Presbyterian History* 57 (Spring 1979): 66-81.

ROBERT L. JOHNSON
CORNELL UNIVERSITY

FELLOWSHIP OF SOUTHERN CHURCHMEN. An organization formed in 1934 to bring about social reform in the South, the first Conference of Younger Churchmen of the South was held in Monteagle TN to discuss ways to involve "liberal and progressive young ministers" in social struggles. The meeting was organized by the Rev. James Dombrowski of the Highlander Folk School in Monteagle and the Rev. HOWARD A. KESTER of the Committee on Economic and Racial Justice in Nashville. Reinhold Niebuhr spoke to the 180 participants; resolutions condemning racial segregation, war, and capitalism were passed. An ongoing organization was created with Kester as secretary and the Rev. Thomas B. Cowan as president; and its name became the Fellowship of Southern Churchmen.

The primary purpose of the Fellowship was to provide support and encouragement to Southern ministers who had progressive but often unpopular views on race, unions, and other social issues. Besides holding annual retreats, the activities of the Fellowship were those of its roughly 200 members in their local parishes and of its secretary, Kester, who organized for the SOUTHERN TENANT FARMERS' UNION and investigated lynchings and cases of peonage for the NAACP and the American Civil Liberties Union. Through its publication, "Prophetic Religion," the Fellowship reported accomp-

lishments in the fields of cooperative living and community change in communities across the South.

The Fellowship was most active in the field of race relations. In 1938 it published a statement signed by 50 prominent Southerners calling for "full citizenship rights" for blacks. In 1943, Nelle Morton replaced Kester as secretary and the Fellowship office moved from Black Mountain to Chapel Hill NC. In cooperation with the Anti-Defamation League, the Fellowship organized campus groups to protest anti-Semitic and Klan activity and held interracial summer work camps in rural and urban settings. The Rev. Charles Jones alternated with Kester as secretary of the Fellowship in the 1950s, but membership declined as the established churches became more active in the area of race relations. The Fellowship's last major project was to present a conference on Christian Faith and Human Relations in Nashville in 1957 which was addressed by the Rev. MARTIN LUTHER KING, JR. In 1964 the Fellowship was reorganized as the COMMITTEE OF SOUTHERN CHURCHMEN under the direction of the Rev. WILL D. CAMPBELL.

See also articles on CHRISTIAN SOCIALISM; SOCIAL GOSPEL.

Bibliography. David Burgess, "The Fellowship of Southern Churchmen, Its History and Promise," *Prophetic Religion* 13 (Spring 1953): 1-11; Anthony P. Dunbar, *Against the Grain: Southern Radicals and Prophets, 1929-59.*

ANTHONY P. DUNBAR
NEW ORLEANS, LOUISIANA

FEMINIST MOVEMENT: *See* ETHICS, CHRISTIAN.

FERRILL, LONDON (OR LOUDIN), (-1854), black Baptist preacher, has origins unknown to history. At the age of 12, while the slave of Anna Winston in Hanover County VA, he experienced religious conversion shortly after being rescued from drowning. A baptized preacher before moving to Kentucky as a freeman, Ferrill had joined the white First Baptist Church in Lexington by 1817 rather than the existing irregular black Baptist congregation led by an unordained former Virginia slave known as Old Captain. Although most older blacks continued to follow Old Captain, many of the younger people supported Ferrill, who acquired a considerable reputation at First Baptist through preaching from the floor.

His followers established a church headed by Ferrill and appealed to the white church for sanction. In 1822, once the Elkhorn Association approved the ordination of a free black, the First Baptist Church helped organize the First African Church, which remained technically its auxiliary. By the 1850s the church had grown from 280 to 1,820 members, making it not only the largest of 17 separate black Baptist churches in Kentucky, but also the largest church of any kind in the state. Ferrill, whose congregation proudly claimed that "he was descended from a royal line of Africans," was described as "more potent" in influence on Lexington's black population than the local police, an influence recognized by city authorities through a subsidy to his salary. He gave 32 years of faithful service not only to his massive black congregation but also, ironically, to the civil authorities.

See also article on BLACK RELIGION.

Bibliography. William J. Simmons, *Men of Mark*; Mechal Sobel, *Trabelin' On: The Slave Journey to an Afro-Baptist Faith*; J. H. Spencer, *History of Kentucky Baptists.*

ROBERT L. HALL
UNIVERSITY OF MARYLAND
BALTIMORE COUNTY

FIRE-BAPTIZED HOLINESS CHURCH (OF GOD OF THE AMERICAS).

A black Pentecostal denomination, it originated through the inspired leadership of Bishop William Edward Fuller, Sr. (1875-1958), and has been guided since 1958 by his son, Bishop W. E. Fuller, Jr. (1921-). The church reports today an adult membership of over 25,000 in 1,050 churches valued at 11 million. It is supervised by three bishops and has well-established mission programs in Jamaica, the Virgin Islands, and Liberia. A denomi-

national newspaper, *True Witness*, has been published since 1909.

In 1898 Fuller read in the *Way of Faith* magazine, published by J. M. Pike of Columbia SC, an announcement of the forthcoming national organizational meeting of the Fire-Baptized Holiness Association—led by Benjamin Hardin Irwin—to be held July 28 to August 28. As a born-again member of the Methodist Church, Fuller had experienced a transforming vision of the fiery divine presence while alone in his cornfield, and this gave him an interest in Irwin's meeting. Fuller rode his mule from Mountville SC to Anderson to attend the meeting. He found himself the only black person there, but he was ordained by a group including the later Bishop JOSEPH H. KING, elected to the general board of the new organization, and sent out to gather churches among the black people.

One report of 1904 shows 500 conversions from Fuller's labors while establishing four congregations in South Carolina and Georgia. By 1908 increasing racial prejudice in the USA led to a mutually agreed upon separation of Fuller and his black followers from the white majority of the denomination at a meeting in Anderson. The black congregations received legal title to their various properties valued at $25,000. Fuller organized his newly independent denomination later that same year at Greer SC with 988 members under the original name of Colored Fire-Baptized Holiness Church, changed in 1922 to the Fire-Baptized Holiness Church of God. In 1926 increasing mission work led to an expansion of the name to include the phrase "of the Americas." Meanwhile, the original inclusive denominational group of whites merged in 1911 with the PENTECOSTAL HOLINESS CHURCH.

The governing authority is located in the General Council that meets every four years, and in the 11-member Executive Council composed of bishops, district elders, and pastors. Doctrinal beliefs continue to include conservative Christian views of conversion, justification, regeneration, sanctification as a second definite work of grace, baptism with the Holy Ghost and fire, speaking in other tongues, divine healing, and the second coming of Christ as imminent, personal, and premillennial. The denomination has accompanied its members northward, having its largest congregations now in such cities as New York, Chicago, Detroit, and Philadelphia.

See also article on PENTECOSTALISM.

Bibliography. Dillard L. Wood and William H. Preskitt, Jr., *Baptized with Fire: A History of the Pentecostal Fire-Baptized Holiness Church.*

DOUGLAS J. NELSON
ARLINGTON, VIRGINIA

FISHER, MILES MARK (1899-1970), Baptist clergyman and scholar, was born in Atlanta GA. The son of a minister, Elijah John, and Florida Neely, he was educated at Morehouse College (B.A., 1918), Northern Baptist Theological Seminary (B.D., 1922), and the University of Chicago Divinity School (Ph.D., 1948). From 1933 until 1965 he was pastor of White Rock Baptist Church in Durham NC and professor of church history at Shaw University Divinity School in Raleigh. He was minister emeritus at White Rock Baptist from 1965 until his death.

Although an outstanding preacher, Fisher is recognized as a pioneer black religious historian. A student of William Warren Sweet at the University of Chicago, Fisher's revised doctoral dissertation, "Negro Slave Songs in the United States," is the best known of his writings. In this work he argued the provocative thesis that many of the slave songs were not simply religious; they were also songs of protest and freedom. The slave songs reveal, he contended, a primary African or Oriental strain in the Negro mind.

Bibliography. Earl E. Thorpe, *Black Historians.*

CLARENCE G. NEWSOME
DUKE UNIVERSITY

FLAGET, BENEDICT JOSEPH (1767-1850), first Catholic bishop in the trans-Appalachian West, was born in France and educated there as a member of the Sulpician order. When the French Revolution threatened to destroy the order, its members, with the blessing of their superior, the Rev. James A. Emery, began to migrate to the New World. Flaget came in 1792, accompanying two other priests and two seminarians, one of whom was STEPHEN T. BADIN. The following year Badin was ordained and sent to Kentucky, there to become the virtual founder of Catholicism in the state. Bishop JOHN CARROLL sent Flaget to the frontier garrison of Post Vincennes where he served until 1795. Then he was called to Washington to teach at Georgetown College, and did so until he was sent in 1798 to Cuba to organize a Sulpician Seminary. He returned to the United States in 1801 and taught for the next eight years at St. Mary's Seminary in Baltimore.

Meanwhile, as a result of Badin's labors, the Catholic community in Kentucky had increased to the point that both Badin and Bishop Carroll realized a new administrative see should be established. When in 1808 Rome organized the see at Bardstown and appointed Flaget bishop, he was overwhelmed. Finally he accepted, and was consecrated on 4 November 1810, arriving in BARDSTOWN the next summer. After his arrival Catholicism flourished in Kentucky, a cathedral was built at Bardstown, several colleges established, charitable orders were begun. Possessed of a sweet disposition, real administrative skill, and an understanding of American ways, Flaget built on the work begun by Badin. Except for a brief interlude in 1832-1833 when his close associate John Baptist Mary David served, Flaget ruled the diocese until 1850. After 1841 the see was located at the growing city of Louisville, and an indicator of Flaget's success was that his successor, MARTIN JOHN SPALDING (1810-1872), was born and educated in Kentucky. No longer did Kentucky Catholics have to look to Europe for leadership.

See also article on ROMAN CATHOLIC CHURCH.

Bibliography. John B. Boles, *Religion in Antebellum Kentucky*; J. Herman Schauinger, *Stephen T. Badin: Priest in the Wilderness*; Martin J. Spalding, *Sketches of the Life, Times, and Character of the Rt. Rev. Benedict Joseph Flaget, First Bishop of Louisville*.

JOHN B. BOLES
RICE UNIVERSITY

FLORIDA. "Is Florida a Southern state?" is an abiding question and one that refers to religious as well as to other dimensions. A negative response to it has greater validity in the 1980s than at any time since La Florida belonged to Spain, but the question has been pertinent since the colonial period. The geographical location of the "Sunshine State," somewhat marginal to the region, puts large distances between its population centers and those of other states. Its tropical climate distinguishes it from every other state not only in the region but also from the entire nation as well. In some respects Florida belongs as much to a warmth-hungry Northeast and Midwest as to the South. Its diverse population, permanent and winter-temporary, reflects that fact.

Florida's history helps explain its uniqueness. And the history of religion is one of the better clues to its special development. The usefulness of religious patterns as a clue is suggested when Florida's social-political units are compared with those of the nation at large. But the uniqueness of its religious patterns are dramatically clear when they are set alongside historical developments in neighboring, and other Southern states.

With a comparative approach in mind, the religious history of Florida can be divided into five chronological periods: (1) Old World Church-State Patterns, 1564-1821; (2) Diversity in Discrete Units, 1821-1879; (3) Southern Patterns Take Over, 1870-1921; (4) Phasing into Radical Pluralism, 1921-1945; (5) Radical Religious Pluralism Prevails, 1945-. The accelerating succession of periods, each shorter than the previous one especially over the past half-century, highlights the complexity of Florida culture in the 1980s.

Old World Church-State Patterns, 1564-1821. Florida did not become a legal part of the United States until 1821 when it was purchased from Spain as a territory. Admitted to statehood in 1845, it was the last of the Southeastern states to enter the Union. From 1565 until 1763 and again between 1783 and 1821 it was La Florida, a colony of Spain. The British period provided a 20-year interlude. From its founding until the Revolutionary era it was on the "rim of Christendom," an isolated, sparsely populated area where cultural patterns remained European longer than in the other seaboard colonies.

Actually Spain had made six attempts to establish settlements for God and King before the first permanent settlement was successfully staked at San Agustín in 1565, five of them on the Gulf coast between Charlotte Harbor and Pensacola, the sixth in the Chesapeake Bay area far to the north of the Atlantic coast but still within Spain's presumed La Florida. The formation of permanent ST. AUGUSTINE itself did not come easily. A year earlier Huguenots had landed at Fort Caroline on the south bank of the St. John's River near present-day Jacksonville to claim the area for France but a skirmish between the French and Spanish a few miles south of San Agustín the next year assured Spain's control of the area. Nombre de Dios was the name given to the site, later to the Mission on the site, by Pedro Menendez de Aviles, on 8 September 1565.

The ascription "Name of God" tells quite a lot. In that political-social climate what was done for country was *ipso facto* done for God. Also at this place Christendom was planted as an extension of Europe's long-held assumption that land, people, and customs all were inextricably bound up with the Church—religion incorporated them all. La Florida was an outpost of Spanish culture, not simply a possession of the Spanish government. From this planting a harvest was meant to be reaped, especially of the souls of the pagan Indians, the area's only inhabitants for many centuries. The Church's tilling of the soil was done rather impressively. The diocese first sponsored these missions to the Indians, then the Jesuits did so, later the Franciscans. And these successive agents went far to fulfill their commissions, all the way north to Virginia and west to Texas. Most importantly, the social policy of these Spanish Christian evangelizers was commendably humane; they sought to instruct and persuade response to Christianity rather than to coerce it. And they sought to leave Indian culture intact. Their policy of respecting indigenous cultures extended to instructing Indian Christians, rather gradually and with some depth, so that they would be in position to catechize other Indians. This was an organized and rather aggressive mission to the native peoples of central and northern La Florida, not the coercive Christianization of heathen people practiced by Catholics and Protestants alike in America and elsewhere.

Such an aggressive style of operation was indeed to occur; in fact, it brought the missionary enterprise largely to an end, but not until the passing of the "golden age of Florida missions," that covered most of the 17th century. From 1595 forward for a century, the Franciscans carried out a successful Christianizing effort with the result that by 1700 some 26,000 Indians had been taught the Christian religion. There was of course some hostility on the part of Indians toward the Christian newcomers and cultural intruders, with 17 priests and lay brothers having been martyred by 1600. However, the undertaking was constructive in both quantity and quality. It should be borne in mind too that the several hundred Spanish settlers, mostly in St. Augustine, made up part of the Catholic population who were served by diocesan priests. In due

course the golden age gave way to a period of sharp decline.

After 1675 good times phased into bad times for the cause of the Christian religion. Paradoxically, this had to do with the encroachment of Christian civilization upon La Florida—a different kind than the Spanish Catholic civilization that had prevailed from the beginning of the European settlement among an uncivilized Indian population. It is likely that the positive state of religion and civilization would soon have eroded from the force of internal conditions anyway. But the rate of deterioration was accelerated by another form of European Christian civilization, the English, that both diverged from and was inimical to Spanish Catholicism. By 1675 English settlers were to be found as far south as Charleston in Carolina; only 25 years later an English hegemony held the territory all the way to the Georgia-La Florida border. This arrangement was soon to spell the beginning of the end of the 150-year Spanish culture in a remote part of the New World. The "rim of Christendom" fell into the field of an inexorably centripetal force. As the British culture permeated American life, there was less and less room for a European alternative.

La Florida's Indian population—a large one—continued to occupy a central role in the drama. These natives abandoned loyalty to the Church rather quickly, most going over to the English side by the time of the War of Spanish Succession (Queen Anne's War) in 1702. After the conflict, Governor James Moore of Carolina attacked St. Augustine and many other villages. A number of churches were destroyed in his raids of 1702-1704. The decline was rapid after that: by 1708 all missions had disappeared; more than 10,000 mission Indians were deported as slaves to Carolina; the number of priests in La Florida dropped to 25 in 1738 and to as few as 10 in 1759. At the time of Spain's cession of Florida to Britain in 1763, no more than eight

Catholics, all lay, lived on the Peninsula, and not many more in the Panhandle. While Florida was not quite on the rim of Christendom any longer, it had moved only a little closer to the expanding civilization of Protestant America. Even though a British colony for 20 years, it shared few qualities with the society with which its future lay.

Although the English government pledged religious freedom to Catholics who remained, many from St. Augustine and Pensacola exiled themselves to Cuba and Mexico. The Church of England appeared, but its ministrations were limited to the few English settlements and garrisons. At one time or another, nine Anglican clergymen were licensed to work in Florida. An Anglican house of worship existed in St. Augustine but neither it nor the cadre of English churchmen lasted long after the Spanish retrocession in 1783. Roman Catholicism did take a new lease on life—small but permanent—with the arrival of a colony of Minorcans in 1768. After 10 years at New Smyrna, a company of some 600 moved up the coast to St. Augustine. Until the great migration from the north in the 1920s, no infusion of Catholics was to occur, with the exception of a Cuban settlement in Key West from 1868 and the Cuban, Spanish, and Italian immigrant settlement in the Tampa area in the late 1800s.

As if a sign of the religious situation to come, a few Protestant settlers straggled into northeast Florida before 1821. They tended to be referred to indiscriminately as Lutherans, but they were mostly Presbyterians, Quakers, and Baptists. The first Baptist church was founded in 1821 in Nassau County, making it the first denomination to form a permanent congregation. Presbyterians followed in 1824. Actually, a sizable proportion of Florida's 10,000 white residents in 1821 (3000 of them in St. Augustine) were of Protestant heritage. And they were accorded a measure of religious freedom,

being required only to have their younger children baptized. In actual practice because of distance and the paucity of priests even this minimal regulation was enforced infrequently.

The closing of the period of "old world patterns" found the population small and the civilization only slightly advanced. But an era had come to an end and the future of Florida was to resemble the culture near it, no longer the Spanish one that had established and sustained it for two and a half centuries.

Diversity in Discrete Units, 1821-1870. When Florida became an American Territory in 1821 and a state in 1845, its incorporation into the United States both mirrored and enhanced its new social and cultural condition. Spain's domination had amounted to little since the beginning of the British period in 1763; indeed it was virtually insignificant throughout the 18th century. Despite its geographical isolation, Florida was certain to be an extension of the United States, politically, socially, and culturally. The last two dimensions included the religious factor. For more than a century it was to be homogeneously American, in fact regionally American. Until its own peculiar forms of population in-migration took place beginning in the 1920s—as late as that, it was quite similar to other Southern states.

But Florida's case is its own. Population was small and scattered. No towns of any size stood within its boundaries and none was approaching urban status. Furthermore little tradition had developed, meaning that no strong sense of identity and pride had appeared. What there was was a sprinkling of farms, villages, and small towns from Pensacola in the west and Tallahassee in middle Florida to St. Augustine on the east, with the peninsula almost totally uninhabited except for some Indians and a Cuban colony at Key West (the state's largest town in 1850). It was a classic frontier society.

The religious life of Florida is described as functioning in discrete units.

What was happening in one area had relatively little bearing on what was happening in other places. Churches existed here, there, and at the next place but with a minimum of interaction. What was true of the church life of Florida was also true of citizen's relations to other dimensions of society. In a manner of speaking there was no Florida, that is, a state with a cohesive life of its own, or anything like a "state of mind" that elicited loyalty and provided identity. Yet this amorphous society had enough public shape to enter the nation as a state and, 16 years later, to secede. Nevertheless the ascription, "frontier society," is powerfully accurate.

But there were people all about and many of them were Christians. Any clustering of adherents to a particular persuasion seemed to organize fairly soon into a congregation. As the local units multiplied, denominational developments appeared: the first presbytery came into being in Tallahassee in 1841; the Florida annual conference of Methodism dates from 1845 at a meeting in the same city; the first Baptist association near Lake City in 1835. But cooperative efforts of these kinds reflect a somewhat later and slightly more fully developed church life. What happened first was the founding of local churches.

The first Baptist church, as we have noted, dates from 1821 in northeast Florida. There had probably been Baptists in the area somewhat earlier, among them runaway slaves from neighboring states. Population growth was small in the counties where the earliest congregations formed. Accordingly Baptist membership was also small, but that planting was to grow to 4,740 in 1870, 2.5 percent of the state's population of just under 200,000. These beginnings, small and simple, befitted a tradition that favored localism, placed low value on education, and attracted the common folk.

Presbyterian beginnings sound more impressive, though they hardly were, owing to the more literate and cultivated sensibilities of Presbyterian people. Scots

filtered into the Panhandle from North Carolina after 1820. The first church was organized in 1824 in St. Augustine (a town with a white population of 300 in 1821, or 10 percent of the territory's). Having appeal to families steeped in the Calvinist heritage, few in numbers they remained but influential. In no Southern state east of the Mississippi River were there so few Presbyterians in the 19th century. In Florida, the least populous of the states at mid-century, 177 organized churches were to be found, only 16 being Presbyterian (compared to 87 Methodist and 56 Baptist churches). Among its public ventures were: a concern to catechize slaves; outspoken hostility to Roman Catholicism; and reasonably close cooperation with the Northern Presbyterian Church.

Methodists, the largest Christian body, can trace their origins to classes and societies in northeast Florida from 1820 on. Expansion and movement were facilitated here as in other states by evangelical zeal and a ministerial system, referred to as circuit-riding, that promoted mobility, a system well suited to demographic conditions. At first attached to the Georgia Conference, Florida's Methodists constituted their own Conference in 1845. The following year when the national church split over slavery, they aligned with their Southern neighbors in the Methodist Episcopal Church, South. Membership totals were impressive, jumping from 6,874 in that year to almost 14,000 in 1860. Also, in Florida as elsewhere, Methodists devoted much energy to the evangelization of the slaves. As the Civil War opened, 6,649 Negro members were reported by the Florida Conference. Eleven years later, not a single Negro belonged; the exodus of black Christians into separate denominations, three of them Methodist incidentally, was rapid and complete. The African Methodist Episcopal Church and the A.M.E., Zion, Church came south and reaped a huge harvest. The Colored Methodist Church was of Southern origins.

The Protestant Episcopal Church made its appearance during the British period but the founding of the first parish church did not occur until 1825 in St. Augustine. Soon thereafter Pensacola and Tallahassee (1827), Key West (1832), and Jacksonville (1834) could point to an Episcopal presence. With roots going back to the first convention in 1838, the Diocese of Florida was formed in 1851 and a bishop was elected. Ten churches could be counted that year and the Episcopal Church was in Florida to stay; however, its effectiveness was largely confined to lifelong Episcopalians, a small company. Alone among Florida's Protestant communions, the Episcopal Church never really divided into Northern and Southern branches, notwithstanding a brief formal affiliation with a symbolic Confederate Church (P.E.C., C.S.A.).

Jews, later to be so strong in numbers and influence, acquired a bit of visibility in this period of diversity in discrete units. Before territorial status was achieved, a few Jews had arrived in Pensacola in 1764 and St. Augustine in 1783, plus a handful of others here and there. As late as 1881, only 722 Jews lived in the state, with a single organized congregation, Pensacola's, dating from 1874. Anti-Semitism, absent in the early decades, had appeared by the 1840s and is thought by some to have contributed to the adding of a last name, Yulee, to "David Levy" the Jew (later a convert to Christianity) who in 1845 became the first Jew to serve as a United States senator.

Southern Patterns Take Over, 1870-1921. After the Civil War, though not directly because of it, an identifiable Florida society took form. Discrete units—in religious terms, Methodist and Baptist, and Presbyterian and Episcopal, with a sprinkling of Catholics and Jews—representing a mild diversity were about to yield to a new configuration. In the place of that simple complex, a recognizable Southern pattern appeared. Now Southern society straddled the boundary Florida shared with Georgia and Alabama. Apart from certain features of flora and fauna and a coastline, Florida differed only in minor ways from the neighboring states.

Not only did cultural cohesion make its first appearance, but the period of 1870 to 1921 marks the era of greatest cohesion ever in Florida's history. For those decades, it was unmistakably a Southern state, society, and culture. Dominant, even normative, patterns prevailed. Peoples and mores were evaluated by standards almost universally accepted inasmuch as they were taken for granted. The peculiar character of the culture of the American South is not to be blamed for this development, since cultural cohesion and dominance are a common human condition. The point is that in Florida this condition made its first appearance and its shape was that of the South.

We should therefore not be surprised that this was also the period of Florida's most hostile response to departures from social norms or challenges thereto. It is the nature of human culture in "sacred" societies that intrusions are resented; "purity" is prized. Impurity in this period of Florida's history was to come in the form of Roman Catholicism—not really from Roman Catholics of whom there were very few.

The traditional denominations remained the largest and most influential. It is not at all accidental that Florida's major Protestant communities were the South's: Methodist, Baptist, Presbyterian, and Episcopal. The state's population had migrated mostly from other Southern states where those were the prominent bodies. Also extension work or domestic missionary activity was carried on by those groups that had strength near by. The near-duplication of the Deep South's patterns by Florida developments is demonstrated by the overtaking of the hitherto largest body, the Methodist, by the Baptists, who surpassed them in size in 1906.

Of greatest importance for the churches in this period was the growth of population in the state. Few settlements of any size existed south of Gainesville and Ocala at the time of the Civil War. But increase and expansion showed signs of promise in the decade of the 1870s and became pronounced by the 1880s. The Methodist Episcopal Church, South, with its circuit riders in the vanguard, pursued the expanding population as it moved southward. As the Tampa and central Florida areas expanded in the 1880s, soon to be followed by the formation of permanent towns down the state's spine, then along both coasts, before and after the turn of the century, Methodists were present to found churches. The largest numerical change took place between 1867 and 1885, there being 12,380 members (all white) in the latter year, up from 6,266 (whites and blacks) in 1867. The membership figures from Reconstruction to 1900 highlight three major developments within Florida Methodism.

First, blacks withdrew or were withdrawn from a previously unified (if unequal) constituency. Always active in missions to the Negroes, the Methodist denomination lost those members to separate black denominations, with no reported Negro membership in the M.E. Church, South, by 1872. Second, growth was substantial before 1890, that is, as long as rural demography and culture patterns remained. Third, statistics leveled off in the 1890s and, in relative terms, decreased, as the "circuit-rider dismounted" and the denomination failed to adjust very sensitively to new conditions. Moreover in this period the Church was challenged by other denominations that had made a belated start in Florida. Even so there were nearly 20,000 members in the main body in 1900, as well as several thousand Negro brothers and sisters and a sprinkling of (sectarian) Methodist Protestants and northern coreligionists (the Methodist Episcopal Church).

Consolidation marks this period. The conference was more maturely structured, districts were organized and developed, church agencies began emerging and taking firm shape. In 1902 in Lakeland, the denomination's educational institution was opened, being named Florida Southern College in 1906. A denomination that had sowed seeds early, broadcast widely, and reaped quite a harvest, was on the landscape as far as the eye could see. Henceforth its rhythms were to be those of stability and ubiquity, not rapid growth or exuberant vitality.

These same traits characterized the early second runners, the Baptists, who have been Florida's largest Protestant community throughout this century (although without the power they have attained in other Southern states). Lacking any kind of connectionalism, the Baptist churches suffered severely in the war's aftermath. The poverty of the Baptist people was reflected in the shortage of ministers and the incapacitation of churches to do anything on an organizational scale. Yet, in spite of severe curtailment of opportunity, churches grew. By using the advantages of the Baptists' associational system, they pooled resources and confronted concerns. It is admirable that so bereft a people could found a college, establish a state paper, and create missionary agencies.

Stetson University was founded at DeLand in 1888. Notwithstanding shortage of funds and depth of financial commitment, the state's Baptists had the vision to found and see to the continuation of a center for the training of the young, lay and clergy alike. The *Florida Baptist Witness* began in 1873 and has enjoyed unbroken service. Local congregations banded together to form area units called associations; in turn, these joined to become a state convention to carry out the will and vision of the smaller units. Of the greatest importance is the decision made in the 1880s to side with the Home Mission Board of the Southern Baptist Convention in preference to the American (Northern) Baptist Home Mission Society that had come on the scene through ministries it undertook on behalf of the recently freed Negroes. Henceforth

Florida's Baptists were to be as solidly in league with the Southern Baptist organization and outlook as those of any other state.

A strong sense of denominational identity was emerging, obviously. These advances on the organizational front mirror that fact. Those in turn are tied to growth in Baptist size. Of the total state population of 520,000 in 1900, Baptist membership stood at 23,136. Twenty years later the figure had increased to 57,078 in a state population just under one million. In this period Baptist growth was greater than the state's growth.

These are Southern Baptist Convention churches' totals, it should be noted. Negro Baptist Churches had begun to dot the Florida landscape from 1880. The reports of 1883 reveal 16,857 members in Negro Baptist congregations—with virtually no racially mixed congregations. Between 1885 and 1920 most of these affiliated with one or another newly organized Negro Baptist denomination.

Presbyterian church life in this period was notably undistinguished. Reeling from the economic blows brought on by the war and its aftermath, Southern Presbyterians talked cooperation with their Northern brothers and sisters, but merger did not occur (nor had it by 1982). The more prosperous Northern body did aid the devastated Southern church financially on a number of occasions.

Florida Episcopalianism appears brighter in this era than Presbyterianism, because being sacramental it externalizes its life. Growth and development were hardly impressive, however. There was a fair amount of work done among the freedmen especially with a view to education and training. The tenure of Bishop JOHN FREEMAN YOUNG (1867-1885) was notable for its efforts to build a strong sense of Churchmanship and mission. But the big news of the period is associated with 1893 when the new "missionary jurisdiction of Southern Florida" saw the light of day. Population was increasing on the southern three-fourths of the peninsula and new parishes and missions were being formed to serve Episcopalians moving there. A glance at the list of congregations existing in the state in the 1890s tells quite a story: (a) Most of them in the territory from Ocala south were to survive and even flourish. (b) In the north and northwest, most of the rural and small town parishes were to remain small or die out, while those in the larger towns were to become the strength of the Church's life in those parts of the state.

Other religious bodies took their place on the Florida scene during this period. A Shaker colony appeared in Osceola County in the 1890s. The Church of the Brethren was in evidence from the 1880s and acquired some strength on the lower half of the peninsula after 1910 as Pennsylvanians, Buckeyes, Hoosiers, and others migrated to the state. Similarly Lutherans and Congregationalists, the latter's presence made notable by its founding of Rollins College in Winter Park in 1885, the state's first institution of higher learning to have a continuing life.

Jews and Catholics continued to be a minority presence. The earliest Jewish congregations were formed in Pensacola (1874), Jacksonville (1882), and Tampa (1894). In 1881, only 772 Jews resided in Florida, of whom 130 were in Jacksonville. Jewish population expansion was to await the immigration, tourist, and economic boom of the 1920s. Roman Catholicism was better represented, there being 24,658 communicants in 1916, less than three percent of the state's population of 921,618. Its fame far outdistanced its size, however. (Notoriety is a more apt description.)

Nativism surfaced in the South much later than it had in the Northeast and Midwest. A function of high-level immigration totals, the nativism that took anti-Catholicism form in the North was vigorous for the 30 years preceding the Civil War. That virulent movement's day in the South occurred during the 1910s as resistance to all sorts of "isms," few making any real impact at all on Southern society. The percentage of Catholics living in Florida was as tiny as that prevailing in other Deep South states. But an ominous threat was seen on the horizon.

Anti-Catholicism in Florida was short-lived, bubbling up by 1913 and mostly out of sight by 1919. Its appearance came to focus in the election of SIDNEY J. CATTS to the governorship in 1916. A Baptist preacher and lawyer recently moved from Alabama to the Panhandle, he ran on the Prohibition Party ticket and won in one of the state's most surprising elections ever. A few proposals passed the House but died in the Senate: e.g., a "garb" bill that would have prohibited priests and nuns from wearing religious clothing or insignia while teaching in public schools; and prohibition acts that would have deprived churches of the use of sacramental wine. Other bills passed were never actually enforced, for example, convent inspection legislation aimed at providing for checking out suspected wrongdoings as "closed" convents and parochial schools. A bill was enacted that prohibited white people from teaching Negroes in white schools (and vice versa); it was enforced once, with the arrest of three sisters teaching at the St. Joseph's school in St. Augustine. Far down state in 1915 popular animosity toward Roman Catholicism was strong enough in Fort Lauderdale to remove a teacher of that faith who had been appointed to a public school position (by a vote of 181 to 7).

Florida, thus, made it into the 20th century a little late and rather gracelessly. Its culture was that of the Deep South, positively and negatively. The Florida that has come to people's minds since World War II is a product of events and developments no older than the years following World War I.

Phasing into Radical Pluralism (1921-1945). Florida's history was typically Southern throughout the 19th century and for the first two decades of the 20th.

Since then it has reverted, in a manner of speaking, to the eccentric character its colonial career manifested. The angle of divergence is of course far smaller for the past half-century. But Florida was becoming a "rim" once again between 1921 and 1945—though perhaps "hub," of the tourist tastes of Eastern Americans is a better image. Still more Southern than anything else or culturally amorphous, Florida was developing its own personality, a complex of people, economy, life-style, and religion, that turned it into a veritable region of its own.

One indicator of its divergence was the early appearance of economic disaster in the 1920s, an occurrence that was Florida's alone. The rest of the country moved ahead in times of relative security and prosperity until the last quarter of the decade's final year, but Florida had already "boomed" and "busted." Americans from the upper Midwest to New England, all the way south to the bordering states were discovering the "Sunshine State." Tourists were coming in ever greater numbers, their forays facilitated by railroads that crisscrossed the state and extended past Miami out to Key West (until a hurricane destroyed some key bridges in 1935). An even greater contributing factor was the construction of a statewide system of public roads. The growing popularity of the family automobile prompted short and long visits to the peninsula over roads that had not existed two or three years earlier.

Some of the tourists and numbers of prospective permanent residents took the bait being dangled by a small army of land developers. "Runaway inflation in land sales" accompanied the crescendo of the Florida fever. But boom turned to bust in 1926. Three years later Florida staggered from the blow of the entire nation's financial calamity. As if those buffetings were not enough, lethal hurricanes struck the southern parts in 1926 and 1935. These major setbacks notwithstanding, Florida became a new society during the 1920s.

Population totals rose from 968,470 in 1920 to 1,468,211 in 1930. The people who came, especially those who stayed, brought their culture with them, their religious affiliations and tastes included.

Radical diversity and radical pluralism happened to Florida almost simultaneously. That is to say, so many newcomers were appearing on the scene, representing such a variety of social and cultural backgrounds, that they swamped the existing complex, especially over the lower two-thirds of the peninsula. In religious terms, Roman Catholics, Jews, and Northern Protestants—Lutheran, Congregational, United Presbyterian, among them—now lived alongside the Southern denominations, diluting their impact and challenging their cultural hegemony. Subtly, Methodism—the closest thing to a "national church"—was coming to reflect Northern as well as Southern traditions and styles. During one and the same era, Florida came to be a conglomerate of peoples and a diffused culture. Southern identity was beginning to give way quite decisively to "Florida culture," a unique, somewhat amorphous, yet locatable version of American life.

Southern culture had not yet been totally forsaken, however (nor has it in the 1980s in the northern tier of counties and the entire northwest). The influence of that way of life was prominent in the 1928 presidential election and campaign that pitted Democratic Governor Alfred E. Smith of New York against Herbert Hoover of the Republican Party. In the South, this amounted to a single issue election, over prohibition and religion, the two fusing into one. Methodist Bishop James Cannon itinerated from Washington throughout the South and beyond to promote the anti-liquor forces against Smith's election. Florida was not left bereft of his services; on 4 August 1928, he journeyed to Jacksonville and departed after organizing "dry Democrats." The Protestant churches gave much support to that cause. Doubtless the Baptist, Metho-dist, Presbyterian, and sect peoples made a major difference in Florida's popular vote. Feelings ran very high, there being many Hoover clubs and anti-Smith clubs. A prominent speaker to such groups and many public rallies was John Roach Straton, fundamentalist pastor of Manhattan's Calvary Baptist Church, who had grown up in Alabama and Georgia and attended a Southern Baptist college and seminary.

Thus, the Hoover *versus* Smith campaign of 1928 reflected the lingering impact of Southern culture, its values and its religion, upon Florida. While it is excessive to speak of these events as the last gasp of regional influence, they do stand as a kind of watershed. The Republican presidential aspirant won in the state, but the rest of the ticket went to the Democrats. Nor did the two-party system return to Florida in that year. It was becoming a steadily less Southern state, but this era witnessed only a "phasing into radical pluralism," not an accomplished social transformation. Sheer population statistics reveal how clear its new course was coming to be, however. Between 1920 and 1930, the percentage of increase was 51.6; during the 1930s it dipped to 29.2. (Then with the Depression past and World War II in process and finished, the percentage of population increase soared to 46.1 in the 1940s.) Since most of these newcomers were from non-Southern states, regional strength was indeed diffused and the old cultural hegemony broken up.

Radical Pluralism Prevails (1945-). The Florida that Americans think of as Florida did not exist before the 1920s and really not until after World War II. Once again the percentage of population increase is revealing. As if the 1940s figure of 46.1 percent were not enough, the 1950s record is overwhelming.

The number of residents in the state rose from 2,778,000 at the beginning of the decade to 4,952,000 in 1960, a growth rate of 78.7 percent. Now what had been incipient from 1920 forward was an accomplished fact. Florida had become unique. It was Southern and not Southern. It resembled other states attractive to retirees and tourists, California and Arizona, yet it was very different from them. It was an amorphous society and culture but it had a kind of shape, tradition, and dynamic of its own. There were at least two units, "the other Florida," from Gainesville north and west, and the mystique-laden peninsular Florida, yet a kind of identity bound all the state's citizens together.

A glance at the religious membership statistics of 1971 affords some clues. (This compilation includes only Christians and not all of that constituency since some black denominations and some other sects were not keeping or reporting detailed records.) In that year 41.2 percent of all Floridians owned some kind of Christian membership. Within that large company the size of three denominations reached double digits, the Roman Catholic Church with 32.8 percent of the total number of Christian adherents, the Southern Baptist Convention with 28.8 percent, and the United Methodist Church with 13.8 percent.

Why these? For one thing, all of them have massive national memberships. In fact, they rank first, second, and third among all American Christian bodies. Are we to infer from this that Florida is a microcosm of American religiosity? Probably not, but the correspondence is striking and suggestive. What it means has two aspects. First, it was predictable that a state that attracted hundreds of thousands of immigrants from the Northeast and Midwest where Catholic numbers are great would show a strong Catholic membership. But it must be remembered also that Florida experiences in-migration from the South as well. New residents especially Cuban, also other Latin citizens, have moved to Florida in large numbers— and these are "99 percent Catholic."

Second, Florida's religious patterns reflect its Southern heritage, with the result that the region's "big two" are prominent in their deepest Southeastern penetration as elsewhere. After all, the Southern patterns that virtually constituted the state down to 1920 were not displaced or replaced, only supplemented. Moreover a healthy proportion of those who have moved into Florida over the past six decades have come from the contiguous region (as did most of the Anglo- and Afro-Americans who settled the area in the early nineteenth century). In the Methodist case, as mentioned earlier, that denomination's size and its general distribution throughout the Northern home territories of new Floridians assured that quite a company of Methodists would be joining their Southern religious cousins in the towns and cities of the Sunshine State. It is thus more intriguing and coincidental than factual that Florida's three largest denominations are also the nation's. Yet we learn quite a lot about both its distant past and its recent history by observing that phenomenon.

Pursuing that point a step further, we note that the nationwide Catholic tendency to be very strong where it is strong at all persists in Florida; similarly the Southern Baptists. In 1971 four counties could claim a Catholic proportion above 50 percent of the total number of Christian adherents. All four—Dade at 62.1 percent, Broward at 58.7, Monroe at 57.7, and Palm Beach at 53.6—are concentrated at the southern tip of the peninsula, closest to Cuba and, in a manner of speaking, also to the Catholic strongholds of Northern areas. (In Florida you "go south to go north.") The obverse is true as well. Where Catholicism is weak, it is almost non-existent. Six Panhandle counties could count fewer than one percent of their residents as members of the Church, and rural Sumter County, some 50 miles north of Tampa, held none.

Southern Baptist Convention size, high and low, is inversely correlated with Catholicism's. All of the state's most Baptist counties are in "the other Florida," the Panhandle mostly. The percentages there are staggering, in the 80s for four, in the 60s and 70s for eight others. The least Southern Baptist counties are all down south in tourist and Northern immigration centers, such as Miami, Key West, Sarasota, West Palm Beach, and St. Petersburg. These percentages range from 10.1 in Broward to 18.1 in Collier.

Methodism's place in Florida is almost routinely akin to its position all over the country: rarely dominant, almost never weak, typically of moderate strength. The greatest proportions (in the 20s) of Methodists appear in such rural counties as Flagler, Franklin, and Jefferson. But they stand between 10 and 20 in almost all the other 65 counties, south and north, urban and rural, coastal and inland. America's "national church" is also Florida's.

From these three to the other denominations the statistical gap is quite wide. The two major Presbyterian bodies account for 6.1 percent of the total number of Christian adherents. The Episcopal Church percentage stands at 5.4 and the three largest Lutheran groups total 4.1. Moreover in the cases of all three, no part of the state reflects a heavy concentration, although Lutherans are mostly found in centers for immigration from Lutheran strongholds.

The picture of Florida's religious culture and the religious dimension of its general culture are misrepresented, however, by exclusive reliance on the size of its largest Christian groups. For one thing, Jews are numerous and their place in the culture is substantial. The estimated Jewish population in the state in 1980 was 455,000 or 5.1 percent of all inhabitants. Only New York and California have a greater number of Jews; in percentage of total population, Florida is surpassed only by New York (12.1), the District of Columbia (6.1), and New Jersey (6.0).

A pronounced pattern of concentration is evident in the state. Miami and Miami Beach are home to 225,000 Jews. Along the rest of the southeast "Gold Coast" totals reach 180,000. Some 17,500 Jews reside in Tampa and St. Petersburg.

Other centers are: Orlando with 12,000, Sarasota with 6,200, and Jacksonville with 6,000. Elsewhere no sum surpasses 1,000 save Daytona Beach's 1,200. Also, quite apart from quantity, the impact of Jewish life on the state may be seen in the extent of its philanthropy and in the increasing scope of its representation in the political life of the state—in the legislature, a recent United States senator, and a recent gubernatorial candidate, for example. Jewish presence and prominence have come a great distance since 1920.

Hardly less significant for the recent religious history of Florida is the rampant diversity that has developed there. One element in the larger picture is secularism; that major force that surely is America's most popular posture since World War II. When defined as the "practice of the absence of God," secularism is readily seen as related to religion, not its denial but rather its nonpractice in the midst of some avowal. Secularism abounds in American society; it is scarcely any stranger to Florida. What is so telling about its strength there is its resemblance to Northern urban life. A curious mixture of Southern rurality and Northern urbanity, Florida is sometimes culturally indistinguishable from New York, Chicago, or Philadelphia. Whereas Southern secularists are often conversant with religious faith and apologetic for their indifference to it, the type associated with a less evangelical and more urban manner of living has simply lost sight of religion, conceptually and experientially—though still without denying it. At bottom, any such view of religion cares too little about it to discredit it any more than to affirm it.

Major Protestant bodies, Roman Catholics, Jews, and secularists are prominent, then, in contemporary Florida society. But they are joined by myriad sects, cults, black denominations, and small religious bodies. A glance at the Saturday religion section of any urban newspaper reveals both a remarkable quantity of religious organizations and an incredible diversity. "You name it, Florida has it," might almost be the state's religious motto. All traditional denominations are present, also Judaism, every conceivable sect and independent congregation, and a plethora of religious science and divine wisdom bodies. It is doubtful that such an abundance in number and variety may be found anywhere else except for southern California. In Florida metropolitan areas, a fantastic confluence occurs: Northeast, Midwest, Southern, and Caribbean; urban, rural, and small town; traditional, recent upstart, and as new (and perhaps as ephemeral) as yesterday; ethnic patterns of all kinds; and so on. Many come to Florida searching; there is plenty to shop for in that remarkable culture, for old and young, for the ill and the adventurous, seemingly for everyone. And secularism is an ever-present force.

One of the surest ways to ascertain a religious body's strength in a locale is to note its commitment to educating its own in that locale. Church colleges were founded by the Congregationalists (Rollins at Winter Park in 1885), the Southern Baptists (Stetson at DeLand three years later), and the Methodists (Florida Southern at Lakeland in 1902). In the 1930s Roman Catholics organized Barry and Biscayne in Miami, but St. Leo's College had been planted in Pasco County in 1889. Florida Presbyterian College (now Eckerd) dates from 1960. Black denominations contributed Edward Waters College in Jacksonville in 1891 (African Methodist Episcopal), Bethune-Cookman in Daytona Beach in 1923 (Methodist), and Florida Memorial College in Miami in 1879 (American Baptist), all springing from earlier foundations. Independent or loosely affiliated Bible colleges and schools dot the state, (noteworthily) at Dunedin, Zellwood, Boca Raton, Temple Terrace (Churches of Christ), and Graceville (Southern Baptist). The Church of God (Anderson, Indiana) has Warner Southern College in Lakeland. Independent Christian schools are to be found statewide, with some offering post-high

school course work. Clearwater is the home of the second largest center of the Church of Scientology for training its leaders and counseling its members. The Krishna and Unification Church movements have made the smallest inroads into Florida but their evangelists may be found in the state's largest airports. And much more.

The story of religion in Florida is fascinating. Never very "normal" by American standards except for its Southern period from 1821 until 1921, it is hardly "normal" now. Yet in certain ways it may be more predictive of things to come in America at large than might have been thought—or than many would like to believe. Florida has become the model of a pluralistic society. In religion, its centers of gravity are Southern traditions, conservative leanings, new movements, and special kinds of immigrants, from Northern states and Caribbean societies. Thus it has its own peculiar forms of pluralism, making for a unique blending. That is why "religion in Florida" as a subject for study demands more attention than it has received. It may be a laboratory for 21st-century America. It certainly is a topic that Floridians need to be well informed about, since knowledge of religious history and patterns could facilitate better human understanding and even aid in the formation of public policy for all the citizens of the state.

See also articles on CARIBBEAN IMMIGRATION; ESTABLISHED RELIGION; INDIANS, SOUTHEAST MISSIONS TO; JEWS; NATIVISM; NEW RELIGIONS; ROMAN CATHOLICS; SANTERÍA; SPANISH INFLUENCE IN LA FLORIDA.

Bibliography. William E. Brooks, ed., *From Saddlebags to Satellites: A History of Florida Methodism*; Joseph D. Cushman, Jr., *A Goodly Heritage: The Episcopal Church in Florida 1821-1892*; *The Sound of Bells: The Episcopal Church in South Florida 1892-1969*; Leonard Dinnerstein and Mary Dale Palsson, ed., *Jews in the South*; Michael V. Gannon, *The Cross in the Sand: The Early Catholic Church in Florida 1513-1870*; *Rebel Bishop: The Life and Era of Augustin Verot*; Douglas W. Johnson, Paul R. Picard, and Bernard Quinn, *Churches and Church Membership in the United States, 1971*; Edward Earl Joiner, *A History of Florida Baptists*; Cooper Clifford Kirk, "A

History of the Southern Presbyterian Church in Florida, 1821-1891," unpublished Ph.D. dissertation, Florida State University, 1966; Charlton W. Tebeau, *A History of Florida.*

SAMUEL S. HILL
UNIVERSITY OF FLORIDA

FOOT WASHING. This ordinance is not practiced by most churches in the larger denominations of the South. Roman Catholic priests in some areas on Maundy Thursday wash the right foot of 12 members of the congregation. In some rural areas, Southern Baptist, Methodist, and Presbyterian wash feet, but this is the exception rather than the rule. Many smaller denominations stress that foot washing should follow the Lord's Supper in accordance with Jesus' command in Jn. 3:1-17. The churches that wash feet in conjunction with communion include many Baptist groups, such as Regular, Old Regular, Duck River, Free Will, Primitive, United, Bible, and Union; also, Churches of God, Church of Christ (Holiness), Pentecostal Holiness Churches, Seventh-Day Adventist, Primitive Advent Christians, Mennonite denominations, Church of the Brethren, and a number of black denominations. The Assembly of God churches do not consider foot washing as an ordinance, although they do wash feet when moved by the Spirit during a revival.

Churches have been led into schism over the question of foot washing. The Primitive Advent Christians came into existence in 1931 in West Virginia so that they could practice this ordinance. The parent denomination, the Advent Christian, does not wash feet. The same kind of schism took place between the Church of Christ and the Church of Christ (Holiness) in West Virginia and has split many Baptist congregations, especially Southern Baptist churches that have decided to abandon the practice. Some whole bodies, the Moravians and a number of black Baptist associations, for example, decided to delete this from their services.

"Foot-Washing" Christians fail to understand other Christians who maintain that foot washing is no more than symbolic or figurative since they regard the observance of baptism and communion as essential. For those who engage in it, foot washing has been a means of fulfilling Christ's command and an expression of reconciliation between Christians as well as a service to one another.

See also articles on APPALACHIAN RELIGION; SACRAMENTS AND ORDINANCES.

RICHARD ALAN HUMPHREY
JOHNSON CITY, TENNESSEE

FRANK, LEO, CASE. This episode of 1913 is undoubtedly the most notorious expression of anti-Semitism in Southern history; its violence had social, political, and symbolic reverberations.

Born in Texas in 1884, Leo Frank was reared in Brooklyn. He earned an engineering degree at Cornell before moving to Atlanta to serve as superintendent of the National Pencil Factory. In 1912 the city's B'nai B'rith lodge elected him its president.

The following year his ordeal began. On 26 April, Confederate Memorial Day, one of Frank's employees, 13-year-old Mary Phagan, the daughter of a dispossessed tenant farmer, was murdered. The superintendent was the last person to admit to having seen her alive; he was indicted on 24 May. Solicitor-General Hugh M. Dorsey of Georgia directed the prosecution, which was based on circumstantial evidence and on the testimony of Jim Conley, the black janitor of the pencil factory who (unlike Frank) had a previous criminal record. The trial, which began on 28 July 1913, was conducted in an atmosphere inflamed by press sensationalism, including that of the anti-Semitic *Jeffersonian*, published by the former Populist Tom Watson. Charges of lascivious behavior toward his female employees were raised against Frank, whose counsel called over 200 witnesses to testify to his character and to the normality of Frank's demeanor on the day of the murder.

The jury required less than four hours to convict him while a crowd estimated at 3,000 gathered outside the Atlanta courtroom and cheered the verdict. A death sentence was pronounced. Several appeals launched on Frank's behalf were directed by Louis Marshall, a noted Constitutional lawyer who headed the American Jewish Committee, and were largely financed by advertising executive Albert D. Lasker. These efforts, which consumed two years, may have deepened the xenophobia of those Georgians convinced of Frank's guilt. The appeals emphasized the prejudice attributed to two of the jurors as well as the mob pressure exerted during the course of the trial. With Justice O. W. Holmes dissenting ("Mob law does not become due process of law by securing the assent of a terrorized jury"), the U.S. Supreme Court in *Frank* v. *Mangum* rejected the writ of *habeas corpus* in 1915 and thus upheld Frank's conviction.

His petition for clemency was supported by over a million signatures (including 10,000 from Georgia). Acknowledging the pertinence of evidence neglected by the defense and privately convinced of Frank's innocence, Gov. John M. Slaton commuted the sentence to life imprisonment and then left the state under mob threats. But Frank himself was abducted from a prison farm by 25 men calling themselves the Knights of Mary Phagan and was hanged near her birthplace on 17 August 1915.

A Jew, a New Yorker, and a factory manager in an agrarian order succumbing to the forces of industrialization and urbanization, Frank had inadvertently aroused the fears of those anxious to preserve regional traditions. In the aftermath of the case, the KU KLUX KLAN was reborn, its nucleus drawn from the Knights of Mary Phagan; and the B'nai B'rith established the Anti-Defamation League to combat such bigotry.

See also articles on JEWS IN THE SOUTH; NATIVISM.

Bibliography. Leonard Dinnerstein, *The Leo Frank Case*;

Steven Hertzberg, *Strangers Within the Gate City: The Jews of Atlanta, 1845-1915.*

STEPHEN J. WHITFIELD
BRANDEIS UNIVERSITY

FRANKLIN SPRINGS, GEORGIA.

A small town in northeast Georgia situated between Athens and Anderson SC, Franklin Springs is associated with Pentecostal history. Named for Benjamin Franklin, the town was known in the 19th century for its springs, which included minerals, sulphur, and freestone. After the Civil War, Franklin Springs was developed as a resort where visitors could come for the "cures" that were attributed to the mineral waters. By the end of the century two large hotels were built near the springs along with several large private residences. With the end of World War I, the springs had lost much of their popularity and the hotels were put up for sale.

The property was bought in 1918 by members of the PENTECOSTAL HOLINESS CHURCH for use as a school or orphanage and for camp meeting grounds. In 1919 the Franklin Springs Institute was established, then in 1933 the school became a junior college and was renamed Emmanuel College.

The church also established its publishing house in Franklin Springs in 1919, now known as Advocate Press. From 1957 to 1969 Franklin Springs also served as the International Headquarters of the Pentecostal Holiness Church.

Because of the huge amount of church literature that is printed and shipped from Franklin Springs, the little town of some 600 inhabitants is well known among Pentecostal people around the world. Emmanuel College by 1980 was a fully accredited liberal-arts junior college with 400 students. A four-year school of Christian Ministries was added to the college in 1973.

See also article on PENTECOSTALISM.

Bibliography. Joseph C. Campbell, *The Pentecostal Holiness Church, 1898-1940*; Joseph H. King and Blanche L. King, *Yet Speaketh*; Vinson Synan, *Emmanuel College.*

VINSON SYNAN
OKLAHOMA CITY, OKLAHOMA

FREDERICA, GEORGIA. Founded in 1735 as a military outpost on the west side of St. Simon's Island, the fort and surrounding community of Frederica thrived briefly in the late 1730s. The town was the Southern defense against Spanish invasion, and soldiers stationed there proved instrumental in defeating the Spanish in the Battle of Bloody Marsh in 1742. During his stay in Georgia, JAMES OGLETHORPE had a residence near Frederica. Part of the town's initial plan was the inclusion of 300 acres as a source of income for an Anglican minister. Frederica's religious importance was secured in 1736 when Charles Wesley, younger brother of John Wesley, was named Commissioner of Indian Affairs, chaplain to the soldiers, and preacher for the town. Charles Wesley's ministry at Frederica preceded his major contributions to Methodism and his service to the town lasted only a few months from March 1736 to May 1736. While there he held services in an oak grove near the town. Wesley's Anglican presence at Frederica was joined by the brief establishment of a German Lutheran Salzburger congregation. Although Frederica declined rapidly as a community after the troop withdrawal in 1742, the planters of St. Simon's Island made the oak grove the location of Christ Church organized in 1807. The church site is an important part of the continuing restoration of Frederica and St. Simon's begun in 1941.

See also articles on COLONIAL PERIOD (in Appendix); METHODIST EPISCOPAL CHURCH, SOUTH; SALZBURGERS.

Bibliography. Kenneth Coleman, *Colonial Georgia*; Charles C. Jones, *The Dead Towns of Georgia*; Burnette Vanstory, *Georgia's Land of the Golden Isles.*

THOMAS F. ARMSTRONG
GEORGIA COLLEGE

FREE WILL BAPTISTS. This Protestant body in the South traces its origin to the GENERAL BAPTISTS of England in the early seventeenth century, who derived their name from their belief that Christ died for all persons, the teaching of general atonement as opposed to the Calvinist view of a limited atonement. The General Baptists grew rapidly during the revolution against Charles I in the 1640s and under Oliver Cromwell in the 1650s. In 1660 they presented a confession to Charles II in hopes of retaining their liberties under the Crown. This document became known as the Standard Confession and is noteworthy for its advocacy of religious freedom. Parliament's passage of a series of laws known as the Clarendon Code brought hardship to Baptists along with all dissenters.

In the late seventeenth century some General Baptists settled in Virginia and Carolina. As early as 1702 a group in North Carolina wrote to their brethren in England requesting a ministry or books, but only the latter could be provided. General Baptist "Messengers" were sent by the Kent Association to Virginia in 1714 and small congregations were established in Isle of Wight and Surrey Counties.

Although General Baptists were living in North Carolina before 1700, there is no documented evidence that churches were constituted until Paul Palmer gathered a congregation in Chowan Precinct in 1727 and another in Pasquotank in 1729. Other General Baptist ministers, among whom Joseph Parker was the most important for later Free Will Baptists, had organized as many as 20 churches in eastern North Carolina by 1755. When John Gano reported to the Philadelphia Baptist Association following his tour of the Carolinas in 1755, they decided to send emissaries to persuade these churches to disband and reorganize because it was alleged that many members of these congregations had been baptized without what was termed "an experience of grace." While the majority of these General Baptist churches were eventually reorganized and became known as Regular Baptists, those churches under the care of Joseph and William Parker refused to submit to such intimidation. Their desire to maintain their heritage amidst the prevailing climate of Calvinist dogma may be seen in their continued use of the Standard Confession of 1660, which they issued in a revised form in 1812. As early as 1800 they had formed a conference and were beginning to be known as Free Will Baptists, though that name was not officially adopted until about 1825.

During the 1820s the number of ministers and churches increased so that the conference agreed to divide in 1830 into the Shiloh and Bethel Conferences. Soon thereafter Thomas and ALEXANDER CAMPBELL gained a few followers among Free Will Baptists. By 1839 these "Disciples" had gained virtual control of the Bethel conference organization and "Free Will Baptist" was dropped from the name of the conference in 1841. The promotion of "Restoration principles" by the Campbellites, as they were called, left many Free Will Baptist churches divided since as many as 25 ministers were persuaded to join them. In 1842 a conference embracing Free Will Baptist principles from both the Shiloh and Bethel Conferences was convened, which became known as the General Conference of Original Free Will Baptists. In the last decades of the 19th century, this conference divided into the Western, Central, and Eastern Conferences.

Other conferences were organized, including the South Carolina Conference in 1831, the Cape Fear in 1855, and the Pee Dee in 1869. Meanwhile as Free Will Baptists migrated from North and South Carolina to other Southern states, churches were organized in Georgia, Alabama, Tennessee, Arkansas, Florida, and Texas. The conferences in North Carolina carried on very little home mission work outside of the state and only limited contact with churches organized elsewhere was maintained. Moreover, there was as yet no organization to embrace these churches in other Southern states in one denomination.

A Northern Free Will Baptist movement that traced its origin to the work of Benjamin Randall in New Hampshire in 1780 made occasional attempts to involve Free Will Baptists of North Carolina in their General Conference, but no union of the two groups was effected.

In 1901 a General Conference was convened at DUNN NC with representatives from local conferences and associations in several states. It was an attempt to unite the Free Will Baptists of the South and a few churches of the Northern movement, but it failed to achieve its purpose. It was again convened in Nashville TN in 1921 after attempts had failed to integrate Free Will Baptists of North Carolina and Tennessee in the Cooperative General Association, organized in 1916 and composed of ministers and churches in the Midwest who refused to support a merger between Northern Free Will Baptists and the Northern Baptist Convention in 1910.

The General Conference (South) met annually until 1935 when agreement was finally reached with the Cooperative General Association (Midwest) to form the National Association of Free Will Baptists. The two groups had separate origins and slightly different traditions in doctrine and church polity. Differences involving the ownership of the Free Will Baptist Press at Ayden NC and the right of a conference in North Carolina to discipline ministers and to settle disputes in a local church caused serious tensions to develop between the North Carolina Convention and the National Association. On 20 March 1962 the North Carolina Convention withdrew from the larger body and has since maintained its own denominational program, including a liberal arts college, a publishing foundation, a children's home, a summer retreat center, home and foreign missions. Its chaplain-endorsing agency is the General Commission on Chaplains, Washington DC. Inclusive membership is 40,000.

In 1963 the General Conference was revived, declaring itself "the continuation and enlargement of the former body of this name." Since it has not developed a program that calls for the active support of local churches, it serves mainly as a fellowship for ministers and representatives of local churches in North Carolina and other states that are not affiliated with the National Association.

The National Association sponsors a Bible College, a home mission program in several states, and foreign missions in several countries. Its headquarters are located in Nashville TN. Its chaplain-endorsing agency is the National Association of Evangelicals. Inclusive membership is 218,000.

Bibliography. Norman Baxter, *History of the Free Will Baptists*; William Davidson, *An Early History of Free Will Baptists*; Damon Dodd, *The Free Will Baptist Story*; Thad Harrison and J. M. Barfield, *History of the Free Will Baptists of North Carolina*; G. W. Paschal, *History of North Carolina Baptists*, vol. 1; A. C. Piepkorn, *Profiles in Belief*, vol. 2.

MICHAEL R. PELT
MOUNT OLIVE COLLEGE

FREE WILL, DOCTRINE OF: *See* ARMINIANISM; CALVINISM.

FREED, ARVY GLENN (1863-1931),

CHURCHES OF CHRIST educator, was born in Saltillo IN and a graduate of Valparaiso University. His mother was a relative of President Rutherford B. Hayes. Early in life he was immersed and associated himself with the DISCIPLES OF CHRIST and began a lifelong career of preaching.

Answering an advertisement in the *Gospel Advocate*, Freed moved to Tennessee in 1889 to operate a school at Essary Springs. During the fall of 1895, Freed moved to Henderson where he became president of West Tennessee Christian College. After two years the school's name was changed to Georgie Robertson Christian College. One of Freed's outstanding students, NICHOLAS BRODIE HARDEMAN, later joined the staff of the college. When the missionary society advocates gained control of the school, Freed and Hardeman resigned. The two men established the National Teachers' Normal and Business College in 1908, the original form of the present-day Freed-Hardeman College.

Freed and Hardeman parted ways in 1923, with Freed joining the faculty of David Lipscomb College in Nashville. He served as vice-president, dean, and high school principal at various times until his death.

Besides his educational endeavors, he was in great demand as an evangelist among Churches of Christ throughout the South. He did little writing, but did publish *Sermons, Chapel Talks*, and *Debates*.

Bibliography. James Marvin Powell and Mary Nelle Hardeman Powers, *N.B.H.: A Biography of Nicholas Brodie Hardeman*.

ROBERT E. HOOPER
DAVID LIPSCOMB COLLEGE

FRENCH HUGUENOTS: *See* HUGUENOTS.

FRENCH INFLUENCE. The earliest

written record of an effort to Christianize the Indians of Louisiana occurred in 1582 when Robert Cavelier, Sieur de LaSalle, and his party of French Canadian explorers floated down the Mississippi to the river's delta. LaSalle laid claim to the entire river valley in the name of Louis XIV of France, and thereby opened up a vast portion of North America to missionary priests from France. During the next century and a half, the religious life in much of the area would be heavily influenced by French Catholicism.

Today, however, the majority of the population found within the Mississippi's drainage basin are at least nominally Protestant, rather than Catholic—the result of the growth and expansion of a dynamic republic over that of a remote and discarded French colony. From the time of the purchase of Louisiana in 1803, remnant features of French Catholicism have been found in various parts of the river valley. The strongest imprints are inside the state of Louisiana. Here, the names of families, church rituals and customs, religious architecture, and continuing cultural ties to France maintain a distinctive cultural enclave within the borders of the South.

Less than a generation after LaSalle's claim, the brothers Pierre Le Moyne, Sieur d'Iberville, and Jean Baptiste Le Moyne de

Bienville established a permanent French settlement at the lower end of the Mississippi River. The French recognized the strategic importance of LaSalle's claim, and they hoped to facilitate communication between the Gulf coast region and Canada. Although initial settlement was at Biloxi in 1699, New Orleans and its environs later became the core area of French colonial activity after 1718 due to advantages in water transport, a richer agricultural hinterland, and strategic defense. Other permanent settlements included Mobile (1710) and Natchitoches (1713).

Religious activity in much of the lower Mississippi River Valley remained largely moribund owing to the small number of priests and administrative difficulties between the church and the French crown. Instead of rounding up the heathen and forcing conversion, the French missionaries normally lived among the Indian villagers and used gentle persuasion, while visiting traders occasionally made brief visits in pursuit of goods or military alliances. But after 1717, the spread of French Catholicism became more noticeable.

Construction of a permanent church building in New Orleans did not occur, however, before 1727. Much of the city's population consisted of convicts, soldiers, and assorted outcasts who were hardly interested in God's spiritual message or the furtherance of religion. Ironically, the second most important center of French Catholicism in Louisiana, Natchitoches, was entirely dependent on the Franciscans at the Spanish colonial post of Los Adayes (Los Adais), 21 miles away. Not until 1728 did the French Capuchins intervene. Other religious orders who entered the territory under French auspices included the Carmelite Fathers and the Jesuits. The arrival of the Ursuline nuns greatly supplemented educational opportunities. Upriver, in the parish of Les Allemands (St. John the Baptist), a settlement of German farmers (1723) created the beginnings of a complicated ethnic mosaic. In 1756, the first Acadian French refugees arrived in New Orleans. During the remainder of the French colonial period, the Church witnessed the eventual suppression of the Jesuits, and new settlements and missions were established in Pointe Coupée (1736), Opelousas (1756), and Le Poste des Attakapas (St. Martinville) in 1756.

With the beginning of the Spanish missionary period as a result of French military defeat at the hands of the British in the Seven Years' (French and Indian) War (1763), Louisiana reluctantly adjusted to a stricter colonial regime. The colony was placed under the administration of the bishop of Santiago de Cuba, and later under the bishop of Havana. The Spanish mission at Los Adayes was abandoned and the center of Catholicism in northwest Louisiana moved to the post of Natchitoches. Spanish Capuchins replaced French Capuchins and proceeded to strengthen Catholicism. A very large proportion of the priests sent to Louisiana were extremely orthodox Irishmen. One of the most colorful ecclesiastics entering New Orleans during the Spanish rule was Fray Antonio de Sedella, popularly known as Père Antoine.

With the arrival of the first bishop of Louisiana, Luis Penalver y Cardenas, in 1795, religious observances among Catholics did not improve and, in fact, remained very lax. Concubinage was common among married and unmarried men, marriage was uncommon among slaves, and a growing spirit of democracy resulted from the recent French Revolution. In the face of these and other difficulties at the time of Louisiana's purchase by the United States, the Church struggled to survive—her clergy understaffed, many of her parishioners unchurched, and priestly authority often usurped by ambitious lay leaders inspired by Voltaire or the French Revolution's anticlerical spirit. For a time, the bishop resided in the upriver city of St. Louis rather than submit to the disorders in New Orleans. Père Antoine's clerical leniency with his parishioners helped to ensure his popularity as it weakened the orthodoxy of Catholicism in the city.

During the administration of the bishop, and later Archbishop Antoine Blanc (1835-1860), Catholicism in the lower Mississippi River Valley experienced a period of rapid growth and acculturation. One of the last major confrontations facing the Church before the Civil War's outbreak was the strong opposition from Louisiana's Know-Nothing (Nativist) political movement, which for a time succeeded in dividing Irish and German Catholic newcomers from the French Creoles. The Civil War brought severe economic hardship and further division among parishioners. In the aftermath of the war the ethnicity of Catholicism in Louisiana was further complicated by the arrival of additional Catholic immigrants from Italy and eastern Europe.

Today, Catholicism in New Orleans and in much of the surrounding Deep South bears only a faint connection with its French origins. However, significant features of the Old Church culture remain. Much of the traditional church architecture in the lower valley is of a neo-Gothic design in the French style; likewise, the crowded cemeteries of New Orleans and other south Louisiana communities retain their above-ground crypt with peculiar French ornamentation. Certain festival days are still observed by Creole descendants in the New Orleans area. Family names, along with Christian names, honoring selected French saints, continue to permeate the cultural landscape. Even some wedding and funeral ceremonies have retained certain customs common to the ancien régime. Mardi Gras, along with other holiday observances, especially those of Holy Week, have strong connections with the early Creole Catholicism of French Louisiana. However, many of the older holiday customs have receded in favor of popular American culture.

See also articles on CAJUN INFLUENCE; HUGUENOTS; LOUISIANA.

Bibliography. Roger Baudier, *The Catholic Church in Louisiana*; Alcee Fortier, *A History of Louisiana*, vols. 1-4;

Charles Gayarre, *History of Louisiana*, vols. 1-4; Lyle Saxon, ed., *Gumbo Ya-Ya: A Collection of Louisiana Folk Tales*; Works Progress Administration, *Louisiana: A Guide to the State.*

TIMOTHY F. REILLY
UNIVERSITY OF SOUTHWEST LOUISIANA

FRIENDS, SOCIETY OF: *See* QUAKERISM; QUAKERS IN THE SOUTH.

FRONTIER, INFLUENCE OF. The development of religion in the South was strongly influenced by the fact that much of the region remained in frontier condition from colonial times through the close of the 19th century. Particularly during the antebellum period, the South's frontier condition would have an impact on the theology, practices, and organization of church life in the region.

The frontier's influence on Southern religion can be dated from the time of the GREAT REVIVAL, which centered on the Southern frontier from about 1795 until about 1805. Indeed, the most obvious product of the frontier's impact, the CAMP MEETING, was a practice that began during that revival and continued to have significance into the 1830s and 1840s. Held outdoors and drawing crowds from a large area, camp meetings comprised a useful adaptation to sparsely settled frontier regions for which the building of meetinghouses would have been impractical.

But the frontier exerted other influences on Southern religion that were both subtler and more profound, growing out of areas of coherence between the needs of frontier people and the main themes of the religion of REVIVALISM, which had developed during the Great Revival. Theologically, this coherence led to an individualism and otherworldliness that dominated religious belief. With roots in an Arminian theology developed most fully by frontier Methodists, and in a traditional Protestant emphasis on CONVERSION and SALVATION, frontier religious belief stressed the importance of each individual's having a direct experience of God's grace, one growing from the individual's choosing to heed and follow the call to salvation that God had made to everyone. This theology quickly outstripped an older Calvinism that had stressed predestination and irresistible grace. At the same time, frontier believers learned to look only to heaven for the fulfillment of salvation, specifically rejecting the possibility of finding rewards in this world.

The needs and tensions of frontier life had much to do with the triumph of such emphases in religious belief. Not only was that life physically hard, but it was characterized by powerful economic and social frustrations as many people moved about the South in search of good lands and an opportunity for prosperity. Good lands were hard to obtain and, for many, this meant a life of economic difficulty and unrealized ambitions. In religious individualism and otherworldliness, however, believers found alternative goals to those which, in this world, were so easily frustrated. The heavenly hope could replace those dreams of worldly success and fulfillment. And, in answering God's call, believers found a way in which they could feel they were making positive decisions for themselves, ones that would, unlike those having to do with worldly matters, reap great rewards (albeit in heaven). Frontier conditions were conducive for creating the kind of alternative represented by the dominant elements of frontier belief.

But frontier life also influenced the ethical and organizational characteristics of frontier denominations. The moral thrust of religion on the frontier was found mainly in strictly administered church disciplines covering all aspects of secular and religious life. The frontier churches have accurately been called "frontier moral courts" because, for their members, they were substituted for secular legal institutions in a broad range of disputes.

The churches took on this role in part as a response to the disorderly nature of frontier communities and to the scarcity of secular institutions. One major result

was to intensify a tendency toward "petty moralism" in the Southern understanding of Christian ethics. Disinclined, given their individualistic and otherworldly theology, to identify sinfulness in deep-seated social ills, the churches chose to fight such private sins as gambling, drinking, dancing, and shady business practices, rather than those that might have represented problems inherent in the social order. Their emphasis was on the individual's living right in a sinful world, so that frontier churches gave little attention to changing the world itself. This moral focus continues to dominate Southern religious life.

Organizationally, the frontier environment strengthened schismatic tendencies in Southern religion. The sparseness of settlement inhibited the growth of strong organizational ties within the major denominations, and the role of church bodies as courts deciding a range of religious and secular issues meant that consensus as well as doctrine came to count heavily in the resolution of even theological differences. The result was that, as frontier believers wrangled over thorny matters of doctrine, dissident groups tended to go their own way in search of cohesion and consensus, forming new organizations. Indeed, such major contemporary denominations as the DISCIPLES OF CHRIST and the CUMBERLAND PRESBYTERIAN CHURCH had their origins in such disputes on the Southern frontier.

No less important was the frontier's influence on the South's religious style, a style that has often been emotional and sometimes anti-intellectual. During the Great Revival, the emotionalism of religion on the frontier had been notable as camp meeting converts, in particular, signaled their experiences of divine grace with such spectacular physical "exercises" as barking, falling, and "the jerks." Although these physical manifestations of grace would be toned down as the antebellum period progressed, the emotional emphasis would continue to characterize evangelical religion in the South.

Anti-intellectualism can go hand in hand with this emotionalism, and sometimes did as frontier church members came to prize experience over ideas as the proper foundation for religious faith. Indeed, many frontier believers strongly opposed the establishment of seminaries and the employment of an educated clergy because of their appreciation of experience over learning. They were supported in this by a pioneer ministry that itself had frontier origins. Like their congregations, these clergymen valued experience and rejected education, beyond a personal reading of the Scriptures, as necessary for effective religious leadership. Known as "Sons of Thunder," they themselves had little formal knowledge of theology and mainly sought, in a plain-spoken yet vivid way, to make the joys of salvation and the horrors of damnation clear and moving. Such men epitomized the simplicity and feeling that would characterize Southern popular religion, especially Southern revivalism, until well into the 20th century.

See also article on EVANGELICALISM.

Bibliography. John B. Boles, *The Great Revival*; Peter Cartwright, *Autobiography*; Charles A. Johnson, *The Frontier Camp Meeting*; T. Scott Miyakawa, *Protestants and Pioneers*; Walter B. Posey, *Frontier Mission*; *Religious Strife on the Southern Frontier*; William Warren Sweet, *Religion on the American Frontier*, 4 vols.

DICKSON D. BRUCE, JR.
UNIVERSITY OF CALIFORNIA, IRVINE

FROST, JAMES MARION (1848-1916), Baptist religious education organizer, was born in Georgetown KY. He graduated from Georgetown College and served numerous churches in Kentucky, Virginia, and Tennessee. While a pastor in Richmond VA, he began to urge the founding of a Sunday School Board for the Southern Baptist Convention. His efforts resulted in such a foundation in 1891, and he moved to Nashville TN to become its first secretary. Opposition and loneliness composed his early experience and after only 18 months he resigned to become

pastor of the First Baptist Church in that city. In 1896 he was persuaded to return to the position as secretary and remained in that position until his death 20 years later.

As first secretary of this board, Frost set the pattern for the board's later growth. He convinced it to become a publishing house and urged a strong curriculum with a graded series of lessons for the various ages. He urged denominational consciousness through the Sunday schools of the churches of the denomination. The board supplied general materials for the local churches and also began to publish books during his tenure of office. He wrote numerous volumes himself.

By the time of his death, the board had prospered enough to erect a building of five floors and dedicate it free of debt in 1914. His pastoral sensitivity, denominational commitment, and unusual business ability combined in a natural way to result in the kind of success that secured denominational consciousness among the Southern Baptists during a period of rapid expansion.

Bibliography. Encyclopedia of Southern Baptists, 1: 512-13; James Marion Frost, *The School and the Church*.

GEORGE SHRIVER
GEORGIA SOUTHERN COLLEGE

FUNDAMENTALISM. This is a powerful, richly connotative but elusive term that begs definition. It does not mean, for example, opposition to all that is modern, nor is it a synonym for religious bigotry or fanaticism, although its adherents sometimes display these traits. If one wished to identify a fundamentalist mentality, its most definitive trait would be militant antimodernism, but Fundamentalism is more than that. By a more precise and historical definition, Fundamentalism is the self-imposed label of an American religious movement that arose in the early twentieth century to promote and defend traditional evangelical beliefs and concerns in response to liberal trends in Protestant churches and secular trends in society. Thus, Fundamentalists are Evangelicals, but not all Evangelicals are Fundamentalists. Evangelicals in America comprise a vast and varied mosaic of traditions of which Fundamentalism is but one.

The fundamentalist movement is most directly rooted in the interdenominational, evangelical network formed in the late nineteenth century by that era's greatest evangelist, Dwight L. Moody, and his colleagues. The early movement drew most of its constituents from the generally Reformed wing of Anglo-American Protestantism: the Baptists, Presbyterians, and Congregationalists. While it has been called a "Bible Belt" phenomenon of the South and Midwest, Fundamentalism was a truly national movement that began in the cities of the North and East. Moody's revivalism included beliefs and concerns that also would characterize the later movement: the primacy of evangelism, the need for an anointing of the Holy Spirit for effective Christian service, the premillennial second coming of Christ, and the verbally inspired, absolutely authoritative Bible. The leaders of this movement did not feel especially defensive about their faith. They knew about liberal theology and the secularizing forces in society, but they believed that evangelical faith would be vindicated by its fruits. Indeed, they were building an impressive network of Bible and missionary training schools, Bible conferences, domestic and foreign mission agencies, and religious magazines.

Moody's successors, however, perceived that the liberal movement was capturing their denominations and eroding commitment to evangelization and biblical authority. Between 1910 and 1915, they published a series of 12 small booklets called *The Fundamentals*, in which widely respected pastors, scholars, and laymen berated liberal theology and critical study of the Bible, reaffirmed evangelism and the promotion of piety as the chief concerns of the church, and defended cardinal evangelical doctrines, notably the inerrancy of the Bible and salvation only by faith in Christ's atoning death. Yet it

would take the cultural shocks brought on by World War I to mobilize these Evangelicals to full-fledged fundamentalist militancy. The wartime sense of threat to American civilization sharpened the conflict between liberals and these "Bible school" people who formed the core of nascent Fundamentalism. Liberals accused them of being disloyal for criticizing the Armageddon-like "war to end all wars" rhetoric. The Fundamentalists replied that Germany's militarism resulted from disbelief in the Bible's authority and acceptance of evolutionary philosophy. These ideas also threatened American civilization, they said, so they formed the World's Christian Fundamentals Association in 1919 to purge them from the churches and the schools.

The outcome of the public controversies engaged by the Fundamentalists and their conservative allies in the 1920s is well known. Their attempts to purge evolution from the schools and to drive liberalism from the denominations met with defeat and growing public ridicule. America was turning its back on God, it seemed, so Fundamentalists became alienated from American public life. In the two denominations hardest hit by controversy in the 1920s, the Northern Baptist Convention and the Presbyterian Church in the U.S.A., separatist movements erupted: the General Association of Regular Baptist Churches in 1932, and the Orthodox Presbyterian Church and BIBLE PRESBYTERIAN CHURCH in 1936 and 1937. Perhaps the greatest number of Fundamentalists, however, remained within the older denominations. Such differing strategies brought fragmentation and enduring grudges. Fundamentalism seemed to be a spent force.

These defeats, however, prompted Fundamentalists to pursue their prior concerns, evangelism, and piety. Over the next two decades, they expanded the network of institutions inherited from Moody's generation, using radio broadcasting to retool their evangelism. During the 1930s their effective communication and salient public position brought Fundamentalism into other traditions, notably that of Scandinavian Evangelicals, the Dutch Reformed, Mennonites, Southern Baptists, and Southern Presbyterians.

In the 1940s Fundamentalists began a major new campaign to save America. The National Association of Evangelicals, founded in 1942, and the Youth for Christ revival of the mid-1940s, initiated an alliance between Fundamentalists and other Evangelicals for bold new evangelistic ventures, including those of BILLY GRAHAM, who achieved national fame by 1950. The goals of the new, pan-evangelical coalition were the same as Fundamentalists' in 1920: a "Christian America." But their new crusades were evangelistic rather than overtly political.

While Fundamentalists seemed to prosper, the old fights between the separatist militants and the nonseparating moderates threatened to split the movement entirely. The irenic posture of the National Association of Evangelicals and Billy Graham marked the determination of one wing of Fundamentalism to sacrifice some militancy in order to cooperate with non-Fundamentalists. This wing's leaders called for new intellectual vigor, social responsibility, and a tolerant spirit. But other Fundamentalists refused to compromise any of their doctrinal scruples or independency; militancy mattered more than respectability to them. They condemned the NAE for admitting Wesleyans and Pentecostals, for refusing to condemn old-line denominations, and for not fighting the liberal Federal Council of Churches.

Carl McIntire, a Bible Presbyterian, led this offensive from the American Council of Christian Churches, which was founded in 1941. Eventually this attack was aimed at Billy Graham, who by 1960 was the leading symbol of evangelical unity and respectability. By that time there were three major divisions in the fundamentalist movement: the "new evangelicals," who supported the NAE, Graham, *Christianity Today* magazine,

and a pan-evangelical coalition; the militant separatists, who sympathized with McIntire and the ACCC and were increasingly isolated from the cultural mainstream; and a large, non-aligned contingent that controlled many of the movement's central institutions, notably the Moody Bible Institute.

One might expect that a movement so splintered would scarcely be able to survive, but all of Fundamentalism's descendants are thriving. The "new Evangelicals" have encouraged a major stirring of evangelical expression and activity since 1960 that ranges from Catholic charismatics to Anabaptist-oriented radicals. The militant separatists are rapidly multiplying, especially in the South where the BAPTIST BIBLE FELLOWSHIP boasts nearly three million members and MORAL MAJORITY leader, Jerry Falwell. The fundamentalist center retains its vigor and has in its Dallas Theological Seminary one of the nation's 10 largest seminaries. The Moral Majority, a fundamentalist-led conservative political coalition, is but one sign of resurgent political activity in the movement. Its constituents are distressed by post-Christian trends in America, but they have pursued a wide variety of positions: from Sen. Mark Hatfield's concern for poverty and hunger to the Moral Majority's anti-abortion, pro-school-prayer positions; from Carl McIntire's obsession with Communism to Billy Graham's pleas for disarmament.

This broad range of temperament, allegiances, and alignments makes it difficult to see how the fundamentalist tradition shows any coherence. The keys to understanding these apparent discrepancies, however, are the paradoxical tensions that form the fundamentalist character. Fundamentalists often take unyielding, conservative stands for old-time religion, old-fashioned morality, and right-wing policies and economics. Yet this rigid, militant mood often conflicts with a flexible, innovative spirit rooted in American revivalism, which tests principles and techniques by their result and asks to be shown from the Bible which is the right position to take. There exists a similar tension between the movement's hopes for the Second Coming and revival. Fundamentalists can be profoundly pessimistic in mood, believing that civilization is decaying and that only Christ's personal return will set things right.

Yet their revival heritage often leads to a conflicting message: America will be saved if her people repent. Consequently, some Fundamentalists will sacrifice militancy for the sake of revival, while others sacrifice revival prospects for a principled, militant stand. Other tensions abound: an inheritance of cultural guardianship and social concern clashes with memories of public ridicule and feelings of alienation. Their search for antidotes to modern crises of authority have prompted hard-line biblical inerrancy and authoritarian styles of leadership, yet Fundamentalists have led populist revolts against ecclesiastical authorities and many of their congregations refuse any outside affiliations. Yet for the sake of evangelism, they will often join in pragmatic, *ad hoc* alliances. These tensions make it difficult to reduce the fundamentalist character to a simple model, but then historians, unlike Fundamentalists, usually find complexity closer to the truth.

See also articles on EVANGELICALISM; EVOLUTION CONTROVERSY; BOB JONES FAMILY; MODERNIST CONTROVERSY; J. FRANK NORRIS.

Bibliography. Joel A. Carpenter, "The Fundamentalist Leaven and the Rise of an Evangelical United Front," *The Evangelical Tradition in America,* ed. Leonard I. Sweet; Paul A. Carter, "The Fundamentalist Defense of the Faith," *Change and Continuity in Twentieth Century America: The 1920s,* ed. John Braeman, et al.; George Dollar, *A History of Fundamentalism in America;* Norman F. Furniss, *The Fundamentalist Controversy, 1918-1931;* Willard B. Gatewood, *Controversy in the Twenties;* George M. Marsden, *Fundamentalism and American Culture;* C. Allyn Russell, *Voices of American Fundamentalism;* Ernest R. Sandeen, *The Roots of Fundamentalism;* Grant Wacker, "The Evangelical Right in Contemporary America," *The Evangelical Tradition in America,* ed. Leonard I. Sweet.

JOEL A. CARPENTER
WHEATON COLLEGE

FUNERALS. The service of worship at the time of death has been among the major rituals of the Southern churches. The predominant EVANGELICALISM shaped regional funerals through the theology and the form of the final rites. Funeral practices varied by social class, racial caste, religious denomination, and rural-urban setting, but shared Southern characteristics existed that represented regional variations from other American death patterns. Southern funerals diverged from Northern ones as far back as the antebellum era, but they differed even more as a result of social changes after the Civil War.

By 1900 the American funeral industry had emerged, bringing the embalming process, elaborate caskets, funeral homes, and a secular funeral service. Professionalization of the funeral industry led to the discouragement of emotional expressions at funerals. These developments mainly affected the Northeastern middle class. The development of the Southern funeral industry lagged because of the low income of Southerners, their rural location, and the persistence of Christian attitudes. Religion, therefore, retained primary influence over the death process far longer in the South than in the rest of the nation.

For most Southerners in most periods of their history a rural Protestant funeral has been typical. A traditional funeral was a community affair, with neighbors and family laying out the body, making the simple pine coffin, sitting up with the body, paying final respects at the deceased's home, and watching over the burial itself. To facilitate attendance, funerals have been frequently held on Sundays, the normal day of religious observance.

As with other aspects of Southern religious life, funerals reflected the evangelical outlook. The concern for conversion and salvation was a central focus of the death process. In the last hours of the dying person's life, efforts were made to insure repentance. After the death, the churches concentrated not on ceremonial attempts to aid the soul of the dead, but rather upon the living. Ministers comforted the family, but even more important was the need to teach relatives and friends of the deceased the necessity for salvation. Funeral hymns and prayers have been comforting portrayals of the peace of HEAVEN, but they also have urged listeners to contemplate their own future. When the hour comes, will the mourners be ready to meet their Lord? In the fundamentalist churches within the region, dying has been seen as evidence of God's hand. Death can be interpreted as a punishment, as the direct result of sin. It can also be seen, though, as a reward for a holy person going to a heavenly afterlife. Southern theology interprets death as a trial, during which faith in God is tested. The afflicted family must confront the most basic questions of human existence and affirm the answers to those questions given by the religious traditions of the region.

Church funeral services have been regarded as essential in the South. Even if the deceased had no religious affiliation nor high moral reputation, a church funeral was still arranged, with a minister associated with a relative of the deceased being asked to conduct services. The presence of a preacher has been another ingredient for any proper Southern funeral, even after professional funeral directors became pervasive. The funeral service itself has been more informal and folksy than elsewhere, reflecting the region's cultural style. Emotional display of grief at funerals has been more likely in the South than in the North, with Pentecostal services more expressive than those of the mainline Southern Protestant groups and black funerals more expressive than white. The contemporary South has moved closer to the American mainstream in funeral patterns, with professional funeral directors arranging and directing the mourning process. Churches, however, continue to be so institutionally vital in the South that they retain a large ritualistic and theological role in managing the human crisis of death.

See also article on CEMETERIES.

Bibliography. Christopher Crocker, "The Southern Way of Death," *The Not So Solid South,* ed. J. Kenneth Morland; James J. Farrell, *Inventing the American Way of Death, 1830-1920*; Charles Hudson, "The Structure of a Fundamentalist Christian Belief System," *Religion and the Solid South,* ed. Samuel S. Hill, Jr.

CHARLES REAGAN WILSON
UNIVERSITY OF MISSISSIPPI

FURMAN, RICHARD (1755-1825), Baptist minister and educator, was born in Esopus NY. The family soon settled near Charleston SC, where young Richard was educated largely by his father. In 1770 the Furmans moved to High Hills, where Richard was converted, joined a Baptist church, began to preach, and in 1774 was ordained. He was such a strong supporter of the American Revolution that he had to flee when the British put a price on his head.

On his return, he was recognized as the outstanding leader of South Carolina's Baptists; in 1787 he was called to the pastorate of the Charleston congregation. He took a central role in the forming of the Charleston Baptist Association, and devoted much attention to educational causes, especially in helping to secure funds so that prospective ministers could get proper schooling. His character and ability were widely recognized; he was chosen as the first president of the Baptist TRIENNIAL CONVENTION, that denomination's first national missionary organization, in 1814. Reelected in 1817, he urged the establishment of a Baptist university in Washington, Columbian College. When the South Carolina Baptist State Convention was organized in 1821, he was chosen to be the first president. At the time of the DENMARK VESEY slave uprising, he spoke for his people in declaring that slaveholding was thoroughly biblical, and therefore moral and Christian. Toward the end of his life, he urged Baptists in the South to establish a collegiate institution; founded the year after his death, it matured into Furman University.

See also articles on EDUCATION, CHRISTIAN HIGHER; SLAVERY.

Bibliography. H. T. Cook, *A Biography of Richard Furman.*

ROBERT T. HANDY
UNION THEOLOGICAL SEMINARY

GAILOR, THOMAS FRANK (1856-1935), a major figure in the Southern episcopal tradition, was born and reared in Memphis. There he observed the trauma of Civil War fighting; his father died during the conflict and Gailor grew up under the influence of his mother, an Irish immigrant, and a series of strong teachers. He attended schools in Memphis, but then went north to college in Wisconsin and to the General Theological Seminary in New York City (1876). Gailor's first ministry was in Pulaski TN (1880-1882), a small town that, he said, regarded him as the mysterious representative of a strange but interesting religion. Ordained to the episcopate in 1893, he served five years as bishop coadjutor and became the fourth bishop of Tennessee upon the death of CHARLES T. QUINTARD.

In 1882 Gailor began his long involvement with the UNIVERSITY OF THE SOUTH. He served there as chaplain, professor of ecclesiastical history, vice-chancellor (1890-1893) and chancellor (1908-1935). He tapped Northerners such as J. P. Morgan and Andrew Carnegie for contributions that enabled the school to expand. Under his administration the SEWANEE TN institution became a focal point for the training of Southern episcopal leaders.

Gailor was widely traveled, including vacations in the Middle East, an official church trip to Japan and China to see missionaries, and frequent visits to England. He served as first president of the National Council of the Episcopal Church and was a frequent lecturer at national church affairs. A Southerner by birth and conviction, he cherished the Confederate memory and valued the Southern sense of traditional values as a compatible accompaniment to the episcopal outlook.

Bibliography. Thomas F. Gailor, *Some Memories*; Charles Reagan Wilson, "Bishop Thomas Frank Gailor: Celebrant of Southern Tradition," *Tennessee Historical Quarterly* 38 (Fall 1979): 322-31.

CHARLES REAGAN WILSON
UNIVERSITY OF MISSISSIPPI

GAMBRELL, JAMES BRUTON (1841-1921), Baptist pastor and denominational leader, was born in South Carolina and reared in Mississippi. In the Civil War he was a scout in Lee's army, and after the war attended the University of Mississippi.

Following a period as a Baptist pastor, Gambrell served as editor of the Mississippi *Baptist Record* from 1877 to 1893.

In 1893 he assumed the presidency of Mercer University, leaving that office in 1896 to become superintendent of missions for Texas Baptists. In 1910 he accepted a position as editor of the Texas *Baptist Standard* and in 1912 became a professor at Southwestern Baptist Theological Seminary in Fort Worth. Gambrell resigned both the editorship and the teaching post in 1914 to become secretary of the Baptist General Convention of Texas, a position he retained until his death. He was also elected president of the SOUTHERN BAPTIST CONVENTION for four terms, 1917 through 1921.

As an editor and denominational leader, Gambrell exercised significant influence upon the development of a strong denominational consciousness among Southern Baptists. While affirming local church autonomy, he urged Southern Baptists to unite in order to achieve global goals in missions and evangelism. He warned Baptists against ecumenical entanglements that might weaken denominational identity and was highly critical of those who opposed cooperative programs for funding missions and denominational agencies. Known as the "Great Commoner," Gambrell sought to communicate Baptist theology and denominational principles to those at the local church level.

See also article on RELIGIOUS PRESS.

Bibliography. James Bruton Gambrell, *Ten Years in Texas*; Bill J. Leonard, "The Southern Baptist Denominational Leader as Theologian," *Baptist History and Heritage* 16 (July 1980): 23-32, 61, 63; E. C. Routh, "Gambrell, James Bruton," *Encyclopedia of Southern Baptists*, vol. 2.

BILL J. LEONARD
SOUTHERN BAPTIST SEMINARY

GARDEN, ALEXANDER (1685-1756), Anglican church leader in colonial South Carolina, was born in Scotland, attended Aberdeen University, was ordained in the Church of England, and served as a curate in London. In 1720 he arrived in Charles Town SC and became the minister of ST. PHILIP'S CHURCH; owing to popular dissatisfaction with the Anglican clergy who had sided with the

proprietors in 1719 when proprietary government was overthrown, Garden was elected rector only in 1725. Henry Compton, bishop of London, appointed Garden his commissary in 1728, and he served in that office for nearly 20 years.

Garden's greatest contribution to South Carolina was to shape a state church that suited the people of the colony rather than one that duplicated the establishment in England. He accepted the power of the colonial laity and the existence of the dissenters. Garden placed a strong emphasis on clerical discipline and converted an ecclesiastical court that suspended one clergyman guilty of drunkenness. Garden also became the champion of the Church of England when he answered the attacks of GEORGE WHITEFIELD on Anglican sacramentalism and good works. His published sermons—*Regeneration, Six Letters to the Rev. George Whitefield, Take Heed How Ye Hear*, and *The Doctrine of Justification*—were widely read throughout the colonies.

Garden retired from St. Philip's in 1753 and died three years later. A combative and even cantankerous person, he was a diligent and able clergyman who won the respect and love of his parishioners. More so than any other single individual, he made Anglicanism the indigenous religion of the South Carolina Low Country.

See also articles on COLONIAL PERIOD (in Appendix); ESTABLISHED RELIGION; SOCIETY FOR THE PROPAGATION OF THE GOSPEL.

Bibliography. S. Charles Bolton, *Southern Anglicanism: The Church of England in Colonial South Carolina*; Frederick Dalcho, *An Historical Account of the Protestant Episcopal Church*; Richard Beale Davis, *Intellectual Life in the Colonial South, 1585-1763*.

S. CHARLES BOLTON
UNIVERSITY OF ARKANSAS
AT LITTLE ROCK

GARRETTSON, FREEBORN (1752-1827), itinerant minister and major figure in the early growth of American Methodism, was born in Maryland. His wealthy

Church of England parents gave him a good elementary education, but died before he was 21 years old. Thrust into managing a household of 20, including several slaves, and still unsatisfied with his religious state, Garrettson heard the preaching of Robert Strawbridge and FRANCIS ASBURY. After a long period of internal agitation, he experienced a Methodist conversion in 1775; immediately he freed his slaves. Reluctantly he became an itinerant preacher, joined the Baltimore Conference in 1776, and for the next 52 years traveled in America and Nova Scotia preaching and establishing churches.

Garrettson rode far and wide, especially through the South, summoning preachers to the CHRISTMAS CONFERENCE (1784) where he was ordained an elder and volunteered for Nova Scotia. After his success almost equalled Wesley's in Europe, the latter's request that Garrettson be superintendent in Nova Scotia and the West Indies was denied by the conference of 1787. Asked by Asbury in 1788 to plant Methodism in New England, Garrettson went to New York where he took the place of an ill minister and remained to establish Methodism along the Hudson, his most important achievement. His most significant publication was his journal, *The Experience and Travels of Mr. Freeborn Garrettson.*

Bibliography. Nathan Bangs, *The Life of the Rev. Freeborn Garrettson;* "Garrettson, Freeborn," *Dictionary of American Biography* 4 (1946): 166-67.

HERMAN E. THOMAS
UNIVERSITY OF NORTH CAROLINA
AT CHARLOTTE

GEFFEN, TOBIAS (1870-1970), dean of Southern Orthodox rabbis, was born in Lithuania, the son of a timber merchant. Because he early demonstrated a keen intellectual curiosity, his parents encouraged him to study in Jewish religious academies. Even after his marriage in 1898, he continued his education while his wife supported the family by running a small store. In 1903 he was ordained as a rabbi; later he would receive a second ordination.

Geffen likely would have remained in Lithuania but for an outbreak of pogroms in Eastern Europe. In 1903 he brought his family to New York, where he accepted the position of rabbi of a small congregation. Four years later he moved to Canton OH. In 1910 he answered an advertisement for Atlanta's Shearith Israel Congregation, which sought a rabbi with the highest form of ordination. Rabbi Geffen was offered the job and spent the remaining 60 years of his life in Atlanta. He was the first Orthodox rabbi to take up permanent residence in Georgia.

Geffen was respected not only for his piety, sincerity, and preaching skill, but also for his remarkable scholarship and knowledge. Orthodox rabbis from all over the South and elsewhere turned to him for assistance in complicated religious questions. He was, for example, considered an expert on the subject of divorce according to Jewish religious law. His most famous judgment, however, concerned Coca Cola. There was some question as to whether the soft drink was kosher for Passover and for all-year usage. Coca Cola officials allowed Geffen to examine the formula used in their product, and he suggested substitution of a few ingredients that would ensure its *kashruth.* The substitution was made and Geffen issued a responsum that Coca Cola was kosher.

Like the leading European Orthodox rabbis of his day, Geffen spent much of his time writing on aspects of the Talmud. He wrote scores of articles and eight books, including his autobiography, *Fooftsik Yahr Rabbanut* (Fifty Years a Rabbi). His reputation in the South resulted mainly from his scholarship and the extensive correspondence he maintained with Jews in all parts of the Southeast.

See also articles on JEWISH IMMIGRATION; JEWS IN THE SOUTH.

ARNOLD SHANKMAN

GENERAL BAPTISTS. This denominational title refers to Baptists who held the Arminian view of an unlimited atonement. Arising in England as early as 1612,

General Baptists antedated by more than two decades Particular Baptists, who held the contrary view of the ATONEMENT.

Although General Baptists were found in the Northern colonies of British North America during the 17th century, they did not appear in the Southern colonies until 1714 when a General Baptist church was organized in Virginia. Some of these Baptists migrated to North Carolina and other parts of the South, where they multiplied. In time, many of them became Calvinists; others called themselves FREEWILL BAPTISTS. As late as 1800 an organized General Baptist movement hardly existed in the United States.

General Baptists reemerged, however, in the fall of 1823 when Benoni Stinson (1798-1869) and others formed the Liberty Baptist Church in Vanderburg County IN. Today it is the oldest General Baptist church in the nation. The Liberty Association of Indiana, which was constituted by four congregations in 1824, became the earliest expression of corporate life among General Baptist churches. By 1830 the presbytery had developed as an agency to control the ordination of ministers and their status as ordained men among the churches.

The General Association of General Baptists was organized at the Harmony Church in Gallatin County IL on 2 November 1870 by representatives of three district associations. At first its goals included union with other Baptist bodies, but within eight years the association had restricted itself to the interests of General Baptist churches.

General Baptists hold to the doctrine that Christ died for all people and not for the elect only. They believe that the security of the Christian is conditioned by a continued faith; hence a believer can fall away from God and be finally lost. These Baptists practice open communion, and a diminishing number of them practice FOOT WASHING. The General Association pronounced in 1980 that two doctrines were unscriptural: glossolalia seen as evidence of the baptism of the Holy Spirit; sanctification interpreted as "a progressive second definite work of grace in God's plan of salvation."

In 1980 the General Association comprised 65 district associations, 899 churches, and 74,466 church members. Sixty-five percent of these communicants are located in Southern states, the greater concentration being in Missouri, Kentucky, and Arkansas. The majority of the members of Northern churches are found in Indiana and Illinois, areas that have been strongly influenced by the South.

The headquarters of the General Association of General Baptists are housed in a new building at Poplar Bluff MO. The oldest agency of the union is its Home Mission Board, established in 1871. It fosters evangelism and the organization of new churches. Foreign missions are carried on in Guam, Saipan, the Philippines, and Jamaica. Other activities of the association include women's work, brotherhood projects, publication of literature for Sunday schools, youth work, operation of a college (at Oakland City IN), maintenance of a nursing home, and aid to ministers. The union has been affiliated with the Baptist World Alliance since 1966.

See also article on ARMINIANISM.

Bibliography. General Association of General Baptists, *Proceedings,* 1980; Ollie Latch, *History of the General Baptists;* A. D. Williams, *Benoni Stinson and the General Baptists.*

CHESTER RAYMOND YOUNG
CUMBERLAND COLLEGE

GEOGRAPHY OF SOUTHERN RELIGION.

Viewed within a national context, the South appears to contain little demographic variation in its religious patterns. Nowhere else does Protestantism, particularly conservative Protestantism, predominate over so large an area. Moreover, the success of the South's two major religious groups, the Baptists and Methodists, has resulted in low religious diversity and high rates of church membership in comparison with other regions of the country. The Baptist dominance of

Southern religion is especially noteworthy, for outside the South this group is a minority almost everywhere. No other part of the country of equal size is as completely dominated by a single denomination. Still, although uniformity is the most essential feature of the South's religious demography, and clearly sets it apart from the rest of the nation, the region possesses a degree of diversity that is worthy of attention.

As noted, Baptists are now the ranking religious group in the South, representing the majority of church members in most of the region's counties. Their imposing presence is the primary fact of Southern religious demography. Although they are numerous everywhere, a major corridor of Baptist strength extends from southern Appalachia, through Georgia, Alabama, and Mississippi, and into northern Louisiana and Texas, and southern Arkansas and Oklahoma. Baptists came to the South in the mid-eighteenth century during the GREAT AWAKENING. They were among the most successful of the several evangelical denominations that attempted to convert the unchurched masses of western Virginia and the Carolina Piedmont, the Southern backcountry of the time. Their great success was partly founded upon the work of farmer-preachers, uneducated men of humble origin who settled and worked among the people they served. Farmer-preachers became especially important figures in the settlement of the trans-Appalachian South following the Revolution. As part of the general westward flow of settlers, they carried the Baptist message wherever people went. Baptist strength east of the mountains was thus transformed into even greater strength in the West.

The Baptists had competition within the Southern missionary field, of course, especially from Methodists. Indeed, early Methodist success rivaled that of the Baptists, and until the first decades of the 20th century the two groups were almost equal in number throughout most of the region. Like the Baptists, the Methodists began their efforts in the South before the Revolution, and moved west with the migrating population. The Methodists differed in that they reached the frontier through a well-coordinated arrangement of circuit riders and regular camp meetings. What the Baptists achieved through the random and spontaneous actions of individuals, the Methodists attained through organization and careful planning. In the last half-century Methodist growth has lagged behind that of the Baptists, possibly because of the latter's continuing commitment to evangelism and the strong regional ties of the SOUTHERN BAPTIST CONVENTION. Methodism is still strong, however. It registers majorities and pluralities in counties scattered across the South, especially in the Carolinas, the Virginias, Maryland, and Tennessee; and large Methodist minorities exist throughout the region.

Together, the Baptists and Methodists form the core of Southern conservative Protestantism. Other representatives of this religious mode include Disciples of Christ, Churches of Christ, Presbyterians, and some members of the larger Pentecostal and Holiness denominations. In the Upper South and the Carolinas, these smaller groups frequently comprise a significant portion of the conservative mainstream. The connections of Disciples and Churches of Christ to the mainstream stem from their origins during the same period of frontier revivalism that led to Baptist and Methodist dominance. Although they began as nondenominational religious movements, their methods and the social background of their membership were very similar to those of the larger two groups. The same was true of Cumberland and other dissenting Presbyterians. The Holiness and Pentecostal movements have developed largely during this century, in part by attracting members from more fundamentalist segments of the conservative mainstream.

Baptists and Methodists have been able to maintain their primacy among religious groups in the South in part because of an absence of extensive extraregional immigration since the early 1800s. Nonetheless, some such immigration did occur, bringing with it important elements of religious diversity. Elsewhere in the South, previously established populations of markedly different religious affiliation also contributed to a degree of variation. Catholic concentrations originating in these ways are the only areas of significant size within the South where a denomination other than Baptists or Methodists contains a majority of church members. Moreover, several of the Catholic subregions are characterized by markedly different patterns of ethnicity than are found elsewhere in the South. They thus provide a strong contrast to the general patterns of Southern religion, although their influence is reduced somewhat by their location on the geographic periphery of the region.

Southern Catholicism is most firmly established where it is associated with large and distinct ethnic groups: southern LOUISIANA and southern TEXAS. The Catholic presence in the former dates back to the early eighteenth century when the French settlements of New Orleans and Mobile were founded. The character of the subregion was most heavily influenced by the arrival in the mid-eighteenth century of the Cajuns, French-speaking Catholics deported by the English from Acadia (colonial French Nova Scotia). Significant contributions also arrived from France and the French West Indies. The history of Catholicism in southern Texas is equally long, beginning in the late 1600s with the establishment of Spanish missions along the northern border of colonial Mexico. The subsequent development, under Spanish, Mexican, and American rule, of a large Spanish-speaking Catholic population in this subregion has made it the most extensive Catholic area within the Southern states. As with Louisiana's Cajuns, Catholicism is a major component of the cultural identity of the Mexican-Americans who numerically dominate southern Texas.

Other smaller areas of Catholic influence include several along the broad northern border zone of the South. One such area, as old as those just discussed but not distinguished by a special ethnic identity, is the western shore of the Chesapeake Bay. Current Catholic majorities in these counties reflect the historic importance of MARYLAND as a center of English-speaking Catholicism and religious tolerance in colonial America. Farther west, the migration of German and Swiss Catholics to the lower Ohio and Missouri rivers during the 19th century is largely responsible for continuing Catholic majorities and pluralities among the counties of east central Missouri and southern Illinois and Indiana. An additional minor zone of Catholic strength in north central Kentucky was founded by Catholic settlers from Maryland. Finally, the most recently developed area of Catholic strength in the South is peninsular Florida. Most Catholics in this subregion are recent immigrants from northern states, part of a general flow of population to Florida during this century. In recent years, Catholicism in southern Florida has developed a distinct ethnic component through the presence of Cuban refugees, particularly in the Miami area.

The above areas of Catholic strength, if the most obvious, are not the only exceptions to Baptist-Methodist hegemony over the religious geography of the South. Subtle variations also exist within the geography of Protestantism. These variations are not highly visible because of the small size of most Protestant denominations in the South relative to the dominant groups. Even when many smaller denominations came together in a particular location to create an island of greater religious diversity, Baptists or Methodists still often claim pluralities of the total church membership. Nonetheless, such areas are an important source of variety within Southern religion, usually indicating a cultural or historical background somewhat different from the mainstream.

Peninsular FLORIDA is a major area of Protestant diversity. Large numbers of Protestants of various persuasions have come to Florida from the Northern states during this century seeking the amenities of the Sun Belt. They joined with the Catholic immigrants and existing Baptists and Methodists to create an area marked by greater religious diversity than any other part of the South. Episcopalians, Lutherans, the Reformed churches, and the United Church of Christ, as well as Disciples, Churches of Christ, and Presbyterians, are all found in greater proportion here than throughout most of the rest of the region. Southern Florida also contains the largest Southern concentrations of Jews, again a result of migration from the North during this century.

Another of the South's distinctively pluralistic religious subregions is the Carolina Piedmont. The development of this complex subregion involved a number of different groups, including the Friends, Lutherans, Moravians, Presbyterians, and the United Church of Christ. Friends have been present in significant numbers in central North Carolina since the late 1600s, when they were attracted by the lack of restrictions against religious nonconformists. During the 18th century, after land had become scarce in southeastern Pennsylvania, settlement began to flow from that state down Virginia's Shenandoah Valley to the Carolina Piedmont, bringing large numbers of Scotch-Irish Presbyterians and a variety of German Protestants, including groups that would later become part of the United Church of Christ. Additional settlers of these and other faiths came directly from the ports of Charleston and Savannah. The presence of the United Church of Christ here is due, in addition to its German members, to the former strength of the CHRISTIAN CHURCH, a later compo-

nent of the United Church of Christ formed in Virginia and North Carolina in the late 1700s by dissenting Methodists.

A distinctive religious subregion located in the hill country of central Texas was formed through the immigration of Germans, Scandinavians, and East Europeans during the mid-nineteenth century. These immigrants brought with them a variety of religious affiliations. Lutherans were and are the most numerous immigrant religious group in the area, claiming pluralities in several counties in 1971. Antecedent groups of the German Evangelical and Reformed Church, now part of the United Church of Christ and the Moravian Church, also came to the hill country during this period of immigration. In addition, a number of German Catholics immigrated, adding variety to the Catholicism already firmly established in Spanish-speaking areas immediately to the south.

A less obvious departure from the norms of Southern religion exists in the Southern highlands. APPALACHIAN RELIGION has a pattern of its own. This region is the birthplace of numerous highly fundamentalist denominations, mainly Pentecostal or Holiness in belief and practice, but far more sectarian than similar, larger groups more fully integrated into the Southern conservative mainstream. Because membership data is not available for many of these small groups, this subregion is less easily distinguished than most. Its presence is signaled throughout most of Appalachia, however, by low rates of membership in the mainstream denominations. The existence of this subregion reflects the individualism, traditionalism, and localism of Appalachian society, as well as its cultural isolation from the rest of the South. Its religious character descends in part from the Separatist-Puritan beliefs of many of its original settlers, and in part from the emotional evangelical region of the 19th-century frontier. Indeed, Appalachian isolation has apparently helped to maintain a religious way of life quite similar in many ways to that of the entire interior South of some 150 years ago.

Finally, a major zone of religious diversity runs along the northern border of the South. Rather than a specific subregion of the South, this area is essentially a broad zone of mixing, in which distinctive elements of Southern religion blend with those of the North. The importance of the Shenandoah Valley as a route for colonial Pennsylvanians migrating to the Carolina Piedmont is still echoed by the large proportions of Presbyterians and German Protestant groups in the valley today. Lutherans, Episcopalians, and the United Church of Christ are other prominent exceptions to Southern norms in Maryland and Virginia. The Disciples, a denomination indigenous to the border zone, form a significant minority and an occasional plurality from Kentucky to Missouri. As described earlier, there are also numerous Catholic concentrations throughout this area.

See also articles on CARIBBEAN IMMIGRATION; MIGRATION, SOUTHWARD (1700-1830); MIGRATION, WESTWARD (1750-1900).

Bibliography. Sidney E. Ahlstrom, *A Religious History of the American People*; Jackson W. Carroll, Douglas W. Johnson and Martin E. Marty, *Religion in America: 1950 to the Present*; Edwin S. Gaustad, *Historical Atlas of American Religion*; "Religious Demography of the South," *Religion and the Solid South*, ed. Samuel S. Hill, Jr.; Samuel S. Hill, Jr., *Southern Churches in Crisis*; Douglas W. Johnson, Paul R. Picard, and Bernard Quinn, *Churches and Church Membership in the United States: 1971*; Terry Jordan, *German Seed in Texas Soil*; John D. Photiadis, ed., *Religion in Appalachia: Theological, Social, and Psychological Dimensions and Correlates*; James R. Shortridge, "A New Regionalization of American Religion," *Journal for the Scientific Study of Religion* 16 (June 1977): 143; "The Pattern of American Catholicism, 1971," *Journal of Geography* 77 (February 1978): 56; "Patterns of Religion in the United States," *Geographical Review* 66 (October 1976): 420; Wilbur Zelinsky, "An Approach to the Religious Geography of the United States: Patterns of Church Membership in 1952," Association of American Geographers *Annals* 51 (June 1961): 139.

ROGER STUMP
STATE UNIVERSITY OF NEW YORK
AT ALBANY
JAMES R. SHORTRIDGE
UNIVERSITY OF KANSAS

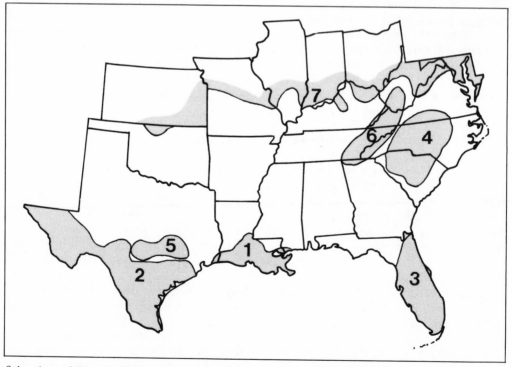

Subregions of Diversity Within Southern Religion: 1) French-speaking Louisiana; 2) Spanish-speaking Texas; 3) peninsular Florida; 4) Carolina piedmont; 5) Texas hill country; 6) Appalachia; 7) northern border zone.

GEORGIA. Among the first inhabitants of the land that was later known as Georgia, everyone was his own priest. The unremitting struggle merely to survive, by requiring all to devote their energies to finding food, prohibited the rise of a priestly class; so, the aborigines, who arrived around 8000 B.C., engaged in individual worship of nature spirits. Within 3,000 years, as the food supply became more dependable, a few people who were paid by others with food were designated as witch-doctors; their function was to control the spirits. Some 5,000 years later, an exalted class emerged as the religious and secular leaders. By 1000 A.D., religious ceremonialism was becoming more sophisticated as great temple mounds were built in the theocratic city-states of Etowah, Ocmulgee, and Kolomoki. After 1300, these societies gave way to the Creek Confederacy, a political rather than a religious unit. Nevertheless, religion remained important among the various tribes comprising the Creek league, and the high priest of each wielded much political power. Paying homage to fire-and-water deities, these Indians celebrated each summer a festival of first fruits during which they performed rites of sacrifice and purification.

Such was the form of worship the Jesuit missionaries of Catholic Spain found when they arrived among the people of Guale, a region of the Georgia coast, in the 1560s. Within six years, the Jesuit effort to make Christians of the Gualeans had failed, the victim of native indifference and Spanish parsimony. In 1573, one year after the last Jesuits had left Guale, Franciscan friars arrived. After a shaky start, the zealous Franciscans, more strongly supported by civil authorities than the Jesuits had been, firmly established their missions. By 1606, having weathered a major Indian revolt, the Franciscans claimed some 1,500 converts. During the next 50 years, the Spanish missions along the coast grew without interruption, and new missions were established to the west in Apalache. With some success, the padres taught the natives European ways. By 1702, however, growing Franciscan complacency and attacks by hostile Indians, pirates, and English settlers in Carolina had caused the nine coastal missions to be abandoned. Twenty-six years later, the Apalache missions fell to Carolinian and Creek depredations.

The Englishmen who settled Georgia shortly after the Spaniards' expulsion were by and large less concerned with the souls of the Indians than with their wampum. Moreover, many of the colony's early clerics soon found that advancing the cause of religion among white Georgians was a hard enough task.

The weakness of the Church of England particularly vexed the colony's officials. Anglican clergymen were partly responsible for that situation. Ministers were few, and of those few many were profane, intemperate, and licentious. Moreover, those priests who were virtuous were often contentious, most notably John Wesley and his brother Charles, who served briefly in the 1730s. Rare was someone like Bartholomew Zouberbuhler, a man of exemplary character who served his SAVANNAH parish effectively for 20 years.

The elitism of the Church of England also turned many Georgians against it. Preaching subordination within a hierarchical social order rather than equality in Christ, Anglican clerics sometimes exhibited contempt for poorer Georgians. The adversarial relationship that often resulted hampered Anglican growth.

The Church of England not only failed to profit from the Great Awakening that aroused many Georgians from spiritual lethargy early in the 1740s but in the long run suffered from that revival of religion. Some Anglican leaders opposed the work of the foremost awakener, GEORGE WHITEFIELD, an Anglican priest in Savannah. Whitefield's Calvinistic theology, his animated style of preaching, and his willingness to associate with those who rejected the Church of England rendered him unacceptable to many of his fellow Anglicans.

Fifteen years after Georgia's settlement, there were only 63 Anglicans in Savannah. Ten years later, the establishment of the Anglican church as the official, tax-supported church failed appreciably to enhance its popularity. As revolutionary fervor intensified in the 1770s, the association of the Anglican church with British authority severely diminished its appeal. By 1775, there were no more than five Anglican churches in the colony.

For much of Georgia's colonial period, those Christians who dissented from the beliefs and practices of the Church of England outnumbered Anglicans. In 1748, there were probably six dissenters for every Anglican in Savannah. On the eve of the American Revolution, dissenters comprised a clear majority of the colony's churchgoers.

Several factors contributed to the growth of dissenting denominations. Although interested in the welfare of Anglicanism, many of the Trustees who supervised Georgia's settlement were just as concerned that their colony grow. Consequently, Georgia was designed to be a haven for persecuted European Protestants. Moreover, the colony's Anglican establishment, even if it had wanted to, was too weak to trouble dissenters, who were allowed to worship freely. Finally, some Georgians, indifferent to religion altogether, did not care what one's faith was. Tolerance was the rule in colonial Georgia.

Some of the European Protestants who came to Georgia stayed only a short time. The Moravians, who began to arrive in 1735, never numbered more than 50; they left in 1740 when civil authorities commanded them to fight the Spanish.

Other Protestants from Europe established themselves permanently. In 1734, Lutherans from Salzburg settled at Ebenezer where they thrived until their leader, the Rev. John Martin Bolzius, died in 1765; thereafter, the SALZBURGERS, numbering about 500, were rent by factionalism. Two years after the founding of Ebenezer, Presbyterians from Scotland established Darien.

Still other Presbyterians came, many from other colonies. In 1752, settlers from South Carolina founded Midway along the coast and built MIDWAY CHURCH (LIBERTY CO.) that, if Congregational in name, was Presbyterian in fact. Three years later, in Savannah, a congregation independent of the Church of Scotland was formed; that church subsequently enjoyed considerable influence because its pastor, John J. Zubly, was the colony's foremost dissenting cleric. By 1770, Scots-Irish had begun to settle the backcountry around Augusta, but a scarcity of pastors and neglect by itinerant preachers retarded the growth of Presbyterian churches there. Five years later, there were some six Presbyterian congregations with 600 members throughout Georgia.

Shortly after Presbyterians came to the backcountry, Baptists arrived there, too. Twenty years earlier, a small group of Regular Baptists had worshipped in Savannah but had left no church. In 1773, a Regular Baptist minister, Edmund Botsford, established a church south of Augusta. A year older than Botsford Church and the first Baptist church in Georgia was Kiokee Church west of Augusta, which was organized by SEPARATE BAPTISTS under the Rev. Daniel Marshall.

The Separates, who came to Georgia from the Carolinas and Virginia, traced their origins to the Great Awakening in New England. Growing out of a revivalistic faction in the Congregational church, Separates restricted membership to those who had undergone the overpowering, specific experience of conversion and maintained that baptism, by mode immersion in water, should be received only by believers who had been born anew in Christ. Moderately Calvinistic, Separates believed that man was innately depraved and could be saved from eternal damnation only by divine grace. Unlike most Regular Baptists and Presbyterians, however, the Separates either denied or ignored the Calvinist doctrines of election and limited atonement. More aggressive and more emotional than the Regulars, the Separates won more converts. In the fluid, harsh society of the Georgia backcountry, the Separates offered settlers comfort and order through the church without condescension. Within three years of the founding of Kiokee Church, there were perhaps 750 Baptists throughout the colony. It was the Separates who "Baptistized" Georgia.

In addition to the Baptists and the Presbyterians along the frontier and the Anglican congregation in Augusta, there was, after 1768, a settlement of Quakers at Wrightsborough in the backcountry. Peopled largely by Friends from North Carolina, Wrightsborough grew into a thriving community of 600 by 1775.

Although many different Christian churches had adherents in colonial Georgia, Roman Catholics were conspicuously absent. Centuries of English hostility toward the Church of Rome coupled with Georgia's proximity to Catholic Florida prompted the Trustees to prohibit the entry of Catholics. In 1747, there were only four Catholics in Georgia, although a few years later the colony was temporarily home for 400 Acadians, who were allowed to worship privately.

Not only did the Trustees wish to keep Catholics out of Georgia, some wanted to ban Jews also. Yet, when 42 Jews arrived in Savannah in 1733, JAMES OGLETHORPE allowed them to stay. Sectarianism soon divided the group, and fear of Spanish invasion prompted mass emigration. That threat ended in 1742, many Jews returned, and Savannah's Jewish community endured, largely because of the leadership of Benjamin of the famous SHEFTALL FAMILY. Although no synagogue was built in the colonial period,

Georgia's Jews worshipped freely in their homes.

If many early Georgians lacked religious commitment, by 1775 religion nevertheless exerted some influence in the life of the colony. Georgia's very settlement resulted in considerable measure from the opportunity most people had to worship freely. Moreover, after 1758, religion had a direct impact on government, for Anglican vestrymen were not only church officers but civil officials as well. Furthermore, the few schools that existed were run by clergymen, the most noteworthy being Whitefield's Bethesda Orphan House near Savannah. Finally, religion imparted to some Georgians a moral code to live by and made them better people.

The American Revolution stopped the progress of organized religion in Georgia. Politics divided denominations, particularly the Anglican, Lutheran, and Presbyterian, each of which contained a substantial minority loyal to the Crown. As fighting intensified in Georgia after 1778, ministers were compelled to flee, congregations were dispersed, and sanctuaries were destroyed. When the fighting ceased in 1782, churches throughout the young state were in disarray.

Nevertheless, developments that would encourage church growth had occurred. The relationship between church and state was fundamentally altered. In 1777, Georgia's first constitution enhanced religious liberty by disestablishing the Anglican church. Subsequent changes in the state's basic law made religious freedom complete. By the end of the century, all religious tests for holding public office had been abolished as had all restrictions on freedom to worship.

The history of religion in Georgia since the Revolution is largely the story of the growth of Evangelical Protestant denominations, especially the Baptist and the Methodist. The denominational diversity that existed in 1775 had been severely diminished by 1800. The Protestant Episcopal Church, the American legatee of the Church of England, had only one active congregation. The Lutheran community at Ebenezer was greatly reduced as a result of wartime division and the subsequent defection of younger members to the Baptists and the Methodists. The Quaker settlement at Wrightsborough fell victim to the war and subsequent developments.

The hegemony of the Evangelicals in Georgia's religious life resulted from their theology, their social ideology, and their methods of spreading the gospel. By the end of the 18th century, theological similarities overshadowed differences among Baptists, Methodists, and Presbyterians. Each denomination—the Methodist with the greatest fidelity—embraced Arminianism, which meliorated the harsh doctrines of Calvinism by espousing the idea of unlimited atonement and by contending that the human will played an active part in the process of salvation.

Although Georgia's Evangelicals emphasized man's depravity, they also stressed the importance of the individual in the sight of God. Even if poor, female, or black, each person was a child of God and, however despised by man, was beloved of Him. The new birth in Jesus Christ made it possible for the reborn to reject social canons in favor of moral understanding founded on religious experience. Extending the kingdom of God on earth became more important than gaining acceptance in the eyes of the world. The Christian might improve the society he lived in by trying to diminish worldly corruption through pious example.

In all likelihood, Evangelical Protestantism attracted Georgians who were dissatisfied with society as they found it and who yearned for an alternative sphere in which to assert themselves. And yet, the primary reason for one's joining an evangelical denomination was not social but religious—to be saved from sin, to live the holy life, and to go to heaven. Fervently, evangelical preachers stressed the urgency of salvation and outlined its plan: conviction of sin, repentance of that sinfulness, and, through God's grace, conversion to a life in Christ. That message was spread in regular church services and, more dramatically, in periodic revivals.

More than anything else, the Great Revival of the early nineteenth century advanced the cause of Evangelical Protestantism in the young state of Georgia. Begun in Kentucky in 1799, that movement reached Georgia two years later. If Presbyterians pioneered the Kentucky awakening, Baptists and Methodists benefited most from the Great Revival in Georgia.

Back in 1786, John Major and Thomas Humphries, Methodist itinerants, had established their church's first congregations in Georgia. Fanning out over the settled portions of the state in the 1790s, Methodist circuit riders took the gospel to frontiersmen who seldom, if ever, had heard it before. These itinerants, who traveled great distances under difficult circumstances for paltry pay, soon seized upon an innovation of the Great Revival to advance Christianity. The camp meeting, though used effectively by Georgia's Baptists, was the stock-in-trade of the state's Methodists in the first half of the 19th century.

Made to order for a scattered population of plain folk, the CAMP MEETINGS provided an occasion for small farmers, who sometimes traveled 50 miles to reach the site, to come together and enjoy the society of one another. Important as the social aspects of the camp meeting were, its prime purpose was to aid in the conversion of sinners. Usually held when crops had been either laid by or harvested, the camp meeting in all its features was designed to keep pressure upon those wrestling with the Holy Spirit. The believers who preached, exhorted, sang, and prayed for the unrepentant with mounting intensity expected the convicted to give evidence of the Spirit's workings. And they usually did by whining, barking, jerking, dancing, and falling to the ground. Thousands of Georgians—men and women, white and black together—attended camp meetings, from the first ones in 1802 until their decline in the 1840s.

The Great Revival swelled the ranks of the Methodists and the Baptists. By 1805, the Baptists, with some 9,500 adherents, had nearly tripled their strength of 1790, and the Methodists, 5,000 strong, had increased threefold their numbers as of 1800. Once the emotional intensity that helped effect these conversions had subsided, many of the newly saved fell away from the church. Nevertheless, the impact of this awakening upon Georgia was lasting, for it further democratized religious life, elevated individual morals, and diminished vices such as brutality, drunkenness, and fornication that were once rife in the backcountry.

With the camp meeting institutionalized and with the number of circuit riders increasing, the Methodist church continued to grow, if occasionally fitfully, after the Great Revival. In 1830, when the Georgia and Florida Conference was formed, the state's Methodists numbered some 20,000. Fifteen years later, at the formation of the Georgia Conference, there were slightly more than 50,000 Methodists. The tenfold increase since 1805 resulted largely from the permanent itineracy used by the church, which was better organized and more effective than the *ad hoc* system employed by Baptists and Presbyterians. By mid-century, 140 Methodist circuit riders carried their message to all parts of the state.

Although the sevenfold increase among Georgia Baptists between 1805-1850 failed to match the rate of Methodist growth, the Baptists achieved those results without the benefit of episcopal organization. Nevertheless, although each Baptist congregation prized its auton-omy, statewide organization emerged in 1822 with the formation of the General Baptist Association, which five years later became the Georgia Baptist Convention. Charged with promoting missions and with coordinating Baptist work, the state convention was built upon voluntary organizations of regional churches, the first of which was the Georgia Association formed in 1784. Composed of two associations at its founding, by 1850 the convention consisted of more than 20 associations with more than 600 churches containing nearly 55,000 members. An additional 15,000 Baptists belonged to churches within associations independent of the state convention.

Georgia's other significant evangelical denomination, the Presbyterian, grew much more slowly than either the Baptist or the Methodist church largely because of Presbyterian insistence upon an educated clergy and reluctance to employ emotionalism. In 1796, when the first presbytery, which included the whole state, was organized, it contained only 14 small churches. The Great Revival, which rejuvenated the Baptists and Methodists, did little for the Presbyterians. In 1810, that church counted just slightly more than 200 communicants, fewer than in 1775. Over the next 20 years, however, vigor replaced dormancy—largely because of the work of a few zealous evangelists such as the Princetonian Remembrance Chamberlain—and by 1830 Presbyterians numbered nearly 3,000. At mid-century, five years after the formation of the Synod of Georgia, the church claimed more than 5,000 communicants.

The 105,000 white Georgians who belonged to the Baptist, Methodist, and Presbyterian churches made up 20 percent of the state's white population in 1850. Therefore, their views on social issues carried considerable weight. In the first half of the 19th century, evangelical leaders saw much in Georgia that needed improving. Although their belief in the separation of church and state caused them to shun direct political action and although they doubted the efficacy of broad social reform without individual regeneration, Georgia's Evangelicals did believe that the improvement of individuals might lead to the betterment of society.

Acting upon that belief, some evangelical ministers in the backcountry, as early as the 1790s, promoted education, notably the Methodist Hope Hull, the Baptist Silas Mercer, and the Presbyterian MOSES WADDEL. Although none of the schools that those men conducted lasted, their very founding showed the intentions of some clerics. As the new century began, church-sponsored schools continued to open and then to close, the most ambitious being the Rev. Henry Holcombe's Baptist academy. Nevertheless, 30 years later, education under Evangelicals achieved permanence in the form of colleges. At the urging of such ministers as Jesse Mercer, Silas's son, and Adiel Sherwood, the Georgia Baptist Convention established Mercer University in 1833. Three years later, Methodists chartered Emory College, and in 1839, assumed control of Wesleyan Female College. A year earlier, Presbyterians, who had dominated the staff of the state university in its early years, opened their own college, Oglethorpe University.

Often, the work at these institutions was hardly of collegiate quality. Yet their faculties included such able people as Augustus Baldwin Longstreet of Emory, a man of many accomplishments; JAMES WOODROW of Oglethorpe, a Harvard-and Heidelberg-trained scientist; and JOHN LEADLEY DAGG of Mercer, an eminent theologian. If the men who established Mercer, Oglethorpe, and Emory did so in part to train ministers, they also hoped to effect the general education of their people and to fashion a social order controlled by Christian leaders.

From the 1820s on through the 1850s, the scope of evangelical benevolence broadened. Churchmen formed anti-dueling societies, supported Sabbatarian-

ism, advocated better treatment of the handicapped, and ministered to the poor. Among the most popular of benevolent enterprises was temperance. Believing intemperance to be a social evil, not just an individual's sin, many Evangelicals worked hard to diminish or to eliminate the use of intoxicating liquors. Baptists in Eatonton led the way in this reform in 1827 by organizing the state's first temperance society. By 1830, Methodists and Presbyterians had begun to join the movement, and more than 40 local societies had been formed. Most Evangelicals refused to mix temperance with politics, however, because to do so would infringe upon the prerogative of the state. As a result, when a Methodist lay preacher ran for governor as the candidate of the Temperance party in 1855, he received only five percent of the vote.

Antebellum Georgia Evangelicals attempted to extend Christ's kingdom and bring about moral improvement not only through the spoken but also through the printed word. Efforts to establish a permanent religious journal that theretofore had failed succeeded in 1833, when Jesse Mercer began publishing the Baptist *Christian Index*, a weekly paper that was among the more significant religious periodicals in the South. Fourteen years later, Georgia's Presbyterians played a major role in establishing the *Southern Presbyterian*, the journal of Southeastern synods, which was usually published in Milledgeville until 1853, when its offices were moved to Charleston. These journals, together with the Methodist paper published out of state, reported denominational activities, appealed for higher pay for ministers, adjured Christians to influence others by living righteously, encouraged benevolence, and promoted missions.

Many Georgia Evangelicals supported organizations to foster missions both in foreign countries and within the state among whites, Indians, and blacks. In the 1830s, Evangelicals began a systematic effort to spread the gospel among Georgia's slaves. Attempts by individuals to evangelize the slaves had long been made. In royal Georgia, the Anglican Zouberbuhler worked zealously in that cause. After the Revolution, Abraham Marshall, Daniel's son, helped organize, with the slave ANDREW BRYAN, the country's first independent Negro Baptist church among Savannah's slaves.

By 1830, nine percent of Georgia's blacks were either Baptists or Methodists. Evangelical Protestantism appealed to black Georgians for many reasons: it contained practices that paralleled African religion; it promised eternal reward or punishment without regard to one's color; it offered blacks one of their few opportunities to associate with whites on a level approaching equality; it imparted hope to a people who had much cause to despair.

After 1830, the mission to slaves received broader support largely because of the efforts of articulate, influential spokesmen. Particularly active in the movement were the Methodist minister JAMES O. ANDREW, elected bishop in 1832, and the Presbyterian divine, CHARLES COLCOCK JONES, SR., the movement's chief theorist. Georgians who supported plantation missions hoped to encourage docility among the slaves, to advance religion among their white masters, to promote better treatment of the slaves, and, what was most important to the mission's leaders, to furnish the slaves the means of salvation. Although race prejudice minimized the success of the mission, it nevertheless contributed to the advance of Christianity among Georgia's blacks. By 1860, roughly 12 percent of the state's Negro population were church members, the great majority being Baptists and Methodists.

Although Jones and Andrew outspokenly advocated worship by whites and blacks together and mixed congregations were common, some Evangelicals of each race favored separate churches in the interests, they said, of space, propriety, and self-determination. Black Baptists had some 25 churches by 1860, the largest

of which, Augusta's Springfield African, had 1,600 members. Close behind was the oldest black congregation, Savannah's First African Baptist, whose pastor of 40 years, ANDREW MARSHALL, was the preeminent black clergyman of the antebellum South.

Because relations between white and black Christians were usually amicable, the state's white Evangelicals were dismayed and angered by the rise of antislavery sentiment among Northern Baptists and Methodists. When Northern Baptists in 1844 refused to appoint a Georgia slaveholder as a denominational missionary, the state's Baptists helped form the Southern Baptist Convention in Augusta the next year. When Northern Methodists, also in 1844, voted to relieve Georgia's James Andrew of his duties as bishop for as long as he owned slaves, Georgian A. B. Longstreet, speaking for Southern Methodists, declared that the vote mandated separation. Not surprisingly, the following year Georgians helped organize the Methodist Episcopal Church, South.

If the mission to slaves, so prized by some Georgia Evangelicals, failed to allay antislavery sentiment in the North and to stay denominational division along sectional lines, the mere issue of missions sparked schism inside the state itself within the largest denomination. As early as the 1820s, some Baptists opposed missions that were supervised not by local churches but by central agencies. Such organization, those Baptists said, was unscriptural and unnecessary. So, too, they believed, was theological education, which would diminish humility and piety among ministers. By the mid-1830s, these conservatives had broken away from the Georgia Baptist Convention to preserve what they believed was pure, primitive Christianity. Within 15 years, antimission associations included almost 400 churches with nearly 12,000 members. Throughout the 1850s, Georgia's Primitive Baptists published the semimonthly *Southern Baptist Messenger*, the most influential Primitive journal in the Deep South.

The mistrust of ecclesiastical authority that provoked division among Baptists, and to a lesser degree among Methodists, also contributed to the appeal of the Campbellite movement, which was even so weaker in Georgia than in states to the north. By 1830, the followers of Alexander Campbell, the Disciples of Christ, numbered nearly 600 in Georgia. Thirty years later, after union with the Christian church, occasional visits by Campbell, and publication at Augusta of the short-lived *Christian Union*, the Disciples numbered 1,100.

In addition to opposing centralized organization and authority, dissident Evangelicals criticized the increasing affluence and refinement of those Georgians within the parent denominations. Between 1830 and 1860, the Baptist, Methodist, and Presbyterian churches changed significantly. Although revivalism remained strong, the camp meeting gave way to the protracted meeting, an event held indoors with less emotionalism. Support of missions and education increased. Solicitude for the welfare of urban churches was more evident among churchmen who theretofore had directed their efforts largely at villagers and country folk.

The urban ministry of the Evangelicals enjoyed much more success than the rural ministry of the leading non-evangelical denomination, the Protestant Episcopal. Despite efforts by a few Episcopalians to broaden the scope of their church's ministry, that church remained confined largely to cities and grew but slowly between 1790 and 1840. In that year, the Diocese of Georgia, organized back in 1823, elected its first bishop, STEPHEN ELLIOTT, JR., who breathed new life into the church. With only six churches and 300 members in 1840, the denomination included almost 30 churches with 2,000 members 20 years later. Even so, Elliott's advice to Episcopal clergy to employ more fervor and less erudition in order to enhance the church's

appeal among rural Georgians met with little support.

Rejected by Georgians at large was the rationalistic message of Unitarianism and Universalism. By 1860, three attempts by Universalists to publish journals had failed, and Georgia's two Unitarian societies were dead.

Greater success greeted the efforts of Roman Catholics, although it can hardly be termed large. After the American Revolution, the Church of Rome benefitted from Georgia's new constitutional guarantees of religious liberty. In 1793, settlers from Maryland established Georgia's first Catholic church at Locust Grove in the backcountry. Seven years later, Catholics in Savannah built a church. In 1850, the Catholic church established the Diocese of Savannah under Bishop Francis X. Gartland to serve the state's eight congregations, virtually all of which were urban.

Georgia's Jews also benefitted from the increased religious liberty after the Revolution. Yet if the Jewish community grew, it was still confined largely to Savannah, which from 1786 to the middle of the next century had the state's only synagogue. Over the following 120 years Georgia's Jewish population would grow to roughly 25,000 and would remain concentrated in the cities, with Atlanta emerging as the chief locus.

As the 1850s advanced, Georgia's churchmen were increasingly caught up in the sectional conflict, despite the efforts of many to avoid involvement in the political disputes between North and South. Nevertheless, because most ministers believed that Scripture sanctioned slavery, they came to view the political conflict in religious terms. Yet, as late as 1861, many clergy, most notably Methodist Bishop George Foster Pierce, hoped that Georgia could remain in the Union. Six of the 10 ministers who sat in the secession convention opposed leaving the Union, but when the convention voted to take Georgia out, a majority of clerical delegates endorsed the decision. So it was in the state at large. Once the issue was decided, most clergy supported Georgia's stand.

After the Civil War began, Georgia's churches worked strenuously for the Confederacy. Congregations collected supplies and distributed them to soldiers. The major denominations jointly published religious literature for the army. Ministers frequently preached bellicose sermons that sometimes characterized the Confederate effort as a holy crusade against the Yankee infidel. Hundreds of clergymen served in the army, and others worked among the soldiers as missionaries or evangelists. Revivals were numerous, fervent, and often lengthy among Confederates fighting in Georgia. Until 1864, the churches enjoyed spiritual growth. Special services occurred frequently, and work among the blacks continued. In the wake of Sherman's march, however, came disruption as some churches were destroyed and others were confiscated for military purposes. The collapse of the Confederacy inflicted hardships upon the churches and the institutions they supported. Ultimately, Oglethorpe University failed to recover and closed in 1872.

Still, the churches endured, and after the war the religious establishment expanded. In 1870, there were 500 more churches than in 1860, and the value of church property had increased by $1,000,000. The pattern of church membership remained unchanged. Baptist and Methodist congregations comprised 70 percent of Georgia's churches in both years.

After the war, the state's religious leaders devoted a good deal of energy to defending their antebellum justification of slavery and to reproving Northern churchmen for being religious carpetbaggers. Ill will was particularly evident within Methodism. Georgia's Methodists of the Southern church accused missionaries of the Northern church of trying to appropriate the pulpits of that state's

Southern churches and of sowing discord among Methodist freedmen.

For their part, the freedmen needed little prodding from Northern missionaries to establish black organizations. The unwillingness of white Christians to associate with free blacks under conditions approaching equality together with the desire of black people to exercise leadership in God's house prompted an exodus of Negroes from churches controlled by whites. Within Methodism some blacks affiliated with the Northern church, but many more joined black organizations. The African Methodist Episcopal Church, which organized its first Southern congregation in Savannah in 1865 and formed a state conference two years later, was especially popular. A smaller number joined with the African Methodist Episcopal, Zion, Church that established a state conference in 1867, or with the Colored Methodist Episcopal Church, the protége of the Methodist Episcopal Church, South, that formed a Georgia Conference in 1870. Black Baptists, while adhering to congregational autonomy like their white counterparts, also left white churches *en masse*. Black Presbyterians, although many fewer in number than Baptists or Methodists, formed the first black presbytery in the United States in 1867. Those blacks, like most other Negro Presbyterians in Georgia, affiliated with the Northern church, from which white Southerners had separated six years before in Augusta.

The evangelical churches provided the principal training ground for black leaders, many of whom served as administrators and faculty of the denominational colleges that were being established in Georgia with the help of Northern churchmen and philanthropists. By 1890, Atlanta, the major center of higher education for blacks in the entire country, housed the following institutions: Atlanta University (founded in 1869, sponsored by the Congregational Church); Clark University (1869, Northern Methodist);

Atlanta Baptist College (1867, later More-house College); Atlanta Baptist Female Seminary (1881, later Spelman College); Gammon Theological Seminary (1883, Northern Methodist); and Morris Brown College (1885, A.M.E.). In Augusta, Paine College (C.M.E.) offered higher education to blacks after 1882.

Although many black religious leaders in the state worked for the improvement of their race, their ideas of how best to achieve advancement varied widely. J. W. E. Bowen of Gammon Seminary advocated accommodation with white leaders; John Hope, president of Atlanta Baptist College, preferred protest to accommodation; HENRY M. TURNER, A. M. E. bishop, endorsed emigration as the only way for blacks to escape oppression.

For thousands of black Georgians, the church provided sustenance during the trying times after emancipation. Church membership, particularly among Baptists and Methodists, increased markedly. By 1890 black Baptists numbered 200,000; black Methodists, 125,000. Adherents of those denominations comprised almost 40 percent of the state's black population.

After the bitterness of Reconstruction had subsided, some white churchmen worked to strengthen the black church. Education, those whites believed, would serve that goal. Acting upon that belief, the Georgia Baptist Convention operated institutes between 1878 and 1895 to train black preachers and deacons. Among Southern Baptists, Georgians, along with Texans, enjoyed the greatest success in that work. In that same period, Georgia Methodism provided the greatest white advocate of black education in the South, the Rev. ATTICUS G. HAYGOOD, who was successively editor of the *Wesleyan Christian Advocate*, president of Emory College, agent of the John F. Slater Fund, and bishop in the Southern Methodist church.

Nevertheless, white evangelical leaders believed that Georgia's blacks should remain subservient. The *Christian Index* defended segregation, denounced social

equality between the races, and, alone among Southern Baptist weeklies at the end of the century, justified lynching under certain conditions. By 1900, professors at Mercer University had characterized black suffrage as a blunder, black education as productive of evil, and the color line as an act of God. As Jim Crow tightened its hold, even Bishop Haygood retreated from his earlier position on the race issue, and Emory College, in 1902, eagerly accepted the resignation of a professor who had written that blacks had rights that whites should be made to respect.

After the Civil War, changes other than black separation from white churches occurred in Georgia religion. Among white Evangelicals, there was a diminution of the discipline that churches meted out to members and an increasing willingness to call upon the state to enact legislation that regulated behavior. By the end of the century, the two largest evangelical denominations were advocating the passage of laws to restrict athletic competition, gambling, worldliness on the Sabbath, and the grounds upon which divorce could be obtained. The greatest evangelical crusade for moral reform was the movement to prohibit the manufacture and sale of alcoholic beverages. That movement received great impetus in Georgia and elsewhere in the South from the persuasive Methodist revivalist, SAMUEL PORTER "SAM" JONES of Cartersville, who believed that Prohibition would cure all of society's ills. Although some evangelical leaders condemned the growing tendency to mix religion with politics and contended that Prohibition was unscriptural, partly because of evangelical pressure, Georgia enacted local-option in 1883 and statewide Prohibition in 1907.

Efforts to persuade the state to sanction evangelical moral precepts by law reflected in some measure the unease that churchmen felt over changes occurring late in the 19th century. Georgia traditionalists feared the effect that the higher criticism, the Darwinian theory of evolution, and the rising industrial ethic might have on religion as they knew it, even though, paradoxically, evangelical leaders sometimes promoted industrialization.

Of those developments, only industrialization had any discernible impact on Georgia, and it did not prove inimical to organized religion. In fact, church membership increased by nearly 30 percent in the latter half of the 19th century. By 1906, 43 percent of all Georgians professed to be church members. Of that number, 92 percent were Baptists and Methodists.

With a view to ministering to the increasing number of members more effectively and to encouraging even further growth, Evangelicals developed more extensive organization. Between 1865 and 1900, the Georgia Baptist Convention, which represented the great majority of white Baptists, created the office of Superintendent of Sunday Schools, established the Board of Missions, organized the Women's Missionary Union and the Baptist Young People's Union, and opened an orphanage. During that same period, similar developments, particularly as regards Sunday school and women's work, occurred within the Southern Methodist church in the state. Moreover, after 1866, two conferences, the North Georgia and the South Georgia, carried out the duties that the Georgia Conference alone had performed since 1830.

Although Baptists and Methodists set the tone of Georgia's religious life at the beginning of the 20th century as they had done through the previous century, other denominations grew significantly between 1850 and 1900. While Georgia's population more than doubled during those years, the growth rate of certain denominations was considerably greater. Membership in the Roman Catholic church increased at least fourfold; in the Presbyterian church, almost fivefold; in the Protestant Episcopal church, nine-

fold; and in the Christian (Disciples) church, thirteenfold. Denominational strength in 1906 was as follows:

Baptist	596,319
Methodist	349,079
Presbyterian	24,040
Roman Catholic	19,273
Christian (Disciples)	13,749
Protestant Episcopal	9,790
All Others	16,787
Total	1,029,037

Not only did the established denominations grow, there were at the end of the century short-lived colonies of Shakers in Southeastern Georgia and Christian socialists near Columbus. Moreover, the seeds had been planted that would yield new sects early in the 20th century.

After the Civil War, division afflicted Georgia's Disciples of Christ. Those poorer Disciples who believed that the denomination was capitulating to fashion, wealth, and unscriptural innovations such as instrumental music and missionary societies broke away and formed the Churches of Christ, which, by 1906, contained more than 1,000 members.

During that same period, largely within Methodism, the Holiness movement gained many followers, making Georgia the banner holiness state in the South. Endorsed in varying degrees by such prominent Methodists as the aged LOVICK PIERCE, the bishop's father, and the young Warren A. Candler, holiness doctrine embraced the Wesleyan idea of Christian perfection that was attained through the post-conversion second blessing of sanctification. Advocates of Holiness formed a state association, published a journal, and established a camp meeting site.

Yet if many Methodist ministers countenanced Holiness, the movement incurred the opposition of Bishop Haygood who, in 1894, prompted the general conference of the Southern church to denounce the Holiness faction. Despite that denunciation, some of Georgia's holiness Methodists remained within the church. Others, joined by the disaffected in other denominations, sought new organizational affiliations, and as a result holiness sects emerged. Prominent among the dissidents was JOSEPH H. KING, erstwhile Methodist minister who became a leader in the PENTECOSTAL HOLINESS CHURCH, which established headquarters at FRANKLIN SPRINGS, began publishing the *Pentecostal Holiness Advocate* in 1917, and two years later founded Emmanuel College. Some years before, in 1907, several Holiness congregations in North Georgia had affiliated with the Church of God based in Tennessee and embraced Pentecostalism. In addition to accepting the doctrine of baptism by the Holy Spirit, a third experience beyond conversion and sanctification, Georgia's Pentecostals believed that evidence of that experience could be shown in the gift of speaking in tongues that were normally unknown to the believer. It seems that the appeal of Pentecostalism was rather like the appeal of Evangelicalism a century earlier. By and large, Georgians who were poor, lonely, anxious, disillusioned with the world around them, and dissatisfied with the religious establishment found the friendship and security offered by Pentecostal fellowship particularly attractive. Pentecostalism would gain many adherents in the course of the 20th century.

The many changes—industrialization urbanization, a rising tide of foreign immigration, new intellectual currents—that weakened traditional religion in much of the country early in the 20th century had less impact in Georgia and the rest of the South. The state's religious establishment remained firmly entrenched. Yet, partly out of fear of the forces of modernity, Georgia, as of the early 1920s, was one of only six states in the nation to require that the Bible be read daily in public schools.

If many of Georgia's Christians welcomed the Bible in the schools, they would bar the spirit of Charles Darwin. In all

likelihood, a majority of Protestant clergy and church members opposed the teaching of the theory of evolution, especially in church-sponsored institutions. A Methodist petition of 1922 charged the dean of the Candler School of Theology with tolerating unchristian instruction. Two years later, Mercer University dismissed an instructor of biology whose stand on evolution was suspect. Nevertheless, no major denomination formally endorsed the proposals of militant fundamentalists to prohibit the teaching of evolution by law. In fact, prominent clerics such as Methodist Bishop Warren A. Candler—whose stout orthodoxy caused him to oppose union with the Northern church because he believed it to be permeated with modernism—and Baptist ministers M. Ashby Jones of Atlanta and John E. White of Savannah denounced attempts to use the church to dictate to the classroom. Partly because of the stand taken by such men, the Georgia legislature by 1925 had twice rejected antievolution bills.

Some Georgians who found aggressive fundamentalism attractive also endorsed the KU KLUX KLAN, although there was no organic connection between the two. Revived and housed in Atlanta after 1915, the Klan succeeded in clothing itself in the mantle of Evangelical Protestantism partly because some churchmen encouraged it to do so in the belief that the Klan's attacks upon foreigners, Roman Catholics, Jews, Negroes, and others who were considered morally deficient would purify America. The incident that adumbrated the revival of the Klan, the lynching of LEO FRANK, an Atlanta Jew, had been obliquely condoned by the Baptist *Christian Index*. In the Klan's imperial city, prominent Baptist ministers and laymen were especially active in the hooded organization, serving as recruiters, national officers, and faculty of short-lived Lanier University, an "All-Southern" institution closely associated with the Invisible Order. Even so, numerous clergymen in Atlanta and elsewhere in the state opposed the Klan, notably Episcopalians C. B. Wilmer and Henry J. Mikell, Methodist Plato Durham, and Baptists M. Ashby Jones and Louie D. Newton, whose subsequent service to his denomination would earn him the title "Mr. Baptist."

By the late 1920s, internal dissension had sapped much of the Klan's strength in Georgia, but the organization remained strong enough to campaign aggressively against Alfred E. Smith, Democratic presidential candidate in 1928. Many Evangelicals outside the Klan also opposed the candidacy of a man who criticized Prohibition and who belonged to the Roman Catholic Church. Nevertheless, other Evangelicals, most notably Bishop Candler, condemned the involvement of their brethren in party politics. Unlike many other Southern states, Georgia remained in the Democratic camp and would likewise do so when another Catholic Democrat ran for president 32 years later.

If some churchmen feared their fellowman, others tried to help him. As the 20th century advanced, many Georgians continued to suffer from poverty and the illness it bred, from ignorance, and from injustice. To fight those evils and to propagate the faith, the churches expanded their benevolent enterprises. Hospitals, orphanages, and homes for the aged were built or enlarged. From the Roman Catholic to the Pentecostal, churches operated schools at varying levels. In higher education, the more notable additions included Bessie Tift College and Shorter College, the former controlled by the Georgia Baptist Convention after 1898, the latter after 1902; Emory University with its Candler School of Theology, which was established in 1914 by a gift from Bishop Candler's brother, Asa, the Coca-Cola magnate; and Agnes Scott College, supported by the Presbyterian Synod of Georgia after 1922, and the Presbyterian Columbia Seminary, which after its move from South Carolina, opened in Decatur in 1927.

Care of the disabled and education of the young received wide support among Georgia's Christians. Less popular was the social gospel, a movement to use the church to change society. Many Christians, particularly Evangelicals, believed that the proper business of the church was to win souls to the Lord and then to encourage pious and moral living in preparation for the hereafter, and not to promote social reform.

Nevertheless, there was an articulate element within Georgia Protestantism that embraced social Christianity. Among Baptists, the Rev. John E. White served as vice-president of the Southern Sociological Congress, an agency organized in 1912 to call special attention to the evils of convict leasing, inadequate education, and racial injustice. The Rev. M. Ashby Jones, the foremost advocate of improved race relations in the Southern Baptist Convention, helped establish the Commission on Interracial Cooperation (CIC) in Atlanta in 1919. The Rev. Edwin C. Dargan served as first chairman of the state convention's Social Service Commission that was created in 1911 to study, among other things, labor conditions and race relations. That commission became ever more aware of social ills under the chairmanship in the 1930s of W. W. Gaines, an Atlanta layman. Baptist women, who were assuming positions of responsibility within the denomination, were also concerned with social problems. Foremost among those women was Isa-Beall Neel, who had long been active in her denomination's benevolent causes and who, when elected in 1931, became the first woman to serve as vice-president of the Southern Baptist Convention. In the 1930s, Neel also served as state chairman of the ASSOCIATION OF SOUTHERN WOMEN FOR THE PREVENTION OF LYNCHING (ASWPL), a Southwide organization based in Atlanta that was composed largely of churchwomen.

Methodists were equally active in spreading the SOCIAL GOSPEL. In 1911, Mary De Bardeleben, the first Southern white woman to engage in such work, established a settlement house for Augusta's blacks. A few years later, the Rev. WILL W. ALEXANDER, having left the pastorate, helped found the CIC and served as its director throughout its 25-year existence. In the 1930s, DOROTHY R. TILLY of Atlanta worked diligently in behalf of the ASWPL. Subsequently, she served on the Southern Regional Council, the successor of the CIC, and organized the Fellowship of the Concerned to monitor the treatment accorded to blacks in the South.

There were also advocates of social Christianity among Presbyterians and Episcopalians. Early in the 20th century, Atlanta Presbyterians began a spiritual and social ministry among blacks in the city's ghetto. Later, the Synod of Georgia established a special committee on moral and social welfare. For a short time in the second decade of the century, Episcopalians operated the La Grange Social Settlement to minister to textile workers. From 1918 to 1940, that denomination supported an industrial school for blacks in Fort Valley.

These attempts to proclaim the social gospel often suffered from popular indifference and inadequate funding. Nevertheless, the very presence of such efforts reflected an increasing willingness on the part of some church members to use religion to advance the cause of social justice.

Social Christianity received its greatest test after World War II. Theretofore, Georgia churchmen attempting to improve both the condition of blacks and relations between the races had refused to challenge the system of racial segregation, in part because they believed that such a radical position would hinder the attainment of their other goals. After 1945, the federal government and civil rights activists increasingly prodded white Georgians to decide whether they would accord the black man his rights under the law or continue to deny him those rights. Many Georgia Christians, victims of their history, opposed the civil rights movement.

The advice of some of the state's religious leaders to comply, in the spirit of Christian love, with the laws of the land sometimes went unheeded. In 1956, a grand jury in Sumter County censured the local ministerial association after the clergymen had condemned the use of violence against members of an integrated commune. Three years later, a Presbyterian pastor in Columbus was dismissed for his liberal stand on the race issue. In the early 1960s, Baptist churches in Atlanta, Macon, and Albany turned away blacks seeking to worship, and townspeople rebuked faculty of denominational colleges that gave succor to civil rights workers. At the end of that decade, the editor of the Atlanta *Presbyterian Survey* was forced to leave his post because he supported the civil rights movement. And so it went.

All the while, however, many religious leaders continued to counsel moderation. When Atlanta was ordered to integrate its public schools in the late 1950s, more than 300 of the city's ministers appealed for obedience and good will. During the same period, the *Christian Index*, seldom before an advocate of the social gospel, denounced violence against the black man, urged respect for his rights, and condemned politicians who sought to close the state's public schools rather than let them be integrated. In the early 1960s, the Georgia Baptist Convention and the North Georgia Conference of the United Methodist Church likewise opposed closing the public schools. Although public schools remained open, a number of churches, angered further by federal prohibition of worship in those schools, abandoned them to establish private institutions where religious instruction was offered to white children only. If the moderation of church leaders was partly responsible for persuading Georgia's white Christians to acquiesce, albeit reluctantly, in the desegregation of secular society, by and large the churches remained segregated.

And they grew. In 1936, roughly 42 percent of the state's population were church members, a figure virtually unchanged since 1906. By 1971, however, at least 60 percent of the population professed allegiance to some Christian church. Denominational membership was as follows:

Baptist	1,792,256
Methodist	501,664
Roman Catholic	103,609
Presbyterian	102,169
Holiness and Pentecostal	78,960
Episcopal	39,780
Others	127,187
Total	2,745,625

Perhaps the major reason for the great increase in church membership since the Second World War is active evangelization on the part of certain denominations, particularly the Baptist. In 1936, Georgia churches within the Southern Baptist Convention had 265,630 members. Thirty-five years later, that number was 1,276,081. In 1971, Baptist dominance pervaded the state; in all but 10 of Georgia's 159 counties, Baptists accounted for a majority of church members.

As church membership increased significantly within the state after 1945, three notable Georgians—one Catholic and two Baptists—demonstrated to the rest of the world what being Christian and Southern might mean. The great Catholic writer, FLANNERY O'CONNOR, showed that both she and the Protestant rustics of whom she wrote were haunted by God. The Rev. Dr. MARTIN LUTHER KING, JR., in the matchless oratory of the black evangelical tradition, stirred millions of people with his dream of social justice. The integrity and compassion of President JIMMY CARTER, who like thousands of his fellow Georgians had been "born again" in Christ, caused millions elsewhere to ponder the meaning of the Christian rebirth that was central to Evangelicalism.

It is that belief in the possibility of Christian rebirth that is the great constant in the history of Georgia religion over the past 200 years. Many changes have occurred during that time: the education of ministers has improved; church buildings have gotten bigger and are more richly appointed; congregations have grown in size and in wealth; worship in the major denominations has become more sedate; groups with little connection to the dominant Protestantism, such as the Mormons and the Jehovah's Witnesses, have appeared; electronic media have carried worship in sermon and song to thousands of homes; some churches have adopted commercial methods to sell themselves; a charismatic movement, akin to Pentecostalism, has emerged; and secular diversions have multiplied.

Through all those changes, some things have stayed the same: revivalism remains vital in many evangelical churches; the ministry of music continues to be an integral part of worship—even Sacred Harp, or shape-note singing, introduced 140 years ago by B. F. White, can yet be heard, particularly in rural churches in South Georgia; the tradition of enthusiastic worship still lives, especially in the Holiness and in the black churches. What is most important, virtually all Georgia Christians, whether farmer or corporation executive, continue, as their forebears did, to believe in an omnipotent and personal God, who through His Son Jesus Christ can save man from sin and give him a heavenly reward.

Georgia's Christians, at their worst, can behave in un-Christian fashion. They can be intolerant of differences, complacent amid wrongs, and smug in their sense of superiority. Yet, at their best, they have fostered learning, benevolence, and good will among men; they have taken seriously the charge to be their brothers' keepers; and in times of distress, of sickness and bereavement, they are a present help indeed. All in all, Georgia is a better place for their presence in it.

See also article on INDIANS, SOUTHEAST MISSIONS TO.

Bibliography. Kenneth K. Bailey, "Protestantism and Afro-Americans in the Old South: Another Look," *Journal of Southern History* 41 (November 1975): 451-72; *Southern White Protestantism in the Twentieth Century*; T. Conn Bryan, "The Churches During the War," *Confederate Georgia*; Emory Stevens Bucke, ed., *The History of American Methodism*, 3 vols.; Harold E. Davis, "Religion," *The Fledgling Province: Social and Cultural Life in Colonial Georgia, 1733-1776*; John Lee Eighmy, *Churches in Cultural Captivity: A History of the Social Attitudes of Southern Baptists*; Hunter Dickinson Farish, *The Circuit Rider Dismounts: A Social History of Southern Methodism 1865-1900*; Douglas W. Johnson, et al., *Churches and Church Membership in the United States: 1971*; John Tate Lanning, *The Spanish Missions of Georgia*; James Adams Lester, *A History of the Georgia Baptist Convention, 1822-1972*; Ronald Wilson Long, "Religious Revivalism in the Carolinas and Georgia, 1740-1805," unpublished Ph.D. dissertation, University of Georgia, 1968; Anne C. Loveland, *Southern Evangelicals and the Social Order, 1800-1860*; Donald G. Mathews, *Religion in the Old South*; William H. Sears, "The Pre-History of Georgia," *Georgia Review* 6 (Winter 1952): 397-408; George G. Smith, Jr., *The History of Methodism in Georgia and Florida, from 1785 to 1865*; Rufus B. Spain, *At Ease in Zion: A Social History of Southern Baptists, 1865-1900*; Henry Smith Stroupe, *The Religious Press in the South Atlantic States, 1802-1865*; Vinson Synan, *The Holiness-Pentecostal Movement in the United States*; Ernest Trice Thompson, *Presbyterians in the South*, 3 vols; U. S. Department of Commerce, Bureau of the Census, *Religious Bodies: 1906-1936*.

WAYNE MIXON
MERCER UNIVERSITY

GERMAN BAPTISTS: *See* CHURCH OF THE BRETHREN.

GILLFIELD BAPTIST CHURCH. One of the oldest black churches in America, the Gillfield Baptist Church (or Second African Church) is traceable to the 18th century. In 1788 a group of blacks and whites in Petersburg VA constituted themselves as the Davenport Baptist Church. A white preacher, the Rev. Mr. P. Black served the church until it disbanded in 1802, apparently for reasons of racial imbalance. While the whites joined various rural churches and later in 1817 established a church in Petersburg, the blacks reconstituted a separate church in 1803.

Originally known as the Church of the Lord Jesus Christ, the congregation did not have a permanent location for six years, but in 1809 settled at Sandy Beach.

In 1810 the Sandy Beach Church, as it was also known, joined the predominantly white Portsmouth Baptist Association. With a membership of more than 300, the congregation moved in 1815 to Gill's Field in Petersburg proper. By 1818 they were widely known as the Gillfield Church.

Throughout the slavery era Gillfield controlled its internal affairs. The church elected two separate groups of deacons, one slave and one free, and a black moderator. During most of the period after the Nat Turner revolt in 1831, their official preachers were white, but unofficially they maintained control over worship, membership, discipline, and finances. In 1837 Gillfield actually defied Virginia law by appointing a black man, Sampson White, as pastor.

White served the church only one year, but through his various pastorates Gillfield was linked to the history of other notable black churches during slavery, namely First Colored Baptist, Washington; Abyssinian Baptist, New York; and Concord Street Baptist, Brooklyn.

In 1865 Gillfield organized the Shiloh Baptist Association of Virginia. In 1867, with a membership of 1,695, the church organized and joined the Virginia State Baptist Convention, Colored.

Bibliography. Luther P. Jackson, *A Short History of the Gillfield Baptist Church of Petersburg, Virginia*.

CLARENCE G. NEWSOME
DUKE UNIVERSITY

GILMAN, SAMUEL (1791-1858), pioneer Unitarian minister, was born in Gloucester MA. He is best remembered as the author of "Fair Harvard," the *alma mater* of the institution from which he was graduated in 1811. Called to the Second Independent Church of CHARLESTON SC in 1819, he served there for the rest of his career, following in the liberal tradition of his predecessor, Anthony Forster. Gilman and his wife became ornaments of Charleston society and were both known for their rather sentimental literary endeavors. (Caroline edited *The Southern Rose* for many years.)

Unlike his Unitarian counterparts in the North, Gilman was a slaveholder, although it is possible that he may have prepared some of his slaves for eventual freedom. He argued for the Union on the issue of nullification, though his political position was characterized as "a constellation of unionism, conservatism, sentimentalism and passivity," possibly arising out of frustration over the contradictions between his Unitarian morality and Southern circumstances.

He wrote rather widely and on a variety of topics: local-color sketches of New England life; an ode on the death of Calhoun; and a number of theological treatises characterized by a shift from the Scottish "common-sense" philosophy to ethical sentimentalism. In general, he represented an emergent style of Southern, urban, middle-class gentility that his published work both reflected and attempted to justify.

See also article on UNITARIAN-UNIVERSALIST ASSOCIATION.

Bibliography. E. Brooks Holifield, *The Gentlemen Theologians: American Theology in Southern Culture, 1795-1860*; Daniel Walker Howe, "A Massachusetts Yankee in Senator Calhoun's Court: Samuel Gilman in South Carolina," *New England Quarterly* 44 (June 1971): 197-200; Douglas C. Stange, "Abolitionism as Maleficence: Southern Unitarians Versus Puritan Fanaticism—1831-1860," *Harvard Library Bulletin* 26 (April 1978): 146-71.

PETER W. WILLIAMS
MIAMI UNIVERSITY

GLOSSOLALIA. An English word compounded from the two Greek words, *glossa* and *lalein*, glossolalia is usually translated as "speaking in tongues" (see 1 Cor. 12-14; Acts 2:3ff.; 10:46; 19:6; Mk. 16:17). In its hybrid form, the word is not found in the New Testament though the two terms from which it is derived do occur there.

In common usage, the term refers to the spontaneous utterance of incomprehensible and seemingly random vocal sounds. The resulting speech appears to be rather effortless in its flow and unusually complex in its structure. The term describes a form of spiritually affected speaking that is of particular value to the believer. Tongues speaking may often sound very much like a chant or calypso.

While it is not uncommon for this kind of speech to reflect some of the characteristics of languages, most linguists consistently maintain that samples of speaking in tongues do not correspond to any known language. The American Bible Society, for instance, analyzed samples of speaking in tongues that had been recorded on tape. Research based on more than 150 aboriginal languages has found no resemblance to any actual language that had ever been treated by linguists. Apparently, then, if communication occurs at all, it does so on a deep psychological level and thus is not contingent upon the identification of the tongues speech with specific human languages.

In the New Testament, tongues speech appears to have evolved out of a desire of religious converts and devotees to have some specific, objective proof of their being possessed by the Spirit of God. Evidently, glossolalia was accepted as an unquestionable evidence.

The phenomenon has been (and continues to be) a feature of religious, especially revivalist, activities at several periods throughout the history of the church. It was not until the late seventeenth century that the phenomenon occurred among numerous peoples of any one locality. In southern France the Cevenols, who lived in constant fear of death, had ecstatic experiences that included speaking in tongues. In the 19th century a major outburst of tongues speaking occurred in England among the followers of Edward Irving, who himself never received the gift. Aside from sporadic instances during the same centuries among several revival movements in England and America, glossolalia was relatively infrequent in its appearance until its phenomenal rise in connection with PENTECOSTALISM in America.

Several Pentecostal revivals sprang up in the United States just after the turn of the 20th century. The earliest recorded instance of glossolalia was in Topeka KS in 1901. By 1906 tongues speaking was being practiced in Los Angeles and by 1960 the movement began to take on international proportions with 26 contemporary church-bodies (with over two million members) tracing their origin to the occurrence in California. By 1960 so many mainline churches had "glossolalist" cliques that a new term, "neo-Pentecostalism," had to be coined.

By far, the greatest boost to glossolalists has come from organizations of lay Christians such as the Full Gospel Businessmen's Fellowship International or the "PTL" club.

See also article on CHARISMATIC.

WATSON E. MILLS
MERCER UNIVERSITY

GOLDEN, HARRY (1902-1981), Jewish humorist, editor, and social critic, was born in the village of Mikulintsy in the Austro-Hungarian Empire. He was one of seven children of Leib Goldhirsch, a Hebrew teacher, and his wife. Immigration officials spelled the family name Goldhurst when the family entered the United States in 1905. Goldhurst later adopted the name Golden as a *nom de plume* and professional name.

Golden attended public schools and high school on the Lower East Side of New York City in the years 1907-1917. Later he was a night student at the City College of New York. He worked as a stockmarket broker in the 1920s and married Genevieve Gallagher, an Irish school teacher from Scranton PA, in 1926.

In the early 1930s Golden served a four-year prison term for mail fraud in connection with illegal stockmarket operation. Forty years later, Richard Nixon granted him a presidential pardon for those early misdeeds.

After a series of jobs as a hotel manager and advertising salesman for news-

papers in New York and Virginia, Golden settled in Charlotte NC, where in 1942 he commenced publication of a personal journal he called the *Carolina Israelite*. This bimonthly paper consisted of short essays on a variety of subjects, but its main themes were the Jewish experience in America, life on the Lower East Side, and the plight of the Southern Negro. Cultural notes of all kinds and homespun philosophy were also staples of Golden's writing. His use of humor in his columns is credited with lessening the potential for racial violence and bitter feeling in his adopted state of North Carolina.

During the peak years of the Civil Rights movement (1954-1968), Golden was considered a spokesman for the liberal or moderate position on race relations in the South. His collected essays, *Only In America* (1957), became the best-selling book of the decade. In all, with considerable assistance from two of his sons, Golden published 18 books, 14 of which were bestsellers.

During his most active period (1957-1967), Golden was adviser to President Kennedy, speech writer for presidential aspirants Adlai Stevenson and Robert Kennedy, and correspondent for *Life* magazine on special assignments to Europe and Israel. Sometimes referred to as the Jewish Mark Twain, Golden was honored by the state of North Carolina near the end of his life for his contributions to improved race relations in the South.

See also article on JEWISH PRESS.

Bibliography. Harry Golden, *The Right Time.*

WILLIAM GOLDHURST
UNIVERSITY OF FLORIDA

GOODPASTURE, BENTON COR-DELL (1895-1977), preacher and editor in the CHURCHES OF CHRIST, was born in Overton County TN. First educated in primitive mountain schools, he continued his education at Burritt College (Spencer TN), Dixie College (now Tennessee Technological University), and Nashville

Bible School (David Lipscomb College). He graduated with highest honors in 1918.

While in college he began preaching for Churches of Christ; his first full-time work was at Shelbyville TN in 1918. Beginning in 1920, he spent 18 years in Atlanta preaching for the West End and Seminole Avenue congregations. Goodpasture took special interest in the ministry of MARSHALL KEEBLE, a black evangelist, who preached to his people throughout the South.

In 1939 Goodpasture became editor of the Nashville-based *Gospel Advocate*, the oldest journal among Churches of Christ. In Nashville he continued his collecting of books and accepted the pulpit of Hillsboro Church of Christ, filling this assignment until 1951. However, he held protracted meetings and gave college lectures. He excelled in biographical sermons, having the capacity for making biblical characters seem to live. His work with the *Advocate* continued until his death. Serving as editor through the 1950s, he had impact during the greatest years of growth among Churches of Christ.

Bibliography. J. E. Choate, *The Anchor That Holds: A Biography of Benton Cordell Goodpasture.*

ROBERT E. HOOPER
DAVID LIPSCOMB COLLEGE

GOSPEL SONGS: *See* MUSIC, RELIGIOUS.

GRACE, CHARLES EMMANUEL ("SWEET DADDY"),

(1881-1960), founder and bishop of the United House of Prayer for All People, was born in Cape Verde Islands off the west African Coast. (His natal name was Marcelino Manoel da Graca.) He came to New Bedford MA around 1908 where he worked as a short-order cook, salesman, and grocer. In 1920 or 1921, after a visit to the Holy Land, Grace established a mission in Wareham and later in New Bedford. Soon he attracted followers, nearly all of them fellow blacks, along the Atlantic Seaboard and built "Houses of Prayer" in Providence, Washington, New York, and Charlotte; the last remains the area of largest membership.

Bishop Grace was noted for healing and mass baptisms. In the early 1920s Grace told a Winston-Salem NC audience that he had raised a sister from the dead. By 1926, his fame having spread, Grace was baptizing hundreds. He believed that his practices went back to "the faith of the early Christians." Lavish in dress with his shoulder-length hair, one-to-three-inch fingernails, and flashy jewelry, "Daddy" Grace traveled about 300 days a year. Though he had problems with the Internal Revenue Service continuously, he was responsible for shepherding a movement that had 111 Houses and missions existed by 1960.

Bibliography. Phil Casey, "The Enigma of Daddy Grace: Did He Play God?," *Washington Post*, 6 March 1960; John Robinson, "A Shout, A Song, A Prayer," *The Black Experience in Religion*, ed. C. Eric Lincoln.

HERMAN E. THOMAS
UNIVERSITY OF NORTH CAROLINA
AT CHARLOTTE

GRAHAM, BILLY (WILLIAM FRANKLIN),

(1918-), preeminent evangelist, was the firstborn of a strict but fair-minded Presbyterian couple of Charlotte NC. He was converted under the impact of the evangelistic preaching of MORDECAI F. HAM in 1934. While attending the Florida Bible Institute and working at a nearby golf course, young Billy came into contact with a variety of visiting evangelists, many of whom stirred him profoundly with stories and sagas of American evangelism. To date, no Christian evangelist has preached to more people than has Billy Graham.

Always sensitive to the changing moods of "middle America" and a growing person himself, his views have ranged from McCarthyism in the 1950s to concern for nuclear arms control in the 1980s. From the time of his rise to fame in 1949 until the middle 1970s, Graham regarded himself as called to a prophetic ministry to deliver "spiritual commentary" on the political and moral state of the world and of the United States in particular. Although a professing premillennialist, Graham for a quarter of a century embodied a residue of the postmillennial belief in America as the land of the new chosen people.

As late as 1972, still with access to American presidents and political figures, Graham professed to appreciate most the prophet Daniel after Christ, because Daniel had combined the role of the prophet with that of the political leader.

By 1975, however, Graham had grown keenly aware of the complexity and unpredictability of political forces. He ceased regarding himself as a prophet commenting on political matters, preferring instead to call himself a New Testament evangelist, offering both salvation for individuals and guidelines for moral reform.

Like other American corporations that grew beyond expectations, the BILLY GRAHAM EVANGELISTIC ASSOCIATION diversified, $22.9 million of its assets being channeled into the World Evangelism and Christian Education Fund. Although this move proved controversial and raised difficult questions about the complexity of corporate evangelism, the association's reputation for financial integrity remains intact.

In the 1980s the seasoned and experienced Graham declined to align himself with the emerging New Religious Right because of its political entanglements and the unsavory fund-raising tactics of some of its leaders.

Although Southern-born and holding membership in Dallas's First Baptist Church, his crusades, contacts, and influence transcend the region and even the nation. He is the quintessential evangelist to the whole world.

See also articles on EVANGELICALISM; PREACHING; REVIVALISM.

Bibliography. Joe E. Barnhart, *The Billy Graham Religion*; Marshall Frady, *Billy Graham, A Parable of American Righteousness*; Richard V. Pierard, "Billy Graham and the U. S. Presidency," *Journal of Church and State* 22 (Winter 1980): 107-27; John Pollock, *Billy Graham: The Authorized Biography*; Lowell D. Streiker and Gerald S. Strober, *Religion and the New Majority: Billy Graham, Middle America, and the Politics of the 1970s*.

JOE E. BARNHART
NORTH TEXAS STATE UNIVERSITY

GRAVES, JAMES ROBINSON (1820-1893), prominent Baptist leader and a founder of the LANDMARK MOVEMENT, was born in Chester VT. As a result of his father's death the year of his birth, Graves was reared in an impoverished home and received little schooling. This deficiency in education he sought to repair by diligent private study. In early manhood he taught school in Ohio and Kentucky, then in 1845 he moved to Nashville TN as a teacher. He was already an ordained minister and soon became pastor of the Second Baptist Church. In 1848 he became senior editor of *The Baptist*, a periodical published in Nashville. He entered the publishing business also, and by the early 1850s books from his presses were reaching a large Baptist readership.

By the outbreak of the Civil War Graves's paper, renamed *The Tennessee Baptist*, had become the most potent Baptist periodical in the mid-South and Southwest, and Graves was the most powerful Baptist personality in that vast region. After the war he became pastor of the First Baptist Church, Memphis, and revived the publication of his paper, again named *The Baptist*.

Graves was the originator and leader of a dynamic high church movement in Baptist ranks that he called "Old Landmarkism." This movement began about 1851 and prospered much beyond Graves's lifetime. The main emphasis of Landmarkism was and is the conviction that only Baptist churches are true churches. Graves supported this view through his paper, his books and publications, and through his powerful leadership of many thousands of convinced followers.

The decisive molding influence that Landmarkism has had upon Southern

Baptist ecclesiology has caused some knowledgable students to claim that Graves was the most influential Southern Baptist of the 19th century.

See also articles on AMERICAN BAPTIST ASSOCIATION; BAPTIST MISSIONARY ASSOCIATION OF AMERICA.

Bibliography. J. R. Graves, *Old Landmarkism—What Is It?*; O. L. Hailey, *J. R. Graves, Life, Times and Teachings.*

JAMES E. TULL
SOUTHEASTERN BAPTIST SEMINARY

GREAT AWAKENING. The first general religious awakening in America, finding earliest expression in the Middle Colonies in 1734, appeared first in the South in Virginia in 1740. In Hanover County, Presbyterian laymen, chief among them Samuel Morris, experienced a spontaneous quickening and appealed to the New Brunswick (NJ) Presbytery for ministerial aid. William Robinson was sent to visit scattered groups of Presbyterians in Virginia and North Carolina. Wherever he went, he stirred a revival spirit as he boldly attacked the decadence of the Anglican church in the region. When he returned to New Jersey, young SAMUEL DAVIES was sent in 1748 to Virginia. Davies evangelized in five counties and firmly established Presbyterianism in eastern Virginia. Leading Presbyterian preachers, Gilbert and William Tennent, Samuel Finley, and Samuel Blair, followed him on evangelizing tours to the South. Two revivalists, Brown and Alexander Craighead, settled in Augusta County and started an awakening among the Scotch-Irish of the Valley of Virginia. Identified with the Presbyterian phase of the Southern awakening was a pioneer effort at evangelizing the black people of the region. Small numbers of black people were won. However, the Presbyterian phase of the Awakening declined after 1750, especially because of a scarcity of ministers.

A Baptist phase of the awakening began in 1754 and 1755 with the arrival in the South of a company of settlers from Connecticut led by Baptist pastors SHUBAL STEARNS and Daniel Marshall. These Baptists were former Congregationalists who had been won to experiential faith through the preaching of GEORGE WHITEFIELD. They had separated from the established churches of New England and adopted believers' baptism as the sign of the regenerate church. They soon came to be known as SEPARATE BAPTISTS. They established themselves at a strategic point on the Southern frontier—SANDY CREEK NC, in Guilford (later Randolph) County—and began aggressively to found churches among newcomers to the region. Their style of preaching as well as the content of their message attracted attention. They called for a radical reorientation of life, a NEW BIRTH, and appealed to the emotions of their hearers. Hindered in North Carolina by political opposition at the time of the Regulator troubles, their movement spread into neighboring colonies and came to largest expression in Virginia after 1768.

Separate Baptist preaching, moderately Calvinistic in theological outlook, addressed the current feelings and needs of the common man. A few prominent citizens, like Colonel Samuel Harris of Pittsylvania and Councillor Robert Carter of Westmoreland, gave their influence to the movement, which became identified in the era of the American Revolution with the popular demand for political and religious freedom.

In Virginia and other areas Baptist evangelists had to contend with the opposition of crude mobs from time to time, but by 1775 the masses began to feel their appeal. Opposition from 1768 to 1775 came chiefly from intolerant local civil authorities. By 1774 there were over 4,000 Separate Baptists in Virginia. Although their revival slowed with the coming of the American Revolution, it flared into new life after the Revolution and flowered between 1785 and 1792, especially in eastern Virginia, north of the James River. By the latter date, Baptists were the most numerous denomination in Virginia.

Meanwhile, a Methodist phase of the awakening had occurred just prior to the Revolutionary War and while Methodists were still regarded as members of the Anglican church. An Anglican clergyman, DEVEREUX JARRATT of Dinwiddie County, espoused the revival interest and worked with Methodist itinerants in southern Virginia after 1773. He introduced the practice of holding testimony and prayer meetings in private homes. Jarratt did not himself leave the established church, but he assisted Methodist preachers to assume leadership of the awakening in southeastern Virginia. The Methodist revival of 1775-1776 found expression particularly in eight counties, an area of about 400 square miles. By 1776 when the Methodist phase flourished, 2,456 Methodists were to be found in Virginia. That number amounted to half of the Methodist membership in the American colonies.

The post-Revolutionary expression of the Awakening chiefly affected the three above-named denominations. Baptists were the chief beneficiaries, but Methodists gained much prominence in the southeastern portion of the state. A new phase of the Methodist awakening appeared first in Prince George County VA in 1787. Its "most remarkable work" was in Sussex and Brunswick circuits. Novel and sometimes extravagant physical and emotional responses marked many meetings. Also, in western Virginia new Methodist circuits arose following revivals in that area in the 1790s. Among Presbyterians, an awakening began at Hampden-Sydney College in 1787 and moved into neighboring counties of central Virginia. William Graham, rector of Liberty Hall Academy, visited Hampden-Sydney in 1789 and returned home to share the revival spirit in the Valley of Virginia. Thence revival spread into the frontier country of Kentucky and Tennessee. The Baptist revival flourished in central and eastern Virginia (especially north of the James) and reached its climax between 1787 and 1789. It was very instrumental in causing Separate and REGULAR BAPTISTS to unite around 1787.

The migration of people from the older settled areas to the Southern frontier carried seeds of the Awakening southward into South Carolina and Georgia as well as westward into Kentucky and Tennessee.

Among special features of the Awakening the following should be mentioned: (1) appeal to the individual conscience in terms of personal responsibility; (2) preaching combining intellectual and emotional appeal; (3) the use of protracted meetings for evangelism; (4) the use of music, especially a hymnody that borrowed heavily from current folk melodies as a primary means of evangelistic appeal; and (5) serious efforts and marked success in evangelizing the black population.

The Great Awakening made important contributions to American democracy, to the development of educational institutions, and to social progress. It hastened the decline of the "formal" or hereditary type of church organization in America and guaranteed the triumph of the "informal" or voluntary type, featuring large-scale lay participation, democracy, and experiential religion. It thus represented a revolt against much for which the established church of the Southern colonies had stood.

See also articles on ANGLICANISM; COLONIAL PERIOD (in Appendix); DISESTABLISHMENT; ESTABLISHED RELIGION; EVANGELICALISM; GREAT REVIVAL; REVIVALISM.

Bibliography. W. M. Gewehr, *The Great Awakening in Virginia, 1740-1790; The Illustrated History of Methodism*; William L. Lumpkin, *Baptist Foundations in the South*; Robert B. Semple, *A History of the Rise and Progress of the Baptists of Virginia*; William Warren Sweet, *The Story of Religion in America*; *Virginia Methodism, A History*; Ernest T. Thompson, *Presbyterians in the South*, 3 vols.; Joseph Tracy, *The Great Awakening*.

WILLIAM L. LUMPKIN
NORFOLK, VIRGINIA

GREAT REVIVAL, THE. A series of religious revivals that swept across the Southern states between 1800 and 1805, this movement is sometimes called the Second Great Awakening in the South. More properly speaking, however, the Great Revival was the South's first *great* awakening.

The First Great Awakening was primarily a movement north of Maryland in the period 1739-1750. A "great" awakening requires certain preconditions: a network of churches and ministers, at least a core of believers, and a perception that the society has fallen away from a better state of religious piety that existed sometime in the past. These preconditions were not widespread enough in the South before the late 1790s to sustain a significant revival. In the mid-eighteenth century there were brief, one-denominational, small revivals in scattered locales, but none ever grew beyond these limitations to merit the term "great" awakening. The tours of GEORGE WHITEFIELD in the South in 1739 and thereafter did not, for example, ignite the kind of religious excitement his New England tours did. Neither the institutions, the leaders, nor the mentality existed for a great awakening in the South.

Between the 1740s and the 1790s these prerequisites were met throughout much of the South. To some degree, the events transpiring in colonial Virginia suggest the historical and social evolution occurring in other colonies. In the 1740s a localized Presbyterian revival began in Hanover County (north of Richmond), flared briefly, then subsided into normal church life. Churches were founded, converts gained, ministers called, and an ideational system established. As the Presbyterian awakening was diminishing, a Baptist revival began in the southern portion of Virginia. Missionaries from the Evangelical and Calvinistic SEPARATE BAPTISTS had brought this strain of Great Awakening piety from Connecticut to North Carolina in 1755. Soon thereafter lay ministers spread the Baptist message into Virginia, where it represented a powerful challenge to the established Anglican church. The small, private community of the local Baptist church, with otherworldly values, sundered the existing society where crown, courthouse, and Anglican church had previously constituted the established community: the result was a subcommunity of Evangelicals who constituted a sort of counterculture.

The unitary society was split even further by the Methodist movement that began in southeastern Virginia in the 1760s. The Baptists had been outsiders who brought their heretical attitudes into the Anglican society. The Methodists were fervent Evangelicals who were initially a wing of the established church, but their outward emotionalism, their antipathy to slavery, and their folk piety made them as disruptive a challenge to the standing order as the Baptists had been. Their period of REVIVALISM was ended by the Revolution, but like their Presbyterian and Baptist counterparts, they succeeded in forming churches, making converts, spreading a belief system, and raising hopes for a different kind of society. These three phases of religious awakening occurred at different times, in separate parts of Virginia, and never expanded enough to qualify as a "great awakening" in the commonly accepted meaning of the term (although the term is sometimes used). Nevertheless, Southern society would eventually be transformed by the popular religion that was taking root.

This story, in general terms, was replicated in the other Southern states before 1790. The Evangelical hope for a reformed society, however, was dampened by a series of events following 1776, when the Revolution, migration westward, and economic, agricultural, and political change disrupted churches and society at large. After an interdenominational revival that flared briefly in Virginia in the late 1780s, a mood of depression set in among clergy and layman, a nagging feeling that religion was declining, or certainly not prospering, as the new nation began to take shape. This sense of despair led to introspection as clergy sought to understand the causes of a relative—and in places an absolute—decline in church membership. Slowly this introspection developed into a form of theodicy, whereby clergy tried to comprehend and justify the much-discussed "declension." Soon, worry about the disappointing state of religion became a belief that God was disciplining the churches for various moral lapses. But once those failures were recognized, acknowledged, and the contrite had asked God for forgiveness—as clergy were arguing by the late 1790s—God would absolve them of their sins and send a reinvigorating revival. Thus the decade of doom became a season of hope, with the remnant of faithful expecting deliverance at the end of the century. Across the region a feeling of expectancy replaced a sense of despondency.

A Presbyterian minister from North Carolina, JAMES MCGREADY, was one of those who confidently prayed for a re-awakening of religious fervor. Having come to Logan County KY in late 1796, he had organized his few parishioners into prayer societies petitioning God for renewal. Gradually his hard-hitting sermons and captivating presence increased his three small congregations. He started holding joint communion services, which began on a Friday with preaching and ended on Sunday afternoon with the sacrament. At one of these services in June 1800, at his Red River church, two visiting ministers, John and William McGee, asked to participate. Because McGready had known William in North Carolina, he allowed them to join in even though John was a Methodist and quite passionate in promoting his denomination. That evening the McGees became extremely aroused, began shouting, and suddenly a spark of excitement leaped from person to person among the normally subdued congregation. With John McGee now shouting that Jesus' spirit was present, a worshiper at the back of the church commenced shouting and crying. Soon many in the crowded church—tired, expectant, feverishly excited—broke out into a religious frenzy. McGready and others present almost instantly interpreted this surprising outbreak of zeal as a clear sign that God in his mysterious way had, right there in frontier Kentucky, begun the long-awaited revival. The next month, an even more spectacular outdoor religious service was held at the Gasper River church—this was the first CAMP MEETING.

Throughout the South clergy and devout laypeople had been waiting for a sign of deliverance and news from Kentucky was heralded as the beginning of a "second pentecost." Quickly, almost like an epidemic, the camp meeting revivals swept across the rural South. Huge crowds, often numbering in the thousands—blacks as well as whites—came to the revival services, prepared to camp out several days if need be, and interdenominational teams of ministers preached. Theological precision was ignored as ministers—caught up in the religious maelstrom—tried to urge listeners to repent and convert. The novelty of these "camp meetings," rather bizarre emotional extremes, and unusual physical manifestations of conviction or conversion (such as falling unconscious or getting spasmodic "jerks"), seemed to legitimate the revival as an act of God. New converts were made, backsliders regained, and piety reinforced.

Throughout the region church membership increased significantly over a two-to-five-year period. Presbyterians soon withdrew from the unruly revivals and, to a degree, Baptists did likewise, leaving the camp meeting a predominantly Methodist institution. But revivalistic religion—emotionally intense, focused on individual conversion, with little awareness of broader social concerns—remained a characteristic of the reinvigorated Protestantism of the South. Churches were established, ministers called, laypeople joined churches by the thousands. A

Baptist-Methodist-Presbyterian trinity of Evangelical churches came to dominate the region. A new sense of religious community resulted, with a system of values and a code of behavior different from the 18th-century Anglican establishment. By the 1830s nearly everyone in the South, rural folk, wealthy planters, and black slaves alike, accepted the particular Evangelical tradition that had emerged during the Great Revival. That tradition became one of the essential ingredients of the historical reification, "the mind of the Old South."

See also articles on FRONTIER, INFLUENCE OF; GREAT AWAKENING.

Bibliography. John B. Boles, *The Great Revival, 1787-1805: The Origins of the Southern Evangelical Mind*; *Religion in Antebellum Kentucky*; Dickson D. Bruce, Jr., *And They All Sang Hallelujah: Plain-Folk Camp-Meeting Religion*; Wesley M. Gewehr, *The Great Awakening in Virginia*; Rhys Isaac, *The Transformation of Virginia, 1740-1790*; Charles A. Johnson, *The Frontier Camp Meeting: Religion's Harvest Time*; Anne C. Loveland, *Southern Evangelicals and the Social Order, 1800-1860*; Donald G. Mathews, *Religion in the Old South*; Walter B. Posey, *Frontier Mission: A History of Religion West of the Southern Appalachians to 1861*.

JOHN B. BOLES
RICE UNIVERSITY

GREEK ORTHODOX CHURCH.

Although the Greek Orthodox Church goes back to the earliest times in the history of Christianity, the legal establishment of the Greek Orthodox Archdiocese of North and South America did not come to pass until 1922 in New York City. However, the first Greek Orthodox Christians came to the Western Hemisphere in 1768. Surprisingly enough, they came to the South, or rather they were brought to the South.

It was at America's oldest city, ST. AUGUSTINE, FLORIDA, that they first landed on 26 June 1768 as part of the 1,500 immigrants from the Mediterranean brought by the Scottish physician, Andrew Turnbull. They were 500 Greek Orthodox men from Smyrna, Asia Minor and Mani, Greece, along with 1,000 men, women, and children from Corsica, Italy, and Minorca, Spain. They did not come as free people, but rather as indigent servants. From St. Augustine, they went southward to the area of Florida that Turnbull named in honor of the birthplace of his Greek wife, Smyrna in Asia Minor. He called his settlement New Smyrna. The Greeks who chose this odyssey to the New World, so as to flee from the tyrannic Ottoman rule, found themselves under servitude in a strange land. In addition to this, they were subjected to deprivation, malaria, and hunger.

The Greek spirit resists enslavement, preferring to be free. In due time, after many petitions to the British Crown, the colonists were granted their freedom and the remaining 100 or so Greek Orthodox men worked their way back to St. Augustine where the first Greek colony in the New World was established. They would gather at the Avero House on historic St. George Street where they would join in prayer, oftentimes led by the Roman Catholic Priest Fr. Pedro Camps, since there was no Greek Orthodox priest in the New World. In 1966 the Avero House was purchased by the Greek Orthodox Archdiocese of North and South America and was designated as a national shrine in honor of the first Greek immigrants who landed on these shores. Named the St. Photios Shrine, it has been restored to its original appearance of 1720, with a chapel added, and its dedication occurring in 1982.

Likewise, it was in 1866 in New Orleans that the first Greek Orthodox Church in North America was founded. The pioneer founders of the Holy Trinity Church were primarily cotton merchants, with Nicholas Marinos Benarchi the leader. Their first parish priest was Archimandrite Agapius Honcharenkos. The church, located on Dorgenois Street, remained intact until 1950 when the General Assembly of the New Orleans parish voted to demolish it and in its place to build a larger church edifice. Recently that structure was sold and the church facilities were relocated.

In 1960 the Eighth Archdiocesan District was established with offices in New Orleans. At the Holy Trinity Cathedral there, the ordination of Bishop Silas of Amphipolis took place in 1960. With the transfer of Bishop Silas to the archdiocese office in New York, Bishop Iacovos of Catania was appointed diocesan bishop of the Eighth District in 1967, and at that time the headquarters were transferred to Houston.

The major wave of Greek immigrants began in the 1890s and continued until the quota system of immigration was established in the 1920s. They came from Asia Minor, the Greek mainland, and the Aegean Islands as well. In 1922 the Greek Orthodox Archdiocese was established under the ecclesiastical jurisdiction of the ecumenical patriarchate whose international headquarters are located in Constantinople.

As the Greek Orthodox Church grew in the South, it became necessary to establish a new diocese; in 1942 the Fifth Archdiocesan District was created with headquarters in Charlotte NC. The first diocesan bishop was Bishop Germanos of Nyssa, followed by Bishop Aimilianos of Harioupolis, Bishop Iacovos of Catania, and Bishop John of Thermon. A diocesan house was built in Charlotte during the episcopacy of Bishop Aimilianos. With the new charter issued by the Holy Synod of the ecumenical patriarchate in 1978, the Fifth District became known as the Diocese of Charlotte and Bishop John became the first bishop of Charlotte in the spring of 1979.

The new charter brought about a restructure and other changes within the archdiocese, which led to the transfer of the diocesan headquarters to Atlanta in 1980, with Bishop John being given the title bishop of Atlanta. The Greek Orthodox Diocese of Atlanta is composed of 48 parishes, nine missions, and the unique Malbis Brotherhood, with its million-dollar church edifice, in Daphne AL. This diocese encompasses the states of North Carolina, South Carolina, Georgia, Florida, Alabama, Mississippi, Louisiana, and the Knoxville area of Tennessee. The clergy in various categories total 60, and the Greek Orthodox communicants total some 50,000. Both the diocesan headquarters and the diocesan cathedral are located in Atlanta, the latter dedicated to the Annunciation of the Theotokos. The diocese youth office is located in Largo FL, with the Olympic Village camp, an affiliated institution of the diocese, nearby in Brooksville.

The largest parishes are those in Atlanta, Charlotte, and Tarpon Springs FL. Nearly half the congregations are in Florida. Those parishes that are 70 or more years in age are Atlanta, Birmingham, Tarpon Springs, Savannah, Pensacola, and Augusta. The Mobile AL and Jacksonville parishes date back some 60 years. Parishes with at least 50 years of history exist in Charlotte, Miami, Raleigh, and Winston-Salem.

Greek Orthodox Churches have become part of the mainstream of American life, finding a general home in this pluralistic nation. Partly because of mixed marriages and conversions to the Greek Orthodox faith, each parish is bilingual and bicultural, at the least. Each parish maintains a catechism school and a Greek language school. The Tampa parish also operates a private day school that is attended primarily by non-Orthodox Christians. Along with these educational programs, each parish maintains a Ladies Philoptochos Society, a junior G.O.Y.A. chapter for its youth, and a Greek Orthodox league for its young adults.

On the diocesan level, the Diocesan Council, appointed by the bishop, serves as an advisory body to him. There is also a Diocese Philoptochos Board that is elected at the biennial Diocesan Philoptochos Conference. The bishop convenes the Diocesan Clergy-Laity Assembly every other year. There are diocesan commissions in areas like youth, religious education, Greek studies, spiritual life, finances, and communications. These, along with various consultants, assist the bishop in the overall life and programs of the diocese.

Over two centuries have passed since the first Greek immigrants landed at St. Augustine. They have continued to increase in number and advance in all professions, contributing to the growth and development of the South, and especially to its spiritual climate.

See also article on NATIVISM.

Bibliography. Rev. William Gaines, *Greek Orthodox Cathedral of Holy Trinity—New Orleans, Louisiana*; Peter T. Kourides, *The Evolution of the Greek Orthodox Church in America and Its Present Problems*; Demetrius Mazacoufa, *The Story of Greeks in America*; Charles C. Moskos, Jr., *Greek Americans*; E. P. Panagopoulos, *New Smyrna—An Eighteenth Century Greek Odyssey*; Nicon Patrinacos, *The Greek Orthodox Community and Its Contribution to America*; Theodore Saloutos, *The Greeks in the United States*; Stephanus Zotos, *Hellenic Presence in America*; Basileos Zoustis, *The Greeks in America* (in Greek).

BISHOP JOHN
ATLANTA, GEORGIA

GRIMKÉ SISTERS. Sarah Moore Grimké (1792-1873) and Angelina Emily Grimké (1805-1879) were born in Charleston SC to a wealthy and socially prominent family. Sarah's precociousness led her father, Judge John Faucherand Grimké, to remark that if Sarah had been a boy she would be the greatest jurist in the country.

In 1829 Sarah took Angelina north with her and away from the slavery system they both detested. In Philadelphia they became Quakers and were immediately involved in numerous causes: prison reform, infant schools, temperance, health clubs, etc. By 1835 they had discovered two issues to champion for the rest of their lives, abolition of slavery and women's rights.

Both somewhat homely, the two women in their plain Quaker dress turned out to be powerful, magnetic speakers and writers. Their unusual minds and courage attracted friends and supporters from the New England intellectual reform-minded community. They were a novelty, drawing large, curious, sometimes hostile crowds. Most churches were closed to them both because they were Quakers and because the belief that a woman in the pulpit was an abomination. Making five or six speeches a week, the sisters spoke to at least 40,000 people and founded dozens of abolition societies.

Angeline married THEODORE WELD, abolitionist leader, on 14 May 1838. Two days later a mob angered by her speech in Philadelphia, rioted and burned the building to the ground. Angelina was so upset she determined to stop speaking but sister Sarah went on. When Sarah caught a severe cold in Boston and could not speak, Angelina substituted and became the first woman to address any state legislature in America on 21 February 1838.

After the Civil War Angelina happened to read about a speech made by a young black man named Grimké at Lincoln College. She wrote young Grimké inquiring if he might be a former slave of one of her brothers. Archibald Henry Grimké replied that he and his two brothers, Francis James and John, were the sons of her brother, Henry, by his slave mistress. Sarah and Angelina's convictions were again tested and again they did not flinch. They accepted the boys as members of their family and sacrificed to educate them.

The Grimké sisters fought their battles for women's rights and racial justice until the end. Newspapers that had attacked them bitterly a half century before hailed them as heroic pioneers in their obituaries.

See also article on ABOLITIONISM.

Bibliography. Allen Johnson and Dumas Malone, eds., *Dictionary of American Biography*, vol. 7; Gerda Lerner, *The Grimké Sisters from South Carolina: Rebels Against Slavery*; Katharine DuPre Lumpkin, *The Emancipation of Angelina Grimké*.

LOUISE PETTUS
WINTHROP COLLEGE

HAM, MORDECAI FOWLER, JR.
(1877-1961), Baptist evangelist known for his anti-Jewish and anti-Catholic crusades, was born in Bowling Green KY the son and grandson of Baptist preachers. At 22, upon the death of his revered grandfather, he abandoned a promising career in business, as well as an offer from a theatrical company, to follow the family's clerical tradition. For more than the first five decades of the 20th century, he held tent and tabernacle revival meetings throughout the South.

Ham specialized in "confrontation" evangelism. In each city where he held a meeting he identified an established "evil" power, most often personified by some well-known individual, to attack and win converts by defeating. His targets included bootleggers, spokesmen for liberal causes, and nebulous rings of Jewish, Catholic, or black conspirators plotting to destroy white Protestant America. One such crusade (Elizabeth City NC, 1924) led to a national scandal earning Ham the racist label that still clouds his memory. Newspaper editor W. O. Saunders proved that Ham's attack upon the Jewish president of Sears-Roebuck, Julius Rosenwald, accusing Rosenwald of operating Chicago houses of prostitution featuring interracial perversions, was merely racist propaganda.

Ham continued preaching, quite successfully, after the scandal for another quarter century. In 1934 in Charlotte, he converted a young man, BILLY GRAHAM, whose fame as an evangelist would far surpass his own. Toward the end of his career, he confined his preaching to the radio, where he continued to strike out at America's enemies both within and without the country.

See also article on NATIVISM.

Bibliography. James T. Baker, "The Battle of Elizabeth City: Christ and Antichrist in North Carolina," *North Carolina Historical Review* 54 (Autumn 1977) 393-408; E. E. Ham, *Fifty Years on the Battle Front with Christ.*

JAMES T. BAKER
WESTERN KENTUCKY UNIVERSITY

HAM, MYTH OF. A widely circulated and embellished story about Noah and his three sons (cf. Gen. 9:18-27) helped white Christians in the antebellum South mediate the contradiction between Christians holding blacks as slaves and the Christian principle of the brotherhood of all people. The biblical tale recounted how Noah cursed Canaan to be a servant because his father, Ham, had seen the patriarch naked; Noah blessed Shem and Japheth for their respect in covering his nakedness. Additionally, Noah pronounced that Japheth would become greater and dwell in Shem's tents with Canaan as his servant.

While there are exegetical difficulties in identifying the enslavement of black people with the curse on Canaan, exponents of the story suggested that there was a textual gloss and that Noah had really cursed "Ham, the father of Canaan"; or alternatively, Canaan as Ham's eldest son metaphorically stood for all of Ham's descendants. The identification of Ham as black had a long history that can be traced from the Babylonian Talmud through medieval writings to English Bible commentaries used by Americans.

The Ham story functioned mythically among white Christians in the antebellum South, because it unified their biblical world view, their racial ethos, and beliefs about America's manifest destiny. By emphasizing Ham's original transgression, white Christians could argue that masters exercised God-given authority over the black race, just as husbands exercised legitimate authority over their wives on account of Eve's original sin. The ambiguity about Ham's offense allowed Southerners to read their racist stereotypes into the biblical account. Ham showed childlike intelligence in mocking his father; Ham's interest in Noah's nakedness suggested the blacks' tendencies toward lasciviousness. As Ham, Japheth, and Shem became archetypes for the black, white, and red races in America, the proponents of slavery could envision that the enslavement of black people and the subjection of the American Indians accorded with God's plan for human progress.

See also articles on SEGREGATION; SLAVERY.

Bibliography. Thomas V. Peterson, *Ham and Japheth: The Mythic World of Whites in the Antebellum South.*

THOMAS VIRGIL PETERSON
ALFRED UNIVERSITY

HARDEMAN, NICHOLAS BRODIE

(1874-1965), early CHURCHES OF CHRIST leader, was born in Milledgeville TN. He was descended from a well-known family. One ancestor, Thomas Hardeman, was a member, along with Andrew Jackson, of the Davidson County delegation to the convention of 1796, which adopted the first constitution of Tennessee. Hardeman entered West Tennessee Christian College at Henderson in 1890. During the same year he was baptized and affiliated with the Christian church. Hardeman received both the B.A. and M.A. degrees from Georgie Robertson Christian College, the new name for the Henderson school.

Even before graduation, Hardeman became involved in education and evangelism. He taught in various schools and was cofounder, along with A. G. FREED, of present-day Freed-Hardeman College. When the missionary society advocates gained control of Georgie Robertson, Freed and Hardeman in 1908 organized the National Teachers' Normal and Business College, later renamed Freed-Hardeman College. Hardeman remained with the school when Freed moved to Nashville in 1923.

Hardeman was in demand as an evangelist and debater. He often debated Ben Bogard, a prominent Baptist. His Nashville debate (1923) with Ira M. Boswell of the Disciples of Christ on the use of the instruments in worship was the high point of his debating career. Although he preached widely, his five Nashville Tabernacle meetings, held over a 20-year period beginning in 1922 and sponsored by the Churches of Christ, are best remembered. Five volumes of *Hardeman Tabernacle Sermons* and the above-mentioned debates have been published.

See also articles on CAMPBELLITE TRADITION; DEBATES, INTERDENOMINATIONAL.

Bibliography. James Marvin Powell and Mary Nelle Hardeman Powers, *N.B.H.: A Biography of Nicholas Brodie Hardeman.*

ROBERT E. HOOPER
DAVID LIPSCOMB COLLEGE

HARDSHELL BAPTISTS: *See* Primitive Baptists.

HARGIS, BILLY JAMES (1925-), archconservative religious-political leader, was born in Texarkana TX. He was ordained to the Disciples of Christ ministry at age 18. In 1948 after a series of pastorates in Arkansas, Missouri, and Oklahoma, he founded the Christian Crusade, with headquarters in TULSA, and soon afterward began to devote full time to the fight against Communism, addressing what he regarded as burning issues in personal appearances, in a plethora of books, pamphlets, and letters, and on broadcasts heard on over 500 radio and 146 television stations at the peak of his popularity in the early 1970s. Dr. Hargis—his honorary degrees were conferred by the Defender Seminary in Puerto Rico and Belin Memorial University in Chillicothe MO—is a spell-binding speaker with great rhetorical skills and exceptional motivational power.

In the mid-1950s, Hargis helped send over a million balloons bearing portions of Scripture behind the Iron Curtain. He also gained wide attention for his strident attacks on the United Nations and the National Council of Churches, which he excoriated as affiliated with various pro-Communist causes and organizations. The intemperance of some of his attacks, coupled with their blatantly political nature, cost Hargis's ministry its tax-exempt status in 1964.

In 1970 Hargis founded American Christian College in Tulsa, but charges that the founder had engaged in sexual relations with both male and female students forced him to sever his ties with the school in 1974 and led to its eventual demise. In 1981 after a period of severe retrenchment—his broadcasts were aired on 20 radio and several cable television outlets late in that year—Hargis obtained a license to own and operate a purchased UHF television station, a move he hoped would stimulate a resurgence of his crusade "for Christ and against Communism."

See also articles on ELECTRONIC CHURCH; FUNDAMENTALISM.

WILLIAM C. MARTIN
RICE UNIVERSITY

HAYGOOD, ATTICUS GREENE (1839-1896), Methodist editor, educator, and bishop, was born in Watkinsville GA. He entered Emory College in 1856, coming under the influence of the LOVICK PIERCE family, and was graduated in 1859.

Haygood was licensed to preach in 1858 and the next year was admitted on trial in the Georgia Conference and assigned as the junior preacher under Lovick Pierce. In the 1860s he served five circuits as a Confederate chaplain, and as a presiding elder.

In 1870 he was elected first Sunday school secretary and six years later was named president of Emory; during the latter years at Emory, he edited the *Wesleyan Christian Advocate*. The best known of his seven books, *Our Brother in Black, His Freedom and His Future*, was published in 1881, and a year later he was one of five bishops elected; but he resigned the office, saying he was called to another work. The next eight years he administered the Slater Fund, which provided money for the education of Southern blacks.

Haygood was again elected a bishop in 1890 and assigned to California, but he returned to Georgia in 1893, broken in health and living until his death as a virtual ward of his one-time student, President Warren A. Candler of Emory.

Haygood was a transition figure between the older Southern Methodism that launched him and the newer Southern Methodism that he sought to shape.

See also article on SEGREGATION.

Bibliography. Elem F. Dempsey, *Atticus Green Haygood, He Took the Kingdom by Violence, Matthew 11:12*; Atticus G. Haygood, *Our Brother in Black, His Freedom and His Future*; Harold W. Mann, *Atticus Greene Haygood: Methodist Bishop, Editor, and Educator.*

JOSEPH MITCHELL
TROY STATE UNIVERSITY

HAYS, BROOKS (1898-1981), Baptist lay leader and statesman, was born in London AR. Except for a brief private law practice, most of his career was devoted to public service. After law school, he joined his father's law firm in Russellville, moving to Little Rock in 1924 when he was named assistant attorney general of Arkansas.

In 1934 he went to Washington to begin a series of assignments under the Roosevelt administration, all of which were related to his lifelong concern for the rural poor. They culminated in a staff position in the Department of Agriculture. In 1942 he was elected to Congress in his home district and served in the House for 16 years.

His selfless courage in attempting to mediate between President Eisenhower and Governor Faubus in the Little Rock desegregation crisis (1957-1958) brought him national attention but also led to his political defeat in a savage campaign that distorted his position as a moderate and inflamed prejudiced voters against him. The defeat, however, opened wider doors for him and brought recognition of his true stature in public life. In succeeding years, he served as a director of the TVA, president of the Southern Baptist Convention, assistant secretary of state, special assistant to three presidents, president of the National Conference of Christians and Jews, visiting professor at two universities, director of the Ecumenical Institute of Wake Forest University, and chairman of the North Carolina Human Relations Committee—to name only a few of many significant posts.

Always a devout churchman, he had a gentle spirit, a well-rounded mind, a quick and native wit, a matchless gift for humor, and an almost endless repertoire of stories, all of which combined to make him one of America's most popular platform speakers, and one of the nation's most beloved statesmen.

Bibliography. Brooks Hays, *Politics Is My Parish*; *This World: A Christian's Workshop*; *A Southern Moderate Speaks.*

CLAUDE U. BROACH
TRYON, NORTH CAROLINA

HEALING, DIVINE: *See* FAITH HEALING.

HEAVEN. In the South, as elsewhere, concepts of Heaven have been shaped considerably by the living conditions and aspirations of the believers. Nineteenth-century and early twentieth-century hymn books often portrayed Heaven as a place of rest, shade, and relief from repressive toil. Southern rural religion in particular placed special emphasis on Heb. 12:1: "Wherefore, seeing we also are compassed about with so great a cloud of witnesses, let us . . . run with patience the race that is set before us." Relatives and friends who had already crossed to the other side served now as an audience of witnesses or spectators, giving encouragement to those still running the race of earthly life. Upon completing the race, the believer immediately joined relatives and friends in the New Jerusalem, thus completing the happy family circle.

A black spiritual captured this theme succinctly, portraying the great chariot sweeping down to take the believer to Heaven to be reunited with loved ones. "Tell all my friends I'm comin', too, comin' for to carry me home." Heaven for Southern rural believers meant, above all, homecoming, when those who had been separated by death would "reunite with loved ones." Preachers and revivalists effectively used this powerful theme of homecoming to gain converts.

Southern religion has never been seriously influenced by concepts of Heaven as mystical absorption. Family and friends are so central to Southern life that Heaven would not be Heaven without them. Instead of absorbing the Southern way of community and social interaction into the mystical being of God, Southern religion retained the family model and turned the members of the Trinity into the most honored and esteemed members of the Great Family. Life without a dynamic social life (no matter how spiritually refined), for most rural

Southerners, could not be regarded as Heaven but as HELL.

As the South became urbanized and industrialized, as the unbroken family circle came under threat, and as members of the same earthly family left for the cities, they became more likely to disengage from the faith of their parents. No popular vivid model of Heaven has emerged in the South to replace the family model. The impact of pluralism, secularization, and urbanization has rendered modern concepts of Heaven colorless and abstract. As communal life gave way to individualism, Heaven as a context for self-realization emerged. But this context is portrayed more in negative terms (as removal of evil influences) than in dynamic positive terms.

Antebellum religion in the South did not conceive of Heaven as a radical break with earth. The popular postmillennial doctrine envisioned a merging of Heaven and earth as the Kingdom of God gradually and steadily infused the earth with righteousness and faith. Hopes ran high that the earth would, in effect, become a colony of Heaven. Earth was often thought of as a kind of new frontier for Heaven, and Christians were exhorted to claim the earth for Heaven.

But wars and other social upheavals destroyed most of this faith, and in its place emerged premillennialism, which portrayed the earth as largely a den of evil awaiting the wrath of God. The saved will be snatched away in the RAPTURE, thus making final the radical destruction of all continuity between Heaven and earth. Even the interim millennium on earth will consist of Heaven's army conquering and occupying enemy territory.

See also articles on CONVERSION; HELL; MILLENNIALISM; PREACHING; REVIVALISM; SALVATION.

JOE E. BARNHART
NORTH TEXAS STATE UNIVERSITY

HELL. Southern religion has produced not only complex theological works on the subject of Hell, but tracts and sermons purporting to describe Hell in graphic and vivid terms. Revivalists became the primary heirs of one side of Jonathan Edwards and his most famous sermon, "Sinners in the Hands of an Angry God." Among believers who have moved from strict FUNDAMENTALISM into a more sophisticated EVANGELICAL PROTESTANTISM, there developed a tendency to forgo descriptions of Hell as literal brimstone and physical torture. Evangelicals and neo-Evangelicals came increasingly to speak of hell in psychological terms. Instead of suffering literal flames, Hell's inmates suffer alienation from all that is good and decent, remorse for the evil done in the past life, excruciating loneliness, and unprecedented grieving.

BILLY GRAHAM represents those revivalists who, growing more sophisticated, could not easily portray God as one who directly tortures his creatures. Hell came to be thought of, therefore, as the quasi-natural consequences of a life lived by one who is naturally evil.

Critics have noted that orthodox Christians tend to define as naturally evil (and therefore worthy of endless Hell) all those adults (at least) who are not Christians. The doctrine of Hell, a stumbling block to many Christians in the South has evoked complex theological explanations and endless qualifications. As a doctrine, it tends to be held by those who regard the Bible as the infallible or inerrant revelation of the Creator. Exceptions are such groups as the JEHOVAH'S WITNESSES and the SEVENTH-DAY ADVENTISTS, who hold to the doctrine of soul-sleep *and* to the doctrine of infallibility.

In the South, black ministers have been prone to picture Hell as a continuation of the troubles of the present world, that is, as the loss of the better life in Heaven.

Critics of the notion of an endless Hell have denounced it as revelation, not of God, but of the most vindictive dimension of human nature. Within each denomination in the South, ministers today differ significantly among themselves regarding the doctrine of Hell.

Those believing in Hell have long been perplexed by the moral question of the eternal state of those who have not heard the Christian gospel. Early nineteenth-century optimism led many religious leaders of the South to anticipate not only the evangelization of the entire globe, but the conversion of great throngs in every section of the world. This twofold vision was a part of the postmillennial dream. But the grandiose vision collapsed on continent after continent. Instead of concluding that the entire notion of Hell as endless punishment was misconceived from the start, however, the orthodox took refuge in the conviction that in Hell some resident there receive a lighter degree of torment than others. Other Christians simply allowed the doctrine of Hell to fade away or be relegated to an obscure part of the theological house, like the insane wife in the attic from the novel *Jane Eyre*.

See also articles on Bible, Inspiration of; Black Religion; Heaven; Millennialism; Preaching; Revivalism.

JOE E. BARNHART
NORTH TEXAS STATE UNIVERSITY

HELM, LUCINDA BARBOUR (1839-1897), prominent Methodist leader, was the founder and guiding spirit of denomination-wide home mission work among Southern Methodist women. She was born near Elizabethtown KY into a prominent family, her father serving as state governor and president of the Louisville and Nashville Railroad. As a child, Helm was both physically frail and religiously devout. She joined the local Methodist church at 18 and soon began religious work in the community, forming societies, most often for youth, to provide biblical instruction and moral guidance. She also became involved in the efforts of Southern Methodist women to support foreign missionaries and was one of the leaders in the formation of the denomination's Woman's Foreign Missionary Society.

However, her major focus was the development of home mission work among women. In 1886, at her urging, the General Conference formed the Woman's Department of the Board of Church Extension to secure funds for parsonages, particularly in the West. As general secretary, she organized hundreds of local societies for this purpose. Her vision, however, included a larger and more active role for women in home mission work and, overcoming considerable opposition, she led the effort to achieve this at the 1890 General Conference with the formation of the Woman's Parsonage and Home Mission Society. Helm was again appointed general secretary. In 1892, she established a periodical, *Our Homes*, to describe and promote the home mission work, advocating causes such as philanthropy among the poor, temperance, and religious instruction among the unchurched. At her death, her sister, Mary, succeeded her as editor.

See also articles on Social Gospel; Women in Religion.

Bibliography. Arabel W. Alexander, *Life and Work of Lucinda B. Helm*; Noreen Dunn Tatum, *A Crown of Service*.

JOHN P. MCDOWELL
ROANOKE, VIRGINIA

HENKEL, PAUL (1754-1825), controversial early Lutheran leader, was born in Davie County NC. He and his wife had nine children, five of whom became ministers. While working as a cooper, he studied theology in Maryland, which led to his licensing in 1783 and his ordination by the Lutheran Ministerium of Pennsylvania in 1792. He lived most of his life in New Market VA, with brief periods of residence in NC (ca. 1800-1805) and Point Pleasant WV, (1811-1813, 1817-1818); but almost every summer he would make missionary tours to preach and to catechize German-speaking people in numerous Southern and Midwestern states. He participated in the organization of three synods: North Carolina (1803), Ohio (1818), and Tennessee (1820). The Tennessee Synod reflected the conservative views of Paul and his sons Philip and David toward the formation of a national General Synod among Lutherans: they opposed its "centralizing" tendency, its vague attitude toward the AUGSBURG CONFESSION, and the revivalist methods of some of its member synods. Through a family printing business, Henkel published a book on baptism and the Lord's Supper (1809), a German hymnal (1810) with many original texts, German and English adaptations of Luther's *Small Catechism*, and several other books of edification.

See also articles on LUTHERAN CHURCH; MIGRATION, SOUTHWARD (1700-1830).

Bibliography. W. E. Eisenberg, *The Lutheran Church in Virginia, 1717-1962*; W. J. Finck, ed. & trans., *A Chronological Life of Paul Henkel, from Journals, Letters, Minutes of Synod*, unpublished typescript; *Life Sketches of Lutheran Ministers, North Carolina and Tennessee Synods, 1773-1965.*

HUGH GEORGE ANDERSON
LUTHER COLLEGE

HIGH CHURCH/LOW CHURCH.

These terms refer to divergent views within the EPISCOPAL CHURCH with respect to doctrinal, sacerdotal, disciplinary, and ritualistic issues. While the lines drawn have historically been fluid, at any given time Episcopalians could refer to a parish, diocese, or priest as tending toward High Church or Low Church.

In the colonial period and including the first half of the 19th century the High Church position accentuated the concept of the church as an organic whole, historically and apostolically continuous with primitive Christianity, with that continuity symbolized and borne by the episcopate. While deeply suspicious of Roman Catholicism, High Churchmen were equally anxious to delineate differences between the Episcopal Church and various Protestant bodies, asserting that the former tended to superstition and the latter to ecclesiastical anarchy, emotional-

ism, and questionable orthodoxy. For example, High Churchmen maintained a "high" view of the eucharistic sacrament rather than a memorialistic understanding, and they understood baptism as regenerative of fallen human nature. Ritually, High Churchmen were distinguished by an insistence upon strict compliance with episcopal and rubrical directions for worship. Their attitude toward other Protestant bodies caused them usually to call attention to differences between them rather than similarities with them. Low Churchmen, by contrast, were more evangelical in spirit and style, often indifferent to rubrical directions, more open to friendly and cooperative ventures with other Protestant bodies, and descendants of a puritanical spirit. In the South, North Carolina had perhaps the greatest High Church representation and Virginia the most Low Church.

The Oxford Movement within the Church of England in the 1840s had its counterpart in the American Episcopal Church, effecting a rift among the High Churchmen as new issues such as private confession were debated. A new faction began to believe and teach that too much Catholic doctrine and practice had been discarded at the time of the English Reformation; and in the American church, disputes were accompanied by occasional trials of clergy for irregularity of belief and ritual practice. Charges were also made that episcopal elections had devolved into partisan contests. Several dozen clergy including one bishop, LEVI S. IVES of North Carolina, left the church in the 1840s and 1850s for Roman Catholicism in the belief that the Episcopal Church was fatally flawed with respect to being properly Catholic in faith and practice. High Churchmen were accused of being "papistical" and puerile, and Low Churchmen were accused of being sectarian and indifferent to Anglicanism's authentic Catholic heritage.

Attempts to legislate against the more militant High Church views failed and these views gradually spread and became commonplace in those dioceses whose bishops were congenial to them. In the middle third of the 19th century this began to affect worship with the gradual introduction in certain parishes of such practically unknown accoutrements as candles and flowers on the altar. Holy Communion was celebrated with more regularity and solemnity, as a puritan plainness gave way to a more romantic and decorative understanding of spirituality. More churches were constructed in the Gothic style and with divided chancels; they were self-consciously designed to be distinctive from Protestant "meeting houses."

In the 1870s ritualism had progressed to the degree that in some few parishes eucharistic vestments, incense, and private confession were regularly in use, and again attempts to legislate nationally against such innovations failed. Thereafter, differences between High and Low Churchmen were contested primarily in episcopal elections, and as a consequence the prevalence of High or Low Churchmanship has tended to vary from diocese to diocese depending upon the views of the diocesan bishop and the clergy whom he has recruited.

Today, a parish that might be described as Low Church would typically celebrate the Holy Communion at an early service each Sunday and once a month at the primary service; the altar would be decorated with a cross, candles, flowers, and vested in colored seasonal frontals; participants in the service would include vested choir and acolytes, with the priest wearing cassock, surplice, and colored stole. Such a parish would have represented the extreme High Church position of 1850, but in the South today this ritual expression is regarded as minimal. The use of eucharistic vestments, while occasionally and rarely seen in 1950, is now widespread to perhaps a majority of parishes. Private confession is generally available though not necessarily at stated, fixed times. The erosion of anti-Roman feeling together with new academic study of liturgics has enabled the introduction of such observances on other than doctrinal, partisan grounds.

In the South today a High Church parish might be nearly indistinguishable from a Low Church parish except by inquiry as to how long a ritualistic devotion has been in use, for what reasons, and how insistently and consistently. While some Southern dioceses are on the whole generally High Church or Low—the dioceses of Virginia, for example, are Low Church in contrast to the High Church dioceses of the southern Florida peninsula—social and doctrinal issues now would be more divisive in the Episcopal Church than sacramental, sacerdotal, and ritualistic ones; and people who in the past decade have left the Episcopal Church to form new episcopal groups are as apt previously to have been High Churchmen as Low Churchmen.

See also articles on ANGLICANISM; LANDMARK MOVEMENT.

Bibliography. George E. DeMille, *The Catholic Movement in the American Episcopal Church.*

MICHAEL T. MALONE
HARTSVILLE, SOUTH CAROLINA

HINES, JOHN ELBRIDGE (1910-), a presiding bishop of the Episcopal Church, served in that capacity from 1965 until 1974. He was born in Seneca SC. His physician-father was president of the South Carolina State Medical Association. After graduating from the UNIVERSITY OF THE SOUTH with a B.A. and from Virginia Theological Seminary with a B.D., Hines was ordained by the Rt. Rev. Kirkman Finlay in 1933.

The Depression had seriously limited the number of positions open to new clergy in South Carolina's Episcopal Church; so he was released by that diocese to begin his ministry in Missouri under Bishop William Scarlett. Scarlett, deeply influenced by Walter Rauschenbusch, the "father of the SOCIAL GOSPEL in America," in turn made a lasting impression on a whole generation of able young Episcopal clergy, including John Hines.

The concerns for political justice and social change had other sources in Hines's case, but his steadfast conviction of their claim on the Christian church was a constant all through his ministry. His 10 years as bishop coadjutor of Texas, 11 years as bishop of Texas, and nine years as presiding bishop were characterized by outspoken, courageous, and often costly witness against racism and all forms of social injustice. His years as presiding bishop coincided with the Viet Nam War and its associated upheavals in society. Sensitive to the times, he called a special meeting of the General Convention at South Bend IN to respond to the current issues. The result was a "General Convention Special Program" (1969), which sought to meet these challenges by funding a wide variety of groups, some controversial, which were dedicated to a more just society.

Bishop Hines retired in 1974 and is currently living in Cashiers NC.

C. FITZSIMMONS ALLISON
CHARLESTON, SOUTH CAROLINA

HISTORICAL PERIODS: *See* COLONIAL SOUTH (in Appendix); RECENT SOUTH (in Appendix).

HOGE, MOSES DRURY (1819-1899), courageous Presbyterian minister and leader, was born in Hampden-Sydney VA. He was educated at Hampden-Sydney College and at the Union Theological Seminary in Virginia.

After a brief stint as assistant to William Swan Plumer, pastor of the First Presbyterian Church of Richmond, Hoge became pastor of the Second Presbyterian Church of that city in 1845. He held this position with distinction until his death 54 years later. Under his guidance the church grew dramatically, becoming the largest congregation in the Synod of Virginia, and one of the most influential Presbyterian churches in the country.

Other prominent Presbyterian churches in Richmond also resulted from his leadership.

During the Civil War Hoge often preached in the army camps near Richmond, and strove to relieve human suffering in the Confederate capital. A shortage of religious literature for soldiers led him to run the Union blockade and sail to England in 1862. There he procured hundreds of thousands of Bibles, New Testaments, Psalms, and other religious books from British Bible societies, and successfully sent them home through the blockade. Like many Southern ministers of his generation, he never ceased paying homage to the LOST CAUSE.

After the war Hoge edited the Richmond *Central Presbyterian* and was a delegate to several international church conferences. In 1890 the people of Richmond proclaimed this popular minister and civic leader the first citizen of the city.

Bibliography. Peyton Harrison Hoge, *Moses Drury Hoge: Life and Letters.*

DANIEL LEE CLOYD
AUBURN UNIVERSITY

HOLINESS. The term "holiness" is applied to God, and in Bible and church history it is associated with purity in the sense of separation from evil. In Judaism and Christianity, specific times and places may be considered holy because of their association with the presence and worship of God. Most important for American religious history, holiness has been perceived as a condition that should characterize those who have established a personal relationship with God.

Puritans devoted their world to purity, emphasizing the progress of SANCTIFICATION as an important part of Christian experience. In general, denominations with roots in the Reformed tradition taught that sanctification—the process in which God made the justified holy—was progressive, lasting throughout life and perfected in eternity.

The most influential conception of holiness for American religious life was that expounded by John Wesley. In *A Plain Account of Christian Perfection*, Wesley took issue with the Reformed perception of the Christian life as a continuing struggle against evil. There was, Wesley asserted, a "habitual disposition of soul" that the Bible termed "holiness." This implied "the being cleansed from sin, 'from all filthiness both of flesh and spirit' and . . . the being so renewed in the image of our mind' as to be 'perfect as our Father in heaven is perfect.' " Wesley counseled Methodists to await this holiness in prayer, faith, fasting, and acts of outward obedience. In some, holiness might be revealed through a process of Christian growth; in others it would be an instantaneous experience. Wesley focused on the content rather than on the timing of the transformation and urged its importance.

In the United States, Wesley's teaching was modified to focus on a sudden crisis experience of inward purity through which the inclination to sin would be eradicated. Holiness became an interdenominational theme that had broad applications to American culture. Out of the religious quest for perfection grew concern for social needs: early nineteenth-century REVIVALISM generated support for social reform.

The extent of American interest in holiness was evidenced in the related concerns of non-Methodist Evangelicals. Charles G. Finney, William Boardman, Charles Cullis, and R. Pearsall Smith were among those who affirmed the availability through entire consecration of "fuller" Christian experience. After the Civil War, D. L. Moody, A. J. Gordon, A. B. Simpson, and R. A. Torrey emphasized in their extensive ministries the necessity of inward purity, stressing the "overcoming" of the sinful nature rather than a definite experience of sanctification. Their affirmation of holiness as process included a focus on the separation of the Christian from various forms of "worldliness." By the late nineteenth century, premillennialism infused their world view,

and gave new urgency to the quest for holiness.

Thus in Methodism and in other denominational contexts as well, the 19th-century stress on holiness, either as sudden crisis or as process, influenced American Evangelicalism widely. It was associated increasingly with separation from "worldliness" and with certain forms of dress and behavior. In the 20th century, the Methodist emphasis was institutionalized in holiness denominations like the CHURCH OF THE NAZARENE or in holiness-pentecostal groups like the PENTECOSTAL HOLINESS CHURCH. The impulse to purity of heart and life continues to be widely felt, particularly in conservative Evangelicalism where eschatology makes it especially compelling. It is reflected in the renewed interest in the person and ministry of the Holy Spirit that is also part of the burgeoning charismatic movement.

See also articles on CHARISMATIC; HOLINESS MOVEMENT; MILLENNIALISM; PENTECOSTALISM; WESLEYAN TRADITION.

Bibliography. W. E. Boardman, *The Higher Christian Life*; R. Newton Flew, *The Idea of Perfection in Christian Theology*; Paul Martin, *The Holy Spirit Today*; A. B. Simpson, *Wholly Sanctified*; R. A. Torrey, *The Baptism with the Holy Spirit*; John Wesley, *A Plain Account of Christian Perfection*.

EDITH L. BLUMHOFER
SOUTHWEST MISSOURI STATE UNIVERSITY

HOLINESS MOVEMENT. This development within conservative Protestantism emerged most directly from a focus within American Methodism on John Wesley's presentation of Christian perfection. Wesley taught that one should pursue experience of perfect love subsequent to one's new birth. This comprised "the loving God with all our heart, mind, soul and strength"; thus "all the thoughts, words and actions" would be controlled by "pure love." Wesley claimed that perfect love took into consideration "creature limitations": one would be freed from the disposition to voluntary transgression, but not from failings rooted in "ignorance" or "infirmity." Wesley called this doctrine "the grand depositum which God has lodged with the people called Methodists." He remained ambiguous as to the precise arrival of perfect love, suggesting both a gradual transformation and a definite crisis experience. Nevertheless, he consistently stressed its importance.

An emphasis on vital religious experience contributed to Methodism's rapid growth in the early American republic. The distinctive emphasis of Methodism's founder was neglected as the movement organized and adapted to the American setting. By the 1830s a minority that focused on this particular teaching and claimed to have the experience succeeded in renewing the denomination's interest in Christian perfection. The experience had many designations: its stress on inward purity made "holiness" a popular, descriptive term. The words "holiness movement" designate a force that, although originating within Methodism, had significant interdenominational appeal, as it focused on the widely felt need for inward cleansing, or holiness, achieved through sudden crisis experience. Particularly influential in revitalizing the call to such perfection were the itinerant efforts of evangelists like Phoebe and Walter Palmer and the publication of literature promoting the theme.

In 1835 weekly prayer meetings to seek holiness were begun by Sarah Lankford in New York City. Continued by Lankford's sister, Phoebe Palmer, these gatherings decisively influenced a core of prominent Methodists and other urban Protestants to proclaim perfect love. The terms used to describe the experience varied: Christian perfection, perfect love, SANCTIFICATION, SECOND BLESSING, HOLINESS. The event to which they referred was regarded as a "present possibility." A shift away from Wesley's willingness to consider the experience as process occurred. The American emphasis focused on sudden crisis. Although leaders stressed their roots in Wesley's teachings, the Holiness Movement developed doctrines and practices that differed significantly from Wesley's presentation. Phoebe Palmer's "altar terminology" summarized the message: God's altar sanctified the sacrifices placed on it. Every human sacrifice "laid on God's altar," then, was made holy. When one had fulfilled the conditions in entire consecration, one could "claim the blessing." Inward sin would be rooted out, replaced by perfect love.

In 1839 Timothy Merritt began a journal, *Guide to Christian Perfection*, which later became the *Guide to Holiness*, an important promotional tool. Phoebe Palmer and others authored books of testimony and exhortation that went through numerous editions. The Palmers's itinerant activities also stimulated the movement's growth. At CAMP MEETINGS and revivals, their teaching won adherents. Like REVIVALISM, it had universal appeal: all who had been justified could find in the second blessing satisfying purity and peace. The message found increasing acceptance outside of Methodism and emerged independently in important non-Methodist contexts until Christian perfection had become a prominent theme in midcentury American culture.

At Oberlin College in Ohio from 1839, Charles Finney and Asa Mahan emphasized perfection as consecration and faith. Terminology again varied: Finney spoke of "entire sanctification," his colleagues of "holiness" or the "baptism of the Holy Ghost." Like their Methodist counterparts, they focused on a second definite experience in the *ordo salutis* through which one could enjoy a "higher" plane of Christian experience.

Another non-Methodist advocate of perfectionist themes was William Edwin Boardman, a Presbyterian who published *The Higher Christian Life* in 1858. In an effort to address his message to those wary of Methodism or Oberlin perfectionism, Boardman used the phrase "higher life" to describe an experience centering around the apprehension by faith of "Christ as All."

Wesley had foreseen potential for disharmony in perfectionist teaching and had warned against spiritual pride and a stress on externals. However, by midcentury variations between the Methodist perfectionist teaching and denominational practice had combined with the issue of slavery to generate controversies from which separate Methodist bodies emerged. The Methodist Episcopal Church, South, had been created in 1844 over the slavery issue. In 1860 dissidents disturbed by the worldliness of the Northern church formed the Free Methodist Church. As the century progressed, a focus on external as well as spiritual evidences of the second blessing would increasingly predominate in the movement.

In 1867 a group of Northern Methodists formed the National Camp Meeting Association for the Promotion of Holiness, an association which, although it welcomed non-Methodist participation, determined to use its meetings to revive Methodism.

Concerned leaders in Southern Methodism also recalled their church to its spiritual heritage. During the 1870s both major branches of Methodism included a strong and vocal element that stressed the holiness experience. In the North thousands attended holiness camp meetings. New periodicals sponsored by both Methodists and independents promulgated holiness doctrines, and for a time it seemed that supporters of the movement might win control of Northern Methodism. In the South as well, the holiness message won support among leading Methodists.

Association crusades in the South drew sufficient local support for the organization of holiness associations within each Southern Methodist district conference; elsewhere, local and state associations also flourished. By 1887 the National Association had conducted 67 national camp meetings, and at least 28 camps authorized by the association were in operation. By 1891 some 304 full-time

holiness evangelists and some 354 "weekday meetings for the promotion of holiness" were listed by the association.

As the movement peaked during the 1880s, controversy over its features and message demanded an evaluation of its role in relation to Methodism. The independence of the associations from denominational control was a central issue. Although Methodists provided national association leadership, that group was interdenominational, listing authorized but non-Methodist evangelists and lending support to many holiness periodicals that were not Methodist. Others charged that the movement had departed from Wesleyanism.

During the mid-1880s radical elements within the Holiness Movement further alienated the denomination by urging supporters to "come out" from the "worldly," "unspiritual" Methodist church. The Church of God (Anderson IN) had been formed in 1880 and holiness bands and missions were organized in the middle West and South where the holiness teaching was particularly influential. Some holiness evangelists also enjoined upon their followers various new doctrines: a stress on external matters like dress and amusements was accompanied in some areas by teaching on sinless perfection, on works of grace subsequent to sanctification (such as third and fourth blessings), on particular evidences of inward holiness, on divine healing, or on the merits of abstinence from pork. Proponents of such special emphases captured the leadership of some local holiness associations.

In the Southern church, ATTICUS HAYGOOD, a Georgia leader, spearheaded the drive to force holiness advocates to acknowledge their relationship to the denomination or to leave the church. Haygood stressed the gradual attainment of sanctification and charged holiness advocates with a focus on "works." Theologians at Vanderbilt made similar charges of Pelagianism; denominational publications supported them. The controversy centered on the basic premises of Methodism, with each side claiming to represent Wesley.

By 1894 the General Conference of the Methodist Episcopal Church, South, issued a statement reflecting the leadership's determination to force holiness advocates either to submit to denominational authority or to separate themselves from the Church. Faced with such a decision, the majority of Methodist holiness advocates eventually chose to remain within the Church where their special emphasis, as in the Northern Church, was gradually absorbed into a broader perspective. Others separated and in the next decade formed over 20 new religious groups, joining holiness advocates with those in other denominations who had never endorsed holiness teaching. Most of these groups appeared in the rural South and the middle West where radical holiness emphases had flourished. The national association did nothing to unify the splintering holiness movement: it urged loyalty to one's original denomination.

Most new groups emerged when response to regional situations made separation advisable. Leaders of independent holiness groups sought to establish pure churches, free from the taint of worldliness and the politics of denominationalism. Among these were the FIRE-BAPTIZED HOLINESS CHURCH, the CHURCH OF THE NAZARENE, the Pilgrim Holiness Church, the Pillar of Fire, the PENTECOSTAL HOLINESS CHURCH, and the CHURCH OF GOD IN CHRIST.

After 1906 PENTECOSTALISM made significant inroads into holiness groups. Some holiness teachers were outspoken opponents of the Pentecostal emphasis, but others, especially in the South, espoused it, regarding Spirit baptism evidenced by GLOSSOLALIA as a third crisis experience following the NEW BIRTH and sanctification. They created the Holiness-Pentecostal Movement, which had its strongest support in the South in groups like the Pentecostal Holiness Church, the CHURCH OF GOD IN CHRIST, and the CHURCH OF GOD (CLEVELAND TN).

The holiness and Holiness-Pentecostal denominations represent today in institutionalized form the rich heritage created by the many 19th-century Methodists and others who sought a "second blessing" in the context of the holiness movement. These groups do not stress the sanctification-of-the-secular theme that the pre-Civil War movement incorporated. Instead, they focus on personal purity in the context of preparation for an imminent second advent.

See also articles on METHODIST CHURCH; WESLEYAN TRADITION.

Bibliography. William E. Boardman, *The Higher Christian Life*; Melvin E. Dieter, *The Holiness Revival of the Nineteenth Century*; Charles G. Finney, *Views on Sanctification*; Charles E. Jones, *Perfectionist Persuasion: The Holiness Movement and American Methodism, 1867-1936*; Phoebe Palmer, *The Way of Holiness*; John L. Peters, *Christian Perfection and American Methodism*; Timothy L. Smith, *Called Unto Holiness*; *Revivalism and Social Reform*; Vinson Synan, *The Holiness-Pentecostal Movement*.

EDITH L. BLUMHOFER
SOUTHWEST MISSOURI STATE UNIVERSITY

HOLY ROLLERS: *See* REVIVALISM.

HOMECOMINGS. The word homecoming is used in the American South to refer to a category of events including annual gatherings of former students at a school, former residents of a community, or former members of a rural church. The term is also used loosely to refer to church anniversaries, cemetery association days, or, less frequently, family reunions. All these events share certain features that influence their grouping into one class: they occur on a regular (usually annual) basis, bringing together to a sacred place of origin people who have been scattered by migration into cities and towns; they are held at rural churches, cemeteries, or camp meeting grounds; they include a communal meal often prepared by mothers of participating families; and they express a set of combined cultural themes enshrining family and religious values.

Church homecomings, church anniversaries, or "founders' days" commemorate the establishment of the church and serve to honor its founding members. The descendants of all the early members gather on this occasion to hear a sermon, and eat a meal together either outdoors "on the grounds" of the church or indoors in the fellowship hall. The gatherings of kinfolk are, in fact, a reunion of several interlinked families, each of whose ancestor was a founder of the church. The assembled kin visit the graves of founding ancestors as a means of honoring the family history; stories are told about the early days of the church and of the illustrious deeds and lives of the founding people. In some rural congregations the group assembles on the Saturday before the homecoming Sunday to clean the cemetery and to put flowers on graves of the kin. These graveyard gatherings also occur independently of the church anniversary or founding Sunday, in which case they are known as "cemetery homecoming," "cemetery association day," or "decoration day."

Homecomings may be timed to coincide with a historically significant date in the church's history, but the great majority are held in the summer months. Reports of early gatherings tie the timing to the cycles of agriculture, stating that May meetings are held "after the roads are passable" and August meetings come "after the crops are laid by." The date is cyclical, for example, the second Sunday in May or the third Sunday in August.

Historically the gatherings can be traced to cultural antecedents in North Britain, namely the outdoor communions in Scotland during the late eighteenth and early nineteenth centuries and, earlier, to Covenanting meetings and field preachings of Reformation times. On the American frontier joint services of several congregations were held when visiting ministers would be in the neighborhood, this feature being especially important to the colonial Presbyterian congregations who depended on the Synod of Philadelphia to supply them with an educated clergy. Other frontier colonial Protestants returned to their congregation of birth as an aspect of summer visiting with kinfolk and for special days celebrating the anniversary of a minister's service or the establishment of the church.

The architecture of rural Southern churches often includes a feature designed to accommodate the homecoming day and also to provide for family reunions—the permanent tables on the church grounds near the building. In some cases these tables are covered with an open-sided cover resembling the arbor of the camp meeting grounds. In many rural churches these tables are in use every Sunday during the summer by one of the large families, who hold separate reunions on Sundays other than that of the congregational homecoming.

Church homecomings, and the symbolic relationship between family and church they signify, are examples of *religious familism*. They restore community to people who have been scattered into cities by the requirements of the modern urban industrial world. In the annual reassembly for the sermon, the hymns, and the shared food, families reaffirm their loyalty to the extended kin group that they have been forced to abandon in order to meet economic needs. They reaffirm a belief in this extended kin group as the "family of faith" and the "people of God" and in the local church of their origin as a sacred place where their ancestors are enshrined. The sacredness of the church and the sacredness of the family are woven together into a web of significance through which individuals find renewal in the face of day-to-day living in isolated nuclear families in an urban, bureaucratic modern world.

See also articles on CAMP MEETINGS; CEMETERIES.

Bibliography. Gwen Kennedy Neville and John H. Westerhoff III, "Folk Liturgies in the American South," *Learning Through Liturgy*; "Community Form and Ceremonial

Life in Three Regions of Scotland," *American Ethnologist* 6 (February 1979): 93-109; "Protestant Pilgrims and Interurban Linkages," *Cities In a Larger Context, 15th Annual Proceedings of the Southern Anthropological Society*, ed. Thomas Collins.

GWEN KENNEDY NEVILLE
SOUTHWESTERN UNIVERSITY

HOSPITALS: *See* SOCIAL SERVICES.

HOT SPRINGS, ARKANSAS. This popular resort was the place where the ASSEMBLIES OF GOD, one of the largest and fastest-growing Pentecostal denominations in the United States, was organized in 1914. Six years earlier, several Wesleyan denominations in the Southeast had been drawn into PENTECOSTALISM, but for ethnic, cultural, or theological reasons many Pentecostals in the central and south-central states had refused to join. About 1910 independent Pentecostal pastors in the south-central region, dismayed by growing doctrinal and financial irregularities, started to promote the idea of a "nonsectarian" organization that would unite these unaffiliated believers. In the summer of 1913 leaders from Texas, Arkansas, Mississippi, and Alabama met at an Interstate Camp Meeting in Eureka Springs AR. Little is known of their activities, but in December *Word and Witness*, an influential newspaper published in Malvern AR, issued a call for a "General Convention of Pentecostal Saints" to meet at the Grand Opera House in nearby Hot Springs, 2-12 April 1914, in order to form a more orderly basis for fellowship.

Hot Springs was chosen for several reasons. Railroads offered off-season fares to the city from distant parts of the region. The old opera house, leased by local Pentecostals, afforded a commodious site for the convention. Most important, the pastor of the Pentecostal following in Hot Springs was Howard A. Goss who, more than anyone, had tirelessly campaigned for a union of like-minded believers. The convention attracted 320 delegates and partisans from 20 states, but Hot Springs seems hardly to have noticed: the local newspaper's only comment was the "Saints" had gathered in the city. The infant denomination did not linger. Its headquarters were soon moved to Findlay OH, then St. Louis MO, then permanently established in SPRINGFIELD MO in 1918. Given the worldwide thrust of the Assemblies of God, the move may have been more than symbolically significant. Hot Springs is nestled on the southern rim of the Ozark Mountains, Springfield on the northern rim.

See also articles on OZARKS RELIGION; WESLEYAN TRADITION.

GRANT WACKER
UNIVERSITY OF NORTH CAROLINA
AT CHAPEL HILL

HOWELL, ROBERT BOYTE CRAW-FORD (1801-1868), Baptist pastor and denominational leader, was born in Wayne County NC to parents of yeoman stock and Episcopal background. He was, however, baptized into Naughunty Baptist Church in 1821 and three weeks later was licensed to preach. His formal education was meager, culminating in two years of study at Columbian College. For years drawn toward law, he agreed to ministerial ordination in 1827 at the request of the Cumberland Street Baptist Church in Norfolk. A successful ministry there terminated in 1834 when he was called to Nashville, the scene of his most remarkable work. Twice pastor of First Church in that city (1835-1850, 1857-1867), his leadership of that congregation was distinguished. During the intervening seven years, he served at Second Baptist in Richmond.

Howell was moderator of associations, president of Tennessee Baptists, vice-president and president of the Southern Baptist Convention. He is remembered as a pioneer in Southern religious journalism and Sunday school development. He was a zealous leader in ministerial education and organized mission work, the latter in an era when antimission sentiments were strong. Active in civic duties, Howell was an officer in the Tennessee Historical Society and a member of the American Baptist Historical Society. His second Nashville pastorate was characterized by conflict with JAMES R. GRAVES and Landmarkism, which had developed in that city and congregation during his Richmond tenure. He wrote numerous articles and a half-dozen books that were instrumental in shaping 19th-century Baptist thought.

See also articles on ANTIMISSION MOVEMENT; LANDMARK MOVEMENT.

Bibliography. J. J. Burnett, *Sketches of Tennessee's Pioneer Baptist Preachers*; Linwood Tyler Horne, "A Study of the Life and Work of R. B. C. Howell," unpublished dissertation at Southern Baptist Theological Seminary, Louisville KY, 1958; Lynn E. May, Jr., *The First Baptist Church of Nashville: 1820-1970.*

WILLIAM ALLEN POE
NORTHWESTERN STATE UNIVERSITY
OF LOUISIANA

HUGUENOTS. Intensified persecution of French Protestants, which began in 1681 and culminated in the revocation of the Edict of Nantes in October 1685, prompted the emigration of about 10 percent of France's Huguenot population, which ranged from one to two million persons. The refugees dispersed throughout Protestant Europe, and the Huguenot population of the colonies, estimated at about 3,000, was largely the result of the subsequent migration of these individuals. Those who migrated to South Carolina as early as 1679, to Ireland in the 1690s, and to Virginia after 1700 came through England, and many stopped at more than one place in the empire before settling in their final destinations. Eighteenth-century wars on the Continent and an uprising in France resulted in another period of emigration, although this migration included Swiss and Palatinate Huguenots, whose parents had been refugees from France one generation earlier.

Religious policy toward the Huguenots and other continental Protestant groups took shape in the late 1600s. As early as the 1660s, Charles II sanctioned the establishment of a French-speaking Protestant congregation in the Savoy (they used Jean Durel's French translation of the Anglican liturgy). The Church of England thus made a place for the refugees within its structure and provided for the reordination of Huguenot ministers. This ultimately facilitated the conforming of the colonial Huguenot congregations to the Anglican church. Both church and state saw in the refugee Protestants a source of social and religious stability and actively encouraged Huguenots to settle in Carolina, Ireland, and Virginia.

The Huguenot settlement at Manakin near the present site of Richmond disintegrated in 1711. Members of this group migrated to the Trent River in North Carolina where they were wiped out in the Tuscarora wars of 1711-1712, and to South Carolina where they joined preexisting settlements in CHARLESTON and in four rural parishes west and north of the city. In the 1700s and 1800s, descendants of these colonists moved south and west into Georgia, Alabama, and Mississippi, following the contours of westward migration. Although once perceived as primarily an urban people, in the South they became farmers and planters.

Of all the Huguenot settlements in the American colonies, only the congregation in Charleston failed to conform to the Church of England, or to the Dutch Reformed Church in the Middle Colonies where this denomination represented the mainstream. Robert Kingdon has interpreted this pattern as evidence of the Huguenots' commitment to the concept of *adiaphora* (nonessentials). Andre LeMercier, Huguenot pastor in Boston, articulated this position most clearly in his *Church History of Geneva in Five Books* (1732); but Paul L'Escot, Francis Guichard, and Pierre Stouppe, all of whom served as pastors of the French congregation in Charleston in the 18th century, echoed this position in their sermons and correspondence or emphasized the fundamental tenets that all Protestants shared. L'Escot set the tone while pastor of the Charleston congregation in the early eighteenth century when the Church of England was established in the colony. In 1711 he wrote the SOCIETY FOR

THE PROPAGATION OF THE GOSPEL IN FOREIGN PARTS to decline their offer of Durel's translation of the Book of Common Prayer. He carefully minimized the differences in outward observances that separated his flock from the Anglicans and indicated that these differences in public worship, although conducive to social order, were distinct from the articles of faith that his parishioners shared with all sincere Protestants. It was a matter of time, he felt, until his congregation adopted the Anglican liturgy as its form of public worship and quietly joined the mainstream.

L'Escot's letter implied that the lay Huguenot population adhered firmly to its practice of CALVINISM and was able to control the direction of the congregation. The lay population in the Anglican parishes was also able to influence the content of the service through the vestry's extensive power over the rector. In the early 1700s Huguenot parishes, which used Durel's translation of the Anglican liturgy, apparently used their power to maintain religious autonomy within the nominally Anglican framework. Commissary Gideon Johnston complained of deviations among Huguenot parishes that had conformed, which included omitting the sign of the cross in baptism and failure to genuflect in the administration of the Lord's Supper. These deviations in ceremony, together with the adherence of the Charleston congregation to the original liturgy, suggest that the Huguenots' Calvinist identification persisted well beyond their conformity to mainstream Anglicanism. By the 1730s, however, contests within the French-speaking parishes concerned the language of the ceremony rather than the content of the rituals, and in 1768 the last French-speaking parish was officially closed.

Early in the life of the French Protestant congregation in Charleston, bequests from its members placed it on an independent financial basis. Ongoing support from the wider community of Huguenots and their descendants maintained its vitality although all prominent Huguenots in the 1700s were also members of the Church of England. Faced with extinction in 1828, the church was reorganized by descendants of Huguenot colonists (mainly Low Country planters), with descent from a Huguenot migrant as the basis for membership. Services were held until 1955, and the church has recently been reopened.

See also articles on ANGLICAN CHURCH; HIGH CHURCH/LOW CHURCH; SOUTH CAROLINA.

Bibliography. Arthur H. Hirsch, *The Huguenots of Colonial South Carolina*; Robert M. Kingdon, "Pourquoi les refugie huguenots aux colonies americaines sont-ils devenus episcopaliens?," *Bulletin de la societe de l'histoire du protestantisme francais* 115 (1969): 532; William Manross, *The Fulham Papers in the Lambeth Palace Library*.

AMY FRIEDLANDER
MARIETTA, GEORGIA

IMMIGRATION: *See* NATIVISM.

IMMIGRATION, CARIBBEAN: *See* CARIBBEAN IMMIGRATION.

INCARNATION. This doctrine that in Christ God took on human flesh is, with the doctrine of the ATONEMENT based on the crucifixion, one of two foci around which Christian theologians have located their interpretation of the atoning work of Jesus Christ. Since the Reformation, at least, the tendency of Roman Catholic and conservative Protestant theologians has been to center attention upon the Incarnation and to extrapolate from its indications of divine-human continuity a high doctrine of the church and its sacraments. By way of contrast, the tendency of radical Protestant and evangelical theologians has been to focus upon the crucifixion, maintaining clear distinctions between the divine and human natures in Christ, and developing low doctrines of the church and the sacraments.

Nurtured in low Anglican and radical Protestant soil, Southern religious traditions largely hung upon the cross. While rarely doubting the Incarnation, their "crucifixation" left Protestant divines ill-defended against the Jeffersonian deist challenge in the late eighteenth century. When reaction came, in the GREAT REVIVAL (Second Great Awakening), the born-again experience rarely led to deep reflection upon the nature of Jesus' birth. Throughout the 19th and 20th centuries, representative Southern evangelical theologians from JAMES H. THORNWELL to EDGAR Y. MULLINS have rarely emphasized and rarely doubted the Incarnation.

In the antebellum South, however, the Incarnation played a key role in theological debates among Presbyterians. That debate, between ROBERT L. DABNEY at Virginia's Union Seminary and JOHN ADGER at South Carolina's Columbia Seminary, largely reflected a similar debate in the North between Princeton's Charles Hodge and Mercersburg's John Williamson Nevin. Nevin had discovered in Calvin lingering elements of a Catholic sense that the Incarnation *was* the atoning event in which God and man were reconciled and made one. In the tradition of Calvinist scholasticism, Hodge and Dabney insisted on the necessity of a radical distinction between the divine and the human in Christ. Although Adger did not share Nevin's philosophical idealism, he took the Incarnation as the starting point of his theology, insisting that it inaugurated the new creation.

Among Episcopalians in the antebellum period, Charleston's JAMES WARLEY MILES did share Nevins's philosophical idealism, though he did not develop it around the doctrine of the Incarnation. That remained for his heir, WILLIAM PORCHER DuBOSE, to do. A student of the continental "mediating theologians," the Oxford movement, and the Mercersburg theologians, DuBose was the South's "incarnational theologian" *par excellence.* Evolution and the Incarnation were so related in his thinking that at the center of his theology was a universal, almost a cosmic, Christology. "The Incarnation, as we know it," DuBose wrote in his earliest and most important work, "is both a generic and a particular fact. Generically, it is the Incarnation of God in man, in humanity; and is still in process, not to be completed until Christ is glorified in His mystical body, the Church. Particularly, it was completed in the ascension of our Lord Himself, and is the incarnation of God in the man Christ Jesus."

See also articles on HIGH CHURCH/LOW CHURCH; SACRAMENTS AND ORDINANCES; THEOLOGY.

Bibliography. William Porcher DuBose, *The Soteriology of the New Testament*; E. Brooks Holifield, "Mercersburg, Princeton, and the South: The Sacramental Controversy in the Nineteenth Century," *Journal of Presbyterian History* 54 (Summer 1976): 238-57; Ralph E. Luker, "Theological Liberalism and Social Conservatism: A Southern Tradition, 1840-1920," *Church History* 50 (June 1981): 193-204.

RALPH E. LUKER
VIRGINIA POLYTECHNIC INSTITUTE
AND STATE UNIVERSITY

INDIANS, SOUTHEAST MISSIONS TO.

Although Protestant sects in the English colonies paid some attention to evangelizing native Americans, it was the Catholic Church that made the earliest, longest, and most intense effort to bring Christianity to the aboriginal inhabitants of the Southeastern United States. Catholic priests established a mission system in Spanish Florida and later in French Louisiana that rimmed the Southeastern coast from Chesapeake Bay to New Orleans and penetrated the interior of many rivers that flowed into the Atlantic Ocean and the Gulf of Mexico. That the missions ultimately failed in the Southeast resulted more from the machinations of international politics and diplomacy than a lack of religious zeal. Once Spain and France were driven out of the modern boundaries of the United States, the missions staffed by their citizens and funded by their governments ceased to exist.

From the beginning, the Spanish missions were always more important than those of the French. French religious efforts among the Southeastern Indians were confined to the 18th century and were a pale reflection of the dynamic work done by the Jesuits in Canada during the 17th century. The Spanish missionary efforts, however, began simultaneously with the first explorers of the Southeast. Juan Ponce de León, Lucas Vásquez de Ayllón, Pánfilo de Narváez, Hernando de Soto, and Tristán de Luna y Arellano all carried priests with their expeditions whose duties included conversion of the natives wherever possible. Credit for the first successful mission, however, rests with Father Sebastian Montero, a clergyman who accompanied Juan Pardo on his wanderings through the backcountry of South Carolina. Working at Guatari, Father Montero maintained a mission to the Wateree Indians from 1556 to 1572. Although this religious work did not endure and was unusual because Father Montero was a secular priest, the South Carolina mission began three centuries of Catholicism among the Southeastern tribes.

The Spanish missions grew very slowly in the 16th century. Early efforts by the Society of Jesus and the Dominicans ended in failure because of Indian hostility. It was not until the last decades of the 16th century when the Franciscans decided to cultivate the heathen fields of Florida that the missions expanded. The Franciscan commitment to Spanish Florida resulted in what some scholars have called the "Golden Age" of missions during the 17th century. At one time or another during this century, the Franciscans worked with the Apalache, Calusa, Ais, Tequesta, Timucua, and Cusabo tribes, claiming some 26,000 to 30,000 converts, and involving 70 missionaries at their peak. Yet by century's end, the mission system collapsed. Spanish Florida came under sharp attack by the new English colonies and their Indian allies in the North. Unable to resist English firepower and numbers, the missions shrank by the 18th century to only those that could be protected by the guns of Spanish forts in St. Augustine and Pensacola. These last Indian missions disappeared in 1763 when Florida was ceded to England. Although Spain regained the province in 1783 and held it until 1821 (when Florida was sold to the United States), religious efforts during the second Spanish period concentrated more on the heretical Protestant immigrants living in Spanish territory than on the few Indians who were left.

Throughout their existence, Indian missions in the Southeast followed a common Spanish pattern. Because of the religious fervor that swept Spain from the 15th to the 17th centuries, missionary work attracted an extraordinarily able element of churchmen. They were willing to die for their faith if need be. Florida received more than its share of these individuals, many of whom were martyred at the hands of American Indians displeased with the presence of outsiders. Among the noted missionaries who labored in Florida at one time or another were Antonio de Montesinos, first champion of Indian rights in the New World, Luis Cancér de Barbastro, fresh from the exciting experiments in Guatemala by the Dominicans to convert the Mayans by peaceful rather than violent means, and Francisco Pareja, a pioneer scholar within the present borders of the United States and a man who studied and published works on Southeastern Indian languages.

As was true throughout the Spanish empire, the bulk of the missionary work was done by members of religious orders.

Proselytizing techniques in Florida were typical of efforts elsewhere. Although some attempt was made to teach Spanish and Latin to the American Indian—efforts that were successful enough to impress numerous outsiders—priests generally taught and preached in the native language of their parishioners. Indeed, one of the first books about the Southeast was a Spanish catechism and dictionary in Timucuan. Missionaries focused great attention on converting Indian leaders, a pattern whose effectiveness in bringing the rest of a group into the Catholic fold had been proven during the conquest of the Moors in Spain and the Aztecs and Incas in the New World. For a time, the Jesuits operated a school in Havana for the children of Florida's Indian royalty. Whenever possible, missionaries congregated tribes into permanent settlements around a mission church, making it easier to serve the faithful and establish a sedentary life-style. Depending upon the location and circumstances, Spanish soldiers were also stationed in mission towns. The Church always recognized the value of pageantry and frequently used both Indian and European varieties for religious occasions. At almost all times, there were far more villages that wanted missionaries and missions than there were clerics available to fill the need. As a result, many priests traveled a circuit from town to town, becoming itinerant missionaries.

For the Indian tribes of the Southeast, the missions were a mixed blessing. Leaving aside the question of Christianity versus indigenous religions, the missions undoubtedly helped prepare the tribes of the Southeast for their later dealings with far more aggressive and ruthless members of Western society. With more time to adjust to the European because of the missions, it was no accident that the major Southeastern tribes survived, although exposed longest to outsiders, while native Americans elsewhere often succumbed in short order. Within the Spanish system, the missionaries frequently interceded on behalf of their charges when trouble occurred with civilian officials. In one famous case, a priest refused to testify against the murderers of five fellow missionaries because such testimony violated ecclesiastical vows to protect one's flock. To the best of their abilities, missionaries promoted a *pax Hispanica* among the converted. In the New World, at least, it made little sense for Catholics to be killing Catholics, especially since these hostilities interfered with the work of the church.

The negative aspects of the mission system cannot be ignored, however. Perhaps the most detrimental effect of this religious work was the unintentional, but deadly, introduction of European diseases. The devastating mortality rate common to native Americans in the rest of the New World when confronted with the European was repeated in the American Southeast. With little or no natural resistance to new diseases, the Indians in this area suffered epidemic after epidemic. Spanish missionaries who reported these natural disasters never realized that they themselves carried the infections from one village to another. With bitter irony, the epidemics struck mission Indians the hardest, leaving their unconverted relatives less likely to be affected.

There were other unpleasant aspects to the missions. New World Indians were required to pay a tribute tax whether they lived in Lima, Mexico City, or Guale (modern Georgia). How onerous these tribute taxes were in Spanish Florida is not clear, but they were paid. The church, moreover, expected the faithful to support their priests with food and labor. There were a few cases, at least, where this obligation resulted in Southeastern Indians being forced to labor hundreds of miles from their homes. What made food contributions and forced labor even more distressing was the Crown's expectation that mission soldiers also be supported in

the same fashion. Should individuals resist such demands or violate certain religious practices, it was not unheard of for missionaries to punish delinquents by whippings or even worse means.

Perhaps the most notorious of the disputes between European churchmen and their New World converts involved Indian culture and customs. As tolerant as most missionaries were by the European standards of the time, there were certain traditional indigenous practices that they chose not to tolerate. Some of these practices could not be incorporated within Christianity under the most liberal interpretations and thus had to be eliminated. The widespread custom of polygamy was a classic example. Other customs, such as certain festivals and traditional sporting events, merely made missionary work harder or offended priestly concepts of dignity. These too were banned. Ecclesiastical abuses combined with mistreatment at the hands of civilian authorities resulted in four serious revolts against Spanish control during the 16th and 17th centuries (1582 in Guale, 1597 the Juanillo Revolt, 1647 in Apalache, and 1656 in Timucua). In the 18th century, some of the mission tribes joined the English and became famous for the zeal with which they persecuted the Franciscans and their diminished followers.

How successful in hindsight was the Spanish mission system among the Southeastern Indians? The answer to this question depends upon many factors, most of them subjective in nature. The missions' role in the ultimate survival of certain tribes cannot be discounted. Moreover, there is no doubt that the missions produced many sincere converts who chose to live under Catholic rule no matter what the cost. When Spain ceded Florida to England in 1763, numbers of Catholic Indians moved to Mexico and Cuba rather than stay behind and live under English (Protestant) rule. By Spanish standards, however, the Southeastern missions had to be judged a failure. While elsewhere in the New World descendants of early mission Indians practice the faith introduced by courageous friars, today the extant mission edifices in Spanish Florida are important only as tourist attractions.

See also articles on COLONIAL PERIOD (in Appendix); FLORIDA; FRENCH INFLUENCE; INDIANS, TEXAS MISSIONS TO; ROMAN CATHOLIC CHURCH; SOCIETY FOR THE PROPAGATION OF THE GOSPEL; SPANISH INFLUENCE; SPANISH INFLUENCE IN LA FLORIDA.

Bibliography. Roger Baudier, *The Catholic Church in Louisiana*; Mark F. Boyd, "Spanish Mission Sites in Florida," *Florida Historical Quarterly* 17 (April 1939): 254-80; Mark F. Boyd, Hale C. Smith, and John W. Griffin, *Here They Once Stood: The Tragic End of the Apalachee Missions*; Michael J. Curley, *Church and State in the Spanish Floridas (1783-1822)*; Jean Delanglez, S.J., *The French Jesuits in Lower Louisiana (1700-1763)*; Michael V. Gannon, *The Cross in the Sand: The Early Catholic Church in Florida: 1513-1870*; "Sebastian Montero, Pioneer American Missionary, 1566-1572," *Catholic Historical Review* 51 (October 1965): 335-53; Maynard Geiger, *Biographical Dictionary of the Franciscans in Spanish Florida and Cuba (1528-1841)*; *The Franciscan Conquest of Florida (1573-1618)*; Alistair Hennessy, *The Frontier in Latin American History*; John Tate Lanning, *The Spanish Missions of Georgia*; Clifford M. Lewis, S.J. and Albert J. Loomie, S.J., *The Spanish Jesuit Mission in Virginia 1570-1572*; Robert Allen Matter, *The Spanish Missions of Florida: The Friars versus the Governors in the "Golden Age," 1606-1690*; Mary Doris Mulvey, O.P., *French Catholic Missionaries in the Present United States (1604-1791)*; Charles Edwards O'Neill, *Church and State in French Colonial Louisiana*; Lucy L. Wenhold, trans. and ed., *A 17th Century Letter of Gabriel Díaz Vara Calderón, Bishop of Cuba, Describing the Indians and Indian Missions of Florida*; Félix Zubillaga, S.I., *La Florida: La misión jesuítica (1566-1572) y la colonización española.*

JAMES A. LEWIS
WESTERN CAROLINA UNIVERSITY

INDIANS, TEXAS MISSIONS TO.

Frontier missions in the Spanish empire always had to serve two masters—the church and the state. Without the support of civilian and ecclesiastical institutions, the religious efforts of the missions could not thrive. Nowhere were the dual pillars of the mission system more evident than in the Spanish attempts to Christianize the Indian tribes of Texas during the 18th century. For reasons that were related but not identical, the viceregal government in Mexico City and the Order of Friars Minors (the Franciscans) developed an interest in the natives of Texas in the closing decades of the 17th century.

Texas became important to Spain because of the French. The Spanish claim to the northern rim of the Gulf of Mexico had been well established by the end of the 16th century, but physical settlement of this area had not occurred. Except for a stretch of Florida coastline on the eastern edge of the Gulf and a series of isolated villages far south of the mouth of the Rio Grande on the western edge, colonists had left the rest of the area alone. With no economic or diplomatic reason to establish colonies along the coast, Spanish neglect of this area was understandable. Unfortunately, the French *fleur-de-lis* shattered Castilian complacency about the Gulf when Frenchmen began to explore the lower Mississippi in the 1680s and established permanent colonies there in the following decade. The threat to Spanish America was obvious. Not only would the new French settlements split the Spanish colonies along the Gulf, but Louis XIV and future Bourbon rulers in Paris could strike at mineral-rich New Spain through one of its weakest approaches, the lightly defended northern frontier. Spanish officials believed that the French had to be pushed out of the region or at least stopped where they were. Such action meant the occupation of Texas and cooperation with authorities in Florida to squeeze the French lodged between them.

Franciscan interest in Texas existed at the same time and grew out of the rich past of that order in New Spain. The Brown Robes were the principal religious order proselytizing along Mexico's northern frontier. In theory, frontier missions lasted only 10 years and were then secularized—property and neophytes (Indian converts) being turned over to parish priests. This process would constantly free missionaries for work in new areas and move the frontier ever farther northward. Although in practice the rotation to secular clerics rarely took place within the prescribed 10 years, the Church never lost sight of that objective and the

Franciscans had pushed their missions as far as the Rio Grande River by the end of the 17th century. Texas was on the horizon.

Reinforcing the Franciscan move into Texas was the availability of an additional number of missionaries looking for a challenge at the end of the 17th century. The Franciscans had created two schools in northern Mexico designed to train priests for the rigors of frontier life. These schools—the Colegio de Misioneros de Propaganda Fide de la Santa Cruz in Querétaro (1683) and the Colegio de Misioneros de Propaganda Fide de Nuestra Señora de Guadalupe in Zacatecas (1707)—had graduates willing to work north of the Rio Grande. Although never numerous, nearly every Franciscan who labored in Texas attended one or the other of these two institutions.

The first effort of the state and the church to establish missions in Texas took place in 1690 in direct response to the ill-fated expedition of La Salle along the Gulf coast. When rumors of the French presence there reached Mexico City, the viceroy (Condé de Galve) ordered an expedition of soldiers and friars from Querétaro to erect a military post (*presidio*) and missions as close to the Mississippi as possible. In 1690 this expedition set up a handful of missions in east Texas along the Neches River staffed with priests and soldiers. These missions only functioned three years and were deserted in 1693 because of their extreme isolation from other Spanish settlements, the hostility of local Indians, and the mistaken impression that the French had given up plans to occupy the lower Mississippi.

The Franciscans and Spanish soldiers did not return to missionary work in Texas until 1716 when once again the specter of France drew them north. This time the French were firmly entrenched along the Mississippi, and there was little Spanish officials could do except to occupy as much of Texas as possible in order to erect a buffer zone between New Spain

and its unwelcomed Gallic neighbors. The east Texas missions were reestablished. The government also built two other mission-*presidio* sites, San Antonio and La Bahiá (the latter chosen to handle coastal Indians and to give Texas access to the sea). Many of these missions functioned until the end of the 18th century when the Texas missions began to be secularized. Thus for Texas the mission period belongs to the 18th century.

The Texas missions followed a traditional Franciscan pattern in working with indigenous populations. The friars strove to convince neophytes to live permanently at mission sites. Once there, life was communal in nature. Mission Indians labored in the fields and tended the large herds of livestock that grazed near the missions. In larger establishments, neophytes learned various handicraft skills needed to keep an agrarian community functioning. In return, the missions provided the converts with food, shelter, protection, religious instruction, and a rudimentary education in Spanish. The Franciscans also introduced Christian Indians to Spanish politics. Each mission elected its own Indian government according to Spanish law.

With the exception of the San Antonio missions, however, the Franciscans in Texas never enjoyed the level of success common to friars elsewhere along the northern frontier. At no time could the Texas missions claim more than a few thousand neophytes for all their sites. Indeed, in some areas missions existed with no converts at all. Scholars attribute the modest accomplishments of the Texas missions in part to conditions in the 18th century. By this time, the Franciscans seemed to have lost the vitality and dedication that characterized their religious work during the two previous centuries. Texas was a province that demanded far more than a cursory, half-hearted effort.

Critics, however, cannot lay all the blame at the feet of the friars. The nature of the Texas Indian played an important role in the comparative lack of missionary success in that area. Earlier mass conversions had always taken place among sedentary peoples whose agricultural habits transferred easily to mission life. This type of native American did not exist in Texas. The Texas Indians were generally nomadic, depending greatly upon hunting for sustenance. The friars were unwilling to roam with their flock during their periodic hunts, and the aboriginal inhabitants of Texas were equally unwilling to court starvation by remaining in a mission environment. As a consequence, little religious instruction and conversion could take place. Only tribes that needed the Franciscans and the *presidios* for protection against powerful enemies settled into mission life. This, of course, automatically placed the friars on the losing side of indigenous politics. It also identified the missions as targets for attack by Apaches and Comanches, the two most powerful tribes in Texas during the 18th century. Despite some interesting attempts, the friars never learned to live in peace with these two giants of the plains.

Although scholars might question the religious accomplishments of the missions in Texas, the labor of the Franciscans certainly bore fruit in other ways. Every mission had a complement of *presidio* soldiers to protect the friars, return runaways, and aid in instructing neophytes. In most cases, the soldiers of these presidial detachments either brought families with them or soon began them. The first cities of Texas evolved around these missions. Although the Franciscan influence on the aboriginal population was slight in the long run, Roman Catholicism never lost its hold over these early European outposts in Texas.

See also articles on FRENCH INFLUENCE; INDIANS, SOUTHEAST MISSIONS TO; ROMAN CATHOLIC CHURCH; SPANISH INFLUENCE; SPANISH INFLUENCE IN LA FLORIDA; TEXAS.

Bibliography. Gerald Ashford, *Spanish Texas: Yesterday and Today*; John Francis Bannon, *The Spanish Border-lands Frontier, 1513-1821*; Herbert Eugene Bolton, *Texas in the Middle Eighteenth Century*; Carlos E. Castañeda, *Our Catholic Heritage in Texas, 1519-1936*; Elizabeth A. H. John, *Storms Brewed in Other Men's Worlds*; Michael B. McCloskey, O.F.M., *The Formative Years of the Missionary College of Santa Cruz of Querétaro, 1683-1733*; Fray Juan Agustín Morfi, *History of Texas, 1673-1779*; Eduardo Enrique Rios, *Life of Fray Antonio Margil, O.F.M.*; David J. Weber, "Failure of a Frontier Institution: The Secular Church in the Borderlands under Independent Mexico, 1821-1846," *Western Historical Quarterly* 12 (April 1981): 125-43; Robert S. Weddle, *San Juan Bautista: Gateway to Spanish Texas*.

JAMES A. LEWIS
WESTERN CAROLINA UNIVERSITY

INFANT BAPTISM: *See* BAPTISM.

INTERDENOMINATIONAL ACTIVITY: *See* ECUMENISM (IN THE SOUTH).

INVISIBLE INSTITUTION. The religion of American slaves has been described as an "invisible institution" for two reasons. First, slaves kept much of their religious life secret from whites. Second, because slaves left few written records, it was assumed that their religion would remain as invisible to the scholar as it was to the master. Within the past decade, however, historical research into slave narratives made the "invisible institution" more visible than formerly seemed possible. Two issues dominate the discussion of slave religion: the influence of African religions and the effect of Christianity upon the attitudes of slaves.

In the United States, African religious influence was less pervasive than in Latin America. There slaves took advantage of Catholic piety to disguise the identities of African gods behind the images and festivals of Catholic saints. Furthermore, greater numbers of Africans entered Latin American slavery over a longer period of the Atlantic trade and outnumbered European colonists by much larger margins than in North America. On this continent, a relatively small number of Africans, dispersed among a large white population, were rapidly outnumbered by a steadily increasing native-born slave population. As a result, continuous and extensive contact with Africa facilitated transmission of African religions in Latin America to a greater extent than was possible in the U. S., with the exception of Louisiana, coastal Georgia, and South Carolina, where the patterns of slave distribution resembled those of the Caribbean.

African religious perspectives and customs did influence the religious life of slaves here, albeit in muted form. West African rituals of spirit possession, for example, transformed the ecstatic behavior of Protestant revivals into the ring-shout, a counterclockwise, circular, religious dance in which the slaves connected African possession performance with the experience of Christian conversion. Similarly, central African medicinal magic informed the practice of conjuration and the cosmology of the Congo determined burial customs of slaves in the U. S.

Christianity, which made little headway among slaves in the colonial period, attracted larger numbers during the evangelical revivals begun in the 1740s and 1790s. By 1800 black preachers were converting and pastoring slaves and free blacks, achieving a status otherwise denied them. Some black Baptists and Methodists even organized their own separate churches in the antebellum South, though most attended churches under white control.

In order to worship God free of white supervision, slaves risked punishment to attend illicit religious meetings in which they rejected the moralistic preaching of white apologists for slavery and stressed the connection between the Christian gospel and freedom. Applying the stories of the Bible to their own history, slaves asserted their belief that God would someday free them as He had the Israelites of old. Individual slaves, profoundly affected by the experience of conversion, affirmed their self-worth despite the dehumanizing conditions of slavery. Though slave religion did not lead necessarily to rebel-

lion, several scholars have seen in the "invisible institution" a form of symbolic protest and resistance against the "peculiar institution."

Out of the "invisible institution" emerged important traditions that would characterize black American culture long after slavery: the spirituals, the shout, the chanted sermon, and the special role of the preacher.

See also articles on Black Religion; Caribbean Immigration; Mission to Slaves; Slavery.

Bibliography. Clifton H. Johnson, ed., *God Struck Me Dead;* Eugene Genovese, *Roll, Jordan, Roll: The World the Slaves Made;* Lawrence W. Levine, *Black Culture and Black Consciousness;* Albert J. Raboteau, *Slave Religion: The "Invisible Institution" in the Antebellum South.*

ALBERT J. RABOTEAU
PRINCETON UNIVERSITY

INVITATION: *See* Altar Call (Invitation).

IVES, LEVI SILLIMAN (1797-1867), controversial High Church priest, was an Episcopal bishop of North Carolina and later a Roman Catholic convert. He was born in Meriden CT but grew up in Turin NY. Raised a Presbyterian, he was educated in the local school and at the Lowville Academy. In 1819 he became an Episcopalian and began the study of theology under Bishop John H. Hobart. He married Rebecca, the bishop's daughter, in 1822. Ordained to the priesthood in 1823, he held successive charges in Batavia NY, Philadelphia PA, New York City, and Lancaster PA. He was consecrated bishop of North Carolina in 1831.

Strongly influenced by the Oxford Movement, Ives's episcopate was one of stormy controversy. He encouraged ceremonial innovations in his diocese and founded a monastic order at Valle Crucis NC. In addition to his High Church views, his genuine concern for Negro education made him unpopular among many elements in North Carolina. By 1850 ecclesiastical pressure had forced him to dissolve his religious order and modify some of his ceremonial practices.

While traveling in Europe on a leave of absence in 1852, Ives shocked the entire Anglican world by making a dramatic submission to Pope Pius IX in Rome on Christmas Day of that year. His spouse became a convert as well. Handicapped by marriage, Ives could not seek orders in the Roman Communion. On returning to the states, he became a lay teacher and publicist in New York, but never attained real stature in his adopted church.

See also articles on EPISCOPAL CHURCH; HIGH CHURCH/LOW CHURCH.

Bibliography. H. G. Batterson, *A Sketch-book of the American Episcopate*; Levi S. Ives, *A Review of the Trials of a Mind in its Progress to Catholicism*; J. J. O'Connell, *Catholicity in the Carolinas and Georgia*.

JOSEPH D. CUSHMAN
UNIVERSITY OF THE SOUTH

JACKSON, JOSEPH HARRISON
(1900-), black Baptist denominational
administrator, was born in Rudyard MS.
Growing up in a rural community without
access to adequate educational facilities,
he taught himself how to read and write.
After working his way through high
school, his thirst for knowledge led him to
Jackson College (now State University)
where he received the A.B. degree in 1926.

He entered the Baptist ministry in
1922 and was named pastor of First Baptist Church in McComb. In 1935 he
accepted an appointment as pastor of
Bethel Baptist Church, Omaha NE. Motivated to further study, he enrolled at Col-
gate Rochester Divinity School, from
which he was graduated in 1932. To that
B.D. degree he added a M.A. from
Creighton University in 1933, which
helped him feel quite secure about his
career in Christian service.

Jackson served as pastor of the Monumental Baptist Church of Philadelphia
from 1934 to 1941. Olivet Baptist Church
in Chicago invited him to come as pastor;
he accepted in 1941 and continues to serve
in that capacity.

Distinction came to Jackson in 1953
upon his election as president of the
NATIONAL BAPTIST CONVENTION, U.S.A.,
INC., (q.v., NATIONAL BAPTISTS) the largest black organization in America with a
membership of more than six million. His
tenure as president ended in September
1982 after nearly 30 years in that office.

While serving as vice-president of the
Baptist World Alliance, he toured Russia,
delivering over 21 addresses. In 1962 he
attended the Second Vatican Council in
Rome, Italy, and had consultations with
Pope John XXIII.

Bibliography. Joseph H. Jackson, *The History of the
National Baptist Convention, U.S.A., Inc.; Many But One:
The Ecumenics of Charity; A Voyage to West Africa and
Some Reflections on Modern Missions.*

HENRY J. YOUNG
GARRETT-EVANGELICAL SEMINARY

JAMESTOWN. The Virginia Company
of London sent three ships, *Sarah Constant, Goodspeed,* and *Discovery,* in 1606
to found a colony in Virginia. The governing council of the colony consisted of Bartholomew Gosnold, Christopher
Newport, John Ratcliffe, John Smith,
Edward Wingfield, John Martin, and
George Kendall. Thirty-two miles up the
James River, on a marshy island, 104 to
108 settlers disembarked on 14 May 1607.
A small fort, rude huts, and a few dugouts

were built. An Indian attack was followed by a siege. Malaria and dysentery claimed 60 lives, but by September the Indians were sending supplies. John Smith went exploring and was captured by Indians. His two companions were killed, but according to tradition Pocahontas saved Smith.

In December, Newport who had previously departed for England, returned with 120 additional settlers. Fire destroyed the village and some colonists died from exposure. On 20 April 1608 another ship arrived with 40 more settlers; October saw another with 70 people including two women, the first in the colony. Famine struck in 1609-1610 and the remnant were actually leaving when Lord Delaware, the new governor, appeared with provisions.

The cultivation of tobacco by John Rolfe in 1612 gave new economic stimulus, but only 351 inhabitants were in the Jamestown area by 1616. In 1619, the first legislative assembly in America met in Jamestown, and a few blacks arrived from Africa. During the Great Massacre in 1622, the fortified village was a refuge. By 1640 the first brick house was built, but during Bacon's Rebellion against Governor William Berkeley in 1676 the town was burned. Although the state house was rebuilt between 1676 and 1684, a fire destroyed it in 1698, which led to the removal of the government to Williamsburg. The persistence of Jamestown's settlers made the colony a symbol of New World determination.

Bibliography. Carl Bridenbaugh, *Jamestown, 1544-1699*; Charles E. Hatch, *The First Seventeen Years At Jamestown, 1607-1624*; E. M. Riley and C. E. Hatch, *James Towne In The Words of Contemporaries.*

FREDERICK V. MILLS, SR.
LA GRANGE COLLEGE

JARRATT, DEVEREUX (1733-1801),

Anglican priest and Methodist-style evangelist, was among the most active and successful evangelical preachers in Virginia and North Carolina during the closing decades of the 18th century. Born in New Kent County VA, he was orphaned early and placed in the care of an older brother. Although he received little formal education, he was fond of study and educated himself sufficiently to become a school teacher.

As a young tutor Jarratt came under the influence of a Presbyterian minister and was "much affected." After an experience of conversion, he considered entering the ministry. His friends encouraged him to do so, but Jarratt had difficulty deciding between the Presbyterian ministry and the Anglican priesthood. In 1762 he opted for the latter, mainly because the two men he admired most, John Wesley and GEORGE WHITEFIELD, were Anglicans. His ordination, first as a deacon by the bishop of London in December 1762 and then as priest by the bishop of Chester in January 1763, took place in England.

Returning to Virginia, Jarratt became rector of Bath parish in Dinwiddie County during 1763. He held that post until he died. A preacher in the mold of the dynamic Whitefield and the fervent New Side Presbyterians, he exhorted his hearers to be saved and to observe a strict morality. Jarratt soon became a popular revivalist in many counties of Virginia and North Carolina, although numerous Anglican (later Episcopal) pulpits were closed to him. Some Anglican clergymen castigated him, labeling him "an enthusiast, fanatic, visionary. . . ." In spite of his frequent itinerating, Jarratt managed to perform faithfully the duties of his own parish. In addition to preaching he wrote and published many of his sermons, as well as a series of letters that were published as his autobiography in 1806.

See also articles on EVANGELICALISM; GREAT AWAKENING; REVIVALISM.

Bibliography. Devereux Jarratt, *The Life of the Reverend Devereux Jarratt* (1806); Harris Elwood Starr, "Devereux Jarratt," *Dictionary of American Biography*, ed. Allen Johnson and Dumas Malone.

DAVID T. MORGAN
UNIVERSITY OF MONTEVALLO

JEFFERSON, THOMAS (1743-1826),

champion of religious freedom, was born at "Shadwell" in Goochland (later Albemarle) County VA and brought up as a member of the established church of the colony, the Church of England. He was educated at lower schools and at the College of William and Mary (1760-1762) by Anglican clergymen. Of them, only his schoolmaster, the Rev. James Maury, received his favorable appraisal. He attributed to the single lay professor at the college, William Small, the fixing of the destinies of his life by giving him his first views of the expansion of science.

Among Jefferson's earliest public offices was that of vestryman of Fredericksville parish in Albemarle County (elected 1767). In 1772, after he moved to Monticello, he was elected to the vestry of St. Anne's. It was his role as a leader of the American Revolution that brought him enduring fame. In the Continental Congress in 1776, he drafted the Declaration of Independence. This he justified by the "laws of nature and of nature's God." "All men are created equal," he wrote, endowed by their creator with the inalienable rights of "life, liberty, and the pursuit of happiness."

Returning to Virginia, he devoted himself to ensuring those rights. As a member of the committee on religion in the House of Delegates, he entered into what he later called the severest contest of his life. This was over the proper relationship between government and religion. In 1777, he drafted a bill guaranteeing the complete separation of church and state. "It does me no injury for my neighbour to say there are twenty gods, or no god," he argued in *Notes on the State of Virginia*. (His book, written in 1781 and first published in 1785, includes a chapter on religion.) The Virginia Statute for Religious Freedom was finally passed in 1786, after it was introduced by JAMES MADISON. Jefferson, who was minister to France at the time, publicized the unique achievement throughout Europe.

In later years, he continued to advance the principle of separation of church and state. While president (1801-1809), he avoided any official observance of religion. The University of Virginia, which he founded in 1819, was the first institution of its kind completely free of religious tests, requirements, or teaching.

Jefferson's principles incited the hatred of many. Much of the opposition to him politically came from the New England states where established churches continued to exist into the 19th century, and where discrimination against those of different faiths remained the law. Likening him to the French revolutionaries, his detractors portrayed him as a potential Bible burner and destroyer of religious institutions. The secular university that he established seemed a threat to the prosperity of the existing church-connected colleges. It was opposed by those who believed that only through enforced religious observance could a moral society be maintained. On the other hand, Jefferson achieved great popularity among liberals in religion and among those who were the objects of discrimination—dissenting Protestants, Roman Catholics, and Jews. They admired him as an apostle of freedom.

Jefferson kept his personal religious beliefs to himself, as he considered they should be. He read widely on the subject, attempting to let reason be his guide, and he recommended the same approach to others. He came to believe that Christianity had through the centuries been corrupted by the influence of heathen mysteries and Platonic philosophy, and more recently by the doctrines of John Calvin. By critical analysis of the New Testament, he tried to get back to the pure ethics of Jesus. In his last decade, he compiled "The Life and Morals of Jesus of Nazareth" by extracting from versions of the Gospels in English, French, Latin, and Greek what he thought to be the authentic passages. He said he was a real Christian, because he followed the teachings of Christ.

Although to a Unitarian in 1822 he predicted the ultimate success of that denomination among Americans, he and his family maintained their membership in the Protestant Episcopal Church of Virginia. As a disciple of the Enlightenment, he rejected the supernatural and was sympathetic to deism, but he said he was a sect by himself. When preachers attacked him for supporting opponents of orthodox religion such as Thomas Paine or THOMAS COOPER, Jefferson was provoked into making harsh anticlerical statements in private correspondence. He was, however, always the friend of churchmen, from BISHOP JAMES MADISON to BISHOP JOHN CARROLL, and the supporter of churches. He attended the services of many different congregations. In the last year of his life, he contributed to and designed the first Episcopal church in Charlottesville. Its rector officiated at his burial at Monticello.

See also articles on CHURCH AND STATE; DISESTABLISHMENT; ESTABLISHED RELIGION.

Bibliography. Thomas Jefferson, *The Life and Morals of Jesus of Nazareth* (sometimes entitled *The Jefferson Bible*); Dumas Malone, *Jefferson and His Time*, 6 vols.; Merrill D. Peterson, *Thomas Jefferson and the New Nation: A Biography*; ed., *The Portable Thomas Jefferson.*

STEVEN H. HOCHMAN
UNIVERSITY OF VIRGINIA

JEHOVAH'S WITNESSES. A conservative and nonorthodox denomination, these people are known internationally for their use of the Old Testament name of God, tireless door-to-door evangelism, conscientious objection, and a refusal to salute the flag or to accept blood transfusions. They are found throughout the South among all social and racial communities, although they are disproportionately numerous among blacks. There is also a large Jehovah's Witness Cuban refugee community in southern Florida.

They regard themselves as the *only* true Christians. They are Arian in theology, deny the doctrine of the immortality of the soul, and believe that only 144,000 plus Christ will attain heavenly immortality. Others who are saved will live eternally on a paradisiacal earth restored to perfection during the millennium.

The Witnesses grew out of the Bible Student movement developed by Charles T. Russell (1852-1916) of Pittsburgh in the early 1870s. In 1876 Russell adopted the Adventist "biblical" chronology of Nelson H. Barbour; it has been basic to the date-setting apocalypticism of Bible Students and Jehovah's Witnesses ever since. In 1881 Russell organized the Watch Tower Society to help carry on his preaching activities. Believing that Jesus had come invisibly in 1874 and that the world would end in 1914, he established a movement throughout much of the Western world.

Russell's successor was a lawyer and former part-time Populist judge, Joseph F. Rutherford (1869-1942) of Booneville MO. Gradually Rutherford recalculated Barbour's chronology, abandoned many of Russell's teachings, and made himself the autocratic head of what he called "the Theocracy." In 1931 he gave the name Jehovah's Witnesses to his supporters. Rutherford was notorious for his vitriolic attacks on "politics, commerce and religion."

Under Nathan H. Knorr the Witnesses became an important international movement with well over 2,000,000 members who continued to expect the imminent end of the world. They now believe that Armageddon must occur before all those who were old enough to witness the beginning of World War I in 1914 die out.

Prior to World War II, the Witnesses were arrested throughout America on charges of violating local ordinances in the distribution of literature. After the U. S. Supreme Court ruled in 1940 that their school children must salute the flag, they became the objects of mob violence throughout the nation, particularly in Texas, Kentucky, Missouri, and Indiana.

To blunt such persecution the Witnesses turned to litigation and won a remarkable string of victories before American courts. In 1943 the U. S. Supreme Court even reversed itself on the flag-salute issue in *West Virginia Board of Education* v. *Barnette*. To date, no denomination has done more to establish guarantees of freedom of religion than the Witnesses.

Recently they had been noted for having marked 1975 as the *probable* date for Armageddon. Paradoxically, too, they are under severe public criticism in the United States and Canada for the maintenance of inquisitorial church courts and for the shunning of excommunicated members.

In 1981 there were 588,503 active Witnesses in the United States. Their international headquarters is in Brooklyn NY.

See also article on MILLENNIALISM.

Bibliography. *Jehovah's Witnesses in the Divine Purpose*; *1975 Yearbook of Jehovahs*; Timothy White, *A People for His Name*.

M. JAMES PENTON
UNIVERSITY OF LETHBRIDGE

JETER, JEREMIAH BELL (1802-1880), a prominent Baptist preacher and editor, was born in Bedford County VA. After undergoing a conversion experience at 19, Jeter became a missionary for the Baptist denomination in Virginia, receiving his ordination in 1824. Jeter held a number of pastorates, mostly in Richmond. From 1836 to 1849 he was pastor of the First Baptist Church in that city; then from 1852 to 1870 he served Grace Church. After resigning from his last pastorate, Jeter edited the *Religious Herald*, the Baptist newspaper in Virginia.

Jeter occupied many positions of leadership in Baptist life. He gave support to its foreign and domestic missions, was president of the Board of Trustees of the Seminary of Richmond College, manager of the Virginia Baptist Education Society, and the first president of the Virginia Baptist Historical Society. Jeter was also instrumental in the formation of the Southern Baptist Convention in 1845. In Virginia he was a leader in the original call for a separate Southern organization and served as the first president of the Foreign Mission Board of the Southern Baptist Convention. Jeter was a staunch defender of Baptist doctrine and polity. In *Campbellism Examined* (1855), he attacked the theological innovations of ALEXANDER CAMPBELL. He also opposed the LANDMARK MOVEMENT, another challenge to Baptist orthodoxy, in the 1870s.

See also article on RELIGIOUS PRESS.

Bibliography. Jeremiah B. Jeter, *The Recollections of a Long Life*.

MITCHELL SNAY
WALTHAM, MASSACHUSETTS

JEWISH CHARITABLE ORGANIZATIONS. The obligation to help the poor and needy is one of the cardinal religious duties required of the Jew. Judaism imposes a demand of being compassionate and humane towards anyone asking for help. Stimulated by this traditional sense of moral responsibility, as well as by a recognition that the welfare of needy Jews rested in the hands of fellow Jews, the charitable activities of the few Southern Jews during the 17th, 18th, and early nineteenth centuries were largely limited to the formal congregation and synagogue. These activities consisted of maintenance of a cemetery, aid to transients and a few local needy individuals, and the freeing of Jewish redemptioners and indentured servants. The first charitable institution apart from the congregation was the Hebrew Orphan Asylum of Charleston SC established in 1802.

During the German-Jewish immigration of the mid-nineteenth century, charitable organizations began operating in New York City. Known as "Aid Societies" or "Benevolent Societies," these organizations institutionalized charitable work as had never been done in the Old Country.

Using the New York organizations as models, similar societies began appearing in Jewish communities throughout the South in the 1850s, proliferating in the region during the first decade after the Civil War. While the purpose behind the creation of these societies in the South paralleled their Northern counterparts, the reasons for their appearance were somewhat different. Because Jews of diverse background living in the Northeastern cities could not unify to meet the needs of developing communal life within the formally organized congregations, it was necessary to "Americanize" charitable activities by aping Christian methods and resorting to structurally separate organizations. In the South, however, the absence of both a formal congregation and a synagogue forced Jews in cities, small towns, and rural communities to seek alternative means of fulfilling the functions of a community center, social club, welfare agency, religious school, and the like, hitherto provided by the synagogue.

Consequently, the Aid Societies, Relief Societies, and Benevolent Societies assumed almost any responsibility dictated by the communities' individual situations, and thereby became the cornerstones of most Southern Jewish communities. These societies became fund-raising organizations for purchasing and maintaining cemeteries and synagogues. They frequently were called upon to fulfill a religiously educational function by organizing, staffing, and running the Sunday and Hebrew schools; in the absence of a Harmony Club or other social organization, these societies frequently assumed the responsibility of providing a cultural atmosphere for the community by putting on dances, plays, and picnics.

The impact of these charitable and fraternal organizations on Jewish life was threefold. First, the activities of the Aid Societies reflect the important and changing role of women in the Jewish community. Due to overbearing economic requirements for survival by men in the New World, the responsibility for the welfare of the family and community more often than not fell on the shoulders of women. Second, many of these societies and fraternal organizations, because of their national connections and emphasis upon uniting and helping all Jews, over-

came the cultural and religious divisions that American and Southern Jewry were experiencing to create a shared sense of Jewishness and eliminate a sense of isolation. And finally, by providing communal needs, these societies helped to create a new outlook for cultural Judaism as opposed to a ritual-religious Judaism and thereby offered viable substitutes to formal congregational affiliation.

By the end of the century, the Jewish charitable activity had coalesced into combined efforts by the great variety of institutions that had appeared. By the end of the first decade of the 20th century, all of the major cities in the South had witnessed the appearance of Jewish Federations, Welfare Funds, or Community Councils.

Currently, there are more than 40 such federation groups raising and distributing funds to over 60 religious, educational, cultural, and service organizations on the local, national, and international levels.

See also article on JEWS IN THE SOUTH.

Bibliography. Secretary Reports, Grandlodge B'nai B'rith, District 5, 1874-present; *Secretary Reports*, Grandlodge B'nai B'rith, District 7, 1878-present; *Free Sons of Israel, National Conference Reports*, 1884, 1888.

LOUIS SCHMIER
VALDOSTA STATE COLLEGE

JEWISH FOLKLORE. Jewish folklore in the South is created out of the union of a common religio-ethnic heritage, experience on Southern soil, and a regional network of family, friends, and acquaintances. With the blending of the Jewish and Southern cultures comes a group of people with some wholly Southern traditions and folklore; some entirely Jewish traditions and folklore; and some traditions and folklore that are a combination of both, that are unique to Southern Jews. Nowhere is the resultant blending of Southern and Jewish traditions more colorfully illustrated than in the culinary hybrid, *matzo* ball gumbo, the featured recipe in a Baton Rouge Jewish cookbook. This fusion of Southern and Jewish traditions is also apparent in the group's oral traditions—anecdotes, jokes, family stories, personal-experience stories, and proverbs; in customary traditions such as holiday and life-cycle customs, and foodways; and in the Southern Jewish world view.

Until very recently, many Southern Jews attempted as much as possible to blend in with their Christian neighbors, neither flaunting nor maintaining Jewish traditions that would appear overtly foreign to other Southerners. Rather than being ethnically and culturally Jewish, they chose to be religiously Jewish, attending temple regularly in the same way that Southern Christians attend church. This basic insecurity of Southern Jews is exhibited in the large number of anecdotes and stories they tell that detail anti-Semitic incidents, and their lack of knowledge about and observance of Jewish traditions.

Southern Jews are united not only by a common religious heritage and a common experience on Southern soil, but also by a network built on close friendships, kinship ties, extensive travel, group celebrations, and use of the media. The scattered nature of Southern Jewry elicits unique events, such as the numerous annually held, weekend-long parties of the early and mid-twentieth century, where Southern Jewish boy met Southern Jewish girl. Today, this socializing is carried out at the regional conclaves and camps sponsored by Jewish organizations. The widespread character of the regional Jewish community also affects the attributes of bar and bat mitzvahs, confirmations, and weddings. For example, the large out-of-town contingent at Southern Jewish weddings, coupled with the Southern and Jewish principles of hospitality, breeds a unique combination of wedding traditions—fruit baskets in guests' rooms, programs listing the endless parties, hospitality rooms, car caravans or bus transportation to parties, and skits roasting the bride and groom.

Although the popular conception of folklore is the study of the traditions of poor, remote, and culturally conservative groups, more and more folklorists are analyzing the traditional customs of urban, middle-class people. Jewish folklorists in the United States have been particularly reticent to study any but the most culturally static Jewish groups—for example, the Hasidim, who have remained the most untouched by American society. Despite the continued emphasis in Jewish folklore on survival of Jewish folklore from the European past, the study of the second, third, fourth, and even fifth generation, upper-middle-class Jews of the South furnishes a more realistic and diverse view of the ever-changing American Jewish culture and folklore.

See also articles on JEWS IN THE SOUTH; JUDAISM.

CAROLYN LIPSON-WALKER
INDIANA UNIVERSITY

JEWISH IMMIGRATION. The coming of Jews to the South went through four ill-defined phases. The first phase, from the middle of the 17th century to the first quarter of the 19th, was characterized by the arrival of Sephardic Jews into the Southern coastal colonies. They generally concentrated in the three coastal cities in which they established congregations: Richmond, Beth Sholom; Charleston, BETH ELOHIM; and Savannah, Mickve Israel. During this period these Southern Jewish communities not only constituted the majority of the Jewish population in America, forming three of the six colonial Jewish congregations, but established many of the religious and social patterns American Jewry as a whole would follow in the years to come. Moreover, during this period and not least in the South, Jews experienced their first emancipation—religious, political, and social—in over 1,000 years.

The next phase, which lasted until the late 1870s, witnessed the arrival of mostly German Jews. It was during this period that the Southern Jewish community was beginning to experience both its numerical eclipse by its Northeastern counterparts and the emergence of a unique Southern Jewish consciousness. While the size of the Jewish population in the coastal cities remained fairly constant, Jewish immigrants individually moved along the Gulf Coast and inland, following the few railroads, rivers, and overland trails. Having established themselves in a myriad of outposts, they were followed by other Jews. Jewish communities were formed, cemeteries were purchased, social services were developed, congregations were organized, and houses of worship were built.

The arrival of the East European Jews formed the third phase of Jewish immigration into the South. During the period when this phase reached its high-water mark, the first decade of the 20th century, the number of Jews coming into the South was hardly a trickle as compared to the millions who remained in the Northeast. One factor that militated against great Jewish immigration into the South was that gentile Southerners were pictured as American pogromists, regardless of the fact that Jews had fought in the ranks of the Confederate armies and held a number of positions of leadership across the region. The South, therefore, did not appear to offer either economic opportunities or physical security—the lack of which had caused the immigrants to flee their ancestral homes initially.

Those Jews who did arrive in the South during these periods, however, found the Gentiles to be receptive to their presence. In many cases Jews came with some fear of rejection and had to overcome their own suspicions of gentile motives. Although they could recall centuries of civil oppression, physical isolation, and religious persecution, in the South Jews pioneered, lived, loved, built, fought, played, and sustained themselves alongside their gentile neighbors. They became political, civic, social, economic, and religious leaders.

Just the same, Jews had to pay a price for entrance into Southern gentile society. Unwilling to accept Jewish cultural separatism, mainline Southerners exerted a pressure upon the Jews to forgo their old ways and adopt Southern life-styles. Generally willing to overlook external disparity, Jews found themselves in the midst of the process of acculturation that always requires a modification of religious life. Accepting the offer of gentile Southern society "to belong," many Jews redefined Judaism in such a way that it depreciated ritual performance and emphasized ethical commitment and charitable activity.

Today, swelled by the fourth wave of immigration, American-born Northerners have discovered the South's climate and economic opportunities. Jews in the South now number about 785,000 or some four percent of the regional population. Most are living in 145 different communities that have more than 100 members worshiping in approximately 200 temples and synagogues, although a sprinkling of Jews are scattered in smaller aggregations throughout the region.

See also article on JEWS IN THE SOUTH.

Bibliography. Myron Berman, *Jews of Richmond*; Stephen Hertzberg, *Strangers in the Gate City: The Jews of Atlanta*; Bertram Korn, *Early Jews of New Orleans*; Louis Schmier, *Reflections of Southern Jewry: The Letters of Charles Wessolowsky, 1878-1879.*

LOUIS SCHMIER
VALDOSTA STATE COLLEGE

JEWISH PRESS. In 1981 the Jewish press in the South consisted of 12 weekly publications, eight biweeklies, and six monthlies with a subscription of approximately 195,000 readers. The oldest of these current periodicals is the *Jewish Herald-Voice* of Houston TX, first published in 1908. Of the remaining newspapers five were begun in the 1920s, two in the 1930s, three in the 1940s, and all but one of the rest in the 1970s.

These publications are the product of a handful of Jewish publications that appeared in Baltimore, Richmond, St. Louis, Atlanta, Mobile, Louisville, Charleston, and New Orleans beginning in the 1850s. Practically all of them were weeklies and monthlies printed variously in German, in German and English, or in English. All of them went through stages of increasing and declining circulation, through rise and fall of status, on their way to ultimate extinction as they struggled to present a point of view and to meet the needs of their ever-changing subscribers.

This activity can be traced back to 1856 in Baltimore when David Einhorn, one of the leaders of the radical branch of the American Jewish Reform Movement, started *Sinai*, a monthly that he edited as an organ to counter the call for moderate reform advocated by Isaac Mayer Wise in his Cincinnati-based weekly *Israelite*. Einhorn's vigorous absolutism forced his departure to Philadelphia in 1861 and his voice ceased to be heard in the South.

During the first 15 years after the Civil War the *Israelite* was the newspaper generally read by Jews in the South. It had a threefold advantage over other Northern-based and local periodicals. First, it was a weekly "family journal" of politics, religion, and literature that contained material of interest to Southern Jews. Second, as a weekly it was more desirable than competing monthlies. Third, it printed a German language supplement, *Deborah*.

In fact, the German-Jewish immigration to the South in the middle of the 19th century gave a pronounced German quality to Southern Jewry. Because German remained the language of many congregations well into the 1870s, Jewish periodicals such as *Sinai* and the St. Louis-based *Die Wahrheit* were published in German. Along with the *Israelite*, other publications issued German supplements to their English edition.

It was not until 1878 that Edward B. M. Browne, rabbi of the Hebrew Benevolent Congregation in Atlanta, attempted to challenge the *Israelite's* influence with an English-language regional newspaper he called the *Jewish South*. The appearances of the *Jewish South* represented a change from the generation of immigrants who tended to think of themselves as part of a larger German-speaking Jewish colony in the United States, to a generation that identified with native America, to a generation that aspired to regional identification.

The *Jewish South* was modeled after the *Israelite*. It quite heavily covered local news on a regional level; it contained a page dealing with national news of Jewish interest as well as a similar page covering overseas events. It carried serialized fiction, feature articles, and extensive editorial comments. Besides such general topics as education, religion, and charity, Browne addressed the newspaper to the problem of identity. He saw his newspaper as an instrument of unity that would promote a sense of common interest among the scattered Jews throughout the South. To this end, he wanted the newspaper to promote a sense of Jewish brotherhood by emphasizing the activities of such fraternal lodges as B'nai B'rith. He aimed for the newspaper to serve as a clearinghouse for news about the activities of Jews and Jewish communities in the South. To cement this sense of regional identity, Browne wanted his newspaper to be a Southern-based and Southern-oriented publication free of influences from New York, Cincinnati, and Philadelphia. At the same time, the *Jewish South* was envisioned as an educational instrument to increase the basic religious knowledge of its readers and to promote increased religious activity within each community, particularly in the Sunday schools. And finally, the newspaper was designed to instruct Gentiles in Jewish ways and thereby eliminate ignorance, hatred, and bigotry.

With the passing of the *Jewish South* in 1882, the one and only real attempt to create a regional Jewish newspaper that would replace the sense of isolation with an information network fostering a sense of unity and mutual aid came to an end. In the decades that followed, Jewish publications abandoned any idea of becoming regional organs and concentrated on local news, becoming increasingly parochial.

Nevertheless, each Jewish publication still adhered to a single goal; namely, promoting a Jewish identity in religious and moral terms while fostering an American identity in social and political terms.

In the 20th century, many of the Jewish newspapers have stood in the forefront on such issues as civil rights, Klan activity, unionism, and anti-Semitism. With the establishment of the Jewish Telegraphic Agency in 1918, as well as the Associated Press and United Press International, many of the local Southern Jewish newspapers were able to obtain extralocal news and address themselves to a range of concerns like the condition of Israel, the establishment of an equitable peace in the Middle East, the plight of Soviet Jewry, and general problems of society.

See also articles on GOLDEN, HARRY; JEWS IN THE SOUTH.

Bibliography. *Jewish South* (Atlanta), 1878-1882; *Southern Israelite* (Atlanta), 1926-present; *Jewish Voice* (St. Louis), 1888-1920; *Sinai* (Baltimore), 1856-1863.

LOUIS SCHMIER
VALDOSTA STATE COLLEGE

JEWS IN THE SOUTH. Nearly everything one concludes from a study of Southern Jewry has its opposite that is equally true. Irony and paradox are constant streams that run throughout any discussion of this people on the fringe of a society immersed in its natural setting, its political and military defeats, its racial ties and convulsions. Nearly everywhere and in nearly everything some Jew has played a part. But it has been a marginal role, even if momentarily as a trailblazer along some frontier of an expanding nation, or as a catalyst of social change in a new era. Indeed, the very deepest paradox may be that of being catalyst and outsider simultaneously.

Jews in America were free of the old ways, free to be like other Americans, though in the South being an American meant becoming a Southerner. Yet the Jew remained forever alien, a foreigner, a non-Christian passing for white, but different from other whites. Conditioned by history to fear the people among whom they lived, the Jews quickly and continuously sensed this difference, and often kept their distance. Their role was largely as intermediaries between white and black, town and country. As shopkeepers and peddlers, they were carriers of news and ideas and fashion, connected as they were by commerce and family to the far reaches of the region and the nation, and beyond. As they confronted this new world, they faced three choices: hold fast to traditions brought from Europe, accommodate through acculturation, or assimilate by complete rejection of their ancestral ways. But whichever choice was made, they absorbed the attitudes of their neighbors and became Southerners—or left.

Jews had come to the New World with Columbus in 1492 (legend and archaeological evidence have led to claims of far earlier arrival), but did not settle in the present territory of the United States until some time later. When exactly is unknown, but individuals positively identified as Jews were present by at least the mid-seventeenth century. (Marranos, or crypto-Jews, may have resided even earlier in Spanish areas.)

Charles II of England rewarded those nobles who had aided his successful attempt at restoring the monarchy after Cromwell's death by granting them all the area between Virginia and Florida. This vast territory—Carolina divided in two in 1729 and Georgia formed three years later—while never governed by John Locke's proposed "Fundamental Constitution for the Government of Carolina," was colonized under its influence and included religious tolerance. Huguenots, Quakers, German dissidents, Roman Catholics, and even Jews were welcomed in an attempt to populate the region. (Catholics would later be prohibited from settling in Georgia under the charter granted Oglethorpe in 1732.) But poor conditions in much of this area led most Jews to settle in the Low Country stretching from Savannah to Georgetown SC. Here ports, rivers, and plantations created a favorable economic climate in the early decades of the 18th century. The few sparse Jewish settlements in North Carolina were soon retarded by anti-Jewish provisions: "that no person who shall deny the being of God or the truth of the Protestant religion, or the divine authority of either the Old or New Testament, or who shall hold religious principles incompatible with the freedom and safety of the state, shall be capable of holding any office or place of trust or profit in the civil department within this state." This restriction was overlooked only once, in 1808, to allow Jacob Henry to sit in the state legislature (having promised to work for the state's welfare, bound as he was by the moral "Law of the Prophets"), and not removed until 1868 when the constitutional convention (which included 13 black delegates) struck down a number of similarly debilitating articles.

Neither was the French territory of Louisiana a stranger to anti-Jewish sentiment, having as part of its 1724 governing charter (the "Code Noir") a provision disallowing all non-Catholic religious worship, and specifically forbidding Jewish settlement. Nevertheless, records indicate that before the territory's purchase by the United States in 1803, Jews were already settled in New Orleans—on a permanent basis by 1758, with the governor's knowledge and in spite of complaints by the Christian populace. It is probable that Jews were living in Natchez, Biloxi, and Mobile, and perhaps in other places in trading areas, particularly along the frontiers where trade with Indians necessitated Spanish language skills, a tongue long familiar to American Jews, many of whom were of Spanish descent. These Jewish communities cannot be said to have flourished, however, until after 1850.

But CHARLESTON (1695) and SAVANNAH (1732) were early centers of Jewish life from which smaller communi-

ties developed in the hinterland and along the coast. (Some Jews went a good deal further west, among them Abraham Mordecai, the first European to settle near what became Montgomery AL, who married an Indian woman in the belief that the American Indians were descendants of the 10 lost tribes of Israel.) Christians objected to Jewish settlers in Savannah, but the presence of a Jewish doctor in the malaria-infested colony won acceptance for the group. Greater tolerance had been shown 100 miles to the north in Charleston and by 1741 Joseph Tobias was able to delete any reference to Christian belief in his oath of citizenship. The first attempt to establish a Savannah Jewish community lasted but a few years, with the majority migrating mostly to Charleston. Adding others from the Caribbean, Charleston Jews boasted a sizable community when it formally incorporated itself as Kahal Kodesh BETH ELOHIM in 1749. By 1800, it was the largest Jewish community in the United States.

Not until 1786, when Jefferson's "Statute of Virginia for Religious Freedom" was passed, were Jews given equal political and religious rights. With some disabilities existing since the colony's founding in 1607, together with the economic and sociopolitical control held by the larger planters, few Jews had much incentive for settling in Virginia. As a staunch opponent of religious intolerance, Jefferson saw his "Statute" as one of his most significant accomplishments. He admitted on one occasion: "the regret that I have ever felt at seeing a sect, the parent and basis of all those of Christendom, singled out by all of them for a persecution and oppression which prove they have profited nothing from the benevolent doctrines of Him whom they profess to make the model of their principles and practice."

America was something new, a breath of fresh air after centuries of oppression and apprehension. Here Jewish immigrants could establish shops in the cities, or carve out territories for themselves as peddlers, often earning enough money to go back to the city to open a shop. Most prospered moderately and became a significant part of the small middle class of the antebellum South. The destitute few were usually supported by the community. Even fewer became wealthy, often as brokers of a wide assortment of commodities, including slaves.

Like their Christian neighbors, Jews supported the ideas of states' rights and nullification of slavery and secession. Rallying to the cause of the Confederacy, they shared in its determination to perpetuate a way of life to which they sought attachment—they could have done little else if they wished to be accepted. Repeating the sentiments of Jews throughout the South just prior to the Civil War, the Hebrew Congregation of Shreveport resolved that "although we might be called Southern rebels, still we solemnly pledge ourselves to stand by, protect, and honor the flag, with its stars and stripes, the Union and the Constitution of the Southern Confederacy with our lives, liberty, and all that is dear to us."

But the very freedom that attracted so many was found by some to be detrimental to the future of their children as Jews. As early as 1791 a Jewish mother living in Virginia wrote to her parents in Germany that in so uncultured an atmosphere, with so few Jewish institutional or personal contacts, it had become nearly impossible to raise her children as Jews. "Here they cannot become anything else [but assimilated]. Jewishness is pushed aside. . . . My children cannot learn anything [Jewish] here." The tension between the immigrant generation and a new world was already being felt.

Compounding this problem were the conflicts carried by the immigrants themselves from Europe. The Sephardim (Jews of Spanish or Portuguese descent, living mostly in the Mediterranean area, Western Europe, and the New World) and Ashkenazim (those of German descent basically, living mostly in Central and Eastern Europe) brought with them a centuries-old division. The experiences of the two groups had been vastly dissimilar and had created a rift between them when circumstances brought them into close contact in Europe. The Ashkenazim, more strictly observant, looked upon their Sephardic coreligionists as overly lax in their ritual observances. The openness and opportunity of America gave further impetus to this move away from the traditions. As each successive group of Ashkenazim arrived, they found an increasingly more acculturated Jewish community, even among the already present Ashkenazim.

Strife was so visible between the 41 Jews in Savannah in 1731 that an Anglican missionary, sent to convert these Jews, noted that there were "two sorts of Jews, Portuguese and Germans. The first having professed Christianity in Portugal or the Brazils are more lax in their ways, and dispense with a great many of their Jewish rites . . . their education in these Countries where they were obliged to appear Christians makes them less rigid and stiff in their way. . . . The German Jews, who are thought the better sort of them, are a great deal more strict in their way and rigid observers of the law."

Three years later, a second clergyman spoke of an even more aggravated situation between the two groups, one not unlike what was experienced in Amsterdam a century earlier, or in Venice a century before that:

> Some Jews in Savannah complained . . . that the Spanish and Portuguese Jews persecute the German Jews in a way no Christian would persecute another Christian.

Though this division was keenly felt, the Sephardic rite was early adopted and maintained by many of these same communities, even when a majority were Ashkenazim (as in Savannah, Charleston, and Richmond). It was a way of attracting the financial support of Sephardic communities in Europe and the Caribbean. More important, it offered a greater atmosphere of decorum than did the more atomistic Ashkenazic pattern of communal worship—something more familiar to their Christian neighbors, and thus more to the liking of those many Jews now seeking acceptance in a new home. Slowly, the impact of America, a land far from the wellsprings of Orthodoxy with its institutions and factotums, converted a sincere attempt at maintaining a traditional Jewish life into a new, Americanized, liberalized Judaism, adhering less and less to ritual and to the ways of daily life known by previous generations.

In these first decades of the Republic, there were no ordained rabbis in America, at least none known to have possessed official credentials. However, those who led these early congregations had some training in Hebrew texts, ritual, and Jewish lore, and often had a higher degree of secular learning, at least enough to qualify them as more knowledgeable than most of their congregants. It was they who set the stage for the Americanized rabbinate, individuals conversant in the ways of two worlds and able to win the respect of Jew and Christian alike.

As early as 1824, 47 members of Charleston's Beth Elohim, a traditional Sephardic congregation, petitioned the "Adjunta" (Trustees) for certain relatively minor changes—a shorter prayer service, conducted in English rather than in Spanish and Hebrew, and a sermon or "English discourse" at each service. No real theological questions were being raised, as they were in Germany; and though perhaps aware of the debates raging across the ocean and of the several reforms occurring there, they took heart from the struggles going on within the city's Congregational church on the part of a group seeking to "rationalize" their religious lives. They did so, and reestablished it as a Unitarian congregation.

When the "Adjunta" refused the requests to loosen the ritual, a dozen dissidents broke away in 1825 to form the Reformed Society of Israelites. Once independent, they felt free to express their deep desire for more radical changes. After all, they were living in a society more pluralistic than their ancestors had ever experienced, and felt justified in their belief that difference and change were legitimate within the Jewish world as well. They used a new prayerbook (compiled by their leader, journalist, playwright, and educator Isaac Harby), called their synagogue a "Temple," and worshiped an old God in a new way, bareheaded and without prayer shawls.

The society survived but a few years before disbanding. A number of its members rejoined Beth Elohim, and when a fire completely destroyed its building in 1838, the question of reform (already under discussion in several other congregations, among them Savannah) was again raised. Paradoxically, religious freedom had destroyed the security enjoyed by the tradition in times of hardship. The devastation of fire rekindled the reformers' desires. An organ was sought to enhance the worship service, and when the "Adjunta" voted against it, they were overturned by a majority vote of the congregation. The introduction of the first synagogue organ in America occasioned a second split in Beth Elohim; but now the traditionalists left, and established their own congregation, Shearith Israel.

Economic differences forced a brief reuniting of the two groups after the Civil War. Their separation was inevitable, however, for by now Beth Elohim had moved further away from the tradition—eliminating second days of holidays, establishing confirmation classes for boys and girls, and rearranging seating with the introduction of family pews, where for centuries men and women had worshiped from segregated areas of the synagogue. So impressed with these changes was Isaac Mayer Wise, organizer of Reform Judaism in America, that he had turned down their offer of a pulpit reluctantly, dissuaded only by fear of yellow fever. In this native reform, largely uninfluenced by the more theologically based movements in Europe, lay the single greatest contribution of Southern Jewry to the religious history of America.

The first German Jews had come to the South early in its colonization. A great wave of immigration was to come in the wake of Napoleon's defeat and later, following the failure of the revolutions of 1848. In both cases repression, denial of economic and professional opportunity, restricted property ownership, and even the prohibition against marriage were left behind in favor of the promise of freedom and opportunity in America.

These German immigrants added much to the growing reform within American Judaism, North and South. While some joined older congregations, others established their own, often retaining cultural ties to their ancestral home both linguistic and ritualistic. The evangelical tenor of Southern society required Jews to establish these religious communities and to build at least some modest structure as an outward sign of their commitment to God. Yet even after the construction of their synagogues, few attended Sabbath services with any regularity. They preferred to celebrate the Sabbath at home, albeit with a nonkosher meal. Sunday schools, however, were nearly always filled, for little else could be done in a small town on Sunday. It was this overt act of going to one's religious house that was often most important; it provided a sense of being integrated into the Southern American scene.

As the 19th century drew to a close, the German congregations adopted more changes in ritual, liturgy, and basic lifestyles. One factor in this development may have been the desire to distinguish themselves from traditional-minded Eastern European Jews whose presence they felt had engendered the growing anti-Semitism they were now experiencing.

The Reform rabbis, often looked up to by Christians as Old Testament prophets, were usually to be found in the forefront of this urge toward acculturation, which sometimes approached assimilation. These developments were dangerous. At the same time, reform has been a major factor in Americanizing Judaism and in making a place within the Jewish community for the many who sought to be more like their Protestant neighbors and yet remain Jews.

This condition has changed slowly since World War I, as Eastern European and German Jews have gradually come together in the synagogue and the family, and as the move toward expressed ethnicity in America has grown. As the new masses of Eastern European Jews moved South in small but significant numbers, older members of local Jewish communities that had resisted reform by establishing more traditional congregations, found these newly arrived coreligionists too Orthodox. This moved them ideologically closer to what became the Conservative movement in America, a position midway between the two. With the passage of the next four decades, the practice of congregants of both groups, Orthodox and Conservative, showed greater resemblance. Those communities having a rabbi tended more often to look to him as a pious model to be revered, though not always followed. But in most cases, the traditional congregations were without adequate leadership. As the desire to be like everyone else grew, and as the arduous task of feeding a family demanded a six-day work week, the fathers, and particularly the second generation, took their families in new directions.

The tightening of immigration laws in the mid-1920s cut off the flow of those additional Eastern European Jews who might have stemmed this movement away from the tradition. The need for an enlarged Jewish population was made more urgent now by a fear of a growing wave of anti-Semitism that tended to isolate Southern Jewry from the larger Jewish community until after World War II. Under these pressures and limitations, Eastern European and German Jews began to create a more cohesive community. Children from the two groups married one another, and this was to have a lasting effect upon Reform Judaism. Reform German temples had begun to lose a sizeable portion of their membership through intermarriage, as had the Sephardim before them. On the other hand, Eastern European Jews seeking to Americanize their Jewish lives found marriage to Reform Germans an acceptable idea. Though pleased with a now-increasing temple membership, they were not totally happy with the unchanging, classical Reform ritual still being practiced throughout the South. Their presence changed the way of life of the remaining German Jews in the coming decades and made them more aware of their own heritage.

The Holocaust and the birth of the state of Israel gave special impetus to this process of growing ethnicity, manifesting itself through the reintroduction of traditionalism into the synagogues and homes of most American Jews. Awareness of this tie to the people of Israel, the Jews as a nation scattered but united, was a new phenomenon in the South, particularly among the Reform Jews and others who wanted to escape the cant of dual loyalty.

Zionism, in the sense of a hoped-for return to the Holy Land by all the people of Israel, is as old as the Diaspora itself, dating to the sixth century B.C.E. Political Zionism, the notion of establishing a Jewish state (as a modern political entity), dates to the late nineteenth century C.E., gaining its first popular expression in the movement defined by Theodore Herzl. It was an attempt to normalize Jewish life by removing the Jews from among the peoples who despised them, and creating a state within which the nation of Israel could dwell in peaceful self-determination.

Reform Judaism, particularly in America, adopted a far different notion of normalization—namely, that Jews were by birth rightful and equal members of the larger nation within which they dwelled, and separated from their neighbors only in matters of religious belief, which many saw as merely a differing expression of faith in the same God. The opposition of Zionism by Reform Jewish leadership crystallized in 1890, when Isaac Mayer Wise, in the name of his Central Conference of American Rabbis (Reform), spoke out against it in unequivocal terms.

Little changed over the next several decades, but as the East European immigrants and their children began to fill the ranks of Reform Jewry's clergy and laity, the pendulum began its slow swing in the opposite direction. The reports of atrocities in Europe in the mid-1940s helped speed this change as many became fearful that it could happen in the United States as well. Reform Jews soon began to join their more traditional coreligionists who had until this time constituted most of whatever small Southern contingent the Zionist movement had during its first half century.

The establishment of the state of Israel in 1948 made much of this opposition moot; even its gentile neighbors applauded the prowess and courage of the tiny state. Only a few members of the American Council for Judaism (an anti-Zionist group having Reform roots) retained their membership as most Reform Jews ended their opposition to the notion of a Jewish homeland. Orthodox and Conservative congregations had, of course, celebrated the new state, having long supported the efforts made to establish a permanent Jewish homeland. Today, little opposition remains among post-Holocaust Jewry, since ties between the two Jewish communities are continuously strengthened through pilgrimage, tourism, cultural links, and financial support.

The struggle to overcome the fear of being seen as a people apart, with loyalty to a country other than the United States, has been a difficult one for American Jewry. Behind it stand two millennia of anti-Semitism, many of its roots lying in Christian beliefs and in the unending attempts to convert Jews to Christianity. Disabilities in several of the Southern states have been noted, but it is especially telling to recall that as late as 1844, the governor of South Carolina (a state with a long history of tolerance) proclaimed Thanksgiving to be a Christian holiday during which thanks was to be given in Christ's name. When 100 prominent Jews in the state objected, he responded by stating how fortunate they were to be in South Carolina, and further, that the United States as a Christian country had chosen to their benefit to tolerate the presence of Jews within its borders.

This sense of being outsiders continued to grow as the Civil War saw the return of the accusation that Jews sought only financial gain from the struggle, and did not participate in the fighting itself. In fact, some 10,000 Jews served the Confederate cause, many as army and navy officers—enough so that General Lee thought it too disruptive to grant Jewish soldiers furloughs so they could observe Rosh Hashanah and Yom Kippur. Anti-Semitic accusations worsened as the war turned in favor of the North. Judah Benjamin's service as secretary of war and secretary of state only aggravated the situation. Of course, it made little difference that similar charges were being made in the North—evidently, the Jews served as a *national* scapegoat.

During the Union occupation of New Orleans, the city's newspapers, in an apparent attempt to curry favor with the occupying forces, singled out the Jews as self-interested and the most incorrigible element in the city. One editor went so far as to insist that "the Jews in New Orleans and all the South ought to be exterminated. They run the blockade and are always to be found at the bottom of every new villainy."

General Grant took this and other (erroneous) charges seriously, particularly when the elimination of potential Jewish trading competition could better

the profits of his non-Jewish commercial associates. With the infamous Order No. 11 of 17 December 1862, Grant expelled all Jews from the Department of Tennessee (which included Kentucky and Mississippi), even forbidding the southern movement of Jewish Union veterans into this area. This, the most blatant, official, governmental anti-Semitic incident in U.S. history, was revoked by President Lincoln upon the first appeal made by a Jew, Cesar Kaskel of Kentucky.

But Grant's order was long remembered in Tennessee, a state that had known anti-Semitism before the war. When he campaigned for the presidency in 1868, a mass meeting of Memphis Jews pledged to employ "every honorable means" to defeat him, "a man unfit for the high position to which he aspires, and incapable of administering the laws to all classes with impartiality and without prejudice." In an unconnected but not unrelated incident that year, the KU KLUX KLAN, founded in Tennessee three years earlier, dragged a Jewish shopkeeper into the streets and shot him as he fled the rope they had prepared for him.

These and similar incidents throughout the South marked an early stage of a phenomenon that was intensified by Reconstruction's scramble for power and economic advancement, and that remained just beneath the surface during the century that followed, to be used by the Klan and others as a means of exercising some control over Southern Jews.

Jews had at first been looked upon as an immigrant source of labor during Reconstruction, needed to replenish the work force depleted by the freeing of slaves. Samuel Weil, a German-born Jew from Atlanta, was named Georgia's commissioner of immigration in 1869, and sent to Europe to find this hoped-for labor force. Though most came as peddlers and dispersed throughout the state, their value to the area was recognized. The Atlanta *Daily Herald* in 1875 noted with pride the obvious prosperity the city was enjoying, pointing to the contribution of the Jews, "Who came with the intention of living with you, and specially as they buy property and build among you, because they are thrifty people who never fail to build up a town they settle in; and again because they make good citizens, pay their obligations promptly, never refuse to pay their taxes and are law-abiding."

But the collapse of the plantation system had transferred the regional center of commerce and political power to the towns and cities. The Jews as businessmen, professionals, mill operators, commodity brokers, and farm owners (usually absentee) slowly gained in influence throughout the South. Reconstruction, the depression of the 1890s, and the general state of economic competition, was too often won by Jews who owned both the tenant farm and the general store, making their offers of tenancy more attractive than those of their gentile competitors. They offered the only real financial alternative to a majority of the region's people through a no-credit, cash-only sale policy, which was attractive by contrast with a farm-supply system of credit backed by a mortgage too easily forfeited when crops failed or prices fell. The Jews' prosperity only served to fan the flames of bigotry.

The FRANK, LEO, CASE in 1915 was the culmination of a long history of anti-Semitic incidents, including castration and tar and feathering. Falsely accused of his female employee's murder and convicted as a result of this rising tide of anti-Semitism, he was lynched—removed from jail and hanged by an angry mob. Theological language found its way into the furor surrounding Leo Frank when Populist demagogue Tom Watson, adding a hint of blood libel to his condemnation of the accused, harangued that "Our Little Girl—ours by the Eternal God—has been pursued to a hideous death and bloody grave by this filthy perverted Jew."

The quarter of a century that ended with the lynching of Frank, the period of growing Populism in the South, had seen anti-Semitism reach serious proportions. Jews had held political office in numerous states during this time, but by 1915 most were gone from political life, or would be by 1920, when the Klan and other virulent anti-Semitic groups and individuals would make of the Jew a social and economic pariah. This image lasted through World War II, only to reemerge during the more heated years of the CIVIL RIGHTS MOVEMENT.

These years proved to be a perplexing time for Jews in the South. On the one hand, many supported the principle of equal rights for religious-ethical reasons. Yet they feared endangering their own positions, even if the hope of racial equality offered the possibility of removing whatever disabilities remained for themselves as well. Faced with this dilemma, some capitulated and remained silent, while others left the more offensive states (particularly Alabama and Arkansas, which lost half of their Jewish population between 1848 and 1980), or the region entirely. A small number, however, soon joined the struggle in Atlanta, Durham, and Jackson, aided by hundreds of Jews who came South as individuals, as members of civil rights groups, or as representatives of national Jewish organizations. As these few brought the reality of personal threats and synagogue bombings to all the Jews of the region, the once largely quiescent communities became more vocal. Some condemned the movement out of fear for their own safety, but many more slowly took an active role in the struggle, seeing it as their moral responsibility and as a means of strengthening their own position (a lesson they had brought from Europe, where in the late eighteenth and nineteenth centuries Jews had advantageously supported liberal and revolutionary movements). The one great exception to this pattern was Miami where, being so large a community, Jews felt secure enough to take a positive stand on civil rights and other issues, without fear of the Klan or White Citizens Councils.

Southern Jews have been few in numbers wherever they resided and, while never fully accepted as a group, have often been perceived on a personal level as much less of a threat than blacks. For most of the Southern Jews who remained, this level of tolerance became an acceptable part of the process through which they hoped to become Americans. Through nearly all of their history, they attempted to maintain the lowest possible profile. For whatever success they achieved in this process they paid dearly, sacrificing much of their tradition and its moral teachings, all for the illusion of security. In many respects, a differing religious expression was all that distinguished the majority of Jews from non-Jews in the pre-World War II South. With most Southern Jewish communities isolated from one another and from the mainstream of American Jewry, the forces at work upon their gentile neighbors tended to play a far greater role in their lives than did the events and ideas affecting their coreligionists in other parts of the country. Modern modes of communication and transportation, World War II and the Holocaust, a changing American society with its growing emphasis upon ethnicity, and the postwar influx of more tradition-minded Northern Jews into the South have permanently altered the lifestyle and aspirations of Southern Jewry. Though some continue to deny their ethnic identity, still fearing a separation from their fellow Southerners, some offsetting factors are present also. A growing sense of Jewishness, developing communal institutions, the deepening concern over intermarriage, and increasing Zionist affiliation and support for Israel are today creating an increasingly stronger Jewish identity and a deepening religious expression, with movement closer and closer to the mainstream traditions that have evolved over the past three millennia.

See also articles on JEWISH IMMIGRATION; JUDAISM; NATIVISM.

Bibliography. Leonard Dinnerstein, *The Leo Frank Case*; Dinnerstein and Mary Dale Palsson, eds., *Jews in the South*; Mark Elovitz, *A Century of Jewish Life in Dixie: the Birmingham Experience*; Barnett Elzas, *The Jews of South Carolina*; Herbert T. Ezekiel and Gaston Lichtenstein, *The History of the Jews of Richmond*; Harry Golden, *A Little Girl is Dead*, *Our Southern Landsman*; Nathan Kaganoff and Melvin Urofsky, eds., *"Turn to the South": Essays on Southern Jewry*; Bertram W. Korn, *American Jewry and the Civil War*, *The Early Jews in New Orleans*; Abraham D. Lavendar, "Shalom with a Southern Accent," *A Coat of Many Colors: Jewish Subcommunities in the United States*, ed. Abraham D. Lavendar; Jacob R. Marcus, *Early American Jews: The Jews of Pennsylvania and the South*; *Memoirs of American Jews*; Charles Reznikoff and Uriah Engleman, *The Jews of Charleston*; Arnold Shankman, "A Temple is Bombed—Atlanta, 1958," *American Jewish Archives* 23 (1971): 125-53; Malcolm Stern, "New Light on the Jewish Settlement of Savannah," *American Jewish Historical Quarterly* 52 (1962-1963): 169-99.

RALPH MELNICK
COLLEGE OF CHARLESTON

JOHNSON, CARRIE PARKS

JOHNSON, CARRIE PARKS (1866-1929), prominent Methodist leader and civil rights worker, was born in Georgia, the daughter of a Methodist minister. She graduated from LaGrange College in 1883, hoping to become a Methodist missionary to China. Her health, however, was too frail to permit such travel. Five years later she married Luke Johnson, a Methodist preacher.

A woman of conviction and ability, she held a variety of posts in the North Georgia Conference of the Woman's Home Missionary Society of her church. Soon she was named secretary to the board of trustees of Scarritt College in Nashville. In her church work she met and joined forces with BELLE BENNETT. These two women led the nine-year successful struggle for laity rights for women in the Methodist Episcopal Church, South. In 1919, a year after the laity rights battle was won, Mrs. Johnson was chosen as a delegate to the first Southern Methodist General Conference open to women.

In 1920 the Women's Missionary Council selected her to head a standing committee to study the race question. Later that year, at the suggestion of WILL ALEXANDER of the COMMISSION ON INTERRACIAL COOPERATION (CIC), she met with black women at Tuskegee to find ways to ease racial tensions. This was followed by a meeting at which black leaders addressed white churchwomen at Memphis. These gatherings persuaded the CIC to admit women as members, and Carrie Johnson was named director of women's work in November 1920.

In her new position she organized CIC women's groups throughout the South. These groups concerned themselves with Negro education, the treatment of Afro-American prisoners, and black health-care needs. Moreover, they forthrightly denounced the practice of lynching. Mrs. Johnson also persuaded scores of Southern women's religious groups to condemn as slander the belief that lynchings were needed to protect the virtue of white women. Mrs. Johnson never openly challenged the concept of segregation, but she insisted that if blacks were to be kept separate, they must truly be treated equally. She is remembered as a crusader for laity rights and as one of the first Southern white women to seek better race relations in Dixie.

ARNOLD SHANKMAN

JOHNSON, CHARLES OSCAR (1886-1965), Baptist preacher and world figure, was born in Anderson City TN. Educated at Carson-Newman College (A.B., 1910) and Southern Baptist Theological Seminary (Th.M., 1920), he was ordained to the ministry in 1909. He was pastor of the following Baptist churches: Newport Beach CA (1910-1911), South Park in Los Angeles CA (1911-1915), Campbellsburg KY (1915-1920), First Baptist Church, Tacoma WA (1920-1931), and Third Baptist Church, St. Louis MO (1931-1958). He was active in national and international Baptist affairs, serving as president of the Northern Baptist Convention (1932-1933), first vice-president of the Southern Baptist Convention (1947-1948), president of the Baptist World Alliance (1947-1950), and trustee of various Baptist institutions, Shurtleff College, Hannibal-LaGrange College, and Missouri Baptist Hospital. Known in St. Louis as "Mr. Baptist" and a community

leader, he served on the St. Louis Board of Education (1946-1952) and was a leader in opposing legalized gambling. Wit, anecdotes, and folksiness characterized his preaching. From the years 1953-1958 came five published volumes containing 186 selected sermons.

G. HUGH WAMBLE
MIDWESTERN BAPTIST SEMINARY

JOHNSON, LYNDON BAINES (1908-1973), thirty-sixth president of the United States, was born in Gillespie County, near Stonewall TX, a descendant of families whose members were prominent in the state's religious and political circles. He was the great-grandson of George Washington Baines, Sr., a Baptist preacher, religious writer and editor, and educator who was president of Baylor University during the Civil War. Johnson's mother, Rebekah Baines Johnson, grew up in this religious milieu and she trained her son well in matters of religion.

Johnson's numerous public references to the Bible, his sometimes ministerial tone in his public speeches, and his sense of righteous indignation at the injustices in society were to a great extent the later manifestations of a pious mother's influence. The Baptist faith of Johnson's mother was not greatly dissimilar to that of the DISCIPLES OF CHRIST, and at about the age of 10—after a summer revival— he joined the First Christian Church of Johnson City. He retained his membership in that denomination for the remainder of his life, even though his wife and daughters were Episcopalians. He attended church quite regularly throughout his life; while in Washington, he most often worshiped at the National City Christian Church, or at St. Mark's or St. John's Episcopal Church.

The greatest influence upon Johnson's political interests and beliefs was exerted by his father, Samuel Ealy Johnson. A member of the Texas state legislature for 12 years who associated with many of the leading state political figures of his time, Johnson's father was as oriented toward politics as his mother was toward religion, and he deliberately included his young son in his political world.

As Johnson matured and then entered a life of public service, his religious values and political decisions inevitably were intertwined. Johnson had a lifelong concern for the brotherhood of all people, and this concern manifested itself in his program of civil rights for blacks. When he was a congressman from Texas's 10th district, he often assured his black supporters that when the time was right and when he had the power, he would advance the status of black Americans. Many believed that Johnson was simply appeasing his black friends and that he was not sincere when he made such statements. In actual fact, in his later years as senator, vice-president, and president, Johnson took a positive stand for black rights and played a significant role in the passage of the Civil Rights Act of 1964 and the Voting Rights Act of 1965. Johnson's entire Great Society program was premised upon his religious conviction that the less fortunate had the right to share in the larger promise of American life. In over 100 pieces of legislation, including medical care for the poor, aid to education, urban assistance programs, antipoverty efforts, a broad housing program, income maintenance for farmers, child nutrition and protection, extended social security coverage, narcotics rehabilitation, and job training for the hardcore unemployed, the Great Society reflected Johnson's Christian concern for people.

Johnson's religious principles were a factor behind his decisions to escalate the war in Viet Nam in order not to surrender American honor on foreign soil, and to halt the spread of world Communism. He was convinced that the United States was the protector of democratic and Christian doctrines throughout the world, and that a retreat from Viet Nam would have been a retreat not only for the nation but also for Christianity itself. Ironically, Johnson's stand on principle resulted in a deepening involvement in Viet Nam at a time when the American people were becoming disenchanted with their nation's presence there. To some extent, Johnson's clinging to religious principles contributed to his demise in the public opinion polls, which in turn helped determine his decision not to seek a second full term as president. For a politician who was known always to operate within the framework of the possible, it is surprising that in the case of Viet Nam, President Johnson allowed principle to determine his stand, and to lead to his fall from political power.

See also articles on CIVIL RIGHTS MOVEMENT; ETHICS, CHRISTIAN; SOCIAL GOSPEL.

Bibliography. Monroe Billington, "Johnson and Blacks," *Journal of Negro History* 62 (January 1977): 26-42; Lyndon B. Johnson Papers, Johnson Library, Austin TX; Rebekah Baines Johnson, *A Family Album*; Alfred Steinberg, *Sam Johnson's Boy.*

MONROE BILLINGTON
NEW MEXICO STATE UNIVERSITY

JOHNSON, WILLIAM BULLEIN

(1782-1862), major figure in the founding of the Southern Baptist Convention, was born on John's Island SC. In 1806 he was ordained and made pastor of the Eutaw Baptist Church.

Later, during the years he was pastor of the First Baptist Church in Savannah (1811-1815), he was active in the founding of the American Baptist Missionary Society, the first national organization among Baptists in the United States; much later (1841) he served a term as its president. In South Carolina he played many founding and leadership roles among Baptists; for example, he served as principal of the Greenville Female Academy and simultaneously founded the First Baptist Church of that city and became its pastor. Further, he also played a major role in the founding of Furman Academy and Theological Institution.

In the 1840s it became inevitable that separation between Northern and Southern Baptists would occur. In 1845 Johnson was a dominant figure in the founding of the SOUTHERN BAPTIST CONVENTION. Significantly, he urged a more centralized ecclesiology than had characterized the TRIENNIAL BAPTIST CONVENTION with its loose societal method. He was elected first president of what has become the largest Protestant denomination in the United States.

One of his unique contributions to religion in the South had to do with female education. Not only did he serve as principal of the Greenville Female Academy and the Edgefield Female Academy, he also led in founding the Johnson Female University. Though without formal education himself, Johnson made a lasting contribution to religious education in the South. His two lifelong concerns were missions and education.

Bibliography. Robert A. Baker, *The Southern Baptist Convention and Its People: 1607-1972*; R. N. Daniel, *Furman University; Encyclopedia of Southern Baptists* 1: 709.

GEORGE SHRIVER
GEORGIA SOUTHERN COLLEGE

JONES, BOB, FAMILY Fundamentalist leaders Robert R. "Bob" Jones, Sr. (1883-1968), Robert R. "Bob" Jones, Jr. (1911-), and Robert R. "Bob" Jones III (1939-), are known for their role in promoting fundamentalist Christianity through preaching, literature, radio broadcasts, films, the arts, and the outreach of Bob Jones University.

Bob Jones, Sr., son of a Confederate soldier, was born on a farm in Skipperville AL. A child of the Reconstructionist period in the South, he became one of the great evangelists of his day, frequently being compared to Billy Sunday. Converted at the age of 11 in a country Methodist church, he received his license to preach at the age of 15. His higher education was limited to two years (1900-1902) at Southern University (later renamed Birmingham-Southern) then at Greensboro AL. Thereafter he preached "old-time" religion in union campaigns in every state of the United States and in 30 foreign countries. It has been claimed that by the age of 42 he had won a million converts to Christianity. He preached an ultraconservative theology and militantly

attacked selected social practices such as dancing, card playing, desecration of the Sabbath, attendance at prizefights, cockfights, and the circus; also starvation wages, the sale and drinking of alcoholic beverages, and "false teaching," meaning theological liberalism, including the Darwinian theory of evolution.

Bob, Sr. founded Bob Jones College at St. Andrews Bay near Panama City FL in 1926. It was moved to Cleveland TN in 1933 and then in 1947, as a university, to Greenville SC. A nondenominational institution, it enrolls some 6,000 students on a 200-acre campus. It has avoided application for accreditation because its leaders wish to have its administrative policies controlled only by "born-again" believers. For many years the school was racially segregated but now "has adopted a non-discriminatory admissions policy, made mandatory by recent court rulings."

Bob Jones, Jr. was graduated from Bob Jones College in 1930 and received the M.A. degree two years later from the University of Pittsburgh. An evangelist and lecturer on Shakespeare, he served as acting president of the college from 1932 to 1947, then as president until 1971 when he became chancellor. He is famous for establishing an internationally known religious art gallery on campus.

Bob Jones III has been president of Bob Jones University since 1971. Prior to that time he was assistant dean of men (1960-1961), professor of speech (1961-1962), assistant to the president (1962-1963), and vice-president (1963-1971).

The Jones family has taken a firm separatist religious posture, criticizing BILLY GRAHAM (who attended Bob Jones College for one semester) for cooperating with nonfundamentalists in his religious crusades, permitting his converts to attend churches of their choice rather than fundamentalist churches, and for his approval of the Revised Standard Version of the Bible. The leaders of Bob Jones University also withdrew their support from the neoevangelical movement,

Youth for Christ, the National Association of evangelicals, and other religious organizations, convinced that by affiliating with such groups they were compromising their religious convictions. The Jones family preferred to work through independent churches and ministers. Their most enduring monument appears to be Bob Jones University, "The world's largest Fundamental Christian School."

See also articles on EVOLUTION CONTROVERSY; FUNDAMENTALISM; MODERNIST CONTROVERSY.

Bibliography. Robert Campbell, O.P., *Spectrum of Protestant Beliefs*; George W. Dollar, *A History of Fundamentalism in America*; R. K. Johnson, *Builder of Bridges*.

C. ALLYN RUSSELL
BOSTON UNIVERSITY

JONES, CHARLES COLCOCK, SR.

(1804-1863), the personification of the Christian slaveholder, was born into the slaveholding oligarchy of Liberty County GA. Educated in the richly textured piety of the MIDWAY CHURCH and the seminaries at Andover and Princeton, he writhed in the moral torments of the slave system. He tried to resolve this inner conflict by forming a Christian church among the slaves of his native county as a model for the entire South. Although sometime professor of church history at Presbyterian Columbia Theological Seminary and secretary of the Board of Domestic Missions of the Presbyterian denomination (Old School), he was most famous as founder of and chief publicist for the Association for the Religious Instruction of the Negro in Liberty County, Georgia.

Jones wrote various catechisms for slaves, *The Religious Instruction of the Negroes in the United States*, and scores of other pieces urging Southerners to form associations similar to his own. With a few other clergymen and wealthy planters he was successful in enlisting a broad network of black religious leaders into an impressive system of religious instruction. Although his moral idealism became a sentimental vindication of the plantation South, he failed in his original

goal—to transform slaves into a self-disciplined and "civilized people" capable of commending themselves to "enlightened" masters as being fit for freedom. He lost his youthful idealism to the realities of his own plantations, representing in his own life the moral sensibility of slaveholders at their best, and the limitations of those sensibilities in coming to terms with the injuries imposed upon black people by the slave system. Although once realizing that the system inflicted those injuries, he could not resolve his moral dilemma because he was so firmly wedded to the necessity of blacks' being subject to whites until they had, in effect, become like their masters.

See also articles on ETHICS, CHRISTIAN; SLAVERY.

Bibliography. Charles Colcock Jones, *The Religious Instruction of Negroes in the United States*; Donald G. Mathews, "Charles Colcock Jones and the Southern Evangelical Crusade to Form a Biracial Community," *Journal of Southern History* 40 (August 1975): 299; Robert Manson Myers, ed., *The Children of Pride*.

DONALD G. MATHEWS
UNIVERSITY OF NORTH CAROLINA
AT CHAPEL HILL

JONES, JOHN WILLIAM (1836-1909),

Confederate religious leader, was born in Louisa County VA. He was educated at the University of Virginia and at the Southern Baptist Theological Seminary.

When Virginia seceded, Jones enlisted in the Thirteenth Virginia Regiment. In 1862 he was commissioned a chaplain; in 1863 he became missionary chaplain of A. P. Hill's corps. He participated avidly in army revivalism.

After the war, Jones pastored churches in Virginia, held important denominational offices, and was chaplain of the University of Virginia and the University of North Carolina.

Jones worked tirelessly to preserve the Confederate experience for posterity. He served as secretary-treasurer of the Southern Historical Society and edited 14 volumes of its papers. For many years he was chaplain-general of the United Confederate Veterans. During his Lexington VA pastorate he came to know Robert E. Lee. Friendship and admiration led him to write *Personal Reminiscences, Anecdotes, and Letters of General Robert E. Lee* (1874), and *Life and Letters of Robert Edward Lee* (1906). Other publications included *Army of Northern Virginia Memorial Volume* (1880); *Christ in the Camp* (1887); *The Davis Memorial Volume* (1889); and *School History of the United States* (1895). Through his lectures, writings, and association with prominent ex-Confederates, he became one of the best-known men in the South. Perhaps more than any other man, Jones fostered the myth of the LOST CAUSE.

See also article on CIVIL WAR.

Bibliography. Charles Reagan Wilson, *Baptized in Blood: The Religion of the Lost Cause, 1865-1920.*

DANIEL LEE CLOYD
AUBURN UNIVERSITY

JONES, SAMUEL PORTER (1847-1906), popular urban revivalist, was born in Chambers County AL. Too young to fight in the Civil War, he studied law briefly with his father and entered practice in 1868. But addiction to alcohol soon ruined his health and career prospects. Jones swore at his father's deathbed to forsake liquor; he accepted Christianity shortly thereafter and preached his first sermon within a week. Between 1872 and 1890 he served as an itinerant minister in the North Georgia Conference of the Methodist Episcopal Church, South. He soon became known as a speaker of uncommon ability and after 1880 assumed the additional task of raising funds for the Methodist Orphan Home in Decatur GA.

Sam Jones's reputation as a vigorous preacher soon led to wider opportunities. In 1885 after an immensely successful revival in Nashville TN, he was acknowledged as a leader in large-scale evangelistic work, earning the title "the Moody of the South." For the next 15 years Jones exerted a national influence, preaching in almost every large city and speaking on the Chautauqua lecture cir-

cuit. Critics censured his slang and folksy humor in the pulpit, but thousands appreciated his eccentric combination of popular entertainment and persuasive zeal.

Jones was convinced that reform was more important than conversion, and he wanted to change moral conduct rather than provide individuals with the comforts of "heart religion." He held that deeds were the test of conversion, that Sinai was more important than Calvary, especially where morality could strike a blow for decency in church and community against such evils as liquor and gambling. Enthusiastic response to his simple dualism of right and wrong made Jones one of the foremost evangelists of his generation. After 1900 he confined his activities to the South, but he remained as energetic as ever.

See also article on REVIVALISM.

HENRY WARNER BOWDEN
RUTGERS UNIVERSITY

JORDAN, CLARENCE (1912-1969), radical Christian leader, was the founder and guiding influence of the KOINONIA FARM. A native of Talbotton GA, he received an undergraduate degree in agriculture from the University of Georgia in 1933 and entered Southern Baptist Theological Seminary in Louisville later that year. During his seminary years, Jordan met and married Florence Kroeger, who shared with him a commitment to personal discipleship by strict adherence to the teachings of the Bible. While doing doctoral work in New Testament and working in an inner-city ministry in Louisville, Jordan began to formulate plans for a Christian communal experiment in the rural South.

In the autumn of 1942, the Jordans and another family purchased a piece of land in Sumter County GA and started the Koinonia Farm. The name for their venture is the Greek word for "communion," which symbolizes their intention to create a New Testament-model community. Jordan's personality was the dominant force in the experiment from the beginning, and his wisdom—agricultural as well as theological—provided the guidelines for the common life. His single-minded commitment to literal New Testament discipleship, including the principle of shared possessions, is reminiscent of the theology of ANABAPTISM.

Although Koinonia Farm was intended by Jordan as a spiritual and agricultural resource for the surrounding citizenry, his advocacy of pacifism and racial equality evoked strong reactions from his white neighbors, culminating in a period of terror and economic boycott in the late 1950s. Jordan gained a hearing, though, in Georgia and beyond through his personal magnetism as a preacher and lecturer. A raconteur in the best Southern tradition, he also communicated his approach to Christianity through his "Cotton Patch" paraphrases of portions of the New Testament, in which he transposed Scripture into the Southern idiom.

As the racial crisis subsided, Jordan participated in the establishment of a new course for Koinonia. Shortly before his death in 1969, Koinonia Partners was formed. This nonprofit organization, which provides low-cost housing for the rural poor, is a continuation of the legacy of Clarence Jordan.

See also articles on ETHICS, CHRISTIAN; UTOPIAN COMMUNITIES.

Bibliography. Joyce Hollyday, "The Legacy of Clarence Jordan," Sojourners 8 (December 1979): 10-19; Clarence Jordan, The Cotton Patch Version of Luke and Acts (and other volumes of CPV on other portions of the New Testament).

JOHN W. KUYKENDALL
AUBURN UNIVERSITY

JUDAISM. Judaism is the religion of the Jewish people. Its roots go back in antiquity to Abraham, Isaac, and Jacob of the Bible. But its ideas and practices have developed and changed throughout the centuries.

Judaism begins with the Exodus-Sinai saga, when a band of Hebrew slaves left Egypt. Their trek brought them to Mt. Sinai, where they received the Torah (God's commandments) and agreed to "hear it and do it" (Deut. 5:24). Judaism has been the religion of this group of people, through both lineal descent and conversion, from that time to this day, with all of the variations in practice and belief that they have manifested in the many lands in which they have dwelled.

The Judaism of modern America is markedly different from the Judaism of the Old Testament. The Hebrew Scriptures detail worship in a Temple in Jerusalem; historic Judaism has worshiped in synagogues found in every Jewish community. They describe a sacrificial mode of worship; historic Judaism has worshiped with words of prayer. They describe the function of a priesthood; historic Judaism has been guided by learned rabbis who have taught and interpreted the teachings of its tradition. Throughout all of the centuries of development, this historic people has been the unifying factor.

Judaism assumes God. The Bible opens with the words, "In the beginning . . ." and this assumption permeates Jewish thought. Numerous times God declares to his people, "I will be your God and you will be my people." (Lev. 26:2; Jer. 11:4; 30:22). The Jewish God is, and his people stand in special relationship to him. This idea is best epitomized in the Sh'ma, found in Deut. 6:4: "Hear, O Israel, the Lord is our God, the Lord is one," a statement repeated morning and evening in Jewish worship, which perhaps best expresses both basic Jewish premises, that God is the God of the Jewish people, and that he is unique.

But one must go beyond this starting point to understand Judaism and its manifestations in contemporary society, the end product of much history. It includes beliefs, holidays, ritual observances, worship, folkways, ethical concepts, and traditions, all of which intertwine to produce the religion of this people, of which no part may be separated out as being paramount.

To a notable degree, Jewish beliefs flow from Jewish religious thought, much of which is postbiblical and called *Aggadah*—the Telling. They tend to describe and not define concepts, since being part of the people, and not simply accepting specific doctrines, brings a person into Judaism. As a result, there is a great deal of freedom to interpret Jewish ideas in ever new and relevant ways to meet a given situation. One can observe the origins of this freedom by reading the Old Testament, the Bible of the Jewish people, where ideas and beliefs are not consistent. They develop and change to meet the contingencies of each new situation in which the people find themselves. Within this wide panoply of theological ideas runs the assumption that the one, universal God of all humanity is concerned for love, mercy, justice; that he is compassionate and caring; the creator of the universe and its ruler; and that he formed humanity in his spiritual likeness, endowing it with his attributes of godliness. Jewish thought in both rabbinic and philosophical literature delves into every possible aspect of God and his relationship with humanity and his world. This approach provides the individual Jew with a wide choice of responses with which to confront the questions of theology, but not with dogmatic answers. As a result, there is a wide latitude of Jewish belief and theological conformity is not a concern.

Far more significant than what the individual Jew believes is the way in which he behaves, how he sanctifies his daily existence. There are ethical principles, holidays, home ceremonies, life-cycle events, and a liturgy that is not only a part of the synagogue rituals, but a part also of one's daily routine at home, work, and leisure. All of these activities are a product of postbiblical Judaism, which expanded upon the biblical injunction, "Ye shall be holy, for I the Lord am holy" (Lev. 19:2), and developed an intricate pattern of *Halachah* (often translated *Law* but more accurately meaning the *Way*—the way in which a Jew should behave in any given situation in order to foster the sense of holiness enjoined upon him). The *Halachah* goes far beyond what are usually considered religious activities, prayer, belief, or holidays. It includes civil and criminal law, regulations dealing with marital relationships (including marriage, divorce, and sexual relations), directions for the rituals of the Temple in Jerusalem (if it should ever be rebuilt), what sort of activity can and cannot be done on the Sabbath, ethical precepts, injunctions dealing with every facet of human behavior. It is a broad and extensive body of literature, attempting to spell out in ever-increasing detail the path to personal piety in life.

Jews celebrate five "major" holidays during the year, "major" not because their message is of greater importance than that of other holidays, but because they are mentioned at least twice in the Pentateuch (Lev. 23:4 ff., Num. 28:16 ff.). These holidays are subdivided into two categories, the High Holidays and the Pilgrim Festivals.

The High Holidays occur in the fall. They are Rosh Hashanah (the New Year) and Yom Kippur (the Day of Atonement), celebrated on the first and second of Tishri and on the 10th of Tishri, respectively. Their themes are similar, both addressing repentance, introspection, forgiveness, and penitence. They are days of worship and prayer and there are special liturgies for the observance of both holidays.

There are three Pilgrim Festivals (Exod. 23:14 ff., Deut. 16:1 ff.). The first is Passover, the holiday marking the redemption of the Jewish people from slavery in Egypt. It is observed by a special meal known as a Seder, in which the saga of the exodus from slavery to freedom is retold with special festivities, with song and prayer, as well as special foods. Shavuot occurs 50 days after Passover, marking the giving of the Decalogue at Mt. Sinai. Sukkot starts five days after Yom

Kippur and is the fall harvest festival, during which Jews erect temporary booths, covered with fall fruits and foliage. The citron and a palm frond with branches of willow and myrtle are also symbols of this celebration. It is an eight-day holiday of thanksgiving and concludes with Simchat Torah, the day on which Jews finish reading from Deuteronomy in the synagogue and immediately start over again reading the account of creation in Genesis. Simchat Torah is a time of joyful praise of God for His gift of the Torah. There are numerous "minor" holidays also, most notably Hanukkah and Purim.

The other important Jewish celebration is a weekly one, the Sabbath, which begins on Friday at sundown and concludes at sundown Saturday. It is traditionally a day of rest in the fullest sense, marked by the cessation of labor for worship and family togetherness. Modern American culture has made inroads into many of the traditional patterns of observance, but many Jews still try to maintain this weekly holiday with attendance at worship.

The Hebrew Scriptures disclose that Jewish worship took place in a Temple, primarily the one in Jerusalem, and that its mode was sacrificial. However, by the time of the New Testament, the synagogue, whose origins are shrouded in mystery, was well established (Mt. 12:9; Lk. 4:16; Acts 13:14; et al.), and Jewish worship occurred also in this people-centered institution that was found wherever there was a Jewish community. The synagogue was so well accepted that when the Temple in Jerusalem was destroyed by the Romans in the year 70 C.E. (A.D.), this democratic house of worship was able to absorb the shock and Judaism survived the trauma. Since that time, Jews have worshiped in synagogues wherever they have lived, dominantly with words, in such forms as prayers, hymns, Bible readings, and sermons.

The synagogue liturgy was originally patterned after the prayers recited in the Temple during the sacrificial offerings (Mishna Tamid 5:1). Over the centuries this liturgy became much more extensive with the addition of new prayers and religious poetry called *piyyutim*. As a result, Judaism developed a set order of worship in a prayerbook called a *Siddur*. This service contains two major sections: the *Sh'ma*, with blessings dealing with God's role in creation, his giving of Torah, and the blessings that follow from observing his teachings, as well as the declaration of God's unity as stated in Deut. 6:4; and the *Amidah*, regularly containing benedictions dealing with God's mastery over life, his holiness, thanksgiving, a prayer for peace, and a hope that one's prayers be acceptable. During the week the *Amidah* contains 13 intermediary blessings—for knowledge, understanding, health, the restoration of the Jewish people to Zion with the coming of the Messiah, among others. On the Sabbath these 13 blessings are removed and a blessing for the gift of the Sabbath replaces them. In addition to the regular weekly and Sabbath worship, the worship for holidays has relevant inserts into the liturgy. The most extensive of these occurs on Yom Kippur, a full day of worship in the synagogue, and a 24-hour fast.

Study is another important aspect of Judaism. It is closely related to worship and there are numerous discussions in rabbinic literature questioning whether the reading of a passage at the time for prayer is to be considered study or prayer. The importance of study is also reflected in the liturgy, as we indicated above with the blessings in the *Amidah* on the theme of knowledge and understanding. It is also seen in the statement by Hillel that the ignorant person cannot be pious because he does not know what is involved (Avot 2:5). Yet another illustration of the place of study is found in the use of the Yiddish word *Shule* (school) as a synonym for synagogue describing one of the three basic functions of this Jewish worship institution.

A salient part of modern Judaism has become political Zionism, the Jewish nationalist movement of the past hundred years to establish a Jewish state in Palestine. The religious hope for the return of the Jewish people to Zion with the coming of the Messiah was regularly repeated after meals, in worship, and on a variety of other occasions by the observant Jew. With the rise of political nationalism in Eastern Europe in the latter half of the 19th century, this hope took on political overtones. Theodor Herzl's book, *The Jewish State*, published in 1896 was the catalyst for the organization of this movement. The following year Herzl successfully called and chaired the First Zionist Congress in Basel, Switzerland. From this small start, the political Zionist movement took root with the eventual establishment of the State of Israel occurring in 1948.

Israel plays a significant role in Jewish life today. It is a Jewish state whose achievements and accomplishments touch Jews the world over. They feel an involvement in its people and their achievements. Its economic stresses and precarious position in world politics are a constant source of concern. It is the recipient of a great deal of Jewish philanthropy and emotional attention. Jews tend to relate to it in a very personal way, especially after the horrors of the Holocaust and the loss of six million Jewish lives during that dark period in modern history. It is simply impossible to understand modern Judaism without a knowledge and appreciation of the prominent place of Israel in the Jewish consciousness, a place that cuts across all partisan lines.

American Judaism is divided into three major religious "sects": Orthodox, Conservative, and Reform. The divisions are primarily based upon the way in which each group looks at the totality of Jewish tradition. Orthodoxy views all of Jewish revelation (Torah in the broadest sense) as being given by God at Mt. Sinai and therefore incumbent upon the responsi-

ble Jew to observe. The Reform Jew sees the same body of tradition as reflecting both God and humanity in various historic circumstances and therefore subject to changing interpretations over the centuries. The Conservative movement follows Reform's openness to change and Orthodoxy's concern for the maintenance of traditional ritual and observance. In addition, the small Reconstructionist movement views Judaism as a "religious civilization" and assumes a sociological orientation to Jewish tradition.

Over and above these groups or schools in modern Judaism are the many "secular" organizations that have no official connection with the synagogue but function within and as a part of the Jewish community and attract a great deal of Jewish time, energy, and concern. Among the more prominent of these groups are B'nai B'rith (a Jewish fraternal order), Hadassah (the women's Zionist organization), the American Jewish Congress, and the American Jewish Committee (agencies devoted to interreligious understanding and Jewish defense against anti-Semitism). These and many more serve a variety of worthy purposes both within the American Jewish community and abroad, as well as in conjunction with many non-Jewish organizations.

Judaism is the religion of the Jewish people. It is multifaceted in its manifestations and far more broad in the aspects of life it incorporates than the common English use of the word "religion" implies, going well beyond the elements of faith or belief, or of synagogue worship and participation. It enters almost every aspect of the life of the individual Jew.

See also article on JEWS IN THE SOUTH.

Bibliography. Leo Baeck, *This People Israel*; Bernard J. Bamberger, *The Story of Judaism*; Hayim H. Donin, *To Be a Jew*; Solomon B. Freehof, *The Responsa Literature*; Evelyn Garfiel, *The Service of the Heart*; Theodor H. Gaster, *Festivals of the Jewish Year*; Arthur Hertzberg, ed., *The Zionist Idea*; George Horowitz, *The Spirit of Jewish Law*; Max Kadushin, *The Rabbinic Mind*; Abraham Millgram, *Jewish Worship*; Ellis Rivkin, *The Uniqueness of Jewish History*, Yearbook of the Central

Conference of American Rabbis; Hayyim Schauss, *The Jewish Festivals*; Milton Steinberg, *Basic Judaism*.

WILLIAM J. LEFFLER II
LEXINGTON, KENTUCKY

JUDAISM IN THE SOUTH: *See* JEWS IN THE SOUTH.

JUNALUSKA: *See* LAKE JUNALUSKA.

JURISDICTION. A geographical division of the United Methodist Church, each consists of the local congregations within about a dozen Annual Conferences in about as many states.

A system of six jurisdictions was originally developed in the 1930s as part of the plan for uniting the Methodist Episcopal Church, the Methodist Protestant Church, and the Methodist Episcopal Church, South. Further, it was a way of preserving regionalism within a national church and a means of incorporating black ministers and black congregations into a predominantly white church without compelling integration at the local level.

There are now five jurisdictions in the United Methodist Church, all based on geographical divisions, with the one jurisdiction, the Central, which was based on racial differences, having been eliminated in 1961. Two of these, the Southeastern and South Central, are in the South. Both of the Southern jurisdictions have developed programs of education, evangelism, and missions to supplement the national and conference programs.

Jurisdictions hold quadrennial conferences of ministerial and lay delegates elected by the various Annual Conferences within the jurisdictions. The primary purpose of these conferences is the election and assignment of bishops to the various Annual Conferences within the jurisdiction.

JOSEPH MITCHELL
TROY STATE UNIVERSITY

JUSTIFICATION. The doctrine of justification, based mainly on Pauline references to the forgiveness by which God makes or pronounces the Christian "righteous," has assumed three promi-nent forms in Southern theology. (1) Roman Catholics argued that justification was a gradual process, initiated in BAPTISM and continued through the instrumentality of faith, love, and the sacramental means of grace in the church, by which the Christian actually became just or righteous. Hence Catholics viewed both justification and SANCTIFICATION as interrelated moments in the same continuous process of transformation. (2) Lutherans believed that justification (an act, not a process) was God's imputing to the believer the righteousness of Christ, hence conferring forgiveness on the faithful, who were thus justified by grace alone through faith. (3) The Reformed theologians, heirs to John Calvin, defined justification as the act by which God accounted the faithful as righteous, but unlike the Lutherans they also emphasized its organic relation to a subsequent gradual process of sanctification, that transformed and renewed the justified believer. They added that God justified only the elect—those who were chosen for salvation from eternity.

Most Southern Presbyterians and Baptists have accepted Reformed interpretations, though sometimes with modifications of the doctrine of election. All Methodists, most Episcopalians, and most Southern churches in the HOLINESS MOVEMENT have denied the doctrine of particular election to salvation but have agreed that justification was a divine act of grace, received through faith alone but integrally related to the subsequent process of sanctification. The Holiness churches, however, along with some in PENTECOSTALISM, have seen justification as only a "first blessing" that is followed by a SECOND BLESSING of HOLINESS, or in some Pentecostal teaching, a "third blessing" of endowment with the power of the Holy Spirit.

The major controversy over justification occurred in the 19th-century encounter between Reformed theologians, mainly Presbyterians and Baptists, and those committed to ARMINIANISM, mainly

Methodists. The various Arminian traditions originated when Jacobus Arminius (1559-1609), a pastor and professor at Leyden in Holland, decided that the "high Calvinist" doctrines of particular election, limited ATONEMENT, and irresistible grace were an affront to the justice and goodness of God. As an alternative, he proposed that God had decreed to justify all believers and that Christ died for all persons, so that grace sufficient for justifying faith was given to all, though not all would evidence the necessary faithfulness. Southern Methodists associated themselves with the revolt of Arminius against Calvinism. Therefore, they insisted that justification did not occur through the imputation of Christ's righteousness to the elect, accounting them righteous despite their fallenness, but rather that God had given all persons sufficient "prevenient grace" to turn from sinfulness to faithfulness and hence to receive in faith the gift of justification. Calvinists accused the Arminians of forgetting that salvation was an unconditioned, merciful gift, and they insisted that Christians could repose in the certainty of God's mercy only if they could believe that God "accounted" them righteous despite their lack of just desert.

The 20th century has seen Protestants move toward a common understanding of justification, though traces of the older differences are still to be found.

Bibliography. Robert L. Dabney, *Syllabus and Notes of the Course of Systematic and Polemic Theology Taught in Union Theological Seminary, Virginia*; E. Brooks Holifield, *The Gentlemen Theologians: American Theology in Southern Culture, 1795-1860*; Thomas Ralston, *Elements of Divinity.*

E. BROOKS HOLIFIELD
EMORY UNIVERSITY

KEEBLE, MARSHALL (1878-1968), evangelist of the CHURCHES OF CHRIST, was born in Murfreesboro TN, a son of former slaves. Baptized in 1892, Keeble began preaching five years later under the influence of his father-in-law, S. W. Womack. But it was not until 1914 that Keeble began traveling as an evangelist. In 1918 he baptized 84 people at Oak Grove, near Henderson TN—the first of more than 200 congregations he would establish. Keeble went on to baptize more than 30,000 people; white preachers who followed in his wake baptized many more who would be converted but not immersed by a black man.

After 1920 Keeble traveled widely throughout the South at the expense of Nashville millionaire A. M. Burton, preaching under tents and in hired halls, baptizing in rivers and stockponds. He was bitterly opposed by preachers of other religious persuasions, threatened by the KU KLUX KLAN, and physically assaulted by white racists. He bore violence and invective with monumental courage and calm; his charm and persuasive rhetoric usually disarmed and often converted his most vehement opponents. He preached in homespun "parables" reflecting expe-riences of his auditors—from the antics of recalcitrant mules to the machinations of installment-loan collectors. Keeble's message emerged from his reading of Scripture; repeatedly he insisted that "the Bible is right." He did not speak out directly against social injustices in his time, but he recruited and trained strong black leaders who did effectively challenge segregation and prejudice. He died in Nashville, the city where he promoted education and the religious press for the Churches of Christ.

Bibliography. J. E. Choate, *Roll, Jordan, Roll: A Biography of Marshall Keeble*; B. C. Goodpasture, ed., *Biography and Sermons of Marshall Keeble, Evangelist*; F. N. Rhodes, "A Study of the Sources of Marshall Keeble's Effectiveness as a Preacher," unpublished Ph.D. dissertation, Southern Illinois University, 1970.

DON HAYMES
MACON, GEORGIA

KEHUKEE BAPTIST ASSOCIA-TION. This organization of Baptist congregations was formed in 1769 at the Kehukey meetinghouse in Halifax County in northeastern North Carolina by five REGULAR BAPTIST churches, and by 1774 it had grown to include 14 congregations including several in nearby southside Virginia. The association split in 1775 over the same issue that had prevented merger

of Regular (Calvinist) and SEPARATE (revivalist) BAPTISTS in North Carolina:
whether to allow persons baptized prior
to conversion to retain church membership. Exacerbating this doctrinal conflict
was the impatience of younger ministers
like Lemuel Burkitt, who chafed at the
dominance of the older Baptist preachers.
Adopting the Separates' position on
church membership, the majority of the
Kehukee Baptists then persuaded four
Separate congregations to join them, thus
creating a new association of 10 churches.

The Kehukees became the model for
other Baptist associations in North
Carolina—notably the Chowan and
Neuse Associations—and this form of
church organization facilitated the rapid
spread of the Baptists in the years that
followed the GREAT REVIVAL (1787-
1805). The associations endowed their
clergy with professional status (even
though the ministers continued to support themselves as farmers); they promulgated official views on faith in
practice in formal annual circular letters,
and maintained fraternal relations with
other associations. Detailed reporting of
baptisms and membership to the association encouraged evangelism not so much
to the unchurched as to backsliders within
existing congregations—indicating the
primary goal of organizing communal life
in an elemental rural culture. The Kehukee Association therefore supported early
Baptist missionary efforts between 1807
and 1811, efforts that would culminate in
the creation of the Baptist State Convention in 1830. But this organized evangelism so alarmed and alienated
congregational purists that by the late
1820s several associations, led by Kehukee, denounced missionaries, temperance
and tract societies, and theological
seminaries—programs often instigated
by Northerners—as Arminian attempts
to undercut God's sovereign control of
salvation and as tainted by the greed and
avarice that accompanied widespread
fund raising. The antimission people
called themselves PRIMITIVE BAPTISTS,

and in 1878 the Kehukee, now numbering
nearly 1,800 members, changed its name
to the Kehukee Primitive Baptist
Association.

See also article on ANTIMISSION
MOVEMENT.

Bibliography. Keith R. Burich, "The Primitive Baptist
Schism in North Carolina: A Study of the Professionaliza-
tion of the Baptist Ministry," unpublished M.A. thesis,
University of North Carolina at Chapel Hill, 1973;
George Washington Paschal, *History of the North Caroli-
na Baptists*; Bertram Wyatt-Brown, "The Antimission
Movement in the Jacksonian South: A Study in Regional
Folk Culture," *Journal of Southern History* 36 (November
1970): 501-29.

ROBERT M. CALHOON
UNIVERSITY OF NORTH CAROLINA
AT GREENSBORO

KENRICK, FRANCIS PATRICK

(1796-1863), pioneer Roman Catholic
priest and major Church figure, was born
in Dublin, Eire. He studied for the priesthood in Dublin and Rome where he was
ordained in 1821. That same year he
volunteered for work in Kentucky, where
he taught at the seminary in BARDSTOWN.
He soon won renown as a preacher and
theologian, and as an author who
defended the Catholic Church against its
critics.

Kenrick attended the 1830 Provincial
Council in Baltimore as theologian to
Bardstown's Bishop BENEDICT FLAGET.
He became secretary to the council and,
soon after, was named coadjutor to the
bishop of Philadelphia. He succeeded to
the see in 1842. Kenrick resolved a bitter
conflict between lay trustees and the episcopacy, and dealt with nativist violence
against Catholic immigrants. He
expanded diocesan facilities to handle a
growing population and founded a
seminary.

In 1852, Kenrick became archbishop
of Baltimore. There he presided over the
Plenary Council of 1853. Caught in
regional conflicts and the slavery debate,
Archbishop Kenrick tried to avoid politicization of the Church. He insisted on
human rights for slaves, but did not condemn slavery as such. He also defended
national loyalty over states' rights.

Among his writings are seven volumes of moral and dogmatic theology. His brother, Peter Richard Kenrick, became the first archbishop of St. Louis.

Bibliography. H. J. Nolan, *The Most Reverend Francis Patrick Kenrick*; J. J. O'Shea, *The Two Kenricks.*

GARY W. MCDONOGH
NEW COLLEGE
UNIVERSITY OF SOUTH FLORIDA

KENTUCKY. It is altogether possible that Kentucky has both the most denominationally diverse and the most religiously homogeneous population of all the Southern states. As is true of the South generally, the Baptist churches have the largest membership in Kentucky. Uncharacteristically Southern, however, is the fact that Kentucky's second largest religious population is Catholic. Surprisingly, much of that is rural Anglo-Saxon; the remainder is centered in the urban areas of Covington and Louisville and made up of the descendants of the German and Irish who migrated to Kentucky before the Civil War. These people blend into the Kentucky cultural landscape with scarcely a discernible difference except for their Catholicism.

By contrast, Baptists and Baptist churches vary greatly with location, region, and social class. Methodists, the various branches of the Christian churches (Campbellite) and Presbyterians show a similar diversity. In fact, individual churches of these denominations may collect congregations as different in style as an Episcopal parish and a Pentecostal sect. While denominational loyalties may be strong, a mountain Baptist and Pentecostal church may be marked more by the common culture of the Applachians, or rural Baptists and Catholics in Washington and Nelson Counties more easily detected by the peculiar characteristics of the "Knob" culture. This cultural homogeneity and religious diversity should not be construed as merely secularism. It reflects more than anything a history that has been more dynamic religiously than culturally or at least in which religion has been formative.

The early settlement of Kentucky was notable for its religious dimension. Unlike colonial settlement patterns in the backwoods areas or the later migration patterns across New York and into the Midwest, many of the earliest Kentuckians arrived in already formed communities and brought their institutions of religion with them. The Baptists, suffering from restrictions under Virginia's establishment, migrated in large numbers in the 1780s. The largest group, known as the "Traveling Church," left Spottsylvania County VA, under the leadership of the Rev. Lewis Craig. The more than 500 persons in this group formed the basis for a large number of Baptist communities in the Bluegrass region of central Kentucky. Maryland Catholics also came to the state in well-organized communities of approximately 25 families. Most of these settled in and around BARDSTOWN in what is now Nelson County. One such group stopped in the Bluegrass and survives to the present as a small but vigorous Catholic minority in Scott County. Presbyterians coming to Kentucky in the earliest period, although not as often in such large groups, tended also to settle contiguous areas. Bourbon County, on the eastern edge of the Baptist settlements in the Bluegrass, was populated almost entirely by Presbyterians. A second area of Presbyterian dominance emerged in the early 1790s with the settlement of Logan County in western Kentucky. On the western fringe of the Bluegrass region along the Salt River, a community of Dutch Reformed settled in the 1780s—a move that represented the second community relocation for these people. Thus the earliest religious landscape of Kentucky featured a significant denominational diversity, but with each denomination living in religiously homogeneous quasi-ethnic, communities.

The termination of the War for Independence from England and military victories over the Indian tribes to the north opened the way for a massive migration to Kentucky that was to disrupt this initial, and, from the point of view of the early settlers, desirable pattern. Virginia rewarded its soldiers of the revolution with warrants for lands in Kentucky. These warrants circulated as currency and produced an interesting pattern of land ownership in Kentucky that influenced both cultural and religious developments in the Commonwealth. Eastern speculators, including a number of Virginia aristocrats, bought these warrants and secured massive tracts of Kentucky land. In addition, the wealthiest of the immigrants who located before 1784, often acting as agents for speculators and absentee owners, were also able to build considerable estates. Among this new aristocracy were many of the earliest religious leaders. The mass of the new immigrants to Kentucky were therefore not of the solid middle-class landowners, but of those less fortunate who were primarily attracted by a common five-year, free-rent plan for clearing the land and building cabins on the claims of both resident and absentee owners. This pattern of land ownership produced a society with two distinct elites, often with conflicting values, a relatively small independent middle class, and a large number of the dependent classes, both slaves and white tenants. The elites may be called the Presbyterian-Nationalist and the Baptist-Localist.

Religiously and culturally the two Kentucky elitist sectors were quite dissimilar. The elite group created from the earliest settlers was primarily rural, poorly educated and otherwise deficient in "higher culture." Most of them migrated from the backwoods areas of the eastern states. Politically their concerns rarely extended beyond their own and neighboring communities, for which they believed that religion should be the primary instrument of social intercourse and order. The largest number of these leaders were Baptists, but the few Methodists in the state and some Presbyterians shared their essential values. The other elite group came more from the coastal plains and represented more old wealth and cultural

sophistication. While land served as a basis of their wealth and they often lived on their estates, this elite was accompanied by a number of urban (town) enterprises, especially commerce and law. Their political interests were national in scope and they looked more to various agencies of government than to the churches as the proper means of social order. Most in this group were Presbyterian, Episcopalian, or Associate Reformed Presbyterian, with by far the largest number being Presbyterian.

During the 1790s the population of Kentucky tripled. Although a number of these new migrants represented the new commercial, manufacturing, artisan, and professional classes that populated the emerging towns, the greatest number were of the rural dependent classes. Most of these were religiously quite indifferent and their presence soon disrupted the religious orderliness that characterized the original settlements. Drunkenness, petty theft, and other activities branded as vices, such as gambling, horse racing, dancing, and "frolicking," rapidly increased. These forms of social disruption were perceived by the religious elites, especially of the Baptist-Localist variety, as a religious problem that could only be solved by an increased attention to religion.

From this set of circumstances came the GREAT REVIVAL. It began in Logan County in western Kentucky in 1799. The problem of maintaining order in this area was so severe in the 1790s that it was called "Rogues Harbor." The "first citizens" of the region, who were primarily Presbyterian but who reflected values similar to those of the central Kentucky Baptists, began praying for a revival in 1797. JAMES MCGREADY was a leading figure in this revival. Two of his three Presbyterian congregations, Red River and Gasper River, experienced mild revivals in 1799. The following summer all these congregations met at Red River in June to observe a communion service. Before the four day affair ended, Logan County experienced a rare religious phenomenon. On the final day, under the preaching of the Methodist William McGee, many people fell semiconscious to the floor under deep religious conviction.

The news of such extraordinary events spread with great rapidity, and elaborate plans were made for a similar meeting the following month at Gasper River. While one of Logan County's wealthiest citizens rode on horseback spreading the news of the forthcoming meeting to adjacent communities, other leading citizens bestirred themselves to Gasper River to prepare the camp-grounds for the large crowds that were expected. This was the first great "camp meeting" in the United States. The greatest meeting of the Kentucky revival came the following year at CANE RIDGE, in Bourbon County just a few miles east of Paris. BARTON W. STONE, the Presbyterian minister, went to Logan County early in the summer of 1801 to investigate and planned a similar event at his church. Eye witnesses estimated the size of the crowd at Cane Ridge at between 12,000 and 25,000—or from 5 to 10 percent of the entire population of Kentucky. At this meeting, preaching ran into the night, people collapsed as if in a coma, others were seized with what was described as the "jerks," while still others barked like dogs. Hundreds pointed to this meeting as the place of their conversion.

The revival produced lasting effects on religion and society in Kentucky, but it also accentuated the denominational diversity and religious homogeneity already observable from the earliest period. The Baptist churches were the largest gainers in the revival, tripling their membership to over 15,000. The Baptist experience illuminates the general tendencies inherent in the revival. The new converts represented an almost perfect cross section of the state's population in 1800. The largest number of converts came therefore from the poor white class and from black slaves. The revival thus integrated this population into the community structure and brought them under the oversight of the Baptist religious, social, and economic elite that continued to dominate the leadership roles in the churches. These leaders concentrated their energies on securing social order through the agency of church discipline. The rate of exclusions as the result of church trials quadrupled in the period after the revival and most of those excluded were among the poor whites and the blacks.

The Methodists, the second-largest gainers among the established denominations, reflected the Baptist pattern in a rather curious way. Although the Methodist polity was centralized and hierarchical, early developments in Kentucky allowed local congregations to function very much like those of the Baptists. While the itinerant ministers provided certain ministerial services to these congregations, the real leaders of the churches were resident laymen who served as class leaders and patrons. These leaders occupied an economic and social status equivalent to the Baptist pastors and deacons. In his two extended tours through Kentucky, Bishop Francis Asbury usually lodged with these leaders, a benefit that gave them additional status as overseers of the social order of their communities.

The Presbyterians, on the other hand, were devastated by the revival, losing at least a third of their 2,700 members by 1810. This also meant a corresponding decline in the power and influence of the social, political, and cultural values of the Presbyterian-Nationalist elite in Kentucky. The Presbyterian clergy, represented by such men as DAVID RICE and John Lyle, were generally highly educated, specialized and professionalized in their ministerial calling, more sensitive to national political and denominational concerns than to those of a particular local community, and suspicious of the genuineness and orthodoxy of the revival. Ultimately they concentrated their attention on attempting to eliminate suspected doctrinal and educational deviation among Presbyterian revivalists. The result was the formation of two new denominations in Kentucky, each reflecting more the concerns of the Baptist elite than those of the Presbyterian elite.

The first new religious group to emerge on Kentucky soil was the Christian churches under the leadership of Barton W. Stone. Stone and several other revivalistic Presbyterian ministers came under the suspicions of the Synod of Kentucky in 1803. They were accused of various excesses, Arminian heresies, and the lowering of educational standards for the ministry. When Richard M'Nemar was tried for heresy, he, Stone, Robert Marshall, John Dunlavy, and John Thompson withdrew to form the Springfield Presbytery which was soon dissolved. Many Presbyterian churches in central Kentucky split between loyal Presbyterians and the followers of Stone, who referred to themselves by the generic term "Christian." In the rural areas the newly formed Christian churches reflected rather precisely the Baptist pattern, even adopting adult immersion. They so strongly insisted upon the autonomy of the local congregation that the first 20 years of their history remains clouded, revealed only in the separate histories of each community. As among the Baptists, however, these churches represented the total spectrum of classes in Kentucky society, with the political and economic leadership of the community clearly reflected in the leadership of the churches. Most of the remaining struggling Presbyterian congregations, however, were made up primarily of representatives of Kentucky's small middle class.

The second new denomination in Kentucky was the CUMBERLAND PRESBYTERIAN CHURCH, formed in 1810 after a lengthy ecclesiastical battle between the Presbyterian revivalists of western Kentucky and the Synod of Kentucky. The revival created an increased demand for preaching and the prorevival Presbytery of Cumberland responded to

this demand by appointing "exhorters" and later by licensing and ordaining ministers not having the education demanded by traditional Presbyterian standards. This group, like the revivalists of central Kentucky, represented the interests of the economic and political elites of the local communities. FINIS EWING, the major figure in the movement, was the eighth and final child of western Kentucky's most prominent family. His older brothers were many times sheriffs, judges, and legislators who were credited with bringing law and order to the entire region. McGready, who ultimately rejoined with the older Presbyterian body, was also a man of property whose lay associates were made up of the region's elite. While the Cumberland Presbyterians did not reflect the ecclesiastical pattern of the Baptist model as clearly as the Christians, the pattern of control by the local elite was pronounced. A loose presbyterial polity featuring circuit riders gave considerable autonomy to the local congregation.

That the Great Revival was primarily a movement of which the major tendency was to promote community order is perhaps most vividly portrayed in the emergence of Shakerism in Kentucky. After 1805 when three Shaker missionaries visited Kentucky, two communities were formed. Those people who became SHAKERS had earlier been participants in and supporters of the revival. In central Kentucky, three of the most prominent ministers in the Stone movement ultimately led most of their congregations into the Shaker commune at Pleasant Hill. The other major community in this village came from the peripatetic Dutch settlement of Mercer County. In western Kentucky, John Rankin, pastor of one of the earliest Presbyterian churches affected by the revival, led his people to form the nucleus of the Shaker commune at South Union. The Shakers pushed community order to its greatest extreme, devising rules and regulations concerning every aspect of life. Although a controversial and often maligned religious group in

Kentucky for a century, the Shakers reflected in microcosm the major tendencies in Kentucky society in the early nineteenth century.

The only major group among the earliest settlers not affected by the Great Revival were the Catholics. Nelson County and the surrounding areas were largely spared the disorder of the 1790s, and the Protestant settlers tended to avoid the area. Catholicism thus prospered. From 1793 to 1797 the 300 Catholic families were served by a single priest, STEPHEN T. BADIN. In 1810 BENEDICT FLAGET was consecrated as the first bishop of the Diocese of Bardstown—which covered an area from Canada to southern Tennessee and from the Alleghenies to the Mississippi River. Under Flaget numerous new churches were built and the state was more adequately supplied with priests. He established St. Thomas Seminary in 1811 and in 1812 the Sisters of Loretto and the Sisters of Charity of Nazareth were founded, thus supplying teachers for the Catholic schools. The consecration of St. Joseph's Cathedral in Bardstown in 1819 symbolized the strength of Catholicism in Kentucky.

Although the revival essentially strengthened the existing power structures in Kentucky, it contained some countervailing tendencies regarding the state's slave population. First, it created a mild antislavery movement. Barton Stone himself became convinced of the evils of slavery and emancipated his few slaves. William Hickman, pioneer Baptist pastor of the Forks of Elkhorn Church, also began preaching emancipation, for which he was dismissed. A small number of Baptist ministers and churches formed the Anti-Slavery Friends of Humanity Association. This movement was never very large and the majority of Kentucky's white religious population defended the institution of slavery. In fact, while religious Kentuckians later supported colonization and African missions, laws passed in the state legislature in 1801 during the height of the revival tightened controls on the state's slave population. Thomas Campbell moved from Boone County in 1820 when he learned, through violations, that Kentucky law prevented the instruction of slaves.

More significantly, the revival stimulated Negro spirituality and increased the desires of blacks to have their own worship services. These were generally perceived by the whites as potentially subversive, and frequently blacks caught preaching were disciplined by the white congregations, in which the blacks had no voice. Black preachers and hearers were so persistent, however, that many of the churches were forced to change tactics and allowed separate, albeit supervised, black services. The first independent black church, also a product of the revival, was established in Lexington. The minister, Peter Duerett, organized the church in 1801 from 50 of his recent converts. The white Baptists refused to ordain him or to recognize the baptism of his converts. He persisted, however, and after his death in 1823, the congregation was admitted into the Elkhorn Association as the First Baptist Church, Lexington, Colored, in 1824. Under the leadership of Elder LONDON FERRILL and Elder Frederick Braxton the congregation grew to over 2,000 by the time of the Civil War. By then there were 17 independent black Baptist churches in the state, most of which, however, were formed in the 1850s.

To some extent the emergence of independent black churches presaged the forces in Kentucky society that were soon to produce not only further denominational diversity but also a social, economic, political, and religious diversity within denominations. The result was that by the time of the Civil War there was often a great deal of diversity within a single denomination but a remarkable similarity of groupings across denominational lines. During the 1820s and 1830s many of the earliest and most fully populated areas of the state developed into mature and relatively stable communities while outlying areas, forced to absorb the bulk of continued population growth, experienced continued disorder. The result was a growing regionalism within the state and a reordering of values and practices of the elites, especially in the more mature communities.

Denominationally this transition was most notable among the Baptists, who in 1820 continued to be the largest group. With over 30,000 members they outnumbered the Methodists two to one. Many second- and third-generation Baptists raised in affluence and positions of leadership began looking beyond the narrow community concerns of their fathers and expressed an interest in state and national affairs. In so doing they adopted a system of values that made them much more compatible with the earlier Presbyterian-National elite. Baptists now became governors, judges, and in 1828 Robert Johnson, son of the Scott County Baptist patriarch, became vice president of the United States. At the same time, the vast number of Baptists remained rural and community oriented.

The tensions inherent in this growing diversity among Baptists expressed themselves most forcefully in the long lasting controversy over missions. When Luther Rice, schooled in the tradition of the New England establishment but becoming Baptist along with Adoniram Judson, visited Kentucky in 1815 to raise funds for the General Convention of the Baptist Denomination in the United States for Foreign Missions, the lines were already clearly formed. The more affluent and better-established Baptists immediately sensed the value of associated activity to foster their recently acquired ambitions while the majority resisted such activity as threatening their limited power in their communities.

The issues became considerably more complex and less focused until the influence of ALEXANDER CAMPBELL began spreading through Kentucky after 1822. Campbell, a Presbyterian become Baptist and starting in 1823 editor of the *Christian Baptist*, initially came to Kentucky to debate baptism with a Presbyterian. His influence among Kentucky Baptists grew to prominence and within a few years became divisive. Campbell advocated the Bible as the only rule of faith and practice, baptism for the remission of sin, weekly communion, the right of any Christian to preach and administer the ordinances, and the supremacy of the local church over associated activities. While Campbell's teachings attracted persons from almost the entire sociological spectrum of Baptists, excluding only the entrenched leadership, they appealed particularly to those of moderate antimission sentiment. Aspiring leaders suspicious of the Baptist drift toward associated activity found a constituency prepared to receive Campbell's ideas. Although General and Regular Baptists had united in 1801 on the basis of the Bible as the only creed, a number of the more powerful churches continued to use the Philadelphia Confession. The general turning away from Calvinism also aided the "reformers," who, significantly, met for the first time the day before the session of the Baptist Missionary Association of Kentucky in 1824.

Before 1830 Baptists were divided into three discernible if overlapping groups—mission, antimission, and followers of Campbell. Beginning in 1828 churches and associations began to divide over the issues raised by Campbell. The antimission Baptists, especially in the outlying areas of eastern Kentucky, the Knobs, and sections of western Kentucky consolidated their positions in those associations, leading the way for a further fragmentation after 1830. Ultimately this strengthened the hands of the mission Baptists in the more established communities of the state because the associations gained greater authority and potential opposition was eliminated.

Alexander Campbell and his followers soon merged with the older Christian churches associated with Barton W. Stone to form yet another distinct denomination, which also incorporated a wide spectrum of religious belief and the

sociological diversity becoming characteristic of denominations in Kentucky. Recognizing their commonalities, the
Christians (Stone) and Disciples (Campbell) of Scott and Fayette counties discussed merger in 1831 and 1832. Both
groups claimed the Bible as the sole rule of
faith and practice, which was now becoming a topic of agreement among most
Kentucky Protestants, and desired to restore the churches to the practice of primitive Christianity. Although each group
was quite persistent in advocating its own
"generic" title and the Disciples opposed
"hired" preachers while the Christians
continued to insist that only ministers
could administer the ordinances, merger
was gradually achieved through a process
of agreement to tolerate differences.

The statistics for enrollment in the
various denominations are approximate
at best, but illustrate something of the
distribution in the state. In 1832 there
were 37,520 Baptists of all varieties with
25 associations, 442 churches and 289
ministers. The Methodists, prospering
without as many internal disputes as the
Baptists, had 77 preachers and a membership of 23,935. Combined, the Disciples
and Christians in various stages of merger
probably had 16,000 members. The Cumberland Presbyterians, now spread
throughout the Midwest, were the fourth
largest denomination in Kentucky with
about 10,000 members. The Presbyterians
had 103 churches, 61 ministers and 7,832
members. The Catholics, having recently
added German immigrants of Louisville
and Cincinnati to their older population,
had 30 priests. In the Episcopal vineyard
five priests were laboring.

The 1830s and early 1840s represented a period of denominational consolidation and expansion. While no new
bodies appeared, the evolution of the
"popular" denominations left many of
their natural constituents uncomfortable
and ready to follow one of the many
evangelical—more precisely, pentecostal-
holiness—sects that emerged after the
Civil War. Activities centered on various

associated missionary and educational
ventures. The earliest church-related
higher education in Kentucky was sponsored by the Presbyterians, who founded
Transylvania University in Lexington in
1797. Initially an institution of some quality, its early history was marked by extensive battles between the Presbyterians
and proponents of "liberal religion" for
control of the school. Liberalism never
secured a firm rooting in Kentucky, however, and in the 1820s Transylvania
returned to more conservative though not
exclusively Presbyterian control. The
Presbyterians chartered Centre College in
Danville in 1825. The missionary (elite)
Baptists by now felt they needed a professional and educated ministerial leadership
and founded Georgetown College in 1829.
The politically and socially aspiring Baptist trustees attempted to secure the aid of
educators of national renown to teach at
the new college. Appearing at the height
of the conflict with the emerging Christian churches, the college became an area
of contention until the Disciples formed
Bacon College in 1836. Initially located in
Georgetown, Bacon College moved to
Harrodsburg in 1839 and was merged
with Transylvania in 1865, with its control passing to the Disciples.

The second phase of denominational
consolidation for Kentucky's largest
groups witnessed the formation of several
associations for missionary and other purposes. The Presbyterians, Cumberland
Presbyterians, and Methodists of the state
already had their machinery by virtue of
their ecclesiastical organization. This was
not the case with the Baptists and Disciples. The Kentucky Baptist Convention
was formed in 1832. Although ultimately
to become the most powerful religious
organization in the state, from the outset
the convention was controlled by a very
small number of ministers. Most of the
members of the 608 churches in the state
were suspicious of such organizations and
refused to support it through contributions or attendance. In an attempt to
secure further support the name was

changed in 1837 to the General Association of Baptists in Kentucky. The association supported Georgetown College and employed agents to preach across the state and raise funds. This change in title had little basic effect and it was not until the 20th century that the General Association consolidated its control of the majority of Baptists in the state.

Christians, even more than Baptists, resisted organizations beyond the level of the local church. Yet certain leaders of this denomination, like their Baptist counterparts, felt that organization was essential to expansion. In 1849 the national American Christian Missionary Society was established and the following year the Kentucky Annual State Meeting was established, with representatives of only 62 of the 400 churches present. In the Christian churches, controversy over such organizations grew and occupied the attention of the denomination after the Civil War.

Consolidation and expansion were followed rapidly by further fragmentation that resulted in even greater denominational diversity. The issues leading to the Civil War and the war itself were more disruptive in Kentucky than in any other state. Although inhabitants of a border state, the vast majority of Kentuckians were proslavery and antiabolitionist in sentiment. In all the denominational schisms previous to the war, most Kentucky churchmen sided with their brethren to the south. Kentucky Presbyterians had historically nurtured a vocal antislavery minority, stemming from David Rice's arguments for a gradual emancipation clause in the Kentucky Constitution of 1792. The Synod of Kentucky in 1834 went so far as to approve, by a vote of 56 to 8, a resolution calling for gradual emancipation. This action was in advance of Kentucky public opinion, however, and the following year some members of the Synod were leaders in the movement to drive the abolitionist James G. Birney, a Presbyterian layman, out of the state. The division of Presbyterianism

in 1837 into Old Side and New Side (OLD SCHOOL/NEW SCHOOL) assemblies was more complex than the later divisions among Methodists and Baptists, but antiabolitionism was at least a significant factor. In the schisms, the Synod of Kentucky joined the South in supporting the Old Side. The Presbyterian antislavery minority continued to be vocal. Their forces were augmented in 1847 when ROBERT JEFFERSON BRECKINRIDGE returned to his native state. A vigorous Old Sider, he gave energy to the small antislavery group and in 1849 he and several other Presbyterians once again tried to have gradual emancipation placed in the Kentucky Constitution. Even the New Side Presbyterians, who at their peak could boast no more than 14 ministers, 22 churches and 1,000 members, resisted the antislavery tendencies of the national General Assembly. The Kentucky delegates to the assembly walked out in 1857 and formed an independent Synod of Kentucky, but within a year most returned to the Old Side.

The Methodist Episcopal Church, South, and the Southern Baptist Convention were both organized in 1845. The primary issue in each case was the debate over the proper role of the church on the issues of slavery and abolitionism. In each case the Kentucky churches stood overwhelmingly with the South. The state's delegates to the national Methodist General Conference in 1844 unanimously supported the South, even though Kentucky Methodist opinion, especially along the state's northern border, was somewhat divided. The South attempted to exert its influence in this region by holding its organizational meeting the following year in Louisville. When the Kentucky Conference of the Methodist Episcopal Church, North, (so it was called in Kentucky) was constituted in 1852, it claimed only 2,183 of Kentucky's approximately 50,000 Methodists. The transition to the Southern Baptist Convention was more easily accomplished among Kentucky Baptists because they had a looser organization and a weaker antislavery heritage. While Kentucky was not represented at the organizational meeting in Augusta GA, in 1845, the General Association of Baptists in Kentucky, meeting later that year at Georgetown, agreed to dissolve its connection with the American Baptist Home Missionary Society and support the newly formed Southern Convention.

The major alteration in Kentucky's religious demography before the Civil War, however, came with the massive German and Irish Catholic migration to Louisville and Covington (greater Cincinnati) in the 1840s and 1850s. While the foreign-born constituted only four percent of the Kentucky population in 1850, almost one third of Louisville's 43,000 residents were of foreign birth, a large percentage of these Catholic. The importance of Louisville as a center of Catholicism was recognized in 1843 when, at the request of Bishop Benedict Flaget, the see was removed from Bardstown to that city. With the leadership of Bishop Flaget and his successor, MARTIN J. SPALDING, Kentucky Catholicism prospered. In 1843 the French Sisters of the Institute of the Good Shepherd came to Louisville and in 1848 the Trappists established Gethsemani in Nelson County. (It was here that Kentucky's best-known religious figure of the 20th century, THOMAS MERTON, lived and wrote.) The following year construction started on the magnificent Louisville Cathedral of the Assumption. By 1853 Catholicism in Kentucky had grown so much that a second diocese was established at Covington.

This rapid growth of German and Irish Catholicism stirred fear among the predominantly Protestant Kentucky population and formed the backdrop of the ugliest episode in Kentucky history. The extremely nativistic Know-Nothing party came to power in Louisville in April of 1855. Previous to the election of August 6 that year, they determined to prevent the foreign born from voting. Riots broke out in both the German and Irish sections of town and a large number of buildings were burned. At least 19 people were killed. Bishop Spalding and Mayor Barbee prevented damage to the Cathedral. Largely because of the immense popularity of Bishop Spalding and the service of the Sisters in caring for the wounded during the Civil War, this form of violent anti-Catholicism subsided in Kentucky.

The coming of the Civil War brought even greater divisions to the state's major denominations. Many Kentucky churchmen who were satisfied with the arrangements forged in the 1840s found themselves faced with the new and more difficult issue of loyalty. Kentucky had the third-largest slave-owning population in the nation and this group dominated Kentucky society and politics. Then, too, the mass of poor whites feared loss of status to freed blacks. Strongly proslavery, the citizens of the Commonwealth were also staunchly prounion. Thus torn, the state attempted to avoid choosing sides by declaring neutrality. Many would have preferred to secede from both North and South. While prounion victories in the congressional election of 1861 kept Kentucky officially in the Union, every Kentuckian was forced to choose sides in a way generally unknown either to the North or South. Families—and their churches—were divided.

In some instances these tensions resulted in the realignment of ecclesiastical allegiances, but the chronicling of these does little justice to the nature and extent of the anguish. Many congregations that did not participate in any of these larger movements struggled through the conflict with their membership divided. The Baptists and the Christian churches, again largely because of their strong congregationalism, experienced the least disruption. The Baptist General Association in 1861 urged an official position of neutrality. Military operations in western Kentucky forced the closing of Bethel College in Russellville in 1861 and the following year Georgetown College suspended its theological school. Methodists were not so fortunate. A number of churches along the northern border of Kentucky were divided and some others joined the Kentucky Conference of the Methodist Episcopal Church, North. The largest confrontation occurred in 1865 when the Kentucky Conference, South voted 35 to 25 to oppose reunion. Fifteen of those ministers were admitted to the Northern branch, which grew to a membership of over 16,000 in Kentucky by 1876.

Kentucky Presbyterians also preferred a course of neutrality. When the national Old School General Assembly declared its allegiance to the Union in 1861, 10 synods in the Confederacy formed the Presbyterian Church in the Confederate States of America. The Kentucky Presbyterians led by the antislavery Breckinridge and proslavery STUART ROBINSON, vehemently opposed the action of the assembly but remained in the Presbyterian Church, USA. As in the case of their Methodist counterparts, the major changes came after the war. When the majority of the Synod of Kentucky was excluded by the Northern body, they joined with the South. The Cumberland Presbyterians, aided by the effective statesmanship of Milton Bird and Richard Beard, managed to avoid formal divisions during the war. Although the Southern delegates were not able to attend the General Assembly during the war, they were enrolled without hesitation in 1866.

Although the Diocese of Kentucky of the Protestant Episcopal Church was relatively unscathed during the war, several churches and ministers in western Kentucky found themselves in an extremely uncomfortable position during periods of Confederate occupation. For which government would one pray during the liturgy? It was perhaps his Kentucky experience, however, that enabled James Crick, president of the House of Deputies in both 1862 and 1865, to lead the Anglicans to a speedy reunion after the war. Thus, except for the Presbyterians and Methodists, most Kentucky denominations passed through the war without further permanent fragmentation. Nevertheless, the war promoted the process of denominational diversity amidst religious homogeneity.

The major impact of the Civil War on the religious configuration of Kentucky came with the rapid emergence of independent black churches after the war. (Formal emancipation did not come to Kentucky until 18 December 1865.) The expectations of the two races were quite different. In politics the legislature of 1866 adopted a provision for black public education and a code of civil rights that was somewhat paternalistic. It also denied black people the right to vote or sit on juries or testify in trials involving whites. A similar view obtained among white religious leadership. The General Association of Baptists in 1866 saw that body's role as one of providing instruction. Viewing the blacks as essentially children, the white Baptists envisioned Sunday schools, day schools, and theological schools for blacks, but concluded that "this work must be done mainly by ourselves." Black Baptists, however, had a different vision. In August of 1865, representatives from 12 of the existing 17 independent Black Baptist churches met in Louisville and formed the State Convention of Colored Baptists in Kentucky. Black Baptists throughout the state began organizing new congregations. By 1869 there were already four black Baptist associations. That same year the State Convention became the General Association of Baptists in Kentucky and claimed 55 churches and 12,620 members. The association continued to grow rapidly. In 1879 it established a school in Louisville, which was ultimately called Simmons University in honor of William J. Simmons, who guided the school from 1880 to 1890. By 1913 the General Association had 371 churches with a membership of over 75,000. Black Methodists, though not so numerous as Baptists, also moved rapidly to form their own churches. The African

Methodist Episcopal Church, initially formed in Philadelphia in 1816, grew rapidly in Kentucky after the war and by 1876 claimed 55 churches and 5,226 members. The African Methodist Episcopal Zion Church sent missionaries to Kentucky and organized a conference in 1863. By 1876 the church had 34 churches and 3,000 members. At this time the Kentucky Conference of the Methodist Episcopal Church, South, had fewer than 200 black members.

By the 1870s, Kentucky churchgoers were members of over 25 denominations, but most of these were of the Baptist, Methodist, Christian, or Presbyterian variety and there was a growing Catholic minority. Even while denominations proliferated, however, there was an ongoing process of religious and cultural homogenization. Kentucky religionists, even of creedal denominations, claimed the Bible to be authoritative. They exposed a general atonement but were fatalistic about the affairs of this life. They were (sometimes militantly) anti-intellectual, dogmatic, and moralistic. Even though petty differences may have at times been exaggerated, they tended to respond more to the personalities of religious leaders than to their particular theologies. While they were intensely concerned about their communities, they were prone to analyze social problems in terms of individual salvation.

Space permits only a few examples of movements in this direction. Baptists had largely abandoned the Philadelphia Confession and Calvinism remained pronounced only in Appalachia. Presbyterian ministers, although still the best educated of the Kentucky clergy, were forced by their congregations to abandon written sermons and were expected to be able to preach at any place on any topic at a moment's notice. Kentucky Episcopalians were strongly evangelical and resisted "formalism." Perhaps of greater significance, however, was the fact that religious controversy was most often among members of a single denomination rather than between denominations.

In the years after 1870, the process of denominational proliferation continued at an even greater rate, but the basic characteristics were only altered slightly. The major intellectual currents of the late nineteenth century, particularly biblical higher criticism and Darwinian evolution, made but little impact on the religious leadership and virtually none on the masses of members. The state's Baptists, who continued to be the dominant religious group, secured the location of the Southern Baptist Theological Seminary in Louisville in 1877 when the young institution moved there from Greenville SC. The small number of Baptists who supported the General Association welcomed the seminary as a means to establish, at least in the county-seat towns, a full-time educated professional ministry. In this way they could extend their influence and further their emphasis on expansion, or "progress," which had become virtually an article of faith.

Some of the things that came with the seminary, however, were not so welcome. The seminary faculty, led by President JAMES P. BOYCE, was representative of the Southern Baptist aristocracy. They were scholarly, dedicated, and conscientious leaders, but socially and theologically conservative, expressing their creativity in the safe realms of homiletics, organization and administration, or grammar. CRAWFORD H. TOY was an exception to this rule. His thinking, and his teaching, was influenced by the theory of evolution and by Pentateuchal criticism. Although irenic of disposition and well loved by his colleagues of a decade and many of his students, Toy was unable to accommodate the requests that he desist in introducing these ideas. As a result he was forced to resign. A major consideration of those critical of Toy was that he would alienate the wealthy supporters of the struggling seminary. While Toy went on to a brilliant career at Harvard, where he became a leading scholar in Old Testament and Semitic studies, Kentucky Baptists had established an enduring pattern that confined their scholars to modes of culturally acceptable thinking. This was emphasized from 1896 to 1899 when WILLIAM H. WHITSITT was forced to resign the presidency of Southern Seminary because of his published studies of Baptist history. The majority of Baptists had come to believe that Baptist churches accurately reflected the New Testament model and some held that there had been a historical succession of such churches from Christ to the present. Whitsitt argued that baptism by immersion emerged in mid-seventeenth-century England. This created a controversy that shook not only Kentucky but the entire Southern Baptist Convention. Although a loyal member of the seminary faculty since 1872, Whitsitt was forced to resign in 1899.

This rejection of intellectual and scientific inquiry was not confined to Baptists in Kentucky but reflected accurately the stance of the overwhelming majority in the state. The Presbyterian seminary, relocated from Danville to Louisville in 1853, followed the norm established by the majority of Presbyterians both North and South, and taught Bible and theology without reference to higher criticism and evolution. The same was true of the Disciples' College of the Bible in Lexington, which was dominated by the conservative president, J. W. MCGARVEY. This institution began to teach aspects of biblical criticism in the early 1920s, however, after the withdrawal of the more conservative Churches of Christ in 1906.

Of far greater impact than scientific discoveries on religion in Kentucky was the popular Holiness movement. The early Holiness movement was of Northern and Midwestern origin but it found a ready constituency in Kentucky. The doctrine of entire sanctification featured the belief that one could experience a second work of the Holy Spirit that could be dated as occurring at a precise moment. While the Holiness movement spread primarily among Methodists, this doctrine was especially appealing to many rural Kentuckians of other denominations. The leaders of the Kentucky phase of the movement were John Wesley Hughes, who in 1890 established Asbury College at Wilmore, and his successor at Asbury, HENRY CLAY MORRISON. Holiness preaching directly attacked the spiritual coldness and formality of the established churches. Combined with various Pentecostal doctrines, especially the premillennial notion of Jesus' imminent return to crush the forces of darkness and install the saints to power, this movement created the most significant changes in the religious configuration of Kentucky in the 20th century.

This was particularly the case in the eastern Kentucky mountains. The Appalachian region of Kentucky had been the bulwark of Calvinism. Whether direct descendants of the strongly antimission Regular or Particular Baptists or members of one of the more exotic snake-handling sects, Kentucky mountain folk staunchly resisted the gradual theological changes taking place in other areas of the state. Notwithstanding their Calvinistic theology, eastern Kentuckians were also fervently emotional in their religious services. They were responsive to holiness and pentecostal emotionalism and their churches grew rapidly in that region. Today one may find a great variety of Churches of God, Holiness, or Nazarene congregations in the same community alongside Primitive, Old School, or Hard Shell Baptist churches. Of whatever sect or denomination, however, the people of this region express a religion that is both pessimistic and fatalistic about the affairs of this world and points to salvation and the world to come as the only hope. They tend to have a significantly higher religiosity than persons from other areas of the state although their participation in formal religious services is significantly lower. They are considerably more tolerant of human weakness and sin, especially among those with kinship or friendship ties, than are the religious of other parts of the state. With variation for regional distinctiveness, however, Appalachia exemplifies the denominational diversity and religious homogenity characteristic of the commonwealth.

The development of religion in Kentucky in the 20th century is more reflective of its 19th-century heritage than it is of major 20th-century movements. One cannot define a Kentucky social-gospel movement, a fundamentalist-modernist controversy, or a dramatic turn to neo-Orthodoxy. What is often described inaccurately as Fundamentalism in Kentucky was nothing more than the persisting moderate folk evangelicalism, which was well defined by 1870. Having nurtured no modernists within its borders, the Commonwealth had no need of an aggressive leadership to lead its citizens back to the fundamentals. Division of opinion among members of all denominations in Kentucky has been along what may more accurately be described as conservative-moderate lines. Actual schisms, reflected in both the Disciples and Cumberland Presbyterian divisions in 1906, were interjected not by new but by very old issues.

This absence of a hard and fast division of Kentucky religions into a "two-party system" allowed for the venting of different opinions, which did not necessarily further fragment a particular denomination. This was especially the case in the controversy in the 1920s over proposed legislation to ban the teaching of evolution in the public schools. All the state's major denominations—Baptist, Methodist, Presbyterian, and Disciples of Christ—had advocates both for and against the bill. Those opposing the bill, however, rarely defended the truth of evolution. E. Y. MULLINS, president of the Baptist seminary in Louisville, was a leading opponent of the legislation but did not personally espouse evolution. The bill was defeated in the 1922 General Assembly by a single vote. Since the religious opinion had not been divided into polar opposites, the issue soon subsided.

In other areas the homogeneity of the state's religious leadership was clearly discernible. In Kentucky the drive for good government, sometimes labeled "the Progressive Movement," was rather clearly an attempt by upper middle-class businessmen and professionals to enforce traditionally Protestant virtues. The two major issues were ultimately prohibition and pari-mutuel gambling. Since Louisville was the largest urban area and most threatened, it quite naturally provided the leadership in these matters. The Louisville Churchmen's Federation, the most significant organization, attracted support from the entire spectrum of religious opinion. Episcopal, Presbyterian, Baptist, Methodist, and Disciples clergy of all leanings cooperated. Among Baptists, for example, everyone from the genteel professors of Southern Seminary to M. P. Hunt, the closest thing to a fundamentalist firebrand to be found in the state, supported the federation's projects. One of the most active leaders was Patrick H. Callahan, the "dry" Catholic who was president of the Louisville Varnish Company. Strangely enough, Callahan paid one-fourth of Hunt's salary, even though the latter was outspoken in his anti-Catholicism. The federation used a diversity of tactics, which included everything from politics to the bringing of Gypsy Smith and Billy Sunday to Louisville for revivalistic crusades. In conjunction with the Anti-Saloon League, these Louisville churchmen were joined by religious leaders around the state, and together they led Kentucky to support the Prohibition Amendment. In 1922 they turned their attention against pari-mutuel gambling. In 1923 Alben W. Barkley, later United States senator and vice-president, picked up this issue and campaigned under the slogan, "Christianity, Morality, and Clean Government."

The pattern of denominational diversity and religious homogeneity and the persistence of conservative Evangelicalism has also influenced more recent 20th-century developments. Kentucky has not been the prolific producer of new denominations nor the location of numerous schisms. If dissension exists, it is usually expressed by the formation of a new congregation of the same denomination. Therefore, an almost infinite variety of churches, often reflecting minute sociological differences, exist in the same denomination. Although in recent decades conservative churches have continued to grow, Kentucky has not been altogether fruitful soil for ultra-rightists, as it has never been for the left. Moreover, this heritage has been particularly suited to promote a limited ecumenism. Kentucky Methodists supported the reunion of 1939. Kentucky Baptists are more prone to associate with Northern Baptists than are their brethren to the south and southwest, and Kentucky Presbyterians, most of whom are dually aligned, may yet hold the key to a long sought Presbyterian merger.

The period of widespread religious revivalism in the 1950s created a national ethos that could be shared by most of the religious people of Kentucky. Billy Graham and evangelists of a similar nature held particular appeal for Kentuckians. Churches of the Southern Baptist Convention, which sponsored a campaign for a "Million More in Fifty-four," grew rapidly during the decade. At the same time, Kentucky became the location of choice for a number of new industrial ventures of corporations whose core of operations was located in the Northeast and Midwest. The transfer to Kentucky of managerial employees, a significant number of whom were Catholic, added both numbers and leadership to Catholicism in Kentucky, especially in growing towns other than the traditional urban Catholic centers of Louisville and Covington.

The "exotic" religions of the 1960s, however, made little impact on the religious demography of Kentucky. To be sure, small congregations of Black Muslims, Satanists, and various cults of varying Near and Far Eastern rootage were formed in the urban and university environs of Louisville, Lexington, and Covington. With the exception of a few Muslim temples, however, these never flourished and have not survived. Likewise, the strong national religious antiwar movement of the late 1960s and early 1970s was but a ripple in the pond of Kentucky's basically conservative evangelical religions.

The latest survey (1971) of Kentucky's religious population confirms the persistence of Kentucky's heritage of denominational diversity and religious homogeneity. The fact that less than 60 percent of Kentuckians, which is somewhat under the national average, are adherents of a particular religion is largely explainable by the reluctance of Appalachian Kentuckians to join even those churches with whom they agree. In several counties in this region, for example, the number of church members is less than 10 percent of the population. The state as a whole remains overwhelmingly Southern Baptist, who make up nearly 50 percent of the religious membership. In the urban centers of Louisville and Covington, and in the traditionally Catholic centers around Bardstown, however, Catholicism is the religion of the majority. For the entire state, the Catholic church has the second largest membership with about 20 percent of the religious population. As a percentage of the church-related population, Methodists have fallen from their strong position of a century ago to a current 12 percent. The various branches of the Christian movement claim about 10 percent, with that being about equally divided between the Disciples and the more conservative Christian Churches and Churches of Christ. Presbyterians and Episcopalians combined number only about five percent. The real strength of various Pentecostal-Holiness denominations in underrepresented in published statistics. Even so, the Church of God (Anderson IN), Church of God (Cleveland TN), Church of the Nazarene, and Assemblies of God also represent approximately five percent of the religious membership in Kentucky. While there are over 50 other Christian denominations or organized religions in Kentucky, these groups each represent less than one percent of the population.

See also articles on ANTIMISSION MOVEMENT; APPALACHIAN RELIGION; CAMP MEETINGS; CAMPBELLITE TRADITION; EVOLUTION CONTROVERSY; FRONTIER, INFLUENCE OF; MIGRATION, WESTWARD (1750-1900); NATIVISM; REVIVALISM; ROMAN CATHOLIC CHURCH.

Bibliography. W. E. Arnold, *A History of Methodism in Kentucky*; Ann B. Bevins, "Sisters of the Visitation: One Hundred Years in Scott County, Mt. Admirabilis and Cardome," *The Register of the Kentucky Historical Society* 74:1 (1976): 30-39; John B Boles, *Religion in AnteBellum Kentucky*; J. W. Cooke, "Stoney Point, 1866-1969," *The Filson Club Historical Quarterly* 50:4 (1976): 337-52; Hoke S. Dickinson, ed., *The Cane Ridge Reader*; William E. Ellis, "The Fundamentalist-Moderate Schism over Evolution in the 1920s," *The Register of the Kentucky Historical Society* 74:2 (April 1976): 112-23; Winfred Ernest Garrison and Alfred T. DeGroot, *The Disciples of Christ: A History*; Fred J. Hood, ed., *Kentucky: Its History and Heritage*; Lester G. McAllister and William E. Tucker, *Journey in Faith: A History of the Christian Church (Disciples of Christ)*; Frank M. Masters, *A History of Baptists in Kentucky*; George Voiers Moore, *Interchurch Cooperation in Kentucky, 1865-1965*; William A. Mueller, *A History of Southern Baptist Theological Seminary*; A. H. Redford, *The History of Methodism in Kentucky*; P. E. Ryan, *History of the Diocese of Covington, Kentucky*; Robert F. Sexton, "The Crusade Against Pari-Mutuel Gambling in Kentucky: A Study of Southern Progressivism in the 1920s," *The Filson Club Historical Quarterly* 50:1 (Jan. 1976): 47-57; J. H. Spencer, *A History of Kentucky Baptists*; M. J. Spalding, *Sketches of the Early Catholic Missions of Kentucky, 1787-1827*; Bill L. Weaver, "Kentucky Baptists' Reaction to the National Evolution Controversy 1922-1926," *The Filson Club Historical Quarterly* 49:3 (July 1975): 266-75; B. J. Webb, *The Centenary of Catholicity in Kentucky*.

FRED J. HOOD
GEORGETOWN COLLEGE

KESTER, HOWARD ANDERSON

(1904-1977), proponent of social justice, was born in Martinsville VA, and a graduate of Lynchburg College and Vanderbilt University's School of Religion. During his student years Kester (always known as "Buck"), through his association with the YMCA and work as youth secretary of the Fellowship of Reconciliation (1927-1929), became deeply involved in the nascent interracial student movement in the South. His work as Southern secretary of the FOR (1929-1934) encompassed not only the region's racial but also its economic problems. While his initial efforts were largely educational, the Depression and capitalism's apparent inability to cope with it persuaded Kester that political action was necessary. In 1931 he joined the Socialist party and the following year he ran for Congress on its Tennessee ticket.

A 1933 dispute over the role of violence in the class struggle cost Kester his position with the pacifist FOR. Reinhold Niebuhr and others who believed he was rendering a useful service in the South sponsored the young Congregational clergyman's work until 1941 when the FELLOWSHIP OF SOUTHERN CHURCHMEN assumed responsibility for his support. During these years Kester investigated lynchings and racial unrest for the NAACP and other national groups; helped organize and publicize the SOUTHERN TENANT FARMERS UNION; and, through the Fellowship of Southern Churchmen, sought to awaken regional Protestantism to its social responsibility.

In 1943 he left the FSC to become principal of the Penn Normal Industrial and Agricultural School in South Carolina where he remained for four years. After working briefly with the relief program of the Congregational church and with the John C. Campbell Folk School in North Carolina, Kester returned to the FSC, serving as its secretary from 1952 until 1957. He spent his later years as a teacher and administrator at Eureka College in Illinois and at Christmount Assembly and Montreat-Anderson College in North Carolina.

See also articles on CHRISTIAN SOCIALISM; SOCIAL GOSPEL.

Bibliography. John Egerton, *A Mind to Stay Here: Profiles from the South*; Howard A. Kester, *Revolt Among the Sharecroppers*; Howard A. Kester Papers, Southern Historical Collection, University of North Carolina Library, Chapel Hill.

ROBERT F. MARTIN
UNIVERSITY OF NORTHERN IOWA

KESWICK MOVEMENT. The Keswick movement was one expression of a yearning for HOLINESS and spiritual power that characterized broad segments of EVANGELICALISM during the last quarter of the 19th century. The movement derives its name from a convention held annually since 1875 in Keswick, England. The teaching associated with Keswick developed from the British ministry of two Americans, Robert Pearsall Smith and William Edwin Boardman. It was given its most popular expression by Hannah Whitall Smith in her classic, *The Christian's Secret of a Happy Life* (1875).

Between 1873 and 1875, Smith and Boardman conducted a series of conferences for the promotion of holiness, stressing the necessity of "death to self" in an experience of "present" salvation. According to their version of this "higher" Christian life, the believer needed only to claim by faith, moment by moment, the reign of Christ within his soul to enter a fuller spiritual experience than most professing Christians enjoyed. After 1875, British Evangelicals, among whom were both prominent Churchmen and non-Conformists, assumed the full leadership of a movement that already attracted international participation. Regional Keswick gatherings as well as periodicals, tracts, and books helped further the emphases identified with the conventions.

Exponents of the Keswick message maintain that they introduce no new teaching but emphasize "old truths, sadly neglected." Central to this claim has been their insistence on the verbal inspiration of Scripture. Handley Moule, bishop of Durham and theologian of Keswick, defined the movement's purpose in words succeeding generations have reiterated: "Keswick stands for . . . a message as old as the Apostles but too much forgotten: the open secret of inward victory for liberty in life and service through the trusted power of an indwelling Christ."

A stress on repeated "fillings of the Holy Spirit" became central both to the notion of living in "victory" over sin and to the Keswick teaching on Christian service. The conventions devote one full day to foreign missions and have encouraged hundreds to consecrate their lives to the cause. In addition, the convention has financed tours to other lands by Keswick missioners who present the movement's distinctive emphasis.

The Keswick movement became directly important to American Evangelicalism from 1892 when D. L. Moody decided to introduce its teaching at his Northfield conferences. Some of Moody's associates, most notably A. J. Gordon and R. A. Torrey, had already committed themselves in their own ministries to similar emphases. As others accepted the message, the 1890s became a decade of rich interchange among such prominent spokesmen and American Evangelicals as F. B. Meyer, Andrew Murray, H. W. Webb-Peploe, A. T. Pierson, and R. A. Torrey. Keswick teachers toured the United States widely and found receptive audiences, especially among non-Wesleyan Evangelicals. Their focus on the "quality" of religious experience rather than on doctrine made their appeal transcend denominational organization and permanently influenced American Evangelicalism. Keswick's motto is "All one in Christ Jesus."

After Moody's death in 1899, the Keswick influence disappeared from the program of his institutions at Northfield. In 1913 Charles Trumbull, editor of the *Sunday School Times*, organized an American Keswick that, from 1923, has been located in Whiting NJ. This and other regional Keswicks have no formal affiliation with the British convention, which remains the most influential regular gathering.

See also articles on HOLINESS MOVEMENT; SECOND BLESSING.

Bibliography. Steven Barabas, *So Great Salvation*; John Pollock, *The Keswick Story*; Herbert Stevenson, ed., *Keswick's Authentic Voice*.

EDITH L. BLUMHOFER
SOUTHWEST MISSOURI STATE UNIVERSITY

KING, JOSEPH HILLERY (1869-1946),
early leader of American PENTECOSTALISM was born in Anderson County SC. The family moved to Franklin County GA in 1885 where young King was converted during a Methodist camp meeting near Carnesville. Shortly thereafter, while attending a Holiness convention led by a Methodist pastor, King testified to receiving an experience of entire SANCTIFICATION.

Feeling a call to the ministry, King joined the Georgia Conference of the Northern Methodist Episcopal Church in 1894 after a short period of service in the U. S. Army. After studying in the school of theology at the U. S. Grant University in Chattanooga, King returned to north Georgia and pastored several Methodist charges.

A staunch supporter of the HOLINESS MOVEMENT in the Methodist Church, King became disillusioned when opposition to the SECOND BLESSING theory began to arise in the church. In 1898 he joined the fledgling FIRE-BAPTIZED HOLINESS CHURCH that was led by Nebraska evangelist B. H. Irwin. King was made vice-president and in 1900 succeeded Irwin as president.

In 1908 King joined the ranks of the fast-spreading Pentecostal movement after having experienced speaking in tongues (q.v., GLOSSOLALIA) in Toccoa GA. He then led his young Holiness denomination into the Pentecostal movement. In 1911 his church merged with the PENTECOSTAL HOLINESS CHURCH of North Carolina while King was on a trip around the world. In 1914 he published his classic theological work entitled *From Passover to Pentecost*. In 1917 King was elected as general superintendent of the Pentecostal Holiness Church and 20 years later he was consecrated as the first bishop of his denomination.

Bibliography. Joseph C. Campbell, *The Pentecostal Holiness Church, 1898-1948*; Joseph H. and Blanche L. King, *Yet Speaketh*; Vinson Synan, *The Old-Time Power*.

VINSON SYNAN
OKLAHOMA CITY, OKLAHOMA

KING, MARTIN LUTHER, JR. (1929-1968),
black minister and civil rights champion, was born in Atlanta GA the son of MARTIN LUTHER KING, SR. and Alberta (Williams) King.

While attending Morehouse College in his native city between 1945 and 1948, he was greatly influenced by BENJAMIN E. MAYS, the school's president. When in search of a vocational career and in doubt about the Christian ministry, King was counseled by Mays to take a deeper look at ministerial work. After making a positive decision, King left in 1948 to attend Crozer Theological Seminary in Chester PA. During his student years he heard Mordecai Wyatt Johnson, president of Howard University, give a lecture on "The Implications of Mohandas K. Gandhi's Philosophy of Nonviolence for the Freedom of Blacks in America." King was so inspired that he became a lifelong student of Gandhi's philosophy of nonviolence.

Graduating from Crozer with a straight A record, King won the Crozer scholarship and enrolled in the Ph.D. program in Systematic Theology at Boston University. Studying under L. Harold DeWolf, Edgar S. Brightman, and Walter Muelder, King was influenced greatly by the philosophy of Personalism. He wrote his dissertation on "A Comparison of the Conception of God from the Thought of Paul Tillich and Henry Nelson Wieman," after which he was awarded the Ph.D. in 1955.

King attracted international attention later that same year. While serving as pastor of Dexter Avenue Baptist Church in Montgomery AL, he led the successful Montgomery bus boycott. In protest against racial discrimination and segregation against blacks, King then led massive civil rights marches throughout the South and in some parts of the North. This activity reached its height in 1963 when King led the greatest civil rights demonstration for freedom in America. In Washington DC, thousands of Americans from diverse ethnic and religious backgrounds demonstrated for freedom. That same year *Time* magazine selected King as its 37th Man of the Year and acclaimed him as one of the most influential people in America. In 1964 he received the Nobel Peace Prize for his service as the single most effective voice for peace in the world.

Because of the demands placed upon him at the national level in the area of human rights, King resigned from the pastorate of Dexter Avenue Baptist Church and accepted a copastorate with his father at Ebenezer Baptist Church in Atlanta. He was the founder and president of the SOUTHERN CHRISTIAN LEADERSHIP CONFERENCE. He published seven books, including *Stride Toward Freedom*, which received the Ainsfield-Wolf Award as the best book in race relations in 1958. During his brief career King received over 400 awards.

He married Coretta Scott, a concert singer and influential leader in her own right. He was assassinated in 1968 in Memphis as he continued his efforts to bring about racial reconciliation and economic justice.

See also articles on BLACK MINISTERIAL PROTEST LEADERSHIP; CIVIL RIGHTS MOVEMENT.

Bibliography. Lerone Bennett, Jr., *What Manner of Man*; Coretta Scott King, *My Life with Martin Luther King, Jr.*; Kenneth L. Smith and Ira G. Zepp, Jr., *Search for the Beloved Community: The Thinking of Martin Luther King, Jr.*.

HENRY J. YOUNG
GARRETT-EVANGELICAL SEMINARY

KING, MARTIN LUTHER, SR.

(1899-), patriarchal black Baptist minister, was born in Stockbridge GA a few miles outside of Atlanta. The son of a sharecropper family, he was one of 10 children. Later to acquire the name Daddy King, he left the rural community very early and moved to Atlanta to seek educational advancement.

Soon thereafter he met and later married the daughter of the pastor of Ebenezer Baptist Church in Atlanta. He worked his way through the Atlanta public school system and later completed the bachelor's degree at Morehouse College. His decision to enter the Christian ministry as a career resulted in Ebenezer Church's inviting him to the pastorate shortly after the death of his father-in-law in 1931. Under his fearless leadership in protesting segregation, second-class citizenship for blacks and discrimination against them, Ebenezer soon became one of the most influential black churches in the South. In 1934 King traveled throughout Europe, the Middle East, and Africa and developed new perspectives on human rights. This led King as early as 1935 to organize direct actions against segregation in Atlanta.

MARTIN LUTHER KING, JR., his internationally famous son, first learned the art of organizing direct protest against the inhumanity of racial discrimination under the tutelage of his father. The senior King nurtured young Martin in self-respect, dignity, and freedom. So in 1955 when history thrust upon the junior King the role of chief spokesperson for the cause of human rights, the foundation had long since been laid for him by his father.

HENRY J. YOUNG
GARRETT-EVANGELICAL SEMINARY

KOINONIA FARM.

Established just outside Americus GA in the autumn of 1942, Koinonia Farm is a Christian community that is intended as a model of the life-style and values of the New Testament Church. The name for the community is the Greek word for "fellowship" or "communion," representative of the members' intention to share material possessions in common.

The idea for Koinonia was developed by CLARENCE JORDAN, a Georgia-born Baptist minister, whose study of the New Testament led him to a strong commitment to pacifism, racial equality, and careful stewardship of the earth's resources. Jordan and his family were joined in the initial Koinonia venture by the Martin Englands, war-furloughed Baptist missionaries to Burma. It was their intention to use the farm as a source of spiritual and agricultural support for the economically depressed region around it.

Jordan's undergraduate training in agriculture undergirded the technical success of the experiment from the outset. Koinonia pioneered in the use of scientific methods for poultry and livestock farming in southwest Georgia and provided assistance for untrained farmers in the area to learn the necessary techniques. In more recent times, the cultivation of pecans, peanuts, and grapes has provided a steady income for Koinonia, as well as a good model for neighboring farmers.

The usual social problems that confront communal ventures were aggravated in Koinonia's case by its forthright advocacy of pacifism and racial integration. During the racial strife of the late 1950s, the members of the Koinonia community were severely harassed by some of their less tolerant neighbors. Acts of physical violence directed at the members of the community and their property were attended by a stringent economic boycott that nearly forced its closing. The assistance of friends, both through direct contributions and through their support of Koinonia's mail-order pecan business, kept the community alive.

A new phase of the Koinonia experiment was begun in the late 1960s with the establishment of Koinonia Partners, an organization dedicated to providing low-cost, interest-free housing for the rural poor. Jordan was joined in the initiation of this project by Millard Fuller, a young Alabama native, who left a lucrative law practice to join the Koinonia community. This new program builds and finances several new houses each year, using construction methods especially developed by the members of the building team, and has recently extended its work to other continents.

At the time of Clarence Jordan's sudden death in 1969, the community was in the midst of a period of numerical growth that continued well into the 1970s. In recent years, there have usually been about 50 people in residence at Koinonia.

See also articles on ETHICS, CHRISTIAN; SEGREGATION; UTOPIAN COMMUNITIES.

Bibliography. Dallas Lee, *The Cotton Patch Evidence*; H. W. Tull, "Koinonia Updated," *Christian Century* 93 (October 13, 1976): 868-72.

JOHN W. KUYKENDALL
AUBURN UNIVERSITY

KORESHANITY. The religion of a small utopian community that called itself Koreshan Unity, was largely the work of a visionary named Cyrus Read Teed (1839-1908). A personal spiritual awakening in 1869 redirected Teed's life from a marginal career in medicine in upstate New York to the leadership of one of the "mind cure" movements that typified late nineteenth-century America.

The name "Koreshan" was Teed's transliteration of the name "Cyrus" from Hebrew. He claimed that his own spirit had once inhabited the body of Cyrus of Persia, as well as many other famous historical personages. Although he used the terminology of orthodox Christianity, Teed's unique personal teachings constituted the essential basis of Koreshanity. Among his more distinctive doctrines was the concept of "cellular cosmogony"—the idea that our world is the convex inner surface of a hollow sphere or globe that faces toward an energy-laden celestial nucleus at the center. Teed claimed to have proven his hypothesis through experiments using a special sighting device called a "rectilineator."

In 1886 Teed was elected president of the National Association of Mental Science. Soon thereafter he began to lay plans for the establishment of a utopian community based on his teachings. After the failure of a grandiose plan to merge several older groups under his leadership, Teed decided to seek a site for an independent community. Eventually, he decided upon a remote but beautiful location just south of Fort Myers FL on the banks of the Estero River, where his

"New Jerusalem" began operation in 1894.

Although Teed claimed a following of 10,000 members throughout the United States, the population of his Florida community never numbered more than 200. The standard of living was somewhat meager, dependent upon small-scale agriculture and orchard activities. Full-fledged members of the Koreshan Unity were expected to adopt a celibate life-style and Teed himself claimed sole right to the education of community children. During the early years of their experiment, the Koreshan group maintained positive relations with the surrounding settlers. In 1906, however, Teed became embroiled in a political dispute with several of the political leaders of the Fort Myers area, and the community fell into local disrepute.

Although Koreshanity survived Teed's death in 1908, its potential for growth was ended. In 1961, the surviving leadership transferred the property to the state of Florida as a state historical site. *See also* article on UTOPIAN COMMUNITIES.

JOHN W. KUYKENDALL
AUBURN UNIVERSITY

KU KLUX KLAN. A terrorist society, revitalization movement, and fraternal lodge, the Klan was founded in the South after the Civil War and recalled to life several times in the 20th century. During Reconstruction it functioned briefly but effectively to overthrow black and Republican political power. The Klan's religious aspect came with its revival as a Protestant lodge in 1915 by former Methodist minister and fraternal organizer, William J. Simmons. "Colonel" Simmons introduced the flaming cross—probably borrowed from the THOMAS DIXON novel *The Clansman* (1906)—and added a religious note to the initiation and ritual. The Klan's white, Protestant, native-born exclusiveness was not unusual among fraternal orders, and it tapped a deep strain of American NATIVISM, enlarged by wartime passions, postwar immigration,

and the changing social world of the 1920s. Klan recruiters, often former ministers, focused their appeal on protection of traditional American values and small-town morality against the outsider-alien, particularly as represented by the ROMAN CATHOLIC CHURCH.

In the 1920s, the Klan spread across America, literally from Maine to California, in the cities as well as small towns. It recruited best among Baptist, Methodists, and Disciples of Christ, and among the Masons and Orange Lodges. The Klan appealed to an America identified with the Anglo-Saxon and Protestant heritage and a sense that that world was under attack. The Klan adopted Rom. 12:1 as "the Klan verse," made church visits and donations, and loudly supported prohibition, law and order, public morality, and school prayer. To many ministers who served as Klan chaplains or welcomed it from the pulpit, the Klan seemed the militant arm of Evangelical Protestantism.

Despite support from individual ministers and Alma White's Pillar of Fire Church, no church convention or major denomination endorsed the Klan. However, support for the Klan was a serious issue and one Methodist bishop felt called upon to warn his fellow clergy that their religion was based on the "Blood of Christ," not Anglo-Saxon blood. Klansmen boycotted Catholic and Jewish merchants, supported immigration controls, prohibition, and a Protestant version of public education. A Klan-promoted law banning parochial schools in Oregon was overturned by the U.S. Supreme Court. Probably at least one out of every 10 native-born, white, Protestant, adult males, belonged to the Klan in the 1920s.

By the later 1920s, Klan violence, immorality, and community divisiveness had thinned its ranks. Even the selection of the Roman Catholic Al Smith as Democratic presidential candidate in 1928 did not bring a revival. In the 1930s, the Klan added concern with Communism and the "Jewish menace" to the "black peril" and somewhat quieted its anti-Catholicism. Klan fortunes waned, and in 1939 the Klan's imperial headquarters in Atlanta were sold to the Roman Catholic Church.

Revived after World War II, but fragmented into competing units, Klansmen bombed synagogues and burned black churches during the civil rights movement of the 1950s and 1960s. Black and many white congregations organized opposition to the Klan. While anti-Catholicism lingered weakly in older Klan organizations, newer Klan empires and a Canadian offspring accepted Roman Catholic members.

See also article on JEWS IN THE SOUTH.

Bibliography. David Chalmers, *Hooded Americanism: The History of the Ku Klux Klan*; Robert M. Miller, "A Note on the Relationship between the Protestant Churches and the Revived Ku Klux Klan," *Journal of Southern History* 22 (August 1956): 355-68.

DAVID CHALMERS
UNIVERSITY OF FLORIDA

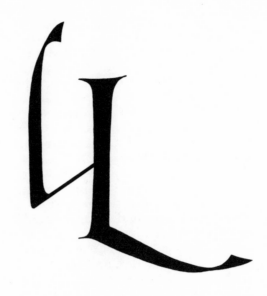

LAKE JUNALUSKA. Lake Junaluska is the most important summer assembly ground in Southern Methodism. Action to establish a place for educational programs, missionary support, and preaching was officially taken in 1908 by the Laymen's Missionary Movement of the Methodist Episcopal Church, South. Bishop James Atkins, George R. Stuart, along with John R. Pepper and JAMES CANNON, JR. were among the most instrumental leaders in establishing the assembly. A site in the Great Smoky Mountains just outside of Waynesville NC was chosen. Construction began in 1912 and the first conference was held in 1913.

The program grew steadily as the Sunday school and missions boards utilized the grounds and built classrooms and increased housing facilities. The Great Depression brought financial troubles resulting in bankruptcy in 1932. Jerry Liner, James Adkins, Jr., W. A. Lambeth, and E. A. Cole were principally responsible for seeing the assembly through to a position of financial stability.

Since 1936, the assembly has grown steadily with summer programs as the focus. In 1955 the World Methodist Council constructed its headquarters at Lake Junaluska and the assembly became the symbolic center for 63 Methodist churches from 90 countries. In 1978 a new Terrace Hotel was built and a year-round program instituted. Presently there are over 500 homes on the grounds with some 250 permanent residences. The assembly continues to be the representative and actual center of southeastern United Methodism.

See also article on METHODIST CHURCH.

Bibliography. Elmer T. Clark, *Junaluska Jubilee*; Mason Crum, *The Story of Lake Junaluska*; Love Branner Atkins Shackford, *The Origin of Lake Junaluska Southern Assembly.*

THOMAS A. LANGFORD
DUKE UNIVERSITY

LANDMARK MOVEMENT. This interpretation of Baptist theology arose in the SOUTHERN BAPTIST CONVENTION near the middle of the 19th century. Called "Old Landmarkism" by its early advocates, the movement was intended to preserve and defend what its leaders thought to be the historic tenets of the Baptist faith.

The originator and dominant figure of Landmarkism was JAMES R. GRAVES (1820-1893), who settled in Nashville TN in 1845 after migrating from Vermont by way of brief residences in Ohio and Kentucky. In 1848 Graves became senior editor of a Baptist publication that he renamed the *Tennessee Baptist*. Graves widened his activities in Nashville by entering the publishing business and by editing a monthly, a quarterly, and an annual, as well as his paper. By the early 1850s his writings and publications were reaching large numbers of Baptists and by 1861 Graves probably was the most powerful Baptist figure in the mid-South and Southwest. Besides his thousands of followers, two men of unusual ability, J. M. Pendleton of Kentucky and A. C. Dayton of Mississippi, joined the Landmark cause. They, with Graves, became known as the "Great Triumvirate" of Landmarkism.

Landmarkism had the character of a rigidly exclusive High Churchism. The claims of the true church, Graves believed, rested upon three biblically based principles: (1) the true church was founded by Christ; (2) it has had a perpetual existence since its founding; and (3) it has possessed the same essential structure throughout its history.

Graves held that all true churches have been interlocked in unbroken historical succession from the time of Christ to the present. A true church is composed, in principle, of believers only. Its members are inducted by baptism, the prescribed marks of which are: a proper subject, a believer; a proper mode, immersion; a proper authority for baptizing, an authentic (that is, a Baptist) church; a proper administrator, a Baptist (usually a minister, but not necessarily) who has himself been baptized on a profession of faith, under the authority of a Baptist church; and a proper design, to declare a salvation already possessed, not to procure salvation in the baptismal act. Authentic baptism is prerequisite to admission to the Lord's Supper. So-called ALIEN IMMERSION (immersions not performed under the auspices of a Baptist church) are not baptisms at all since they lack the

authorization of true churches. Communion services are spurious unless conducted under the sponsorship of a Baptist church. Non-Baptist ministers, since they lack ordination by true churches, are not authorized to preach. The church is local in character. Each church is self-governing under Christ. God gave authority in the church to the congregation itself, not to a ministerial class within the church. True churches have never persecuted and never apostatized.

If a "religious society" lacks any of the requirements stated above Graves thought, it is not, and cannot be, a church.

Graves, in defining "church succession," naively held that Baptist churches could be traced back to the first century through the history of dissent. It is doubtful that any knowledgeable historian would give any credence to this theory today.

The Civil War interrupted the advance of Landmarkism, but the movement made a strong resurgence after the war. Before Graves died, it had become a prevailing Baptist ideology in Tennessee, southwest Kentucky, northern Alabama, Arkansas, Mississippi, Texas, and Louisiana. Pockets of Landmarkism during the 20th century appeared in all the Southern states and indeed as far north and west as Hawaii and Alaska.

Landmarkism has by no means been confined to the Southern Baptist Convention. In the Southwest two sizable Landmark Baptist denominations flourish today: the AMERICAN BAPTIST ASSOCIATION and the BAPTIST MISSIONARY ASSOCIATION OF AMERICA. Their collective membership totals over one million people.

The Landmark Movement was unable to preserve its original synthesis of elements as formulated by Graves. Though now in considerable decline, it is still identifiable among Southern Baptists in the virtual disappearance of the doctrine of the universal church, in a negative attitude towards "alien" immersions, and in the hostility of many Southern Baptists towards the ecumenical movement.

The principal importance of Land-markism is that it became perhaps the dominant ECCLESIOLOGY of Southern Baptists during the latter half of the 19th century and through at least the first third of the 20th century. It still affects profoundly the ecclesiology and polity of the Southern Baptist Convention.

See also articles on HIGH CHURCH/LOW CHURCH; RELIGIOUS PRESS; SACRAMENTS AND ORDINANCES.

Bibliography. J. R. Graves, *Old Landmarkism—What Is It?*

JAMES E. TULL
SOUTHEASTERN BAPTIST SEMINARY

LATTER-DAY SAINTS: *See* MORMONS IN THE SOUTH; REORGANIZED CHURCH OF JESUS CHRIST OF LATTER-DAY SAINTS.

LEAVELL FAMILY. Distinguished Baptist leaders, this family is descended from George Washington Leavell (1844-1905), a native of Pontotoc County MS, ex-Confederate soldier and businessman, and his wife, Corra Alice (Berry) Leavell (1851-1913). Through their family of nine sons, they have left a remarkable legacy of leadership to Southern Baptists.

The oldest, Landrum Pinson (1874-1929), was a gifted organizer and promoter of Sunday school and youth work. He was field secretary of the Southern Baptist Sunday School Board, first secretary of the Baptist Young Peoples Union, and teacher (1915-1920) of Sunday school pedagogy at the Southern Baptist Theological Seminary.

Frank Hartwell (1884-1949), pioneer leader of Southern Baptist campus ministries, was secretary of the Department of Student Work of the Sunday School Board from 1928 until his death, and in 1926 initiated the annual student retreat at Ridgecrest Baptist Assembly.

Roland Quinche (1891-1963) was a pastor of Baptist churches in Mississippi, Georgia, and Florida; superintendent of

Evangelism of the Home Mission Board of the Southern Baptist Convention (1937-1942); and president of New Orleans Baptist Theological Seminary (1946-1958). During his administration the seminary was moved from its Washington Avenue site to its present 75-acre campus in the Gentilly section.

The other sons were Arnaud Bruce (1877-1949), a dentist and Baptist layman; James Berry (1880-1933), bank cashier, pastor, and evangelist; George Walne (1882-1957), medical missionary to China; Clarence Stanley (1889-1968), state Sunday school secretary; Ullin Whitney (1894-1960), college professor and educational missionary to China; and Leonard O. (1886-1952), state Sunday school secretary and pastor. His legacy has been carried on through his son, Landrum Pinson II (1926-), a pastor of Baptist churches in Mississippi and Texas, first vice-president of the Southern Baptist Convention (1967-1968), president of the Southern Baptist Pastors' Conference (1970-1971), president of the Baptist General Convention of Texas (1971-1973), and since 1975 president of New Orleans Baptist Theological Seminary.

Bibliography. Charlotte Henry Leavell, ed., *Genealogy of the Nine Leavell Brothers of Oxford, Mississippi* (1957); L. P. Leavell, *Mr. and Mrs. George W. Leavell* (1927); C. B. Hamlet III, "Leavell, George Washington," *Encyclopedia of Southern Baptists*, 2: 782; C. Aubrey Hearn, "Leavell, Landrum Pinson," *Encyclopedia of Southern Baptists*, 2: 782; J. Hardee Kennedy, "Leavell, Roland Quinche," *Encyclopedia of Southern Baptists*, 3: 1804; William Hall Preston, "Leavell, Frank Hartwell," *Encyclopedia of Southern Baptists*, 2: 781-82.

DANIEL HOLCOMB
NEW ORLEANS BAPTIST SEMINARY

LECTURESHIPS (CHURCHES OF CHRIST). This is a form of religious education that has served as a rallying center for CHURCHES OF CHRIST unity and orthodoxy. Emerging from the dissension that splintered the Disciples of Christ in the decades following the Civil War, members of the new movement found themselves at the beginning of the 20th century an impoverished, if impassioned, minority. Outside middle Tennessee, almost all meetinghouses and schools were in the hands of "digressives." Communication among a scattered remnant was left primarily to weekly journals that regularly attacked the "digressives," the "sects," and indeed any deviation, real or imagined, from a closely guarded consensus. "State meetings," which had brought evangelists and leading members together in earlier times, were now seen as seedbeds in which support of missionary societies, use of instrumental music in worship, and other abhorrent "innovations" had been cultivated. Isolated and embittered in tiny clusters of true believers, church leaders found few opportunities for the face-to-face dialogue or spiritual and intellectual enrichment they had previously enjoyed in large gatherings for preaching and discussion.

As church leaders set about recreating "loyal" schools, they sought ways to serve struggling congregations while promoting "Christian education." Shortly after its founding, Childers Classical Institute brought university-trained evangelist George A. Klingman to Abilene TX for a series of lectures in 1907, attended by students and preachers from the area. As the expanding school became Abilene Christian College, the program became "a short course in the Bible" and then a "preachers' meeting" with lectures by several distinguished evangelists. By 1918 Abilene Christian had assembled its first annual "Bible lecture week" with six days of speeches.

Such gatherings were not new; West Tennessee Christian College—soon disbanded as the Disciples divided—had scheduled just such a "lecture course" as early as 1892. But Abilene Christian was the first school in the movement to concentrate its lectureship in a single week of the academic year; and in 1919, it was the first to publish its annual lectures in a book. This program continues to draw 10,000 visitors to Abilene each year the last week in February. Other Southern schools related to the Churches of Christ followed Abilene's example: Harding

College in 1924, Freed-Hardeman College in 1937, Alabama Christian in 1943, Oklahoma Christian in 1950, Lubbock Christian in 1957, then Fort Worth Christian in 1960. David Lipscomb College inaugurated a lectureship in 1947, coincident with its expansion to four-year college status, but its program has not continued annually. Symposia, seminars, panel discussions, and open forums have become regular features of lectureships, along with displays of products and services related to church activity. More recently, local churches have begun sponsoring lectureships to scrutinize issues in which they are particularly interested.

While the influence and importance of lectureships, particularly at Abilene, may have been exaggerated by William Banowsky in *The Mirror of a Movement*, his book about that enterprise, many observers would agree with the verdict of the eminent minister-editor Reuel Lemmons in 1959: "The lectures delivered at our Christian colleges have become accepted everywhere as the very best in brotherhood thinking and presentation." From the beginning, lectureships have promoted "Christian education," defined and resolved areas of conflict, presented challenges for action, and broadened the intellectual-theological consensus of Churches of Christ.

Bibliography. William S. Banowsky, *The Mirror of a Movement.*

DON HAYMES
MACON, GEORGIA

LEE, JESSE (1758-1816), early Methodist evangelist, stands second only to FRANCIS ASBURY for leadership achievements in the first 50 years of American Methodist history. Born in Prince George County VA, into a family won to evangelical faith by the Anglican DEVEREUX JARRATT, he experienced conversion in 1774. Lee was an eyewitness of the Methodist revival in his native area in 1775 and 1776. He served briefly in the Continental Army in 1880. A local preacher for a time, he was the first native Virginian to enter the Methodist ministry. Asbury found him in Salisbury NC in 1785. Connected with the Baltimore Circuit by 1788, he shared in the great Methodist revival that began in Virginia in 1787. Chosen by Asbury to make a frontal attack on New England, he was appointed to begin work in the Stamford CT area in 1789. At Stratfield that same year he organized the first Methodist society in New England. For 10 years, he ministered in all of the states of New England.

In 1801 Lee returned to Virginia to serve as presiding elder of the Norfolk District. He was nominated for bishop in 1800, but Whatcoat was chosen over him. His later ministry was in the Virginia and the Baltimore Conferences. He published a history of United States Methodists in 1810. Lee was chaplain of the United States House of Representatives from 1809 to 1815.

See also articles on GREAT REVIVAL; REVIVALISM.

Bibliography. Emory S. Bucke, ed., *The History of American Methodism; Illustrated History of Methodism*; William Warren Sweet, *Virginia Methodism, A History.*

WILLIAM L. LUMPKIN
NORFOLK, VIRGINIA

LEE, ROBERT GREENE (1886-1978),

classical Southern religious orator, was born in York County SC, the son of a sharecropping family. A symbol of his climb from obscurity and poverty to fame and affluence is the transfer of the log cabin where he was born to the Cardova Baptist Encampment near Memphis TN where he spent the major part of his ministerial career.

Converted and baptized a Southern Baptist at the age of 12, Lee almost immediately wanted to be a preacher and demonstrated remarkable oratorical skills but remained at home to help his parents on their farm until his 21st birthday. The years 1907-1908 he spent working on the construction of the Panama Canal, earning enough money to begin his college career at Furman University where he was graduated in 1913.

Lee served several Baptist churches in South Carolina before becoming pastor of the First Baptist Church of New Orleans (1922-1925). After a brief return to South Carolina to serve a church in Charleston, he became pastor of the promising Bellevue Baptist Church in Memphis in 1927 and remained there until his retirement in 1960. His fame and prestige grew steadily over the years, and he served four terms as president of the Tennessee Baptist Convention and three times as president of the SOUTHERN BAPTIST CONVENTION (1948-1951).

The most famous of Lee's sermons is "Pay Day Someday," which he repeated over 1,260 times. His theological emphasis was spiritual more than social and his ECCLESIOLOGY strictly denominational.

See also article on PREACHING.

Bibliography. E. Schuyler English, *Robert G. Lee, A Chosen Vessel*; Robert G. Lee, *Payday Everyday.*

JAMES T. BAKER
WESTERN KENTUCKY UNIVERSITY

LELAND, JOHN (1754-1841), advocate

of religious liberty and sometimes confused with an English minister of the same name and era, merits the distinction of having served as the staunchest figure in that cause among Baptists in America. Although a resident of Massachusetts for much of his life, Leland served as an itinerant minister in Virginia from 1776-1791 and was regarded by the Virginia Baptist historian ROBERT B. SEMPLE as "probably the most popular" preacher of that era and "unquestionably a man of fertile genius."

The concerted agitation by Leland and others for complete religious freedom met with success in 1786 with the passage of the bill written by THOMAS JEFFERSON for Establishing Religious Freedom in Virginia. In 1788, Virginia Baptists became convinced that the proposed Federal Constitution did not adequately provide for religious liberty. As a result, Leland announced his candidacy for the Virginia Convention as an opponent of ratification. However, upon being assured by JAMES MADISON that this shortcoming would be rectified, he threw his support to Madison, who was easily elected. Madison's resultant proposal of the Bill of Rights provided the necessary safeguard for religious liberty in the First Amendment.

Civil liberty as well as religious liberty was of paramount concern to Leland. At the meeting of the General Committee of Virginia Baptists held in Richmond on 8 August 1789, Leland drafted the resolution condemning SLAVERY as "a violent deprivation of the rights of nature, and inconsistent with a republican government" and recommending the use of "every legal measure to extirpate this horrid evil from the land."

Returning to Massachusetts in 1791, Leland continued the struggle for religious liberty both as a minister in Cheshire and later as an elected representative to that state's House of Representatives from Berkshire County. Perhaps the best known incident in Leland's life was the presentation in 1801 of an enormous cheese weighing 1,235 pounds to Thomas Jefferson, the newly elected president of the United States. The gift was prepared by the women of the Cheshire congregation as a result of Leland's admiration for Jefferson's position on religious liberty. Shortly before his death, Leland's efforts for religious liberty resulted in 1833 in the disestablishment of the church in Massachusetts, the last state establishment to be eliminated, and the provision by law for complete religious liberty.

See also articles on CHURCH AND STATE; DISESTABLISHMENT.

Bibliography. L. F. Greene, ed., *The Writings of the Late Elder John Leland*; Robert B. Semple, *A History of the Rise and Progress of the Baptists in Virginia.*

BERNARD H. COCHRAN
MEREDITH COLLEGE

LIBERAL RELIGION: *See* UNITARIANS IN THE SOUTH.

LIELE, GEORGE (1750-?), pioneer black preacher, served during the formative years of black church development. He was perceived by many very early as an orator of extraordinary magnitude. Born in Virginia in 1750, he moved with his master, Henry Sharpe, to Burke County GA. He attended a local Baptist church with his master regularly. After being baptized he decided upon the ministry as a career. His unusual gift as an orator enabled him to preach frequently to both black and white congregations. He was in great demand as a preacher and found himself traveling extensively throughout the Savannah area.

The response to George Liele's gift as a preacher by black and white people alike led to his master's decision to free him. His freedom provided him with the opportunity to make a full-time commitment to the Christian ministry. Among his many converts was ANDREW BRYAN, an influential black Baptist preacher. Also, although the SILVER BLUFF BAPTIST CHURCH originated under the leadership of the Reverend Mr. Palmer, its major development flourished under George Liele. It is reported to be the first independent black Baptist church in America.

Liele's ministerial work flourished until it was interrupted by the Revolutionary War, during which his master was killed. Heirs of Henry Sharpe's estate did not agree to Liele's manumission and, therefore, had him imprisoned in the expectation that he would be reenslaved. Because Colonel Kirkland of the British Army had him released, when the British evacuated Savannah, Liele went to Jamaica indentured to Kirkland for a brief period.

Liele worked to secure money to pay off his indenture and obtained a certificate of manumission in 1784. He then began full-time ministerial work in Kingston, Jamaica, which resulted in the establishment of a congregation of over 500 members and the building of a large church. His ministerial work in both the Savannah and Kingston areas proved to be among the most progressive accomplishments of his day.

HENRY J. YOUNG
GARRETT-EVANGELICAL SEMINARY

LINCOLN, ABRAHAM (1809-1865), sixteenth president of the United States, was born near present-day Hodgenville KY. He grew up, by his account, "in the most humble walks of life" in Kentucky and Indiana. Aside from brief stints in country schools, he was self-educated.

After moving with his family to Illinois, Lincoln settled in New Salem in 1831. There he held various jobs, read law, and developed a keen interest in politics. Elected as a Whig to the state legislature in 1834, he served four terms, eventually becoming his party's floor leader. Like his hero, Henry Clay, he favored a strong national government, government-supported internal improvements, and the Bank of the United States. He believed slavery to be wrong, but he was no abolitionist.

Lincoln moved to Springfield in 1837 and, having been admitted to the bar, began practicing law. In 1846 he was elected to Congress. His one term in the House of Representatives was undistinguished save for his actions concerning the Mexican War and slavery. His "spot resolutions" implied that President Polk had needlessly provoked the war, and he proposed the gradual abolition of slavery in the nation's capital. He returned to Springfield in 1849 and resumed his increasingly successful law practice.

His opposition to the Kansas-Nebraska Act brought Lincoln back to politics as a candidate. He ran unsuccessfully for the United States Senate in 1855. Soon thereafter he joined the new Republican party. Campaigning again for the Senate in 1858, he delivered his famous "house divided" address and engaged with Democratic opponent Stephen A. Douglas in a series of debates that failed to put him in the Senate but won him national prominence.

When other candidates proved unacceptable in 1860, the Republicans gave Lincoln their presidential nomination. His election caused seven states to secede and form a Southern confederacy. Though Lincoln privately told Southerners that their institutions would not be assailed, his determination to preserve the Union, to keep slavery out of the territories, and to hold federal property in the South led to war and the secession of four more states. Lincoln prosecuted the war vigorously, assuming broad powers and looking always to restore the Union. Through the Emancipation Proclamation of 1 January 1863, freedom for Southern slaves effectively became a war aim. Lincoln died before his plans for Reconstruction matured, but his Louisiana experiment, pocket veto of the Wade-Davis bill, and second inaugural address indicated that he wanted few conditions placed on the South beyond acceptance of the Thirteenth Amendment.

Although he had a fatalistic belief in God, Lincoln never joined a church. During the war he increasingly viewed himself as an instrument of God, and he became a quasi-messiah in the minds of Southern slaves and freedmen. His martyrdom at the hands of John Wilkes Booth helped enshrine him in the pantheon of American civil religion.

See also articles on CIVIL WAR; SLAVERY.

Bibliography. Roy P. Basler, ed., *Collected Works of Abraham Lincoln*, 9 vols.; James Garfield Randall, *Lincoln the President*, 4 vols.; Benjamin P. Thomas, *Abraham Lincoln*.

DANIEL LEE CLOYD
AUBURN UNIVERSITY

LIPSCOMB, DAVID (1831-1917), early CHURCHES OF CHRIST leader, was born in Franklin County TN. Educated at Franklin College, Nashville, he enrolled in 1846 and graduated in 1849. While in college he was baptized by TOLBERT FANNING and became a member of the DISCIPLES OF CHRIST. His plans did not include preaching and other public Christian work, but he began preaching before the Civil War. During the war he became concerned with the question of war and the Christian's participation in civil government. He accepted the basic Mennonite views of government.

At the conclusion of the Civil War, Lipscomb and Tolbert Fanning reissued the *Gospel Advocate.* For the next 47 years Lipscomb served as the editor of the paper. He emphasized a very literal interpretation of the Bible. Consequently, he believed the silence of the Scriptures must be respected. He opposed the missionary society movement among Disciples and was against the use of instruments in worship. He became the most important leader of the conservative Disciples. As the years of the 19th century progressed, he and others of like persuasion began using the name Churches of Christ to designate this group. By 1906 the Churches of Christ and the Disciples of Christ were two separate groups.

Always interested in education, he was responsible for organizing the Fanning Orphan School in 1884. With James A. Harding, Lipscomb founded the Nashville Bible School, now David Lipscomb College, in 1891. He was never the president of either school, but served each as chairman of the board of trustees.

Besides his editing, Lipscomb wrote *Civil Government, Biography and Sermons of Jesse Sewell,* and several commentaries on New Testament books. Articles and questions and answers from the *Advocate* have been compiled into other volumes.

See also articles on ANTIMISSION MOVEMENT; CAMPBELLITE TRADITION; RELIGIOUS PRESS.

Bibliography. Robert E. Hooper, *Crying in the Wilderness: A Biography of David Lipscomb*; Earl West, *Life and Times of David Lipscomb.*

ROBERT E. HOOPER
DAVID LIPSCOMB COLLEGE

LITERATURE AND RELIGION. The
American South has long been characterized by the richness of its literary tradition and the fervor of its religious faith. An understanding of either one of these aspects of Southern culture might easily (and in some cases necessarily) entail an awareness of and sensitivity to the other. If FLANNERY O'CONNOR is correct in

asserting that "The larger social context is simply left out of much current fiction, but it cannot be left out by the Southern writer," neither can it be left out by the critic of Southern fiction. A crucial component of this larger context is the role that Protestantism has played in the region. As C. Vann Woodward argues, not "learning nor literature of the secular sort could compare with religion in power and influence over the mind and spirit of the South." The importance of each of these cultural elements, then, has been well established, and a relationship between the two can be presumed; the nature of that relationship, however, remains open to discussion.

To speak of Southern religion and Southern literature in the same breath is to acknowledge *ab initio* a relationship in some way posited by a shared cultural background. This is not to assert that either of these cultural strains lacks an integrity of its own or that its form is somehow entirely fashioned by its social setting. Nevertheless, together Southern religion and literature share certain structural components and thematic elements that allow them, when viewed in tandem, to shed light on one another and to reveal new insights into Southern culture. As separate and distinct strands in the elaborate tapestry of Southern life, this region's religion and its literature have moved at times along parallel paths and at other times along intersecting ones.

At their most fundamental level, religion and literature both seek to establish or render an order on what otherwise appear to be arbitrary human actions and random natural occurrences. Religion serves to endow ordinary events with an extraordinary or divine significance and to provide a pattern of meaning for life; literature imposes a fictive order that beckons the reader to enter and that then exerts its own force as it intrudes upon consciousness and eventually upon everyday reality. In the South, a culture dependent not only on certain established concepts of order developed throughout its history—as are all cultures—but long preoccupied with the notion of order itself, religion and literature have both played conspicuous roles in the creating, reflecting, and interpreting of that order. Moreover, such tasks have been achieved largely through their mutual reliance on the same source: the written and spoken word or, more specifically, the story. Because human beings give shape and meaning to life through language, the story—as the fundamental narrative structure—acts to impose order on experience. It is the germ of religious expression as well as of literary art from which all else springs. Southern religion and Southern literature both rely heavily on the oral traditions of storytelling, and this mutual dependence informs their content, provides their primary structure, and creates the ground for their interaction.

A yearning for order has manifested itself in a variety of ways from the earliest days of the South to the present. Such a preoccupation—indeed at times an obsession—can be most clearly seen in the religious life of the region. If the Anglicanism established in Virginia and some of the other Southern colonies lacked popular appeal and an enthusiastic following, it did serve to lend stability and a sense of order to those early precarious ventures. But it was not until the revival era, a period often considered to be plagued by confusion and disarray, that the ordering impulses of what came to be known as "Southern religion" began to be felt fully in this region.

The post-Revolutionary and antebellum South was not by any means isolated from the ideals of Enlightenment rationalism that permeated the Western world. Virginia-bred Thomas Jefferson and his associates exerted a significant influence on Southern society. A belief in the unity of truth, the orderliness of the universe, and the reasonableness of Christian faith realized itself in the evangelical REVIVALISM of the rural areas just as it did in the decorum of the urban congregations. The popular perception of South-

ern revivals as disorganized displays of emotion that developed almost without warning is not an entirely accurate representation of the times. Though revivalistic enthusiasm often appeared chaotic (and at times did become so), there were definite rules of order that governed the existence and enabled the success of the CAMP MEETINGS. Furthermore, even though the revivalists of the early nineteenth century loudly heralded the free expression of religious feeling, a certain orderly progression of behavior and emotion leading to Christian conversion was prescribed. While they might have differed on the exact nature of this process and the precise chronology of events, most denominations regarded religious life to be an essentially inward, orderly affair that paralleled the orderliness of the universe and the Divine Will.

A dearth of educational facilities, the lack of widespread literacy, and the often meager academic achievements of ministers impelled Southern religion to depend on a direct means of access to religious truth. As a consequence, doctrinal statements were often stripped of all outer layers of theological accretion and expressed in simple story form. The stories of God's grandeur in the creation of the world, the sinfulness of Adam and Eve, and the grace of God as demonstrated in the birth and resurrection of Jesus provided the shape and substance of popular Southern religious faith. These biblical stories were translated into a rural idiom and then transmitted by word of mouth from preacher to preacher and then to congregations. Such stories proved particularly effective in supporting Southern revivalism as they became appropriated by individuals and disclosed in the form of witnessing at revivals or church services. Hence the biblical story furnished a pattern for the understanding of the particular events of human life just as it endowed a sense of meaning on human history. Gradually, as would be expected, these stories became intermingled with the story of the region—its history and its interpretation of that history—and part of a distinctively Southern world view. Thus by the early 1800s there emerged a sense of regional identity that relied on the peculiarity of the Southern experience supported by the simple yet compelling nature of the biblical stories.

If the religion of this region played an important part in the ordering of Southern life and the establishing of a sense of cultural identity, then the literature of the region played an equally important role in the maintaining of that order and identity. With the arrival of the 19th century came the blossoming of a distinctively Southern literature. What the revivals had already accomplished in forging a somewhat coherent world view was fortified by the fiction of the times. These developments in the South were pushed forward even further by the emergence of the slavery issue and the forthcoming war. The polarization of North and South made it imperative that each side see its own position as holy and just. As a result, the cause of sectional self-defense usurped all others and literary as well as religious figures played an important role in this endeavor. Frequently, then, literature was created and measured by standards other than aesthetic ones, and writers saw themselves not only as representatives of, but just as often apologists for, their culture.

Among the most convincing ways that writers of this era served in the struggle for Southern self-justification was through the telling and embellishing of the story of the region. Historical romances, in the tradition established by the ever-popular Sir Walter Scott, became the standard format for the literature of the times. In his novel *Swallow Barn: Or Life in the Old Dominion* (1831), John Pendleton Kennedy created a romanticized version of plantation life with masters and slaves living together in a pastoral setting and mutually benefiting from the arrangement. This depiction of the tranquil plantation ambience later became a model for literary renditions and popular conceptions of life in the Old South. But it

was William Gilmore Simms, a prolific writer of this era, to whom the task fell of blending the style of Sir Walter Scott with the Southern experience and, in the process, of creating a literature uniquely responsive to the times.

Simms, an enthusiastic proponent for the establishment of a Southern profession of letters, had an all-consuming interest in history that resulted in numerous essays, biographies, and historical novels. For the most part, his fiction relied on the historical romance to provide a glorious past for the region—most notably in his seven novels of the Revolutionary War. Yet his interest in the past was not merely based on an abstract, intellectual curiosity. Rather, it originated in a strong personal belief, largely motivated by prevailing social conditions, in the necessity of relating the experience of the past to the trials of the present. In this effort he utilized the historical documents in his vast library, but he also depended on the lingering memories of people who had participated in past events. A personal source for these oral traditions was his grandmother who, according to Simms, "had in store a thousand legends ... which served to beguile me from sleep many and many a long winter night." Simms firmly believed that these stories, accompanied by official accounts and molded into fiction, would give Southerners a strong sense of tradition and supply the basis for an orderly way of life.

This dependence on the oral traditions of storytelling also formed the foundation of the literary subgenre of Southwestern Humor. Writers such as Augustus Baldwin Longstreet, George Washington Harris, and Johnson Jones Hooper were educated men—usually of prominent Southern families—who poked fun at rural folkways and, at the same time, used their countrified heroes to mock the pretenses of the more genteel culture. Harris's Sut Lovingood, a "nat'ral born durn'd fool," was always getting himself into trouble by laughing at long-winded preachers and short-sighted politicians. Although the writers of these stories were essentially collectors of Southern folk legends and took themselves less seriously than did Kennedy, Simms, and the like, their attention to the mores of the common people and their reliance on the oral traditions of storytelling helped to unite Southerners of all classes through the fashioning of a shared comedy of their life.

Both religion and literature, then, were significant components in the development of a regional consciousness and the legitimation of regional institutions. Together these two cultural forces created and drew upon a story that romanticized the region and that allowed Southerners to develop a view of themselves as honorable and righteous members of a now-threatened social order. A regional orthodoxy emerged that depended on religion and literature to buttress it and withal scarcely permitted dissension. Yet few were the Southerners who could unequivocally resolve the principles of democracy and equality struggled for in the not-too-distant war against England with the brutal facts of slavery. Thus cracks in this supposedly united armor appeared and permitted, although certainly did not encourage, a writer such as Edgar Allen Poe to spring from this milieu and create an art informed but not dictated by his culture.

Following the Civil War this defeated region was forced to find meaning in and justification for its way of life. Religious institutions served this purpose by relating the glories of the antebellum days and by sustaining the theology of that time. It was hoped that by reiterating the biblical and regional stories of the past, the enclaves of religious life prevalent in the revival era could be reestablished. And indeed, the individualistic, pietistic religion of earlier days became further fused with the Southern life-style in the postwar decades. Literature, too, played its own part in the reinforcing of this world view. With the growth of cities throughout the country, and the associated prob-

lems of industrialization, there evolved an increased interest in the more simple ways of the past. Southern local color artists were able to take advantage of this new attention and gain a national audience. They employed many of the techniques of their prewar colleagues, but were able to merge the oral traditions of the tall tales with the aristocratic tendencies of the historical romance to form an interpretation of a Confederacy characterized by chivalry and graciousness. The plantation novel, earlier formulated by John Pendleton Kennedy, now reached the apex of its popularity as it lovingly rendered a world of aristocratic stability. Thomas Nelson Page of Virginia best exemplified this nostalgia as he wrote about plantations full of dashing young planters, faithful black slaves, and delicate Southern ladies.

Even in the midst of this romantic infatuation with the Old South, a few writers were able to draw upon these same techniques and yet shape them in ways that transcended the literary fashions of the era. Charles Waddell Chesnutt, a black writer from North Carolina, relied on the tall tales of the Southern frontier, but provided an ironic twist to them. Ever so subtly he was able to change the tone of these stories from one of glorification of the old days to one of searching scrutiny. In *The Conjure Woman* (1899), Chesnutt used the frame story to have a former slave tell his white audience how slavery felt to those who were oppressed by it. In a similar but more powerful manner, Mark Twain was able to transform the narcissistic proclivities of the plantation novels, as well as the exaggerated aspects of the stories of the Southwest humorists, into an art that was derived from the oral traditions of the South but capable of perceptive criticism. He went several steps further than merely poking fun at foibles of the common folk; he raised questions hitherto unarticulated in successful Southern literature. Through Huckleberry Finn, who drifts down the Mississippi River with Jim, the runaway slave, Twain called into question the supposedly civilized ways of the people from the towns along the shore. But this criticism was not solely directed at Southern society; it implied a critique of all societies that exhibit hypocrisy and injustice. Thus for the first time in Twain's work, Southern literature draws upon its heritage of storytelling and yet also achieves universal stature. As a result, the regnant orthodox story of Southern life sacrifices some of its formerly immutable and sacrosanct character and becomes part of a living, breathing tradition.

The perpetuation of a culturally sacred story supported by the combined forces of a defensive religious and literary tradition provided a supportive environment to members of Southern society. Edgar T. Thompson, a Southerner by birth and sociologist by profession, has explained the appeal of such a world to a young child: "In it I was located and knew who I was supposed to be and what I was expected to do and to think." The Southern way of life offered order and security. Yet as the 20th century gave rise to new developments, it became a difficult task to sustain a culturally isolated posture. The effects of mass transportation and communication could not be ignored. Although the South did not experience a large influx of immigrants as occurred in the Northeast, technological advances established a type of pluralism; most Southerners encountered other ways of life, and thereby a multiplicity of cultural stories, at some time or another.

The one story of life as experienced in the South and buttressed by an idiosyncratic view of the Scriptures no longer sufficed to explain all. Southern pietism continued to flourish, but the rug of social integration was pulled out from underneath it—at first gradually and then more rapidly. Although Southern churches were able to unite and fight together for causes involving personal morality, they began to lose their hold on the society and the individual consciousness. The personalistic bias of Southern religion remained intact; but while the individual conversion experience had always been at the center of Southern religiosity, now numerous competing individual stories took the place of a dominant societal one. This is not to say that Southerners easily let go of the heritage of the past. The use of biblical verses to uphold traditional concepts of morality and stoke the raging EVOLUTION CONTROVERSY indicate otherwise. Previously, however, the biblical narratives had merged with Southern history to create a common story of the region. Now, with the increasing availability of educational facilities and expanding urban centers, Southern religion became dependent on a means of survival other than that of the oral transmission of cultural legends.

This state of regional and religious uncertainty set the stage, perhaps ironically, for the appearance of a vital literature with staggering universal dimensions. In the midst of much anxiety, there developed an art form that was built on the traditions of the past but far surpassed earlier literary efforts. The absence of an accepted story as the authoritative interpretation of all of life did not diminish the concern about such matters; rather, this vacuum drew Southern writers to a serious consideration of the meaning of the history of their region. Accordingly, the successful literature of this century has grown out of a sense of community placed under sharp scrutiny. In contrast to their more provincial colleagues of the past, many modern Southern literary artists left the region for awhile and then returned—alienated from but nevertheless a part of their homeland. As a result, it has been possible for such writers to be critical and appreciative of the South as a region, in terms of both its unique and its universal qualities. Until recently, the South has remained a traditional community or group of communities that had a somewhat unified story to tell about victory, defeat, love, meaning, and value. This background has sustained modern writers who, steeped in the oral traditions of their heritage though often partially estranged from them, have combined humor, irony, and warmth with an intense sense of tragedy in their works.

There has been no writer more adept at bringing the traditions of the past into the present than WILLIAM FAULKNER. The mythic county of Yoknapatawpha is bound together by the stories of the region and the time. In some ultimately inexplicable manner, Faulkner was able to interweave the experience of the Sartorises with that of the Compsons, Sutpens, Snopeses, and others to create what Malcolm Cowley has called a "legend" of the South. All of his works draw upon the larger story of Southern life but render it in specific ways. The tall tales of the Southwest humorists enliven numerous Faulkner short stories and novels. History, its uses and abuses, permeates the Faulkner corpus; it forms the central theme in *Light in August* and *Absalom, Absalom!*. Not only do time, history, and stories provide the focus for Faulkner's works, these themes also supply the texture of them. In *The Sound and the Fury*, Faulkner charts the decline of the Compson household by telling about the same basic events from four different perspectives. The points of view range from that of the moronic Benjy to that of the abstracted Quentin to that of the ruthless Jason and finally to that of a more distant narrator who concentrates on the humanity of the black servant Dilsey. No one perspective could tell the whole story; when all four are taken together they begin to reveal the meaning of the tragedy of the Compson family. In this disintegrating universe, with bonds between persons and the past being severed haphazardly, no single story could suffice. It takes a plurality of stories to explain events but, as in all of Faulkner's works, the presence of the larger cultural story is relied upon, probed, and unraveled.

Faulkner is not unique among 20th-century Southern writers in his dependence on the oral tradition of storytelling or in his use of modern narrative techniques to approach the story of the region. Robert Penn Warren is another artist who has done so repeatedly over his long and versatile career. In his novels *All the King's Men, At Heaven's Gate,* and *Night Rider,* among others, he has relied on the history of the region to inform his work. In his narrative poetry he has fused the experience of the South with the story of his own life. Black writers, too, have exhibited many of these same tendencies. In the works of Zora Neale Hurston and Margaret Walker, fictional accounts of slavery and its after-effects divulge the vitality and variety of the Southern black experience. More recently, Eudora Welty has demonstrated her dependence on the use of stories. Her novel *Losing Battles* is a work based on this fundamental human storytelling propensity. Through her powerful use of the story, Welty brings an expansive, sprawling, but rather ordinary family to life and endows them with extraordinary warmth, humor, and strength. Each member of this family has a story to tell, and through the interweaving of the individual stories a larger, grander one emerges.

For Welty, stories provide both the structure and substance of the novel. Her work serves as an indicator of how stories have been used in Southern literature from its beginnings to the present. In a manner that has been at times restraining and at other times liberating, stories have tied Southern literature to the culture from which it springs. They have tied literature to the religious traditions of the region as well. Religious metaphors abound in Southern poetry and fiction, and many writers self-consciously address theological questions—most notable in this century, FLANNERY O'CONNOR and WALKER PERCY. But it is through the story, the germ of both religious reflection and literary creation, that Southern religion and literature merge and are granted perspective. An examination of either religion or literature tells the story of the region in part; an examination of them both together through the multistoried layers of art and faith reveals much about the region, a great deal about its history, and even more about the human drive to create and maintain order.

See also articles on CALDWELL, ERSKINE; PERCY, WILLIAM ALEXANDER; SMITH, LILLIAN; TATE, ALLEN.

Bibliography. John B. Boles, *The Great Revival, 1787-1805*; Malcolm Cowley, "Introduction," *The Portable Faulkner*, rev. ed.; Giles Gunn, *The Interpretation of Otherness: Literature, Religion and the American Imagination*; E. Brooks Holifield, *The Gentlemen Theologians: American Theology in Southern Culture, 1795-1860*; C. Hugh Holman, *The Immoderate Past: The Southern Writer and History*; Donald G. Mathews, "The Second Great Awakening as an Organizing Process, 1780-1830: An Hypothesis," *American Quarterly* 21 (1969): 23-43; Perry Miller, "Religion and Society in the Early Literature of Virginia," *Errand Into the Wilderness*; Flannery O'Connor, *Mystery and Manners*; Louis D. Rubin, Jr., *The Faraway Country: Writers of the Modern South*; William Gilmore Simms, *The Wigwam and the Cabin*, rev. ed.; Lewis P. Simpson, *The Dispossessed Garden: Pastoral and History in Southern Literature*; Allen Tate, "The Profession of Letters in the South," *Essays of Four Decades*; Edgar T. Thompson, "God and the Southern Plantation System," *Religion and the Solid South*, ed. Samuel S. Hill; C. Vann Woodward, *Origins of the New South*; "Why the Southern Renaissance?" *Virginia Quarterly Review* 51 (1975): 222-39.

ROSEMARY M. MAGEE
ROBERT DETWEILER
EMORY UNIVERSITY

LORD'S SUPPER: *See* SACRAMENTS AND ORDINANCES.

LOST CAUSE, THE. This distinctively regional term refers to the South's post-Civil War attitude toward the Confederacy. It developed into one of the region's central myths, with a ritualistic structure of public celebrations honoring the wartime efforts. Southern Memorial Day, funerals of Confederate heroes, the dedication of Confederate monuments, and gatherings of Confederate veterans' groups were the occasions for the expression of Southern sentiment about the sacred past.

The Lost Cause had religious connotations because ministers and churches played a central role in the formal, organized attempts to maintain the Confederacy as a spiritual force in postbellum Southern life. Preachers applied Christian imagery and theological concepts to the Confederacy and shaped the Lost Cause into the image of evangelical Protestantism. They portrayed the Confederate effort as a moral-religious crusade, but after the CIVIL WAR Southerners worried that their society and its churches would fall into decline due to the evils stemming from Confederate defeat. They used the Lost Cause movement to reinforce what they saw as endangered spiritual values. Religious leaders used the behavior of the Confederates as parables of Christian conduct. Lost Cause heroes had sacrificed and died for the South, symbolically purifying it through their blood sacrifice.

The Lost Cause as an organized movement was closely connected with the region's churches. Preachers used the agencies, publications, and ritual events of the Lost Cause to instill religious and moral instruction. Regional denominations in turn publicized the latter-day Confederate organizations and their message. Lost Cause activities promoted interdenominationalism. Rituals honoring the cause frequently took place in Christian churches and most religious groups cooperated in these community affairs. Each denomination contributed its distinctive religious outlook and spirit to shaping the Lost Cause.

The theological concerns of Southern Protestantism were expressed in the Lost Cause. Confederate defeat raised fundamental questions concerning the relationship of Southerners to God. Central to this relationship was the idea of Southerners as a chosen people. During the Civil War, Southern ministers had argued that the conflict was a holy war, but with defeat they faced the task of explaining defeat in a crusade. How could a righteous cause be frustrated when a just God ruled the universe? In interpreting the results of the war, Southern religious leaders elaborated on a traditional Christian interpretation of history that looked toward the future. Adversity such as the Confederate failure was a way to greater faith. God's mysterious ways were beyond human understanding, but the divinity had a place for the South in his plans. Each event in Southern history, as in all things, worked to bring the Christian plan to fulfillment. The duty of Southern Christians after the war was to be patient in their wilderness of defeat. The Confederate defeat came to be seen as a form of discipline from God, who was preparing his chosen people for future greatness. Participants in the events of the Lost Cause learned that the South must be preserved as a spiritual bastion. God had sent Confederate defeat as a test for His people and if they passed it they would be prepared for future battles with evil. The religious aspects of the Lost Cause thus helped pave the way for postbellum Southern religious crusades against any form of evil.

Bibliography. Rollin Osterweis, *The Myth of the Lost Cause*; Charles Reagan Wilson, *Baptized in Blood: The Religion of the Lost Cause, 1865-1920.*

CHARLES REAGAN WILSON
UNIVERSITY OF MISSISSIPPI

LOUISIANA.

Beginnings. The territory now making up the state of Louisiana was once a section of the vast Mississippi Valley claimed by Robert Cavalier de La Salle for France (1682) and named Louisiana in honor of King Louis XIV. It was controlled successively by Antoine Crozat (1712-1717), John Law's Company on the West (1717-1731), the French (1731-1763) and Spanish (1763-1800) Crowns. Returned to France (1800-1803), it was sold to the United States as a territory (1803-1812). The extreme southern part of the Louisiana Purchase became the 18th state admitted to the Union (30 April 1812).

The Mississippi River, discovered in 1541 by Hernando De Soto, a Spanish explorer, was the major artery used in the settlement and colonization of what became Louisiana. In 1699 Pierre Le Moyne Sieur d'Iberville proceeded from the Gulf of Mexico up the river beyond the site of the later state capital, Baton Rouge. In 1718, Jean Baptiste Le Moyne Sieur d'Bienville, a younger brother of Iberville, founded a city on the banks of the Mississippi and named it New Orleans in honor of the Duke of Orleans. In 1722, he moved the capital of French Louisiana from Biloxi on the Gulf Coast to New Orleans, located on a crescent-shaped bend in the river, hence its sobriquet of "Crescent City."

Franciscan missionaries Zeno Membré and Anastase Douay accompanied La Salle on his historic voyage down the Mississippi River to its mouth. Priests were sent by the Quebec Seminary in Canada to evangelize the Indians in lower Louisiana at the beginning of the 18th century. Jean Francois Buisson de St. Cosme, possibly the first American-born missionary martyr, was slain by Chitimacha Indians near the late site of Donaldsonville on the Mississippi River in 1706. Jesuits, Capuchines, Carmelites, and other pioneer missionaries made their way up and down the river, moving downstream to its mouth and upstream as far as Pointe Coupée organizing missions, out of which came parishes at a later time. They also traveled extensively on winding bayous and picturesque lakes in search of converts among the Indians. Probably the first chapel in the Lower Mississippi Valley was built by the Bayagoula Indians under the direction of a Jesuit missionary, Paul du Ru, in 1700 at what is now Bayou Goula in Iberville Parish. It was named in honor of St. Francis Xavier. The first Mass celebrated in Natchitoches, the oldest town (1715) in later Louisiana, was offered by Antonio Margil. New Orleans had a "substantial church building" in 1727, the same year the Ursuline Nuns opened an academy that has the longest uninterrupted history of any Catholic school in America.

Perspective. One glance at a map depicting the religious bodies in the state of Louisiana discloses the sharp division between Protestantism in the north and

Roman Catholicism in the south. The difference is not merely a matter of religion but also of culture. The northern part of the state is characterized by a Puritan ethos and a strong pietistic strain, whereas south Louisiana, except in the southeast (once known as "West Florida"), exhibits a French and Spanish Catholic mentality, in which the Anglo-Saxon, Puritan, and pietistic heritage of Protestantism is quite subordinate.

There are some subtle and some sharp differences in the life-styles of the regions. North Louisiana is characterized by a conservative and rather traditional pattern, with strong legalistic and moralistic elements, a viewpoint that puts a large premium upon personal behavior in conformity with church and community standards. In south Louisiana, the relationship between religious teaching and life-style is less clear. The Catholic conception of culture is more concerned with basic moral issues as seen by the Church and less with specific codes of conduct. For example, *Mardi Gras*, the last day before Lent, which is celebrated in New Orleans, is a significant holiday for only a few in Shreveport.

Generalizations about sectionalism in Louisiana in recent years, however, must take into account the homogenizing impact of the mass media, especially television, and tendencies toward conformity to a secular outlook in the state as well as increasing penetration of Protestantism throughout south Louisiana and some Roman Catholic growth in the central and northern parts of the state, largely in Avoyelles, Rapides, and Natchitoches paishes. Nevertheless, the predominantly Anglo-Saxon Protestant North and the strong Catholic South represent different viewpoints. An additional element in the religious and cultural schism is Anglo-Saxon versus immigrant values, the culture of the South being more open to the latter.

Cosmopolitan New Orleans, a mixture of Creole, Acadian (Cajun), and "American" cultures, is distinguishable from a triangular shaped section of the state that runs from Lake Charles in the Southwest, to the "Crescent City" in the East, to Alexandria in central Louisiana. The Acadian French people who were expelled from Nova Scotia by the English in the mid-eighteenth century predominate in this area and constitute a culture that differs from the more syncretistic community in New Orleans.

Roman Catholic Expansion. Acadian settlements were formed at St. Martinville on Bayou Teche, in the Opelousas region, and along the Mississippi River above and below Baton Rouge, notably in Iberville Parish at St. Gabriel, where the historically important Parish Registers of St. Charles Church were deposited at Grand Pré (1688-1755). Despite a shortage of priests and churches, the Cajuns retained their Catholic religion and established a cluster of parishes in St. Martinville (1765), Opelousas (1777), Grand Coteau (1819), Lafayette, formerly Vermillionville (1821), and New Iberia (1838). They continue their devotion to a colorful and traditional Catholicism, in which veneration of the Virgin Mary and invocation of the saints are fused with "the sacred heart of Jesus," pictures of which can be seen on the walls of many a cottage in south Louisiana. The Blessing of the Shrimp Fleet just before it sails out into the Gulf of Mexico for the first catch of the season by priests in elaborate vestments is for them both a social occasion and a deeply felt religious experience. The Blessing of the Sugar Cane also carries a profound religious meaning for these faithful Catholics. The priest begins his walk between the rows of sugar cane just before work begins in the fields accompanied by acolytes, choristers, and a crucifer. "As he progresses," Frances Parkinson Keyes once wrote, "the Cleric bestows his blessing on everyone and everything he passes. He prays that the workers may be industrious, the mules patient and enduring, the knives sharp, the carts strong, the harvest plentiful." The Sugar Cane Festival in New Iberia, the Rice Festival in Crowley, the Dairy Festival in Abbeville, and the Jambalaya Festival in Gonzales are begun with solemn Masses.

The Cajun expresses his love of life by staging big Saturday night dances (*fais-dodos*) and pirogue races on Bayou Barataria, by cooking a delectable concoction called gumbo and a mysterious and highly seasoned mixture of crawfish, rice, and "what have you" called jambalaya, by brewing strong black coffee (French-drip) and making much of family ties (*la famille*). His church teaches him that life can be lived in a "state of grace," sustained by contrition and then confession to his friendly priest, who provides penances to counterbalance his moral lapses and offers the serene certainty of absolution. He does not brood about the mysteries of life and death, mortal and venial sins, which he leaves to his church. His conversation is sprinkled with stories passed down to him by his forebears. He speaks in a delightful French dialect or equally captivating English with a Cajun accent. He laughs a lot, enjoys his distinctive culture, and does not take himself too seriously. In other words, for the Cajun the sacred and the secular tend to merge into a single way of life.

The Cajuns have been called country folk in contrast to Creoles, who have been described as city folk. This geographic distinction, which had a certain validity in the past, has been tempered by population mobility and intermarriage. Strictly speaking, the Creoles are the white descendants of the French and Spanish settlers of the Colonial period. The Cajuns, as already indicated, came to Louisiana in the mid-eighteenth century, largely from Canada. Both groups and the Italians who settled in the state during the last century are predominantly Roman Catholic.

The French and Spanish cultures from which Catholicism in New Orleans is derived are reflected in place (French Quarter) and street (Almonaster) names, in colorful celebrations (All Saints' Day), in historic buildings (the Cabildo), even in the menus of restaurants (crawfish *étouffé*, shrimp Arnaud). The St. Louis Cathedral (named for Louis IX, the crusading King of France), founded in 1793, is one of the genuinely historic buildings in the nation. Another carryover of Catholicism is the designation of the civil subdivisions of the state as "parishes" instead of "counties." Also, many parishes are named for Saints.

The concentration of Roman Catholics in south Louisiana, mainly along the Mississippi River, Bayou Lafourche, and other streams, posed serious problems. Inundations, tropical hurricanes, yellow fever epidemics, and the toll of typhoid fever resulted in shifts and depletion of population. After the Civil War, heavy debt created a precarious situation. Pew rentals and revenue from parish fairs were insufficient supplements to the depleted resources of the church. Nevertheless, the faithful labor of obscure priests and nuns stabilized the church and, after the stresses of the Reconstruction period (1865-1877) had passed, Catholicism moved forward again. In 1918, the Diocese of Lafayette was established, giving the state three jurisdictions: the Archdiocese of New Orleans (1850), the Diocese of Alexandria (formerly Natchitoches, 1853), and Lafayette. The Diocese of Baton Rouge was created in 1961. More than one million Catholics are concentrated in south Louisiana and constitute about 33 percent of the total population of the state. Lafayette has a higher proportion of Catholics (61 percent) and more black Catholic adherents than any other diocese in the United States (80,500). There are 72,000 black Catholics in the Archdiocese of New Orleans. The large number of blacks who adhere to the Catholic faith grows out of the fact that most slave owners who supervised sugar plantations in south Louisiana were Roman Catholics. Another reason for the concentration of black Catholics in the state comes out of the *Code Noir*, formulated by Bienville in 1724, whose prescriptions required that slaves be baptized into the Catholic Church. Separate Catholic churches for blacks are rather recent: St. Katherine's (1895) in New Orleans was the first congregation of this kind. In 1981, there were more than 100 separate black Catholic churches in the state.

Education has occupied an important place in the policy of the Catholic Church in Louisiana since 1725, when a school for boys was established by Capuchin Raphael de Luxembourg. There are two Catholic universities in New Orleans—Loyola of the South (Jesuit) and Xavier of Louisiana, the latter being the only Catholic university in the United States specifically designed for blacks. St. Mary's Dominican College, also in New Orleans, is a school for women. Each diocese has a school board supervising Catholic elementary and secondary education, the earliest of which was organized in Alexandria in 1889. Joseph F. Rummel, for whom a Catholic high school in New Orleans was named, served as Archbishop of New Orleans from 1935 until his death in 1964. He was succeeded by John Cody, who after a brief tenure became archbishop of Chicago. Philip Hannan was appointed archbishop of New Orleans in 1965.

Protestant Episcopal Church. Roman Catholicism was the only organized Christian community in New Orleans until the founding of Christ's Church, a predominantly Episcopal congregation also called the New Orleans Protestant Church, whose first service was held in the Cabildo in November, 1805. Philander Chase, who later became rector of the church, described attendants at this service as "numerous and of the most respectable Americans, and very decorous in their deportment." It is possible, though unlikely, that on this occasion Chase preached the first Protestant sermon to an organized congregation in the whole area purchased by the United States in 1803. This church, now Christ Church Cathedral, was not only the first non-Roman Catholic Church in the city but probably in what became the state of Loui-

siana in 1812. Six years before that it had become officially a Protestant Episcopal congregation.

Three of the leading Episcopal churches of New Orleans were organized within a period of 10 years beginning with St. Paul's in 1838 and followed by Annunciation in 1844 and Trinity in 1848. Leonidas Polk, the first Bishop of Louisiana, was also Rector of Trinity Church from 1856 to 1861. He had served as a Missionary Bishop of the Southwest from the time of that diocese's formation in 1838. The Episcopal Church in Louisiana was part of this jurisdiction. Under his guidance, churches were organized in Shreveport, Plaquemine, Opelousas, Thibodaux, Napoleonville, Donaldsonville, along Red River, and Bayous Lafourche and Teche. He spent his energies unstintingly, "gathering congregations, holding services, preaching, baptizing, confirming, and celebrating the sacrament wherever and whenever he could find an opportunity," as his son wrote. A specific example of his courage was an occurrence at Shreveport, where on Sunday 24 March 1839 he led what has been called "the first religious service ever held in that primitive settlement of rivermen" despite the fact he was told "we have never had any preaching here, and we don't want any." He rented a house, borrowed a table to serve as a pulpit, secured a hand-bell that he rang to advertise the service, and proceeded to preach anyway.

Polk became bishop of Louisiana in 1841. He and Bishop Stephen Elliott of Georgia initiated a movement that eventuated in the organization of the University of the South at Sewanee TN. Known as the "Fighting Bishop," Polk served as a lieutenant colonel in the Confederate army and lost his life at Pine Mountain, Marietta GA in 1864.

William Thomas Leacock became rector of Christ Church in 1852 and served with uncommon devotion for 32 years. An Englishman and a graduate of Queen's College, Oxford, he was familiar with the formalism of the Church of England and yet he was equally aware of the rather informal church life in the Mississippi Valley, where he had served pioneer congregations prior to his ministry in New Orleans. His varied background as a churchman enabled him to strike a balance between high and low church tendencies. For this and other reasons he was greatly loved.

Christ Church in New Orleans, built in 1886, became Christ Church Cathedral in 1892. This change was brought about despite opposition by the older parish churches in the diocese, especially in New Orleans, and in the face of a negative attitude on the part of some low churchmen toward the increase in Episcopal prestige symbolized by the creation of the Cathedral. Davis Sessums, who had become rector of Christ Church in 1887, was elevated to the Episcopate in 1891. Believing "a Bishop needed a church," as he expressed it, he was chiefly responsible for changing the oldest parish church in the diocese into a cathedral.

During the early years of his episcopacy, Bishop Sessums provided vigorous leadership, especially in the areas of missions, the involvement of laymen in the life of the church, and the bearing of the Gospel upon society. A serious illness, from which he never recovered completely, cast its shadow over the last two decades of his episcopacy. The Davis Sessums Memorial Student Center, constructed by the Diocese of Louisiana on the campus of Louisiana State University in 1929, was one of the first facilities of this kind established by any church in the United States and probably the first by any denomination in Louisiana.

When James Craik Morris became bishop in 1930, the diocese counted 12,592 communicants, about half of whom lived in New Orleans where there were eight churches. Bishop Morris struggled with staggering financial problems during the depression of the 1930s. Though his energies were devoted largely to administrative affairs, he found "nothing disconcerting in the process" by which Christ Church Cathedral was brought in eight years from "the lowest low churchmanship to what earlier would have been rejected as impossibly high." Dean William H. Nes (1927-1947) was chiefly responsible for transforming "Low Church Protestantism" into what was probably the first large Anglo-Catholic Parish in the South. Dean Nes sought "to make the Cathedral authentically Anglican," as he put it. He instituted daily Eucharists, replaced the communion table with an altar, introduced Eucharistic vestments, reserved Holy Communion so that it could be taken into sickrooms, and heard confessions on Saturday afternoons.

Communicants in the Episcopal Church in Louisiana in 1955 amounted to 20,622, organized into 45 parishes. In 1980, the Western Diocese of Louisiana was formed with 13,000 communicants and Willis R. Henton was elected bishop. The Diocese of Louisiana retained 16,000 communicants. No single factor accounts for the slow rate of growth of Episcopalianism in the state. Few Episcopalians migrated to Louisiana because they belonged to the upper economic bracket and were, therefore, not inclined to move from the Atlantic seaboard in search of a better life. Those who came were not of strong missionary and evangelistic inclination. The present bishop is James B. Brown, who was elected in 1977.

Presbyterian Church. Sylvester Larned, a young Presbyterian minister from Massachusetts, found one Protestant church when he arrived in New Orleans in 1818. It was Christ Church (Episcopal), that worked harmoniously with a small group of Presbyterians led by Larned, who built a house of worship in 1819 and solidified the Presbyterian witness. This community formed the nucleus of the First Presbyterian Church in the city, organized in November, 1823.

Larned's untimely death in 1820 left the young congregation without clerical leadership at a time of serious financial crisis. The church's debt was substantial, $45,000. THEODORE CLAPP, a Congregationalist, who arrived in New Orleans in 1822 when the Plan of Union bound the two denominations, agreed to become pastor of the church provided the financial problem could be solved. A lottery, legal at that time, raised $25,000 and the rest of the debt was absorbed by Judah Touro, a Jewish philanthropist and merchant, who thereby assumed ownership of the church. As a consequence of these circumstances, a Jew came into possession of a Presbyterian church with a Congregational minister in a predominantly Roman Catholic city.

Clapp's ministry was a stormy one from the beginning owing to personal conflicts between the pastor and some of his parishioners and his growing inability to support biblically what he called "the distinguishing tenets of Calvinism." It is not surprising that Clapp was deposed from the ministry by the Presbytery of Mississippi in 1833 and became the founder of the "First Congregational Church in the City and Parish of New Orleans," which continued to worship in the edifice Larned had constructed in 1819. Clapp's church was Unitarian from the outset of his new ministry in 1833, though the designation "First Congregational Unitarian Church" was not used until 1853. The first Unitarian Church of New Orleans, a descendant of this congregation, celebrated its 125th anniversary in 1958. It has been said that for more than three decades New Orleans was noted for "the American Theatre, the French Opera, and Parson Clapp's Church."

In spite of difficulties associated with the Presbyterian Church in New Orleans and a paucity of preachers, "no more than seven or eight" in the state, Presbyterianism expanded steadily if not spectacularly throughout Louisiana. Churches were organized in Baton Rouge (1827), Alexandria (1844), and Shreveport (1845). The Second and Third Presbyterian Churches in New Orleans were established in 1845 and 1847, respectively. The Presbytery of New Orleans (1844-1845) was renewed in 1855. A year earlier, the Red River Presbytery in north Louisiana had been formed.

The famous BENJAMIN MORGAN PALMER, who served as pastor of the First Presbyterian Church in New Orleans from 1856 until his death in 1902, became the outstanding figure in Louisiana Presbyterianism and a leader of his church in the South. He shared with JAMES HENLEY THORNWELL leadership in crystallizing the influence of antebellum Southern Presbyterianism in favor of the Confederacy. At the formation of the Presbyterian Church of the Confederate States of America in Augusta GA on 4 December 1861, he was unanimously chosen to preach the opening sermon and elected moderator. Someone has remarked that he did "more for the Confederate cause than a regiment of soldiers."

The Synod of Louisiana, which resulted from the division of the Synod of Mississippi into two synods in 1901, is one of the smaller synods, numerically and geographically, of the Presbyterian Church in the United States. There were 105 churches in the synod with about 6,000 members in 1901. In 1959, there were 123 churches with over 30,000 communicants. Though the increase in total number of churches has been minimal, total membership increased five times in the 1901-1959 period. Since then membership has increased modestly.

It should be said that, although size is hardly unimportant, the impact of a church upon the culture in which it functions cannot be calculated adequately in quantitative terms. Judged by the quality of its influence, the Presbyterian Church in Louisiana has wrought well. Early Presbyterian ministers and churches played a major role in civilizing the Louisiana frontier. Presbyterian policy, always insistent upon an educated ministry and the importance of Christian culture, has provided a significant counterpoise to the anti-intellectualism that has sometimes passed for theology in some sectors of Southern religion. (What has been said here about Presbyterianism can be said equally concerning the Episcopal Church in Louisiana.)

Baptists. Baptists first appeared in Louisiana toward the end of the 18th century. The first known Baptist in the area was John Coulter, who arrived with his family at Ft. Miro, later named Monroe, in April 1797. Nothing is known of his activities as a Baptist until he moved to Wilkinson County MS in 1807, where he served as treasurer of the Mississippi Association for several years.

Bailey E. Chaney, a member of the Salem Church in Mississippi and a licensed minister, probably preached the first Baptist sermon in what is now East Feliciana Parish of the state of Louisiana. That event may have occurred in 1798 but more likely it took place early in the 19th century. There is no evidence that he organized a church.

The initial Baptist church in Louisiana was founded on a bluff overlooking the Bogue Chitto River in present-day Washington Parish. It bore the name of Half Moon Bluff Baptist Church and was accepted for membership in the Mississippi Association on 17 October 1812.

Edmund J. Reis, a Frenchman from Nova Scotia, was probably the first Baptist missionary to enter New Orleans. He arrived in late 1812 and remained for about six months, during which he distributed Bibles and preached with little success. Without question, he was the first French-speaking Baptist minister to visit Louisiana. Benjamin Davis served as an agent of the Louisiana Bible Society in New Orleans from December 1815 to March 1816. He returned to the Crescent City in 1818 and was chiefly responsible for organizing a church, that also affiliated with the Mississippi Association. Davis was probably the first Baptist to administer the ordinance of baptism in the city. It was also the first baptism by immersion ever witnessed by most of the curious crowd gathered on the banks of the Mississippi River in front of the Custom House. James A. Ronaldson arrived

in New Orleans in 1816, finding a few Baptists already on the scene, Cornelius Paulding among them. In a commodious house owned by Paulding, a place to hold services was provided. Ronaldson left New Orleans in 1817 and later (1830s) was accused of adopting the restorationist views of the Campbellite movement.

William B. Johnson, a South Carolinian who subsequently achieved the distinction of serving as president of both the Triennial Convention and the Southern Baptist Convention, was invited to visit New Orleans by Paulding early in 1817. During his brief visit to the city, Johnson preached in Paulding's house and on board a ship. By permission of Antonio de Sella (known also as Father Antoine), he gave an address in the St. Louis Cathedral in behalf of the Poydras Orphan Asylum. In 1980, this writer (a Baptist) preached in the Cathedral to the participants in a national meeting of the Association of Clinical Pastoral Education, evidence of an ecumenical spirit that characterizes the major Christian bodies in the state today.

Several efforts to establish Baptist churches in New Orleans (1818, 1826, 1841) did not succeed. The scattered Baptists were eventually unified by Russell Holman, a missionary sent by the American Baptist Home Mission Society, and T. J. Fisher, an evangelist from Kentucky. The church known now as the First Baptist Church, organized on 28 December 1843, was the result. After an unsuccessful effort to establish a church in Baton Rouge (1838), what is now the First Baptist Church of that city was founded in 1874. It is now the largest church cooperating with the Louisiana Baptist Convention.

Penetration of Baptists into central and north Louisiana came about in the 1816-1820 period. In 1816, the Beulah Baptist Church was organized in Cheneyville in central Louisiana. Two years later, the Louisiana Association, the first in the state, was formed in the Cheneyville church. Joseph Willis, who had been instrumental in the formation of the first Baptist church west of the Mississippi River, Calvary, on Bayou Chicot near Opelousas on 13 November 1812, was deeply involved in the formation of the Beulah Church and the Louisiana Association.

James Brinson, who came to Louisiana from Tennessee in 1820, was probably the first Baptist minister to settle in north Louisiana west of the Ouachita River. He was chiefly responsible for the organization in 1821 of the Pine Hills Baptist Church, which within a year joined the Louisiana Association. Assisted by John Impson, Brinson extended the Baptist witness westward into what was then the northern section of Natchitoches Parish. Near what is now Minden, they discovered a group of Baptists, including Newitt Drew, son of the governor of Arkansas. Black Lake Baptist Church was established in 1823. A Baptist church was organized in Shreveport on 14 February 1845. The pastor was John Bryce, former associate pastor of the First Baptist Church in Richmond VA, who had come to Louisiana to serve as collector of taxes on imports from the Republic of Texas.

In 1837 a colony made up mostly of Baptists from South Carolina settled in the Mt. Lebanon community in present day Bienville Parish. The Rehoboth Church, which was founded almost immediately, became the center of Baptist work in central and north Louisiana. The Louisiana Baptist Convention was organized there in 1848 and a college was begun in 1856.

J. R. Graves (1820-1893), leader of the LANDMARK MOVEMENT, exercised a significant influence upon Louisiana Baptist life as editor of the *Tennessee Baptist*, which for some years after 1869 served as the official paper for Louisiana as well as for Tennessee. Also he traveled throughout the South, including Louisiana, and cultivated loyal followers who occupied strategic positions among the state's Baptists. For example, A. J. Rutherford could write after the Civil War that the "[Baptist] Churches of Louisiana . . . are stand-

ing on the fore and aft line of Landmarkism, contending earnestly for one Lord, one Faith, one Baptism, and the only true and evangelical *church* and *ministry*." The impact of the Landmark view was confirmed by Hanson Lee: "The churches . . . in Louisiana . . . are a unit on the communion question. [They] reject Campbellite and Pedobaptist immersions and would not commune with a church that would tolerate them. We never knew an 'open communion' Baptist or a Pedobaptist or Campbellite immersion to be recognized, though exceptional cases . . . may have existed." After the death of Graves and the challenge of the Landmark ecclesiology and methodology by Baptist historians like W. H. Whitsitt, Landmarkism split off from the Southern and the Louisiana Baptist Conventions and became a separate historical entity. In 1905 Landmark churches formed the General Association that became the American Baptist Association in 1924. It divided (1950) to form the North American Baptist Association, which since 1969 has been called the Baptist Missionary Association of America. The Landmark ideology lingered among Louisiana Baptists but ceased to be dominant. There were approximately 135 Landmark (also called "Missionary") Baptist churches in Louisiana in 1981.

Recovery from the ravages of the Civil War was a slow but steady process for Louisiana Baptists. There were times of deep despair as suggested by the report in 1869 of the "Domestic Missions Committee" of the State Convention that "nothing has been done, nothing is being done, nor do we see that much can be done without means." But such notes of discouragement were not typical. In retrospect, the growing unity of Baptists in the state is evident. The three Baptist churches in New Orleans, which were oriented toward Mississippi until the early 1890s, became actively involved in the Louisiana Baptist Convention and entered the 20th century in full cooperation with Baptists in central and north

Louisiana. It is not surprising that Louisiana College was founded in this period of consolidation. The school grew out of a resolution offered by E. O. Ware in 1898 and opened its doors in Pineville in 1906. Ware, who served briefly as the first president of the college, also led Louisiana Baptists as State Secretary for two periods, 1892-1906 and 1910-1912. Claybrook Cottingham, a member of the original faculty, became head of the college in 1910, a position he filled with distinction for 31 years. Mention must be made of H. M. Weathersby who was Dean of the college for over 40 years. The solidity and strength of Louisiana Baptists are rooted as much in this institution as in the State Convention itself.

Sporadic efforts to provide a state Baptist paper go back to 1847, when the short-lived *Southwestern Baptist Chronicle* was first published. In 1919, the Louisiana Baptist Convention purchased the *Chronicle* from E. O. Ware and the name was changed to the *Baptist Message*, which continues to serve as a unifying factor in Louisiana Baptist life.

Three Louisiana Baptists have served as presidents of the Southern Baptist Convention: M. E. Dodd (1934-1936), pastor of the First Baptist Church in Shreveport; W. W. Hamilton, Sr. (1941-1944), president of the Baptist Bible Institute (founded in 1916 and since 1946 the New Orleans Baptist Theological Seminary); and J. D. Grey (1952-1954), pastor of the First Baptist Church in New Orleans. Grey, widely known as "Mr. Baptist" in the Crescent City, serves as a symbol of the significant growth and influence of Baptists in South Louisiana in recent decades.

The Southern Baptist Hospital in New Orleans, though no longer under the auspices of the Southern Baptist Convention, was proposed at a meeting of the Orleans-Tammany Association in New Orleans in 1919. Louis J. Bristow, the first "Superintendent" (1924), laid the foundations for what has become one of the leading private hospitals of the nation.

A small group of Baptists entered what became Louisiana at the beginning of the 19th century. By 1860, Baptists in the state numbered about 10,000 and by 1900 they had grown to 35,000. In 1948, the figure reached 260,000. In 1981, there were more than 500,000 members of about 1,300 churches associated with the Louisiana Baptist Convention that has headquarters in Alexandria. Black Baptists numbered about 600,000 and were related to several conventions.

Methodist Church. Methodist beginnings in Louisiana are associated with several colorful figures. Lorenzo Dow, "an eccentric evangelist," was probably the first Methodist to preach in the territory. Early in 1803, he crossed the Mississippi River from Natchez in order to hold "religious meetings." Leander Blackman, presiding elder at Natchez (1805-1807), was apparently the first itinerant Methodist minister to visit Louisiana. Elisha Bowman sought unsuccessfully to organize a church in New Orleans, that he described as an "ungodly city" where he preached to a few "straggling people in the open street," but managed to establish a congregation in Opelousas in 1806. James Axley, whose "pet aversions were Masonry, slavery, whiskey, tobacco, and [what he called] the fashions," was a preacher of unusual power and a person of rare versatility. He erected with his own hands probably the first Protestant church building in Louisiana in 1808 near Catahoula Lake.

In 1815 New Orleans was visited for the first time by a Methodist bishop, William McKendree. But it was not until 1825 that a Methodist church was finally organized by Benjamin M. Drake. In the next two decades Methodism manifested increasing vigor. By 1847 there were 13 churches with 1,328 white and 1,280 black members in the Crescent City.

The General Conference of the (national) Methodist Church in 1844 voted 111 to 60 to ask Bishop James O. Andrew of Georgia to desist from his episcopal labors until he should divest himself of several household slaves he acquired by a second marriage. The Southerners refused to accept this judgment and submitted a plan of separation that was implemented in a Convention of the Southern Churches at Louisville, Kentucky, on 1 May 1845. In this manner the Methodist Episcopal Church, South, was born.

Until 1846, Methodist work in Louisiana was under the jurisdiction of the Mississippi Conference except for a short period when the churches west of the Mississippi River were part of the Arkansas Conference. The Louisiana Conference of the Methodist Episcopal Church, South, was created in 1845 and included 8,101 members, of whom 3,329 were black. It covered the territory west of the Mississippi River and the cities of Baton Rouge and New Orleans on the east side. In 1849 the remainder of the churches east of the river affiliated with the Louisiana Conference. During the 1853 session, the Louisiana Conference adopted a resolution supporting representation by laymen in Methodist conferences, one of the first steps in this direction in Southern Methodism.

Centenary College was founded by the Mississippi Conference at Brandon Springs in 1841. It was moved to a more suitable site in Jackson LA in 1845 on property purchased from the College of Louisiana by Judge Edward McGhee, an ardent Methodist, who then gave the buildings and grounds, that he greatly improved, to Centenary College. During the Civil War, the college was closed and served as a Confederate hospital; later during the conflict it was occupied by Federal troops. The school reopened in 1865. Centenary was moved to Shreveport in 1908 and continues as a strong Methodist liberal arts college.

The Louisiana Conference also operates Glenwood Hospital (West Monroe), Methodist Hospital (New Orleans), and a children's home (Ruston). The *New Orleans Christian Advocate*, established in 1850, continued publication until 1946 when Mississippi Methodists terminated support of it in order to publish their own paper. The *Louisiana Methodist* has been issued in conjunction with The *Arkansas Methodist* in Little Rock since 1949. Wesley Foundations are maintained at eight colleges and universities.

In 1939, when the Northern and Southern branches of Methodism were unified, the Louisiana Conference that belonged to the Methodist Episcopal Church, South, brought into the Methodist Church 189 ministers and 70,787 members. A second Louisiana Conference, associated with the Northern wing of Methodism, was organized in Wesley Chapel in New Orleans in 1869. It was composed of black and white ministers and churches. In 1939, it shared in the merger movement by bringing 18 ministers and 3,278 members into the unified church. A third Louisiana Conference that supervised the Methodist Protestant Church was formed in 1846. It brought 48 ministers and 3,529 members into the Methodist Church in 1939. At that time membership in the Methodist Church in Louisiana amounted to 77,594. In 1981, there were 137,077 members and 550 churches in the United Methodist Church—its name since 1968—in the state.

Disciples of Christ. The first sermon preached in Louisiana for the Disciples of Christ was by Jacob Creath near Bayou Sara on the Mississippi River in October, 1826. Creath was a resident of Mississippi but visited Louisiana frequently as the pioneer missionary of a new movement on the frontier started by Thomas and Alexander Campbell.

Jackson was the site of the first congregation in the state formed in April of 1836. James Shannon, president of the College of Louisiana there (and later president of the University of Missouri), presided at this historic meeting of a little band of five members and thereby elicited interest and curiosity on the part of people in Louisiana in the Disciples movement and conferred a certain prestige upon the teachings of the Campbells. During a tour in 1839, Alexander Campbell delivered eight lectures in Jackson.

A second congregation was formed at Cheneyville in 1843 made up of 20 members who withdrew from the Beulah Baptist Church largely as a consequence of reading Campbell's periodical, the *Millennial Harbinger*. Through the medium of his paper, as well as in his preaching, lectures, and debates, Campbell attacked every denominational belief and practice for which he found no authority in the New Testament: "missionary societies, Bible societies, associations, synods, presbyteries, creeds, confessions, church constitutions, bishops, reverends, doctors of divinity," Calvinistic theology, the use of instrumental music in public worship, quarterly rather than weekly observance of the Lord's Supper, baptism as a symbol of salvation already received rather than "for the remission of sins," and a host of other "innovations." Because of certain superficial similarities between Baptists and the Disciples, especially in the beginning, Baptist churches were uniquely vulnerable to Campbell's attacks, of which the split in the Beulah Church is an example.

A strange and curious feature of the Disciples congregation at Cheneyville was the baptistry, that "consisted of a dry compartment for the minister alongside the one filled with water for the candidate." This could be the first compartmentalized baptistry for immersion in the history of Christianity! The pulpit used by Alexander Campbell when he preached at Cheneyville has been preserved and was installed in the new church building.

The Disciples church at Cheneyville, supported by wealthy planters, had slave members, who as the custom was in most churches before the Civil War sat on a balcony especially designed for them. One of the slaves, William "O'Neil," a barrel-maker, accumulated $1,000 toward the price of his freedom by working far beyond what was required of him by his owners. A friend, C. G. McCormick, who hired O'Neil and his wife, Ellen, from their owners to work with blacks in religious matters, provided an additional $2,000 and took the required legal steps to secure his freedom. Then he earned enough to buy liberty for his wife. William and Ellen were among only several blacks who continued in the Cheneyville Church after the Civil War, when most former slaves formed their own separate churches.

A congregation (which did not survive the Civil War) was organized in New Orleans in 1845. Alexander Campbell, an inveterate traveler in his tireless efforts to propagate his restorationist faith, lectured in a brick building housing the church in 1857. He continued his journey to Baton Rouge, where he was the guest of Governor Wickliffe, and lectured in the church that had been organized in 1848. By 1860, there were approximately 600 members of Disciples of Christ congregations in Louisiana.

After the Civil War, growing tensions in the Disciples of Christ movement developed. This was predictable in light of the fact that "all Disciples, conservatives and progressives alike, . . . aimed to restore New Testament Christianity in order to unite the church for the purpose of winning the world to Jesus Christ." The effort "to restore New Testament Christianity" clashed with the ideal "to unite the church." In other words, the effort to restore primitive Christianity tended to militate against the ideal of unity in the church and the ideal of church unity tended to militate against the effort to restore the "pure" Christianity of the past. Ecumenism and restorationism tended to pull people in opposite directions and the result was growing discord within the Disciples movement that led to division at the turn of the century. The split, which was formally accepted in 1906, was officially confirmed on 22 June 1907 by David Lipscomb, who responding to an inquiry by the United States Census Bureau, wrote: "There is a distinct people taking the word of God as their only and sufficient rule of faith, calling their churches 'Churches of Christ', ... distinct and separate in name, work, and rule of faith from all other bodies and peoples."

At the time of the schism, Churches of Christ were made up of 159,658 members, about two-thirds of whom came from the 11 states that had formed the Confederacy. "The sectional bifurcation of the Disciples of Christ," suggests one historian, "is one of the most vivid American examples of the bending of the Christian ethos to fit the presupposition of the community."

In 1981, the Churches of Christ showed their greatest strength, numerically and geographically, in the northern and western parts of the state. Accurate statistics are difficult to secure for these churches, a fact that is due largely to the emphasis placed upon the independence of the local congregation by the Churches of Christ and a corresponding lack of intercongregational organization. According to a rough estimate, there were in 1981 about 250 churches with 15,000 members in Louisiana. At that time, the Disciples of Christ ("Christian Churches") had 25 congregations and 5,800 members in the state.

Lutheran Church. Before the Louisiana Purchase (1803), Protestantism had no legal existence in this region. A few German immigrants in the colony sought to sustain their Lutheran heritage through informal organizations, out of which came some of the later Lutheran churches.

After the War of 1812 large numbers of German immigrants came to New Orleans by ship, most of whom continued their trips north by river steamboats to various western and northern destinations. Some of them remained in New Orleans. In the absence of a Lutheran church, many settlers worshiped in the German Protestant Church (now the First Evangelical Church) founded in 1826.

A glimpse of the early history of Lutheranism in Louisiana is provided by a report made by Jacob Zinck to the Tennessee Synod soon after he made a missionary tour of the state, on which tour he baptized 28 infants and adults. St. Paul's Lutheran Church was organized in New Orleans in 1840, perhaps partly as a result of Zinck's efforts. The Zion congregation was started in 1847. The St. John's Church, formed in 1852, was the first Lutheran church in the city to become affiliated with the Missouri Synod. At this time, there were three Lutheran churches in the Crescent City.

The Missouri Synod reported 58 churches and 19,713 members in Louisiana in 1964, and a slight increase in membership took place in the 1970s. In 1981 25 congregations, some of which were black, were located in New Orleans. The Missouri Synod supported the Bethlehem Lutheran Welfare Association and the Bethlehem Orphan's Home in New Orleans. In 1964, the American Lutheran Church had seven congregations with 2,011 members and the Lutheran Church in America had five congregations with 892 members in Louisiana. In 1981, membership in Lutheran Churches in Louisiana reached about 24,000.

United Pentecostal Church. Pentecostalism is a movement of considerable variety and, therefore, cannot be treated fully in this article. One expression of this faith, that is reasonably strong in Louisiana, is the United Pentecostal Church, formed in 1945 through a merger of the Pentecostal Church, Inc. and the Pentecostal Assemblies of Jesus Christ.

This form of Pentecostalism is the largest "unitarian" or "Oneness" group within the Pentecostal movement. Pentecostals in the United Church believe that "there is only one person in the Godhead—Jesus Christ." "Baptism in water by immersion [is, therefore] in the name of the Lord Jesus Christ for the remission of sins." They are sometimes called "Jesus Only" Pentecostals and in this respect differ from the so-called normative Pentecostal denominations. The

United Pentecostal Church shares in the general Pentecostal movement in most other respects, including baptism of the Holy Spirit and glossolalia.

In 1981, there were 272 United Pentecostal Churches and 600 pastors, missionaries, and evangelists in the state; Sunday school attendance reached about 30,000. The Louisiana District headquarters is located in Tioga.

Mennonites. The first Mennonites to arrive in Louisiana were probably immigrants from Alsace-Lorraine, who landed in New Orleans. In 1839, for example, Christian Reeser, his two brothers and a sister settled in that city. A few Mennonites, with whom John F. Funk had correspondence, were residents of New Orleans in 1874.

In 1898, a Mennonite church was organized in Lake Charles in southwest Louisiana, made up of 40 members at one time. Only one family was left in 1955 because of a decline in rice farming in which they were engaged. In 1918, a Mennonite congregation that did not survive was formed at Des Allemands, west of New Orleans. However, in 1936, three Mennonite families reestablished a church at Des Allemands, which now has 45 members. An outgrowth of this church is a congregation at Akers, north of New Orleans, organized in 1942. In 1955, there were 20 members of this church, largely French-speaking.

Judaism. Jews appeared first in what became the state of Louisiana in the late 1750s. By January 1779, there were six Jews in New Orleans. One of these was Isaac Rodriguez Monsanto, a Dutch merchant, who moved his headquarters from Curacao to New Orleans. A gifted entrepreneur, Monsanto and his entourage, including three brothers, conducted business operations with merchants throughout the boundaries of the later state of Louisiana and beyond. Though they were known to be Jews, they shared in Catholic worship without baptism.

Judah Touro settled in New Orleans in 1801 or 1802 and through his industrious attitude and frugal living became a wealthy man. Indifferent to Judaism until his later years, he was persuaded by Gershom Kursheedt to build a synagogue for the second New Orleans congregation in 1845. Touro's attitude toward Judaism was typical of the early Jewish settlers, who were for the most part equally indifferent to the cultivation of Jewish identity. There is a story about a rabbi who unable to find a Jewish maiden to his fancy married a Catholic lady. When the rabbi died, much persuasion was required to restrain the weeping widow from putting a crucifix into her husband's coffin.

The first congregation, Shaarei Chassed, was established in New Orleans in 1827. It was not only the first synagogue in Louisiana but probably in the Gulf Coast region and in the Mississippi Valley south of Cincinnati. Manis Jacobs was its first president. What is now Touro Synagogue was organized in 1847. In 1850, Sharbay Tefilah Congregation was formed in New Orleans. Judaism, however, did not prosper owing to lukewarm support by people of wealth and extensive intermarriage that occurred "perhaps more [frequently] than in any [other] major city in the United States," it has been stated.

German Jews especially fanned out from New Orleans into small towns and rural areas. They served as artisans, merchants, and traders. Benevolent societies, cemeteries, and congregations in Alexandria (1854), Donaldsonville (1856), and Monroe (1861) resulted from their labors. Except for New Orleans, Shreveport had the largest Jewish community in the state by mid-century. Synagogues were established there in 1859 and 1892. B'nai B'rith, Zionist, and other groups were formed to further Jewish interests and embody the culture as well as the religion of Judaism. Though Jews settled in Baton Rouge around 1800, a congregation was not formed until 1858; it became B'nai

Israel in 1879. Jewish communities were also organized in Bogalusa, Lafayette, Lake Charles, Morgan City, Natchitoches, New Iberia, and Opelousas.

The most important Jewish institution created in the state was the Association for the Relief of Jewish Widows and Orphans of New Orleans (1854), probably the first agency of this sort in the United States. Frequent deaths due to recurring yellow fever epidemics in the New Orleans area made this association essential. It was supported by assimilated Jews, "who demonstrated no other concern with their Jewish identity."

Until the late nineteenth century, the full participation and integration of Jews in the life of New Orleans were encouraged by the cosmopolitan spirit of the city and furthered by widespread intermarriage of Jews and Christians. The first King (Rex) of Mardi Gras, in 1872, was a Jew, Louis J. Salomon. Other distinguished Jews were JUDAH P. BENJAMIN, United States senator (1853-1861), Henry W. Hyams, lieutenant governor of Louisiana (1859), and Edward Warren Moise, speaker of the Louisiana legislature in the 1850s and later attorney general, all of them assimilationists.

Rabbi James K. Gutheim was the major Jewish leader in New Orleans after the Civil War. Initially discouraged by the poor prospects of Jewry in the city after the war, he moved to New York City in 1868. A group of his friends who founded a Reform Congregation, Temple Sinai, encouraged him to return to New Orleans in 1872. By 1885, Reform Judaism was a significant force in the city. Rabbi Julian B. Feibelman served Temple Sinai for over 40 years (1935-1980).

The total Jewish population in Louisiana declined after 1940 when the number of Jews peaked at about 16,000, of whom about 10,000 lived in New Orleans and 2,000 in Shreveport. But Jews have continued to exhibit leadership far beyond what their small proportion of the population would suggest. For example, Jewish

mayors have served in New Orleans, Alexandria, Monroe, Crowley, Donaldsonville, and Morgan City. In the 20th century, assimilationist tendencies have abated and, though Jews still share widely in the social and political life of the state, there is now a deeper sense of historical and psychological identity in the Jewish community than was the case in the 19th century.

Voodooism. Though Voodooism in and of itself would hardly qualify for inclusion in this article, justification for including it lies in the fact that it became intertwined with a broad spectrum of religious cults and exerted some influence upon Catholic and Protestant Christianity, especially but not exclusively among blacks in New Orleans. Catholic ritual, incense, and flickering candles that cast an eerie glow in subdued light characterize most of the temples, led by a usually self-appointed "Mother" or "Father" who wields unusual power. Sometimes Protestant hymns but more frequently gospel songs are sung to the accompaniment of vigorous hand clapping and foot stamping. There is a good deal of "falling out," talking in "unknown tongues," alleged communion with the spirits of departed relatives, and belief in demons poised to do their deadly work unless they are properly placated. These phenomena, of course, have a multiplicity of sources, of which Voodooism is only one. Nevertheless, Voodooism provides a distinctive quality to what it touches and must be taken into account in any estimate of the more spontaneous expressions of religion in the area of which New Orleans is the center. Marie Laveau, a free mulatto, who served as Queen of the Voodoos for more than three decades in the mid-nineteenth century, revised the ceremony of her cult to bring in veneration of the Virgin Mary and adoration of the saints "so that Voodooism became a curious mixture of West Indian fetish-worship and perverted Catholicism."

Voodooism derives from an African cult in which cosmic powers, usually powers of evil, were symbolized, placated, and "worshipped in the form of a large snake." For almost two centuries, most blacks and many whites in south Louisiana felt the influence of this strange practice. Voodoo rites seem to have been especially attractive to slaves. Emotional excesses and occasional violence drove the movement underground and it is difficult to witness a Voodoo ceremony now. However, Voodoo charms are still available. There are sources from which one can secure "Love Powders, Get-Together Drops, Boss-Fix-Powder, Easy Life Powder, Come to Me Powder, Devil Oil, Controlling Oil, and Dice Special" and the celebrated *gris-gris*, a small bag filled with bits of reptile skin, cayenne pepper, and other exotic elements, the most feared and costliest of Voodoo magic.

See also articles on BLACK CATHOLICISM; CAJUN INFLUENCE; FRENCH INFLUENCE; ROMAN CATHOLIC CHURCH; SPANISH INFLUENCE.

Bibliography. H. C. Bezou, "Louisiana," *New Catholic Encyclopedia*, vol. 7; J. H. Bowdon and F. E. Maser, "Louisiana," *The Encyclopedia of World Methodism*, vol. 2; Hodding Carter and Betty Werlein Carter, *So Great a Good: A History of the Episcopal Church in Louisiana and of Christ Church Cathedral*; John T. Christian, *A History of the Baptists in Louisiana*; John Duffy, ed., *Parson Clapp of the Strangers' Church of New Orleans*; Winfred Ernest Garrison and Alfred T. DeGroot, *The Disciples of Christ: A History*; Melvin Gingerich, "Louisiana," *The Mennonite Encyclopedia*, vol. 3; Glen Lee Greene, *House Upon a Rock: About Southern Baptists in Louisiana*; R. H. Harper, *Louisiana Methodism*; Frances Parkinson Keyes, *All This Is Louisiana*; Bertram W. Korn and Edward L. Greenstein, "Louisiana," *Encyclopedia Judaica*, vol. 11; Lester G. McAllister and William E. Tucker, *Journey in Faith: A History of the Christian Church (Disciples of Christ)*; Benjamin H. Pershing, "Louisiana," *The Encyclopedia of the Lutheran Church*, vol. 2; Penrose C. St. Amant, *A History of the Presbyterian Church in Louisiana*; *A Short History of Louisiana Baptists*; Lyle Saxon, State Supervisor, Louisiana, *A Guide to the State*.

PENROSE ST. AMANT
SOUTHERN BAPTIST SEMINARY

LOVE FEAST. This term is used to refer to the Communion service as it has been practiced in the CHURCH OF THE BRETHREN. The Church began in 1708 because of the conviction of eight people that they ought to be a part of a church that practiced literally the sacraments of the Christian church. From their study of the New Testament and of recently published church histories, they were convinced that Christians of every generation ought to wash one another's feet and eat a meal together as well as breaking the bread and drinking the wine.

For many years during the 19th century, this service was held on a Saturday evening once a year. It became a feast of love, for Brethren gathered from many neighboring congregations to participate. It was a closed service with only members of the Church participating, although the Brethren welcomed visitors.

The Church of the Brethren has changed in many ways in the 20th century. Although the Church is congregational in organization and great variety exists in the denomination, most Brethren congregations have opened their Love Feast service to any Christian who wishes to participate. Many congregations have introduced a Sunday morning bread-and-cup communion, on a once or twice a year basis, in addition to the Sunday evening (or sometimes Maundy Thursday) Love Feast service. Perhaps a few congregations no longer have any Love Feast service. Historically, however, it was the Brethren addition of the washing of feet and the eating of a meal of love that made the Love Feast a distinctive service.

ROGER E. SAPPINGTON
BRIDGEWATER COLLEGE

LOVELY LANE CHAPEL. One of the earliest churches built by colonial followers of John Wesley, this congregation opened for services in 1774 in the heart of the city of Baltimore. Although Pennsylvania and New York had small Methodist communities, the Baltimore area was an early center of the evangelical Anglican movement. FRANCIS ASBURY, the great early leader of the Wesleyan movement in America, regularly visited Maryland, especially concentrating his efforts on Baltimore. The city's first Wesleyan church was built on Strawberry Alley in 1773. The next year, two of Asbury's converts, William Moore and Philip Rogers, helped found the second Baltimore church for the congregation, the chapel on Lovely Lane. Baltimore became the first city in the New World with two churches for Evangelicals, and the neighboring countryside held several more.

The Lovely Lane Chapel was an unimposing stone building with two simple entrances in the front. Initially it was lit only by arched windows. Reflecting the poverty of the evangelical movement, the appointments inside were primitive. The seats lacked backs and the building had no heating system.

By 1784 when John Wesley had agreed that more attention had to be paid to the American mission, Baltimore had clearly become the center of American evangelical Anglicanism. When Francis Asbury organized the meeting to discuss the future of American Wesleyanism, the obvious location was Baltimore. On 24 December 1784 the CHRISTMAS CONFERENCE convened at the Lovely Lane Chapel and created the new denomination, the Methodist Episcopal Church of the United States. The chapel itself was spruced up a bit for the meeting; now many of the seats had backs, and a stove warmed the room.

The meeting was the chapel's last moment of glory, however. The following year Bishop THOMAS COKE authorized its sale when the congregation moved to a new building on Light Street. The next year the Lovely Lane Chapel burned to the ground.

See also article on METHODIST CHURCH.

DAVID T. BAILEY
MICHIGAN STATE UNIVERSITY

LOW CHURCH/HIGH CHURCH:
See HIGH CHURCH/LOW CHURCH.

LUNENBERG LETTER: *See* CHURCHES OF CHRIST.

LUTHERAN CHURCH.

Colonial Period, 1607-1789. Lutherans entered the Southern states by two routes: migration from Pennsylvania into the valley of Virginia and the Piedmont of North Carolina, and through the ports of Savannah and Charleston. In 1717 a group of Germans settled in Orange County VA and then moved to Madison County where they established Hebron Church. In 1740 they built a frame church, part of which remains today. Their first pastor was John Caspar Stoever, Sr.

The first Lutherans in North Carolina were from the Palatinate and settled at New Bern. They were sent by Queen Anne in 1710 but were wiped out by an Indian massacre. Later migrations from Pennsylvania resulted in the establishment of several congregations, but they had no pastor until 1773 when Adolphus Nussman arrived. Palatine Lutherans settled in South Carolina as early as 1732, and in 1755 a Lutheran congregation was organized in Charleston.

In 1734 Lutheran refugees from Salzburg, Austria, settled in Georgia at Ebenezer. These SALZBURGERS had been driven from their homes by the Roman Catholic archbishops, and through the help of the English were able to migrate to the New World. Their two pastors were John Martin Boltzius and Israel Christian Gronau. The first governor of Georgia, John Adam Truetlen, was a Salzburger. Henry Melchior Muhlenberg, the "Patriarch of American Lutheranism," visited these Southern congregations as part of his pastoral supervision of American Lutherans.

National Period, 1789-1865. During this period three issues concerned Southern Lutherans: home missions, the organization of synods, and the formation of a national body. Home missionaries such as John Stauch, PAUL HENKEL and Jacob Scherer worked in the Southern states. In 1803 the "mother synod of the South," the North Carolina Synod, was organized at Salisbury. In 1820 four pastors of this synod, including Paul Henkel and two of his sons, Philip and David, who wanted strict subscription to all the articles of the AUGSBURG CONFESSION and who opposed the formation of a national body, formed the Tennessee Synod. As early as 1793 the Virginia Special Conference of the Ministerium of Pennsylvania was formed. In 1820 it was organized into the Synod of Maryland and Virginia, which subdivided into two synods in 1829. In 1824 the South Carolina Synod was organized out of the North Carolina Synod. In 1820 the first general organization of American Lutherans was created at Hagerstown MD, the General Synod, with representatives from North Carolina and Virginia participating.

Between 1830 and 1860 four new Southern synods were formed: Southwestern Virginia, 1842; Mississippi, 1855; Georgia, 1860; and Holston, 1860. Of the eight Southern synods, only North Carolina, Virginia and Southwestern Virginia belonged to the General Synod.

The leading figure of Southern Lutheranism during this period and through Reconstruction was JOHN BACHMAN, pastor of St. John's Church, Charleston. He was instrumental in the founding of the Lutheran Theological Southern Seminary (1830) at Columbia SC and Newberry College (1858) at nearby Newberry. In 1842 Roanoke College was established in Virginia.

The major theological controversy of 19th-century Lutheranism was the conflict between "American Lutheranism" and "Old Lutheranism." John Bachman and many of the South Carolina clergy supported "American Lutheranism," and the Henkels and many of the Tennessee clergy supported "Old Lutheranism." None of the Southern synods adopted the "Definite Synodical Platform," 1855, that American Lutheranism produced, which suggested some revisions of the Augsburg Confession.

The Lutheran Church was the last of the major American denominations to split into Northern and Southern bodies, and this split was not over slavery prior to the war, but came after the war began and was the practical result of political division. In 1861 the Lutheran synods in the South began to withdraw from the General Synod, and five of them (Virginia, Southwestern Virginia, North Carolina, South Carolina, and Georgia) formed the General Synod of the Evangelical Lutheran Church in the Confederate States of America in 1863. The Tennessee, Holston, and Mississippi synods did not participate.

Modern Period, 1865-1980. From Reconstruction to World War I the Southern Lutheran Church was primarily concerned with forming a more inclusive Southern body and with reuniting the General Synod. In 1866 the General Synod CSA changed its name to the Evangelical Lutheran General Synod in North America. Through a series of "Diets" the United Synod of the Evangelical Lutheran Church in the South was formed in 1886, and included all eight Southern synods.

Not only did the Southern synods withdraw from the General Synod, but in 1866 other synods withdrew over theological issues and formed the General Council of the Evangelical Lutheran Church in North America (1867). The Southern United Synod took the initiative in bringing these three bodies back together by proposing a "Common Service" and a common hymnal. Furthermore, the "General Synod South" had a median doctrinal position on which the General Synod and General Council could reunite. In 1918 the United Synod in the South, the General Council, and the General Synod reunited to form the United Lutheran Church in America.

Southern Lutherans did limited work among black Americans. The Synodical Conference (1872), composed of more conservative bodies, led the way here, and as a result two black colleges were founded—Emmanuel Lutheran College in Greensboro NC and Luther College in New Orleans. In 1889 several black Lutheran pastors and congregations from the North Carolina Synod formed the Alpha Synod of the Evangelical Lutheran Church of Freedmen in America.

Twentieth-century American Lutheranism is primarily the history of synodical realignment, mergers, and the creation of cooperative agencies. In 1921 the Tennessee and North Carolina synods merged as the North Carolina Synod, and in 1922 the Virginia, Southwestern Virginia, and Holston synods merged into the Virginia Synod. In 1960 the Southwestern Synod was created covering the states of Tennessee, Alabama, Georgia, and Mississippi. The Lutheran Church in America, formed in 1962 and including the United Lutheran Church in America, is the strongest Lutheran body in the Southern states. The American Lutheran Church, formed in 1960, is not strong in the South, nor is the Lutheran Church-Missouri Synod (1847). Most Southern Lutherans have participated in the two cooperative agencies formed in this century, the National Lutheran Council (1918) and the Lutheran Council in the United States of America (1967).

See also article on LUTHERANISM.

Bibliography. H. George Anderson, *Lutheranism in the Southeastern United States, 1860-1886: A Social History*; Donald S. Armentrout, "John Jacob Scherer, Jr.: A Type of Southern Lutheran," unpublished Ph.D. dissertation, Vanderbilt University, 1970; G. D. Bernheim and G. H. Cox, *The History of the Evangelical Lutheran Synod and Ministerium of North Carolina, in Commemoration of the Completion of the First Century of Its Existence*; Raymond M. Bost, "The Reverend John Bachman and the Development of Southern Lutheranism," unpublished Ph.D. dissertation, Yale University, 1963; William E. Eisenberg, *The Lutheran Church in Virginia, 1717-1962*; Charles W. Hethcote, *The Lutheran Church and the Civil War*; Paul E. Monroe, Jr., "A History of Southern Lutheranism," unpublished S.T.M. thesis, Hamma Divinity School, n.d.; E. Clifford Nelson, ed., *The Lutherans in North America*; Gordon W. Ward, Jr., "The Formation of the Lutheran General Synod, South During the Civil War," *The Lutheran Quarterly* 13 (May 1961): 132-54; *A History of the Lutheran Church in South Carolina*.

DONALD S. ARMENTROUT
UNIVERSITY OF THE SOUTH

LUTHERANISM. This Protestant family originated as a reform movement within the Western part of the Catholic Church. Martin Luther (1483-1546) became the leader of the movement when in 1517 he called for a public disputation on the abuse of "indulgences"—the practice of the church to forgive particular sins by receiving money offerings rather than by demanding confession to the priest. By 1520 Luther began to question the entire hierarchical-sacramental system of ecclesiastical authority, contending that Scripture and the early postbiblical tradition did not justify the hierarchical structure of Roman Catholicism.

Echoing St. Paul's Epistle to the Romans' rejection of the salvific power of Jewish law, Luther rallied "Lutherans" (the name given his supporters by opponents) around the "chief article of faith," the doctrine of "justification by faith alone, through grace, without the works of law" (Rom. 3:24; 28). This doctrine, Luther contended, was not just one among many, but rather the norm for all teachings in the church by which the Christian faith is to be communicated. According to Luther, one becomes right with God, "justified," by complete trust in what God did in Jesus Christ for the atonement of all sins, not by trying to appease God through doing good works, "law." God offers salvation as a gift, "by grace" not affected by good works of love, even though God will reward such works. Christians ought to direct their moral efforts to helping the neighbor in need without any ulterior motive.

Despite the pope's and the emperor's condemnation of Luther in 1521, Lutheranism spread rapidly, first throughout Germany and Scandinavia, then to territories now known as Poland, Czechoslovakia, Hungary, and Rumania. Many territorial princes who, as feudal landlords, had control over their citizens' religion, joined the Lutheran movement, more often than not because they wanted independence from the pope and emperor. Faced with these domestic problems and military threat of the Islamic Turks from the South, Emperor Charles V agreed to hear the Lutheran case at the Diet of Augsburg in 1530. However, he rejected the Lutheran AUGSBURG CONFESSION that had been drafted by the lay theologian Philip Melanchthon of Wittenberg when it was submitted. All attempts to settle the controversy through theological dialogue failed.

By 1547, the year after Luther's death, the Lutheran military Smalcald League and Catholic territorial forces led by the ruler of Bavaria and supported by both pope and emperor went to war. Although the Smalcald League lost the war one year later, Emperor Charles V did agree to tolerate "the churches of the Augsburg Confession," as the 1555 Peace of Augsburg called them, with the proviso that an ecumenical council was to deal with these religious problems before a final political settlement would be reached. But the Council of Trent (1545-1563) refused to admit the Lutherans to their deliberations, and rejected the basic Lutheran teachings.

Lutheranism, which had created a number of territorial churches by the 1550s, nevertheless continued to gain political strength. In 1580, Lutheran teachings were collected and published as the *Book of Concord*. It contained Luther's Large and Small Catechisms of 1529; the *Augsburg Confession* and its defense in the *Apology* of 1530; Luther's *Smalcald Articles* of 1537; and the *Formula of Concord* of 1577, which had been drafted by several churchmen to resolve intra-Lutheran controversies in Germany. Lutheran territorial churches adopted the basic features of Luther's catechetical and liturgical programs. As state churches, they cooperated closely with their territorial rulers. By 1600, a majority of German territories had become Lutheran, together with the kingdom of Denmark and Sweden, which controlled the regions of Norway and Finland. The Thirty-Years' War (1618-1648) finally forced a political settlement of the religious issues. The Peace of Westphalia in 1648 recognized the churches of the *Augsburg Confession* as separate but equal entities under the law in the Holy Roman Empire.

Lutheranism, as either a movement or an institution, was decisively affected by cultural and political changes in Europe. Philosophical rationalism influenced the Lutheran theological faculties at state universities. A number of Lutheran territorial churches in Germany tried to oppose both rationalism and Roman Catholicism with a "Lutheran orthodoxy" in the 17th century. Lutheran dogmaticians devised systems of thought and morals, anchored in the doctrine of an inspired inerrant Scripture, which were enforced by political laws. "Pietists," as their opponents nicknamed them, criticized this "religion of the head" and began a reform movement of their own in 1675. The movement stressed a "religion of the heart," the main features of which were Bible study, individual conversion, lay ministry, and "non-worldly" morals. Much more successful than the "orthodox," Pietists shaped much of church and political life in 18th-century Germany and Scandinavia.

In the 19th century, the Pietist spirit helped create the Lutheran "inner mission" movement, which designed effective social welfare programs, created the female diaconate, started prison reforms, and founded a number of church hospitals under the leadership of the churchman and politician John H. Wichern (1808-1881). Lutheran Bible societies and foreign mission workers joined non-Lutherans in efforts for mission and Protestant unity. Yet when Prussia advocated a union between Lutheran and Reformed (Calvinist) churches in 1817, on the 300th anniversary of the publication of Luther's Ninety-Five Theses, conservative Lutherans opposed such a move. Many of them went to the United States and organized the Lutheran Church Missouri Synod in 1847.

Many German and Scandinavian Lutheran churches experienced heavy political pressure and sometimes persecution during the reign of Adolf Hitler (1933-1945). In Germany, a minority of German Lutherans resisted Hitler and formed what they called "the Confessing Church" in opposition to the strong majority who called themselves "German Christians" and acceded to Hitler's demand to coordinate Nazism and Lutheranism. Danish and Norwegian Lutheran churches, which refused to cooperate with Nazism, were not heavily persecuted by German occupation forces during the 1940s.

The Lutheran World Federation was founded in 1947 in an attempt to provide a common platform for about 80 million Lutherans belonging to churches in Europe, North America, Latin America, Africa, and parts of Asia, especially Indonesia. The federation has no authority over member churches, but it holds regular world assemblies and initiates a variety of programs that frequently lead to common social and political action. The federation is also in close contact with the World Council of Churches, to which most Lutheran denominations belong.

Since Lutheranism began as a reform movement within Roman Catholicism, dialogue with Catholics has been important to Lutherans. Although little, if any, contact was maintained between the two traditions for more than 400 years, the Second Vatican Council has moved Roman Catholics towards realistic dialogue with other churches, including Lutherans. Lutherans and Catholics have been engaged in an ongoing dialogue in the United States and on an international level since the 1960s with the objective of ascertaining the differences and similarities between them. The dialogue in the United States, which is sponsored by the Secretariat for Unity and the Conference of Catholic Bishops in the United States as well as by the Lutheran World Federation and its National Committee in the United States, has dealt with a series of thorny doctrinal issues ranging from baptism to papal infallibility. There are also Lutheran dialogues with the Greek Orthodox church on an international level, and with representative Baptists, Presbyterians, and other Protestant groups in the United States.

The tension between Lutheranism as a reform movement within the Catholic Church and the Lutheran denominations around the world is manifested in church polities. Scandinavian churches are governed by an episcopal system that makes them state churches. German Lutherans have developed a combination of episcopal and synodical polities in the various territorial churches which, as a federation, are led by a bishop (one in East Germany and one in West Germany). American Lutheran denominations have adopted the synodical system, but have accepted the title "bishop" for many of the synodical presidents who head the synods. The highest legislative authority for U.S. Lutherans is a national convention. Lutheran churches in Latin America, Africa, and Asia prefer the episcopal system, even though the notion that bishops are the authentic successors of the first apostles is not generally accepted.

Almost all Lutheran churches around the world subscribe, in one form or another, to the *Augsburg Confession* and to Luther's *Small Catechism* as the decisive teachings of the Lutheran tradition. Thus Lutheranism is strongly committed to the Western liturgical tradition that is chiefly embodied in the Roman Mass. Recent Lutheran hymnals disclose a strengthening of this tradition with a renewed emphasis on ritual, congregational singing, and a general appreciation of music.

Ethnic differences that, especially in the United States, formerly separated various Lutheran groups, have given way to an increasing appreciation for Christian unity. One indication of that appreciation is the formal agreement between the Lutheran Church in America and the American Lutheran Church (the two counting about six million members) and the Anglican community in the United States to share their altars and pulpits on an interim basis. Such an agreement signals the ecumenical commitment of Lutheranism, expressed in a healthy tension between unity and diversity.

See also articles on LUTHERAN CHURCH (IN THE SOUTH); MIGRATION, SOUTHWARD (1700-1830); PIETISM; PROTESTANT REFORMATION.

Bibliography. Paul Althaus, *The Theology of Martin Luther; The Ethics of Martin Luther;* Conrad J. Bergendoff, *The Church of the Lutheran Reformation*; Wilhelm Dantine, *The Justification of the Ungodly*; Werner Elert, *The Structure of Lutheranism*; Gerhard O. Forde, *Justification By Faith*; Eric W. Gritsch and Robert W. Jenson, *Lutheranism*; Clifford E. Nelson, *The Rise of World Lutheranism*; Luther D. Reed, *The Lutheran Liturgy*;

Theodore G. Tappert, *The Book of Concord*; *The Encyclopedia of the Lutheran Church*.

ERIC W. GRITSCH
LUTHERAN THEOLOGICAL SEMINARY

MCBEE, SILAS (1854-1924), Episcopal editor and ecumenist, was born in Lincolnton NC, received his early education in Lincolnton and entered the UNIVERSITY OF THE SOUTH in 1873. There he came under the influence of the chaplain, WILLIAM PORCHER DUBOSE, who became his teacher in theology for life. Graduated in 1876, McBee joined the administrative staff of the university. In 1883 he became principal of the Fairmont School for Girls at nearby Monteagle. There he developed an unsuspected talent for wood carving into a study of ecclesiastical architecture in which he became an expert among Episcopal laymen.

From 1896 to 1912 McBee was editor of the New York *Churchman*, the semi-official newspaper of American Episcopalians. In that capacity and as vice-president of the Brotherhood of St. Andrew and of the Laymen's Missionary Movement, he became a leading denominational spokesman in the ecumenical movement. His international tour on its behalf in 1910 is recounted in *An Eirenic Itinerary* and led to the founding of the *Constructive Quarterly* two years later. An impressive venture in world ecumenism, with an editorial board representing four continents and all major Christian traditions, the *Quarterly* was crippled by the outbreak of World War I. McBee continued to publish the journal until 1922 when, after a troubled decade, ill health forced him to discontinue it.

See also article on ECUMENISM.

Bibliography. Norman C. Duncan, "Silas McBee, *Churchman* Editor," *Churchman* 178 (June 1964): 24; Silas McBee, *An Eirenic Itinerary: Impressions of Our Tour with Addresses and Papers on the Unity of Christian Churches*; "Obituary," *New York Times*, September 4, 1924.

RALPH E. LUKER
VIRGINIA POLYTECHNIC INSTITUTE
AND STATE UNIVERSITY

MCDANIEL, GEORGE WHITE (1875-1927), Baptist pastor, author, and denominational leader, was a native of Texas and a graduate of Baylor University and Southern Baptist Theological Seminary, Louisville KY. Ordained a minister in 1899, he held pastorates in Kentucky and Texas before coming to First Baptist Church, Richmond VA in 1905. There McDaniel gained the admiration of Virginia Baptists for his forceful preaching and his administrative ability. During his 22-year tenure, First Baptist, already the largest congregation in the city, doubled its membership. McDaniel reached further prominence by championing PROHIBITION and repeatedly opposing proposed state laws requiring Bible reading in public schools. He held numerous state denominational positions, including the presidency of the Baptist General Association of Virginia. He wrote six books, mostly about Baptist history and beliefs. In *The Supernatural Jesus* (1924), he issued a blistering critique of modernism and defended conservative theology.

Between 1924 and 1927 McDaniel served as president of the Southern Baptist Convention. Following a series of controversies about evolution, some Baptist leaders wanted the convention to repudiate evolution and prohibit the teaching of it in denominational schools, colleges, and seminaries. Although an outspoken critic of evolution, McDaniel played a crucial role in preventing a bitter and divisive fight over that issue at the 1926 meeting of the SBC. He concluded his presidential speech with a statement rejecting evolution and affirming that man was a special creation of God. The convention endorsed his statement in a resolution and largely put aside the evolution question during the rest of the meeting.

See also articles on CHURCH AND STATE; EVOLUTION CONTROVERSY; MODERNIST CONTROVERSY.

Bibliography. Douglass Scarborough McDaniel, *George White McDaniel.*

SAMUEL C. SHEPHERD, JR.
CENTENARY COLLEGE

MCGARVEY, JOHN W. (1829-1911),

clergyman, educator, and editor among the DISCIPLES OF CHRIST, was a dominant influence in the development of that denomination's ministerial education and a vigorous polemicist in the denomination's debates on ecclesiology, the use of instrumental music in worship, and biblical criticism. A native of Kentucky, McGarvey matriculated in 1847 at Bethany College where he studied under ALEXANDER CAMPBELL and other Disciple luminaries, was baptized, and determined to become a preacher. After

graduation in 1850, he settled in Fayette MO, taught school, continued study for the ministry, married, and established a home of his own. He preached for nine years at Dover before Civil War hostilities and his own pacifism created a need to relocate. Invited to the pastorate of the Disciples church in Lexington KY, he spent the remainder of his life working in that city.

McGarvey was instrumental in the formation of a College of the Bible within Kentucky University in 1865 and became the professor of sacred history. Except for a brief period in the 1870s, he held this position until his death. He became president of the college in 1895. Having earlier written for other journals, he edited the *Apostolic Times* (later renamed *Apostolic Guide*) from 1869 to 1893 and wrote a column on biblical criticism for the *Christian Standard* after 1893.

McGarvey advocated a thorough grounding in biblical study for ministerial candidates and a rather narrow, legalistic use of Scripture in dealing with religious questions of the day. He supported the organization of missionary societies among the Disciples but vigorously opposed as unscriptural the use of instrumental music in services of worship. Through his journal and books such as *Evidences of Christianity* and *Authorship of the Book of Deuteronomy* as well as his classroom instruction, McGarvey provided intellectual leadership for a generation of Disciple clergy. However, his methods of inquiry and his concern for context reflected in his *Lands of the Bible* led many of his students into paths far more liberal than McGarvey's own.

See also articles on CHURCHES OF CHRIST; RELIGIOUS PRESS; THEOLOGICAL EDUCATION.

Bibliography. J. W. McGarvey, *The Autobiography of J. W. McGarvey (1829-1911)*; William C. Morro, *Brother McGarvey*; Dwight E. Stevenson, *Lexington Theological Seminary, 1865-1965: The College of the Bible Century.*

SAMUEL C. PEARSON
SOUTHERN ILLINOIS UNIVERSITY
AT EDWARDSVILLE

MCGARY, AUSTIN (1846-1927), an influential leader among Texas CHURCHES OF CHRIST, was born in Huntsville TX. Young McGary grew up with Sam Houston's children and when the Civil War began, he and Sam Houston, Jr. joined the "Huntsville Grays" together. After the war McGary distinguished himself as a frontier Texas sheriff. Around 1880 he became interested in religion through the writings of ALEXANDER CAMPBELL, became a member of the Church of Christ, and was soon preaching for churches around Austin.

The 1880s were a time of controversy for Churches of Christ. "Progressives" and "conservatives" were arguing about whether missionary societies and instrumental music were in harmony with their professed goal of restoring the New Testament church. McGary stood with the "conservatives" and established the *Firm Foundation* in 1884, assuring readers that it would "assume a stern air" in opposing innovations in the church. McGary was also concerned about baptism, and he and DAVID LIPSCOMB, editor of the *Gospel Advocate*, continued an editorial debate on this subject for nearly a decade. The *Firm Foundation* barely survived through its early years, but by 1889 it had 5,000 subscribers and became a weekly. (It continues as a widely read journal in the 1980s.)

When Churches of Christ and Disciples of Christ finally divided, Texas was one of the few states where Churches of Christ were stronger than Disciples. The *Firm Foundation* and its bellicose editor had made the difference; his editing of that journal stands as his most enduring work.

See also article on RELIGIOUS PRESS.

B. J. HUMBLE
ABILENE CHRISTIAN UNIVERSITY

MCGREADY, JAMES (1760-1817), frontier Presbyterian revivalist, was born in western Pennsylvania. He moved with his parents to Guilford County NC in 1778, but returned to his native state in the mid-1780s to study for the ministry under the tutelage of two New Light (New Side) Presbyterian revivalists, John McMillan and Joseph Smith. On 13 August 1788 McGready was licensed to preach by the Redstone Presbytery of Pennsylvania, and that fall decided to return to North Carolina to pursue his ministerial career. En route he visited Hampden-Sydney College where a spirited student revival was underway, and was further convinced of the efficacy of revivalistic preaching. Once back in North Carolina he focused his powerful oratorical skills on the materialism, violence, and drinking of the slaveowning society, and he met instant opposition.

He gained new converts, several of whom later became ministers, but the rising opposition, including threats against his life, led McGready to leave North Carolina and move to Logan County KY in August 1796. The following January McGready took charge of three small churches—Red River, Gasper River, and Muddy River congregations—and quickly attempted to revive their members. His zeal and inspirational leadership began immediately to take effect; many of the communicants signed a pledge to unite in weekly prayer for revival. The decade of the 1790s across the South was marked by religious decline, both real and perceived. But many ministers, like McGready, had come to expect a "season of revival." Such hope contributed to an outpouring of religious enthusiasm, beginning in the summers of 1799 and 1800 at McGready's three churches. The frontier CAMP MEETING is said to have originated at his Gasper River church in July 1800.

From McGready's churches the revival flame spread across the South, constituting the so-called GREAT REVIVAL (Second Great Awakening) of 1800-1805. Although interdenominational unity was the desire and first fruit of the revival, division and schism soon followed. McGready was identified with the revival faction, but when the wildly dissenting

SHAKERS arrived and more fervent revivalists splintered to form the CUMBERLAND PRESBYTERIAN CHURCH, McGready hesitated to join them. After several years of disciplinary probation he was readmitted to the orthodox Transylvania Presbytery in 1810. The next year he was sent to Southern Indiana to help establish Presbyterian churches, and spent the remainder of his life in similar missionary activities. He died at his home in Henderson KY. His letters published in various missionary magazines at the beginning of the century document the Great Revival, and his sermons reveal surprising theological sophistication. He is best remembered as the father of the Great Revival.

See also articles on FRONTIER, INFLUENCE OF; REVIVALISM.

Bibliography. John B. Boles, *The Great Revival, 1787-1805: The Origins of the Southern Evangelical Mind*; James McGready, *The Posthumous Works of the Reverend and Pious James M. McGready* (2 vols., 1831-1833), ed. James Smith; John Opie, Jr., "James McGready: Theologian of Frontier Revivalism," *Church History* 36 (December 1965): 445-56.

JOHN B. BOLES
RICE UNIVERSITY

MCKELWAY, ALEXANDER JEFFREY

(1866-1918), social reform leader, was born in Sadsburyville PA. His father, a Presbyterian minister, moved the family to Virginia one year after his son's birth. Educated at Hampden-Sydney College and Union Theological Seminary in Virginia, he entered the Presbyterian ministry and between 1891 and 1898 served as pastor of churches in Virginia and North Carolina. From 1898 until 1905 he edited the *North Carolina Presbyterian*.

Like a number of other religious editors in the state, McKelway participated openly in public affairs. In 1898 he endorsed the Democrats' virulent disfranchisement campaign and defended the violent actions of whites in the Wilmington race riot. On the other hand, editor McKelway championed a number of "progressive" reforms, particularly the abolition of child labor. In 1905 he left denominational work to join the National Child Labor Committee, recently formed under the leadership of EDGAR GARDNER MURPHY. McKelway crisscrossed the South—lecturing, lobbying, and writing on behalf of child-labor reform.

Despite some legislative successes, McKelway came to believe that the problems of child labor could only be resolved by federal legislation. In 1909 McKelway became chief Washington lobbyist for the NCLC. His work paid off in 1912 with the establishment of a federal Children's Bureau.

McKelway belonged to the network of college-trained, religiously oriented social reformers who helped set the tone of Southern progressivism. Although unable to transcend his own culture in matters of race, he helped introduce into Southern and national politics an element of humanitarian concern for a helpless segment of an industrial society.

See also article on SOCIAL GOSPEL.

Bibliography. Betty J. Brandon, "McKelway," unpublished Ph.D. dissertation, University of North Carolina, 1969; "A Wilsonian Progressive—Alexander J. McKelway," *Journal of Presbyterian History* 48 (1970): 2-16; Herbert J. Doherty, "Alexander J. McKelway: Preacher to Progressive," *Journal of Southern History* 24 (1958): 177-90.

ROBERT C. MCMATH, JR.
GEORGIA INSTITUTE OF TECHNOLOGY

MACLACHLAN, HUGH DAVID CATHCART

(1869-1929), Disciples of Christ minister and community leader, was born in Scotland where he earned A.M. and B.L. degrees from the University of Glasgow. After arriving in the United States in 1894, he survived as a Texas cowpuncher and newspaper editor before attending Transylvania College and studying philosophy and religion at the University of Chicago. In 1904 he became an American citizen, was ordained as a minister in the DISCIPLES OF CHRIST, and began his ministerial career at a church in Shelbyville KY.

From 1908 to 1929 Maclachlan served as pastor of Seventh Street Christian Church in Richmond VA where he promoted interdenominational cooperation. He helped to organize the Richmond Council of Churches and he exchanged pulpits with other ministers as well as with Rabbi Edward N. Calisch. In 1927 Maclachlan arranged a goodwill dinner for city Protestants, Catholics, and Jews. His peers esteemed him for his breadth of scholarship evidenced in sermons, articles for *Christian Century*, and lectures delivered at the University of Chicago. Deploring intellectual narrowness and religious intolerance, he criticized fundamentalist leaders and opposed such measures as state censorship of movies.

A consistent advocate of social reform, Maclachlan backed such causes as labor legislation, women's suffrage, and world peace. He helped to create the Richmond Juvenile Court, and as president of the Juvenile Protective Association of Virginia he contributed to the development of the state's juvenile court system. He was one of the founders of the Richmond School of Social Work and Public Health, a forerunner of Virginia Commonwealth University.

See also articles on ECUMENISM; SOCIAL GOSPEL.

Bibliography. H. D. C. Maclachlan Papers, Disciples of Christ Historical Society, Nashville, Tennessee.

SAMUEL C. SHEPHERD, JR.
CENTENARY COLLEGE

MCTYEIRE, HOLLAND NIMMONS

(1824-1889), Methodist editor, bishop, and educator, was born on a plantation in Barnwell County SC. The family later moved to Alabama and Holland was educated by tutors and in private schools. He graduated from Randolph-Macon College in 1844, the same year he was licensed to preach. Joining the Virginia Conference of the Methodist Episcopal Church, South, in 1845, he was assigned to Williamsburg.

McTyeire was transferred in 1846 to Mobile where he met, and later married, Amelia Townsend, whose father was editor of the *Mobile Register*. He moved to Demopolis, then to Columbus MS, and in 1849 to New Orleans where, in addition to serving churches, he became the first editor of the *New Orleans Christian Advocate*. In 1858 McTyeire was elected editor of the *Nashville Christian Advocate*, a position he held until forced by Federal troops to leave Nashville in March 1862. The McTyeire family spent the rest of the war in Alabama, with Holland preaching in Montgomery.

A delegate to the 1854 and 1858 General Conferences, he was also a member of the 1866 General Conference that chose him as one of the four new bishops, thus giving episcopal representation to the progressive wing of the church.

McTyeire's episcopacy spanned 23 years, during which the most important accomplishment was the establishment of Vanderbilt University. Instrumental in securing the gift that made this possible was Mrs. McTyeire, whose cousin was Commodore Vanderbilt's second wife.

See also articles on EDUCATION, CHRISTIAN HIGHER; RELIGIOUS PRESS.

Bibliography. Edwin Mims, *The History of Vanderbilt University*; John J. Tigert IV, *Bishop Holland Nimmons McTyeire: Ecclesiastical and Educational Architect.*

JOSEPH MITCHELL
TROY STATE UNIVERSITY

MADISON, BISHOP JAMES (1749-

1812), first Episcopal bishop of Virginia, and cousin of President James Madison, was born in Augusta County VA. Graduated with distinction from the COLLEGE OF WILLIAM AND MARY in 1772, he soon joined its faculty. Ordained into the Anglican priesthood in 1775, he supported the cause of the colonies and became president of the college at the start of the Revolution. Simultaneously, he served as rector of James City Parish and (from 1790 on) as bishop of Virginia.

Judicious in temperament and popular among his contemporaries, Madison guided William and Mary skillfully during a difficult period. He was principally an educator, scientist, and political philosopher. He led the Virginia astronomers who extended the Mason-Dixon line, designed a standard map of Virginia, and was elected to the American Philosophical Society. Thomas Jefferson, Benjamin Rush, Joel Barlow, and dozens of William and Mary graduates who served in the legislatures and Congress of the new republic were among his correspondents. He was also a noted orator.

Historical judgments blaming Madison for the collapse of the EPISCOPAL CHURCH in Virginia lack perspective. Madison faced major obstacles: the loss of the clergy's state salaries and glebe lands; the defections not only of the common people to the Baptists, Methodists, and Presbyterians, but also of the male gentry to the Deists; the depletion of the clergy following the Revolution; the tainted reputation of Anglicanism; and the westward migration of Episcopalian families. In addition, though Virginia was larger than England, Madison was obliged to hold simultaneously the four jobs of rector, professor, president, and bishop. Yet until the years and the defeats took their toll, Madison's episcopal activities rivaled those of any of his contemporaries.

Bibliography. George MacL. Brydon, *Virginia's Mother Church*, vol. 2; Edward L. Goodwin, *The Colonial Church in Virginia*; David L. Holmes, "The Decline and Revival of the Church in Virginia," *Up From Independence: The Episcopal Church in Virginia*, ed. Brewster S. Ford and Harold S. Sniffen.

DAVID L. HOLMES
COLLEGE OF WILLIAM AND MARY

MADISON, JAMES (1751-1836), fourth president of the United States (1809-1817), was the son of an Anglican planter in Orange County VA. Throughout a life that spanned eight decades, Madison remained a nominal Anglican and maintained an intellectual interest in theology. As a statesman his primary contribution to American religion was his consistent advocacy of separation of CHURCH AND STATE. He was educated first in plantation schools staffed by Anglican clergymen, then at the College of New Jersey (now Princeton University) under John Witherspoon, a Calvinist exponent of the Scottish Enlightenment. Graduat-

ing in 1771, Madison stayed on at Princeton for six months to study Hebrew and ethics with Witherspoon, who in Scotland had resisted the authority of the established Presbyterian Kirk.

In Virginia Madison witnessed the harassment of DISSENTERS by the established Anglican church. This experience contributed to his support of the revolution against British rule. The 1776 Virginia convention adopted his resolution asserting religious freedom, rather than mere toleration, in the Declaration of Rights. When the Virginia House of Delegates considered a General Assessment bill to subsidize the teaching of religion, he anonymously wrote the *Memorial and Remonstrance against Religious Assessments* (1785), which aroused public opinion and contributed to the measure's defeat. In the House he was floor manager of the Statute of Religious Freedom (written by his political confidant, THOMAS JEFFERSON), which completed the DISESTABLISHMENT of the Anglican church in Virginia. Following the ratification of the federal Constitution, he won a closely contested election as a congressman in 1789 in part by assuring Baptists in his constituency that their religious freedom would be preserved. In the First Federal Congress he fulfilled a campaign pledge by introducing the Bill of Rights, including the First Amendment, which prohibited establishment of religion. He was convinced that the most effective guarantee of religious freedom was not constitutional measures but the multiplicity of competing sects that would never allow any single denomination to gain supremacy in America.

Madison's assertion of religious freedom was not hostile to religion itself; he considered that church and state flourished best when separated. As Jefferson's secretary of state and then as president, he corresponded with many religious leaders, including his second cousin, JAMES MADISON, the first Episcopal bishop of Virginia. Madison attended St. John's

Church, across Lafayette Square from the White House. In retirement he was asked by Jefferson to draw up a list of books on theology to be acquired by the library at the newly founded University of Virginia, which Madison served as visitor and rector. His list gave most detailed coverage of patristic writings but also demonstrated his familiarity with works of the Reformation and Enlightenment. Throughout his life Madison was economically dependent on the labor of slaves but favored gradual, compensated emancipation. He was a founder of the AMERICAN COLONIZATION SOCIETY yet, because of increasing financial difficulties, could never manumit his own slaves, even in his will. Probably America's most theologically knowledgeable president, Madison was also the nation's most effective guarantor of religious freedom.

See also articles on ANGLICAN CHURCH; COLONIAL PERIOD (in Appendix).

Bibliography. Irving Brant, *James Madison*; William T. Hutchinson et al., eds., *The Papers of James Madison*; Ralph Ketcham, *James Madison: A Biography*.

THOMAS A. MASON
UNIVERSITY OF VIRGINIA

MAKEMIE, FRANCIS (c. 1658-1708), pioneer American Presbyterian, was born of Scottish parentage near Ramelton, County Donegal, Ulster, and grew up amid the persecution of Presbyterians in Ulster and Scotland after the Restoration in 1660. He attended Glasgow University, was ordained to the ministry in 1682, and arrived in the American colonies as a missionary in 1683. There he labored on the Eastern Shore in Virginia, Maryland, and Delaware, and in Barbados. He married the daughter of a wealthy merchant in Accomack, which finally became his home.

Concerned for the social as well as the religious growth of the colonies, he published his *Plain and Friendly Persuasive* (1705) to encourage citizens of Maryland and Virginia to form towns and centers of commerce and to persuade others to settle in the area. Although making his living in trade, his chief concern was the planting of Presbyterian congregations and the expansion of the church's influence. In 1706 he was the chief architect of the Presbytery of Philadelphia, the first Presbyterian court on this side of the Atlantic. Organized in part to show Presbyterian strength in a hostile Anglican climate, it was composed of seven ministers. Some of these had New England backgrounds, but all had Presbyterian sympathies rather than Congregationalist. Makemie was elected the first moderator of this body.

In 1707 Makemie became involved in a court fight in New York with Lord Cornbury, the governor, in which he defended successfully his right to preach under the Act of Toleration in 1689, although he also argued that the establishment of the Church of England did not extend to the colonies. He won his case, but Cornbury forced him to pay for the costs. Makemie left a *Narrative* (1707) of his imprisonment that contained some of the earliest arguments for the rights of dissenters in America. Among Makemie's other extant writings is a defense of the CALVINISM of the WESTMINSTER CONFESSION OF FAITH against the Quakers in an *Answer to George Keith's Libel* (1693), and *Truths in a True Light* (1699). In these Makemie tried to show how close Anglicans and Presbyterians were in their faith, and how they both differed from Roman Catholics.

See also articles on CHURCH AND STATE; DISSENTERS; ESTABLISHED RELIGION.

Bibliography. Boyd S. Schlenther, *The Life and Writings of Francis Makemie*.

JAMES H. SMYLIE
UNION THEOLOGICAL SEMINARY
IN VIRGINIA

MANLY, BASIL, JR. (1825-1892), Baptist theological educator, was born in Red Bank SC, grew up in Charleston, and in 1837 moved with his family to Tuscaloosa AL. He was educated at the University of Alabama, from which he graduated with first honors in 1843; at Newton Theological Institution in Massachusetts; and at Princeton Theological Seminary, from which he graduated in 1847.

After his ordination in 1848, Manly served Baptist churches in Alabama and Mississippi. In 1850 he became pastor of the First Baptist Church of Richmond VA. He held that prestigious post until 1854 when he became president of the Richmond Female Institute.

Manly devoted himself and most of his career to the Southern Baptist Theological Seminary in both Greenville SC and Louisville. He authored its Articles of Faith and was on its first faculty. During the Civil War, when the seminary closed, he preached in rural churches. In 1871, after working hard to rebuild the seminary, he became president of Georgetown College in Kentucky. Soon after the seminary was moved to Louisville, however, he rejoined its faculty, and remained with that institution for the rest of his life.

Manly contributed richly to Baptist life. He composed many hymns and with his father he compiled the popular *Baptist Psalmody* (1850). He also published another hymnbook, *Manly's Choice* (1891). He was instrumental in the 1863 founding of the Southern Baptist Sunday School Board, and he edited the publication *Kind Words*, which was used in Sunday schools for decades. His most important scholarly works were *A Call to the Ministry* (1867), and *The Bible Doctrine of Inspiration* (1888).

See also article on THEOLOGICAL EDUCATION.

Bibliography. Louise Manly, *The Manly Family.*

DANIEL LEE CLOYD
AUBURN UNIVERSITY

MANLY, BASIL, SR. (1798-1868), pioneer Baptist educator, was born near Pittsboro NC. He was educated at the Bingham School, at a Baptist college in Beaufort SC, and at South Carolina College from which he graduated first in his class in 1821. He was the father of eight children, one a famous Baptist educator in his own right, BASIL MANLY, JR.

Manly was licensed to preach in 1818 and ordained to the Baptist ministry in 1822. While serving congregations in and near Edgefield SC in the early 1820s, he helped found the forerunner of Furman University. In 1826 he became pastor of the prestigious First Baptist Church of Charleston.

In 1837 Manly accepted the presidency of the University of Alabama. He bought a plantation near Tuscaloosa, helped establish the Alabama Historical Society, and was instrumental in the founding of Judson and Howard colleges as Baptist institutions.

Manly returned to Charleston in 1855 to become pastor of the Wentworth Street Church. He actively promoted the Southern Baptist Theological Seminary, presiding over the three conventions (1856, 1857, 1858) that established the institution. He went back to Alabama in 1859 as an evangelist for the Baptist State Convention, but soon became pastor of the Baptist church in Montgomery.

In 1860 Manly condemned the federal government and was an unsuccessful secessionist candidate for the legislature. In February 1861 he delivered the prayer at the inauguration of Confederate President Jefferson Davis. A stroke in 1864 left him partially paralyzed; he died in Greenville SC.

See also article on EDUCATION, CHRISTIAN HIGHER.

Bibliography. Louise Manly, *The Manly Family.*

DANIEL LEE CLOYD
AUBURN UNIVERSITY

MARNEY, CARLYLE (1916-1978), prominent ecumenical Baptist preacher, pastor, and theologian, was born in Harriman TN. He graduated from Carson-Newman College in 1938 and matriculated at Southern Baptist Theological Seminary in Louisville. He received the Th.M. degree in 1941 and the Th.D. degree in church history from that institution in 1946. His doctoral dissertation, never published, was on "The Rise of Ecclesiological Externalism to 337 A.D."

Marney served Immanuel Baptist Church in Paducah KY from 1946-1948, and then accepted a call to the First Baptist Church of Austin TX. It was during his pastorate there (1948-1958) that he became regionally prominent as a preacher and writer. His first book to attract national attention was *These Things Remain* (1953). During most of his Austin years he also served as adjunct professor of Christian Ethics at Austin Presbyterian Theological Seminary. In 1958 Marney accepted a call from the Myers Park Baptist Church in Charlotte NC, serving there until 1967. During this period he wrote *Structures of Prejudice* (1961) and *The Recovery of the Person* (1963), and published various books of sermons. His frequent appearances in college and university chapels enhanced his growing national reputation as a preacher.

Marney's resignation from the Myers Park Church was precipitated by health problems. Seeking an alternate form of ministry he founded in 1967 the Interpreter's House, a retreat center for clergy, at Lake Junaluska NC. The last decade of his life was dedicated to this special ministry, although Marney continued to make frequent talks at church assemblies and pastors' schools, and was an adjunct professor of homiletics at Duke Divinity School from 1972-1978. During his Interpreter's House years he published *The Coming Faith* (1970) and *Priests to Each Other* (1974). This period also marked a shift in Marney's thought to broader ecumenical and interfaith interests.

Marney was active with both the National and World Council of Churches, and served on the editorial boards of such prominent ecumenical journals as *Theology Today* and *Religion in Life*. He was awarded several honorary degrees, including the D.D. from the University of Glasgow in 1976. He had been invited to give the Lyman Beecher Lectures at Yale Divinity School in 1979. Recognized during his lifetime as a gifted and colorful preacher, recent appraisals of his thought have clarified his creative contributions as an ecumenical theologian.

See also articles on ECUMENISM; PREACHING.

Bibliography. John J. Carey, *Carlyle Marney: A Pilgrim's Progress*.

JOHN J. CAREY
FLORIDA STATE UNIVERSITY

MARSHALL, ANDREW (1775-1856), early black Baptist preacher, was born in Bryan County GA as a slave. His progression toward the ministry began in 1785 when he was converted and baptized by his uncle, ANDREW BRYAN, then pastor of the First African Baptist Church of Savannah. After purchasing his freedom, Marshall succeeded Bryan as that church's minister in 1815 and remained in that capacity until his own death 41 years later.

His most notable pastoral experience involved a doctrinal dispute that resulted in the cleavage of his church and its expulsion from the white-controlled Sunsbury Association. The tumult began in 1832 when he allowed ALEXANDER CAMPBELL to preach from his pulpit "new doctrines" that advocated the replacement of existing ecclesiastical structures with ones directly modeled after the primitive church described in Acts. When Marshall made statements that seemed to sanction such tenets, some church members strongly objected. He broke with the dissenters, took most of the congregation with him, and retained as his group's name, First African Baptist Church.

The Sunsbury Association voted to silence him and consider his church dissolved. Nevertheless, his congregation continued to exist as a Baptist body because it insisted upon its right to remain sovereign in spiritual matters (by grounding its policies upon the Bible) and in ministerial leadership (by retaining him as pastor, in spite of continued clerical and civil objections). After Marshall disavowed any Campbellite leanings, he and his congregation were reinstated in the Sunsbury Association in 1837. That the church members remained and their minister retained his pulpit in this segregationist antebellum era was a tribute to his leadership. A black contemporary observed that at Marshall's death the mile-long funeral procession in Savannah was "unequalled by anything of the kind in that city or region where a colored person was concerned."

See also articles on BLACK RELIGION; INVISIBLE INSTITUTION.

Bibliography. E. K. Love, History of the First African Baptist Church; Albert J. Raboteau, Slave Religion: The "Invisible Institution" in the Antebellum South; James M. Simms, The First Colored Baptist Church in North America.

EDWARD L. MOORE
NASHVILLE, TENNESSEE

MARTIN, THOMAS THEODORE

(1862-1939), Baptist evangelist and polemicist, was born in Smith County MS. He was educated at Mississippi College (A.B., 1886) and Southern Baptist Theological Seminary (Th.M., 1896), then taught natural sciences at Baylor Female Institute, Belton TX (1886-1888). Ordained to the Baptist ministry in 1888, he was pastor in Kentucky at Glenview and Beattyville, then in Colorado at Leadville, Canon City, and Cripple Creek, before becoming a full-time evangelist in 1900. In addition to holding evangelistic meetings for the rest of his life, he organized the Blue Mountain (MS) Evangelists, served as dean of Union University's School of Evangelism (1919-1930), and founded the American School of Evangelism (1930). He published over two dozen books and pamphlets. In early writings he focused on personal conversion and devotion, salvation by faith, and superiority of Baptist doctrines: Gems From The Sick Room (1897), God's Plan With Men (1912), Redemption and The New Birth (1913), and The New Testament Church (1917). In later writings he defended prohibition and opposed modernism and evolution.

See also article on MODERNIST CONTROVERSY.

G. HUGH WAMBLE
MIDWESTERN BAPTIST SEMINARY

MARX, DAVID (1872-1962), prominent Reform rabbi and civic leader, was born in New Orleans. The son of German immigrants, he was educated in public and private schools in New Orleans and Cincinnati. Upon graduation from high school he simultaneously enrolled at the University of Cincinnati and Hebrew Union College. In 1894 he received a B.A. degree from the former and was ordained at the latter by Isaac Mayer Wise, the founder of American Reform Judaism.

Rabbi Marx accepted a position at Temple Emanuel in Birmingham AL in 1894 but left one year later to become rabbi of the Hebrew Benevolent Congregation (The Temple) in Atlanta. Rabbi of The Temple for 51 years, Marx was one of the most influential Jewish leaders in the South. He regularly delivered guest sermons in Protestant houses of worship, including Afro-American churches. He also published a Sunday column for the Atlanta Journal. Never one to shun controversy, he was clergyman for Leo Frank (q.v., FRANK, LEO, CASE) and he openly protested against the teaching of Shakespeare's The Merchant of Venice in public schools on the grounds that it fostered anti-Semitism.

In Atlanta Marx helped organize the Hebrew Orphans' Home, the Schoen Free Kindergarten, the Federation of Jewish Charities, and the Jewish Educational Alliance. On the regional and national level, he served as vice-president of the Southern Rabbinical Association, president of the Southeastern Jewish Religious School Union, trustee of the National Jewish Hospital in Denver, and treasurer of the Central Conference of American Rabbis.

An avid Mason, Marx was quite active in Atlanta's civic life. The first Jew admitted to the Atlanta Rotary Club, he served on the board of trustees of more than a dozen city organizations. He was a leader in the effort to promote better race relations and was a member of the COMMISSION ON INTERRACIAL COOP-

ERATION and its successor, the Southern Regional Council. He was a founder of the Unity Club, which promoted interfaith and racial cooperation.

Marx, however, was controversial because of his unyielding opposition to Zionism, which he refused to moderate even after the Holocaust. He was an honorary vice-president of the American Council for Judaism, the most important Jewish group opposed to Zionism, a fact that offended many Atlanta Jews.

See also article on JEWS IN THE SOUTH.

                                    ARNOLD SHANKMAN

MARYLAND.

Geography. Geography has been significant in the religious history of Maryland. Located between Pennsylvania and Virginia, Maryland has been influenced by religious developments in the middle states and in the South. Although small—only 10,577 square miles—Maryland has four regions: the Eastern Shore's lowlands, the Western Shore's rolling hills, the mountains, and the Baltimore area. Baltimore is located at the intersection of the deep waters of the Chesapeake Bay and the fall line of the Piedmont.

Early Development. Maryland was planned by George Calvert (1580-1632), an English convert to Catholicism, who had participated in the Virginia Company and in the ill-fated experiment at Avalon. The charter was granted to his son, Cecil Calvert (1604-1675), the Second Lord Baltimore. The Calverts believed in the ordered society of the medieval period and envisioned a land of country manors supporting a feudal order in which different classes had different obligations. The colony was named for Charles I's queen, Henrietta Maria.

The colony was to be partially a refuge for wealthy Catholics. When the *Ark* and the *Dove* sailed in 1633, the ships had 128 passengers who had taken the Test Oath; however, an additional 72 persons joined the expedition at Crews, Isle of Wight. These included three Jesuits: Father

Andrew White, Father John Altham, and Brother Thomas Gervase. On 25 March 1634, the ships landed at St. Clement's Island, and Father White celebrated Maryland's first Mass. White, the leader of the Jesuits until his deportation to England, conducted an active ministry to the Piscataway, Patuxent, and Anacosta Indians. He wrote two works about the colony: *Declaratio coloniae Domini Baronis de Baltimore* and *Relatio Itinerio in Marylandus* as well as a grammar, dictionary, and catechism in the Indian language.

Religious conflict was a mark of the colony from its founding to the American Revolution. The colonists on Kent Island, led by William Claiborne, resented the presence of Catholics in the new colony as well as their own inclusion in Baltimore's domains. In 1635 and 1638, force had to be used to incorporate the earlier settlement into Maryland, and the Kent Islanders invaded Maryland in 1645, forcing the governor into temporary exile.

Some of Maryland's early problems can be attributed to the lack of a definite policy on religion. The Charter, which reserved ecclesiastical patronage to the Baltimores, implied that the colony was to be Anglican, but Baltimore supported a policy of toleration. In 1636, an oath was imposed on the governor that prohibited interference with any Christian on account of religion. During the English Civil War, perhaps to forestall more radical action, Baltimore instructed his governor, William Stone, to secure a toleration act that would protect his coreligionists. In 1649, the law, "An Act Concerning Religion," was passed. It provided for the toleration of all trinitarian Christian groups and imposed heavy penalties for disturbing the religious peace.

The Act was ineffective. The Puritans who had settled "Providence"—the region near Annapolis on the Patuxent River—supported Cromwell's government, and when William Stone supported the claims of Charles II, they revolted and joined the Kent Islanders in an armed force that defeated Stone at the Battle of the Severn, on 25 May 1655. From 1655 to 1658, when Baltimore regained control, Catholics were persecuted and some of their priests forced to leave the colony.

Although such Jesuits as Thomas Copley (d. 1652) secured a strong financial base for the church by purchasing such lands as St. Thomas Manor, 17th-century Maryland had a chronic shortage of priests. In 1669, Lord Baltimore complained to Rome about the problem, and in 1673, Father Thomas Massey established a Franciscan mission that grew to four priests in 1677. Additional Jesuits were also sent to the colony.

The problem of providing Catholic education was pressing. Maryland's pattern of large farms and plantations scattered the population, and priests taught the catechism by traveling house to house. In 1677, Father Michael Foster, S.J., established a classical academy at New Town that would have been the second oldest college in the United States had it survived the Glorious Revolution.

Anglicanism had been in Maryland before Baltimore's colony. The Rev. Richard Stone served Kent Island from 1631 to 1638, and the chapel at St. Mary's was shared by Catholics and Anglicans until 1638. The growth of the Church of England, however, dates from the Restoration when Anglicanism began to replace Puritanism on the Western Shore. By 1676, there were four Anglican congregations in Maryland: Trinity Creek, St. George's, St. Paul's, and Kent Island, and such laymen as Jeremiah Eaton and Roger Coger had begun to leave property for glebes to support the ministry.

Seventeenth-century Anglicanism, lacking wealth and government support, did not have the means to support an active ministry. The few priests who came to the colony came more for secular than religious reasons. Another deleterious factor was the scattered location of such churches as there were. The faith was carried primarily by the family, although anti-Catholicism does seem to have strengthened some people's determination to remain Anglican.

In 1657, the Quaker Elizabeth Harris began to preach in the area around Annapolis and on Kent Island. Although Maryland passed laws against Quakers in 1657 and 1658, the movement made progress and by 1665, Quakers were beginning to attain positions in local government. In 1668, the legislature passed a bill permitting affirmation to replace the oath. The community was strengthened by visits from John Burnyeat, William Edmundson, and George Fox in the 1670s.

Lord Baltimore, who owned sizable property in Ireland, encouraged immigration from that land to Maryland. In the 17th century, these Scotch-Irish pioneers began to settle on the Eastern Shore and in the Annapolis area. The Rev. Thomas Wilson and the Rev. Robert Lawson worked as itinerant preachers in the area, but the first permanent Presbyterian ministry was on the lands of Ninian Beall, a Scot, who made his fortune in the colonial trade. On his landed estate, located between Patuxent and Washington City, 200 Scots and Scotch-Irish were gathered into a church by the Rev. Matthew Hill (d. 1679). Francis Makemie (c. 1658-1708), who was appointed as a missionary to the New World by the Presbytery of Laggan, Ireland, began his ministry in 1683 on the Eastern Shore where he established the Snow Hill congregation among others. In 1706, these churches joined with other Presbyterian churches in Delaware and Pennsylvania in the first presbytery in the United States.

Judaism was not tolerated under Maryland's laws. Jacob Lumbrozo, the first Jew in Maryland, was tried on 23 February 1658 for denying the divinity of Christ. Although he was acquitted of the capital charge, he wisely left the colony.

In England, the period from the Restoration (1660) to the Glorious Revolution (1688) was a time of increasing religious conflict as the royal family drifted toward the open Catholicism of James II. Louis XIV of France revoked the Edict of Nantes in 1685, raising fears about similar acts in England. Finally, James II was deposed by the Glorious Revolution and William and Mary assumed the throne.

In Maryland, these tensions were magnified by Protestant dislike of the Catholic proprietor and by prejudice against the local Catholic minority. Anti-Catholic agitation increased the local Catholic minority. Because of its growing strength throughout the period, in 1681 John Coode attempted a Protestant revolution. When news of the overthrow of James II arrived in the colony, another army, led by Coode, expelled Baltimore's governor. On 26 August 1691, Lionel Capley was appointed as the royal governor of Maryland with instructions to see that the Book of Common Prayer was used in the colony.

The Age of Establishment. From 1692 to 1701, the Maryland legislature passed laws establishing the Church of England. The laws of 1692, 1694, and 1696 were disallowed, because their wording was ambiguous. Largely through the efforts of THOMAS BRAY (1656-1730), the commissary for Maryland, the bill of 1701 was approved. The law created 30 parishes to be served by an elected vestry of six members, two church wardens, a clerk, a registrar, and a minister. The priest was supported by a poll tax of 40 pounds of tobacco from which he was to pay the clerk 1,000 pounds. Marriage was regulated, and the minister was to be paid a set fee for every service performed. Significantly, the law made no provision for clerical discipline or for the education of future pastors.

Bray was the most important figure in the early history of the establishment. In 1696, he was appointed commissary by Bishop Campton of London. Although there was no colonial chapter, a commissary did the work of a dean in the Established Church: visitations, supervision of the clergy, and administration of diocesan affairs. There was some hope in 1697 that Bray might be appointed as suffragan allowing the church to have confirmations and ordinations, but King William, who depended on the nonconformists politically, vetoed the promotion. Bray spent less than a year in his charge and conducted only one visitation. In part, his role was ceremonial. When Annapolis was designated as the capital, Bray represented the crown in the gift of communion silver to the new parish of St. Anne's. His efforts were largely unsuccessful, however, in the area of church discipline and administration where his good intentions were largely ignored by the local clergy.

Bray's primary contributions to Maryland's establishment were made in London. He recruited clergy for the new church, and in 1699, he established The Society for Promoting Christian Knowledge to supply parishes with ministerial libraries. These libraries included works in classics, divinity, philosophy, and natural science. With their help, a local minister could establish a school or prepare a candidate for Holy Orders.

After Bray, the commissary system disintegrated. Although in 1716 Jacob Henderson and Christopher Wilkenson were appointed as commissaries for the eastern and western shores, neither was able to discipline the clergy. After their deaths, no further commissaries were appointed. As a result of the failure of the commissary system, the Church of Maryland became little more than a federation of churches sharing a common liturgy and having rights at law.

The Church of Maryland was a success in the area of evangelism. After establishment, it acquired a popular base on the western shore and displaced the Puritans in the Annapolis area. The parishes of the church maintained a more lively sacramental life than was customary among Southern Anglicans. Four parishes observed Holy Communion three times a year; four celebrated four times a year;

three celebrated eight times a year as well as on major festivals, and seven had monthly communion as well as celebrations on all major festivals.

Throughout the 18th century, complaints were lodged against the quality or morals of the Maryland clergy. In the absence of any form of church discipline, it is impossible to pass judgment on those charges. Colonial ministers, whose parishes covered vast areas and who were isolated from other clergy, may have used alcohol to help ease the pains of settlement—as other colonists did—and the link between the establishment and the aristocracy could encourage the hurting parson. Yet, some of the worse abuses in the Church of England were avoided in the New World. The incomes of clergy were adequate, and there were no poor parishes where a priest might be impoverished. Nonresidence, the most serious problem in England, was prohibited in Maryland by law.

The return of the Baltimore family to power in the colony in 1713 created additional problems for Maryland's Anglicans. Under the charter, the proprietor had the right to all ecclesiastical patronage. During the era of Frederick Calvert, 1731-1771, Fourth Lord Baltimore, this right was abused. Frederick was a rake who continually bombarded the governor with requests for the appointment of his companions to sinecures. His most notorious appointment was Richard Allen who had written a pamphlet defending his Lordship from a charge of rape in 1768. Allen was rewarded with St. Anne's parish, Annapolis, as well as other positions.

Unlike other Southern Anglicans, Maryland's priests supported the appointment of a colonial bishop. However, the colony's political leaders, especially William Paca and Samuel Chase, put together a coalition that blocked the proposed office in 1773.

Although Maryland granted complete toleration to Protestant dissenters in 1702, Catholics were not granted civil rights in the 18th century. The new government imposed the Test Oath in 1692, and despite the efforts of the former attorney general, Charles Carroll, the law was allowed in London. In 1704, Father William Hunter and Father Robert Brooke, the latter the first Marylander ordained as a priest, were tried for violating the establishment acts and ordered to cease their priestly activities. In the same year, the legislature passed its "Act to Prevent the Growth of Popery." Catholic worship was prohibited in the state as was the baptism of a non-Catholic child, and Catholics were prohibited from establishing or teaching in schools. In 1707, under pressure from England, laws were passed permitting private masses, but laws were added against the importation of Irish Catholics as servants. In 1708, a census of the Catholic population was ordered as a protection for the province. The last anti-Catholic legislation was passed during the French and Indian Wars when a double tax was imposed on Catholics in lieu of military service. Wealthy Catholics such as the Carroll family threatened to leave the colony unless such laws were changed.

The penal laws affected Catholic religious life. Catholic chapels were closed, and services were held in rooms attached to private homes. Naturally, such services were extremely plain. The absence of a bishop or vicar apostolic limited sacramental life since neither confirmation nor Holy Orders could be received. In 1720, the Franciscans were withdrawn, and the mission placed entirely in the hands of the Jesuits. The Jesuits were stationed at various manors and farms throughout the state, and they would say Mass twice a month at their stations and then ride a circuit to bring the sacraments to their flocks. Often a priest served an area of more than 500 square miles. The missionary priests were very effective as evangelists of the slave population, with the result that Afro-Americans made up a third of the communicants.

Persecution forced the Jesuits to establish for their order a center that was geographically distant from most of Maryland's population. In 1706, they purchased St. Xavier's Manor on the Little and Great Bohemian rivers. By 1745, the Jesuits had established a classical school at the Manor that was equivalent to a modern high school or junior college. Among its students were Robert and Edward Neale, James Heath, Robert Brent, Charles Carroll of Carrollton, and JOHN CARROLL, later to be bishop of Baltimore.

In 1748, after driving the French from the Canadian coast, the English deported the Acadian population. About 900 refugees were assigned to Maryland, and their presence caused a wave of anti-Catholic hysteria and a law prohibiting local Catholics from aiding their settlement was passed. About 40 French families settled in Baltimore Town where Father John Ashton, chaplain to Carroll of Carrollton, gathered them into a small congregation.

In 1773, Pope Clement XIV issued *Dominus ac Redemptor* suppressing the Jesuits everywhere except Russia, and on 6 October 1773, the American Jesuits were ordered to present their written submission to the decree. The future of the Church was in doubt since the Jesuits had supplied the financial support as well as priests for the Church.

The Denominational State. In 1776, the legislature passed the Declaration of Rights that disestablished the Anglican church and declared all Christian churches equal before the law. The act was hardly hostile to religion: the legislature reserved the right to tax citizens for the support of the church of their choice and protected the property of the Anglican churches from confiscation. It further assumed that the Christian churches were public corporations entitled to support from the state. This favorable attitude promoted the growth of various denominations whose individual congregations were incorporated by the legislature.

The Episcopal Church. During the Revolution, Episcopal (from 1785) ministers were required to take an oath of allegiance to the state. Since the new oath conflicted with an earlier ordination vow to be loyal to the king, many Church of Maryland pastors were caught in an ethical dilemma. Some, such as Hugh Neill of St. Paul's, Queen Anne, refused the oath without abandoning their posts; others, like John Scott of Stepney, Sommerset, refused the oath and went into exile. While we cannot determine how many of the 14 Anglican clergy who left the state or how many of the five who retired did so because of the oath, it may have been a factor in their decisions.

The war demoralized and disorganized the Episcopal churches. The Rev. William Smith (1727-1803), first provost of the College of Philadelphia, became rector of St. Paul's and Chester parishes, Kent County, in 1779 and used his position to direct an Anglican recovery. In 1780, he called a clerical convention to settle the affairs of the church; it adopted a new name, Protestant Episcopal Church. In the same year, he helped organize Washington College to train a native ministry. In 1783, he led the clergy to secure the right from the legislature to change the Book of Common Prayer. These activities culminated in his election as bishop of Maryland and in instruction to seek consecration in England.

The revision of the Prayer Book caused controversy and weakened Smith's position. Proposed by William White and Charles Warton, in collaboration with Smith, it showed the influence of the Enlightenment understanding of faith and modified many customary practices. In 1786, Thomas Cradock and Samuel Johnson accused Smith of public drunkenness, and while the charge was never established, the Episcopal General Convention of 1789 failed to approve his consecration. By the time that Smith left the state to resume his duties in Philadelphia in 1789, the Protestant Episcopal Church had weathered the storm of the revolution and was organized as a free church. In 1792, Thomas Claggett, a less colorful man, was consecrated as the first bishop of Maryland.

While the Eastern Shore churches (that were to be organized as the Diocese of Easton in 1861) have tended toward a more evangelical nature, the churches on the Western Shore and in Baltimore have manifested a more High Church orientation. The leader in the High Church development was St. Paul's, Baltimore. By 1790, the Rev. Joseph Bent had introduced liturgical changes, and the Rev. Edward Watt, rector from 1827-1864, was the first Episcopal priest to wear Eucharistic garments in the United States; he also practiced the reservation of the Sacrament. The Rt. Rev. William Robinson Whittingham, bishop from 1840 to 1879—the longest term in Maryland's episcopal history—was firmly committed to a high church policy. Although his tenure was marked by controversies over liturgy and theology, these did not inhibit the growth of the church. Nine new parishes were formed in Baltimore alone during the 1850s.

Maryland's Episcopal parishes have been centers of benevolence. In 1789, St. Paul's, Baltimore, led in the establishment of the Maryland Society for the Abolition of Slavery and the Relief of Free Negroes. During the 1820s, individual parishes created local missionary societies and Sunday schools. A number of churches established in the late nineteenth century offered a broad range of services to their communities. English influence was seen in such special organizations as the choir school at St. Paul's that were directly related to Oxford Movement concerns. In both world wars, Maryland Anglicans led in providing religious and social services for the troops stationed in the state.

Establishment religious values have continued into the 20th century in the form of a strong sense of the role of place in religious life. In the 1960s, as racial and urban tensions mounted in Baltimore, St. Paul's had to decide whether it would join the flight to the suburbs. The church decided to remain in the central city and to adapt its style of ministry to the changed conditions. St. Paul's response was typical of many Maryland Episcopal institutions that decided to stay in difficult, but traditional, locations.

Lutherans. Although Lutherans entered Maryland in 1649 when Swedes established a colony in Cecil County, the largest numbers of Lutheran settlers began to enter the colony in the late eighteenth century. German settlers used Western Maryland as a highway from Pennsylvania to the Valley of Virginia, and Lord Baltimore, who needed people to fill his Western claims, offered them attractive terms to establish residence there. Western Maryland assumed many of the social characteristics of German Pennsylvania.

There were few pastors among the German settlers, and many who claimed that title had little or no religious training. These irregular pastors caused serious disruptions, and appeals for help to Henry Muhlenberg in Philadelphia were common. In the absence of regular ministers, school teachers often preserved Lutheran traditions by conducting services of morning prayer and by encouraging the reading of the Luther Bible. As in the case of many other immigrant groups, cemeteries were often founded before churches could be erected.

Early Lutherans in the West were often served by itinerants. John Casper Stoever, whose circuit reached from New Holland to York PA, came to Monocracy in 1733 to baptize the children; in the next year, a congregation agreed to share its pulpit with any Reformed pastor in the area. When Stoever resigned from his circuit, he ordained David Chandler, a teacher from Conewego, to serve the charge.

One of the most important centers of Lutheranism in the West was the town of Frederick where a church was established in 1745. Two years later Muhlenberg visited there to attempt to correct problems caused by the irregular ministers, Carl Rudolph and Empiricus Schmidt.

Muhlenberg led the congregation in the making of a covenant in which they agreed to support Lutheran doctrine and to exclude the Moravians from fellowship. Such covenants were common in the formative period. In 1752, the Rev. Bernhard Hausihl, who arrived in the area with a company of Palatine Germans, became pastor of the congregation. The broad church type of Lutheranism that was characteristic of the Palatinate was to have considerable influence on that denomination's life in Maryland.

From 1750 to 1794, a score of Lutheran churches was founded in Washington, Frederick, and Carroll counties. By this time, most new German settlers were entering Maryland through Baltimore and pushing west from there. One of the significant churches founded by these immigrants was the Evangelical Lutheran Congregation in Cumberland established by Frederick Lange, an itinerant clergyman, and which served as a missionary center for the far western part of the state.

In 1750, after Baltimore began its growth as a port, Germans established a joint Lutheran and Reformed Congregation. The union did not last. In 1756, under the leadership of John Christian Faber, the Reformed members were able to erect a meetinghouse of their own. The High German Evangelical Lutheran Congregation, established in 1755, was unable to secure a meetinghouse until 1762.

Pastor John Daniel Kurtz (1763-1856) was the first full-time minister to serve the Baltimore congregation. Kurtz had been born in America, and he studied divinity at the school of the prophets maintained by Henry Ernst Muhlenberg at Lancaster PA. Strongly influenced by the theology of the Awakenings, Kurtz led in the establishment of the Maryland Bible Society and of the seminary at Gettysburg. In 1820, he was one of the leaders in the establishment of the Synod of Maryland and Virginia and served four terms as its president.

The establishment of the synod provided Maryland's older Lutheran communities with stability. Maryland's practice of incorporating congregations rather than denominations meant that the synod was a voluntary society that pastors and churches might join, if they chose. It had no doctrinal requirements before 1829, when the Augsburg Confession was adopted, and in its first half century, the synod functioned more as a coordinating agency for church benevolences than as an ecclesiastical body. Liturgically, the synod tended toward a German service somewhat similar to the Book of Common Prayer. At the same time revivalism was practiced, though not as commonly as among other Protestant groups.

In the 1820s a new wave of German immigration began to enter Baltimore, which made the city one of the most heavily teutonic in the East. Language problems among Lutherans became acute as the newer immigrants entered the older German churches. In 1828, the First English Lutheran Congregation was established in Baltimore, and in 1840, the Second English Lutheran Church was formed in response to the revival of 1839-1840.

The clash between older and newer Germans, however, was more than a "language dispute." Maryland's older Lutherans were committed to a different style of faith. Conscious of their own frontier roots, Maryland Lutherans sent circuit riders, such as C. F. Heyer, Jacob Medtart, and N. B. Little, deep into Ohio and Indiana. Debates were held over the continued use of wine in the communion services, and strong support was given to the temperance movement. Theologically, Maryland's older Lutherans tended to follow the American Lutheranism popularized by Samuel Schmucker at Gettysburg Seminary where many of Maryland's pastors were trained.

The newer immigrants were not drawn to the frontier kind of life and tended to settle in urban ghettos in Baltimore. For them, the church was one of the primary supports of their culture. Theologically, the immigrant pastors brought the German disputes between rationalists, confessionalists, and mediators with them into their new environment. In 1845, F. C. D. Wynken led his congregation into the confessional Missouri Synod which was popular with conservative immigrants. Even more typical was St. Stephen's Lutheran, Baltimore, established by the Rev. Charles A. Meister in 1849. The parish church was complemented by a host of German organizations as well as a strongly confessional parochial school.

The Rev. Henry Scheib (1801-1897) represented the more radical form of immigrant Lutheranism. Scheib was called to Zion Lutheran Church in 1835. Deeply influenced by rationalism and biblical criticism, he led the congregation to a virtual German Unitarianism. During his pastorate, the church maintained no synodical connections. Scheib was perhaps the most creative religious educator of his day. His parochial school allowed students and a faculty to share in the formulation of policy, and from 1838 had an active P.T.A. The program of studies was based on a developmental understanding of childhood. Scheib's successor, Julius Hofmann, who came in 1889, also represented European theology. An admirer of the German theologian Schleiermacher, Hofmann led the church back into the synod. World War I presented the great crisis of Hofmann's ministry, and he was able to convince his church to be active in support of the American position in the conflict.

The Civil War had little impact on Maryland's Lutherans who were more concerned with the problems of the immigrants than they were with national politics. Local congregations, while occasionally disturbed by individuals with strong views, maintained a steady course.

Maryland Lutheranism's social concern grew out of both a frontier setting and its German background. Such charities as the Lutheran Pastor's Fund, established in 1839, Sunday Schools, and Women's Sewing and Missionary Socie-

ties, were rooted in American Evangelicalism. Two very successful charities, the Deaconesses, whose Mother House was established in Baltimore in 1895, and the Inner Mission, founded in 1913, were based on German understanding of home missions; these have remained active in the inner city.

The rapid growth of the Washington-Baltimore corridor has produced a significant growth among Lutherans. As new job opportunities have drawn Lutherans of different synodical, theological, and geographical backgrounds, the state's Lutheran bodies have assumed a more rational character. In architecture, many of the new churches have abandoned the gothic so common in the past in favor of modern and ultra-modern styles.

The Catholic Church. The Catholic Church in Maryland emerged from the Revolution in an unsettled condition. John Carroll (1735-1815), an ex-Jesuit missionary at Rock Creek, took the lead in reorganizing the Church. In 1782, he formed the remaining priests into the Select Body of Clergy that was incorporated by the state as the legal successor to the property of the Jesuit order, and in 1784, Carroll was appointed as Vicar Apostolic for the United States. Five years later, the clergy elected him as bishop. Significantly, he elected to reside in Baltimore rather than the more heavily Catholic, rural St. Mary's.

Carroll was deeply concerned with Catholic education. In 1791, Georgetown College was opened in the District of Columbia, and in that same year, the Sulpician Fathers opened the first major seminary in the United States, St. Mary's, at the Nine Mile Tavern in Baltimore. A French order of priests dedicated to theological education, this group made considerable impact. Unlike some other orders, the Sulpicians historically have concentrated their efforts on the religious formation of the seminarian. Accordingly, they gave Maryland's Catholics much of their intellectual leadership in the early nineteenth century, and two from their number, Ambrose Marechal (served 1817-1834) and Samuel Eccleston (served 1834-1851), became archbishops of Baltimore.

Maryland became a center for many American religious orders. In 1790, Carmelite nuns established a contemplative convent at Port Tobacco, and in 1808, the restored Jesuit order made Maryland its headquarters. But the most significant religious order founded in the state was the Sisters of Charity of St. Joseph. Elizabeth Ann Seton (1774-1815), a Catholic convert, came to Baltimore in 1808, and in 1809, she and a small group of women opened a school in Emmitsburg. Officially recognized in 1812, the Sisters of Charity have been a major teaching order in Maryland, and their schools have contributed much to the character of Catholic Maryland.

John Carroll's cathedral in Baltimore was old St. Peter's Church. In this church, the first ordination to the priesthood (Stephen Badin in 1793) took place, also the first episcopal consecration (Leonard Neall in 1800). In 1806, Archbishop Carroll laid the cornerstone for the new Cathedral of the Assumption of the Blessed Virgin Mary, a basilica designed by the prominent church architect, Henry Latrobe. However, the poverty of the archdiocese kept the new church in debt and unconsecrated until 1876. The Plenary Councils of the American Catholic Church met here in 1852, 1866, and 1884. In 1959, the Cathedral of Mary Our Queen was opened in a more residential section of the city.

The diocese that elected John Carroll bishop was largely composed of old American stock; by the time of Archbishop Neale's era, the archbishopric was in the midst of a social revolution. Immigrants were pouring into Baltimore. The Irish, who were the largest group, quickly assimilated themselves to the American church; however, the Germans insisted on separate ethnic parishes such as St. Alphonsus, built in 1842. Later, Italian, Polish, and Ukrainian parishes were founded. Maryland became a locus of different Catholic traditions sustained by the parochial schools that taught the immigrants' language as well as English.

In the 1850s, Baltimore was the center of Know-Nothing agitation in the state. Mobs roved the streets attacking the immigrants and often beating priests. Every effort was made to keep the new citizens from the polls. James (to be Cardinal) Gibbons experienced this terror as a young priest in an immigrant parish, and his later attempts to provide an American foundation for the Church may have stemmed from these experiences.

Although sectional feeling ran high in Maryland, the Catholic community maintained an official policy of neutrality. The only disruption of church services that occurred was at St. Ignatius, Baltimore. When Union troops arrived in 1861 during Father Charles King's Solemn High Mass, the entire congregation as well as the deacon, subdeacon, and altarboy fled. Father King finished the service as a low Mass.

Catholic parishes in Maryland have been complex organizations housing a variety of benevolent and social activities; Confraternities of Christian Doctrine, Holy Name Societies, St. Vincent de Paul Societies, Legions of Mary, and the Knights of Columbus have been widespread. These societies have not only provided opportunities for fellowship and spiritual growth; they have often been the backbone of the financial programs of their parishes. A yearly "bull roast" to help support the school, sponsored by the various groups in the parish, is an abiding tradition.

The rural parishes in St. Mary's County and on the Eastern Shore have their own traditions. Many of them were served by missionary priests who rode a circuit until the 20th century. Often the priest would leave his parish church with his missionary kit and deliver the sacraments to those too far from the church for regular attendance. Religious education was conducted by individual catechetical sessions at different homes on the circuit. In St. John's, Hollywood, such visitations did not cease until 1935, and priestly ministry continued to have a traveling component until the 1950s.

Twentieth-century developments changed the patterns of Eastern Shore Catholicism much as immigration had changed Western Shore Catholicism in an earlier epoch. The advent of the automobile made possible the growth of parochial schools in the 1920s and helped to introduce the complex organizational patterns of urban Catholics to a hitherto rural society.

Vatican II has hastened changes. Notwithstanding their immigrant heritage, Maryland's Catholics have been in the forefront of efforts to Americanize the Church. James Cardinal Gibbons, archbishop from 1877 to 1921, established Catholic University in Washington to open the Church to modern culture, and James Courtney Murray, the great Catholic theorist of Church-State relations, taught at Woodstock. In one sense, the Council simply affirmed the direction that the state's Catholics had been taking. The most visible changes in the Church have been in the area of worship. Not only are Masses in English, often with modern music, but new churches tend to be simple in their construction. In many older parishes, the old statues and side altars have been replaced by plain iconographic presentations.

Although the archdiocese lost many priests in the aftermath of the Council, the introduction of new associations of priests has strengthened the vocations of those who have remained. The most striking changes have been in theological education. The Jesuits moved their training center from Woodstock to New York, and the Sulpician Fathers have appointed Protestants to their faculty at St. Mary's. In addition, St. Mary's has been accredited by the American Association of Theological Schools and has experimented with a new curriculum that stresses scriptural studies and field education. The Catholic Church in Maryland continues to change as the full implications of the new directions in theology and ministry are drawn out on the parish level.

The Methodists. In Maryland, the evangelical impulse of American Protestant life was expressed primarily through the Methodist movement. Although George Whitefield visited the colony in 1740 and 1746, there was little response to his preaching. The first Methodist preacher in the colony was Robert Strawbridge (d. 1781), an Irish convert. He arrived between 1760 and 1766 and purchased a farm in Frederick County to use as a base for his evangelistic tours. Strawbridge traveled throughout the colony, including the Eastern Shore, establishing chapels and winning converts. The areas visited by him were the heart of the great Methodist revivals of 1780-1781 on the Eastern Shore and 1789-1793 on the Western Shore. Strawbridge was unconcerned with church order and insisted on celebrating the sacraments. Largely as a result of his labors, almost half of the Methodists in the colonies in 1773 were Marylanders.

Early Maryland Methodism depended on the class leader and local preacher who conducted extensive programs of lay witness and education. These men kept the Methodist revival alive during the long periods of absence of the traveling ministry and provided much of the pastoral care for the newly awakened converts. When the representatives of British Methodism, such as Joseph Pilmoor, THOMAS COKE, and FRANCIS ASBURY arrived, they stressed the role of the itinerant minister who was to admit new members to classes, regularize societies, and supervise the local ministry.

The Methodist revival was closely connected to the resurgence of pietism among the German Reformed. The Reformed were strongly influenced by the Dutch precisionist movement and by the work of Spener. Most Reformed immigrants brought a belief in the religion of the heart with them from Germany.

Benedict Schwobe, pastor of the German Reformed Church in Baltimore, was a warm friend of Robert Strawbridge and Francis Asbury.

Philip William Otterbein (1726-1813) was another important Methodist ally among the Reformed. In 1754, Otterbein had an experience of conversion that opened his heart to new forms of ministry, and when he came to Baltimore in 1774, his preaching led to a major revival among the German Protestants. The congregation outgrew its small building, and a new church, symbolically constructed from the bricks used as ballast in ships bringing immigrants from Germany, was constructed for him. The bells of the new church were to be rung whenever a ship from Germany arrived in the harbor, although Otterbein prohibited their use on Good Friday. In 1800, Otterbein and Martin Boehm, a former Mennonite, founded the United Brethren to spread revival among the Germans.

Although many itinerants were imprisoned or beaten because of their refusal to take the loyalty oath from 1776 to 1781, the Methodists were gradually displacing the Church of England in many counties. The latter was more seriously disrupted by the movement for independence than the Methodists, and many Christians, especially on the Eastern Shore, turned to the chapel in the absence of their regular clergy. Maryland, curiously enough, recognized the denominational independence of Methodism before official action was taken: in 1781, a law was passed exempting Methodists, but not Anglicans, from the loyalty oath.

In 1784, the famous CHRISTMAS CONFERENCE held at LOVELY LANE CHAPEL in Baltimore recognized the independence of American Methodism. John Wesley had appointed Thomas Coke and Francis Asbury superintendents of the new church, and they were formally elected. Asbury was ordained and, following the adoption of the Discipline and a liturgy, assignments to circuits were made. John Andrews and William West,

Episcopal rectors in Baltimore, met with Asbury and Coke to attempt to persuade them to remain within the Anglican church but their pleas were in vain.

The Christmas Conference also authorized the founding of Cokesbury College. When the school opened in 1787 at Abingdon under Levi Heath, it was clear that the new denomination had overextended itself. Money was not available for such a venture. When the original buildings burned, the school was reopened as an academy in Baltimore in 1796; when those buildings were destroyed as well, the venture was abandoned. The experiment had cost between $710,000 and $720,000. It was not until 1832, when the Baltimore Conference purchased Dickinson College in Pennsylvania, that Methodists in Maryland had a center for higher education.

The Great Methodist Revival of 1780-1820 began on the Eastern Shore and gradually moved west. At its height in 1789-1792, the churches were adding 1,000 members annually. The smallpox epidemic of 1792-1793 slowed the rate of growth, but the movement was not to be contained. In 1800, 1,232 converts were made in Baltimore; 382 in Frederick County; 330 in Montgomery; and 60 in Harford. In the same year, black membership in Calvert County went from 814 to 1,664.

In 1803, the CAMP MEETING was introduced by Henry Smith on the Winchester circuit. This new technique spread rapidly, with Nicholas Snethen attracting between 1,000 and 2,000 to his 1803 meeting in Reisterstown. In 1806, 579 were converted and 118 sanctified at a Baltimore County camp. The new style of evangelism, however, was harder to discipline than the older techniques, and in 1811, the conference agreed that camp meetings had to be approved by the presiding elder. Symptomatic of the problem was a Maryland law, passed in 1812, that prohibited the sale of liquor within two miles of a camp meeting. In 1820, Snethen and Alexander McCaine demanded lay representation in the conference and were opposed by the bishops and presiding elders. Through the *Wesleyan Repository* and its successor, *Mutual Rights*, the dispute was carried into the congregations where Union Societies of itinerants, local preachers, and laypeople were formed. After the expulsion of the Baltimore Union Society in 1828, schism was inevitable. In 1830, the resultant new denomination took the name the Methodist Protestant Church.

Although polity was the stated reason for the split, the need for the new church was occasioned by other social factors. The Methodist Protestant people favored a warmer style of evangelism than the Methodist Episcopal Church, especially the expanded use of the camp meeting, and they were strongest in the west and on the Eastern Shore—areas that were removed from the growth of the Western Shore and the city of Baltimore. By 1867, the new church was strong enough to establish Western Methodist College in Westminster and, in 1887, to create Westminster Theological Seminary. Following the reunion of the two churches, the Protestant Methodist and the Methodist Episcopal in 1939, the seminary was taken over by the newly united body and in 1958 relocated in Washington, acquiring the name Wesley Seminary.

The Civil War disrupted Maryland's Methodists more than it did the other religious groups in the state. Although Maryland had remained with the North in 1844, the "new chapter" on slavery, which was added to the Discipline in 1860, created an uproar. Rival conferences were created, and several independent Methodist societies were formed. After the war, the church extension boards of the Northern and Southern churches stole members from each other and founded competing churches in the area of the other denomination's strength. The Methodist Episcopal Church, South, won many of these battles, and when the two were reunited in 1939, it was able to bring almost 100,000 members into the new body.

The most important change in the state's Methodism after the Civil War was the gradual but steady increase in the number of seminary trained pastors. As a result, the churches moved in the direction of a more liberal theology and of a transformation of the older holiness ideal into modern concepts of social service. Harris Franklin Rall, pastor of First Methodist (Lovely Lane) from 1905 to 1910, was an organizer of the Methodist Federation for Social Service in 1907, and an important spokesman for the Social Creed, adopted by the Northern church in 1908. The Baltimore Conference opposed Negro disenfranchisement in 1915, and the work of the conference was one of the primary reasons for the defeat of a referendum on Afro-American voting in 1910.

The greatest period of post-Civil growth was 1945-1965 when a national religious revival coincided with the expansion of the Washington-Baltimore suburbs. This was also a period of rising ecumenical interest. In 1966, the Baltimore Conference merged with the Washington Conference (Black), and in 1969, union was effected with the United Brethren. In 1970, a joint ordination service was held in Washington Cathedral in which William F. Creighton, the Episcopal Bishop of Washington, joined with Bishops Love, Lord, and Leddin of the United Methodist Church in ordaining new elders for the Baltimore Conference. Methodism remains the largest Protestant denomination in the state; on the Eastern Shore it continues to comprise more than half the total population.

The Baptists. Despite strong missionary efforts, Baptists have never been as numerous in Maryland as in other Southern and border states. The GREAT AWAKENING, that laid the foundations of Baptist growth further south, did not occur in the state, and Methodism dominated the GREAT REVIVAL (Second Great Awakening). Further, the moderate form of aristocracy in Maryland did not spark the sharp Baptist democratic reaction that other forms of aristocracy, such as Virginia's, provoked.

The first Baptist church in Maryland was a General Baptist congregation established at Chestnut Ridge, Baltimore County, in 1742. By 1754 this congregation had divided, and a Particular Baptist church was gathered and admitted into the Philadelphia Association. Elder John Davis (1712-1808) served this Chestnut Ridge congregation for 60 years; he traveled as an itinerant throughout the Western Shore region, and his labors resulted in the establishment of many churches in the area. The First Church in Baltimore was one of these. Established about 1773, the church called Lewis Richards, a graduate of Lady Huntington's school at Trevecca, as its first full-time pastor. The Second Baptist Church in the city migrated as a body from England under the leadership of John Heally, a new connection Baptist. This church may have had the first Sunday school in the state. In 1793, the churches on the Western Shore united to form the Baltimore Association.

Elijah Baker and Philip Hughes, itinerants from Virginia, established the first Baptist churches on the Eastern Shore at Salisbury, Broad Creek, Fowling Creek, and Fishing Creek. In 1782, these churches formed the Salisbury Association.

The antimissionary movement sharply divided Maryland Baptists from 1820 to 1836. The issue was particularly heated on the Western Shore, and in 1836 the Baptist Union of Maryland was formed from those churches that supported missions and evangelism. There were fewer than 2,000 Baptists in the state at the time of the schism. Maryland was the only state where Baptists with a strong alliance with the Philadelphia Association resisted the new movements in missions and benevolence.

After the schism, Baptist efforts in Maryland turned towards the new city evangelism that had been developed in the North. In 1834, William F. Broadus, William T. Brantley Sr., and J. O. Choules conducted a protracted meeting at First Baptist, Baltimore, and in 1834, 1839, and 1856 Baptists invited Jacob Knapp, an evangelist who modelled his ministry on that of Charles Finney, to conduct revivals in the city. In 1879, Baptists were among the leaders in extending an invitation to D. L. Moody to conduct a revival in the city. Although these citywide efforts benefited other denominations as much or more than they benefited the Baptists, they did establish a strong Baptist presence in the city. In 1905, the Baltimore Baptist Training School was organized to help evangelize the city through lay witness and religious surveys.

The other approach to evangelism taken by Maryland Baptists was to invite prominent Baptists from other states to serve Maryland churches. William Crane (1790-1866), a wealthy Baptist layman from Virginia, moved to Baltimore in 1834 to help bolster Baptist fortunes. In 1847, Richard Fuller, the popular pastor of First Baptist, Beaufort SC accepted a call to Seventh Baptist, Baltimore, as a missionary duty and through energetic evangelism increased the membership from 87 to 1,200. The socially prominent Eutaw Street Baptist Church was formed by Richard Fuller and members of Seventh who had moved into that area in 1871. W. T. Brantley Jr., (1816-1852) came to Seventh Church in 1871 for reasons similar to those that had brought Fuller there earlier. Under his leadership, the Young Men's City Mission began the Sunday school that would later become the Brantley Baptist Church. Rising young Baptists leaders, such as E. Y. Mullins and Curtis Lee Laws also felt drawn to the city that presented such a challenge.

Despite their small size, Maryland Baptists have played important roles in Southern Baptist history. During the Civil War, when Southern Baptists were cut off from their missions abroad, Baltimore Baptists provided money and leadership to sustain the enterprise. After the war, Maryland women led by Anne Graves, Alice Armstrong, ANNIE ARMSTRONG, and Mrs. A. J. Rowland, helped to establish the Woman's Missionary Union to support Southern Baptist work. The Week of Prayer for Foreign Missions and the Christmas Offering, now convention-wide endeavors, originated in their work. Joshua Levering (1845-1935), layman and philanthropist, helped to restore financial order to the Southern Convention in the dark days of the late nineteenth century when it appeared that the enterprise would go bankrupt. He served as president of the convention and as chairman of the Trustees of Southern Seminary, Louisville.

Although Maryland Baptists made modest gains in the thriving suburbs of Washington after World War II, social changes in the Baltimore area in that same period have weakened the heart of Maryland Baptist work. Efforts have been made to establish new churches in Baltimore's suburbs, and some congregations, such as Seventh, have decided to stay in the inner city and experiment with multiracial forms of congregational life.

The Presbyterians. Despite firm colonial foundations, Presbyterianism in Maryland has remained relatively small. The heavy Scotch-Irish immigration of the late eighteenth and early nineteenth centuries tended to settle north or south of the state where more western lands were available, and few of the 19th-century German immigrants had a Reformed background. The identification of revivalism and Methodism in Maryland further weakened Presbyterian efforts at growth.

In 1763, Patrick Allison, a Princeton graduate, became the first Presbyterian pastor in Baltimore. John Glendy, a Scotch-Irish immigrant trained at the University of Glasgow, was the first pastor at Second Presbyterian. Apparently, Glendy's preaching had unitarian overtones. In 1817, the presbytery warned against the denial of the trinity, and when

John Breckinridge, another Princeton graduate, became associate pastor in 1826, the church had to dismiss half its membership for non-trinitarianism.

Maryland Presbyterian life was conservative. Although Sunday schools were added to the churches, the first in 1802, denominational societies were strongly preferred. The only non-presbyterian organization to have widespread support was the American Colonization Society. It was introduced at Second Presbyterian by that church's third pastor, ROBERT J. BRECKINRIDGE. Maryland's Presbyterians adhered to the Old School in 1837, and, although four pastors supported the Southern church during the Civil War, remained loyal to that position until the merger of Old and New School in 1869. By and large, pastors in the state have been drawn from Princeton Seminary and have reflected its style of leadership.

Maryland Presbyterianism has been prosperous and stable. The most controversial product of the church was J. Gresham Machen, the son of an old Baltimore family, who led the conservative forces against modernism in the 1920s. Significantly, J. Ross Stevenson, whose reforms at Princeton contributed to Machen's withdrawal from Presbyterianism, came to the presidency of the Seminary from the pulpit of Brown Memorial Church in Baltimore. Today, three presbyteries serve the state: Baltimore, New Castle (Eastern Shore), and the National Capitol Union, which is a joint effort with the Southern church.

Afro-American Religion. In Maryland, slavery rarely involved the large commerical plantation, and blacks and whites lived more intimately than in the deep South. Further, some religious traditions served to ameliorate the conditions of the slaves. The Quakers maintained a strong antislavery tradition, and many Methodists were opposed to slave holding on principle. Roman Catholicism, while not campaigning against slavery, insisted that slavery was only an economic condition and did not affect the slave's relationship to God. Further, Maryland had a large free black population in the 19th century that was numerically equal to the slave population at the time of emancipation. This older free black community, which was intensely interested in education and social advancement, tended to set the standards for the Afro-American community in religious as well as social matters.

Catholic missionary work among the slaves began as soon as they arrived in the colony. The Jesuits saw the Africans as a natural extension of their charter to conduct Indian missions, and Catholic planters, unlike many Protestants, recognized an obligation to convert their servants. Although massive immigration from Europe deflected Catholic energies, concern with the religious needs of black Catholics continued. In 1829, the Oblate Sisters, the Church's first black religious order, arrived from Santo Domingo and established St. Francis School for Colored Girls. Their mission quickly expanded to include Sunday schools and catechetical instruction for those Negro children who could not attend parochial schools. As the parish school became a mark of Maryland's Catholics, the Oblates established new schools in predominantly black parishes.

Although blacks were rarely as segregated from whites in Catholicism as in Protestantism, the Catholic Church in the 19th century moved toward the establishment of black ethnic churches. In 1859, Father Peter Miller, S. J., was appointed as a missionary to the blacks of Baltimore. His church, St. Francis Xavier, originally met in the basement of St. Ignatius' Church, but in 1863, Archbishop Spalding dedicated a new building for the congregation. In 1871, the Afro-American mission was transferred from the Jesuits to the newly formed Josephites.

In addition to launching St. Francis Xavier, the Josephites, who had been founded in England to work with the freedmen, established a minor seminary at Walbrook and a major seminary in Washington DC. Although Afro-Americans had been ordained earlier in Europe, Charles Uncles (1859-1933) was the first black priest ordained in the United States. He attended the Oblate Sisters' School at St. Francis Xavier and the Baltimore Normal School before his baptism in 1879. When he decided to enter the priesthood four years later, he followed other Afro-American candidates to St. Hyacinthe's College in Quebec. In 1888 he applied to St. Mary's Seminary, and after a meeting of the student body to vote on his admission, was the first Negro admitted to the school. In 1891, he was ordained and began a teaching ministry with the Josephites at Walbrook; when the school moved to New York in 1920, he left Maryland to continue his duties there.

One of the crusaders for justice among black Catholics was Father John Henry Dorsey, S. S. J. (1873-1926). He served as an altar boy at St. Francis Xavier, and was educated at St. Thomas (Minneapolis), Walbrook, and St. Mary's, Baltimore. Following his ordination in 1902, he became a missionary to poor whites and blacks in Alabama. When his work there became too controversial in 1923, he was made pastor of St. Monnica's, a poor black parish in Baltimore. In 1926, he was killed by a parishioner whose apparent motive was robbery.

The Methodist revival attacked large numbers of Afro-Americans, especially in the city of Baltimore that had approximately 9,000 free black residents in 1800. In 1802, Lovely Lane Methodist Church helped to establish Sharp Street Methodist for its black members. Sharp Street was an early center of black activism: money was raised to purchase the freedom of slaves; reading and writing were taught in the Sunday school; the Liberian colonization plan was studied, and abolitionist speakers, especially those active among Maryland's Methodists, were invited to speak. Since Maryland had no laws prohibiting the education of free blacks, the church was able to establish an influential private school.

More racially conscious Afro-Americans had founded a Colored Methodist Society in 1782, and in 1802, the African Methodist Bethel Society, as it was then known, called Daniel Coker as their pastor. Coker had been a slave on the Eastern Shore and was a convert of Robert Strawbridge. He had escaped to New York, and with the aid of Francis Asbury had earned enough to purchase his freedom. Under his leadership, Bethel left the parent Methodist organization. The church was a center for the publication of attacks on slavery and for the education of free blacks. Coker himself became disillusioned with the changes for racial improvement in Maryland and emigrated to Africa. Bethel has remained a key Afro-American pulpit, and 14 of its pastors, including DANIEL PAYNE, the historian, have served the African Methodist Episcopal Church as bishops.

The third early Afro-American pastor in Baltimore was William Livingston. Born in New York, he was ordained by Bishop William White of Philadelphia, and in 1824, established St. James' First African Episcopal Church. Although related to the Church of England, St. James' maintained a style of ministry that was similar to that of the black Methodists in the city.

In 1848 Sharp Street and Asbury Station Methodist churches petitioned the General Conference for a separate Negro Conference, but this request was denied until after emancipation in 1864. In that year, the Methodist established the Washington Conference that united black Methodists in Maryland and the District of Columbia. In 1940, A. P. Shaw became the first Afro-American to serve the conference as its bishop, and in 1956, Emma Birrell was ordained by the Washington Conference. She was the first woman ordained as a Methodist elder in the state. In 1965, after a century of leadership among black Marylanders, the Washington Conference was merged with the formerly all white Baltimore Conference, and Afro-Americans and whites shared the positions of leadership in the new body.

The period after 1864 was the beginning of a half century of steady growth. By 1890, the Methodist Episcopal Church had expanded to include 7,000 black members and black Methodist owned property valued at $225,000. In that same period, the African Methodist Episcopal Church grew to 5,000 members and owned property valued at $200,000. Since both denominations had strict membership requirements, average attendance was probably twice the reported membership. Afro-American Methodists were more than twice the size of their nearest Protestant rival, the Baptists, who reported only 5,700 members at the same date.

Higher education was a major concern of Maryland's Afro-American Methodist community. In 1867, the Centenary Biblical Institute was opened to train black pastors. The growth of the segregated public school system offered new opportunities for educated blacks, and in 1876 a normal department was opened. Many Methodist ministers appear to have combined ministry with school teaching. In 1890, the name of the school was changed to Morgan College, and in 1939 the school was purchased by the state. Afro-American Methodists, however, were allowed to retain facilities on the campus.

Black Baptists, like their white counterparts, have not been as influential in Maryland as in other Southern states. In part, this has been due to the pattern of white evangelization. The areas of heaviest slave owning in Maryland were in the Southern counties and on the Eastern Shore where Catholics, Episcopalians, and Methodists were dominant.

In 1834, Moses Clayton formed the First Colored Baptist Church, and in 1836, the church was admitted to the Maryland Baptist Union. In that same year, William Crane purchased the freedom of Noah Davis, a slave preacher, and he traveled the state preaching to slave and free. In

1848, Seventh Baptist dismissed its black members to form the Second Colored Baptist Church. Both First and Second Colored Churches were active in the Maryland Baptist Union until 1864 when they withdrew to establish the Maryland State Convention.

The most remarkable of Baltimore's black Baptist churches was Union Baptist, which was formed by the merger of two small congregations in 1866. The congregation purchased the old Disciples' Meeting House, and in 1872 called the Rev. Harvey Johnson as its pastor. Johnson, a graduate of Wayland, made the church a center of black education and evangelism. By 1885, Union had 2,000 members who formed the base of the Brotherhood of Liberty that fought discriminatory legislation in the state. The outreach of Union resulted in the formation of Macedonian, Calvary, Perkins Square, Frederick, Winfield, and Westminster Baptist churches. Significantly, Union refused to ordain a candidate for the ministry who had not acquired some formal education, and the congregation provided money and other forms of support for students at Wayland and Howard Colleges.

Afro-American Christians in Maryland were active participants in the civil rights struggles of the 1960s. In the 1970s, however, the black denominations began to face two different problems. On the one hand, there was a new Afro-American immigration into Baltimore that put increased pressure on very limited resources. On the other hand, the new opportunities for blacks that they had done so much to create were producing a middle class that was moving to the suburbs. Whether the black denominations will be able to meet the demands of this exodus or whether these newly established people will turn to the mainstream denominations is not clear.

Unitarians. Unitarianism has not played a significant role in Maryland's religious history. First Unitarian Church, Baltimore, was constructed in 1817 to serve the needs of immigrants from New England to the city. In 1819, William Ellery Channing preached his famous sermon, "Unitarian Christianity," at the ordination of Jared Sparks there. The sermon made almost no impression on Baltimore. The most successful Unitarian minister to serve in Maryland was the Rev. John Ware who preached to crowds of 2,000 at Ford's Opera House during the Civil War. The spread of liberalism, however, among other Protestant churches, especially the Methodist, prevented those gains from becoming permanent. Enoch Pratt (d. 1896) was the leading 19th-century Unitarian layman. His gift of $1,200,000 to the city established the Enoch Pratt Library, one of the leading public libraries in the United States.

Judaism. Judaism grew slowly in Maryland in the years immediately following the American Revolution. The state's constitution and laws assumed that Maryland was a Christian state and, although a cemetery was purchased in Baltimore, it was not clear whether a Jewish organization could be incorporated. From 1818 to 1826, bills were introduced in the legislature to extend civil rights to Jews. Thomas Kennedy (1776-1832), a Presbyterian immigrant from Ireland, led the battle, and the final law allowed Jews to be admitted to the courts and to vote on an oath of belief in God. The last civil rights bill for Jews was passed in 1847 when the state's prohibition against black suits of "white Christians" was changed simply to "whites."

Baltimore's early Jewish community was largely composed of immigrants from Bavaria and in 1830, *Nidlei Israel*, later Baltimore Hebrew Congregation, was established. Abraham Rice (1800-1862), who came in 1840 as rabbi, was the first person with full rabbinic training to settle in the United States. From the beginning of his ministry, Rice faced the problem of Americanization in his congregation. Despite a heavy program of fines and an attempt to exclude Sabbath breakers from the reading of the Torah in the services, Rice was unable to bring his congregation into line with his convictions. In 1849 he resigned and was followed by Henry Hochheimer, a graduate of the University of Munich, who continued to attempt to maintain orthodoxy. In 1870, however, the congregation formally acknowledged the Reform position of many of its members, and the Chizuk Emunah Congregation was formed in reaction to the changes.

The first Reform Synagogue in Baltimore was Har Sinai, which was established after Rabbi Abraham Rice protested the use of Masonic rites at the funeral of Jacob Ahrens in 1842. David Einhorn (1809-1879) was called to the synagogue as rabbi in 1855. Einhorn, one of the founders of Reform Judaism in Europe and a radical on secular as well as religious subjects, was forced to flee from Baltimore in 1861 because of his uncompromising position on slavery.

Oheb Shalom Congregation was established in 1853 as an alternative to the orthodoxy of Baltimore Hebrew and to the radicalism of Har Sinai. In 1859, the synagogue secured the services of Rabbi Benjamin Szold (1829-1902) who had been trained both in European rabbinical schools and at the University of Breslau. Szold was one of the leading advocates of Conservative Judaism in America.

The renewal of persecution in Eastern Europe radically changed Baltimore's Jewish community. The newcomers were not comfortable in German-speaking congregations, and they tended to form small Orthodox synagogues composed of their fellow countrymen. In 1909, for example, there were 25 congregations of Russian Jews within the city. The new immigrants were poor, and the pattern of German Jewish owners and Eastern European Jewish workers quickly developed in Baltimore's garment industry. Further, the Eastern Jews created a different culture composed of night schools, unions, Zionist organizations, and cultural activities that made East Baltimore the scene of countless, unending debates. Despite their differences from either the older Jewish or the Gentile communities, Eastern immigrants in Baltimore made rapid social progress, and by the early 1920s they had begun to leave the ghetto.

Although Judaism in Maryland has often seemed to function like one of the Christian denominations, there have been significant differences. As important as the synagogues have been, especially for the German Jews, Jewish charities and organizations have provided more of the cement that has held the community together than has worship. The first charity had the improbable name, Irish *Chevra*, and it was followed by a long list of organizations that included the Hebrew Benevolence Society (1856), the Hebrew Orphanage Society (1872), the Free Burial Society (1869), the Jewish Consumptive Hospital (1909), and the Jewish Educational Alliance (1890). In 1920, the Associated Jewish Charities was formed to coordinate the work of German and Jewish charities.

The need of Jewish education has also united the community. Early Jewish education was conducted in the synagogue where the rabbi taught secular and religious subjects. In 1856, the small Sephardic congregation experimented with a Sunday school for those students attending public schools, and the institution spread. In 1900, Samson Benderly (1876-1944) came to Baltimore as the principal of the Hebrew school maintained by the Hebrew Educational Society. Under his leadership, the school adopted progressive education and stressed the integration of play and learning. Benderly's school highlighted the need for trained teachers and in 1902 Hebrew College was established to train men and women to work in Jewish education. In 1910, Benderly left Baltimore to take a similar position in New York, and Hebrew College was temporarily closed. The school reopened in 1919 with a broader curriculum designed to train people in all areas of Jewish life and history.

Baltimore Jews supported fellow Jews in Israel before the modern Zionist movement. In 1847, Jehiel Cohen collected funds for the Jewish settlements there, and in that same year, Rabbi Rice organized a group to provide regular aid. Although few Jews from Maryland had immigrated to the Holy Land, Zionist organizations of all types have been supported. In 1897, Rabbi Schepel Schafer attended the First Zionist Congress, and Henrietta Szold (1860-1945), the founder of Hadassah, was the daughter of one of Baltimore's leading rabbis. The rise of Nazism and the subsequent establishment of the state of Israel have intensified the Baltimore community's commitment to Israel and have had the effect of creating a deeper appreciation of Jewish faith and customs. Like the charities and Jewish education, Israel is a major object of the support of Jews in the state.

Summary. Maryland's religious patterns have remained stable over a significant period of time. The primary changes in that pattern have come from immigration into the state; however, immigration has often changed particular denominations more than it has changed the pattern of denominational loyalty. Even the rapid expansion of the Washington suburbs has had less influence than one might have supposed. Maryland appears to be basically content with its patterns of religious diversity. Although the ecumenical movement has had some impact, especially among Methodists, denominationalism will probably continue to dominate the state's religion in the future. Maryland's denominations serve many social functions: religious, ethnic, educational, and charitable. And these functions have built for the churches a firm foundation in the life of the state.

See also articles on BLACK CATHOLICISM; CALVERT FAMILY; CHURCH AND STATE; DISESTABLISHMENT; ESTABLISHED RELIGION; METHODIST CHURCH; NATIVISM; ROMAN CATHOLIC CHURCH.

Bibliography. Patrick Allison, *First Presbyterian Church, Baltimore, Maryland*; Gordon P. Baker, *Those Incredible Methodists: A History of the Baltimore Conference of the United Methodist Church*; Thomas Beaenkoph, et al., *Moody in Baltimore*; L. P. Bowen, *The Days of Makemie*; Isaac M. Fein, *The Making of An American Jewish Community: The History of Baltimore Jewry from 1773 to 1920*; Theodore Gambrall, *Church Life in Colonial Maryland*; Rufus Jones, *The Quakers in the American Colonies*; J. J. Johnson, *Historical Summary of the Shrines, Churches, Chapels, and Homes of the Priests in St. Mary's County since 1634*; Charles G. Herbermann, *The Sulpicians in the United States*; Julius Hofman, *A History of Zion Church of the City of Baltimore, 1755-1897*; Anabelle M. Melville, *John Carroll of Baltimore*; Nelson Rightmeyer, *Maryland's Established Church*; Joseph Watts, *The Rise and Progress of Maryland Baptists*; Adel Ross Wentz, *History of the Evangelical Lutheran Synod of Maryland of the United Lutheran Church in America, 1820-1920*; Albert Werline, *Problems of Church and State in Maryland*; Blanche Sydnor White, *Our Heritage: History of the Women's Missionary Union, Auxiliary to the Maryland Baptist Union, 1742-1958.*

GLENN T. MILLER
SOUTHEASTERN BAPTIST SEMINARY

MASON, CHARLES HARRISON

(1866-1961), black cofounder of the CHURCH OF GOD IN CHRIST, was born near Memphis in Shelby County TN. In 1895 Mason and C. P. Jones, missionary Baptist ministers in the Lexington MS area, accepted the HOLINESS doctrine of entire SANCTIFICATION and began preaching it in black Baptist churches. The local Baptist association soon expelled the two clergymen for their heterodoxy. Mason and Jones began a holiness revival in Lexington in February 1897, out of which evolved the Church of God in Christ.

Late in 1897 the new sect was incorporated in Memphis, becoming the South's first chartered organization in the HOLINESS MOVEMENT. The church's legal status entitled its ministers to clergy rates on the railroads, and to perform marriages, privileges prompting unaffiliated white Holiness ministers to seek and receive ordination in the predominantly black organization.

In March 1907 Mason and two associates attended the Pentecostal revival then underway in Los Angeles. Five weeks later the three returned to Memphis, professing to have received the BAPTISM OF THE SPIRIT. Mason's conversion to PENTECOSTALISM precipitated a profound division within the Church of God in Christ since C. P. Jones, general overseer and presiding elder, rejected the doctrine.

The rift between their followers resulted in a schism in the sect in August 1907. Mason and his Pentecostal neophytes retained the name Church of God in Christ while Jones and the Holiness faction adopted the name Church of Christ (Holiness) U.S.A.

The soft-spoken but firm Mason presided over his church until his death. Under his leadership the Church of God in Christ became the largest black Pentecostal body in the United States.

Bibliography. Klaud Kendrick, *The Promise Fulfilled: A History of the American Pentecostal Movement*; Mary Mason, *The History and Life Work of Bishop C. H. Mason, Chief Apostle, and his Co-laborers*; Vinson Synan, *The Holiness-Pentecostal Movement in the United States.*

ROBERT F. MARTIN
UNIVERSITY OF NORTHERN IOWA

MASTERS, VICTOR IRVINE (1867-1954), Baptist journalist, was born in Anderson County SC. He was educated at Furman University (A.B., 1888; A.M., 1889) and Southern Baptist Theological Seminary (Th.M., 1889) and ordained a Baptist minister in 1889. He served briefly as pastor of Baptist churches in Yorkshire and Rock Hill SC (1893-1894) and Pocahontas VA (1894-1896). His major contribution, however, was as a Baptist journalist and writer. He was associate editor of the *Baptist Courier* of SC (1896-1905); owner-editor of the *Baptist Press* of South Carolina (1905-1907); associate editor of the *Religious Herald* of Virginia (1908-1909); superintendent of publicity of the Home Mission Board of the Southern Baptist Convention (1909-1921); editor of the board's *The Home Field* (1909-1917), and editor of the *Western Recorder* of Kentucky (1921-1942). He wrote several books on Southern Baptists' home-mission work between 1912 and 1921, showing special concern over the presence of Catholics and other aliens in the South. He took emphatic and usually conservative editorial positions on theological, program-related, and institutional issues debated by Kentucky and other Southern Baptists. His major theo-logical book was *Re-Thinking Baptist Doctrines* (1937).

See also articles on NATIVISM; RELIGIOUS PRESS.

G. HUGH WAMBLE
MIDWESTERN BAPTIST SEMINARY

MAYS, BENJAMIN ELIJAH (1895-), nationally known educator and advocate of racial integration, was born in Epworth SC. Though reared in the rural South, his accomplishments at Bates College (A.B., 1920) and the University of Chicago (M.A., 1925; Ph.D., 1935) prepared him for a distinguished academic career. Before that, Mays served at various posts: minister of Shiloh Baptist Church in Atlanta GA, instructor in mathematics and English, executive for the Urban League and YMCA, and director of studies about black churches. As dean of the School of Religion at Howard University from 1934 to 1940, he attracted national attention by improving standards enough to qualify for an "A" rating from the American Association of Theological Schools. In 1940 he became president of Morehouse College and showed for 27 years that hard work and learning could enhance competence and self-respect among Southern blacks.

Mays viewed racism and segregation as constant enemies. Neither an extremist nor a militant agitator, he called for peaceful reforms within existing American structures. He thought the present democratic system provided for universal suffrage, equal justice before the law, and fair practice in jobs, education, and health services. The challenge was to secure what was already possible. Mays used his position at Morehouse to meet that challenge, producing graduates with sufficient integrity and resourcefulness to warrant racial parity. From a religious perspective, Mays sought integration more than desegregation. He envisioned goals of spiritual wholeness and mutual love that overcame artificial barriers, not pragmatic compromises won through violence or factionalism. After retiring in 1967, Mays served as consultant and committee member on dozens of boards including HEW, UNESCO, and the Ford Foundation. He worked with the Baptist World Alliance and both Federal and World Councils of Churches to foster increased human dignity and greater social harmony through Christian principles.

See also articles on BLACK RELIGION; CIVIL RIGHTS MOVEMENT; ETHICS, CHRISTIAN.

Bibliography. Benjamin E. Mays, *Born to Rebel: An Autobiography, Lord, the People Have Driven Me On.*

HENRY WARNER BOWDEN
RUTGERS UNIVERSITY

MEADE, WILLIAM (1789-1862), third Episcopal bishop of Virginia, was born in Frederick (now Clarke) County during the period of the collapse of the Anglican tradition in Virginia. His mother influenced him to attend the orthodox College of New Jersey.

Graduating in 1808, Meade briefly studied for the ministry in Maryland under an uncompromising Anglican Evangelical, Walter Dulany Addison. Ordained by Bishop JAMES MADISON in 1811, when the former Established Church of Virginia had lost all of its glebe lands, most of its clergy and churches, and all but a few hundred of its active laity, Meade immediately began a lifelong mission of returning Virginia's mother church to its former strength. Working with such like-minded clergy as RICHARD CHANNING MOORE and William Holland Wilmer, and utilizing evangelical techniques pioneered in Virginia by DEVEREUX JARRATT, he achieved a remarkable revival. Elected assistant bishop in 1829, Meade succeeded Moore as bishop of Virginia in 1841.

In the national affairs of his denomination, Meade became a leader of the Evangelical (or Low Church) party and one of the principal American critics of the Oxford Movement. He was among the most scholarly and prolific of the antebellum Episcopal clergy, though his theological works display a resistance to new ideas.

His occasionally inaccurate *Old Churches, Ministers and Families of Virginia* (1857) remains notable as a museum of facts about Virginia history. Active in voluntary societies, Meade is best described as the "nursing father" of the Protestant Episcopal Theological Seminary in Alexandria VA. Initially opposed to secession, he subsequently served as presiding bishop of the PROTESTANT EPISCOPAL CHURCH IN THE CONFEDERATE STATES OF AMERICA. Spartan in life-style, stern in manner, and disciplined in the manner of John Wesley, Meade personified a school of Episcopalianism that was at once staunchly Protestant, thoroughly evangelical, and loyally Anglican.

Bibliography. David L. Holmes, "The Decline and Revival of the Church of Virginia," *Up From Independence: The Episcopal Church in Virginia,* ed. Brewster S. Ford and Harold S. Sniffen; John Johns, *A Memoir of the Life of the Right Rev. William Meade*; Robert Nelson, *Reminiscences of the Rt. Rev. William Meade.*

DAVID L. HOLMES
COLLEGE OF WILLIAM AND MARY

MENCKEN, HENRY LEWIS (1880-1956), journalist and critic of conservative religion, was born in Baltimore. Although he was a lifelong resident of the South, his vigorous, colorful prose and combativeness won him national recognition. During the 1920s he was the best-known newspaperman in the country as a reporter for the Baltimore *Sun* and also the most influential editor in the country, first with the *Smart Set* and later with the *American Mercury*. He also produced literary studies and in 1919 published the first version of *The American Language*, a monument of American scholarship.

In 1920 his assessment of the lack of culture in the South, "The Sahara of the Bozart," caused a storm of protest throughout the region. Mencken continued his attacks almost monthly in his magazines. In 1925 he helped to secure Clarence Darrow for the defense of JOHN T. SCOPES, the Tennessee school teacher who had defied the law by teaching evolution. Mencken gleefully reported on the "monkey trial" for the *Sun* and other papers, and when WILLIAM JENNINGS BRYAN, the special prosecutor of Scopes, died exhausted five days after the close of the trial, he published probably the cruelest obituary ever written in English.

But his major targets during the period transcended the South. Mencken was fiercely opposed to a constellation of ideas that he called Puritanism. He led the national counterattack by intellectuals on three aspects of that mind-set: prohibition, censorship, and fundamentalist theology. He did believe, however, that Puritanism in its most virulent form was a Southern phenomenon, and so pursued it most energetically there.

See also article on SCOPES TRIAL.

Bibliography. Fred C. Hobson, Jr., *Serpent in Eden: H. L. Mencken and the South*; H. L. Mencken, *Prejudices*; *Treatise on the Gods.*

STEPHEN S. CONROY
UNIVERSITY OF FLORIDA

MEREDITH, THOMAS (1795-1850), versatile Baptist leader, served as educator, minister, editor of a religious weekly magazine, college trustee, and denominational servant. For that reason he was regarded in his own time as North Carolina Baptists' single most influential figure. A "missionary" to North Carolina, Meredith was born in Bucks County PA. He was educated at the University of Pennsylvania and shortly thereafter began a career that, except for a brief pastorate in Savannah GA, was spent entirely in North Carolina. After brief service as a schoolteacher, Meredith served on two separate occasions as minister of the Baptist church in New Bern and for nine years in Edenton.

In 1830, as one of the 14 founders of the North Carolina Baptist State Convention, he helped draft its original constitution. His continuing contribution was rendered on different occasions as secretary, vice-president, and president of that organization.

Having founded the *Biblical Recorder* in 1835, it was as editor of that denominational weekly that Meredith's greatest influence on North Carolina Baptists was felt. He regarded slavery as "an evil of great magnitude" and attempted to cause Baptists to confront this and other social ills through the pages of the *Biblical Recorder*. Indebtedness, which plagued the paper from its inception, and his untimely death in 1850 unfortunately limited the scope of his achievement.

An early advocate of women's education, Meredith served on three separate committees that had been appointed by the North Carolina Baptist Convention in response to a motion "to consider the establishment of a female seminary of high order." Although a half century was to elapse after his death before this proposal was to become a reality, the Baptist Female University, which was established in 1899, was later to bear his name in recognition of his efforts in its behalf.

See also articles on RELIGIOUS PRESS; WOMEN IN RELIGION.

Bibliography. Mary Lynch Johnson, *A History of Meredith College*; W. B. Sprague, *Annals of the American Pulpit.*

BERNARD H. COCHRAN
MEREDITH COLLEGE

MERTON, THOMAS (1915-1968), famous Roman Catholic author and mystic, was born in Prades, France, the son of artists. He grew up and attended schools in France, Britain, and the United States, where his maternal grandparents made a home for him after both his mother and father died.

He was a student at Columbia University in 1938 when he became a Roman Catholic; and he was a teacher and published poet when in 1941 he entered the Trappist (Order of Cistercians of the Strict Observance) Abbey of Gethsemani in Kentucky. During his 27 years at Gethsemani he wrote more than 50 books, the most famous being the 1949 best-seller *The Seven Storey Mountain*. Other well-received and influential books were *Seeds of Contemplation* (1949), *The Sign of Jonas* (1953), *Disputed Questions*(1953), *Seeds of Destruction* (1961), *Conjectures of a Guilty Bystander* (1966), and *Faith and Violence* (1968).

Merton was applauded and honored for the beauty of his poetry, the wisdom of his spiritual writings, and the power and perception of his social criticism. Cloistered as he was, he nevertheless introduced a great deal of secular thought into the American Catholic monastic movement and a great deal of Catholic monastic thought into the secular social movements of the turbulent American 1960s. He spoke in behalf of peace, social justice, and racial harmony, using his position as a recognized literary figure and religious leader to good effect.

In 1968 Merton spent three months, his first extended absence from Gethsemani, in the Far East addressing Catholic orders, attending ecumenical meetings, and studying Buddhist monasticism. Exactly 27 years to the day after becoming a monk, he retired to his Bangkok hotel room following a meeting with Asian religious leaders. After a bath, with his feet still wet, he touched a defective fan and was electrocuted.

Bibliography. James T. Baker, *Thomas Merton, Social Critic*; Monica Furlong, *Merton, A Biography.*

JAMES T. BAKER
WESTERN KENTUCKY UNIVERSITY

METHODISM: *See* WESLEYAN TRADITION.

METHODIST CHURCH, THE. Methodism first came to the South when JOHN WESLEY arrived in Georgia in February 1736 as chaplain to the colony. He was followed by his brother Charles, who came as secretary to JAMES OGLETHORPE. In Georgia John first met the MORAVIANS who influenced him greatly, as seen in his organization of a religious society he later described as (after Oxford) "the second rise of Methodism." Disillusioned with a lack of response, both John and Charles left Savannah in 1737. The next year GEORGE WHITEFIELD, their friend and coworker at Oxford, arrived in Georgia and founded Bethesda Orphan House. In 1739-1740 he inaugurated the GREAT AWAKENING in the South on a tour up the Atlantic seaboard, preaching from Savannah northward.

The later Methodist movement, established by John Wesley in England in 1739, reached the South between 1760 and 1766 with the preaching of the fiery Irish lay preacher, Robert Strawbridge, who had immigrated to Maryland. By 1766 there seems to have been a Methodist society in Leesburg VA. In 1769 Wesley began to send preachers to America; in 1772 one of them, Joseph Pilmoor, toured the Atlantic states, preaching from Maryland to Georgia. By 1776 there were circuits in Maryland, Virginia, and North Carolina. Southern membership grew from 600 in 1773 to 3,348 in 1776—46 percent of the total American membership. During the Revolution Wesley's preachers returned to England, except for FRANCIS ASBURY. They were replaced with Americans, largely Southerners. By 1783, 89 percent of the Methodists lived below the Mason-Dixon line.

Methodist Episcopal Church: In 1784 Wesley ordained THOMAS COKE a superintendent for the Methodists in America and directed him to ordain Francis Asbury. On 24 December 1784, the CHRISTMAS CONFERENCE met in Baltimore and organized the Methodist Episcopal Church. It adopted Wesley's recension of the Anglican Articles of Religion, his *Notes on the New Testament*, and standard sermons as its doctrinal foundation. Soon Coke and Asbury were addressed as bishop.

In 1785 Asbury led a group of preachers into South Carolina and sent others to Georgia. By 1786 Methodism had expanded into western North Carolina, Tennessee, and Kentucky. Until his death in 1816 Asbury annually visited churches, held conferences, and controlled the denomination. In 1800 Tobias Gibson began work in Mississippi. Expansion into Alabama, Florida, and Texas followed by the 1820s. Eventually separate annual conferences were organized in states or regions. A quadrennial General

Conference adopted the *Discipline*, the book of church order. A Book Concern, founded in 1789, provided the church with literature.

Four schisms divided the young church. As early as 1786 black Methodists in Baltimore disapproved segregation in worship and formed a separate society. In 1816 they joined Richard Allen in Philadelphia in organizing the AFRICAN METHODIST EPISCOPAL CHURCH. In 1792 JAMES O'KELLY in North Carolina challenged episcopal autocracy and established the Republican Methodist Church (later the CHRISTIAN CHURCH, which merged into the Congregational-Christian, now the UNITED CHURCH OF CHRIST). In Charleston in 1792 William Hammett organized the Primitive Methodist Church, but after his death in 1803 it languished. In 1830 the Methodist Protestant Church was organized to protest clerical control, and by the 1840s it had congregations in most Southern states.

Methodism began to grow dramatically during the GREAT REVIVAL (Second Great Awakening). After Presbyterian JAMES MCGREADY pioneered the frontier CAMP MEETING in Kentucky in 1800, joint Methodist, Baptist, and Presbyterian meetings were held. By 1807 Asbury wrote that "camp meetings prevail generally." As denominational rivalry increased, however, bitterness deepened and separate camp meetings were held. To provide leadership for the church and to bolster self-consciousness, Methodists and the others began to establish schools and colleges. In 1830 Randolph-Macon was founded in Virginia, the earliest that has survived to the present.

From the beginning the institution of slavery was a problem. Large numbers of blacks joined Methodist churches. The Christmas Conference in 1784 prohibited slaveholding wherever emancipation was legal. But by 1808 Southerners prevailed on the General Conference to allow each Annual Conference to rule on whether members could buy and sell slaves. In 1836 New Englanders began to push for a

return to the earlier position. Methodist abolitionists brought bitter reaction from Southern churchmen, who defended slavery from a biblical basis. South Carolina led in organizing missions to slaves. Finally, in the 1844 General Conference a debate over the ownership of slaves by Georgia Bishop JAMES O. ANDREW, who was prohibited by law from freeing them, resulted in a division of the denomination into Northern and Southern churches.

Later in 1863 as Union armies moved southward, Northern bishops sent missionaries to seize vacated churches. For freedmen they organized churches, annual conferences, schools, and colleges. The Freedmen's Aid Society directed Northern charity southward. Likewise, the AME and AMERICAN METHODIST EPISCOPAL ZION churches established congregations across the South.

Methodist Episcopal Church, South: On 1 May 1845 delegates from the Southern conferences met in Louisville KY and voted to establish the ME Church, South. Its first General Conference met in Petersburg VA in May 1846. The church campaigned aggressively on its northern border for members and established mission churches in Kansas, New Mexico, and California, then established foreign missions too, with the first in China. WILLIAM CAPERS, who had pioneered the South Carolina effort, was appointed to develop a denominational MISSION TO SLAVES on plantations. A publishing house opened in Nashville TN and a series of *Christian Advocates* provided church news to Methodist families. Leaders began to distinguish between Northern Methodism (a "political" church) and Southern Methodism (with a "strictly Scriptural mission").

In 1861 the church numbered 750,000 (including 208,000 blacks). It embraced the Confederacy and hundreds of chaplains and missionaries accompanied the armies in the field. Bible and tract societies furnished soldiers with literature. In the wake of defeat, the church lay in disarray. Leaders were embittered by Reconstruction and the ecclesiastical imperialism of the ME Church. The church lost 250,000 members by 1866; black membership dropped to 70,000. In 1866 the General Conference began to rebuild by granting lay representation in Annual Conferences and establishing District Conferences as regional rallying points within conferences. It continued to work with blacks, but gradually urged them to unite with the Colored (now CHRISTIAN) METHODIST EPISCOPAL CHURCH.

By 1869 membership equalled its prewar size; by 1900 it numbered 1,412,000. Schools and colleges reopened, and in 1873 Vanderbilt became the church's central university. In 1878 the Woman's Missionary Society was organized to promote missions. REVIVALISM was the central tool of evangelism and "worldly amusements" such as gambling and dancing occupied the social conscience of the church. In the 1880s the HOLINESS MOVEMENT attracted some church members; they founded Asbury College in Kentucky. But in a theologically conservative church, FUNDAMENTALISM made little headway.

Layman Henry Grady promoted a vision of "the New South," blessed by later Bishop ATTICUS G. HAYGOOD in *Our Brother in Black*. By 1914 the church adopted the Social Creed and broadened its social witness. Its major crusade was fought in favor of prohibition, led by Bishop JAMES CANNON, JR. By the 1930s some leaders were advocating better race relations.

In 1914 the church withdrew support from Vanderbilt and founded two new universities—Southern Methodist in Dallas and Emory in Atlanta. In 1924 James B. Duke established Duke University in Durham NC, with the largest gift ever made to Christian higher education.

Efforts at reunion with the ME Church began in 1869 with an exchange of fraternal delegates, first in meetings of bishops and then in the General Conferences. In 1876 a joint commission met at Cape May NJ to begin conversations. In the 1890s a Commission on Federation was joined by the Methodist Protestant Church. A joint hymnal was published and in 1916 a Joint Commission on Unification met. Major roadblocks were desired by Southerners to maintain regional identity in a new church and to insure racial segregation. A plan of union proposed five regional jurisdictions that would elect the bishops and a Central Jurisdiction that included black churches. After several efforts, the plan was finally adopted. On 10 May 1939 in Kansas City the three churches became the Methodist Church.

Disgruntled Southerners, led by Bishop Collins Denny and a lay organization, established the Southern Methodist Church. It included racial segregation in its Articles of Religion. In 1960 it reported 4,608 members.

The Methodist Church: In the new church the Southern states were divided at the Mississippi River into the Southeastern and South Central Jurisdictions. Of the six jurisdictions only the two white Southern ones became viable organizations. The SE Jurisdiction, for example, gained title to both Emory University and the Lake Junaluska Assembly. It created a series of boards and agencies.

The CIVIL RIGHTS MOVEMENT brought increasing pressure on the segregated church. In 1956 the General Conference adopted Amendment 9 to its constitution to provide voluntary integration of the Central Jurisdiction (made up of black churches) into the regional ones.

In 1968 the Methodist Church united with the Evangelical United Brethren Church, which had few congregations in the South, to form the United Methodist Church.

The United Methodist Church: The united church came into being in April 1968 over the opposition of many Southerners who did not favor the racial integration favored by the majority. The new church adopted 1972 as the target date by which the 12 remaining black Annual Conferences would be merged with white ones. Finally, the General Conference adopted 1 July 1973 as a mandatory date for the mergers. A major priority of Southern Annual Conferences in the 1970s was making a merger work. By 1979 the merged conferences in the SE Jurisdiction contained 2,931,000 members, the SC Jurisdiction 1,957,000. Only in the 1980s have they seriously turned to other matters.

See also articles on METHODIST EPISCOPAL CHURCH, SOUTH; WESLEYAN TRADITION.

Bibliography. Emory S. Bucke, ed., *History of American Methodism*, 3 vols.; Hunter D. Farish, *The Circuit Rider Dismounts: A Social History of Southern Methodism, 1865-1900*; Frederick A. Norwood, *The Story of American Methodism*; Robert W. Sledge, *Hands on the Ark: The Struggle for Change in the Methodist Episcopal Church, South, 1914-1939*.

A. V. HUFF, JR.
FURMAN UNIVERSITY

METHODIST EPISCOPAL CHURCH: *See* ASBURY, FRANCIS; CHRISTMAS CONFERENCE; COKE, THOMAS; LOVELY LANE METHODIST CHURCH; METHODIST CHURCH, THE; METHODIST EPISCOPAL CHURCH, SOUTH.

METHODIST EPISCOPAL CHURCH, SOUTH. The Methodist movement began in the South between 1760 and 1766 with the work of Robert Strawbridge in Maryland. By 1783, 89 percent of American Methodists lived in the South. During the GREAT REVIVAL after 1800 Methodism began to grow dramatically.

At its beginning American Methodism remained faithful to the antislavery teachings of John Wesley. In 1808, however, the Southern Annual Conferences secured the right to judge whether church members could hold slaves. When abolitionists pressed for a return to the earlier practice, Southern leaders opposed them and established missions to slaves. A confrontation occurred during the General Conference of 1844 when Bishop JAMES O. ANDREW of Georgia, a slaveholder through marriage, was ordered to "desist from the exercise of [his] office so long as this impediment remains." A Plan of Separation provided for the division of the church into two sectional denominations.

On 1 May 1845, delegates from 15 annual conferences (Kentucky, Missouri, Holston, Tennessee, North Carolina, Memphis, Arkansas, Virginia, Mississippi, Texas, Alabama, Georgia, South Carolina, Florida, Indian Mission) met in Louisville KY and established the ME Church, South. The first General Conference met in Petersburg VA in 1846. Bitterness ensued over ownership of the Book Concern and rivalry took root in the border states. Mission churches were established in Kansas, New Mexico, California, and foreign missions begun in China. Leaders began to distinguish between Northern Methodism (a "political" church) and Southern Methodism (with a "strictly Scriptural mission"). In 1861 the church numbered 750,000, including 208,000 blacks.

Southern Methodism embraced the Confederacy and sent hundreds of chaplains and missionaries to the armies; Bible and tract societies provided the region with literature. But at the Civil War's end, the church lay in disarray. Its leaders were embittered by Reconstruction and the ecclesiastical imperialism of the Methodist Episcopal Church (Northern). By 1866 the church had lost 250,000 members; black membership dropped to 70,000. The 1866 General Conference began rebuilding by granting lay representation in Annual Conferences and establishing District Conferences as regional rallying points within conferences. Most black members joined all-black denominations or churches.

In 1869 membership equalled its prewar numbers; by 1900 it was 1,412,000. Schools and colleges reopened, and in 1873 Vanderbilt became the church's central university. In 1878 the Woman's Missionary Society began to promote missions. REVIVALISM was the major tool of evangelism, and "worldly amusements," such as gambling and dancing occupied the social conscience of many churchmen. In the 1880s the HOLINESS MOVEMENT attracted some; they founded Asbury College in Kentucky. However,

FUNDAMENTALISM made little headway in the theologically conservative Southern church.

Layman Henry Grady promoted the "New South," blessed by later Bishop ATTICUS G. HAYGOOD in *Our Brother in Black*. In 1886 church women widened the social witness of the denomination by establishing the Woman's Home Missionary Society, which developed city missions and settlement work. In 1914 the General Conference adopted the Social Creed. Bishop JAMES CANNON JR. was in the forefront of the crusade for prohibition. But social activism was strongly opposed by many, including the influential Bishop Warren A. Candler of Georgia, who advised: "Let politics alone!"

In 1914 the church withdrew support from Vanderbilt after a bitter controversy and established two universities—Southern Methodist in Dallas and Emory in Atlanta. In 1924, James B. Duke established Duke University in Durham NC with the largest gift ever made to church higher education. Total church membership in 1925 reached 2,478,623.

Efforts at reunion with the ME Church began in 1869 with exchanges of fraternal delegates, first among bishops, then in General Conferences. In 1876 a joint commission met at Cape May NJ. In the 1890s a Commission on Federation was joined by the Methodist Protestant Church. Major roadblocks to union were the desires of the Southerners to maintain regional identity and racial segregation in a new structure. A Plan of Union proposed five regional jurisdictions and a Central Jurisdiction for blacks. After several unsuccessful efforts, the plan was adopted. On 10 May 1939, the ME Church, South, became part of the reunited Methodist Church.

See also articles on METHODIST CHURCH, THE; WESLEYAN TRADITION.

Bibliography. Emory S. Bucke, ed., *History of American Methodism*, 3 vols.; Hunter D. Farish, *The Circuit Rider Dismounts: A Social History of Southern Methodism, 1865-1900*; John P. McDowell, *The Social Gospel in the South: The Woman's Home Mission Movement in the Methodist Episcopal Church, South, 1886-1939*.

A. V. HUFF, JR.
FURMAN UNIVERSITY

MIDWAY CHURCH (LIBERTY COUNTY, GEORGIA). Few Georgia churches can claim the importance of the Midway Church. Located halfway between Darien and Savannah, the church originated as a mission of the Congregational Church in the 18th century. After initial settlement in Dorchester MA, the congregation migrated to Dorchester SC in 1695. A part of the congregation moved to Georgia and took residence in St. John's Parish (Liberty County) in 1752. White Congregationalists brought a slave culture with them and the church became the center of a wealthy rice plantation district.

Midway was the focus of revolutionary ferment along the Georgia coast. The church took the lead in sending representatives—including Button Gwinnett and Lyman Hall—north to argue for independence. In 1792, members built the existing white frame structure. There in the 1830s, the pastorate of the Rev. CHARLES COLCOCK JONES was noted throughout the South for its attention to formal Christian services for slaves. Although slaves were segregated in the balcony, blacks and whites worshiped together through the war years. War-related devastation in the county led to the dispersal of white church members and the Midway Church became a center of black Protestantism in 1868. For a time black Presbyterians and black Congregationalists sponsored by the AMERICAN MISSIONARY ASSOCIATION shared the church. In 1874, the Congregationalists built their own church at nearby Golding's Grove. The black Presbyterians continued to use Midway until the 1890s. In 1889 black Protestants from the church area joined in a summer-long millenarian revival known as the Christ Craze. Although in disrepair in the early twentieth century, the church has since been restored. Regular meetings of the Midway Society are held at the church.

Bibliography. Thomas F. Armstrong, "The Christ Craze of 1889," *Southern Communities in the Nineteenth Century,* Vernon Burton and Robert McMath, eds.; George Rogers and Frank Saunders, "The American Missionary Association in Liberty County, Georgia: An Invasion of Light and Love," *Georgia Historical Quarterly* 62 (Winter 1978): 306-15; James Stacy, *History of the Midway Congregational Church, Liberty County, Georgia.*

THOMAS F. ARMSTRONG
GEORGIA COLLEGE

MIGRATION, SOUTHWARD (1700-1830).

The colonial South was the site of one of two great demographic upheavals in American history. During the half century prior to the Revolution nearly a million people—the majority Scottish or German rather than English—traveled up the Shenandoah Valley, some settling there and many others coming farther south into the Carolina Piedmont and Georgia backcountry. While the majority of these settlers came from Pennsylvania, a significant minority originated in the Chesapeake and a smaller number entered the colonies as immigrants at Southern ports like Wilmington (especially the highland Scots who settled the upper Cape Fear Valley of North Carolina) and Charles Town and Savannah (for example, the German-speaking SALZBURGERS on the Georgia frontier).

Along with its Northern counterpart—the movement of some 250,000 New Englanders up the Connecticut River Valley into the northern New England frontier—this migration had a profound impact on the development of American society in the late eighteenth and early nineteenth centuries. Both served as immediate preludes to the 19th-century settlement of the American hinterland: New England Yankees stamping western New York, the Western Reserve, and much of the Northwest territory with antislavery politics, millenarian expectation; and small-town business enterprise and farmers and planters carrying into the new Southwest a peculiarly Southern culture of familial clannishness, touchy honor, volatile self-assertiveness, decentralized cultural authority, and racial apprehension.

Indeed, the late eighteenth-century settlement of the Southern backcountry and the expansion of Southern agriculture into the trans-Appalachian West during the half century following the Revolution were coterminous with the creation of the South as a self-conscious region. As historians reconstruct the emergence of sectional awareness, the interaction of low-country planters and backcountry farmers in post-Revolutionary politics was the crux of a distinctively Southern way of life. Though initially estranged, the two subregions rapidly coalesced. An elite, usually composed of Presbyterian lawyers, politicians, and landowners, emerged by the time of the Revolution with the best land, with a network of schools and colleges linked informally to the College of New Jersey at Princeton, and with an ideology of duty, diligence, and principled opportunism. That elite then could deal with the older, Episcopalian, low-country planter elite that had dominated the coastal society since the late seventeenth century. Especially in South Carolina the two elites intermarried and coalesced in the legislature. The creation of plantations and the purchase of large numbers of slaves in the backcountry served to knit together the two regions. Slavery indeed became the key to regional consciousness. From the South Carolina low country with its black majority to the mountain communities like Burke County NC where less than five percent of the population was black, a flourishing domestic slave trade and a conviction that slavery was an essential precondition to the preservation of order gave slaveowners at every level of the white social order a common stake in the preservation of the peculiar institution.

The Louisiana Purchase and the securing of an American port at New Orleans, coupled with population pressures within the backcountry and a burgeoning world demand for cotton, then combined to trigger the settlement of the new Southwest during the early nineteenth century—especially between 1815 and 1830. The immense fertility of the belt of land in Alabama and Mississippi known as "the black belt" enabled upstart land speculators and frontier farmers to amass immense wealth in cotton production and to create a kind of hothouse variety of plantation culture in which gambling, aristocratic living, and political competition attained a frenzied level of intensity, heightening and expanding proclivities inherent and potential in the older cultures of the backcountry and the colonial aristocracy.

At every point in the process of population movement and regional transformation, religion played a crucial role in the formation of culture and in the people's perception of experience. During the colonial period the creation of a moral order in many ways preceded the attainment of political order. People moved in groups tied together by common church affiliation: Pennsylvania English-stock QUAKERS, Scotch-Irish PRESBYTERIANS, Dunkers (CHURCH OF THE BRETHREN), MORAVIANS, German Reformed and LUTHERANS, SEPARATE BAPTISTS from Connecticut, and after 1784, Methodists. The fertility and cheapness of the land attracted them, but even more magnetizing was its place in their imaginations as a New Canaan where their children could live in harmony with others and PIETY toward God impelled them to enter and tame a new land. When contracting land scales, rising taxes, and parasitic officeholders from the low country in the 1760s provoked the Regulator uprising of 1770, observers on both sides of the uprising saw it in religious terms: with the Baptists in the vanguard of the movement, Presbyterians trying to achieve political compromise, and Quakers torn between their grievances against the colonial government and their commitment to political quietism. Herman Husband, a former Quaker and articulator of Regulator grievances, voiced a stark, primitive Christian radicalism and millenarianism. Similarly, in South Carolina the Regulators in the 1760s were led by Presbyterian landowners who took the law into their own hands when the assembly in Charles Town proved unable and unwilling to create the machinery of law and order in the backcountry.

During the post-Revolutionary and early national periods, the use of circuit riders by the Methodists and the proliferation of Baptist associations accompanied and fostered a decentralized society in which local churches, elites, and county courthouse officials became arbiters of social behavior. Accordingly, the South developed what Bertram Wyatt-Brown calls "an ascriptive culture" in which people carried with them a set of moral and social credentials—family name and connections, church membership, body language, verbal manner and style, poise and demeanor—that signified virtue and responsibility. Increasingly concerned with the struggle between the forces of darkness and light, initially divided over the issue of slavery and then compelled by lay pressure to acquiesce in a proslavery ideology, and serving as the principal institution in a rural rudimentary cultural setting, Protestant churches played a crucial role in giving rootedness to the children of the great southwestward and westward migrations of the late colonial and early national epochs.

See also articles on GEOGRAPHY; MIGRATION, WESTWARD (1750-1900); WELSH INFLUENCE.

Bibliography. Richard J. Hooker, ed., *The Carolina Backcountry on the Eve of the Revolution: The Journal and other Writings of Charles Woodmason, Anglican Itinerant*; Robert D. Mitchell, *Commercialism and Frontier: Perspectives on the Early Shenandoah Valley*; Edward W. Phifer, "Slavery in Microcosm: Burke County, North Carolina," *Journal of Southern History* 28 (May 1962): 137-60; Robert W. Ramsey, *Carolina Cradle: Settlement of the Northwest Carolina Frontier, 1747-1762*; Bertram Wyatt-Brown, "The Ideal Typology and Antebellum Southern History: A Testing of a New Hypothesis," *Societas* 5 (Winter 1975): 1-29.

ROBERT M. CALHOON
UNIVERSITY OF NORTH CAROLINA
AT GREENSBORO

MIGRATION, WESTWARD (1750-1900). The pace of frontier settlement in the South increased rapidly with the passage of time. After nearly a century of occupation, colonists in 1700 still were huddled close to the Tidewater. Fifty years later they had advanced to the Appalachian mountains on a broad front, and in 50 more, despite the disruptions of two wars, they were deep into Kentucky and Tennessee. Another half century saw the frontier virtually extinguished.

Chesapeake Bay was the focus of early English settlement activity. Tobacco, the economic underpinning of the region, grew well and was easily exported through numerous excellent harbors. Growers desired wharves of their own and, as a result, settlement expansion was directed around the bay rather than westward. For about 200 miles south of Virginia, offshore sandbars and shallow harbors limited activities in the Carolina Grant. A small group on Albemarle Sound were forced into a largely self-sufficient existence by these conditions. South of the sandbars, colonies existed on the lower Cape Fear River and at Charles Town (Charleston) after 1670. Farthest south, in Spanish Florida, lay ST. AUGUSTINE, founded in 1565 but possessing only a few hundred people.

Rates of expansion westward varied tremendously from the various tidewater beachheads. Virginians and Marylanders pushed entirely across the Piedmont and into the Shenandoah Valley by 1740. Expansion was checked occasionally by Indian raids, but good tobacco markets and active land speculation generally favored advance. After 1730 people drifting south from Pennsylvania in search of cheaper land increased the pace of settlement. The Pennsylvania stream soon filled the Shenandoah Valley and began to spread into the unoccupied North Carolina Piedmont.

Settlement advance in South Carolina and Georgia was only moderate. Attempts to move due westward brought contact with the large Creek and Choctaw nations. Spanish and French outposts were nearby as well, and with alliances constantly shifting among these groups, everyone

ventured to extend their frontiers only with caution. Georgia, for example, was established in large part to be a buffer colony between South Carolina and the Spanish, and was peopled with English debtors and unsuspecting immigrants from all over Europe. South Carolina used similar buffer tactics on its own frontier, bringing to the colony groups of Scotch-Irish Presbyterians, Welsh Baptists, German Lutherans, and others.

By 1750 the Southern colonies were much more diverse religiously than they had been a half century earlier. The Anglican church still dominated, but in Georgia non-English settlers outnumbered the English, and all the other colonies had significant religious minorities. English Catholics were numerous in eastern Maryland because of early religious tolerance there. French HUGUENOTS constituted perhaps one-sixth of South Carolina's population in 1700 and the frontier colonies mentioned above greatly augmented the diversity. The largest contributors to the non-Anglican population of the South were German and Scotch-Irish groups, plus English Quakers, all of whom filtered south from Pennsylvania. These peoples dominated western Maryland, comprised two-thirds of the population in Virginia's Shenandoah Valley, and were the principal groups settling the North Carolina Piedmont. In addition, French Catholic settlers at this time were occupying the Mississippi River levees from New Orleans to Baton Rouge, creating additional diversity for the future United States. Slavery added a further dimension, especially in the Chesapeake and South Carolina coastal areas.

Land speculation had been so lucrative for Virginians in the 1730s and 1740s that by midcentury strong pressure existed to open lands across the Appalachian divide. The frontier turmoil of the French and Indian War curtailed such activity until 1763, but a boom developed immediately after the Treaty of Paris was signed. The French threat in the Ohio Valley was eliminated and considerable Cherokee land was opened for settlement, a punishment for this tribe's alliance with the French. The Potomac route all the way to Pittsburgh was occupied in the early 1760s; by 1768, when a treaty officially opened Indian lands south and east of the Ohio River, numerous settlements existed in eastern Tennessee and the Kanawha Valley. Land speculators became active in the Bluegrass Basin of Kentucky by 1770, soon after Daniel Boone had laid out a connecting route from Cumberland Gap. The Revolutionary War halted the surge into the interior for a few years, but activity resumed in 1779. North Carolina settlers occupied the rich Nashville Basin and Kentucky reportedly had 20,000 residents by the fall of 1780. The Piedmont of the Carolinas filled at this time as well, but there was little advance by Georgians into Creek lands.

The large populations of Virginia, Maryland, and eastern Pennsylvania partially explain the early pattern of trans-Appalachian expansion. The easiest routes from all three places focused on the Potomac River and Cumberland Gap region. Land speculation among Virginians was another factor. Political pressure and promotion from this source helped to direct attention to Kentucky. Finally, Indian problems were minimal in this area. Kentucky was central to no powerful group, whereas to both the north and the south lay homelands of sophisticated tribes.

Between 1790 and the War of 1812 pioneers consolidated settlements already founded on the western fringes. North Carolina had opened all of Tennessee for settlement at low prices in 1783, before pressure mounted to cede its western lands to the new national government. The region boomed. After the Louisiana Purchase in 1803 the Kentucky-Tennessee tongue of settlement extended itself even farther west, into Missouri. The lures were lead mines and trading possibilities inherent at the mouths of the Ohio and Missouri rivers.

The frontier in the lowland South barely moved at all during this time period. Georgians advanced westward a bit to the Oconee River after the Creeks ceded this territory in 1790, but no one placed real pressure on the Indian groups. Cheap, Indian-free land existed in nearby Tennessee, and Spain continued to control the entire Gulf coast eastward of the Mississippi River. This control restricted American access to Mississippi Territory. The major rivers, the routes any exports from the new territory logically would take, all flowed south into Spanish soil. By 1810 Mississippi Territory and western Georgia constituted an empty "island," unoccupied by Euro-Americans.

Southerners saw the War of 1812 as a boon to the frontier. Farmers hoped victory would open European markets for their products and many people observed that, because Spain was allied with England, victory might include the American occupation of the Spanish Gulf coast. This occupation was now highly desirable because Southerners were beginning to realize the economic consequences of Eli Whitney's cotton gin. Plantations had been well established on the Piedmont by 1800; now growers were eager to push westward into Mississippi territory.

The war produced the results cotton growers had expected. West Florida was seized in 1813 and the easternmost of the major Indian groups, the Creeks, conveniently provided land-hungry Americans with an excuse for attack by siding with the British. Victories over the Creeks were easy, showing how vulnerable the dissension-ridden tribes were. Between 1816 and 1821 the government forced nearly all Indian groups to cede lands, but the rapid rate at which the newly opened tracts were settled quickly prompted a policy of complete Indian removal. By 1830 the relocation process beyond the Mississippi River was well underway. The last of the Creek and Cherokee lands along the Georgia-Alabama border were being occupied at this time as were the remnant Choctaw and Chickasaw holdings in northern Mississippi.

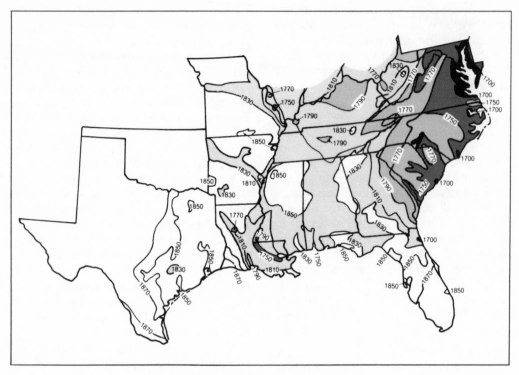

The Expansion of the Settlement Frontier

A land boom continued across the South in the 1830s. Planters and their slaves occupied the best lands: the Piedmont, the Alabama "black belt" and, after levee construction in the 1840s, the Mississippi floodplains. Herdsmen and small farmers settled elsewhere, passing over only large sections of the coastal zone, including most of Florida. The Gulf coast was too rainy to produce cotton reliably and the soils often were poor. Even as one group of Southerners occupied the last of the Indian lands in Mississippi and Alabama another group advanced along a broad front into trans-Mississippi territories. From earlier settlements on the Missouri, Arkansas, Ouachita, and Red Rivers they moved by 1850 into all but the roughest of the upland areas.

Indians in Missouri and Arkansas had been moved out prior to Euro-American expansion, so the settlement process there was generally regular, rapid, and without incident. Indians became a factor again after 1840, however, as the "per-

manent" Indian Territory created a decade earlier in present-day OKLAHOMA and Kansas blocked further westward movement. Restless upland Southerners trekked to the southwest, joining the cotton growers in a joint advance on Texas, the only remaining Southern frontier.

Americans actually had begun settlement in TEXAS in 1820, when the region was Mexican territory. Mexico encouraged this activity, reasoning that colonization might be the best way to hold its claim. As the pace of American immigration quickened, Mexico changed its policies. Tensions eventually led to Texas independence in 1836 and then to American annexation. Generous land policies encouraged many to come, including colonies of German and Slavic peoples.

Nearly all the South had passed through the frontier stage by 1850. The area now known as Oklahoma had no official white settlers, but through the presence there of Cherokee, Creek, Choctaw, and other Southeastern tribes, this area too was Southern in many senses. Extreme southern Florida remained unsettled until after 1900.

See also articles on GEOGRAPHY; MIGRATION, SOUTHWARD (1700-1830).

Bibliography. Thomas P. Abernethy, *The Formative Period in Alabama, 1815-1828;* Harriette S. Arnow, *Seedtime on the Cumberland;* Ray A. Billington, *Westward Expansion: A History of the American Frontier;* Avery O. Craven, *Soil Exhaustion as a Factor in the Agricultural History of Virginia and Maryland, 1606-1860;* Michael F. Doran, "The Origins of Culture Areas in Oklahoma, 1830-1900," unpublished Ph.D. dissertation, University of Oregon, 1974; Herman R. Friis, "A Series of Population Dot Maps of the Colonies and the United States, 1625-1790," *Geographical Review* 30 (July 1940): 463; Lewis C. Gray, *History of Agriculture in the Southern United States to 1860,* 2 vols.; Sam B. Hilliard, "Indian Land Cessions," Association of American Geographers *Annals* 62 (June 1972): map supplement 16; Terry G. Jordan, "The Imprint of the Upper and Lower South on Mid-Nineteenth-Century Texas," Association of American Geographers *Annals* 57 (December 1967): 667; William O. Lynch, "The Westward Flow of Southern Colonists before 1861," *Journal of Southern History* 9 (August 1943): 303; Harry R. Merrens, *Colonial North Carolina in the Eighteenth Century;* Frank L. Owsley, "The Pattern of Migration and Settlement on the Southern Frontier," *Journal of Southern History* 11 (May 1945): 147; W. Stitt Robinson, *The Southern Colonial Frontier, 1607-1763;* Randall D. Sale and Edwin D. Karn, *American Expansion: A Book of Maps;* James R. Shortridge, "The Expansion of the Settlement Frontier in Missouri," *Missouri Historical Review* 75 (October 1980): 64; Robert B. Walz, "Migration into Arkansas, 1820-1880: Incentives and Means of Travel," *Arkansas Historical Quarterly* 17 (Winter 1958): 309; Wilbur Zelinsky, "An Isochronic Map of Georgia Settlement, 1750-1850," *Georgia Historical Quarterly* 35 (September 1951): 191.

JAMES R. SHORTRIDGE
UNIVERSITY OF KANSAS
ROGER STUMP
STATE UNIVERSITY OF NEW YORK
AT ALBANY

MILES, JAMES WARLEY (1818-1875), Episcopal philosopher, was born on a plantation near Orangeburg SC, and educated at Willington Academy, South Carolina College, and General Theological Seminary. After brief service in South Carolina parishes, he joined Horatio Southgate's Episcopal mission to Constantinople in 1843 where he labored for four years. Returning to Charleston, he published his most important work, *Philosophic Theology,* while serving interim parish appointments. Elected professor of the history of philosophy and Greek literature at the College of Charleston in 1850,

Miles published some 40 public addresses and scholarly articles as pamphlets and also wrote for the *Southern Quarterly Review,* the *College of Charleston Magazine,* and *Russell's Magazine.*

Miles was a philosophical idealist and theological liberal who wrote under the influence of Schleiermacher's followers of the mediating school in German theology and Coleridge's disciples among the English broad churchmen. An accomplished linguist, he exploited contemporary biblical criticism in his effort to justify the racial subordination in the South's peculiar institution. After study in Europe from 1854 to 1856, Miles returned as a librarian to the College of Charleston, where except for a brief period of exile from war-torn Charleston, he remained until resigning in 1871.

Bibliography. E. Brooks Holifield, *The Gentlemen Theologians: American Theology in Southern Culture, 1795-1865;* Ralph E. Luker, "God, Man and the World of James Warley Miles, Charleston's Transcendentalist," *Historical Magazine of the Protestant Episcopal Church* 39 (June 1970): 101-106; James Warley Miles, *Philosophic Theology; or, Ultimate Ground of All Religious Belief Based on Reason.*

RALPH E. LUKER
VIRGINIA POLYTECHNIC INSTITUTE
AND STATE UNIVERSITY

MILLENNIALISM. This movement, which is based on Christian doctrine, derives from the belief that history will culminate in a golden age. Although comparable ideas have existed outside Christianity, the term itself comes from Rev. 20, which predicts a thousand years (hence "millennium") of felicity at the end of time. Among Christians, the millennial era has been associated with the Second Coming, an event generally expected to occur before the millennium (premillennialism) or immediately thereafter (postmillennialism). Because of the ambiguity of this symbolism, believers have conceived the millennium in various ways—some stressing its continuity with the present, others emphasizing its cataclysmic intrusion into history, and many drawing elements from both visions.

Millennial symbols have played a major role in American thought. They helped to form the notion of the United States as the Redeemer Nation, to spawn sectarian movements, to inspire evangelical crusades and revivals, and to shape the emerging FUNDAMENTALISM of the late nineteenth and early twentieth centuries. Although millennialism in the South has not received the attention it merits, enough research has been done to suggest that it has occupied there a similarly important place and has performed equally diverse functions. Its social uses have included sanctification of the status quo, promotion of melioristic reform, and radical rejection of the existing order.

The revivals around 1800 marked the first major upsurge of millennialism in the South. Widespread conversions convinced many that the Kingdom of God on earth was at hand. A few sectarians like Richard McNemar, whose spiritual odyssey carried him from Presbyterianism to the Shaker faith, concluded that Christ had already come and the millennium had commenced. Some anticipated an imminent physical return of Christ; but like most Northerners, the majority of antebellum Southern clergymen appear to have been postmillennialists who expected a progressive evangelical conquest of the world rather than an early Second Coming. Southern postmillennialism, however, differed from its Northern counterpart in one important particular. Whereas the latter was frequently allied with a free-labor capitalism, the former increasingly made a virtue of slavery. Especially among Presbyterians, many ministers envisioned the gradual expansion throughout the world of a Christian civilization that included slavery. The Civil War deepened these contrasting, but in some respects strikingly similar, senses of mission. Both sides viewed their respective nations as the embodiment of the ideal millennial order, and each portrayed the conflict as an apocalyptic contest between good and evil.

After the Civil War, millennialism appeared in several guises. Populists in the 1890s sometimes employed the image of millennial perfection as a critique of the existing social order and as an incentive to its renovation. While this motif constituted only a minor theme in Populism, it did represent one of the few attempts in Southern religion to harness eschatological symbols to radical social reform. More common in postwar thought was a new gradualist postmillennialism that, shorn of its explicit proslavery philosophy though not of its nostalgia for the LOST CAUSE, served as a religious gloss to the New South ideology. The postbellum period also brought the growth of a strident premillennialism, frequently in dispensational form. Premised upon biblical inerrancy and literalism, dispensationalism pronounced this age hopelessly corrupt, awaited the early return of Christ, and in most of its variants promised true believers removal from earth (THE RAPTURE) before the tribulations of the last days. This eschatology tapped Southern disillusionment over Confederate defeat but also drew on sentiments shared with conservatives elsewhere: biblicism, distrust of liberal theology, and anxiety about the direction of modern civilization.

Although historians have viewed dispensationalism as a largely Northern phenomenon in its early stages, Southerners played an important role in its dissemination. James H. Brookes, a St. Louis minister, was an early dispensational leader; and Cyrus I. Scofield, adopted son of Tennessee and former Confederate soldier, edited the 1909 Reference Bible that bears his name and is still the indispensable textbook of the movement. Since 1924, Dallas Theological Seminary in Texas has been a major purveyor of the dispensational viewpoint. Likewise, premillennial views gained currency among various holiness and later Pentecostal groups that flourished in the South after the 1880s, especially in the subcultures of Appalachia, the Piedmont, and the Ozark Plateau.

Millennialism in black religion was complex. Under the slave regime, the spirituals promised deliverance and a final judgment when the last would be first. This rhetoric hovered in a realm of ambiguity between this-worldly and otherworldly fulfillment. Although most slaves appear to have adopted a premillennial quietism, awaiting deliverance from the hand of God, their millennial symbols always possessed the latent possibility of other interpretations. Thus the black preacher Nat Turner, inspired by an apocalyptic vision of "white spirits and black spirits engaged in battle" while "blood flowed in streams," launched the most famous American slave insurrection in 1831; and the freedmen at the close of the Civil War heralded emancipation as the long-awaited Day of Jubilee. Similarly, a black exodus to Kansas in 1879 took on the character of a folk migration to a millennial kingdom.

Albeit in somewhat secularized form, the most complete synthesis of Southern millennialism's disparate strands was perhaps achieved in the utterances of MARTIN LUTHER KING, JR. He converted a quasieschatological vision of transcendent justice and moral judgment into an effective instrument of social reform. Moreover, he successfully fused the best ideals of the white majority, long accustomed to viewing its institutions as virtually the polity of the millennium, with the yearning of his own people for deliverance.

See also articles on HOLINESS MOVEMENT; PENTECOSTALISM.

Bibliography. John B. Boles, *The Great Revival, 1787-1805*; Jack P. Maddex, Jr., "Proslavery Millennialism: Social Eschatology in Antebellum Southern Calvinism," *American Quarterly* 31 (Spring 1979): 46-62; George M. Marsden, *Fundamentalism and American Culture*; Donald Mathews, *Religion in the Old South*; Nell Irvin Painter, "Millenarian Aspects of the Exodus to Kansas of 1879," *Journal of Social History* 9 (Spring 1976): 331-38; Bruce Palmer, *"Man Over Money": The Southern Populist Critique of American Capitalism*; Albert J. Raboteau, *Slave Religion*; Charles Reagan Wilson, *Baptized in Blood: The Religion of the Lost Cause, 1865-1920*.

JAMES H. MOORHEAD
NORTH CAROLINA STATE UNIVERSITY

MILLER, ROBERT JOHNSTON

(1758-1834), early liturgical Protestant leader, was first a Methodist itinerant, then an Episcopalian ordained by and serving North Carolina Lutherans, and finally an Episcopal priest. Miller exemplified the affinity that liturgical churches had for one another and the intense yearning of these bodies to bring spiritual suasion to isolated rural settlers.

Born and reared in Scotland in a Scottish Episcopal family, he emigrated to Massachusetts in 1774, served in the Continental Army, and was mustered out in Virginia after the Battle of Yorktown. He became a Methodist itinerant and was assigned to the Tar River Circuit, which included western North Carolina, but left the Methodists in 1784. Disheartened by the failure of an attempt to organize an Episcopal diocese in North Carolina in 1793-1794, he sought and secured ordination by five North Carolina Lutheran pastors in 1794—not as a Lutheran but as an Episcopalian. Nevertheless, he was among the founders, and was first secretary of the North Carolina Lutheran Synod in 1803; made extensive missionary journeys to South Carolina and Virginia in 1811 and 1813; and served Lutheran parishes at Troutman and Dutchman's Creek from 1815-1821 as well as the Episcopal church in White Haven NC. Between 1813 and 1821, he explored the possibilities of fraternal union between Lutherans and Episcopalians in the state. In 1821 he left the Lutherans to affiliate with the recently formed Episcopal Diocese of North Carolina. Throughout the 1820s Bishop JOHN STARK RAVENSCROFT sought Miller's support for more aggressive competition with other denominations, especially Presbyterians, but Miller apparently expressed some discomfiture with the bishop's belligerence. Miller's skill as a catechist, reflecting his Lutheran and Episcopal experience, permeated his *Introduction to the Knowledge of the Christian Religion* (1799).

See also articles on ECUMENISM; LUTHERAN CHURCH.

Bibliography. George MacLaren Brydon, "The Ministry of the Rev. Robert Johnston Miller in North Carolina," unpublished MS in George M. Brydon Papers, Virginia Historical Society, Richmond; Robert M. Calhoon, "Lutheranism in Early Southern Culture," *"A Truly Efficient School of Theology": The Lutheran Theological Southern Seminary in Historical Context, 1830-1980,* ed. by H. G. Anderson and R. M. Calhoon; John B. Weaver, "Robert Johnston Miller," *Dictionary of North Carolina Biography,* ed. William S. Powell.

ROBERT M. CALHOON
UNIVERSITY OF NORTH CAROLINA
AT GREENSBORO

MINISTER. In Latin the word "minister" means an attendant or servant, a doer of the little things, as opposed to the magistrate who exercises authority. The minister is thus under the orders of another, attending the wants and needs of others.

As a general designation for any clergyman in church circles, it is used especially in nonepiscopal bodies. Contrary to theoretical Protestant understandings of the ministry of the whole people of God, the title is used most often as a professional designation, so that one can say that one's profession is "minister"—he or she is "in the ministry"—and most people will understand what is meant.

Commonly in the South, this is an "uptown" designation for the clergy. It has about it the sound of a fine organ, the color of stained glass, the implication of well-constructed and illustrated sermons in a quiet, reserved setting. A clergyman (or woman) who is referred to as a minister has probably graduated from seminary, may belong to a good civic club in the town, and is expected to play a role in the community as a part of the established leadership, in addition to congregational and denominational duties.

WILLIAM C. SMITH, JR.
GREENSBORO, NORTH CAROLINA

MISSION TO SLAVES. This instrument for the Christianization of slaves was an ideal of Southern white Protestantism that was institutionalized in various ways. Before the Revolutionary period, the SOCIETY FOR THE PROPAGATION OF THE GOSPEL of the Church of England attempted to proselytize slaves with only modest results.

Through the explosive and sporadic Baptist-Methodist revivals of the 1760s and 1790s, however, blacks came into evangelical churches in impressive numbers; black Methodists in coastal South Carolina on occasion outnumbered white coreligionists by a ratio of 10 to 1. There was even a handful of independent black Baptist churches in the South by 1800, and by 1821 autonomous black Methodist churches had been established in Baltimore and Charleston. Most converted blacks, though, were in congregations or societies linked in some way—sometimes only nominally—with biracial churches managed by whites.

By the 1830s, prominent whites began to lobby churches for special missions to reach blacks left unaffected by the moral-religious life of local churches. There were several reasons for this new impetus, but the most obvious one was political. In 1822 and 1831 black insurrectionaries had emerged from the unsupervised religious life of a few Afro-American communities. Black revolution could be linked directly with increased antislavery activity in the North, where a new generation of reformers was beginning to reaffirm the earlier, Revolutionary critique of slavery, insisting that Christian responsibility left believers with no alternative but to renounce slaveholding and to abolish slavery.

Since Southern religious leaders could not surrender to Yankees their definition of whites' moral responsibilities, they attempted to develop widespread support for special missions to slaves. Conversion and not liberty was the essence of Christian ethics. Most successful in establishing specific missions were the South Carolina conference of the Methodist Episcopal Church under the leadership of WILLIAM CAPERS and a few county missionary societies such as that sponsored by an evangelical coalition in Liberty County GA under the aegis of CHARLES COLCOCK JONES SR., a wealthy minister-planter educated at Princeton. Capers and Jones were the chief publicists for the missionary ideal.

Despite their efforts and those of idealists very much like them, the mission was not very successful, affecting only a few thousand slaves. Most Christian blacks belonged to local churches or societies rather than to the mission itself.

The purpose of missions was threefold. First of all, they were to bond master and slave into a religious unity. Through ritualistic acknowledgment of a common condition with mutual respect and obligations, Christians could theoretically bridge the chasm between white and black. Second, in attempting to teach those suffering in ignorance and sin about the redemptive personal balm of a Christian faith, the missions were to prevent the politicization of the black community and to teach young blacks a world view that could legitimize white hegemony. The goal of that program would have been the internalization of an evangelical, individualistic self-discipline, emphasizing sexual restraint, respect for property, deference and obedience to authority, and personal honesty. For a few idealists such as Jones, a third goal was the development of such a superhuman moral discipline among blacks designed to elicit from masters an acknowledgment of the slaves' humanity that could, in turn, help to loosen and eventually to corrode completely the chains of slavery. Such romanticism led Southern white apologists after the Civil War to interpret the mission as the white South's finest effort on behalf of slaves. If so, it was not nearly so effective in converting blacks as Afro-American ministers preaching a gospel of hope, love, and justice that transformed the slaves' suffering not into the legitimization of slavery, but a triumphant juxtaposition of judgment and liberty.

See also article on BLACK RELIGION.

Bibliography. Charles Colcock Jones, *The Religious Instruction of the Negroes in the United States*; D. G. Mathews, "Charles Colcock Jones and the Southern Evangelical Crusade to Form a Biracial Community," *Journal of Southern History* 40 (August 1975): 299-320; *Slavery and Methodism.*

DONALD G. MATHEWS
UNIVERSITY OF NORTH CAROLINA
AT CHAPEL HILL

MISSISSIPPI. Religious folks in the community shunned him. After all, everybody knew of his fondness for whiskey, the many hours he spent swapping tall tales around checker games on the town square, and his inability to hold down a steady job. But when Bill Faulkner won the Nobel Prize, he became interpreter by default of Mississippi culture—including religion. When a University of Virginia student asked him if the tall convict in *Old Man* believed in God, Faulkner must have smiled quizzically as he replied, "His background would be the bucolic, provincial, Southern Baptist; and it may be a debatable question whether that sort of Baptist believes in God or not."

A bucolic, provincial Southern Baptist, committing the fallacy of generalizing from the particular, might roundly criticize WILLIAM FAULKNER for such an unorthodox statement; but few knowledgeable persons would challenge Faulkner's understanding and use of Mississippi religion in his works. Faulkner himself was well aware of the role religion had on his writing. Replying to another Virginia inquisitor, he stated, "Remember, the writer must write out of his background. He must write out of what he knows and the Christian legend is part of any Christian's background, especially the background of a country boy, a Southern country boy." Academicians often lament that Southern Christianity is more Southern than Christian. But just as religion permeates the narrative and symbols of William Faulkner and WALKER PERCY, so it permeates the lives and touchstones of black and white Mississippians. Mississippi culture and religion have been so interwoven that an effort to extract the thread of religion from the fabric cannot avoid incompleteness and falsification of social reality. Even so the effort must be undertaken.

An unstated assumption in Faulkner's Virginia dialogue was that whenever a people search for meaning in life, religion becomes a part of, often directs, that search. Therefore, religion in Mississippi began with the first human beings to inhabit the area, the American Indians. Admittedly, little is known of their culture. The writings of archaeologists and anthropologists indicate that the Mississippi Indian groups, especially the Muskogean-speaking peoples, were a part of what is known as the Southern Ceremonial Complex. The complex consisted of a set of natural and abstract symbols based on an understanding of nature. In their worship, the sun, the Great Holy Fire Above, played a crucial role. Each household was able to share its warmth and power with a ceremonial fire. Rites of passage, especially birth and burial, were events that emphasized both man's relationship to the larger cosmos and his dependence on its rhythm and flow.

This culture was challenged by the entrance of the European into the area in 1540, with the De Soto expedition. Although the Catholic nations of France and Spain were to dominate the area for the next two and a half centuries, there is little evidence that religion gained anymore than a toehold in what would become Mississippi. Natchez, the center of economic and governmental activity, had a Catholic church, but that outpost of civilization had the only Christian religious edifice in the area. The conquistadors were interested in power and wealth; they had no time for spiritual dialogue with savages. The inadvertent introduction of European diseases, resulting in epidemics among the Indians, had a greater impact on the tragic fate of the Mississippi Indian than either the presence of the sword or the absence of the cross.

Christians largely ignored the Indian until the Protestant evangelical efforts of the Jeffersonian Era. The ancient cultural practices of the Indian, religious and otherwise, had largely crumbled because of a decline in the network of clan society. There are many explanations for the disintegration of a viable Indian culture: disease, warfare, mixed-marriages,

Europeanization, and other cultural and demographic forces both within and without the Indian society. The first Protestant missionary among the Indians was Joseph Bullen. Vermont bred and Yale educated, he came to the Mississippi frontier in 1799. Over the next four years he made several tours through the Choctaw and Chickasaw nations. Bullen was followed in his efforts by the work of Presbyterian, Baptist, and Methodist groups during the first three decades of the 19th century. Presbyterian missionaries Cyrus Byington and Cyrus Kingsbury translated hymnals and other religious material into the Choctaw language during the 1820s. With the Indian removals of the 1830s and the attendant attitudes of alienation, Protestant activity among the Indians lost its former fervor. Although sporadic efforts continued, especially in the frontier camp meeting tradition, the Indian became generally an object of white derision.

During the period from 1763 to 1798 Mississippi was a Spanish colony. The colonial authorities relaxed their pro-Catholic qualifications for citizenship and worship in order to attract more Americans to the Natchez area. Protestants were allowed to worship as they chose, but they were not to hold public meetings or proselytize. Although Spanish Catholics considered this to be a fair compromise, Evangelical Protestants were not disposed to cater to such constraints. In 1791 a Baptist minister named Richard Curtis began his ministry at Coles Creek, north of Natchez. Four years later, following a series of violations of local religious rules, the Spanish authorities sought to arrest him after he performed a Protestant marriage ceremony. He went into self-exile until the United States acquired the territory in 1798. The following year the first Protestant missionary activity began in the area with the arrival of a minister, Tobias Gibson, who had been sent by South Carolina Methodists to evangelize the frontier. First, he established a church at Washington, north of Natchez; within a year Gibson had established the Natchez Circuit with as many as nine churches.

The Presbyterians began their missionary activity in the Mississippi territory in 1800 with the sending of three missionaries, the impetus again coming from the Carolinas. During their eight-month stay in Mississippi they were able to establish nine preaching stations, five that eventually became churches. It should be noted that these sporadic mission activities were neither the beginning of Protestantism in the area since Protestants had already moved into Mississippi nor did they produce the permanent establishment of ecclesiastical institutions.

During the first decades of the 19th century Mississippi was a part of frontier, known (along with Alabama) as the Old Southwest. For most if not all of the antebellum period, Mississippi remained a rough and tumble place, the saw-toothed cutting edge for an expanding society. Religious observances were sporadic: a circuit rider coming through every four weeks or so; a fall camp meeting that the people could attend or ignore; or the biweekly visitations of a rural farmer-minister, that is, provided a local church had been established. For the most part, the preachers arose from the folk. To use the term "clergy" for "the frontier parson" broadens—and distorts—the traditional image of both.

There were two basic types of ministers in Mississippi, the educated and the uneducated. The Episcopal and Presbyterian denominations required a trained clergy, a condition that hindered these groups on the frontier. The generation of a trained clergy took time, money, and patience, three necessities in short supply on the frontier. The predominant Baptist and Methodist denominations made no educational requirement of their ministers. In fact, there was a strong anti-intellectual attitude on the frontier, a value that was sometimes expressed openly. One Primitive Baptist gathering

in Mississippi was so adamantly opposed to an educated ministry that it officially challenged "the learned world to show any divine authority for sending a man to school after God called him to enter the ministry. If He wants a learned Moses or Saul of Tarsus, He will have them qualified before He calls them into his work." Although other groups were not so dogmatic in their attitudes, the basic motive of Evangelicals on the frontier was the conversion of the sinner, not the intellectual cultivation of the saint.

In rural Mississippi, laymen have often stated with good humor that more preachers are called *from* the field than *to* the ministry. In frontier Mississippi, that joke would not have possessed enough realism to elicit a smile. The life of the frontier preacher was anything but a life of ease. In 1816 the standard salary of a Methodist circuit rider was $100 a year, plus his expenses. Owing to the hardships incurred, he was expected to remain single. Baptists, and other groups without an hierarchy, decided on a church-by-church basis how a pastor was to be paid. Since most of these pastors were also farmers and usually served more than one congregation, churches were often able to rationalize inadequate compensation or even, at times, to pay nothing at all. During the antebellum period Baptist churches voted annually on the calling of a pastor. Since he was in God's service, it was considered bad form to ask about compensation. Therefore, for many, service in the ministry stood as a financial liability. Of all religious groups, only Presbyterians and Episcopalians paid their clergymen an adequate salary. But financial compensation was not why these men were in the ministry; the hardships of the Methodist circuit riders attest to that most dramatically.

On the American frontier, there were several ways denominational leaders could choose to minister to their flocks. The method most representative of the frontier style is that of the Methodist circuit rider—other denominations, especially the Cumberland Presbyterian, used the same system. The basic pattern was to designate a group of churches as a circuit, thereby allowing a single minister to visit with each congregation at least once every six weeks.

The circuit rider daily contended with the ruggedness of life on the frontier. When Milton H. Jones was riding the Carroll Circuit in 1836, his horse had to outrun a panther on a ridge between the Big Black and Yalobusha rivers. There being few roads and bridges, a rider had to be resourceful. John D. Shaw spent a portion of his ministry in the lowlands of the Mississippi Delta where at times "he would mount his canoe instead of a horse" as he threaded through the many rivers, lakes, bayous, and swamps in the area of his circuit. Once he finally arrived at his destination, the preacher would find the accommodations to be meager. Sometimes with the onset of dusk, he would prevail upon a frontiersman to allow him to spend a night in a half-finished cabin. Even the finished cabins of host families could be difficult to adjust to, as George Shaeffer discovered. For in the standard one-room cabins, all the family and any guests slept in the same area. Shaeffer recalled that "I felt considerably embarrassed the first time I had to retire under such circumstances, but I soon adapted myself to the usages of the people."

Not all single Methodist circuit riders were willing to adapt to all the rigors of the circuit, however. By 1825, the conference was accepting married ministers. Some of these married clergymen boarded their wives during their journeys; others took their wives with them. Arrangements made did not always meet with acclaim within the circuit. The Louisville Circuit complained of the 1838 appointment of Lorenzo Langford: "Mr. Langford had a family; and they lived a considerable distance from the circuit, how was he to render the circuit full service?" Just as basic was the question as to how these men were to provide financial support for their families. By the 1850s, a married

circuit rider received only $150 a year plus a supplement of $100 if he had children at home.

As mentioned before, to the Evangelical the winning of people's souls was the first duty of the preacher on the Mississippi frontier. For many churchmen, the best method to attain that goal was through camp meetings. Although the excesses of the Cane Ridge (Kentucky) revival period beginning in 1801 had largely passed by the time Protestantism became established in Mississippi, the CAMP MEETINGS offered preachers opportunities to evangelize the dispersed population of the state quickly—or so it seemed. These events, at least in the beginning, were community-wide with most denominations participating, and with as many as 20 preachers present at a single event. Presbyterians had started the tradition in Mississippi, but by 1810 they had turned over that promising strategem to others. The Methodists reaped the greatest numerical harvests, with Baptists not far behind.

The camp meetings of the late summer and early fall were as much social affairs as religious gatherings. They perpetuated the myth of the leveling effect of the frontier by often making it a reality. Prevailing social and economic divisions were eroded by the tides of emotion. Within the context of revivalism, some continued to be "more equal" than others: blacks and Indians were not only allowed to participate but were actively encouraged to do so—so long as Indians worshipped away from whites and blacks worshipped only in the presence of whites.

The boundaries between races were frequently violated during periods of REVIVALISM. The first revival meeting in Yalobusha County had only one preacher, a black man. Pompey, a slave of the Rawls family of Marion County, exhorted throughout the state. One white participant in the Yalobusha meeting reported that Pompey was the best praying preacher he had ever heard. When the black preacher had gotten the audience's emotion to a fever pitch, he sat down, exclaiming (as the white observer stated), "When de Lord preaches, Pompey stops."

The first decade of the 19th century witnessed the introduction of hierarchical structures for the major Evangelical Protestant groups. Because Baptist "hierarchies" are grassroots organizations, it is no surprise that the people of that denomination were able to organize at the associational level at an early date. In 1806 six local churches banded together to form the Mississippi Baptist Association. As with other religious activity in the territory at the time, the association was located in the Natchez District, that being Adams and surrounding counties. By 1819, two other Baptist associations, Union and Pearl River, had been organized as the edge of the frontier pushed eastward from the Mississippi River.

In 1813 the Mississippi Conference of the Methodist Church officially met for the first time in Spring Hill; it comprised a few churches from Louisiana as well. Not until 1816, however, was a bishop able to be in attendance for the annual conference. That conference ordained WILLIAM WINANS as a local preacher, marking the beginning of his long and notable career as a frontier spokesman. The next year after Mississippi attained statehood (1817), there were six Mississippi circuits with 2,235 members, one-fifth of the membership being black.

Presbyterians were able to organize a Mississippi presbytery in 1816, under the sponsorship of the Kentucky synod. The particular style of Presbyterian organization is immediately apparent when one notes that the seven congregations with a total membership of only 200 persons had five full-time resident ministers. Throughout the antebellum period Presbyterians, along with Episcopalians, were to remain smaller but at the same time better organized than their Baptist and Methodist counterparts. Much of this was due to the emphasis on a trained clergy. But organization and education were not

highly sought religious goals on the Mississippi frontier. Frederick Law Olmstead, in his travels along the Southern frontier, recorded overhearing the following conversation:

"Uncle John's an Episcopalian, ain't he?"
"Yes."
"Well, there ain't no religion in that no how."
"No, there ain't."

Frontier religion preferred a more emotional expression.

An American stereotype of today has the rural preacher breathing fire against personal morality's sinful triplets: drinking, dancing, and gambling. The preachers of the Mississippi frontier graphically depicted these vices before their audiences, but with varying degrees of enthusiasm. For example, the subject of alcohol consumption was not a well-defined issue on the American frontier. Not to offer a guest a dram of your favorite whiskey was downright inhospitable. The frontier minister was as likely as not to be a regular if moderate imbiber.

Thus, it should come as no surprise that most pastoral sermonizing against drinking during the antebellum period was directed toward a call for moderation rather than for abstinence. A brief survey of changing Baptist attitudes is instructive. The Mississippi Association, at its gathering in 1827 resolved:

That this Convention considers drunkeness one of the most injurious and worst of vices in the community, and we deeply deplore the destructive ravages made in our country and churches by the excessive and improper use of ardent spirits.

Three years later, the Pearl River Association indicated that the problem was rather close to home when it declared: "Resolved, that the church and friends in general provide no ardent spirits for the association when she may hereafter meet, as we do not want it." The following year the host church acceded to the request. As civilization challenged the Mississippi frontier, the pronouncements of Baptist groups became bolder. The chairman of the Baptist Committee on Temperance stated in 1847, "The fashionable and inordinate use of intoxicating drinks is a great evil—a curse in the land—the bane of society, morals, and religion." But it was not until 1853 that Southern Baptists in Mississippi called for prohibition as the proper remedy for the problem of drink. Even then, the flexible mind of the frontier Christian was able to condemn the seller of liquor while having little to say concerning the consumer.

The campaigns for the soul and against personal sin paid numerical dividends for Evangelical Protestantism. Methodists reaped the greatest harvests during the antebellum period. From their 1818 membership of 2,235 members, the Methodists grew to 10,949 by 1846, almost a thousand of them black. Owing to the continued success of the circuit riders and camp meetings, by the eve of the Civil War there were 50,000 whites and over 11,000 blacks in the denomination. Much of this phenomenal growth was due to the ability of Methodism to attract Mississippians from every class of society. In many ways, the Methodist churches came to mirror the society around them.

Baptist growth was not far behind. By 1824 Baptists in the state were able to organize their first state convention; it was disbanded in 1829, however, because of internal opposition to so "hierarchical" a body. Baptists were divided along mission/antimission and other lines. Also, the appearance of the primitive Christian, or restoration, movement cut into Baptist numerical strength as Primitive Baptists and the Disciples of Christ (also called Christians or Churches of Christ) gained a following in the state.

Offsetting some of the losses due to this factionalism was the opening of new territory to white settlement when the Choctaw and Chickasaw cessions were made in 1830 and 1832. With the northern half of the state available for white relocation, Baptists exhibited tremendous growth. In 1835 there were 10 Baptist associations with 107 churches having almost 5,000 members. Ten years later, the number of associations had doubled, the number of churches and membership had increased almost fourfold. By 1860 there were 41,482 Baptists with 305 ordained ministers and 596 churches.

The established denominations began to have new competition in the 1830s when, as just mentioned, the Campbellite movement entered the state. Actually some work had been done in the 1820s by these followers of Alexander Campbell. They were seen by other Protestants, especially the Baptists and Methodists, as troubling the Mississippi calm with "seeds of heresy, discord and disaffection." Although it is true that there were many debates and some tract writing among the various groups involved, much of the fight against Campbellism was simply for power and prestige. In fact, a number of Baptists, including William E. Matthews, became Disciples during the course of the period. Matthews had come from Alabama as a Baptist minister in 1828, but within a year had become a Disciple and had convinced three Baptist churches to follow Campbell's teaching. By 1860, there were almost 2,500 Disciples in the state in 24 churches.

Presbyterians and Episcopalians represented the High Church Protestant tradition in Mississippi. By 1829, the Mississippi Presbytery had grown enough to justify the creation of the Synod of Mississippi and South Alabama. This was followed six years later with the creation of the Synod of Mississippi with 24 churches having 800 to 900 members. Although the Presbyterians did not have the tremendous numerical increase of the Baptists and Methodists, by 1860 there were 148 Presbyterian churches, excluding those of the Cumberland Presbyterian movement.

Reaching out from the hills of Tennessee, the first Mississippi presbytery among the Cumberlands was organized in 1832. In many ways, Cumberland Presbyterians were more similar to Baptists and Methodists than to their fellow Presbyterians. They used a circuit-riding system and eschewed a trained ministry. By 1860, there were 60 Cumberland Presbyterian churches in Mississippi.

Much closer to regular Presbyterians in class and order were the Episcopalians. Their work in Mississippi had begun in 1790 with the work of Adam Cloud in Natchez. Even he came into conflict with the Catholic authorities for "preaching, baptizing, and marrying people contrary to the laws of the existing Government." Therefore, in 1795 his property was confiscated, and he was arrested and sent to New Orleans. There is no recording of further Episcopal work in Mississippi until 1820, when Christ Church at Church Hill in Jefferson County was organized by Cloud. Six years later the Episcopal Diocese of Mississippi was organized with four churches, five clergymen, and 100 communicants. The diocese became self-governing in 1849. Although never large in number, the Episcopal Church, under the able leadership of William Mercer Green, steadily grew during the last decade before the Civil War. By 1855 there were 30 clergymen, 33 parishes, and 941 communicants.

From the beginning of the 19th century until the 1840s, Mississippi Catholics were few in number. When Mississippi became a state in 1817, there was only one Catholic church in the state. The clergymen of the church were poorly compensated; usually foreign-born, few of them were able to speak English well enough to minister to the needs of their parishioners. As the Irish migration of the 1840s and 1850s took place, the Catholic population in Mississippi also began to increase. By the mid-1850s there were at least six Catholic churches in the state. Although the times continued to be difficult, Mississippi was beginning to attract some American-born priests. By 1852 there were 6,000 Catholics in Mississippi and 11 priests.

The institutions of religion and slavery were in constant tension on the Mississippi frontier. The white Christian's "responsibility" for the slave's soul posed a vexing problem. There was little debate that the black person should be made aware of the Word of God, but the issue was how to present this message selectively. For the most part, masters encouraged their slaves to attend church with them in order to learn about God's admonition that servants should be obedient to their masters. Since by 1840 blacks made up a majority of Mississippi's population, this practice led to some rather one-sided statistics. In 1846 a Natchez Baptist church had only 62 whites out of 442 members and at Grand Gulf the comparable numbers were eight and 113.

At an early date blacks in towns began to seek acceptable alternatives to the repression the white churches imposed upon them. One of the most successful movements occurred in Natchez. There blacks attending the Wall Street Baptist Church first began to meet as a part of the church, but in a separate building with white observers present. A little later they established the Rose Hill Baptist Church and began worshipping without white intrusion.

The Rose Hill story was not typical, however. Legal measures were taken to insure that blacks did not become too independent. The Poindexter Code of 1821 provided that blacks could only assemble to worship with their master's written permission and at least two white persons present. The code also forbade free blacks and mulattoes from serving as ministers. In practice, however, its provisions regarding slavery were seldom honored until abolitionist attacks on slavery began in the 1830s.

Throughout the antebellum era, white urban churches manifested quite a bit of flexibility in their dealings with blacks. One story coming from the period concerned the conversion of Prior Lee, a prominent white member of the Jackson community who was converted at a black revival meeting. He was so grateful that he had his slaves make bricks that he then donated for the erection of a white church. He made sure that blacks were allowed to use the basement for their worship services. Other communities had similar arrangements for black worship. In urban areas to some extent, but especially in the more prevalent rural churches, blacks had their most meaningful worship experiences in "prayer meetings," at some remove from the glances of prying whites. As one former slave in Simpson County recalled during the 1930s, blacks would often slip away to an arbor for their religious gatherings so that "we could sing praises and shout all us wanted to." There can be little doubt that they also added to the selective biblical canon that whites had given them.

In spite of white efforts to control the type of Christianity practiced by blacks, by the Civil War period black Christianity was far different from the white version. As Eugene Genovese indicates in *Roll, Jordan, Roll*, blacks throughout the South had taken Christianity, merged it with African antecedents, and made a religion that served their purposes and needs. Whites misinterpreted what had happened. In 1860 Southern Baptists in Mississippi officially acclaimed separate black worship—supervised by whites—as a laudable goal. This concern sprang from the failure of masters to instruct their slaves in the mere rudiments of Christianity. What the Baptists failed to understand was that *blacks* were instructing blacks in the type of Christianity they needed to understand in order to survive in this world.

When Northern abolitionists began to attack the institution of slavery during the 1830s some Southern churchmen immediately came to its defense. James Smylie, a Mississippi Presbyterian, was one of the earliest defenders of the institution. He published his pamphlet on the subject in 1836, probably prompted by the fact that he was the owner of 53 persons, making him the third-largest slaveholder in Amite County. The positive-good the-

ories of Smylie gained widespread acceptance in Mississippi religious circles. In 1837 the Mississippi Baptist Convention declared that abolitionism was an attempt "to detract from the social, civil, and religious privileges of the slave population." As abolitionist attacks continued, however, others began to express doubts about the amount of "positive good" that had been exercised. In 1847 the Choctaw Baptist Association accepted a committee report that stated: "We feel that we cannot too earnestly recommend the utmost attention on the part of the ministers, churches, and christian owners to the *religious improvement of their servants*." This direct reaction to abolitionist statements also called for plantation owners with at least 10 adult slaves to build houses of worship for them.

The most prevalent reaction to abolitionism was to distance the church from the problem. William Winans argued that ideally slavery should be done away with; but he added that man should not interfere with the workings of God who in his own time would end it. Jesus would destroy slavery at the Second Coming, which Winans estimated would occur around the year 2000. Another Methodist minister made much the same point, arguing "that with the abstract subject of slavery, we have nothing to do, nor do we regard it as a subject on which the church has the right to legislate."

The period of the Civil War and Reconstruction caused a basic shift in Mississippi religion. Institutionally, Southern churches formally separated from their national groups. Baptists and Methodists parted company with their kinsmen during the 1840s; Presbyterians had their break in 1861. Although other groups did not experience formal rupture, either because of regionalism (Cumberland Presbyterians) or universalism (Catholics), regional loyalty took precedence over religious ties. Although exceptions can be mentioned, members of the clergy seldom took part in political affairs. Once the Civil War did begin, however, churchmen wholeheartedly supported the Southern cause. At Mississippi College, a Baptist school for young men, the entire student body became privates and the professors officers as they organized the Mississippi College Rifles. Clergymen often became infantry officers. Mark P. Lowery, founder of Blue Mountain College and father of a family of Baptist pastors, was a general during the conflict.

With the ending of the conflict, whites returned home determined that the church would be one aspect of Southern life that would not be reconstructed along Northern lines. Although some black membership continued in white churches, blacks were not given any authority in church governance. In some cases, blacks were evicted from white churches. But in most instances blacks were more concerned with independence in their religious worship than they were in taking over white edifices. Whites and blacks alike contributed to the formation of racially separate congregations and denominations.

Northern religious organizations were helpful in assisting black institutions during the Reconstruction era. In the field of education, Northern Methodists organized Shaw University (later changed to Rust College) in Holly Springs and a number of academies throughout the state at both elementary and secondary levels. The AMERICAN MISSIONARY ASSOCIATION founded Tougaloo College just north of Jackson; it became a nationally renowned liberal arts institution.

Northern Methodist organizations also assisted in the establishment of black local churches in Mississippi. The African Methodist Episcopal Church sent organizers to the South. The Colored Episcopal Church was organized with support from both Northern and Southern church organizations, although financial support was almost exclusively from Northern groups. Some church organizers, such as Thomas Stringer in Vicksburg, adroitly combined their religious functions with successful Reconstruction political careers.

One group of Mississippi black Baptists organized the General Baptist Missionary Convention. Most of the churches in this convention were small; Mt. Horeb in Greenville having 810 members and Rose Hill in Natchez with 400 members became the largest congregations. The proceedings of the annual meetings of the convention did not show evidence of any great distinction being made between urban and rural churches. All black churches were struggling, despite the aid provided by Northern friends. The greatest problem faced by black churches during the post-Civil War era was an uneducated ministry. Churches were often warned to be wary of unlicensed ministers. Educational institutions for ministerial training such as Natchez College, Jackson College, and Roger Williams University (in Memphis) were supported insofar as a poor constituency could manage with the assistance of subsidies from the American Baptist Home Mission Society throughout the late nineteenth century.

There were frequent conflicts within the black Baptist churches during these decades. An item from the 1884 convention report is indicative of the problems black churches faced during this trying period: "The missionaries made good reports this year, financial and otherwise. No 'bogus conventions,' church troubles or 'imposters' were reported." In 1890 the General Baptist Missionary Convention, which by then included portions of Louisiana and Arkansas, united with the General Baptist Convention of Mississippi to form the General Baptist Missionary Convention of Mississippi. The newly consolidated convention consisted of 900 churches with 79,732 members.

In the post-Civil War period, white ethnic groups added to the changing religious complexion of the state. Aside from ethnic Catholics, Jews were the largest white minority ethnic group. French governor Bienville's Black Code of 1724 had prohibited Jewish settlement in the Mississippi area and the Spanish authorities later pursued similar policies. But the relative religious tolerance of the United States enabled Jewish merchants and peddlers to move into Mississippi during the early decades of the 19th century. By 1820, 100 Jews lived in the state. Anti-Semitism, which seems to surface during crises, occurred during the Union occupation of Mississippi. General U. S. Grant, noting the speculation and black marketing of cotton in the area under his control, promulgated an order demanding that all Jews leave the area. This singling out of an ethnic group was done in spite of a general knowledge that many businessmen were involved in the trade, and further that not all Jews who were businessmen were so involved. After the war, conditions improved for the Jewish communities in Mississippi with congregations being established in Jackson, Vicksburg, Columbus, and other urban areas. The congregations being quite small, usually both Reform and Orthodox services would be performed at the same synagogue.

Other ethnic groups playing a role in Mississippi religion were Greeks and Syrians, both embracing the Eastern Orthodox faith. Their organizational development was similar to that of the Jews in that they first organized social and cultural clubs. When the group became financially strong enough to build an edifice and support a priest, a church would be organized. Depending on the size of the ethnic community, Greeks would sometimes worship at the Syrian Orthodox Church, as they did in Vicksburg, or the Syrians at the Greek church, as in Jackson.

Mississippi never achieved the heterogeneous religious environment of Florida, Louisiana, or even Alabama. This was due partly to the state's continued reliance on an agricultural economy among white and black Protestant farmers and small businessmen. Even the numerous sectar-

ian divisions prevalent in contiguous areas of Alabama, Tennessee, and Arkansas were lacking in Mississippi. The state continued to be a remarkably homogeneous Baptist/Methodist state.

The subject of "demon rum" tended to unite all the white Evangelical Protestants of Mississippi. Because their attitude toward drinking changed after the Civil War, they saw drinking as a sin in and of itself rather than seeing drink as an activity that could lead to the sin of drunkenness. Baptists led the fight. In 1882 a prohibition convention was held in Jackson, presided over by W. S. Webb, the president of Mississippi College. Frances E. Willard visited Corinth the same year, organizing the Mississippi Woman's Christian Temperance Union. Roderic Gambrell, son of *Baptist Record* editor J. B. GAMBRELL, edited *The Sword and Shield*, a prohibitionist journal. These efforts successfully led to the passage of a local-option law in 1886. Since Mississippi was still a semicivilized frontier in the 1880s, feuds being settled by violent means, an antiprohibitionist assassinated Roderic Gambrell in 1887. This influenced his uncle, J. H. Gambrell, to become a fervent evangelist on the temperance circuit.

Prohibitionists thought they were on the side of the angels, for by 1890 it was apparent that "a war between rum and righteousness raged, with the general movement in favor of the prohibition cause." While the counties of Mississippi's interior quickly voted "dry," the Mississippi River counties and those along the Gulf Coast remained "wet." This made hill-country whites increasingly suspicious of blacks and white ethnics whose votes thwarted prohibition in those areas.

Possibly because of a hierarchical structure that tended to hold in check ministers intent on division, Methodists did not seem to have the internal division of Southern Baptists, Primitive Baptists, and the Christian Church. But these last three had to contend with two areas of friction throughout the 19th century; one was local church order, the other primacy of local organization over centralizing tendencies. The first of these, although causing some local churches to split, rarely became the source of major controversy; but it did indicate the need of decentralized church structures to avoid anarchistic tendencies.

Primitive Baptists adhered to strict church discipline long after other organizations had loosened most formal procedures. Letters from sister Baptist churches were not always honored; investigations of belief systems were sometimes made. Disfellowship of persons found to be in violation of the church's stands occurred most often in cases where personal moral codes were involved. In 1879, a member of a black Primitive Baptist church was disfellowshipped when he overstepped the bounds of his newly found freedom: he had two wives. In the New Chapel Church in 1880, one of the sisters in the congregation stood up during a service, pointed her finger at a prominent man of the community, and stated she had accepted his offer to live in adultery. They were both excluded from fellowship. Merely charging someone with evil deeds did not mean that a kangaroo court was immediately formed, however. In 1877 at the Middletown Creek Church a young lady accused a young man of "horsing around" on a horseback date. The witnesses she had identified were not forthcoming at the hearing and charges were dismissed.

Moral grounds were not always the reason for disfellowship. The Elam Church at Water Valley excluded a female member in 1898 for "getting malicious with the church." A woman was excluded from the Middleton Creek Church in 1882 for "slandering her husband." Often family rifts were repaired through the intervention of the church.

Primitive Baptists, along with other groups, had taken stands against secret orders during the anti-Masonic period before the Civil War. Therefore, many members of secret labor unions and farm protest movements of the 1870s and 1880s were disfellowshipped. Once the secretive organizations either dissolved or came into the open, their members were not discriminated against in church membership.

The great theological struggle among Primitive Baptists late in the century was the Absolutist versus Conditionalist controversy. This had been an undercurrent in the church since its beginnings in the 1830s and 1840s; but it did not surface until the 1890s. Although referred to by other groups as "hardshells" because of their predestinarian views, Primitive Baptists came out of this period as Conditionalists. This meant that they allowed persons a greater role in their own salvation; this placed greater responsibility for personal actions on every individual.

Because of its decentralized structure, the Disciples of Christ movement does not lend itself to easy analysis. By 1891 there were 60 Disciples churches meeting in Mississippi, one-half with their own houses of worship. There were between 5,000 and 6,000 whites and 3,000 blacks in the denomination, with 32 white and 32 black ministers. But around the turn of the century a schism occurred over the issues of centralization and musical instruments. The former issue revolved around how best to marshal resources for missionary activities. The cooperationists argued that churches should band together for such activities but not through the use of missionary societies, since the societies tended to acquire a centralizing tendency of their own. Many people saw the use of musical instruments as another example of the modern church's apostasy from the purity of the New Testament church. During this period most antimission and anti-instrument forces joined under the banner of the Churches of Christ, with those of more liberal persuasion in the Christian Church (or Disciples of Christ). The 1906 religious census shows that more in Mississippi—again unlike the mountainous neighboring states—were members of the Christian Church than of the Churches of Christ.

Mississippi was a crossroads for Southern Baptist controversies of the 19th century. From the 1850s forward, Mississippi was one of the three states, along with Tennessee and Alabama, strongly influenced by the LANDMARK MOVEMENT. Its leading proponent, JAMES R. GRAVES, was personally popular throughout Mississippi Baptist circles, often preaching in revivals or debating spokesmen from other denominations concerning his exclusivistic doctrines of church polity. During the post-Civil War era, J. B. Gambrell, a much more moderate leader, became the most active spokesman for Baptist causes. As editor of *The Baptist Record*, Gambrell was able to sound the alarm on issues ranging from prohibition to centralization. His opposition to centralizing tendencies did not reach full fruition until later in the Texas phase of his career when he became prominent during the convention-wide debate over the formation of a Sunday School Board.

"Martinism" was the great controversy among Mississippi Baptists during the 1890s, riveting their attention for at least five years. They had been a party to a convention-wide struggle during that decade, having refused financial support to the Southern Baptist Theological Seminary in Louisville when its president, W. H. Whitsitt, would not "admit" that Baptists preceded the Protestant Reformation. Maybe because Whitsitt attended the 1897 Mississippi Baptist Convention at Grenada, there was no official talk of the controversy surrounding him. A person's presence at the particular gathering, however, was not a guarantee of reconciliation. M. T. Martin was indeed there, sitting quietly while a storm erupted around his doctrinal views. Referred to as "Professor," Martin had been a mathematics teacher at Mississippi College during the 1870s. Beginning in 1893, he preached throughout the state of a need for persons to be "re-baptized," since their earlier professions of faith may have been "inaccurate." This doctrine of "re-baptism," which was to become known as

"Martinism," smacked of the Methodist belief in backsliding.

The "Martinism" controversy had been spread across the pages of *The Baptist Record* and associational minutes since 1895. Orthodox opponents of this doctrine were determined to stop the heresy in Grenada. A committee presented an unanimous report to the convention: "Resolved, that this Convention does not endorse, but condemns, the doctrinal views of Prof. M. T. Martin, as these views are set forth by himself and published over his own name in his pamphlet entitled 'The Doctrinal Views of M. T. Martin.'" Although this statement seems to have been the climax of the controversy, delegates to the 1905 meeting of the convention still heard faint echoes of the "Martinism" period. As for Whitsitt, he resigned his presidency in 1898, and Mississippi renewed its support of the seminary.

The anti-intellectual attitude of many Mississippians did not always translate into an anti-institutional bias. Churches were responsible for establishing the first viable institutions of higher education in Mississippi. In general, the earliest efforts were intended for the elevation of young women in female institutes, that were usually secondary schools or finishing schools. Both Baptists and Methodists were prominent in this phase of educational life.

In 1826, Hampstead Academy was founded in Clinton. By 1830 it had become Mississippi College, functioning under Presbyberian auspices. In order to help the struggling school financially, Presbyterians organized a lottery. This device did not solve long-term problems, however, and Clinton gave the school to Mississippi Baptists in 1850.

Methodists had established Centenary College at Brandon Springs in 1841; but four years later it moved to Jackson LA. Although it was still a part of the Mississippi Conference, those ties loosened over time until Millsaps College was established in Jackson in 1892. Under the guidance of its founder, Harvard-educated Major Reuben Millsaps, the school quickly established itself as one of the outstanding Methodist colleges in the South. Before the founding of Emory University and Southern Methodist University, Millsaps ranked second to Trinity (Duke) among Southern Methodist colleges in the size of endowment.

Although academies and colleges of all types were established by church groups, female colleges continued to be especially popular among the denominations down into the 20th century. Baptists were given Blue Mountain College in 1920; it had been a private college since 1873. In 1912 Baptists also opened Mississippi Woman's College of Hattiesburg. It eventually became William Carey College, a coeducational institution. Among Methodists, Whitworth College (1859) in Brookhaven continued to be their largest postsecondary institution until financial problems during the Great Depression forced it to close. The state's Presbyterians relied on Southwestern College (1875) in Memphis for male education, since that institution was supported by the synods of five Southern states, including Mississippi. Belhaven College was established in 1893 in Jackson as a Presbyterian female college; it became coeducational in 1954. All of these institutions—male, female, and coeducational—offered both religious training for people going into church-related vocations and liberal arts instruction in a Christian setting.

The beginnings of the 20th century marked the maturation of Protestantism in Mississippi. It is true that Protestant denominations continued to grow numerically, at times phenomenally, during the course of the century; but the last vestiges of the frontier were disappearing. Although the camp-meeting tradition continued, it was now more of a social than a religious event. One participant at the Seashore camp meeting of 1900 stated, "It looks to us as if Methodist preachers have well nigh forgotten, or are

fast forgetting, how to say 'Amen.' The responses we heard were few and feeble." The reports of the results of the round of camp meetings in 1902 were not encouraging: "They were not having success at conversions as they had formerly experienced." By the eve of World War I, denominational walls that had surrounded camp meetings were disintegrating as union meetings, usually sponsored by Presbyterians, Methodists, and "Campbellites," became the standard of the day.

This did not herald the beginnings of modernism in Mississippi churches, let it be noted emphatically. During the Progressive Era, Mississippi religious groups rarely enlisted in the cause for social betterment. Not only did they not support crucial social legislation with general social purposes, they were not even able to get a statewide prohibition law until 1918. But social concern was being shown outside the political arena. Baptists in the state supported the building of a hospital in Jackson and a tri-state facility in Memphis; Methodists were engaged in similar building programs during the era. Both groups upgraded the orphanages they had long supported. The major efforts of Evangelical Protestants continued to be on evangelism and numerical growth.

The rallying cries of Evangelical Protestantism in 20th-century Mississippi were the three "E's": Expansion, Enlistment, and Enlargement. The religious census from 1906 through 1936 showed Southern Baptists winning the numbers game over Methodists. Trends within the decentralized black religious community were not as readily apparent since the religious statistics were unreliable. Almost certainly, the growth of black denominational institutions was at a standstill.

During recent years, Southern Baptists have so dominated the growth within white denominations as to claim an uncontested victory. A 1971 religious survey indicated that Southern Baptists were a majority of the religious adherents in 68 of the state's 82 counties. In only three counties, two predominantly black and the third on the Gulf Coast, did Southern Baptists fail to place first among denominational bodies.

Race relations continued to be the Achilles' heel of Mississippi's religious bodies. During the 1960s, a white culture that had failed to wrestle with Christian social ethics all along, began under the stress of crisis to dictate its own terms. The leadership of black churches, with its relative freedom from the oppression of the segregated society, began to exercise its role as the catalyst of a freedom movement. As a result, black churches were often bombed or burned. Meanwhile, many well-meaning white ministers were either quiet or left the state. The White Citizens Councils were proving to be rather adept at silencing the men of God in their pulpits. Many promising ministerial careers were shattered—from the fertile fields of the Delta to the state's large urban churches. As Jewish leaders spoke out in favor of human rights, the anti-Semitism of the KU KLUX KLAN gave rise to the bombing of a rabbi's home and temples in Jackson and Meridian. Although the civil rights movement in Mississippi had begun with a strong religious underpinning, young blacks were especially frustrated by the reaction of white churchmen and began to turn to alternative world views, such as black separatism and Marxism. In white churches, the world was so out of kilter that moderation was seen as a sign of courage.

Both Mississippi culture, black and white, and Mississippi religion survived the tumult of the 1960s. The exact nature of the survival is more difficult to determine. Sunday morning church services are still the most segregated events in the state. There is still a strong current of religious conservatism, as exemplified several years ago when five Episcopal priests, having become disenchanted with the liberalization of the church, took vows in the Eastern Orthodox tradition and entered a Mississippi monastery for

instruction. But there also seems to be a new tolerance for diverging religious views in Mississippi—pluralism, if you will. During the 1970s many Baptists supported the conservative television evangelism of James Robison while others listened attentively to John Claypool, liberal minister of the Northminster Church in Jackson. Pentecostal groups, one of the fastest-growing movements in the state, received implicit establishment recognition with the election of one of their own, Cliff Finch, as governor in 1975. For the most part, the 1970s were years of quiet introspection.

The story of religion in Mississippi has been one full of faith—and fatalism; brotherhood—and bigotry; peace—and platitudes; kindness—and the Klan. The tragedies of the past, especially the recent past, lead one to search for a prophetic voice that may give hope for the future. What Mississippians need now is reconciliation. A native son, WILL CAMPBELL, has been in such a "business" for many years. He grew up in Amite County, but not in the same world as that of the antebellum slaveholding Presbyterian James Smylie. Campbell has been at the forefront of the human rights struggle while at the same time attempting to heal the wounds of divisiveness. He recently recounted many of his experiences in *Brother to a Dragonfly*. To many, the allegory of his friend P. D. East is appropriate for the religious condition of Mississippi. According to East's story, an Easter chicken was born different from the other chicks in the barnyard; but over time it became just like everyone else. East, an atheist, was rather fond of jesting Campbell concerning his Christian beliefs. Finally, East asked him to state the essence of the Christian message—in 10 words or less! After thinking for a moment, Will replied, "We're all bastards but God loves us anyway." Man is the leveler; God is the elevator. Godless humanism is not what Mississippi, the buckle of the Bible belt, should fear most, but un-Christlike Christianity. If Campbell's prophetic voice is heeded, Mississippi will not only endure, it will prevail.

See also articles on CIVIL RIGHTS MOVEMENT; FRENCH INFLUENCE; FRONTIER, INFLUENCE OF.

Bibliography. Jessie L. Boyd, *A Popular History of the Baptists in Mississippi*; Janice Byrd, "A History of the Jews in Mississippi," M.A. thesis, Mississippi College, 1979; J. B. Cain, *Methodism in the Mississippi Conference, 1846-1870*; Edward Riley Crowther, "Mississippi Baptists, Slavery and Secession: A Study in Religious Ideology," M.A. thesis, Mississippi College, 1981; Charles Conrad Di Michele, "The History of the Eastern Orthodox Church in Mississippi," M.A. thesis, Mississippi College, 1968; Fred R. Graves, compiler, *The Presbyterian Work in Mississippi*; W. L. Hamrick, *The Mississippi Conference of the Methodist Protestant Church, 1829-1939*; John G. Jones, *A Complete History of Methodism as Connected With the Mississippi Conference*, vols. 1 & 2 (1799-1845); W. B. Jones, *Methodism in the Mississippi Conference, 1870-1894*; Lewis G. Jordan, *Negro Baptist History, U.S.A., 1750-1930*; J. Allen Lindsey, *Methodism in the Mississippi Conference (1894-1919)*; Charles Howard Lucas, "History of the Church of Christ in Mississippi," M.A. thesis, Mississippi College, 1964; B. W. McDonald, *History of the Cumberland Presbyterian Church*; Richard Aubrey McLemore, *A History of Mississippi Baptists, 1780-1970*; Gene Ramsey Miller, *A History of North Mississippi Methodism, 1820-1900*; James J. Pillar, *The Catholic Church in Mississippi, 1837-1865*; "Religious and Cultural Life, 1817-1860," Richard A. McLemore, ed., *A History of Mississippi*, vol. 1; Patrick H. Thompson, *The History of Negro Baptists in Mississippi*; Ernest Trice Thompson, *Presbyterians in the South*, 3 vols.

EDWARD NELSON AKIN
MISSISSIPPI COLLEGE

MISSOURI.

MISSOURI. Strategically located at the heart of the North American continent, Missouri is near the confluence of three great rivers. It has thus been historically shaped by cultural influences from both the North and the South.

The first human inhabitants were Indians. They hunted its great forests and fertile plains, fished its clear streams, cultivated its productive soil, and fought for possession of its land. Since they left no written records, our knowledge of their religion is limited. But through archeological investigation, oral tradition, and the reports of early travelers and traders we can know something.

While there were differences among the various tribes that lived in this area, in general it may be said that in their view, the world was inhabited by invisible spirits. They could be good, bad, or simply mischievous. These spirits could be controlled to some extent by the secret lore of medicine men. There were fetishes that could ward off evil or promote good, and there were signs and omens that should be followed. From time to time prophets emerged who could predict the future. They marked with religious rites the great moments in each individual's life—birth, puberty, marriage, and death. At death it was believed the soul of the individual entered into the life of another world. Their worship was more danced out than thought out. They observed certain taboos in accordance with sacred tradition. There were also sacred times, such as the corn harvest, sacred places, such as a high hill, and sacred objects, such as a curiously shaped stone. In the world around them they sensed the power of a tremendous, mysterious force or excellence known in some tribes as "orenda" or "wakenda"— the "power that moves." This sense of the Holy, or the numinous, as it has been called, aroused in them overpowering feelings of both fascination and fear, as well as awe and wonder. Closely related to this sense of the Holy was their belief in a high god, generally known as the Great Spirit, and called Wah'kon-tah by the Osages, who ruled over all.

The religion of these earliest inhabitants of Missouri had in it a great deal of magic, superstition and fear, and lacked a coherent view of the world. But whatever may have been the weaknesses or failures of their faith, it enabled them to live harmoniously with nature, and there was much that was beautiful in their view of the land, the sky and the Great Spirit.

Missouri enters into the full light of history with the coming of French explorers, traders and missionaries in the last half of the 17th century. These intrepid men were motivated to endure the hardships and dangers of the wilderness by a desire to claim the vast Mississippi Valley for France, by a drive for personal adventure and wealth, and last, but not necessarily least, by a concern for the conversion of the Indians to Christianity.

Among these adventurers were a number of missionary priests, such as Father Jacques Marquette (1637-1675), who in 1673 explored the Mississippi, and Father Louis Hennepin (1640-1701) of the Recollets who in 1679 further explored the region. From about 1700 to 1703 a Jesuit mission station near what is now St. Louis was in operation, and the first church in Missouri was built. About 1735 the first permanent settlement was made at St. Genevieve. In 1764 St. Louis was established and it quickly became the dominant town in the French territory of Louisiana, which included most of the area drained by the Mississippi River.

Thus the first settlements in what is now Missouri were founded by Roman Catholics and the influence of French culture was strong. Although the Louisiana territory was under the rule of France, which recognized the Catholic Church as the only approved faith, and though Protestants were by law prohibited from conducting public worship, marriages, and funerals, in actual practice the French authorities pursued a rather tolerant policy in matters of religion. The founders of St. Louis—Pierre Laclede and Auguste Chouteau—for example, read and enjoyed the works of Rousseau, Diderot, and Voltaire, and other writings that reflected the secular, humanist influence of the Enlightenment. Further, settlers were needed if the territory was to grow and flourish. So Protestant settlers entered the area in growing numbers and freely followed their faith.

In 1762 France ceded the Louisiana territory to Spain, gave it back to France in 1800, and then in 1803 Napoleon sold this magnificent realm to the United States. In accordance with the United States Constitution and the Bill of Rights, religious freedom for all was then officially established, though in practice this ideal was not always faithfully followed. In any event, the population grew and in 1821, after much controversy, Missouri was admitted to the Union as a state and, further, as a slave state.

At about this time Roman Catholic immigrants—mostly from Ireland and Germany—began to settle in Missouri in large numbers. Earlier, Bishop DuBourg formed the first diocese in the state, built a cathedral (now a familiar landmark in St. Louis), and led in a renewal of Catholic life. Schools were established, usually under the rule of nuns, who also founded orphanages and hospitals. St. Louis University was chartered in 1832 under the leadership of the Jesuits. Missions to the Indians, seminaries, monasteries, and convents were also brought into being. As it developed into one of the strongly Catholic cities in America, the diocese of St. Louis in time became an archdiocese. Throughout this time of steady growth the hierarchy and priesthood of the Catholic Church deserve great credit for the ways in which they ministered to their immigrant people as they struggled through the trauma of leaving their homeland and adjusting to life in a new and different world. Thus the Roman Catholic Church became the largest religious body in Missouri, as well as the first.

Through most of the 19th century, wave after wave of Americans also poured into Missouri. The first great wave was made up largely of settlers from the states of the upper South—Kentucky, Tennessee, Virginia, and North Carolina—and they gave to the state a definite Southern character. They were also mainly Protestant in background, and of the denominations that evangelized, among them the Baptists, Methodists, Presbyterians, and Disciples were especially effective.

Baptists began to come into Missouri late in the 18th century, and it was a Baptist preacher from Kentucky who preached in February of 1794 what was probably the first Protestant sermon in what is now Missouri. But it was not until

1805 that a Baptist preacher from Virginia, David Green, formed near Cape Girardeau the first Protestant church.

Though some of their preachers, such as John Mason Peck, were well-educated men, most of them were "farmer preachers" who largely supported themselves and had only a minimal education. They shared the hard life of their people. They labored during the week at clearing the land, plowing, planting, and cultivating their corn patch, splitting rails and, if need be, helping a neighbor build a cabin or barn. Then on Sundays or during PROTRACTED MEETINGS, they travelled on horseback to preach the Gospel. They preached with fervent conviction that Jesus Christ brings to penitent believers forgiveness and new and everlasting life. The congregations they formed were covenant communities in which the members agreed to walk together and help one another live the Christian life. Errant members were subject to exclusion from their fellowship if they failed to reform their lives. Many, like the preachers Abraham Lincoln heard as a boy in Kentucky and Indiana, were inclined to believe the Calvinistic doctrine of predestination. But such dogma did not keep them from being aggressive evangelists and the Baptists (most of whom are now Southern Baptists) became in time the largest Protestant body in Missouri. They were also instrumental in founding several colleges, including William Jewell, Hannibal-La Grange, and Southwest Baptist College.

The Methodists, led by their circuit-riding preachers, also grew rapidly under the difficult and demanding conditions of the Missouri frontier. Their ministers are famed for their courage and hardihood in braving the elements and the many dangers of the wilderness in order to bring the Gospel to a rough and undisciplined folk. These preachers too, many of them, had been converted from a rough and turbulent life; they too, often had very little formal education, but they had the Bible, the Hymn Book, and the Book of Discipline in their saddlebags, whose contents they taught and used, and in addition they encouraged the reading of books from the Methodist Book Concern. Appointed by their bishops to serve a circuit of churches and to form new ones, they preached as opportunity afforded—in cabins, taverns, under brush arbors, or wherever a group could be gathered. Many of their converts came from camp meetings in which people camped together for a week or so to socialize, sing and pray, and listen to the heart-felt preaching that sought to celebrate the grace of God and move the unregenerate to find pardon and new life in Christ. The doctrine they taught was Arminian—God's grace is freely available to all through Christ for all humanity. Perhaps their doctrine was best communicated through the great hymns they sang. Both Methodists and Baptists have established substantial seminaries in Kansas City. Today they constitute the second-largest Protestant body in Missouri.

The people of the Christian Church (Disciples of Christ) also came into Missouri with the tide of immigrants from the East and South early in the 19th century. Theirs was a noncreedal faith that sought to bring about the unity of all Christians through a return to "simple New Testament Christianity." Like the Baptists they were led mainly by lay preachers, with little distinction being made between clergy and laity.

Elders Thomas McBride, T. M. Allen, and Joel Haden, all from Kentucky, were among the earliest Disciples preachers in Missouri. McBride founded what was probably the first Disciples church on Salt Creek in the "little Dixie" area of central Missouri in 1817.

Along with their commitment to the restoration of New Testament Christianity as the way to Christian unity, they developed the idea that salvation is not so much an event as a process—a process of logical steps that included faith, repentance, believer's baptism by immersion, growth in Christ through regular worship, and the celebration of the Lord's Supper each Lord's Day.

Although led by lay preachers, Disciples ministers were frequently men who respected learning, and so it was natural that they should found colleges as well as churches. Among the schools that they founded that have survived are Culver Stockton, William Woods, Columbia, and the Missouri School of Religion, and since 1909 they have shared with the United Church of Christ in the support of Drury College.

But among the Protestants it has been the Presbyterians who have provided the most distinguished intellectual leadership to the churches and the culture of Missouri, and this from an early date. In 1816 one of the first Presbyterian churches in the state was formed by Salman Giddings near Potosi with the help of four elders who had moved there from North Carolina. Additional congregations were soon established and in 1819 the first presbytery was formed, and 10 years later the first synod.

Many of these Presbyterian ministers were commissioned and supported by missionary societies back east. Well educated, they tended to be young and idealistic and were shocked by the crudity and squalor of frontier life. In time, however, they came to understand and appreciate the good qualities of the people whom they sought to serve. Timothy Flint, for example, a Harvard graduate, came to the St. Louis area and found it to be a godless place in which swearing, drunkenness, sabbath-breaking, slovenliness, and violence abounded. But 10 years later his attitude had changed: without ceasing to deplore the drudgery and crudity of their lives, he could now see, and warmly praise, their hardihood, courage, generosity, and honesty.

With their insistence upon a learned ministry and their concern for education, the Presbyterians founded numerous colleges. Among those that have survived are Westminster, Park, Tarkio, Missouri Valley, the School of the Ozarks, and Lindenwood. They also shared with the Dutch Reformed and Associate Reformed Presbyterian churches in the establishment of a mission school—Harmony Mission—for the Osage Indians.

In the 19th century the Congregationalists, working mostly through the AMERICAN MISSIONARY ASSOCIATION, founded a considerable number of congregations in Missouri. But they remained small and in the 19th century most of them faded away, perhaps because there was not a heavy migration of people from New England and the upper middle west into Missouri.

There was, however, some migration from the Northeast, and it tended to be made up largely of teachers, merchants, and other professional people. Among these sons and daughters of the Puritans were some Unitarians. William Greenleaf Eliot, grandfather of the poet, T. S. Eliot, came out to St. Louis shortly after his graduation from the Harvard Divinity School and organized the first Unitarian church in the state in 1834. Then, a little later, he founded a school that developed into Washington University.

Another influential New Englander was W. T. Harris, a Connecticut school master, who came to St. Louis where in time he became superintendent of schools. Enamoured of the Idealist tradition in philosophy, especially as manifested in the thought of Hegel, he led in forming the Saint Louis Philosophical Society and in publishing the *Journal of Speculative Philosophy*, whose first issue came out in 1867. It was the first philosophical periodical in the English language.

Harris was especially attracted to Hegel's idea that history is a process of development, through struggle, towards a better human society. In this struggle the individual is gradually being liberated from the control of the group to which he belongs. Back of this progressive advance is the World Spirit and this Spirit is imminent in all things. From this Harris concluded that America, with its freedom and individualism and other democratic principles, represents the culmination of history. Against the atheism of Marx and the agnosticism of Spencer, Harris thus posited a power that works for good. He found in Hegel what he believed to be an essentially religious view of the world's meaning. To Americans, at least, it could also mean that this is the best of all possible worlds.

It was in St. Louis that the first Episcopal parish, Christ Church, was formed in 1819. Its rector was Jackson Kemper who would later become the first Missionary Bishop of the Episcopal Church in America. In 1844 the first diocese was formed with Cicero Hawks as its bishop, and in 1859 a beautiful cathedral was built. Eventually Episcopal parishes were established in every part of the state, though not so much in rural areas. With its strong sense of history, its concern for order and beauty in worship, and its leadership in the quest for Christian unity, the Episcopal Church exercised considerable influence on the religious life of the state.

Another religious group with a strong and poignant sense of history is Judaism. Jews were not allowed to enter the Louisiana Territory while it was under French and Spanish rule, but after it became a part of the United States a growing Jewish community came into being that was made up largely of immigrants from Germany and Poland. It was not until 1836, however, that regular worship services were conducted. Three years later these services led to the organization of the first synagogue in Missouri—Acduth Israel. In the course of the 19th and 20th centuries other synogogues were formed, in St. Louis, Kansas City, St. Joseph, Sedalia, Springfield, and elsewhere. Like their Christian counterparts, the Jewish religious community has divided along Orthodox (conservative), Conservative (moderate), and Reform (liberal) lines.

German settlers from the east and from abroad came into Missouri very early in its history. Indeed, the first resident Protestant minister in the state was probably Samuel Weyburg, a German Reformed pastor from North Carolina, who settled near Cape Girardeau in the 1800s. The settlers from the east were mainly the descendants of Germans who had settled in Pennsylvania and then in succeeding generations had moved to Ohio and Indiana or the Carolinas and then to Missouri. This migration included Lutheran, German Reformed, Evangelical (a union in Germany of Reformed and Lutheran churches), Moravian, Mennonite, and Church of the Brethren traditions. Then, through much of the 19th century there was a great wave of immigrants from Germany into Missouri. In religion, they included Roman Catholics (destined to become the largest religious group in Missouri), liberal intellectuals who were leaving what they believed to be oppressive conditions in their homeland, moderate members of the Evangelical church, Lutherans, and an ultraconservative group from Saxony that in this country developed into the Lutheran Church Missouri Synod. This latter church is not confined to Missouri—it is to be found in most parts of the country as well as abroad—but its great strength is in the Midwest.

Influenced by pietism, its members have also sought to maintain strict fidelity to traditional Lutheran doctrine. Where liberals had left Germany because they felt it was too bound by ecclesiastical and political despotism, the Missouri Synod Lutherans had left their homeland because of what they believed to be its growing drift towards rationalism and liberalism.

Arriving in the St. Louis area in 1839, their first years were difficult. But they found a strong leader in Carl Walther, and they became in time a growing and dynamic church.

With their concern for scholarship and for purity of doctrine, they quickly devoted themselves to founding educational institutions. In the same year as their arrival, 1839, they established Concordia Theological Seminary in St. Louis for the training of their ministers. Colleges and parochial schools for the proper education of their people soon followed. From these schools have come some of the outstanding scholars in the fields of biblical and historical studies.

Traditionally, they have held themselves aloof from other denominations. The central theological issue for them has been the nature of the inspiration and authority of the Bible, and it was over this issue, primarily, that they have in recent years suffered through a division that grew out of repeated clashes between conservatives and moderates.

The great immigration from Germany in the early and middle years of the 19th century made St. Louis a national center of Lutheran education, scholarship, and publication. But it is also true that many of these immigrants were farmers who sought and settled on land in every part of the state, although the spires and towers of their churches are especially to be seen on the prairies of western Missouri and in the villages and towns in the central part of the state. They frequently created communities known for their stability, and strong family ties, with the church as the center of their life. The Missouri Synod church at Freistatt, for example, has won national recognition for its effectiveness in creating a wholesome community in which religion and life are meaningfully joined together.

In all of this movement of diverse peoples into Missouri, we can see that a rich diversity is becoming a hallmark of its religious life. No one form of religion dominates the scene. And learning to live with this diversity did not come easily for those who were involved in it. There were denominational rivalries that at times became heated and bitter. This was especially true in the case of the Mormons.

As a young man of 18 living in upstate New York in an area known for its revivals and religious excitement, Joseph Smith Jr. began to report visions of an angel who directed him to a place in a field where he dug up some writings on golden plates that he translated—with divine help—into the Book of Mormon. This was in 1827. He and some friends began to sell the book from door to door. The next step was the formation of a religious organization—the CHURCH OF JESUS CHRIST OF LATTER-DAY SAINTS, with Smith as the leader. As they grew they experienced the hostility of neighbors so they moved to Kirtland OH. Here also they encountered suspicion and threats so that in the early 1830s they moved again, this time to Independence MS, which Smith declared to be the "promised land," the "new Zion." But relations between "the saints" and the "gentiles" soon soured. The Mormons were accused of practicing polygamy and committing sacrilege. As they continued to grow they aroused the fear that they would eventually gain control of the area. Further, they were abolitionists, and this aroused the ire of the proslavery people who feared that they would incite slaves to rebellion.

Threats and some violence caused the Mormons to move out of the Independence area to Clay and Caldwell counties, and from there to Illinois where the familiar pattern of suspicion and hatred repeated itself. Smith was jailed, and then shot to death by a mob. After this, most of the Mormons, led by Brigham Young made a heroic trek in 1846 across the plains and mountains to their new Zion in the desert country of what is now Utah. However, the Reorganized Church of Jesus Christ of Latter-day Saints, a smaller body produced by a division over leadership, has a number of churches in Missouri and continues to make Independence its national headquarters.

The history of black people in Missouri is, in an even more profound way, a story of suffering. For they came as slaves, first during the French and Spanish eras, and then in much greater numbers with the tide of immigration from the South. They worked in the lead and zinc mines, they labored to clear, plow, plant, and harvest the fields, they built fences, loaded and unloaded the steamboats, and in general provided much of the labor that was needed to transform a wilderness into thriving farms, towns, and cities. In 1821 Missouri was, after much controversy, admitted into the Union as a slave state. In 1860, on the eve of the Civil War, blacks constituted about 10 percent of the population.

Most of the slaves in Missouri did not work in gangs under an overseer, but rather worked with their owners, who typically owned only two or three slaves. This made for a more human and personal relationship. But in spite of the intention of many white masters to be just and good masters, the fact remains that families were separated and black people were subjected to the degradation of the slave system with its trade in human flesh.

For these reasons, and many others as well, the institution of slavery was a source of controversy among white church people almost from its beginning, and this controversy increased in intensity and violence—especially as slaves became more valuable. In Missouri, as in other border states, families, churches, and society in general were torn by dissension.

An ominous sign of the gathering storm may be seen in the murder of Elijah Lovejoy, a Presbyterian minister and editor. His strong antislavery articles in a paper he published in St. Louis so enraged proslavery sentiment that a mob destroyed his printing shop in 1836. Undaunted, he moved across the river to the free soil of Alton IL, from which he continued his attack on slavery. Again a mob destroyed his presses and this time murdered him as well.

Other signs followed. Church people opposed to slavery were increasingly willing to defy laws that established or perpetuated slavery. So, in the name of what they believed to be a higher law, they organized to help slaves escape to Canada and freedom via the "underground railroad." In 1841 two ministerial students and a young friend were tried, convicted,

and sentenced to from three to five years for encouraging and helping blacks to escape from slavery.

In the 1850s a vicious border warfare broke out along the Missouri-Kansas line, with proslavery partisans making raids into Kansas to kill and burn, and equally bloody raids into Missouri by abolitionists. John Brown became nationally known as a violent abolitionist, and received guns and other support from church people in the north and east.

In this explosive atmosphere churches were torn apart. The Presbyterian, Methodist, and Baptist churches divided over the issue of slavery and so far only the Methodists have been able to find their way back to unity.

The controversy in the churches was by no means a simple matter of being for or against slavery. There was in it a tangle of other issues—such as the preservation of the Union—and in the churches several categories of people might be found. There were fire-eaters like James Shannon who defended slavery on arguments drawn from nature and the Bible; there were moderates who sought to find a gradual way by which slavery might be abolished without recourse to war; and there were abolitionists who in the name of God demanded an immediate end to slavery, whatever the cost.

The rising tide of anger and conflict finally erupted into civil war in the spring of 1861. It continued for four long years, and Missouri endured her share of violence and disruption.

In their travail the black people of Missouri learned how to cope and how to endure. In this process they sometimes developed an inner strength and compassion that is impressive. Mark Twain (Samuel Clemens) knew blacks as he grew up in Hannibal, and when he worked with them as a riverboat pilot on the Mississippi. There is good reason to believe that his sympathetic portrayal of Jim, the friend and companion of Huckleberry

Finn in his novel of that name, was drawn from life. A further illustration is that of George Washington Carver, who was born a slave in southwestern Missouri, but overcame severe handicaps to become an outstanding scientist, committed to helping poor farmers grow better crops.

In their years of bondage many black people became Christians, and after the Civil War they left the churches of their former masters and formed their own churches (mostly Baptist and Methodist) led by black preachers. These churches provided consolation and faith in times of adversity as well as a sense of dignity and worth. Their preachers were frequently men of natural ability who found in the church a place where they could exercise their talents and leadership. Indeed, the church offered not only spiritual guidance, but also music, some opportunity and incentive to learn to read and write, and support and counselling in time of crisis.

In the 20th century, secularism has bit deeply into the religious faith and practice of both blacks and whites, especially as they left farm and village to live in crowded city ghettos. But in these cities, such as Kansas City and St. Louis, black musicians created a new form of music—jazz, especially the blues—that sometimes expresses a religious dimension—a feeling of loneliness, abandonment, and sadness in powerful ways.

The Civil War represents a kind of continental divide in American history in the sense that after 1865 the United States became a different kind of nation. The frontier faded and increasing numbers of Americans lived in cities. New waves of immigration from central and eastern Europe helped to fill the burgeoning urban areas. The rise of universities with their humanistic and scientific point of view, the historical and critical study of the Bible, the Darwinian theory of evolution, the growing encounter with other religions, the technological revolution that annihilated space and time and made the world a neighborhood—these are only some of the forces that were creating a new kind of world with new problems and challenges to religion.

One of the leading characteristics of this post-Civil War era was the increasing pluralism of American religious life. Although this diversity was often due to ethnic and cultural differences, there were also, in many instances, theological conflicts, especially those that might be broadly categorized as a clash between liberal and conservative points of view. For example, in the late nineteenth century the holiness issue was a major factor in some splits away from the Methodist church. The Holiness movement was made up largely of people who believed that the Methodist church had become too worldly and liberal and had departed too much from the teachings of the founder, John Wesley. They were especially concerned to keep his doctrine of holiness, or Christian perfection, in which it was taught that a Christian should seek to receive a second blessing of entire sanctification, a state of being in which one's whole life might be centered on the love of God. A number of Holiness churches were formed out of this controversy, but in Missouri the CHURCH OF THE NAZARENE has been especially strong, its international headquarters being in Kansas City.

The Pentecostal movement generally held to the doctrine of holiness, but in addition advocated the experience of glossolalia, or speaking in tongues. They further believed in faith healing and, like most Fundamentalists, held to the inerrancy of Scripture. The Pentecostal movement has divided over various issues, but one of the largest of these divisions is that of the Assemblies of God. It makes SPRINGFIELD its world headquarters, and in addition maintains there a publishing house, a graduate seminary, a training school called Central Bible Institute, and Evangel, a liberal arts college. Other Pentecostal bodies have headquarters in St. Louis and Joplin.

Missouri, like the rest of the nation, has also experienced an upsurge of interest in religious movements influenced by Asian religions, particularly forms of Hinduism and Buddhism. In some instances this influence has been mediated by the transcendentalist ideas of Emerson and Thoreau. Some aspects of this strain of thought may be seen in the teachings of the Church of Christ, Scientist, which founded congregations in Missouri. This movement in turn influenced the founders of the Unity School of Christianity begun in 1889 in Kansas City by Charles and Myrtle Fillmore. The movement they launched grew and prospered, and a 1,300-acre farm near Lees Summit, in the Kansas City area, was purchased and beautifully developed into a publishing, learning, and worship center. Unity accepts the reality of the physical world, and holds to a belief in reincarnation, but its aims are not so much theoretical as practical: it seeks to show people through the power of constructive thought the way to more abundant living.

If Missouri's growing religious pluralism has been due to some basic theological differences—as well as ethnic and social differences—then much of this conflict may be reduced to the fundamental conflict between liberalism and conservatism. These terms are notoriously difficult to define. That they are also relative terms is indicated by the fact that Southern Baptists are generally regarded as conservative by liberal Protestants, but to the independent Baptists (BAPTIST BIBLE FELLOWSHIP), who have built some of the largest congregations in the state, the Southern Baptist Convention is regarded as tainted with liberalism, or as harboring "modernists."

But these slippery terms may have some usefulness in considering the differing ways in which religious people reacted to the modern world. Liberals, for example, have tended to be more open to the culture of the 20th century, more willing to accept the scientific world view, while conservatives have been more resistant to change, more critical of science— especially Darwinian evolution—and more loyal to the traditional beliefs and practices of their faith.

Conflicts over these and other issues troubled nearly all forms of religion in the post-Civil War era, and these conflicts have continued up to the present. In 1889, for example, a Disciples minister in St. Louis, R. L. Cave, preached a series of sermons in which he stated that he could no longer believe in the virgin birth or physical resurrection of Jesus. Forced to resign by a majority of the church members, he led a minority in founding one of the first community churches in America. A little later, another Disciples minister, Burris Jenkins, developed a community church that became one of the most controversial congregations in the state.

In some cases liberal-conservative tensions led to disruption, as when the Disciples divided into the Churches of Christ, the Independent Christian Churches, and the Christian Church (Disciples of Christ), or, most recently, when the Lutheran Church (Missouri Synod), the Presbyterian Church U.S. and the Episcopal Church, suffered through the trauma of division (the last two in less major ways).

It should be remembered, however, that these and other divisions are counterbalanced by a strong and sometimes dramatic surge towards Christian unity in which Roman Catholics, Episcopalians, Methodists, Presbyterians, and Disciples have given conspicuous leadership. The cause of Christian unity was also served by the Missouri School of Religion in Columbia, that offered courses in religion at the University of Missouri, and for awhile won national recognition for its efforts to bring small churches in rural communities together to form one strong church that could more effectively serve the needs of the people. (It was replaced in 1981 by a Department of Religion.)

But by and large Missouri remains a rather conservative state and is generally considered to be a part of the Bible Belt that reaches across much of the South. This conservatism is especially marked in the Ozark hill country, as is illustrated by the extreme case of the small town of Liberal MO. Founded in 1880 by G. H. Walser to be a refuge for free-thinkers, the founder boasted that the village had no priests, preachers, or peace officers, no churches or saloons, and no loafers or beggars. When some Protestants tried to settle at the edge of his town Walser built a fence to try to keep them out. But in the course of time the enterprise began to fail financially, the founder became a convert to spiritualism, several Protestant churches moved in, and the whole episode is largely forgotten except as it may appear in sermon illustrations.

On a more significant level, Missouri was the birthplace of one of the nation's greatest theologians, Reinhold Niebuhr. Born in Wright City, where his father was the pastor of the local Evangelical and Reformed church, Niebuhr studied at Elmhurst College, Eden Theological Seminary, and the Yale Divinity School, and then became pastor of a small mission church in Detroit. There he became aware of the plight of the industrial worker whose cause he subsequently championed. He became nationally known as a prophetic speaker and writer. In the late 1920s Niebuhr became a member of the faculty of Union Theological Seminary in New York where he lived out the busy years of his distinguished career.

In his early years Niebuhr had been a liberal, a socialist, and a pacifist, but the rise of the Nazis to power in Germany led him to a new consciousness of the inherent and inescapable sinfulness of human nature. There was for him no possibility that a utopia might be established on earth. Yet man must act and shoulder the responsibilities that must be borne. The Bible, which he took seriously but not literally, provides a more realistic and profound view of human existence than did other religions and ideologies. At the end, he believed that the Bible also offered hope and the promise of forgiveness through a God who is the transcendent Lord of all life and history. Thus he found both liberalism and conservatism inadequate, and found in biblical religion that Word of God that brings both judgment and mercy.

In retrospect, we can see that the history of religion in Missouri is one in which, as Niebuhr might have taught, there is a mingling of vision, courage, pride, tragedy, and new beginnings. It is also, as this sampler might suggest, a history in which there is constant change and elaboration. As to the future, of only one thing can we be sure: like one of the clear, fast flowing streams of the Ozark hill country, movement and some surprising turns will continue to mark the history of this state and its people.

See also articles on FRENCH INFLUENCE; MIGRATION, WESTWARD (1750-1900); MORMONS IN THE SOUTH; OZARKS RELIGION; ROMAN CATHOLIC CHURCH.

Bibliography. Sydney Ahlstrom, *A Religious History of the American People*; Everett Dick, *The Dixie Frontier*; William E. Foley, *A History of Missouri, 1673-1820*; Samuel S. Hill, Jr., *Southern Churches in Crisis*; John Joseph Matthews, *The Osages: Children of the Middle Border*; Duane Meyer, *The Heritage of Missouri: A History*; *Missouri: A Guide to the "Show Me State,"* compiled, Writers' Program of the Works Project Administration, Missouri; Perry McCandless, *A History of Missouri, 1820-1860*; Edwin C. McReynolds, *Missouri: A History of the Cross-Roads State*; Paul C. Nagel, *Missouri*; William E. Parrish, *A History of Missouri, 1860-1875*; Henry A. Pochman, *German Culture in America*; *Reinhold Niebuhr: His Religious, Social and Political Thought*, ed., Charles W. Kegley and Robert W. Bretall; Earl T. Sechler, *Our Religious Heritage: Church History of the Ozarks, 1806-1906*.

RICHARD M. POPE
LEXINGTON THEOLOGICAL SEMINARY

MODERN REVIVALISM: *See* PROTRACTED MEETINGS; REVIVALISM.

MODERNISM: *See* SECULARIZATION.

MODERNIST CONTROVERSY.
Modernism is an understanding of the relationship between faith and reason. More a method than a body of thought, it values change over stability in the formu-

lations of faith and prefers challenging understandings rooted in revelation to questioning knowledge derived from science. Within Southern history, the Modernist Controversy refers to the argument over the teaching of evolution that drew national and worldwide attention to the region and its religion during the 1920s.

Even before that decade, several 19th-century incidents signaled Southern preference for orthodoxy. Between 1878 and 1888, for example, each of the major denominations purged scholars who allowed their scientific knowledge to influence their religious understanding, as the stories of ALEXANDER WINCHELL, CRAWFORD H. TOY, and JAMES WOODROW testify. In this era, however, similar cases issued in not dissimilar outcomes in the North.

Early in the 20th century, the context changed. In the South, the failures of both New South rhetoric and Populist politics combined with Southern racial attitudes to reinforce the region in its condition of economic and social provincialism and to exclude from it immigrants with their diversities. The nation as a whole, meanwhile, impelled by industrialization and immigration, sought in Progressivism either revision or restatement of its understanding of "American." Despite the trauma of World War I and its aftermath, most outside the South still carried into the 1920s optimism about human potential and faith in the possibilities of prosperity. Southerners, drawing on their own historical experience and a more consistently conservative religious vision, brought a different insight when they joined the postwar effort.

In a world of mind-numbing change, many who yearned for some anchor of stability sought it in their Christian faith. Especially Southern religious apologists, disposed to premillennialism by their religious insight no less than by their social and economic circumstances, pointed to Germany and Russia as proof of the de-

structive effects of too great a faith in human potential. Led generally by Baptists who understood their tradition as most faithful to primitive Christianity, concerned people strove to meet the time's challenge by restoring faith in "fundamentals."

They identified Darwinian evolution as the greatest threat to the fundamentals of faith, with its apparent glorification of change and demeaning of both divine and human dignity. Evolution not only challenged the authority of the Bible by contradicting its inspired account of human origins, it also substituted belief in the rise of humanity from a baser condition to a fuller life for the biblical teaching of humanity's fall from a state of innocence. With a single stroke evolution seemed to shatter scriptural inerrancy, to eliminate the need as well as the hope for salvation, and to void the eschatological promise of the Second Coming of Christ.

The teaching of evolution emerged as the central issue between those who preeminently valued scientific knowledge and those who primarily prized religious wisdom. If biblical literalists found in evolution a challenge to their faith, intellectuals saw in strictures on evolution's teaching a violation of their freedom. But the most significant conflict did not come at the seminary level. In the United States, parents entrust to the public schools their children's growth in both knowledge and wisdom; the young are to learn in school both the timeless wisdom of their elders and the latest knowledge of a technologically mobile society. Education should lead to knowing more but not to thinking differently. Wary of such dichotomizing, modernists challenged this assumption, reposing their hope in the faith that knowing more inevitably leads to thinking differently.

Political pressures as well as economic interests contributed to the focus on the public schools. Urged on by enthusiasts such as WILLIAM JENNINGS BRYAN, who proclaimed it more important that school children know the Rock of Ages than that they study the age of rocks, various political bodies prohibited the teaching of evolution in tax-supported institutions. The prosecution of JOHN T. SCOPES made Tennessee's law the most infamous, but similar measures were enacted before that trial in Oklahoma and Florida, and after it in Mississippi and Arkansas. Elsewhere, local school boards followed the example of Texas in banning textbooks that discussed evolution.

In spite of all this flurry, within five years of Scopes's conviction the Modernist Controversy had been largely forgotten. Many factors contributed to this outcome: Bryan's death and the demise of other fundamentalist stalwarts; intradenominational political maneuverings; the economic crash of 1929; and the reemergence in 1928 of Prohibition as the primary fundamentalist concern. Yet even in the 1940s many teachers feared to mention evolution, and the early 1980s witnessed several Southern legislatures debating requirements to teach "creationscience" in the public schools.

Was the Modernist Controversy of the 1920s then of no importance? Not precisely, for in two ways its significance proved profound. More than any other 20th-century episode, the antievolution crusade was seized upon to dramatize the conservative religious temper of the South and to vulgarize its "Bible Belt" stereotype. The resulting ridicule solidified Southerners, activating defenses that ranged from the Agrarians' "stand" in the 1930s to the perceptive stories of FLANNERY O'CONNOR in the 1960s. More deeply, the significance of the Modernist Controversy lies in its effect on religious thought in the South. The acrimony of the argument imposed an equation between orthodoxy and fundamentalism that smothered conservative religious thinking. Ironically, the muteness that resulted contributed as much as did the modernist onslaught to the effect of rendering all thought irreligious. The Modernist Controversy of the 1920s thus obfuscated the very question it supposedly aimed to clarify—the relationship between piety and reason in the lives of those who, following Christian tradition, value both.

See also articles on EVOLUTION CONTROVERSY; FUNDAMENTALISM; SCOPES TRIAL.

Bibliography. Kenneth K. Bailey, *Southern White Protestantism in the Twentieth Century*; Paul A. Carter, "The Fundamentalist Defense of the Faith," *Change and Continuity in 20th-Century America: the 1920s*, ed. John Braeman et al.; Norman F. Furniss, *The Fundamentalist Controversy, 1918-1931*; Willard B. Gatewood, Jr., ed., *Controversy in the Twenties: Fundamentalism, Modernism, and Evolution*; Robert T. Handy, "Fundamentalism and Modernism in Perspective," *Religion in Life* 24 (Summer 1955): 381-94; "The American Religious Depression, 1925-1935," *Church History* 24 (March 1960): 3-16; William R. Hutchison, *The Modernist Impulse in American Protestantism*; George M. Marsden, *Fundamentalism and American Culture*; Ernest R. Sandeen, *The Roots of Fundamentalism*; James J. Thompson, Jr., *Tried as by Fire*.

ERNEST KURTZ
ATHENS, GEORGIA

MOISE, PENINA (1797-1880), celebrated poet and Jewish author, was born in Charleston SC, her parents being refugees from the Santo Domingo revolt. Her father, a native of Alsace, ran a small shop in Charleston. Following his death in 1809, Penina had to end her formal education and make lace and embroidery to help the family pay its bills.

Moise had a talent for poetry and was encouraged in this endeavor by friends. As early as 1819 she was writing poetry, and before her death she had authored at least 350 poems. These appeared not only in Charleston newspapers, but also in the Boston, Washington, and New Orleans press, in *Godey's Lady's Book*, and in Jewish periodicals. Most of her work concerned secular subjects, but a significant number had Jewish themes. In 1833 she published *Fancy's Sketch Book*, which featured 60 of her poems. This was the first book written by an American Jewess.

Never married, she was devoutly religious and a faithful congregant of BETH ELOHIM, the second-oldest synagogue in the United States. In 1842 she became superintendent of that temple's Sunday school. The great majority of the selections in *Hymns Written for the Use of Congregation Beth Elohim*, the first American Jewish hymnal, were her compositions. In 1846 she published *Hymns Written for the Use of Hebrew Congregations*. Several of these hymns are used in Reform temples today.

Hers was a hard life. She devoted her early years to caring for her paralyzed mother. In 1854 she spent months nursing victims of a yellow fever outbreak in Charleston. An avid secessionist, she fled to Sumter SC during the Civil War. By 1865 her eyesight was failing. Nonetheless, she continued to write poems on a slate, which were transcribed by a niece. She also helped run a girls' school and orally taught classes in literature. On Fridays she held a salon at her house that attracted Charleston's literary lights.

In 1911 the Charleston section of the National Council of Jewish women published *Secular and Religious Works of Penina Moise.*

See also article on JEWS IN THE SOUTH.

ARNOLD SHANKMAN

MOLLEGEN, ALBERT (1906-), Episcopal theologian, was born in McComb MS. A convert to the Episcopal Church, and with a background in engineering, "Molle," as he was always called by everyone from bishops to students, graduated from Virginia Theological Seminary in 1931. After ordination in Mississippi he did graduate work at Union Theological Seminary, receiving his S.T.M. degree there in 1936. He enjoyed a close relationship over the years with the faculty at Union, becoming a personal friend of Reinhold Niebuhr and Paul Tillich. The latter had an especially strong influence upon Mollegen, who vigorously defended Tillich's Christology, but began to be critical of Tillich's directions in the late 1950s.

Mollegen taught at Virginia Theological Seminary in Alexandria from 1936 until retirement in 1974. He brought to Virginia the rigors of the historical-critical method and the stringent political

realism of neo-orthodoxy. He taught New Testament and Christian Ethics, but was even more widely influential in apologetics. He traveled widely, speaking at universities, clergy conferences, and ecumenical gatherings. He helped start a Lay School of Religion in Washington that drew many illustrious people, including James Pike, later a bishop.

As a teacher, conference leader, pastor, General Convention delegate, and advisor to bishops, he was one of the outstanding leaders of the Episcopal Church in his generation. Among his many writings are: *Christianity and Modern Man, Christianity and St. Paul,* and *Christ and Everyman.* Characteristic of his teaching was the constant relating of Christianity to politics, medicine, psychiatry, philosophy, and contemporary literature.

See also article on THEOLOGY.

C. FITZSIMMONS ALLISON
CHARLESTON, SOUTH CAROLINA

MONK: *See* BROTHER.

MONKEY TRIAL: *See* SCOPES, JOHN T.; SCOPES TRIAL.

MONSIGNOR. This is a title used as a term of honor or respect in reference to patriarchs, archbishops, and bishops; it is also applied to certain priests especially honored by the Holy See in Rome.

In the United States the title is commonly reserved for those priests who are recognized by the pope, generally for their learning, piety, apostolic zeal, or particular service to the Church. Priests so honored hold membership in the pontifical household and certain prerogatives in liturgical celebrations and clerical dress. The honor is not of a sacramental nature, nor does it imply any special jurisdiction, as in the case of a bishop.

While Monsignor is for the most part an honorific title, its bestowal is one way of recognizing significant contributions by individual priests, since they are their united to the ministry and household of the pope.

In the reforms Pope Paul VI made of papal honors and household offices in 1968 (*Motu Proprio "Pontificalis Domus"*), efforts were undertaken to "select from institutions and customs handed down . . . those which appear to be essential and most important." In so doing, the following factors were stressed: the "preeminence of matters spiritual," "the demands of truth," "the value of public discipline," "the pursuit of the practical," and the functional and reasonable effectiveness of customs or institutions in preference to their mere nominal, decorative, or ostentatious use.

In the Catholic Church of the South, it is not uncommon to meet priests bearing the honors referred to above. Given the informality of the South, it is also not uncommon to find that many of these priests prefer to be addressed simply as "father."

ROBERT J. BAKER
ST. VINCENT DE PAUL
REGIONAL SEMINARY

MONTREAT, NORTH CAROLINA.

This community, located two miles from Black Mountain, is the site of a Presbyterian summer community dating to the turn of the century. The name is derived from Mountain Retreat Association, the title of a private corporation administered by a board of governors associated closely with the Presbyterian Church in the United States, known regionally as "Southern Presbyterian." Located in a mountain cove near the convergence of the Black Mountains with the Blue Ridge, the community includes a winter component affiliated with the Montreat-Anderson College, a summer conference center that uses the college buildings for religious conferences and seminars, and a cluster of over 400 privately owned residences known as "cottages," used primarily in summer for family gatherings and vacations.

Montreat is the hub of ceremonial life in Southern Presbyterianism, with the total summer population at times reaching as many as three to four thousand.

Conference meetings are held in college classrooms and in a large central auditorium; conferees are housed in a dormitory, a hotel operated by the association, one of the many guest houses, or in a rented cottage. Conference themes include women's concerns, family life, ministry and mission, music, the Bible, youth, and other topical issues within Christian education or ethics. These assemblies and their programs combine aspects of the historical CAMP MEETING with those of the Chatauqua or summer institute, framing modern questions within traditional frameworks of social gathering, worship, and study. College students are hired every year to staff a children's program known as "the clubs" and to serve as maintenance and domestic staff for the center.

Members of the cottage-owning community are closely tied in a network of kinship, friendship, and shared cultural ancestry of Scottish Presbyterianism. Many houses are owned jointly by extended families, some having been in one family for three to four generations. The cottage families begin to assemble in early summer; often the mother comes to Montreat with children and the father joins the group for weekends and vacation. Reunions are held here, and daughters bring their children home to mother for long visits with their sisters and friends. Kinship ties among the cottage families are reinforced by marriage within the denomination, the Presbyterian colleges, and the community of Montreat.

In addition to the social function of forging and continuing networks among scattered people, Montreat provides a symbolic enactment of the meanings and values held by Southern Presbyterians. It is a ritual statement of a way of life. Through this gathering, traditional values of family and church can be restated annually and new meanings and values can be generated out of existing cultural forms. As a social and symbolic form, Montreat is similar to the church HOMECOMING, the family reunion, and the camp meeting of the rural South and to the Covenanting meeting and the Communion Season of Scotland. As an institutional form it is similar to Protestant denominational conferences in the South and elsewhere. It is distinctive because of its symbolic importance to Southern Presbyterians and because of its role as a preserver of a Scottish Presbyterian cultural core within the seemingly "mainstream" Protestant South.

Bibliography. Robert C. Anderson, *The Story of Montreat From Its Beginning 1897-1947;* Gwen Kennedy Neville, "Annual Assemblages as Related to the Persistence of Culture Patterns: An Anthropological Study of a Summer Community," University Microfilms; "Kinfolks and the Covenant: Ethnic Community Among Southern Presbyterians," *The New Ethnicity—Perspectives From Ethnology; 1973 Proceedings of the American Ethnological Society,* ed. John Bennett.

GWEN KENNEDY NEVILLE
SOUTHWESTERN UNIVERSITY

MOON, LOTTIE (CHARLOTTE DIGGES)

(1840-1912), a pioneer Southern Baptist missionary to China and symbol of that denomination's devotion to foreign missions, was born near Charlottesville VA. She grew up in an atmosphere of privilege, piety, and high idealism. In 1861 she graduated from Albemarle Female Institute with a master's degree in classics and a marked interest in foreign languages and cultures. Her family's financial circumstances having deteriorated, she supported herself after the Civil War by school teaching. In 1873, dissatisfied with her life and feeling a call to missionary service, Miss Moon joined the Southern Baptist station at Tengchow in northeast China. From that point to her death in 1912 she worked as an evangelist and teacher in east Shantung province.

Lottie Moon's most notable work was done in the years 1885-1890. An ardent proponent of the professional role and rights of unmarried female missionaries, she lived at that time under independent but trying conditions in an interior district called P'ingtu. By hard work and adaptability she was instrumental in establishing the base for an important evangelistic center. Her P'ingtu work also attracted attention among Southern Baptists in America. One of her reports inspired an 1888 Christmas offering that was ostensibly for the purpose of sending aid for her and her work. More important, the offering provided a focus for organizing the Woman's Missionary Union, an agency that has provided massive and indispensable support to SBC missions ever since.

The last 20 years of Miss Moon's life were spent mostly in educational and evangelistic work at Tengchow. She was remarkable for her fortitude and charity, her advocacy of missionary "woman's work," and for her open-minded devotion to China. Tiny in stature, she was a woman of considerable intellectual attainments and increasingly introspective spirituality. In 1918, to honor her memory and as part of a general upgrading of the SBC mission effort, the offering begun in 1888 was designated the Lottie Moon Christmas Offering for Foreign Missions. Subsequent promotional efforts have apotheosized Miss Moon as a heroine and attracted substantial contributions to mission work. Through 1979 the offering had raised $445,400,453 and had a Christmas 1980 goal of $45,000,000.

See also articles on SOUTHERN BAPTIST CONVENTION; WOMEN IN RELIGION.

Bibliography. Catherine B. Allen, *The New Lottie Moon Story;* Irwin T. Hyatt, Jr., *Our Ordered Lives Confess: Three Nineteenth-Century American Missionaries in East Shantung;* Una Roberts Lawrence, *Lottie Moon.*

IRWIN T. HYATT
EMORY UNIVERSITY

MOORE, RICHARD CHANNING

(1762-1841), the second Episcopal bishop of Virginia, was elected in May 1814. Seven clergymen were present for that convention; at the last diocesan convention over which Bishop Moore presided in May 1841, 89 Virginia clergymen attended. The intervening years witnessed a resurrection of the EPISCOPAL CHURCH in Virginia following a period of severe decline between 1770 and 1810.

Twelve years before Moore's arrival the diocese had been decimated by Virginia's Glebe Act of 1802, which gave to the state all property of parishes then without a clergyman or whenever an incumbent clergyman vacated. This action, which followed DISESTABLISHMENT, led to the closing in the following decade of nearly two-thirds of the 107 parishes that survived the Revolution.

Before going to Virginia, Moore was for 27 years minister of three churches in Rye, Staten Island, and New York City. His success as pastor and preacher attracted the attention of evangelical Episcopalians dominating the Virginia diocesan Standing Committee. The vestry of the new Monumental Church in Richmond was persuaded to call Moore as their minister, and the diocese elected him bishop.

Moore's oratorical skill in stirring emotions, his evangelical preaching and prayer meetings, his reluctance to initiate disturbing change, his kind and gentle personal ways, and his widespread travels in the diocese, all contributed to extensive church growth and the erection of buildings throughout the diocese. He gained, too, with the help of the diocesan Standing Committee, and the effective leadership of William Meade, who became assistant bishop in 1829. Long before Moore died, he was widely revered by Episcopalians and other church people throughout the Commonwealth.

JAMES L. MCALLISTER, JR.
MARY BALDWIN COLLEGE

MORAL MAJORITY. A political-action group based upon fundamentalist Christian moral principles, the Moral Majority was the flagship group in the resurgence of conservative Christian political activity beginning in the mid-1970s. Although the organization was not founded until June 1979, its genesis was stimulated by previously existing conservative organizations.

Some leaders of secular right-wing political groups became alarmed over the leftward drift of America and resolved to bring it back to its previous glory. They realized that there was a great pool of politically inactive, conservative Christians in the country who needed to be mobilized in the rescuing of America. They asked Jerry Falwell, pastor of the Thomas Road Baptist Church in Lynchburg VA, to head the religious phase of the movement. Falwell, already disturbed by pornography, abortion, the gay rights movement, the agitation for the Equal Rights Amendment, government interference with Christian schools, and the lack of prayer in the public schools—all evidences of "secular humanism"—agreed to form the Moral Majority. Since he already had developed a widely syndicated television show, "The Old-Time Gospel Hour," he was able to give the new political emphasis great visibility.

The Moral Majority is made up of essentially autonomous chapters distributed all across the country. The largest and most active of these chapters were on the East and West Coasts, particularly California, although Falwell's TV ministry had the highest percentage of its viewers in the South. Just prior to the 1980 election it was estimated that the organization had two to three million members, although as late as May 1982 the *Moral Majority Report*, a monthly newspaper, had a circulation of only 900,000. Falwell asserted that his organization was not just a fundamentalist Christian group, since it also included conservative Catholics, Orthodox Jews, Mormons, and even some people who professed no religion.

In the presidential election of 1980 the New Christian Right, of which the Moral Majority was a major component, claimed that it made the difference in electing Ronald Reagan and defeating several liberal congressmen. Some analysts doubted that it was the deciding factor, but all agreed that it played a significant role. Prior to the midterm election of 1982 great effort was being made to enlarge its membership and sweep more conservative candidates into office. Falwell proclaimed that the Moral Majority intended to be a permanent influence in American politics.

The Moral Majority is subjected to three principal criticisms. Some Fundamentalists argue it should only preach Christ, not be involved in politics. Some, such as BILLY GRAHAM, criticized it for allying itself too closely with secular right-wing politics. Moderates and liberals criticized it because it tried to impose its own moral standards and political views on the entire country, to create a Christian America, and thus annul the religious pluralism of the nation. Falwell denied the latter, saying that he valued a religiously pluralistic society and the First Amendment right of religious freedom. But he also said that he and his organization would struggle to drive corruption from America.

See also article on FUNDAMENTALISM.

Bibliography. Gabriel Fackre, *The Religious Right and Christian Faith*; Jeffrey K. Hadden and Charles E. Swann, *Prime Time Preachers: The Rising Power of Televangelism*; Samuel S. Hill and Dennis E. Owen, *The New Religious/Political Right in America*.

RONALD B. FLOWERS
TEXAS CHRISTIAN UNIVERSITY

MORALITY, CHRISTIAN: *See* ETHICS, CHRISTIAN.

MORAVIAN CHURCH.

This Protestant body traces its origins to the 15th-century Hussite Reformation and the founding of the Unitas Fratrum (Unity of the Brethren) in 1457 at Kunvald, Bohemia. While deriving much of their theology, polity, and life-style from John Hus (1369-1415), the Unitas also incorporated elements of the Utraquist and Taborite factions of the Hussite movement. Basically rural in nature, the Unitas developed as a pacifist and quietist sect influenced by the perfectionism and New Testament orientation of Peter Chelcický (1390-1460). Eventually the Unitas became the major Protestant movement in Bohemia and Moravia in the 16th and 17th centuries. Its leaders like Lukas of Prague and

John Amos Comenius guided the sect toward becoming a more liturgical, educational, and mainline Protestant tradition as evidenced in the Confessio Bohemica, 1575. The Unitas is remembered for its contributions of Bohemian hymnody, the Kralitz Bible, and a rich heritage of devotional literature.

By 1620-1621 the shifts in religious and secular power and the spirit of the Catholic Reformation in Central Europe led to the repression of the Brethren. The movement scattered in exile to Poland and the Baltic region, as well as going underground in Moravia. During this period, called the "Hidden Seed" by Moravians, Bishop Comenius (1592-1670), the distinguished educator and humanist, kept alive the spirit and organizational heritage of the Unitas Fratrum.

Remnants of the old or Ancient Unity found their way to the Saxon estate of Count Nicholas Zinzendorf (1700-1760) in 1722. Establishing their village, Herrnhut, on the count's estate, the Moravians reconstituted their church as the incorporated Unitas Fratrum. Zinzendorf's patronage combined his Pietist and Lutheran concepts with their Hussite heritage. What emerged was a highly experimental movement with an intense heart religion, a quietist ethic, and an ecumenical polity. Zinzendorf saw the Moravians as a "church within the church" and developed Moravian congregation towns with a theocratic and communal polity. This Renewed Moravian Church sent out missionaries to neglected areas such as the Caribbean (1732), Surinam (1735), South Africa (1737), and Labrador (1771). Part of this broad vision sent the first group of Moravians to SAVANNAH GA in 1735. Led by Bishop August Spangenberg (1704-1792), a Pietist and associate of Zinzendorf, this group traveled with Charles and John Wesley to Savannah.

The Moravian experience in Georgia (1735-1740) was complicated by their pietism, their pacifism, and their evangelical interest in the Creek and Cherokee

Indians as well as the black slaves of the Carolinas. A school and mission station was started for the Creeks at Irene, an island in the Savannah River. Peter Böhler and George Schulius projected work among black people at Purysburg. Moravian missions in America, given shape by men like David Zeisberger and John Heckewelder, sought an understanding of the indigenous Indian culture. Stressing a simple Christ-centered faith and ethic, the Moravians also established educational and other helping ministries. Caught by their pacifism and at odds with the Savannah community over religious freedom, the Brethren concluded their Georgia work in 1740. Several of these Moravians moved to the GEORGE WHITEFIELD tract in Pennsylvania, which became the Moravian town of Nazareth. It was adjacent to the larger Bethlehem congregation town founded in 1741.

In 1747 and 1748 Moravians made exploratory mission trips into the Virginia backcountry with limited success. The next organized phase of Moravian work in the South began with the London negotiations with Lord Granville and the purchase of a hundred thousand acre tract in North Carolina. The 1752 survey party picked a tract in the Yadkin Valley that was named Wachovia. A small, selected group of Moravians traveled down the Great Wagon Road from Pennsylvania to settle Bethabara (House of Passage) in 1753 as a temporary congregation town until Salem, the central town for Wachovia, could be established. Bethabara as an outpost in the Carolina backcountry provided a small farming and artisan community as a base for missions to the Creeks and Cherokees. Its careful planning, literate life-style, and theocratic organization reflected an intense experiential piety generated in Europe and transferred to the Southern frontier.

The second town, Bethania (1759), was followed by the founding of Salem in 1766 as the center for Wachovia. Under the leadership of men such as Frederick

William Marshall, this town became a trade and craft center for the South, exhibiting the best aspects of a planned town in terms of architecture and industry. Its communal economy, choir system (a grouping of Moravians according to age, sex, and marital status complementing regular family life), craft industries, cultural life, and educational institutions embodied a practical and viable utopian vision. At the dawn of the 19th century the Moravian evangelical faith spread to several country congregations with Salem and its Home Moravian Church as their center. Its schools were represented by the Salem Boarding School (1802), which became Salem Academy and College, a center for the education of Southern women in the 19th and 20th centuries. Mission work among the Cherokees was begun in 1800 at Springplace GA. Much of this earlier legacy is reflected today in the restored town of Old Salem.

The Moravian Church gradually expanded and changed in character. Its pacifism, which proved difficult in the American Revolution, gave way to a gradual accommodation in the War of 1812. The communal economy was adjusted and eventually dismantled by midcentury. By the 1840s German was no longer used in official records. With the secularization of Wachovia's towns, the Church moved toward American denominational patterns and a more flexible ethic while retaining many of its earlier traditions of worship, lovefeasts, music, and mission consciousness. More recent periods of renewal and church extension were marked by Moravian growth to over 50 congregations of about 21,000 members in the Winston-Salem area, the state of North Carolina, and other areas of the South. While the contemporary Southern province of the Moravian Church is active in the Protestant mainstream, it retains its ties, by way of its conferential polity, to the worldwide Unity. Today, two-thirds of the membership of the Unitas Fratrum is in the areas where Moravians initiated mission work.

See also articles on MISSIONS TO THE INDIANS, SOUTHEAST; NORTH CAROLINA; PIETISM; PROTESTANT REFORMATION.

Bibliography. J. Taylor Hamilton, *History of the Moravian Church*; Hunter James, *The Quiet People of the Land*; Howard Kaminsky, *A History of the Hussite Revolution*; *Records of the Moravians in North Carolina*, vols. 1-9; *The Three Forks of Muddy Creek*, vols. 1-7, Old Salem Incorporated; Jarold Zeman, *The Hussite Movement, A Bibliographical Study Guide*.

CLARK A. THOMPSON
SALEM COLLEGE

MORMONS (THE CHURCH OF JESUS CHRIST OF LATTER-DAY SAINTS).

Itinerant missionaries brought the doctrines of the Church of Jesus Christ of Latter-day Saints, the Mormons, into the South soon after the founding of the church at Fayette NY in April 1830 by Joseph Smith, Jr. Smith said that as early as 1820 he began receiving revelations that told him all existing churches had strayed from the teachings of Christ. He claimed that in 1823 an angel named Moroni revealed to him the hiding place of some golden plates, or tablets, containing writings in a strange language. In 1827 the angel permitted him to take the plates from their hiding place and by peering into seer stones found with the plates he was able to translate the inscriptions into English. The finished work was called the *Book of Mormon* and Smith and his followers asserted that with divine guidance and authority they had reestablished the original New Testament church founded by Christ and the apostles.

The *Book of Mormon*, considered a sacred text equal in authority to the Bible by members of the church, tells of some ancient Hebrew people led by a prophet named Lehi. Following God's directions they left Jerusalem about 600 B.C. and traveled eastward by land and water until they reached the Land Bountiful— America. Here they divided into opposing factions, the Nephites and the Lamanites. Eventually all the Nephites were killed except the prophet Mormon and his son Moroni. They wrote their history on the golden plates and after his death on earth the angel Moroni guarded them until they were revealed to Smith. Mormons believe that Smith was permitted to translate about one-third of the material on the golden plates before they were returned to the angel Moroni. They also believe that the American Indians are descendants of the ancient Lamanites, and from its inception the church has carried on missionary activities among the Indians to try to bring them back to the faith of their ancestors.

At first Smith attracted few followers, so in 1831 he moved with his family and a handful of converts from New York to Kirtland OH. Shortly after this move occurred, some of the more zealous of Smith's converts crossed the Ohio River to engage in missionary activities in the Southern states. The first branch of the Mormon Church in the South seems to have been founded in Cabell County (now West) VA in 1832, and in the years immediately thereafter a number of other small, struggling branches were established in Kentucky, Tennessee, Mississippi, Arkansas, Maryland, North Carolina, and South Carolina. There seems to have been little hostility to the Mormons in the South at this time.

All of the branches in the South were tiny, usually consisting of no more than 8 to 10 members each. Most were not permanent owing to the influence that the Mormon doctrine of The Gathering had on church members. Briefly stated, this millennial doctrine, based on revelations received by Smith, held that Mormons should remove themselves as much as possible from the sinful world and gather together with their fellow church members to prepare for the return of Christ. Under the influence of this doctrine, most early converts to the church in the South and other places left their homes and resettled near the Prophet Joseph Smith and their fellow churchmen to await the millennium.

Mormon missionary activities in the South were interrupted by the outbreak of the Civil War but were gradually resumed after the cessation of hostilities. In 1875 church officials in Salt Lake City formally organized the Southern States Mission consisting of the states of Tennessee, Arkansas, Alabama, Georgia, Mississippi, and Virginia. Later North and South Carolina, Kentucky, Maryland, Texas, Florida, Louisiana, and Ohio were added to the mission.

Because of widespread opposition to the Mormon belief in polygamy and the fear that Mormon elders were trying to lure Southern women to be wives in the harems of Mormon patriarchs, the church's missionaries encountered much violent opposition in the Southern states in the post-Civil War period. Mormon missionaries were often seized and whipped and several were murdered, the first being Elder Joseph Standing who was shot and killed by members of an anti-Mormon mob near Varnell's Station GA in July 1879. The culprits of these crimes were rarely brought to justice.

Despite the persecution, Mormons persevered in the Southern states and near the end of the century church officials began printing a weekly newspaper at the headquarters of the Southern States Mission in Chattanooga TN. Known as the *Southern Star*, the paper was published from December 1898 to December 1900 in an effort to disseminate Mormon beliefs in the Southern states and maintain morale among church members. It appears that during the late nineteenth century the Mormon Church never had more than some 1,000 members at anytime in the South.

In 1920 the headquarters of the Southern States Mission were transferred to Atlanta. Recently the single regional Mission has been replaced by a number of area Missions. With the abandonment of polygamy by church officials in the 1890s, the gradual liberalizing of Southern religious views, and the emergence of a slightly more tolerant spirit among many Southerners, violent opposition to the Mormons lessened during the early twentieth century. As the arable areas of the Far West were rapidly populated in the late nineteenth century, Mormon Church officials began deemphasizing The Gathering and instead urged Mormons to live righteous, godly lives where they were. As a consequence of this changing emphasis, the migration of Mormon converts from the South declined and today the Mormon Church has approximately 196,000 members in the South. Like Mormons everywhere, they believe in such things as life before birth, baptism for the dead, marriage for all eternity, and God's continuing revelations given to the prophet of the church.

See also articles on REORGANIZED CHURCH OF JESUS CHRIST OF LATTER-DAY SAINTS; RESTORATIONISM.

Bibliography. James B. Allen and Glen M. Leonard, *The Story of the Latter-day Saints;* Leonard J. Arrington and Davis Bitton, *The Mormon Experience: A History of the Latter-day Saints;* LaMar C. Berrett, "History of the Southern States Mission 1831-1861," unpublished M.A. thesis, Brigham Young University, 1960; Fawn Brodie, *No Man Knows My History—The Life of Joseph Smith the Prophet;* Samuel G. Ellsworth, "A History of Mormon Missions in the United States and Canada, 1830-1860," unpublished Ph.D. dissertation, University of California, Berkeley, 1951; William W. Hatch, "A History of Mormon Civil Relations in the Southern States, 1865-1905," unpublished M.A. thesis, Utah State University, 1965; Andrew Jenson, *Encyclopedic History of the Church of Jesus Christ of Latter-day Saints;* Thomas F. O'Dea, *The Mormons;* Brigham H. Roberts, *A Comprehensive History of the Church of Jesus Christ of Latter-day Saints,* vol. 5.

DAVID BUICE
LOUISIANA TECH UNIVERSITY

MORRISON, HENRY CLAY (1857-1942),

evangelical Methodist leader, was born at Bedford KY, and orphaned as a child. After education at Ewing Institute in Perryville KY and a year at Vanderbilt University, he was ordained in 1887 as an elder in the Kentucky Conference of the Methodist Episcopal Church, South. In 1890 the conference released him from pastoral service to do full-time evangelism.

Morrison's zeal as an evangelist and a leader in the HOLINESS MOVEMENT in Southern Methodism brought him to trial in his home conference in 1897 for "contumacious conduct." Cleared of the charges, he was subsequently elected as delegate to five General Conferences and the Ecumenical Methodist Conference in London in 1921. Vanderbilt University also granted him an honorary D.D.

Morrison's career, spanning more than 60 years, was full and diverse. The Christian Century recognized him in his own time as one of the 50 great preachers in America. Morrison was intensely devoted to any cause he espoused. His successful holiness revivalism provided a constituency that allowed him to promote vigorously the Wesleyan doctrine of Christian perfection or entire SANCTIFICATION in Methodism. To further this cause he founded the influential *Pentecostal Herald* in 1890 and edited it for almost 35 years. Morrison's most lasting influence on American and particularly Southern religion was exercised through Asbury College and Asbury Theological Seminary at Wilmore in his home state. He was president of Asbury College from 1910-1925 and 1933-1940. In 1923 he founded Asbury Theological Seminary, now one of the largest seminaries in the United States.

See also articles on EVANGELICALISM; HOLINESS; THEOLOGICAL EDUCATION.

Bibliography. P. A. Wesche, *Henry Clay Morrison; Who's Who in America; Who's Who in the Clergy*, vol. 1; C. F. Wimberly, *A Biographical Sketch of Henry Clay Morrison.*

MELVIN E. DIETER
ASBURY THEOLOGICAL SEMINARY

MOSELEY, SARA BERNICE (1917-), Presbyterian agency leader and moderator, was born in Anson TX and educated at Texas State College for Women, doing further study at the University of Michigan and University of Texas at Austin. Her service as a lay leader in the Presbyterian Church, U.S., began at the local church level where she served as a church school teacher, youth advisor, choir director, and president of the Women of the Church. She subsequently was president of the presbytery's Women's Council, moderator of Covenant Presbytery, and chairperson of the presbytery's Division of Ministers. At the assembly level she served for 13 years on the denomination's

top governing board and chaired the Board of Women's Work and the Division of International Mission. But her career was climaxed in 1978 when she was elected the first woman moderator of her denomination at the 118th General Assembly, the church's highest court. She had earlier been the first chairperson of the denomination's Mission Board elected by the General Assembly, and the first woman ordained an elder by her home church, the First Presbyterian Church of Sherman TX.

She is especially remembered for her sensitive and judicious leadership of the 1978 Consultation on the Overseas and Domestic Mission of the PCUS, a critical gathering that charted the course of the denomination's mission effort for the coming decade. As moderator of the General Assembly, Moseley won the admiration of clergy and lay persons throughout the South because of her ability to reconcile divergent factions and to humanize institutional structures and procedures.

She is married to John D. Moseley, longtime president of Austin College. In recognition of her outstanding leadership in the church, she has been awarded honorary degrees by three colleges.

See also article on WOMEN IN RELIGION.

HARRY E. SMITH
AUSTIN COLLEGE

MOUNTAIN RELIGION: *See* APPALACHIAN RELIGION.

MOURNERS' BENCH: *See* ALTAR CALL (INVITATION).

MULLINS, EDGAR YOUNG (1860-1928), Baptist leader and theologian, was born in Franklin County MS. Graduating from Texas A&M College, he completed his studies at the Southern Baptist Theological Seminary in 1885. Following pastorates at Harrodsburg KY and Lee Street Baptist Church in Baltimore, he became associate secretary of the Foreign Mission Board of the Southern Baptist Convention in 1895. After four months he resigned and accepted the pastorate of the Baptist church in Newton Center MA. He was one of the last Southern Baptists to have a national career.

In 1899 Mullins was elected president of the Southern Baptist Theological Seminary. There he became professor of theology in addition to his administrative duties. Through his leadership the seminary campus was moved from a crowded, downtown location in Louisville to its present spacious site in 1926.

During the controversy over evolution in the 1920s, Mullins was called on to help resolve conflicting views within the denomination. In 1924 he was made chairman of a Southern Baptist Convention committee to draft a statement of the Baptist faith and message. The committee's report was adopted by the Convention in 1925. He served as president of the Convention from 1921 to 1924. In 1905 Mullins participated in the organizational meeting of the Baptist World Alliance and served as president of that body in 1928.

His published writings, which have won wide acceptance, include 12 books, 29 pamphlets and booklets, 400 articles, addresses, and reports, and 190 book reviews. His best-known books are: *Why Is Christianity True?* (1905); *The Axioms of Religion* (1908); *Baptist Beliefs* (1912); *Freedom and Authority in Religion* (1913); and *Christianity at the Crossroads* (1924). His monumental work is *The Christian Religion in Its Doctrinal Expression* (1917), a systematic treatment of theology.

See also article on THEOLOGY.

Bibliography. *Baptist History and Heritage,* 15: 3: 15-22; W. W. Barnes, *The Southern Baptist Convention, 1845-1953; Encyclopedia of Southern Baptists.*

JOHN S. MOORE
LEXINGTON, VIRGINIA

MURPHY, EDGAR GARDNER

(1869-1913), Episcopal clergyman and social reformer, was born near Fort Smith AR, educated at the UNIVERSITY OF THE SOUTH, and the General Theological Seminary, New York City. In 1893, the year of his ordination, he accepted a rectorship in Laredo TX where he protested the lynching of a black murderer and thus began his lifelong crusade for racial justice. Never robust in health, he was forced by illness to move to pastorates in Ohio and New York, but in 1898 he welcomed the opportunity to return to his beloved South through St. John's parish, Montgomery AL.

Three of the major social problems burdening the "New South" were of intense concern to this "gentle progressive": "the Negro question" (as it was then called), child labor, and popular education. In 1900 Murphy formed the Southern Society for the Promotion of the Study of Race Conditions and Problems in the South, and this organization sponsored an important conference in Montgomery that year. The fact that no black leaders were invited to speak and that he could inform his friend, Booker T. Washington, that the movement for racial justice would only be impeded by the participation of Southern blacks and Northern liberals, illuminates Murphy's posture of benevolent paternalism. The society's collapse illuminates the limitations to his understanding of the depths of racism. Still, in a time of growing caste his was one of few voices raised in protest. Murphy also led the way in founding the Alabama Child Labor Committee, the first state committee in the nation. Although his Southern heritage prevented him from supporting federal regulatory legislation, his gallant efforts did prick the national conscience and as a result the abomination of sweated children was brought under limited state control.

In 1903 Murphy withdrew from the ministry to become executive secretary of the Southern Education Board, explaining that this action, far from being a repudiation of Christianity, was "my best response to God's will, and to the needs of our church and our country." He devoted the remaining years of declining strength to the cause of the education of children, black and white, in the South.

See also article on SOCIAL GOSPEL.

Bibliography. Hugh C. Bailey, *Edgar Gardner Murphy, Gentle Progressive*; Maud King Murphy, *Edgar Gardner Murphy, From Records and Memories*; Ronald C. White, "Beyond the Sacred: Edgar Gardner Murphy and a Ministry of Social Reform," *Historical Magazine of the Protestant Episcopal Church* 44 (March 1980): 51-69.

ROBERT MOATS MILLER
UNIVERSITY OF NORTH CAROLINA
AT CHAPEL HILL

MUSIC, RELIGIOUS, OF THE PROTESTANT SOUTH.

Religious music accompanied the founding of the Southern colonies and the settling of the Southern frontier; it has ever since remained central to the Southern experience. While colonists below the Mason-Dixon line veered dramatically in their religious practices from their brethren to the North, their musical inheritance was very much the same. Psalmody prevailed in the Anglican churches of the South just as it did among the Puritan congregations of New England. John Calvin's insistence that Christians sing only the metrical versions of the Psalms of David affected the song preferences of British Protestants everywhere.

Seaboard Southerners, however, proved much more responsive to new songs and styles and to instruments in the church than did New Englanders or their brethren in the Southern backcountry. Calvinist influence soon waned within the established churches, but remained strong among the dissenting groups who pushed westward toward the Piedmont, or southward through the Great Valley of Virginia. The venerable art of "lining the hymn," whereby a congregation sings a verse of a song in response to the sing-song declamation of a song leader, was preserved by some Scotch-Irish Presbyterians but more often by frontier Baptists. The practice was necessary for people who were often illiterate, or who had few available songbooks, but it was preserved long after it had lost any practical utility. Lining became a tradition too strongly cherished to be abandoned. Today, white PRIMITIVE BAPTISTS and some black Baptist congregations retain the practice.

While ancient British hymns and carols moved into the Southern backcountry as part of the cultural baggage of the earliest settlers, the practice of hymn singing owes most of its modern popularity to the innovations made by Isaac Watts and to the dissemination promoted by the Wesleyan evangelical movement. Watts was the most popular of several musical reformers whose religious poetry inspired a resurgence of hymnmaking and diminished the hold that psalmody exercised over the minds of Protestants. Watts's groundbreaking *Hymns and Spiritual Songs* (1707) was published in America as early as 1739, but individual songs from the collection had appeared here long before that. Watts's hymns found a receptive audience among both black and white Southerners, especially during the years of the GREAT AWAKENING. In 1735 Charles and John Wesley arrived in Georgia and two years later they published a collection of psalms and hymns. Strongly influenced by the pietistic and musical MORAVIANS, the emotion-laden songs favored by the Wesleys proved indispensable in winning converts to Methodism. By the time of the American Revolution, Methodism had established a strong foothold in the Southern colonies, and the songs of Charles Wesley and other Methodist poets such as John Newton ("Amazing Grace") and William Cowper ("There is a Fountain Filled With Blood") had moved into the permanent consciousness of Southern Christians.

There is no evidence that either of the Wesleys made the statement attributed to them, "Why should the Devil have all the good tunes?," but their songs did often employ folk and popular melodies. The line between secular and spiritual music has always been a tenuous one, and religious composers have often borrowed from worldly sources. As the Southern folk pushed into the upland western counties and down through the Appalachian passes and on into the new regions of

Kentucky and Tennessee, they took with them a large body of "folk spirituals"— songs generally wedded to folk tunes that had grown up on the American frontier, or that had survived the Atlantic transit. No phenomenon was more important in changing the nature and style of Southern religious music than the famous CAMP MEETINGS. The GREAT REVIVAL of the early 1800s did much to tame the southwestern frontier, to diminish the power of Calvinism while democratizing religion, and also to shape the Southern mind.

Camp meetings also influenced the texture and tone of Southern religious music. Camp meeting evangelists used the older hymns, but songbooks were rare, and their pages soon became tattered and worn as they were passed from singer to singer. To encourage mass participation, spirited melodies were used and refrains and choruses were added to the older songs. Through the repetition of phrases and refrains, and through the employment of "wandering verses" that appeared frequently in various songs, singing was made easier for large groups of people who generally had no songbooks and who often could not have read them anyway. The meetings were not only ecumenical (promoted by Presbyterians, Baptists, and Methodists), they were also biracial; black and white Southerners had ample opportunities to learn from each other. Songs that came out of the Kentucky revivals, or that were otherwise identified with them, began to appear in print as early as 1805. According to Dickson Bruce in *And They All Sang Hallelujah*, the choruses of the songs that he assumes came directly out of the camp meeting experiences are important repositories of plain-folk theology. The choruses sing of the soul's pilgrimage through an unfriendly world, the assurances of a heavenly reward, and of a HEAVEN that is defined in contrast to the world's limitations.

By the mid-nineteenth century the religious repertory of the Southern folk encompassed a wide variety of song types:

psalms, Watts and Wesleyan hymns, formally composed American hymns (of the Lowell Mason and Thomas Hastings variety), folk spirituals, and camp meeting songs. Such songs circulated by word of mouth, but many of them were included in "tune books" such as John Wyeth's *Repository of Sacred Music, Part 2* (1813), or Ananias Davisson's *Kentucky Harmony* (1817). Whatever the song type, and from whatever source, Southern material invariably circulated in shape-note form. The shape-note system of notation was introduced in New England about 1800 by William Little and William Smith in *The Easy Instructor* as a method that would facilitate sight reading among semiliterate people. The shape of the note, independent of its position on the staff, indicated its musical pitch (fa was represented by a triangle, sol by a circle, la by a square, and mi by a diamond). The method was transported into the South by singing school teachers who came down out of Pennsylvania into the Shenandoah Valley. These itinerant singing masters were hardy souls who became as well known, and as warmly welcomed, as peddlers or Methodist circuit riders. They came into a community, held their schools for 10 days, and then left for another community where they once again taught their method.

Joseph Funk, a Mennonite immigrant from Pennsylvania, compiled one of the earliest Southern shape-note tunebooks (*Choral Music*, 1816), and the singing "normal" school founded by his descendants at Singers Glen VA became a training ground and point of debarkation for singing teachers who wandered through the rural South. Songbooks employing the shape-note methodology proliferated in the mid-nineteenth century, but among the more renowned were *Southern Harmony* (1835), *Hesperian Harp* (1848), *Social Harp* (1855), and *Christian Harmony* (1866). The most famous, primarily because of its amazing endurance, is Benjamin F. White's and E. J. King's *Sacred Harp* (1844). Unlike most of the other books that moved rather quickly toward the acceptance of the seven-note "do-re-mi" style (Jesse Aitken, *The Christian Minstrel* (1846), was the first significant acceptance), *The Sacred Harp* adhered to the use of the four-note style of solmization ("fa-sol-la-mi"). The book is now in its eighth revision and is still revered by thousands of Southerners as second only to the Bible. Periodically, sacred harp singers still meet in various locations in the Deep South to sing songs from the cherished old book. Seated in a hollow square arranged according to the four voice parts, the singers sing in a cappella fashion as they follow their song leaders, first through the notes of the song and then through the words. The surging four-part harmony of the "fasola" singers, displayed in such songs as "Come Thou Fount of Every Blessing," is an emotional experience not soon forgotten.

Black religious music assumed forms dramatically different from those of white music; nevertheless, the music of the two racial groups cannot be discussed apart from each other. Slaves frequently attended white churches in the antebellum South and were present in great numbers at the camp meetings of the early nineteenth century. The music of evangelism moved among the blacks along with the sermons of the preachers, and the hymns of Watts were introduced to the slaves as early as 1756. If black people of necessity absorbed much of the culture of their masters, theirs was nonetheless a world lived apart, and even clandestinely, from whites. In the all-black sphere of the quarters at night or when work was done, at funerals or midnight praise sessions, the slaves built a community of their own. Indeed, Lawrence Levine (*Black Culture and Black Consciousness*) argues that the slaves preserved the sense of a "sacred world," which enabled them to survive the rigors of racial oppression and to attain a degree of liberation within the confines of bondage.

Religious music, then, played a central role in the lives of antebellum blacks, who sang such songs at work and play, as well as in church contexts. It is fruitless to speculate on the origins or even the forms of the spirituals since they were not systematically collected until the Civil War era, and it is probably irrelevant to do so. Whether white-derived or black-created, the songs became the possession of the blacks and were performed in styles that were only remotely related to white European tradition. A few of the songs appeared earlier in Northern magazines, but most were introduced to the American public in an 1867 publication, *Slave Songs of the United States*, compiled by three Northern missionaries who had gone to work among the freedmen in Port Royal SC. The songs evoked a flurry of interest among Northern abolitionists and Congregationalists, but the real vogue for spirituals came after 1871 when nine student-singers from Fisk University in Nashville traveled north for a series of concerts to raise money for their school. Seeking to impress their white, middle-class audiences, the young men and women sang semiclassical compositions, patriotic airs, and Stephen Foster "plantation" songs. But under the prodding of their listeners, they began singing the spirituals. In subsequent trips to the North and to Europe the Fisk Jubilee Singers set off a profound interest in the spirituals that lasted to the end of the century. Cultivated musicians seized upon these songs for artistic exploitation, and Anton Dvorák, the great Czech composer, was not alone in suggesting that the spirituals be used as the basis for a national "high art" music.

While the patrons of classical or "serious" music eagerly stressed the artistic potential of the black spirituals, the Southern people, black and white, sought musical sustenance wherever they could find it and were largely oblivious to whether their musical choices fit someone else's aesthetic standards or not. The vogue for the spirituals came in the context of a national burgeoning of evangelistic music. This new music was indebted in many respects to camp meeting hymnody, but it projected a more urban ambiance and seemed peculiarly attuned to the needs of a developing middle-class civilization. The urban society that took shape in the three decades after 1865 was one that remained acutely conscious of its rural roots. Nostalgia, then, often accompanied the sense of liberation rural people might have felt in the city. Many people, too, felt a sense of disquietude about the materialism that swept the country in the aftermath of the war. The urge to get back to God was paralleled by the fear that a new generation would be lost in the impersonal city. The Sunday School Movement, the YMCA, and the Salvation Army each utilized music to reach a transient and unchurched urban population.

Overshadowing them all, however, as sources of religious songs, were the big-city revivals of the late nineteenth century. Every evangelist from Dwight Moody to Billy Sunday traveled with a songleader who soothed or warmed up the crowd before the preacher gave his sermon. From Ira Sankey to Homer Rodeheaver in the 19th century, to George Beverley Shea in our own time, songleaders have generally utilized the popular musical currents of the day. The sounds of ragtime, blues, and even rock, have been enlisted in the service of religious music. Such songwriters as George F. Root, P. P. Bliss, Charles Gabriel, W. H. Doane, and Fanny Crosby, who could just as easily have written for the genteel parlor trade (as indeed some of them did), contributed a profusion of songs to the evangelistic crusades. In 1875 Ira Sankey and Philip Bliss collaborated on a collection of songs that became the nucleus of the very popular *Gospel Hymns, no's. 1 to 6* (1875-1894). This was the first apparent usage of the word "gospel" to describe the developing musical genre. While martial songs appeared often in gospel collections, the visions of a comforting Savior and a pastoral heaven, as well as nostalgic evocations of country churches, loving parents, and family firesides, appeared more often

in the songs. Such classic songs as "Blessed Assurance," "Softly and Tenderly," "Pass Me Not," "Beautiful Isle of Somewhere," and "In the Garden" found great favor in the South, making their way into both the convention paperback hymnals and the denominational hymnbooks where many of them have remained. The most famous gospel composers were from the North, but such Southerners as Charles Tillman, A. J. Showalter, and J. W. Vaughan also made vital contributions to the genre.

By 1900 a host of publishing houses dotted the Southern landscape, most of them specializing in shape-note notation and issuing an average of two paperback hymnals per year. The songbooks were often used in country churches, but more often at weekend singing conventions, the famous "all-day-singings with dinner-on-the-grounds." The prime movers behind the post-Civil War surge of Southern songmaking were two descendants of Joseph Funk—his grandson, Aldine Kieffer, and another grandson by marriage, James H. Ruebush. The Ruebush-Kieffer Company, founded in 1865 in Dayton VA, was not only a major supplier of songbooks, but its Virginia Normal Music School (headed by Benjamin S. Unseld) furnished teachers for the rest of the South, and its magazine, *Musical Million*, contained a compendium of information about singers and singing schools. Another product of Virginia's Funk family, Anthony J. Showalter, the composer of "Leaning on the Everlasting Arms," established a publishing house in Dalton GA in 1885. Before he died in 1924 Showalter saw many of his students become famous throughout the South as composers, teachers, and publishers.

The Holiness-Pentecostal movement was still another force that colored the religious music of the South. The urge to restore a sense of Wesleyan piety to the Methodist church was part of a larger dissatisfaction with the alleged coldness and formality of the established churches at the end of the 19th century. By stressing once again a "religion of the heart," the Holiness people opened up the floodgates of emotionalism, appealing to poor and repressed people who could feel at home neither in the world nor in the churches. The holiness impulse soon inspired a search for the "third blessing," the baptism of the Holy Spirit whose evidence would be manifested in "speaking in tongues." The Pentecostals were not afraid of emotion; they actively sought it and viewed it as evidence of the Holy Spirit's presence. And they have been receptive to all types of musical rhythms and instruments from tambourines and horns to electric guitars. Whether conveyed in the throbbing, hypnotic, tom-tom rhythm of the mountain SNAKE HANDLERS, or in the orchestral jazz of the black sanctified churches, Pentecostal music permitted an expressiveness and abandon not available to poor people in the outside world. The Holiness-Pentecostal movement (or sanctified movement, as it is known in black religion) put music back into the congregations, whence it had been persistently removed by "better music" people ever since the days of Lowell Mason. Pentecostal sects were highly receptive to the paperback hymnals that poured from the Southern shape-note publishing houses, and anonymous Pentecostal composers were also responsible for such enduring songs as "This World Is Not My Home," "When the Saints Go Marching In," and "Great Speckled Bird." Pentecostalism as a musical force deserves further study, for a wide range of significant American musicians from Elvis Presley and Jerry Lee Lewis to Mahalia Jackson, Andrae Crouch, and the Blackwood Brothers either grew up in a Pentecostal-sanctified church environment or have acknowledged the influence of that tradition.

The 20th century has witnessed both the commercialization and the nationalization of Southern religious music. While a commercial intent certainly accompanied (and sometimes dwarfed) the missionary impulse of the writers and publishers of the 19th century, full-fledged commercialization did not come (perhaps was not possible) until the era of radio and recording. The commercial exploitation of Southern religious music occurred at roughly the same time and in the same manner as did the discovery of secular folk music. The appearance of radio stations in the South after 1920 provided performance outlets for all kinds of musicians. Stimulated in part by the competition posed by radio, the phonograph industry also began paying closer attention to heretofore neglected grassroots entertainers. Some Southern religious performers had been recorded earlier, but it was not until the 1920s that such music systematically began to appear on phonograph recordings.

The modern history of Southern religious music begins with James D. Vaughan. When Vaughan established his publishing house in Lawrenceburg TN in 1905, his holiness missionary zeal burned brightly. But Vaughan was also an astute businessman who pioneered in techniques that became standard in white gospel music. He appears to have been the first publisher to employ traveling quartets to market his songbooks; he chartered the first radio station in Tennessee (WOAN, 1922) and used it to advertise his business. One of his quartets made the first commercial recordings of such music in 1922. The Vaughan company remained the dominant shape-note publishing house east of the Mississippi River through the 1930s, but west of the river its leadership was challenged by the Stamps-Baxter Company, organized by Virgil O. Stamps of Jacksonville TX and Jesse R. Baxter of Chattanooga. In 1928 a quartet headed by Stamps's brother Frank, and called the Stamps All-Star Quartet, recorded for the Victor label in Atlanta. One of the group's initial recordings was of a song called "Give the World a Smile," a tune made immensely popular by its use of an after-beat rhythm (a syncopated response made by the other singers to the bass singer's lead). Most quartets thereafter affiliated with the Stamps company, or bore the Stamps name as part of their title, using "Give the World a Smile" as their theme song.

The recording success of the Stamps All-Star Quartet was a milestone in gospel quartet history; the group was the first to free itself from exclusive affiliation with publishing house activities. The members sold songbooks, but they did not work in the publishing houses, and they booked themselves independently. By the mid-1930s gospel quartets had become fixtures on radio stations throughout the South. Another Stamps Quartet began a long-standing tenure on KRLD in Dallas in 1937, where their noon and Sunday broadcasts made them household words in the Southwest. The Blackwood Brothers from Mississippi began their radio career in 1936. A Texas family group, D. P. Carter and his children (Jim, Rose, and Anna), began broadcasting in 1936 on WBAP in Fort Worth as the Chuck Wagon Gang. Their recording career for Columbia, lasting from 1936 until 1977, was the longest enjoyed by any singers of religious songs. The radio and recording activities of the quartets encouraged the rise of new songwriters, men and women who built upon the old shape-note foundations. Preeminent, perhaps, was Albert E. Brumley, from Powell MO, a protégé of Eugene M. Bartlett of Hartford Music Company. Brumley's "Turn Your Radio On" (1937) illustrated the crucial role played by the broadcasting medium in popularizing gospel music. Brumley wrote over 600 songs of both the traditional gospel variety and sentimental nostalgic songs that commemorated declining rural values. His "I'll Fly Away" (1932) has been one of the most performed songs in gospel music history.

Black gospel music followed similar paths of commercialization. Beginning with Virginia's Norfolk Jubilee Quartet, several quartets made records during the 1920s. Most of them performed a cappella and were called "jubilee quartets," probably because of the impact made earlier by the Fisk Jubilee Singers. The newer quartets, however, performed in styles significantly different from the Fisk group, projecting a down-home sound and image far removed from the cultivated approach of the Nashville singers. By the mid-1930s several quartets, such as the Fairfield Four, the Dixie Hummingbirds, the Five Blind Boys, and the Swan Silvertones, had attained wide followings within the black community; at least two, the Charioteers and the Golden Gate Quartet, had become known to white audiences also. The black quartets became famous for their extraordinary sense of rhythm (achieved usually without the benefit of instrumental accompaniment) and for their vocal excellence. Most of the quartets had brilliant soloists, such as Claude Jeter of the Swan Silvertones, R. H. Harris of the Soul Stirrers, and Ira Tucker of the Dixie Hummingbirds, whose remarkable vocal control and range affected the styles of singers far removed from the gospel field.

The quartets made up only one part of a much larger black religious genre. Adherents of black religious music might also choose the guitar-accompanied, blues-gospel sound of Blind Willie Johnson, the jazzy piano renditions of the sanctified singer Arizona Dranes, or even the half-spoken, half-sung sermons of men like the Rev. J. M. Gates. Sermons have continued to sell extensively to this day. Though it is rooted in the spirituals and Southern rural experience of black people, modern black gospel music is intimately interrelated to the movement of black people to the cities and to the North. Residence in Northern black ghettos brought oppression, but it also inspired a sense of liberation. Black churches were forums of self-expression and religious music a means of emotional release and personal statement. Though gospel music partisans would vigorously deny it, black religious music frequently utilized the styles and instruments of secular music. With the sanctified churches in the lead, the saints joyously applied the rhythms of jazz and blues to spiritual songs. In the years before World War I, Charles Tindley, an African Methodist Episcopal Church minister from Philadelphia, became the first great black gospel composer. Such blues-tinged songs as "Stand By Me," "We'll Understand It Better By and By," and "Leave It There" moved into the repertories of both black and white singers and were frequently included in the white shape-note hymnals.

Tindley's most apt student (though not a direct protégé) was Thomas Dorsey, universally recognized as the father of modern black gospel music. Born in Villa Rica GA, Dorsey had been a successful blues musician and composer in the 1920s and a pianist for such singers as Ma Rainey. Dorsey was the son of a Baptist minister and his thoughts were never far from the church even when he was recording risqué songs like "It's Tight Like That." He moved to Chicago in 1918 but did not commit himself wholly to religious music until about 1930. Along with Sallie Martin, he organized the Gospel Singers Convention and began traveling to churches around the country training choirs and soloists. Dorsey did much to shape the piano style that is now so characteristic of black gospel music and he helped launch the careers of many of the genre's greatest stylists, most notably Mahalia Jackson who traveled with him from 1939 to 1945. Above all, Dorsey wrote some of the great songs of gospel music, including "Peace in the Valley" and "Precious Lord, Take My Hand." "Precious Lord" was written in 1932 shortly after the death of his wife and infant son. The song has sustained millions of people through their own weariness and grief.

In the years since World War II, Southern religious music has burgeoned commercially and has moved beyond its regional parameters to a national and international audience. If anything, religious music has become even more pervasive in American life than it was before the war. But as it has become increasingly commercialized and nationalized, it has also become shorn of sectarian associations and, some would say, of theological content. Most modern gospel music, black and white, is designed for popular consumption and is aimed at the largest possible audience. Gospel music, as always, reflects the secular culture in which it thrives. Consequently, gospel vocal and instrumental styles borrow heavily from country, soul, rock, and jazz music.

During the late 1940s and early 1950s the gospel groups moved away from the church and school circuits and into the major auditoriums. The big gospel buses became a familiar part of the American landscape as they rolled down the highways, bearing on their sides such names as the Blackwood Brothers, the Statesmen, the Singing Rambos, the LeFevres, the Speer Family, the Happy Goodman Family, or the Florida Boys. Gospel fans could often hear several acts on one "package" show, a format pioneered by promoter Wally Fowler in 1948. Fowler, the founder of the Oak Ridge Quartet, also specialized in "all-night gospel singings," a phenomenon actually introduced by V. O. Stamps to close out his annual singing schools in Dallas.

Quartets still claimed a spiritual mission in the immediate postwar years, but "show business" intruded persistently, and they employed numerous devices to win favor over each other. The singers vied to be the highest tenors or the lowest basses, or they adopted the smooth, pear-shaped tones of the pop quartets. The white quartet business gained its greatest exposure in national popular culture after 1954 when the Blackwood Brothers of Memphis won first place on CBS's Arthur Godfrey Talent Show and then saw one of their recordings, "Have You Talked To the Man Upstairs," climb into the top-ten popularity chart. The personnel of the group has changed dramatically through the years, but James Blackwood, a charter member since 1934, has remained one of the superstars of gospel music.

Elvis Presley's emergence as the king of rock and roll brought additional national exposure to the gospel quartets. Although the influence is often over-looked, Presley's style drew heavily upon those of the gospel singers whom he had heard often in and near Memphis. His contributions to gospel popularization, however, went much farther than his own personal style. He was accompanied on his early RCA recordings and on many of his concerts by the Jordanaires, and later by J. D. Sumner and the Stamps Quartet. The Nashville-based Jordanaires also appeared as background voices on many of the successful country records that came out of that city in the late 1950s and early 1960s; they, in fact, made vital con-tributions to the shaping of what became known as the "Nashville Sound."

The white gospel business as a whole has become as firmly identified with Nashville as has country music. There is now a Gospel Music Hall of Fame in Nashville, as well as a Gospel Music Asso-ciation that each year presents Dove awards to a lengthy list of "best" per-formers and songs in a variety of catego-ries. The GMA has made tentative attempts to recognize the close relation-ship between white and black gospel music, and some black singers such as Mahalia Jackson have been named to the Hall of Fame along with white musicians such as Albert Brumley and James D. Vaughan. On the whole, though, the two forms of music have maintained separate identities and concert audiences generally remain segregated. Black gospel singers like James Cleveland, Dorothy Love Coates, Shirley Caesar, the Dixie Hum-mingbirds, and the Mighty Clouds of Joy appear regularly in auditoriums and churches throughout America, but few white people ever see them. On occasion, black performers have won recognition far beyond the ghettos. Andrae Crouch, for instance, a pianist and vocalist with a soft, crooning style, is a fixture on televi-sion evangelistic shows. The two singers who did the most to popularize black gos-pel music in mainstream America were Sister Rosetta Tharpe from Cotton Plant

AR, and Mahalia Jackson from New Orleans. Tharpe was an exponent of "hot" gospel music, a swinging, synco-pated style that seemed reflective of both the juke joint and the sanctified church. Such songs as "Strange Things Happen-ing Every Day," featuring her lusty sing-ing and dynamic, single-string guitar playing, were prominently featured on radio programs in the late 1940s and early 1950s.

Surpassing all gospel singers in both quality and popular appeal was Mahalia Jackson, who became virtually an institu-tion in American life before her death in 1972. Mahalia's music came from the churches of New Orleans, but her style showed more than a little influence from the records of Bessie Smith. Her rise to fame came after she moved to Chicago and became part of the burgeoning gospel scene there. She became a periodic partici-pant on television specials and talk shows after World War II and, because of her recognizable fusion of blues and gospel vocal techniques, she was even invited to sing at the Newport Jazz Festival in 1958. Mahalia, though, resisted all efforts to lure her from religious music, and while she often sang "pop gospel" songs that were far removed from her down-home origins, her style never really strayed from that of the churches of her youth.

Gospel music today is both a big busi-ness and a sustaining force for millions of people. Spiritual commitment obviously varies widely among the professional musicians. Some are evangelists; some will move on to other styles of music once the potential for profit is established else-where. Though many gospel singers pas-sionately affirm their distinction from secular singers, stylistically they differ lit-tle, and usually not at all, from other types of musicians. Generally it is the lyrics alone, or the social contexts in which they are performed, that set gospel performan-ces apart from other types of music. The gospel songs themselves still evoke responses similar to those aroused in the late nineteenth century. Their advocates find them uplifting; their detractors dismiss them as trash. They have firmly ensconced themselves in American popular culture, but only a few will ever receive more than a condescending glance from the "good music" people and few will ever make their way into the approved church hymnals. Although the old songs are still deeply cherished by Southerners, very few of them—"The Old Rugged Cross" or "Precious Memories," for example—now appear in the repertories of the gospel quartets. The gospel singers, like pop singers everywhere, perform newly composed songs designed for the broadest popular appeal. Consequently, the songs seldom concentrate on the grim or tragic side of human existence, or even upon the sufferings of Christ (the venerable "blood songs" now have little appeal). Modern gospel songs generally present a soothing or upbeat picture of life.

Nevertheless, the older musical culture of the rural South survives. Sacred Harp singings still convene somewhere in the South almost every Sunday and singing conventions are held in county courthouses and small-town churches throughout the year, particularly in north Georgia and Alabama. The tradition of family gospel singing is still strong among rural Southerners, and groups perform at home and in church, and sometimes on local radio stations, while remaining unknown to the larger American public.

Commercial country music is in many respects a stronger repository of fundamentalist values and traditional religious music styles than is mainline gospel music. Virtually all country singers include religious pieces in their repertories; and such superstars as Willie Nelson, Merle Haggard, and Emmylou Harris have in fact contributed most to the preservation and dissemination of old-time gospel songs (such as "The Uncloudy Day" and "Will the Circle Be Unbroken?") through the inclusion of such numbers in their concerts and recordings. In the subgenre known as bluegrass, where singers like Ralph Stanley, the Lewis Family, and the Sullivan Family perform religious material as often as secular numbers, one can hear songs that predate the gospel era and styles that echo the a cappella harmonies of the Primitive Baptist Church and the rousing rhythms of a brush arbor meeting or a Holiness revival. Among bluegrass and old-time country singers one finds no reticence concerning the blood songs and songs considered quaint or old-fashioned in other music circles, such as the world-rejection songs or those describing the soul's pilgrimage through the world. Fundamentalist assumptions strongly color the lyrics of country gospel songs, and a tendency to equate vanishing rural values with godly virtues is a constant theme of the music.

Religious music remains an integral and vital facet of Southern culture. Southern-born musicians have taken their versions of gospel music around the world, and in so doing have made gospel one of the most commercially viable musical genres in America. But commercial success has inevitably diminished both the distinctiveness and Southernness of the music. Nevertheless, the music of the old-time Protestant South still lives among such performers as the Sacred Harp singers who have resisted the tide of modernism, and among the country musicians who remain faithful to the music of their childhood.

See also articles on BLACK RELIGION; EVANGELICALISM; HOLINESS MOVEMENT; PENTECOSTALISM.

Bibliography. Lois Blackwell, *The Wings of the Dove: The Story of Gospel Music in America*; Stanley Brobston, "A Brief History of White Southern Gospel Music," unpublished Ph.D. dissertation, New York University, 1977; Dickson Bruce, *And They All Sang Hallelujah*; Buell E. Cobb, Jr., *The Sacred Harp*; James C. Downey, "The Music of American Revivalism," unpublished Ph.D. dissertation, Tulane University, 1968; Charles Linwood Ellington, "The Sacred Harp Tradition of the South," unpublished Ph.D. dissertation, Florida State University, 1970; Dena J. Epstein, *Sinful Tunes and Spirituals*; Harry Eskew, "Shape-Note Hymnody in the Shenandoah Valley, 1816-60," unpublished Ph. D. dissertation, Tulane University, 1966; Jo Lee Fleming, "James D. Vaughan,

Music Publisher," unpublished S.M.D. dissertation, Union Theological Seminary, 1972; Tony Heilbut, *The Gospel Sound*; George Pullen Jackson, *White Spirituals in the Southern Uplands*; Lawrence Levine, *Black Culture and Black Consciousness*; J. B. T. Marsh, *The Story of the Jubilee Singers*; William C. Martin, "At the Corner of Glory Avenue and Hallelujah Street," *Harper's* 244 (January 1972): 95-99; Charles Wolfe, ed., *The Gospel Ship*.

BILL C. MALONE
TULANE UNIVERSITY

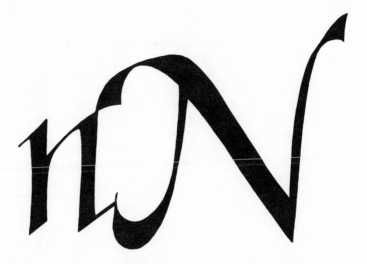

NASHVILLE, TENNESSEE. The decade that witnessed the birth of the federal constitution saw Methodism reach Nashville as part of its frontier thrust. By 1787 a Methodist church had been founded there. Today's McKendree Church (named for the pioneer, William McKendree) is the outgrowth of this beginning. James Robertson and his wife early joined the church in what proved to be a harbinger of the next two centuries as prominent citizens found a spiritual home there. Early in the 19th century FRANCIS ASBURY visited the church, finding not less than a thousand people.

Presbyterians were active in the vicinity earlier, but had no organized church in Nashville before 1814, when Gideon Blackburn constituted the work with seven members. In 1849 the church erected its third building, since two had burned. This new structure represented a strong trend toward a revival of Egyptian architecture. Almost a century later in 1955, a majority of the members moved to a new location and continued as First Church. A minority retained the old building to become Downtown Presbyterian Church. An earlier 19th-century split within Presbyterian ranks gave rise to the CUMBERLAND PRESBYTERIAN CHURCH, which developed strength in Nashville and the area around it.

By 1820 the Sunday school movement reached Nashville. The first school met in what is now McKendree Methodist Church, but was a union school involving Methodists and Presbyterians. Mrs. Felix Grundy, a Presbyterian, was a guiding spirit in the undertaking. Initially there was opposition to the school. However, it was the adumbration of a movement destined to make Nashville the home of religious publishing houses on a grand scale. A far-reaching step was taken in 1854 when the METHODIST CHURCH, broken into Northern and Southern branches, located the Methodist Publishing House there; this was to become the South's first major publishing enterprise.

In the third decade of the 19th century Episcopal and Roman Catholic interest in Nashville commenced. The first Episcopal church was established in 1829; two years later Christ Church was erected. Its present building, opened in 1894, is listed on the National Register of Historic Places. Mass was offered in Nashville as early as 1821; within the decade a building was erected for the first Catholic church in the state. When Nashville finally became the state's capital city, the church sold its original site on Campbell Hill for a state house. The Know-Nothing party helped curtail the growth of Catholicism. Before 1860 religious conflict between Protestants and Catholics, and prejudice within Protestantism and within particular denominations asserted itself in Nashville. This chapter in the city's religious history was the 19th-century parallel to the 20th-century conflict over Liberalism and Fundamentalism, which loomed large in the first quarter of the new century.

Baptist beginnings in Nashville were checkered, owing in part to a schism that developed around ALEXANDER CAMPBELL and BARTON W. STONE. For a decade Campbell was identified with REGULAR BAPTISTS but separated from them in the 1820s. In 1832 Stone merged his congregations with Campbell's, creating the Disciples of Christ. By 1849 Disciples had constructed a handsome building in Nashville and published the *Christian Review* there. Many early Baptists joined this movement. R. C. B. HOWELL had started *The Baptist* in 1835, the first stable Baptist paper in the new West. (The attractiveness of the city for religious journalism was a major factor in shaping Nashville's prominent place as a religious capital.) It was during Howell's two pastorates there (1835-1850, 1857-1867) at First Baptist Church that the work of this denomination was solidified. His second pastorate was marked by controversy with JAMES R. GRAVES and the LANDMARK MOVEMENT. Following the Civil War Baptists and Methodists gained a position of religious dominance. By 1891 the SOUTHERN BAPTIST CONVENTION had organized its second Sunday School Board, the new board being located in Nashville. J. M. FROST gave distinctive service as its secretary well into the 20th century. Under other long-tenured secretaries the board has grown to embrace numerous programs and operations.

After 1865 distinct black Methodist and Baptist churches developed more rapidly. Some of the black Baptist conventions have made Nashville their headquarters. Other groups to emerge included the CHURCHES OF CHRIST, the conservative branch of the Campbellite movement. DAVID LIPSCOMB became their outstanding leader, as their Nashville-based college signifies. Another denomination with headquarters here is the FREE WILL BAPTISTS, which maintains a Bible college in the city.

A significant educational development was the chartering of a university in 1872, soon called Vanderbilt, connected with the Methodist Church. Recognized as a leading school in the South, Vanderbilt became a center of controversy over new theological interpretations growing out of 19th-century developments. Along with numerous smaller church-related colleges, it earned for Nashville the appellation "Athens of the South."

See also article on TENNESSEE.

Bibliography. Robert A. Baker, *The Southern Baptist Convention and Its People: 1607-1972*; F. Garvin Davenport, *Cultural Life in Nashville on the Eve of the Civil War*; Downtown Presbyterian Church, "A Brief History"; Stanley J. Folmsbee, Robert E. Corlew, and Enoch L. Mitchell, *Tennessee: A Short History*; Lynn E. May, Jr., *The First Baptist Church of Nashville: 1820-1970*; McKendree United Methodist Church, "A Brief History"; Methodist Publishing House, *About United Methodism in Nashville*; Lucy Ray, et al., "Christ Church"; William Waller, *Nashville in the 1890s*.

WILLIAM ALLEN POE
NORTHWESTERN STATE UNIVERSITY
OF LOUISIANA

NATIONAL BAPTISTS. The name shared by the three largest black Baptist denominations, National Baptists refers to a constituency numbering between nine and ten million. The National Baptist Convention, U.S.A., Inc. is the oldest, dating from 1895, and has a membership above six million. The National Baptist Convention, USA, was founded in 1915 and reported 2,668,779 members in 1982. Organized in 1961, the Progressive National Baptist Convention is the most recent and in size exceeds a half-million.

Black Baptists hold to the classic themes and features of the historic Baptist communion. In particular, they emphasize the independence of local congregations and the view that baptism (thus church membership) is reserved for "adult believers." The expressive style of black Baptist worship is a natural outgrowth of insistence on personal faith, the process of knowing it and feeling it for one's self. In addition, it reflects the history of Afro-Americans' adaptations of the European Baptist heritage as that had been modified in the white Baptist life of the South.

Afro-Americans did not come under the influence of Christianity on any widespread basis until the late eighteenth century. One reason for its development then was the emergence of evangelical forms of the Christian faith after mid-century among Southern whites. This occurred through the arrival, then rapid expansion, of SEPARATE BAPTISTS from New England. The later birth and growth of the Methodist communion was also influential in this regard. In both cases, warmhearted personal faith was a hallmark. This new religious force in the Southern region generated aggressive missionary activity throughout the population, among blacks as well as whites.

By the era of the Civil War, black Baptist numbers had swelled to some 400,000 while Methodist size had increased to 210,000. This dramatic growth reflected large numbers of blacks in independent black churches and as members of mixed congregations (in which blacks often had some say). In addition, thousands of black men and women met to worship, pray, and sing in the INVISIBLE INSTITUTION that is, in brush arbors or in the slave quarters on plantations.

Once emancipation was law, black churches sprang into existence in a remarkably short period of time. The church was the one social organization in which black people had had direct participation. Self-determination was a telling force in religious life as nowhere else. About two-thirds of the new independent constituency was Baptist; that same proportion continues to the present. The largest percentage of black Christians are Baptist and the largest percentage of black Baptists are National Baptists (the total of the three denominations bearing that name).

Between 1865 and 1879, black separatism became the pervasive ideology of Afro-American Baptist leaders. The first national association formed was the Consolidated American Baptist Missionary Convention, but it dissolved in 1879 from internal conflict rooted partly in a class consciousness over prewar social status. Unity was only delayed, however. In 1895 in Atlanta the National Baptist Convention, U.S.A., Inc., was organized as a merger of missionary, educational, and publishing societies.

The "unincorporated" body of National Baptists was organized in 1915 when a split occurred around the issue of the ownership of the Convention's publishing house. The focal point of the conflict was the Rev. Robert H. Boyd, the corresponding secretary of the publication board, who owned the property on which the publishing agency stood and in whose name all its materials had been copyrighted. Boyd withdrew the publishing house from the Convention and he and his colleagues moved out to form the "unincorporated" body.

The Progressive National Baptist Convention, Inc., appeared in 1961 as a result of controversy within the "incorporated" body: how national officers are to be elected was the issue. The new body insisted on a limited tenure prescribed by constitution for its presidents, a policy that had been adopted by the "incorporated" group in 1953. However, when J. H. JACKSON refused to step down from the incorporated body's presidency at the end of his set term, a segment led by the Rev. L. Venchael Booth withdrew to form the "Progressive" group.

This new denomination has taken an active role in American political life, especially in the CIVIL RIGHTS MOVEMENT. (MARTIN LUTHER KING, JR., affiliated with this body.) The incorporated body has begun to show signs of greater interest in political involvement in the early 1980s.

A major force among black citizens in the United States, National Baptist life symbolizes much of the richness and anguish of the Afro-American past. It continues to be a voice, a refuge, and a forum for action for its nearly 10-million-member constituency and for black Americans generally.

Bibliography. Mark Miles Fisher, *A Short History of the Baptist Denomination*; Owen D. Pelt and Ralph Lee Smith, *The Story of the National Baptists*; Albert J. Raboteau, *Slave Religion*; Edward Starr, ed., *A Baptist Bibliography*; James M. Washington, *The Origins of Black Baptist Separatism, 1863-1897.*

NATIONAL COUNCIL OF CHURCH-ES: *See* ECUMENISM (IN THE SOUTH).

NATIVISM. The Southern religious experience has been shaped by nativist fears of foreign immigrants, especially those who have been Catholics or Jews. For the South, as for the nation as a whole, xenophobic concerns have oscillated in intensity and character, but they have existed almost from the beginning of European settlement in America. Nativism has been as complex a phenomenon as it has been long-lived. Yet, as John Higham has observed, some form of defensive nationalism has rested at the core of all brands of antiforeign agitation. Occasionally Southerners have perceived immigrant religions as threats to their cherished social patterns. Indeed, of various nativist traditions, those centering on religious antipathies have perhaps been the most long-lasting and divisive.

Though heterogeneous in population by world standards, the South has not received a large-scale foreign immigration relative to other sections of the Uni-

ted States. Still, the South has shared in the nativist turmoils periodically troubling the nation. There is ample psychological evidence to suggest that a danger removed from immediate scrutiny is very often most feared. In practice, the region seldom has originated nativist outbursts. Rather, the South has resonated to impulses initiated elsewhere.

Historically, religious nativism has adopted two principal guises: anti-Catholicism and anti-Semitism. The first of these two is by far the most important and long-standing. Colonial Americans, for example, transported a cluster of anti-Catholic prejudices from the Old World. The sensitivity of Southern colonialists was heightened by the threatening presence of nearby Spanish possessions. These negative dispositions induced some administrators to enact laws curbing immigration and controlling the free exercise of Catholicism. Xenophobic anxieties, however, were never at the center of colonial attention. The tendency to experiment with legislative restrictions nevertheless persisted, as exemplified in short-lived provisions in the Georgia and North Carolina constitutions that barred Catholics from state offices.

The full development of anti-Catholicism awaited the massive influx of Irish and German immigrants in the period 1830-1860. Faced with a rapidly expanding Catholic Church, and torn by the mounting sectional crisis, Americans increasingly listened to nativist explanations of their problems. Tales of Popish plots against the nation's liberty, with immigrants acting as agents, were coupled with fantastic stories of priestly immorality and treachery. The most vivid political manifestation of these patterns was the rise of the Know-Nothing party in the 1850s. Representing the culmination of two decades of growing anti-Catholic sentiment, the party ran numerous candidates.

In the South, a few coastal cities such as Charleston and New Orleans and the states of Louisiana and Maryland were most affected. Here anti-Catholic campaigners succeeded in capturing political office and establishing nativist newspapers and organizations (e.g., the New Orleans *Protestant* and the Louisiana Native-American Association). As concern over slavery intensified, and Know-Nothingism lost momentum to Republicanism, the party became essentially a Southern entity. In the election of 1856, Millard Fillmore, the Know-Nothing candidate, received his greatest support from the South. A more violent side to this agitation existed as anti-Catholic mobs attacked convents in New Orleans, Galveston, and Charleston. The Civil War soon diverted the attention of all Americans from such concerns.

Nativism rekindled with the mass migrations of Southern and Southeastern Europeans after 1880. The main contours of this new xenophobia were not centered on religion, but rather on issues surrounding race and radicalism. Another outbreak of anti-Catholicism did occur around 1910, with the South providing something of a leadership role. Located in rural, small-town America generally, this religious nativism coincided with the rise of FUNDAMENTALISM. No more articulate spokesman for this cause existed than the Populist leader Tom Watson of Georgia, who spread a message of papal intrigue. Wilbur Franklin Phelps's *The Menace*, published in Aurora MO, reached circulation of one million by 1914 on the strength of a virulent anti-Catholicism that soon spilled over into politics. Watson became a U. S. senator in 1920; SIDNEY J. CATTS captured the Florida governorship in 1916 with a blatantly nativist campaign.

The rebirth of the KU KLUX KLAN after 1915 revealed most clearly a renewed Southern attachment to anti-Catholicism. Klan ideology drew heavily on the rural, fundamentalist perspectives underpinning much of anti-Catholic sentiment. Among its "noble" missions, the Klan dedicated itself to advancing Protestant Christianity. As such, it was naturally drawn to "No-Popery." As the Klan gathered strength in the South (and elsewhere), it gave organized direction to rising anti-Catholicism in the 1920s. Klan support went to candidates endorsing nativist platforms in various local and state elections. Violence, as always, accompanied the agitation, with the most Catholic of Southern states, Louisiana, again leading the way. By 1925, however, the Klan reached its zenith and its influence began to spiral downward.

Anti-Catholicism remained after the Klan's decline, although without a significant institutional base. Various anti-Catholic tracts and beliefs circulated in the South, periodically assuming importance during such events as the 1928 and 1960 presidential races of Catholic candidates Al Smith and John F. Kennedy. The forthright explanations of his religion by Kennedy and, more important, his election and service as president, did much to dispel religious fears. Catholicism in high public office had been put to the test.

Anti-Semitism in the South has been more diffuse than anti-Catholicism. Antipathy toward Jews has usually taken the form of negative stereotypes picturing Jews as cunning, avaricious Shylocks who combined moral depravity with social vulgarity. During the Populist era some Southerners supported the view that Jews were part of an international financial conspiracy, charges given further credibility after 1918 by the spurious Protocols of the Elders of Zion. These concerns, however, lacked a clear religious dimension, and anti-Semitism always occupied a lesser rank in the lexicon of Southern nativist fears.

The South has had specific instances of anti-Semitic behavior, ranging from social discrimination to acts of violence. Southern locations were among the first in the nation to experience substantial anti-Semitic demonstrations. In the late

1880s and early 1890s parts of the lower South witnessed instances of home burning, store wrecking, and physical beatings directed against Jewish merchants by debt-ridden farmers. The brutal 1914 lynching of an Atlanta Jew (q.v., the FRANK, LEO, CASE) captured national headlines. The Ku Klux Klan also included Jews among their enemies and engaged in periodic acts of intimidation. Yet these crusades were of secondary importance to the interests of both the Klan and the region as a whole.

Bibliography. Gordon Allport, *The Nature of Prejudice;* Ray Allen Billington, *The Protestant Crusade, 1800-1860;* David M. Chalmers, *Hooded Americanism: The History of the Ku Klux Klan;* David A. Gerber, "Cutting Out Shylock: Elite Anti-Semitism and the Quest for Moral Order in the mid-Nineteenth Century American Market Place," *Journal of American History* 69 (December 1982): 615-37; John Higham, *Strangers in the Land: Patterns of American Nativism, 1860-1925;* Carey McWilliams, *A Mask for Privilege: Anti-Semitism in America.*

GEORGE E. POZZETTA
UNIVERSITY OF FLORIDA

NEGROES, RELIGION OF: *See* BLACK RELIGION.

NEW BIRTH. The Christian idea of the New Birth is first found in the New Testament book of the Gospel of John. There rebirth takes place from "below," the realm of flesh, to "above," the realm of spirit. The Johannine author transmutes the future age of regeneration (Mt. 19:28) to present spiritual experience. To be a "child of God" is to receive new life from God himself, not through natural procreation but by a miracle of grace.

In the New Testament, there generally is a sharp contrast between the two orders of existence, that of the old creation and that of the new. The metaphors of passing from death into life and from darkness into light express the radical change wrought by the grace of God. The Johannine passage on new birth (3:1-8) links the birth from above with baptism and the Spirit of God. Although Paul employs the idea of adoption rather than "new birth" in the context of Roman law,

he too associates faith and the Spirit with the beginning of the new life symbolized in baptism. The new birth marks one's entry into the Christian life; it also connotes the new state or relationship to God. The book of 1 John in particular emphasizes the ethical aspects of the spiritual birth. The Pauline contrast between old and new being, outward and inward, and flesh and Spirit highlights the continuing moral conflict in the life of the Christian.

The various branches of the Christian church differ in their opinions on the connection between baptism and new birth. In the Roman Catholic Church and in "High" Anglicanism, the sacrament of baptism is identified with regeneration. Similarly, for Luther baptism meant dying to sin and being born to new life. The Holy Spirit effects regeneration through baptism; baptism is also the assurance of God's constant readiness to forgive sins. But unlike the Roman doctrine of baptism, Luther's view stressed the element of conversion. To John Calvin, regeneration was identical with repentance, the work of the Holy Spirit. Other Protestant churches see CONVERSION rather than baptism as the sacrament of regeneration. Baptists embrace "believer's baptism," seeing it as a sign rather than a sacrament of regeneration.

In the early Protestant writings on conversion, there is constant reference to the three basic elements of faith, repentance, and the renewal of the will. Luther tended to identify conversion with faith, Calvin with repentance, and Melancthon with the renewal of the will. But all three agreed in seeing the work of conversion, regeneration, or new birth as the work of God. The personal accounts of conversion by many Christian leaders from Augustine through Luther and Calvin to the present day recount experiences of illumination after a time of anxiety, guilt, or fear, followed by a sense of release, peace, and joy. For some the conversion is sudden, for others gradual. Yet the accounts consistently focus not on the psychological and emotional aspects of the experience but on its spiritual and scriptural meaning.

Popular revival movements in America, from the time of the GREAT AWAKENING to the present day, have made conversion and regeneration central in preaching and Christian experience. Southern evangelical churches have stressed the necessity of being "born again," typically associating spiritual regeneration with certain kinds of moral behavior as signs of the new life. In this they are in line with the major Protestant theological traditions, though they may codify morality in a somewhat external fashion. For the Protestant Reformers, conversion marked the beginning of sanctification, as a state of justification and a growth in faith, love, and hope. The struggle to conform the mind of the believer to the mind of Christ is lifelong, but the new birth signifies to Christians the assurance of final victory.

See also articles on EVANGELICALISM; REVIVALISM.

Bibliography. Alan Richardson, ed., *A Theological Word Book of the Bible*; Reinhold Seeberg, *Text-Book of the History of Doctrines.*

THOMAS E. MCCOLLOUGH
DUKE UNIVERSITY

NEW HAMPSHIRE CONFESSION OF FAITH.

After 1780 the theological views of Calvinistic Baptists in New Hampshire were considerably moderated by the influence of the FREE WILL BAPTIST movement, led by Benjamin Randall (1741-1808). In 1830 the Baptist Convention of New Hampshire appointed a committee to prepare a confession that would be "agreeable and consistent with the views of all our churches in this state." The confession in finished form was presented to the board of the convention in 1833 and was submitted to the churches for its adoption. It has been known as the New Hampshire Confession.

J. Newton Brown, a member of the committee for drafting the confession, became editorial secretary of the American Baptist Publication Society. In 1853 he published the confession on his own authority, with alterations, in the *Baptist Church Manual*. In the course of time the moderate CALVINISM of the New Hampshire Confession made it more popular among Baptists both inside and beyond New England than the strongly Calvinistic Philadelphia Confession.

The widening influence of the confession may be seen by noting several historical developments. In 1867 J. M. Pendleton, who had been a leader of the LANDMARK MOVEMENT, incorporated the confession in his *Church Manual*. The confession's silence on the doctrine of the universal church caused its widespread adoption in churches influenced by Landmarkism. In 1894 Edward Hiscox incorporated the confession in what became a standard church manual in the 19th century, *The New Directory for Baptist Churches*. In 1933, 50 churches withdrew from the Northern Baptist Convention because of the supposed theological liberalism of that body, and formed the General Association of Regular Baptist Churches. With slight modifications they adopted the New Hampshire Confession. In 1925 the SOUTHERN BAPTIST CONVENTION adopted a confession closely modeled upon the New Hampshire Confession except for the addition of 10 articles. In 1963 the same convention issued another confession that took as its models the New Hampshire Confession and the confession of 1925, with a few minor alterations.

The New Hampshire Confession has become among Baptists of the South the most influential confession of their history. Much of its popularity has been due to its emphasis upon the local church and its strong assertion of the inerrancy of the Scriptures.

JAMES E. TULL
SOUTHEASTERN BAPTIST SEMINARY

NEWELL, BERTHA PAYNE

(1867-1953), social reform advocate, was born in Wisconsin in 1867, a native of the North who became very active in a variety of activities in the South. She was educated at the University of Chicago and from 1901-1909 was head of the Department of Kindergarten Education in the university's School of Education. While in Chicago, she was influenced by the settlement house work of Jane Addams. In 1909 she married William A. Newell, a minister of the Methodist Episcopal Church, South, and moved with him to the Western North Carolina Conference. Soon she became very active in the work of the Woman's Missionary Council of the M. E. Church, South. In 1920, she became superintendent of the council's Bureau of Social Service (reorganized in 1930 as the Bureau of Christian Social Relations), a position she held for 18 years. As superintendent, she assumed a major role in urging the women's missionary societies in the local churches to support various social reform projects.

She was particularly active in promoting interracial work. Although encountering opposition and indifference from inside and outside the women's organization, she was quite successful in encouraging local missionary societies to investigate conditions for blacks in their communities and to support better schools, improved housing, and equal justice. She demonstrated a commitment to eradicate violent crimes against blacks by serving as secretary of the ASSOCIATION OF SOUTHERN WOMEN FOR THE PREVENTION OF LYNCHING. Though most active in interracial concerns, Newell also worked on behalf of a number of other social reforms, including child labor, world peace, and women's rights.

See also articles on METHODIST CHURCH; SOCIAL GOSPEL; WOMEN IN RELIGION.

Bibliography. Jacquelyn Dowd Hall, *Revolt Against Chivalry*; Noreen Dunn Tatum, *A Crown of Service*.

JOHN P. MCDOWELL
ROANOKE, VIRGINIA

NOAH, CURSE OF: *See* HAM, MYTH OF.

NORRIS, J(OHN) FRANK(LYN) (1877-1952), Fundamentalist pastor and polemicist, was born in Dadeville AL but moved with his family at the age of 11 to Texas. Norris was graduated from Baylor University in 1903 and from the Southern Baptist Theological Seminary in 1905. After a student pastorate in Texas he became minister of the McKinney Avenue Baptist Church in Dallas from 1905 to 1908. From 1907 to 1909 he was editor and eventually owner of the *Baptist Standard*, the newspaper of Southern Baptists in Texas.

The churches Norris served simultaneously, First Baptist in Fort Worth (1909-1952) and Temple Baptist in Detroit (1935-1951), grew to be among the world's largest with 15,000 and 10,000 members, respectively. They were, however, basically preaching centers built upon the cornerstone of his own personality. His dominating, independent spirit; his sensationalist tactics; and his "drive" for positions of leadership linked with his theological dogmatism led to many controversies. The most memorable occurred in 1926. In the midst of anti-Roman Catholic feelings in Fort Worth, which he had been instrumental in precipitating, Norris shot and killed an unarmed man who had invaded Norris's study to defend the mayor of the city against Norris's accusations. On a change of venue to Austin, Norris was found "not guilty" on the first ballot, the jury believing that the minister had acted in self-defense when a stranger provided an "apparent danger."

Norris's debates with the leaders of the Southern Baptist Convention were lengthy and bitter. He charged the denomination with failure to respect the independence of the local church and with theological liberalism. The Pastor's Conference at Fort Worth expelled him in 1914 because of his radically independent spirit and his constant criticism of fellow ministers; the Tarrant County Baptist Association excluded him in 1922 for being a threat to the "peace, harmony, and unity" of that body; and in 1924 the Baptist General Convention of Texas ousted both Norris and his church for "unBaptistic and noncooperative" actions.

As a forceful speaker, Norris campaigned arduously throughout Texas in 1928 on behalf of Herbert Hoover, against the presidential candidacy of Alfred E. Smith, and he was credited with a major role in Hoover's victory. The basic issue, Norris affirmed, was the "Roman Catholic question." In the 1930s, Norris was influential in the conversion of John Birch, a student at Mercer University, and namesake of the John Birch Society. Young Birch followed Norris to Fort Worth, joined his church, studied in his seminary, and went to China under Norris's personal sponsorship. During the last years of his life, Norris stepped up his attacks against Russian Communism, vilifying the movement itself as well as the many persons whom he believed were Communist sympathizers.

See also articles on FUNDAMENTALISM; NATIVISM.

Bibliography. C. Allyn Russell, "J. Frank Norris, Violent Fundamentalist," Voices of American Fundamentalism; Mark G. Toulouse, "A Case Study in Schism: J. Frank Norris and the Southern Baptist Convention," Foundations 26 (January-March, 1981): 32-53.

C. ALLYN RUSSELL
BOSTON UNIVERSITY

NORTH CAROLINA. Religious activity in colonial North Carolina dates from the Ralph Lane Colony that sailed from Plymouth, England, in 1585. A clergyman accompanied this and subsequent groups. The Lane Colony returned to England with Sir Francis Drake in 1586. The next year another colony was sent out under John White; they returned to Roanoke Island in July 1587. Within two weeks the first recorded Protestant baptism in the New World took place when a friendly Croatan Indian, Manteo, was baptized. This has come to be known as the famous "Lost Colony" because it disappeared.

The first permanent settlers in the state followed the streams in southeastern Virginia that emptied into the Albemarle Sound in northeastern North Carolina. There were already well-established settlers in this area when Charles II granted a charter to the eight Lords Proprietor in 1663. The proprietors were to have "the advowsons and patronage of churches" and were authorized to grant liberty of conscience to all persons who should conform to the practices and beliefs of the Anglican Church.

Although the intent of the Royal Charter and subsequent instructions to the Royal governors were for the Church of England to be the established church in North Carolina, its inaction and neglect played into the hands of dissenting groups, notably the QUAKERS. This group had become very influential in political affairs in the Albemarle region. According to one history, they constituted only about one-seventh of the total population but were better organized than any other religious body.

In 1704, John Blair, an Anglican missionary, described the religious sentiment in the colony when he wrote:

> The country may be divided into four sorts of people: first the Quakers, who are the most powerful enemies to church government, but a people very ignorant of what they profess. The second sort are a great many who have no religion, but would be Quakers, if by that they were not obliged to lead a more moral life than they are willing to comply to. A third sort, something like the Presbyterians which sort is upheld by some idle fellows who have left their lawful employment, and preach and baptize through the country without any manner of orders from any sect or pretended Church. A fourth sort, who are really zealous for the interest of the Church are the fewest in number, but the better sort of people. And would do very much for the settlement of the Church government

there, if not opposed by these three precedent sects: and though they be all three of different pretensions, yet they all concur together in one common cause to prevent any thing that will be chargable to them, as they allege Church government will be, if once established by law.

In 1701 the colony's first church law, the Vestry Act, was passed. This legislation provided for the laying out of parishes, the organization of vestries, the erection of churches, and a poll tax on all tithables for the support of the clergy. In 1703 an act providing that an oath be taken by members of the General Assembly that they were communicants of the Church of England repealed the right of affirmation that the Quakers had enjoyed for years. The dissenters continued to be opposed to these various acts, but the government continued to pass laws and vestry acts in 1758, 1760, 1761, and 1762. Finally in 1765 a vestry act was agreed upon. William Tryon, Royal governor and zealous churchman, kept requesting that clergy be sent from England to assist the Established Church.

In 1776 North Carolina adopted a new constitution. There would be no established church, no compulsory attendance at religious worship, or compulsory support of any religious organization. All citizens would be at liberty to exercise their own "mode of worship." Clergymen could not serve in the General Assembly while still exercising their pastoral functions. No person "who should deny the being of God or the truth of the Protestant Religion, or the Divine Authority of the Old or New Testament, or who shall hold Religious Principles incompatible with the Freedom and Safety of the State" would be eligible for public office.

These provisions caused some problems in later years. John Culpeper and William Taylor in 1801 and Joshuah Crudup in 1820 were expelled from the legislature because they were practicing ministers. This was an unpopular cause

since both Culpeper and Crudup were elected to the national Congress. An effort to expel Joseph Henry, a Jew from Carteret County, failed in 1809. In 1833 William Gaston, a Roman Catholic, was elected to the Supreme Court of North Carolina. The Constitutional Convention of 1835 met to redress this problem and others. Despite a two-day address by William Gaston against religious tests for office, the convention only substituted "Christian" for Protestant in the clause, thus removing the test for Roman Catholics but not for Jews. It was not until the Constitution of 1868 that this was changed and then only atheists were barred from holding public office.

Despite governmental support for the Anglican Church, the Society of Friends (Quakers) was the most important religious group in the colony before 1700. The earliest-recorded missionary to North Carolina was the Quaker William Edmundson, founder of the Quaker faith in Ireland. He first came to America in 1672 with George Fox, founder of the Society. By May 1672, Edmundson was preaching his first sermon near present-day Hertford in Perquimans County. If his observations were correct, the settlers of the Albemarle Sound area at that time had "little or no religion." They did attend his preaching and he won two converts. Later in November of the same year George Fox visited the area and did evangelistic work for 18 days. Fox came again in 1676-1677 and found the Friends to be "finely settled."

According to William P. Johnson the signing of the Carolina Charter in 1663 probably served as an impetus to migration, as hundreds of settlers began to pour into the northeast in the 1660s and 1670s. A large number came from lower Virginia into the Albemarle area. In the western part of the state, New Garden meeting in Guilford County was established in 1754 and populated largely by New England Quakers from Nantucket. This became the most important Quaker settlement in North Carolina.

By the end of the American Revolution, the Friends' opposition to the war had cost them in both numbers and growth. They had also retired from public life; as a result their political influence declined. They did continue to pioneer in prison reform and the care of the insane. From the beginning North Carolina Friends were deeply involved in the antislavery movements. It was this last fact that caused many families to leave the state and its slave-holding society for the lure of fertile farmland and greater freedom in the Northwest Territory. They migrated to Indiana and other Midwestern states.

The state's Quakers were organized in a series of meetings. The First Day meetings for worship; the Monthly Meetings for congregational business; Quarterly Meetings combined worship and business for a group of congregations in a specific geographical area; Yearly Meetings were and are the units of Quaker jurisdiction over a given geographic area. The North Carolina Yearly Meeting of the Religious Society of Friends dates from 1698. By the 1860s there were 25 monthly meetings established in North Carolina.

The Friends suffered further during the Civil War because of their opposition to war and their antislavery sentiments. Many were conscripted to work in the state salt works on the coast. Others paid substitutes in lieu of military service. After the Civil War they received financial support and other materials from coreligionists from other states.

The Friends had a deep interest in the support of education. Guilford College was chartered in 1833 as New Garden Boarding School. It opened in 1837 and unlike the state university and other denominational schools Guilford was coeducational from its beginning. After the Civil War, concern was shown for the emancipated blacks. Schools were established to serve them, these often being operated by volunteers.

Return migration from the Midwest helped the Friends to grow. Former North Carolinians and their families came back from southern Ohio and Indiana. By 1876 membership had climbed to 5,500. Clothing and encouragement had been sent by Baltimore Friends to assist people devastated by war. With outside assistance, schools were established and schoolhouses rebuilt. Then in 1874 the Society of Friends experienced a great revival. Eleven years later the first Woman's Missionary Society met at New Garden. Publication of a newspaper, *The Friends Messenger* began in 1904 and lasted until 1932, to be replaced by *The Friends News Letter*, now the chief means of communication for North Carolina Friends. According to 1971 statistics the Friends have 73 churches with a total membership of 12,511, most of them concentrated in the central Piedmont.

The first missionary sent to North Carolina by England's SOCIETY FOR THE PROPAGATION OF THE GOSPEL (S.P.G.) was Daniel Brett, who probably arrived in the year 1700. Little is known of his work. Following Brett, the Rev. John Blair came by way of Virginia, arriving among the people of the Albemarle in 1704. The S.P.G. that sent these missionaries was the missionary arm of the Church of England. It provided financial and moral support for some 37 missionaries who served in North Carolina between 1701 and 1775. The most promising young men, however, did not come to the wilderness of North Carolina. The Rev. C. E. Taylor wrote of his parish and predecessor: "I have therefore settled myself for a while in St. George's Parish, Northampton County, void by the Resignation of Mr. Barnet, one of the Society's Missionaries who I am informed has fled into Virginia being charged with crimes too base to be mentioned."

Despite being the state religion, encouraged and supported by government officials, the Church of England did not enjoy the favor of a majority of the inhabitants of North Carolina. The people of this province and colony were more concerned with conquering a frontier and having ample provisions in store than with supporting an established clergy.

By the close of the Proprietary period in 1729, the S.P.G. had sent a few missionaries, and provided a library. Also several chapels had been erected but little else had been done. In 1739 Governor Gabriel Johnston called the assembly's attention to the fact that there were only two places in the Province where divine services of the Established Church were regularly performed. By the end of Governor Tryon's term in 1770 there were ministers in 18 of the 22 parishes.

The American Revolution ended any influence that the Church of England may have had in North Carolina. The 1776 State Constitution did away with the idea of an established church. Many of the ministers left the state because of their understanding of the oath they had taken to the king. Chapels and meeting places were abandoned or taken over by other denominations. It was many years before the Protestant Episcopal Church with any significant effect was to take the place of the Church of England.

Baptists were among the first permanent settlers of North Carolina. The first record of their presence in the colony was contained in a letter written by John Urmstone, an Anglican minister, on 12 June 1714, in which he complained that two of his vestrymen in the Chowan Precinct were "professed Anabaptists." The first Baptist minister of record was Paul Palmer, a native of Maryland, who was living in Perquimans Precinct in 1720. His missionary endeavors led to the formation of North Carolina's first Baptist church in 1727 in Chowan County. This church existed for several years and then disappeared. Palmer was also the founder two years later of Shiloh Church in Camden County. This church is the oldest extant Baptist church in the state.

Seventeen General Baptist churches had been formed in the eastern part of the state by 1754, according to one historian.

The next year many of these churches transferred to the Particular Baptist persuasion, largely through the efforts of Benjamin Miller and Peter P. Vanhorn, evangelists from the Philadelphia Baptist Association. The Jersey Settlement and Baptist Church under the leaderships of Benjamin Miller and John Gano was the Particular Baptist enterprise that influenced the piedmont section of the state.

The same year, 1755, saw the founding of Sandy Creek Baptist Church south of Greensboro by SHUBAL STEARNS and Daniel Marshall. The coming of the "New Lights" or SEPARATE BAPTISTS, and the formation of Sandy Creek was to prove the most significant event in North Carolina Baptist history. This congregation was to become not only the mother of other local churches but the mother of all Separate Baptists in the Southern states. In the first 17 years of the church's existence, Morgan Edwards wrote, 42 churches and 125 ministers had "sprung from the parent church." They were called "New Lights" because of their belief in the possibility of individual inspiration and enlightenment through the Holy Spirit. They were called "Separates" because of their desire to separate themselves from the Congregational Church and organize independent societies.

In the eastern part of the state the Particular Baptists began to call themselves "Regular Baptists" to emphasize the distinctiveness from Separates. Most of the eastern North Carolina Baptist churches had been members of the Charleston (SC) Baptist Association from its beginning in 1751 but the distance from the main body made this affiliation impractical. Therefore, on 6 November 1769, the delegates from five churches formed the KEHUKEE BAPTIST ASSOCIATION, the second-oldest association in North Carolina, and the first in which the Separate and Regular Baptist churches united. Distinctions between the two soon were obliterated. The Kehukee Association included all the Baptist churches in eastern North Carolina with the exception of two or three of the Free Will order.

During the 75 years immediately following the organization of Shiloh in 1729, Baptists had spread from the Atlantic Ocean to the Tennessee border and had organized these churches into associations for cooperative activities. According to David Benedict there were 11 associations, about 200 churches, and some 13,000 Baptists in North Carolina by 1812.

By 1805 Baptists under the leadership of Martin Ross began to take an interest in the support of missionary activities. A "Baptist Philanthropic Missionary Society" was organized in 1805. In 1811 a corresponding body called the "General Meeting of Correspondence" was organized. This body lasted until 1821 when it was supplanted by the North Carolina Baptist Society for Foreign Missions (later Foreign and Domestic Missions) that had been formed in 1814. Again Martin Ross took the initiative and introduced a resolution in the 1826 annual meeting of the Chowan Baptist Association, calling for the formation of a Baptist state convention. Unfortunately he died before plans could be completed for this statewide unification of Baptists.

In 1820 Joshua Lawrence presented a document entitled "Declaration of the Reformed Baptists in North Carolina" to the Kehukee Association. A year later the majority of the 35 churches in the Kehukee had endorsed Lawrence's proposal to "discard all Missionary Societies, Bible Societies, and Theological Seminaries, and the products heretofore resorted to for their support, in begging from the public." The mission-minded churches began to withdraw from the Kehukee Association. Several churches in the Kehukee and other associations split over the issue of supporting missions. Shortly thereafter the antimission elements adopted the name of Kehukee Primitive Baptists.

The friends of Martin Ross and of missions sought to revive organized Baptist work in the state. On 10 February 1829, several ministers and laymen met in Greenville and formed the North Carolina Baptist Benevolent Society. When they convened the next year they adopted the following resolution: "That this Society be transformed into a State Convention." At this time there were 14 Baptist associations, 272 churches, and "upwards of 15,360 members," according to Thomas Meredith. They were interested in supporting state missions and soon realized that this involved the development of a state newspaper, a college, and Sunday schools.

Early in 1835, THOMAS MEREDITH's new periodical, the *Biblical Recorder*, was issued after a trial issue the year before. This became the voice of the missionary Baptists in the state; except for the year 1842 and a short suspension in 1865 the *Biblical Recorder* has been published continuously.

In 1833 Wake Forest Manual Labor Institute was chartered. Its doors were opened for the education of young ministers in 1834, with 72 students attending the first session. The institute was rechartered as a college in 1838. In 1956 it moved from its first location in Wake County to Winston-Salem and 10 years later it became Wake Forest University.

Delegates from west of the Blue Ridge Mountains found it difficult to participate because of the difficulties of travel. That largely accounts for the formation of the Western Baptist Convention in 1845. It organized three boards and supported Judson College and Mars Hill College as educational institutions, and several newspapers as well. When travel became easier these Baptists of the West sought to reunite with the state convention, accomplishing that goal in 1898.

Sunday school activities were not neglected. In 1845 the North Carolina Baptist Sunday School and Publication Society was organized to promote the work. The state convention organized a Sunday school board in 1863 that took over the society's work.

In 1860 North Carolina Baptists had 780 congregations with a total of some 65,000 members—already the largest denomination in the state. During the Civil War Baptists were very active in supplying tracts and Bibles to the Confederate soldiers.

During the 1870s the Convention began to show an interest in new fields of activity, among which were the care of orphans and the work of women's missionary societies. The Thomasville Orphanage was finally opened in 1894 under John H. Mills. The scattered woman's societies came together in a state organization in 1877 as the Central Committee, later the Woman's Missionary Union. Fannie Exile Scudder Heck, its first president (1886-1887), later became president of the Woman's Missionary Union of the Southern Baptist Convention. In this same period, the education of women became a concern of the convention when the Baptist Female University was chartered in 1891. This became Meredith College, located in Raleigh, in 1909. In 1899 the former Chowan Baptist Female Academy (now Chowan College) joined the convention's other schools.

After World War I a cooperative endeavor with the Southern Baptist Convention to raise 75 million dollars led to the formation of the Unified Program, that became the Cooperative Program. Another result was the establishment of the North Carolina Baptist Hospital in Winston-Salem that opened its doors to patients in 1923.

The Convention took over the operation of Mars Hill College in 1911; Campbell College (now University) in 1925; Gardner-Webb College in 1948; and Wingate College in 1949.

The Baptist Children's Homes and the Baptist Homes for the Aging have also expanded their activities and presence over the state. A new headquarters build-

ing was completed in Raleigh in 1955 and at present plans are being made for an expanded state headquarters complex on the outskirts of Raleigh.

North Carolina Baptists continue to be the largest Protestant denomination in the state. In 1981 that body reported 3,452 churches and a total membership of 1,129,735.

After the Civil War black Baptists generally withdrew to form their own churches, associations, and even denominations. The American Baptist Home Mission Society (Northern) sent workers and financial assistance into the state. Shaw University was established in Raleigh, largely through the efforts of H. M. Tupper. Other Baptist schools and academies for blacks were supported. The Baptist Educational and Missionary Convention of North Carolina (now the General Baptist Convention) was organized in Goldsboro in 1867. A century later, in the 1970s and 1980s, both the General Baptist Convention and the Baptist State Convention of North Carolina had joint annual meetings. A few black churches have affiliated with white associations. Black Baptists have established the *Baptist Informer* as their state newspaper.

FREE WILL BAPTISTS in North Carolina began their history with the work of Paul Palmer (1692-1763), a General Baptist preacher, whose threefold doctrine consisted of free grace, free will, and free salvation. He first organized the "church in Chowan" in 1727, and then Shiloh in 1729. Both Missionary and Free Will Baptists trace their beginnings to this church. By 1750 other churches had been organized in eastern North Carolina and northeastern South Carolina. Some of these churches were those that Benjamin Miller and Peter P. Vanhorn could not convert from General to Particular in 1755. Joseph and William Parker are given the credit for saving these five churches for the Free Will Baptists.

By 1800 total membership was reported at 25,000. Eastern North Carolina was and remains the stronghold of the denomination. The General Conference of Free Will Baptists was meeting as early as 1807 according to one historian. This conference divided into the Bethel and Shiloh Conferences that met until 1842 when they reunited into the General Conference. In 1886 they split into the Eastern and Western Conferences. Cape Fear Conference was formed in 1855, the Pee Dee in 1869, and Central in 1895. In 1839 the General Conference listed 2,006 members and 32 preachers. The Conference of 1884 listed 7,649 members and 82 ministers in 111 churches. In 1913 the State Conference was organized. They began the Free Will Baptist Press (dating to 1873); an orphanage at Middlesex (1920); Cragmont Assembly at Black Mountain; a seminary (founded in 1896); Eureka College (founded in 1925); and Mount Olive College (1952). A split came in the North Carolina Free Will Baptist ranks in 1958 over the recognition of a minority by the Western Conference. As a result the General Conference of Original Free Will Baptists was organized in 1961, and the North Carolina Association of Free Will Baptists came into being in June of 1962.

In the colonial period the Presbyterian Church in North Carolina, like the Episcopal Church, enjoyed a prestige far out of proportion to the number of its followers. Its ministers had the reputation for education and leadership and its layman for sobriety and industry that made Presbyterianism a term of approbation. Organized Presbyterian work came into the piedmont areas of North Carolina from the 1730s to 1770s when the Scotch-Irish swarmed into the piedmont from Pennsylvania, then down the Valley of Virginia to settle on the edge of the North Carolina frontier. They quickly appealed to the synods of New York and Philadelphia for missionaries and ministers, and these synods responded to their call.

In the eastern part of the state there were Scotch-Irish Presbyterians on the Henry McCulloh grants in Duplin and New Hanover counties as early as 1736. The first large group of Highlanders from Scotland made their way up the Cape Fear River and settled in the Cross Creek area (now Fayetteville) in 1746. They scattered themselves over an area that now includes Bladen, Cumberland, Sampson, Moore, Robeson, Richmond, and Anson counties; a section that to this day is a stronghold of Presbyterianism. These Scottish Highlanders spoke only Gaelic, a fact that protected them from nearby Baptists and others, and kept them faithful to the Calvinist tradition even when they had no pastors.

In 1770 the Orange Presbytery held its first meeting at Hawfields. By 1788 the Synod of the Carolinas was composed of three presbyteries, namely Orange, South Carolina, and Abingdon. In 1795 Concord Presbytery was set off from Orange. Then in 1812 the General Assembly of the Presbyterian Church was petitioned to establish the Synod of North Carolina, the new synod boasting 31 ministers, 85 churches, and about 4,000 communicants the next year.

According to one historian "a coldness and want of energy" had pervaded the Presbyterian Church in North Carolina. There had been ruptures in the denomination, of which the 1837 split was felt the most, involving the Old School and the New School. Between 1838 and 1849 Presbyterians were increasing at the rate of less than 100 per year, but in the 1850s a new spirit arose in the church. As a result the denomination increased its interest and support in contributions, foreign and domestic missions, and evangelism. This last activity came too late for the Presbyterians to compete with the Baptist and Methodist denominations, however. From 1813 to 1860 the number of churches had increased by only 99. They were generally in the principal towns and villages of the piedmont and Cape Fear sections of the state. In the west there were churches at Wilkesboro, Lenoir, Asheville, Morganton, Marion, and Statesville, but the denomination had scarcely penetrated the Northeast.

On 1 November 1861, the Synod of North Carolina meeting in Raleigh, voted to join the formation of the General Assembly of the Presbyterian Church in the Confederate States. During the Civil War chaplains were supplied to the soldiers, and collections were taken for the benefit of orphans, and the education of children of deceased soldiers. In this four-year period the Presbyterian Church in North Carolina gained only eight ministers and five churches, and lost more than 2,000 communicants.

The 1870s and later decades saw the denomination turning to evangelizing as the country became more settled. The denomination even had a "Committee on Aggressiveness" to further its evangelizing efforts but synodical Home Mission endeavors did not begin until 1887. One of the immediate results was the establishment of a home for orphans, now at Barium Springs.

The Presbyterians were the first denomination in the state to attempt the establishment of a college with the founding of short-lived Queen's College in the 1770s in Charlotte. Individual Presbyterians had been prominent in the early history of the University of North Carolina, but they were not successful in founding a permanent college until 1837 when Davidson College opened its doors to young men; it was chartered by the state legislature late in 1838.

The North Carolina Synod of the Presbyterian Church in the United States was composed of seven presbyteries in 1975, with 677 churches and 821 ministers. Most of the black churches, located primarily in the Cape Fear area, belonged to the Northern branch of the Presbyterian Church.

The interpretation has been offered that "the fact that Presbyterians considered it a mark of vulgarity not to be able to read or repeat the Shorter Catechism in a time when half the people of the State

were illiterate was sufficient to set them apart from the adherents of other denominations." The gentry and middle class dominated the membership at a time when the other denominations in the state were making great numerical gains. The discipline within the family and the church's continued efforts to educate its youth has been a significant contribution to the state through the years.

The first Lutherans in the original colony of North Carolina were wiped out by the Indians in 1711. Permanent Lutheran congregational life in the state can be said to date from the mid-eighteenth-century flow of German immigrants from Pennsylvania. They came down the Shenandoah Valley into piedmont North Carolina bringing their German language and customs. This movement is reflected today in the large concentration of Lutheran churches in the central and western parts of the state.

A congregation was reported on the Haw River as early as 1745. This early congregation and others that were soon established needed pastors. Pastor Adolph Nussmann was sent from Germany, along with John Arends as teacher, to assist the early congregations. During the American Revolution there were only two Lutheran pastors in the state. After the war other denominations began making inroads into the Lutheran congregations. PAUL HENKEL made this report in 1802: "There were many immersionists (Baptists) in the audience . . . . These found my sermon so contrary to their taste that they strongly disapproved . . . one of the company who carried a large club in his hand stepped up to the pulpit and interrupted my sermon."

The Lutherans also distrusted the revivalistic methods that appealed to North Carolinians in the frontier area. The dominant trend among them was toward a stricter orthodoxy. This led to the establishment of a synodical organization, the North Carolina Synod being formed in Salisbury in 1803. Most of the Lutheran synods in the South have derived from this body. Its constitution did not contain any references to the confessional writings of the Lutheran Church. This fact, and the new synod's control over the licensing and other requirements, led to their first crisis. David Henkel was placed on probation and his license was withdrawn in 1819. His father, Paul Henkel, and others withdrew and organized the Tennessee Synod in 1820. This new synod covered the same area as the North Carolina Synod. The two synods existed side-by-side until 1921 when they merged to form the United Evangelical Synod of North Carolina.

The Civil War deeply affected North Carolina Lutherans. Southern Lutherans met in Concord in 1863 and formed the General Synod of the Evangelical Lutheran Church in the Confederate States of America, later altered to the United Synod of the South. It took a half century, until 1918, for the state's Lutherans and other Southern Lutherans to join in a national organization. As a result of the Civil War the small number of blacks withdrew to found the Alpha Synod of the Evangelical Lutheran Church of Freedmen in America in 1889. It dissolved a few years later. A rival Lutheran denomination, the Missouri Synod Church, began to assist the black congregations in the state. Immanuel College, founded in Concord in 1903, later moved to Greensboro where it continued to educate blacks for about 50 years.

After several educational institutions had failed, Lenoir-Rhyne College in Hickory was organized in 1891 (as Lenoir College), and it continues as the state's only Lutheran school. The Women's Missionary Society was organized in 1885. In 1923 the *North Carolina Lutheran* was founded as the denominational newspapers. The American Lutheran Church and Lutheran Church in America both recognize Sipes Orchard Home (boys) at Conover. The LCA owns the North Carolina Homes, Inc. at Hickory.

In 1860 Lutherans were the fourth-largest denomination in North Carolina with 3,942 members and 38 congregations. Today Lutheran churches in North Carolina are divided among three national bodies: the ALC, the Lutheran Church-Missouri Synod, and the LCA. The LCA embraces the North Carolina Synod of seven districts. In 1971 the total membership was 98,184 in 265 congregations. The largest membership is in the Central District with congregations in China Grove, Salisbury, and Statesville.

The first members of the Reformed tradition of Protestantism came into the Pamlico section of North Carolina from Virginia in 1690. They had no minister and no organized congregation. They were members of the Reformed Church of France. Other Swiss and Palatine Reformed members settled in the New Bern area in 1710, but the majority of this group were killed by the Indians in 1711 and the survivors went into the Presbyterian Church.

The high tide of German immigration into North Carolina was from 1745 to 1755, these representing the Reformed, Lutheran, and Moravian churches. All three groups settled in the piedmont area of the state. Often the Lutheran and Reformed members built union churches. The greatest problem experienced by these ethnic churches was a lack of ministers, but several made their way into the colony from South Carolina and Europe.

The Rev. Samuel Suther began his ministry in North Carolina in June 1768, and served Reformed churches until 1786. He was credited with organizing most of the Reformed congregations still in existence where the North Carolina Classis was organized in 1831. From brush arbors to substantial churches the Reformed churches developed their ministry among the German settlers. The need for more ministers persisted, however, there being only one pastor left in the state by 1812. The German Reformed Synod meeting in Pennsylvania responded to the need in North Carolina by sending ministers on several occasions.

After the Civil War blacks began to form their own Reformed congregations. A black congregation was admitted to the classis in 1868 but was not listed after two years. The classis went on record as favoring Sunday schools and prayer meetings. They were against the evils of intemperance and in 1858 took an advanced stand for that time, when they resolved "that the making or distillation for the purpose of indiscriminate sale of intoxicating liquors, its use as a beverage, the practice of giving it to hands invited to log-rollings, huskings, raisings, etc., is immoral in its tendencies and justifies the exercise of discipline."

Most denominations in the South divided with their Northern counterparts over the question of slavery but not the Reformed Church. The Classis of North Carolina did secede, however, but over the "Mercersburg Theology", a question of the soundness of theology taught in that Pennsylvania seminary. The regional factions were reconciled in 1866.

The Classis of North Carolina's involvement in education saw its culmination with the founding of Catawba College in 1851. Benevolent activities resulted in the formation of the Nazareth Orphan's Home in 1906. The Woman's Missionary Society was organized in 1897. Beginning in March 1894, J. L. Murphy and T. C. Leonard began publishing the *Corinthian*, that was subsequently endorsed by the Classis and became the *Reformed Church Standard*.

After several years of preliminary meetings the Evangelical Synod of North America and the Reformed Church in the United States united in 1934 as the General Synod of the Evangelical and Reformed Church. A committee met in 1939 at First Church, Salisbury, and organized the Southern Synod of the Evangelical and Reformed Church.

The German Reformed denomination in North Carolina has never been large. In 1860 it consisted of 15 congregations. In 1971, after merging with the Congrega-tional Christian Churches to form the UNITED CHURCH OF CHRIST, 255 congregations were reported with 53,839 adherents.

Better organized than the other German religious groups that came to North Carolina and smaller in numbers than the Lutherans, the Unitas Fratrum (United Brethren), or MORAVIANS, purchased the huge Wachovia tract (almost 99,000 acres) in what is now Forsyth County. Bethabara was first settled in 1753, nearby Bethania was begun in 1759, and the construction of Salem (now Winston-Salem) was underway by 1766. During the early years, the Wachovia settlement was governed by Moravian church boards abroad, although the state's Brethren also maintained close ties with the Pennsylvania settlements.

From the beginning Salem was a planned community organized on a communal basis with the congregation's governing boards controlling the civil, business, and religious matters. The lease system was installed to keep undesirable citizens and businesses out of the community. It is worth remembering that congregational and business records were kept in German. In 1849 the congregation gave up its supervision of businesses and in 1856 the lease system was abolished.

Moravianism was more than a religion—it was also a way of life. The community was organized into a choir system, individuals grouped according to their age, sex, and marital status. The various groups lived in separate quarters with their own separate officers. When a member died he or she was buried in a cemetery site set aside for the choir of which he or she was a member.

The Brethren did not emphasize conversion to Moravian tenets, but were interested in preaching the Gospel to all, a practice pursued by hardly any other denomination. From earliest years, the Brethren were sending missionaries to the Indians. Records that they carefully preserved give present-day historians a glimpse of their life and activities as well as information on other denominations and ministers in piedmont North Carolina with which the Moravians came into contact.

During times of war this company of hardy Christians suffered greatly, particularly during the American Revolution. Their refusal to bear arms for either side led to raids on their communities and farms by both Loyalists and American forces interested in locating foodstuff and livestock. They took a strong stand to help everyone and to fight no one. By the time of the Civil War ideas had changed so much that the Salem congregation band became the regimental band of the 26th North Carolina Infantry, CSA; it still exists and enjoys wide popularity. The Moravian Music Foundation of Winston-Salem is the principal repository for music scores used by Moravians worldwide.

The Academy for Girls was established in Salem in 1772 with one teacher and two pupils. It continued to grow and was opened to non-Moravians in 1802. This early school is continued at present in the work done by Salem College and Salem Academy. Moravians were also interested in foreign missions and spreading the faith to non-Moravian areas. In 1825 the state's Moravians established work in Indiana and then in Illinois. In 1850 another group left for Iowa. Congregations also were established in the larger communities and cities: Raleigh in 1903, Greensboro in 1908, Charlotte in 1920, and Mt. Airy in 1925. Their congregations are still confined largely to the piedmont area of the state, however. The Southern Province of the Moravian Church in America, founded in 1771, has its headquarters in Winston-Salem. In 1971 there were 43 congregations with 2,000 members.

Methodists were the last major Protestant body to appear in colonial North Carolina. Preaching had begun in 1772 when Joseph Pilmoor preached in the eastern area of the state. The first permanent foothold of Methodism in the colony, however, resulted from the preaching of Robert Williams of Brunswick County VA, leading to the formation of the first North Carolina circuit in 1776 with 683 members. Methodists began to spread rapidly over the state; only three years later there were three circuits with 1,467 members. Other circuits were formed and ministers came on horseback from Virginia mostly and went as far west as the Blue Ridge. Thus, with few areas excepted Methodists had succeeded in covering the entire state of North Carolina in little less than a decade.

The Methodist Episcopal Church in the United States was organized in Baltimore in 1784. The first annual meeting in the state was held in the home of Green Hill, near Louisburg, the next year, conducted by Francis Asbury and Thomas Coke, the two major figures in early American Methodism. In 1836 the North Carolina Conference was formed by dividing the Virginia Conference. The Methodist ranks have experienced several divisions. The first came in 1792 when JAMES O'KELLY and his associates left the General Conference and formed the Christian Church, now a part of the United Church of Christ. In the 1820s the Methodist Protestant Church was formed from dissidents within the Methodist Episcopal Church. They created a separate conference in 1828. Strains created by the approach of the Civil War resulted in the formation of the Methodist Episcopal Church, South in 1844. Three national branches, the Methodist Episcopal Church (Northern), the Methodist Episcopal Church, South, and the Methodist Protestant Church effected unification in 1939 as The Methodist Church. In 1968 another merger, this one with the Evangelical United Brethren (EUB), occasioned the changing of its name to the United Methodist Church. The vast majority of North Carolina Methodist churches are United Methodist.

By the end of the 1850s Methodists had established a newspaper, the *North Carolina Christian Advocate*. Trinity College (now Duke University) had been founded a few years earlier. Commitment to higher education was continued in the 1950s with the establishment of Methodist College at Fayetteville and North Carolina Wesleyan College at Rocky Mount. Homes for the orphans and elderly have been part of Methodist life for over a century.

However, smaller groups of Methodists have also split away over the years. The Wesleyan Methodist Church was formed in the 1840s, as was the Primitive Methodist Church; the Free Methodists came into being in the 1860s. In 1968 the Wesleyan Methodists merged with the Pilgrim Holiness Church to form the WESLEYAN CHURCH. After the Civil War, the Methodist Episcopal Church (Northern) organized many black congregations in North Carolina. But other black congregations were organized independently at black initiative: the African Methodist Episcopal Zion Church (AME-Zion) as early as 1865; the African Methodist Episcopal Church (AME) by 1868; and the Colored Methodist Episcopal Church (CME) that became the Christian Methodist Episcopal Church in 1956.

Figures for 1971 for all Methodists in North Carolina credit the denomination with 2,018 churches and 534,721 total adherents, making it the second largest denomination in the state.

The CHRISTIAN CHURCH in North Carolina was founded largely through the efforts of James O'Kelly, a Methodist lay preacher and later elder. He was assigned to the Tar River Circuit on the Virginia-North Carolina border. O'Kelly and his followers withdrew from the Methodist Episcopal Church in 1792, desiring to have "a free constitution and a pure church." Prior to 1831 some of the churches practiced baptism by immersion only, and rejected infant baptism, a practice that led to a split in the denomination in 1810. The followers of William Guirey,

with the majority of the Virginia churches, withdrew and formed the Independent Christian Baptist Church. O'Kelly and the North Carolina churches formed the Old North State Conference. By this time his followers were also known as O'Kellyites; the North Carolina churches that did not join the O'Kellyites were known as Christian Baptists.

After preliminary planning the Virginia and North Carolina Christians were united in 1825. O'Kelly, the founder, died the next year and was buried in Chatham County. In 1844 the denomination began publishing the *Christian Sun*, in Raleigh and Pittsboro, until the Civil War years. Several reorganizations took place in the 19th century. Then in July 1961 the Congregational Christian Churches merged with the Evangelical and Reformed Church to form the United Church of Christ. In 1971 that body reported 255 congregations and 53,839 adherents in North Carolina.

What of the Established Church of the colonial period? The American Revolution intensified prejudices against the Church of England that persisted for many decades. Episcopal clergymen continued to preach after the Revolution but it was not until 5 June 1790 that the Rev. Charles Pettigrew, the Rev. James L. Wilson, and two laymen, John Leigh and William Clements, met in Tarboro to provide some organization for the Episcopal Church in North Carolina. In 1817 the state's Diocese was organized. By 1830 there were only 11 ministers and 31 congregations, most of them concentrated in the East, with two in Orange County, and two farther west in Rowan County.

When the North Carolina convention was held in Salisbury in 1823 the clerical deputies unanimously elected JOHN STARK RAVENSCROFT of Virginia as the first Episcopal bishop of the diocese. One historian wrote:

> Thus at last, after years of struggle the church in North Carolina was firmly established—not on the old basis of state support, in which it

had failed, but on a new basis of an independent, voluntary church supported by the desires, energy, and labors of its clergy and its congregations.

The clergy that served the scattered congregations in the state were also very active in preaching and ministering to the blacks prior to the Civil War. Several plantations had separate services for their slaves. A mission school was established at Valle Crucis in the northwestern mountains in 1844. Bishop LEVI S. IVES, who served from 1831 to 1851, was torn by conflicting religious beliefs. He was first a Presbyterian, then an Episcopalian, and then a Roman Catholic.

North Carolina Episcopalians were members of the Protestant Episcopal Church in the Confederate States during the Civil War period. Twelve Episcopal chaplains served with the soldiers and one served the military post at Wilmington. Losses in church membership and wartime damages to churches had to be repaired, and Bishop Thomas Atkinson gave leadership. His endeavors increased the clergy from 36 to 66, and the number of communicants from 1,778 to 5,889 by 1881.

A Missionary District of Asheville was formed in 1895. The Diocese of Western North Carolina was formed in 1922. In 1883 the Diocese of East Carolina was established—both of these dioceses coming out of the Diocese of North Carolina. The Rt. Rev. Henry Beard Delaney was consecrated Bishop Suffragan of the Diocese of North Carolina in 1918, with the responsibility of working with blacks in North and South Carolina.

Saint Mary's College was founded in Raleigh in 1842 by Albert Smedes as an Episcopal school for girls. Saint Augustine's College was founded there in 1867 to educate blacks. Christ School, Arden, began its work in 1900. Patterson School, Lenoir, is the only preparatory school for boys owned by the Episcopal Church in the state of North Carolina.

The 1971 statistics list 223 churches and 65,665 adherents in the three dioceses that now cover the state. Comments made by an antebellum historian on the Episcopal Church in the pre-Civil War era could probably still apply today. He wrote: "The Episcopal Church was far more influential in the state than its small number of adherents would indicate. Most of the church buildings were located in the towns, substantial buildings supported by substantial citizens, merchants, planters, professional men, [and] government officials." The church was not popular with the common people and "its real influence had scarcely stirred beyond the coastal plain, its chief field during Colonial times."

The Disciples of Christ began their work in North Carolina largely through the efforts of some former Presbyterians. BARTON WARREN STONE, while serving in Kentucky, began to advocate that the various denominations discard all formal discipline and return to the Bible as the all-sufficient rule of faith, so that all Christians might unite in brotherly love. Alexander Campbell was also advocating much the same position. David Purviance, a former Presbyterian from Iredell County, was the first to preach the faith of the "Restoration Movement" in North Carolina.

Alexander Campbell first visited North Carolina in 1833. During his stay in the state for some six months, entire Baptist congregations went over to the "Campbellites," as his followers were then being called. Later visits in 1838 and 1845 were also productive in winning adherents.

The Bethel Free-Will Baptist Conference of the Disciples of Christ was organized in 1841. They soon became the Annual Conference of the Disciples of Christ in North Carolina. Because of the exceedingly democratic and individualistic polity of the church it is difficult to estimate the numbers of the Disciples in North Carolina during the formative years. Their strength prior to the Civil

War appeared to be in the East. After the Civil War most of the Union Baptists, an Open-Communion group numbering more than 3,000, were largely absorbed by the Disciples.

The 1870s were marked by an aggressive expansion of the North Carolina Disciples of Christ. Women's work began to be recognized and in 1871 "Sisters' Beneficent Societies" began to be formed. By 1892 there were 20 auxiliaries in the state. In 1877 the North Carolina Christian Missionary Society was formed to spread the Gospel within the state. In 1878 a State Evangelist was selected and began his work. In 1902 Atlantic Christian College was incorporated in Wilson. The *North Carolina Christian* began publication in 1920.

Growth came slowly to the Disciples but they were increasing their ranks in a methodical manner. In 1971 they reported 334 congregations and 46,310 adherents.

Catholic immigrants first settled in the Pamlico Sound region in eastern North Carolina as early as 1737. But Catholics were few in number and their organizational life limited. From 1790 until 1829 they were under the jurisdiction of the Diocese/Archdiocese of Baltimore. In 1820 the Diocese of Charleston was formed and North Carolina Catholics were served by clergy from South Carolina. Its bishop, John England, made many visits into the state from Charleston between 1821 and 1824.

By 1830 Catholics in New Bern had a church building. In 1832 the first Mass was celebrated in Raleigh. In 1838 the Very Rev. Thomas Murphy was stationed in Fayetteville, the first Catholic pastor in North Carolina, and served in the eastern part of the state until 1844. After a year in Georgia he returned to Wilmington, where he continued to serve until his death in 1863.

Catholic missionary endeavors in the western part of the state began with the opening of the gold mines in the Mecklen-

burg County area around 1830. Churches were built in Gaston County in 1843, in Charlotte in 1852, in Asheville in 1869, and in Concord in 1870. These stations were largely served by clergy from South Carolina and Georgia until the 1850s. On the eve of the Civil War there were seven congregations containing 350 members in the state.

In 1868 the state of North Carolina became a separate vicariate, the famous Bishop James Gibbons being the first Vicar Apostolic of North Carolina. In 1868, according to his biographer, "He found only two or three priests, about the same number of humble churches, and a thousand Catholics scattered at different points all over North Carolina." He "traveled night and day, and by all modes of conveyance, new and obsolete." Gibbons administered the sacraments in such secret places as garrets and basements, and knew all the adult Catholics in North Carolina personally. He established the Benedictine Order at Belmont Abbey, the Sisters of Mercy in Wilmington, ordained some dozen priests, erected a half-dozen new churches, and opened several schools.

The state's Catholic population amounted to 1,700 in 1878. In 1924 the Diocese of North Carolina was formed. It was later divided into the Raleigh Diocese, serving the eastern portion of the state and the Charlotte Diocese, serving the western portion of the state. By 1971 North Carolina Catholics were reporting 157 churches with a membership of 69,133.

The Seventh-Day Adventists denomination was organized 21 May 1863, with 125 churches and 3,500 members into a General Conference. The states of North and South Carolina are in the Carolinas Conference, first organized in 1901, and reorganized in 1918. In 1971 North Carolina Adventists had 71 churches and 8,739 total adherents.

North Carolina was among the first of the original 13 colonies to welcome Jewish settlement explicitly. The Fundamental Constitutions for the Carolinas stated that the colony was open to settlement by "Jews, heathens, and other dissenters." The first Jewish settlers came into the state from Barbados, and were of Spanish-Portuguese origin. Wilmington seems to have had a Jewish community as early as 1738. The earliest Jewish name on record appears to be Aaron Moses who witnessed a will in 1740. Others came into the state with some becoming quite prominent. Jacob Henry was elected to the state legislature in 1808. He successfully kept his challenged seat but it was not until 1868 that the state constitution officially gave Jews the right to hold public office in the state.

The Jews who came into the state in the second half of the 19th century were mostly immigrants from Germany. They turned to the one profession universally open to them, peddling. (The Cherokee Indians referred to such Jews as "egg-eaters." The probable reason for this term was the strict adherence to the Jewish dietary laws. The peddlers avoided meat of any kind until they returned home on Friday evening in time to observe the Sabbath.) "Way Stations" were established in Wilmington, Albemarle, and Yanceyville where they could resupply and where they could be "home for the Sabbath." Isaac Harby estimated that there were 44 Jews in the state in 1826. In 1860 the Jews of Wilmington were advertising for a cantor to serve them.

It was not until 1867 that North Carolina's first congregation was established in Wilmington. This was formally incorporated as Temple of Israel in 1873. Other towns and communities began to organize their resident Jews in the post-Civil War years. Asheville had two congregations, Durham one; Goldsboro established a congregation in 1883; New Bern had a congregation, Tarboro had a congregation by 1872; and in 1883 Statesville formed a congregation. After 1880 the East-European Jews began to settle in the state—principally in the mill towns and the larger cities and communities. The largest group of Jews settled in the piedmont area with the largest congregation in Greensboro. In 1970 there were 27 synagogues in the state. North Carolina could also boast of having the only "circuit rider," a Jewish lay leader who visited the scattered communities unable to maintain a synagogue or a rabbi on their own. *The American Jewish Time-Outlook* began publishing in Greensboro in 1935 and Harry Golden founded the *Carolina Israelite* in Charlotte in 1940.

In any brief resumé of religion in North Carolina a number of extant and extinct denominations alike must be omitted, owing largely to the lack of information sources. These groups, too, have made contributions to the religious life of the state.

Religion has played a very important role in the history of the state of North Carolina from the Colonial era to the present. The various strands of denominationalism have been tightly interwoven with the secular history of the state. Denominations provided the stability on the frontier before civil and judicial authorities arrived. They were in the forefront, often being the first to provide educational opportunities, orphanages for the children, and homes for the aging. Leaders in denominational life have often been the leaders in political, social, and public arenas as well. Most of the surviving denominations in our state have suffered one or more splits in their ranks but in most circumstances this division has led to larger memberships and greater growth for all concerned. Religion and denominationalism continue to exert a wholesome and much-needed influence on North Carolinians of today.

See also articles on ANGLICAN CHURCH; MIGRATION, SOUTHWARD (1700-1830).

Bibliography. George H. Anderson, *The North Carolina Synod Through 175 Years (1803-1978)*; Francis C. Anscombe, *I Have Called You Friend: The Story of Quakerism in North Carolina*; Lawrence F. Brewster, *A Short History of the Diocese of East Carolina, 1883-1972, With Its Background In the History of the Anglican Church in the*

Colony and The Protestant Episcopal Church in North Carolina; Elmer T. Clark, *Methodism in Western North Carolina*; Wallace R. Draughan, *History of the Church of Jesus Christ of Latter-day Saints in North Carolina;* Adelaide Fries, J. J. Hamilton, D. L. Rights, and M. J. Smith, ed., *The Records of The Moravians in North Carolina*, 11 vols.; Cardinal James Gibbons, *Reminiscences of Catholicity in North Carolina*; Harry Golden, *Jewish Roots in The Carolinas*; Thaddeus F. Harrison and J. M. Barfield, *History of the Free Will Baptists of North Carolina*, 2 vols.; Cushing B. Hassell, *History of the Church of God From The Creation to AD 1885: Including Especially the History of the Kehukee Primitive Baptist Association*; Guion Johnson, "Religious Denominations," *Antebellum North Carolina: A Social History*; Donald Keyser, ed., Abstracts and index of articles in *The North Carolina Historical Review*; Jacob C. Leonard, *The Southern Synod of the Evangelical and Reformed Church*; George W. Paschal, *History of North Carolina Baptists*, 2 vols.; Jethro Rumple, *The History of Presbyterianism in North Carolina*; Durwood T. Stokes and William T. Scott, *A History of The Christian Church in the South*; Robert H. Stone, *A History of the Orange Presbytery, 1770-1970*; Charles C. Ware, *North Carolina Disciples of Christ: A History of Their Rise and Progress.*

JOHN R. WOODARD
WAKE FOREST UNIVERSITY

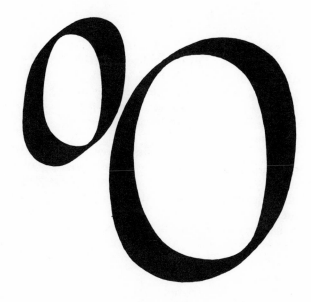

O'CONNOR, MARY FLANNERY
(1925-1964), Roman Catholic short-story writer and novelist, was born in Savannah GA. At the age of 13 she moved with her family to Milledgeville. In 1941 her father died of a hereditary disease (Lupus) that would later claim the life of his daughter. After graduating in 1945 from the Georgia State College for Women, O'Connor went to the State University of Iowa where she received her M.A. in 1947. For a brief time she lived in New York but returned to Milledgeville to live on a farm with her mother. Except for a series of brief lecture tours in this country and a European pilgrimage to Lourdes and Rome, she remained in that town until her premature death at the age of 39.

During her active writing career (1948 to 1964), O'Connor published three volumes of fiction with a fourth published posthumously: *Wise Blood* (1952); *A Good Man is Hard to Find & Other Stories* (1955); *The Violent Bear It Away* (1960); *Everything That Rises Must Converge & Other Stories* (1965). Her short stories were all combined in the National Book Award-winning *The Complete Stories* (1971). Her nonfiction prose has been collected and edited by Sally and Robert Fitzgerald under the title *Mystery and Manners* (1969). Sally Fitzgerald has also edited a generous selection of her letters in 1979: *The Habit of Being: The Letters of Flannery O'Connor.*

This relatively modest literary output has evoked an intense scrutiny of her work by critics since her death. There is a general critical consensus about the high quality of her writing but agreement about the nature of it has not been as unanimous. O'Connor wrote from an orthodox Roman Catholic point of view ("I see from the viewpoint of Christian orthodoxy . . . for me the meaning of life is centered in the redemption of Christ and that what I see in the world, I see in relation to that") but her novellas and short stories were centered in the life of the rural South. Her stories are populated with misfits, cripples, fanatical holiness preachers, gaunt farmers, drifters, and other such characters from the Southern *demi-monde.* Her fiction was meant to shock the reader into religious recognition, but it was only by indirection and allusion that her Christian orthodoxy strikes home. The very parabolic quality of her writing creates paradoxes and what she means to say is often conveyed by what she does not say directly or openly.

It is difficult to generalize about the structure of her stories, but one principle does seem to operate rather regularly: her characters move inexorably from a plane of false consciousness to a moment of revelation. In many of her stories characters who proclaim that "they know who they are" or that "they see clearly" are rudely, and often violently, awakened to a new vision or a deepened insight into their human condition. O'Connor has called this awakening that occurs as one moves from false consciousness into insight the movement from "manners to mystery."

True to her Catholic sense of sacramentalism, nature, often particularized into sunsets or tree lines, is a living witness to the mystery of Christ in the world. Her emphasis on the presence of Christ in the cosmos as a palpable reality and her fascination with consciousness enlarged by that presence made her sympathetic to the ideas of Teilhard de Chardin. When she began to read his newly translated works in the late 1950s, she found in his theological vision a view of the world not dissimilar to her own. The title of her last volume (*Everything that Rises Must Converge*) was a conscious tribute to his influence.

Although the majority of her stories are set in the milieu of the rural South, she vigorously eschewed the notion that she was a regional writer. Her links to the Southern literary tradition are patent, but her juxtaposition of comedy and tragedy ties her equally to writers like Nathanael West in this country and Franz Kafka on the Continent. Her evocation of violence reflects her strong conviction that the world has within it the presence of the demonic, which wars against modernity's too facile optimism about the nature of evil in the world. Violence in her fiction, however, is neither random or aleatory. Her early novella *Wise Blood* was, in fact, a passionate rejection of Sartrean existentialism. Echoing certain Sophoclean themes, her benighted hero in *Wise Blood*

gains vision in blindness by finally understanding that his relativized world without ultimate significance is a treacherous lie. For O'Connor the world, paradoxically enough, is both redeemed and "thrown off balance" by the redemptive work of Christ. That paradox is explored in a range of stories from the early "A Good Man is Hard to Find" to "Parker's Back," a story she wrote during her final illness.

O'Connor's unabashed Christian orthodoxy has struck many contemporary critics as alien territory, but she never flagged in presenting this viewpoint in her work. In fact, she felt that the strangeness of the Christian vision compelled her to write in such a manner to compel the attention of her readers. As she once said: "For the blind you write large and for the deaf you shout."

See also articles on LITERATURE AND RELIGION; ROMAN CATHOLICISM.

Bibliography. David Eggenschwiler, *The Christian Humanism of Flannery O'Connor*; John R. May, *The Pruning Word: The Parables of Flannery O'Connor*; Gilbert Muller, *Nightmares and Visions: Flannery O'Connor and The Catholic Grotesque.*

LAWRENCE S. CUNNINGHAM
FLORIDA STATE UNIVERSITY

OGLETHORPE, JAMES (1696-1785), a major figure in colonial Georgia, was born in England, the youngest child of a staunch Jacobite family. Although sent to Oxford, he expressed an early preference for a military career that eventually would give him fame and be instrumental in the founding of Georgia in 1733. After fighting with Prince Eugen of Savoy against the Turks in 1717, Oglethorpe temporarily joined his siblings in Jacobite exile. He returned to England in 1722 and began a 32-year parliamentary career as representative from Haslemere. Oglethorpe pursued legislation that helped outline a British mercantilist empire. His work for sailors' rights and for debtors expressed his sympathy for the oppressed. Building upon his parliamentary and philanthropic sympathies, Oglethorpe joined with the associates of the late THOMAS BRAY and Viscount Percival to promote the colony of Georgia both as a military buffer and as a humanitarian endeavor. Without defensive success against the Spanish, humanitarian concerns would be of little account. To effect the defense of Georgia, Oglethorpe founded FREDERICA as a military outpost and encouraged a wide-ranging, settler-recruitment policy. Although he was Anglican, Oglethorpe promoted the migration of many religious groups during his 10 years in the colony. Because of his efforts, Georgia came to represent ethnic and religious diversity, including Anglican, Methodist, German Lutheran, Scotch Presbyterian, and Sephardic Jews. In keeping with his religious sentiments, Oglethorpe was a leader of the Georgia trustees in restricting the use of rum and the introduction of slavery. After several successful but controversial years as aggressive representative of the trustees in Georgia, Oglethorpe retired from active colonization to England where, in 1743, he married Elizabeth Wright and lived out his remaining years as a member of an English Enlightenment circle including literary figures James Boswell, Samuel Johnson, and Hannah More.

See also article on GEORGIA.

Bibliography. Amos A. Ettinger, *James Edward Oglethorpe*; Phinizy Spalding, *Oglethorpe in America*.

THOMAS F. ARMSTRONG
GEORGIA COLLEGE

O'KELLY, JAMES (1738-1826), early reformer of church polity, was a schismatic Methodist itinerant whose North Carolina and Virginia followers were the principal founders of the Southern CHRISTIAN CHURCH. Born in Virginia and self-educated, he became a trial Methodist itinerant in 1778. From the outset he clashed with FRANCIS ASBURY over the location of ecclesiastical authority. O'Kelly insisted on the absolute right of the itinerants to govern their collective ministry while Asbury and the majority of the Methodist clergy believed that "the discipline . . . published by Mr. Wesley," which placed substantial supervisory power in Asbury's hands, was essential to the well-being of a growing denomination.

By 1792, however, O'Kelly and a minority of like-minded itinerants insisted on a totally democratic ministry. After Asbury repeatedly refused to discuss the matter with them and in 1793 invited them either to acquiesce in Methodist discipline or leave the church, O'Kelly and his cohorts considered themselves involuntarily excluded. Accordingly, "we formed our ministers on an equality," O'Kelly explained, "gave the laymembers a balance of power in the legislature; and left the executive business in the church collectively." Though accused of Unitarian heterodoxy by one detractor, O'Kelly was thoroughly trinitarian. However, his highly Christocentric conception of God reinforced his antihierarchical views on church polity. Insisting that every believer had direct access to the ear of the Savior, O'Kelly believed that Christians from all denominations should come together with a minimum of structure and joyfully announce the simple teachings of Scripture—"I am for Bible government, Christian equality, and the Christian name," he declared. In keeping with this stark confession, he published in 1789 an *Essay on Negro Slavery* that condemned the rapaciousness of English commerical expansion, argued that slavery debased and contaminated the soul of masters and overseers, cited biblical denunciations of human "pride, idleness, violence, spoil, and oppression," and lamented the offense slavery represented to a suffering Savior.

Bibliography. Nathan O. Hatch, "The Christian Movement and the Demand for a Theology of the People," *Journal of American History* 67 (December 1980): 545-67; Charles Franklin Kilgore, *The James O'Kelly Schism in the Methodist Episcopal Church*; Durward T. Stokes and William T. Scott, *A History of the Christian Church in the South*.

ROBERT M. CALHOON
UNIVERSITY OF NORTH CAROLINA
AT GREENSBORO

OKLAHOMA. Oklahoma was one of the latest areas to be identified with the South, an action that came about more by accident than by plan. Before 1820 the area was populated by the Plains Indians. The picture began to change after 1820 when the Choctaw Indians purchased land in what was to become Oklahoma; these were the first Eastern Indians to acquire land in the region. Between 1820 and 1842 the Five Civilized Tribes (Cherokees, Choctaws, Chickasaws, Creeks, and Seminoles) were mostly removed from the Southeastern states into Indian Territory. Following the Civil War, during which the Indian Nations were aligned with the Southern cause, the population pattern began to change again with the intrusion of white settlers. Eventually the Indian Nations were dissolved and the state of Oklahoma was established. For almost a century Oklahoma served as an Indian colonization zone; nearly 60 tribes were settled within its borders in that time. Much of Oklahoma history is Indian history.

Early History of Oklahoma: 1541—1817. European influence in Oklahoma began with the Spanish explorers. Francisco Vásquez de Coronado started his expedition northward from Mexico in 1541 and crossed western Oklahoma during his journey. Possibly Hernando de Soto traveled across northeastern Oklahoma during his three year expedition in North America (1539-1542). Juan de Oñate entered Oklahoma in 1601. Claims of the lands explored were made for Spain, but no permanent settlements were established.

Oklahoma was also claimed by the English and French. English charters extending all the way from the Atlantic to the Pacific were granted to commercial companies as a result of their exploration of the Atlantic coast. René Robert Cavelier, Sieur de la Salle, laid claim to all the territory drained by the Mississippi River for France. The region was awarded to Spain as a part of Louisiana by the treaties of 1762-1763 culminating the Seven Years War.

French traders settled among the Indians and frequently intermarried. Lively trade was carried on between the French and the Caddoans before 1700. Trade villages were established, and Ferdinandina, a trading post west of the Arkansas River in what is now Kay County, has been called the first white settlement in Oklahoma.

After Louisiana was retroceded to France by Spain in 1800, President Thomas Jefferson offered to purchase the Isle of Orleans. A counteroffer was made by the French to sell the entire province of Louisiana. Louisiana was transferred to the United States on 3 November 1803. All of Louisiana north of the 33rd parallel was designated the District of Louisiana and placed under the administration of Indiana Territory in 1804. The next year the Territory of Louisiana was organized with the seat of government at St. Louis.

American exploration of Oklahoma took place during the years 1806-1821 beginning with James B. Wilkinson. Seven expeditions were conducted to explore the region. One of the notable explorers was Thomas Nuttall, the English botanist whose journal describes the flora and fauna of the region as well as the Indians encountered. Six more explorations were conducted in the period 1832-1853.

Soon after Louisiana was purchased from France, President Jefferson drew up a proposal to exchange land occupied by Indians in the eastern states for "equivalent portions" in Louisiana, and Indian removal became a policy of the United States government. Some voluntary migrations occurred between 1817, when the Cherokees signed a removal treaty and obtained land in Arkansas, and the passage of the Indian Removal Act in 1830. The removal of Choctaws from Arkansas led to the establishment of a permanent border between Arkansas and Oklahoma in 1825. Arkansas Territory was created in 1819 and included all that is now Oklahoma with the exception of a strip between 36° and 36° 30' south latitudes.

The removal of the Five Civilized Tribes to Oklahoma was a process that lasted more than 20 years, beginning in 1825 and ending with efforts to comb the Seminoles out of the Florida swamps in the 1840s. For all the Indians involved in the removal the experience entailed great hardship and suffering, as the term "Trail of Tears" indicates. Many people, especially infants and the elderly, died along the trails. In the case of the Creeks and Seminoles warfare occurred because of the resistance of some to removal. The most costly of these was to the Seminoles whose numbers were reduced by one-third as a result of war and the hardships of journey from Florida to Indian Territory.

Establishment of the Indian Nations: 1817-1890. The first substantial formal Indian colonization of the trans-Mississippi West occurred among the Cherokees. They originally occupied an area extending over western North Carolina, eastern Tennessee and Kentucky, northern Georgia, and northeastern Alabama. Very early they came under the influence of traders from the coastal English settlements. Many, especially the mixed-bloods, adopted the ways of their white neighbors. Two factions arose among the Cherokees when the question of removal was posed: some favored relocation in order to continue the old ways of life, and others were opposed to relocation, preferring to remain on their ancestral land as planters and stock raisers.

The first Cherokee removal occurred in 1817 on a voluntary basis when the tribe ceded about one-third of its lands in the East for equal acreage between the White and Arkansas rivers in Arkansas. This territory was traded for land in northeastern Oklahoma in 1828.

The treaty of 1828 provided for the removal of white persons resident in the new Cherokee Nation, compensation of the Cherokees for the improvements they had made on their Arkansas lands, payment of the sum of $50,000 for the inconvenience the move caused them, provision of a printing press and type, an annual payment of $2,000 for 10 years for the support of schools, and subsidization of the removal of the remaining eastern Cherokees including the cost of subsistence for one year. The treaty contained the promise: "Under the most solemn guarantee of the United States, [this land shall] be and remain theirs forever—a home that shall never, in all future time, be embarrassed by having extended around it the lines, or placed over it the jurisdiction of a Territory or State, nor be pressed upon by the extension, in any way, of any of the limits of any existing Territory or State."

The Treaty of New Echota (Georgia) in 1835 provided for the removal of all the remaining Cherokees to the assigned Cherokee lands west of Arkansas and Missouri. The treaty also provided for the settlement of friendly tribes, including the Osages, Kaws, Pawnees, Poncas, Nez Percés, and Oto-Missouris on surplus Cherokee lands.

As part of the removal policy, Indian tribes purchased or were assigned land in Indian Territory. The first of the tribes to acquire land was the Choctaws who purchased the area south of the Canadian and Arkansas rivers. In 1825 the Choctaws ceded their lands in Arkansas to the United States and were promised an annual sum of $6,000 per year "forever," the removal of white settlers from the newly defined Choctaw nation, and no future settlement of United States citizens on Choctaw lands.

Most of the Chickasaws moved into their district in southern Indian Territory by the end of 1840. Their presence was resented by the Kiowas and Comanches who had occupied the land before, and intertribal strife occurred. Intratribal warfare marked the removal of the Creeks. The Seminoles had to be moved by force.

As a consequence of the various removal treaties, Indian Territory contained five semi-autonomous Indian republics. These Indians had been strongly influenced by their white neighbors while in the East and adopted the republican constitutional system of government. The first constitutional government among the Five Civilized Tribes was that of the Choctaws who adopted a written code of laws prior to 1820 and, in 1826, enacted a constitution that provided for the election of their district chiefs and council. After their arrival in Indian Territory, each of the Five Civilized Tribes established a government and four adopted written constitutions. The Seminoles observed an unwritten code.

The tribal constitutions had common features and were a mixture of Indian and Anglo-Saxon usages. Generally the constitutions were characterized by their liberal rules of eligibility for office, the recognition of the fundamental right of people to change their laws, the equality of free citizens, and the separation of governmental powers. The Choctaw and Cherokee constitutions each had a bill of rights. The final forms of the constitutions were adopted by four tribes between 1839 and 1867 in the following order: Cherokee (1839), Chickasaw (1856), Choctaw (1860), and Creek (1867). The capitals of the Indian nations were located in Tahlequah (Cherokee), Tuskahoma (Choctaw), Tishomingo (Chickasaw), Okmulgee (Creek), and Wewoka (Seminole).

The period 1830-1861 may be called the Golden Years for the Five Civilized Tribes. It was a time of respite from the demands of settlers for their lands and progress in taming the wilderness. They organized their governments, and established towns, farms, ranches, and plantations. Newspapers, books, and magazines were published. An extensive school system was established that, in most of the Indian nations, made it possible for every child to attend school through the academy level and, in some cases, the first two years of college.

By 1885 Oklahoma was divided into two large Indian communities. The eastern half was occupied by the Five Civilized Tribes and the western half by more culturally deprived tribes. The Medicine Lodge Council in 1867 set up 21 separate reser-

vations administered by eight agencies. Each of the agencies had at least two tribes under its jurisdiction, and several had five tribes or more.

All of Oklahoma except the Panhandle remained Indian Territory until 1889 after which successive areas in western Oklahoma were opened to homesteaders. By means of the Organic Act of 2 May 1890 Oklahoma Territory was formed out of the Unassigned Lands and No Man's Land (the Panhandle) plus lands that were added by land openings. The Organic Act divided Oklahoma into two areas: Oklahoma Territory, being the western portion, and Indian Territory, the eastern. The federal census of 1890 showed the population of the Twin Territories to be 78,475 in Oklahoma Territory and 180,182 in Indian Territory. In 1907 the Twin Territories were fused into the state of Oklahoma.

Education and Missions in Indian Territory. Efforts to achieve social and religious progress in Indian Territory were a part of the settlement of the Indians in Oklahoma. Missionaries had been active among the Five Civilized Tribes while they were in the southeastern United States, and those efforts continued after the removal.

The earliest organized missionary efforts among the Five Civilized Tribes were undertaken by the Moravians, who established a school and mission for the Cherokees at Spring Place GA in 1801. When the Cherokees moved west the Moravian missionaries went with them and constructed a mission center called New Spring Place.

The United Foreign Missionary Society was organized on 25 July 1817 by the General Assembly of the Presbyterian Church, the General Assembly of the Dutch Reformed Presbyterian Church, and the General Synod of the Associate Reformed Church. The Society was responsible for organizing schools and missions in the Indian Territory. In 1826 the American Board of Commissioners for Foreign Missions, an ecumenical board supported by the Presbyterians and Congregationalists, absorbed the United Foreign Missionary Society. Work among the Five Civilized Tribes was begun in 1817 in the eastern United States, and teachers and missionaries accompanied the Indians on their journey to Indian Territory.

The UFMS sent two Presbyterian missionaries, Epaphras Chapman and John P. Vinal, to explore the possibility of establishing a mission among the Cherokees of Arkansas in 1819. However, because the American Board had already made plans for a station among the Cherokees, Chapman and Vinal traveled further west into the Osage country and selected a site for a mission. After Vinal died on the return trip to New York, Chapman organized a missionary party and, along with William F. Vaill, led a group of 17 adults and four children to Indian Territory where Union Mission was established in 1821. The missionaries organized a church in May 1821 and erected a school building. They admitted four Osage students in August of the same year. Union Mission was the first Indian school in Oklahoma.

The Creek removal to the Indian Territory began in 1827, and 3,000 Creeks were living in their designated national boundaries by 1830. The Creeks wanted a mission and a school, and Union was the mission that could serve them. Later the Creeks asked for their own school for their children.

Union Mission closed early in 1833 and remained closed until the summer of 1835 when Samuel Austin Worcester, a Congregational missionary sent out by the American Board, installed a printing press at Union. Worcester had established a newspaper, the *Cherokee Phoenix*, at New Echota in 1828 and printed the newspaper and other Cherokee items in the syllabary composed by George Guess (also known as Sequoyah). Worcester was forced to leave Georgia in 1834, and the American Board decided to continue his work in the West. Worcester installed his printing press, which he moved from New Echota at Union Mission in 1835. In 1837 Worcester chose Park Hill as the permanent location for his press because of its more favorable location.

The missionaries in the Creek Nation faced growing hostility and were forced out in late 1836. During the time the missionaries were banned from the Creek Nation, the Presbyterian Church divided into the "old school" and "new school" factions. The "old school" renewed its mission work, and in 1841 the Board of Foreign Missions sent Robert M. Loughridge to visit leaders in the Creek Nation. He was granted permission to establish a school and to preach, but in the school only. Loughridge returned to his home in Alabama to raise money for the new mission and established the Kowetah Manual Labor Boarding School for Creek Indians in 1843.

A new treaty between the United States and the Creeks in 1845 included a provision for the education of Creek children; the monies were referred to as the Creek National School Fund. An agreement was made between the Presbyterian board and the Creek government for the expansion of the Kowetah Mission, the allocation of $75 a year for each student, and a new school of manual labor. The new school opened in 1848 as the Tullahassee Manual Labor School with Loughridge as its superintendent.

The Tullahassee school enjoyed the advantage of a good location and the educational program was successful for 10 years. The Civil War, however, divided the Creek Nation into two factions, and both the Tullahassee and Kowetah Missions were seized by the Creek government in 1861.

The Tullahassee Mission reopened in 1868 upon the return of William Robertson, who had been principal at the school under Loughridge. The school burned in 1880, but neither the Creek government nor the Board of Missions encouraged Robertson to rebuild because of a shift in population. The mission came to an end after Robertson's death on 26 June 1881.

Robertson's daughter Alice went to the East to raise money for a new mission. She was successful and began Nuyaka Mission near Okmulgee, the Creek capital, in 1884. Later Alice Robertson was appointed head of the Presbyterian School for Indian Girls in Muskogee.

The Methodists carried on mission work among the Five Civilized Tribes before the removal. Their work was conducted through Methodist conferences adjacent to the nations rather than a missions board. The Missouri Methodist Conference and later the Arkansas Methodist Conference assumed the responsibility for serving the Indians in Indian Territory. The Methodists relied on house-to-house visitation and circuit-rider preachers rather than fixed religious centers and schools. The Methodists gave little attention to schools among the Five Civilized Tribes until the 1840s.

Methodist preaching to the Indians in the Oklahoma-Arkansas area is first recorded as taking place about 1820 by the Rev. William Stevenson. The Asbury Manual Labor School near North Fork Town was established in 1850.

The Baptists worked among the Five Civilized Tribes before removal beginning in 1817, and several missionaries accompanied the Indians to Oklahoma. The first Cherokee Baptists in Oklahoma arrived in 1832 when 80 families led by Duncan O'Briant established a settlement 70 miles north of Fort Smith. Evan Jones, an immigrant from Wales, and Jesse Bushyhead, a Cherokee, each led a party of Cherokees to Indian Territory where they settled at Pleasant Hill, also known as Baptist Mission. In 1845, Jones was furnished with a press and type by the Baptist Mission Board of Boston. The Baptist Mission Press was responsible for some important imprints including the *Cherokee Messenger*, the first magazine published in Oklahoma. The paper was devoted to religious and temperance topics printed almost entirely in Cherokee characters. The Baptist Mission Press also printed the book of Genesis, about half of the New Testament, and English and Creek hymnals, among other publications.

Roman Catholic work among the Indians in Oklahoma on a continuing basis did not begin until 1840 when some Jesuit Fathers began to establish mission stations in Indian Territory and built the first church at Atoka in 1874. Some Spanish missionaries who accompanied the first explorers reached some Indians. French trappers and traders also came into contact with them, but no permanent missions resulted from those efforts.

The first permanent resident priest was the French Benedictine, Isidore Robot, who was appointed Prefect Apostolic of the Indian Territory in 1876 with his residence at the Benedictine Abbey of the Sacred Heart. He established a college and, in 1880, an academy for girls. Fr. Ignatius Jean followed Robot as the second and only other Prefect Apostolic in 1880. Jean founded the first and only pre-1900 Catholic periodical in Oklahoma, *The Indian Advocate*, in January 1889. After the opening of No Man's Land for settlement, secular priests were needed in addition to the Benedictines already serving. Fr. Theophile Meerschaert was sent to Oklahoma as the first bishop of the newly created diocese of Oklahoma in 1905.

Missionary efforts by the Christian Church first occurred in 1856 when James J. Trott, a missionary appointed by the American Christian Missionary Society who worked among the Cherokees in North Carolina and Georgia, went on a preaching tour that included the Cherokee Nation in 1856. It was his hope to begin a mission in Indian Territory, but with the prospects of war looming by 1860 the ACMS decided to retrench rather than expand its efforts. There were no permanent congregations established by Trott's efforts in the Cherokee Nation.

Other Christian Church preachers worked among the Indians during the 1870s, but it was not until 1884 that a missionary was engaged by the ACMS to work with them. Isaac Mode began working among the Creeks in 1885 but was transferred to the Cherokee Nation because of language difficulties. A mission among the Choctaws was begun about 1884 by R. W. Officer who received permission to open a mission and training school at Atoka. Officer was the first Christian Church missionary to engage in the training school activities characteristic of most of the other missionary groups.

The greatest influx of Christian Church ministers and the founding of permanent churches did not occur until the opening of Indian lands for white settlement. At that time, for example, J. H. Monroe, a minister, joined the homesteaders and established a church in Guthrie less than two weeks after the opening of the Cheyenne and Arapaho territories. Another minister, E. F. Boggess, staked a claim for a church lot in Perry when the Cherokee Strip was opened. Other preachers and members followed so that before statehood there was a Christian Church in every town with a population of 1,000 and in every county seat except two.

Mission work by the Mennonites began in 1880 when the General Conference Mennonite Mission Board began working among the Arapahos and later the Cheyennes and others. The first missionary was Samuel S. Haury. He was scheduled to begin work in the Indian Territory in April 1878 but was unable to go until September. When he arrived he found that a Quaker missionary had already arrived and the field was no longer open. The next year the Indian agent at Darlington, a Quaker, informed Haury that the Quakers would work only among the Cheyennes and urged the Mennonites to begin work among the Arapahos. The Quakers also turned the Cheyenne work over to the Mennonites in 1884.

The Mennonite mission at Darlington opened in 1880. Word was received that year that the military post at Cantonment, 65 miles northwest of Darlington, would be abandoned, and the buildings were offered for missionary work. Haury went to Cantonment. As the Indians began to scatter after 1890 other stations were occupied. When the government began to build Indian schools to replace the mission schools, Darlington and Cantonment closed, in 1898 and 1901 respectively.

The end of the missionary work among the Indians as carried on in the missions described was brought about by the building of Indian training schools by the government, the break-up of the reservations, the allotment of land that the Indians were required to occupy, and the intrusion of large numbers of white settlers. New approaches were needed to meet the demands of a changing territory.

The earliest formal education in Oklahoma was that provided by the Indian schools. As stated before, some of the schools were established by churches and combined religious teaching with instruction in basic subjects. Among the notable academies that grew out of the missions were Sacred Heart, Asbury, Tullahassee, Wheelock, and Bloomfield.

Congress established an annual fund of $10,000 on 13 March 1819 to be used to "civilize" the American Indians and gave it to missionary organizations to administer. The missionaries were to use the money to employ "persons of good moral character to instruct the Indians in reading, writing, and arithmetic." The funds were insufficient for the task and monies from private sources were raised to build schools in the Indian nations. The tribes also appropriated funds for the support of public schools and to subsidize the mission schools. The theories of manual labor of Johann Heinrich Pestallozzi interested the missionaries, and they applied them to the education of the Indians as schools of manual labor for Indians were established. The missions were a powerful factor in the transformation of the Indian culture, not only because of the religious training given but also the general and manual education provided.

Dwight Mission, established in 1830, was the oldest school in Oklahoma although Union Mission was established earlier. Prior to 1890, 37 missions were established and 13 more during 1890 or after. Most of the earlier missions were in the northeast part of Indian Territory between the Arkansas border and the Grand River and in the southeast near the Texas border. Missions were not established in the central area until later.

The Cherokees supported public schools independent of the missionary schools. Despite the extensive educational activities established by the various missionary societies for the Cherokees, far more Indian children were involved in the Cherokee Nation's public schools than in the mission schools.

The Creeks had no public school system but supported the mission schools. The Creeks tried to ban Christian worship between 1834 and 1842, but rescinded that action, and the Presbyterians were invited to return and reopen the Kowetah Mission.

The Choctaws were among the most enlightened tribes and maintained an excellent educational system. The schools were supported by funds from the sale of their eastern lands. The tribe allowed missionaries to evangelize only if they furnished qualified teachers equal to the number of preachers. The schools were constructed by tribal funds, but churches were required to supply teachers. The American Board was active in supplying teachers and had as many as 10 schools under their care. The Methodists also assisted in operating Choctaw schools.

After the Chickasaws moved west in 1842, W. H. Duncan of the Indian Methodist Conference established a school at Pleasant Grove. The Chickasaws used money from the sale of their land in Mississippi to establish a system of schools,

and Methodist and Presbyterian missionaries served as teachers.

The Seminoles developed educational programs belatedly and had no funds from the United States government for the support of their schools. Not until after 1844 were mission schools established. A mission to the Seminoles was established by the Presbyterians at Oak Ridge after 1848 by John Bemo, a Seminole, and John Lilley, a Presbyterian missionary. Joseph S. Murrow, a Baptist missionary and teacher, arrived in the Seminole Nation in 1857.

Dissolution of the Indian Nations: 1890—1906. The Indian cultures in Oklahoma were quite diverse. Between 1820 and 1880 over 60 tribes were colonized, joining the tribes that had claimed the area as their home before. Some tribes were sedentary, agricultural, and peaceful; others were migratory, hunting and gathering, and warlike. Each tribe was an independent self-contained social unit with its own system of government.

At the outbreak of the Civil War the Five Civilized Tribes found themselves in an unfavorable situation. At an intertribal council held in 1861, John Ross, a chief of the Cherokees, counselled neutrality in the conflict. In fact, many of the tribal leaders favored neutrality; however, most of the United States officials who had been assigned to the Five Civilized Tribes were from the South. A bad impression was made on the Indian Nations by the withdrawal of federal troops from Indian Territory at the outbreak of war and the hesitation of officials of the Indian Bureau to pay annuities when due, especially through the agents who were Southern men. The situation of the Indians is defined by Roy Gittinger in *The Formation of the State of Oklahoma*: "The position of the Five Civilized Tribes on the border, not their sympathy for the Southern Confederacy, caused them to take part in the war between Union and secession. The abandonment of the Indian Territory by the United States and its occupation by the Confederacy made it necessary for the Indians to recognize the authority of the Confederate government or opposed it unaided."

Citizens of the Five Civilized Tribes were sharply divided on the question of support for the Confederacy at the outbreak of the Civil War. Partisan conflict stemming from disputes over westward removal influenced the attitudes of many. Nearly all Choctaws and Chickasaws supported the Confederacy until its destruction; but the Cherokees, Creeks, and Seminoles were divided into hostile parties. Some Indians enlisted in the armies, and eventually the Creeks numbered 1,575 men in the Confederate Army and 1,675 in the Union forces. Union Cherokee soldiers totalled 2,200 in contrast to 1,400 Confederates. Seminoles in the Union army outnumbered those of the Confederacy.

Although there were no great battles in the Indian Territory comparable to those in the East, fierce fighting did occur with the irregular fighting of partisan groups being most destructive. Heavy losses were suffered by the Cherokee, Creek, and Seminole tribes, among whom bitter internal strife added to the destruction of large-scale war.

The most costly aspect of the Civil War, however, was the aftermath. Although the citizens of the Indian Nations had not been solidly for the Confederacy, the federal government used the commitment of the tribal governments to alliances with the Confederacy as an excuse to force the tribes into acceptance of the dissolution of their republics. The Indian nations were regarded as having been in rebellion against the Union and the treaties by which they had been formed therefore nullified.

The Reconstruction plan for the Indian territory was worked out by the two senators from Kansas, James Lane and Samuel Pomeroy. Basically, the Lane-Pomeroy plan authorized the president to suspend treaties with the Five Civilized Tribes, appropriate portions of their domain, and direct removal of the tribes from Kansas to Indian Territory. During 1866 the Five Civilized Tribes submitted to the Reconstruction Treaties that included the cession of tribal lands as proposed by Lane and Pomeroy. These treaties provided for the abolition of slavery, the recognition of citizens' rights for the freedmen of the Indian tribes, and the settlement of tribes from Kansas, Nebraska, and elsewhere in land in the western part of Indian Territory. Land ceded by the Creeks and Seminoles was limited to "such other civilized tribes as the United States may choose to settle thereon."

Between 1865 and 1889 drastic social, economic, and political changes occurred in Indian Territory causing it to become a kaleidoscope of tribal and ethnic cultures. During that period railroad construction brought about a revolution of transportation of people and goods and promoted new enterprises. As the railroads spread across Oklahoma, pressure built up for the opening of Indian Territory to homesteaders. The railroad interests claimed they were entitled to large land subsidies as a reward for their risk in developing the railroads. To their demands were added the voices of mining, lumbering, and ranching interests. A class of professional promoters called "Boomers" appeared in 1879 dedicated to pushing the cause of opening the land to homesteaders.

The pressure for change was increased by the influx of new immigrants. The white population increased steadily in Indian Territory after 1865 in what was referred to as the "Silent Migration."

Between 1879 and 1884 Boomer raids were made into Indian Territory and white settlements established. On 3 March 1889 a rider known as the Springer Amendment was attached to the Indian Appropriations Bill that provided for opening the unassigned lands for settlement, and President Benjamin Harrison issued a proclamation that the unassigned lands would be opened 22 April 1889. Probably the total of persons who made the run on this date was over 50,000. Other Indian lands were occupied by white settlers through runs or lottery between 1872 and 1901. The Curtis Act passed by Congress in 1898 provided for the compulsory liquidation of the Five Civilized Tribes. Surplus land in the Cheyenne-Arapaho country was made available for homesteaders on 19 April 1892, and on 16 September 1893 the Cherokee Outlet was opened. The last remaining Indian land in western Oklahoma was opened in August 1901. None of the lands in the national territory of the Five Civilized Tribes were opened to runs.

The Dawes Commission began meeting in 1894 and concluded its work in 1905. Through the Dawes Commission's negotiations with the Five Civilized Tribes it was agreed that all tribal governments were to cease operation during 1906. The territory of the Five Civilized Tribes was allocated to members of the tribes.

The question of single or double statehood was settled by the 58th Congress. Bills were introduced in the House of Representatives and the Senate in 1905 calling for the admission of the state of Sequoyah, the territory of the Five Civilized Tribes, but both were tabled. President Theodore Roosevelt signed the Enabling Act that provided for the creation of a single state from the "Twin Territories" in June 1906. Oklahoma was admitted to the Union as the 46th state on 16 November 1907.

The effect of the "Silent Migration," the Boomer settlements and the land runs is seen in the fact that when Oklahoma Territory and Indian Territory were fused into a single state the population stood at about 1.5 million. Of the 750,000 in Indian Territory the ratio of non-Indians to Indians was at least seven to one. The population of Oklahoma increased dramatically; from 180,182 in Indian Territory and 78,475 in Oklahoma Territory in 1890 to 392,000 in Indian Territory and 398,331 in Oklahoma Territory in 1900.

Developments After Statehood: 1907—1981. After statehood was achieved attention was focused on bringing order to the state and developing industry, exploiting the mineral deposits, expanding agriculture, and stabilizing social customs.

A sidelight to the story of the development of the economy, but illustrative of the development of social concern, is seen in the decision of the citizens of the new state to have a PROHIBITION clause in the state constitution. Regulations regarding alcoholic beverages differed in Oklahoma Territory and Indian Territory. When Indian Territory was formed, Congress passed an act that stated: "If any person shall sell, exchange, or give, barter, or dispose of any spirituous liquor or wine to an Indian . . . such person shall pay the sum of five hundred dollars." In Oklahoma Territory licenses for the sale of liquor could be granted by the Board of County Commissioners.

As plans for statehood developed in the 1890s the WOMAN'S CHRISTIAN TEMPERANCE UNION and the Anti-Saloon League, in alliance with Protestant churches, began to organize and campaign for constitutional prohibition. The Anti-Saloon League was especially influential and prided itself as "the church in action." Carrie Nation visited Guthrie in 1905 and founded a branch of the Prohibition Federation.

Much of the attention of the prohibitionists was directed toward Congress. They reasoned that, since the United States government had a moral responsibility to the Indians and the treaties had guaranteed the tribes protection against alcohol, it would be legal for Congress to outlaw the manufacture and sale of liquor in all parts of the new state.

The Oklahoma Enabling Act passed by Congress in 1906 declared for single statehood and required continuation of prohibition within Indian Territory for 21 years after the admission of the new state. No restriction was placed on Oklahoma Territory except for the former Osage Nation. The state was permitted to establish an agency to supervise the sale of liquor for medical and other prescribed purposes. On 11 September 1907 approval was given to constitutional prohibition for the entire state. Prohibition lasted until 1959 when the state constitution was amended to permit regulated sales of liquor.

The constitutional prohibition on the manufacture and sale of liquor was not considered by some to be strong enough and efforts were made to enact "Bone Dry" legislation. A bill was passed in 1917 that made it "unlawful for any person in the state to possess any liquors received directly or indirectly from a common or other carrier" with the exception of pure grain alcohol intended for scientific or medical purposes. Because the Webb-Kenyon Act of 1913 forbade the interstate shipment of alcohol in violation of state laws, possession was outlawed. A problem arose with the law in that it did not exempt sacramental wine. No effort had been exerted by the Catholics during the formation of the law for an exemption for religious purposes. Some sacramental wine was confiscated in Norman in August 1917, and the attorney general issued an interpretation of the law that sacramental wine was prohibited. A test case was filed on behalf of the Catholic Church in Guthrie after the MKT Railroad refused to transport eight quarts of sacramental wine from Kansas to Oklahoma, and the court upheld the law. The national attention that this case focused on the plight of the Catholic Church in Oklahoma caused concern on the part of prohibition forces because, even if the Catholics were not numerous in Oklahoma, the Catholic vote would be necessary to pass the Eighteenth Amendment in other states. Some defeats of the prohibition election in New York were attrib-

uted to the Oklahoma situation, with the result that even "dry" leaders attempted to force a change in the Oklahoma ban on sacramental wine. The Oklahoma Supreme Court ruled that sacramental wine was exempted from the law in May 1918. The sale of liquor was finally legalized in 1959 after more than 50 years of prohibition.

The period of World War I produced significant social changes. War-generated urbanization developed rapidly in the greater Southwest, and between 1910 and 1920 the urban population of Oklahoma increased almost 69 percent as compared to the national average of 29 percent. During the World War II years more of the population was drawn to the larger communities. The trend has continued so that the 1980 United States Census reports that 58.6 percent of the total population live in four Standard Metropolitan Statistical Areas (Enid, Lawton, Tulsa, and Oklahoma City). The Tulsa and Oklahoma City SMSA's account for 51 percent of the total population.

A wide variety of racial and ethnic strains have contributed to the population of Oklahoma. This became especially conspicuous beginning in the 1870s with the mining boom and the influx of Europeans into the Choctaw Nation. The immigrants included Italian, Welsh, Irish, Slavic, Greek, Polish, and Russian miners. Later the land rushes saw homesteaders from Mexico, England, France, Canada, and even China and Japan coming into the region. Farming attracted Czechs and German Mennonites.

Those settlers from abroad did not stream into Oklahoma in such multitudes as they did in other states, but the numbers were significant. At the time of statehood approximately eight percent of the population was composed of foreign-born people and their children. The immigrants brought with them their own languages, social customs, and religious practices. Many of the foreign-born tended to concentrate in certain localities, a fact that gave them disproportionate influence.

Seven European countries sent more than 1,000 immigrants. The Germans were the largest group, numbering about 10,000. They included both those born in Germany and Russian-born Germans. Religiously they consisted of two distinct groups: Mennonites and Lutherans. In the number of immigrants represented, the Poles and Lithuanians were the next largest groups.

The first Jewish settlers entered Indian Territory following the Civil War. They began to come in substantial numbers after the opening of the unassigned lands in 1889, the year in which the first permanently organized Jewish community was established at Ardmore. The majority of Oklahoma Jews appear to have come from Germany or Austria although some were from Russia.

Negroes were among the earliest settlers in Oklahoma. A large percentage of Oklahoma's Negroes are descendants of slaves who belonged to the Five Civilized Tribes, although there was a limited migration from the South to Indian Territory immediately after the Civil War. Others came to Oklahoma during the land runs beginning in 1889. Today about seven percent of the population of the state is black.

Through this admixture of Indian, European, and non-European immigrants Oklahoma attained a highly diverse set of ethnic cultures and religions. The presence of Roman Catholic, Greek Orthodox, Episcopal, Lutheran, and Mennonite churches attests to the variety of European immigration, and a reflection of the European immigration to the mining camps in the Choctaw Nation is found at Hartshorne where one of the few Russian Orthodox Churches in the entire Trans-Mississippi West is located. But even in the face of the variety of immigration into the state there has been a trend toward uniformity in the religious picture.

The development of oil resources in the state was the cause of much change and the catalyst for new urban troubles. Crime became a sensational and widely noted aspect of life in the boomtowns. The seeming inability of the law enforcement agencies and politicians to arrest social change caused many Oklahomans to turn to the KU KLUX KLAN to enforce both laws and moral behavior. The KKK represented for them a force to oppose the perceived threats of Negroes, Catholics, and Jews and sustain old social values. Because the Klan's primary role in Oklahoma seemed to be the restoration of moral authority, the membership even included some non-Protestants and non-whites. By 1922 some 70,000 Oklahomans had joined the Klan. Following Klan-inspired violence in 1922 the Klan lost much of its prestige and faded as a power in the Oklahoma political scene by the close of that decade.

The popularity of the Klan demonstrated a religious and social attitude that has characterized Oklahoma through much of its history as a state. That is, there is a tendency toward uniformity of religious expression, as evidenced by the predominance of a relatively small number of denominations in the state and the conservation of old, or traditional, values. The state presents an overall countenance of religious conservatism and seems to be particularly hospitable to Fundamentalism. Two examples are seen in the prominence of ORAL ROBERTS and BILLY JAMES HARGIS in the religious scene.

Oral Roberts is one of the best known religious personalities in the United States. His career has included that of an evangelist with a faith-healing ministry, president of an evangelistic organization, founder and president of a university, and founder of a health-care facility of large proportions. Roberts was born in 1918 in Ada OK, the son of a Pentecostal preacher. Roberts entered the ministry in 1935 and for the next 12 years served in general evangelistic work and as pastor of churches in Enid and Shawnee, then in Toccoa GA, and Fuquay Springs NC. He took courses at Oklahoma Baptist University and also attended Phillips University. He holds an honorary doctorate of laws from Centenary College. He began his healing ministry in TULSA in 1947 and by 1955 was travelling with his "cathedral tent" that, with all the campaign equipment for his crusades, required eight truck trailers to carry it. He established Healing Waters in 1956; later this organization became the Oral Roberts Evangelistic Association. Roberts is now an ordained elder of the United Methodist Church.

Oral Roberts University officially opened in 1965 with a student body of 300 students, and by 1981 the number had risen to 4,000. The university is described as being committed to the "historic Christian faith" and standing for the authority of the Bible as the Word of God. The baptism in the Holy Spirit and the gifts of the Spirit are stated to be the distinctive charismatic dimension of the university. The City of Faith Medical and Research Center, a diagnostic center, hospital, and clinical research center, is located adjacent to the university campus. The hospital opened in 1981 and will provide 777 beds according to plans.

The Christian Crusade was founded in 1948 by Billy James Hargis who was serving at the time as minister of a Christian Church in Sapulpa. The Crusade was organized to safeguard and perserve "conservative Christian ideals," to oppose persons or organizations who endorse socialist or Communist philosophies, and to oppose U.S. participation in the United Nations, among other goals. Hargis had been ordained at the Rose Hill Christian Church in Texarkana and served as a minister for Christian Churches in Sallisaw then Granby MO, before going to Sapulpa in 1946. He was educated at the Ozark Bible College, that was located at Bentonville AK, at the time, and was the recipient of an honorary doctorate from Bob Jones University in 1961.

Hargis began to devote his full-time efforts to the Christian Crusade in 1950 and became a leader in the right wing political movement of the early to mid-1960s. In 1966 the Church of the Christian Crusade was founded. Also associated with the Christian Crusade were the David Livingstone Missionary Foundation and the American Christian College of Tulsa. The church and its associated ministries suffered a setback in the mid-1970s when Hargis was charged with sexual immorality and the board of the college asked for his resignation as president. In October 1974 Hargis resigned his position with the college and retired from the church and the associated ministries. Six months later, however, Hargis came out of retirement and regained control of the church and the allied ministries except for the college.

A significant exception to this assertion of the Protestant dominance in the religious scene of Oklahoma is the persistence of the primitive Indian religion. Such historic observances as the Sun Dance and Ghost Dance have been vital spiritual forces among the tribes of western Oklahoma, and the Native American Church is a faith recognized by state charter.

The Native American Church dates to 1906 when an intertribal association of peyote groups in Oklahoma and Nebraska was formed. The name Union Church was adopted in 1909. The Bureau of Indian Affairs began a campaign in 1918 to declare peyote illegal, and in reaction the Native American Church was incorporated. The practices of the Native American Church vary widely but a common feature is the peyote ritual. Legal battles have surrounded the use of peyote since 1899 when its use was outlawed in Oklahoma. The law was repealed in 1907. When psychedelic drugs were declared illegal by federal law in 1966, peyote and the Native American Church were excluded by the law.

The character of religion in Oklahoma is demonstrated by the religious institutions. Primarily, the institutions of higher education supported by religious bodies and the relative strength of the various denominations provide such a picture. Religious support of higher education dates from 1894 when Henry Kendall College was founded in Muskogee by the Presbyterians. Later the college became Tulsa University. Other colleges and universities supported by religious bodies are:

INSTITUTION (FOUNDING NAME AND/OR DATE)	LOCATION	SPONSORING BODY
Bethany Nazarene College (Oklahoma Holiness College, 1899)	Bethany	Church of the Nazarene
Oklahoma City University (Epworth College, 1904)	Oklahoma City	United Methodist
Oklahoma Baptist University (1906)	Shawnee	Southern Baptist
Phillips University (Oklahoma Christian University, 1907)	Enid	Christian Church (Disciples of Christ)
St. Gregory's College (1915)	Shawnee	Roman Catholic
Midwest Christian College (1946)	Oklahoma City	Christian
Southwestern College (1946)	Oklahoma City	Pentecostal-Holiness
Oklahoma Christian College (Central Christian College, 1949)	Edmond	Church of Christ
Bartlesville Wesleyan College (Central Pilgrim College, 1959)	Bartlesville	Wesleyan Methodist
Oral Roberts University (1963)	Tulsa	Independent
Hillsdale Free Will Baptist College (1964)	Moore	Baptist General Conference in America
American Christian College (1907)	Tulsa	Independent

Graduate theological programs are offered at Phillips University and Oral Roberts University. Both of these programs are accredited by the Association of Theological Schools.

Maps displaying the distribution of churches in 13 religious denominations or families of denominations are presented in *Religion in America: 1950 to the Present*. The maps indicate the size and concentration of these churches in terms of their respective percentage membership of the total population, based on the 1970 United States census. The census reported 2,559,463 people in 77 counties in the state of Oklahoma.

Twelve of the denominations analyzed are represented in Oklahoma. The percentages of the total population in the seven most heavily populated counties in the state are presented in the following table:

Church Membership in Terms of Percentage of Total Population of the Seven Most Populous Counties							
DENOMINATION	COUNTY (Population in 1,000s)						
	Payne	Garfield	Musko-gee	Cleve-land	Coman-che	Tulsa	Okla-homa
	(50)	(56)	(81)	(59)	(108)	(399)	(527)
	%	%	%	%	%	%	%
Baptist	15-24.9	15-24.9	25-49.9	15-24.9	15-24.9	15-24.9	15-24.9
Methodist	5-14.9	5-14.9	5-14.9	5-14.9	5-14.9	5-14.9	5-14.9
Roman Catholic	1-4.9	1-4.9	1-4.9	5-14.9	1-4.9	5-14.9	1-4.9
Presbyterian	1-4.9	1-4.9	1-4.9	1-4.9	1-4.9	1-4.9	1-4.9
Christian*	5-14.9	1-4.9	1-4.9	0-.9	0-.9	1-4.9	1-4.9
Episcopal	0	1-4.9	1-4.9	1-4.9	0-.9	1-4.9	1-4.9
Lutheran	1-4.9	5-14.9	0-.9	1-4.9	0-.9	1-4.9	1-4.9
Pentecostal	0	0-.9	0-.9	0-.9	0-.9	0-.9	0-.9
Adventist	0-.9	0-.9	0-.9	0	0-.9	0-.9	0-.9
United Church of Christ	0	0-.9	0	0	0-.9	0-.9	0-.9
Reformed	0	0	0	0	0-.9	0	0
Mennonite	0	0-.9	0	0	0	0	0

*[Includes Christian Church (Disciples of Christ), Christian Church, and Churches of Christ as a family of denominations.]

The strength of these denominations statewide is indicated by the following tabulation:

Church Membership in Terms of Percentage of Total Population by Number of Counties							
DENOMINATION	UNDER 0%	1%	1-4.9 %	5-14.9 %	15-24.9 %	25-49.9 %	OVER 50%
Baptist				4	23	47	3
Methodist			2	51	21	3	
Christian	5	9	41	19	3		
Roman Catholic	2	17	46	12			
Presbyterian	12	16	47	2			
Lutheran	34	16	25	2			
Pentecostal	19	34	24				
Episcopal	34	30	13				
Adventist	37	37	3				
Mennonite	65	3	8	1			
United Church of Christ	65	10	2				
Reformed	75	2					

The preceding tables demonstrate that only the Baptists and Methodists are represented in all counties in the state. The most numerous churches in order are Baptists, Methodists, Christian Churches (denominational family), Roman Catholics, Presbyterians, and Lutherans. The Episcopal, United Church of Christ, Adventist, Reformed, and Pentecostal churches constitute less than five percent of the total population in any county.

The distribution of the churches is important. The northeastern quarter of the state (the area within a line beginning at the southern boundary of Cleveland County and running eastward to Arkansas and a line at the western border of Okla-

homa County running northward to Kansas) contains 29 counties. Thirteen of the counties in this section of the state account for approximately 56 percent of the total population; and, of these 13 counties, three account for approximately 25 percent of the state's population. Overall, 68 percent of the population is urban and 32 percent rural.

In summary, these statistics demonstrate that in the counties with the highest population, Baptist churches have the largest membership by a significant margin over the other denominations in all parts of the state. Second in size of membership are the Methodists, who show a consistent strength throughout the state.

Also, these statistics indicate that the religious picture is dominated by seven denominations, and that the character of religion in the state is mainly conservative.

See also articles on INDIANS, TEXAS MISSIONS TO; LANDMARK MOVEMENT.

Bibliography. Thomas E. Brown, *Bible Belt Catholicism: A History of the Roman Catholic Church in Oklahoma, 1905-1945;* "Oklahoma's 'Bone-Dry Law' and the Roman Catholic Church," *Chronicles of Oklahoma* 52 (Summer 1974): 316; Jackson W. Carroll, et al., *Religion in America, 1950 to the Present;* Leland Clegg and William B. Oden, *Oklahoma Methodism in the Twentieth Century;* Herbert M. Dalke, "Seventy-five Years of Missions in Oklahoma," *Mennonite Life* 10 (July 1955): 100; Stephen J. England, *Oklahoma Christians: A History of Christian Churches and of the Start of the Christian Church (Disciples of Christ) in Oklahoma;* Grant Foreman, *Beginnings of Protestant Christian Work in Indian Territory; The Five Civilized Tribes;* Arrell M. Gibson, *Oklahoma: A History of Five Centuries;* Roy Gittinger, *Formation of the State of Oklahoma, 1803-1906;* Douglas Hale, "European Immigrants in Oklahoma: A Survey," *Chronicles of Oklahoma* 53 (Summer 1975): 179; Richard H. Harper, "The Missionary Work of the Reformed (Dutch) Church in America Oklahoma," *Chronicles of Oklahoma,* 18 (September 1940): 252; Charles J. Kappler, *Indian Affairs: Laws and Treaties, II;* Christian Krehbiel, "The Beginnings of Missions in Oklahoma," *Mennonite Life,* 10 (July 1955): 108; H. Wayne Morgan and Anne H. Morgan, *Oklahoma: A Bicentennial History;* John W. Morris, et al., *Historical Atlas of Oklahoma;* Jesse Rader and Edward E. Dale, *Readings in Oklahoma History;* E. C. Routh, "Early Missionaries to the Cherokees," *Chronicles of Oklahoma,* 15 (December 1937): 449; Walter N. Vernon, "Beginnings of Indian Methodism in Oklahoma," *Methodist History,* 18 (April 1979): 127; Fred G. Watts, "A Brief History of Early Higher Education Among the Baptists of Oklahoma," *Chronicles of Oklahoma* 17 (March 1939): 26.

JAMES K. ZINK
SOUTHEAST MISSOURI STATE UNIVERSITY

OLD REGULAR BAPTISTS. Carrying a self-designated name, this denomination is located principally in southern Appalachia. It descends from United Baptists, a merger of SEPARATE BAPTISTS and Regular Baptists of the late eighteenth century. The term, Regular, according to one associational clerk, differentiates the current group from Baptists "who have departed from the teachings of the scriptures, in so large a measure." It "stands for soundness in doctrine, faith and practice."

New Salem Association, constituted in 1825 in eastern Kentucky, was the first union among the present-day denomination to use the designation, Regular. It changed its name from United to Regular in 1854 and added the word, *Old,* in 1870. It has "given an arm" to form seven associations, two being identified now with PRIMITIVE BAPTISTS. Almost all the 24 associations in this denomination derive from New Salem or its offshoots. Statistics available for 20 of them reveal 362 churches and 19,359 members. These churches are found mostly in Kentucky, Virginia, West Virginia, and North Carolina.

Each congregation conducts public worship one Sunday a month. The simply structured service consists of singing, preaching, and praying.

The hymnody is sung without instrumental accompaniment. A precentor lines out the hymnal text, often using a tuneless song book. Following a 17th-century technique, he sings the first line of the text and melody in the hymn's usual tempo; the congregation joins him as soon as it recognizes the words and tune. Then the leader rapidly chants the next line, and the singers follow him in a slow, ornamented way. Such precenting and responding continue until the song is finished.

Sermons are spontaneously preached under the inspiration of the moment. One preacher "introduces" the service with a brief address. Two or more others preach before the meeting ends. Old Regular preaching often turns into powerful, sentimental chanting. It probably resembles that of 18th-century Separates as closely as any practiced today. A member now and then encourages the minister in his delivery. One may cry, "Now take your time and preach." Another may call out, "Preach till you get tired," or "You don't hear that kind of preaching every day." The preacher often reminds his hearers to pray for him, "because I can't preach unless the Lord blesses me."

Old Regular Baptist polity is congregational. One preacher put it this way: "The governance of our church is [con-

trolled by] the entire male membership."
The unsalaried leader of a congregation is
the moderator; he is an elder, the title
given to every ordained preacher.

In the meetinghouse, the members,
segregated from the visitors, are seated on
each side of the preaching stand, men to
the left, women to the right of the elders,
who sit directly behind the pulpit. Visitors
face the pulpit from their pews.

Old Regular Baptists do not hold to
particular election, having embraced the
Arminianism of Separate Baptists. In
their doctrinal statements many Old Regular associations reject any biblical interpretation that makes "God partial,
directly or indirectly . . ." These Baptists
immerse in natural streams only. Their
sacramental service includes foot washing
as well as the taking of bread and "the
fruit of the vine."

Among Old Regular Baptists, conversion is defined as an adult experience; it
usually occurs after a person undergoes an
extended period of "deep conviction of
heart and mind because of his sins . . ."
The penitent travels from sin to grace,
agonizing until God produces spiritual
birth. Such personal confrontation of sin
is like the endurance of "terrors" by 18th-
century Separate Baptists.

See also articles on Appalachian
Religion; Music, Religious.

Bibliography. Loyal Jones, "Old-Time Baptists and Mainline Christianity," in J. W. Williamson, ed., *An Appalachian Symposium: Essays Written in Honor of Cratis D.
Williams*; Rufus Perrigan, *History of Regular Baptist[s]
and Their Ancestors and Accessors*; Arthur Carl Piepkorn, *Profiles in Belief: The Religious Bodies of the United States and Canada*, 2: 441-42; William Tallmadge,
"Baptist Monophonic and Heterophonic Hymnody in
Southern Appalachia," *Yearbook for Inter-American
Musical Research*, 11 (1975): 106-36.

CHESTER RAYMOND YOUNG
CUMBERLAND COLLEGE

OLD SCHOOL/NEW SCHOOL. These
are the names given to the factions that
divided the Presbyterians in the middle
third of the 19th century. The New School
grew out of the liberalization of Congregationalism, the nondenominational
societies of "the benevolent empire," and

"new measures" revivalism. The Old
School developed from Calvinist traditions independent of New England Puritanism, the predestinarianism of
Princeton Theological Seminary, and a
growing sense of Presbyterian
particularity.

Theologically, the New School owed
much to "the New Divinity" formulated
before 1800 by Joseph Bellamy and
Samuel Hopkins. Reconciling the Calvinist schema with contemporary ethical
ideas, they taught inheritance of a disposition to sin but not of the penalty of Adam
and Eve's sin. Hopkins understood "conversion" as a voluntary change following
God's action of "regeneration." In the
1820s "the New Haven theology" of
Nathaniel W. Taylor interpreted even
regeneration as essentially voluntary. Old
School Presbyterians wished to exclude
Hopkins and Taylor's teachings from
their church. New School Presbyterians
found the teachings tolerable, and some
adopted them. The New School welcomed
the "new measures" in evangelism, but
the Old saw "practical Pelagianism" in
them.

The controversy concerned church
government as well as doctrine. Under
the Plan of Union (1801), Presbyterians
and Congregationalists cooperated to
found churches in the West. New England
seminarians entered the Presbyterian
ministry and organized congregations
that might follow either system of polity.
Strict Presbyterians found that the polity
anomalies of the Northwestern synods
made it hard to discipline ministers for
doctrinal errors. The New School supported Congregationalist-dominated
benevolent societies, but the Old tried to
build up Presbyterian denominational
boards.

In the North, the New School prevailed in New York and the upper Midwest, and the Old in New Jersey,
Pennsylvania, and the lower Midwest. In
the South, Hezekiah Balch introduced
Hopkinsianism into East Tennessee in
the 1790s, and Maryville College perpe-

tuated it. The New School influenced the mixed Congregational-Presbyterian churches in coastal South Carolina, but inland churches in the Carolinas rallied to the Old School. Virginia leaders initially assumed an irenic stance.

In the 1830s the controversy dominated Presbyterian church politics. The Old School was usually a minority in the General Assembly, but it organized and agitated actively. Two thousand Presbyterians in 1834 signed its "Act and Testimony" against New School errors. At the 1835 Assembly, an Old School majority initiated new policies, but in 1836 a New School majority blocked implementation.

At the Assembly of 1837, a large Old School majority abrogated the Plan of Union as contrary to the church constitution and committed the body to church boards instead of "societies." More drastically, it exscinded from the church four synods that had been organized under the plan. Old School leaders hoped to reclaim all "sound" Presbyterians, but many sided with the New School against the excision. The 1838 Assembly split, forming two churches that claimed the title of "the Presbyterian Church in the United States of America."

The split coincided with active antislavery agitation in the church and some charged that the excision was directed against New School antislavery activity. That concern did not inspire the Old School movement, but it may have helped to draw some wavering Southerners into it. At the 1837 Assembly Southerners overwhelmingly supported the Old School, and Virginians originated the excision proposal. Some pointed out that the Old School constituency in the North was more conservative on slavery than the New. New School members in the South replied that antislavery feeling was general in the North and that slaveholders must rely on limits on national church power. They therefore considered the Old School more dangerous because of its actions in 1837.

After the split, a large majority of Southern Presbyterians adhered to the Old School. The New School predominated in East Tennessee and adjacent Appalachian areas of Virginia and Alabama, and counted significant numbers in the rest of Virginia and in Mississippi, Kentucky, and Missouri. In South Carolina, Charleston Union Presbytery sympathized with the New School on doctrine and polity, but declared independence of both national churches on proslavery grounds. It initially hoped to unite Southern Presbyterians in a sectional church, but in 1852 it joined the Old School.

In the 1850s the New School church, which was becoming more "Presbyterian" in polity, regularly adopted antislavery pronouncements despite Southern opposition. In 1857 the Southern New School presbyteries resolved that members might hold slaves not only in exceptional circumstances but "from principle," "believing it to be according to Bible right." When their assembly condemned that position, they separated and formed the United Synod of the Presbyterian Church. Only in Missouri and the District of Columbia did Southern churches side with the Northern majority. The United Synod, free from Northern connection, then claimed to be the only safe church for proslavery Presbyterians. It noted signs that Northerners in the Old School disagreed with the Southern defenders of slavery.

The Civil War facilitated Presbyterian realignment. The Old School presbyteries in the Confederacy formed the Presbyterian Church in the Confederate States of America. Presbyterians supported their governments' war efforts and ecumenical cooperation followed the battle lines. In 1863 committees drafted a plan to unite the PCCSA and the United Synod. Because of doctrinal opposition, the PCCSA agreed instead to receive the New School churches into its structure. The Synod's presbyteries agreed and the union occurred harmoniously in 1864. In East Tennessee, however, some Unionist Presbyterians returned to the Northern New School church during military occupation. In 1870, when the two "schools" united in the North, there were again two churches—but they were Northern and Southern, not Old and New School.

After 1870 PCUS leaders attached polemical value to the Old School heritage, claiming that the large New School element in the PCUSA compromised its Calvinism. Some regarded the PCUS as the true continuation of the Old School. They argued that their church union of 1864, unlike the Northern union of 1870, had preserved an Old School basis. The difference was actually one of degree—of proportions of members rather than basis of union. "The war of the schools" ended, but its memory persisted.

See also articles on PRESBYTERIAN CHURCH IN THE UNITED STATES; PRESBYTERIANISM; UNITED PRESBYTERIAN CHURCH.

Bibliography. Fred J. Hood, *Reformed America*; George M. Marsden, *The Evangelical Mind and the New School Presbyterian Experience*; Harold M. Parker, Jr., *Studies in Southern Presbyterian History*; *Presbyterian Re-Union Memorial Volume, 1837-1871*; Ernest Trice Thompson, *Presbyterians in the South*, vols. 1 and 2; Robert Ellis Thompson, *A History of the Presbyterian Churches in the United States*.

JACK P. MADDEX, JR.
UNIVERSITY OF OREGON

ONENESS POSITION, THE: *See* PENTECOSTALISM.

ORDINANCES: *See* BAPTISM; SACRAMENTS AND ORDINANCES.

ORPHANAGES: *See* SOCIAL SERVICES.

ORTHODOX CHURCH: *See* GREEK ORTHODOX CHURCH.

ORTHODOX JUDAISM: *See* JUDAISM.

OTEY, JAMES HERVEY (1800-1863), first Episcopal bishop of Tennessee and a founder of the UNIVERSITY OF THE SOUTH, was born in Bedford County VA. He graduated from the University of North Carolina in 1820. In 1821 he became headmaster of the Warrenton Academy in North Carolina. It was in Warrenton that he was prepared for baptism, confirmation, and eventually the priesthood by the local rector, the Rev. William Mercer Green. He was ordained by Bishop JOHN STARK RAVENSCROFT in 1827. Through that prelate he was imbued with Catholic tradition, which he combined with his own evangelical zeal. The same year he settled in Franklin TN, where he organized a congregation and opened a boys' school. Within a short time he also established churches in Nashville and Columbia. In 1834 Otey was consecrated bishop of Tennessee, the state's first. A forceful preacher, within six years he increased the number of clergy in the diocese from 6 to 21, and confirmed more than 6,000 people during his episcopate.

Always interested in higher education, Bishop Otey made a tour of Europe in 1851, visiting the major English and European universities. In 1857 he united with Bishops LEONIDAS POLK of Louisiana and STEPHEN ELLIOTT of Georgia to found the University of the South at Sewanee. He was a staunch unionist during the hectic decade that preceded the Civil War and strove for the reconciliation of the estranged sections. The shock of war plus his arduous labors broke his health, resulting in his death in 1863.

See also article on EPISCOPAL CHURCH.

Bibliography. George R. Fairbanks, *A History of The University of The South*; William M. Green, *A Memoir of The Rt. Rev. James Hervey Otey, D.D., LL.D., The First Bishop of Tennessee*; Arthur H. Noll, *A History of The Church in The Diocese of Tennessee*.

JOSEPH D. CUSHMAN
UNIVERSITY OF THE SOUTH

OUTLER, ALBERT COOK (1908-), prominent Methodist theologian and ecumenist, was born on 17 November 1908 in Thomasville GA and grew up in Methodist parsonages. Educational experiences at Wofford College (B.A., 1928), Emory (B.D., 1933), and Yale (Ph.D., 1938) shaped his vocational interests more toward historical and pastoral theology than the parish ministry. As professor of theology at major universities (Duke, 1938-1945; Yale, 1945-1951; Southern

Methodist, 1951-1979), he made diverse and influential contributions to both religious learning and ecclesiastical reform. Outler was instrumental in reshaping Perkins School of Theology at SMU, making it an outstanding center of scholarly research as well as of ministerial preparation. As a dedicated churchman, he attended Methodist quadrennial general conferences for decades and served on numerous task forces. In 1972 the denomination adopted a report from his study commission that for the first time in this century officially clarified its doctrinal heritage.

Outler pursued excellence in a wide range of areas, including psychotherapy and pastoral care, theology, patristics, and Wesleyan studies; but perhaps his greatest contribution was in ecumenical activity. A pivotal spokesman on the Faith and Order Commission of the World Council of Churches after 1952, he made timely proposals to aid mutual discovery and appreciation among churches. Many of his publications demonstrated how people with different perspectives could appropriate wider views of Scripture and the various traditions shared by all Christians as a common history. Whether working on interfaith committees or serving as official observer at the Second Vatican Council, Outler sought to enhance the goal of Christian unity through mutual understanding. Teacher, scholar, and ecumenical churchman, he served as a model for and a representative voice of American Methodism.

See also articles on ECUMENISM; METHODIST CHURCH; THEOLOGICAL EDUCATION; WESLEYAN TRADITION.

Bibliography. Albert C. Outler, *The Christian Tradition and the Unity We Seek*; *Methodist Observer at Vatican II*; *Theology in the Wesleyan Spirit*.

HENRY WARNER BOWDEN
RUTGERS UNIVERSITY

OZARKS RELIGION. Religion in the Ozarks is integrated with the history of Ozarks culture as a whole. Culture in turn has been almost invariably related to the region's geography and its natural resource base. The Ozarks is here defined as the highland bound by the Missouri, Arkansas, and Mississippi rivers, the lowland delta of eastern Arkansas and southeast Missouri, and the prairie plains of western Missouri, Kansas, and Oklahoma. The Ozarks has been historically isolated, an isolation caused both by its geography and by the culture of its founding white populations.

French Catholic traders, miners, and villagers created a special town life in Ste. Genevieve, St. Louis, and St. Charles on Ozarks borders before the American Revolution. Creole-Catholic culture dominated those towns long enough to dictate that when centers of British-American Protestant culture were established on the Old Ozarks Frontier, they would be dispersed and characteristically rural.

The foundation population was Protestant Scotch-Irish with some German and English admixture, who came from the southern highlands to the east for a century and a half after the Revolution. Tennessee, Kentucky, the Carolinas, and Virginia were primary states of origin; but the migration stretched back to Ulster in the early eighteenth century and the Scottish lowlands in the 17th. An Ozarks pioneer yet alive in 1900 might have had parents born in Tennessee, grandparents in Pennsylvania, great-grandparents in Ireland, and great-great-grandparents in semibarbaric Scotland. All may have lived relatively traditional lives in circumstances and locales isolated from the cultural mainstreams of modernity and the Enlightenment. The religion of the Scotch-Irish was influenced by tradition, migration, sojourning in new lands, and isolation upon perpetuated frontiers.

The religion of the Ozarks Scotch-Irish was in the tradition of Scottish Presbyterianism. But other traditions, elements of primitive and barbaric religions—magic, conjures, power doctors, touches of animism and pantheism—persist even to the present. A resistance to the institutionalization of religion, a desire to have one's name entered only in the Lamb's Book of Life, and not in "The Book" of the churches of men is characteristic. One young woman revivalist explained that she was not in violation of the Pauline injunction that women should keep silent in the churches. "This is not church," she said simply. RE-VIVALISM, PENTECOSTALISM, and FUNDA-MENTALISM are effective allies in a perpetual watch kept against the Enlight-enment and modernity, those twins of the humanistic spirit that would replace tradi-tion with innovation, provincial culture with cosmopolitan culture, and a sacred world view with a secular one. Resistance to new ways has not fully succeeded; but the will to resist has remained strong and tenacious. It lives on inside the churches embraced by the children, and continues to be a source of conservatism and reaction.

The archetypal British-American church in the Ozarks has been the rural union church. Normally termed "non-denominational," it is really predenomi-national, and anti-institutional. One such church, or "chapel," built by a prosperous Methodist in the 1880s, was by charter open to preaching by any and all Chris-tians except Mormons. Another such chapel continues to be guarded by its elderly neighborhood trustees against denominational takeover. A documentary film crew was denied entry because an octogenerian matriarch trustee suspected that they were really "from the Method-ists." Such churches are living museums of old folkways and traditions and are a locus of the power and influence of families that "own" them.

Germans and Scotch-Irish have often lived side by side in the American South; and the Ozarks is no exception. Ozarks Germans of Mennonite tradition from Pennsylvania came to the Missouri River border in the 1850s. More numerous and better-known groups came directly from Germany between the 1830s and World War I. The Saxon Lutheran colony in Perry County near the Mississippi (1839) became the Missouri Synod. German Catholics superseded the French as chief occupants of Ste. Genevieve. Germans made the Ozarks counties along the south bank of the Missouri and west bank of the Mississippi peculiarly their own. The steep but fertile Loess slopes there have become distinctively German: great churches built in native ochre limestone rise on Ozarks ridges above narrow wind-ing old-world streets, thrifty gardens, butcher shops, and pin-neat farms. "Sanc-tissimo Cordi Jesu, MDCCCLXXIX." Catholics and Lutherans both have spread such landscapes across northern and east-ern Ozarks borders, dramatic monuments to the 19th-century dream of *Germania in Amerika*.

Post-Civil War Reconstruction in the Ozarks was a phenomenon of moderniza-tion, abetted by an influx of new Yankee immigrants. Towns sprouted along the new railroads, and with them the denomi-nations, products of the new modernity and bourgeois life-styles. The most numerous finally are Southern Baptist, Methodist, and the Churches of Christ, with the Assemblies of God and other Pentecostal and fundamentalist groups of the 20th century also prominent. (The rural Presbyterian Church of Caledonia, Washington County MO was founded in 1816 in the interior Belleview Valley, and was a center of Scotch-Irish Protestantism for a century, sending out missionaries even to Catholic St. Louis.) Denomina-tions here as elsewhere in the South have been crucibles for fiery struggles over modernity and secularism. The oldest Campbellite congregation of SPRINGFIELD MO (1834) split into the Church of Christ and the Christian Church (Disciples of Christ) ostensibly over organ music; but deeper issues were life-style, taste, author-ity, epistemology, and the nature of Scrip-ture and of the congregation.

The Ozarks has been peculiarly conge-nial to a kind of patriarchal "Father Abra-ham" phenomenon. Authoritarian, sometimes messianic and apocalyptic, individuals and groups come to the Ozarks (whether as to Eden or to the Wilderness) to live, prepare, and wait. The Order of the Sons of Zion, a quasi-Mormon colony, and Yahweh City, a cabalistic group believing in the special power of pyramids, are current examples of the work of charismatic patriarchal leaders. A different expression is in the Amish and other Mennonite groups that have come to the Ozarks in the past generation. They are attracted by low land prices, low population density, rurality, low levels of social control, tolerance of eccentricity, and a traditional, provincial cultural milieu.

Ozarkers in the late twentieth century remain essentially rural and small-town people, overwhelmingly white, British- and German-descended, and despite important islands of Catholicism, largely Protestant. Lately an explosive immigration abets a process that is here as elsewhere drawing the province into the international cosmopolitan superculture. Nevertheless, religiosity and a sacred world view remain alive and well in the Ozarks.

See also article on APPALACHIAN RELIGION.

ROBERT FLANDERS
SOUTHWEST MISSOURI STATE UNIVERSITY

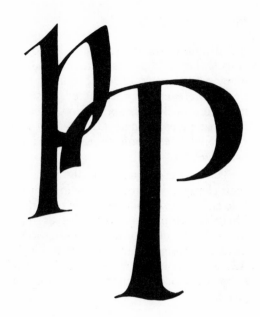

PACIFISM: *See* ETHICS, CHRISTIAN; JORDAN, CLARENCE; KOINONIA FARM.

PALMER, BENJAMIN MORGAN (1818-1902), Presbyterian preacher and Southern regionalist, was born in Charleston SC. As the son of one Presbyterian minister and the nephew of another (whose name he bore), Palmer made an early commitment to the ministry. Following two years at Amherst College, he transferred to the University of Georgia, graduating in 1838. His ministerial education was completed at the Presbyterian Theological Seminary in Columbia SC in 1841.

After a brief pastorate in Savannah, Palmer returned to Columbia to become pastor of First Presbyterian Church in 1843. In 1853, he was appointed to a teaching post in the seminary there. Palmer moved to First Presbyterian Church in New Orleans in 1856, where he remained until his death, except for his years as chaplain to the Confederate forces during the Civil War.

Palmer quickly attained the reputation of "pulpit orator." His widely reprinted Thanksgiving sermon of 29 November 1860 advocated the secession of the South to defend its "providential trust" to perpetuate slavery; and in 1861, he was elected moderator of the first General Assembly of the Presbyterian Church in the Confederate States of America.

Palmer's theological stance was essentially an extension of the conservative thought of JAMES H. THORNWELL, changing little during his lifetime. In addition to the ministry, Palmer became deeply involved in social issues, particularly the development of higher education in Louisiana.

See also article on PREACHING.

Bibliography. Thomas Cary Johnson, *The Life and Letters of Benjamin Morgan Palmer.*

DORALYN J. HICKEY
NORTH TEXAS STATE UNIVERSITY

PAROCHIAL SCHOOLS: *See* ROMAN CATHOLIC CHURCH IN THE SOUTH.

PASTOR. This is a word rich in biblical imagery, for it is the Latin word for "shepherd," a frequently used metaphor for God in the Old Testament, and for Jesus in the Gospel of John.

This title is often used of a "minister," one who is in the profession of the ministry, who serves a local congregation, although some expand the term to include all (such as institutional chaplains) who spend time in the care and cure of souls. "Pastoral care" thus has come to mean in many circles the counseling ministry of clergy wherever they are situated. As such, this is one of the functions of local clergy, one that gives primary identity to their vocational lives alongside their work as preachers.

Lutherans characteristically refer to their clergy as "pastor," this being both a title and a form of address, much as other Christians employ the word "Reverend." In the South most other denominations, including Roman Catholicism, use this title as a synonym for "minister." Evangelical Christians frequently speak of "my pastor."

WILLIAM C. SMITH, JR.
GREENSBORO, NORTH CAROLINA

PASTORAL CARE. Pastoral care reflects a way of seeing and understanding. It consists of acts of healing, sustaining, guiding, and reconciling performed by representatives of the religious community in relation to issues of ultimate concern. But the substance of these acts, the way need is perceived and ministered to, takes its cue from the prevailing theological orientation and the sociocultural setting. Regional characteristics of the South and of Southern people, together with a particular understanding of the nature of the Christian life, have meant that churches and ministers in the area have always had a deep commitment to pastoral care. The demand to love and care for one's neighbor has always formed an essential part of the design of Southern church life.

Acknowledgment of the theological and cultural underpinnings of pastoral care makes it possible to speak of it in Southern churches generally. Regardless of nuances of denominational difference, there has been a sameness to the theological orientation of the dominant denominations in the South. A consensus seems to have existed among Methodists, Baptists, and Presbyterians that care begins with a personal relation to God in Christ

and is established through the direct action of the Holy Spirit. The experience is understood as profoundly emotional, eventuating in a holy life characterized by devotion, discipline, and zeal. The black church and other Protestant denominations have been at times in accord with the majority and at times unique. But the region itself has been permeated with an evangelical theological perspective.

Pastoral care's development in Southern churches may be described in three stages. The initial period from 1750 to 1850 was a time of communal care. The world was perceived to be uncaring, but a conversion experience provided a new basis for personal worth, one stemming from the direct activity of God and attested by life in a community of "watchful care." The vehicle for this care was a disciplined attentiveness to individual life that sought to insure freedom from worldly taint and safe passage to an eternal home.

In Methodist class meetings, Baptist testimonials, and Presbyterian love feasts, members attempted to bind up the wounds of their brothers and sisters, to see them through times of temptation, loneliness, and doubt, to reclaim the erring and help them to become strong. Family responsibility to prepare children to hear and receive the gospel was emphasized, and widows and orphans received special attention. Ministers functioned primarily as evangelists, guides, and protectors. They proclaimed the need for conversion and stood faithfully with the community in their quest for salvation and holiness.

The aftermath of the Civil War saw this communal discipline and care all but disappear. The second stage placed an emphasis on the individual's relation to God, assurance of that relation, and conformity of behavior. The change was not so much one of belief as of the churches' self-understanding. As members became socially influential, the church tended to identify its interests with those of the region and to participate in its general defensiveness. From 1850 to 1940 pastors continued to visit, to comfort, and to encourage. They sought conversions still, but their understandings of the Christian life became individualistic and moralistic and reflected social norms of respectability. Moreover, views of guilt and assurance were only incidentally informed by the region's tragedy, pathos, and poverty and focused instead on an individual's relation to God and acts of personal kindness and piety. Thus the individual's status before God became the dominating motif of pastoral care. Evangelism, exhortation, and the ordering of life according to biblical norms, even by law if necessary, became the primary work of the caring pastor.

A decided shift—the third stage—has taken place in the understanding of pastoral care in Southern churches since 1940. As the region emerged from its isolation, pastors found themselves dealing with unfamiliar problems with undependable guidelines from the past. This was accompanied by a different theological climate, in that the authority of Scripture was questioned by many. Finally, the influence of the secular psychological and psychotherapeutic communities was keenly felt and its possibilities for pastoral care clearly discerned.

This more recent period may be characterized in several ways. It has involved, first, a new way of seeing. Attention shifted from norms and social conventions to persons, their actual experiences and perplexities. Second, a somewhat different way of understanding emerged, more broadly based and striving to comprehend the intrapsychic and interpersonal dynamics of persons. Motivation replaced behavior as the object of understanding and care, and simple, one-cause theories of human dilemmas became suspect. Again, pastors began to seek new ways to help. The emphasis shifted to listening, acceptance, and compassion as opposed to judging, evaluating, and con-

frontation. These developments in turn placed pastors in a new relation to their parishioners. Authoritarian guides became fellow sufferers dedicated to consulting with persons about the distresses and directions of their lives and the ways in which grace might be realized. Finally, a new way of training in pastoral care appeared. Actual cases provided the basis for collaboration between pastors and skilled supervisors as clergy sought to learn of people and of ways to care.

Between 1945 and 1960 all of the major seminaries in the South added faculty members in the field of pastoral care who reflected this or similar orientations. Among the leaders in this movement are: William Oglesby at Union Seminary (Presbyterian) in Richmond; Wayne Oates at the Southern Baptist Seminary in Louisville; Charles Kemp at Brite Divinity School (Disciples of Christ) in Fort Worth; and Russell Dicks at Duke Divinity School. The curricula they fashioned were far removed from the "hints and helps for pastoral visitation" that had previously characterized pastoral care education. Moreover, clinical facilities in general and mental hospitals sprang up throughout the South. Clinical pastoral education became an important development as students and active pastors sought to enhance their pastoral skill and understanding in such settings under careful supervision. Obert Kempson in South Carolina, Richard Young in North Carolina, Charles Gerkin in Georgia, and Dawson Bryant in Texas are but a few of the scores of chaplains who established such programs. Together these seminary faculty people and chaplain supervisors began to set new standards as to the meaning of care.

The more conservative denominations and Bible Schools, though caught up in the emphasis on pastoral care, added faculty members and instituted curriculum change more slowly, if at all. Often they felt the innovators were forsaking the Bible and setting aside a right understanding of Christian life. Thus the Church of God (Cleveland TN), the Churches of Christ, the Cumberland Presbyterians, and various Pentecostal groups continued to reflect the biblical literalism of the earlier period and to avoid accommodating their theological stance to the newer counseling emphasis. Yet there was considerable interest and several of the more adventurous sought secular degrees in psychology and counseling to supplement their theological training. More recently, these muted voices have begun to articulate an evangelical pastoral care.

Within the black church community the approach to pastoral care has reflected the earlier communal care. Thus the church has been a locus of affirmation in the midst of which one was sustained as one endured the turmoil and oppression of this life. Only in the last decade has there appeared an interest in the more recent developments in pastoral care, including the development of faculty in black seminaries and the enrollment of black pastors in clinical pastoral education programs. Edward Wimberly of Atlanta is a leader in this field and has published its first book, appropriately entitled, *Pastoral Care in the Black Church.*

The significance of these developments in pastoral care for Southern churches centers on ministry and understanding. A better trained and more psychologically aware ministry now serves Southern churches. Frequently the result of this training is a more humane and compassionate minister. Moreover, Southern pastors, professors, and chaplains have assumed positions of national leadership in this field and so have been able to contribute to the larger church's ministry in important ways. Such work has also enlarged pastoral understanding. Teaching in pastoral care has influenced, for example, theological anthropology. Dynamic understandings of the person and awareness of personality development led away from body-soul dichoto-

mies and to an appreciation of human wholeness. These understandings, coupled with proximity to human life, fostered broader understandings of religious experience and an appreciation for individual differences. Finally, pastoral care has confronted the Southern pastor and church in a new way with the complexity of human motivation. Simple sin and goodness lose their economic value as explanations or interpretations of human life. One fruit of the work in pastoral care in the South has been to plunge us back into an appreciation for the ambiguities of life and a new awareness of the depth of both sin and grace.

There is a certain logic and consistency about the role pastoral care has played in Southern life. It may be argued that its acceptance was the fruit of the revival tradition that emphasized personal religious experience and the ordering of life. Certainly it did not seem to pose the threat that the Civil Rights Movement or higher criticism did. Instead, pastoral care picked up perennial themes from the theology and ecclesiology of Southern religion and cast them in a new mold. It has found a place and been at home in the South because it acknowledged the tragedy and pathos of life, arose in a time of social turmoil and disenchantment, and approached its task in a way familiar to Southern people.

See also article on THEOLOGICAL EDUCATION.

Bibliography. William A. Clebsch and Charles R. Jaekle, *Pastoral Care in Historical Perspective;* Donald G. Mathews, *Religion in the Old South;* Liston O. Mills, "The Relation of Discipline to Pastoral Care in Frontier Churches, 1800-1850," *Pastoral Psychology* 16 (December 1965): 22-34; Wayne E. Oates, *Protestant Pastoral Counseling;* Edward P. Wimberly, *Pastoral Care in the Black Church.*

LISTON O. MILLS
VANDERBILT DIVINITY SCHOOL

PAYNE, DANIEL ALEXANDER (1811-1893), black church leader, was born of free black parents in Charleston SC. He attended Minor's Moralist Society School (founded by free blacks) and was tutored by Thomas Bonneau in mathematics, English, Greek, and French. In 1829, having become skilled not only in academics but also in carpentry and other trades, Payne founded a successful school for black children in Charleston. In 1835 local authorities closed his school pursuant to an 1834 state law imposing fines and whippings on free blacks keeping schools where literacy was taught to blacks, slave or free. Thus exiled, Payne, a Methodist since the 1820s, entered Lutheran Theological Seminary in Gettysburg PA. At an 1839 address in Fordsboro NY on the occasion of his ordination by the Franckean Synod of the Lutheran Church, he delivered a blistering indictment of slavery.

Finding no Lutheran congregation to serve, he briefly pastored a Presbyterian congregation in East Troy NY before moving to Philadelphia where he opened a school (1840), joined the AFRICAN METHODIST EPISCOPAL CHURCH (1841), and became a minister in that church (1842). Within 10 years after becoming an AME minister, Payne had become the denomination's official historiographer (1848) and its bishop (1852). Intervening duties such as the editorship of the *Repository of Religion, Science, and Literature*, the presidency of Wilberforce University, and vigorous research delayed publication of his history of the church until 1891. Perhaps the greatest personal triumph of his career was returning to Charleston in 1865, 30 years from the day he had left, to organize the first South Carolina Annual Conference of the AME Church.

See also article on BLACK RELIGION.

Bibliography. Josephus R. Coan, *Daniel Alexander Payne, Christian Educator.*

ROBERT L. HALL
UNIVERSITY OF MARYLAND
BALTIMORE COUNTY

PENNINGTON, JAMES W. C. (1809-1870), fugitive slave, abolitionist, and churchman, was born in Maryland. A trained blacksmith, he escaped from his slave condition in 1827, and settled in Newtown, Long Island, where he embraced Christianity. In 1830 Pennington attended the first National Convention of Colored People as an abolitionist and anti-colonizationist. He taught school in Newtown and later in New Haven, where he studied theology with a tutor and listened to lectures at Yale Divinity School. Several pastorates followed: at the black Presbyterian Church in Newtown (1838-1840); Fifth (Talcott Street) Congregational in Hartford (1840-1847); and First (Shiloh) Presbyterian in New York City (1847-1855).

At Hartford, Pennington organized the Union Missionary Society, forerunner of the AMERICAN MISSIONARY ASSOCIATION; became the first black president of the Hartford Central Association of Congregational Ministers; and was a delegate to the World's Anti-Slavery Convention in London (1843). While serving as the first minister of Shiloh, Pennington's autobiographical sketch, *The Fugitive Blacksmith* (1849), was published in London. He had previously published *A Text Book History of . . . Colored People* (1841), as well as sermons and articles. In recognition of these accomplishments and as a symbol of his race's potential, the University of Heidelberg, Germany, conferred the D.D. degree upon Pennington in 1849. Two years later he was declared legally a free man in America. He was elected president of the Convention of Colored People in 1853. He was labeled an alcoholic in 1854 but recovered, continued as an abolitionist, and published two notable articles before dying in Florida. His writings and influence were known and were an inspiration to black Americans, South and North alike.

See also article on ABOLITIONISM.

Bibliography. "Pennington, J. W. C.," *Dictionary of American Biography*, 1946, 13:441-42; Herman E. Thomas, "An Analysis of the Life and Work of James W. C. Pennington, A Black Churchman and Abolitionist," unpublished Ph.D. dissertation, Hartford Seminary Foundation, 1978.

HERMAN E. THOMAS
UNIVERSITY OF NORTH CAROLINA
AT CHARLOTTE

PENTECOSTAL HOLINESS CHURCH.
This denomination owes its existence to

the holiness revival that swept across American Protestantism after the Civil War. Doctrinal sources include the theology of John Wesley as promoted through the National Holiness Association, which began in Vineland NJ in 1867. Though the NHA was led largely by Methodists, the movement was interdenominational and was spread mainly through the agency of the "Holiness Camp Meeting."

The basic teaching of the HOLINESS MOVEMENT was that Christians should seek a SECOND BLESSING of entire SANCTIFICATION after conversion. Many holiness teachers insisted on an instant experience that brought the believer into a state of Christian perfection, resulting in a radically changed life-style. This included deliverance from tobacco, liquor, and all forms of worldliness. Holiness worship styles were exuberant and emotional.

In 1894 the Methodist Episcopal Church, South, adopted a statement opposing the holiness movement in the church. Within the next 10 years, some two dozen holiness denominations sprang up across the United States and in several foreign countries. The Pentecostal Holiness Church represents a merger of three of these groups.

The first organization was the FIRE-BAPTIZED HOLINESS CHURCH with origins in Iowa in 1895. This group was formed by a Baptist lawyer turned holiness preacher named Benjamin Hardin Irwin of Lincoln NE. Basing his teachings on the writings of Wesley's colleague, John Fletcher, Irwin taught that the "baptism of fire" was an experience subsequent to the sanctification experience. This baptism was accompanied by extraordinary manifestations of shouting, dancing, ecstasies, and visions. This teaching was widely denounced in the holiness press as the "third blessing heresy." To promote his movement, Irwin began publication of a periodical entitled *Live Coals of Fire.*

In August 1898, Irwin organized the Fire-Baptized Holiness Church in Ander-son SC with conferences in eight Southern and Western states and two Canadian provinces. In 1900 Irwin left the church he had founded, turning the leadership over to JOSEPH H. KING, a former Methodist pastor from Georgia, who subsequently became the church's most important leader until his death in 1946.

The second organization was the Pentecostal Holiness Church of North Carolina, which was founded by Methodist minister ABNER BLACKMON CRUMPLER of Clinton. In 1890 Crumpler received the second blessing while living in Missouri and returned to his home state determined to begin a holiness revival among North Carolina Methodists. In 1893 he succeeded in organizing the North Carolina Holiness Association. He then conducted a whirlwind tour of tent revivals that raised the ire of his Methodist superiors because of his denunciations of the church.

In 1899 Crumpler was tried in a Methodist Church court near Elizabeth City NC for preaching in a local circuit against the wishes of the local pastor. Although he was acquitted of the charges, Crumpler left the Methodist Church and later organized the first local Pentecostal Holiness congregation on the courthouse square in Goldsboro. By 1900 Crumpler was publishing a paper entitled the *Holiness Advocate* and was able to convene a conference in Fayetteville that adopted a *Discipline* for the new denomination, which used Methodist models for its theology and government.

The third group that merged with the Pentecostal Holiness Church was the Tabernacle Pentecostal Church of Greenville SC, which began in 1898. Known originally as the Brewerton Presbyterian Church, this body of some 15 churches was begun by Nickles John Holmes, a Presbyterian pastor from Greenville. In 1896 Holmes had received the "second blessing" under the ministry of D. L. Moody in Northfield MA. Returning to South Carolina, Holmes began a Bible

College and church that taught the basic tenets of the turn-of-the-century holiness movement.

By 1900 all three churches had accepted some doctrines that had become widespread among holiness and other "higher life" advocates in England and America. These included instant divine healing "as in the atonement" in answer to prayer, and the imminent, premillennial, personal second coming of Christ.

From 1906 to 1908 all three groups were swept into the ranks of the Pentecostal Movement through the influence of the Azusa Street revival in Los Angeles. The new "Pentecostals" in California were led by a Texas black man, WILLIAM J. SEYMOUR, who taught a "third blessing" of BAPTISM OF THE SPIRIT accompanied by speaking in tongues (GLOSSOLALIA) as the "initial evidence."

Pentecostalism was brought to the South by GASTON BARNABAS CASHWELL of DUNN NC, who was a member of Crumpler's church. In 1906 Cashwell went to Los Angeles and received his tongues-attested Pentecostal baptism. Returning to Dunn he led a month-long revival in a tobacco warehouse that resulted in the conversion of most of the ministers of the aforesaid three groups to the Pentecostal Movement. On later trips to Birmingham in 1907 and CLEVELAND TN in 1908, Cashwell led important leaders of the CHURCH OF GOD and the future ASSEMBLIES OF GOD into the Pentecostal camp. By 1908, both the Pentecostal Holiness Church and the Fire-Baptized Holiness Churches had adopted Pentecostal articles of faith.

A move to unite the churches followed the Pentecostal revivals of 1906-1908. As a result, the Fire-Baptized Holiness and Pentecostal Holiness Churches merged in 1911 on the grounds of the Falcon camp meeting in North Carolina. In 1915 the Tabernacle Pentecostal Church also merged with the Pentecostal Holiness Church. At the time of these mergers, the united body numbered some 5,000 members in about 200 churches.

Since 1915 the denomination has spread from its Southern base to become a national and, through its World Missions program, an international church. Early missions efforts included China (1909), Africa (1913), and India (1921). By 1980 overseas membership had surpassed that in the United States.

Beginning in 1967 the Pentecostal Holiness Church began a policy of affiliating with like Wesleyan-Pentecostal bodies. In that year an affiliation was effected with the Pentecostal Methodist Church of Chile, which claimed some 320,000 adult baptized members. This church boasted the largest Protestant congregation in the world (Santiago's Jotabeche Church with 90,000 members). In the United States, affiliations were effected with the predominantly Black Original United Holy Church of the World, the Congregational Holiness Church, and the Pentecostal Free-Will Baptist Church. With its U. S. and overseas affiliates, the church numbered some 622,000 members in 1981.

Perhaps the most famous and influential minister in the history of the church is evangelist ORAL ROBERTS, who from 1935 to 1969 was a member of the East Oklahoma Conference. Considered the world's leading Pentecostal preacher, Roberts joined the United Methodist Church after founding Oral Roberts University in Tulsa in 1965.

A leading participant in Pentecostal ecumenical enterprises, the Pentecostal Holiness Church joined the World Pentecostal Conference in Zurich in 1947 and the Pentecostal Fellowship of North America in 1948. It also was a charter member of the National Association of Evangelicals, which was formed in 1943. *See also* articles on HOLINESS; METHODIST CHURCH; MILLENNIALISM; PENTECOSTALISM.

Bibliography. Emory Stevens Bucke, ed., *The History of American Methodism*; Joseph E. Campbell, *The Pente-*

costal Holiness Church, 1898 to 1940; Charles E. Jones, The Perfectionist Persuasion; Joseph H. King and Blanche L. King, Yet Speaketh; Harold Paul, From Printer's Devil to Bishop; Vinson Synan, The Holiness-Pentecostal Movement in the United States; The Old-Time Power; George Floyd Taylor, "Our Church History," The Pentecostal Holiness Advocate (20 Jan. 1921–14 April 1921).

VINSON SYNAN
OKLAHOMA CITY, OKLAHOMA

PENTECOSTALISM. As an organized religious movement, Pentecostalism is a 20th-century phenomenon. Its roots, however, are in Hebrew history. Pentecost originally referred to the Jewish Feast of Weeks that was celebrated 50 days after Passover (Deut. 16:9-11). On the day of Pentecost in the Hebrew calendar, Jesus' disciples "were all filled with the Holy Spirit" (Acts 2:4). This "baptism" was marked by an ability "to speak in other tongues" and was understood as an endowment with power that would make possible the fulfillment of the "great commission" (Acts 1:8; Mt. 28:20). Contemporary Pentecostals maintain that all believers should experience a definite "baptism with the Holy Spirit" (Acts 1:5): their theological background determines whether they regard this as a second or a third stage in the *ordo salutis*. They accept GLOSSOLALIA as the evidence of such baptism.

Because of its stress on charismatic experience, Pentecostalism can be perceived as a "third force" that emerges in many Christian communions. In this context, it is best defined as a belief that Spirit-baptism, evidenced by glossolalia, is an experience contemporary Christians can enjoy. Traditionally, Evangelicals have understood the Acts 2 account as describing a phenomenon unique in Christian history, in which the Holy Spirit permanently entered the church: Spirit-baptism, then, was a nonrecurrent apostolic endowment with both immediate and symbolic significance. Glossolalic utterances virtually disappeared from mainstream Christianity after the first century.

During the late nineteenth century, a concern for HOLINESS and spiritual power characterized American Evangelicalism and focused attention on the Holy Spirit. In Methodism, this was expressed in an emphasis on John Wesley's notion of Christian perfection. Growing Wesleyan-oriented holiness associations included non-Wesleyans who shared the desire for an instantaneous crisis experience of cleansing from inward sin, an experience also termed the "second definite work of grace," a SECOND BLESSING, BAPTISM OF THE SPIRIT, entire SANCTIFICATION, or Christian perfection. The associations were not subject to denominational jurisdiction, and tension within the Methodist hierarchy led to the disavowal in the 1894 General Conference of the Methodist Episcopal Church, South, of the independent features of the HOLINESS MOVEMENT. Under pressure, the majority of Methodist holiness advocates chose to remain with the denomination; others withdrew to form independent holiness churches. Between 1893 and 1900, 23 holiness groups were formed, most in the South and Midwest.

During the same years, D. L. Moody and other prominent Evangelicals with Congregational, Presbyterian, and Baptist backgrounds accepted the premillennial view of Christ's return. The belief in the imminent second coming was fundamental to the *Weltanschauung* of leaders like R. A. Torrey, A. J. Gordon, and A. T. Pierson. Their yearning for holiness reflected their perception of the relationship between holiness and preparedness for the second advent. Their quest for "enduement with power for service" evidenced their conviction that the time remaining to proclaim the gospel was short.

This wide-reaching focus on holiness and endowment created the context in which Pentecostalism emerged. In 1901, Charles Parham, an itinerant Midwestern holiness evangelist, introduced the teaching that the biblical initial evidence of Spirit-baptism was glossolalia. This assertion, in effect, created the Pentecostal movement. After receiving the experience, Parham began to proclaim in the southern Midwest the restoration to Christianity of the apostolic gifts, including tongues. Stressing the continuity between his message and primitive Christianity, he called his work the Apostolic Faith.

Parham remained committed to the holiness teaching on a definite experience of sanctification but rejected the holiness identification of the "second blessing" with Spirit-baptism. He considered the baptism with the Holy Spirit a third crisis experience in the *ordo salutis*, one which he associated with "power for service." His teaching on tongues as a "sign gift"— evidence of the Holy Spirit's endowment—remained largely confined to a small area of the Midwest until 1906 when its presentation in Los Angeles initiated a revival that evoked widespread response.

Among the visitors to Los Angeles where WILLIAM J. SEYMOUR, a black holiness preacher, supervised the revival meetings were representatives of Southern holiness groups. The holiness movement was particularly affected by the Los Angeles revival: from its ranks came some of the strongest supporters and the staunchest opponents of early Pentecostalism. The promulgation of the doctrine of tongues as a "sign gift" would divide holiness ranks.

Two whose Los Angeles visits would be particularly significant to the growth of Southern Pentecostalism were G. B. CASHWELL of DUNN NC, a former Methodist who in 1903 had joined the Holiness Church of North Carolina, and CHARLES H. MASON, coleader of the Memphis-based CHURCH OF GOD IN CHRIST, the first legally chartered Southern holiness group.

In Los Angeles late in 1906, Cashwell received baptism with the Holy Spirit. He returned to Dunn and presented Pentecostal teaching at a series of revival meetings to which he invited local holiness ministers, many of whom accepted his message. In 1908, Cashwell's group became the Pentecostal Holiness Church of North Carolina. In 1911, this group merged with the FIRE-BAPTIZED HOLINESS CHURCH and became the PENTECOSTAL HOLINESS CHURCH, an important Southern Pentecostal denomination.

From 1907, Cashwell preached throughout the South. During his ministry in CLEVELAND TN in January 1908, A. J. TOMLINSON, general overseer of the Church of God, received Spirit-baptism. The Church of God had grown out of the Christian Union, a holiness gathering begun in Camp Creek NC in 1886. Since an 1896 local revival, glossolalia had been experienced in the group, although no doctrine relating glossolalia to Spirit-baptism was promulgated. Tomlinson had joined the church in 1903, and his preaching and administrative ability had assured him a position of leadership. By 1908, the group had adopted the name Church of God and had grown to include small rural congregations in the mountain region where Tennessee, North Carolina, and Georgia converge. Tomlinson's acceptance of Pentecostal teaching brought the Church of God into the Pentecostal movement.

Reports from Los Angeles drew Charles Mason of the black holiness group, the Church of God in Christ. He received baptism with the Holy Spirit and brought Pentecostal teaching into his denomination where, despite opposition from the group's founder, Charles Price Jones, it was accepted by a majority of the denomination's ministers and membership. These, following Mason's leadership, withdrew from the General Assembly, retaining the name of Church of God in Christ; Jones renamed his non-Pentecostal faction The Church of Christ (Holiness) USA.

By 1908, then, these independent Southern holiness groups had embraced Pentecostalism. In the holiness tradition, they continued to affirm an experience of instantaneous sanctification, which they regard as discrete from baptism with the Holy Spirit. Together with several small, regional Apostolic Faith groups, the Pentecostal Holiness Church, the CHURCH OF GOD (CLEVELAND TN), and the Church of God in Christ compose the major part of the holiness Pentecostal movement which, though not confined to the South, continues to find its largest following in that region.

In contrast to this Southern pattern in which previously organized groups incorporated a new doctrine into an established framework were hundreds of independent Pentecostal missions across the country. Increasingly the need for order and fellowship was perceived in this part of the movement outside the holiness ranks. In April 1914 at a General Council in HOT SPRINGS AR, a fellowship of independent congregations known as the ASSEMBLIES OF GOD was formed. A move toward denominational organization came in 1916 when a serious theological challenge from within led to the adoption of a statement of faith.

Since 1913, various Pentecostals had claimed the unity of the Godhead, asserting that there was "only one person in the Godhead—Jesus Christ." Those who espoused this emphasis were rebaptized "in the name of Jesus." Over one-third of the 585 ministers then associated with the Assemblies of God endorsed the "oneness" position. Holiness Pentecostal groups were virtually unaffected by the teaching, but the Assemblies of God was forced clearly to define its faith. Its 1916 "Statement of Fundamental Truth" disavowed "oneness," affirming commitment to evangelical trinitarianism. It also identified the Assemblies of God with the Reformed view of sanctification as a progressive process, thus recognizing the division of Pentecostalism—with respect to the doctrine of sanctification—into two

segments. In this framework, reflecting the influence on Pentecostalism of the late nineteenth-century premillennialist and Keswickian focus on the Holy Spirit, Spirit-baptism was regarded as a second crisis experience in the *ordo salutis*. The Assemblies of God is the largest Pentecostal denomination; 32 percent of its churches are in the South.

The Assemblies of God was numerically weakened by the withdrawal of the "oneness" faction in 1916. Organized independently, "oneness" Pentecostal denominations like the UNITED PENTECOSTAL CHURCH and the Pentecostal Assemblies of the World have experienced considerable growth while continuing to evoke the criticism of the major Pentecostal bodies.

Their espousal of glossolalia and divine healing at first made Pentecostals unwelcome in the broader evangelical community. Formal acceptance came in 1941 when Pentecostals were received into the National Association of Evangelicals. Regular meetings of the Pentecostal Fellowship of North America and triennial World Pentecostal Conferences recognize the shared heritage of the many Pentecostal denominations. Because they cannot subscribe to a trinitarian statement of faith, oneness groups remain excluded from these associations.

The denominations provide structure and stability in a movement prone to enthusiasm. In spite of the emergence of Neo-Pentecostalism in both Protestantism and Catholicism, distinctive doctrines give denominational Pentecostalism continued reason for separate existence.

See also articles on KESWICK MOVEMENT; MILLENNIALISM; REVIVALISM.

Bibliography. Robert M. Anderson, *Vision of the Disinherited: The Making of American Pentecostalism;* Charles Conn, *Like a Mighty Army Moves the Church of God;* Fred Foster, *Think It Not Strange: A History of the Oneness Movement;* Donald Gee, *All With One Accord;* Wade Horton, ed., *The Glossolalia Phenomenon;* Klaude Kendrick, *The Promise Fulfilled: A History of the Modern Pentecostal Movement;* William Menzies, *Anointed to Serve;* John T. Nichol, *Pentecostalism;* Ralph Riggs, *The Spirit Himself;* Vinson Synan, *The Holiness-*

Pentecostal Movement; The Old-Time Religion: A History of the Pentecostal Holiness Church; George H. Williams and Edith L. Waldvogel, "A History of Speaking in Tongues and Related Gifts," The Charismatic Movement, ed. Michael Hamilton.

EDITH L. BLUMHOFER
SOUTHWEST MISSOURI STATE UNIVERSITY

PERCY, WALKER (1916-), novelist and essayist, was born in Birmingham AL. Since both of his parents died before he was 14, he and his two brothers moved to Greenville MS to live with their father's first cousin, WILLIAM ALEXANDER PERCY, known by them as "Uncle Will." In the culturally rich atmosphere of their new home, they learned to love poetry and classical music. Literary personages frequently visited the house; WILLIAM FAULKNER even played tennis there occasionally. Young Walker later wrote of the elder Percy: "What was to be listened to, dwelled on, pondered over was, of course, . . . the man himself, the unique human being." Uncle Will profoundly influenced his young cousin's development as a writer, everything he did was "usually in *relation* to him whether with him or against him."

Following public school years in Greenville, Walker Percy entered the University of North Carolina at Chapel Hill. Although he displayed some interest in writing while in college, he pursued a degree in chemistry because he was convinced at the time that "scientific truth was the only truth worth pursuing." He then entered the College of Physicians and Surgeons at Columbia and received his M.D. degree in 1941. He did not like medical school much and began to question the capacity of the scientific method to identify truth. Among his observations was the remark that "science can say everything about a man except what he is in himself." Such insight influenced his thinking and writing from that time forward.

While interning in pathology at Belleview Hospital, Percy contracted tuberculosis and soon found himself isolated at a sanitorium at Saranac Lake. He later said of this period of his life, "TB liberated me." During his confinement, he became acquainted with the Danish theologian, Søren Kierkegaard, and read extensively the works of modern European existentialist writers. After an attempt to return to pathology following his release from the sanitorium, he suffered a relapse and gave up medicine altogether. Uncle Will had died in the meantime and left his young cousin enough money to move back south to New Orleans where he was free "to think about the curiousness of man's condition." Soon after his marriage in 1946, he and his wife converted to Catholicism.

Percy's route to becoming a novelist was long and somewhat torturous. From the time he moved to Louisiana until 1961, when his first novel appeared, he wrote a series of essays that were carried in various scholarly journals. In the 1950s, Percy wrote two full-length novels that never reached publication. But in 1961, with the careful assistance of a Knopf editor, he published *The Moviegoer*, which won the National Book Award the next year. Since then, other novels have followed: *The Last Gentleman* (1966); *Love in the Ruins*, subtitled, "The adventures of a bad Catholic at a time near the end of the world" (1971), winner of the National Catholic Book Award; *Lancelot* (1977); and *The Second Coming* (1980). He published a series of essays in *The Message in the Bottle* (1975).

Percy's novels, which are suffused with a comic cynicism, actually find their ground in the classical doctrines of Christianity, as expressed by writers like Sartre and Camus, whom he encountered during his bout with tuberculosis. Percy is, however, no mere novelist of ideas. He manages to tell stories of believable complexity about ordinary characters who are attempting to find their way out of the malaise of contemporary life. Nor are the novels saturated with religious symbolism. When theological or religious language is used, it is used in a gently ironic way to expose the emptiness of the conventional religious institutions in our society, or it is used in a painfully straightforward way to force the protagonist to come to terms with his own life. Percy's characters eventually discover that the answers they so desperately seek are to be found, not in some exotic or heroic religious activity, but by coming to terms with and accepting the circumstances of their own lives and by choosing and loving the persons who are almost always nearest to them. Although the later novels are bleaker in tone and theme, their ideational structure remains grounded in religiousness.

As a native Southerner, Percy makes use of the typically Southern stratagems of irony, humor, and exaggeration to explore and penetrate the habits, mores, and customs of the figures who inhabit the novels. No pretension is left intact, no social convention is left unexamined, and it is all done in great good humor. Thus Walker Percy, a writer who is both Southern and Catholic, has displayed a remarkable dexterity by appropriating from both traditions those elements that, when placed in juxtaposition with one another, create a highly original fictional world of universal dimensions.

See also article on LITERATURE AND RELIGION.

Bibliography. Panthea Reid Broughton, ed., *The Art of Walker Percy: Stratagems for Being*; Robert Coles, *Walker Percy: An American Search*; Martin Luschei, *The Sovereign Wayfarer: Walker Percy's Diagnosis of the Malaise*; Jac Tharpe, ed., *Walker Percy: Art and Ethics.*

GEORGE C. BEDELL
TALLAHASSEE, FLORIDA

PERCY, WILLIAM ALEXANDER

(1885-1942), planter, lawyer, and writer, was born in Greenville MS. His maternal grandparents were French Roman Catholics who migrated from New Orleans to the Mississippi Delta country following the Civil War. The Percys, by contrast, traced their lineage to Charles B. Percy, an Englishman who moved to Mississippi in the 1770s.

Young Percy was educated at a convent school in Greenville and by private tutors. Reared a Catholic, he nonetheless sought his undergraduate education at his father's alma mater, the UNIVERSITY OF THE SOUTH at Sewanee TN, an Episcopal school, from which he received a B.A. in English literature in 1904. He received a law degree from the Harvard Law School in 1908 and returned to Greenville where he practiced law with his father. He maintained a summer place at Sewanee, and in 1939 the university awarded him a D.Litt.

Percy, who traveled extensively throughout his life, was in Europe when war broke out in 1914. He returned to Greenville but headed back to Belgium in 1916 to assist in the work of the Hoover Relief Commission. King Albert later decorated him for his service to the Belgian people. In spite of his small stature, he won a commission in the U. S. Army and joined the 37th Division in France soon after the U. S. entered the war. He ended military service as a captain and was awarded the Croix de Guerre with a gold and a silver star.

Active in civic and political affairs in Greenville throughout his adult life, Percy vigorously opposed the KU KLUX KLAN. Although his attitude toward black people seems paternalistic and even racist to later generations, he was considered progressive by most of his contemporaries, a "nigger lover" by some. As chairman of the local Red Cross chapter, he oversaw the rescue operations that cared for the 120,000 persons left homeless by the great flood of 1927.

Although the practice of law and oversight of his vast plantation required a great deal of his time, Percy liked to think of himself primarily as a poet. Greatly influenced by the ancient Stoic tradition, his treatment of specifically Christian themes was tempered by heroic resignation and agnosticism. "His Peace," a poem published in 1924, was adapted and set to music by David McK. Williams in 1941 and is published in the 1940 Hymnal of the Episcopal Church. The last stanza of the hymn well demonstrates Percy's basic religious orientation:

The peace of God, it is no peace,
But strife closed in the sod.
Yet, brothers, pray for but one
thing—
The marvelous peace of God.

Sappho and Levkas, a collection of poems, was published in 1915, followed by *In April Once* in 1920, *Enzio's Kingdom* in 1924, and *Selected Poems* in 1930. Following Percy's death, *The Collected Poems*, to which Roark Bradford wrote an introduction, was published in 1943.

In 1941 Percy published *Lanterns on the Levee: Recollections of a Planter's Son*, a gentle and nostalgic view of the Old South, a civilization that he believed was being destroyed, not merely by "outside agitators," but also by the rise of meretricious politicians in the South. In a chapter on his undergraduate years at Sewanee, Percy described the beginnings of his agnosticism. Following an unsuccessful attempt to prepare himself for confession at the Catholic parish church in nearby Winchester, he wrote that he "rode back to the leafy mountain mournful and unregretful, knowing thenceforth I should breathe a starker and colder air, with no place to go when I was tired."

At the time of his death in Greenville, his family consisted of three younger first cousins who had come to live with him in 1931, following their mother's death. WALKER PERCY was the eldest of the three.

See also article on LITERATURE AND RELIGION.

                          GEORGE C. BEDELL
                       TALLAHASSEE, FLORIDA

PERFECTION, CHRISTIAN: *See* PENTECOSTALISM; WESLEYAN TRADITION.

PIERCE, LOVICK (1785-1879), pioneer Methodist leader, was born in Martin County NC. He grew up in South Carolina and was converted under the preaching of a Methodist circuit rider in 1803. Pierce joined the South Carolina Conference in 1805 and was assigned to the Great Pee

Dee Circuit. The following year he went to the Apalachee Circuit, and in 1809 was made a presiding elder. The Pierces had eight children, one of whom, George Foster, became a bishop in the METHODIST EPISCOPAL CHURCH, SOUTH.

Pierce served as a chaplain in the War of 1812 and then stopped preaching and earned a medical degree at the University of Pennsylvania, practicing in Greensboro GA until 1823. Having assured his family's financial security by his medical practice and by farming, Pierce returned to the ministry, serving appointments near his farm in west-central Georgia.

He was a charter member of the Georgia and South Georgia Conferences and was elected to the first delegated General Conference of 1812 and to 14 other General Conferences of the Methodist Episcopal Church and the Methodist Episcopal Church, South.

More liberal on such issues as education for women and theological education for ministers than his son, the bishop, Lovick Pierce's life bore fruit in another Georgia bishop, ATTICUS HAYGOOD, whom he taught to love theology and to prepare sermons carefully.

When Pierce died in 1879, his life had spanned almost the entire first century of American Methodism.

Bibliography. William R. Cannon, "The Pierces: Father and Son," *Methodist History* 17 (October 1978): 3-15; Harold W. Mann, *Atticus Greene Haygood, Methodist Bishop, Editor, and Educator.*

                          JOSEPH MITCHELL
                       TROY STATE UNIVERSITY

PIETISM: *See* PIETY.

PIETY. The term now signifies habitual reverence and obedience to God. Originally, the Latin *pietas* meant the natural affection of parents and children for each other, including faithfulness to familial duties and roles. The warmth of a genuine, intimate happiness and regard characterized original "piety."

The Latin family meaning carried over into Western Christian monastic practice. In the Benedictine house, from the sixth century A.D., the abbot served as *pius pater*, pious father, similar to the father of the noble Roman family. The dutiful father cared for his children; so the abbot saw his monks as sons in his care. Thus *pietas* also began to mean "pity." The Italian, *pieta* (a representation of Mary holding the body of the dead Jesus, as in the renowned piece by Michelangelo), shows this quality of caring piety, or pity.

Roman usage also considered piety the appropriate attitude toward the gods. Seneca, in terms strikingly parallel to the Old Testament prophets, enjoined obedience and faithful devotion to the gods, rather than vain, ritualistic practices. His work was studied and edited centuries later by the young John Calvin. Cicero also spoke of piety as justice toward the gods. Augustine of Hippo, Catholic father and devoted student of Cicero, tells in his *Confessions* of the *pietas* of his mother, Monica, or her devotional duty to faith.

Such Christian piety continued an element of the original family meaning, suggesting a filial affection for God. One Catholic authority speaks of piety as a gift of the Holy Spirit that enables the fulfillment of religious obligations with happiness. Thus piety as filial affection is not only a virtue, but the source of all virtue. A special gladness informs the notion of true piety, since affection for God naturally and unpretentiously makes life both happy and faithful.

This simple concept, with its suggestion of dignity and warmth of attitude, has undergone important changes through religious history. To understand the meaning of piety in the religion of the South requires attention to these complicated changes.

First, piety has often indicated an affected, false piety, an attitude of holiness that is an empty conceit, assumed outwardly and perhaps hypocritically. In such cases, piety, a spontaneous attitude, yields its name to opposite qualities that are artificial and self-imposed.

Second, piety has become associated with a particular Protestant movement called "Pietism," an outgrowth of the Reformation in Germany. Philipp Jakob Spener (1635-1705), the acknowledged father of the movement, was a student of history at Strasburg who became interested in the vitality of Luther's writings and hope for a renewed laity in the church. In the orthodox Lutheran church, Spener saw a merely objective attachment to doctrine, routine participation in the sacraments, and little concern for growth in Christian love. He became zealous for a true personal faith of the heart nourished in small house-groups of laity, and for a conversion experience for clergy. About two generations after Spener, the Wesleyan revival, a parallel movement in England, proclaimed a heart-felt relation to Christ as personal Savior, along with newness of life both individual and corporate.

Pietism gave a particular meaning to piety. Not only affectionate loyalty to God, but a special conversion to Christ, biblical nurture within a small *collegium*, and adoption of a strict personal morality became its marks, along with contemplation of Christ's death as the astonishing price of one's personal salvation. At its worst, Pietism has been narrow, judgmental, and emotionally excessive. At its best, it has afforded individuals and groups dignity and hope, generated loyal fellowship, and performed extensive social service.

Piety in the religion of the South, whether black or white, has been largely exercised through the form of Protestant Pietism. One strand, the New Light Presbyterian and Separate Baptist, a Puritan piety, extended through revivals southward from New England during the latter half of the 18th century. Another, the Methodist, appeared in the South early in the 19th century. REVIVALISM and the call to intense personal faith in Christ have at times reflected true piety and at times have become a mechanical convention or even a charade. Consider Sinclair Lewis's *Elmer Gantry* or Flannery O'Connor's Onnie Jay Holy and Asa Hawks (in *Wise Blood*). On the other hand, a true, animating Southern piety has flourished, if not as serene filial affection, then as dramatic wonder that the story of Christ and the form of individual, interior experience closely cohere. The devotion of a Dilsey in William Faulkner's *The Sound and the Fury* is an example. So also are the lines from "Cheerful," a Sacred Harp melody of Appalachia:

O how I have long'd for the coming of God.
And sought him by praying and searching his word;
With watching and fasting my soul was opprest,
Nor would I give over, till Jesus had bless'd.

See also articles on EVANGELICAL PROTESTANTISM; EVANGELICALISM (IN THE SOUTH).

Bibliography. J. H. Nichols, *History of Christianity, 1650-1950*; G. Schnürer, *Church and Culture in the Middle Ages.*

WILLIAM MALLARD
EMORY UNIVERSITY

PILGRIM HOLINESS CHURCH: *See* WESLEYAN CHURCH, THE.

PITT, ROBERT HEALY (1853-1937),
Baptist pastor, editor, and denominational leader, was born in Middlesex County VA and attended Richmond College. Ordained a minister in 1877, he served a number of congregations, mainly in Richmond. In 1888 he began his 49-year career with the *Religious Herald*, Virginia's state Baptist newspaper. After becoming editor and sole owner in 1906, Pitt took strong stands on social issues and denominational policies. He authored rigorous critiques of American capitalism, called for fairer treatment of Virginia's blacks, opposed capital punishment, and advocated lay rights for Baptist women. For 12 years he headed the Virginia Anti-Saloon League and he vigorously opposed

the presidential candidacy of Al Smith in 1928.

During the 1920s Pitt eloquently articulated traditional Baptist support of religious liberty. He used his influence to defeat a proposed state antievolution law and a measure requiring Bible reading in public schools. He condemned fundamentalist preachers for trying to dictate their beliefs to other Christians. As a member of the 1925 Southern Baptist Convention Committee on Baptist Faith and Message, he protested that the committee's report, subsequently adopted by the convention, constituted a creed and thereby departed from the denomination's historic position.

Pitt held various state denominational offices. He was instrumental in securing vital funds for Richmond College and Westhampton College for women, which now form the University of Richmond. For more than 40 years he served as a member of the Foreign Mission Board of the SBC and as the American Secretary of the Baptist World Alliance.

See also articles on CHURCH AND STATE; PROHIBITION; RELIGIOUS PRESS.

SAMUEL C. SHEPHERD, JR.
CENTENARY COLLEGE

POLK, LEONIDAS (1806-1864), versatile Episcopal Church leader, was the first bishop of Louisiana, lieutenant general, Confederate States of America, and a founder of the University of the South. He was born in Raleigh NC, and educated at both the University of North Carolina and West Point, where he graduated in 1827. The following year he resigned his commission to enter Virginia Seminary at Alexandria. He was ordained to the priesthood in 1831. He served for some time as curate of Monumental Church, Richmond VA, but his health failed and he resigned his post to travel in Europe. He was made missionary bishop of the Southwest in 1838. In 1841, he was translated as first bishop of Louisiana. During his episcopate, the church exhibited much growth.

Always concerned with higher education, Bishop Polk envisioned a great Southern university that would enlighten the aristocracy and prepare future leaders to move towards the gradual emancipation of the Negro slaves. He united with Bishops STEPHEN ELLIOT of Georgia and JAMES H. OTEY of Tennessee to found the UNIVERSITY OF THE SOUTH at Sewanee TN in 1857.

When the Civil War broke out in 1861, Polk reluctantly accepted the commission of major general, C.S.A., and "buckled the sword over the gown." In 1862 he was promoted to lieutenant general, serving as second in command under Generals Johnston and Bragg in the West. His major engagements were Shiloh, Perryville, Murfreesboro, and Chickamauga. Polk was killed by cannon fire at Pine Mountain GA.

Bibliography. George R. Fairbanks, *A History of the University of the South*; Joseph H. Parks, *General Leonidas Polk C.S.A., The Fighting Bishop*; William M. Polk, *Leonidas Polk, Bishop and General*, 2 vols.

JOSEPH D. CUSHMAN
UNIVERSITY OF THE SOUTH

POPE, LISTON (1909-1974), theological educator and author, was born in Thomasville NC. He devoted his career as a theologian and church leader to bridging the gulf, traditional in the South, between personal and social religion. After graduation from Duke Divinity School in 1932, he served a Methodist congregation in High Point NC and in 1935 began doctoral study at Yale. In 1940 he received the university's Porter Prize for his thesis, published in 1942 as *Millhands and Preachers: A Study of Gastonia.*

He was a member of the Yale Divinity School faculty from 1938 to 1973. He became known worldwide as a founder of a discipline largely associated with American seminaries, Christian Social Ethics. He traveled widely as a leader of the World Council of Churches; and, while the civil rights movement was beginning, published *The Kingdom Beyond Caste.* As the Gilbert L. Stark Professor of Social Ethics and as dean of YDS, he helped train

hundreds of future ministers and teachers to combine "hard social analysis" with "transcendent ethical standards." His pioneering work on Gastonia centered on the great textile strike of 1929. Through historical, sociological, economic, and theological analysis, he dealt a stunning intellectual blow to the Southern religious tradition that separated "spiritual" and "social." "Overtly, religion in mill churches appears to be indifferent to economic conditions; actually, it is in part a product of those conditions and, by diverting attention from them, is indirectly a sanction on them."

Pope sought to show Southern churchgoers how to become careful critics, rather than innocent captives of their society. His book on Gastonia remains a classic of the economic, cultural, and institutional church history of the South.

See also articles on ETHICS, CHRISTIAN; SOCIAL GOSPEL.

DONALD W. SHRIVER, JR.
UNION THEOLOGICAL SEMINARY

PREACHER. This is the title most commonly employed in the South for Protestant clergy and, by extension, may be used even for Catholic priests and Jewish rabbis. When the name of the clergyman (or woman) is unknown or not remembered, "preacher" is regarded as sufficient designation, even as the doctor suffices under similar situations for the physician.

It is likely that this designation commonly holds across the region because the most public work of the clergy is in their role as leaders of worship. Moreover, within the most popular types of worship service, the sermon is the central and lengthiest component. Indeed, the service of worship is frequently referred to as the "preaching service" and, to cite a graphic example, the "six-point record system" of the region's largest Christian body (the Southern Baptist Convention) credits 20 percent to Sunday school attendees who "attend preaching."

However, the preacher is more than a proclaimer of the Gospel; this individual is also assumed to be the moral monitor, whose presence puts a damper on profanity and obscenity and whose visits elicit discussions of religious subjects. The preacher is also invited to be present at public events, to bless them by prayer and his presence. For some, this seems to be a hollow symbolization, lacking in any real religious meaning. For others, this is viewed as a sign of the conviction that God is in and cares for the world, and the preacher is the one given the opportunity to incarnate that reality.

WILLIAM C. SMITH, JR.
GREENSBORO, NORTH CAROLINA

PREACHING (IN THE SOUTH). It is impossible to understand the character of religion in the South without exploring the soul and psyche of the Southern preacher. In a region where religion is more than a single thread that can be tugged from the fabric of culture, but rather is the frame upon which much of the culture is woven, it has been preaching as much as any other single force that has shaped the patterns and textures of the cultural cloth.

There was a time in Southern religious history when religious impulses focused upon other objects (the intellectual abstractions of Deism, for example, or the eucharistic emphasis of Anglicanism), but these approaches were finally and vigorously swept aside in favor of a pulpit-centered faith more suited to the passionate temperament of the region. There is truth amid exaggeration in W. J. Cash's claim that "what [the] Southerner required . . . was a faith as simple and emotional as himself. A faith to draw men together in hordes, to terrify them with Apocalyptic rhetoric, to cast them into the pit, rescue them, and at last bring them shouting into the fold of Grace."

In the first third of the 19th century what has been termed a "left-wing, Low Church, Protestant orthodoxy" forged a theological and ecclesiastical consensus in the South that endured virtually intact for 150 years. The official centerpiece of this consensus was the Bible—often a literal, even fundamentalistic, understanding of the Bible. Yet in actual practice, the energy for this movement was provided by the incarnation of the Bible in the personalities of the preachers and the sermons they preached. Southerners still favor the term PREACHER over more general titles like PASTOR or MINISTER ("Preacher Jones visited me today"), an indication that every ministerial function (education, pastoral care, evangelism, etc.) comes to focus and gains legitimacy in the primary function of preaching.

A remarkable feature of Southern religious life has been the presence of a commonly held understanding of the role and importance of the preacher, an understanding that transcends racial and denominational distinctions. In the preachers of the South three primal and formative biblical images come together in a powerful fusion: prophet, sage, and evangelist. Southern preachers have been understood, and have understood themselves (though not always self-consciously), as the synthesis of these three biblical prototypes. Southern preachers have been Moses, Solomon, and Paul; lawgiver, wise teacher, and revivalist. They have been caretakers of the sacred traditions as well as chief huntsmen of the Hound of Heaven. From this synthesis, the changing political, social, and theological realities of Southern life have, at various times and in various places, called first one, then another, of these images into prominence, making it possible and profitable to explore separately these three strands of Southern preaching.

The Southern Preacher as Sage. Whenever one form of religious expression becomes dominant in a region, as has been the case in the South, the goals and values of the religious life become mingled with those of the "cultured" life. Southerners, according to JAMES M. DABBS, have manifested a tendency "to replace religion with politics, and to make politics, religion, and the moral life one."

When the religious, political, moral, and social spheres of society merge, that convergence evokes a style of ministerial leadership that can prosper only in this rare climate. Under these conditions the ministry is not forced to be prophetic, calling for social reformation, nor is it called to be evangelistic, urging personal transformation. The minister, rather, has the privilege of functioning as sage: the one who stands *in* culture, not over against it; the one who confirms what is wise in life and calls for mastery of it.

Southern preachers have at many times and in many ways fulfilled the role of sage. Like the Old Testament wise men before them, they have told stories and propounded wise proverbs. They have translated Christian ethics into "Christian manners." They have spoken, not of the scandal of the faith, but of the "reasonableness" of it. They have often equated the "Southern Way of Life" with the Christian way of life and defended that equation with great effort, and sometimes at great cost.

When Southern preachers have been "sages," their preaching style has been one of polished rhetoric and eloquent phrases. This is a confident and positive style, full of flourishes, often ornate, a style that develops its rhythms out of an assured view of the inner harmony of God and human life.

At no point in Southern history did the image of the preacher as sage achieve sharper definition than it did during the time of the "gentlemen theologians," the antebellum and Civil War period. E. Brooks Holifield describes these ministers as "the proponents of clerical gentility, a small and elite body . . . [who] articulated the 'orthodox' religious thought of the Old South."

Like all true sages, these preachers represented, according to Holifield, the blending of "the religious sentiments of the common folk," on the one hand, and the "image of the minister as gentleman, exalted and elevated through character,

erudition, and professional status," on the other. Their populist-oriented critics "bemoaned their 'chaste and classic' sermons fashioned 'to please the refined ears and cultivated tastes of the age,'" and yet the content of those very sermons, more often than not, was aimed at demonstrating the common-sense rationality of the widely held religious views of Southerners.

An example of this can be seen in BENJAMIN M. PALMER (1818-1902), a Presbyterian and one of the "gentlemen theologians" who was at one time termed the "glory of the Southern pulpit." On the one hand, Palmer had little affection for the simple, practical pulpit style prized by ordinary folk, as he was noted for his ornate, doctrinal sermons, strenuous intellectual exercises that lasted as long as an hour and a half. On the other hand, his sermons were essentially attempts to justify prevalent religious attitudes on the basis of appeals to scriptural proof-texts and common sense.

Given the inclination of the sage to provide religious explanations and justifications for cultural realities, it is not surprising to discover, in the preaching of the "gentlemen theologians" and others like them in the Civil War period, attempts to justify slavery theologically. For example, James Smylie, a Presbyterian minister in Mississippi, built upon the foundations of God's law and natural law to preach that slaveholding was justified and that Christians had no moral obligation to seek its abolition. Similarly, the Methodist Samuel Dunwoody declared, in a sermon published in 1837, "that God made express biblical provision for perpetual slavery and condemned the Negro race to continued existence in slavery." In the many sermons of this type preached in the South, the argument was essentially that the law of God and the law of nature had found natural and reasonable expression in the slavery laws of the Southern states.

One of the most articulate and visible of the preacher-sages of the South was

JAMES H. THORNWELL. A South Carolinian, Thornwell studied at Andover Seminary and at Harvard Divinity School, but he rejected the liberalism and "infidelity" of both and returned to the South. Not a Presbyterian by birth, he joined that denomination in 1832 because he was impressed by the precise logic of the WESTMINSTER CONFESSION OF FAITH. His intellectual prowess and rhetorical skill soon pushed him to a position of prominence in Southern religious life. He served as a university president and a seminary professor, but he gained his greatest fame as a preacher and a defender of Southern moral and religious values. His sermons, like the other expressions of his thought, were appeals to both the tenets of orthodox Christianity and to the "laws of the mind," an article of the philosophy of Common Sense Realism prevalent in 18th-century Scottish universities. Perhaps the most quoted of Thornwell's sermons is "The Rights and the Duties of Masters," preached in May 1850 at Charleston. This sermon, based on Col. 4:1 ("Masters, give unto your servants that which is just and equal; knowing that ye also have a master in Heaven"), argues that, while the ultimate goal of the gospel includes the removal of the institution of slavery, under the present circumstances of a fallen world, slavery is supported by the gospel as a means of encouraging the spiritual progress of slaves. In a key section of the sermon Thornwell maintains, "Slavery is not repugnant to the spirit of the Gospel, in its present relations to our race. It is one of the conditions in which God is conducting the moral probations of man—a condition not incompatible with the highest moral freedom, the true glory of the race, and, therefore, not unfit for the moral and spiritual discipline which Christianity has instituted."

It would be a mistake, however, to assume that the energies of the Southern preacher-sages have always been applied to the defense of morally bankrupt causes or rigid orthodoxy. Seeking wisdom in faith and culture, Southern preachers have also called for true piety and honesty in business affairs, for the embodiment of Christian love in everyday relationships, and for the control of passion and aggression by the rule of reason and the power of the spirit. Southern life has afforded the possibility, sometimes real and sometimes illusory, that the cultural ideal and the religious ideal could be one and the same. In such a climate "Wisdom calls in the street" and the pulpit becomes the sacred desk of the sage.

The Southern Preacher as Prophet. For decades there has been a deep fissure in the moral life of the South. On the one hand, Southern society has been confident, open, relaxed, and self-assured. It has poured its democratic and aristocratic energies into a theocratic mold, and its ideal has been a society at one with itself and with God. On the other hand, there has been the all-encompassing issue of race, and along with it the conviction, in what Cash calls the "secret heart" of the South, that the South has been morally wrong, in slavery and segregation in particular, and in racial relations in general. "The Old South," claimed Cash, "in short, was a society beset by the specters of defeat, of shame, of guilt—a society driven by the need to bolster its morale, to nerve its arm against waxing odds, to justify itself in its own eyes and in those of the world."

If it is the sage who assumes the task of social maintenance and self-justification, it is the prophet who seizes the imperative of moral failure and issues that call for social regeneration. The prophetic preaching tradition in the South has spoken to the South's "secret heart." Even when Southern preachers have raised prophetic voices on issues like the wages of sanitation workers or the need for public housing, Southerners have sensed, correctly, that the fundamental question has almost always been that of justice in racial relationships.

It should be noted that prophetic preaching does not always take the form of highly visible public pronouncements. There have been, of course, preachers in the South like MARTIN LUTHER KING, JR., whose prophetic sermons were delivered in the context of the publicly prominent civil rights movement of the 1950s and 1960s. Much of the South's prophetic preaching, however, has been less conspicuous and more local. Walter Brueggemann, having examined the biblical prophetic tradition, maintains that "the task of prophetic ministry is to nurture, nourish, and evoke a consciousness and perception alternate to the consciousness and perception of the dominant culture around us." Here and there in the history of Southern preaching, its contours sometimes barely discernible beneath the traditional theological vocabulary that it has employed, can be found a strand of preaching that has quietly nourished an alternate consciousness, the prophetic vision of a new and just South.

The prophetic dream of a radically different way of viewing social relationships can clearly be seen in some of the preaching of the plantation slave ministers of the 18th and 19th centuries. Describing the special place of the preacher in black culture, W. E. B. DuBois maintained, "The Preacher is the most unique personality developed by the Negro on American soil. A leader, a politician, an orator, a boss, an intriguer, an idealist—all these he is. . . . "

Contrary to their reputation in some areas, the slave preachers were often literate and skilled, and as Eugene D. Genovese has claimed, competent slave preachers "existed in sufficient numbers to guarantee that most slaves heard reasonably well-trained and well-educated black preachers once in a while."

On the surface, the message of the slave preachers was rarely social or political and most often took the form of direct biblical exposition, as was the case in white preaching. This " 'straight preachin' from the Bible," according to Genovese, "does not suggest political fireworks, but neither does it suggest

ideological neutrality." There was an unstated, but nonetheless sharp, contrast made between the white-dominated world and the biblical view of the world in which God was "no respecter of persons."

In his autobiography, black minister HOWARD THURMAN described the effect of a typical sermon of a slave preacher: "When the slave preacher told the Calvary narrative to my grandmother and the other slaves, it had the same effect on them as it would later have on their descendants. But this preacher, when he had finished, would pause, his eyes scrutinizing every face in the congregation, and he would tell them, 'You are not niggers! You are not slaves! You are God's children!' "

Though some of the slave preaching was admittedly devoid of social content, Genovese finds other examples of the revolutionary impact of the "nonpolitical" preaching of the slave preachers. For example, a preacher who addressed his slave congregation as "sirs and madams," a simple sermon on the parable of the "sheep and the goats" to a slave gathering for whom "goat" was a term applied to whites, and countless sermons on "freedom in Jesus." What many of the slave preachers did was to allow the gospel to be heard on its own terms, highlighting the themes of personal dignity, worth, and equality. In the context of the slaveholding South, this was nothing less than a call for social transformation; in short, prophetic preaching.

White response to the slave preachers was quite varied. Many antebellum whites protected and encouraged the plantation preachers, even received spiritual counsel from them on occasion. There were other times, especially during periods of relative unrest (for example, after the Nat Turner revolt), when the slave preachers were forbidden to preach and sternly punished for doing so. The Rev. CHARLES C. JONES, a white preacher of the 19th century who supported the ministry of slave preachers, reported that a slave preacher named ANDREW BRYAN—"a man of good sense, great zeal, and some natural elocution"—was strictly forbidden to preach or lead in worship. His services were broken up and those in attendance whipped. Other reports indicate that a slave preacher was burned alive near the courthouse at Greenville SC because he preached in defiance of his master's prohibition and fled to escape the announced punishment of 500 lashes.

These reports stand in contrast, of course, to the many accounts of deep support and generosity for the slave preachers from whites; and it is surely true, as Genovese has indicated, that "white toleration of the preachers, which always existed in uneasy balance with repression and abuse, became part of a growing tendency to promote religious segregation."

In many ways the preaching of the black church in the South today is a direct descendant of the plantation slave preaching, in its strong biblical base, its use of stories, striking images and emotion, and its vigorous prophetic zeal. King's "I Have a Dream" sermon preached at the Lincoln Memorial in Washington in 1963 is perhaps the most famous example of the contemporary black prophetic style, but it is not an atypical one.

Prophetic preaching in the South has not been restricted, however, to the black church. Concern for justice and social transformation has been a consistent, though sometimes muted, theme of white preaching as well. There were white preachers in the antebellum period who nudged white consciences on the issue of slavery, and after the Civil War, the erection of the walls of racial segregation did not find universal support in white pulpits.

In the late nineteenth century there was, especially among Methodists, some movement, however slight, toward the SOCIAL GOSPEL that was being advocated in the Northern churches. Occasionally this trend in theology found its way to the pulpit, as it did in the preaching of ATTICUS G. HAYGOOD. Haygood, presi-

dent of Emory University and later a Methodist bishop, preached a Thanksgiving Day sermon in 1880 entitled "The New South," which was built on Henry Grady's use of that phrase. Haygood's vision in this sermon was a prophetic one: a South transformed, facing its racial responsibilities and opening its economy to the wider world.

The most vivid, and in many ways the most courageous, examples of white prophetic preaching resulted from the civil rights struggle of the 1950s and 1960s. In the cities, towns, and villages of the South there were white ministers of all denominations who brought the struggle for civil rights into their pulpits. They did so at some risk, but also with great effect. Commenting on the role of the ministry in the Little Rock AR school crisis of 1957, Ernest Q. Campbell and Thomas F. Pettigrew maintained that "the Protestant ministry is potentially the most effective agent of social change in the South in the decade ahead." Donald W. Shriver, Jr., who edited a collection of sermons preached in the context of the civil rights movement, questions the notion that ministers were "the single most effective agent of social change," but nonetheless sees the prophetic preaching of this period as one among several factors that influenced the profound social changes that occurred in the South. The question faced by progressive white ministers of the day, according to Shriver, was, "How can one execute the difficult maneuver of seeking to modify a culture while standing within it?"

Presbyterian minister John Lyles, in a 1957 sermon entitled "Amos Diagnoses Our Southern Sickness," attempted precisely that "difficult maneuver": to stand, as a pastor, within the culture of the South while, at the same time, allowing the biblical message to call that culture into question. His sermon, similar to many others preached during this period, said in part: "God has brought us to this hour. In our sickness he is at work. In the midst of turmoil he is calling his people to stand firmly for justice, equality, and love. From this sickness our church and the South will either recover and move into a period of robust good health in race relations or go into a relapse whose course cannot be predicted."

That quote comes from the first of two sermons Lyles had planned to preach to his congregation, the Marion (SC) Presbyterian Church. After the first sermon was preached, however, the leaders of the congregation met with Lyles and together they agreed to issue this statement in the following week's church bulletin:

> Although the Session does not agree with Mr. Lyles' sermon last Sunday, we affirm his rights to preach the Gospel as God leads him to do. However, because of present conditions in our church, and without in any way restricting the freedom of the pulpit, we have asked him not to preach his second sermon on race relations and he has concurred.

Strained pastoral relationships like those experienced by Lyles were not uncommon among white Southern ministers who spoke prophetically on racial matters, but congregations varied widely in their responses to prophetic preaching. There have been, in fact, three types of responses to the prophetic preaching tradition in the South. Some Southerners have embraced the prophetic message along with all of its impulses against the dominant Southern culture. Indeed, there are in the South today congregations, black and white, that have self-consciously gathered around such preaching and have gained their congregational identity over against the prevalent cultural and religious pattern of attitudes and values.

The second type of response has been outright rejection of the prophetic tendency. Sometimes this resistance comes in the form of the doctrine of the SPIRITUALITY OF THE CHURCH, a radical separation of the affairs of this world from the affairs of the world-to-come. A companion view is that the Christian faith is a "personal matter" rather than a corporate or social reality. Dabbs suggests another reason why many Southerners do not want politics and public matters brought into the pulpit: During the Civil War Southern preachers made "a terrible mistake" when they claimed from the pulpit that God was blessing both slavery and the Southern cause. Though Southerners have generally forgotten the origins of their strong tendencies toward church-state separation, claims Dabbs, the effects of defeat and moral humiliation linger powerfully.

There has been, however, a third and more common response by Southerners to prophetic preaching. This is the response of ambivalence, the kind of ambivalence shown by the leaders of the Marion Presbyterian Church. While resisting the prophetic voice, Southerners still hear it speaking to their "secret heart," feel the words touching the crevices of moral self-doubt. God who redeems the land also judges the land. Southerners have believed this more deeply, perhaps, than the people of any other region; and this has placed them in the complex, sometimes incomprehensible, position of both opposing and respecting, defying and nourishing the prophetic word. For Southerners, the deepest truth is that the prophetic voice is a troubling voice, but it is God's voice and it must never be stilled.

The Southern Preacher as Evangelist. Southern preachers have functioned in the role of sage, explicating the common values of religion and culture, and they have been prophets, calling the culture into question. The oldest, and still the most prevalent, image for Southern preachers has been that of evangelist: the one who calls for personal repentance, conversion, and loyalty to the cause of Christ.

Those accustomed to viewing the South as the evangelical "Bible Belt" of the nation often find it difficult to grasp that, prior to the 19th century, the South was not a particularly religious region.

The Episcopal Church, which Cash has described as "an exotic in America," found itself somewhat out of touch with the needs and the emotions of the common people of the South. As a result, its influence was largely confined to the older, more sophisticated coastal settlements, while in the back country of the South, religious tolerance, or perhaps indifference, prevailed.

In England, however, the Wesleys and their "Methodist Movement" had made an evangelical impact upon Anglicanism, and Anglican missionaries to America provided the South with some of its earliest evangelistic preaching. Among these early evangelists was GEORGE WHITEFIELD, who was widely considered to be the most influential preacher of his day. Between 1737 and 1770 Whitefield traveled to America seven times, preaching not only in the South, but in New England as well. Though Calvinistic in theology, Whitefield was passionate and enthusiastic in style and spirit and his preaching services had a revivalistic flavor. "I know that many of you come here out of curiosity: though you come only to see the congregation," Whitefield once preached. "Yet if you come to Jesus Christ, Christ will accept you."

The initial impact of Whitefield and other preachers like him was felt most keenly in New England, especially in the revival movements known collectively as the GREAT AWAKENING. The South did not experience the full power of these evangelistic stirrings until the turn of the 19th century. Between 1797 and 1805 a wave of religious fervor began to spread across the Southern frontier. The center of this activity was Logan County KY, a place once so notorious that it was known as "Rouges' Harbor." There, under the leadership of a Princeton-trained minister named JAMES MCGREADY, emotional, camp-meeting-style revivals were held. McGready had many converts: the laity were converted by his evangelistic message; the ministers present were converted to his evangelistic methods and

promptly adopted them in their own locales. Thus the fires of revival spread into Virginia and the Carolinas.

The most spectacular of the camp meeting revivals in the South was, without a doubt, the one held in August 1801 at CANE RIDGE in Kentucky. Organized by a Presbyterian minister named BARTON WARREN STONE, who was himself converted by the preaching of McGready, the Cane Ridge meeting was attended by a huge crowd, variously estimated at between 10 and 25 thousand people. This is to be viewed in light of the fact that the population of Lexington, then Kentucky's largest city, was barely two thousand.

What happened at Cane Ridge, in the words of Sydney E. Ahlstrom, "has challenged the descriptive powers of many historians, yet none has risen fully to the occasion." Thousands were caught up in the persuasive preaching and in the evangelistic enthusiasm of the crowds and hundreds responded with an outpouring of bodily jerks, frenzied dancing, barks and screams, uncontrollable laughter, and singing.

The events at Cane Ridge were controversial at the time and they remain so today. Some referred to it as "the greatest outpouring of the Spirit since Pentecost." While others, noting the presence of fleshly passions among the spiritual ones, alleged that "more souls were begat than saved." However the occurrences at Cane Ridge and at the other camp meeting revivals are judged, it is clear that they symbolized a new era and theme for religion in America, especially in the South. As Ahlstrom puts it, "The most important fact about Cane Ridge is that it was an unforgettable revival of revivalism, at a strategic time and a place where it could become both symbol and impetus for the century-long process by which the greater part of American evangelical Protestantism became revivalized."

What separates the South and Southern preaching from the rest of American religious life is not the *presence* of revivalism, but the *persistence* of it as a prominent characteristic of worship. The South has been distinctive as a region, according to Samuel S. Hill, Jr., by virtue of its "retaining, entrenching, and institutionalizing the frontier tradition of revivalism, during a time when Christianity in the North and West were being subjected to numerous modifying factors."

It probably cannot be said with certainty why the South has clung to the revivalist form of worship, and along with it the evangelistic form of preaching. Perhaps it is a product of the natural conservatism of a rural region, composed of few cities and many small farms. It may also be that the revivalist preacher appeals to a sense of deep personal guilt and to the need for the power of the Cross, religious expressions more vitally related to the Southern historical experience than they are to the history of any other part of America. Historian C. Vann Woodward has observed that, "The experience of evil and the experience of tragedy are parts of the Southern heritage that are as difficult to reconcile with the American legend of innocence and social felicity as the experience of poverty and defeat are to reconcile with the legends of abundance and success."

Whether or not it is true, as Louis Hartz has claimed, that the South in relation to the rest of the nation has been "an alien child in a liberal family, tortured and confused, driven to a fantasy life," it is certainly true that many Southerners have been driven to the altar of repentance. The South's tragic sense of history was reinforced, sometimes replaced, with a profound sense of personal guilt. The result was the rapid growth in the South of those denominations, black and white, whose preachers proclaimed a simple message of guilt and sin, blood and salvation, and whose worship, even when conducted behind stained glass and in fine brick buildings, still echoed the brush arbor and the camp meeting. There were several such groups, but the most prevalent were, and remain, the Methodists and the Baptists.

Among the Baptists, there were a number of preachers who rode the crest of the evangelical swell in the 19th century, but none was more notable than JOHN A. BROADUS. A Virginian born to Welsh parents in 1827, Broadus was converted at a revival meeting in the 1840s and soon left the profession of teaching to become pastor of a Baptist congregation in Charlottesville. Broadus's eloquent and evangelistic pulpit style brought him fame throughout the South. He blended the revivalist message with a deep and scholarly concern for expository, biblical preaching. He ended his career as a professor of homiletics and finally as president at the Baptist seminary in Louisville. For decades his textbook on preaching was used in the seminaries of several evangelical denominations and a revised edition is still used in a few seminaries today.

A 19th-century Methodist preacher who gained recognition throughout the South for his evangelistic preaching was SAMUEL P. JONES (1847-1906). Jones, an attorney turned minister, was noted for his vigorous condemnation of the "vices" of alcohol and cardplaying. "The law is what ought to be preached first," he maintained, "that conviction might follow." He conducted evangelistic meetings in many Southern towns and, ultimately, in public auditoriums in several Northern cities as well.

In the contemporary South, the image of the preacher as evangelist endures in many ways. It persists, first of all, in the regular worship services of the "low-church" denominations, as preachers routinely present the "plan of salvation" and call for the conversion and rededication of the hearers. Moreover, many congregations in the South continue the tradition of special revival "seasons" involving several days of preaching services with guest evangelists doing the preaching. Although briefer now than in the past, and not the townwide events they once were, these revival services are still the showcase for a type of evangelistic preacher reminiscent of frontier revivalism. In *Killers of the Dream*, LILLIAN SMITH remembers the visiting evangelists of her childhood as "remarkable storytellers, with a warm, near-riotous sense of humor; brilliantly adept with words. . . . We admired them and were influenced by them, for they had two of the essential qualities of leadership: They were free of personal anxiety, and they were close to their instinctual feelings. . . ."

The evangelistic impulse also can be discovered in the preaching of the textile congregations and the "non-mainline" denominations, such as the holiness groups and the Church of God. The preachers in these groups almost invariably "preach for the verdict" of conversion and their sermons sometimes are delivered in chanted form, rhythmic and songlike. Bruce A. Rosenberg, who has studied this preaching style, maintains that some of these sermons are often chanted to a rigorous metric and tonal formula and, as such, bear the marks of an authentic "folk art."

Finally, the evangelistic style can be seen beyond the boundaries of local congregations in the form of "professional evangelists," like BILLY GRAHAM, who conduct modern versions of the camp meetings in football stadiums and high school gymnasiums. Graham, who is perhaps the best-known minister in America, has exported his evangelistic preaching and revival methods, cultivated in the South, all over the world. Raised as a Presbyterian, Graham later joined the Baptists, a group more accepting of his own conversion experience and more amenable to his sense of evangelistic calling and conversion-oriented style of preaching. Graham's preaching, now adapted to the demands of the electronic media and often criticized for its lack of social concern, still embodies the essential characteristics of Southern revivalism: an

appeal to a personal sense of guilt and sinfulness, a call for repentance, and the invitation to make a "decision for Christ."

Sage, prophet, and evangelist—these are the indelible images of the Southern preacher. Even as one image gains ascendancy, as is inevitably the case, the others remain, waiting their own time, hidden in the fabric of the gospel that is preached and in the consciousness of the preachers who serve that gospel. The differences in preaching styles and emphases have been noted and explored, but what must finally be observed and wondered at is the commonality. For Southerners—white and black, slave and free, Presbyterian, Methodist, and Baptist—the sage, the prophet, and the evangelist have come together in a remarkable alloy: the personality of the preacher.

See also articles on EVANGELICAL PROTESTANTISM; EVANGELICALISM; PURITANISM; THEOLOGY.

Bibliography. Sydney E. Ahlstrom, *A Religious History of the American People*; Walter Brueggemann, *The Prophetic Imagination*; Ernest Q. Campbell and Thomas F. Pettigrew, *Christians in Racial Crisis: A Study of Little Rock's Ministry*; W. J. Cash, *The Mind of the South*; James McBride Dabbs, *Who Speaks for the South?*; Eugene D. Genovese, *Roll Jordan Roll*; Samuel S. Hill, Jr., *Southern Churches in Crisis*; E. Brooks Holifield, *The Gentlemen Theologians: American Theology in Southern Culture*; Charles C. Jones, *The Religious Instruction of the Negro in the United States*; Bruce A. Rosenberg, *The Art of the American Folk Preacher*; Donald W. Shriver, Jr., ed., *The Unsilent South: Prophetic Preaching in Racial Crisis*; Francis Butler Simkins, *The South, Old and New: A History*; Lillian Smith, *Killers of the Dream*; Hubert Vance Taylor, "Preaching on Slavery, 1931-1961," *Preaching in American History*, ed. Dewitte Holland; F. R. Webber, *A History of Preaching in Britain and America*, vol. 3; C. Vann Woodward, *The Burden of Southern History*.

THOMAS G. LONG
PRINCETON THEOLOGICAL SEMINARY

PREDESTINATION. In the history of Christianity no doctrine has caused more controversy than predestination. This controversy reached such a heated level in the 18th century that John Wesley ordered the Methodist clergy not to preach it. The Southern part of the United States has not been exempt from this controversy. Unfortunately many people abstracted predestination from its proper framework, the salvation given by God, to that of a metaphysical argument. Sometimes argument over this issue within a given denomination (Baptist, Methodist, and Presbyterian) has been as intense and divisive as it has been between different denominations.

In the American South, Christians have tended to be Calvinist, of one variety or another (infralapsarian, supralapsarian, or hypothetical universalist), or Arminian (prevenient grace, free will, or synergist). Calvin's classic statement of the doctrine is: "Predestination we call the eternal decree of God, by which he has determined in himself, what he would have to become of every individual of mankind. For they are not all created with a similar destiny; but eternal life is foreordained for some, and eternal damnation for others. Every man, therefore, being created for one or the other of these ends, is, we say, predestined either to life or to death." (*Institutes*, 3:xxi:5)

Calvin's influence in the South has been greatest among Particular, Regular, United, Primitive, and other "hard shell" Baptists and among Scotch-Irish Presbyterians. The doctrine was stated for these groups even more vigorously by Calvin's friend, the Scot, John Knox. Many Baptists and Presbyterians came into the South in the 18th century with a belief in absolute unconditional double predestination within the context of the doctrines of original sin, total depravity, and grace through Christ's vicarious sacrifice. This doctrinal emphasis fit into the Calvinist scheme of salvation, which glorified the Creator and assessed the creature in lowly, or even harsh, terms. Calvin's disciples split over whether God decreed each individual's destiny before creation (supralapsarianism) or after the fall of Adam in the Garden of Eden (infralapsarianism).

Not all the Christians who moved into the South were Calvinist, however. General Baptists, Methodists, Episcopalians, and others were very critical of the harshness of the Calvinist doctrine. They thought it made God the author of sin and, further, was prone towards antinomianism. These Christians, through teaching that Christ died for all sinners and that each person through the gift of prevenient grace can freely choose salvation, believe that in so doing they protect God's attributes of love and justice and protect each individual's dignity and freedom. Some others emphasize that God conditionally offers salvation to all men, foreknowing who would accept it or reject it. Still others, especially PRIMITIVE BAPTISTS, state that we must preach the hope and the promise of the Gospel, which is "Jesus came into the world to save all of humanity from sin." Even to mention reprobation is to go beyond the Gospel.

Throughout the South the debate goes on between election and/or reprobation, particular and general atonement, determinism and free will, absolute and conditional predestination, and God's glory and the happiness of human beings.

See also articles on ARMINIANISM; ATONEMENT; CALVINISM; PRESBYTERIANISM; SALVATION.

RICHARD ALAN HUMPHREY
JOHNSON CITY, TENNESSEE

PRESBYTER. The word presbyter comes from the Greek *presbuteros*, "older person" or "elder." The word is used in the New Testament to refer to an administrative office in the early church (Acts 11:30, 14:23, 15:22). Different forms of church government emerged in the history of the church as a result of the question whether this office was identical with or distinguished from that of *episcopos*, "overseer," "superintendent," or "bishop" (Acts 20:28, Phil. 1:1). Presbyterian churches believe that these offices were the same and appeal to their original identity to defend representative rather than hierarchical church government.

In Presbyterian churches a presbyter is a person elected to participate in the legislative and judicial work of the various "courts" of the church—PRESBYTERY (a court composed of presbyters from all the individual churches in a district), SYNOD (a court composed of presbyters from all the presbyteries in a larger area), and GENERAL ASSEMBLY (the highest court, composed of presbyters from each presbytery in the denomination). Presbyters are called COMMISSIONERS rather than "representatives" because they are sent not to serve the wishes of those who elected them but to discover the will of God in the debates and consensus of an assembled court. They are ministers, sometimes called teaching elders, and laymen and women who are elected by a congregation to be ruling elders. Clergy and laity have equal representation and authority in a church court. Although a presbyter is an "elder," it is not advanced age but maturity, moral and spiritual integrity, competence, and commitment that qualify one for the office.

See also article on PRESBYTERIANISM.

SHIRLEY C. GUTHRIE, JR.
COLUMBIA THEOLOGICAL SEMINARY

PRESBYTERIAN BODIES: See UNITED PRESBYTERIAN CHURCH.

PRESBYTERIAN CHURCH IN AMERICA. This conservative denomination was formed in December 1973 chiefly from dissenting people and congregations that had belonged to the PRESBYTERIAN CHURCH, U.S. For its first year, the denomination called itself the National Presbyterian Church. At its origin the PCA claimed 75,000 members and 200 congregations. In 1979 it reported 82,095 members in 440 congregations served by 584 ministers.

The denomination has perceived itself as "a strongly Scriptural, evangelical, and Reformed witness to Christ." Its directory listed congregations and missions throughout many states beyond the South than its parent body, the PCUS.

A portion of the PCUS, since at least the time of Reconstruction, had articulated an understanding of the spirituality of the church, which sought to resist corporate statements or other forms of support for any social or political movements. Some Presbyterians with conviction, for example, resisted the temperance movement on this ground—that it interfered with social practice in the name of religion. More frequently, though, the spirituality doctrine served to excuse believers from seeking social change or political reform. Many saw no conflict between the doctrine and American patriotism, Anglo-Saxon racism, or other ingredients in U.S. conservatism.

When the struggle began to obtain civil rights for black people in this country, the PCUS took sometimes hesitant but nevertheless definite steps in favor of efforts to integrate the schools and churches in the South. Proponents of spirituality resisted this stance and considered it a violation of the rightful place of the church in society. The Presbyterian Journal (1942-) argued that the PCUS in this and other issues had departed from its historic tradition. Subsequent decisions in the PCUS to ordain women as ruling elders, then as ministers, and to cooperate in the ecumenical movement were also condemned. The Journal called for another direction in the denomination and threatened withdrawal if the "social teachings" did not change.

In 1964, Concerned Presbyterians, Inc. began gathering similarly minded groups as a focus for PCUS "conservatism." Its leadership overlapped with that of the Journal, and it tried to extricate the PCUS from ecumenical affiliations, and its involvement in such "affairs of the world." Declaring that it espoused "plenary, verbal inspiration" of the Bible and a return to the Westminster Standards, the Concerned Presbyterians moved to separate institutionally from the PCUS when union talks with the UNITED PRESBYTERIAN CHURCH IN THE UNITED STATES OF AMERICA took place, and when the PCUS began contemplating a narrative "Declaration of Faith."

Other groups urging withdrawal from the PCUS were a Presbyterian Evangelical Fellowship and Presbyterian Churchmen United.

According to ecumenical sources, the PCA is a member of the North American Presbyterian and Reformed Council. It cooperates with the Orthodox Presbyterian Church in some publications.

A "Vanguard Presbytery" was formed in 1972 of independent congregations and several particular churches seeking to withdraw from the PCUS. This provisional judicatory convoked conferences that prepared for the 1973 meeting of the new General Assembly. A number of congregations have joined from other Presbyterian bodies and the PCA has budgeted funds for mission efforts in American cities. Significant leaders in the formation of the PCA have included G. Aiken Taylor, longtime editor of the *Presbyterian Journal* and Kenneth S. Keyes, president of the Concerned Presbyterians, Inc. at its inception. In 1979, the PCA voted not to engage in talks that could lead to merger with the Orthodox Presbyterian Church or other such bodies.

LOUIS WEEKS
LOUISVILLE PRESBYTERIAN SEMINARY

PRESBYTERIAN CHURCH IN THE UNITED STATES (PCUS). Originally the Presbyterian Church in the Confederate States of America (PCCSA), this denomination was formed in 1861 as a result of the Civil War. In an 1861 address to the Christians of the world, the denomination claimed a special mission to witness to the "spirituality" of the Church. It remained separated from the parent body for 122 years, the Presbyterian Church in the United States of America (PCUSA; since 1958, the United Presbyterian Church in the United States of America, UPCUSA). Merger was approved in 1983, to be effective in 1987. This was so in part because of the bitterness of Reconstruction politics and because Presbyterians in the North violated this "spirituality" by an inappropriate involvement in the political processes. The PCCSA itself vigorously supported slavery and the

Confederacy. The PCUS is now found in the Southeast with many congregations in border states and in Texas. Its Constitution includes Confessions and provisions about Order, Discipline, and Worship.

Doctrine: Although named for its polity, theologically the denomination shares with Protestant Christians the view that the Scriptures of the Old and New Testaments are the only "rule of faith and practice," and accepts the Trinitarian and Christological formulas of the early Christian councils. As a subordinate standard to the Bible, the PCUS adopted and its officers subscribe to the WESTMINSTER CONFESSION OF FAITH (1646) and the Larger and Shorter Catechisms. Certain teachings have been modified or amplified over the years. In 1788, for example, American Presbyterians removed the Erastian position of the original Confession when they organized a General Assembly in the United States. In 1942 (following confessional revisions made by the PCUSA in 1903), the PCUS adopted amendments to the Confession on the work of the Holy Spirit and of God's love for the whole world, placing in a larger perspective the concept of predestination, an emphasis of an earlier Calvinism. JAMES HENLEY THORNWELL (1818-1862), ROBERT LEWIS DABNEY (1820-1898), and JAMES WOODROW (1828-1907) made formative impacts upon the thought of the denomination, the latter being disciplined for his moderate acceptance of evolution in the 1880s. Basically conservative, the PCUS escaped bruising theological controversy in the 1920s. Along with other leaders, church historian Ernest Trice Thompson (1894-) and biblical scholar John Bright (1908-) helped members to deal with recent intellectual currents. In 1975-1976 an effort was made to modify the confessional stand with the adoption of a Book of Confessions along with a contemporary statement entitled "A Declaration of Faith." A General Assembly committee headed by Albert C. Winn (1921-) led a denominationwide discussion, but the proposal failed to gain the three-fourths vote of the presbyteries needed for the change. The Declaration is widely used throughout the church, however.

Polity: The polity of the PCUS is presbyterian, and its provisions are found in the *Book of Church Order*, which contains the Form of Government and the Rules of Discipline. This order was first adopted in 1879 after many years of debate and revised significantly in 1925, 1945, and 1961. It is a representative system with a graded court structure—an intermediate position between congregationalism and episcopacy. Congregations elect pastors, elders, and deacons who are ordained in the name of the Trinity and with the laying on of hands. Pastors are ordained to the ministry of the word and sacraments; elders, to aid in governing the church; deacons, to the ministry of sympathy and service. Congregations are organized in presbyteries made up of pastors and elders; presbyteries are organized in synods and a General Assembly, the highest court, with responsibilities for review and the general welfare of the whole body. The latter usually meets once a year and is made up of pastors and elders elected by the presbyteries. The PCUS has expanded the importance of the elder, who now participates in the ordination of pastors. The elder may serve as moderator of the three highest courts, and under certain conditions preach and administer the sacraments. Since 1963 women have been ordained to all these offices.

In 1861 the General Assembly, eager to control its own functions between meetings, created executive committees for domestic and foreign missions, education and publication, and to deal with its pension system. In 1949 this work, including women's activities, was finally organized under boards. Since a 1972 restructuring, the General Assembly Mission Board has coordinated the denomination's concerns in these areas. The moderators of the church's courts and the leaders of these agencies have a functional and not a sacerdotal status. STUART ROBINSON (1814-1881), BENJAMIN M. PALMER (1818-1902), and MOSES DRURY HOGE (1818-1899) were pastors who gave considerable leadership to the denomination, while in the 20th century John J. Eagan (1870-1924) and Francis Pickens Miller (1895-1978) played leading roles as laymen. In 1963 Rachel Henderlite (1905-) became the first woman to be ordained as a minister by the denomination.

Worship: Since the Westminster Assembly in the 1640s Presbyterians have been suspicious of fixed forms of worship. The "Directory for the Worship and Work of the Church" adopted in 1963 followed a pattern of giving counsel that was established in the Westminster Assembly's *Directory of Worship*. The *Directory* was modified by American Presbyterians in 1788 and numerous times thereafter. Presbyterians have encouraged worship in ways that are biblically sound, simple, intelligible, and spiritually edifying. His emphasis has been on the reading and interpretation of the Scripture through the sermon, the two sacraments of baptism and the Lord's Supper. Infants as well as adults are baptized, usually by sprinkling. The Lord's Supper is celebrated at least quarterly and sometimes more often. The bread and the cup are served by pastors and elders and usually passed from one communicant to another. Directions are also given for the work of evangelism, education, stewardship of possessions, and the service of God in daily occupations. Throughout its history, the PCUS has resisted aspects of REVIVALISM so prevalent in the South, and also high church tendencies popular in the 19th century. In 1903 the PCUSA commended for "voluntary use" a *Book of Common Worship*, and in 1932 the PCUS followed suit and allowed the use of the *Book* by congregations seeking an enrichment of liturgical practices. Since 1903, the *Book* has been revised considerably. For many years Presbyterians sang nothing but the Psalms, but in the 18th and 19th centuries hymns of "human composure" were introduced into worship. The most widely used volume of hymns is *The Hymnbook* (1955), which has a range of verses and music, as well as many Psalms.

Mission: In the years following the Civil War the denomination placed an emphasis on rebuilding damaged institutions and on planting churches throughout the South, including those among blacks and Indians. Moreover, under the leadership of J. Leighton Wilson (1809-1886) and others, it developed missions in China, Japan, Korea, Columbia, Brazil, Mexico, Africa, Greece, and Italy. Among its most noted missionaries were Hampden C. DuBose (1845-1910), who opposed the opium trade in the East; W. M. Morrison (1867-1918) and William H. Sheppard (1865-1927), who protested injustices to black people in the Belgian Congo (Zaire); John Leighton Stuart (1876-1962), ambassador to China after World War II; and L. Nelson Bell (1894-1973), medical missionary and prominent layman who helped to found *Christianity Today*.

The denomination has also engaged in educational work, founding four theological seminaries—Union, Richmond VA (1823); Columbia, Decatur GA (1928); Louisville (1901); and Austin (1902); and several liberal arts colleges, the oldest being Hampden-Sydney (1776) and Stillman for blacks (1876-1877). In 1914 the General Assembly organized a training school in Richmond for purposes of teaching religious education. It is now known as the Presbyterian School of Christian Education. The *Presbyterian Survey* (1911-) has served as the official magazine and the John Knox Press has published popular and scholarly books under the auspices of the denomination. *Interpretation*, began in 1947, is a widely circulated quarterly of Bible and theology published by Union Theological Seminary in Richmond.

Long associated with the Sunday school movement, the PCUS experimented with the Covenant Life Curriculum in 1963, a venture in cooperation with other denominations. LEWIS SHERRILL (1882-1957) was one of the denomination's leading educators. Gradually the denomination gave a broader interpretation to the meaning of the "spirituality" of the church under the leadership of such people as Walter L. Lingle (1868-1956), president of Davidson College, and E. T. Thompson. The General Assembly established a Committee on Moral and Social Welfare in 1934 during the Depression years. This committee, under different names, in succeeding years has instructed the consciences of the members about larger societal problems, such as war, poverty, race, and human sexuality. The PCUS has taken a strong stand against segregation and racism in the South and the nation.

Gradually drawn out of its regional isolation into ecumenism, the denomination became a member of a pan-Presbyterian organization called the World Alliance of Reformed Churches in 1876-1877, the Federal Council of Churches, 1912, the National Council of Churches, 1950, and the World Council of Churches in 1948, although its association with the last three bodies has been uneasy at times. During the Civil War it united with several smaller Presbyterian bodies, yet it has been unable to reunite with the body from which it separated in 1861. Fraternal relations were finally established in 1883, and the two denominations began to practice comity arrangements. In the 1930s they began to discuss reunion and plans were submitted to the presbyteries in 1954-1955. These plans were defeated because they failed to gain the three-fourth vote of the presbyteries needed for such a union. In 1969 the constitution was amended to allow joint PCUS and UPCUSA presbyteries. A number of union presbyteries exist in border areas. Black congregations of the UPCUSA exist within the bounds of the PCUS—a result of mission work after the Civil War—and the presence of these churches complicates the quest for reunion. Another attempt was being made to bring together the churches on the basis of a common confession. Then in 1983 merger was approved.

Although largely white, middle and upper class, and professionally oriented, the denomination does embrace a variety of other races and classes of people within its constituency. As of 1979, it listed 852,711 communicant members, 4,067 churches, and 5,431 ministers.

See also articles on CALVINISM; PRESBYTERIANISM; UNITED PRESBYTERIAN CHURCH.

Bibliography. Ernest Trice Thompson, *Presbyterians in the South*, 3 vols.

JAMES H. SMYLIE
UNION SEMINARY IN VIRGINIA

PRESBYTERIAN CHURCH (U.S.A.).

In 1983 a new Presbyterian body came into being. On 10 June of that year, the 122-year-old separation of the Presbyterian Church in the United States (Southern) and the United Presbyterian Church in the United States of America (Northern) was brought to an end.

The newly created denomination had a total membership of 3,166,050 with 21,255 ministers nationwide. The PCUS (Southern) boasted 814,931 members and 6,077 ordained ministers were from that body. Some Presbyterians living in the South had belonged to synods of the UPCUSA, inasmuch as the Northern church had maintained some pre-1961 congregations in the South, most notably in East Tennessee and northern Alabama. Dually affiliated presbyteries existed in several places, such as Texas, Oklahoma, Missouri, and Kentucky.

Here and there black congregations belonged to the Northern Church. All told, about 40 percent of the 3.16 million members live in the area of the former PCUS, the South. Among the several national concentrations of Presbyterians, some are in the South, in Virginia, North Carolina, Florida, and Texas.

Reasons for the long separation, now overcome, are many and complex. How-

ever, the two most salient are: (1) surviving sectional attitudes, once hostile but more recently habitual and provincial; (2) a tendency on the part of the Northern body to take more liberal positions than the South liked. Even so, when the vote was taken, 53 PCUS presbyteries approved and only eight opposed. On the second point, the Presbyterian Church in America (PCA) was organized in 1973 in protest against liberalism in the PCUS and, no doubt, in anticipation of the merger consummated in 1983.

10 June 1983, in Atlanta, was a red-letter day for most American Presbyterians. Some 15,000 people were present for the communion service uniting South and North, with many thousands of others participating through a nationwide television link.

PRESBYTERIANISM.

The Presbyterian denomination includes those churches throughout the world that are Calvinistic in theology and Presbyterian in church government. Rooted in the Reformed (or Swiss) branch of the Reformation, the denomination is generally called "Reformed" on the continent of Europe and "Presbyterian" in the British Isles. Although preceded and influenced by Huldreich Zwingli (1484-1531) of Zurich and others, the chief architect of Presbyterianism was John Calvin (1509-1564) who led the Reformation in Geneva, making it an international center of Protestantism.

Presbyterian theology, or CALVINISM, is based on the major tenets of the PROTESTANT REFORMATION: the final authority of the Bible for faith and practice, salvation by faith in God's grace rather than one's works, and the priesthood of believers. Calvin stressed the glory and sovereignty of God, which he understood in relation to God's holy and loving purposes. He interpreted the sovereignty of God as a practical teaching that assured believers living in difficult times that God is in control of events and reminded them that their own lives and the life of the church and society are to be brought into conformity with God's will. Believers are to understand that faith bears fruit in a life of active love toward God and neighbor and of moral purity. Efforts to reform the church centered on worship and church government and rested on two fundamental convictions: (1) that Christ is the only head of the church and thus that the church is to be conformed to his will as revealed in Scripture; (2) that the church consists of all believers rather than an elite priesthood.

Substantial reform of worship took place under the leadership of Zwingli, Calvin, John Knox, and others. These reforms stressed those elements that address worshipers' intellects and consciences rather than their senses and feelings, yet Presbyterian worship has often been deeply moving. Two sacraments, baptism and the Lord's Supper, were recognized, but were not to be celebrated apart from preaching. Further, it was insisted that the Lord's Supper is not a sacrifice made to God, but rather is a gift of God to the church through Jesus Christ. While these basic principles regarding worship have been stressed, congregations have been permitted considerable freedom in the forms of worship used. On the continent of Europe, Presbyterian worship has tended to be more formal than in the British Isles and America.

The Presbyterian church is governed by PRESBYTERS (from the Greek "presbyteros"), or elders, which is the origin of the name "Presbyterian." Calvin enunciated the basic principles of Presbyterian church government in his *Ecclesiastical Ordinances* and *Institutes of the Christian Religion.* Presbyterian polity provides that the communing members elect officials who govern the church in a graded series of "courts" or judicatories. The local congregation is governed internally by the SESSION, which is composed of the PASTOR (or teaching elder) and ruling elders who are elected from the laity. DEACONS, also elected from the laity, care for the

needy and administer the church's money and property, but are not part of the session. The PRESBYTERY, composed of all the pastors and one or more ruling elder from each church, supervises the churches of a district. At the regional level there is a SYNOD, consisting of three or more presbyteries; at the national level, there is the GENERAL ASSEMBLY. While details and terminology may differ, the foregoing is representative of Presbyterian polity.

Even before Calvin's death the impact of the Genevan Reformation was being felt in other parts of Europe. At a synod in Paris in 1559, the HUGUENOTS, as the Presbyterians of France are called, organized a national church on the basis of Presbyterian polity, thereby setting a pattern that was to be influential in the Netherlands, Scotland, and America. By 1571 there were 2,150 Huguenot congregations in France, but they experienced severe opposition which, with some periods of remission, lasted into the 18th century. Persecutions in the late seventeenth and early eighteenth century caused thousands of Huguenots to become refugees in the Netherlands and many other lands, including America. The Huguenot Church in France has remained vigorous but has not been numerically large.

Reformed (Presbyterian) congregations were associated with the cause of the Dutch provinces in their struggle for independence from Spanish rule that began in the 1560s. The Dutch Reformed Church was formed during this struggle, becoming the established church of the Netherlands. During the 17th century Calvinistic refugees from Scotland, England, and France found a haven in the Netherlands. Further, Dutch colonists took their faith with them to America, South Africa, and the Dutch possessions in the Pacific, Caribbean, and the Atlantic, thus spreading Presbyterianism.

The early strength of the Reformed (Presbyterian) Church in Germany was in the Palatinate where in 1563 the Heidelburg Catechism was produced. Although the Reformed Church spread to other territories, it remained a minority in Germany. However, the Reformed League's Barmen Synod in 1934 contributed to the formation of the Confessing Church, which maintained a witness independent of Hitler's regime. Despite some early successes the Reformed (Presbyterian) movement failed to establish sizable permanent communities in Eastern and Southern Europe, except in Hungary and areas of present Romania.

In Scotland, Protestantism triumphed under the leadership of John Knox (c. 1510-1572), a disciple of Calvin. Although Scotland was to become the center of Presbyterianism in the British Isles, it was only after a prolonged struggle that the Church of Scotland, in 1690, was established in Presbyterian form. This event, however, did not subdue concern among the Covenanters and Seceders about the state's interference in the appointment of pastors and alleged laxity in doctrine, which led to several secessions from the Church of Scotland. More unitive influences began to work in the mid-nineteenth century with the result that most Scottish Presbyterians now belong to the national church.

Presbyterianism, developed as part of the Puritan movement in England, has been a tiny minority in that nation since the late seventeenth century. Nevertheless, when Parliament convened Westminster Assembly in 1643, the English Presbyterians, supported by delegates from Scotland, dominated the Assembly, which composed the WESTMINSTER CONFESSION OF FAITH, the Larger and Shorter Catechisms, and the Directory of Worship. These documents were adopted by the Church of Scotland and later by Presbyterian bodies in America.

Presbyterianism was brought to Northern Ireland in the 17th century by Scottish settlers whose influence was augmented by English Puritan and French Huguenot immigrants. The Presbyterian Church had been the dominant ecclesiastical body there since that time. A small but vigorous Presbyterian church, the Welsh Calvinistic Methodist Church, which is Presbyterian in polity and Calvinistic in theology, developed in Wales in the 18th and 19th centuries. Further, Presbyterianism was spread to North America, Australia, New Zealand, and other parts of the British Empire.

In the 19th century Scottish immigrants brought Presbyterianism to Canada. Although Presbyterians joined Methodists and Congregationalists in forming the United Church of Canada in 1925, a minority preserved a denominational body, the Presbyterian Church in Canada.

The first presbytery of the largest Presbyterian Church in America was established by FRANCIS MAKEMIE of Northern Ireland in 1706, probably in Philadelphia. The first synod was established in 1716 and the General Assembly of the Presbyterian Church in the United States of America was founded in 1788. By 1800 the denomination was one of the most influential church bodies in the nation, not only because of its increasing membership but also its learned ministry, its contributions to education, and the service rendered by its ministers and members to the Revolutionary cause. Rapid growth in the 18th and 19th centuries resulted from the influx of immigrants with Presbyterian heritages from Northern Ireland, Scotland, England, and the continent of Europe, from the impetus provided by the great revivals, and by vigorous educational and missionary work, often carried out in close cooperation with the Congregationalists. The changing social, political, and intellectual environment of America contributed to controversies and, sometimes, schisms, including the Old Side/ New Side schism of 1741-1758, and the OLD SCHOOL/NEW SCHOOL schism of 1837/38-1869. At the beginning of the Civil War in 1861, Southern presbyteries withdrew to form the present PRESBYTERIAN CHURCH IN THE UNITED STATES (the Southern Presbyterian Church). Although American Presbyterians in the 20th century have continued to experience differences and even divisions over theology, biblical interpretation, and the role of the church in society, unitive forces have been at work as well.

While the largest number of American Presbyterians belong to what was originally the UNITED PRESBYTERIAN CHURCH IN THE UNITED STATES OF AMERICA, or churches that grew out of it, there are two other branches of the Presbyterian family of churches in America. One of these branches has its roots in the Covenanter and Secession churches of Scotland and includes, among others, the General Synod of the ASSOCIATE REFORMED PRESBYTERIAN CHURCH, located in the South, and included the former United Presbyterian Church of North America. The latter body merged with the Presbyterian Church in the United States of America in 1958 to form the United Presbyterian Church in the United States of America. The other branch of Presbyterianism comprises churches from the continent of Europe, the largest being the Reformed (Dutch) Church of America, which dates from the organization of its first congregation in New Amsterdam in 1628.

The influence of Presbyterianism has reached beyond strictly religious concerns to many areas of life, particularly to education, politics, and economics. Presbyterians have stressed education in order to equip ministers to preach and lay persons to read the Bible, and to prepare people to be useful in the community. Further, they have believed that all truth, including that found through science and philosophy, is from God and thus is worthy of study. Following Calvin's example of founding the academy in Geneva, Presbyterians have supported public education and founded educational institutions in many lands. Before the Civil War in America, Presbyterians founded 49 colleges, more than any other denomination.

In politics, fundamental Presbyterian beliefs about God and humanity contributed to the development of democratic

ideals and institutions. Absolutism, whether in church or state, has been opposed as a usurpation of God's sovereignty and an injustice to the people. Belief in the universality of sin has contributed to the establishment of constitutional monarchies and democratic states with checks and balances in order that the self-interest of those in power might be restrained. Further, since these beliefs found early expression in the Presbyterian form of church government, Presbyterians often have been predisposed to support similar structures in the state.

Much research remains to be done regarding the complex relationships between Calvinism and the rise of capitalism. While Calvin did teach that one should do one's work with diligence, this must not be for private advantage, as in later free enterprise theories, but for the sake of community, especially for those in need. However, societies in which Calvinism has been strong have been marked by the energy and diligence of their people and generally have been in the forefront of commercial, industrial, scientific, and technological developments.

Calvin's insistence that all of life should be conformed to the will of God has given Presbyterians a strong sense of responsibility for the health of society, and when the biblical emphases of the Reformation period have been remembered there has been special concern for the poor and helpless. Thus while Presbyterians have taken various positions regarding social issues, many of them have played important roles in most reform efforts, including abolition, the Social Gospel, civil and women's rights movements, as well as the more recent peace movements.

Vigorous missionary work in large areas of Asia, Africa, Central and South America, and the Pacific Islands has made Presbyterianism a worldwide denomination. Some churches in former missionary lands, such as the Presbyterian Church in the Republic of Korea, are now large and active bodies. Presbyterianism is worldwide in another sense as well, in that many of its member churches have supported and provided key leadership for the modern ecumenical movement. W. A. Visser't Hooft of the Reformed Churches of the Netherlands was the first general secretary of the World Council of Churches, a post in which he was succeeded by Eugene Carson Blake of the United Presbyterian Church in the United States of America.

Bibliography. Maurice W. Armstrong, Lefferts A. Loetscher, and Charles A. Anderson, eds., *The Presbyterian Enterprise: Sources of American Presbyterian History*; Roland H. Bainton, *The Reformation of the Sixteenth Century*; Theodore H. Bozeman, *Protestants in an Age of Science: The Baconian Ideal and Antebellum American Religious Thought*; Arthur Dakin, *Calvinism*; Harold J. Grimm, *The Reformation Era: 1500-1650*; George D. Henderson, *Presbyterianism*; John H. Leith, *Introduction to the Reformed Tradition*; Lefferts A. Loetscher, *A Brief History of Presbyterianism*; John T. McNeill, *The History and Character of Calvinism*; William T. Maxwell, *An Outline of Christian Worship: Its Development and Forms*; James Moffatt, *The Presbyterian Churches*; James Hastings Nichols, *Corporate Worship in the Reformed Tradition*; Wilhelm Niesel, *The Theology of Calvin*; Elwyn A. Smith, *The Presbyterian Ministry in American Culture*; William W. Sweet, *Religion on the American Frontier: The Presbyterians*; Leonard J. Trinterud, *The Forming of an American Tradition: A Re-examination of Colonial Presbyterianism*.

WILLIAM R. HOYT
BERRY COLLEGE

PRESBYTERY. A presbytery is the central legislative and judicial body in Presbyterian churches. It is composed of all the ministers in a district together with lay men and women from each congregation who have been elected ruling elders in their congregation and are chosen by the session of their congregation to represent it at an assembly of the presbytery. (A SESSION is the governing body of an individual congregation composed of the minister and ministers, sometimes called teaching elders, and the ruling elders.) Ministers and lay people have equal authority. Both are called PRESBYTERS or COMMISSIONERS (the latter rather than "representatives" because they are charged not to represent the opinions and wishes of their congregations but are commissioned to seek at the presbytery meeting a consensus concerning the will of God).

Some of the most important functions of the presbytery are: (1) to exercise oversight over all the congregations under its jurisdiction; (2) to ordain ministers, approve their call to a particular congregation (the call itself being issued by majority vote of the congregation), supervise their work and if necessary dissolve the pastoral relationship between a minister and a congregation; (3) to act as an appeal court from sessions of individual churches; (4) to address petitions and overtures to higher courts (the SYNOD, a court composed of commissioners from a group of presbyteries, and the GENERAL ASSEMBLY, composed of commissioners from each of the presbyteries in the denomination); (5) to act on proposed changes in the polity and confessional standards of the denomination and on matters of faith, ethics, and public policy referred to the presbyteries by the general assembly, a stipulated percentage of positive votes from the presbyteries being necessary to approve the general assembly's recommendations or decisions.

See also article on PRESBYTERIANISM.

SHIRLEY C. GUTHRIE, JR.
COLUMBIA THEOLOGICAL SEMINARY

PRESIDENTS FROM THE SOUTH: *See* CARTER, JAMES EARL; JEFFERSON, THOMAS; JOHNSON, LYNDON B.; LINCOLN, ABRAHAM; MADISON, JAMES; TRUMAN, HARRY S; WILSON WOODROW.

PRIEST. This is the title given to the primary functioning officers of the several "catholic" churches. By virtue of ordination through laying on of hands, the priest is one designated and empowered to be minister of word and sacrament, teacher of the faith, and leader of the local Christian community.

In the Roman Catholic, Orthodox, and Anglican faiths, the priest is understood to belong to one of three grades of sacramental ministry referred to as "Holy Orders," those grades or orders being the diaconate, priesthood, and episcopacy (bishopric). In all three faiths the term "priest" belongs principally and primordially to Christ, as does the term "sacrament." The ordained priesthood is seen as a sacramental manifestation or actualization of the priesthood of Jesus Christ.

Since the Church itself is a kind of sacrament, the priestly ministry, in its proclamation of the Good News and celebration of the Sacraments of Christ, may be seen as actualizing and expressing the broad sacramental reality of the Church. The priest's ministry also has specific reference to the Sacraments, whether the number is regarded as seven or two.

It would seem that Jesus avoided applying the term "priest" to himself. His own life and mission, while being essentially priestly, was not linked to a particular priestly tribe or to a hereditary caste. In that sense his priesthood was a radically new kind of priesthood, as seen most clearly in the Book of Hebrews. In the New Testament the term "priest" is nowhere applied to the disciples of Jesus either, reflecting similarly the radical departure from the priesthood existing before Jesus. By the end of the second century, when Christian terminology of the Eucharist as "sacrifice" came into use, the term "priest" began to be applied in reference to the bishop. Gradually the term was applied to the presbyters, the priests of the second grade.

The Orthodox and Roman Catholic faiths and some theologians among the Anglican faith hold to the necessity of an unbroken continuity with Christ through the apostles and the generations of their successors. This is the doctrine of Apostolic Succession. The office of bishop is the agency of continuity and authority; thus a bishop must ordain.

Published reports from several recent ecumenical consultations have addressed themselves to the topic of ordained ministry: Lutheran-Roman Catholic, Methodist-Roman Catholic, Orthodox-Roman Catholic, Anglican-Roman Catholic, and Presbyterian/Reformed-Roman Catholic. A surprising amount of agreement has been reached on areas formerly subject to controversy. Areas where

different doctrinal positions are held center around such topics as the possibility of ordination of women, apostolic succession, and different understandings of what constitutes sacramentality.

See also article on ROMAN CATHOLICISM.

Bibliography. Raymond Brown, *Priest and Bishop*; Bishop Dmitri, *Orthodox Christian Teaching: An Introduction to the Orthodox Faith*; Jean Galot, *Un Nuovo Volto del Prete*; Richard P. McBrien, *Catholicism*, vol. 2; John Macquarrie, *Principles of Christian Theology*; Jerome Quinn, "Ministry in the New Testament," *Lutherans and Catholics in Dialogue IV: Eucharist and Ministry*; Timothy Ware, *The Orthodox Church*.

ROBERT J. BAKER
ST. VINCENT DE PAUL
REGIONAL SEMINARY

PRIMITIVE BAPTISTS. A conservative religious denomination strongly concentrated in the South but rather widely dispersed throughout the nation. The ANTIMISSION MOVEMENT of the early nineteenth century gave rise to this group, which represents a protest against "man-made" organizations in the churches. Before the advent of mission societies, Baptists of the South had been almost uniformly committed to the doctrine of particular election. The appearance after 1820 of mission organizations, seminaries, and Sunday schools introduced into many churches and associations a controversy related to this tenet. Opponents argued that such institutions did not exist in apostolic times and, therefore, were unjustifiable. They also regarded the centralization of power in them as inconsistent with the spirit of the gospel.

Among the associations in which this dissent first erupted was the KEHUKEE ASSOCIATION of North Carolina. In 1827 it discarded "all Missionary Societies, Bible Societies and Theological Seminaries, and the practices heretofore resorted to for their support, in begging money from the public" and characterized such agencies as "not warranted from the word of God." Here and there other associations took the same action or broke into two parts. By 1840 the Baptist garment had been rent. Churches and associations that objected to these "human inventions" generally called themselves Old-School Baptists and in time Primitive Baptists.

Primitive Baptists hold firmly to the doctrine of predestination. The atonement of Christ is seen as limited. The sovereign God elected the saints for salvation before the foundation of the world. By his Holy Spirit he effectually calls them from their sins, regenerates them, and causes them to persevere in grace. These Baptists consider their doctrine Calvinistic but contend that its origin antedates Calvin and derives from a biblical position. Also, they do not believe all that the reformer taught.

In polity, Primitive Baptists are congregational. The only biblical officers of the church are elders and deacons. Baptism is administered by immersion. Only the baptized may participate in the Lord's Supper, which is observed at stated intervals by the use of red wine and unleavened bread. Probably half the Southern churches practice the washing of the saints' feet. Most congregations are affiliated with a district association.

Within this nationwide communion there are at least four identifiable divisions. The largest segment of communicants holds to the traditional doctrines and practices of Primitive Baptists. It numbers about 53,000 members in 1,565 churches. Its greatest strengths are found in Georgia and Alabama.

The second group is marked by a belief in the absolute predestination of all things that come to pass, whether good or evil. Its some 7,000 members are organized into 390 congregations and are more numerous in North Carolina and Virginia than in any other states.

A "Progressive" element—composed of 162 churches and about 10,000 members—maintains Sunday schools and youth organizations and uses instrumental music in worship. Its greatest numbers are located in Georgia and Florida.

A fourth division consists of black people whose churches are associated with the National Primitive Baptist Convention of the United States of America, organized in 1907.

See also articles on CALVINISM; FOOTWASHING; PREDESTINATION.

Bibliography. A. B. Hall, *Primitive Baptist Statistics, 1974*, 2 vols.; Cushing Biggs Hassell and Sylvester Hassell, *History of the Church of God..., Including Especially the History of the Kehukee Primitive Baptist Association*; Byron Cecil Lambert, *The Rise of the Anti-Mission Baptists: Sources and Leaders, 1800-1840*; Jerry A. Newsome, *A Modest History of [Progressive] Primitive Baptists in the United States*; Arthur Carl Piepkorn, "The Primitive Baptists of North America," *Concordia Theological Monthly* 42 (May 1971): 297-314.

CHESTER RAYMOND YOUNG
CUMBERLAND COLLEGE

PRIMITIVE CHRISTIANITY: *See* RESTORATIONISM.

PROHIBITION. Rum, cider, and later distilled whiskey were regular parts of the diet of most American colonists, including Southerners, many of whom believed that beverage alcohol was necessary or desirable for digestion and good health. In the colonial period, TEMPERANCE (moderation) rather than prohibition (total abstinence) characterized the appeals of those who called for some kind of liquor restrictions. Even though clergymen as a group were probably more immoderate than their parishioners, some colonial ministers preached against the sin of drunkenness, and most colonial laws relating to intoxicating spirits were directed against the misuse of "the good creature of God." Some colonies, including Georgia, restricted the liquor traffic generally, while others limited the sale of ardent spirits to the Indians.

The Prohibition movement is usually assumed to have begun while the American Revolution was in progress. In a strongly worded document, Dr. Benjamin Rush, surgeon general of the Continental army, called for total abstinence, arguing that alcohol had no food value, that it aggravated diseases, and that even its moderate use led inevitably to drunkenness and destruction. Because of Rush's reputation and the apparent scientific

basis for his arguments, the wide circulation of his ideas in pamphlet form may
have reduced alcohol consumption in the
new nation. However, between the formation of the Constitution and about
1820, total alcohol consumption rose
quite rapidly, in part because of the changing nature of the society in that formative
period of the nation's history.

The 1820s witnessed the beginning of
a widespread temperance-prohibition
effort in the United States. This movement, a reaction to the great national
binge, was built upon earlier sporadic
actions. It was an expression of Christian
fervor growing out of a great religious
awakening, and was a part of a general
humanitarian movement dedicated to
improving American society. Founded in
1826, the American Temperance Society
(later American Temperance Union) was
one of many national, regional, and local
organizations working to reduce the consumption of alcohol, most reformers
opposing liquor on moral grounds. During the 1830s and 1840s several states and
territorial legislatures passed a variety of
local-option, temperance-prohibition
laws. In 1851 the Maine legislature
enacted a strongly worded statewide prohibition law espoused by reformer Neal
Dow; several Northern states followed
suit before the end of the decade. Before
the Civil War began, however, most of the
states had repealed their prohibition laws,
primarily in the face of the great masses of
alcohol-drinking immigrants who were
coming into the United States in the
prewar years.

The temperance-prohibition movement was lethargic in the immediate postwar era. In 1869 the National Prohibition
party was formed and beginning in 1872 it
regularly ran presidential and lesser candidates. While it was unsuccessful as an
organized party, it helped to politicize the
prohibition issue. In 1874 Frances Willard
founded the Woman's Christian Temperance Union, an organization militantly
dedicated to alcohol reform. The Anti-
Saloon League, founded in 1895, became a

powerful force for reform in the early
twentieth century. It called itself "the
church in action against the saloon," and it
worked hard to enlist Protestant churches
(especially the Methodists and Baptists,
the largest Protestant denominations in
the nation and the two groups dominating
the Southern religious scene) in behalf of
the cause. While the churches had been
involved in the temperance-prohibition
movement since colonial days, in fact
their voices had never been well organized. Overcoming doubts about the relationship of church and state, after about
1890 the churches came to play a leading
role in the antiliquor drive. The efforts of
the secular organizations and churches
resulted in a second wave of state prohibition laws. In the 1880s and 1890s several
states, including Georgia, Mississippi,
Virginia, Florida, and Missouri, passed a
variety of local-option laws. Attempts to
pass statewide prohibition failed in North
Carolina, Tennessee, Texas, and West
Virginia. South Carolina, Virginia, North
Carolina, and Alabama experimented
with state monopolies of liquor sales. In
1900 five states in the nation had statewide prohibition and 36 others allowed
some form of local option.

In the early twentieth century, when
the Progressive movement expressed
concern for and attention to remedying
the shortcomings of American government and society, the prohibitionists tied
the outlawing of alcohol to Progressivism.
In 1913 nine Southern states (including
Georgia, Mississippi, North Carolina,
Tennessee, and West Virginia) were
under statewide prohibitory legislation,
and 31 other states operated under local-
option laws, causing one-half of all Americans to be living under prohibition laws
in about 70 percent of the land area of the
United States. Ten more states (including
Virginia, Arkansas, South Carolina, Alabama, and Florida) adopted prohibition
during World War I. As a patriotic gesture
to help win the war, the national Congress
provided for temporary wartime prohibition when it prevented the manufacture

of beverage liquor in order to conserve scarce food supplies. Led by the militant Anti-Saloon League and supported by many Protestant churches, prohibitionists stepped up their demands for a constitutional amendment providing for permanent national prohibition. In late 1917 the Congress easily passed the EIGHTEENTH AMENDMENT and by January 1919 the required number of states had ratified it. One year later national prohibition ("an experiment—noble in purpose") began.

In the 1920s many otherwise law-abiding citizens drank liquor, much of it manufactured in illegal stills in the Southern mountains, in defiance of what they considered intrusion upon their personal freedom, although the number of drinkers and the amount of alcohol consumed was less in the 1920s than in the 10 years preceding or following that decade.

Enforcement became the greatest problem associated with national prohibition. In the post-World War I moral let-down, in an increasingly open and urbanized society, in a period of high prosperity, and at a time when rapid transportation was making great strides, opposition to and violation of national prohibition seemed to characterize the generation of the 1920s. Law-defying gangs and their leaders, including the notorious Al Capone of Chicago, profited from the control and distribution of illegal booze. Neither the national government nor the states nor a combination of the two possessed or committed the resources to combat the criminal activity. Several groups, including the Association Against the Prohibition Amendment, the American Legion, and some organized labor unions came out for repeal, arguing that national prohibition was unenforceable. The South had been and remained the country's strongest supporter of a dry society; but in the late 1920s a shift in national public opinion, increased political pressures, and the onset of the Great Depression stimulated repeal sentiment. The Congress passed a repeal amendment

in early 1933, and before the year was out, the Twenty-first Amendment had been ratified by popularly elected conventions in three-fourths of the states, including 11 in the South.

When the effort for a nationwide uniform code of conduct ended, this complex question was returned to the jurisdiction of the separate states. Some states again passed statewide prohibition, and the remainder provided for a variety of local options, including state-owned or privately owned package stores, limited numbers of liquor-selling licenses, county or municipal regulations, and restricted hours for sales. In 1980 at least 15 dry organizations, continuing to hold to the dogmas of earlier prohibition groups, coordinated their activities through the National Temperance and Prohibition Council. The Prohibition party still existed and the Anti-Saloon League had been renamed the American Council on Alcohol Problems. Of the surviving prohibitionist militants, the Woman's Christian Temperance Union retained the greatest vitality.

Throughout American history, many arguments for not drinking beverage alcohol have been given: that it was harmful to the body, that it adversely affected family relationships, that it reduced the productivity of laborers, that it was sinful, and that it encouraged immoral and criminal activity. Historically the temperance-prohibition movement had its roots in the Puritan ethic (with its unswerving belief in the virtues of hard work, honesty, thrift, piety, and sobriety), a deep-seated American humanitarian reform impulse, religious fundamentalism with its emphasis upon personal morality, a fear of foreign immigrants who brought with them supposedly alien religions (Roman Catholicism and Judaism) and supposedly alien drinking habits, and a rural society repelled by a growing city culture that was associated with hard drink and its attendant evils. Many organizations had been responsible for the movement's momentum, not the least of which were the nation's Protestant denominations. By the end of the 19th century prohibition had become a part of the religious faith of the nation. This is not to say that prohibition was the creature of the "rural-evangelical virus"; rather it is to say that it was in accord with basic American religious values—values nutured all over the nation and particularly in the Southern states.

See also articles on CHURCH AND STATE; EIGHTEENTH AMENDMENT; ETHICS, CHRISTIAN; NATIVISM; SOCIAL GOSPEL.

Bibliography. Herbert Asbury, *The Great Illusion: An Informal History of Prohibition*; Ernest H. Cherrington, *The Evolution of Prohibition in the United States of America*; Norman H. Clark, *Deliver Us from Evil: An Interpretation of American Prohibition*; D. Leigh Colvin, *Prohibition in the United States*; Charles Merz, *The Dry Decade*; James H. Timberlake, *Prohibition and the Progressive Movement, 1900-1920.*

MONROE BILLINGTON
NEW MEXICO STATE UNIVERSITY

PROTESTANT EPISCOPAL CHURCH: *See* EPISCOPAL CHURCH.

PROTESTANT EPISCOPAL CHURCH IN THE CONFEDERATE STATES OF AMERICA. The secession of Southern states in 1861 created a crisis for the Episcopal churches within them. Unlike the Baptist, Methodist, and Presbyterian denominations, the EPISCOPAL CHURCH had not been divided by the tensions that led to the CIVIL WAR. The 1859 General Convention held in Richmond had been harmonious. After the political secession, however, the movement to alter the relations between North and South began with a letter dated 23 March 1861 written to the bishops of the South by the bishops of Georgia and Louisiana, calling for a consultation to be held in Montgomery, 3 July 1861.

These two church leaders, STEPHEN ELLIOTT and LEONIDAS POLK, while declaring their happiness with the national Episcopal Church, cited the difficulties presented by secession as a reason for meeting. Their fellows soon were convinced and the consultation met as scheduled, with four bishops and

representatives from six dioceses present. Major decisions were deferred until a convention could be held in the summer of 1862. A committee was formed to prepare a proposed constitution and canons to be considered at an adjourned session to meet in October. Measures were taken to sustain the missionary work already underway in the South and a committee was appointed to make plans for continuing it. At the adjourned meeting at Columbia SC on 16 October, attendance was large. All of the Southern bishops were present except Polk, who was serving as a general with the Confederate army. All of the dioceses except Texas were represented in the House of Deputies.

The constitution was presented and debated; the form in which it was sent out to the dioceses was almost identical to that of the undivided Church, except for references to the nation and its officers. The attempt to change the name of the Church to "The Reformed Catholic Church" was defeated, as was the effort to drop "Protestant" from the name, but the name of the national gathering was changed from "Convention" to "Council." Intensified work among black people was urged upon the dioceses. A further problem considered was Alabama's need to elect a bishop to succeed the deceased Nicholas Hamner Cobbs. No specific action was taken, so the diocese elected the Rev. RICHARD HOOKER WILMER of Virginia, who was consecrated in Richmond by Bishops WILLIAM MEADE and Johns of Virginia and Elliott of Georgia.

The constitution was adopted by the dioceses of Virginia, South Carolina, North Carolina, Georgia, Alabama, Mississippi, and Texas within a few months and the first General Council was summoned. It met in Augusta GA for 10 days, beginning on 12 November 1862. The council's action left the *Book of Common Prayer* untouched except for references to states and made few canonical changes.

After the war the 1865 General Convention welcomed the dioceses of the

South back to the convention; the bishops of North Carolina and Arkansas, and deputies from Texas and Tennessee were represented. The General Council of the Confederate Church met in Augusta GA 8 November 1865 and in effect dissolved itself. The Protestant Episcopal Church in the United States of America was reunited by that act.

Bibliography. Joseph Blount Cheshire, *The Church in the Confederate States;* William A. Clebsch, ed., *Journals of the Protestant Episcopal Church in the Confederate States of America;* Edgar L. Pennington, "The Organization of the Protestant Episcopal Church in the Confederate States of America," *Historical Magazine of the Protestant Episcopal Church* 17 (December 1948): 308-38.

LAWRENCE L. BROWN
EPISCOPAL SEMINARY OF THE SOUTHWEST

PROTESTANT REFORMATION.

The Protestant Reformation began by stages as a limited, fragmentary attempt at reform within the structure of European Catholicism. At length, through varieties of direct and indirect political and economic support, the movement broadened its social base and supplied several alternative models of ecclesiastical and political polity in Europe and America. In the early sixteenth century the immediate issue of reform in the abused system of indulgences widened into the more general issue of ecclesiastical authority. Notably under Martin Luther, John Calvin, Philip Melanchthon, and Ulrich Zwingli, the prevailing medieval authority of pope and tradition was challenged and then supplanted by the twofold individualistic principle of authority as *sola fides, sola scriptura* (faith only, Scripture only). A central theological issue that concerned both right-wing and left-wing reformers was the question of the distribution of God's grace to men. The classic position defined by Calvin was the restriction of the distribution of grace to the elect; the left-wing position associated with the name and writings of Jacob Arminius (1560-1609) assumed a universal distribution and accessibility of grace.

The deeper issue of the Protestant Reformation was not the question of authority or penance, but was instead the means of grace: how is man related to God, by what means is God's grace for salvation delivered to man? In medieval thought the edifice of Christendom—the hierarchical church and the developed sacramental system—functioned as the mediating structure of man's relation to God through which grace became available to man. Though bountiful, though as wide as providence, grace was nonetheless mediated to man through the social-institutional form of the church and its sacraments. The Reformation here reorders the cosmic locus of man; it displaces and effectively sets aside the traditional mediating structures of grace. In this sense the Reformation in retrospect may be seen as nothing short of a religious revolution of the most radical type. The several summary principles of *sola gratia,* (grace), *sola fides, sola scriptura* are benign under the pen of Luther or Calvin but once set free from the constraints of ecclesiology and theological system, these open the door to a vast universe of religious possibilities not yet plumbed in the pluralism of Western sects. For the early reformers these principles were limited levers of assault upon a limited issue, ecclesiastical authority. Set loose from the strictures of formal theological and ecclesiological system, they bring into question all religious institutional structures and culminate in the religious equivalent of solipsism: pietism. It is a long way from Luther and Calvin to current sectarian pluralism in America, but the Reformation is the first step.

As the social institutionalization of Reformation ideas widened, two general streams of theological influence emerged, CALVINISM and ARMINIANISM. The general emphasis of their respective namesakes has been preserved, but the details of their writings have been left behind. In America the Calvinist and Arminian positions become the unacknowledged but real determinants that vitalized the development of American religion in the colonial and early national periods.

Although vigorously defended in New England during the GREAT AWAKENING by presbyterian exponents, the strict Calvinist position was increasingly challenged and eventually supplanted by nearly ubiquitous assent to Arminian principles. Although Calvinism was preserved as a formal feature of the doctrinal posture of some Congregationalists, Presbyterians, Methodists, and Regular Baptists, the tenor of American Protestantism, indeed of American religion, becomes more and more Arminian. Although the name of Jacob Arminius was almost unknown among Baptists and Methodists during the GREAT REVIVAL, the success of these groups in evoking allegiance in the South is confirmation of Arminian thought.

The Protestant Reformation was more than a movement of theological and religious simplification and reform. Its success was due as much to the support of political and economic interests as to the acceptance of Luther's ideas. After the initial theological controversy, the Reformation quickly leaves matters of personality behind as it becomes a broad-fronted cultural revision. Treating the Reformation as a simple theological controversy in a distant period of church history is somewhat like treating the Copernican revolution, which is roughly contemporary with the Reformation, as a finished episode in the history of science without considering the consequences that continue to flow from it.

This theological controversy widened into a broad movement of cultural reformation that massively reordered the premises of Western culture. By relocating the drama of salvation in the individual conscience before God, the Reformation accomplished a de facto SECULARIZATION of society that could not have been accomplished through direct secular confrontation. In the dismantling of ecclesiastical authority consequent upon the Reformation the way is paved for sectarian pluralism, but the attendant premise

of secularization is perhaps the more important consequence.

See also articles on ANABAPTISM; LUTHERANISM; PROTESTANTISM.

Bibliography. Roland H. Bainton, *The Age of the Reformation*; Owen Chadwick, *The Reformation Era, 1500-1650*; Hans J. Hillerbrand, *Christendom Divided: the Protestant Reformation*; *The World of the Reformation*; Wilhelm Pauck, *The Heritage of the Reformation*; George H. Williams, *The Radical Reformation*.

GERALD L. SMITH
UNIVERSITY OF THE SOUTH

PROTESTANTISM. The word *protestant* (Latin, *protestans*) was as early as 1529 applied to certain German princes and cities committed to Luther's critique and revolt against the "indulgence traffic" of Rome, the penitential system, and so, the way of salvation prescribed by late Medieval Catholicism. In common usage the protest gave currency to the descriptive noun "Protestantism" as a covering term for the reform movement better denoted as the 16th-century PROTESTANT REFORMATION.

The negative force of the word is misleading in that it obscures the vast positive theological insight of the reform movement, which had slumbered in Western Medieval Catholicism, not without forerunners, from the 14th century onwards. Of the positive import of the Reformation these words of Philip Schaff remain suggestive: "It went, through the intervening ages of ecclesiasticism, back to the fountainhead of Christianity itself. . . It was a deeper plunge into the meaning of the Gospel than even St. Augustine had made. It brought out from this fountain a new phase and type of Christianity that had never as yet been fully understood and appreciated in the Church at large." However significant the socioeconomic and political factors were that attended the 16th-century revolution of Christendom, the revolution was basically spiritual and doctrinal—a regenerative impulse at the heart of Christianity and a renovation of the human spirit.

The final cleavage between Eastern and Western Roman Catholicism in 1054

A.D. had divided Christendom in two main streams. The 16th-century Reformation, precipitated by Luther and advanced by Zwingli, Bucer, Cranmer, Calvin, and others, made Protestantism the third principal stream of organized Christianity, itself dividing through succeeding centuries into many Protestant denominations. Viewed from one perspective, the Reformation, or post-Reformation churches and Eastern Catholicism (Orthodoxy) have something in common: they alike dissent from the absolute claim of Rome to the primacy of Christendom; that is, to the hierarchical order and *magisterium* of the See of Rome that, historically, claimed final authority in the supreme teaching office and governance of Christ's Church. Accordingly, Protestantism and Eastern Orthodoxy have traditionally been in protest. For them, the alleged supremacy of the See of Peter as divinely appointed Master of the Keys has always lacked sufficient complementation by the Pauline "sword of the Spirit." This is symbolic for the point that, for both Protestantism and Eastern Orthodoxy, the Church Universal is so conceived that the God in Christ, through the working of his Holy Spirit, remains always the immediate Lord of his Church. It is for this reason that it is cogently claimed of Luther's protest that, in substance, it is Luther's own plea: "Let God be God!" In like manner, Eastern Catholicism has, through two millennia, declined to attribute supremacy to any patriarchal church. It may be said that both of the dissenting traditions protest a certain, (and until quite lately) unacknowledged subordination of pneumatology to ecclesiology, or of the Holy Spirit to the *historical* Holy Mother Church, and as a doctrinal slant deeply ingrained in the Roman tradition. In its inception, therefore, Reformation theology, especially in Lutheran usage, was radically Trinitarian and can hardly be properly understood save as a repristination of the Spirit, that is, the Third Person of the Godhead, who is God constantly at work in the human world for its salvation. In Protestantism

accordingly, the Church, while both the creation and instrument of God's Holy Spirit, is never viewed as so possessed of the Spirit that the workings of the latter are in any way at its calculated disposal, either through preaching or sacraments or dogmatic decree.

An underlying kinship between Orthodoxy and Protestantism was already sensed by the English Reformers and the 17th-century Anglican divines whose resort to the Greek fathers on current controversial issues is manifest from Cranmer or Jewel to Pearson and Jeremy Taylor. Both traditions, for instance, subscribe in principle to an ecclesiology in which episcopal rule is seen not as the *esse* but only as the *bene esse* of the Church. The standing difference and dispute between East and West over the "procession" of the Holy Spirit from the Father *and the Son (filioque)*—an interpolation of the Nicene-Constantinopolitan Creed in the West first authorized by the Third Council of Toledo (589 A.D.)—is indicative of the refusal of Eastern Catholicism to allow any subordinate status to the Third Person of the Trinity. For the East, God the Father, through the Holy Spirit, is immediately at work equally in creation and redemption. This insistence fosters a doctrine of the Church and of the "means of grace" resistant to the more rigorously channelized "means of grace" in the keeping of the Church of Rome and was therefore far more acceptable to the English Reformers. In degree it also nurtures a standpoint in sacramental theology closer to the views of several churches of the Reformation, whether Lutheran or Reformed.

Moreover, this perceptible tendency of Eastern Catholicism to emancipate the Holy Spirit places the stress upon the Divine initiative. So also it complements the major thrust of Luther's recovery of the Pauline soteriology: by grace *alone* through faith *alone*. Schaff was on target in the judgment that the Reformation "was, in fact, a new proclamation of the free Gospel of St. Paul, as laid down in the Epistles to the Romans and Galatians." In Luther's republication of salvation by grace through faith, the accent upon divine grace is reassertion of the antecedence of God's gracious act in Christ but also upon the moving Spirit of God, for example, "that we might receive the promise of the Spirit through faith" (Gal. 3:14. Cf. Rom. 8:9f.). This is the Pauline "sword of the Spirit" (Eph. 6:17). There is, in a measure, a sense in which Eastern Orthodoxy and Reformation Protestantism were and are agreed upon liberating the sovereign "freedom of God for man" in the work of human salvation which, alike, distinguished them both from late Western Medieval Catholicism. Luther was in revolt from the latter because of his perception of its unreserved claim to custodianship of the Keys and, therewith, the means of sacramental grace at its arbitrary disposal. Luther, as Protestant, startled as he also angered his contemporaries in voicing his novel perception that the Medieval Church of Rome had domesticated God.

While it was long smoldering before coming to flame, Reformation Protestantism was ignited precisely by Luther's *Ninety-five Theses* nailed to the doors of the Wittenberg Church in 1517. Enlightened by his Pauline studies, Luther perceived the system of reparation as salvation by the prescribed works of men under the tutelage of the Church rather than by God's grace through *faith alone* as enabled by "the Spirit of the living God" (2 Cor. 3:3). The keynote of the Lutheran Reformation was, of course, Rom. 3. There St. Paul proclaims to his contemporaries—Jew and Gentile at Rome—God's, not man's, way to restored community. It is the way neither of Greek *arete*, nor of Jewish "righteousness of the law." Rather, it is a "righteousness of God"—indeed, both of and from God— "manifested apart from the law, although the law and the prophets bear witness to it." It is "the righteousness of God" through faith in Jesus Christ for all who

believe" (Rom. 3:21, 22). But closing with the "righteousness of God" through faith is God's doing also, and through the present working of his holy Spirit. It is then in virtue of the divine approach and initiative manifested in Jesus Christ as the "revelation of the mystery . . . kept secret for long ages but now disclosed . . . to all nations" that God's own way of human redemption is to be recognized and claimed by faith. This is the Pauline gospel that Luther republished in the 16th century. Accordingly, Luther's protest in the *Ninety-five Theses* and thereafter is that salvation is God's intervention on behalf of mankind as a whole and is not as such to be codified, reserved, or dispensed as if it were in the keeping or at the decree of Holy Mother Church.

But Luther was not simply in protest toward Rome. The positive teaching of the entire Reformation is that, in the ordeal of redemption or cure of the gone-wrongness of human existence—quite as surely as in the creation of the environing world—the resultant is the constant working of God's sovereign grace, which moves among humanity to restore a lost community broken by human waywardness that declines to accept its divine destiny. For the restoration of communion God has revealed himself in the Mediator Jesus Christ. Faith, therefore, is acceptance of God's acceptance of sinful men divinely warranted through Christ. To be related to Christ in faith is *eo ipso* God-acceptance as moved by "the Spirit of God" (Rom. 8:14). The outcome in St. Paul's gospel is the "new creation" and/or "newness of life" (2 Cor. 5:17; Rom. 6:4). This final Pauline consummation was fully adopted neither by Luther nor by the Reformed wing of the Reformation. *Simul justus et peccator*, justified but yet sinner—or, "God reigns but sin remains"—seemed to limit "Christian perfection." Only with Spener and the pietists, the Moravians, and the Wesleys was Christian perfection or entire sanctification of life an allowable expectation of the renovation of man.

Justification by grace alone through faith alone, however, became the central positive affirmation of the Lutheran and Reformed wings of continental European Protestantism. It was attended by several corollaries: (1) the way of salvation is afforded only through Scripture as God's own Word; (2) the sum of that Word is Jesus Christ—the Word made flesh for man's salvation through faith; (3) the historical Church is always in need of reformation measured by the norm of Scripture and not tradition; (4) of the right understanding of God's Word, "God is his own interpreter" by way of the inner witness of the Holy Spirit—the *testimonium Spiritus Sancti internum* (Calvin); (5) consequently, effectual understanding of the Word is in God's keeping and cannot finally be determined by any ecclesial tribunal *ex officio*, thence proposed for the assent of the faithful; (6) thus the Reformers do not look to an infallible *magisterium* or teaching office; rather, the doctrinal norm tends to become the *consensus fidelium* of the believing community, those justified by faith; (7) accordingly, apodictic truth in doctrine is relinquished; objective certainty is declined along with dogma in the Roman sense. In its place the corporate mind, ideally considered, is expressed in the form of confessions of faith beginning with the AUGSBURG CONFESSION of 1530 to be succeeded by regional or national confessions such as the Heidelburg, Gallican, Scottish, or the Thirty-nine Articles of the Church of England.

In classical Protestantism, the knowledge of God and the service of God is then a concomitant of justification by grace through faith. The latter is really the condition *sine qua non* either of the true knowledge or the proper service of God. In consequence, a distinguishing mark of Protestant Christianity, in its classical expression, has been the indispensability of justifying personal, appropriating faith. This, however, also tended to locate the norm of verity in personal experience even if corporately shared and made it, to

that extent, admissable of control and possible correction. Whenever that happens, the way is opened for individualism in Christian confession, understanding, and practice. This has been productive of the actual historical proliferation of the mainstream of Protestantism into its many ecclesial bodies. Here, Protestantism faces a dilemma: the price of justifying faith (*fides qua creditur*) as a personal *realization* has the potential for both intramural and extramural pluralization rather than for a unity of Christ's Church. It is true that, in the Lutheran, Reformed, and Anglican traditions, historic confessional norms have exercised a check upon intramural and extramural proliferation, setting bounds to individual theological spontaneity.

Whenever Protestant doctrinal reflection has found its focus more nearly in the dictum *sola Scriptura* (as in the 17th-century Protestant scholasticism) than in the watchword, salvation by *sola gratia* through *sola fides*, tendencies toward a dogmatic fideism have appeared. In more recent times this tendency has earned the name of "fundamentalism." It may be judged that this recurrent and resilient Protestant phenomenon derives its warrant from the 16th-century Reformers who, in their contest with medieval traditionalism, made Holy Scripture the sole and sufficient ground of both faith and practice "requisite or necessary to salvation." For the Reformers, God is, from Scripture, his own interpreter by way of the "internal witness of the Holy Spirit," and already in Luther there is all but explicit denial of identity between the canon of Scripture and its *essence*, namely, Jesus Christ, savior by God's grace through faith. More than a century of "scientific" biblical criticism, however, has precipitated a situation now, by comparison, that renders ambiguous the meaning of "the Word of God" in Scripture that has led undoubtedly to a genuine crisis in Protestantism. This is especially the case where a simple equation is made between the sum of the written canon and the Word of God, a claim that goes beyond the Reformers, who could not have envisioned the issue in its modern setting. In no sense did the early Reformers suppose that God, through his Holy Spirit, is not quite as truly Lord of the Scriptures and their interpretation as also he was Lord of his Church.

This latter is a standpoint hardly surviving or comprehensible to the modern mind, especially to minds long accustomed to the exercise of critical historical method—a logic in probing ancient documents of the past, including the Bible—who credit only those findings as truth that square with the same historical methodology. This is not the kind of vehicle of evangelical understanding contemplated either by the Reformers of 16th-century Protestantism, or by a succession of more discerning commentators on the distinction between *fides historica* and *fides salvifica*. The latter presupposes awareness of a distinction early recognized by Luther and Melanchthon but largely obscured by the Reformed wing of the Reformation and greatly neglected elsewhere, namely, the distinction first made explicit by St. Augustine concerning two kinds of faith. Faith in the primary sense is *fides qua creditur*—the faith *by which* is believed what is believed. The other is *fides quae creditur*—the faith that is believed, namely, the creed or confession. The latter is derivative and dependent upon the former. When understood and honored, the *fides qua creditur*, presupposing as it does the work of God in the human spirit, is *fides salvifica*, saving faith. It is grace, not of man's working. Melanchthon struggled to define the faith in Article 20 of the Augsburg Confession, although he attained to a more successful statement in the later editions of his *Loci Communes*. Concerning faith the Confession reads: "It does not only signify a knowledge of the history" [that is, of the biblical story of our redemption through Christ] "but it signifies a faith that believes, not only the history, but also the *effect of the history*; to wit . . . that by

Christ *we* have grace, righteousness and remission of sins. . . . " So Melanchthon strove to communicate Luther's understanding of the grace and work of Christ *pro nobis* through the present working of the Holy Spirit as existential appropriation. It may be judged that precisely in this recovery of *fides qua creditur*—long obscured in Medieval Christianity, save in a Bernard of Clairvaux or Jean Gerson—is the point of renewed meeting between Lutheran Reformers and Western Catholicism. Here, the Reformation understanding of the knowledge of God by aid of Scripture—but not really *alone*—joins hands with the deepest thought of Western Catholicism in the teaching, first of Augustine and then of Anselm: Except *you* believe you will in no wise understand, or *Credo ut intelligam*—I believe, *in order* to understand. Salvation by grace alone through faith alone, then, vindicates itself as a common witness of perception and testimony. In the latter, this perception became obscured with the 13th-century ascendancy of the Aristotelian-Thomistic standpoint over the Augustinian inheritance.

See also articles on BIBLE, AUTHORITY OF; CALVINISM; EVANGELICALISM; LUTHERANISM; PRESBYTERIANISM; ROMAN CATHOLICISM.

Bibliography. Elmer Arndt, *The Heritage of the Reformation*; Roland H. Bainton, *Here I Stand*; John H. Bratt, *The Heritage of John Calvin*; W. R. Estep, *The Anabaptist Story*; Thomas Evans, *A Concise Account of the Religious Society Called Quakers*; Robert T. Handy, *A Christian America*; H. J. Hillerbrand, *The Protestant Reformation*; Charles A. Jenkens, *Baptist Doctrines*; Julius Köstlin, *Life of Luther*; C. L. Manschreck, *Melanchthon The Quiet Reformer*; James H. Nichols, *A Primer For Protestants*; Philip Schaff, *Creeds of Christendom*, vol. 3; H. Shelton Smith, et al., *American Christianity*, 2 vols.; William W. Sweet, *The Story of Religion in America*; J. S. Whale, *The Protestant Tradition*; John Wesley, *Journal. Works*, vols. 1-4; D. Elizabeth Winslow, *Jonathan Edwards*; B. L. Woolf, *Reformation Writings of Martin Luther*, vol. 1.

ROBERT E. CUSHMAN
DUKE UNIVERSITY

PROTRACTED MEETING. The name given to a series of revival services held in a church and conducted over a period of several days, "protracted meeting" had its greatest currency during the 19th century. Protracted meetings were held annually in many communities in the United States. Developed as early as the period of the GREAT REVIVAL (1787-1805), the protracted meeting was an outgrowth of the CAMP MEETING, an outdoor revival meeting form developed on the Southern frontier. Protracted meetings received their most sustained development, however, between 1825 and 1835 in their use by the western New York revivalist Charles Grandison Finney. Such meetings began to achieve significant popularity in the South during the 1830s and 1840s among both the Methodists and Baptists, although the Baptists had most to do with the development of the form in the South.

The protracted meeting in the South was a significant manifestation of changes in the region during the first half of the 19th century. The earlier, outdoor camp meeting had been a response to a frontier environment in which permanent church facilities were scarce and in which the population was widely scattered. However, as frontier areas became more settled and church buildings available, such outdoor gatherings no longer seemed necessary. Hence, while camp meetings would continue to be held for some time, by the mid-nineteenth century the protracted meetings would come to dominate revival efforts in the region.

Protracted meetings varied greatly in length and character. Although the earliest meetings tended (like camp meetings) to last for three or four days, one week to 10 days became the norm as the form developed, with some extending to two weeks or even a month depending on the size of the crowds and their enthusiasm. Because they were held indoors, protracted meetings were scheduled at all times of the year, although late summer and early fall were the favored seasons. In the earliest period, protracted meeting services took place at regular intervals during the day and at night; but later, services tended to be confined to the evenings when they would not disrupt the normal daily activities of most participants.

A protracted meeting was a major religious event, frequently involving ministers of several congregations, traveling together to the churches in a community and holding services as a group. Some protracted meetings were even interdenominational, with local Methodists and Baptists cooperating to carry forward the work of the revival. Protracted meeting services could be highly emotional, but the level of emotionalism tended to lessen after the Civil War, as the meetings' Methodist and Baptist sponsors achieved greater affluence and sought more decorum in their religious activities.

Protracted meetings continued to have some importance in the South and elsewhere into the early years of the 20th century, but beginning even in the antebellum period, the form underwent major changes. Increasingly, the term itself came to be replaced by the more generic label "revival meeting," and local ministers often turned over the services to outside evangelists who specialized in conducting revivals.

See also articles on FRONTIER, INFLUENCE OF; REVIVALISM.

Bibliography. John B. Boles, Religion in Antebellum Kentucky; William G. McLoughlin, Modern Revivalism; Francis Butler Simkins and Robert H. Woody, South Carolina During Reconstruction.

DICKSON D. BRUCE, JR.
UNIVERSITY OF CALIFORNIA, IRVINE

PROVINCE. As used by churches, this term has a geographical and administrative reference. A province is the confederation of several neighboring dioceses, individually independent, yet united for cooperation and common pastoral action, (in the Episcopal and Roman Catholic Churches).

A Roman Catholic province is presided over by a Metropolitan, who is the archbishop of a particular diocese, to which the office of Metropolitan is automatically attached. The responsibilities of an archbishop are limited and carefully defined by the Roman Catholic Code of Canon Law (numbers 436 and 442).

Churches of the Anglican (Episcopal) communion are bound together "not by a central legislation and executive authority but by common consultation and mutual loyalty" (Lambeth Conference, 1908 Encyclical Letter). Though certain bishops of the Episcopal Church throughout the world hold the title of archbishop (such as Canterbury, whose archbishop is also referred to as the Primate of All England), such is not the practice in the United States.

The term *province* also applies to different houses of a religious or secular institute, united in a certain region, with their own territories of responsibility, boundaries, and provincial leaders (referred to by various titles). The authority to establish or alter in any way Roman Catholic archdiocesan provinces resides with the Apostolic See in Rome and can take place at the recommendation of the national conference of bishops (number 433).

ROBERT J. BAKER
ST. VINCENT DE PAUL
REGIONAL SEMINARY

PUNISHMENT: *See* HELL.

PURITANICAL: *See* PURITANISM.

PURITANISM. "Puritanism" is one of the more abused words in the taxonomy of American religion. It is most often used to describe phenomena entirely unrelated to the original meaning of the word. Four main uses of the word—ecclesiastical puritanism, ideological puritanism, moralistic puritanism, and epithetic puritanism—supply a convenient typology of puritanism.

(1) Ecclesiastical puritanism refers to the program of liturgical and theological purification issuing from principles of the Calvinist reformation. Its purpose was to divest churches of Roman Catholic influences in liturgy, theology, ARCHITECTURE, decoration, and vestments. Strongly Calvinist in theological stance, early ecclesiastical puritanism became an important sociopolitical force in England, Holland and, to a lesser extent in France and Switzerland. Appealing to Scripture alone as the entire guide for faith, practice, and public order, radical puritans in England sought to reform civil as well as ecclesiastical polity and to repudiate statutory, positive (that is, human) law and to replace it with the divine law of Scripture. Led by Thomas Cartwright, William Travers, and others, ecclesiastical puritanism infected English public life from the mid-sixteenth to mid-seventeenth centuries, culminating briefly in an antimonarchical puritan commonwealth. Richard Hooker, William Laud, and John Whitgift formulated the classic defense of the Established Church in the 16th century against the Puritans. Puritans' ideas survived for many years in popular form in the writings of John Bunyan and John Milton.

Ecclesiastical puritanism was transplanted to North America early in the 17th century with the establishment of the New England colonies. Characterized more by intolerance of nonpuritan worship than by religious freedom, puritans attempted to establish commonwealths of pure religion free of Roman Catholic elements and beyond the reach of English royal and episcopal interference. Difficulties of settlement and expansion and the continual influence of dissent, loss of fervor, and new emigrants seriously undermined puritan theocracy. In time, the rigid puritan ecclesiology was tempered in the direction of CONGREGATIONALISM and its Calvinist theology was inherited by Congregationalist, Presbyterian, Methodist, and regular Baptist groups. After 1700 ecclesiastical puritanism tends to degenerate into the other types of puritanism described below. A small but legitimate inheritance of ecclesiastical puritanism continues to be seen in the South in the general opposition to Roman Catholicism and, in particular, to the use of crucifixes and crosses among Baptists and rural Methodists.

(2) Ideological puritanism is a religious philosophy of radical other-

worldliness. It is characterized by an underlying dualism of reality and knowledge reflected in disjunctions such as soul-body, spirit-flesh, church-world, salvation-damnation, beatitude-sin, righteousness-unrighteousness, God-man, Christ-Satan, heaven-hell, etc. These polarities are not inherently dualistic or puritan, but become so when the polarity is dissolved pejoratively through a cultivated bias against the latter elements of each pair. Ideological puritanism has been the driving force in the sectarian division of the original Protestant positions, and is currently reflected in the cultic pluralism of Europe, America, and Asia. This type of puritanism has little historical connection with ecclesiastical puritanism and may be traced ultimately to the various gnostic dualisms of Asia and the Middle East. Ideological puritanism appears in Southern religion in the crypto-metaphysical apparatus of REVIVALISM, evangelical preaching, and the nurtured alienation of the sects and cults of the oppressed.

(3) Moralistic puritanism is ethical rather than theological opposition to the "things of the world and the flesh." It is an indirect descendant of colonial ecclesiastical puritanism, but it has little in common with the earlier European form. In fact, the accepted social practices of English and Continental ecclesiastical puritans—for example May-pole revelry, consumption of beer, and dancing—were antithetical to the attitudes of moralistic puritanism. The historical link between moralistic and ecclesiastical puritanism is firmer in the colonial period in as much as the original "blue laws" of Connecticut, Massachusetts, and New York were the product of second and third generation ecclesiastical puritans. This historical link is obscured, however, in the development of moralistic puritanism in the South. Moralistic puritanism is seen in the Southern equivalent of blue laws such as Sunday closing laws, restricted Sunday sales, and the closing of retail businesses during church hours. It is seen also in the opposition of "mixed" bathing, "social"

dancing, and in the Southern Protestant opposition to alcoholic beverages and "liquor-by-the-drink." Recently this type of puritanism is found in the attitudes of church constituencies that oppose the liberalization of sexual morality, in concern over clothing styles (particularly of women), and in the religious opposition to the use of tobacco, cosmetics, and jewelry. It is occasionally reflected in the attitudes of religious lobby groups opposing abortion, pornography, and sex education in public schools. Moralistic puritanism attempts to establish a normative private and social morality of a conservative type. Moralistic puritanism is given selective scriptural support, but is widely enough endorsed outside of churches in some regions to form a self-validating moral consensus.

(4) Epithetic puritanism refers to the loose use of the unqualified term "puritan" to describe social and moral attitudes that are viewed as illiberal, restrictive, conservative, quaint, nonprogressive, or "old-fashioned." Typically the use of the term reflects the bias of the user against the strictures of the practices thus designated. Most of the content of moralistic puritanism would be described epithetically as "puritan" by an unsympathetic observer. This use of the term "puritan" is perhaps the most widely employed in common conversation and successfully obscures the other legitimate meanings of the word. The *locus classicus* of epithetical puritanism with reference to the South and Southern religion is the essays of H. L. MENCKEN.

See also articles on BIBLE, AUTHORITY OF; CALVINISM; ETHICS, CHRISTIAN; PREACHING.

Bibliography. P. Collinson, *The Elizabethan Puritan Movement*; Everett H. Emerson, *English Puritanism from John Hooper to John Milton*; David D. Hall, ed., *Puritanism in Seventeenth-Century Massachusetts;* M. M. Knappen, *Tudor Puritanism*; Perry Miller and Thomas H. Johnson, *The Puritans*; Alan Simpson, *Puritanism in Old and New England*; Leonard J. Trinterud, ed., *Elizabethan Puritanism*.

GERALD L. SMITH
UNIVERSITY OF THE SOUTH

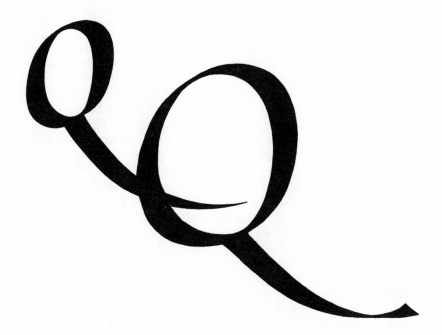

QUAKERISM. The Religious Society of Friends, more commonly known as Quakers, has its roots in the English Commonwealth and dates itself from the illuminating experience of George Fox on "Pendle Hill," southeast of Lancaster, in 1652. He was joined by influential fellow "seekers of the Light," among whom were Francis Howgill, William Dewsbury, Elizabeth Hooten, Richard Farnsworth, Margaret Fell (later Fox), James Nayler, William Penn, and Robert Barclay, who aided in the rapid expansion of this radical sect within England's Protestant Reformation.

The movement spread from Lancashire and Westmoreland in the Northwest of England back to London, then over to Norwich in the East and to Bristol in the West. The story of Quakerism from 1652 to the death of George Fox in 1691 was at first one of tragic persecution, imprisonment, and at times death; but it ended with eventual triumph and expansion from the days of Cromwell through the reigns of Charles II and James II, and finally, after the Toleration Act of 1689 was passed, to enlarged freedom for all religions in England under William and Mary.

Quakers arrived in America in the 1660s bearing their faith. Various internal forces, indigenous to its first generation, resulted in the growth of several factions, especially since the Great Schism of 1827-1828 in Philadelphia and that of 1845 in New England. Two dominant types emerged, generally referred to as the Evangelical and Pastoral Friends (the Friends United Meeting and the Evangelical Friends Alliance), and the Orthodox, unprogrammed, nonpastoral Friends (London Yearly Meeting and the Friends General Conference). The former groups were inspired by the leadership and preaching of Thomas Shillitoe and Joseph John Gurney, and the latter by Elias Hicks and John Wilbur, and their followers. While a few regional yearly meetings continue independently, most yearly meetings of these diverse types are now associated and work together cooperatively under the aegis of the Friends World Committee for Consultation, with a small, central world office in London. Many of these yearly meetings join in broader national programs, especially in the worldwide work of the British Friends Service Council and the American Friends Service Committee in programs aimed at world peace, the elimination of war, interracial reconciliation, right sharing of the world's resources, relief, and rehabilitation.

There have been various attempts to define Quaker theology, notably in George Fox's famous "Letter to the Governor of Barbadoes," written in 1671; in Robert Barclay's *An Apology for the True Christian Divinity* published in 1676; and in the "Richmond (Indiana) Declaration of Faith" of 1887. It remains the practice of Friends everywhere, however, to seek their own understanding and interpretation of theology. Nearly all Yearly Meetings have developed books of discipline, usually referred to as "Christian Faith and Practice," that give brief summary statements and examples of Friends' beliefs and practices. These books of "Faith and Practice" are in effect a continuing effort to reflect as accurately as possible both the theology and the ethics of Quakerism, but they do not include creedal statements. Instead, they provide a set of "queries" to guide the individual conscience and in turn to quicken the Inner Light.

With respect to the central matters of faith, there is remarkable consensus among Friends today, in harmony with the group's founders, that each individual person must seek within himself the meaning of divinity, the significance of Jesus of Nazareth as a man and of Christ as the Eternal revelation of God; for the witness of the Scriptures as God's Word; for the existence and nature of evil and good; and for the way to atonement and salvation.

Quakerism was at the experiential, mystical end of the Reformation spectrum in England and remains there today. Friends wanted to be free of all outward authorities: whether the Torah and its rabbinical interpretations; the Vatican and the pope; the Church of England and the king; the New Testament; ordained priests and preachers; or the state and its social and political control. They set themselves, therefore, to their own intense study of the Bible, their commit-

ment to service in the name and spirit of Jesus, their dedication to a way of life that would eliminate the causes of war, discrimination, and inequality. They rejected outward ceremonies and rituals of distinction and declared that all life is sacred, thus advocating a totally sacramental view of life in the family, the place of work, the community, and the world. Exemplifying this joining of theology with first-hand experience in a communitarian ethics were the lives of Margaret Fell Fox, as the unifying figure for the work of the "Valiant Sixty" at Swarthmore Hall; William Penn in the establishment of Pennsylvania; Elizabeth Fry, the great prison reformer at Earlham Hall; and John Woolman, the voice of freedom from war and slavery in 18th-century America.

In spite of such intellectually competent Quakers as Robert Barclay, Rufus Jones, Howard Brinton, Henry Cadbury, Elton Trueblood, and Douglas Steere, Quakers remain largely committed to the belief that the most meaningful pathway to the Divine is through experience and feeling, augmented by the practical guide of reason, but always in response to the Divine Light Within. Friends have always accepted science, knowledge, and reason as part of natural revelation, but always in harmony with the manifestation of the Divine. They were very slow and often negative, however, in the acceptance of the aesthetic revelation of the Divine, especially in drama, fiction, music, and the arts in general. Slowly this attitude has changed, so that the role of creative arts and crafts has become one of the most marked developments in 20th-century Quakerism.

At the heart of Quakerism today, whether in England, America, Kenya, Japan, or Peru, are two distinct but related meetings. One is for worship, whether based on waiting in silence for the divine spark or responding to the witness of an evangelist. The other is the meeting for business, whose decisions take Friends out into the world, calling all men to a way of peace, within themselves, their families, their communities, in all the arenas of economic, social, and political life. There is, in short, no required, crystallized creed. Quakerism was in the beginning and still is the individual search within the worshiping community for God's will and the group effort to put it into practice.

See also article on QUAKERS IN THE SOUTH.

Bibliography. Robert Barclay, *An Apology for the True Christian Divinity*; Howard Brinton, *Friends for Three Hundred Years*; Elfrida V. B. Fould, *The Story of Quakerism*; London Yearly Meeting; *Christian Faith and Practice*; Elbert Russell, *A History of Quakerism*.

J. FLOYD MOORE
GUILFORD COLLEGE

QUAKERS (IN THE SOUTH). The Religious Society of Friends (Quakers) dates from the illuminating experience of George Fox, its principal founder, on Pendle Hill in Lancashire, England, in 1652. By 1656 Friend Elizabeth Harris visited Maryland. William Edmondson and George Fox visited the Carolinas in 1672, laying the foundation for establishment of North Carolina Yearly Meeting in 1698.

QUAKERISM became the first organized religion in the Carolinas under the leadership of John Archdale, a Quaker, as acting governor in 1685-1686 and as governor in Charleston, 1695-1696. It stressed firsthand, direct revelation of Christ within each individual and each worshiping group rather than authority of church, Scriptures, sacraments, or clergy. It also developed two strong social testimonies, a pacifist witness against war and opposition to human slavery, both of which created suffering and imprisonment during the American Revolution and Civil War.

During the Colonial period Friends Meetings settled primarily near the coasts of Virginia, the Carolinas, and as far south as Charleston. Economic and political conditions soon pushed these settlers west into the Piedmont. Even more important was the wave of immigration from Pennsylvania and Nantucket, down through Maryland to western Virginia, along the Shenandoah Valley, into the Piedmont Carolinas and Georgia in the mid-eighteenth century. Virginia Yearly Meeting was held for 142 years from 1702 to 1844. Friends in northern Virginia now belong to Baltimore Yearly Meeting. Friends in South Carolina and Georgia belonged to North Carolina Yearly Meeting until their meetings were laid down mostly by northwestern migration in the 19th century.

The strength of Quakerism in the South began to emerge in Piedmont North Carolina in the areas of Cane Creek, New Garden, Centre, Deep River, and Springfield Meetings.

Friends provided strong leadership in the abolition of slavery, whether by manumission societies, Underground Railroad, or resettlement in Africa, in the lives of such men as Charles Osborn and three members of the Coffin family, Vestal, Levi, and Addison. They also migrated in large numbers, sometimes an entire community, to slave-free territories in the Northwest, especially in Ohio and Indiana. North Carolina Yearly Meeting had substantially eliminated slaveholding from its membership by 1814.

While the westward migration of Friends nearly decimated Quaker leadership in the Carolinas, its central stronghold continued to evolve around its innovative coeducational New Garden Boarding School, founded just west of Greensboro in 1837. As a center for education, outreach, and leadership, the school helped Friends survive slavery, the Civil War, and Reconstruction by the influence of such figures as Nathan Hunt, Jeremiah Hubbard, and Nereus Mendenhall, along with timely aid from the Baltimore Friends Association and Francis T. King. In 1888 it became Guilford College.

From 1865 to the mid-twentieth century, Quakerism in the South slowly regained its strength, expanding again into Tennessee, Georgia, South Carolina, Florida, and the Southwest. But it did so only after the fervor of evangelical and revivalistic Protestantism of the Reconstruction period had penetrated the small, surviving Friends communities. Gradually they began to give up their testimony against "the hireling ministry" in favor of the Protestant pastoral system. This resulted in a minor split of North Carolina Friends into two Yearly Meetings in 1903.

The pendulum has swung back during the 20th century toward the earlier social concerns in response to two world wars, Korea, Vietnam, and the struggle for racial equality. At the heart of this resurgence has been North Carolina Yearly Meeting, Guilford College, the Southeastern office of the American Friends Service Committee (founded in 1917), and the influence of many effective leaders such as Lyndon and Mary Mendenhall Hobbs, Raymond and Helen Binford, Elbert Russell, Clyde Milner, Algie Newlin, and Claude Shotts. Migration of Friends from nonpastoral Yearly Meetings also aided in the establishment of three new Yearly Meetings in the past two decades: Southern Appalachian, Southeastern, and South Central, extending from Kentucky to Florida and Texas.

One of the most important events in Southern Quaker history was the coming of the Fourth World Conference of Friends to the campus of Guilford College for 10 days in 1967. About 1,200 Friends from 35 nations evaluated their faith and action and set international goals for the coming years. At the largest world gathering in Quaker history, U Thant, secretary-general of the United Nations, addressed an audience of about 7,500 in Greensboro, challenging Friends to work even harder for the human factor in world peace at a time of crisis in Vietnam and Israel.

By 1980 there were 229 Friends Meetings in 14 Southern states and the District of Columbia. North Carolina had 93 Meetings and a membership of about 14,000, followed by Virginia with 29; Oklahoma, 21; Florida, 20; Texas, 19; Maryland, 14; and Tennessee with 13. There are five or fewer Meetings in Georgia, Kentucky, Arkansas, West Virginia, Louisiana, South Carolina, and District of Columbia. Mississippi has none.

In addition to Guilford College, there are six schools affiliated with Friends in the area: Baltimore Friends and Sandy Spring in Maryland; Sidwell Friends in Washington; Virginia Beach Friends; and New Garden and Carolina Friends in Durham and Greensboro NC. Friends retirement communities are located at Sandy Spring MD and Greensboro. Friends operate Quaker Lake, a year-round conference center and camp near Greensboro, and Quaker House, the only counseling center for conscientious objectors in military camps at Fayetteville near Fort Bragg and other installations in North Carolina. The Southeastern regional office of the American Friends Service Committee is located in Atlanta with branch offices in North Carolina and Florida. The North Carolina Friends Historical Collection is located at Guilford College.

See also articles on ABOLITIONISM; EVANGELICALISM; MIGRATION, SOUTHWARD (1700-1830); NORTH CAROLINA.

Bibliography. Kenneth L. Carroll, *Quakerism on the Eastern Shore*; Fernando G. Cartland, *Southern Heroes or Friends in War Time; Handbook of the Society of Friends* (1977); Rufus M. Jones, *Quakers in the American Colonies*; J. Floyd Moore, *Friends in the Carolinas*; Elbert Russell, *A History of Quakerism*; Stephen B. Weeks, *Southern Quakers and Slavery.*

J. FLOYD MOORE
GUILFORD COLLEGE

QUINTARD, CHARLES TODD

(1824-1898), Episcopal chaplain and bishop, was born in Stamford CT. He grew up in comfortable surroundings and attended school in New York City, including graduation from medical school in 1847. He moved south to Georgia in 1848 and three years later began teaching medicine in Memphis, where he formed a close friendship with Bishop JAMES H. OTEY. In 1854 he became a candidate for the Episcopal priesthood, eventually serving as a rector in Memphis and Nashville. A believer in the Oxford Movement, he referred to himself as a "high churchman" and a "ritualist" to describe his veneration of the church's liturgical tradition.

When the Civil War began, the volunteers of a unit of the First Tennessee Regiment picked the previously Unionist Quintard as their chaplain and he accompanied them when they left Nashville in 1861. He stayed with the unit as chaplain and surgeon until the end of the war. Quintard became a symbol of the national reconciliation of Episcopalians after the Civil War. Bishop Otey died in 1863 and Quintard was chosen as his successor in 1865. His confirmation as bishop of the Tennessee Diocese by Northern and Southern bishops gathered in Philadelphia for the 1865 General Convention of the Prostestant Episcopal Church was a sign of regional cooperation in the church. He quickly launched rebuilding efforts in his diocese, which had been materially and emotionally damaged by the war.

Quintard worked also to insure the survival of the UNIVERSITY OF THE SOUTH at the end of the Civil War. As vice-chancellor he sponsored the establishment of a diocesan training school at SEWANEE TN in 1866 and laid the cornerstone for St. Augustine Chapel in 1867. He energetically raised money for the institution in the North and in England, where he visited three times. While having his official ecclesiastical residence in Memphis, he retained a home in Sewanee and made its school the scholastic center for Southern Episcopalians. Resigning as vice-chancellor in 1868, he continued fund raising and promotional work for the school until his death.

See also article on HIGH CHURCH/LOW CHURCH.

Bibliography. Arthur H. Noll, ed., *Doctor Quintard: Chaplain C. S. A. and Second Bishop of Tennessee.*

CHARLES REAGAN WILSON
UNIVERSITY OF MISSISSIPPI

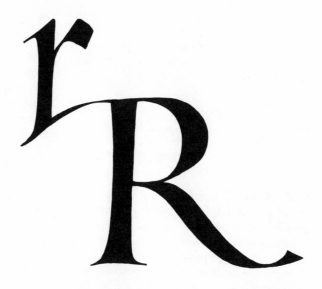

RADICAL REFORMATION: *See* ANABAPTISM.

RADIO MINISTRIES: *See* ELECTRONIC CHURCH.

RANKIN, M(ILLEDGE) THERON (1894-1953), Baptist missionary statesman, was born in Newberry County SC, and was graduated from Wake Forest in 1918, Southern Baptist Theological Seminary, (Th.M.) in 1921 and (Ph.D.) in 1928.

He was appointed missionary to China in 1921 by the Foreign Mission Board of the Southern Baptist Convention. His wife had grown up in China as the daughter of missionaries and went to China as a missionary one year before her husband-to-be. Rankin was teacher, then president, of Graves Theological Seminary to 1935. These were difficult years because of a decline of financial support for missionary work due to the Great Depression. In China they were years of internal political struggle and of Japanese invasion as well.

Rankin was his board's Secretary for the Orient from 1935 to 1944, with headquarters in Shanghai from 1936. The family was interned in Hong Kong after Pearl Harbor and returned home on the *Gripsholm* in 1942. He was the unanimous choice of the board in May 1944 to become its executive secretary, a position he held until his death.

As a denominational executive, Rankin emerged as a statesman of stature. A Baptist by heritage and conviction, his vision transcended his denomination and region. He saw the need for the Chinese and Japanese (and all other) indigenous churches to develop with independence and freedom. Though converted by the Southern Baptists, they were Christians at work in their own setting.

Rankin was a world-Christian. He placed everything in the Baptist work, doctrine, attitude, purpose, and practice, under the test of its relation to and its fitness for the Christian world mission. The doing of this required consolidating the healthy purpose of the denomination, broadening the horizons of understanding in the churches, and seeking to match profession with enlightened commitment.

With such a spirit and vision, Rankin became, in his time, not only Southern Baptists' most credible voice, but a spokesman of the faith heard and appreciated by believers of all names. Ecumenical statesmen have not been numerous in his denomination; unmistakably he was one.

See also article on ECUMENISM.

Bibliography. J. B. Weatherspoon, *M. Theron Rankin, Apostle of Advance.*

THERON D. PRICE
FURMAN UNIVERSITY

RAPTURE. A term used in dispensational premillennial eschatology, rapture denotes the catching up of Christian believers to be with Christ in the heavens. This event is preparatory to the Second Coming of Christ with His saints to bring in the millennial period of peace to the earth. In premillennial theology the seven-year period from the rapture of the church to the Second Coming is known as the Marriage Supper of the Lamb. On earth the seven-year period is represented as the period of the Great Tribulation. Although the term "rapture" is not found in the New Testament, the passage in 1 Thes. 4:17 is used as a proof-text for the word.

The "rapture" concept has become increasingly fixed as an end-time motif in evangelical understanding and preaching because of the rapid spread of dispensational premillennialism among conservative Evangelicals since the late nineteenth century. The word first entered contemporary theology through the teachings of J. N. Darby and the Plymouth Brethren (DARBYITE MOVEMENT) in mid-nineteenth-century England. Darby wrote extensively about the events surrounding the Second Coming of Christ, spreading his premillennial philosophy of history throughout British nonconformist churches. There has been recent controversy over the origin of the rapture concept in Darby's thought. Some recent scholarship attributes its rise to a vision by a member of the Irvingite movement earlier in the century.

In America the term and the premillennial theology that supports it were popularized by the rise of the prophetic conference movement in the last quarter of the 19th century. The conversion of the famous evangelist, Dwight L. Moody, to the premillennial view encouraged the growing conservative-fundamentalist movement in American Evangelicalism to do the same. The influence of C. I. Scofield was even more significant; his popular annotated editions of the King James Version of the Bible introduced the rapture concept to the millions of Americans who purchased them. The strong premillennial theology of Scofield's notes stood very close to the inspiration of the Bible itself for many of the users of "the Scofield Bible." Popular religious novels such as *In the Twinkling of an Eye* and *The Mark of the Beast* by Sydney Watson also helped to fix the rapture image upon the growing fundamentalist movement. The spectacular nature of the rapture event in which millions of believers suddenly were to be separated from worldly society became a part of popular American religious imagery.

The centrality of the rapture in premillennial theology has given rise to increasing controversy among Evangelicals concerning the time frame of the event. The prevailing majority still hold to the traditional position that the believing church is raptured just before the beginning of the seven-year tribulation period that precedes the Second Coming of Christ to set up the millennial reign. This is known as the pretribulation rapture. In more recent times, an increasing sentiment has arisen supporting a midtribulation rapture of the church at the point at which the most drastic oppression of the tribulation period begins. The third or post-tribulation position holds that the church will be part of the sufferings of the whole tribulation period and be snatched away just before the great battle of Armageddon that ushers in Christ's millennial reign.

The rapture theme continues to inspire popular religious writing, such as Hal Lindsay's *The Late Great Planet Earth*. Dallas Theological Seminary and the theological journal, *Bibliotheca Sacra*, are the foremost representatives of the historic pretribulation position in contemporary Evangelicalism.

See also articles on EVANGELICAL PROTESTANTISM; HEAVEN; MILLENNIALISM.

Bibliography. Lewis Sperry Chafer, *Systematic Theology*, vol. 4; Millard J. Erickson, *Contemporary Options in Eschatology*; John F. Walvoord, *The Blessed Hope and the Tribulation*.

MELVIN E. DIETER
ASBURY THEOLOGICAL SEMINARY

RATIONALISM (RELIGIOUS).

Rationalism, defined as the power of *a priori* reason to grasp the substantial truths of religion, approaches religion in a scholastic or Thomistic method. Consequently, it tends to view God, humanity, and especially the Bible in an ordered, Aristotelian manner. Joined with this method is a Lockean rationalism, a religious reductionism that pares down the essential elements of doctrine to those that are simple and knowable by all, and a greater stress on the cognitive and intellectual faculties than on the effective and psychological faculties. This particular kind of rationalism, rather popular in the South, verges more on the common sense variety rather than the detailed and extended qualifications of medieval scholasticism. Very rarely does it produce the fine distinctions or technical terms that characterize forensic sciences, philosophy, or law.

Religious knowledge is determined by syllogisms, direct inferences, approved apostolic examples, logical deductions, and directions from the biblical text. Belief in the Enlightenment dictum that individuals are more similar than unique makes it imperative that everyone be able to—and must—possess a uniform biblical understanding of the will of God, both in generalities and in particulars. In such an epistemology salvation is as much the result of one's reasoning ability as the practice of virtue.

The Bible is seen as revealed propositions that are normative or prescriptive, rather than merely descriptive. In the manner of Aristotle, Scripture is viewed as a collection of individual works whose authors are teaching particular truths. The words of the Bible are equated with what the Bible means. The Bible means what it says.

Since Southern theology generally tends to underplay the *imago dei* within human personalities, one is thrown back on Scripture as the only infallible source of knowledge about God. This results in the frequent attempt at creating a need for God by exposing people to the saving knowledge found only in Scripture. God does not draw people to a knowledge of truth; rather, people learn of God themselves.

With such a lofty conception of the importance and sufficiency of human perception, the exegetical function of the interpreter of Scripture is crucial. In this rationalized approach to the Bible, in which every piece of doctrine becomes a *fides explicita*, a necessary stress is put on correct biblical understanding (as opposed to religious experience or churchly authority). Since Scripture operates *ex opere operato*, its self-evident truths need only be clearly stated to be believed and obeyed. Since right belief was epistemologically possible, it was religiously necessary.

In this context every fine point of doctrine becomes crucial, which results in disagreement, little use for gradations of truth, division with those who cannot reason alike, a near deification of knowledge, and a battery of tightly reasoned differential dogmas. The Bible is viewed as a compilation of individual puzzle pieces that can be removed and rearranged.

Since religion is no mystery, there is no need for a learned clergy to interpret the Bible. Where Luther and Calvin believed that a special illumination of the Spirit was necessary for a correct understanding of the truths of salvation, in the case of Southern rationalism the opposite is true. Everyone has the capacity to perceive and interpret.

Many such sermons, organized along the dialectical method, with a heavy use of argumentation, polemics, rhetorical questions, persuasion, exhortation, and examples, verge on being unabridged concordances where every verse that contains the key word, like pearls on a string, is indiscriminately linked together. Scripture, after all, is a collection of separate entities, with a great stress put on their arrangement and ordering. This approach is found most commonly in the CHURCHES OF CHRIST movement within the CAMPBELLITE TRADITION.

Southern rationalism stresses the individual conscience and will as the determiners of religion and history. The social environment as a barrier to free will is deemphasized. Human free will determines its own actions. The ultimate controlling power lies in the reasoner, however, and not in reason.

The logical result of this quite optimistic estimation of benevolence and a corresponding underestimation on impulses such as tradition, faith, and motivation, is a weak conception of grace. A Pelagian concept of sin conceives of it as an act or action, rather than as an organic defect. This is so because in order for sin to be regarded as sinful, it must proceed from a will that is essentially free. Sin's origin, then, lies more in laziness than in egocentricity.

In such an individualistic conception of sin, religious good works with a social orientation become moments of self-perfection or self-aggrandizement motivated more by self-elevation and mastery than by community aims. Religious life becomes a legalistic interpretation of do's and don'ts.

See also articles on BIBLE, INTERPRETATION OF; THOMISM.

Bibliography. F. Roy Coad, *A History of the Brethren Movement*; C. Norman Kraus, *Dispensationalism in America*; Ernest R. Sandeen, *The Roots of Fundamentalism.*

CAREY J. GIFFORD
NASHVILLE, TENNESSEE

RAVENSCROFT, JOHN STARK

(1772-1829), first bishop of the Episcopal Diocese of North Carolina, was born in Prince George County VA. The family moved to Scotland, his mother's home, the same year, and young John was educated there and in England. Ravenscroft returned to Virginia after the Revolutionary War to recover the family estate. After attending the College of William and Mary to study law, he settled down as a country gentleman.

Despairing of his inability to break the habit of swearing, he was converted to Christianity and became a lay preacher of the Republican Methodist Church (see CHRISTIAN CHURCH). As he came to doubt his authority to minister, he consulted with Bishop R. C. Moore of Virginia, and was led to seek ordination. He became a believer in apostolic succession. After ordination he became rector of St. James' Church, Mecklenburg County, where he built a strong congregation.

He declined several calls to large churches before being elected bishop of North Carolina in 1823. His first sermon before his diocese, "On the Church," set forth in uncompromising manner his belief in the divine origin and exclusive authority of the church. To this and to some statements in his "Farewell Discourse" to St. James' Church, John Rice, a Presbyterian theologian, took exception in a published review. Ravenscroft replied in print and a lengthy controversy ensued. He was also challenged by Low Churchmen of his own communion, among them WILLIAM MEADE, later second bishop of Virginia.

Ravenscroft was an untiring pastor, lovingly attentive to clergy and laity under his charge. His health declined because of the rigors of constant travel and he died after only seven years as bishop. His influence upon thinkers of the church was strong and he was revered as an able High Church theologian.

See also article on HIGH CHURCH/LOW CHURCH.

Bibliography. Frank M. McClain, "The Theology of Bishops Ravenscroft, Otey and Green Concerning the Church, the Ministry and the Sacraments," *Historical Magazine of the Protestant Episcopal Church* 33 (1964): 103-36; John N. Norton, *The Life of Bishop Ravenscroft*; John V. Van Ingil, ed., *The Works of the Right Rev. John Stark Ravenscroft*, 2 vols.

LAWRENCE L. BROWN
EPISCOPAL SEMINARY OF THE SOUTHWEST

REDEMPTION: *See* SALVATION.

REFORM JUDAISM: *See* JUDAISM.

REFORMATION: *See* PROTESTANT REFORMATION.

REFORMED PROTESTANTISM: *See* CALVINISM.

REFORMED TRADITION: *See* JUSTIFICATION; PRESBYTERIANISM; WESTMINSTER CONFESSION OF FAITH.

REGULAR BAPTISTS: *See* OLD REGULAR BAPTISTS.

RELIGIOUS EXPERIENCE: *See* PIETY.

RELIGIOUS LIBERTY: *See* CHURCH AND STATE; JEFFERSON, THOMAS; LELAND, JOHN.

RELIGIOUS PRESS. Ever since the days of Martin Luther, churchmen have used the printing press to inform and instruct the faithful; to enlist followers in their cause; to combat evil, error, and superstition; and to promote and strengthen sectarian loyalties. Church leaders in the South, as have their co-religionists in other areas, have been firm believers in the "power of the press," devoting considerable energy and resources to publication.

Although sectional or Southern ecclesiastical organizations were not formed until the 1840s, the religious press in the region dates from 1802 when Henry Holcombe, a Baptist in Savannah, published *The Georgia Analytical Repository*. Holcombe's publication, like many of this genre, survived only a brief time; however, by the 1830s the religious press was an established institution in the South. By this decade weekly newspapers and magazines representing the Baptists, Disciples of Christ, Methodists, Episcopalians, Presbyterians, Roman Catholics, and others were published in the region.

By 1861 at least 25 religious weeklies were published in the South. Baptist papers were printed in every state except Florida, and Methodist papers were published at Richmond, Raleigh, Columbia, Nashville, Memphis, Louisville, St. Louis, New Orleans, and Galveston. Presbyterian weeklies emanated from Richmond, Fayetteville, Charleston, and New Orleans. An Associate Reformed Presbyterian paper was published at Due West SC; Disciples of Christ papers were published at Richmond and Bethany (later West) VA; the *Christian Sun*, representing the Southern Christian Convention, was printed at Suffolk VA; and the *Methodist Protestant* was published at Baltimore. Newspapers representing the Protestant Episcopal Church were published in Richmond and Raleigh; and Roman Catholic papers were printed at Charleston, Baltimore, St. Louis, Louisville, and Bardstown (KY). A Lutheran family operated the Henkel Press (established in 1808) at New Market VA and published childrens' books, catechisms, minutes of ecclesiastical organizations, hymn books, and other items. A church weekly, the *Lutheran Observer*, was published in Baltimore.

The editors of the religious newspapers usually were clergymen who were appointed by a denominational committee of the state or regional organization. However, some of the papers were privately owned and operated; in these instances the editors were dependent upon denominational support and were expected to be loyal to the tenets of the denomination. Most of the religious newspapers consisted of four pages and had an average circulation (in 1860) of 3,590. The contents and makeup of the different papers were similar and consisted of news of the denomination and its various agencies; excerpts from secular newspapers, including foreign ones; essays on theological subjects and Christian conduct; editorial comments on current events; varying degrees of sectarian polemical commentary; poetry and devotional or inspirational items; and advertisements.

At one time or another during the Civil War all religious newspapers in the South suspended publication; however, a few months after Appomattox the religious press resumed operation. Most of the prewar papers continued and were soon joined by new ones. Among the principal additions were: the *Lutheran Visitor*, published at Columbia where the Lutherans later established a publishing house; the first Jewish publication in the region, the *Spectator* (1885); and a number of papers that represented the various black denominations that flourished in the area. Perhaps the earliest of the Negro papers was the *Southwestern Christian Advocate*, published at New Orleans from 1866. The next year the *Christian Index*, a Baptist paper, was published in Tennessee, and the *Star of Zion*, an African Methodist Episcopal, Zion, church paper began publication in North Carolina. During the 1870s the *Afro-American Presbyterian* was published at Wilmington NC and the *Baptist Pioneer* at Selma AL. Although the fatality rate for black newspapers was high, many survived and by the 1970s they were published in various places throughout the South, such as Nashville, Atlanta, Shreveport, Charlotte, Little Rock, Memphis, and Dallas.

By the opening years of the 20th century all of the principal denominations and numerous small sects, both black and white, were represented by religious publications. Most of the major denominations provided papers for their constituency in each state or diocese, and some were represented by several papers. For example, there were 60 Baptist publications in the region, of which seven were located in the state of Texas. As the Roman Catholic Church in the area grew in membership, its religious publications increased. Each diocese sought to provide a paper for its territory, and by the mid-twentieth century more than 20 weeklies were published for Catholics in the South.

Missionary societies of the different denominations also published magazines and pamphlets to inform their constituency of the missionary enterprise and to elicit support for the denomination's mission program. At San Antonio the Methodist Church published a German-language missionary journal, *Der Missions Freund*.

Although numerous religious publications began in the South, few had a continuous history. Frequently those that endured did so by changing their name and merging with other publications. For example, the *Presbyterian Outlook* is the successor of the *Central Presbyterian*, the *Presbyterian Standard*, the *Southern Presbyterian*, the *Southwestern Presbyterian*, and the *Presbyterian of the South*. Among the denominational papers that have retained their antebellum titles are the *Religious Herald* (Virginia), the *Christian Index* (Georgia), the *Christian Observer* (Richmond and Louisville), and the *Christian Advocate* (Nashville). The circulation of religious weeklies in the 1970s ranged from less than 2,500 to over 375,000; the *Lutheran Witness*, published by the Missouri Synod and for a national constituency, reported a circulation of more than 600,000.

In addition to newspapers, Sunday school literature, youth magazines, and various missionary periodicals, several religious quarterlies or journals were published by the churches in the South. Perhaps the two most respected of these began publication in the antebellum era. The year 1847 marked the appearance of the first issue of both the *Southern Presbyterian Review* and the *Methodist Quarterly Review*. In the 1880s the *Southern Presbyterian Review* was superseded by the *Union Seminary Review*, a publication that continued until 1945 when it was transformed into *Interpretation: A Theo-*

logical and Biblical Quarterly. The *Methodist Quarterly Review* was published until the 1930s; after the reunification of Methodism's two regional bodies in 1939, the principal journal of the church became *Religion in Life*.

The first denomination in the South to establish a publishing enterprise was the Methodist Episcopal Church, South. In 1854 leaders in this church formed the Southern Methodist Publishing House and established headquarters at Nashville. It printed Sunday school literature, tracts, devotional items, hymnals, the *Methodist Book of Discipline*, and other religious books. Until 1924 all publications were under the imprint of the Southern Methodist Publishing House; in that year it began publication of books of general Christian interest under the imprint of the Cokesbury Press. After the reunion of 1939, the denomination's publishing house was named the Abingdon-Cokesbury Press. This combined the names of the publishing agencies of the Methodist Episcopal Church and the Methodist Episcopal Church, South. Nashville was chosen as headquarters for this press. In 1954 the church adopted a single name for its press, Abingdon; Cokesbury became the name of Methodist book stores throughout the nation. By the 1970s the publishing activities of the Methodist Church had offices in 14 metropolitan areas of the nation and annually published more than 100 titles. One of its principal items in recent decades was the multivolume *Interpreter's Bible* (1952-1957).

During the Civil War, Presbyterians in the South created the church's Committee on Publications with offices in Richmond. The purpose of this committee was to publish and circulate religious literature and books for the church's constituency. The committee's offices were destroyed by fire in April 1865, but under the leadership of E. T. Baird, church publications were revived. Within five years the committee published 18 million pages of tracts and other religious materials. In 1872 it began the publication of the writings of JAMES HENLEY THORNWELL and other church leaders. Until 1955 publications of the Presbyterian Church in the United States appeared under the imprint of denominational committees. In that year the John Knox Press was formed as the publishing house of the church. Until 1974 when its operations were moved to Atlanta, the John Knox Press was located in Richmond.

The last of the major Southern denominations to form a publishing agency was the Southern Baptist Convention. Shortly after the Civil War the Sunday School Board of the Southern Baptist Convention began the publication of literature for use in Sunday schools. Until the 1890s most Sunday school items and other religious books that were used by Southern Baptists were obtained from the American Baptist Publication Society in Philadelphia. In the 1890s the Southern Baptist Convention decided to publish more of its own literature; the agency for this undertaking was the Sunday School Board, which was located in Nashville. Until 1934 all of its publications carried the imprint of the Sunday School Board; in that year the board expanded its publishing activities to include books of a general Christian interest, publishing them through the Broadman Press. Twenty years later the Broadman catalogue listed more than 200 titles in print. Included were books for children, youth, and adults; for preachers and other church leaders; and in such categories as Bible study, missions, sermons, fiction, inspiration, personal Christian living, biography, doctrine, religious education, ethics, recreation, and music.

Two other denominational publishing establishments located in Nashville are those sponsored by the Cumberland Presbyterian Church and the Churches of Christ. The Disciples of Christ publishing house, the Bethany Press, is located in St. Louis. Like their counterparts in secular publishing, the religious presses in recent decades have made most of their books

restoration of the apostolic ordinances of baptism and communion, with Servetus setting forth an elaborate theology of baptism, in which he insisted that only believer's baptism by immersion is scriptural. To be saved, he contended, one must both believe and be baptized. While Campanus had a broader view as to where truth might be found, calling as he did for a "Catholic restitution" that sought truth "among the sects and all the heretics," he nonetheless revealed an attitude that usually characterizes restorationists: that what they have "restored" is the true church, while others are sects consisting of heretics.

This "restoration motif," as historians identify it, was so prevalent among the Anabaptists that George H. Williams has concluded: "So widespread was restorationism (restitutionism) as the 16th-century version of primitivism that it may be said to be one of the marks of the Radical Reformation." Franklin H. Littell, another authority on the underground Reformation, has suggested that the best term to describe ANABAPTISM is "the Restitution."

The Anabaptists have many heirs in the modern church, such as the Amish, Mennonites, Quakers, Plymouth Brethren, and Church of the Brethren, who stress various motifs of primitivism, whether pacifism, FOOT WASHING, holy kiss, or austere means of dress and transportation. But restorationism has also made its way in varying degrees across a large section of Protestantism. One historian counts 176 restorationist sects, each claiming to be the true "restored" church, and asks the embarrassing question, "What kind of book is our Bible that it could yield 176 different conceptions of the Church of Christ, each deemed of such importance that it required a separate church to be founded upon it?"

Restorationists in the South include three churches of the CAMPBELLITE TRADITION: CHRISTIAN CHURCH (DISCIPLES OF CHRIST), CHRISTIAN CHURCHES AND CHURCHES OF CHRIST, and CHURCHES OF

CHRIST (often distinguished by lack of instrumental music, another primitivism). The Disciples of Christ have in recent years all but discarded the restoration ideal in favor of ecumenicity, believing that unity and restoration are inimical to each other, though both motifs are admittedly a part of their heritage. The other two fellowships, being more conservative theologically, are adamantly restorationist, insisting that the restoration of primitive Christianity is the means to unity. But even these two churches are not in fellowship with each other, disagreeing on what constitutes restoration, such as the question of instrumental music. This is typical of restorationism, which tends to be polarizing. This was evident from the beginning with the various sects of the Anabaptists, who could not even ride together on the same boat when they came to the New World.

ALEXANDER CAMPBELL, the principal founder of these churches that identify themselves as "the Restoration Movement," was actually within the Reformed (Calvinist) tradition rather than the restorationist, calling his unity movement the "New Reformation," which he saw as a continuation of the work of Luther and Calvin. Unlike the Anabaptists and restorationists generally, who believe the church ceased to exist, Campbell believed in the inviolability of the church, even though it may always need reform. It was typical of him, therefore, to say, "Let us see a reformation in fact—a reformation in sentiment, in practice—a reformation in faith and manners." While he spoke of restoration, especially "the restoration of the ancient order," it was in reference to restoring *to* the church, which he believed existed in his time, things he thought were neglected, rather than restoring the church itself, as if it did not exist, which is a basic premise of restorationism.

See also articles on LANDMARK MOVEMENT; PRIMITIVE BAPTISTS.

Bibliography. Erwin Iserloh, et al., *Reformation and Counter Reformation*; Franklin H. Littell, *Anabaptist View of the Church*; C. C. Morrison, *The Unfinished*

Reformation; Earl I. West, *The Search for the Ancient Order*, 3 vols.; George H. Williams, *The Radical Reformation*.

LEROY GARRETT
DENTON, TEXAS

REVIVALISM. This is a method for recruiting converts based on a theology that stresses the importance of a CONVERSION experience, a definite time and place in which one accepts Jesus Christ as Savior from sin and Lord of life. Originally the Puritans considered it an adult experience, but for many it has become youth's initiation into the religious community.

Revivals are periods of religious fervor during which an unusual number of conversions take place. Originally considered miraculous outpourings of God's grace, they became routinized in the 19th century and individual preachers or "revivalists" traveled around "holding revivals." In the South they also became institutionalized and localized in the CAMP MEETING. Today many Southern churches hold annual "revivals" or "camp meetings" during which a visiting minister reminds church members of their past commitments and recalls those who have strayed.

William McLoughlin makes the distinction between awakenings ("periods of cultural revitalization that begin in a general crisis of beliefs and values" and end a generation later with a "profound reorientation") and the religious revivals that have been related to them. He cites five awakenings in American history: Puritan, 1610-1640; First, 1730-1760; Second, 1800-1830; Third, 1890-1920; and Fourth, 1960-1990(?).

Though the South was not settled primarily by English Puritans, Baptists and Presbyterians owe their origins to that movement. During the First GREAT AWAKENING, GEORGE WHITEFIELD stopped in Savannah and Charleston on his way north, but he did not draw great crowds as he did in New England.

The Second Great Awakening is usually said to have begun with the GREAT REVIVAL of 1800 in Kentucky and Tennessee. This spontaneous eruption of religious emotion, characterized by its unusual physical manifestations, began at Gasper River and CANE RIDGE before spreading like wildfire into the Virginias and Carolinas. Its lasting effects were felt by Methodists, Baptists, and Presbyterians.

An outbreak of revival enthusiasm among troops during the Civil War and subsequent preaching of Wesleyan Holiness ideas, particularly in north Georgia, laid the groundwork for the Third Awakening, during which the HOLINESS MOVEMENT and PENTECOSTALISM sprang up among whites and blacks across the region, forming numerous new denominations. These revivals should not, however, be confused with FUNDAMENTALISM, a theological movement of the same period that also shaped Southern religion.

The only Southern revivalists of national reputation had been the Methodist SAM P. JONES, born in Alabama in 1847 and based in Cartersville GA during his career in the 1880s and BILLY GRAHAM. Jones stressed the need to "draw the line" on moral issues and urged people to "Quit your meanness!" Paralleled by Billy Sunday in the North, Jones shifted the emphasis from a relationship with God to moral legalism.

While revivalism has helped to shape Southern religion, the churches have grown, not so much through waves of revival fervor, but through consistent evangelism.

See also articles on EVANGELICALISM; PROTRACTED MEETINGS.

Bibliography. John B. Boles, *The Great Revival, 1787-1805: The Origins of the Southern Evangelical Mind*; William G. McLoughlin, *Revivals, Awakenings, and Reform*; Donald G. Mathews, *Religion in the Old South*.

NANCY A. HARDESTY
ATLANTA, GEORGIA

RICE, DAVID (1733-1816), pioneer Presbyterian minister and early opponent of slavery in Kentucky, was born in Hanover County VA. Although his family was devoted to the Church of England, Rice converted to Presbyterianism under the influence of SAMUEL DAVIES. He attended the College of New Jersey when Davies became its president. A year after his graduation in 1761, he was licensed to preach in Hanover Presbytery. He was ordained in 1763, and about the same time married Mary Blair, daughter of the New Side Presbyterian pastor Samuel Blair.

Rice served with mixed results the congregations that Davies had vacated in Hanover County. After a longer and more productive ministry at Peaks of Otter in Bedford County, he moved in 1783 to Kentucky where he organized the congregations forming at Danville, Cane Run, and Fork of Dix River, the first churches in the area. He presided over the formation of Transylvania Presbytery (1786) and he promoted the Transylvania Seminary (University) in Lexington.

Rice's parents had opposed slavery and he in turn worked against its spread into Kentucky. As a delegate to the State Constitutional Convention of 1792, he sought but failed to achieve adoption of an antislavery article. His tract, *Slavery Inconsistent with Justice and Good Policy* (1792), on the subject received considerable attention. He was chosen to preach at the formation of the Synod of Kentucky in 1802.

See also article on ABOLITIONISM.

LOUIS WEEKS
LOUISVILLE PRESBYTERIAN SEMINARY

RICE, LUTHER (1783-1836), founder of Baptist foreign missions in America, was born in Northborough MA. In 1802 he joined a Congregational church. Entering Williams College in 1807, he participated in the famous "Haystack Prayer Meeting" the next year. The convictions emanating from that experience led him and five others, including Adoniram Judson, to seek appointment as foreign missionaries. This resulted in the organization of the American Board of Commissioners for Foreign Missions by the Congregationalists. Rice was among five men sent in 1811 to work in Asia.

After his arrival in India, Rice adopted the Baptist position and was baptized by immersion in November 1812. Judson and his wife formally became Baptists after arriving in India. Now separated from the Congregationalists and without any means of support, the three young Baptists agreed for Rice to return to America to seek financial support from the Baptists.

Arriving in America in 1813, Rice traveled the Eastern Seaboard from Boston to Savannah informing churches of the need for foreign missions. After conceiving a plan for a general missionary society made up of representatives of smaller societies, he led in the organization of the TRIENNIAL CONVENTION in May 1814. He was instrumental in the publication of the *Columbian Star*, the first Baptist weekly in America, begun in 1818. He also led in establishing Columbian College (now George Washington University) that was opened in Washington DC in 1822 for training ministers and missionaries.

Bibliography. Garnett Ryland, *The Baptists of Virginia, 1699-1926*; Evelyn Wingo Thompson, *Luther Rice: Believer in Tomorrow.*

JOHN S. MOORE
LEXINGTON, VIRGINIA

RIDGECREST, NORTH CAROLINA. For almost three quarters of a century this village has been home for a Southern Baptist Convention assembly. It is located two miles east of Black Mountain. Bernard W. Spilman is credited with originating the idea of such an assembly, being a pioneer Sunday school worker in North Carolina. The North Carolina Baptist Convention purchased almost 1,000 acres for an encampment, the assembly being chartered in 1907 and bearing the title Ridgecrest Baptist Assembly from 1912. As early as 1907 the SBC in its annual meeting endorsed the assembly with moral support but did not at the time offer financial aid. By the end of World War I Ridgecrest was becoming a convention-sponsored project.

The early years of Ridgecrest were marred by many vicissitudes with frequent change of managers. Fires and tornadoes destroyed much of the early property. In the second quarter of the century Ridgecrest was fully stabilized, having been placed under the Sunday School Board of the SBC in 1944. More and more the board gave financial support while steering the assembly toward denominational purposes. It became popular as a center for denominational gatherings; down to 1952 it remained the convention's only such site (when Glorieta NM assembly was established). Camp Ridgecrest for Boys became a new operation in 1930; Camp Crestridge for Girls opened in 1955.

The quarter of a century prior to 1980 proved to be an era of remarkable expansion, which witnessed constant building and modernization of facilities. By the 1950s attendance surpassed 25,000 annually. Attendance reached 38,000 at the end of the next decade. Continued development is seen in that by 1980 Ridgecrest Conference Center guest day attendance exceeded 234,000.

Conferences offered cover every phase of church and denominational work. These range from highly practical to inspirational. Thousands have encountered profound religious experiences at Ridgecrest, a claim attested by the large number who repeatedly return. Its programs attract national and international speakers and other participants.

Bibliography. Robert A. Baker, *The Southern Baptist Convention and Its People: 1607-1972*; William Wright Barnes, *The Southern Baptist Convention: 1845-1953*; R. L. Middleton, "Ridgecrest Baptist Assembly," *Encyclopedia of Southern Baptists.*

WILLIAM ALLEN POE
NORTHWESTERN STATE UNIVERSITY
OF LOUISIANA

ROADSIDE SIGNS. Across the South, but especially in the mountainous areas of the Appalachians and the Ozarks, travelers in cars see signs by the roadside proclaiming religious messages. Sometimes they are homemade or even rough-hewn;

they can also be sturdily constructed and professionally painted or sculpted.

The Bible phrases or concise sayings on them are typically evangelistic, warning the sinful person to "get right with God" or "prepare to meet thy God" or to consider "where will you spend eternity?" Their pronouncements are less often devotional or ethical in nature. In the absence of any research to date, one hypothesizes that they are offered as ministry to hell-bound sinners by sectarian Christians, most likely from Holiness or Pentecostal or independent Fundamentalist quarters.

Evidence informally acquired does suggest that such signs are more common in the mountain regions than elsewhere. Perhaps they are one reaction to the process of modernization. When outsiders began to travel through hitherto isolated territory and their ways were perceived as strange at best and evil at worst, a number of resident Christians saw an opportunity and a responsibility. It can be argued that the signs are a creative act, even a folk art.

The religious roadside-sign phenomenon invites comparison with the religious bumper-sticker craze of the 1970s and 1980s. It may be that, though separated by time and place, these phenomena have analogous features. But this too is a conjecture. This feature of religion in the South is now sufficiently common and significant to warrant investigation.

ROBERTS, ORAL (1918-), the most famous and successful of all Pentecostal preachers to date, was born in Oklahoma, the fifth son of a small-town preacher. Healed of apparent tuberculosis at age 17, Roberts was ordained a few weeks later by the PENTECOSTAL HOLINESS CHURCH and began a career as a traveling evangelist. At 20 he married "his darling wife Evelyn" and for almost a decade they lived an itinerant existence as Roberts held revivals and pastored small churches in the South and Southwest.

In 1947, after a dramatic service in which the gift of healing he had long expected finally manifested itself, Roberts became a full-time evangelist. He moved to TULSA in 1948 and established a non-profit ministry known as Healing Waters, Inc., the forerunner of the present Oral Roberts Evangelistic Association. Within less than five years, over 1,500,000 people were hearing him preach under his great tent each year, countless others heard his radio broadcasts over a network of 300 stations, and his *Healing Waters* magazine had a circulation of over 250,000. In 1954 he began filming his revival services for television and by 1958 was preaching and praying for the sick and afflicted over 136 stations.

Roberts has used his exceptional success to unify and strengthen the Pentecostal community. He has been a moving spirit in the Full Gospel Businessmen's Fellowship International, and Oral Roberts University, which opened its doors in 1965, is the most impressive educational institution in the Pentecostal world. In 1968 Roberts joined the United Methodist Church, a move variously interpreted as a cynical attempt to broaden his base of financial support, an exercise in upward social mobility, or part of a genuine effort to identify with a Christian world beyond a narrow Pentecostalism.

Though he ended his healing crusades in 1968, Roberts returned to television in 1969 with a format that featured slick production techniques, the World Action Singers of ORU, and guest appearances by celebrities. His quarterly specials and his syndicated weekly program, seen over approximately 175 stations, made him the most widely viewed television preacher in the closing years of the 1970s. During that decade Roberts gave great emphasis to the principles of "Seed-Faith," whose essence is that those who give generously to God, perchance through his servant, Oral Roberts, can expect a miraculous return on their investment. Seed-Faith and attention to positive thinking and material abundance seemed to overshadow the earlier healing message until,

in 1977, Roberts announced a bold effort to combine medicine and prayer in a multimillion-dollar city of Faith Medical and Research Center, to be constructed on the ORU campus. After much opposition and a serious financial crisis exacerbated by a loss of approximately 40 percent of his television audience—at the end of 1980 he was being seen by an average weekly audience of approximately 2,351,000 over 177 stations—Roberts opened the complex in November 1981. Much remained unfinished, however, and some observers foresaw continuing financial difficulties for the institution.

For several years, Roberts's son, Richard, has assumed an increasingly prominent role in the ministry and the OREA, but it appears doubtful he possesses the intellectual or administrative gifts necessary to head the empire his father has built.

See also articles on ELECTRONIC CHURCH; FAITH HEALING; PENTECOSTALISM.

Bibliography. David E. Harrell, *All Things Are Possible*; Oral Roberts, *The Call*.

WILLIAM C. MARTIN
RICE UNIVERSITY

ROBERTSON, ARCHIBALD THOMAS

(1863-1934), renowned Baptist scholar, was born near Chatham VA. He received the A.M. degree in 1885 from Wake Forest College, then completed the Th.M. degree at Southern Baptist Theological Seminary in 1888. From that date until his death, he was associated with his seminary alma mater where he served as a professor in the New Testament field.

The author of more than 40 books, Robertson is best known for his original research in the area of the Greek New Testament. His "big grammar" (*A Grammar of the Greek New Testament in the Light of Historical Research*, 1914) is perhaps his best-known work. He was the author of a six-volume commentary entitled *Word Pictures in the New Testament*. Throughout all of his research and writings, he emphasized the importance of word studies, particularly etymology, for the task of New Testament interpretation. He sought to demonstrate how a knowledge of the intricacies of the Greek New Testament actually clarifies much of historical theology. Robertson was concerned with the significance of nonbiblical philology and syntax as these affect the understanding of New Testament language and thought. His contribution to the knowledge of the Greek New Testament, and his theories concerning the centrality of exegesis for an understanding of biblical theology, continue today to influence both Greek grammarians and theologians alike. He ranks as one of the foremost scholars given to the world by the Baptists of the South.

See also articles on BIBLICAL INTERPRETATION; THEOLOGICAL EDUCATION.

WATSON E. MILLS
MERCER UNIVERSITY

ROBINSON, STUART (1814-1881), Presbyterian pastor and editor, was born in Ireland, immigrating to the United States at the age of five. He grew up in the home of a Presbyterian clergyman, James Brown, and decided that he too should become a minister. He studied liberal arts at Amherst College, then undertook theological education at Union Seminary in Virginia and at Princeton Seminary.

Ordained in West Virginia in 1842, he served churches in Kanawha-Salines (1841-1846), in Frankfort KY (1846-1852), and at the Second Presbyterian Church, Louisville (1858-1881). Robinson also filled the chair in Church Government and Pastoral Theology at the fledgling Danville Seminary (1856-1858). While at Danville, an Old School institution, Robinson focused dissent against the pro-Union views of ROBERT J. BRECKINRIDGE. Robinson voiced a doctrine of the SPIRITUALITY OF THE CHURCH that maintained that religion should tend to the soul while social institutions cared for the body. This doctrine, more radical than previous formulations with the same title, prevailed among Southern Presbyterians and many other evangelical

denominations for several decades. After the Civil War Robinson led a majority of Presbyterians from the border states into the Presbyterian Church in the United States. He was moderator of that assembly in 1869.

Robinson's sermons and articles, together with books such as *The Church of God* (1858) and *Discourses of Redemption* (1868) made him a focal figure in evangelical Protestantism during the 1870s. Through wise dealings in real estate Robinson became wealthy. He gave sums to begin a pension program in the PCUS, to support orphanages, and to start new congregations.

LOUIS B. WEEKS
LOUISVILLE PRESBYTERIAN SEMINARY

ROMAN CATHOLIC CHURCH (IN THE SOUTH). Even before there was a "South," Catholicism existed in the region. In 1565 the Spanish established a Catholic mission at ST. AUGUSTINE, and later Spanish and French priests seeded missions and European settlements in the Mississippi Valley and Gulf areas. With the founding of Mobile in 1706 and New Orleans in 1718, French Catholics gained a strong foothold in the Gulf. But time and the thin Spanish and French numerical presence eroded the early Catholic imprint further inland. Only along the Gulf did French Catholicism survive as a visible cultural and religious influence on later Southern society.

The roots of "American Catholicism" went back to 1634, when a band of English Catholics under the leadership of the CALVERT FAMILY landed in Maryland. There, the Calverts attempted to build a refuge for Catholics fleeing persecution and handicaps in England. Aided by Jesuit missionaries, the small Catholic population kept its faith alive, but it lost effective political and social control of the colony to Protestant settlers by the end of the 17th century. To protect itself from the visceral anti-Catholicism of the English Protestant settlers, the Catholic minority espoused the principle of religious toleration. The American Revolution and the quelled the rebellions, and when church councils called for uniform church practices and obedience, they asserted their control over the ecclesiastical communities.

Southern Catholic lay people have generally assumed a passive role in the church since the mid-nineteenth century. A brief resurgence of lay activity occurred in the 1880s and 1890s, but it was largely confined to a few Catholic intellectuals critical of the American church's submission to Irish Catholic religious and social norms. Vatican II, which invited self-criticism and openness in the church, altered church discipline, promoted a vigorous devotional life, and bred a more demanding and critical laity in the American church. In the 1960s and 1970s increased lay initiatives and independence from clerical control resurfaced, as evident in burgeoning lay organizations. In some instances prominent lay leaders even clashed with church policy, as in questions of unions and race. Still, most Southern Catholics seek approval from their bishops and operate within the circle of accepted Catholic action.

Catholic religious and social life exists in the parish, turning on the twin axes of church and school. Attendance at Mass, sacraments, and weekly devotions, the types and activities of parochial organizations, religious vocations coming from the parish, the functioning of the parochial schools, adherence to Catholic morality— all measure Catholic conduct and commitment.

As the highest executive in the diocese, the bishop is personally responsible for all Catholic units in his territory. Southern bishops are overburdened with administration, largely because of poor management. For the most part, bishops use only clergy as assistants, and consequently, they call on individuals trained in theology or church history or philosophy to oversee expensive building programs or to administer charities. The shortage of priests compounds the problem of finding qualified specialists to run Catholic pro-

grams. In 1963 Bishop Richard O. Gerow of the Natchez-Jackson diocese tried to remedy his staffing problems by opening advisory positions on his diocesan commissions to lay professionals who could counsel him on lay activities, music and liturgy, and building. Necessity has forced other bishops to continue Gerow's experiment, but most Southern prelates prefer to run their complex bureaucracies in the old manner. Overtaxed bishops have developed "bricks and mortar" mentalities preoccupied with internal ecclesiastical and financial matters and wary of involvement in potentially distracting and disruptive social issues. As organization men within Southern society, the bishops have generally promoted cooperation and consensus.

Ethnic differences within the church have threatened Catholic unity in the South. Almost alone of regional religions, Catholicism has been an immigrant church. Immigrants carried their Old World antagonisms to their new Southern world and to their church. American- and French-born Catholics in Maryland clashed with Irish immigrant priests and congregations in Norfolk and Charleston in the early nineteenth century. The Creoles of Louisiana resisted growing Irish influence in the American church in the 1850s. Irish and German immigrants in New Orleans jockeyed for nationality parishes with their own countrymen as priests. At the same time, however, the church served as a social and cultural barrier against an alien and sometimes hostile Protestant world. Catholic immigrants, Creoles, Cajuns, and free people of color walled themselves inside a Catholic culture, building schools, associations, and charitable institutions that paralleled those of the Protestants. New waves of Catholic immigrants, especially the Italians who came to Louisiana in the late nineteenth century and the Spanish-speaking peoples who have migrated to Florida and the Gulf area after World War II, have reenacted the pattern of internal ethnic tension while Catholic closure morality—opposing abortion, for example—has dovetailed so neatly with evangelical Protestant positions that Catholics have become sought-after allies in recent efforts to impose a conservative morality on the nation. The election of Jeremiah Denton, a Catholic, to the United States Senate from Alabama in 1980 suggests the "acceptability" of Southern-born Catholics in public life today. The extent to which anti-Catholicism existed, however, intensified Catholic group consciousness in the South.

Patterns of settlement also affected Catholic consciousness and group cohesion. Catholics have always remained a numerical minority in the South, but they have been highly concentrated wherever they settled in numbers. Until 1960, Louisiana generally accounted for more than half the Southern Catholic population. Today, Catholics continue to occupy the geographic fringes of the South, with Catholics largely congregated in Maryland, Florida, Louisiana, and parts of Texas. Outside of Louisiana, Catholicism has been an urban religion. The Southern Catholic population swelled with the arrival of Irish and Germans in the 19th century and Italians in Louisiana in the late nineteenth century. Between 1870 and 1970 the Southern Catholic population multiplied six times and new concentrations of Catholics emerged in the dioceses of Richmond, Miami, Lafayette, and San Antonio. Since World War II Catholic population growth has derived significantly from the movement of Spanish-speaking and Northern-born Catholics into the South. Still, in 1970 only four percent of the Southern population was Catholic.

In the 20th century Catholic efforts to win converts scored modest success at best, with conversion rates per thousand between 3.5 in 1930 and 4.8 in 1960. Interestingly, the conversion rates are highest in the dioceses where Catholic population is the smallest. In areas of high Catholic concentration, approximately three-quarters of the converts enter the church because of marriage to Catholics. Southern Catholics follow the national trend toward increased exogamy in recent years. The intermarriage of the Catholic social minority with members of the social majority underscores the overall acceptance of Southern Catholics in society. The church discourages intermarriage, but dispersed, isolated Catholics in the region have had little choice except to seek partners outside the faith. In 1970, in the dioceses of Raleigh, Charleston, Savannah, Atlanta, Nashville, and Little Rock, where Catholics constituted only two percent of the total population, mixed marriages ranged from 56 percent to almost 80 percent. Under such circumstances, Catholic group consciousness has been difficult to maintain.

Since World War II the church has recorded a steady erosion of Catholic identity and observance of religious duties, although Vatican II shows signs of arresting this trend. Indicative of habits and trends underway before Vatican II was the experience of "St. Mary's Parish," an urban, ethnically diverse (Irish, French, German, Italian) parish in New Orleans studied closely by Joseph Fichter, S.J., in 1950. Fichter learned that only about one-third of the parishioners met their religious duties of attending Mass, receiving the sacraments, and observing holy days. Catholic women were more conscientious than men. Although a "fairly good" number of practicing Catholics entered the vocations, overall spiritual activism was low. About 40 percent of the parishioners neglected their religious duties altogether, and ethnic and secular intrusions corrupted religious practices. The local pastor particularly frowned on the Italians' excessive devotion to the Feast of Saint Joseph's. "Christening parties" after baptism obscured the religious meaning of the sacrament. Allegiance to church teachings on contraception, divorce, intermarriage, and required attendance at Catholic schools had weakened perceptibly, although Catholics still adhered generally to church teaching on abortion and euthanasia. Only slightly more than half the Catholics believed that the devil was real. In interpretive areas of morality, such as race relations, almost all Catholics shared the world view of their Protestant counterparts. Studies of the Catholics in the 1960s confirm the patterns Fichter observed in his New Orleans sample, but also note that marginal Catholics isolated in heavily Protestant areas tend to have little identity with the church or with Southern society in general, largely because they are newcomers to the South.

Even so, Southern Catholics are more religious than their Northern counterparts. Recent comparative studies suggest that Southern Catholics are more likely to pray daily, to consider entering religious life, and to maintain friendly relations with the clergy. In that sense, Southern Catholics conform to the regional patterns generally of high religiosity.

As a matter of policy, the church has absolved itself of moral responsibility for Catholics' civil welfare. The church has stressed individual salvation rather than social reform. In the South the church cultivated the inner spiritual kingdom, and until Vatican II largely eschewed ventures in public policy, except to support Southern positions.

In matters of race, the litmus test of Southern identity, Catholics aligned with the white Protestant churches. According to church teaching, slavery did not violate church law, natural law, or divine will. Church spokesmen rebuked masters for abusing slaves, and they instructed them to bring their slaves into the Christian fold, to honor the sacrament of marriage among them, and to meet their slaves' physical needs. Beyond that, the church adopted a proslavery stance. In his widely circulated writings, Bishop England put aside his personal distaste for slavery to attack abolitionist meddling in Southern affairs and to uphold the right of masters to keep their human property. During the secession winter Augustin Verot of Savannah delivered a sermon, subse-

quently printed and distributed throughout the South, in which he blamed the North for destroying the union by its threats to Southern property and security. Verot also reminded Catholic masters of their Christian obligations to the slaves. His theme of SLAVERY as a duty and a burden for masters coincided with Protestant arguments on the subject. Catholic slaveholders, who included the Jesuits up to 1836, treated their slaves no differently than Protestant slaveholders, which suggests that Catholicism forged no distinctive morality concerning bondage.

Southern Catholics endorsed secession, enlisted in the Rebel army, and prayed for Confederate victories. The churchmen also clashed, in print, with Northern churchmen over the slavery, secession, and war issues. But slavery and secession did not rive the church along sectional lines as they did several Protestant denominations. Catholic unity was rooted in religious dogma, not public policy. The church's unity showed in 1866 at the meeting of 45 American bishops at the Second Plenary Council in Baltimore. Southern and Northern bishops expressed a common concern for the spiritual and physical plight of the ex-slaves. They urged priests and laymen to embark upon a new ministry to the blacks but, except in Georgia and Florida, their plans failed. The massive immigrant tide sweeping the United States after the war overwhelmed the church's resources and saturated its attention.

In the Catholic church the pattern of segregation developed more slowly than it did in Southern Protestant churches. The Second Plenary Council had recommended that bishops build separate churches for blacks, but the decision was left to each bishop in his own diocese. The Catholic principle of universality, the lack of priests, and the reluctance of many blacks to depart slowed the process of SEGREGATION. Still, segregation was underway. An all-black church, St. Francis Xavier Church, opened in Baltimore in

1864. Two religious communities of colored nuns (the Oblate Sisters of Providence, founded in Baltimore in 1829, and the Sisters of the Holy Family, founded in New Orleans in 1842) worked with blacks exclusively. In 1871 an English group of Josephite Fathers from Mill Hill began their ministry to American blacks. At the close of the 19th century Mother Katharine Drexel established the Sisters of the Blessed Sacrament, a community that developed an extensive network of schools for blacks. Other orders have also withstood the scorn of white Catholics to work among blacks. The lack of black priests retarded segregation. As late as 1964, a mere 115 black priests served about three-quarters of a million black Catholics in the United States. Southern black Catholics had to wait until 1965 for an American-born black to become a bishop in the South, when Harold R. Perry became auxiliary bishop of New Orleans. The problem of recruiting black priests has been related to the lack of educational facilities for black Catholics. The only major seminary for blacks was St. Augustine's at Bay St. Louis MS, although all dioceses now accept black candidates for the priesthood.

White racism had driven many blacks out of the Catholic church by the 20th century. In the South, blacks were refused access to Catholic schools, hospitals, and orphanages, and most bishops acquiesced in the general movement toward segregation. The church's practice of permitting national parishes for European immigrant groups provided the model for the creation of separate black and white Southern parishes. The pace of segregation varied according to place. New Orleans was among the last to accept separate parishes because affluent colored Creoles were woven into the Creole Catholic cultural and social fabric and resisted being lumped together with black Catholics. In time each Southern diocese ran two separate systems of schools, orphanages, hospitals, and religious socie-

ties. Blacks even got their own university, Xavier University in New Orleans.

From its beginning, segregation evoked anger among some Catholics. Black Catholics attacked racial prejudice and they organized lobbies such as the Federated Colored Catholics to push reform within the church. In 1933 several white priests joined the black protesters to form the Clergy Conference on Negro Welfare, which intended to make priests and nuns "color conscious by every available form of publicity." Chapters soon cropped up in Mobile, Richmond, and Raleigh. These early groups were short-lived, but they provided the philosophical and organizational foundation for modern Catholic involvement in the CIVIL RIGHTS MOVEMENT and in church reform.

Pressure from outside the South largely accounted for shifts in the church's racial policies during the civil rights era. Catholic and interfaith committees on race prodded the church to end school segregation in the South. In 1962, for example, a Southern field office of the National Conference for Interracial Justice was added in New Orleans to direct the dismantling of Jim Crow in the archdiocese with the largest black Catholic population.

Individual clergy broke the longtime Catholic resistance to racial justice. For many years Archbishop Joseph Rummel of New Orleans had invested his prestige in appeals for moderation, but most of the early action occurred in the upper South and focused on the schools. In 1947-1948 Archbishop Joseph Ritter of St. Louis and Archbishop Patrick O'Boyle of Washington desegregated their archdiocesan schools. In 1953 Virginia-born Bishop Vincent Waters of Raleigh faced down a mob to integrate Catholic schools and hospitals. In 1954 Bishop William Adrian of Nashville defied local ordinances to integrate the Catholic parochial schools.

In 1958 Rome declared that "the heart of the race question is moral and religious" and that "segregation cannot be reconciled with the Christian view of our fellow man." Many Southern Catholics were slow to accept this new directive. Region triumphed over religion on matters of race, particularly in the Deep South where Southern Catholics opposed integration as a matter of course. But the momentum of the civil rights movement in the nation and calls for racial justice emanating from Vatican II put Catholic segregationists on the defensive. By the autumn of 1962 Southern bishops had integrated Catholic elementary and secondary schools everywhere but in Alabama and Mississippi. In so doing, they moved the pace of desegregation ahead of the public schools. Hospitals and other church institutions opened to blacks in the wake of school desegregation. In worship, however, segregation survived because of customs nurtured during the Jim Crow era, and in schools de facto segregation exists still because of residential patterns and parental preferences.

However reluctantly, the Southern church meted out penalties to Catholics who continually or violently opposed the church's teaching on race relations. But the prominence of threats of internal discipline and external political pressures in demands for Catholic desegregation obscured the moral and spiritual dimensions of the conflict and reduced it to a power struggle. Catholics generally share regional attitudes concerning race. Some Catholics, such as Leander Perez, the longtime political boss of Plaquemines Parish, Louisiana, even suffered excommunication rather than submit to the new church policy. The undiminished political power of the excommunicated Perez in a heavily Catholic parish attested to the church's inability to alter deeply ingrained social and cultural attitudes and practices.

In the civil rights crusade some Catholics particularly resented the "invasion" of Northern-born Catholics in local Southern affairs. Bishop Thomas J. Toolen of Mobile-Birmingham forbade Catholic priests and nuns to participate in

the civil rights marches of 1963, and he railed against carpetbagger priests. The civil rights issue tore away at traditional lines of authority in the church as individual priests and nuns marched in Selma without obtaining the customary permission of the local bishop to "work" in his diocese. Indeed, the civil rights movement commingled with Vatican II to foster an independent spirit among Catholic clerics and nuns, the radical implications of which are only beginning to be understood in the Southern church.

The church is changing with the times. The presence of a tough-minded antiracist like Archbishop Oscar Lipscomb of Mobile, himself a native of Mobile, reflects a rising social liberalism in the Southern church. The liberalism of Southern clerics has assumed many forms, even that of criticism of American involvement in Vietnam when Archbishop Hallinan of Atlanta and others swam against the tide of Southern, and Catholic, opinion in 1964 to oppose American military involvement in Southeast Asia. In Appalachia Catholic nuns have fought to prevent the closing of coal mines. The migration of more politically liberal, Northern-born Catholics into Southern cities in the 1960s and 1970s has introduced new ideas and potentially new proponents for social change into the Southern church.

The most important attempt to mobilize Catholic influence in Southern public affairs was the Catholic Committee of the South (CCS), founded in 1939 and the product of Southern, not Northern, social concerns. The CCS attempted to operate within both Southern and Catholic contexts, drawing its support from Southern Catholics committed to a regional approach in solving social and economic problems. The CCS attacked rural peonage, racial violence, political corruption, antilabor attitudes, illiteracy, and poverty in the South—all social ills related to racism. By the early 1950s the CCS was concentrating its efforts in Louisiana, where it joined a few prolabor priests, Archbishop Rummel, and H. L. Mitchell's National Farm Labor Union to battle the American Sugar Cane League, Senator Allen J. Ellender, and antiunionists in the sugarcane fields. In 1953 the sugarcane workers' strike grew out of Catholic involvement in labor organizing. Its failure, however, exposed the church's inability to force its members to submit to the hierarchy's definition of ethical responsibility, and because several Catholic churchmen opposed the union, it illustrated the church's inability to stand united in the area of social justice.

The Southern Catholics' responses to race, labor, and other social issues parallel those of the region's Protestants. This fact suggests that, however much Southern Catholics diverged from the regional norms in matters of religious ritual and theology, they converged in matters of social belief and culture. Southern Catholics remained Southern. Their adaptation to their social environment grew out of Catholicism's introverted theology, which fixed on personal salvation through the sacraments rather than ethical responsibility. In many ways, the Southern Catholics' ability to separate the sacred and profane in the South has allowed them to live with the seeming contradiction of being both Southern and Catholic, of accepting both regional social values and a universal faith.

See also articles on BLACK CATHOLICISM; CHURCH AND STATE; FRENCH INFLUENCE; GEOGRAPHY; ROMAN CATHOLICISM; SPANISH INFLUENCE; SPANISH INFLUENCE IN LA FLORIDA.

Bibliography. Roger Baudier, *The Catholic Church in Louisiana*; Thomas Becnal, *Labor, Church, and the Sugar Establishment*; John Tracy Ellis, *American Catholicism* 2nd ed.; *The Life of James Cardinal Gibbons, Archbishop of Baltimore*; Joseph H. Fichter, *Southern Parish: Dynamics of a City Church*; Fichter and George L. Maddox, "Religion in the South, Old and New," *The South in Continuity and Change*, ed. John C. McKinney and Edgar Thompson; Michael V. Gannon, *Rebel Bishop: The Life and Era of Augustin Verot*; Philip Gleason, ed., *Contemporary Catholicism in the United States*; Andrew M. Greeley, *The Catholic Experience: An Interpretation of the History of American Catholicism*; Peter Guilday, *The Life and Times of John Carroll, Archbishop of Baltimore*; *The Life and Times of John England, First Bishop of Charleston*; Alfred O. Hero, Jr., *The Southerner and World Affairs*; Thomas T. McAvoy, "The Formation of the Catholic Minority in the United States, 1820-1860," *Review of Politics* 10 (1948): 13-34; Randall M. Miller and Jon Wakelyn, eds., *The Catholic Church in the Old South*; Vincent J. O'Connell, "The Church in the South," *The American Apostolate: American Catholics in the Twentieth Century*, ed. Leo R. Ward; William A. Osborne, *The Segregated Covenant: Race Relations and American Catholics*; James J. Pillar, *The Catholic Church in Mississippi*; Walter B. Posey, *Frontier Mission: A History of Religion West of the Southern Appalachians to 1861*; Madeleine H. Rice, *American Catholic Opinion in the Slavery Controversy*; Edward Wakin and Joseph F. Scheur, *The De-Romanization of the American Catholic Church*.

RANDALL M. MILLER
ST. JOSEPH'S UNIVERSITY

ROMAN CATHOLICISM. This historic institution may be simply defined as that Christian body that acknowledges the spiritual authority of the bishop of Rome (known more familiarly as the pope) and the other bishops who are in communion with him. Those Christians may be members of the predominant Latin rite, as are the vast majority of American Roman Catholics, or they may belong to one of the many Eastern rites (Ruthenian, Syrian, Coptic, Italo-Albanian, etc.) who acknowledge the primacy of the pope. The adjective "Roman," while used in official documents of the Catholic church from the time of the Council of Trent in the 16th century, was mainly popularized in the last century by Anglican writers who desired to distinguish the Roman Catholic church from the other two branches of historic Catholicism, the Orthodox and the Anglican. The term is in common usage today both outside and within the Roman Catholic church.

Roman Catholicism is complex both in its historical development and its current actuality. Certain distinguishing characteristics in its own self-understanding help to define it as a distinctive ecclesial reality distinct from, but not entirely at odds with, the Protestant and Orthodox ecclesial tradition.

First, and most obvious, is the Petrine ministry. The Roman Catholic church professes its belief that the present pope is the legitimate and historical successor of Saint Peter, the head of the apostles. As such, the pope is the "permanent and visible source and foundation of unity and fellowship." (Vatican Councils I and II)

It is solemn Catholic teaching that the pope is infallible, whether he teaches the church authoritatively as an individual or in concert with the other bishops of the church in an ecumenical council, on matters directly pertaining to faith or morals. The charisma of papal infallibility does not mean that the pope is impeccable (incapable of personal sin or error in conduct or thought) or a source of new revelation (the pope cannot create a new doctrine not already found in the historical witness of the Christian tradition or in the Scriptures). Papal infallibility must be understood as an essentially negative charisma. It means that the pope in his role as supreme teacher of the church will not lead the church into error on a matter of what is to be believed as part of the deposit of faith or in a course of moral action. Catholic theologians, whether liberal or conservative, all agree that popes historically have exercised the charisma of personal infallibility most rarely in the course of the church's history.

The notion of Petrine ministry is intimately linked with the doctrine of apostolic succession, a teaching held in common with both the Anglican and Orthodox churches. The bishops of the Catholic church regard themselves as the legitimate successors of the first apostles. As such, the bishops are called upon to "teach, rule, and sanctify" that portion of the church under their jurisdiction. Individual bishops do not enjoy the gift of personal infallibility but their corporate teaching expressed in universal (that is, ecumenical) councils is regarded as infallible. According to Roman Catholic teaching, the full unity of the church of Christ is best expressed by the body of bishops who are in union with the head of the apostolic college, the successor of Saint Peter.

The quotidian administration of the Roman Catholic church reflects its affirmation of both the Petrine ministry and the doctrine of apostolic succession. The papacy, with its various congregations and offices in the Vatican, oversees the administration of the global church. Bishops ordinarily oversee a specific territory (called a DIOCESE or a see), which is usually further subdivided into territorial parishes under the care of a priest who is designated as a pastor. This basic administrative model, reflecting a church order based on the episcopacy, is further modified, according to exigencies, by national conferences of bishops, groupings of individual dioceses under the guidance of a metropolitan or archbishop and, at the more local level, by the constitution of parishes not on territorial, but ethnic or special need lines.

Another characteristic of Roman Catholicism is its strong emphasis on SACRAMENTALISM. In its most general sense a sacrament may be defined as an external visible sign of an inward grace. In that broad sense the Catholic church does not hesitate to call Christ himself a sacrament since the church affirms the God-man to be a visible sign of God's grace in the world. Likewise, the church itself is often called a sacrament in that it is the visible sign in the world of the invisible saving grace of Christ in the world.

More technically the sacraments are those visible signs in the life of the church that mediate the grace of Christ to the believer. Roman Catholicism (in common with Orthodoxy) affirms seven such signs of divine institution: Baptism, Confirmation, Holy Eucharist, Penance, Holy Orders, Matrimony, and the Anointing of the Sick. "The purpose of the sacraments is to sanctify men, to build up the body of Christ, and, finally, to give worship to God. Because they are signs they also instruct." (Vatican Council II)

The sharing of the Holy Eucharist, in which Catholics profess Christ to be truly present under the gifts of bread and wine, "shows itself to be the source and apex of the whole work of the preaching of the gospel." (Vatican Council II) The Holy Eucharist is celebrated in the Mass, the central liturgical rite of the Roman Catholic church. The Mass as a liturgical rite has undergone a complex historical development over the centuries. Nonetheless, the structure of the Mass reflects two basic components: the proclamation of God's word by Scripture readings, responsorial prayer based on the psalms, and preaching and the celebration of the Eucharist through the offerings of bread and wine, their consecration, and reception in holy communion. The liturgical reforms of the Second Vatican Council (1962-1965) were undertaken for the precise purpose of underscoring the basic structure of the Mass, which is based on word and sacrament.

The broad sympathy that the Roman Catholic church has for sacramental religion has also made it amenable to the notion of a sacramental revelation of God understood in the broadest of terms. Historically Catholicism has insisted that the presence of God can be detected, however imperfectly, in the world of nature around us. Furthermore, the church has traditionally encouraged the use of art, ritual, architecture, external symbols, hieratic gestures, and other visible means to foster PIETY and devotion. Such usages reflect Catholicism's understanding that the materials of the world, properly utilized, lift the heart and the mind to God. The highly externalized religious practices of historical Catholicism are partially explained in terms of the cultural matrix out of which Catholicism was born in conjunction with the Catholic conviction that the visible can mediate the invisible. Mediation is a key idea in Catholic theology. For Catholics, as Richard McBrien has said, "The universe of grace is a mediated reality: mediated principally by Christ, and secondarily by the church and by other signs and instruments outside and beyond the church."

Another key characteristic of the Roman Catholic church is its profound appreciation of tradition. The term tradition as used by Catholic theologians has both an involved technical theological use

and a generalized meaning. We can, in fact, distinguish Tradition and tradition(s) in Catholic thought.

By Tradition, the Roman Catholic church means the Gospel as it was received by the apostles from Christ and as that Gospel was handed down (tradition means a "handing down") by them and their legitimate successors. This Apostolic Tradition is "expressed in a special way in the inspired books" (Vatican Council II) but also includes the constant preaching and teaching of the church throughout history. There is but one Christian revelation, which is the Word of God handed down by the church and contained preeminently in the sacred Scriptures, which are received as canonical in the church. Since this Word of God is entrusted to the church, she is its only authentic and final interpreter. The Second Vatican Council teaches, however, that the teaching office of the church (called the *magisterium*) is not "above the Word of God, but serves it teaching only what is handed on, listening to it devoutly, guarding it scrupulously, and explaining it faithfully by divine commission, and with the help of the Holy Spirit; it draws from this one deposit of faith everything which it presents for belief as divinely revealed."

As distinct from Tradition are those traditions that came into the church as certain historical moments. These traditions may be very much a part of the de facto look of contemporary Catholicism, but they are not immutable and/or irreformable. Thus the celibacy of the Latin rite clergy is a tradition with deep roots in Christian asceticism, but the sacramental character of the priesthood is part of the Catholic Tradition. It follows that the Catholic church could have a married priesthood (in fact, there is a married clergy in the Eastern rite church), but it could never abolish the priesthood itself. Similarly, it is the teaching of the Catholic church that matrimony is a sacrament but only part of its legal tradition that a Catholic must marry before a priest and two witnesses. The historical traditions of the church are always open to change. Catholicism's recent history demonstrates that change can come despite the essentially conservative nature of an institution that prides itself on its fidelity to its historical traditions.

Finally, the Roman Catholic church puts a strong emphasis on the church as more than an earthly institution. This emphasis is affirmed in the historical creeds as the "communion of saints." In that belief the church affirms its solidarity with the dead who await the vision of God in heaven (hence the doctrine of purgatory, praying for the repose of souls, and so forth) and those who already stand before the throne of God. Roman Catholic devotion to the saints, and preeminently to Mary the *Theotokos*, must be understood in the light of this doctrine. Traditional Catholic theology and spirituality have always insisted that the living faithful stand in prayerful union with those friends of God who already enjoy the vision of heaven and whose lives stand as exemplars for those on earth.

This sense of solidarity with those who are "beyond the vale of tears" also points to the strong eschatological nature of Catholicism's self-understanding. Catholicism points itself to the absolute future. The Second Vatican Council described the church as a "pilgrim church." As such, Catholicism sees itself as moving, however hesitantly, to that final consummation of all things in Christ. Current debates in Roman Catholic circles about the church's relationship to political and/or social structures, especially as those debates are being shaped by liberation theologians, are seen by many as correctives to those thinkers in the church who in the past so emphasized the eschatological nature of Catholicism that they ignored or downplayed the incarnational view of eschatology as the working out of the kingdom of God in the here and now.

The common image of Roman Catholicism as a highly structured, monolithic, and essentially conservative ecclesial organization does not hold up under close scrutiny. Although Roman Catholicism does have a complex and disciplined structure and a certain historically reinforced bias against rapid or large-scale change (a resistance now rather weakened), it has traditionally sheltered within its walls great diversity. Styles of spiritual expression go from the folk religion of Latin American shrines to the austere simplicity of Trappist abbeys. Intellectual currents range over a vast area of sophistication and influence: there are Catholic thinkers who utilize the work of Karl Marx and others who breathe fire against all modern culture. The very character of Catholicism is also diversified according to the cultural matrix in which it finds itself. The Catholicism of Ireland is quite different from that of Africa. The extensive growth of Catholicism in Africa and Southeast Asia, together with the influence of other non-European expressions of Catholicism, should add further diversity to the ancient institution of Roman Catholicism in the not-too-distant future.

See also articles on PROTESTANTISM; ROMAN CATHOLIC CHURCH (IN THE SOUTH); SACRAMENTS AND ORDINANCES.

Bibliography. John Dolan and Hubert Jedin, *History of the Church,* 8 vols.; Avery Dulles, *Models of the Church*; Langdon Gilkey, *Catholicism Confronts Modernity*; Patrick Granfield, *The Papacy in Transition*; Gustavo Gutierrez, *A Theology of Liberation*; John Hardon, *The Catholic Catechism*; Hans Kung, *The Church*; Richard McBrien, *Catholicism,* 2 vols.; Karl Rahner, *Foundations of Christian Faith*; ed., *Sacramentum Mundi,* 6 vols.; *The Documents of Vatican Two,* ed. Abbott et al.; *The New Catholic Encyclopedia,* 15 vols.

LAWRENCE CUNNINGHAM
FLORIDA STATE UNIVERSITY

ROTHSCHILD, JACOB M. (1911-1973), a prominent Reform rabbi and civil rights advocate, was born in Pittsburgh. Growing up in a family strongly devoted to Reform Judaism, he early decided to become a rabbi. In 1932 he graduated from the University of Cincinnati; four years later he was ordained at Hebrew Union College. Prior to World War II he held posts in Davenport IA and Pittsburgh. After the attack on Pearl Harbor he resolved to become a military chaplain and was sent to the South Pacific. It is believed he was the first American rabbi to minister to a combat unit in World War II.

In 1946 Rothschild accepted the position of rabbi at Atlanta's Hebrew Benevolent Congregation (The Temple), succeeding David Marx. A supporter of the republic of Israel, he had some difficulties with his predecessor, an avowed foe of Zionism.

Rothschild was best known for his efforts to promote interfaith dialogue and civil rights. In 1947 he established the Institute for the Christian Clergy to promote Christian study of aspects of Jewish life and thought. In 1948 Rothschild boldly attacked segregation, and his synagogue was the first in Georgia to invite blacks to attend integrated affairs. Increasingly bold in his attacks on segregation, the rabbi strongly supported the *Brown v. Topeka* Supreme Court decision of 1954. In 1958 The Temple was bombed by segregationists. The bombing inspired Ralph McGill to write a newspaper column that was later awarded the Pulitzer Prize.

Rothschild befriended MARTIN LUTHER KING, JR., and in 1964, when King won the Nobel Peace Prize, the rabbi and his wife organized a movement to hold a dinner in honor of the Nobel laureate. In 1968 after King's assassination, Rothschild was selected by the Atlanta area clergy to deliver a special memorial address in behalf of the slain civil rights leader.

Rothschild held a variety of important posts within the Atlanta Jewish community. He was best known as a bold and fearless critic of bigotry and racial prejudice and as a proponent of interfaith dialogue.

See also article on JEWS IN THE SOUTH.

ARNOLD SHANKMAN

RUFFNER, HENRY (1790-1861), Presbyterian minister and political and educational reformer, was born in Page County VA. As a small boy he moved with his mother and father from the Shenandoah Valley to the wild territory of what is now Kanawha County WV. With his father, Henry helped operate the family saltworks, the first in the region.

Ruffner was attracted to scholarship and Presbyterianism while a student at the classical academy of the Rev. John McElhenney at Lewisburg. He undertook his college studies at Washington College (now Washington and Lee University) in nearby Lexington VA. He taught at this Presbyterian college's grammar school and, upon graduation in 1813, he studied theology with the president of the college. Licensed to preach in 1815, he returned to the Kanawha country as a missionary to the area's impoverished mountaineers.

Ruffner became professor of ancient languages at Washington College and eventually its sixth president (1836-1848). As professor and president, Ruffner instituted various educational innovations, maintained his well-known preaching skills at nearby Timber Ridge Church, and wrote a variety of theological works. In one of his rare attempts at fiction, Ruffner described the harm caused by religious bigotry in *Judith Bensaddi* (1839).

Ruffner's fame as a political and agricultural reformer centered around his argument in the renowned "Ruffner Pamphlet" (1847) for the removal of slavery west of the Blue Ridge and the partition of Virginia into two states. He was an early, active proponent of public education, and his influence in this area rivaled that of Jefferson. Ruffner's adamant liberal stance on the slavery issue and in educational matters, as well as his involvement in local denominational disputes, led to his resignation from the presidency of Washington College.

Bibliography. Henry Ruffner, *Address to the People of West Virginia Shewing That Slavery is Injurious to the Public Welfare*; "Proposed Plan for the Organization and Support of Common Schools in Virginia," *The Fathers of the Desert; or, an Account of the Origin and Practice of Monkery*, 2 vols.

J. MICHAEL PEMBERTON
UNIVERSITY OF TENNESSEE, KNOXVILLE

SABBATARIANISM: *See* ETHICS, CHRISTIAN; PURITANISM; SEVENTH-DAY BAPTISTS.

SACRAMENTS AND ORDINANCES. Southern churches have maintained a wide spectrum of doctrinal positions. Roman Catholics affirmed seven sacraments (Baptism, Confirmation, the Eucharist, Penance, Extreme Unction, Ordination, and Matrimony) which, in accord with the Council of Trent (1545-1563), they defined as efficacious and necessary means of grace designed to initiate or continue the process of justification. Protestants accepted only Baptism and the Eucharist/Lord's Supper, which they defined in various ways, though often with covenantal imagery taken from Gen. 17:1-27 and Mk. 14:24.

The doctrinal spectrum revealed the interconnection between sacramental views and wider presuppositions about religious experience, the church, and the valuation of the material world. Specifically, a "high" doctrine of sacramental efficacy presupposed a view of religious experience as participation in the divine service of a visible community, a doctrine of the church as the extension of the incarnation of Christ, and a confidence that external and material realities enhanced the religious life. A "low" view of the sacraments—or a preference for the word "ordinance" to designate BAPTISM and the Lord's Supper—presupposed a notion of religious experience as a moment or process of inward conversion, a doctrine of the church as a pure community of the faithful, and a conviction that in religious matters the "flesh profiteth nothing" (Jn. 6:63).

The spectrum can be illustrated with the doctrine of Baptism. At one end stood Roman Catholics, who believed that Baptism contained and conferred the grace of justification. High Church Episcopalians said that only by admitting infants into the church covenant and hence changing their "outward condition" did the sacrament confer "regeneration" (their Low Church Episcopal colleagues believed that Baptism merely "sealed" a conditional covenant requiring future repentance and faith). Confessional Lutherans viewed Baptism as a convenantal promise of life and thus as a means of regeneration (Lutheran Evangelicals viewed the rite only as a "visible Word" filled with doctrinal meaning and designed to move the mind and emotions through its symbolism). Methodists and Presbyterians occupied the middle position on the spectrum. Most Methodists viewed Baptism as the "seal" of a universal but conditional covenant, requiring future faith and repentance, and as the means of entrance into the church, though some Methodists viewed the sacrament merely as a parental pledge. Presbyterians usually agreed that the rite sealed a conditional covenant—requiring future faith—for all infants and adults who were baptized, but they added that it also sealed an "absolute" covenant, ensuring salvation, though only for God's elect. Presbyterians differed as to whether Baptism served as a means of church membership or as a symbolic recognition of the prior membership conferred through a covenantal relation. The Holiness and Pentecostal churches of the late nineteenth century usually considered Baptism in water as an outward symbol of an inner Baptism in the Spirit, or as a parental pledge to nurture faith in their children. Baptists preferred to speak of Baptism as an "ordinance," commanded or "ordained" by Christ as a "sign" of obedience and inner faith. In short, groups that emphasized inward experiences and defined the Church as a voluntary community of the faithful have tended to move away from any view of Baptism as an efficacious rite.

A similar spectrum has marked doctrinal views of the Eucharist or Lord's Supper. Roman Catholics believed that through the miracle of transubstantiation the elements of bread and wine actually became in substance the real body and blood of Christ, who was then sacrificed in the Mass. A few High-Church Episcopalians accepted a doctrine of transubstantiation; most affirmed a real spiritual presence of Christ. A few confessional Lutherans insisted on a mysterious corporeal presence of Christ the Word; their "evangelical" counterparts abandoned the doctrine of a real physical presence. In the other denominations, the issue was whether to accept a doctrine of the true spiritual presence of Christ or to claim

only that the Lord's Supper served as a rite of commemoration. Again, the churches that accented inward experience, like the Baptists, who designated the Lord's Supper as another "ordinance," tended to adopt a commemorative view. The prevalence of a conversionist spirituality in Southern Protestantism has helped to popularize the notion of the Lord's Supper as a rite of remembrance, designed to evoke appropriate assent and feeling. Indeed, the open debates over the Lord's Supper have usually had little to do with the older issue of Christ's presence: the divisive problem has been admission. The policy of "close communion," whereby many congregations, especially among the Baptists, admitted only their own faithful members, has provoked controversy since the 18th century.

Debates over sacraments and ordinances have informed both the organization and the self-consciousness of the Southern denominations. Following the 18th-century GREAT AWAKENING, controversies over the nature, mode, and subjects of Baptism shaped popular understandings of the Baptist movement. Distress about the unavailability of the Lord's Supper helped provoke the Methodist break from the Church of England in 1784. Sacramental quarrels marked—and often defined—the divisions between confessional and evangelical parties, especially among Lutherans and Episcopalians. ALEXANDER CAMPBELL attracted converts to his Christian Movement (known later as the CAMPBELLITE TRADITION) by preaching that the aim of Baptism was "remission of sins" even though the rite was only a formal sign expressing the attitude of God toward faithful adults and deriving its value from faith. The "Old Landmark" Baptists of the mid-nineteenth century argued that the only true churches were local institutions that practiced believer's Baptism by immersion. Their position left a lasting mark on the Southern Baptist Convention, even after many from the LANDMARK MOVEMENT persuasion withdrew. And the claim advanced after 1913 by "one-ness" Pentecostal groups that churches could baptize only in the name of Jesus Christ rather than with the Trinitarian formula created an enduring division in the Pentecostal traditions. Hence on a popular level, sacramental practice has often defined denominational identity.

Sacramental themes have also been interwoven with broader cultural and religious patterns. Their cultural meaning was especially clear in the 18th-century disagreements about the propriety of baptizing African slaves. Only after securing legal confirmation that Baptism could not confer temporal liberty—and often inserting such a disclaimer in the baptismal ceremony—did the clergy gradually gain free access to the slaves. The broader religious import of sacramental patterns was manifest, moreover, when a series of "sacramental meetings" in 1799 helped spark the GREAT REVIVAL (Second Great Awakening) in the South, giving rise to the CAMP MEETING as a standard institution on the frontier.

The prevalence of a conversionist spirituality within Southern REVIVALISM has created a tendency in the region's Protestant churches to minimize the efficacy of sacraments and ordinances and to accent their function as signs of faith and obedience or aids to inner devotion.

Bibliography. John Boles, *The Great Revival, 1787-1805*; Samuel S. Hill, *Southern Churches in Crisis*; E. Brooks Holifield, *The Gentlemen Theologians: American Theology in Southern Culture 1795-1860*; Donald G. Mathews, *Religion in the Old South.*

E. BROOKS HOLIFIELD
EMORY UNIVERSITY

SACRED PLACES: *See* AUGUSTA STONE CHURCH; BARDSTOWN KY; BETH ELOHIM; BETHANY WV; CANE RIDGE KY; CHARLESTON SC; DUNN NC; FRANKLIN SPRINGS GA; FREDERICA GA; HOT SPRINGS AR; JAMESTOWN; MIDWAY CHURCH; MONTREAT NC; NASHVILLE TN; RIDGECREST NC; ST. AUGUSTINE FL; ST. PAULS, RICHMOND; ST. PHILIP'S CHURCH (CHARLESTON); SANDY CREEK NC; SAVANNAH; SILVER BLUFF CHURCH; SPRINGFIELD MO; TULSA OK.

ST. AUGUSTINE, FLORIDA. Founded on 8 September 1565, it is the oldest city of Western and Christian origin in the continental United States. The city received its name from Pedro Menéndez de Avilés, leader of the founding expedition, who made his landfall in Florida on 28 August, the Feast of St. Augustine of Hippo. Pioneer pastor Francisco López de Mendoza Grajales celebrated on 8 September the first Mass in a permanent U. S. settlement. He and other secular priests with Menéndez established a parish church (San Agustín) and a mission to the Indians (Nombre de Dios). The parish has had a continuous history to the present, except for a 21-year period (1763-1784) when the Floridas were under British rule. The mission became the anchor of a chain of Franciscan missions which, in the 17th century, stretched north along the Georgia coastal islands and west through the interior as far as the Apalachicola River. St. Augustine also was the site (in the early 1600s) of the country's first seminary for the education of priests (Franciscan).

The Florida colony never prospered as Menéndez and his successors had hoped and the capital city of St. Augustine remained throughout the Spanish periods (1565-1763, 1784-1821) a sparsely populated garrison town. The Indian missions collapsed in 1702-1704 following damaging raids by the English from Carolina. Catholic life concentrated thereafter on the parish, which received an infusion of new life in the 1770s from Minorcan survivors of an ill-fated British indigo plantation at New Smyrna; many descendants of the Minorcan families reside in the city at this date.

Prior to the Reconstruction period St. Augustine and Florida were under the ecclesiastic jurisdiction, successively, of the dioceses of Santiago de Cuba (1565-1787); San Cristobal de Habana (1787-1793); Louisiana and the Floridas (1793-1825); the Vicariate of Alabama and the Floridas (1825-1829); the Diocese of Mobile (1829-1850); the Diocese of

Savannah (1850-1857); and the Vicariate Apostolic of Florida (1857-1870). In 1870 St. Augustine was erected a separate see, a position that it retains at this date as a suffragan of the metropolitan see of Miami. The Spanish parish church completed in 1797 serves as the Cathedral of St. Augustine.

See also article on SPANISH INFLUENCE IN LA FLORIDA.

Bibliography. Michael V. Gannon, *The Cross in the Sand*; Thomas Graham, *The Awakening of St. Augustine*; Eugene Lyon, *The Enterprise of Florida.*

MICHAEL V. GANNON
UNIVERSITY OF FLORIDA

ST. PAUL'S EPISCOPAL CHURCH, RICHMOND, VIRGINIA.

This downtown church has shared and symbolized the city's history. Dedicated in 1845, the building is notable for its Greek Revival architecture. St. Paul's intricately designed sanctuary ceiling features a star radiating from the symbol of the Trinity which, in turn, encloses the Hebrew inscription for Jehovah. Later the church added stained-glass windows and a reredos that is a copy of DaVinci's *Last Supper.*

St. Paul's early history is closely linked with the Confederacy. Robert E. Lee and Jefferson Davis were members and many other Confederate leaders regularly worshiped there. During the Civil War, women of the church transformed its lecture room into a sewing room where they made uniforms, blankets, and sandbags for fortifications. On a long-remembered Sunday morning, 2 April 1865, Jefferson Davis was abruptly summoned from his pew by a courier with a message from General Lee, advising Davis of the need to evacuate Richmond. In the 1890s St. Paul's memoralized both Lee and Davis with windows of Tiffany glass. Alluding to Lee's loyalty to the South, the Lee window portrays Moses leaving Pharaoh's court and includes the inscription: "By faith Moses refused to be called the Son of Pharaoh's daughter; choosing rather to suffer the affliction with the children of God, for he endured as seeing Him who is invisible." The Davis window depicts Paul standing before Herod Agrippa II and cites Acts 26:31, "This man doeth nothing worthy of death or of bonds. ..."

Throughout the 20th century the rectors and the members of St. Paul's have led campaigns for community reforms. The church's most notable work has been on behalf of interdenominational and interracial cooperation. In recent years St. Paul's has originated a number of social welfare projects, which have subsequently been supported by the city of Richmond.

Bibliography. Elizabeth Wright Weddell, *St. Paul's Church, Richmond, Virginia, Its Historic Years and Memorials.*

SAMUEL C. SHEPHERD, JR.
CENTENARY COLLEGE

ST. PHILIP'S CHURCH, CHARLESTON, SOUTH CAROLINA.

The first St. Philip's church, a wooden structure, was built in Charles Town in the early 1680s. After the establishment of the Church of England in 1706, Anglicans in Charles Town felt the need of a larger, more permanent, and grander church. Legislation was passed in 1711, and construction began sometime after; the second St. Philip's, located several blocks from the first, was probably open for services in the late 1720s and was completed in 1733.

The new brick St. Philip's was an imposing structure. The Anglican clergy called the unfinished edifice in 1723 "the greatest ornament of this City and an Honor to the whole province," and 30 years later the *Gentleman's Magazine* carried a picture of St. Philip's and pronounced it "one of the most regular and complete structures of the kind in America." Frederick Dalcho left a detailed description. "The front of the Church is adorned with a Portico, composed of four Tuscan Columns supporting a double pediment. ... The Roof is arched, except over the Gallaries; two rows of Tuscan Pillars support five arches on each side and the Gallaries. ... There is no Chancel; the Communion Table stands within the body of the Church. ... There are 88 Pews on the Ground Floor and 60 in the gallaries." St. Philip's also had a wooden, octagonal, domed steeple that rose to a height of 80 feet and contained a clock and two bells. An English organ provided music.

For a quarter of a century after its opening, St. Philip's was the focal point of Anglicanism in South Carolina. Commissary ALEXANDER GARDEN was the rector in those years and his presence made St. Philip's the administrative center as well as the architectural pride of the established church. According to the vestry, 600 to 700 people worshiped on Sundays in the 1750s; church pews, owned by individuals, were valuable pieces of property. During and after the American Revolution, the rector of St. Philip's was the Rev. Robert Smith, a prominent patriot who later became the first Episcopal bishop of South Carolina.

St. Philip's became somewhat less significant when St. Michael's, a second and equally magnificent church, opened in 1762. St. Philip's continued to serve its parishioners, however, until 1835 when it succumbed to fire. A third church, modeled on the second, was quickly built and it stands today.

See also article on ARCHITECTURE.

Bibliography. S. Charles Bolton, *Southern Anglicanism: The Church of England in Colonial South Carolina*; Frederick Dalcho, *An Historical Account of the Protestant Episcopal Church In South Carolina*; Albert Sidney Thomas, *A Historical Account of the Protestant Episcopal Church in South Carolina, 1820-1957*.

S. CHARLES BOLTON
UNIVERSITY OF ARKANSAS
AT LITTLE ROCK

SALVATION. If one single Christian body has had as much influence as the Baptists on religion in the South, it is the Methodists. For both, personal salvation has been central. The Methodist emphasis upon "heart-felt religion" and an intense conversion experience dovetailed with the Baptist rejection of religion by parental proxy. These two denominations were the warp and woof of especially Southern frontier religion, the Baptists emphasizing individualism, and the Methodists taking up the radical gospel of free will to promote social ministries.

Southern Baptists, under the impact of zealous Methodists and the frontier mentality, surrendered a major doctrine from the Calvinism of the PARTICULAR BAPTISTS of Europe. God no longer predetermined some for salvation and others for damnation. Salvation was a gift to all, and human free will rather than God cast the deciding vote. Before the Civil War, the South cherished high hopes and plans to convert the entire world to Christianity, since God had prearranged to deny the offer of salvation to no one. Even slaves, denied open doors on earth, were declared free to enter the gates of heaven. Freedom was the theme of the new nation with its new frontier, and free salvation with free grace was nowhere proclaimed more persistently and fervently than in the South.

There was one central doctrine that Methodists and Baptists remained unable to agree upon. The Baptists joyously clung to the one doctrine of Calvinism that meant most to them, the doctrine of Eternal Security. Despite numerous and varied arguments thrown against this doctrine, Baptists never budged from their belief that once individuals have received the free gift of salvation, nothing in HEAVEN, earth, or HELL could cause them to lose their salvation. Hence the Baptists' motto, "Once saved, always saved."

Methodists and most "Campbellites" argued that the Christian could "fall from grace," but Baptists insisted that the saved could never be lost again once the Spirit of God had begun his special work of grace in the heart.

In the 20th century, salvation for a large percentage of Methodists came to be understood as social responsibility and personal piety. The idea of salvation as escape from hell changed, partly because hell itself became "demythologized," no longer to be seen as external torment. Salvation, therefore, became escape from one's own evil heart, character, and deeds. The resurgence of FUNDAMENTALISM and EVANGELICALISM in the South in the

1970s and 1980s represents a reaction to the steady impact of both religious humanism and the historical-critical method, each of which has caused a number of Christians to think of salvation in a radically new way.

See also articles on ARMINIANISM; CONVERSION; HEAVEN; HELL; PREDESTINATION; SIN.

Bibliography. Carlyle Marney, *The Recovery of the Person: A Christian Humanism*; E. Y. Mullins, *The Christian Religion in Its Doctrinal Expression*.

JOE E. BARNHART
NORTH TEXAS STATE UNIVERSITY

SALZBURGERS. This extremely active, useful, and pious group of German Lutherans settled in the colony of Georgia, beginning in 1734, under the sponsorship of the Society for the Promotion of Christian Knowledge (SPCK) and the Trustees for Establishing the Colony of Georgia. The prime catalysts in this migration were Samuel Urlsperger, a corresponding member of the SPCK and minister of St. Anne's Church in Augsburg, and Henry Newman, secretary of the SPCK in London.

In 1731 the Roman Catholic archbishop of Salzburg, Count Anton von Firmian, peremptorily expelled Protestants from his realm. The decision created much sympathetic feeling in Britain, particularly within the SPCK, which has been active for a number of years in relocating and/or supporting persecuted Protestants on the European continent. Newman and the SPCK brought the plight of these German Lutherans to the attention of the Trustees of Georgia, who heard of their predicament with sympathy and interest. Ultimately the first shipment of Salzburgers was transported to Rotterdam under the financial aegis of the SPCK; later this group paid the salaries of the Salzburger ministers in Georgia. The Georgia Trustees, anxious to bring to reality the early ideal of their colony as a haven for persecuted Protestants, paid the expenses of the transport to Georgia and supported the group until it could stand on its own.

Under the leadership of their effective young ministers, Johann Martin Boltzius and Israel Christian Gronau, the first transport of Salzburgers reached America in March 1734. JAMES EDWARD OGLETHORPE escorted them to the site of their initial town, dubbed Ebenezer (Rock of Help), and laid it out for them. Although the location of Ebenezer was moved to Red Bluff on the Savannah River in 1736, the town was the center of the Salzburger effort in Georgia from the start.

The Salzburger community was a well-organized, tightly controlled world dominated by the ministers. Boltzius in particular wielded close control and worked carefully with Oglethorpe and the Trustees until his death in 1765. Owing to their thrifty and hard-working ways, these German Lutherans developed Ebenezer into the most prosperous settlement in Georgia. Subsequent migrations founded Salzburger colonies on St. Simons Island, at Goshen and Bethany, and in other locations. Jerusalem church at Ebenezer, constructed of brick in the 1760s, is Georgia's oldest surviving religious structure. The Salzburgers, who held on to their German language and traditions for many years, were particularly successful in the production of silk. This operation reached its zenith in the 1760s and early 1770s.

The Salzburgers' rugged determination and sincere pietism acted as an inspiration for later generations of Georgians. The group provided Georgia with one of its earliest painters and sketchers in the person of Baron Philip von Reck. His vivid drawings of the colony's flora and fauna are supplemented by fascinating sketches that depict in some detail the lives, customs, and dress of the Indians in and around Ebenezer.

Dissent and controversy, introduced into the Salzburger settlements by two opposing clergymen about the time of the American Revolution, boded ill for the independent, self-conscious Salzburger community. Ebenezer itself was torn between Loyalism, Whiggery, and a neutral stance; the Salzburger settlement later produced one of Georgia's first chief executives when John Adam Treutlen became governor in 1777. However, occupation of Ebenezer and the surrounding area by the British early in 1779 disrupted community life, and although efforts were made to reestablish pre-Revolutionary Salzburger society after the war, these attempts failed. Following the Revolution, the Salzburger Lutherans fanned out over Georgia and the South. By 1800 the town of Ebenezer had lost its standing as one of the main centers in Georgia. By 1855 an observer reported that the community had but two inhabitants.

See also articles on GEORGIA; LUTHERAN CHURCH.

Bibliography. Louis De Vorsey, Jr., ed., *De Brahm's Report of the General Survey in the Southern District of North America*; Kristian Hvidt, ed., *Von Reck's Voyage. Drawings and Journal of Philip Georg Friedrich von Reck*; Charles Colcock Jones, Jr., *The Dead Towns of Georgia*; George Fenwick Jones et al., eds. and trans., *Detailed Reports on the Salzburger Emigrants Who Settled in America . . .* , six vols. to date; ed. and trans., *Henry Newman's Salzburger Letterbooks*; P. A. Strobel, *The Salzburgers and Their Descendants.*

PHINIZY SPALDING
UNIVERSITY OF GEORGIA

SANCTIFICATION. Southern churches have advanced at least six interpretations of the doctrine of sanctification or HOLINESS. Roman Catholics viewed sanctification and justification as interrelated in a single process through which the Christian gradually moved from original sin to righteousness; they taught that sanctifying grace, which gradually produced inner renewal, was imparted at BAPTISM, increased by means of the other SACRAMENTS (AND ORDINANCES), and then further augmented through meritorious works of faith and love. Lutheran churches spoke of sanctification not as a cumulative process of spiritual renewal and growth but as a gift conferred on the faithful when God mercifully regarded their faith "as righteousness." The Presbyterians and Baptists in the Reformed tradition joined John Calvin in returning to the notion of sanctification as a process

through which the old self gradually died and a renewed self emerged, but like Calvin they insisted that the process began only after the divine act of justification had occurred. Episcopal and Methodist theologians adopted much of the Reformed imagery, but the Methodists, following John Wesley, diverged from the older Protestant patterns in claiming that God's grace was sufficient to produce "entire sanctification" or "Christian perfection," a disposition of pure love. The WESLEYAN TRADITION, in turn, deeply informed the mainstream of the HOLINESS MOVEMENT in the South, which tended to define sanctification as an instantaneous SECOND BLESSING, issuing in Christian perfection, subsequent to the "first blessing" of justification and regeneration. Many Holiness groups insisted, like early Methodists, on strict standards of dress and behavior as a witness to the sanctifying experience. And finally, the portion of PENTECOSTALISM that grew out of the Holiness tradition valued sanctification especially as a necessary prelude to a "third blessing" of empowerment by the Holy Spirit, evidenced by speaking in tongues.

Eighteenth-century Methodists brought the doctrine to the forefront of theological discussion. The "perfectionist renaissance" of the 1840s and 1850s, however, also attracted adherents in other denominations, primarily Northern and Calvinist, which frequently joined the Methodists in associating the theme of sanctification with social as well as individual reform. By that time, the doctrine was contributing to controversy and ecclesiastical splits in the North. Was sanctification gradual or instantaneous? Was it essential that the sanctified believer attest to the experience? Was a specifiable experience of sanctification necessary for salvation? Following the Civil War and the emergence, initially in the Northeast, of a series of CAMP MEETINGS and other small gatherings to promote holiness, such questions began to occasion bitter debate and finally separations, especially from the Methodist Church, whose bishops, North and South, condemned the burgeoning holiness "party." By the 1890s, separate Holiness churches were beginning to gather strength in the South and Southwest. The CHURCH OF THE NAZARENE is the largest of the denominations with a considerable Southern membership that continues to accent the centrality of sanctification.

Bibliography. Charles E. Jones, *A Guide to the Study of the Holiness Movement*; *Perfectionist Persuasion*; George Marsden, *Fundamentalism and American Culture*; Leland Peters, *Christian Perfection and American Methodism*; T. L. Smith, *Revivalism and Social Reform*; Vinson Synan, *The Holiness-Pentecostal Movement in the United States.*

E. BROOKS HOLIFIELD
EMORY UNIVERSITY

SANDY CREEK, NORTH CAROLINA. The strategic site for his settlement in North Carolina chosen in 1755 by SHUBAL STEARNS, founder of the SEPARATE BAPTISTS, was Sandy Creek in Guilford (later Randolph) County. Three wilderness roads converged there. The "Settlers Road" ran from north to south, connecting Pennsylvania with Georgia. Another, later called "Boone Trail," went from Wilmington on the coast to settlements on the Yadkin. A third, known as the "Trading Path," ran from southeastern Virginia to the Waxhaw country. Where the roads crossed, Stearns built his meetinghouse. All who came that way would be called to hear the musical voice and the compelling message of the dynamic preacher.

There were but 16 members of the church in the beginning, all newly arrived from eastern Connecticut. The preacher had two assistants, Daniel Marshall and Joseph Breed. Widespread attention was soon given to the "zealous, animating manner" of Stearns's preaching. Calls for preaching came from nearby settlements of the growing frontier population. Stearns and his assistants responded to the calls and itinerated as far as the coast of the colony.

Daniel Marshall gathered and organized a daughter church at Abbott's Creek by 1757. Philip Mulkey led in forming the Deep Creek Church later that year. Numbers of young evangelists began to go out from Sandy Creek and the daughter churches. In 1758 representatives of the three churches met at Sandy Creek and formed the Sandy Creek Baptist Association in order "to impart stability, regularity and uniformity to the whole." This was the first Separate Baptist Association.

Within a few years the mother church at Sandy Creek had over 600 members. Its branches spread in all directions, from Virginia to Georgia. By 1772, 42 churches had been planted from Sandy Creek's ministry and 125 ministers had been raised up.

The Regulator troubles around 1771 caused most of the early Sandy Creek members to disperse into other regions of the South.

See also articles on EVANGELICALISM; GREAT AWAKENING; SOUTHERN BAPTIST CONVENTION.

Bibliography. William L. Lumpkin, *Baptist Foundations in the South*; G. W. Paschal, *History of North Carolina Baptists*; Robert B. Semple, *A History of the Rise and Progress of the Baptists in Virginia.*

WILLIAM L. LUMPKIN
NORFOLK, VIRGINIA

SANTERIA. A religious tradition of African origin that was developed in Cuba, it was brought to the United States by exiles from the revolution of 1959. The tradition began in the 19th century when hundreds of thousands of men and women of the Yoruba people from what is now Nigeria and Benin were carried to Cuba to labor in the island's booming sugar industry. Thrust into an alien and brutal world, these slaves forged a subtle and complex system of correspondences between the religious life of their African past and the Catholic Christianity they were enjoined to adopt. Originally a religious response to enslavement and deculturation, Cuban santeria evolved into an Afro-Cuban folk religion that has touched all levels of Cuban society, though the preponderance of its devotees continues to be poor and black.

The name santeria—"the way of the saints"—is derived from the symbiotic relationship that the devotees find between Catholic saints and Yoruba spirits called "orishas." Each of the Catholic saints is said to have an African identity as an orisha and may be most effectively petitioned by worship in the African manner with songs and prayers in the Yoruba language, ecstatic dancing, and vegetable and animal sacrifices. The pantheon of orishas forms a rich taxonomy of the entire cosmos as each orisha has his or her special realm in the mineral, vegetable, animal, and human worlds.

As the devotee grows in a mutual relationship with the orishas, one will reveal him or herself to be the devotee's special patron. At an elaborate and costly ceremony of initiation, this patron is "seated in the head" of the devotee, thus establishing a mystical bond in which the orisha functions as the devotee's "deepest nature." The ultimate identity of orisha and human being is dramatically played out in ceremonial spirit possession where, triggered by percussive cues, the orisha emerges or "descends" to overcome the personality of the devotee-medium and dance and speak with the congregation. This ceremonial presence of the orisha among the community is the climax of the ritual life of santeria since it brings human and divine into joyous and healing contact.

Since the Cuban revolution of 1959 nearly one million Cubans have come to the United States, bringing santeria to all the major American cities where they have settled, particularly in south Florida. Due to its many parallels with other African-derived religious traditions of the American South such as voodoo and hoodoo, santeria has inspired many American blacks to reawaken their awareness of their own half-forgotten African roots. Most notable of these Afro-American religious experiments is the Yoruba community of Beaufort SC, a self-contained village where Yoruba social and religious life is conscientiously recreated and revivified.

Bibliography. Roger Bastide, *African Civilizations in the New World*; Lydia Cabrera, *El Monte*; Pierre Verger, *Notes sur le culte des Orisa et Vodun*.

JOSEPH MURPHY
GEORGETOWN UNIVERSITY

SAVANNAH, GEORGIA. More so than New England, the South was marked by religious diversity. Savannah, known for contributions to urban planning, is also important as an example of that regional religious trait. Central to colonial Georgia's military mission was the recruitment of settlers. JAMES OGLETHORPE, notwithstanding his and the trustees' Anglican affiliations, included many religious outlooks among the migrants he sponsored. The result was a city that proved home to many faiths and showed a de facto toleration. Relying on aid from the SOCIETY FOR THE PROPAGATION OF THE GOSPEL, the Society for the Promotion of Christian Knowledge, and income from trustee lands, the services of John Wesley were secured as missionary to the Indians and as Anglican priest in 1736. Wesley's tenure in Savannah was largely unsuccessful. He left after 22 months amidst charges of unprofessional conduct. Wesley's efforts were followed in 1738 by those of GEORGE WHITEFIELD, who not only made Savannah his base for several GREAT AWAKENING tours in the 1740s, but founded Bethesda Orphanage near Savannah in 1740. The Savannah contributions of both Wesley and Whitefield were prelude to later triumphs, but did secure Anglicanism in Georgia. Other faiths were found in the town. A Jewish doctor disembarked in 1733 and Savannah became a center of Sephardic Judaism. In the 1730s, too, MORAVIANS under Augustus Gottlieb Spangenburg settled briefly near Savannah before moving to Pennsylvania. Lutheran SALZBURGERS founded the town of Ebenezer near Savannah. In 1759 a Lutheran church was established in the city. John Zubly's Independent Presbyterian Church (ca. 1745) provided a Calvinist orientation. In the 1770s, Savannah witnessed some of the earliest expressions of separate black churches, and the efforts of ex-slaves GEORGE LIELE and ANDREW BRYAN led to the founding of the First African Baptist Church in 1779. For all of the denominational diversity manifest in Savannah, religion in Georgia's 18th century remained what historian Sidney Ahlstrom has termed "desultory and rather sad."

See also articles on BLACK RELIGION; JEWS (IN THE SOUTH).

Bibliography. Harold Davis, *Fledgling Province*; Edwin Scott Gaustad, *Historical Atlas of Religion in America*; Albert Raboteau, *Slave Religion: The "Invisible Institution" in the Ante-Bellum South.*

THOMAS F. ARMSTRONG
GEORGIA COLLEGE

SAWDUST TRAIL: *See* ALTAR CALL (INVITATION); REVIVALISM.

SCARBOROUGH, LEE RUTLAND (1870-1945), Baptist preacher, teacher, and administrator, was born in Colfax LA. One of nine children, he lived in Mississippi and Tennessee, moving in 1874 to Texas where his father was a Baptist farmer-preacher. At age 18 he entered Baylor University to prepare for a law career. After receiving a B.A. in 1892, Scarborough entered Yale, graduating in 1896 with Phi Beta Kappa honors. In 1896 he was ordained and became pastor of First Baptist Church, Cameron TX. From 1899-1900 he attended the Southern Baptist Theological Seminary in Louisville. He then served as pastor of First Church, Abilene TX, from 1901 to 1908, where he established a reputation as an evangelist.

In 1908 Scarborough became professor of evangelism at the Southwestern Seminary in Fort Worth, at the invitation of B. H. CARROLL, president of the school. In 1915 he succeeded Carroll, continuing to teach evangelism until his retirement in 1942. Scarborough's commitment to personal evangelism shaped many of the theological and pastoral concerns of the seminary.

A tireless fundraiser, he promoted numerous financial programs, even serving as director of the denomination's 75 Million Campaign in 1919. He was president of the Convention for two years, 1939 and 1940. A conservative, he nonetheless opposed efforts of Fundamentalists to divide the denomination in the 1930s. Scarborough wrote numerous books on preaching and evangelism. These include *With Christ After the Lost, Endued to Win, How Jesus Won Men,* and *Prepare to Meet God.*

See also articles on SOUTHERN BAPTIST CONVENTION; THEOLOGICAL EDUCATION.

Bibliography. C. C. Goen, "Scarborough, Lee Rutland" in *Dictionary of American Biography*, supplement three; Lee Rutland Scarborough, *How Jesus Won Men*; Franklin M. Segler, "Scarborough, Lee Rutland," in *Encyclopedia of Southern Baptists*, vol. 2.

BILL J. LEONARD
SOUTHERN BAPTIST SEMINARY

SCIENCE AND RELIGION. Beginning with the publication in 1927 of Samuel Eliot Morison's harsh indictment of the Old South for having destroyed all kinds of creative thought, including science, a battle has raged over the issue. Those who continue to argue that the Southern mind in the antebellum period was essentially unscientific or antiscientific are aware of the well-known Southern eminence in science during the colonial and early national period. They generally claim, however, that a marked hardening of "the religious and proslavery orthodoxies" during the 20 years preceding the war caused a reduction in support for science, if not an outright hostility to it.

There can be no argument about the basic facts. Certainly throughout the 18th century very few scientists of note lived further north than Philadelphia, and the slave states were disproportionately represented in the scientific community. By the 1850s Philadelphia had become the southernmost outpost of scientific eminence, and the slave states were underrepresented by any measure that one wishes to use for scientific activity. While such a transformation may seem to give a surface validity to Morison's original claim, it need not necessarily be interpreted that way.

In the earlier period, when "science" really meant "natural history exploration," the longer collecting season more than compensated for the sparse population and the lack of cities in the South. Southern scientists, severely feeling their isolation, were more highly motivated to join, by correspondence, in the international natural history circle then being directed from European centers. All of Linnaeus's correspondents, for example, lived either in Philadelphia or the South. The lack of educational opportunities in the South further tied the literate Southern colonial to Europe and kept him (and his sons) exposed to contemporary European and English thought. When the young Southerner went to Europe, the seat of culture, for his higher education, he could secure a level of learning superior to that of Harvard or Yale, which in the 18th century served either religious or provincial concerns and, paradoxically, helped keep literate New Englanders intellectually isolated.

By the middle decades of the 19th century, however, both the conditions in the country and in science had changed drastically and Southern advantages either had vanished or were turned into disadvantages. Once the initial history surveys had been made, attention turned to as yet unexplored areas. Most important, as Americans began to develop their own scientific institutions—associations, libraries, herbaria, museums—and their own capacity for scientific education, most of this new activity depended upon a population density found nowhere in the South except for Charleston and New Orleans. Although these two cities maintained a flourishing intellectual life, they were too remote from other populous areas for their local scientific communities to be actively integrated within the developing national community. Thus one should not be surprised upon learning that Southerners were rare in the membership of the American Association for the Advancement of Science. The shifting of dominance in science to the Northern seaboard appears to have had nothing to do with either slavery or religious "orthodoxies." The most accurate statement about the antebellum Southern mind is probably, judging from all the statistical studies available, that at most it was "only relatively—not essentially—unscientific." The relative lack of scientific activity can no doubt be explained by reference to the state of science, demographic factors, and especially the lack of an urban culture, meaning the agricultural orientation of the region.

The question of "science and religion in the South," however, is not exhausted by such considerations. Because Southerners shared in the general conviction of the antebellum period that science and religion were very closely connected, they conducted scientific study as part of their overall interest in religious matters. Before the Darwinian revolution, American Protestantism was generally united in the secure belief that science and religion each in its own way proclaimed the glory of God and gave insight into his plan. Natural theology, understood as the effort to prove the existence and display the attributes of God by evidences from nature, was regarded as a kind of *scientia scientiarum*, and the foundations of religion were thought to rest upon the same sure basis in observation as were those of, say, mineralogy or zoology. "The course of nature," wrote one Old South minister, "is nothing but the will of God producing certain effects, in a constant and uniform manner."

The vehicle through which the Protestant orthodoxy was transmitted was the Scottish philosophy of common sense that dominated American colleges for the first 60 years of the 19th century. Beginning in the Eastern colleges of Princeton, Harvard, Andover, and Yale, it was carried to Hampden-Sydney College in Virginia by Samuel Stanhope Smith and was soon entrenched in such Deep South institutions as the College of South Carolina and the University of Georgia. Smith, an early leader in the movement, tried to show that "scientific investigation rightly conducted will never lead to conclusions that contradict the written Word of God."

Since the facts of science were thought to lead directly to a better understanding of God and his ways, it followed that a good many clergymen would actively pursue the study of science. JOHN BACHMAN, distinguished zoologist, collaborator with Audubon, and long-time pastor of St. John's Lutheran Church in Charleston could have been speaking for a large number of his Southern colleagues when he reported that he felt compelled by his clerical duty to investigate the natural sciences. Believing, like all orthodox Protestants in the first half of the 19th century, that the same method of study was appropriate for both science and theology, Southern clergymen also agreed that the study of theology was a scientific activity in the same sense that geological or chemical study were scientific undertakings. In such a climate, it seemed natural for Yale geologist and founding editor of the *American Journal of Sciences*, Benjamin Silliman, to give his lectures on chemistry and geology in the First Presbyterian Church of New Orleans.

A recent study of 100 clerical leaders of the Old South found that at least 13 of them taught science or mathematics in Southern colleges. A major purpose of the new church-sponsored colleges springing up in the South in the 1840s and 1850s was to demonstrate the harmony of religion and science by offering courses in chemistry, natural philosophy, and sometimes other sciences. As Jesse Mercer explained the curriculum at the Baptists' new university in Georgia, each of the academic disciplines offered the chance to study "the works of God, in creation, and providence, and grace." Bacon College, founded in Kentucky by the Disciples of Christ in 1836, was even named in honor of the founder of "the inductive method of reasoning and the new science"; Methodists agreed with the Disciples that the "patient inquiry into facts" appropriate for biblical studies was closely related to

"the scientific method" and had probably led to its discovery. Luther, Calvin, and Sir Francis Bacon were listed by one writer in the Southern *Methodist Quarterly Review* as important figures in the birth of modern science. Samuel Taylor, a Maryland attorney and foremost exponent of a pure Baconianism in America at the time, was labeled in 1859 the "first philosopher in America" by the *Southern Presbyterian Review*.

The commitment to science was so strong that in some jurisdictions, especially among the Presbyterians, prospective clerics were actually required to pass examinations on scientific subjects, and the various Southern theological journals regularly included items of "scientific intelligence," full-length articles on science, and reviews of scientific books. Beginning in 1824, instruction in science was provided to every young ministerial student at the Presbyterian Seminary in Virginia so that they could be armed to answer "the cavils and objections of infidels," which the president assured his new professor of theology had become more readily answerable in proportion to the enlargement of the natural sciences.

In their celebration of natural theology, Southern religious writers were probably quite similar to their Northern colleagues. In both sections the conviction that "entire harmony" would be the final outcome of all studies of science and religion—the certainty that any discoveries of science were bound to confirm the traditional dogmas of Christianity—permitted most theologians and scientists to view themselves as allies. Likewise, since the view undoubtedly worked to the benefit of a young scientific community struggling for legitimacy (in both sections), scientists themselves were among the leading proponents of the doctrine. The colleges and universities throughout the Old South invariably included courses in the natural sciences in their curricula. They were, to be sure, inclined to be quite elementary and they tended to include as much preachment as science, but on both counts they simply reflected the times, not the section. According to all the evidence, instructional materials and "philosophical apparatus" were severely lacking throughout the country in the first half of the 19th century. It is equally true that one could study geology, for example, nowhere in America without extensive exposure to Silliman's religious ideas, for his particular reconciliation of "Genesis and geology" filled the lengthy introduction and the footnotes to his edition of *Bakewell's Geology*, by far the most widely used text in America. Textbooks in other fields were likewise replete with "evidences" and religious meanings.

While Southern colleges hardly qualified as "liberal enclaves," still the theological climate in many Southern institutions seemed to be slightly more tolerant than in the typical Northern college. THOMAS COOPER, president of South Carolina College, roundly denounced Silliman's work and another Southern writer proclaimed it to be "at least twenty years behind the knowledge of the day," being particularly outraged by the lengths to which the Yale geologist was willing to carry the reconciliation effort. It is true that Cooper was brought up on charges by the trustees of South Carolina College for his views on theology, but probably even more significant is the fact that he secured acquittal by convincing the jury that his personal views were irrelevant to his capacities as president. Equally worthy of comment is the fact that William Barton Rogers was teaching an evolutionary view of natural history at the University of Virginia before 1845, and that the great debate joining the question of the origin of the human race with the inspiration of the Old Testament was touched off by a "radical Southerner from Mobile" in a pair of lectures from the chair of political economy at the University of Louisiana in 1848.

There was always a potential for conflict in the insistence that science and theology inevitably led to the same conclusions. As long as scientists concentrated on the here and now, and contented themselves with description, arrangement, and classification, no occasion for conflict need arise; but by the middle of the 19th century, scientists were beginning to ask questions of origin and process, being driven to ever more tortuous mental convolutions in order to show "harmony." Benjamin Silliman's argument that each of the seven "days" in the Genesis account was a geological period of indefinite length was widely accepted, but it always carried the implication that the natural sciences were to become the standard for biblical interpretation—an implication that, no doubt, helps account for the angry rejection by the writer in the *Southern Review*, and which certainly became explicit in the conservative classicist Tayler Lewis's well-known rejection of science in his argument with the geologist James Dwight Dana. On the other hand, the belief that "whatever goes by the name of science" and contradicts the revealed truth is "only false philosophy," as one apologist put it, raised the possibility of seriously limiting the range of permissible explanation in science.

Although Southerners generally went along with some form of stretching the seven "days" of Genesis, they were entirely too committed to the Bible to accept another well-known "reconciliation" effort of the antebellum period, even though it might have provided an excellent rationalization for the existence of black slavery. In order to continue working within the biblical short chronology (about 6,000 years) and still explain how the races of man had been distributed about the earth from the Garden of Eden, a number of American scientists, including the popular Louis Agassiz, postulated that the races of man, like the races of lower animals, had been separately created and especially fitted for their conditions of existence. Despite the apparent scientific assistance being offered to the defenders of slavery, almost to a man Southern scientists and theologians refused to accept it. The outstanding opponent of the separate creation school, in fact, was John Bachman of Charleston, who published a refutation of the theory on strictly scientific grounds, while holding on to his proslavery beliefs by a more-or-less literal reading of the Bible.

It was publication of Darwin's theory, of course, that drove the greatest wedge between science and religion. Yet the rift that was created in the closing decades of the 19th century and that grew into the bitter fundamentalist controversy of the 20th century does not appear to have anything to do with sectional divisions. A reaction to the growth of liberalism in religion, FUNDAMENTALISM, like its 19th-century precursors, cut across all denominations and all sections. The alarm raised by a presbytery in Mississippi against the new forces in religion was symptomatic, and the prescription symbolized the passing of the old era: "Whereas, we live in an age in which the most insidious attacks are made upon revealed religion through the natural sciences, and as it behooves the church, at all times to have men capable of defending the faith once delivered to the Saints, therefore, *Resolved* that the Presbytery recommend the endowment of a professorship of the natural sciences, as connected with revealed religion in one or more of our theological seminaries."

In 1861 such a professorship was established at the seminary in Columbia SC and JAMES WOODROW was appointed to the chair. His dismissal in 1888 following a four-year controversy over his acceptance of evolution, was followed by the New York Presbyterians' dismissal of Charles A. Briggs from Union Theological Seminary in 1893 for his espousal of liberalism, and of Henry Preserved Smith from Lane Seminary in the following year. Earlier, the Methodists had fired ALEXANDER WINCHELL from Vanderbilt for teaching that man had descended from pre-Adamic stock, and the Disciples were continuously embroiled in controversy over various issues of liberalism. Among the Baptists, the issue did not arise until

the 20th century, and when it did, it was a nationwide phenomenon. Indeed, 20th-century Fundamentalism, contrary to the assentions of earlier students, was initiated as a movement of Northern Baptists and Presbyterians, and theologically its strength remained in the Northern half of the country and the far West, as is indicated by the sites of its first national conventions: Philadelphia (1919), Chicago (1920), Denver (1921), Los Angeles (1922). The fifth annual convention, in fact, was held in Fort Worth as a deliberate attempt to stimulate the interest of Southern churchmen. The legislative success of Fundamentalism in three Southern states during the 1920s and its near-success in Arkansas and Louisiana during the 1980s, is better explained by the rural domination of the legislatures than by any sectional considerations. Whatever distinctiveness there appears to be can still be traced to the same demographic differences as existed in the antebellum period. Science and religion in the South, in the 20th century as in the antebellum period, is best viewed as a particular manifestation of national—if not international—concerns, and the shifting relationships were parts of broader intellectual movements.

See also articles on EDUCATION, CHRISTIAN HIGHER; EVOLUTION CONTROVERSY.

Bibliography. Stewart G. Cole, *The History of Fundamentalism*; E. Merton Coulter, "Why John and Joseph LeConte Left the University of Georgia, 1855-1856," *Georgia Historical Quarterly*, 53 (1969): 16-40; George H. Daniels, *American Science in the Age of Jackson*; Clement Eaton, *The Mind of the Old South*; Norman F. Furniss, *The Fundamentalist Controversy, 1918-1931*; Charles C. Gillispie, *Genesis and Geology*; E. Brooks Holifield, *The Gentleman Theologians: American Theology in Southern Culture, 1795-1860*; Herbert Hovenkamp, *Science and Religion in America, 1800-1860*; Thomas Cary Johnson, *Scientific Interests in the Old South*; Sally G. Kohlstadt, *The Formation of the American Scientific Community*; Ronald L. Numbers and Janet S. Numbers, "Science in the Old South: A Reappraisal," *Journal of Southern History*, 48 (May 1982): 163-84; Milton Rudnick, *Fundamentalism and the Missouri Synod*; Morgan B. Sherwood, "Genesis, Evolution, and Geology in America before Darwin: The Dana-Lewis Controversy, 1856-1857," in *Toward a History of Geology*, ed. Cecil J. Schneer; William Stanton, *The Leopard's Spots: Scientific Attitudes Toward Race in America, 1815-59*; Donald G.

Tewksbury, *The Founding of American Colleges and Universities Before the Civil War.*

GEORGE H. DANIELS
UNIVERSITY OF SOUTH ALABAMA

SCOPES, JOHN THOMAS (1900-1970), is known to history as the defendant in the famous Tennessee vs. Scopes trial, which resulted in the upholding of a Tennessee statute forbidding state public school teachers from teaching the theory of evolution. Born in Paducah KY, young Scopes indifferently attended various Protestant churches, including the Presbyterian church of his parents. While attending public schools in Kentucky and Illinois, he was exposed to the Darwinian theory of evolution. That exposure continued at the University of Kentucky, where he took more physical science courses before graduating in 1924 with a bachelor's degree in Arts-Law. He was then hired to teach science and to coach football in the public high school in Dayton TN.

During the spring of 1925, this mild-mannered and retiring young teacher agreed to violate the antievolution law in order to test its constitutionality. After the trial, Scopes accepted a scholarship for advanced study in geology at the University of Chicago. Upon completing two years of graduate study, he was hired by Gulf Oil of South America and sent to Venezuela. While there he was baptized in the Roman Catholic Church, the only church with which he ever had any formal relationship. After a third year of study in geology at the University of Chicago, he took a job in 1933 with United Gas Corporation as a company field geologist in the Houston TX area. He was transferred to Shreveport LA in 1940, working there until his retirement in 1964, and continuing to live there until his death.

See also articles on EVOLUTION CONTROVERSY; FUNDAMENTALISM; SCOPES TRIAL.

Bibliography. John T. Scopes and James Presley, *Center of the Storm*; Jerry Tompkins, *D-Days at Dayton.*

MONROE BILLINGTON
NEW MEXICO STATE UNIVERSITY

SCOPES TRIAL. In early 1925 the Tennessee state legislature enacted a statute stating that "it shall be unlawful for any teacher in any of the . . . public schools of the state . . . to teach any theory that denies the story of the Divine Creation of man as taught in the Bible, and to teach instead that man has descended from a lower order of animals." Believing that this law violated a teacher's right to "teach the truth," the leaders of the New York City-based American Civil Liberties Union (ACLU) immediately announced that their organization would raise a special fund to finance a test case and would hire distinguished lawyers to argue it if a Tennessee teacher was willing to cooperate. Stimulated by the ACLU's announcement, a small group of citizens in Dayton TN decided the law should be challenged, believing that the resulting publicity of a trial would be good for their small town's economy and civic image. They convinced JOHN THOMAS SCOPES, a young science teacher and football coach at the local high school, that he should be willing to be tried for violation of this law. After his arrest, preliminary hearing, and indictment in May, Scopes was then brought to trial on 10 July. WILLIAM JENNINGS BRYAN, three-time presidential candidate, former secretary of state, and outspoken conservative Protestant, led the prosecution. Clarence Darrow, well-known criminal attorney from Chicago, headed the team of lawyers that the ACLU provided for Scopes's defense.

Newspapers sent dozens of reporters and photographers to this "monkey trial," giving the events national publicity and contributing to the circus atmosphere that engulfed the trial and the city for eight exciting days. Scopes himself became incidental to the trial; he was not even called to testify. It was a battle between Darrow and Bryan, with Bryan arguing that the law was a valid exercise in Tennessee's police power to protect school children from scientific theory that contradicted the teachings of the Bible, and Darrow arguing that the Tennessee law was unconstitutional, since a teacher had every right to teach scientific theory. After Judge John T. Raulston refused to allow expert testimony from eminent American scientists, the jury accepted the argument of the prosecution. Since the defense had admitted that Scopes had violated the law, the jury found Scopes guilty and Raulston fined him $100. In January 1927 the ACLU appealed this decision to the Tennessee supreme court, which later upheld the antievolution law, so that it remained on the statute books for many years. The decision of the trial judge and the supreme court reflected the pervasiveness of the fundamentalist religious milieu in the American South in the early twentieth century. Historically, the Scopes trial became a symbol of the continuing conflict between science and religion.

See also articles on EVOLUTION CONTROVERSY; FUNDAMENTALISM; SCIENCE AND RELIGION.

Bibliography. L. Sprague de Camp, *The Great Monkey Trial*; Ray Ginger, *Six Days or Forever?*.

MONROE BILLINGTON
NEW MEXICO STATE UNIVERSITY

SECOND BLESSING. A term, second blessing, is commonly used by Holiness, Pentecostal, and Higher Life movements to denote a critical religious experience of Spirit cleansing and filling subsequent to the initial experience of Christian justification and new birth. The term relates particularly to the teaching of John Wesley concerning Christian perfection or entire SANCTIFICATION. Wesley taught that by God's grace the heart of the regenerate Christian could be cleansed of its constant inclination to sin and be liberated to a readiness to love God and every person. Because this "cleansing of the heart" came to individuals through faith and the work of God rather than their own works, the experience became known as a "second blessing," especially in American Holiness-Higher Life circles.

After 1835 Charles G. Finney and Asa Mahan, New School Calvinists, joined Methodists who were already promoting Wesley's doctrine of Christian perfection in promoting a "second blessing" revival in the American churches. The revivalist's methods of direct address, specific call to response, and public confession of need, which had characterized Finney's preaching to unbelievers, were now used to call Christian believers to a higher level of Christian experience and whole-hearted commitment to God's will. Among Calvinistic churches this sanctification experience was often known as a "second conversion," the "rest of faith," or "entire consecration." By the close of the 19th century all Holiness-Higher Life groups tended to use the term BAPTISM OF THE SPIRIT or "fullness of the Spirit" for the experience.

Critics of the teaching charged that it tended to deprecate the significance of the experience of justification—the initial work of God's grace in an individual's heart. The hope for Christian perfection of any kind, they contended, was too optimistic and too susceptible to spiritual pride.

Beginning with Wesley, proponents of the teaching maintained that the Scriptures and the experience of the church supported their position. Perfection of the heart in love by faith in Christ and the power of the indwelling Holy Spirit was not only promised but possible to all Christians. The outward expression of that inner perfection of intention, however, was never capable of absolute expression because of the fallenness of the human race and all creation. Nevertheless, Christians who had experienced "the second blessing" would seek with their whole heart to demonstrate God's love in all of life—above all in active concern for the spiritual and temporal needs of others.

Borne on the waves of REVIVALISM, which swept the North and South after the Civil War, the preaching of second-blessing theology gave birth to new movements and institutions in American religion. Among these were the Church of God (Anderson IN), the CHURCH OF THE

NAZARENE, the Pilgrim Holiness Church (now the WESLEYAN CHURCH), and Holiness-Pentecostal churches such as the PENTECOSTAL HOLINESS CHURCH. Interdenominational centers such as Asbury College and Theological Seminary in Wilmore KY are products of the ecumenical thrust of the movement. Numerous denominational colleges were also founded by the new Holiness or Pentecostal churches, which sprang from the revival milieu: Trevecca College in Nashville, and Bethany Nazarene College in Bethany OK (Nazarene), Central College, Central SC (the Wesleyan Church), and Lee College, Cleveland TN (CHURCH OF GOD, CLEVELAND TN).

The movement spread to England and the Continent. The Salvation Army, the Keswick Conventions, and several small Holiness sects came into existence out of the revival there. The Christian Holiness Association, organized in 1867 as the National Camp Meeting Association for the Promotion of Holiness, continues to act as an interdenominational forum for many of the groups who hold "second blessing" teaching as central to their understanding of Christian experience. The most contemporary expression of a "second blessing" theological motif is to be found in many of the new charismatic fellowships that have sprung up across broad segments of the Christian denominations since 1960.

See also articles on HOLINESS MOVEMENT; KESWICK MOVEMENT; OLD SCHOOL/NEW SCHOOL; PENTECOSTALISM.

Bibliography. Melvin Easterday Dieter, *The Holiness Revival of the Nineteenth Century*; Charles Edwin Jones, *Perfectionist Persuasion*; Timothy L. Smith, *Revivalism and Social Reform in Mid-nineteenth Century America*; Vinson Synan, *The Holiness-Pentecostal Movement*; B. B. Warfield, *Perfectionism*.

MELVIN E. DIETER
ASBURY THEOLOGICAL SEMINARY

SECOND COMING OF CHRIST: *See* MILLENNIALISM; RAPTURE.

SECOND CUMBERLAND PRESBYTERIAN CHURCH.

This black denomination consists of 6,494 communicants in four synods, 15 presbyteries, and 143 congregations. It is located in 10 states, mostly Southern. There are 131 ordained ministers, 16 of whom are women.

The church came into existence following the Civil War. Historians estimate that in 1860 there were 20,000 black Cumberland Presbyterians in the churches of their white masters. Following the war both the white and black Cumberland Presbyterians expressed their desire for separate churches. In the late 1860s several conventions were held for black Cumberland Presbyterians. In 1869 one was called and hosted in Murfreesboro TN by the General Assembly of the white church. The decision to form a separate black church was made at that time.

The first "colored" presbytery, at Elk River TN, was organized in 1869. In 1871 the first synod was organized in nearby Fayetteville. A General Assembly was organized in Nashville in 1874 with 46 ministers and 3,000 communicants. This completed the organization of the "Cumberland Presbyterian Church, Colored." In 1958 the name was changed to "Cumberland Presbyterian Church in the U.S. and Liberia, Africa," as a consequence of affiliation with a group of churches in Liberia. This relationship was short-lived and in 1960 the name was changed to "Second Cumberland Presbyterian Church."

During the decade of 1957-1967 an effort was made to unite the two churches. The General Assembly of the Cumberland Presbyterian Church voted for union, but the Second Church rejected it by the vote of one presbytery.

The two bodies continue to explore ways of expressing their acknowledged unity: they share the same Confession of Faith and form of government; the General Assemblies exchange fraternal greetings and delegates; a Federated Board of Christian Education serves both churches; the Board of Finance of the white church lends financial assistance to the black churches by means of loans; several joint youth camps are held each year; and the white church helps provide leadership for the annual National Sunday School Convention of the black church. Leaders of the black church are trained in Bethel College in McKenzie TN and the Memphis Theological Seminary.

The women and youth of the Second Cumberland Presbyterian Church are actively involved in such organizations as the National Sunday School Convention, the National Women's Organization, the National Junior Missionary Society, and the National Youth Work.

Since 1958 the Second Cumberland Presbyterian Church has been a member of the World Alliance of Reformed Churches. In 1978 a significant joint work was begun by the two Cumberland Presbyterian Churches on a revised Confession of Faith. It is expected that both churches will vote on the revised Confession in 1984. This joint project is regarded by both churches as a major step toward organic union.

In 1976 new headquarter facilities for the Second Cumberland Presbyterian Church were built in Huntsville AL with the assistance of the Board of Finance of the white church. It is here that the chief literary organ of the church, the *Cumberland Flag*, is published.

See also article on CUMBERLAND PRESBYTERIAN CHURCH.

Bibliography. Ben Barrus, Milton Baughn, Thomas Campbell, *A People Called Cumberland Presbyterians*; *Directory of Second Cumberland Presbyterian Church, 1981*; John Jenkins, *Souvenir History of the Colored Cumberland Presbyterian Church*.

JOE BEN IRBY
MCKENZIE, TENNESSEE

SECOND GREAT AWAKENING: *See* GREAT REVIVAL.

SECULARIZATION.
This is the process by which society and the individual come to sustain themselves through the rational, temporal, and technical resources of the world (the *saeculum*) rather than by supernatural, religious resources, or an eternal destiny. The term first appeared in approximately its present sense in the Treaty of Westphalia at the end of the Thirty Years' War (1648), where it referred to church lands handed over to princes.

The most important period of secularization in history has been that of the modern West, granted its significant roots in ancient Greek and Israelite culture. The clearest token of Western secularity has been the development of science and technology, though the accompanying philosophical and religious changes have been equally significant. Seventeenth-century physics began to look upon matter not as the element of potentiality within dynamically changing entities (Aristotle), but as separable, objective material to be measured and controlled through advanced knowledge. Science, therefore, opened the way for technology to pursue the utilitarian goal of an earth conformed to human need and design. The results in modern production, communication, and medicine, both positive and negative, are clear.

Parallel to these developments there emerged a sense of autonomy, leading both individuals and institutions to posit their own rational authority and capacity for self-governance. The modern world became a realm where reason, accountable only to itself, was hailed as king. Work in philosophy by such figures as Descartes, Spinoza, Bacon, and Kant as well as the science of Newton, the economics of Adam Smith, the later dialectic thought of Hegel and Marx, and even the psychology of Freud, announced in various ways the self-sufficiency of secular reason in the world's affairs. In the political arena, the rise of the modern state, visible certainly since England's Henry II (12th century) and France's Philip IV (14th century), broke the unity of medieval Christendom into widespread national sovereignties. With the further demolition of the divine right of kings in the French Revolution and tolerance of religious dissent in various nations (including the disestablishment of state Christianity in some, as in the United States), the basis for government became secularized across the West.

Religion obviously played a role in these developments and in turn was significantly influenced by the secularizing trend. Not only did religion represent the past against which secularizers inveighed, but also secularization seems to have constituted a paradoxical form of religious decision and posture. That is, secular thought translated the divine object, God, into the modern, objective world, a world manipulable by reason and technology, while itself assuming the old God-role. Thus the secular move may have been covertly a religious move. On the other hand, recognized religious thought as such from the 18th to 20th centuries deliberately incorporated secular elements. Liberal Protestantism, as in Ritschl, Harnack, and Rauschenbusch, found the Kingdom of God immanent within human moral process, and the Gospel a description of natural spiritual potential. Neo-orthodox thinkers like Bultmann, Gogarten, and Bonhoeffer have seen secularizing as one fruit of Christ's work; in rejecting salvation by works and self-righteousness, Christ freed the world from preoccupation with supernatural, heavenly reward. He offered instead simple trust toward himself and his sacrifice, and secular, ethical accountability in the world. Still, theologians have opposed secularity where it has meant the selfish worship of one's own worldly powers.

The South has experienced wide incursions of secularity through urbanization, commerce, industry, and the various media. Where religion has been associated with older social and economic patterns (as was often the case with racial segregation), the dissolution of those patterns has resulted either in religious decline or emergence of liberal religious views and churches. Secularity in the form of liberal religion has meant that the values and procedures of the surrounding secular culture heavily inform and guide the life of any given congregation. At times, older ways of exclusivism and privilege have often translated themselves into newer, more subtle forms, such as privileged patterns of housing or private schools.

On the other hand, secularized social and religious patterns have often produced a withdrawn religious reaction. Neo-fundamentalism has responded to growing secular influences by asserting a firm objective barrier (the inerrant Bible) against liberal, secular tendencies, in favor of the perceived orthodoxy of Christian faith.

In some instances, the freer, more open relationships of secularization have combined with inherited religious patterns of piety, worship, and song to produce a church life both progressive and traditional. Here historic Southern elements of gentleness and loyal conservatism have combined with a commitment to justice in the new secular arena.

Bibliography. Peter L. Berger, *The Sacred Canopy*; *A Rumor of Angels*; Dietrich Bonhoeffer, *Ethics, Letters and Papers from Prison*; Christopher Lasch, "The Cultural Civil War and the Crisis of Faith," *Katallagete* 8 (Summer 1982): 12-18; Larry Shiner, *The Secularization of History*.

WILLIAM MALLARD
EMORY UNIVERSITY

SEGREGATION. This pattern of arranging relations between black people and white people became normative in the 20th-century South. The region acquired a reputation as the home of Jim Crow laws and attitudes, and the Bible Belt as segregation and EVANGELICALISM established a powerful hold over the society. Most white Southerners perceived no irony in the situation and rather easily reconciled their religious beliefs and racial practices. In fact, formal segregation developed earlier and persisted longer in the churches than in other institutions. Southern religion, nevertheless, appeared more the captive than the sponsor of Jim Crow.

The adaptation of religious values to racial needs had a long history in the region. In the 1660s white Virginians overcame their qualms and ruled that conversion of a slave to Christianity did not necessitate emancipation. Over the next two centuries, Afro-Americans entered the Christian community with no change in their secular status. By 1860 many had joined white congregations and denominations, but the apparent institutional unity concealed tendencies toward separation. White churches almost always relegated blacks to special sections of the meeting place or even held separate services for them. The slaves, on the other hand, did not passively accept the Christianity of their white masters but transformed it into a theology of equality and deliverance. In a few areas, independent black congregations formed and throughout the South religious practices within the slave community came to constitute the INVISIBLE INSTITUTION.

Once emancipation had occurred tendencies toward separation soon became strict segregation. Almost immediately after the war, an exodus of blacks from white churches began and within a year or two few integrated congregations remained. Most of the freedmen withdrew to join or organize Baptist or Methodist churches. The Methodist congregations usually affiliated with Northern Methodists or the Northern black denominations, the AFRICAN METHODIST EPISCOPAL CHURCH, and the AFRICAN METHODIST EPISCOPAL, ZION, CHURCH. The black Baptists started organizing all-black state conventions as early as 1866 but did not succeed in forming the National Baptist Convention of America (q.v., National Baptists), a denominational structure, until 1895.

Contemporaries and historians have differed over how to interpret the rapid withdrawal of blacks from white churches. Certainly discriminatory treatment by white church members forced black Christians to choose between leaving white churches or accepting second-class citizenship in the Kingdom of God. The whites who claimed that the freedmen left voluntarily, however, had a point. The blacks did not always or only flee from white insult but also chose to establish institutions in which to develop their own forms of worship and theology. With its roots in the religion of the slave community, the black church was more than simply a refuge from white racism; it was a sanctuary for a distinctive black faith.

Fearful that biracial participation in churches might lead to social equality, whites hardly mourned the departure of the freedmen. In fact, whites soon took the initiative in segregating religious institutions. In 1870 the Methodist Episcopal Church, South, formed an all-black church, the Colored (later CHRISTIAN) METHODIST EPISCOPAL CHURCH, for those blacks who had not left the denomination. By 1884 even the Northern Methodist church condoned the separation of the races in its Southern work.

By the mid-1880s white agitation for greater racial separation had also emerged in the Presbyterian and Episcopal churches, both of which had already lost many of their black communicants to the more popular denominations. In 1874 the General Assembly of the Presbyterian Church in the United States adopted as a goal the establishment of an independent black communion. With continued white encouragement, black Presbyterians in 1898 formed the Afro-American Presbyterian Church. It gained little tangible support from white or black Presbyterians, however, and in 1916 it became an all-black synod within the General Assembly of the white church. For almost three decades the Episcopalians debated various forms of institutional separation of the races. In the early twentieth century, that denomination's General Convention refused to establish a separate jurisdiction but approved the appointment of special bishops for the work among blacks. Only two such bishops were ever appointed. Presbyterians and Episcopalians, therefore, escaped permanent denominational segregation, possibly because they had a stronger tradition of racial paternalism than Methodists and Baptists, stemming from the fact that they had fewer black members. Even the united denominations had segregated congregations.

By the early twentieth century, whites had completed the task of segregating the Southern religious community. The numerically dominant Methodists and Baptists had organized segregated denominations and the small, but socially influential, Presbyterians and Episcopalians had adopted forms of internal separation. Most of the less-prominent denominations also practiced segregation. Even the Pentecostal sects that began as biracial movements usually segregated as they established more formal structures. The Roman Catholic Church maintained its commitment to unity but conducted only a limited ministry among blacks, had few black members, and ordained almost no black priests. In its parishes, blacks usually sat in special sections. Even such partially integrated sanctuaries were rare; whites and blacks seldom worshiped together in the South.

Within the segregated churches, whites did not maintain even a "separate but equal" concern for blacks. The major white denominations provided only limited support for the education of black ministers and displayed little other interest in their religious welfare. Shortly after 1900 one Atlanta minister claimed that the white churches had "spent probably a hundred times as much money since the Civil War . . . to evangelise the people of China, Japan, India, South America, Africa, Mexico, and Cuba, as they" had "to give the Gospel to the Negroes. . . ." The white churches proved even less concerned about the secular welfare and social status of blacks than about their souls. Southern Protestantism's emphasis on personal salvation and piety rather than on social responsibilities supported white inactivity. Almost singularly among Southern whites, George W. Cable found that his faith helped propel him toward a critique of the South's racial practices.

The Southern religious community, in fact, more often gave aid and comfort to the forces that adopted disfranchisement, legal segregation, and proscription between 1885 and 1915. In his novel *The Leopard's Spots*, former Baptist minister THOMAS DIXON, JR., cast a minister as the guiding spirit of the campaign to establish white supremacy. In some states religious leaders did participate in disfranchisement, but religious values were not really the driving force behind the creation of a biracial society. Denominational bodies and individual members nevertheless supported the new racial order, although at times they did gently question the resort to racial violence. Some Southerners, like Dixon himself, even invoked religion in defense of white supremacy.

Once strict segregation had been established in Southern churches and society, no significant white dissent emerged until after the Second World War. Christian principles influenced the small band of Southern racial reformers of the interwar years, but only the more radical of them attacked segregation. Except for an occasional mild plea for tolerance, the mainline denominations and the majority of church people accepted or even defended the racial status quo. In the 1930s Southern Methodists refused to merge with their Northern brethren until the plan of union included the creation of a segregated Central Jurisdiction for blacks.

During World War II the nation's churches reconsidered racial issues and in 1946 the Federal Council of Churches of Christ in America urged its members to renounce segregation. After that prodding and the 1954 Supreme Court decision on school desegregation, most of the major denominational bodies in the South called for an end to segregation. Some pastors took heroic stands in support of integration of both church and society—often at the cost of their pulpits. Local congregations usually dissented from, if not openly defied, the leaders' call for racial change. In the battle to end segregation, the white church often remained trapped by its limited view of the church's role in society, its ties to its culture, and its institutional dependence on its members and community.

Racial separation remained the practice even though some steps were taken to end segregation within the churches. In the 1960s many congregations adopted open membership policies. In 1968 a reorganization of Methodist churches led to the abolition of the Central Jurisdiction. Yet as late as 1980 the Southern Presbyterian church reported that only six percent of its members were black and the Southern Baptist Convention claimed no black communicants. Most blacks remained in, apparently preferring, all-black churches and denominations. In a 1977 Gallup Poll, only 34 percent of white churchgoers in the South said blacks attended their churches. The same whites split almost equally over whether or not they would like to see more blacks attend. As MARTIN LUTHER KING, JR., had observed earlier, 11 o'clock on Sunday morning was still one of the most segregated hours of the week.

Racial segregation within the Southern churches, rooted in the tendencies toward separation in the antebellum years and institutionalized after the war, persisted in the 1980s. The segregated white church had done little for blacks and had rarely challenged segregation in society. For most of the post-Civil War era, restricted by an emphasis on salvation and personal piety and restrained by the social fetters on institutional churches, Southern Protestantism condoned segregation in society and embraced it in its own affairs.

See also articles on CIVIL RIGHTS MOVEMENT; SLAVERY.

Bibliography. Kenneth K. Bailey, "The Post-Civil War Racial Separations in Southern Protestantism," Church History 46 (December 1977): 453-73; Southern White Protestantism in the Twentieth Century; Ernest Q. Campbell and Thomas F. Pettigrew, Christians in Racial Crisis: A Study of Little Rock's Ministry; John L. Eighmy, Churches in Cultural Captivity: A History of the Social Attitudes of Southern Baptists; Hunter D. Farish, The Circuit Rider Dismounts: A Social History of Southern Methodism, 1865-1900; George M. Fredrickson, The Black Image in the White Mind: The Debate on Afro-American Character and Destiny, 1817-1914; David E. Harrell, Jr., White Sects and Black Men in the Recent South; Samuel S. Hill, Jr., Southern Churches in Crisis; E. Franklin Frazier, The Negro Church in America; C. Eric Lincoln, The Black Church Since Frazier; Frank S. Loescher, The Protestant Church and the Negro: A Pattern of Segregation; Robert M. Miller, "Southern White Protestantism and the Negro, 1865-1965," The Negro in the South Since 1865, ed. Charles E. Wynes; Andrew E. Murray, Presbyterians and the Negro—A History; I. A. Newby, Jim Crow's Defense: Anti-Negro Thought in America, 1900-1930; David M. Reimers, White Protestantism and the Negro; H. Shelton Smith, In His Image, But . . . Racism in Southern Religion, 1780-1910; Rufus B. Spain, At Ease in Zion: Social History of Southern Baptists, 1865-1900; Ernest T. Thompson, Presbyterians in the South, 3 vols.; C. Vann Woodward, The Strange Career of Jim Crow.

GAINES M. FOSTER
LOUISIANA STATE UNIVERSITY

SEMPLE, ROBERT BAYLOR (1769-1831), early statesman among Baptists in America, was born in King and Queen County VA, the son of an immigrant lawyer from Scotland. Although in early life "strongly tinctured with the sentiments of infidelity," he underwent conversion, rejecting the Episcopalianism of his mother for membership in the Upper King and Queen Baptist Church. Later ordained, he became pastor of the newly constituted Bruington Church, serving it along with a number of other Baptist churches in Virginia until his death. Apparently not an eloquent pulpiteer, he was, nevertheless, a gifted and energetic leader. In addition to ministerial duties Semple established a classical academy at the family farm, "Mordington," where he taught for a number of years.

Semple's influence was not limited to Virginia but included service among Baptists on a national scale. At various and often concurrent times, he served as moderator of the Dover Association, president of the Virginia Baptist Missionary Society, business manager and also president of the Trustees of Columbian College (later George Washington University). He also served as the second president of the important TRIENNIAL CONVENTION of Baptists in the United States, being reelected to that post at each succeeding meeting until his death.

His writings included circular letters for the Dover Association, contributions to the *Religious Herald*, catechetical instructions for children, and a biography of Samuel L. Straughan. His most noteworthy achievement was the publication of an invaluable repository of early Baptist materials entitled *A History of the Rise and Progress of the Baptists in Virginia* (1810).

Bibliography. Garnett Ryland, *The Baptists of Virginia, 1699-1926*, Robert B. Semple, *A History of the Rise and Progress of the Baptists in Virginia*; James B. Taylor, *Virginia Baptist Ministers*, series 1.

BERNARD H. COCHRAN
MEREDITH COLLEGE

SEPARATE BAPTISTS. The earliest Separate Baptists were first called "Separates." Arising out of the Edwards-Whitefield revival in New England, the "Separates" were so named when they withdrew from or were excluded by the state churches (Congregational). Spiritual life in the churches established by law was at a low ebb when the GREAT AWAKENING arrived in the region in the 1740s. Only a minority of church members were directly affected by the awakening, and they were often made uncomfortable in the churches when experiential religion was stressed as essential. Many of the revived people withdrew to form communities espousing the doctrine of the "pure" church of believers. These groups appeared in numbers in eastern Connecticut. Near at hand already existed a few Baptist churches, holding to the ideal of the pure church but at first rejecting the awakening because of its appearance among state-church people. Occasional contacts with Baptists resulted in adoption by many Separates of the baptism of believers as the sign of the regenerate church. Thus entire communities and many individual Separates became "Separate Baptists." Some of the older Baptist churches contracted the revival enthusiasm. Between 1740 and 1768, Baptist churches in New England increased from 23 to 69, in spite of the generally hostile religious and social climate of the region.

In New England the two kinds of Baptists quickly made common cause, and the Separate Baptists did not form a distinct denomination. However, in August 1754, SHUBAL STEARNS of Tolland CT led a part of his congregation to the frontier of the Southern colonies. Settling at SANDY CREEK NC, a crossroads point in Guilford (later Randolph) County NC, he organized a new church of 16 members and began an aggressive program of witnessing to that region. His church grew to a membership of 600 within a few years and other churches were planted. In 1758 three of the churches formed the Sandy Creek Baptist Association, which enlarged its membership into South Carolina and Virginia in the years 1760-1765. By 1770 the association divided along colony lines into three associations. The movement flourished most in Virginia, where there were 55 churches by 1774.

The Separate Baptists were mildly Calvinistic in theology and zealously revivalistic in practice. Everywhere they preached the need for an experience of radical conversion, a "new-birth." They appealed to the emotions of their hearers. Their worship was informal and spontaneous. Lay men and women witnessed publicly to their faith. Their churches were firmly disciplined.

Early efforts of the REGULAR BAPTISTS of Virginia to arrange a union with the Separates proved abortive. However, the struggle for civil and religious liberty brought the two kinds of Baptists together. They united in Virginia in 1787 and in other states shortly afterward.

In Kentucky the union was delayed until 1801. Even then some isolated churches kept alive the name of the oldest association, the South Kentucky, and remained aloof from the main body of Kentucky Baptists. As members of these churches moved westward they formed new Separate Baptist churches and associations. In 1812 the several associations were bound together in the General Association of Separate Baptists.

See also articles on EVANGELICALISM; GREAT AWAKENING; REVIVALISM.

Bibliography. William L. Lumpkin, *Baptists' Foundations in the South*; Robert B. Semple, *A History of the Rise and Progress of the Baptists of Virginia.*

WILLIAM L. LUMPKIN
NORFOLK, VIRGINIA

SEPARATION OF CHURCH AND STATE: *See* CHURCH AND STATE; JEFFERSON, THOMAS.

SERPENT HANDLERS: *See* SNAKE HANDLERS.

SESSION.

A session is the governing body of a Presbyterian congregation. It is the lowest "court" in the Presbyterian system of representative judicatories that moves from the session to the presbytery (all ministers and congregations in a district) to the synod (a group of presbyteries) to the general assembly (commissioners from each presbytery). The session consists of the minister or ministers (sometimes called teaching elders) who are called by vote of the congregation with the approval of the presbytery to which it belongs, and lay men and women (ruling elders) elected by the congregation. Its task is to supervise the congregation's worship, educational program, spiritual and moral life, and in cases where there is no board of deacons, its financial affairs and ministry to the sick and needy.

Ministers and lay people on sessions (as on all other courts of the church) have equal authority, though a minister is ordinarily the moderator or chairperson. While a session is chosen by the congregation, its responsibility (like that of the other courts) is to seek and administer the will of God, not the popular will of the people. A session is not an autonomous body but is bound by the constitution (polity manual and confessional standards) of the denomination, and subject to the supervision and decisions of the higher courts of the church.

See also article on PRESBYTERIANISM.

SHIRLEY C. GUTHRIE, JR.
COLUMBIA THEOLOGICAL SEMINARY

SEVENTH-DAY ADVENTISTS.

This sectarian Protestant body is one of the most rapidly growing Christian bodies in the world today, especially in the Southern region of the United States, where it claims over 200,000 adherents out of a national total of 588,538 and a worldwide count of 3,000,000. Aggressive evangelism with an emphasis on tithing undergirds this growth. Seventh-day Adventists regularly lead American per-capita giving records, averaging $784 per person, over three times that of the Southern Baptists, who also are taught to tithe.

Such fiscal devotion has resulted in a widespread ministry in North America, including 10 liberal arts colleges, two universities, and a theological seminary. The worldwide zeal is reflected in over 3,000 weekly radio broadcasts in 75 languages (including the popular "Voice of Prophecy" program), a weekly TV program—"Faith for Today"—viewed on 125 outlets, 49 publishing houses, 400 magazines that advance the church's work in 590 languages, and over 6,000,000 students enrolled in Bible correspondence schools.

Adventists regard the human body as the temple of God and are known for their emphasis on health, practicing vegetarianism, and abstaining from the use of alcohol and tobacco while discouraging the use of coffee and tea. Through the leadership of W. K. Kellogg, an early leader in one of their medical centers, Battle Creek MI has become the cereal capital of the world. They operate over 500 medical stations, including a medical school, over 100 hospitals, and 42 sanitoriums.

Adventism, a Christian doctrine emphasizing the view that the Second Coming of Jesus is near, has found many followers in every age of Christian history. Adventism was very prominent among American denominations during the first half of the 19th century. The roots of the Seventh-day Adventist Church can be traced to William Miller

(1782-1849), a radical Jeffersonian and deist from Vermont who was converted during the GREAT REVIVAL and eventually became an ordained Baptist minister. Biblical chronology that anticipated the end of the age absorbed his interest. He believed that precise dates for specific events could be found through a prophetic use of Bible numbers and dates. Using Bishop Ussher's dates, he believed he had located the time for the Second Coming sometime between 21 March 1843 and 21 March 1844. Miller developed a considerable following with the enthusiastic aid of a Boston minister, Joshua Himes. The date was changed to 22 October 1844 when the first date passed unfulfilled. The uneventful October date became the "Great Disappointment."

The movement was revived when a New York Millerite farmer, Hiram Edson, had a vision that the "cleansing of the sanctuary" had actually occurred on the predicted October date, but *in heaven*, not on earth. This resulted in a key Adventist doctrine, which holds that the cleansing of the sanctuary in heaven marked the beginning of the "Investigative Judgment" of all persons before Christ comes in his glory. Using the standard of the Decalogue, Christ began judging all his people in 1844.

There were many divisions and some association with the SEVENTH DAY BAPTISTS, who emphasized Sabbath observance on Saturday. Unity was secured through the leadership of a young woman, Ellen Harmon (1827-1915), who married a Millerite elder, James White. She had over 2,000 visions, including one vision of the Ten Commandments with a halo around the Sabbath commandment. Ellen White, the "Adventist Prophetess," became a prolific writer and her writings are accepted by Seventh-day Adventists as "inspired counsels of the Lord." The new church established headquarters in Battle Creek MI in 1855, adopted the name "Seventh-day Adventists" in 1860, and moved its headquarters to Washington DC in 1903.

Seventh-day Adventists practice believer's baptism by immersion, along with converts agreeing strictly to such practices as tithing, Sabbath observance, and total abstinence. The Lord's Supper is a memorial observed quarterly, often after a foot-washing ceremony in another room. Church government is highly representative and offers a great deal of autonomy. Overall, they are governed by an executive committee of the General Conference chosen by delegates from the various church groups. There are three conference levels. Pastors and other workers are paid out of a central conference fund after assignment by the conference.

Seventh-day Adventists are much like other fundamentalist groups in America. Their distinctive beliefs include the "Investigative Judgment," the sanctuary, the "Spirit of Prophecy as a gift of the spirit promised in the last days," and the observance of the Sabbath on Saturday. Strict legalistic approaches preclude much cooperation with other bodies. Although "professing no creed but the Bible," the denominational *Yearbook* publishes 22 "Fundamental Beliefs" said to set forth the "principal features" of their belief.

See also articles on FUNDAMENTALISM; MILLENNIALISM.

Bibliography. Edwin S. Gaustad, ed., *The Rise of Adventism*; Walter R. Martin, *The Truth about Seventh-day Adventism*; *Seventh-day Adventists Answer Questions on Doctrine: An Explanation of Certain Major Aspects of Seventh-day Adventist Belief*; A. W. Spalding, *Origin and History of Seventh-day Adventists*, 4 vols.; Ellen G. White, *The Great Controversy between Christ and Satan*.

CARLTON T. MITCHELL
WAKE FOREST UNIVERSITY

SEVENTH DAY BAPTISTS. The first Seventh Day Baptist Church was organized in Newport RI in 1671 with 15 covenanting members. William Davis, the first minister of the congregation, had initially come from England to join William Penn's colony. After separating himself from the Quakers, he eventually joined a Baptist congregation and began advocating that Christians should keep the Sabbath on the seventh day because the Ten Commandments were moral laws that stood for all time. Both Davis and later Sabbatarians argued that Protestants compromised scriptural authority by following the papist tradition of worshiping on Sunday. One group of Seventh Day Baptists in Washington NH influenced Adventists to adopt the Old Testament Sabbath.

The Seventh Day Baptists migrated westward in the late eighteenth century. A small congregation in Shrewsbury NJ under the leadership of William Davis's grandson, Jacob Davis, Sr., moved en masse to western Virginia in 1789. They settled on land owned by Samuel Fitz Randolph in the watershed of the Monongahela River, forming a church in New Salem VA (now Salem WV). Through active revivalism, the denomination established 10 churches in this area during the 19th century. Nationwide, membership peaked around 10,000 in 1895, declining to less than 5,000 today. Successful foreign missions, however, have added approximately 13,000 members to the denomination.

In the antebellum period Northerners and Southerners alike promoted temperance and unequivocally condemned slavery. Although one member of the Lost Creek Church in Virginia inherited a black woman and her son, he publicly affirmed that his "ownership" was a legal fiction since Virginia law did not allow emancipation. Both blacks were full members of the Seventh Day Baptist congregation whose minister, Samuel D. Davis, frequently argued abolitionism. The Seventh Day Baptists founded educational academies wherever they settled in large numbers; three have become coeducational colleges, currently operating as small, nondenominational, private schools. They are Alfred University in upstate New York, founded in 1836; Milton College in Wisconsin, 1867; Salem College in West Virginia, 1888.

Bibliography. Corliss F. Randolph, *A History of Seventh Day Baptists in West Virginia*; Albert N. Rogers, *Seventh Day Baptists in Europe and America, 1900-1955*; Seventh Day Baptist General Conference, *Seventh Day Baptists in Europe and America: Historical Papers*, 2 vols.

THOMAS VIRGIL PETERSON
ALFRED UNIVERSITY

SEYMOUR, WILLIAM JOSEPH

(1870-1922), pioneer black Pentecostal bishop, was born to former slave parents in Centerville LA. He was the leader of the unusual Azusa Street revival whose peak years of 1906-1909 in Los Angeles CA launched the global Pentecostal-charismatic movement of the 20th century. By 1982 this movement numbered 51 million members worldwide, with 11 million more Christians of similar persuasion in the traditional "mainline" denominations.

Seymour believed that his revival recaptured two elements of early apostolic practice: (1) speaking in unknown tongues along with certain other spiritual gifts, and (2) Christian togetherness and unity transcending barriers of race, nationality, status, or sex. He brought together in his own compelling personality the 19th-century emphasis upon HOLINESS and the American heritage of black-slave faith, producing out of this a new Pentecostal spirituality thought to be the second great contribution of black Christians to the church universal, the first being their religious music. Although white leaders of the movement later disregarded Seymour's emphasis upon racial inclusiveness, its explosive growth particularly in Africa and Latin America is an important factor in the expectation that Christianity in the 21st century will be located predominantly in the Third World among nonwhite and Pentecostal believers.

Lacking in opportunity for formal education, Seymour taught himself to read and write. After caring for his family until his mid-twenties, he traveled to Indianapolis, where he served as a waiter and joined the Simpson Chapel Methodist Church. Moving to Cincinnati in 1900, he studied with the prominent Methodist evangelist, Martin Wells Knapp, for a year. Smallpox robbed Seymour of sight in his left eye, and left a disfigurement that was largely concealed by a handsome beard. He received ordination as an evangelist with the "Evening Light Saints," later known as the Church of God Reformation Movement (Anderson IN).

Going on to Houston to evangelize and search for relatives lost during slavery days, he settled there with his family but traveled widely to preach and work with other black holiness leaders such as the later bishops Charles Price Jones and CHARLES HARRISON MASON. In December 1905, by sitting alone in segregation outside the classroom door, Seymour attended the Houston Bible School of the white evangelist, Charles Fox Parham, who stressed speaking in unknown tongues as an important part of Christian experience.

In January 1906 Seymour moved to Los Angeles to accept the pastorship of a small black holiness mission church with a record of interracial cooperation. Within one week he found himself summarily dismissed because of his outspoken advocacy of speaking in unknown tongues, although he had never essayed it. Soon after, he formed a small black prayer group at 214 North Bonnie Brae Street that often attracted white visitors. Suddenly, from 9-12 April an explosive outburst of speaking in unknown tongues erupted in this prayer group with such force that it immediately gained the attention of the entire city of Los Angeles.Within days huge crowds arrived that were mostly white and forced a move to larger quarters. Seymour found a large but ramshackle old former black church building in the downtown slum area at 312 Azusa Street. The "Azusa Street Mission" became a legend in its own time as the site of continual services where throngs of people attended not only from the varied ethnic and racial groups of the city but from all over the nation and world, as far away as China. Overseas missionaries and church leaders often made special pilgrimages to see for themselves what was happening. Seymour's quiet but effective leadership presided over this often unruly but always fascinating worship event. Within two years of these activities the Pentecostal Movement—as Seymour dubbed it—took root in over 50 nations.

After 1909 Seymour's ministry diminished rapidly in influence due to the rising climate of racial prejudice in the nation, and the increasing withdrawal of white Pentecostals into ever more racially exclusive groups and denominations. He felt such obvious pain at the renewed separation of the races that had once come together so powerfully, and at what he considered to be a loss of brotherly love, that when he died suddenly of a massive coronary occlusion in 1922 while dictating a letter, his followers believed that he had died of a broken heart.

See also articles on GLOSSOLALIA; HOLINESS MOVEMENT; PENTECOSTALISM.

Bibliography. Fred T. Corum, *Like As of Fire*; Douglas J. Nelson, "For Such A Time As This: The Story of Bishop William J. Seymour and the Azusa Street Revival," unpublished Ph.D. dissertation, University of Birmingham (U.K.), 1981; William J. Seymour, *The Doctrines and Disciplines of the Azusa Street Faith Mission.*

DOUGLAS J. NELSON
ARLINGTON, VIRGINIA

SHAKERS. The United Society of Believers in Christ's Second Appearing— the Christian people usually known as Shakers—has proved to be the most successful and longest-lived of the American utopian, millennial religious experiments.

Although English in origin and a radical branch of Quakerism with roots in the 16th-century French Comisard movement, the sect attracted few adherents until "Mother" Ann Lee and eight followers emigrated to America in 1774 to settle near Albany NY. A series of religious revivals in the area attracted thousands of converts who found in Shakerism a workable scheme for expressing their religious fervor. A pattern of communal living based upon self-denial evolved to foster their newfound faith. The Shaker way aspired to human perfection, and advocated a life designed to eliminate those human frailties that set people at odds with one another, such as sex, fame, money, and war. The life-style generated sought to embody their convictions; even their buildings and furniture reflected their striving for simplicity, economy, and orderliness.

The Shakers affirmed the dual aspect (the Mother/Father nature) of God, the perfectibility of human nature, and the imminence of the millennium. Members were required to confess their sins, to lead celibate lives, and to separate themselves from ordinary society into communities based on the common ownership of property. Persecuted by hostile relatives and neighbors, they withdrew from the "world" into "society order" on isolated tracts of farmland. Complex written covenants reinforced their separateness. With the passage of time, the original spontaneity of their personal religion yielded to prescribed routine. In later years, even the ecstatic dancing and shaking—the activities that gave the group its name—turned into a close-order drill exercise performed at weekly meetings.

In the early nineteenth century, the Kentucky revivals established the Shakers in the South just as the New York revivals had planted Shaker villages throughout New England and New York. The New Lebanon Society dispatched three of its most gifted leaders—Issachar Bates, Joseph Meacham, and Benjamin Youngs—to establish colonies in Ohio, Kentucky, and Indiana. Many early members were recruited from the ranks of New Light Presbyterians who were attracted by the leadership of strong schismatic ministers. In Kentucky, they settled at South Union, 15 miles north of the Tennessee border, and at Pleasant Hill in the heart of the Bluegrass area near Lexington. Shakerism attained its greatest strength in the 1830s when the membership reached 6,000 in 18 societies in eight states.

Theoretically, each society functioned as a unit of the whole, but the Southern societies did exhibit some regional differences. Pleasant Hill had some Swedish members and South Union had a number of blacks, slaves freed when their owners became Shakers. During the Civil War, the Southern villages suffered heavy property damage and financial loss. Pleasant Hill's stone and brick buildings are especially fine examples of Shaker architecture, and the Kentucky societies benefited by able leadership from Youngs, Richard McNemar, and John Dunlavy. The Shakers engaged in silk culture and manufacture, raised fine livestock, and packaged and marketed garden seeds. The influence of the Shakers began to wane by midcentury. Pleasant Hill closed in 1910, South Union in 1922.

In the 1890s, in an effort to augment their dwindling numbers, the Shakers established colonies at White Oak GA and near Kissimmee FL. Both colonies proved to be successful at farming, but unsuccessful in attracting converts, so they disbanded, sold their property, and divided the proceeds among the colonists, most of whom returned to Shaker villages in the North.

See also articles on Great Revival; Utopian Communities.

Bibliography. Edward D. Andrews, *The People Called Shakers: A Search for the Perfect Society*; Marguerite F. Melcher, *The Shaker Adventure*; Charles Nordhoff, *The Communistic Societies of the United States.*

SHEFTALL FAMILY. The Sheftalls were the best-known, if not the outstanding, Jewish family in colonial Georgia. The patriarch of the family, Benjamin Sheftall (1692-1765), had come over from London with the first group of Spanish-Portuguese Jews in 1733. He was a German Jew, a native of Bavaria or Frankfort-on-Main, who spoke English and German-yiddish, which he taught to his oldest son, Mordecai.

Benjamin was active in the establishment of congregation Mikveh Israel in

SAVANNAH in 1735 in which he seems to have served as sexton and *schochet* (ritual slaughterer). He had two sons, Mordecai by his first wife, Perla, and Levi by his second wife, Hannah. Benjamin kept the congregation's vital records, a task carried on by his son Levi. In 1748, he sent to England for *tifillin* (phylacteries) and prayer books for Mordecai's bar mitzvah, the first recorded observance of this rite in America. In 1750, he joined a group of Christians in creating Georgia's first philanthropic organization, the St. George Society, to assist widows and orphans.

Mordecai Sheftall (1735-1797), like his father, was an observant Jew. His substantial position and economic social status in the Savannah community was not secured at the cost of religious indifference. By 1762 he was in the front ranks of the Georgia Jews' attempt to secure legislative confirmation of their cemetery on the Savannah common, which had been deeded by JAMES OGLETHORPE in 1733. A similar attempt eight years later also failed. On 2 August 1773, Mordecai Sheftall gave the six Jewish families living in Savannah a few acres to serve as a burying ground and as a building lot for a synagogue; the cemetery remained in use until 1850. On the eve of the Day of Atonement in 1774, he used a room in his home for worship. That marked the third effort to organize a permanent Jewish congregation in Savannah with Mordecai serving as the *mohel* and as one of the religious leaders.

Supporting the American Revolution, he became chairman of the parish committee and subsequently served as colonel in the Georgia brigade and as commissary general of purchases and issues to the state militia. He was captured, paroled, recaptured and paroled again. With the end of the war, after having made his way to Philadelphia where he became active in that city's Jewish community, he returned to Savannah and remained there. His son Levi (1739-1809) helped reestablish the Jewish congregation in Savannah in 1790,

serving as its president in 1789 and keeping the congregation's vital records as did his uncle and grandfather before him.

See also article on JEWS IN THE SOUTH.

LOUIS SCHMIER
VALDOSTA STATE COLLEGE

SHERRILL, LEWIS JOSEPH (1892-1957), Presbyterian leader in pastoral care, was born in Haskell TX. He received his formal education there and at Austin College (A.B., 1916), Louisville Presbyterian Seminary (B.D., 1921), and Yale University (Ph.D., 1929). While in seminary Sherrill became intrigued with the new discipline of psychology and its relationship to Christian education. Called to the faculty of Louisville Seminary in 1925 in Religious Education, he produced a number of works in that discipline, *Religious Education in the Church* (1936) the best known. As a member of the faculty and later dean of the seminary (1930-1950), Sherrill worked with denominational leaders of both the Presbyterian Church in the United States and the United Presbyterian Church in the United States to incorporate in curriculum and program materials the latest insights in pedagogy.

Sherrill's interest in psychology led to his writing *Guilt and Redemption* (1945), and after his call to Union Theological Seminary, New York, he continued with *The Struggle of the Soul* (1951) and *The Gift of Power* (1955). These three works pioneered in the application of depth psychology to traditional Christian doctrines and piety. His work opened especially the PCUS to the issues and opportunities of the new "sciences" of the 20th century. The historian of Southern Presbyterianism, E. T. Thompson, called Sherrill the "pioneer theologian of the twentieth century" for that communion. Sherrill also helped form the American Association of Theological Schools, the accrediting agency of U. S. seminaries, and served as its first executive secretary (1935-1938) and its president (1938-1940). He was married to Helen Hartwick Sherrill, a social worker and writer, who coauthored some books with him.

See also article on PASTORAL CARE.

LOUIS B. WEEKS
LOUISVILLE PRESBYTERIAN SEMINARY

SILVER BLUFF CHURCH. The first independent, black Baptist church in America originated in the year 1773 at Silver Bluff, located 11 miles downriver from Augusta GA. It was formed by the Reverend Mr. Palmer in the colony of South Carolina. George Galphin, slavemaster of the Silver Bluff congregation, became one of its members. He facilitated the growth of the congregation by allowing David George, a local minister, to be ordained in the congregation. He also permitted GEORGE LIELE to preach to the congregation during its early development.

When Savannah was evacuated by the Americans in 1778, the Silver Bluff Church was forced into exile. During this period of war between the British and Americans, George Galphin abandoned the Silver Bluff congregation in an effort to flee from the British. David George and 50 slaves of this congregation aligned themselves with the British in Savannah and were freed.

After peace was established in 1783, the Silver Bluff Baptist Church was revived under the able leadership of Jesse Peter who remained a slave in South Carolina following the British evacuation of Savannah in 1782. Taking upon itself various names and locations during its brief duration, the Silver Bluff Baptist Church lasted from 1773 to 1793.

HENRY J. YOUNG
GARRETT-EVANGELICAL SEMINARY

SIN. In the English Bible the word sin translates a variety of words in the original Hebrew and Greek: disobedience, iniquity, rebellion, wickedness, crookedness, faithlessness, and missing the mark. In the Old Testament, sin is a breach of covenant, whether it is injuring one's brother, committing adultery, or refusing to give the laborer his or her due.

The deepest insight into sin in the Old Testament is embodied in the story of "the Fall" (Gen. 3). In remarkably vivid and terse language, "original" sin is pictured as disobedience to the Creator, the source of life. In the New Testament, Paul stressed the universality of sin, expressed in the mystic unity of the race in the "first Adam" (Rom. 5:12-21). Sin is not only a state of disobedience and disbelief, it is an external power that enslaves humankind and from which deliverance can only come through the redemptive act of God in Christ.

In the history of the church, the theological view of sin has often been obscured and sometimes eclipsed by a moralistic view of sin. The Protestant Reformation was launched when Martin Luther, through his own religious struggle and profound study of the Bible in its original languages, rediscovered the theological meaning of sin as the willful alienation of the creature from the Creator. Pinpointing the Pauline statement, "The just shall live by faith" (Rom. 1:17), Luther focused the theological meaning of sin as unfaith, the turning away from God to self in pride and self-centeredness. The opposite of sin was not righteousness but faith; through faith one was righteous, that is, in a right relation with God.

The tendency to think of sin primarily in moralistic rather than theological terms, as bad or socially condemned attitudes and actions rather than as unbelief, has been prominent in American Protestantism, as recently manifested in the pronouncements of the MORAL MAJORITY. But Christians generally agree that persons cannot save themselves from the power and effects of sin by their own attempts at righteousness. In the death and resurrection of Christ, God initiates salvation, to which the appropriate response is faith and loving obedience.

See also articles on ATONEMENT; SALVATION.

Bibliography. Edward La B. Cherbonnier, *Hardness of Heart*; J. R. Coates, trans. and ed., *Bible Key Words.*

THOMAS E. MCCOLLOUGH
DUKE UNIVERSITY

SISTER. A woman referred to by this title is one who seeks to pursue her Christian vocation in the context of a religious community, through a life that is centered in prayer, some form of Christian ministry, and the practice of the evangelical counsels of poverty, chastity, and obedience that have been publicly professed by vow.

Some religious institutes of women are of a contemplative nature (e.g., cloistered Carmelites, Cistercians, and Poor Clares). Their principal objective is to praise God and intercede by prayer for their fellow men and women, in conjunction with daily community labors within the monastery. The 16th-century contemplative St. Teresa of Avila and the 19th-century saint Therese of Lisieux are examples of women dedicated to such a ministry. Technically, the term "nun" is associated with these women to distinguish them from women engaged in active pastoral ministries outside the monastery or cloister (to whom the title of "sister" is more properly attached).

Other religious institutes, in addition to focusing on prayer, are oriented to ministries that are directed to education (e.g., Sister of Notre Dame), health care (e.g., Daughters of Charity), parish ministry (e.g., Parish Visitors of Mary Immaculate), and social service (e.g., Sisters of Social Service). Many communities are involved in ministries that touch all these areas (e.g., Dominican Sisters) and involve such specialized fields of service as adult education, religious education; pastoral care of the sick, elderly, and physically and mentally handicapped; and community organization—staffing centers of peace and justice, ministry to prison inmates, ministries with the rural and urban poor. Mother Teresa of Calcutta is an example of a sister whose ministry has spanned teaching and Christian charitable service. She left teaching in 1948 and founded an order dedicated to service of the poor (Missionaries of Charity).

Various religious orders of women have distinguished themselves for their work in the Southern United States. Such orders as the Daughters of Charity and Sisters of Mercy were outstanding in their nursing care of Union and Confederate troops during the Civil War. The Sisters of St. Joseph of St. Augustine FL, Sisters of St. Francis, Sisters of the Holy Names of Jesus and Mary, the Oblate Sisters of Providence, and Sisters of the Blessed Sacrament are noted for their ministry to Indians and blacks in the South.

While the term "sister" is commonly, though not exclusively, used by Roman Catholics, Orthodox, and Episcopalians in the above, more restrictive sense, Free Church communities prefer to apply the term in the broader sense of Matt. 12:50: "Whoever does the will of my heavenly Father is brother and sister and mother to me."

ROBERT J. BAKER
ST. VINCENT DE PAUL
REGIONAL SEMINARY

SLAVERY. Unlike Latin America and the Caribbean islands where plantations routinely consisted of hundreds of slaves, more than one-half of the slaves in the antebellum South lived on family farms. Small plantations with 20 to 50 slaves accounted for another quarter. These small agricultural units encouraged whites to adopt patriarchal attitudes toward the men and women that they held in bondage. Slaveowners in Virginia in the 18th century frequently pictured themselves in pastoral settings as modern-day Patriarchs, charged with governing large extended families that included their bondmen and bondwomen.

Although the introduction of black slaves into North America was clearly based on economic considerations, patriarchal attitudes of planters coupled with the Puritan religious legacy raised questions about the slaveowners' responsibility for converting the Africans to Christianity. Clergymen and English governmental officials encouraged Christian MISSION TO THE SLAVES in the English colonies. Yet these efforts frequently met resistance from slaveowners. The greatest fear centered on the question of whether or not baptized slaves could be kept in perpetual bondage. The longer slaveowners resisted Christian missionary activity among their slaves, the greater was the tendency for ministers to make assurances that they were only concerned about the spiritual salvation of the blacks. In 1689 Cotton Mather, a leading Puritan clergyman in New England, clearly stated that baptism would not mean emancipation; six colonial legislatures enacted statutes backing this position between 1664 and 1706.

Slaveowners, however, faced a dilemma. On the one hand, they often justified slavery on the grounds that it would facilitate the Africans' liberation from heathenism and their acceptance of Christianity; on the other hand, they clearly saw that Christian equality could be used as a wedge by those who opposed all forms of human bondage.

Clergymen in the mid-eighteenth century did, in fact, argue both positions. The Methodist revivalist GEORGE WHITEFIELD, although clearly opposed to the slave trade, wrote that there was no necessity to link the slaves' spiritual salvation to their emancipation. Scandalized that slaveowners did not place a high priority on converting blacks to Christianity, he argued, as Mather had a century earlier, that true Christianity would make Africans better servants by encouraging such virtues as honesty, obedience, and love. On the other hand, John Woolman, the leading Quaker advocate against slavery, held that the institution of slavery clearly contravened Christian principles of the brotherhood of all humans and the Golden Rule.

As the revolutionary spirit of 1776 augmented the missionary zeal of the Great Awakening, other clergymen joined Woolman's campaign against slavery. FRANCIS ASBURY and THOMAS COKE (Methodist bishops), JOHN LELAND and David Barrow (Baptists), DAVID RICE and George Bourne (Presbyterians) contended that Christianity could not compromise with slavery. Strong antislavery resolutions were passed at Methodist Conferences in 1780 and 1784, but opposition from laity in the South forced church leaders to suspend indefinitely their execution. Slavery's opponents among the Baptists and Presbyterians made little progress convincing Southerners in their denominations to promote emancipation. Only the Quakers ultimately convinced their meetings that slavery was incompatible with membership. Gradually the clerical opponents of slavery were forced to mute their attacks or leave; many left the slaveholding states to continue their agitation in the North.

The conditions of slavery in the South influenced the religious beliefs and practices of both white people and black people. During the Great Revival early in the 19th century evangelical religion gained ascendancy in America. Revivalists preached a personal religion, convicting individuals of sin so that they could experience a joyful salvation in Christ. Yet revivalism was not devoid of all social theory; Evangelicals believed that as individuals turned to God, society itself would become perfected. Revivals did, in fact, spawn the temperance movement, prison reform, and even antislavery groups that frequently promoted sending emancipated slaves to Liberia.

After 1830, however, both Northerners and Southerners came to realize that colonization schemes were impractical. As Northern Evangelicals such as THEODORE WELD and Albert Barnes became more strident in promoting ABOLITIONISM, slaveowners became increasingly suspicious of revivalism's social thrust, and Southern preachers began to assure them that Christianity could accommodate the "peculiar institution." In recasting Southern religion to fit the reality of slavery, white Southerners developed a religious world view based on four fundamentals. First, the core of true religion was the individual's conversion experience, not the restructuring of society. Second, civil institutions such as marriage, the family, and slavery were necessary to restrain human beings tainted by original sin. Third, Christianity's appropriate role was to ameliorate the improper uses of authority by encouraging personal piety, not to challenge valid social structures. Fourth, a literal reading of the Bible was the sole means for judging the legitimacy of all institutions.

White Christians in the antebellum South therefore accommodated themselves to their peculiar institution by formulating religious principles with one eye cast on the realities of slavery. They read the Bible literally to show that God permitted and even ordained slavery. Assimilating racist views, they argued that slavery was necessary to control the sinful predispositions of an inherently inferior race. They believed that by converting both slaveowners and slaves to Christ, they could encourage masters to exert their authority with compassion. To avoid the animosity of slaveowners, missionaries preached to slaves a gospel of personal morality that stressed obedience, thrift, and honesty.

The religion of black people in the South was also influenced by slavery. From the earliest times slaveholders in the American colonies sought to eradicate all elements of African language and culture by systematically separating members of the same tribe on different farms and plantations. Naturally, Africans were prohibited from practicing their native religions because masters feared that gatherings of slaves for "heathenish" purposes could lead to rebellion. The Africans' religious heritage was fairly easily uprooted in North America (except on the sea islands off South Carolina and in Louisiana) because of the small ratio of blacks to whites and because procreation made the importation of large numbers of slaves from Africa unnecessary.

Although the black population became Christianized in large numbers during the general awakenings, their position as slaves affected their own religious perceptions. As slaves they could easily discern their masters' self-interest in promoting a morality that stressed obedience and trust. While the masters used Christianity to encourage docility among slaves, historians generally contend that there were few "Uncle Toms" who truly felt contrite for "stealing" a little extra food. But the harsh conditions of slavery did reinforce a religion of hope among the slaves. At times that hope took an other-worldly form where slaves believed they would be compensated in heaven for injustice in this world; at other times biblical stories such as the Exodus account created hopes for liberation from human bondage. In a few instances, at least, this hopefulness took on an apocalyptic cast: slave revolts, led by Gabriel Prosser, DENMARK VESEY, and Nat Turner in the first three decades of the 19th century, combined visionary revelations with physical revolt. While the compensatory religious hopes of the slaves for rewards in the next life dovetailed with the slaveowners' interests, a thin line existed between spiritual liberation and political emancipation in the slaves' religion. The "spirituals," sung by the plantation slaves, clearly show Christianity's double-edged sword: "O my Lord delivered Daniel O why not deliver me too."

See also articles on ETHICS, CHRISTIAN; SEGREGATION.

Bibliography. John W. Blassingame, *The Slave Community*; E. Franklin Frazier, *The Negro Church in America*; Eugene D. Genovese, *Roll Jordan Roll*; Winthrop D. Jordan, *White over Black*; Donald G. Mathews, *Religion in the Old South*; Gerald W. Mullin, *Flight and Rebellion*; Thomas V. Peterson, *Ham and Japheth*; Albert J. Raboteau, *Slave Religion*; Milton C. Sernett, *Black Religion and American Evangelism*; H. Shelton Smith, *In His Image, But . . .* ; Kenneth M. Stampp, *The Peculiar Institution*.

THOMAS VIRGIL PETERSON
ALFRED UNIVERSITY

SLAVES, MISSION TO: *See* MISSION
TO SLAVES.

SMITH, BENJAMIN MOSBY, Presbyterian seminary professor, was born in
Powhatan County VA. He graduated from
Hampden-Sydney College in 1829, and
taught briefly in Milton NC. He studied at
Union Theological Seminary in Virginia
from 1831 to 1833, and remained there as
assistant instructor until 1836, being
ordained a minister in 1835. In 1836 and
1837 he traveled and studied in Europe.

Smith held several pastorates in Virginia, at Danville (1838-1840), Tinkling
Spring and Waynesboro (1840-1845), and
Staunton (1845-1853). He helped to
organize societies to promote public education in 1831, and in 1839 he reported to
the governor of Virginia on the Prussian
school system as a model. In 1853 and
1854 he was executive secretary of the
(Old School) Presbyterian Board of
Publication.

In 1854 Smith became professor of
Oriental literature at Union Seminary in
Virginia. He held that position until
retirement in 1889. From 1858 to 1874 he
was also copastor of the College Church at
Hampden-Sydney. As a moderate on slavery and Southern rights, Smith came into
his own after the Confederacy fell.
Renewing old contacts, he raised funds in
the North and border states to revive his
seminary. Union outdistanced its sister,
Presbyterian Seminary, Columbia, and
Smith's role at Union grew.

In 1876 Smith was moderator of the
Presbyterian Church in the United States
General Assembly. He proved relatively
open to rapprochement with Northern
Presbyterians. From 1871 to 1882 he
served as public school superintendent of
Prince Edward County. He wrote *Family
Religion* (1859) and guides to Bible study.
See also article on THEOLOGICAL
EDUCATION.

Bibliography. Francis R. Flournoy, *Benjamin Mosby
Smith (1811-1893)*; Eugene C. Scott, *Ministerial Directory of the Presbyterian Church, U. S., 1861-1941.*

                         JACK P. MADDEX, JR.
                         UNIVERSITY OF OREGON

SMITH, H(ILRIE) SHELTON(1893-),
major figure in religious and theological
education and an ecumenist, was born
near Greensboro NC. A graduate of Elon
College (1917), he served as a chaplain in
World War I. In 1923 he received his
Ph.D. from Yale and over the next five
years was director of leadership education
of the International Council of Religious
Education. Between 1928 and 1931 he
taught briefly at Columbia and Yale, after
which he taught for 32 years at Duke
where his instruction included philosophy
of religious education (1931-1940), Christian ethics (1940-1945), and American
religious thought (1945-1963). In 1953 he
was appointed James B. Duke professor of
American religious thought.

Combining intellectual integrity and
practical realism, Smith pursued scholarship to increase wisdom and to serve the
common good. In curricular affairs he
broke new ground by establishing the
study of American Christianity as an academic field at a Southern university. In
1935 he also encouraged local ecumenical
activity by founding and serving as first
president of the North Carolina Council
of Churches. In that organization and in
general education he tried to increase
mutual trust among churchmen in worship and work. Smith thought that critical
inquiry into the Christian community's
historical experiences could yield new
theological insights and wider opportunities for religious witness. Through his lectures, counsel, and personal example he
showed that a better understanding of the
American past could help improve contemporary values. Colleagues around the
country recognized his scholarly eminence by electing him president of the
American Society of Church History in
1957 and president of the American
Theological Society the following year. Of
all his honors, perhaps none was more
fitting than the NC Council of Churches'
citation of 1978 that recognized Smith's
distinguished service in the cause of ecumenical Christianity.
See also articles on ECUMENISM;
THEOLOGICAL EDUCATION.

Bibliography. H. Shelton Smith, *Changing Conceptions of Original Sin: A Study in American Theology Since 1750; In His Image, But . . .: Racism in Southern Religion, 1780-1910,* ed. with R. T. Handy and L. A. Loetscher; *American Christianity: An Historical Interpretation with Representative Documents.*

HENRY WARNER BOWDEN
RUTGERS UNIVERSITY

SMITH, LILLIAN EUGENIA (1897-1966),

novelist and spokeswoman for racial justice, was born in Jasper FL. The seventh of nine children of parents who descended from old slaveowning families, she grew up in a typical Deep South community that would later provide the setting for her writings.

Her father had made a fortune producing naval stores, and her upbringing, which included black servants, devout Methodism, and an emphasis on culture and education, was not uncommon for upper-class white Southerners of her generation. Lillian Smith aspired to a career as a pianist and spent 1917-1918 studying at the Peabody Conservatory in Baltimore, but the drastic decline of her father's financial situation, brought about by the collapse of the European market for naval stores during World War I, forced her to return to the South. Her father had purchased land in Rabun County near Clayton in the north Georgia mountains originally as a summer home for his large family, but had moved there permanently in 1915 to operate a summer hotel and girls camp on Old Screamer Mountain, the site of the Smith home. Smith helped her father and also worked as a school teacher.

In 1922 she accepted a position at a Methodist missionary school in Huchow, China, where she taught music for three years. While in China she read extensively about Freudian psychology and also became familiar with Gandhi's ideas. Smith returned to Georgia in 1925 and took over from her aging father the directorship of his girls camp and, with the assistance of another Georgia woman, Paula Snelling, turned it into a place where some of the white South's wealthiest families regularly sent their daughters.

Although primarily occupied in running the camp, the income from which was used to pay off family debts, Smith also undertook creative writing. Some initial rejection of her work by publishers probably contributed to her and Snelling's decision in 1935 to begin publishing a small magazine devoted to literature, poetry, criticism, and the South. They called it *Pseudopodia* (later changed to *North Georgia Review* and then to *South Today*), and the new journal was immediately hailed as one of the most sparkling and provocative to come out of the South in years. In addition to serving as a vehicle for Smith and Snelling's own writings, the magazine included contributions by the then still largely unknown Southern journalist, W. J. Cash, and by black writers such as W. E. B. Du Bois and Sterling Brown. Increasingly, it began to reflect Smith's preoccupation with the origins and consequences of caste segregation. In 1938, she and Snelling traveled to Brazil where Smith wrote much of what eventually became *Strange Fruit*, the novel that would make her famous. Fellowships from the Rosenwald Fund also helped her devote time to studying and writing.

During World War II, Smith became more explicitly critical of white supremacy and what it meant for the South. In 1943 she declared in *South Today* that fighting for freedom while maintaining Jim Crow was like "trying to buy a new world with old Confederate bills." She was especially critical of what she perceived as the timidity of Southern liberals and hoped that her soon-to-be-completed novel would stimulate them to take bolder action.

Strange Fruit finally appeared in 1944. It dealt with the tragic consequences of an interracial love affair between a white man and black woman in a small Southern town. Provocative in theme, explicit in language, and psychologically probing, *Strange Fruit*, quite to the surprise of its author, became a bestseller. It was banned in Boston and produced as a play on Broadway. Eventually it sold over three million copies and was translated into 16 languages, turning Smith overnight into the white South's most prominent critic of segregation. Her point was that segregation was psychologically injurious to both whites and blacks and that the South could neither prosper nor remain true to its Christian heritage as long as it existed. She conveyed this message repeatedly in lectures, radio talks, and articles in national magazines.

In 1949 Smith published her autobiography, *Killers of the Dream*. The book examined the triumph of white supremacy in the South and its connection to religious beliefs, sexual attitudes, and child-rearing practices. It further enhanced her reputation as the most outspoken white Southern critic of segregation and she received numerous awards from religious and civil-rights groups. Two later books, *Now is the Time* (1955) and *Our Faces, Our Words* (1964), were passionate statements on behalf of the civil rights movement. Smith's other writings include *The Journey* (1954), a volume of personal reminiscences growing out of her own struggle against cancer, which testified to the dignity and triumph of the human spirit, and *Memory of a Large Christmas* (1961), another autobiographical work. Her only other published novel, *One Hour* (1959), dealt with the themes of sin, guilt, and false accusation.

See also article on LITERATURE AND RELIGION.

Bibliography. Louise Blackwell and Frances Clay, *Lillian Smith*; Richard H. King, *A Southern Renaissance: The Cultural Awakening of the American South, 1930-1955*; Morton Sosna, *In Search of the Silent South: Southern Liberals and the Race Issue*; Helen White and Redding S. Sugg, Jr., eds., *From the Mountain*.

MORTON SOSNA
STANFORD HUMANITIES CENTER

SMYTH, THOMAS (1808-1873), a leading Presbyterian divine in the Old South, was born in Belfast, Ireland and educated at Belfast College and Highbury College in London. He came to the United States in 1830 and shortly thereafter received a degree from Princeton Theological Seminary. In 1832 he accepted a pastorate at the Second Presbyterian Church in CHARLESTON SC where he remained for 38 years. Besides his pastoral duties, Smyth took a special interest in missions, serving for many years as chairman of the Committee on Foreign Missions in the Synod of South Carolina.

With a powerful intellect and an excellent knowledge of church polity, Smyth became a prominent defender of the orthodox principles of Old School Presbyterianism. During the schism of 1837, he represented the Old School minority in the Charleston Union Presbytery. In the *Prelatical Doctrine of Apostolical Succession* (1841) and *Ecclesiastical Republicanism* (1843), Smyth attacked the High Church doctrines of the Episcopal Church and extolled the virtues of Presbyterian polity. Both works enjoyed wide circulation in America and Europe. He opposed a union between the United Synod of the South and the Presbyterian Church because of the New School views of the former body. Along with JAMES H. THORNWELL and BENJAMIN M. PALMER, Smyth was a leading contributor to the influential *Southern Presbyterian Review*.

See also article on OLD SCHOOL/NEW SCHOOL.

Bibliography. Thomas Smyth, *Autobiographical Notes, Letters and Reflections*; *Complete Works of Rev. Thomas Smyth*.

MITCHELL SNAY
WALTHAM, MASSACHUSETTS

SNAKE HANDLERS. This variety of conservative Protestants comprises men and women who belong to churches commonly designated as "Holiness" and "Pentecostal." They handle poisonous snakes in the conviction that they are acting under the guidance and protection of the Holy Ghost. Their system of ritual and belief is based upon a literal interpretation of the King James Version of the Bible, which they regard as a "roadmap from earth to Heaven." Mark 16:18 ("They shall take up serpents") is the principal text invoked in justification of their use of snakes.

Most snake handlers are Appalachian mountaineers, the descendants of English and Scotch-Irish pioneers who settled the region in the period between 1780 and 1840. They are characterized by a low level of formal education. Some of the older members can neither read nor write. The men earn their living as coal miners, mill hands, and factory workers. The women spend their days in the performance of domestic chores.

At least two nights each week snake handlers assemble for religious services. At the emotional peak of a meeting, to the accompaniment of vigorously strummed guitars, clashing cymbals and tambourines, shouting and singing, clapping and stamping, devotees remove rattlesnakes and copperheads from their wooden boxes and begin to handle them. Sometimes they place the snakes on top of their heads, or wrap them around their necks, or thrust them inside their shirts, or rub them over their faces, or "tread" on them with bare feet, or toss them to other worshipers.

Only rarely do the serpents strike their handlers. A painful bite is generally seen as evidence that the worshiper experienced a "wavering" of faith or failed to follow the "leading" of the Spirit. Most devotees reject the idea of seeking medical aid for a bite, believing that true children of God look to the Lord for their healing. At least 63 people have died as a consequence of snake bites suffered in religious meetings.

Snake handling was initiated about 1913 by George W. Hensley, an illiterate preacher from the hills of eastern Tennessee. The practice won adherents all across the South, especially in the coal-mining regions of the Appalachians. In time, with the northward migration of mountaineers in search of jobs, snake handling became established in Ohio, Michigan, and Indiana as well.

Between 1936 and 1953 snake handling was outlawed by state statute in Kentucky, Georgia, Virginia, Tennessee, North Carolina, and Alabama, and by municipal ordinance in Bartow FL and Greenville SC. These laws did virtually nothing to abate the practice. (The Georgia law was repealed in 1968.)

Snake-handling religion has proven itself to be a movement of considerable vitality and durability. It continues to attract new devotees even today. The vast majority of new members are sons and daughters of veteran followers of the movement. In a number of families snake handling has been carried on for three generations or more. Ties of kinship have been a factor of crucial importance in both the diffusion and the persistence of the snake-handling faith.

See also articles on APPALACHIAN RELIGION; HOLINESS MOVEMENT; PENTECOSTALISM.

Bibliography. Steven M. Kane, "Holy Ghost People: The Snake-Handlers of Southern Appalachia," *Appalachian Journal* 1 (Spring 1974):255-62; "Ritual Possession in a Southern Appalachian Religious Sect," *Journal of American Folklore* 87 (October-December 1974):293-302; "Holiness Ritual Fire Handling: Ethnographic and Psychophysiological Considerations," *Ethos* 10 (1982):369-84.

STEVEN M. KANE
BROWN UNIVERSITY

SOCIAL GOSPEL. Long before the Progressive Era, Protestants in America had practiced acts of charity, concerned themselves with social issues, and labored to bring about the millennium of a redeemed Christian republic, Southerners as well as Northerners were much implicated in these evangelical enterprises. The Social Gospel was a mood and movement rooted in this earlier evangelical tradition (and informed by European and British example), yet it had an identity of its own distinguishing it from both antebellum social Christianity and later Protestant social activism. It was a late nineteenth-century response to the challenges of industrialization, urbanization, and immigration, supported by the liberal New

Theology (though the connection was never one-to-one), and inspired by the older dream of a "Christianized America" given new expression by Walter Rauschenbusch's "Kingdom of God" vision. It flowered in the decade preceding the Great War, knew a kind of Indian Summer in the 1920s, and then was radically transformed under the impact of the Great Depression and World War II and the concurrent ascendancy of Neo-Orthodoxy.

Some historians have argued that the Social Gospel deeply penetrated the South. They are unpersuasive. It did not, and for clear reasons. The challenges confronting the North were not seen as immediate by a South that remained primarily agrarian, rural, Anglo-Saxon, Protestant, poor, and burdened with its own "problem," the massive presence of blacks. The Social Gospel was strongest in affluent institutional churches and among educated clergymen; both were scarce in the South. Moreover, the continuing conservative Southern theological soil failed to provide needed nourishment. Finally, Southern traditions of individualism and localism were inimical to the Social Gospel's bureaucratic, centralizing tendencies.

Still, it was not totally absent. Evangelists of the dispossessed were found in the ranks of the Alliance and Populist and other movements protesting the crucifixion of farmers and laborers on a cross of gold. Every major denomination sought to eliminate the evils (correctly perceived as social as well as personal) of drinking, gambling, prostitution, sabbath desecration, and also such enormities as lynching, convict lease labor, and child labor. Every major denomination also possessed a few authentic champions of Christian justice. The Episcopal priest EDGAR GARDNER MURPHY courageously, if gently, labored for educational reform, the protection of sweated children, and racial equity. The Presbyterian minister ALEXANDER J. MCKELWAY in blunter fashion fought the good fight for many reform causes. Meth-odist Bishop ATTICUS HAYGOOD early spoke on behalf of blacks, and the Methodist minister WILL ALEXANDER was a founder of the COMMISSION ON INTERRACIAL COOPERATION, an organization largely composed of Southern churchmen. The Mississippi Baptist minister Charles Otken wrote one of the first critical exposés of Southern economic conditions; a Tennessee preacher was in the vanguard of convict-lease-system critics; and in Atlanta the Baptist minister M. Ashby Jones won fame as a reformer. In 1912 the SOUTHERN SOCIOLOGICAL CONGRESS was formed to study social problems and its composition was heavily clerical. Later the important ASSOCIATION OF SOUTHERN WOMEN FOR THE PREVENTION OF LYNCHING was fueled by Christian compassion. In the Progressive Era such racial reformers as WILLIS D. WEATHERFORD and Francis Pickens Miller, both associated with the YMCA, began their illustrious careers. Wake Forest President WILLIAM LOUIS POTEAT and Richmond's Union Theological Seminary Professor Walter Lingle stood as examples of social Christianity's presence in Southern church schools.

Christian teachings inspired these and more individuals and movements questing for social and racial justice in the South. If Southern Protestantism was only partially penetrated by the Social Gospel during the period of its flowering in the North, the faith proclaimed by the churches did inspire and sustain reform and humanitarian enterprises.

See also articles on CHRISTIAN SOCIALISM; SOCIAL SERVICES.

Bibliography. Kenneth K. Bailey, *Southern White Protestantism in the Twentieth Century*; Robert Moats Miller, "Fourteen Points on the Social Gospel in the South," *Southern Humanities Review* 1 (Summer 1967): 126-40; Ronald White, Jr. and C. Howard Hopkins, *The Social Gospel.*

ROBERT MOATS MILLER
UNIVERSITY OF NORTH CAROLINA
AT CHAPEL HILL

SOCIAL SERVICES. Church-sponsored social services in the South exist at three levels. First, there are those projects supported by a single church or a small group of churches often on the initiative of some interested layman or minister. They are of great variety and may include, for example, services to prisoners or to refugees, counseling on problem pregnancies or where rape has occurred, "hot-line" telephone counseling on drug abuse, domestic violence, or suicide, preventive services such as "Mother's morning out," nighttime shelter for "street people," group homes for troubled adolescents, neighborhood centers and day care centers that serve the community as well as church members. These services are largely staffed by volunteers, although there is increasing awareness of the need for training and professional guidance. A few churches employ professional social workers on their staffs.

The number and quality of such services has increased greatly in the last 20 years. They have arisen not so much from any theological change as from the heightened awareness of social problems that characterized the 1960s and enlarged community conscience. Such programs are often innovative, on the cutting edge of social services, and are rarely directly evangelistic; rather, they express human compassion in the hope that those they serve may become open to a relationship with the Divine.

Second, in some communities, churches of all denominations have come together to create an interchurch or interfaith agency, often with professional leadership, to meet the unmet needs in the community. Such agencies may deal with emergencies that fall outside the purview of the public welfare system or may undertake community projects of their own, such as housing developments. They show an ecumenical spirit that has too often been lacking in church-sponsored work. Again, this is a fairly recent development.

At a third level, that of the diocese, synod, convention, or conference, churches have traditionally maintained children's agencies or homes. Some of

these are of considerable antiquity, such as the Ursuline Convent in New Orleans, dating from 1727, although it was not strictly a children's home but a shelter for entire families. Most of the larger denominations founded homes in the years after the Civil War—a few before—and many new homes were built in the first quarter of this century. The children under their care were largely orphans who otherwise would have entered the workhouse or become "little wanderers" on their own. They were reared entirely in the orphanage, were expected to show gratitude— they were dismissed if they did not—and were trained to be self-supporting, pious, and well behaved.

In the 1930s and 1940s the number of orphans needing care declined sharply due to advances in public health. Institutional care came under a great deal of criticism with governmental child welfare agencies developing foster family care as the preferred method of caring for dependent children, who were now mostly the victims of family breakdown. In the North many institutions closed and others became residential treatment centers for the emotionally disturbed. In the South, however, where governmental programs grew more slowly, children's institutions were still needed for the dependent child. Church children's homes, faced with caring for children with many more problems than before and in response to newer concepts of child care, humanized and individualized their programs. The number of children in any one living unit fell from an average of 25 to eight or nine; "house-fathers" were introduced; children were sent to community schools; institutions employed social workers; child-care staff were given training; some homes developed foster family as well as group care and others decentralized their operation and either dispersed their campuses or added to them by establishing community-based group homes. The most important change, however, was the beginning of active work with the children's homes, particularly in the

South. This effort led to much shorter stays in institutions.

In the face of another anti-institutional wave in the 1970s and a growing belief in the importance of permanency in children's lives, many church homes began to specialize in specific task-oriented programs, such as family clarification, behavior change, supplemental (but not substitute) parenting, and crisis care, for which group care is particularly effective. This trend is likely to continue.

Church children's homes in the South have been, on the whole, far less dependent than those in the North on payments for care from public sources. In Texas, for example, 70 percent of placements are made directly by families. Despite sharply rising costs—treatment in a residential center runs into tens of thousands of dollars per child per year—some denominations hold firmly to the principle of the separation of church and state.

In the 1950s and 1960s many denominations became interested in homes for the aging and many of these were established. Although in general, unlike the children's homes, these tended to serve principally church members and often depended largely on payments by residents, most have opened their doors to recipients of Supplemental Social Insurance and Medicare. The better homes offer guaranteed care until death, with the possible exception of hospitalization.

Another recent development has been the establishment of family life centers, offering marital counseling and parental education. Some of these are outgrowths of children's homes, signifying their interest in the whole family.

Social services have, on the whole, taken third place in the interest of denominations, behind colleges and hospitals with which they compete for funds, but may become a major concern if the movement to return social services to the private sector continues. This will be a tremendous challenge. Not only will there have to be a major increase in giving but

an enlargement of the concept of justice (rather than charity) away from its debased modern sense, or perhaps a return to its original sense of thinking well of others, if human needs are to be met.

See also articles on ECUMENISM; SOCIAL GOSPEL.

Bibliography. Robert R. Gillogy, ed., *Sacred Shelters*; Alan Keith-Lucas, *The Church Children's Home in a Changing World*; *The Church and Social Welfare*; Diane Mercer, "The Social Mission of the Church," *Social Work and Christianity* 7 (February 1980): 7-15; F. Ellen Netting, "Social Work and Religious Values in Church-related Social Agencies," *Social Work and Christianity* 9 (Spring-Fall 1982): 4-20; William J. Reid, "Sectarian Agencies," *Encyclopedia of Social Work* 17th issue, 1977: 1244-54.

ALAN KEITH-LUCAS
UNIVERSITY OF NORTH CAROLINA
AT CHAPEL HILL

SOCIETY FOR THE PROPAGATION OF THE GOSPEL IN FOREIGN PARTS. Chartered in 1701, the Society for the Propagation of the Gospel in Foreign Parts (S.P.G.) was a private corporation consisting of clergy and laity in England and the colonies. THOMAS BRAY, already a member of the Society for the Promotion of Christian Knowledge (S.P.C.K.), led the movement to organize the S.P.G. after a brief sojourn in Maryland convinced him of the religious and social disarray in the colonies. The S.P.G. represented the Anglican equivalent to general Protestant reform societies that characterized England at the turn of the 18th century, which tended to be too broadly based for Anglican clerics. Its membership included the archbishop of Canterbury and the bishop of London, who was also one of the Lords Commissioner of Trade and Plantations. Although its instructions to its missionaries took a determinedly apolitical position, its leadership was well placed to play an influential role in the administration of the empire.

In practice, the society supported its missionaries through stipends and allotments of books and materials. Its missionaries simultaneously occupied state-supported parishes in the Southern colonies, and the financial support of the S.P.G. might have attenuated some of the influence the vestries exercised over the incumbents. Regular complaints of poverty and arrogant parishioners from the missionaries to the secretary of the society suggest, however, that the stipends were insufficient to counter the effect of the powerful laity.

The society envisioned its missionaries as educators of the population and sent schoolmasters as well as ministers. In many cases, the minister was both teacher and priest for his parish. The educational policy of the S.P.G. in both pulpit and classroom consisted of instilling in the laity the precepts of appropriate obedience to secular and religious authority. Its clientele encompassed not only the professed Anglicans but also the refugee Protestants, Dissenters of all sorts, Indians, and slaves. Consequently, the society made French translations of the Book of Common Prayer available to the nonconforming French congregation in Charleston as well as German and Dutch editions for other non-English groups. Narrowly confining its support only to its own missionaries, however, meant that the S.P.G. did not offer stipends to the incumbents of the French-speaking Anglican parishes in South Carolina who were not missionaries sent out by the society, and in this way the society rendered those rectors more vulnerable to the dictates of influential vestries.

A broad interpretation of its clientele brought the S.P.G. missionaries into frequent contact with Indians and slaves early in the 18th century. Although both nonwhite groups were found in all of the colonies, the size of the Indian population in the Southern colonies and the extent of slavery created a special set of circumstances for missionaries in this region. Francis LeJau of the parish of St. James, Goose Creek SC, proved a keen observer of Indian practices during the period in which the native cultures were decimated along the coast. Like other missionaries,

he was sympathetic to the Indians' plight and explored facets of their religion that seemed compatible with primitive Christianity. These customs included circumcision, a legend of a great flood, and the concept of a single Great Spirit. Other missionaries in Carolina encouraged Indians to place their children in Christian households for education in white civilization, and when this policy failed, at least one missionary bought Indian slaves whom he then included as members of his household. Commissary Gideon Johnston sent the son of a Yamassee chief to England to be educated by the society, although the chief himself was expelled from the colony after the Yamassee War of 1716-1717.

Early eighteenth-century missionaries met substantial resistance from the laity in their efforts among the Indians since white traders felt that Christianity interfered with their conduct of the Indian trade, which significantly included traffic in slaves. Even deeper resistance, however, greeted the S.P.G.'s work among the plantation slaves. The society perceived no conflict between the institution of SLAVERY and the content of Christianity and itself became a slaveholder with the acquisition of Codrington Plantation on Barbados in 1710. The S.P.G. believed that its purpose among the slaves was to educate them in the precepts of order and place, so instilling obedience and increasing their productivity that it hoped to instill in the white population just deference among the different social orders. Slaveowners, however, slowly accepted the society's work among the slaves and cooperated only after the oath of baptism for slaves included a phrase explicitly rejecting the notion that baptism changed a Christian slave's earthly condition. In addition, laws were passed between 1664 and 1710 in Virginia, Maryland, North Carolina, and South Carolina that affirmed this position on the baptism of slaves.

In a broader spirit, Commissary ALEXANDER GARDEN founded a school for free blacks in Charleston in 1743 with the support of the society, and the society committed itself to a school for training black teachers in Charleston. The Charleston Negro School declined before the Revolution, however, as a result of the lack of suitably trained black teachers.

On the whole, in well-settled, stable colonies such as South Carolina, where the church enjoyed state support and achieved a measure of influence, the S.P.G. successfully contributed to the maintenance of the establishment. In areas such as North Carolina where the church was less successful, the influence of the society's missionaries was weak.

See also articles on ANGLICAN CHURCH; INDIANS, SOUTHEAST MISSIONS TO.

Bibliography. John Calam, *Parsons and Pedagogues*; David Humphreys, *An Historical Account of the Incorporated Society for the Propagation of the Gospel in Foreign Parts; Letter Books of the Society for the Propagation of the Gospel in Foreign Parts.*

AMY FRIEDLANDER
MARIETTA, GEORGIA

SOCIETY OF FRIENDS: *See* QUAKERS IN THE SOUTH.

SOUTH CAROLINA. Founded as an English proprietary colony in 1670, South Carolina has had a religious history dominated by Protestants (Baptists, Methodists, Presbyterians, Episcopalians, Lutherans) but marked by religious tolerance. Until the present century, leading churches have usually reflected a conservative theology and supported the views and mores of "the establishment" and of society rather than moulding them or guiding them in new directions. In a state with a black majority for so long, race has been a major factor in church history.

Started as a venture for profit, the seven Proprietors offered religious tolerance as a lure for settlers, and very quickly dissenters constituted a majority. Newcomers were supposed to "acknowledge a God," and any seven persons were authorized to form a church and worship as they pleased. The Church of England was depicted as the "National Religion" and the Carolina parliament was authorized to "establish" it and tax the people for its support, a step not taken until 1706. The large Anglican minority was disproportionately influential, including many colonial leaders in a society marked by an identifiable aristocracy.

The first 10 years on the west bank of the Ashley River were difficult and tenuous. Soon after the arrival of the first minister and after the colony had been moved to the peninsula between the Ashley and Cooper rivers (present CHARLESTON), a church (Anglican) was organized and built (ca. 1681) on the site of the present St. Michael's. As historically significant was the "White Meeting House" begun about 1690 by Calvinists of various sorts—from New England, northern Ireland, and Scotland. Sometimes called "the Independent Church," from it ultimately sprang Congregationalists, Presbyterians, and Unitarians. The Baptists—today the most numerous group—began with a migration led from New England by William Screven in 1696 and the building by 1701 of their first meeting house in Charles Town. Not numerous but to become very influential in state history were French HUGUENOTS who came following the revocation of the Edict of Nantes (1685) and who had a church in Charles Town by 1687. Often successful in the business community and shrewd in politics, Huguenots soon tended to join the church of King and Proprietors who had given them refuge and thus they helped undergird the special position of Anglicanism.

Particularly important was the 1702 arrival of the first missionaries of the SOCIETY FOR THE PROPAGATION OF THE GOSPEL IN FOREIGN PARTS (SPG), destined to provide about two-fifths of the always understaffed ministry of the Anglican establishment, to spread the Church beyond the confines of Charles Town, to promote education, and to be the first whites to show much humanitarian concern about Indians and Negroes. Planters (many from Barbados, of which Carolina to a degree was an offshoot) were reluctant to have slaves converted lest such would alter their status (based on a theory that one should not own "baptized property"). A statute of 1712 reassured planters (and their consciences?) on that point, but still for many generations planters and other colonial leaders did little to encourage Christianizing blacks.

As an SPG missionary viewed early Carolinians, "Religion was the thing about which they troubled themselves the least." But some Anglican colonists troubled themselves considerably about their dissenter neighbors after 1700—as much over economic and political rivalry as over their theological views. In 1704 an act that would have severely reduced dissenters' political participation and would have subjected Anglican ministers to a lay commission was disallowed in England, but the Church Act of 1706 was both an ecclesiastical and political landmark: Anglicanism was established as the state church to receive fiscal support from government, and parishes were laid out that had civil as well as church functions and were to be the basis of representation in the Low Country until 1865. Non-Anglicans, however, could continue to vote and to serve in the Assembly.

In the parish system, the vestry—called by one scholar "the real seat of power in the establishment"—reflected American distrust of distant tyranny so that the prestigious merchants and planters of the Carolina aristocracy through the vestry dominated the Anglican Church and its ministers with a "congregationalist attitude." It was a latter-day manifestation of "the spirit of the Puritan Revolution."

With no local episcopal authority to restrain strong-willed Anglican clergy, the Bishop of London appointed "commissaries" to represent his office and to exercise jurisdiction where he could not visit in person. The Rev. Gideon Johnson, the first commissary (1708-1716), soon described his flocks as "the vilest race of men on earth," though ultimately he saw things less darkly once he reconciled himself to an Anglicanism quite different from that in England. A more famed commissary was the Rev. ALEXANDER GARDEN, also rector of ST. PHILIP'S CHURCH (the oldest congregation of Charles Town), who in 1740 became embroiled in an acrimonious controversy with GEORGE WHITEFIELD whose unconventional and emotional preaching in South Carolina seemed much too radical and irregular to Garden. Nevertheless, Whitefield's emphasis on the salvation of the individual soul by effective evangelism was to be a format and doctrine most widely embraced and preached by those denominations which thereafter became dominant in South Carolina religious history. Whitefield's appeal was such that had he stayed in the colony, the church that contained about 45 percent of the churched might well have been disestablished.

The "White Meeting" (so called from the color of the meeting house) containing Scots, Scotch-Irish, English dissenters, and even French Huguenots was the grandmother church for many congregations. The groups tolerated each other harmoniously, but Scots disposed to Presbyterianism left in 1732 to form the "Scots Presbyterian Church" (later called by some the First Presbyterian Church). A group of congregationalist-minded souls moved from Meeting Street to Archdale Street to form the "Second Congregational Church," and then migrated even further philosophically by becoming a strong Unitarian Church in the 19th century. In the original church, Congregationalists and Presbyterians stayed together for years (of the first six ministers, four were Congregationalists and two were Presbyterians, including the famed William Tennent). Ultimately the church was the leading Congregationalist group in the state.

The tolerance of the Carolina colony was most evident in its acceptance of Jews who established the second American congregation (Beth Elohim) in Charles Town in 1750. Not only was this group accepted, but also became proportionately one of the largest communities of Jews in America by 1800, making up about five percent of the Charleston white population. One scholar has stressed their early right to vote in the colony and states that the first Jew in America, if not in the modern world, to be elected to public office was Francis Salvador, chosen for the Provincial Congress of 1775.

In the 1730s the colonial government sought to populate the inland area by promoting establishment of townships (across the "midlands" of the present state). Although the scheme as envisioned had mixed results, it began a population movement of immigrants from abroad and the North who drastically altered the religious complexion of the colony. Certainly the Anglican population shrank proportionately as Welsh Baptists poured down from Delaware to the banks of the Pee Dee, Scotch-Irish Presbyterians to Black River, and Germans and Swiss (both Lutheran and Reform groups) to various areas.

All suffered by not having a supply of pastors to accompany them, perhaps the Germans most of all. Factionalism further plagued the Germans, some—like Huguenots—becoming Anglicans as they followed a remarkable preacher, John Ulrich Giessendanner II. Earliest of these (1732) were the German Swiss on the lower Savannah at Purrysburgh, which evaporated after a few trying years. Largest German influx was to the Saxe-Gotha area (modern Lexington County) with a spillover into the "Dutch Fork" between the Broad and Saluda rivers, all of which is still plainly evident in local names and Lutheran concentration. By the 1750s Germans were settling in Charles Town and there organized the mother Lutheran church of the state, St. John's, in 1755, to be finally stabilized in the 1770s during the pastorate of Henry Melchior Muhlenburg.

The Baptists who came south to the Welsh Neck on the Pee Dee, later moving across the river to Society Hill, built their first meetinghouse in 1744. Like Puritans, they undertook (as Baptists were to do for a century) to police and punish the morals of their own community. Establishing contacts with English Baptists in Oliver Hart's Charles Town church, they formed the first Baptist "association" in the South. The Charleston Association, to be the model for others and also for the conventions yet to come, stabilized scattered Baptist churches, provided criteria and guidance, and yet was no threat to the independence in congregationalism. At the time when South Carolina had not yet produced a Baptist minister from its own ranks, Hart won into the fold RICHARD FURMAN, his disciple and successor who in many respects was the dominant founding father of Southern Baptistism.

After 1750 came the big wave of newcomers to the Back Country. One group, originally moving out of New England, were the SEPARATE BAPTISTS, so called because they had separated from Congregationalists as the "New Lights" after coming under the influence of Jonathan Edwards and the GREAT AWAKENING. Pouring into the piedmont with the Rev. Philip Mulkey in the vanguard, they appeared to Hart and the Charles Town Baptists as an intense, rigid group—often also rude and unlettered. Gradually the Low Country faction became reconciled to the Separates and their zealous religion.

Among the major "firsts" of South Carolina Baptists was the formation of the first all Negro congregation in America at SILVER BLUFF (near Augusta) between 1773 and 1775.

After 1750 the largest tide broke upon the piedmont Back Country from Virginia and Pennsylvania. Some were Separate Baptists with a mild Calvinistic flavor, but many were inclined to Presbyterianism. Rude subsistence farmers, unsophisticated and often high-strung, this scattered population above the fall line jumped from 22,000 to 83,000 during 1765-1775—to four-fifths of the colony's white population. In 1768 there were 38 Presbyterian settlements in the colony. Like early Lutherans, few Presbyterian groups had ministers and depended on synods of the North for occasional missionaries; there were only three settled Presbyterian pastors in the vast hinterlands when Revolution came. This problem that long plagued Presbyterians stemmed partially from their insistence on an educated ministry—a limited supply amid a growing population, a factor that worked to the benefit of Separate Baptists. Emphasis on liturgy or anything smacking of "Romanism" thwarted the bold SPG missionaries, especially the famed and vitriolic Charles Woodmason, who detested the "Pack of vile levelling common wealth Presbyterians" whose "roving Teachers ... stir up the Minds of the People ..." But then he was no more complimentary of his prospective converts, "a Sett of Vile unaccountable Wretches." At least Anglicans had nearly all of their 22 parishes staffed in 1776.

Unlike some colonies, Anglicanism in South Carolina was not a major force for Loyalism in the Revolution; only 5 of 23 Anglican ministers stuck with Great Britain, and many of the major leaders of the cause came from St. Philip's Church. Until 1780 the Back Country was largely Loyalist or neutralist, resisting a barnstorming 1775 tour by William Tennent and Oliver Hart, leading Presbyterian and Baptist divines of Charles Town, who sought recruits for the Revolutionary cause. After British conquest of the coast in 1780 and oppressive measures of some military leaders, the state became more committed to secession. Dissenters won a victory in 1778 with disestablishment of Anglicanism, equal rights being extended then to all Protestants and in 1790 to Catholics and Jews.

Among latecomers, Methodists had the biggest impact. Although John Wesley himself had visited South Caro-

lina (his "Charleston Hymn Book" was printed there in 1737) and Whitefield in 1740, probably the first later Methodist was Joseph Pilmoor in 1773 although no preacher was stationed in South Carolina until a visit by FRANCIS ASBURY in 1785, after which Charles Town Baptists let Methodists use their meetinghouse.

In 1787 South Carolina Methodism formally began with the first annual conference presided over by Bishops Francis Asbury and Thomas Coke at the "Blue Meeting House" (to distinguish it from Congregationalists' "White Meeting") on Cumberland Street. The first conference assigned three presiding elders over seven circuits containing 2,071 white and 141 Negro Methodists. In the state, the church enjoyed meteoric growth (484 churches by 1850) explained by organization and theology. The former was built around an itinerancy based on circuit riders assisted by local preachers, certainty of services at designated places and times, Methodist "classes" under zealous lay leaders, and a firm discipline under an authoritarian system. The theology stressed the gospel of free will and free grace available to all, a view appealing to listeners who sought to be masters of their own destiny. Rather than hoping to establish a church once there was a sufficiently large congregation to call a pastor if one was available, frontier folk might find the Methodist circuit rider there before the population or the congregation, his task being to greet the newcomers and to make Methodists out of them.

As Methodism flourished after 1785, Presbyterians entered a relative decline—still handicapped by a paucity of ministers. They further dissipated their strength by heresies and theological controversies, "the Scotch mind," as D. D. Wallace put it, "seeming to take a mournful pleasure in making itself miserable in that way." One such division produced the ASSOCIATE REFORMED PRESBYTERIAN CHURCH (ARP) who organized a separate presbytery in 1790 and in 1803 their own synod with 2,000 members, a conservative psalm-singing band of "seceders" who have remained strong in the state but not numerous.

The post-Revolution years for South Carolina Baptists centered around the Rev. Richard Furman who took the Charleston pulpit in 1787 and did much to shape Southern Baptist life in general. His church had been the first Baptist church in the South; the Charleston Association was the first in the South (preceded only by Philadelphia); the first Baptist state convention was established in the state in 1821, with Furman as president; and the TRIENNIAL CONVENTION of all Baptists was formed in Philadelphia in 1814, with Furman as first president. Despite the charge that Baptists had little concern for an educated ministry, its leadership in the state—Oliver Hart, Richard Furman, and John M. Roberts—stressed and encouraged it. Furman had organized the first children's society in the state, the first Baptist college in the South (at Greenville) was to be named after him, and the first general Baptist seminary in the South was to begin there. Long before such institutions, the Charleston Association in 1755 had established a fund and society to assist the education of needy young men seeking ministerial training.

Just as the Baptists' maturing rotated around Richard Furman, so did the Lutherans emerge to order and stability with a notable leader, JOHN BACHMAN. After decades of too few churches and no strong cohesive organization, the formation of the South Carolina Synod in 1824 with Bachman as its president portended a new day. Coming to St. John's, Charleston, in 1815, he began a ministry that was to last over 50 years; practically defunct in 1815, St. John's was soon one of the most dynamic congregations in the state. Bachman was also a major force in establishment of the seminary that began in 1830.

Just as Bachman was famed as a naturalist, the key personality in Unitarianism was a leading literary figure in Charleston, SAMUEL GILMAN, who presided (1819-

1858) over what was an influential church.

Catholic history in the state virtually began in 1821 with the arrival of Bishop JOHN ENGLAND to head the new Diocese of Charleston. During his time the best-known Catholic leader in the nation, this native of Ireland was a controversial figure of great intellect and ability. Although a few tactful Catholics may have settled in the state in earlier days, there was no priest until 1788. When the bishop arrived, there were only a few small churches with a few communicants (estimates vary from 1,000 to 5,000). Although the diocese included North Carolina and Georgia, Bishop England concentrated his attention upon the Charleston area where he soon got an academy started, a new convent established, and an orphanage launched. In 1822 he founded the *U. S. Catholic Miscellany*, the first Catholic paper of strictly religious nature in the country. By 1842 there were 7,000 Catholics (mostly Irish in background) in the large diocese scattered among 65 churches that had 21 priests; in 1850 there were 14 South Carolina churches, the strongest area (then as now) being Charleston. Although the colonial doctrine of religious liberty had specifically excluded "papists," the Constitution of 1790 granted them the right to vote.

Church practices and appearances varied greatly. Some stately Anglican churches could almost match the classical 18th-century London structures on which they were modeled. In the hands of Robert Mills, the Independent Church (Charleston) came to be known as the Circular Church, when "rectangular box" would have been an appropriate label for scores of meetinghouses. Music varied from Bach to bedlam. "Singing Billy" Walker's *Southern Harmony*, published in Spartanburg in 1835, not only set publishing records but also shaped the singing habits and tastes of thousands.

Sermons—especially among non-Episcopalians—were long and often loud, with favorite topics repentance, damnation, salvation, and the millennium. Individual humility was supposed to precede salvation of the individual who then expected an experience of grace to be followed by regeneration. The larger and growing denominations maintained strict watch over the conduct of members by frequent discipline and even expulsion—perhaps socially useful where law and government had not kept up with settlement. The object of greatest concern seemed to be drinking, followed by neglect of church. In the region where increasingly religion was more concerned with individual salvation than with improvement of society, at least churches were involved with individual conduct that was detrimental to social order. Fighting, mistreatment of spouses and children, breach of contract—all were fit subjects for churches to punish but also to mediate or arbitrate. Unfortunately, amusements of every variety were viewed as Satan's playground, Methodists even frowning on "idle visits" on the Sabbath. A Welsh Neck church enjoined good Baptists to keep children from "wicked company and vain pleasures, such as playing at cards" because "lovers of pleasure are not lovers of God." In church discipline cases, women were usually expected to remain silent.

Economic distinctions were clearer in 1800-1860: South Carolina Episcopalians were more affluent and perhaps best educated; Presbyterians increasingly spread across a broad spectrum (more affluent along the coast); and Baptists and Methodists were the poorest economically. (Methodists complained that if they converted wealthy sinners in the summer by winter they were Episcopalians or Presbyterians.) Preachers in these two had to accept an austere existence (though many Baptist pastors held other jobs). In 1800, Methodist salaries were $80 a year; South Carolina Lutheran pastors were said to be the most poorly paid of that group in the nation in 1849—only two making as much as $250 a year. Average salary for Presbyterian clergy in 1850 was $300. Never at home, Methodist circuit riders almost had to be bachelors and to put much of their meager income into one valuable and necessary possession: a horse.

The rapid growth of Baptists, Methodists, and Presbyterians came from constant evangelism and frequent REVIVALISM that all sponsored and in which they sometimes cooperated. Highlight of the church year was the PROTRACTED MEETING (dubbed by the irreverent "distracted meeting") unless they had a camp meeting in the area—the fruition of the GREAT REVIVAL (Second Great Awakening). Emotional extravaganzas, exercises in mass hypnosis, social event of the season, or "the most sublime . . . scenes on this side of eternity": camp meetings were thus variously depicted by South Carolinians who soared off into rhapsody or unconsciousness while "jerking," "wheeling," or "barking" in the holy "exercises" or "under impression." Gradually decorum drew many dour Presbyterians apart and left the excessive joys to shouting Methodists who had dozens of such "camp grounds" and "tabernacles." (One observer lists 42 "prominent" ones.) As one South Carolina Methodist reported to Asbury, "Hell is trembling, and Satan's kingdom falling."

In a state with poor education (no "public schools" in the modern sense), all churches bestirred themselves. Beginning in 1711, Anglicans and successor Episcopalians long had Sunday schools for underprivileged and Negro children, and the Independent Church had two sessions on the Sabbath. Much time went to catechisms and Bible memorizing, but some basic literate skills were also lightly touched. By 1828 Cumberland Street Methodist Church had 400 Negroes in Sunday school (pastor was James O. Andrew, over whom the Methodist Church split in 1844 when he was bishop), and by 1846 there were 265 Methodist Sunday schools in the state. All denominations were thus engaged, the first Baptist convention (1821) having made them a major emphasis.

Comparable to "middle schools" or secondary schools were church academies and "seminaries," both in towns and rural regions, supplemented by many run privately by preachers (especially Presbyterians). A few academies were notable, although most were not. Some examples: Mt. Bethel (Methodist, 1794); Tabernacle (c. 1820), predecessor to Cokesbury Conference School (Methodist, 1834-1918); Willington, most famous one run by the Rev. MOSES WADDEL, Presbyterian; Lexington Institute (Lutheran); and Reidville Male and Female High Schools (1857), run by a Presbyterian minister.

South Carolina has been birthplace and graveyard for a number of colleges, many church-related. Several reasons explain denominational efforts in antebellum days: the need for an educated ministry; a proper function for the church to render to society; education safe from heretical influences of THOMAS COOPER at South Carolina College; tuition cheaper than state colleges (strange sounding today); means for evangelism and good public relations. Although parents were assured that sons could go to Cokesbury, for example, "without risk to their morals," the danger was perhaps no greater one place than another. Curricula were similar in all types. (S. C. College faculty had its share of Presbyterian and Episcopal ministers.) Unfortunately, most of the denominational colleges prior to 1860 had poor standards, facilities, and libraries. Erskine (ARP) began at Due West in 1839, Furman (Baptist) at Greenville in 1851 (having gone through several metamorphoses beginning at Edgefield in 1827), Wofford (Methodist) at Spartanburg in 1854, and Newberry (Lutheran) at Newberry in 1856. In 1854 Baptists and Methodists began female colleges in Greenville and Columbia, respectively, and ARPs began one in Due West in 1859. (Omitted are academies and seminaries that called themselves colleges.)

In the history of theological training in the South, South Carolina has played a small but significant role. Despite Methodist emphasis on education, prior to 1860 they founded no seminary and some leaders staunchly opposed such. In 1827 the first property that the new state Baptist convention acquired was for the training of preachers: the Furman Academy and Theological Institution, which was to have a checkered and migrant career until the 1850s. Once the SOUTHERN BAPTIST CONVENTION was formed in 1845, the new Furman University served its needs until the formation of the Southern Baptist Seminary in Greenville in 1859—transplanted to Louisville in 1877. The ARP denomination in 1837 planted its seminary in Due West where it has remained. Another still flourishing was the first Lutheran seminary in the South, begun in 1830 peregrinating even more than Furman as it wandered through the wilderness to various places from its start until establishment in Columbia in 1911. Plagued by having to go elsewhere for training, Presbyterians opened their seminary in Columbia in 1830 because there "was concentrated the most wealth, literary advantages, and moral force"—and because it might be a bulwark against "infidel principles" emanating from Thomas Cooper's neighboring institution. Housed in a Robert Mills-designed residence (today a restored showplace), it had a notable faculty before 1860 (including JAMES H. THORNWELL, BENJAMIN M. PALMER, JOHN B. ADGER, CHARLES COLCOCK JONES, and John L. Girardeau) who stressed the Bible's total infallibility, written by God and being a book of science, history, and astronomy as well as theology and ethics.

After 1830, with the exception of the few Quakers, reactions of South Carolina churches to slavery varied little. Most clergy accepted the system of slavery and raised no serious or discomforting questions about its propriety. In earlier days there were sharp Methodist exceptions: Wesley and Asbury minced no words in condemning the institution, and early Methodism in the state suffered ostracism and resentment because of its "integrated" status (4,529 black members by 1791) and concern for "lower classes" and "the spiritual welfare of the colored people." To many, Methodism was a misfit in South Carolina Low Country society, especially after the 1790 General Conference had held that slaveholding was contrary to the laws of God and man.

Gradually South Carolina Methodists softened such views and thereafter had less difficulty winning converts. By the 1830s because of cotton prosperity, phobias caused by abolitionists' attacks, and fear of slave revolts, all South Carolina hierarchies provided religious rationale to defend the institution that the laity wanted preserved. Planters no longer worried about the propriety of owning a Christian. Partially to salve their own consciences and partially to refute strident Northern voices charging them with sinful ways and unconcern for Negroes' souls, all denominations began doing mission work to bring black converts into a special second-class status within their congregations and to provide Sunday schools for black children. This South Carolina holier-than-thou counterattack was probably sincere and it certainly was impressively energetic.

Slaveholders encouraged mission work, sometimes claiming that devout slaves were more docile and hence better as workers. The synod directed South Carolina Lutherans to provide facilities so that Negroes would be "prepared and fitted for full acceptance . . ., according to their situation in society." (Bachman's Negro Sunday school had 32 teachers and 150 pupils.) Some churches put their black members in balconies or held separate services for them. Some sent missionaries to plantations, a project most ambitious after 1829 with Methodists who by 1855 had 32 preachers thus assigned and were raising $25,000 for this mission work.

One concern beset whites: their fear of free blacks' association with slaves in churches stirring discontent or worse. Especially did this fear arise after

the DENMARK VESEY Rebellion (1822). Despite this, in 1849 Second Presbyterian Church, Charleston, erected a second building for their Negro members, a step so popular that a separate church soon had to be built, the largest church structure in Charleston for this black flock and their popular white preacher. (They did have a gallery for whites.) Bethel Methodist, Charleston, turned its old building over to its black members; in 1880 the building was moved again by its Negro congregation that today therefore has the oldest Methodist church building (1797) in the state—"Old Bethel." Thus blacks were a part—a separate-but-not-equal part—of white churches. Richard Fuller, distinguished Baptist preacher of Beaufort, had 2,000 Negro members; in 1860 there were 3,166 white Episcopalians and 2,960 black Episcopalians; white Baptists attracted 21,911 blacks into their church by 1858; the "white" Methodist church of 1860 had more blacks than whites— 42,469 to 34,357.

Whites saw their church efforts as "moral and spiritual progress without any threat, open or implied, to . . . the established order." But Negro churches run by Negroes they viewed askance. In 1817, MORRIS BROWN, a free Negro affiliated with the African Methodist Episcopal Church, started the Emmanuel Church in Charleston, the mother church of that denomination in the South. Quickly it attracted 1,000 members, but white pressures and intimidation (arrests for "disorderly conduct") threatened it, and after the Vesey affair it was closed down by public authorities. (Brown went north and became the second AME bishop.)

After division in the national church bodies, South Carolina ministers became strident defenders of the peculiar institution as a "positive good" that was blessed by God. Most notable were two Presbyterians: James H. Thornwell and Benjamin M. Palmer. Earlier Richard Furman had defended it as not "contrary to the genius of Christianity," and WILLIAM CAPERS, leader of the Methodists' mission work, found it quite harmonious with the Gospel. Most did stress the responsibility of masters to be humane. The rigid South Carolina proslavery position spread by emigration: in 1860, 291,300 whites lived in South Carolina while 470,257 who had been born in the state then lived elsewhere.

Even as disruption of the Union approached, churchmen did not flinch in the regional paranoia. Convinced that it was the unfolding of the work of Divine Providence that would protect the South and its institutions if war came, Thornwell said, "We are prepared to meet it with unshaken confidence in the God of battles." The state Baptist Convention in 1861 asserted that God approved of the South's action and "the wickedness of the wicked will return on their own heads." Perhaps ironically, the Secession Convention held its first session in Columbia's Baptist Church.

Most churches suffered deeply during the Civil War years. Catholics lost their cathedral, two orphanages, two convents; Episcopalians had 10 churches burned and 23 parishes suspended; Baptist ministers declined from 540 to 302; church schools were defunct or virtually so. The 53 Presbyterian congregations had only 28 ministers.

At war's end, churches panicked at the invasion of Northern missionaries who had first come to the sea islands in 1862 and came in larger numbers in 1865. Northern churches sought conversions and new members with mixed success, but they did found and support Negro schools and colleges, including Benedict (Baptist) in Columbia (1871), Claflin (Methodist) in Orangeburg (1869), and Allen (AME) in Columbia (1870).

Proud of their prewar evangelization of Negroes, white churches expected to keep their Negro converts (72,349 in 1860, compared to 70,729 white members)—but still in a secondary status. Whites were disappointed and surprised when blacks departed en masse for new churches of their own: Southern Methodist black enrollment plummeted from 42,469 to 653 between 1860 and 1873. Some went to the South Carolina Missionary Conference set up by the Northern Methodists (43,000 by 1890), a group to enter the "Central Jurisdiction" in 1939 and to merge with the South Carolina Conference in 1972. The Baptist convention invited "their" Negroes to stay but on the old basis of inequality; instead they made a mass exodus and in "congregational bliss" started scores of their own churches with no organization or convention for several years. Presbyterians alienated most of their 1860 black constituency by implying that Negroes were not competent to run their own affairs; many of these became Methodists or Baptists, but in 1906 some 8,000 belonged to the Northern Presbyterian Church. The liturgical Episcopalians watched 2,698 of their 2,960 black members defect, but retained St. Mark's, Charleston, as their "mother church" there, though with a white pastor, a situation that caused lengthy controversy in the diocese.

Ultimately white churches accepted realistically that blacks' new allegiance would be to their own churches under their own leaders—the major institution that they henceforth could control. Some new congregations were blocs of blacks who seceded together from white churches and started their own—easiest to do in the Baptist system. The South Carolina Southern Baptists contained 29,211 Negroes in 1858, but only 1,614 in 1874; by 1886, the new black convention (Baptist Educational Missionary and Sunday-School Convention) had 100,286 members. The new Colored Methodist Episcopal Church (CME), sponsored somewhat as a client by white Southern Methodists, failed to hold the allegiance of blacks, getting only 3,468 members in the state by 1890—perhaps suspect because of its origins.

Particularly effective was the revival of the AME Church in Charleston that

Morris Brown had started prior to the Vesey Rebellion. Led by the Rev. Richard H. Cain, charismatic AME Northern preacher, a South Carolina conference was organized in 1865 at a meeting held in Zion Presbyterian Church. As pastor of the restored Emmanuel Church, Cain soon had the largest congregation (about 3,000) of the AME Church in the South. Indication of the lack of bitterness was that Trinity Methodist (white) let Emmanuel meet in their church until the new AME building was completed. Like many Negro preachers—by definition leaders in the race's one large institution, Cain played many roles: member of Constitutional Convention, state senator, and member of Congress. After leaving South Carolina, he was elected an AME bishop.

That oldest black denomination (AME) expanded rapidly: By 1866 it had 22,388 members and 13 ministers; in 1878 it divided the state into two conferences; and by 1898 it had more members in South Carolina than in any other state. (AME membership statistics disconcert: If a communicant does not pay during the year, he is not counted.) The AME, Zion blacks formed a South Carolina conference also in 1867 and within 20 years it had about 100 churches, mostly along the North Carolina border.

The generation following Reconstruction was the most formative one for "main line" South Carolina churches. Attitudes and habits that were to shape several generations were then fixed—as were political, social, and economic attitudes and outlooks of South Carolinians. To many later, this "Bourbon Era" was made to appear the "good old days."

The era of 1875-1914 was also a paradoxical period: Church bodies seemed bustling and statistics growing, church administration becoming more efficient and effective, new programs and institutions starting, and revivals claiming great conquests. On the other hand, despite such obvious changes, the church was itself not changing greatly in response to the changes and problems of the society

that enveloped it. As the major all-Southern institutions remaining after the Confederacy, churches embraced the Bourbon and LOST CAUSE concept that Utopia lay somewhere in a South now gone, that the "Southern way of life" (whatever that was) was superior and that as much of it as possible should be preserved. (Historians often suggest that "the South" did not die at Appomattox, but was born there.) Hence ecclesiastical organizations that appeared to be bustling and changing were often quite dedicated to maintenance of much of the status quo, to a conservative religious orthodoxy suspicious of innovation or of anyone slightly skeptical. The Southern clergy have been called "the most radical of sectionalists," and the church had become a prisoner of the South that it had done so much to create and now to perpetuate. Religiosity was fused with regionalism. In such cultural isolationism, fear of change and alliance with "the establishment" meant that the church was not disposed to examine that society with critical eye nor to commit the heresy of advocating changes in it. Much that was good was guarded and protected in that stance; much that was bad was tolerated and pickled by that stance. Such was not altogether new: South Carolina churches had long "gone along"—most notably by providing theological defense of slavery when that pleased the lay flock. For decades they had preached against individual sin and promoted individual salvation rather than identifying factors in the environment that shaped or oppressed individuals or suggesting ways of applying Christian principles to social problems. To a large extent, the church continued on that same path in the New South.

During 1875-1914, the "social gospel" came to the North, concerned particularly with problems connected with large-scale industrialization, urbanization, and immigration. South Carolina did not have quite the same problems. But it too had problems: abject poverty in agriculture and share-cropping, drab life in the new cot-

ton-mill villages, inhumane evils in the
convict-lease system, the demeaning status of the Negro, and the perennial problem of racial tension. On all these, the
church spoke—occasionally, discreetly,
and in muted tones. In general, the South
Carolina church had its old emphasis—
"the old time religion" with stress on such
sins as card playing and dancing.

Even so, churches did not altogether
"pass by on the other side of the road" and
they engaged in activities that later could
be and were expanded in ways to make for
a healthier society and a healthier church.

South Carolina churches had been
mission-minded before the war, and
although now they virtually ceased their
mission work to Negroes (though the
South Carolina AME Church sent a missionary to Liberia), "missionary societies"
sprang up like onions. After a dormant
period, the state's Methodist Conference
in 1881 made this a major thrust and
ultimately a large number of South Carolinians went abroad to many countries,
Brazil and China leading the list. Baptists
did the same, but South Carolina Presbyterians lagged behind their fellow Presbyterians elsewhere. Lutherans did home
mission work with new German groups
arriving in the state, thereby adding new
congregations (seven of which were
German-speaking).

Two important spin-offs resulted.
The first was the establishment of all
kinds of "societies" by which enthusiasm
could be generated for a "cause" and
machinery provided to further it—
missions at first, but then temperance,
youth work, and other concerns of the
church. Second, the missionary societies
began the emancipation of women, providing acceptable and available opportunities for involvement outside the
household, for self-awareness and self-
assertion. The response of South Carolina
women in 1868 was described by one as
"truly magnificent." In 1878, South Carolina Methodist women in the state had 83
missionary societies—even before the

General Conference gave official sanction
to such. Baptist women had done missionary work in the Sea Islands as early as
1811, but in 1881 they organized their
first missionary society and soon were
supporting a Shanghai hospital.

Sunday schools were not new, but
statewide organization of them was, as
was affiliation with the American Sunday
School Union that standardized procedures, provided a uniform lesson plan,
and made literature available. Congregations sometimes coordinated efforts in
"union schools" or with teachers' meetings on Saturday night where there was
ecumenical study together of the same
lesson. The flourishing of this wing of the
church brought more lay people than
ever—including women—into "church
work." South Carolina Lutherans had
more Sunday schools than they did
churches, discovering that as a good way
to incubate new congregations. In 1894
the Baptist Convention put pressure on
its churches for the schools, admitting
that many earlier efforts had involved
"aimless unconcern" and "vague glitter-
ing generalities." The Methodist Conference of 1900 reported 705 Sunday schools.

Akin to "societies" was the upsurge of
organizations for youth—maybe because
of denominational misgivings about such
non-church movements as the YMCA and
Christian Endeavor. The Luther League
started at Newberry in 1895; the Baptist
Convention pushed the BYPU beginning
in 1894; and the Methodists started the
Epworth League in the state in 1891 and
had 47 operating by the end of the decade.
Episcopalians had many youth involved
and organized in the 1920s.

"Spreading the gospel" and keeping
the constituency informed involved many
publications, organized in various ways.
The *Sunday Visitor* of South Carolina
Episcopalians claimed to be the first such
magazine in the United States (1818), followed by the more ambitious *Gospel Messenger*. John England's *U. S. Catholic
Miscellany* initiated such publication

among American Catholics. The second Methodist periodical in America was the *Wesleyan Journal* begun in 1825 with William Capers as editor, though it soon merged with the *Christian Advocate* of New York. With the growth of Southern self-consciousness, the *Southern Christian Advocate* began in Charleston in 1837 with Capers as editor—an organ that once served several conferences but ultimately came to be the state's paper. Baptists began their highly successful *Baptist Courier* in 1877—like some of its predecessors, a private venture rather than an official organ but one endorsed by the Convention, that did buy it in 1920 and make it the voice of the denomination. Since 1879 it has been published at Greenville, "the Baptist capital." In 1847 James H. Thornwell founded the *Southern Presbyterian Review*, and in 1831 the *Lutheran Observer* began, but the first journal just for the South Carolina Synod was the *Lutheran Messenger* (1922), renamed later (1938) the *S. C. Lutheran*.

Expansion of church institutions characterized the 1875-1914 period and began with the Presbyterians' opening Thornwell Orphanage at Clinton in 1875 with eight children. Chief founder was William P. Jacobs, Clinton pastor, who named it for his friend and teacher. The *Baptist Courier* then reminded its readers that they had ignored that field, a gap filled in 1892 when the first child entered their Connie Maxwell Orphanage in Greenwood. In 1894 Methodists did go and do likewise—setting aside talk of a hospital—and opened Epworth Orphanage in Columbia in 1895. (All are today called children's homes.) After 1909, Episcopalians concentrated their efforts of this nature in a Children's Home in York. South Carolina Lutherans support one in Salem VA.

Only Baptists and Catholics have entered the hospital field: the former now have a large one in Columbia, opened in 1914, and another in Easley (1958). Roman Catholics maintain hospitals in Charleston, Columbia, Greenville, York, and Dillon.

The antebellum church maintenance of schools and academies continued into the 20th century. As public education came following Reconstruction, many still had reservations about it. The *Baptist Courier* in 1882 opposed compulsory education, perhaps in an adverse mood because of the fear and friction then raging between state and denominational colleges. Ministers—both with and without parishes—were still also school teachers, and in the day before public high schools, there were numerous church-related forerunners of such. These varied widely, as did the nature and extent of church control and governance. Samples of some of the long-forgotten citadels of learning that dotted the landscape are Harmony "College" at Bradford Springs and Parochial School of Arsenal Hill Church (both Presbyterian); Six-Mile Academy and Ridgedale Academy (Baptist); Leesville English and Classical Institute, and Summerland College (Lutheran). Church colleges owned or cooperated with "fitting" or preparatory schools to train budding scholars for freshman level. For example, Furman had Spartan Academy (at Landrum) and its own fitting school, and Wofford had Carlisle School (Bamberg), ties with Cokesbury, and its own fitting school in Spartanburg.

The denominational colleges founded before 1860 (see above) survived the war, and in 1880 were joined by Presbyterian College in Clinton, another Jacobs venture. Two common denominators existed: poverty and the goal of providing some ministers. Joining the three women's colleges started before the war were some new but not strong ones that had varying degrees of closeness with their churches: Coker College at Hartsville (1908), Anderson at Anderson (1912), Limestone at Gaffney. (Coker and Limestone are now independent.) The Presbyterian venture at Clinton was a success, unlike their College for Women at Columbia (1893), that was combined with their Chicora (1906) of Greenville in 1916, and then later the combination moved to Charlotte with Queens College. The Wesleyan Church began Central Wesleyan in 1906. The Negro colleges of Reconstruction did survive but not thrive. Other four-year black colleges were also started: Morris (1908) of the Baptist Educational and Missionary Convention and Voorhees (1897), taken over by the Protestant Episcopal Church in the 1920s. Latest college additions have been Baptist College at Charleston (1960) and one that labels itself properly the "world's most unusual university," the large and fundamentalist Bob Jones University, that moved to Greenville in 1947. Also unusual were two that had characteristics of the "manual labor schools" of the 19th century: Ferguson-Williams Industrial College, one under Presbyterian auspices (1903-1920) that provided industrial training for Negroes at Abbeville till 1920; and the Textile Industrial Institute (1911) at Spartanburg (now Spartanburg Methodist College), that maintained two student bodies rotating with each other, one in class for a period while the other worked in mills earning school costs.

The seminaries (already noted) were marked by stability at Erskine, great strengthening by the Lutherans once they settled in Columbia (1911), and near-suicide by Presbyterians (also in Columbia) in their controversy over Professor James Woodrow and evolution in the 1880s (a spectacle precipitated by weakness and small enrollment that finally led to reestablishment in Decatur GA in 1927).

The noisiest theological controversy was the one that roared about evolution, itself tied to the bigger issue of inerrancy of scripture read literally. The Fundamentalists alarmed by Darwin were also usually the same group favoring rigid rules about social conduct. Though widespread, the issue was highlighted by the JAMES WOODROW case at Columbia Seminary

and the efforts to unseat this professor who had been brought there in 1859 to a new professorship designed to deal with the relations between religion and science. After two decades when this moderate compromiser said the conflicts between the two were "apparent" but "not real," he alarmed the conservatives who were also upset by his statement that the relationship of science and religion was more "one of noncontradiction" than one of harmony. After furious debate during 1883-1888, he was removed not for the fallacy of his statements or interpretation but for discussing these matters at the seminary that were "contrary to our church's interpretation of the Bible, and to her prevailing and recognized views." He was personally respected, and even chosen moderator of the South Carolina Synod in 1901. After the imbroglio, he was elected president of the University of South Carolina, and the commotion was virtually forgotten by the time of his death in 1907.

Another theological row of 1880-1910 centered about the HOLINESS MOVEMENT rooted in John Wesley's theology. The Methodist founder had preached justification, or "being saved" by faith at the time of "conversion" and commitment—an "experience" emphasized in revivals. But Wesley also went on to define a "second blessing" in which one may later be purified of his sinful nature and thus surrender his will to God—this conceived of as a transcendent, purifying experience that in effect puts one beyond the reach of sin. Those rare persons who achieved this second step—that is, sanctification, or holiness of hearts—perceived this as the ultimate goal of religious experience—or holiness. Holiness groups thus sought to stress and reach this "second blessing," or Christian perfection, a sanctification of one's life thereafter free of sin.

With reforming zeal returning to Methodism about 1870, many pietists stressed this doctrine and formed "holiness associations," within the Methodist Conference and sometimes in other churches, usually amid considerable emotionalism. Not surprisingly, factionalism within traditional churches resulted, and from this came over a score of holiness denominations after 1894. One significant group began in Iowa in 1895 but was organized in Anderson in 1898 as a denomination, "The Fire-Baptized Holiness Church." South Carolina had met the Holiness movement not only among troubled Methodists (with the Rev. R. C. Oliver maybe the best known one), but in other forms as well: in Benjamin Hardin Irwin, an evangelist at the Wesleyan Methodist Church in Piedmont in 1896; in a holiness paper, *Way of Faith*, published at the Oliver Gospel Mission in Columbia and circulating all over the nation; in the *Way of Holiness*, published in Spartanburg; and in the career of N. J. Holmes, a Presbyterian preacher. About the turn of the century a number of Holiness adherents moved on to embrace PENTECOSTALISM, that to most involved a third "step" or blessing, that of speaking in tongues as a mark of progression.

With this came a number of additional congregations. Holmes, who received pentecostal baptism in 1907, established a "Bible and Missionary Institute" in 1898 that moved about the state but finally settled in Greenville as the Holmes Theological Seminary where it became—and is—an important force in the pentecostal movement in the nation, exercising a conservative influence and "discouraging extremism and excessive emotionalism." As a seminary, it has produced hundreds of preachers, especially for the PENTECOSTAL HOLINESS CHURCH, a successor of the FIRE-BAPTIZED HOLINESS CHURCH. Although holiness and pentecostal groups are often considered to be limited to "socially disinherited and economically underprivileged," such stereotyping may be unwise. As one scholar put it, they "rejected a society that they felt wicked and corrupt, and that social order rejected them as unstable, backward, and self-righteous." Some holiness people are probably correct to say that they are closer

to Wesley's theology than are many modern Methodists. One might also see in the group of 1890-1910 adumbrations of the charismatic movement of the 1970s.

Interesting was the original absence of racism in the movement: Present and accepted in the 1893 Fire-Baptized Holiness Church was a Negro, W. E. Fuller, of Mountville, who became a leader and brought in others to the new denomination. In Greer in 1908, however, he formed a new black pentecostal denomination, "The Fire-Baptized Church of God of the Americas" that continues with headquarters in Greenville at the Fuller Normal and Industrial Institute.

While the holiness movement was emerging, there was also underway a new "Awakening" marked by nationally known "princes of the pulpit" such as Dwight L. Moody, Billy Sunday, and others who brought to revivalism the tactics of big business: efficient organization, salesmanship, and shrewd public relations. Insofar as revivals can be measured by statistics, they were fabulously successful. Most of these dynamic preachers did not tour the South, perhaps because the region still had its own revivalism in its own "protracted meetings," CAMP MEETINGS (less numerous now), union services, and its own evangelists—SAM JONES, MORDECAI HAM, "Cyclone Mack" McLendon, and others who played the opera houses, tents, and "tabernacles" apart from the regular sanctuaries. Many delighted in it; perhaps many of the dejected got their minds off the ills of this world, even those existing in Henry Grady's much touted New South.

Amid revivals, South Carolina churches could be expected to continue pursuing the old villains of sin—and they did. Baptists noted that the "cardinal sin" (drinking) kept growing. The presbytery blamed the Yankees: "The gloom and despondency caused by the downfall of the Confederacy no doubt tended to lead many young people especially into unusual and excessive dissipation." In this mood, Calvinists also lambasted "promiscuous dancing, card playing and theatrical performances as worldly folly" and charged that "The Lord's Day was desecrated by worldly pursuits, profane swearing and drunkenness." A Baptist paper found itself on the horns of a dilemma since the creation of a third party, the Prohibitionists, "would imperil white supremacy." The Methodists in 1887 called theaters "traveling cess-pools" and one preacher warned against "promiscuously" indulging in the "fascinating art" of dancing that would "lead to dissipation and lasciviousness." Lutherans moved in gingerly fashion, maybe because some of their new Germans were accustomed to a "continental Sabbath." The unfortunate legacy of these "Gloomy Guses" was the stereotype created among the young who long after saw such as the chief characteristics and value system of "the church."

South Carolina reactions to the issues that concerned Northerners involved in the Social Gospel were both positive and negative. On the matters connected with rapid industrialization, Carolinians were ambivalent. Rejecting Darwin on biological evolution, they nevertheless tended to embrace Social Darwinism—the gospel of laissez-faire and the worship of "free enterprise." Echoing Henry Grady and New South boosterism, churchmen welcomed cotton mills, singing hosannas for entrepreneurs, and cooperating with their paternalism. In the mill-built instant communities, here were potential instant-congregations. As mill owners attracted workers with low-rent houses, credit at the company store, subsidies for schools, and other forms of "welfare capitalism," so did they aid with church construction and contributions toward ministerial salaries. All this led one Methodist pastor to see "the hand of God" in the coming of the mills and to "think of Southern industry as a spiritual movement." At least 161 churches were built either entirely or in part by new mill companies. The population explosion on new "mill hills" provided an opportunity for church expansion and also for missionary challenge. Lutherans issued warnings in 1909 lest labor unrest and strife ("ruinous, anarchistic") accompany the transformation. Lutherans and Presbyterians talked about problems to be assuaged, but most of the expansion with mill churches was that of Baptists and Methodists, with holiness and pentecostal groups soon involved.

Still strongly rural, Protestantism showed little concern about urban problems or immigrants, far less than the North did, though the Baptist Convention in 1895 deplored "sinful" cities and immigrants, proclaiming, "We must evangelize them, or they will overcome us," the "they" being foreigners who "bring along with them their anarchy, their Romanism, and their want of morals."

But in the Progressive Era and the early twentieth century, the church was not totally ossified. Although church papers frowned on women's suffrage, the church encouraged education for women more than the state did. Although the church did little to change the basics of a white supremacy society, it did condemn gross injustice and begin to acknowledge that the problems had not been "solved." Women's groups concerned themselves with problems of children (not just in their orphanages), formed organizations for various causes, advocated efforts to improve race relations, and faced "relevant" issues. In 1889, Sally Chapin of Charleston in a national convention of the WOMAN'S CHRISTIAN TEMPERANCE UNION (WCTU) lashed out at the convict-lease system ("a disgrace to the civilization of the nineteenth century") and pled for reducing the work week for men. At the time, the Spartanburg WCTU was running an employment bureau for women needing work.

Maybe the church had not turned society wrong-side-out, but church agencies were beginning to "view with alarm" several vexing conditions. In 1906, a presbytery fumed about the need for the church to work in mill villages, lumber camps, and areas laden with other neglected unfortunates. In 1914, the Baptist Convention established a new committee to encourage interdenominational efforts to solve community problems, particularly those of race and labor relations. Maybe this was talk and not action—but earlier the talk had not noted this direction. In 1928, the Episcopal Department of Christian Social Service set out to awaken the diocese to the problems of interracial relations and continuing child labor problems, and as the Depression came advocated a public welfare program for the state.

While the larger denominations were moving slowly in those directions, newer denominations—many of them offshoots of Wesleyan pietism—grew and flourished as they declaimed the old-time religion of anathemas about personal conduct, fundamentalism, and revivalism. "The church"—in the broadest sense— was embarked simultaneously on two different courses: the larger, older denominations on a new one; the newer denominations on one which the big denominations were beginning to abandon after so many generations.

Some tenuous generalizations about religion in South Carolina since 1914 are, in order:

1. In 1980 the six largest denominational groupings, in order, are Baptist, Methodist, Presbyterian, Catholic, Lutheran, Episcopal. Of these, Catholics were showing fastest growth: 42 percent in 12 years, and 22.8 percent for the last four years, largely from in-migration.

2. Main-line churches have not been growing (statistically) as fast as the population has.

3. Most notable recent expansion of institutions has been in the development of homes for the aging by all major denominations.

4. As the "mill village" as a detached, homogeneous community passes from the scene, the future of the "mill church" becomes a challenge and underscores a possible role for an industrial chaplaincy.

5. The problem of rural churches in a rapidly urbanizing society has not been solved. The ARPs present a classic case of the dilemma. A similar problem is that of numerous small and weak churches in a day of easier transportation.

6. Dozens of small churches and sects abound, despite the preceding paragraphs concentrating on six major groups. The "church directory" in a typical Saturday newspaper may include 30 or more varieties.

7. Among the large denominations, church harmony and cooperation have become quite marked. One factor has been Vatican II. Another has been the South Carolina Christian Action Council, formed in 1933 and made up of 17 denominations (Protestant and Catholic). Starting with temperance emphasis, it has gradually broadened to issues of people and society: voting rights, death penalty, race relations, drug problems, and particularly the moral implications of political decisions. In the latter, many state officials have been involved and show sensitive concern.

8. In the era of changing race relations, church leaders have not followed the crowd, as in the 19th century, but have sometimes courted unpopularity by supporting social change. Methodists have generally been in the lead; black and white annual conferences merged in 1972; Wofford was the first white college to desegregate voluntarily. The contrast with 19th century churches and their defense of slavery as a "positive good" has been a sharp one.

9. Long the leaders of the Negro community, black ministers have declined somewhat in relative influence and status as leaders from other occupations and professions have emerged amid the changes in society.

10. Leadership and many parishioners in major churches have accepted these and other social changes and have deemphasized the old stress on "individual sin" as the chief concern of religion. Baptists in 1965, for example, shunned efforts to get

them to revive the opposition to teaching of evolution. Social justice and public problems have been accepted as proper matters for church concern. In so doing, church voices have not always echoed the "popular" side or the view of powerful vested interests. Maybe this explains why South Carolina churches have not "grown" much in statistics, but they nevertheless may have been growing in other ways.

See also articles on ESTABLISHED RELIGION; LUTHERAN CHURCH; MIGRATION, SOUTHWARD (1700-1830); MISSION TO THE SLAVES.

Bibliography. Hugh George Anderson, Lutheranism in the Southeastern States, 1860-1886: A Social History; Albert D. Betts, History of South Carolina Methodism; Barnett A. Elzas, Jews of South Carolina; History of the Lutheran Church in South Carolina; Abran V. Goodman, "South Carolina From Shaftesbury to Salvador," Jews in the South, Leonard Dinnerstein and Mary D. Palsson, eds.; F. D. Jones and W. H. Mills, History of the Presbyterian Church in South Carolina Since 1850; Joe M. King, History of South Carolina Baptists; Ernest M. Lander, Jr., A History of South Carolina, 1865-1960, ch. 6; Loulie Latimer Owens, Saints of Clay: The Shaping of South Carolina Baptists; George C. Rogers, Jr., Church and State in Eighteenth-Century South Carolina; Vinson Synan, The Holiness-Pentecostal Movement in the United States; Francis B. Simkins and Robert H. Woody, South Carolina During Reconstruction, chs. 14, 15; Rosser H. Taylor, Ante-Bellum South Carolina: A Social and Cultural History, ch. 10; Albert S. Thomas, Historical Acount of the Protestant Episcopal Church in South Carolina, 1820-1957; George B. Tindall, South Carolina Negroes, 1877-1900, ch. 10; Leah Townsend, South Carolina Baptists, 1670-1805; Ernest Trice Thompson, Presbyterians in the South, 3 vols.; David Duncan Wallace, Historical Background of Religion in South Carolina; History of South Carolina, 3 vols.

LEWIS P. JONES
WOFFORD COLLEGE

SOUTHERN BAPTIST CONVENTION.

Baptists of the Southern states organized the Southern Baptist Convention 8-12 May 1845 in Augusta GA. Geographically restricted to the Confederate states, the SBC began with a total membership of 351,951 in 4,126 local Baptist churches. In 1981 the SBC had churches in every state of the United States and had become the largest Protestant denomination in the country with a total membership of nearly 14 million.

Baptists of the South, 1680-1845. Though the SBC was not formed until 1845, Baptists had been in the South since the last two decades of the 17th century. Much of what later could be described as the Southern Baptist identity took shape during the period from 1680-1845. Four factors were of particular importance.

The first of these was the synthesizing of diverse Baptist traditions, especially the PARTICULAR BAPTIST and the SEPARATE BAPTIST traditions. Calvinistic in theology, the Particular Baptists developed out of English Baptist life and planted the first Baptist churches in the South near Charleston SC. Characterized by pietistic Puritanism, Calvinistic confessionalism, denominational connectionalism, and concern for ministerial education, this group left an important mark on Baptists of the South. RICHARD FURMAN, pastor of the First Baptist Church, Charleston SC from 1787-1825, personalized this early Baptist tradition in the region.

Separate Baptists, on the other hand, emerged out of revivalistic New England CONGREGATIONALISM and migrated to North Carolina in 1755. Led by SHUBAL STEARNS, the Separate Baptist legacy was primarily one of personal evangelism and REVIVALISM. Beginning in the 1780s the Separate Baptists and the Particular Baptists began consolidating, and by the end of the first decade of the 19th century the process was virtually completed. Baptists in the South were shaped by both the evangelistic emphases of the Separates and the more churchly emphases of the Particulars.

A second factor shaping the denomination prior to the formation of the SBC was the westward migration. Following the American Revolution, numerous Baptists joined the trek away from the Atlantic seaboard onto the newly opened trans-Appalachian frontier. The frontier became fertile soil for Baptist growth, intensifying Baptist individualism in ethics, congregationalism in church life;

revivalism in ministry style, and simplicity in worship patterns. Moreover, the frontier further identified Baptists in the South as an agrarian people related primarily to the common people.

The rise of the modern missionary movement was a third factor that shaped Baptists in the South prior to 1845. Under the leadership of LUTHER RICE, Baptists in the United States organized the TRIENNIAL CONVENTION in 1814. This was their first national body in America and its purpose was to undergird foreign missions. By 1832 the American Baptist Home Mission Society had been founded. Before 1845 Baptists of the region, ardent advocates of foreign and home missions, played a prominent role in the Triennial Convention and the ABHMS. When the SBC was organized in 1845, it was structured around a commitment to missions, both foreign and domestic.

Slavery and regionalism comprised the fourth shaping influence on the Baptists who were to become the SBC. Before the invention of the cotton gin in 1793, a few Baptists had condemned SLAVERY. Most, however, had viewed slavery as a biblically sanctioned institution. During the heated abolition conflict of the 1830s, this latter attitude intensified and hardened.

The Southern Baptist Convention, 1845-1900. Baptists of the South separated from the Triennial Convention and the ABHMS in 1845 over the issue of slavery. With the growing abolition sentiment of the 1830s and 1840s, both Baptist mission societies were faced with the question of appointing slaveholders as missionaries. In the early 1840s the mission societies affirmed and reaffirmed positions of neutrality on slavery. These Baptists had good reason for questioning the genuineness of that neutrality. They feared, among other things, that they were perceived as second-rate Christians because of their proslavery posture.

Baptists in Alabama forced the issue on 25 November 1844 when they addressed a fateful letter to the Board of Managers of the Triennial Convention. The Alabama Baptists resolved "that our duty at this crisis requires us to demand from the proper authorities in all those bodies to whose funds we have contributed, or with whom we have in any way been connected, the distinct, explicit, avowal that slaveholders are eligible, and entitled, equally with non-slaveholders, to all the privileges and immunities of their several unions; and especially to receive any agency, mission, or other appointment, which may run within the scope of their operation or duties."

The Board of Managers of the Triennial Convention issued a frank and stinging reply. "If," they said, "any one should offer himself as a missionary, having slaves, and should insist on retaining them as his property, we could not appoint him." To avoid ambiguity the board said, "One thing is certain: we can never be a party to any arrangement which would imply approbation of slavery."

In response to this clear repudiation of slavery, 293 "delegates" representing diverse Baptist bodies such as local churches, state conventions, educational institutions, and missionary societies met in Augusta 8-12 May 1845 and organized the SBC. W. B. JOHNSON, prominent South Carolina pastor, was the "father" of the SBC. He was primarily responsible for drafting both the "Constitution" of the SBC and a "Public Address" that explained why the SBC was organized.

These two central SBC documents have several important emphases. First, Baptists in the South believed that the formation of the SBC was mandated by questions surrounding the slavery issue. Theological or ecclesiological differences had nothing to do with the denominational division. Second, the "extent of this disunion" involved only the Foreign and Home Mission enterprises. These Baptists did not separate from the Publication Society, for example. Third, Southern

Baptists formed a new kind of denominational structure, one that was more centralized, more connectional, and more cooperative than any heretofore known among Baptists anywhere, in Europe or America. They forsook the decentralized, societal approach of the North and formed one convention with two boards, home and foreign. Fourth, the SBC unity was to be found in functional missionary endeavors and not in doctrinal or theological creedalism. The SBC cemented the new denomination, not around doctrinal uniformity, but by "organizing a plan for eliciting, combining and directing the energies of the whole denomination in one sacred effort, for the propagation of the gospel."

Following the organization of the SBC, a denominationalizing process began among Southern Baptists that continued throughout the 19th century. At least three factors contributed to this sharpening of Southern Baptist identity. The first of these was cultural/political. The "Southernness" of Southern Baptist life had been initiated by sectionalism and slavery, but it was intensified by Southern Baptist attitudes toward secession, the Confederacy, the Civil War, and Reconstruction. When the SBC met 10-13 May 1861 in Savannah GA the delegates clearly identified with secessionism and everything Southern. They defended the right of secession, pledged themselves to the Confederacy, and substituted "Southern States of North America" for "United States" in the SBC constitution. In the 19th century Baptists *of* the South became *Southern* Baptists. The region impressed a discernible cultural identity on the SBC.

A second factor increasing the Southern Baptist consciousness in the 19th century was LANDMARKISM, essentially an ecclesiology fathered by JAMES R. GRAVES in Nashville TN. With a view of history that stressed local Baptist church successionism back to the New Testament, Landmarkism claimed exclusive validity for Baptist churches, Baptist ministers, and Baptist ordinances. Landmarkism

gave Southern Baptists an identity and left a legacy of antiecumenism, sectarianism, and authoritarianism in its churches. It did, however, provide the Southern Baptists of the 19th century with an ecclesiological identity.

Institutional developments constituted the third factor that intensified the denominationalizing process among Southern Baptists in the 19th century. When the separation by region occurred in 1845, only the mission societies were involved. By 1891, however, the SBC had organized the Baptist Sunday School Board, which displaced the older American Baptist Publication Society. Other forces were driving a more decisive wedge between the two major white Baptist denominations in America. By the turn of the 20th century there were few significant points of contact between them.

In addition to the formation of the BSSB, Southern Baptists had strengthened the Foreign and Home Mission Boards, founded Baptist colleges, and organized the Southern Baptist Theological Seminary (1859) and the Woman's Missionary Union (1888).

The Southern Baptist Convention, 1900-1980. Southern Baptists have known phenomenal growth in the 20th century. In 1900 they reported a total membership of 1,657,996 in 19,558 churches. By 1950 those figures had increased to 7,079,889 and 27,788. By 1981 total church membership was 13,789,580 and the total number of churches was 36,079.

The growth of the SBC institutions also mushroomed in the first half of the century. In 1900 the SBC had only three boards (foreign, 1845; home, 1845; Sunday school, 1891) and one theological seminary (Southern Baptist Theological Seminary, 1859). By 1951 the convention had added one board (Annuity, 1918), four theological seminaries (Southwestern, 1908; New Orleans, 1917; Golden Gate, 1951; Southeastern, 1951), and six commissions (Brotherhood, 1907; Christian Life, 1913; Education, 1916; American Baptist Theological Seminary Commission, 1924; Radio and Television, 1946; Historical, 1951). Since 1951 only one seminary (Midwestern, 1957) and one commission (Stewardship, 1960) have been organized. Thus most of the SBC institutional development came in the first half of the 20th century.

Three internal developments in the SBC in the 1920s have emerged over the years as pivotal points in the denomination's history. One was organizational, the second was financial, and the third theological. In 1927 the Executive Committee of the SBC was created in recognition of the fact that the convention needed a coordinating body to act for the SBC between annual sessions. This committee is the fiscal agent of the denomination and has accumulated significant power over the years. In 1925 the SBC launched the Cooperative Program, a financial arrangement between state conventions and the SBC that undergirds the entire denominational mission. The program is the economic lifeline of the SBC. Also in 1925, the SBC adopted their first doctrinal statement. Known as "The Baptist Faith and Message," the statement was designed as a consensus of theological affirmation and not as a binding creed on individuals, churches, and convention institutions.

Throughout the 20th century the SBC has been an aggressive evangelistic and missionary denomination. In fact, evangelism has been the salient denominational characteristic in this century. While it has known internal skirmishes, apart from the Fundamentalist Controversy of the 1920s, the SBC has not been racked by controversy during the middle decades of the century. Since that time, however, noticeable stress points have appeared in the life of the denomination.

One of those has been the geographical expansion of Southern Baptists. Until World War II, the SBC base remained fairly constant, centered in the Southeast, South, and Southwest. Between 1845 and 1942 only six additional states were added to the original 14 state conventions affiliated with the SBC. By 1982, 34 state conventions had identified with the SBC, with churches in all 50 states. This expansion has placed pressure on the "Southernness" of Southern Baptist life. Geographical expansion has produced a growing and menacing cultural pluralism. Cultural diversity has also derived at the SBC from the civil rights struggle of the 1960s with its focus on ministry to black people and the human rights struggle of the 1970s with its focus on the emerging new roles for women.

Another stress point is theological. Since the early 1960s, the SBC has been involved in three very decisive doctrinal disputes. While each of the conflicts had its own particular features, underneath all of them has been a growing and threatening theological diversity in Southern Baptist life.

One of the greatest stresses in recent years is that of denominational loyalty. "Cooperation" has, over the years, almost been a theological maxim for Southern Baptists. Today some believe that an erosion of the SBC cooperative mentality is taking place. The issue is focused for several years to come: How much diversity can a denomination sustain and yet maintain unity?

See also article on FRONTIER, INFLUENCE OF.

Bibliography. Robert A. Baker, *A Baptist Source Book*; *The First Southern Baptists*; *Relations Between Northern and Southern Baptists*; "Southern Baptist Convention," *Baptist Advance*, ed. Davis C. Woolley; *The Southern Baptist Convention and Its People*; *Baptist History and Heritage* 16 (April 1981); William Wright Barnes, *The Southern Baptist Convention, 1845-1953*; John Lee Eighmy, *Churches in Cultural Captivity: A History of the Social Attitudes of Southern Baptists*; *Encyclopedia of Southern Baptists*, 4 vols.; Brooks Hays and John E. Steely, *The Baptist Way of Life*; Samuel S. Hill and Robert G. Torbet, *Baptists North and South*; George B. Kelsey, *Social Ethics Among Southern Baptists, 1917-1969*; W. L. Lumpkin, *Baptist Foundations in the South*; Walter B. Shurden, *Not a Silent People: Controversies That Have Shaped Southern Baptists*; *Southern Baptist Convention Annual*, 1845-Present; Rufus B. Spain, *At Ease in Zion: A Social History of Southern Baptists*; William Warren Sweet, *Religion on the American Frontier: The Baptists*; Robert G. Torbet, *A History of the*

Baptists; G. Hugh Wamble, "Baptists of the South," *Baptists and the American Experience*, ed. James E. Wood, Jr.

WALTER B. SHURDEN
MERCER UNIVERSITY

SOUTHERN CHRISTIAN LEADERSHIP CONFERENCE (SCLC).

First organized early in 1957 by MARTIN LUTHER KING, JR., and other young Southern black ministers who had become active in local civil rights protest efforts throughout the South, the SCLC served as the primary organizational vehicle through which the Southern black church made its crucial contributions to the modern CIVIL RIGHTS MOVEMENT.

Although viewed by many as simply a larger reflection of King's individual role as the symbolic leader of that movement, the SCLC actually served a much broader function. First, in the late 1950s it drew together ministers who believed the black church had a responsibility to act in the political arena and who sought a means for expressing that latent activism. Later, in the years from 1962 through 1968, the SCLC organized the protest campaigns in cities such as Birmingham and Selma AL, which brought the civil rights movement to the forefront of national attention and won the enactment of legislative milestones such as the Civil Rights Acts of 1964 and the Voting Rights Act of 1965.

Three major influences shaped SCLC's founding. The first was the Montgomery AL bus boycott of 1955-1956, a local protest effort that brought King to national attention and made him the symbol of the new black activism in the South. Second, young black ministers in other Southern cities sought to emulate the Montgomery example and bus protests patterned after the Montgomery one emerged in cities such as Birmingham, Tallahassee, New Orleans, and Atlanta. Many of these activists were seeking a forum for exchanging ideas and experiences. Third, a number of New York-based civil rights advocates, such as Bayard Rustin, Ella Baker, and Stanley Levison, who previously had helped raise funds and organize Northern publicity for the Montgomery protest, were drawn in. They also advocated the formation of a regional organization in the South that could spread the influence of Montgomery's mass movement and provide King a larger platform.

Initially labeled the "Southern Negro Leaders Conference on Transportation and Nonviolent Integration" by King and Rustin, the conference met three times in 1957 before finally adopting the present name, with the word "Christian" added at the personal insistence of King. Seeking to avoid competition and conflict with the NAACP, SCLC chose to be composed not of individual members but of local organization "affiliates," usually civic leagues, ministerial alliances, or individual churches. Looking for a goal beyond that of desegregating city bus lines, King and the other young ministers leading the conference—C. K. Steele of Tallahassee, Fred L. Shuttlesworth of Birmingham, Joseph E. Lowery of Mobile, and Ralph D. Abernathy of Montgomery—focused on the right to vote and sought to develop a program, staff, and financial resources with which to pursue it. Until 1960, however, their efforts largely floundered, in part because of the many other demands upon King's time and energy, but also because of personnel problems on the small staff and relatively meager finances.

Transformation of SCLC into an aggressive, protest-oriented organization began in 1960 with King's own move from Montgomery to Atlanta and his appointment of a dynamic new executive director, the Rev. Wyatt T. Walker of Peterburg's Gillfield Baptist Church. Coupling his organizational skills with King's prowess as a speaker and inspirational leader, Walker soon brought about a seven-fold expansion of SCLC's staff, budget, and program. While some staff members concentrated on voter registration efforts and others on citizenship-training programs funded by Northern foundations, Walker and King set out to design a frontal assault on Southern segregation. Stymied initially in 1961-

1962 in the southwest Georgia city of Albany, Walker and King chose the notorious segregation stronghold of Birmingham as their next target. In a series of aggressive demonstrations throughout April and May of 1963, SCLC put the violent excesses of racist Southern lawmen on the front pages of newspapers throughout the world. Civil rights rose to the top of the national agenda and, within little more than a year's time, the Civil Rights Act of 1964 began altering Southern race relations.

Following King's much-heralded success at the March on Washington and his receipt of the Nobel Peace Prize, SCLC repeated the Birmingham scenario with an even more successful protest campaign in early 1965 in Selma, focusing upon the right to vote. Out of this effort emerged the Voting Rights Act of 1965. Subsequent SCLC efforts in Chicago, Louisville, and Cleveland in 1966-1967 involving issues of housing and jobs were judged far less successful. Late in 1967 the conference began planning a massive "Poor People's Campaign" to confront the issue of poverty in America, but after King's assassination in April 1968, the effort all but collapsed in confusion. Lacking King's renown, SCLC's resources and staff shrank precipitously in the years following his death. Internal tensions surrounding King's successor, Ralph D. Abernathy, and wider changes in the civil rights movement further contributed to the conference's decline. Only in the late 1970s, when another of the original founders, Joseph E. Lowery, assumed the SCLC presidency, did it appear at all possible that the organization might once again play the invaluable role that it had orchestrated between 1957 and 1968.

Bibliography. Adam Fairclough, "The Southern Christian Leadership Conference and the Second Reconstruction, 1957-1963," *South Atlantic Quarterly* 80 (Spring 1981): 177-94; "A Study of the Southern Christian Leadership Conference and the Rise and Fall of the Nonviolent Civil Rights Movement," unpublished Ph.D. dissertation, University of Keele (U.K.); Martin Luther King, Jr., Papers, King Center for Nonviolent Social Change, Atlanta; Papers, Mugar Library, Boston University; David L. Lewis, *King: A Critical Biography*; Lawrence D. Reddick, *Crusader Without Violence: A Biography of Martin Luther King, Jr.*; Southern Christian Leadership Conference Papers, King Center for Nonviolent Social Change, Atlanta; Eugene P. Walker, "A History of the Southern Christian Leadership Conference, 1955-1965: The Evolution of a Southern Strategy for Social Change," unpublished Ph.D. dissertation, Duke University, 1978.

DAVID J. GARROW
UNIVERSITY OF NORTH CAROLINA
AT CHAPEL HILL

SOUTHERN PRESBYTERIAN CHURCH: *See* PRESBYTERIAN CHURCH IN THE UNITED STATES.

SOUTHERN SOCIOLOGICAL CONGRESS. This annual gathering of socially concerned Southerners that met between 1912 and 1920 marked the furthest advance of SOCIAL GOSPEL thinking in the South. The idea for a congress that would unite ministers, educators, and social workers originated with Kate Barnard, Oklahoma's Commissioner of Charities and Corrections. Barnard urged her idea on Ben W. Hooper, reform-oriented governor of Tennessee, who drew upon the intellectual resources of Vanderbilt University and the financial support of Mrs. E. W. Cole in convening the first meeting of the congress in Nashville in 1912. At Nashville and at Altanta in 1913, outstanding Social Gospel leaders and sociologists, both Northern and Southern, addressed the membership, grown from 700 to over 1,200 in that single year.

Initially the SSC's organizers sought to bring research and motivation to bear upon a wide range of problems. Announced aims emphasized perceived Southern needs: prison reform, especially of the convict-lease system; improved care of "defectives"; remedying educational backwardness and racial injustice. Particularly at the 1913 Atlanta meeting, blacks participated as equals, members such as MARY MCLEOD BETHUNE demonstrated insight on interracial matters and on how the congress's concerns affected the South's black population.

Beginning in 1914, when the congress met at Memphis jointly with the National Conference of Charities and Correction, presentations became more inspirational than factual, leading the more practical and scholarly members to shift allegiance to other nationally based groups. The SSC moved its headquarters to Washington in 1916, and in 1920 changed its name to the Southern Cooperative League of Education and Social Service.

Outside forces such as World War I with its shattered idealisms and the growth of available alternatives certainly contributed to the demise of the SSC, but the effort it represented also harbored internal flaws. Members lacked the ability or the willingness to confront the South's major problem, its poverty. Reliance on the churches in an era when Southern religion was largely rejecting social emphasis in favor of restatement of the need for individual salvation further undercut the vision that had inspired the congress's beginnings.

The main significance of the movement is thus its revelation of the limits inherent in the South's response to the Social Gospel. Neither the economic reality nor the religion of the region provided hospitable ground for social insight, and the myriad ways in which that insight could be smothered are amply demonstrated by the brief history of the Southern Sociological Congress.

Bibliography. Lee M. Brooks and Alvin L. Bertrand, *History of the Southern Sociological Society*; E. Charles Chatfield, "The Southern Sociological Congress: Organization of Uplift," *Tennessee Historical Quarterly* 19 (December 1960): 328-47; "The Southern Sociological Congress: Rationale of Uplift," *Tennessee Historical Quarterly* 20 (March 1961): 51-64; James E. McCulloch, ed., *The Call of the New South*.

ERNEST KURTZ
ATHENS, GEORGIA

SOUTHERN TENANT FARMERS' UNION. This organization of agricultural workers was founded in the spring of 1934 in a schoolhouse near Tyronza AR by black and white sharecroppers who had been evicted from their plantation homes. It was intended to be an interracial organization representing the oppressed class of Southern agriculture: sharecroppers, wage laborers, even small-farm owners. Some of the union's far-reaching goals

reflected socialist influence: "land for the landless" was a rallying cry, and as interpreted by the union theorists, it meant breaking up the plantations and redistributing the land to those who worked it and to workers' cooperatives. Other goals—the commitment to interracial cooperation and nonviolence—reflected the influence of the many ministers, untutored and seminary-trained, who formed most of the STFU leadership.

The main activities of the STFU, however, were resisting the wholesale displacement of tenant families in the wake of the Agricultural Adjustment Act and other New Deal policies designed to force tobacco and cotton lands out of production. This implied the housing and feeding of its members who were evicted and building a defense from attacks by local landowners.

Although headquartered in Memphis for safety reasons, the STFU was most active in Arkansas where at one time it claimed 212 locals. The union had a substantial following in Oklahoma and Missouri, with scattered locals in Texas, Mississippi, and Tennessee. Each local represented a portion or all of the workers on a single plantation, and they were occasionally organized separately by race and sex. Local leadership was predominantly black; approximately one-half of the elected officers were women. All groups shared equally in making policy at conventions held in Arkansas and Oklahoma between 1936 and 1939. The union claimed 30,827 members in 1937. Church and socialist leaders from the South provided most of the direct leadership, but other people and groups lent support, for example, the Socialist party, and individuals like Sherwood Eddy, Reinhold Niebuhr, and Norman Thomas.

Strikes in Arkansas, Oklahoma, and Missouri were less successful than the union's first "general strike" during the cotton harvest of 1935, although they too provoked violent resistance. Only a handful of collective bargaining agreements were obtained, but the STFU was an effective advocate for tenant farmers seeking their share of crop support benefits and public works jobs. By testifying frequently before Congress the STFU contributed substantially to the design of the Farm Security Administration and to the effective administration of its programs in parts of the South. Its distribution of relief supplies made survival possible for many sharecroppers, as did its sponsorship of the Delta Cooperative Farm, founded as a haven for evicted sharecroppers in Bolivar County MS. Its most important contribution, however, may have been the example of interracial cooperation it provided the labor and civil rights movements to come.

Internal conflict between Communist and Socialist sympathizers surfaced in 1937 when the STFU, after being spurned by the American Federation of Labor, became a founding member of the communist-influenced United Cannery, Agricultural, Packing, and Allied Workers of America (CIO). Political differences and the difficulty of imposing traditional union practices upon sharecroppers caused the STFU to disintegrate rapidly in 1939.

It revived in 1942 to transport cotton field workers to the Southwest under the authority of the War Manpower Commission and cannery workers to the north under the first interstate migrant plan ever arranged between a union and an employer. In 1946, the STFU was awarded a charter by the AF of L, changed its name to the National Farm Labor Union, shifting most of its activities to the vineyards of California.

See also articles on CHRISTIAN SOCIALISM; KESTER, HOWARD A.; SOCIAL GOSPEL.

Bibliography. Anthony P. Dunbar, *Against the Grain: Southern Radicals and Prophets, 1929-1959*; Donald H. Grubbs, *Cry From the Cotton: The Southern Tenant Farmers' Union and the New Deal*; Howard Kester, *Revolt Among the Sharecroppers*; H. L. Mitchell, *Mean Things Happening in This Land.*

ANTHONY P. DUNBAR
NEW ORLEANS, LOUISIANA

SPALDING, MARTIN JOHN (1810-1872), early Roman Catholic priest and bishop, was born in Rolling Fork KY. His ancestors had arrived in Maryland in 1657, and the family moved to Kentucky in 1791. Spalding entered seminary in 1826, studying in BARDSTOWN KY, and Rome. He returned to Kentucky as priest and teacher in 1835. Within a decade he won fame as an author as well. In his works Spalding responded to criticism or ignorance of the Catholic Church. He also wrote a history of Kentucky Catholicism, among other books.

In 1848, Spalding was consecrated coadjutor to the bishop of Louisville. Two years later he succeeded to the See. In Louisville, Bishop Spalding dealt with anti-Catholic riots in the 1850s. He built new parishes and expanded Catholic education. Although he held Southern sympathies, he sought peace and a neutral role for the Church during the Civil War.

In 1864, Spalding became archbishop of Baltimore. There he was the guiding spirit behind the Second Plenary Council (1865), which set rules and organization for American Catholicism. In Baltimore, Spalding was concerned about black Catholics and brought the Josephites from England to serve them. He also founded St. Mary's Industrial School.

In 1869-1870, Archbishop Spalding was a leader in the American delegation to the First Vatican Council. At first he did not favor defining papal infallibility, but later reconsidered and supported the dogma in a pastoral.

Bibliography. Clyde Crews, *Presence and Possibility: Louisville Catholicism and its Cathedral*; John L. Spalding, *The Life of the Most Rev. M. J. Spalding, D.D., Archbishop of Baltimore*; Thomas Spalding, *Martin John Spalding: American Churchman.*

GARY W. MCDONOGH
NEW COLLEGE
UNIVERSITY OF SOUTH FLORIDA

SPANISH INFLUENCE. Governor Alexander O'Reilly established Spanish religious policy in LOUISIANA in 1770 when he followed suggestions of the Capuchin Father Dagobert in creating 11 parishes served by 18 priests as follows: six for New Orleans and environs; one each for the German Coast parishes of St. Charles and St. John the Baptist; one each for the Acadian Coast parishes of Ca-Bahan-Nosé, La Fourche de Chetimachas, and Iberville; two for the Upper Louisiana parishes at St. Louis and Ste. Genèvieve; and one each for Pointe Coupée, Opelousas, Attakapas, Rapides and Natchitoches. Louisiana's major problem was a chronic shortage of qualified priests, defying secular and religious efforts to provide them.

From medieval times, as a result of the reconquest of Spain from the Moors, the Crown had special privileges, which included the creation of parishes and bishoprics and the appointment of priests and members of the hierarchy. This *Patronato Real* enabled Spanish governors in Louisiana to name priests and to remove those found lacking, such as, for example, Father Juan Delvaux who was removed because of his pro-Jacobin activities in Natchitoches during 1795. In turn, the Crown subsidized the church by paying the salaries of its priests and bishops, and by paying for the expense of building churches and equipping them. Members of the parish were not required to tithe, although some did (such as Andrés Almonester y Roxas, who rebuilt the St. Louis parish church after its destruction in the 1788 New Orleans fire).

Father Cirillo de Barcelona, chaplain with the Gálvez forces conquering British West Florida (1780-1781), acted as auxiliary bishop of Cuba until 1787, when the provinces of Louisiana and the Floridas came under the control of the Diocese of St. Christopher of Havana. During a pastoral visit in the West Florida parishes of Pensacola and Mobile he performed various sacraments such as first communion, baptism, and marriage, and compiled census reports showing that Pensacola's 572 settlers included 292 white Catholics and 47 white Protestants, 119 black Catholics and 114 black Protestants. Mobile's 1791 population of 733 included 258 whites, not broken down as to religion. Father

Cirillo also visited the settlements of San Esteban de Tombecbé and the Tensaw and noted 348 and 493 settlers respectively, the majority of them new settlers from the United States. These were souls the church sought to win to the Catholic church by gentle persuasion rather than by force.

The radical departure from traditional exclusivism by the Spanish crown indicated both expediency and an enlightened policy aimed at attracting settlers to the sparsely settled Spanish-American frontier. Private exercise of the Protestant faith was permitted by order of the Supreme Council of State as a result of suggestions made by Governor Esteban Miró in 1785. This policy continued until Manuel Gayoso de Lemos decreed in 1798 that the policy of toleration extended only to the first generation; the children of Protestant settlers were expected to become Catholics, and those objecting were expelled from the provinces of Louisiana and West Florida.

Because the settlers enjoyed a good sermon, English-speaking Irish priests, educated at the University of Salamanca's *Colegio de Irlandeses*, arrived to serve the two parishes at Natchez (Cole's Creek, 18 miles north of the fort, and the parish of Our Savior of the World, in Natchez itself, where a new church was dedicated 12 June 1791); St. Michael's Parish of Pensacola; the Purest Conception at Mobile; and the Church of the Transfiguration at San Esteban de Tombecbé (St. Stephens of the Tombigbee). Two separate groups of Irish priests arrived and included Father Michael Lamport in the Mobile District, Constantine Mackenna, William Savage, Gregorio White, Frances Lennan, and the Carmelite, Father John Brady.

Protestant ministers such as the Presbyterian John Bolls, Episcopalian Adam Cloud, and Baptist Richard Curtis, Sr., violated the ban on public preaching and were either imprisoned or expelled from the Natchez District. Religious and political liberty, ever entwined, were the goals of settlers attempting to overthrow

Spanish rule in 1797. Jews did not suffer proscription, however, except when three were expelled by O'Reilly from New Orleans in 1769 for both religious and smuggling reasons.

In the Mobile District Father Constantine Mackenna formally blessed the new church on 30 May 1793 with a solemn mass and the customary procession. Victories of Gálvez in the American Revolution were celebrated by *Te Deum* masses in the St. Louis Parish church at New Orleans, later to become a cathedral.

Priests took an active role in educating the youth, but proposals in 1795 for a religious seminary in New Orleans were opposed by Governor Carondelet because the creole young were too wild and used to their hunting along the bayous. A popular New Orleans schoolteacher at the Spanish school was Father Luis de Quintanilla, a Capuchin from Spain. Governors preferred Spanish Capuchins to the French ones because of the traditional respect for monarchy.

Catholic clergy alone were entitled to officiate at marriages after 1792, and priests such as Father Lennan maintained separate records for the non-Catholic unions he blessed. Because of the frontier situation, a priest would sometimes visit a remote area and marry the parents and baptize their children on the same day. According to the historian, John F. H. Claiborne, "There was more religious freedom and toleration for Protestants in the Natchez district, than Catholics and dissenters from the ruling denomination, enjoyed in either Old or New England.... It was a community of Protestants under a strictly Catholic dynasty, in an age of intolerance."

Pope Pius VI created a separate diocese for Louisiana and the Floridas on 25 April 1793, and Bishop Luis Ignacio Mariá de Peñalver y Cárdenas arrived at New Orleans on 17 July 1795. After a formal visitation he reported that the provinces were filled with bastardy, concubinage, and miscegenation. Atheists and Protestants set bad examples that affected the Catholic parishioners adversely. Despite his vigorous efforts, moral laxity continued to plague secular and religious officials alike throughout the Spanish domination.

See also articles on CHURCH AND STATE; FRENCH INFLUENCE; ROMAN CATHOLIC CHURCH; SPANISH INFLUENCE IN LA FLORIDA.

Bibliography. Roger Baudier, *The Catholic Church in Louisiana*; Clarence W. Bishpam, "Fray Antonio de Sedella, An Appreciation," *Louisiana Historical Quarterly* 2 (January 1919): 24-37; (July 1919): 237-47; Caroline Maude Burson, *Stewardship of Don Esteban Miró, 1782-1792*; Jack D. L. Holmes, "Andrés Almonester y Roxas: Saint or Scoundrel?" *Louisiana Studies* 7 (Spring 1968): 47-64; "*Dramatis Personae* in Spanish Louisiana," *Louisiana Studies* 6 (Summer 1967): 149-52; "Father Francis Lennan and His Activities in Spanish Louisiana and West Florida," *Louisiana Studies* 5 (Winter 1966): 255-68; *Gayoso, The Life of a Spanish Governor in the Mississippi Valley, 1789-1799*; "Irish Priests in Spanish Natchez," *Journal of Mississippi History* 29 (August 1967): 169-80; "Spanish Religious Policy in West Florida: Enlightened or Expedient?" *Journal of Church and State* 15 (Spring 1973): 259-69; Bertram Wallace Korn, *The Early Jews of New Orleans*.

SIR JACK D. L. HOLMES
BIRMINGHAM, ALABAMA

SPANISH INFLUENCE IN LA FLORIDA. Spanish Roman Catholics were the first representatives of Western religion to explore, settle, and evangelize territory now part of the United States. Juan Ponce de León, lately governor of Puerto Rico, discovered the continental land mass at its southeastern extremity in Easter Season, 1513, and gave it the name *Pascua florida*, flowery Easter. Contracted to La Florida, the name soon afterwards would be used to designate Spanish claims not only in the Florida peninsula where Ponce landed but in territory north as far as Newfoundland and west indefinitely from the Atlantic.

The use of a religious term for the land's name was in keeping with Spanish practice in the New World: in another example, Ponce named the Florida keys, which he circled, the *Mártires* because they resembled to him Christian martyrs lying dead in an ancient arena. Ponce returned to the gulf coast of the peninsula in 1521 hoping to plant a permanent settlement and Christian mission, but was driven off by Indian attacks in which he himself was fatally wounded. The 1521 expedition is important, however, as the first positively authenticated instance of the presence of Catholic priests, both secular and religious, on the U. S. mainland.

Of equal significance was the expedition of Lucas Vásquez de Ayllon to the north Georgia coast in 1526 where he and his settlers founded a colony and built a church, both dedicated to St. Michael (*San Miguel*). That first U. S. parish would last only three months, however, owing to sickness and starvation, and the surviving colonists with their priests withdrew to Santo Domingo whence they came. Other ill-fated expeditions followed: those of Pánfilo de Narváez in 1528-1537 and Hernando de Soto in 1539-1543, with secular and religious priests, wandered far across the continent but without lasting result. In 1549 a priest of the Dominican order, Luis Cáncer de Barbastro, came to Florida's lower gulf coast hoping to duplicate his earlier missionary successes in Guatemala. Slaughtered by Indians before he could do much more than hold aloft his crucifix, Cáncer is remembered as the country's first-known Christian pacifist and martyr. The district of Pensacola was settled under Tristán de Luna in 1559, but that ambitious attempt to plant permanently the Spanish cross and flag failed after three years of struggle.

The first successful and permanent Christian settlement in North America was established by Pedro Menéndez de Avilés at a site on the upper east coast of the Florida peninsula to which Menéndez gave the name ST. AUGUSTINE (*San Agustín*). The date of foundation was 8 September 1565, 40 years before the English Jamestown and 55 years before Plymouth Rock. Thus St. Augustine became the cradle of Western culture and religion in the United States, as it also became the origin and headquarters of the first Indian mission system.

A secular priest named Sebastian Montero, working in the Carolina back-country (*Orista*), had the first-recorded missionary success with the American Indians in 1566-1572. Priests and lay brothers of the Society of Jesus (Jesuits) had less success in the same time period at missions in Florida and Virginia. After suffering numerous violent deaths at the hands of their Indian charges, the Jesuits withdrew from La Florida. Members of the Order of Friars Minor (Franciscans) took their place beginning in 1573 and concentrated their first labors around St. Augustine and among the Indians of the Georgia coastal islands. A half century later they had built additional missions across the interior as far as present-day Tallahassee and the Apalachicola River. In 1655 the Franciscan friars counted 26,000 baptized Indians in 38 missions.

The high point of the mission epoch was 1675 when 40 friars were in the field teaching the catechism and rudiments of European arts and crafts. Lacking sufficient stone, the missionaries constructed their churches and compounds from wattle and daub, with the result that only occasional wood post foundations and clay wall fragments remain today. Convert instruction was conservative and the friars' correspondence reveals that they worried constantly that they were merely applying a Christian veneer over persistent aboriginal beliefs. Certainly a quasi-Spanish veneer characterized the mission culture where Indians, *muy españolados*—very Hispanicized— addressed each other as *don* and sang the Latin hymns of Catholic Europe.

The missions came to an end in 1702-1704 when English forces with Indian allies from Carolina destroyed the Georgia and Florida compounds, killing many of the Christian converts and taking others to Charleston as slaves. The Spanish missions would not be successfully revived and for the remainder of the Spanish periods in Florida (1704-1763, 1784-1821) Catholic religious life contracted around the *gobierno* at St. Augustine and the *comandancia* at Pensacola.

See also articles on FLORIDA; INDIANS, SOUTHEAST MISSIONS TO; SPANISH INFLUENCE.

Bibliography. Michael V. Gannon, *The Cross in the Sand*; Maynard Geiger, O.F.M., *The Franciscan Conquest of Florida*; John Tate Lanning, *The Spanish Missions of Georgia*; John Jay TePaske, *The Governorship of Spanish Florida*.

MICHAEL V. GANNON
UNIVERSITY OF FLORIDA

SPEAKING IN TONGUES: *See* CHARISMATIC; CHARISMATIC MOVEMENTS; GLOSSOLALIA.

SPIRITUALITY OF THE CHURCH.

The doctrine of the spirituality of the church, an attempt to relate the church to culture and a variant of types that have a long history in the church, was a fundamental conviction of many Presbyterian theologians in the South especially during the century from the 1830s to the Second World War. Its most powerful advocate was JAMES HENLEY THORNWELL who, as chairman of the Committee on Bills and Overtures for the 1848 Presbyterian General Assembly (Old School), defined the doctrine in a statement giving the position of the church on the "New York City Temperance Society Organized on Christian Principles."

The Church of Jesus Christ is a spiritual body, to which have been given the ministry, oracles and ordinances of God, for the gathering and perfecting of the saints in this life, to the end of the world. It is the great instrumentality of the Saviour, through which, by his eternal Spirit, He dispenses salvation to the objects of His love. Its ends are holiness and life, to the manifestation of the riches and glory of Divine grace, and not simply morality, decency and good order, which may to some extent be secured without faith in the Redeemer, or the transforming efficacy of the Holy Spirit. The laws of the Church are the authoritative injunctions of Christ, and not the covenants, however benevolent in their origin and aim, which men have instituted of their own will; and the ground of obligation which the Church, as such, inculcates is the authority of God speaking in His Word, and not pledges of honour which create, measure and define the peculiar duties of all voluntary associations. (*Collected Writings*, 4:469)

The report went on to argue that "no court of Christ can exact of His people to unite with the Temperance, Moral Reform, Colonization, or any other Society which may seek their aid. Connection with such institutions is a matter of Christian liberty." The church has a right and under certain circumstances is bound to bear testimony in favor of or to condemn such societies. Yet the church is limited by the authority of Scripture and cannot identify ambiguous political and social causes with the will of God. Individual Christians have the liberty to sponsor causes that as the church they cannot advocate. The doctrine does not separate Christian faith from political, social, and economic life. It does deny the church the role of advocate for secular causes or the right to go beyond what is perceived to be the explicit teaching of Scripture in its proclamations.

The doctrine of the spirituality of the church was corrupted by the pressures of racial and economic issues into an escape from social responsibility. This has kept it from receiving the attention it deserved as one way of relating church and culture.

Bibliography. E. T. Thompson, *Presbyterians in the South*; James Henley Thornwell, *Collected Writings*, vol. 4.

JOHN H. LEITH
UNION SEMINARY IN VIRGINIA

SPIRITUALS: *See* MUSIC, RELIGIOUS.

SPRINGFIELD, MISSOURI. Spring-

field continues to be called "the buckle on the Bible Belt." The metaphor is grotesque; but its continuance suggests a persistent descriptive utility for a secular and cosmopolitan society. Religious culture in Springfield rests upon foundations of evangelical and primitive Protestantism. Although most of the religious winds of the past century have stirred the locale, Fundamentalism and Pentecostalism may have stirred it the most.

Springfield is the largest city in the Ozarks area and is an important center for the historic institutionalization of religion in it. The ASSEMBLIES OF GOD brought its General Council and Gospel Publishing House (1918), Central Bible College (1922), and the AG Graduate School (1973). The BAPTIST BIBLE FELLOWSHIP (BBF), an association of some 3,000 independent fundamentalist congregations, located its headquarters and Baptist Bible College in Springfield in 1950. High Street Baptist Church of the BBF claims the largest Sunday school in Missouri. Yankee Congregationalist newcomers to Springfield established Drury College (1874), a center of elite high eastern culture in a town struggling to create a public school system. The two large hospitals are St. John's Regional Health Center of the Sisters of Mercy, and the Lester A. Cox Regional Medical Center, formerly Burge Protestant Hospital. Although the city is predominantly Protestant, the headquarters of the Springfield-Cape Girardeau Diocese, Roman Catholic Church is located there.

Springfield is in religious culture a city of the upper South and of the Ozarks. Ninety-eight percent white and over-whelmingly of English and Scotch-Irish southern highland descent, Springfield-ians tend to be very "religious." It is a religiosity Protestant and Southern, from Episcopal through Southern Baptist to union churches and churches that deny that they are churches. At Southwest Missouri State University (15,000 students), the first academic department of Religious Studies of any public college or university in Missouri enrolls some thousand students per year in elective religion courses.

See also article on OZARKS RELIGION.

ROBERT FLANDERS
SOUTHWEST MISSOURI STATE UNIVERSITY

SPRINGFIELD WILL AND TESTA-MENT.

Properly termed *Last Will and Testament of Springfield Presbytery*, this is a basic historical document of the Christian Church (Disciples of Christ), the Churches of Christ, the Christian Churches, and the United Church of Christ. It was signed in June 1804 by the founders of the Christian Church in the West, including Richard McNemar and BARTON W. STONE. All six of the founders were promoters of the GREAT REVIVAL in the West (1797-1805) in northern Kentucky and southern Ohio. In September 1803, four of the original five signatories had withdrawn from the jurisdiction of the Synod of Kentucky rather than face censure for rejecting the doctrine of election. Following this action, they had constituted themselves as Springfield Presbytery, taking the name Springfield from a town in southern Ohio.

In the *Last Will and Testament*, written by McNemar, the signers willed that: their presbytery "die, be dissolved, and sink into union with the Body of Christ at large"; the name of their presbytery be forgotten; their power of making laws for the church cease; the church itself try candidates for the ministry; particular churches choose their own ministers; the Bible alone be accepted as a "sure guide to heaven"; Christians cultivate a spirit of mutual forbearance; people who might have wished to make the Springfield Presbytery their king look to Jesus instead; the Synod of Kentucky suspend all persons suspected of heresy; people who accused them of dividing the church examine the matter more carefully and that their "sister bodies read their Bibles carefully, that they may see their fate there determined and prepare for death." They explained that they had taken this action from the conviction that Christians were divided because of the adoption of human creeds and forms of government.

Division was a blot upon the cause of Jesus that prevented sinners from coming to the Lord.

The document breathes a spirit of millennial expectation. The signers called for all Christians to join them in crying to God to "remove the obstacles which stand in the way of his work, and give him no rest till he make Jerusalem a praise in the earth." They expressed the fond hope that the Great Revival in the West would terminate in the universal spread of the gospel and the unity of the church. Though dissolving their presbytery, they did announce at the end of the document that they would continue to preach, to assist in ordaining ministers, and to strengthen each other in the work of ministry. Shortly after signing the document, McNemar and John Dunlavy accepted the testimony of the SHAKERS that the millennium had begun in the life of Mother Ann Lee. In fact, of the original six, only Stone and one other, David, remained identified with the Christian Church.

See also article on CAMPBELLITE TRADITION.

D. NEWELL WILLIAMS
BRITE DIVINITY SCHOOL

STEARNS, SHUBAL (1706-1771), founding pastor of the mother church of Southern Baptist revivalism, was born in Boston MA and reared there and in Tolland CT. His career reminds us that the evangelical and emotional religion with which the South has long been closely identified was, for the most part, brought in from outside. For many years a Congregationalist, he was inspired to greater spiritual devotion in 1745 through the preaching of GEORGE WHITEFIELD. Along with other sympathizers of the GREAT AWAKENING, Stearns soon abandoned Congregationalism and formed a "Separate" church.

Following a split in the Separate church over infant baptism in 1751, Stearns was ordained a Baptist minister and served as pastor of a "Separate Baptist" church, which he had recently orga-

nized. In 1754 he moved to Virginia, resided briefly before moving to a place in Guilford County NC called SANDY CREEK, a more promising field for his evangelistic efforts. At Sandy Creek, with the help of Daniel Marshall (Stearns's brother-in-law), he established the Sandy Creek Baptist Church in 1755.

Proclaiming a modified Calvinistic theology and the need for everyone to have an emotional experience of conversion, the SEPARATE BAPTISTS of Sandy Creek evangelized the backcountry of the Carolinas, Virginia, and Georgia. Seven Separate Baptist churches of North Carolina and Virginia, led by Stearns, formed the Sandy Creek Baptist Association in 1760. Stearns's church at Sandy Creek grew to over 600 members before it was disrupted in 1771 as a result of the Regulator movement.

See also article on SOUTHERN BAPTIST CONVENTION.

Bibliography. Morgan Edwards, "Materials Towards a History of the Baptists in the Provinces of Maryland, Virginia, North Carolina, South Carolina, and Georgia" (original manuscript in the Furman University Library); Clarence C. Goen, *Revivalism and Separatism in New England, 1740-1800*; David T. Morgan, "The Great Awakening in North Carolina, 1740-1775: The Baptist Phase," *North Carolina Historical Review* 45 (July 1968): 264-83.

DAVID T. MORGAN
UNIVERSITY OF MONTEVALLO

STEWARD. An officer of a local Methodist congregation who has the responsibility of leading the congregation in the meeting of its obligations, primarily financial, to the pastor and to the larger church. Persons are chosen for this position because of their interest in, and concern for, the affairs of the church and because of their potential for supporting the program of the church financially. Stewards are elected annually by the quarterly conference meeting under the presidency of the district superintendent and following the guidelines in the *Discipline.*

Stewards are often highly visible since they frequently usher, take up the offering, and lead the congregation in prayer.

These officers are the chief supporters of the local pastor and the connecting links between the local congregation and the larger church in such matters as changes in pastoral leadership.

Stewards are organized into boards that meet regularly to plan the programs of the local congregation within the guidelines adopted by the General Conference.

In recent years the term "steward," which was first used by John Wesley, has virtually disappeared from the *Discipline* of the United Methodist Church, but continues to be used, at least informally, within most of Methodism.

JOSEPH MITCHELL
TROY STATE UNIVERSITY

STONE, BARTON WARREN (1772-1844), a multidenominational founder, was born in Port Tobacco MD. A descendant of the first Protestant governor of Maryland, he spent his early years there and in Virginia. Though he grew up in the Church of England, he professed to be "converted" under Presbyterian preaching while a student at David Caldwell's Academy in Guilford County NC. In 1798 he became pastor of the Presbyterian churches at CANE RIDGE and Concord KY where he was active in promoting the GREAT REVIVAL in the West (1787-1805).

In 1803 he and four other promoters of the Revival withdrew from the jurisdiction of the Synod of Kentucky rather than face censure for rejecting the doctrine of election. Taking the name Springfield Presbytery from a town in southern Ohio where they had met, they published an apology that called for the rejection of creeds as tests of fellowship. In 1804, having come to believe that denominational names and institutions were a hindrance to Christian union, they adopted the name *Christian* and dissolved their presbytery. Within a year, two of the original members of the Springfield Presbytery became SHAKERS; in 1811, another two returned to the Presbyterians. Thus Stone assumed sole leadership of the Christians.

In the 1830s he guided the majority of the group into union with the Disciples led by Thomas and ALEXANDER CAMPBELL. Stone's theological position was deeply influenced by Enlightenment thought, which left no place for paradox. He believed the doctrine of predestination contradicted the gospel of God's love for sinners. He also believed that the orthodox doctrines of the trinity and the atonement contained serious contradictions. Stone articulated his theology at length in *An Address to the Christian Churches in Kentucky, Tennessee and Ohio on Several Important Doctrines of Religion* (1821). He is claimed as a founding figure by the CHRISTIAN CHURCH (DISCIPLES OF CHRIST), the CHURCHES OF CHRIST, the CHRISTIAN CHURCHES AND CHURCHES OF CHRIST, and the UNITED CHURCH OF CHRIST.

See also article on CAMPBELLITE TRADITION.

D. NEWELL WILLIAMS
BRITE DIVINITY SCHOOL

STUDENT MINISTRIES: *See* CAMPUS MINISTRY.

SUFFRAGAN. In the Episcopal Church this refers to a bishop who assists the diocesan bishop in the performance of episcopal and administrative duties; but unlike a bishop coadjutor, a suffragan does not automatically succeed the diocesan bishop at his death or resignation. A suffragan bishop is elected by the diocese at the request of the diocesan bishop and with the approval of the General Convention. He holds his position in the diocese until death or resignation, although he may accept election as the bishop coadjutor, the successor to his own diocesan bishop, or to a position in another diocese.

No diocese may have more than two suffragan bishops at one time, except with the approval of the General Convention. A diocesan bishop may, however, obtain from his diocese the right to appoint an assistant bishop from among those bishops in the Church who by canon are eligible for such an appointment.

Although the duties of an assistant bishop may be identical to those of a suffragan bishop, the former's term of office expires with the termination of the appointing bishop's jurisdiction. (In the Roman Catholic Church, a bishop who assists a diocesan bishop is usually called an auxiliary bishop.)

HERBERT S. WENTZ
UNIVERSITY OF THE SOUTH

SUMMER ASSEMBLIES: *See* LAKE JUNALUSKA; MONTREAT NC; RIDGECREST NC.

SUPERINTENDENT. An ordained elder of a Methodist church who has been appointed by a bishop to administer the affairs of the denomination in a district, such as officer is referred to as a "District Superintendent" (or D.S.). Superintendents serve as pastors to the local pastors within their district and as the bishop's representatives in all matters regarding the local congregation's connection to the denomination.

They are usually appointed from among the more experienced elders in an Annual Conference and are limited by the *Discipline* to terms of no more than six years in length.

Superintendents make at least annual visits to the local churches within their districts to preach and preside over business meetings, at which the officers of the local congregation are elected and at which the congregation voices its support of the denomination's program by voting on the apportionments.

One of the most important responsibilities of superintendents is assisting in the appointment of pastors to the congregations under his (or her) care. In carrying out this duty the superintendents consult with pastors, lay representatives of the local churches, and other superintendents, and advise the bishop, who has final responsibility for such appointments.

Superintendents are often elected to Jurisdictional and General Conferences and thus share in the shaping of the church's national program and in the election of bishops. "Superintendent" replaced the older Methodist term, "presiding elder," in the 20th century.

JOSEPH MITCHELL
TROY STATE UNIVERSITY

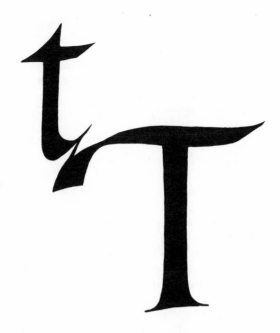

TANT, FANNING YATER (1908-),
CHURCHES OF CHRIST editor and evange-
list, was born in Macon TN, and at pres-
ent resides in Birmingham AL. Son of a
well-known Texas preacher, J. D. Tant, he
was baptized by his father in 1919. He
began preaching among Churches of
Christ in 1926. He began his education at
David Lipscomb College and continued at
the University of Louisville, Louisville
Presbyterian Theological Seminary,
Northwestern University, University of
Colorado, University of Oklahoma, and
Stephen F. Austin University.

He has preached for churches in
Louisville, Denver, Chicago, Oklahoma
City, and Birmingham, and has been in
great demand as an evangelist throughout
his preaching career. He is best known,
however, for his editorship of the *Gospel
Guardian* (1949-1971) and *Vanguard*
(1975-). Tant sees himself as among the
"conservative brethren." He wrote in the
Gospel Guardian on 19 May 1949: "The
development of institutionalism, centralized elderships, doctrinal weaknesses in
the missionary situations are but a few of
the more apparent issues crying for correction." The first issue of *Vanguard* (9
January 1975) stated: "For twenty-five
years the Lord's faithful disciples have
been fighting a sort of 'rear-guard' action
against the onrushing tides of liberalism
and institutionalism."

He is the author of two books, *J. D.
Tant: Texas Preacher* and *Old Testament
History*. He debated the scripturalness of
congregational cooperation on two different occasions. For five years he was the
director of the Bible chair at Stephen F.
Austin University.

See also article on RELIGIOUS PRESS.

ROBERT E. HOOPER
DAVID LIPSCOMB COLLEGE

TANT, J. D. (1861-1941), famous
CHURCHES OF CHRIST preacher, was born
in Paulding County GA. Having lost all
its possessions during the Civil War,
the William Tant family moved to Texas
in 1876. Reared a Methodist, Tant became
a Methodist preacher at the age of 14. In
Texas he attended school for four years,
then became a circuit rider in north Texas.
His religious beliefs were disturbed in
1881 by two "Campbellite" preachers.
Even though he began preaching among
Churches of Christ, he was not convinced
of a need for rebaptism until 1885.
Throughout his preaching career, he sup-

ported himself, usually by farming. Tant was a frontier preacher. Whether preaching or debating, his method was attack. During his lifetime he engaged in more than 200 debates, most often with Baptists.

From his two marriages, 10 children were born, Fanning Yater being the best known. Making Hamilton TX home for 15 years, the family began moving to make a living; they lived variously in New Mexico, Arkansas, Tennessee, and Mississippi. Much of the farm work was left to Nannie while Tant preached and debated.

Having fought the missionary society movement and the instrument in worship for many years, his last years were filled with warnings: "Brethren, we are drifting." Along with AUSTIN MCGARY, editor of the *Firm Foundation*, Tant represents the frontier approach to religion prevalent in late nineteenth-century Texas.

See also article on DEBATES, INTERDENOMINATIONAL.

Bibliography. Fanning Yater Tant, *J. D. Tant—Texas Preacher.*

ROBERT E. HOOPER
DAVID LIPSCOMB COLLEGE

TATE, ALLEN (1899-1979), novelist, essayist, and critic, was born in Winchester KY. He was a paradoxical figure: the Southerner who lived much of his life in the North, the Protestant who converted to Roman Catholicism, and the classicist who understood modern poetry, of which he produced stunning examples himself.

Early in his life he became spokesman for the Southern heritage that was his by birthright and commitment. While still a student at Vanderbilt University, he associated with a group known as the Fugitives, who sought to understand cultural problems by reference to Southern history and experience. Long before the environmental cause emerged, they recognized the threat of an industrialized, plastic age and mourned the forsaking of the agrarian life. It was not that they all wanted to be farmers, but that they sought return to values that they identified with an earlier

time when culture was largely agrarian. Accordingly, they rejected the South's culture of recent past. In 1930 a few of the group (Tate being one), together with other sympathetic writers, announced their position in a manifesto, *I'll Take My Stand*, a collection of essays commending virtues of the tradition. What they recommended for the South, they recommended for all.

Essentially Tate regarded the stance as classical rather than romantic, a position typified in the mythical Aeneas, who fled the wreckage of Troy and sought to fulfill his destiny by founding a new nation oriented to values that Tate thought identical to those of the antebellum South. Tate argued that by choosing industrialism, America had capitulated to machines, thereby insuring the decay of intellectual thought. Concerned with humanity's ends and purposes, he saw modern society as a world of wonders, but as lost nevertheless because values were lost. Devoid of a sense of sin, humanity suffers from an illness more easily deplored than remedied. Rejecting the effort of the new humanists to set up an ethic divorced from tradition and religion, Tate constantly opted for the traditional and conservative.

His perspective is clearly set forth in his most famous poem, "Ode to the Confederate Dead," in which a man stands at the gate of a Confederate cemetery and understands that those who lie there had found a meaning in life that he is powerless to achieve, although he longs for the kind of certainty they had. The nostalgia for that certainty and the suggestion that it can be found in religion are recurrent motifs in Tate's work.

Professionally he taught at Southwestern College in Memphis, North Carolina Woman's College, New York University, and for 17 years at the University of Minnesota. In addition, he lectured widely at home and abroad, edited the *Sewanee Review* for a season (1944-1946), and for several years was poet in residence at Princeton University. He was one of the group of literary figures who worked for the release of Ezra Pound from the mental institution where he had been committed after his pro-Axis broadcasts during World War II.

See also article on LITERATURE AND RELIGION.

Bibliography. Radcliffe Squires, *Allen Tate: A Literary Biography*; Allen Tate, *Collected Poems, 1919-1976.*

STUART C. HENRY
DUKE UNIVERSITY

TELEVISION MINISTRIES: *See* ELECTRONIC CHURCH.

TEMPERANCE.

The temperance movement began in the United States in 1784 when Dr. Benjamin Rush warned that distilled liquor could harm health. The Philadelphia physician advocated weak beer as a substitute for rum, brandy, gin, and whiskey. While Rush's medical students carried his plea across the country, most Americans continued to drink alcoholic beverages, especially whiskey. Southerners liked peach brandy; one devout Georgia Methodist said his health required at least a quart a day.

Around 1810 New England ministers discovered that a moral argument against liquor had wide appeal. In all regions revivalists required converts to evangelical Christianity to offer visible proof of salvation by giving up the "demon rum." Between 1825 and 1840 alcohol consumption plummeted. The South was less committed to this early temperance movement than New England, perhaps because Southerners were suspicious of "Yankee reformers" who often denounced both liquor and slavery. Southern leaders of the cause included Virginia planter John Cocke, Georgia Baptist minister Adiel Sherwood, and Alabama planter James Birney, later an abolitionist.

After 1840 mainline Protestant churches required members to pledge abstinence from all alcoholic beverages, and grape juice replaced communion wine. The 1840s also witnessed the formation of voluntary associations, such as the Knights of Good Templars, Sons of Temperance, and Rechabites, which brought nondrinkers together for social purposes. The most important new group was the Washingtonians, an organization of self-declared reclaimed alcoholics who used Alcoholics Anonymous-type fellowship to reinforce abstinence.

By the 1850s the temperance movement, as leaders called their intemperate antiliquor crusade, shifted from using moral suasion to coax the individual to give up drink for righteousness' sake to using the law to ban the sale of alcohol. Several Northern states adopted statewide or local-option PROHIBITION, but in the South, only Delaware had a state prohibition law, and it was soon repealed. In Georgia B. H. Overby, a prohibitionist candidate for governor in 1855, received only six percent of the vote.

The Civil War led the federal government to tax distilled liquor for the first time since the War of 1812. Some prohibitionists opposed the tax as government participation in sin; others favored it as an effective way to raise the price of liquor and reduce consumption. Brewers did not oppose a tax on whiskey, and after the war brewers became powerful as beer-drinking immigrant factory workers filled the nation's cities. In the South where long, hot summers made brewing unprofitable, whiskey predominated, but the federal excise was not always paid.

By 1900 the WOMAN'S CHRISTIAN TEMPERANCE UNION and Anti-Saloon League had gained statewide or local-option laws in most states, and more than half the country was legally dry. However, prohibitionists realized that a single wet city, county, or state filtered liquor into surrounding dry territory. Prohibitionists pushed for a federal constitutional amendment to ban alcoholic beverages. In 1919 they succeeded through the passage of the EIGHTEENTH AMENDMENT, in part because of antiliquor teachers and propaganda in the public schools, and partly because of claims that prohibition would end crime, poverty, and prostitution. Nor did the connection between saloons and corrupt political machines help the cause of liquor. But the main reason prohibition came was that World War I destroyed the credibility of the only effective opponents, the brewers, virtually all of them of German origin.

Throughout its history, the temperance movement has an especial appeal to women, who as wives and daughters were often victims of crime, poverty, and domestic violence perpetrated by drunken husbands and fathers. As early as the 1830s women were a majority of the members of temperance societies, and the tide of prohibition at the end of the century was linked closely to the power of the WCTU, rising female political lobbying and participation, and the view of many progressives that prohibition and women's rights were twin reforms.

Prohibition reduced but did not end alcohol consumption, which during the 1920s became associated with organized crime. After repeal in 1933, when the issue was left to state control, prohibition waned, even in the South. In 1966 Mississippi became the last state to give up statewide prohibition; by the 1970s Texas allowed bars to sell liquor by the drink; and in the early 1980s Georgia permitted Sunday sales in hotels and restaurants. Yet the century-old connection between temperance and evangelical religion remained strong. Not only did electronic revivalists tell viewers that drink was the devil's brew, but in Tennessee only a handful of counties were legally wet. In 1982 among the remaining dry counties in the state was the one containing Lynchburg, home of a well-known liquor.

Bibliography. Norman H. Clark, *Deliver Us from Evil*; John A. Krout, *The Origins of Prohibition*; C. C. Pearson and J. Edwin Hendricks, *Liquor and Anti-Liquor in Virginia*; W. J. Rorabaugh, *The Alcoholic Republic*; H. A. Scomp, *King Alcohol in the Realm of King Cotton*; Ian R. Tyrrell, *Sobering Up*.

W. J. RORABAUGH
UNIVERSITY OF WASHINGTON

TEMPLIN, TERAH (1742-1818), pioneer Presbyterian minister in Kentucky, was born in Bedford County VA. He studied theology under DAVID RICE and at Liberty Hall Academy after the death of his fiancée. Licensed as an evangelist by Hanover Presbytery in 1780, he traveled into the Bluegrass area and preached several times. His father John moved permanently to Danville in 1781, and his son took residence with him.

Templin helped form the first Presbyterian congregations in the area, serving with his former teacher David Rice. Templin received final ordination (1785) as the first act in the forming of Transylvania Presbytery, which he helped lead. He served churches in Jefferson County (Beargrass and Pennsylvania Run), Nelson County (Bardstown), and Washington County (Springfield). He moved in 1799 to Livingston County in western Kentucky as first pastor of the Livingston and Donaldson churches. He participated in the forming of the Cumberland Presbytery in that area in 1803, and his absence from subsequent meetings of the judicatory may have helped precipitate the crisis that led finally to the formation of the CUMBERLAND PRESBYTERIAN CHURCH. He was asked to moderate the first meeting of Muhlenburg Presbytery (1810), which contained Synod of Kentucky "loyalists." Templin died near Bardstown, having remained a bachelor, a rare occurrence for Presbyterian ministers in the early nineteenth century.

LOUIS B. WEEKS
LOUISVILLE PRESBYTERIAN SEMINARY

TENNESSEE. Early in its history, Tennessee became an important center of denominational headquarters and boards. The Southern Methodist Church located its publishing house in NASHVILLE in 1858, and the city is now the home of several agencies of the United Methodist Church, including the United Methodist Publishing House, the Board of Education and Ministry, and the Board of Discipleship. Nashville also houses the Executive Offices of the Southern Baptist Convention, along with that church's Sunday School Board, Education Commission, and other major agencies. The city has long been a center of religious education.

Among the accredited four-year colleges in Nashville in 1980 were: Belmont College (Baptist), Scarritt College for Christian Workers (Methodist), Trevecca Nazarene College (Nazarene), and David Lipscomb College (Churches of Christ). Vanderbilt University was the pride of Southern Methodism until a majority of the trustees, over the protest of the bishops, dissolved the university's ties with the church in 1914, resulting in a controversial court case.

Not only has Tennessee been important in the history of the major Southern churches, it has also been the most prolific breeding ground for new sects in the United States. A recent survey of sects in the United States indicated that Tennessee was the headquarters of more sects per million inhabitants than any other state in the country. The diversity of religion is indicated by a listing of the other major colleges in the state with historical religious ties: Carson-Newman and Union (Southern Baptist); Lambuth and Tennessee Wesleyan (United Methodist); the University of the South (Episcopal); King College and Southwestern at Memphis (Presbyterian in the United States); Knoxville, Maryville, and Tusculum (United Presbyterian Church in the United States of America); Bethel (Cumberland Presbyterian); (Reformed Presbyterian); Lane (Christian Methodist Episcopal); LeMoyne-Owen (United Church of Christ and Tennessee Baptist Missionary and Educational Convention); Christian Brothers (Roman Catholic); Lee (Church of God, Cleveland, Tennessee); Milligan (Christian Church); Southern Missionary (Seventh-day Adventist); Tennessee Temple (Independent Baptist); and Bryan College (Fundamentalist). Numerous other junior colleges and unaccredited schools represent such churches as the Free Will Baptists, the Church of God of Prophecy, and the United Christian Church and Ministerial Association.

The times were not auspicious for the future of religion when the first Scotch-Irish Presbyterian ministers arrived in Tennessee just before the American Revolution. A few years later, in 1790, the first national census listed only five percent of the nation's population as church members. Few travelers into the West failed to comment on the moral and spiritual backwardness of the area. The moral laxity of the hardy Celtic and English frontier settlers in East Tennessee shocked and disturbed the early evangelists in the area. One Tennessee minister reported finding his entire congregation so drunk they could not listen to him; another told of repeated encounters with "refugees from justice"; gambling, horse-racing, fighting, and other "popular sins" were constant targets of frontier preaching.

Perhaps the greatest obstacle to establishing organized religion in early Tennessee was the physical isolation of the settlers. Churches were difficult to sustain among the scattered frontiersmen, and few ministers were eager to venture into the wilderness where dangers were real and support uncertain.

Early Tennesseeans also imbibed of the rationalism of their age. The state was settled during the euphoric days of the Revolution and was admitted to the union in 1796, only seven years after ratification of the constitution. Many of the new nation's intellectuals had replaced faith in a personal Christian God with a respect for reason and an adoration of Nature and Nature's God. Rationalism combined with the dissatisfaction of the "dissenting" sects to bring an end to established religion in the South by the end of the Revolution. The Tennessee Constitution was drafted in 1796 when the disestablishment debate was still fresh, and that document not only forbade religious establishment, but also provided that "no minister of the gospel or priest" could be elected to the legislature of the state, a ban that remained in force until struck down by the state Supreme Court in 1978.

In the midst of this hostile environment, however, religion made modest headway in Tennessee's earliest history. Small numbers of church members, infrequent occasions for formal worship, and the apparent immorality on the frontier obscured the residual Christian faith that most of the settlers brought with them across the mountains. Organized religion came close on the heels of the first settlers into the Southwest Territory in the 1770s. From the earliest days, frequent appeals were sent back to the East for ministerial help. In a few instances, entire congregations in North Carolina moved west to Tennessee.

Excluding the likely ministrations of Catholic priests in the company of the De Soto expedition and early French traders, and an Anglican chaplain who accompanied William Byrd into the territory, the first ministers to hold services in Tennessee were Presbyterians. The early religious history of the state was dominated by the three great evangelical churches of the frontier: Presbyterian, Baptist, and Methodist. Each of these churches expanded rapidly in early Tennessee history, and the Methodists became particularly adept at bringing religion to the settlers who fanned out across the state in the antebellum period.

A few hardy and independent Scotch-Irish Presbyterian ministers followed their countrymen down the valleys of the Appalachians into Tennessee in the last quarter of the 19th century. As early as 1773 at least two Presbyterian congregations had been formed, and in answer to a request from 130 families, Charles Cummings, the first settled minister in southwest Virginia, visited Tennessee to preach. Another Presbyterian, Samuel Doak, became the first minister to settle permanently in the territory in October 1777. Educated at Princeton and for a time a member of the faculty of Hampden-Sydney College, Doak followed a pattern typical of Presbyterian clergymen in the South when in 1785 he established Martin Academy (later Washington College) in Washington County. The school was reputed to be the first educational institu-

tion west of the mountains. Other ministers soon joined Doak, and by the time Tennessee became a state in 1796, 27 congregations had been established stretching as far west as Nashville. The Presbyterian ministers brought with them a respect for education and refinement that earned them a lasting reputation as the cultural leaders of the state.

Baptists were the second important religious group in the early history of Tennessee. Two Baptist congregations were established in the territory as early as 1765, but they did not survive the Indian wars that preceded the Revolution. Among the earliest permanent settlers in the Southwest Territory, however, were Separate Baptists from North Carolina. In 1779 a congregation of North Carolina Baptists migrated along with its minister, Tidence Lane, and built the Buffalo Ridge Church near Boone's Creek, probably the first permanent Baptist church in the territory. In 1781 the Holston Association began meeting as a branch of the Sandy Creek Association of North Carolina, and in 1786 it became an independent association with seven member churches. By the time Tennessee was admitted to statehood a second association had been established in the central part of the state.

Early Tennessee Baptists brought with them a missionary zeal inherited from their Separate Baptist heritage in the GREAT AWAKENING. In addition, the Baptist belief in independence was well suited to frontier conditions. Most helpful to early Baptist expansion was the system by which each congregation "called" its own minister, generally one of the more energetic and devoted local members. These innovative and self-supporting ministers (early Tennessee Baptists generally disapproved of "hireling" clergymen) placed the church on a firm footing by the time of statehood.

The only other religious body to play a significant role in the early history of the Southwest Territory was the Methodist Episcopal Church. Although the church was not formally founded until the famous Christmas Conference in 1784, Methodist missionaries had been active in forming societies in America since 1766. Most Methodist work had been along the coast, but by 1783 the Holston Conference of Methodist societies had been formed. Jeremiah Lambert became the first traveling preacher in the territory. In 1788, Bishop FRANCIS ASBURY made his first trip into the territory, meticulously recording his impressions of the religious life of the area and laying plans for the expansion of the church.

The Methodist circuit riders who worked in the territory before 1796 statehood made slow progress, although in 1790 the Methodists erected in Nashville the first stone meetinghouse in the territory. In 1796 the church still counted only about 550 members in Tennessee. But the Methodists were poised for expansion at the turn of the century. The church had completed a period of reorganization after its break from Anglicanism, had an aggressive and dedicated leader in Bishop Asbury, had firmly established the circuit-rider system that made possible the supply of ministers to widely scattered congregations, and espoused an Arminian theology that seemed perfectly suited to the intellectual climate of the frontier.

As settlers poured into Tennessee in the wake of statehood, the basic religious structure of the state was shaken and reformed by the eruption of the GREAT REVIVAL in the West. The revival was triggered by the fervent preaching of Presbyterian JAMES MCGREADY who moved to Logan County KY in 1796. In 1799 McGready's churches began to experience fervent revival and a similar stirring broke out in the Presbyterian congregation of William McGee in Sumner County TN. In 1800, William McGee and his brother John (who was a Methodist minister) visited and participated in a meeting held at one of McGready's congregations. By the fall of 1800, the full revival fervor had been transferred to Tennessee and spread rapidly through the Presbyterian and Methodist churches of the state. In 1801, in an ecumenical fervor that was short-lived, the Baptists joined with the other two churches and revival fires swept across the state. Religious meetings frequently attracted 5,000 listeners.

Tennessee revivals were accompanied by all of the physical manifestations that came to be known as "acrobatic Christianity" in the East. Perhaps the most curious "exercise" was the "jerks." LORENZO DOW, one of the most famous itinerant evangelists on the frontier, recorded his impressions of the "jerks" while on a tour of East Tennessee in 1801: "I spoke in Knoxville to hundreds more than could get into the courthouse, the Governor being present: about one hundred and fifty appeared to have jerking exercises.... I have seen Presbyterians, Methodists, Quakers, Baptists, Church of England, and Independents, exercised with the *jerks*; Gentleman and Lady, black and white, the aged and the young, rich and poor, . . . from which I infer . . . that it is no trifling matter. . . . I passed by a meeting-house where I observed the undergrowth had been cut up for a camp meeting, and from fifty to one hundred saplings, left breast high . . . and left for the people to jerk by.... I went over the ground . . . and found where the people had laid hold of them and jerked so powerfully, that they had kicked up the earth as a horse stamping flies."

Perhaps the most important religious innovation connected with the revival was the CAMP MEETING. The first camp meeting in Tennessee was apparently held in August 1800 under the leadership of John McGee, a Smith County Methodist known as "the father of camp meetings in America." The early camp meetings were spontaneous affairs, but within a few years they became regularized. Permanent campgrounds were built, though many still camped in tents and wagons, and a more formal routine was followed. The meetings also became less ecumenical. First the Baptists cooled because of theological reservations and sectarian inhibitions; by the end of the first decade of the 19th century, Presbyterians began to question the emotional excesses and the leadership of "lay" ministers often associated with the meetings.

Of the three denominations present in the state at the outbreak of the revival, the Methodists clearly profited most from the new religious enthusiasm. Camp meeting techniques—including emotional appeals to come to the mourner's bench—meshed well with Methodist Arminianism. The revival combined with the efficient circuit-rider and class-meeting systems to greatly expand the influence of Methodism. In 1800, WILLIAM MCKENDREE, a Virginia convert to Methodism, came to Tennessee as "presiding elder" over the work in the West. In 1808, McKendree became the first American-born bishop appointed in the young church's history. He continued to live in Nashville and wielded a tremendous influence on Tennessee Methodism until his death in 1835. By 1800 the Methodist church claimed over 10,000 members in the state and had become the largest religious body in the state. In 1824 the state was divided into two conferences, Holston and Tennessee, and in 1840 the Memphis Conference was added. By 1830 the Tennessee Methodist church counted 35,000 members and far outnumbered its nearest competitor.

When the great revival began in Tennessee the Baptists were reluctant participants. Within a few years most Baptists had abandoned the camp meeting, with its alleged excesses, in favor of PROTRACTED MEETINGS. More important in retarding Baptist growth in the first half of the 19th century, however, were a series of internal struggles within the denomination. Independent in the extreme, Tennessee Baptists proved to be among the most obstinate critics of an emerging national denominational consciousness that found institutional expression in the formation of the General Missionary Convention in 1814. Although pioneer missionary Luther Rice visited Tennessee several times in the years after 1815, cooperative

mission work was seriously retarded in the state by antimission preachers, the most famous of whom was Daniel Parker. Until 1821 Parker preached at the New Hopewell Church in Middle Tennessee. Throughout the 1820s and 1830s the antimission controversy plagued Tennessee; many new Primitive Baptist associations were formed and probably a majority of the state associations tried to take a neutral position in the controversy. In 1840 the West Tennessee Association included the following statement in its articles of belief: "We believe, from experience, the Missionary, Bible, Temperance, Tract, and Masonic Societies, S. S. Unions and theological seminaries to make preachers for the Lord, are destructive to the peace and fellowship of the baptist church. . . . But all almsdeeds any member is at liberty to perform; *Provided* he does not let his *left hand* know what his *right* doeth." In 1833 the Tennessee Baptist Convention was organized by supporters of missions, but it remained weak and disbanded in 1842. Between 1842 and 1874 Baptist churches in the state met in their sectional conventions and went through a period of internal strife described as "the darkest in Tennessee Baptist history."

A second major controversy racked Tennessee Baptists in the 1840s, centering around the personality and teaching of James R. Graves who became editor of the *Tennessee Baptist* in 1847. Graves soon made the paper a stronghold for "Landmarkism," a doctrine that claimed the historical continuity of Baptist churches from Bible times and emphasized the independence of local churches. Graves and Landmarkism were bitterly opposed by respected Nashville minister R. B. C. Howell, but Landmarkism had a powerful conservative influence on the churches of Tennessee and elsewhere in the South.

In spite of this internal strife, and to some degree aided by the extreme independence of the local churches, Tennessee Baptists increased in numbers dramatically during the antebellum years, though not at the same rate as the Methodists. In 1790 Baptists had one association, 18 churches, 21 preachers, and 889 members in the state. By 1814 those numbers had increased to seven associations, 174 churches, 133 preachers, and 12,194 members. By 1845 Tennessee Baptists numbered 32,159; in 1860 the churches reported 46,564 members.

The third major denomination in Tennessee at the time of the great revival, the Presbyterians, suffered a series of crippling setbacks in the years before the Civil War. Presbyterian ministers remained important to the educational system of the state, but the church's emphasis on ministerial training proved to be a hindrance to expansion. When some Presbyterian leaders began to criticize camp-meeting revivalism in the second decade of the 19th century, open dissension broke out in the church. The major issues were the revival's softening impact on Presbyterian Calvinism and a growing disregard of the traditional educational requirements for ministerial ordination. Accused of wrongdoing on both of the questions, in 1814 the Cumberland Presbytery in West Tennessee became independent, and in 1829 the CUMBERLAND PRESBYTERIAN CHURCH was formed. That body quickly became the largest Presbyterian body in the state. In 1830 the *Presbyterian Advocate* reported that the Presbyterian church in Tennessee had only 97 churches, 76 ministers, and 7,374 members.

Presbyterian development was hindered further by continued doctrinal strife after the Cumberland schism. Southern Presbyterians remained strict Calvinists and, as a result of growing theological liberalism and antislavery sentiment in Northern Presbyterianism, a national division into OLD SCHOOL and NEW SCHOOL churches occurred in 1838. Presbyterian churches in Middle and West Tennessee were overwhelmingly loyal to the Old School General Assembly, but many of the churches in East Tennessee revealed an antislavery disposition by joining the New School. The coming of the Civil War brought a complicated and general reshuffling of the churches. In 1858, the Southern New School synods, including Holston Presbytery in Tennessee, withdrew from that church because of its increasingly radical abolitionism and formed the United Synod of the Presbyterian Church in the United States of America. In 1861, the Old School church divided along sectional lines, resulting in the formation of the Presbyterian Church in the Confederate States. The Confederate church courted the United Synod Presbyterians in the South during the war years, and in 1864 a union was negotiated. Outside of Tennessee this merger was completed with little incident, but in East Tennessee confusion and strong passion continued well into the Reconstruction period. Union sympathizers in East Tennessee denounced the union with the Confederate church and voted to unite with the General Assembly of the Presbyterian Church in the United States of America (New School). The struggle for local churches was bitter and sometimes violent; the disposition of numerous church buildings was decided by the courts. The conflicting claims of the two groups made the statistics of the period unreliable, but the churches of East Tennessee were probably divided about equally. One presbytery report sadly noted: "Sad division and bitter alienations among God's people furnish the world an opportunity of taunting and reproaching by saying 'see how these Christians hate one another.'" In 1861 the Southern Presbyterians claimed only about 150 churches in Tennessee with around 8,500 members; perhaps 50 congregations were affiliated with the Northern church. The 1860 census of "church accommodations" placed the Presbyterian church fourth in the state with 78,655 seats, far behind the Methodists with a reported 288,460 and surpassed also by the Baptists and the Cumberland Presbyterians.

These were years of bitter sectarian competition in Tennessee, marked by vituperative religious journalism and public debate. The most noted Methodist antagonist was "Parson" William Brownlow of Knoxville who was editor of the *Knoxville Whig*, and in 1865 was elected Republican governor of Tennessee. Brownlow's Baptist counterpart was JAMES R. GRAVES, who in a series of books, as well as through the columns of the *Tennessee Baptist*, regularly scorned Methodism, Presbyterianism, and the "Campbellites." The other two major participants in this rough and tumble struggle for the religious loyalty of antebellum Tennesseeans were the Cumberland Presbyterians and the DISCIPLES OF CHRIST. Both of these new churches were born amidst the revival fervor of the early nineteenth century and both spread rapidly in Tennessee.

The Cumberland Presbyterian schism had begun in 1805 when the Synod of Kentucky questioned the laxity of the Cumberland Presbytery, including James McGready, in the appointment of new ministers. After several abortive attempts at compromise, a dissident group led by minister Finis Ewing formed an independent Presbytery in 1811 and the General Assembly of the Cumberland Presbyterian church in 1825. The Cumberland church was strongly revivalistic and experienced remarkable growth. Cumberland Presbyterians were particularly adept at capturing and establishing churches in rural areas. In 1861, about 35,000 of the Church's 100,000 members were in Tennessee.

The second important new church to enter Tennessee in the wake of the great revival was the Disciples of Christ. The Disciples, generally known at the congregational level as the Christian Church or the Church of Christ, grew out of the combined reform of Alexander Campbell of western Virginia and Barton Stone of Kentucky calling for the "restoration of New Testament Christianity." Both Campbell and Stone had been Presbyterian ministers, but more important in Tennessee was Campbell's association with

the Baptist cause. Campbell was a Baptist for a number of years before launching an independent movement, and from 1823 to 1830 edited an influential magazine named the *Christian Baptist*. When the Disciples became independent in the 1830s, they ravaged the Baptist church in Tennessee. The Disciples began in Tennessee as a result of the work of Philip Fall. Fall became pastor of the First Baptist Church in Nashville about 1830 and subsequently led nearly the entire congregation into the Christian church. The Concord Baptist Association was reduced from 49 churches with 3,399 members to 11 churches with 805 members as a result of Disciple defections. The dominant figure in early Disciples' history in Tennessee was TOLBERT FANNING who edited the *Christian Review* in the 1840s and the *Gospel Advocate* beginning in 1853. By 1860 the Disciples had an estimated membership of over 12,000 in the state in 106 churches.

While these five evangelical churches played dominant roles in the development of religion in antebellum Tennessee, other religious groups slowly established themselves in Tennessee. By 1860 Episcopalianism, Catholicism, Lutheranism, and Judaism had small memberships in the state.

It seems remarkable (in view of its long establishment in the colonial South) that the Episcopal Church did not have a congregation in Tennessee until 1827. But the Episcopal church had been crushed by the events of the Revolution and preoccupied with internal problems in the early nineteenth century. JAMES HERVEY OTEY, an extraordinarily able and zealous convert to Episcopalianism, established the first church in Franklin in 1827, St. Paul's. Otey was an energetic missionary, and within a few years, preaching to small groups in rented halls, he established Christ Church in Nashville, St. Peter's Church in Columbia, and Trinity Church in Clarksville. In 1834, Otey was consecrated as the first bishop of the Diocese of Tennessee at the age of 34. He was a vigorous bishop, but by 1860 the church still claimed only 26 parishes, 27 clergymen, and about 1,500 communicants in the state.

It is not clear when the first English-speaking Roman Catholics entered Tennessee, but it is likely that some began to spill over from the Catholic settlements in Kentucky around the turn of the century. Between 1808 and 1810 Father Stephen Badin, pioneer Kentucky priest, made four trips into Tennessee to visit Catholics. Kentucky priests continued to make occasional forays into Tennessee, and a church was apparently built in Nashville shortly after 1820, but it was not until 1830 that the first parish was formed in Nashville. In 1837 the Diocese of Tennessee was formed, and the Rt. Rev. Richard Pius Miles, a native American Catholic, was consecrated as the first bishop. Bishop Miles, known as the father of Catholicism in Tennessee, aggressively expanded the church in Tennessee. During the 1850s Catholics endured severe persecution with the outbreak of Know-Nothing enthusiasm. Violence erupted in Knoxville, Nashville, Murfreesboro, Franklin, Pulaski, and other places where Catholics had churches. According to one early estimate, the Nashville diocese still had only 11 churches in 1858.

A few German Lutherans entered Tennessee during the very early years of the state. The first church in the state was organized about 1795, but it was not until 1820 that the Tennessee Synod was formed. The church grew slowly because of its dependence on German immigrants and because of a lack of ministers. In 1860 it claimed only 18 churches, mostly in the eastern counties.

According to one contemporary estimate, the state of Tennessee had about 2,500 "Israelites" in 1858 and two synagogues, one in Nashville and the other in Memphis. The first Jewish settlers were apparently Germans, but the first rabbi in the state was Alexander Iser, a Russian Pole, and both of the early synagogues were Orthodox. In 1862, a Reform congregation was established in Nashville, and by 1867 synagogues had been established in Chattanooga and Knoxville.

Most of the Tennessee churches were active in social and benevolent causes in the antebellum period, supporting Bible, tract, and education societies, and fervently denouncing drinking, dancing, and other "popular sins." But one social issue dominated their attention and that of their fellow Southern Christians—the relationship of Christianity to slaveholding. In their earliest days, all three of the evangelical churches in Tennessee were antislavery. Prior to 1830 most Methodists and Baptists were nonslaveholding whites. The churches of East Tennessee remained moderately antislavery throughout the antebellum period. As attitudes hardened in the country after 1830, Tennessee churches followed sectional loyalties. Then the major evangelical churches divided, when most Tennessee churches remained loyal to the South.

To some extent, the peculiar geography of Tennessee, that set East Tennessee apart economically, socially, and politically, complicated the religious divisions within the state. As has already been noted, East Tennessee became a battleground for competing Presbyterian churches. However, most Tennessee churches supported the South prior to the war. When the Southern Baptist Convention was founded in 1845, Tennessee churches uniformly supported the new convention. When the Methodist Episcopal Church, South was formed in the same year, all of the conferences in Tennessee united with the Southern church. The Protestant Episcopal Church finally divided under the pressure of war in 1861, and the Tennessee Diocese joined the Confederate church without controversy (unity was restored in 1865). Both the Disciples of Christ and the Cumberland Presbyterian Church escaped division over slavery and Civil War. Most of the members of both churches were in the border states, and the leaders of each body tried to take moderate, non-divisive stands on slavery.

The conversion of blacks to Christianity took place in two spurts in Tennessee. The first, a result of the general evangelical fervor of the great revival and the antislavery sentiment that accompanied it, established the ascendancy of the Methodist and Baptist churches among blacks. In 1836, however, the Methodist Church still reported only 7,500 black members in the state. A second spurt of missionary activity among the slaves followed the establishment of the independent Southern churches. Self-conscious about their relation to slavery, Southern Baptists and Methodists made extraordinary efforts to convert slaves, and one historian has estimated that 90 percent of the black population of Tennessee was Christian by 1860.

Most blacks worshipped with and held membership in white congregations. Church record books generally noted "that there were colored members" and chronicled their achievements and trials alongside those of white members. Sometimes black members had separate Sunday schools; probably typical was the arrangement in the Christian Church in Nashville: "There are two colored Sunday Schools under the immediate control of colored members; but over which the Church exercises general superintendence." Independent black congregations were less common; however, a few black Baptist churches appear to have existed in the state before the Civil War. An ordained black minister named Nelson Merry presided over the large quasi-independent Spruce Street Colored Church in Nashville beginning in 1853. Methodist black "mission" churches operating under the supervision of a white church were common.

The Civil War had a devastating effect on organized religion throughout the South, but the impact was particularly severe in Tennessee because of the military activity within the state and because of the animosity between the Unionists in East Tennessee and the Confederate majority in the remainder of the state. The Methodists and Baptist churches lost perhaps a third of their members during the Civil War, and other churches suffered similar disruption. Church buildings were frequently seized by the government and used for military purposes. In the early years of the war clergymen who were Union sympathizers were persecuted in a variety of ways and some were expelled by their churches. By 1863 the tide was reversed in Tennessee, and with Union forces in control of the state, radicals like Brownlow called for retribution against the "rebel church." The only substantial pacifist statement by Tennessee ministers during the war was made by a group of Middle Tennessee Disciples led by DAVID LIPSCOMB and Tolbert Fanning. Their position was ignored by the civil authorities and apparently was not widely endorsed by the members of their own church in Tennessee.

The occupation of Tennessee by Federal troops also made the state a field for missionary work by the Northern churches. Led by Brownlow, the Northern Methodists established the Holston Conference in 1865 to compete with the Southern conference, and with the support of the army many Southern churches were seized. Secretary of War Edwin Stanton ordered all Baptist churches in the state turned over to the American Baptist Home Mission Society if the churches were not presided over by a "loyal" minister. Although President Johnson ordered all buildings returned in 1865, bitter disputes continued.

A third major development during the Civil War and Reconstruction was the separation of blacks into independent churches. Whether mostly at the instigation of the liberated freedmen or of Southern whites, blacks quickly moved out of the white churches. Immediately after the war, the two most successful black churches were the African Methodist Episcopal Church and the African Methodist Episcopal Zion Church that had been established in 1816 and 1821 in the North and began organizing churches in Tennessee before the war was over. Southern Methodists apparently gave encouragement to the new churches in order to diminish the influence of the Methodist Episcopal missionaries among the freedmen. By 1863 both of the black churches had sufficient members in Tennessee to organize a conference. Southern Methodists encouraged the segregation of their remaining blacks into separate churches, and in 1870, in a meeting in Jackson, those churches were organized as the Colored (now CHRISTIAN) METHODIST EPISCOPAL CHURCH OF AMERICA. The Methodist Episcopal Church also made vigorous efforts to attract blacks and probably 10 percent of that church's membership in the state was black at the end of Reconstruction.

The Baptist denomination gained increasing numbers of blacks after the Civil War, many attracted by the congregational independence of the Baptists. While segregation of the races into separate congregations went on rapidly after the Civil War, black Baptists retained an adjunct relationship to the regular associations until the 1890s. In 1865, the Primitive Baptists of the state separated their black congregations into the Negro Primitive Baptist Church, and in 1869 the Cumberland Presbyterians, in a meeting in Murfreesboro, organized the Colored (now SECOND CUMBERLAND PRESBYTERIAN CHURCH. Both Southern Presbyterians and Disciples of Christ continued to include their black congregations as a part of their denominations, but neither church had a significant number of black members.

Equally as important as the establishment of the black churches was the educational and benevolent work of the Northern churches. The Methodist Episcopal Church founded an educational institution in Nashville in 1866 that subsequently became Meharry Medical School. The Congregational Church, through the AMERICAN MISSIONARY ASSOCIATION, established schools for blacks throughout the South, including Fisk in

Nashville and LeMoyne in Memphis. Schools were also operated in Tennessee by the Northern Baptists and the Presbyterian Church in the United States of America.

The dominant white evangelical churches in Tennessee went through a generation of rebuilding in the wake of the Civil War. The Baptist State Convention was finally organized in 1874, and in 1889 the *Baptist and Reflector* became its official organ. The Methodists took a major step forward in 1876 when, under the leadership of Bishop HOLLAND MCTYEIRE, Vanderbilt University was established. Nashville once again became a major publishing center. Competition for new members was keen among the major evangelical churches, and the Baptists and Methodists were extraordinarily successful in rebuilding their memberships by 1900. The intense sectarian rivalry of the late nineteenth century was only slightly less acrimonious than that of earlier years.

At the same time, the post-Civil War years were marked by a powerful Southern civil religion. Southern church leaders, including Catholics and Jews, united on countless public occasions to memorialize the "lost cause" and to explain in religious terms the tragedy of Southern history. No institution was more central to this religion of the lost cause than the University of the South, which opened its doors in 1865 in SEWANEE through the efforts of Bishop CHARLES QUINTARD of the Protestant Episcopal Church. The school had been planned in 1856 by Bishop LEONIDAS POLK. When the dream was resurrected in 1867 by Confederate veteran Quintard, the school quickly became the "stronghold of the Southern aristocracy," as well as a distinguished educational institution.

By 1900 the denominational shuffling caused by sectional tensions and the organization of independent black churches had been completed. The most spectacular single development at the turn of the century was the growth of the

Baptists. Between 1880 and 1900 the Southern Baptists passed the Methodist Episcopal Church, South, as the leading denomination in the state and surged far into the advance in the 20th century. Methodist growth slowed, partly as a result of the bitter fight in Tennessee between the Northern and Southern churches and partly because of a diminishing evangelical zeal. According to the 1906 religious census, the largest denominations in Tennessee were: Southern Baptist, 159,838; Methodist Episcopal Church, South, 140,308; National (Negro) Baptist Convention, 93,303; Methodist Episcopal Church, 46,180; Cumberland Presbyterian Church, 42,464; Churches of Christ, 41,411; African Methodist Episcopal, 23,377; Presbyterian Church in the United States, 21,390; Colored Methodist Episcopal, 20,634; Roman Catholic, 17,252; Disciples of Christ, 14,904; Primitive Baptist, 10,204; Protestant Episcopal Church, 7,874; Presbyterian Church in the United States of America, 6,786; African Methodist Episcopal Zion Church, 6,651; and Colored Cumberland Presbyterian, 6,640.

The major denominations present in Tennessee had changed little since the 1830s (with the exception of the separation of the black churches), although there were variations in the vitality of each group. In the years from 1890 to 1910, however, each of the four largest white churches in the state—the Baptists, Methodists, Disciples, and Cumberland Presbyterians—suffered divisions. Each of the divisions was national in scope, but Tennessee played a central role in all of them. This new religious ferment combined with an increased influx of non-Southern churches to bring a new diversity to Tennessee religion. All of the divisions reflected the changing economic and social conditions in the state, particularly the growth of the middle class and increased rural-urban tensions.

Perhaps the clearest example of social and economic religious tensions was the division within the Disciples of Christ. In the religious census of 1906, the most theologically conservative Disciples churches were separated from the remainder of the movement and listed as CHURCHES OF CHRIST. The doctrinal basis of the division was disagreement over the use of instrumental music in worship and organized missionary societies. At the national level the Churches of Christ captured only 159,658 of the movement's total membership while the more liberal Christian church listed 982,701 members. The South, particularly Tennessee, was the stronghold of the Churches of Christ. Even within Tennessee the division was sectional; a majority of the churches in East Tennessee became Christian churches while in both Middle and West Tennessee an overwhelming majority were Churches of Christ. But the division also had clear rural-urban characteristics. In every major city in the state with the exception of Nashville, the Christian church won far more members than the Churches of Christ. A second division in the Disciples of Christ occurred in the 1920s leading to the establishment of a liberal, ecumenical denomination, the General Assembly of Christian Churches (Disciples of Christ) and the evangelical (but instrumental and cooperative) undenominational fellowship of CHRISTIAN CHURCHES AND CHURCHES OF CHRIST. This division was also sectional. Most of the urban churches joined the liberal General Assembly, while in East Tennessee the rural congregations that had refused to join the Churches of Christ formed their own fellowship and retained control of Milligan College.

In 1971 the liberal Christian church listed 17,849 members in 88 congregations in Tennessee. The conservative Christian churches listed 22,379 in 148 churches, mostly in East Tennessee. In the 20th century the Churches of Christ grew rapidly in the state, listing 72,015 members and 978 congregations in the census of 1926. A loose collection of local churches, the Churches of Christ have not reported membership statistics in recent years, but the group's aggressive evangelism has probably made it the second- or third-largest religious body in the state. This movement's membership is concentrated heavily in Middle Tennessee. Davidson County listed over 120 Churches of Christ by 1980, and the Madison Church of Christ claimed over 5,300 members. The *Gospel Advocate*, published in Nashville and edited by the minister of the Madison Church, Ira North, probably has the largest circulation of any periodical among the Churches of Christ.

The Cumberland Presbyterian division resulted from the refusal of about one-third of the churches in the denomination to accept union with the Presbyterian Church in the United States of America in 1906. The way opened for union when the Northern Presbyterians further diluted their Calvinistic beliefs around the turn of the century. Many of the Southern churches, however, reflecting pride in their Cumberland heritage as well as fear of the influence of blacks in the united church, refused to participate. In Tennessee, the Cumberland Presbyterian church reported 536 congregations with 42,464 members in 1906; in 1916, after the merger, those figures declined to 398 congregations and 27,631 members. The division was also sociological. The congregations that remained Cumberland were mostly rural; the church was virtually devoid of urban congregations until well into the 20th century. In 1980, the Cumberland Presbyterian Church's main denominational offices were in Memphis where the *Cumberland Presbyterian* was published. In 1971, the church listed a membership of 38,246 in Tennessee.

Baptist growth in the late nineteenth and early twentieth centuries was rapid, but the church continued to be troubled by Landmark resistance to organized mission work. James R. Graves's influence remained strong in Tennessee until his death in 1893, and Landmarkism pushed the entire denomination in a conservative direction until the 1960s. Nevertheless, some Landmarkers became so dissatisfied with what they believed to be organizational encroachments on the local churches that they bolted the Southern Baptist Convention in 1905 and formed the American Baptist Association. While this new church was strongest in Arkansas and the Southwest, in 1936 the Landmarkers listed 5,582 members in Tennessee in 37 churches, almost all in rural areas.

More serious were the divisions within Southern Methodism around the turn of the century. The HOLINESS MOVEMENT erupted first among Northern Methodists shortly after the Civil War and had a divisive influence in that section in the late nineteenth century. For the most part, however, Southern Methodism captured the Holiness movement, welcoming the reopening of campgrounds and encouraging the renewed emphasis on perfectionism. B. F. Haynes, editor of the *Tennessee Methodist* in the 1890s, was an ardent advocate of Holiness and subsequently left the church over the question. The influence of the separatist Holiness churches did not appear in the census until 1916, and in that year the most influential of them, the Church of the Nazarene, reported only 24 churches with 1,903 members in Tennessee. The Nazarenes grew slowly to a membership of 5,416 in 1936 and 11,767 in 1971.

More important was the growth of PENTECOSTALISM in Tennessee. In the 1890s the Holiness movement developed an increasingly radical extreme wing that urged pushing on to deeper and deeper spiritual experiences. At the same time the Methodist church began to try to control the influence of the movement. The radical Holiness movement became Pentecostal around the turn of the century when the "baptism of the Holy Spirit," accompanied by speaking in tongues, spread across the nation. Cleveland TN became one of the centers of Pentecostalism. A. J. TOMLINSON was the most prominent leader of a group of Holiness churches in western North Carolina and East Tennessee near the end of the 19th century, and from 1903 to 1923 he served as General Overseer of the Church of God. In 1908 the movement turned Pentecostal, adopted the name Church of God, and established its general offices in Cleveland. The Church of God, along with other Pentecostal groups, was extremely schismatic because of its dependence on charismatic leaders and because of its extreme conservatism in matters of doctrine and personal morality. The Church of God suffered a major split in 1923 involving Tomlinson's autocratic management of church affairs, and Tomlinson took about one-third of the membership into the CHURCH OF GOD OF PROPHECY. In 1957 Grady R. Kent led a small group out of that church to form The Church of God (Jerusalem Acres) based on a prophetic concept of "New Testament Judaism." Also headquartered in Cleveland was the United Christian Church and Ministerial Alliance, formed in 1958 by H. Richard Hall, a tent revivalist and former minister in the Church of God of Prophecy. Jellico TN became the headquarters of the Church of God of the Mountain Assembly, Inc., founded in 1906.

Pentecostalism remained a vital movement in Tennessee in modern times. The CHURCH OF GOD (CLEVELAND TN) had 23,936 members in the state in 1971 and had completed a modern headquarters building in CLEVELAND. In 1952 the Church of God of Prophecy reported 3,577 members in the state. In addition, other major Pentecostal groups entered the state and grew during the charismatic boom of the 1970s. At the same time, the creative cutting edge of Pentecostalism continued to generate new sects among the poor of the state, including the Church of God with Signs Following, a group of loosely connected rural churches that continued to arouse the periodic interest of the press with snake-handling services.

In the midst of this sectarian caldron, many of the mainline churches experienced great growth in Tennessee, particularly during the national religious boom in the 1950s. Southern Baptist membership in the state grew from 226,896 in 1936 to 900,743 in 1971. Baptist churches also expanded their social vision in a variety of ways, particularly after the 1950s. Throughout the 20th century the churches of the state were liberal supporters of such institutions as the Baptist Memorial Hospital in Memphis, the Baptist Hospital in Nashville, and a number of other benevolent institutions. More than anything else, however, Baptists emphasized missions, and state churches liberally supported both the foreign and home mission boards. The state convention underwent a general reorganization in 1957 to bring greater efficiency. In 1980, four Baptist churches in Tennessee—Highland Park in Chattanooga (independent), Park Avenue in Nashville, and Bellevue and Broadway in Memphis—were listed among the 100 largest churches in the nation.

A small but old Baptist group that made significant gains in Tennessee in the post-World War II period was the FREE WILL BAPTISTS. The descendant of Arminian Baptists who came to North Carolina in 1727, the church remained alive in isolated rural congregations throughout the 19th century. The church reported only about 3,000 members in Tennessee in 1906, but by 1971 it had grown to 20,801. A conservative evangelical group with a strong sense of its own history, the church has its national headquarters and a Bible College in Nashville.

The Methodist Church in the state grew to a membership of 360,749 in 1971, but most of its increase resulted from the union of the Northern and Southern Methodist bodies in 1939. In spite of its slowed rate of growth, the Methodist church remained an important influence in the state, and, increasingly, a liberal influence. Southern Methodists were among the founding members of the Federal Council of Churches in America in 1908, and Bishop E. R. Hendrix was the council's first president.

The Presbyterian Church in the United States grew from 34,255 members in

1936 to 63,259 in 1971, obviously profiting from the growth in the mainline churches after World War II. The church became increasingly urban; by 1926 over half of its members lived in Memphis and Nashville. In the 1970s most Southern Presbyterians remained theologically conservative and a part of the evangelical establishment of the state. The Cumberland Presbyterian Church during the same years increased its membership from 19,556 to 38,246 and slowly began to establish churches in the major cities of the state. The Presbyterian Church in the United States of America gained from its acquisition of many Cumberland churches and in 1971 reported 18,146 members in the state.

The Protestant Episcopal Church grew from 14,156 members in 1936 to 30,679 in 1971. Like the other moderate Protestant denominations in the state, the Episcopal Church slowed in growth in the 1960s and 1970s and faced yearly budget strains. Along with Methodists and Presbyterians, Tennessee Episcopalians made the boldest social statements in the post-World War II years, especially in their advocacy of the rights of blacks and women.

The appearance of small numbers of Unitarians, Mormons, and Seventh-day Adventists in recent religious polls in the state reflect the growing heterogeneity of the state's population. More significant, however, was the large growth of the Roman Catholic Church and Jewish synagogues in the 20th century. The number of Roman Catholics in Tennessee grew from 31,985 in 1936 to 92,577 in 1971. In 1963, the Catholic Church in Tennessee was operating 67 elementary schools, 13 high schools, and three colleges with a total student population of 21,506. In spite of its substantial growth, Roman Catholicism remained largely an urban phenomenon in Tennessee. The growth of the Church in the state led to the establishment of a second diocese in Memphis in 1971.

The growth of Judaism in Tennessee was even more dramatic. The religious census of 1906 reported only 919 Jews in the state, almost all living in the state's four urban centers. By 1936, the Jewish congregations in the state listed 23,275 members. Much of the increase came from a large influx of Orthodox Jews around the turn of the century, but the early twentieth century also witnessed the appearance of important Reform rabbis in Tennessee, including Julian Mark in Nashville, Abraham Feinstein in Chattanooga, and Harry W. Ettelson in Memphis. Jews, as well as Catholics, suffered from nativist agitation in Tennessee, particularly during the 1920s, but they were remarkably visible in the cultural and political life of the state throughout the 20th century.

By far the most powerful black religious group in Tennessee in the 20th century was the Baptists. In 1936 the combined membership of black Baptist churches in the state was over 140,000. The National Baptist Convention, U.S.A., Inc., maintained its BTU Board in Nashville and its Educational Board in Memphis. The African Methodist Episcopal Church published its national paper, the *A.M.E. Recorder*, in Nashville where it maintained its education and publication departments. In addition, several black Pentecostal churches grew rapidly in the 20th century. Perhaps the most important was the Church of God in Christ that was founded in Memphis in 1906 by Bishop Charles Harrison Mason. In 1980 the church reported a national membership of 425,000 and maintained its headquarters in Memphis, the home of Presiding Bishop J. O. Patterson.

The evangelical churches of Tennessee in the 20th century, in spite of their sectarian competition and splintering, formed a nearly solid conservative Protestant Establishment in the state. While some urban Episcopal, Presbyterian, and Methodist pastors and professors were probably embarrassed by the fundamentalist reputation in Tennessee in the

1920s, most of the Protestants in the state were firm supporters of the antievolution law passed by the state legislature in 1925. The law, introduced by Representative J. W. Butler, a farmer and a Primitive Baptist from Macon County, was tested in the famous trial of JOHN T. SCOPES in Dayton in July 1925. When WILLIAM JENNINGS BRYAN came to Dayton to help prosecute the "infidel" Scopes, he received the unanimous support of the ministers of that small town.

The Protestant Establishment of the state also united in countless conservative social crusades and mass revivals during the 1920s and 1930s. Beginning in the 1920s, the state hosted countless mass revivals conducted by Billy Sunday, MORDECAI HAM, and such lesser revivalists as J. C. Bishop, "the Yodeling Cowboy Evangelist." In the 1950s that massive company Establishment reacted enthusiastically to Billy Graham's crusades. The issues most often discussed in such revivals and in most Protestant pulpits and papers were soul-saving, prohibition, the dangers of evolution, dancing, and political radicalism. The nomination of Al Smith for the presidency in 1928 roused the Protestant Establishment to new heights of concerted political action. Smith's opposition to prohibition, in addition to his Roman Catholic faith, set off a religious-political campaign that led Tennessee into the Republican camp for the first time in the 20th century. The Smith campaign also climaxed a renewed outbreak of anti-Catholicism that put tremendous pressure on the 25,000 Catholics in the state.

Since World War II the evolution of the churches has brought considerably more diversity to Tennessee religion. Not only has the number of Roman Catholics and Jews continued to increase, but also the mainstream Protestant denominations have become increasingly liberal and linked with the mainstream churches outside the South. Southern Episcopalians, Presbyterians, and Methodists spawned important social agencies in the post-World War II period. In Tennessee these three denominations led in the establishment of ministerial alliances and other ecumenical agencies in the state's major cities. Many local churches expanded the role of women and the young in their programs.

Tennessee Baptists remained much more conservative. Nevertheless, many Southern Baptists in the years after World War II became increasingly concerned about the social involvement of such agencies as the Christian Life Commission and the Baptist Joint Committee on Public Affairs. Many feared that liberalism had invaded the church's theological seminaries. When conservative Southern Baptists launched a concerted campaign in 1979 to win the presidency of the Southern Baptist Convention, their candidate was Adrian Rogers, pastor of the 11,500-member Bellevue Church in Memphis. Many Tennessee Baptists became convinced in the 1950s that the Southern Baptist church was beyond rescue and joined the mushrooming independent Baptist movement. The Southwide Fellowship of Independent Baptist churches, centered around the Highland Park Baptist Church and Tennessee Temple University in Chattanooga, was one of the most important national centers of that movement. Lee Roberson, pastor of Highland Park, built a church in the postwar years that had a total membership of nearly 55,000 in 1980.

In summary, religion in Tennessee has been influenced by all of the forces that shaped religion in the South: the ethnic homogeneity of the state's early settlers, the heritage of the great revival, the presence of large numbers of blacks, the Civil War, the economic backwardness of the state in the aftermath of the Civil War, and the slow Americanization of the state in the 20th century. In addition, Tennessee religion has been shaped in some unique ways. The Disciples of Christ and Cumberland Presbyterians were important in Tennessee because they entered the state before 1830; after that date religion in the South tended to freeze along the denominational lines that then existed. Neither church successfully spread to the East or South after 1830, though both moved West. Tennessee was composed of three economically and culturally diverse sections. The presence of the mountain white population in the East greatly complicated the denominational history of the state. Finally, Tennessee's central location in the Upper South and its early reputation as a center of culture and education made it an ideal place to establish denominational headquarters and church colleges.

See also articles on CAMPBELLITE TRADITION; EVOLUTION CONTROVERSY; FRONTIER, INFLUENCE OF; LANDMARK MOVEMENT; RESTORATIONISM; SCOPES TRIAL.

Bibliography. John Alexander, *The Synod of Tennessee*; Cullen Carter, *Methodism in the Wilderness, 1786-1836*; James W. Carty, *Nashville as a World Religious Center*; J. E. Choate, *Roll Jordan Roll: A Biography of Marshall Keeble*; J. B. Collins, *Tennessee Snake Handlers*; Charles W. Conn, *Like a Mighty Army Moves the Church of God, 1886-1955*; E. Merton Coulter, *William G. Brownlow: Fighting Parson of the Southern Highlands*; George Flanigan, ed., *Catholicity in Tennessee*; Thomas O. Fuller, *History of the Negro Baptists of Tennessee*; Ray Ginger, *Six Days or Forever?*; David E. Harrell, Jr., "The Disciples of Christ and Social Force in Tennessee, 1865-1900," The East Tennessee Historical Society's *Publications* 38 (1966): 48-61; C. W. Heishell, *Pioneer Presbyterians in Tennessee*; Robert E. Hooper, *Crying in the Wilderness: A Biography of David Lipscomb*; Paul Isaac, *Prohibition and Politics: Turbulent Decades in Tennessee, 1885-1920*; W. Fred Kendall, *A History of the Tennessee Baptist Convention*; Isaac Martin, *History of Methodism in Holston Conference*; Herman Norton, *Religion in Tennessee, 1777-1945*; *Tennessee Christians*; Oury Taylor, *Early Tennessee Baptists, 1769-1832*; James R. Wilburn, *The Hazard of the Die: Tolbert Fanning and the Restoration Movement*; William Woodson, *Standing for Their Faith: A History of Churches of Christ in Tennessee, 1900-1950*.

DAVID E. HARRELL, JR.
UNIVERSITY OF ARKANSAS

TENT REVIVALS: *See* ALTAR CALL (INVITATION).

TEXAS. In 1807 the American explorer Zebulon Pike, who was being escorted by Spanish officials to the Spanish-American border at Natchitoches LA, recorded his impressions of the scruffy, scattered settlements in what is now east Texas. He noted, among other things, that the religion of Spanish Texas was Catholic—"but much relaxed." Pike's pithy phrase aptly described the religious life of Texas during the years before 1836 in which it was a province, first of Spain and then, briefly, of Mexico.

The settlements Pike visited originated in the second quarter of the 18th century as military outposts to guard against the French and as missions to the region's peaceful Hasinai and Caddo tribes. That missionary impetus had failed, though, by 1807. The white man's diseases eventually decimated the small native populations, and those Indians who survived could not be forced to remain affixed to the several struggling missions in northeast Texas. To the southwest, San Antonio de Bexar, the principal Spanish settlement in Texas, was no more successful. By 1800 only a few dozen converted Indians and a handful of rag-tag clerics could be found at San Antonio. After 75 years of colonizing efforts, there were at the turn of the 19th century fewer than 3,000 settlers in Spanish Texas. Growth was inhibited by the vast wasteland between the Nueces River and the Rio Grande that separated Spanish Texas from northern Mexico and by the Spanish refusal to allow trade with the French in Louisiana. More important, in the early eighteenth century the awesome Comanches swept southward onto the Llano Estacado, the "Staked Plains" of west Texas. Mounted, these "Lords of the Plains" were among the most effective warriors in history. They were, in fact, the only American aborigines to halt for any length of time—more than a century—the white man's advance in the New World.

In 1821 the first Anglo-Americans began to appear in the vacuum of Spanish Texas. This vanguard of the boisterous young republic's "manifest destiny" to march to the western sea was led first by Moses Austin, a Connecticut Yankee who came to Texas by way of Virginia and Upper Louisiana, and then by his son,

Stephen F. Austin, the "father of Texas." Austin's colonists settled in present-day Austin and Washington counties on the Brazos River, where they were tolerated with guarded suspicion by Spanish and Mexican officials. There for 15 years they lived under an established Catholic Church. Moses Austin had already dealt with the problem of an established church in Upper Louisiana, which from 1764 to 1800 was controlled by the Spanish. Between 1783 and 1798 the Spanish had granted religious toleration to Protestants, whom they actively endeavored to attract to the area. In 1798, the year Austin arrived in Spanish territory from Virginia, the Spanish restricted toleration to the first generation of settlers. Austin, however, found it easy enough to be considered "un bon catholique" by vaguely affirming his adherence to the Church. And when he petitioned the Spanish government in Mexico for permission to bring settlers to Texas in 1820, he stated that he was a Catholic.

His son, the person who actually established the colony, was at great pains to advise prospective settlers of the Catholic establishment in Texas. Between 1821 and 1824 Stephen Austin attempted to comply with the stipulation that colonists certify their Catholicism, and as many as a quarter of the first male settlers may have done so. It is clear, though, that most did not and that no Spanish or Mexican official seemed to mind. The attention of those officials was distracted by the Mexican efforts to achieve independence from Spain, which efforts proved successful in 1824. The constitution framed for Mexico after independence was modeled on the "liberal" Spanish constitution of 1812. It established a republican government, that, in turn, expelled all Spanish priests and confiscated the Church's extensive properties. But the constitution also established the Roman Church and prohibited "the exercise of any other whatsoever." In Texas Stephen Austin was not unduly disturbed. He had informally advised some of the Mexican offi-

cials who had framed the constitution, and he was confident that the "natural operations" of republican principles soon would make possible the free exercise of all religions.

In the meantime, while republicanism spread "its fostering arms over the vast domains of Mexico," Austin insisted that his colonists acquiesce in the Catholic establishment—at least publicly. He forbade non-Catholic services, he performed provisional civil marriages himself and then bound the couples to be married by a priest when one arrived, and he urged Mexican officials to send such a priest to Texas. And continually he sought to keep evangelical preachers out of Texas.

Stephen Austin was a late product of the American Enlightenment. He attended between 1808 and 1810 Transylvania University in Lexington KY, that at the time was arguably the most liberal institution of higher learning in the republic. There he imbibed the religious skepticism currently fashionable in Kentucky, that Jeffersonian Virginia at one remove. He then brought with him to Texas the prejudices of that skepticism—an anti-Catholicism, that he managed usually to conceal, and a loathing of Methodist preachers especially, which he publicly proclaimed. He believed evangelical preachers to be fanatics whose presence would do more harm to the colony "than a dozen horse thieves," no light charge in a society absolutely dependent upon the horse. He denounced in typically Jeffersonian terms the denominational bickering he believed inevitably would follow evangelists to Texas and that would just as surely provoke Mexican officials to enforce ecclesiastical regulations they had been content to ignore. Like Jefferson, Austin believed that no one religious group could demonstrate the superiority of its dogma to any other. Indeed, one suspects that the father of Texas may have welcomed the rather innocuous Catholic establishment because it made impossible the sectarian squabbles Austin so abhorred. (It is perhaps worth noting that most of the Mexican officials with whom Austin dealt were Freemasons who probably shared his religious skepticism and distaste for theological debate.)

Austin was not entirely successful in excluding Protestant ministers from his own colony, and, of course, he had no authority to keep them out of other areas of Texas. Between 1820 and 1836, then, the founders of Protestantism in Texas arrived. By the later date, there were 12 Methodist, 13 Baptist, at least one Disciples of Christ, three Presbyterian, and three Cumberland Presbyterian ministers in the area. The earliest of these settled around Nacogdoches and San Augustine in northeast Texas. The second area of concentration was around the Austin colony on the Brazos. And the last group of preachers to arrive in the colonial period gravitated toward Houston and the nearby island settlement of Galveston.

Virtually all of these men were itinerants. Some of them organized churches during the colonial period, but public worship in them was quite rare before 1836. Since Mexican officials consistently refused to send priests to the area, there was, in effect, no organized religious activity in Texas before it gained its independence. Ministers—and some lay people—were astounded by the almost complete lack of religious exercises in an area that gave the Sabbath over to "visiting, driving stock, and breaking mustangs," which was what Texans apparently did on the other six days of the week also. One Methodist minister could find nothing in 1834 to cheer him on his Texas circuit, where most Methodists he encountered were either "backslidden," or were going to dancing school, or worst of all, had "joined the Baptists."

This frustrated comment notwithstanding, there was in fact little proselytizing among the Protestant denominations during the colonial period. Of course, proselytizing would not be expected from groups that officially were proscribed. But it is also true that many of

the early Protestant preachers and their followers in Texas tended to be of the "hard-shell" variety. Like, for instance, T.J. Pilgrim's church of Predestinarian Baptists, a surprisingly large number of early Methodist, Presbyterian, Disciples, and Baptist settlers did not believe in organized missionary efforts, were predestinarian, and seemed more interested in maintaining congregational purity than in poaching on other denominational preserves.

Because any preaching efforts threatened always to get them expelled from Texas, these early evangelists tended to emphasize the educational aspects of the ministry. Their first activities often were in founding Sunday schools and primary schools. Later they would be among the founders of an astounding number and variety of denominational colleges in Texas. Gradually, the reputations of these early evangels improved, even among the secular-minded men emerging as the leaders of the developing Anglo-Texas culture. William B. Travis, soon to die at the Alamo, in 1835 even issued a call for American Methodists to send more ministers to Texas, realizing as he did that the churches they would create were simply essential to the success of that culture. And, by and large, Mexican officials left the Protestant evangelists alone. For instance, in 1832 an official in Nacogdoches complained about a nearby camp meeting to his commandant, a Col. Piedras. "Are they stealing horses?" the colonel inquired. No. "Are they killing anyone?" No, again. "Then let them alone," Piedras wisely concluded.

The Americans in Texas encountered a religious culture very unlike the one that produced them. The young American republic was dominated increasingly by an Evangelical Protestantism that was divided into highly competitive denominational voluntary associations to propagate varying versions of religious truth. And Protestant America was aggressively insistent upon the natural superiority of that denominational voluntaryism to all other forms of religious organization. In Spanish Texas all of those beliefs had to be repressed before 1836. That early repression perhaps explains in part the force with which these ideas suddenly appeared in the Republic of Texas.

The alienation of Texas from Mexico after 1824 was probably as inevitable as historians are allowed to designate any historical development. Like the British after 1763, Mexican officials between 1830 and 1835 attempted to impose controls over colonists too long neglected. And, with self-conscious reference to the 18th-century crisis of the British empire, the ever-growing number of Americans in Texas resisted those efforts. The events of the Texas Revolution—at least the story of the defense of the Alamo—now inform the nation's mythology and need not be recounted here. Suffice it to say that the dead of the Alamo were avenged in April of 1836 by the Texas victory at the Battle of San Jacinto. Though Mexico continued to contest the point, Texas existed as a sovereign republic until 1845, when, after much controversy, she was admitted into the American union.

Religion seems not to have played a significant role in the crisis of 1835-1836 that led to the Texas Revolution. Protestant Texans fared no worse under Mexican rule after 1824 than they had under previous Spanish regimes, and they apparently understood that. Still, the Declaration of Independence of 1836 indicted Mexico with establishing a "national religion" and with supporting a standing army and a tyrannous priesthood, both equally "the eternal enemies of civil liberty." The Republic's constitution guaranteed complete religious freedom and, moreover, prohibited ecclesiastics of all descriptions from holding public office.

It was axiomatic in 18th-century republican theory that the essential character of any new nation was set irretrievably by first impressions. In an almost mechanistic sense, the political philosophy of first the American and then the Texas republic held that a society would reflect forever the character of its first citizens and the institutions they created. Protestant ministers in the Republic of Texas were determined to influence in significant ways that process. In language that harked back to the early days of the American republic, the Baptists of Washington-on-the-Brazos, the Republic's birthplace, in 1837 urged their brothers in America, "our mother country," to send missionaries to Texas. The Methodists and Presbyterians had already embraced "the favored hour," the Baptists warned. "They know that society is now being formed. They know that early impressions are the most lasting. . . ." The Baptists must not delay.

The denominations of the "mother country" did not quite know how to respond to appeals from an independent nation populated largely by Americans. The late 1830s was one of the high points of Protestant "home" missionary activities on the western frontier, and it was a period that saw most of the major American denominations enthusiastically embarked on "foreign" missionary endeavors also. An independent Texas presented those Protestants with a dilemma: was the new western republic to be considered a "home" or a "foreign" field? The question was not an idle one. The answer determined the part of the denominational hierarchy that would have charge of Texas missions. The Texans themselves certainly were unsure of their status. The Baptists at Washington-on-the-Brazos directed the appeal mentioned above to the American Baptists' Foreign Mission Society. But the appeal was taken up by the Home Mission Society, that arranged for Georgia Baptists to "adopt" the Texans, thereby creating an important and long-lived connection between Texas and Georgia Baptists. In much the same fashion, Texas Methodists during the Republic were in the charge of Mississippi Methodists, who never quite decided if Texas was a home or a foreign field. During the life of the Republic the House of Bishops of the Episcopal Church debated the issue of mission work in Texas along with plans for evangelizing efforts in China, Africa, and Greece. But those discussions were not resolved until 1844 because canons allowing for the support of missions outside the United States had to be drafted and approved. Consequently, organized Episcopal work in Texas did not begin until after the Republic ended. The Presbyterians, though, had the most difficulty in resolving the issue of Texas' status. The Texas Presbyterians during the Republic would not decide whether to join the American hierarchy, and the Americans, in turn, could not decide the conditions under which such a union might be possible.

Clearly, the uncertainty of Texas' present and future status dampened the enthusiasm of American Protestants for mission efforts in the decade of the Republic. Those efforts were hindered further by floods, by recurring attacks of yellow fever and red men, and especially, by the alarming if unsuccessful Mexican invasion of 1842. And finally, one suspects that the appeals for aid from nearby Texas were simply not as enticing to Americans as were the calls from the more exotic fields of Hawaii, the Far East, and darkest Africa.

Still, Texas Protestants established during the Republic the organizational foundations of most of the major denominations: the Cumberland Presbyterians' Texas Presbytery (1839); the Presbyterians' Brazos Presbytery (1840); and the Baptists' Union Association (1840). These pioneer judicatories lay between the Austin colony and Nacogdoches/San Augustine, the area in which Protestantism had germinated during the colonial period. More so than in the colonial period, denominational strife—especially conflict between denominational schools—appeared during the Republic. As early as 1843 the students of the Presbyterian school at San Augustine engaged in sharp theological debates with students at the Methodist institution at Ruters-

ville. And a Methodist circuit rider might rail against "the watery tribe" (the Baptists), while the Baptists would join the Methodists in castigating all "Campbellites." But, as had been true in the colonial period, disagreements *within* denominations over missions, an educated ministry, and central versus local authority were often more intense than disputes among the denominations themselves.

The principal denominations sometimes overcame their differences in efforts to elevate the moral climate of the Texas Republic. Fewer than one-eighth of the 100,000 whites numbered in the first census in 1847 were members of any church. Perhaps even more disturbing to ministers than that statistic, though, was the ease with which unlicensed and uncontrolled preachers circulated in the Republic. One notorious example was one "Daddy Spraggins," a hard-shell Baptist who patronized the saloons of Velasco both before and after haranguing sinners. His unconventional ministrations led Presbyterian, Methodist, and Baptist ministers to establish in Houston in May of 1837 the "Ecclesiastical Committee of Vigilance for Texas," that declared its intention to locate and expose religious imposters. The Episcopalians of Galveston even endeavored to protect their church from undesirable members by resolving in 1843 to admit to communion only those who "enjoy the confidence of the rectors at the time of their emigration" and who brought to Texas "satisfactory testimonials for Christian character . . ." Occasionally the Protestants banded together literally to do battle for the Lord, as when in 1838 the Baptist, Methodist, and Cumberland Presbyterian ministers of Washington-on-the-Brazos joined forces and persuaded reluctant gamblers to allow sacred services in an empty billiards room.

Travelers in the Republic of Texas commented frequently upon the sudden visibility of an ever-growing band of Protestant preachers after 1836. One Josiah Whipple in 1843 observed that "the backwoodsman has gone into the forest, and the panther is scarcely more keen scented for his blood than the Methodist preacher is for his soul." And a young visitor to Houston in 1845 was impressed by the variety of religious services available in the rough bayou settlement. He awoke one Sunday to the bells of a Catholic Mass, went to a Methodist Sunday School before hearing a Baptist sermon, took in a Presbyterian Bible class in the afternoon, and topped the day off with an evening lay sermon back at the Methodist meeting-house. But, in fact, the Protestant clergymen in the Republic were a tiny handful of men very much aware of their precarious position in an aggressively impious land. Despite their concerns about its moral condition during the Republic, they did not mount extensive campaigns aimed at reforming Texas and Texans.

An independent Texas presented the Roman Catholic Church with problems quite different from those encountered by the various Protestant denominations. For instance, none of those groups had to wrestle with the question of recognizing the independence of Texas. The Vatican diplomatically avoided explicitly addressing the question until annexation rendered it moot, but Rome did take actions before 1845 that granted *de facto* recognition to the Republic. Soon after San Jacinto, the Vatican began activities that, in effect, severed Texas' historical relationship with the Spanish/Mexican /Franciscan continuum in the Church's missionary activities and, instead, pointed Texas Catholicism toward the French Vincentians in American Louisiana. Unlike the experience of Protestants during the Republic, then, the question of the interaction between Texas and American Catholics was determined by a third party, the Vatican.

In 1838 Rome directed Father John Timon, the Visitor of the American Vincentian Province, to survey the Church's work in Texas. Timon, who was stationed in New Orleans, chose to reach Texas by sea by way of Galveston rather than by going overland through east Texas, which was the route whereby Protestantism, by and large, entered the Republic. In Texas Timon entranced the Republic's legislators with an expansive, genial sermon that went a long way toward defusing the still potent anti-Catholic sentiment among the Republic's leaders. Back in New Orleans Timon prepared nine Vincentians who had been recruited in Europe for work in Texas. That work began in 1840 when he was appointed Prefect-Apostolic of Texas. Supervising an enormous jurisdiction now independent of Monterrey, Timon had effectively all the powers of a resident bishop. He appointed as his vice-prefect John Odin, whom he sent to Texas to perform the actual supervision of the new efforts. In 1841 Texas became a full vicariate, and Odin became Vicar under Timon, who simultaneously became the bishop of New Orleans. Finally, in 1847, Texas was elevated to a diocese and Odin became its first bishop. Significantly, he was not seated in Spanish San Antonio but in Galveston, a city with many connections with the United States. Odin was given jurisdiction over the disputed area between the Nueces River and the Rio Grande, but he did not exercise power there until the American victory in the Mexican War settled the question of the southern border of Texas. At the same time he endeavored to recruit from Europe German-speaking priests to serve the growing number of German colonies in Texas. The "father of Texas Catholicism," Bishop Odin reported in 1847 that there were 10,000 Catholics in the new state, located primarily in and around San Antonio and these German colonies.

The growth of that German presence was one of the more important developments in Texas between annexation and secession. From 1840 to 1860 more than 30,000 Europeans arrived in Texas, almost invariably through the port of Galveston. They included virtually no potato-famine Irish and were, for the most part, Germans and Czechs from Bohemia and

Moravia. These European settlers usually avoided areas of Anglo concentration. The early "Adelsverein" colonies, for instance, put down German roots in and around New Braunfels. Later settlers pushed into the "Hill Country" of central Texas and there created German communities as far west as the Llano River valley, the first successful white settlements above the Balcones Escarpment. The Europeans who came to Texas were overwhelmingly Catholic. In some early communities the Germans and Czechs shared a single house of worship; later they would be differentiated by language. In response to the growing number of these European Catholics in Texas, Rome in 1859 dispatched members of the Benedictine order into the state and focused their efforts in central Texas.

Of course not all European immigrants to 19th-century Texas were Roman Catholics—a substantial portion of them were Lutherans of varying national origin. Taken together, the Lutherans have constituted a major component of the rich ethnic and religious mixture of Central Texas especially. Swedish Lutheranism had its origins in several small settlements in and around the exposed capital at Austin in the 1830s and 1840s. Permanently settled ministers did not arrive to serve the Swedes, however, until the 1870s, when the Augustana Synod was organized (1875). The first Norwegian Lutherans came to Texas during the Mexican War. They tended to settle to the north of the Swedes, in Henderson and Bosque Counties. In 1900 they joined the Norwegian Lutheran Church of America. These Norwegian and Swedish settlements were very small, but German Lutherans settled in 19th-century Texas in considerable numbers. There were a few German Lutherans in colonial Texas, and their numbers increased substantially in the period between annexation and the Civil War. Concentrated in the area between Houston and Austin and finally in the Hill Country to the west of the capital, the

Germans organized the First Evangelical Lutheran Synod of Texas in 1851 and years later joined the Lutheran General Synod, a connection that lasted until 1868. There began then a series of shifting alignments with several national groups that continued to agitate the German community in Texas well into the 20th century.

The antebellum period was also a significant period in the history of Jewry in Texas. Individual Jews had been active in Texas as early as 1821 and were among Austin's original Old Three Hundred colonists. And in the mid-1840s Henry Castro had created a thriving colony on the Medina River, the first successful settlement between San Antonio and the Rio Grande. But the emergence of organized Jewish life in the state awaited the period between annexation and secession. The first Jewish cemetery in Texas was established in 1844 in Houston, where the first synagogue was built a decade later. Other cemeteries and places of worship were created before 1876 in Austin, San Antonio, Waco, and Dallas.

During the antebellum years the attention of Texans appears not to have been concentrated on the sectional crisis and the attendant debate over slavery that dominated politics at the national level. The state was preoccupied with paying its debts, determining its boundary with New Mexico, and defending its frontier. Texas was the only state admitted to the Union with unconquered Indian tribes still living within its border, and that fact was perhaps the most important concern of the state for at least a full generation after annexation. But, finally, even the distracted Texans had to deal with the explosive issues that were tearing at the Union.

Fully one-quarter of the 600,000 people counted in the 1860 Texas census were slaves. There seems to have been nothing unique about slavery in the Lone Star state. The Texans, like Southerners everywhere, used biblical arguments to justify slavery. The 1848 report of the Baptist

State Convention on "The Religious Condition of the Colored People" rehearsed the traditional interpretation of slavery as the way in which a wise Deity provided for the eventual redemption of Africa by allowing some of her children to be brought—albeit involuntarily—to the land of light and Christian republicanism. The report directed that all congregations should make the blacks under their care "familiar with the Bible by reading and directing their minds to those simple, plain and important parts that appertain to their soul's eternal welfare and future destiny." As they did throughout the South, slaves in Texas most frequently attended services with their master. Separate services for blacks, under white supervision, were held if numbers warranted them. There are records, for instance, of an Episcopal Sunday school, brush arbor meetings, and baptisms exclusively for blacks in Matagorda in the 1850s. And the Baptist Colorado Association in 1854 even accepted an all-black congregation into its membership. However, the Union Association of the same denomination rejected the application of an all-black group in the next year.

Texas is not usually thought of as a "border" state, but the Red River was, after 1854, part of the Northern boundary of slavery. Along that border in 1859 and 1860 occurred several outbreaks of violence between Protestant opponents and supporters of slavery that eventuated in the hanging of a missionary of the Methodist Church. When that denomination divided over the issue of slave-holding bishops in 1844, each side had agreed not to send missionaries into the other's territory. That agreement had broken down as early as 1848. In 1858 Anthony Bewley, an antislavery Southern Methodist lay elder, was assigned by the Missouri Conference of the Northern branch of the church to do mission work along the Red River in Texas. The Conference sent other preachers to Dallas. North Texas in the 1850s was rife with rumors of fires set and whites murdered by slaves enflamed by

abolitionist agitators—like the Methodist missionaries, it was charged. Bewley was attacked in particular, especially after the news of John Brown's raid on Harper's Ferry raced through the increasingly alarmed region in 1859. Applauded by the editor of the Methodist *Texas Christian Advocate*, citizens of Dallas drove two Methodist missionaries from Dallas, severely beating at least one of them in the process. A mob was then raised against Bewley, who fled with his family to Arkansas. A posse pursued them, though, and brought the preacher back to Fort Worth, where he was hanged after a mock trial.

This astounding development notwithstanding, the fact is that the Protestant denominations of Texas rarely contended over the issue of slavery during the antebellum period. The overwhelming majority of Texas Methodists supported the ecclesiastical schism of the 1840s as easily as they would the 1861 political division that it foretold. The Southern Baptist Convention was born in the year Texas entered the Union, and Texas Baptists by and large supported the drive toward secession that at least temporarily ended that union. The fact of the matter is that Texas Methodists and Baptists in the antebellum period were never part of ecclesiastical unions that crossed the Mason-Dixon line; instead what they entered were the regional unions of "Southern" Methodists and "Southern" Baptists. The Disciples of Christ were strongest in the border states and had learned how to finesse discussions of slavery, that continually threatened that denomination's emphasis on Christian unity. Alone among the major denominations, the Disciples were able to turn back efforts to make "correct views" on slavery prerequisites for communion. And they survived the sectional crisis and war intact. Indeed, the Episcopal Church was the only major denomination that divided as the union dissolved. Among Texas Episcopalians, there were occasional divisions over slavery, as when Austin's

Church of the Epiphany split in 1856, in large measure over the issue. But even in that case, the two parts reunited in 1859 to create the present-day St. David's Parish. After Texas seceded, the state's Episcopal Convention joined the rest of the South in a separate Episcopal Church simply by adopting "a principle of Catholic usage . . . the existence of a National Church in every separate Nation. . . ." That logic, of course, made equally simple the return of the Southern Episcopalians to a single American church after the war determined that the South would not be a separate nation.

The debate over slavery, the sectional crisis, and the resulting war involved one religious group in a unique way. The American Catholic Church, of course, did not divide over the issue of slavery. But many of Texas' growing number of German Catholics became increasingly critical of slavery in the fifties. In 1854 Germans attending the annual singing festival at San Antonio adopted a resolution that condemned slavery on moral grounds and called for federal assistance in ending the institution in Texas. Inevitably, the resolution intensified the Anglo-Texans' suspicions about the Germans' loyalty to the South and its "peculiar institution." Early in the Civil War 75 German settlers sympathetic to the Union left Kerr County in west Texas determined to find new homes in Mexico. The band was intercepted by Texas forces and defeated in the Battle of the Nueces in August of 1862. Martial law was then established in the German counties of central Texas, a situation that persisted intermittently through the war. Many German Texans, of course, were loyal to the Confederate cause, and several German priests served as chaplains to Texas troops.

The postwar period in Texas, as in the rest of the defeated South, saw the complete segregation of the races. That process was nowhere as complete as in the state's churches. It is true that a few white churchmen endeavored to preserve antebellum patterns of racially mixed worship, but even they apparently sensed the inevitability of change. The Episcopal Bishop Alexander Gregg urged only that the "principle of separation" should not "have place" any further "than is necessary." Again, the Baptist instance is instructive. Black Baptists began withdrawing from white churches at the war's conclusion. Some of their new congregations, though, did petition for membership in the state's Baptist associations. The petitions drew a mixed response. In 1866 the Union Association recommended that a petitioning black congregation be accepted only if it would select its moderator, clerk, and delegates to the Association from the white members of the First Baptist Church of Houston. In the same year the minority of the Colorado Association advocated black congregations' being admitted to the Association under similar "safeguards." But the Association's majority favored complete separation of black and white Baptists, perhaps because of their own eagerness to be done with the freedmen, perhaps because they realized that no group of blacks would now submit to such limitations.

By 1869 the majority of the state's black Baptists belonged to segregated congregations. In the 1870s and 1880s white Christians gladly allowed the blacks to go their own way, emphasizing at all times the freedmen's desire to worship apart from their former masters. Some denominations, the Disciples for instance, made no effort whatever to minister to blacks. Most, however, undertook at least token efforts at outreach. Catholics, for example, established in 1884 the Catholic Missions for the Colored People and the Indians, that in the eighties and nineties established black congregations in the more settled areas of the state, beginning in 1888 with Houston's Holy Rosary Parish. For their part, blacks went about establishing the Texas branches of the great black denominations that flourished in the postwar period, most importantly the Texas Conference of the African

Methodist Episcopal Zion Church, organized in 1883.

As black and white Christians withdrew into segregated fellowships in the late nineteenth century, the United States Army waged a finally successful campaign against the last free-ranging Indians in Texas. With the removal of the Indian threat—and with the coming of the railroads and the windmill—the white man's borders in Texas began to advance to the south, west, and north. Texans thereafter had always to contend with the distance—the vast space—that for most outsiders has been the most memorable thing about the Lone Star state. The state's size has been a constant source of amazement and comment. In the Episcopal General Conference of 1874 Texas' Bishop Gregg used a map of Texas to strengthen his appeal for more bishops for the state. An astonished Bishop Wilmer, from adjacent Louisiana, confessed his ignorance of Texas' size: "I never realized before how big your Diocese was," he said. "You can have all the Bishops you want."

The denominations of Texas responded to the state's vastness in varying ways, but the necessity for that response has been until the very recent past one of the two or three most important variables in the religious life of Texans. The Episcopalians early on devised perhaps the most effective means of dealing with those distances by providing for "missionary districts" for north, south, and west Texas. Those districts facilitated the extension of the denomination's hierarchy throughout the state in an ordered, regular fashion. Equally effective was the work of the Methodists' mission conferences, especially among the German settlements of central Texas and, gradually, among the Mexican-Americans south of the Nueces. Predictably, the mission efforts of the aggressively congregational Baptists were less systematic. But after 1876 even the Baptists supported what was called "home" mission work among the Germans, first, and then in the Catholic strongholds of El Paso, Corpus

Christi, and San Antonio. It is easy, however, to give too much weight to these Protestant mission endeavors in north, west, and south Texas. To be reminded of their limits, one need only note that as late as 1888 there was *no* minister—of any description—in the area around the raw Panhandle town of Amarillo.

Like Texas Protestants, Catholics in the late nineteenth century moved west, north, and south of the state's antebellum boundaries of settlement. In the south and southwest of the state Catholic mission endeavors culminated in 1912 in the creation of the huge Diocese of Corpus Christi, at 88,000 square miles larger than either Utah or Minnesota. Of the area's 158,000 inhabitants, 83,000 were Catholic; of those, 70,000 were of Mexican descent. In north and west Texas Catholic incursions produced settlements that in the late twentieth century are still among the least expected features of the Texas landscape. Sometimes organized by the church, but more often led by individual Catholic entrepreneurs, small groups of Catholics, many of them from the Catholic German belt of central Texas, created in the midst of a Protestant sea what one geographer has called Catholic "folk-islands." Muenster in the Blackland Prairie, Windthorst in the Cross Timbers, and Nazareth on the High Plains, among others, remain today almost entirely Catholic, testimony to both the audacity and the perseverance of their 19th-century Catholic founders.

The distances with which Texans contended threatened at all times to intensify the basically congregational nature of all religions in the state. In the late nineteenth and early twentieth centuries two institutions emerged that were intended to counteract the centrifugal force of all that space: the denominational periodical and college. Each remains in the late twentieth century a crucial element in the life of most Texas denominations. The *Texas Presbyterian*, the *Firm Foundation* (Disciples, later Churches of Christ), the *Texas Catholic*, *The Churchman* (Episcopal), the *Texas Baptist Herald* and the *Baptist Standard,* and perhaps most significantly, the Methodists' *Texas Christian Advocate,* were each established to inform, unify, and occasionally mobilize the denominational community that supported it. There appears, in fact, to have been a correlation between the congregational nature of a denominational community and the importance it placed on its periodical. For instance, the intensely congregational Baptists supported the *Texas Baptist Herald* as early as 1855. But apparently the two most hierarchical of the state's denominations did not sense the need for periodicals to augment the unifying force of their hierarchies until the 1890s. The *Texas Catholic* appeared only in 1890, and the Episcopalians' *Diocese of Texas* was first published in the same year, ceased appearing in 1898, and did not surface again—as *The Churchman*—until 1906, a full half-century after the first Baptist publication.

Equally important as prospective instruments of denominational unification were the colleges created by Texas religious groups between 1840 and 1920. During that period Texas Christians established more than three dozen senior denominational colleges that have survived to the present. Denominational colleges, of course, have been important everywhere in American religious culture. But they seem to have played an unusually significant role in the religious history of the Lone Star state. Perhaps the distances that separate the communicants of the supporting denominations explain in part their importance. Some of the state's religious colleges and universities have attained in the 20th century national reputations—Texas Christian University, Baylor University, Southern Methodist University, the Presbyterians' Austin College in Sherman, and Trinity University in San Antonio come most readily to mind. Others, such as the Church of Christ's Abilene Christian University, are less well known. A.C.U. is only one of three denominational schools—the Bap-

tists' Hardin-Simmons University and the Methodists' McMurry College are the others—located in the west Texas city of Abilene, a community so thoroughly dominated by the mainline Protestant denominations as to have evolved something of a regional folklore around its rigorously religious atmosphere. The same is true of Waco, home of Baylor University, the largest of the Southern Baptists' institutions of higher learning.

Several of the surviving denominational colleges are institutions established for blacks by both black and white Christians. They include the Methodists' Wiley College in Marshall, the oldest black college west of the Mississippi; Austin's Huston-Tillotson College, now sponsored jointly by the Methodists and the United Church of Christ; the Christian Church's Jarvis College in Hawkins; the AME's Paul Quinn College, now in Waco; the two Baptist schools, Bishop College in Marshall and Butler College in Tyler; and the Christian Methodist Episcopal Church's Texas College, also in Tyler.

The urge to solidify denominational communities was even more evident in the creation of a large number of seminaries that in the late twentieth century remain significant elements in the religious life of Texas. The Roman Catholics support three such institutions: Holy Trinity in Dallas, Assumption in San Antonio, and St. Mary's in Houston. Two of the more important Protestant seminaries, Austin Presbyterian Seminary and the Episcopal Theological Seminary of the Southwest are in the capital. But the "Metroplex" of Dallas-Fort Worth has become the center of theological education in Texas. The Disciples' Brite Divinity School at Fort Worth's Texas Christian University and the Perkins School of Theology at Dallas's Southern Methodist University are both well regarded. Also located in Dallas is the Dallas Theological Seminary and Graduate School of Theology, that remains today the aggressive center of the dispensationalism of its founder, Cyrus I. Scofield. And in Fort

Worth the Southern Baptist Convention maintains the largest theological seminary in the world, Southwestern Baptist Theological Seminary.

Ironically, the journalistic and educational institutions created to foster denominational unity have often contributed to intradenominational conflict. The history of three bodies, the Disciples, the Methodists, and the Baptists, in the late nineteenth and early twentieth centuries was marked by seemingly unrelenting internal warfare. The Baptists, for instance, supported between 1845 and 1885 *two* competing colleges, one at Waco and the other at Independence. It is clear now that most of the bitter divisions between two apparently irreconcilable groups of Baptists can be reduced to a dispute between the supporters of the two schools. They were united in Waco in 1886, and the resulting Baylor University was thereafter as effective an instrument of denominational unification as its two predecessors had been sources of contention. That is not to say that the divisions among the state's Baptists ceased; the focus of the divisions simply shifted from the colleges to the denomination's paper. Between 1890 and 1915 the Baptists contested among themselves for control of the *Texas Baptist Herald*, a debate that finally saw the two principal antagonists involved in a gunfight! At the same time the state's Methodists were embroiled in the "holiness" controversy occasioned by the teachings of HENRY C. MORRISON of Kentucky. Partisans of Morrison and their foes each endeavored mightily to win the *Texas Christian Advocate* over to their side and, in the doing, turned the journal into a battlefield. The same was true of the *Firm Foundation* when the Disciples began to debate in the late nineteenth century the scriptural basis of instrumental music in Christian worship and the proper way of supporting mission work.

In the 20th century an ever-widening gap has developed between a mythical and the real Texas. The myths about the state,

of course, have been by and large the creations of Texans, who have acquired over the years a well-deserved reputation—or notoriety—for exaggerating the attributes of their state. The main outlines of the myths are well known: everything is bigger and better in Texas than anywhere else, and no sane person would wish to live elsewhere; all Texans have at least one oil well and live on ranches of baronial dimensions; and so forth. Although it is not quite mythic in proportion, a firm popular perception about the state's religious culture has emerged in the 20th century also. In that popular view Texas is the buckle of the Bible belt, a homogeneous land of flamboyant fundamentalist preachers who periodically galvanize their huge congregations into remarkably potent instruments of political conservatism and social repression.

But a real Texas has developed in the 20th century that is considerably more complex than the Texas of myths. Since the Civil War the most important constant in the history of the state has been the steady growth of its population. In each of the years between 1870 and 1880, for instance, 100,000 hard-pressed Southerners—black and white—moved to Texas, some of them simply scrawling "GTT"—"Gone to Texas"—on their dilapidated shacks as they left. After the upheavals in Mexico in the 1910s, the number of immigrants from across the Rio Grande increased dramatically; it has never abated. Hundreds of thousands of Americans in the 20th century got to know Texas as the sweltering site of their basic military training. After World War II a remarkable number of them returned to retire, in San Antonio and Austin especially, where retired veterans have become significant parts of the population. More recently, the veterans have been joined by the "snowbirds" of the "frostbelt," who are attracted by the state's climate, relatively low tax structures, and employment opportunities. These later migrations have been made possible by perhaps the most significant invention in the state's history: air conditioning. And this immigration into Texas has coincided—especially since 1950—with an important intrastate shift of population from the countryside to the state's major cities. By 1980 Texas, the mythic land of wide open spaces and rugged individualism, was ranked among the three most heavily urbanized states in the nation, and three of its cities—Houston, Dallas, and San Antonio—were ranked among the eleven most populous in the United States.

If the realities of Texas' population are increasingly at odds with the myths about the state, there seems, superficially at least, to be much to support the popular impressions about its religious culture. It is undeniably true that the mainstream Protestant churches in general and the Southern Baptist and Methodist churches specifically are dominant in Texas. And those denominations have been, and remain, politically active. The Methodists and their *Texas Christian Advocate* were the most powerful force in the crusade to "dry up" Texas early in the 20th century. And Baptist and Methodist voters continue to vote to keep officially dry Texas counties that are in reality awash in liquor obtained just across county lines or in "private clubs." The high point—or the nadir, of one prefers—of religious involvement in politics came in the 1960 crusade led by E. S. James, the courtly editor of the enormously influential *Baptist Standard*, against the presidential candidacy of Catholic John Kennedy. And it is obviously true that some highly visible congregations, such as Dallas's huge First Baptist Church, are dominated by colorful figures like W. A. CRISWELL, men whose strong personalities reinforce constantly the still basically congregational and individualistic tendency of most Protestant denominations in the state.

But there is much more than this to religion in Texas in the late twentieth century. The stereotype of a homogeneous Protestant culture vastly oversimplifies a society that is becoming as diverse and complex as any in the nation. It most obviously ignores the fact that the Catholics constitute the largest single group in the state. And it overlooks a significant if subtle transformation. By the 1970s virtually all of the Protestant denominations—as well as the Catholics—had institutionalized some form of outreach program that gave social and communal dimensions to endeavors that might remain essentially individualistic in their primary focus. And if those efforts, such as the Baptists' Christian Life Commission, do not yet constitute precisely a "social gospel," they do call into question any view of religion in contemporary Texas that emphasizes exclusively its individualistic essence. Moreover, any description of religion in Texas that stops with the Baptists and Methodists errs in ignoring the phenomenal growth since 1945 of the CHURCHES OF CHRIST in the state. Among the most rigorously congregational of all religious groups in America, since 1906 the Churches of Christ have been counted as a separate denomination that since World War II has been among the fastest growing of American denominations. Its greatest growth has been in Texas, where it is strong in the northern and, especially, western areas.

The stereotype of religious homogeneity in Texas has been challenged further by the recent proliferation of exotic religious groups in the state. This has been particularly true in the new frontier of urban Texas that rapidly has replaced the wide open spaces as the scene of opportunity, stimulation, and violence in the state. One of the largest Krishna Consciousness groups in the seventies gathered not in Los Angeles or in New York City but in Dallas. In Houston a bombastic, superpatriotic colonel presided with spiritual close-order drills over the Berachah Church, preaching an astoundingly militaristic gospel that seems a caricature of the 19th-century Texas gospel of competitive individualism. And everywhere in the state one finds the residue of the revivals of the

1970s. A small group of "messianic" Jews gathered briefly on, of all places, the shores of Possum Kingdom Lake near the small Cross Timbers town of Graham. Charismatics were to be found in virtually all denominations. The Church of the Redeemer in Houston became an important and controversial center of the movement within the Episcopal Church. Not even the Southern Baptists were immune. In that decade the Baptist General Convention of Texas found it necessary to investigate and then expel from its membership two rather large congregations whose ministers proved receptive to the revival of interest in the "gifts." Perhaps the most impressive result of that revival has been the increase in the number of "independent" and "Bible" churches that draw a growing portion of their members from disaffected communicants of the mainstream denominations. This increase appears particularly strong in the captial city of Austin, where the University of Texas is rapidly becoming one of the national centers of the revival of fundamental religion among young people of college age.

In 1986 Texas will celebrate the sesquicentennial of its independence from Mexico. As the state prepares to mark that milestone in its history, the developments that in the recent past have been transforming its religious landscape continue apace. Its rural and village churches die along with the small farms and ranches to which they were once organically connected. The farm folk who tilled the land and ran a few head of cattle have leased their mineral rights to distant corporations and have moved to the county seat, there to die in one of the "old folks' homes" that are becoming one of the most important businesses in those towns. The churches of those centers are growing in numbers, sophistication, and complexity. The towns near the booming major cities find that, virtually overnight, they are suburbs with most of the problems of the city and none of the solaces of the countryside. "First" churches accustomed to serving stable communities of 20,000 find themselves struggling to even comprehend—much less serve—the needs of an ever changing population of 100,000. And the great cities themselves continue to grow more rapidly than almost any others in the nation. And as Dallas and Fort Worth, Houston, San Antonio, and Austin approach the populations of America's 19th-century metropolises, they begin to behave as those earlier cities did. The great downtown churches and synagogues abandon the inner cities first to black and brown people and then to gentrification and follow their congregations to the suburbs. There they erect physical plants on a true Texas scale and in them attempt to develop programs that will provide for those communicants a spiritual center, a place of fixity in the midst of what has become in the last 25 years one of the most arresting cultural transformations in the history of the American republic, the passing of the great Southwest from one frontier into another.

See also articles on GEOGRAPHY; INDIANS, TEXAS MISSIONS TO; MIGRATION, WESTWARD (1750-1900); ROMAN CATHOLIC CHURCH; SPANISH INFLUENCE.

Bibliography. Robert A. Baker, *The Blossoming Desert: A Concise History of Texas Baptists*; Carter Boren, *Religion on the Texas Frontier*; R. Douglas Brackenridge, *Voice in the Wilderness: A History of the Cumberland Presbyterian Church in Texas*; Lawrence L. Brown, *The Episcopal Church in Texas, 1838-1874*; Carlos E. Castañeda, *Our Catholic Heritage in Texas, 1519-1950*, 7 vols.; Henry Cohen, et al., *One Hundred Years of Jewry in Texas*; Joseph M. Dawson, *A Century with Texas Baptists*; *The Spiritual Conquest of the Southwest*; Stephen Eckstein, *A History of the Churches of Christ in Texas*; William Ransom Hogan, *The Texas Republic: A Social and Economic History*; Richard B. Hughes, "Old School Presbyterians in Texas, 1830-1861," unpublished Ph.D. dissertation, University of Texas at Austin, 1963; R. E. Ledbetter, "The Planting and Growth of Protestant Denominations in Texas Prior to 1850," unpublished Ph.D. dissertation, University of Chicago, 1950; DuBose Murphy, *A Short History of the Protestant Episcopal Church in Texas*; Olin W. Nail, ed., *Texas Methodism, 1900-1960*; George H. Paschal, Jr., and Judith A. Besmer, *One Hundred Years of the Synod of Texas of the United Presbyterian Church in the U.S.A.*; Macum Phelan, *A History of Early Methodism in Texas, 1817-1866*; William Stuart Red, *A History of the Presbyterian Church in Texas*; *The Texas Colonists and Religion, 1821-1836*;

Jesse Guy Smith, *Heroes of the Saddle Bags: A History of Christian Denominations in the Republic of Texas*; Walter Prescott Webb, editor-in-chief, *The Handbook of Texas*, 3 vols.

HOWARD MILLER
UNIVERSITY OF TEXAS
AT AUSTIN

THEOLOGICAL EDUCATION. This enterprise in the South had its beginnings in the recognition of the need for Anglican (Spanish, English, and French) clergy during the settling of the Southern portion of the country, and the obvious lack of available, qualified ministers. The expansion of colonies both in population and in area made necessary the securing of additional clergy, trained in the homelands or in the newly established educational institutions of the New World. The COLLEGE OF WILLIAM AND MARY was opened in 1694 for the purpose of providing an educated clergy for the established (Anglican) church. It was more significant and successful as the first Southern college of arts and sciences than it was as the center for training clergy of the church.

No similar colleges were established in the Southern colonies for education or for the training of clergy for the Roman Catholic priesthood or the Protestant clergy during the remainder of the 17th or during most of the 18th century. Clergy came as needed from the homelands and communions, or were trained in one of the newly established Eastern theological colleges, such as those at Harvard, Yale, King's College (now Columbia University), and the College of New Jersey (now Princeton), if they did not receive their clerical preparation in association with an experienced, practicing clergyman. This latter arrangement—training for a fee under an able clergyman—probably was the preferred arrangement for many of the communions. As evangelical Christianity spread throughout the land, many groups looked upon a direct call of God, with confirmation by a given congregation, as the essential preparation for the exercise of the Christian ministry. Some groups were highly suspicious of overly educated clergy who were thought to lack the evangelical zeal demanded for a successful ministry. Baptists in particular demanded men called by God and prepared by the Spirit for their clerical vocation. This preference for persons touched by the Spirit was widespread throughout the South, both before and after the American Revolution.

In the early years following America's independence from England, many of the clergy still came from overseas, often accompanying the immigrating groups or coming specifically from the homeland of the immigrants to join them in the New World. After independence, the supply of clergy was cut off from Great Britain. Soon there developed, however, an interest in having clergy who shared the outlook of citizens of the new states through having been reared among them. The adoption of the principle of separation of church and state demanded that theological training in America follow a pattern somewhat different from that found in Europe or in Great Britain. Denominational theological colleges were established in the Eastern states during the late eighteenth and the early nineteenth centuries, and these schools flourished, providing for the clerical needs of many Southern congregations. Among the strongest of these were Harvard, Yale, New Brunswick, Andover, General, Newton, and Princeton. New universities in Virginia and North Carolina had no theological colleges and the College of William and Mary was not a very congenial place for the training of Episcopal priests.

The beginnings of theological education in the South are Roman Catholic. Bishop JOHN CARROLL of Maryland worked with great determination to provide a theological seminary in the New World. Maryland's Georgetown University was established in 1789 as a Roman Catholic college. Some priests received their training there, but Bishop Carroll wished to have a seminary for the purpose of training priests who would know how to fulfill their ministry in the new circumstances of American life. He was finally able to get the Sulpician order to open St. Mary's Seminary in 1791, the first theological school in the South. It continues to flourish.

The spread of Catholicism to Charleston, BARDSTOWN (KY), New Orleans, St. Louis, and Cincinnati made necessary the opening of theological schools in those localities in the early nineteenth century. JOHN ENGLAND, bishop of Charleston, was successful in opening a small school there in 1822, which by 1833 had sent 20 priests into the diocese. St. Thomas Seminary in Bardstown began in 1808 with the establishment of the diocese, but it was a struggling and tiny enterprise. A seminary in St. Louis was established by the Sulpicians in 1818; New Orleans had to wait some considerable time for a seminary of its own. Cincinnati had its seminary by 1829. Most of these theological schools were supported by small colleges where the sons of congregation members received general education, often with the seminarians as their teachers. The college fees helped to support the seminary.

Episcopal, Presbyterian, Baptist, and Lutheran theological education came to the South at about the same general period of time, rather early in the 19th century, although the Presbyterians had attempted earlier to establish seminaries, one of them at Maryville TN. In 1807, the Presbyterians began a theological school in connection with Hampden-Sydney College in Virginia. From this effort, the Union Theological Seminary in Richmond developed; its date of founding is 1812. The Columbia Theological Seminary has its origins in 1828 at the Presbyterian Church of Lexington GA. It was moved to Columbia SC and again in the current century to its present location in Decatur GA. In Kentucky, initial efforts began at the turn of the 19th century in connection with the establishment of Transylvania College in central Kentucky, but it was not until 1853 that the Danville Theological Seminary, now the Louisville Presbyterian Theological Seminary, was established.

Baptist seminary education has its impetus in the South from the initiatives of LUTHER RICE in Washington DC. In 1821 the Columbian College was opened there for the training of men and women for mission service and for the ministry. In 1832 the Baptists then established the University of Richmond as their first Southern college for the education of ministers and others. Baptist seminary work then moved from Richmond to South Carolina, and by 1859 the first Southern Baptist Theological Seminary was founded in Greenville. On the Greenville faculty was one of the most distinguished biblical scholars of Southern Baptist history, C. H. TOY, who went on to Louisville when the seminary moved there in 1877, and then took up his teaching at Harvard Divinity School when conflict over his theology broke out in Louisville.

The education of Episcopal priests was concentrated for several decades in the General Theological Seminary in New York, which had been founded in 1817. But already by 1823 a group of laypersons from Maryland, the District of Columbia, and Virginia were bent upon opening a theological school that would be more attentive to American and evangelical influences. They established a theological school in association with the College of William and Mary in that year, but this arrangement proved unsatisfactory; the college did not seem hospitable to the purposes of the seminary's founders. Accordingly, they moved the seminary to its present location in Alexandria as the Protestant Episcopal Theological Seminary of Virginia.

Episcopal seminary education in Kentucky began in Lexington in 1832 and continued for a few years. The charter for an Episcopal theological school was recently reactivated (1951) and theological education, especially for the candidates for the priesthood who have had a secular vocation for some time, continues in Lexington at the Episcopal Theological Seminary in Kentucky.

In Tennessee, the UNIVERSITY OF THE SOUTH was founded in 1860, intended as a major university with a school of theology for the education of clergy for the Southern Episcopal Church. Created at the initiative of many of the dioceses of the Episcopal Church, the St. Luke's School of Theology of the University of the South has always had a small enrollment, but its alumni have been highly influential church leaders through the years.

Lutheran theological education in the South began in Virginia and moved to South Carolina, as the Lutheran population was enlarged by new arrivals from Europe or moved down from Pennsylvania through western Maryland and Virginia through western Maryland and Virginia to the Carolinas and Georgia (between was established in 1830 in Pomaria SC and opened its doors the next year. It was moved to various locations during the next decades, including the campus of Newberry College in the town of that name. After the Civil War, the seminary had a 12-year location on the campus of Roanoke College in Salem VA before moving back to South Carolina in 1884.

Methodism had a somewhat later beginning in theological education. The General Conference of 1820 authorized the founding of literary institutions, and by the end of the 1830s several colleges had been established where the study of theology took place. In the South, these colleges were Randolph-Macon in Virginia, Emory in Georgia, Holston in Tennessee, and Emory and Henry in southwestern Virginia. Trinity College was soon to come (1859), tracing its origins to a school in Randolph County founded in 1838, and developing into Duke University.

The oldest of the Methodist theological schools is Boston University School of Theology, founded in 1839 as the New England Bible Institute. Garrett (in Evanston) came next, in 1854. A formally organized Methodist theological school in the South came into existence in Nashville with the founding of Vanderbilt University in 1873 and the opening of its Biblical Department in 1875. The Methodists withdrew recognition from Vanderbilt in 1914 after controversy had developed over procedures for electing members of the Board of Trust. Perkins School of Theology of Southern Methodist University was founded in 1911, Candler School of Theology of Emory University began in 1914, and Duke University's Divinity School began its work in 1926 on the newly created university campus.

Lexington Theological Seminary, the first Disciples of Christ seminary formally organized, opened its doors in 1865 as the College of the Bible. Disciples educators had been pioneers, however, in the creation of Bethany and Transylvania Colleges already at the end of the 18th century. Disciples would go on to found many colleges and seminaries, as well as numerous Bible chairs, in the South and Southwest.

Until the 1830s, Protestant and Catholic Christianity were nearly unanimous in their opposition to slavery. But the opposition began to diminish as the numbers of slaves increased through the South and as more and more leading members of the Christian congregations saw their livelihood heavily dependent upon the institution of slavery. The issue of slavery had divided the churches of North and South to such an extent by the 1840s that many of the church bodies formally separated into Northern and Southern churches. Some of these divisions still have not been overcome and the legacy of slavery still affects Christianity in the South.

Blacks and whites worshiped together for some years in the 18th and the early nineteenth centuries. The first black Baptist congregation formed in the United States was organized at SILVER BLUFF CHURCH on the Savannah River in South Carolina in 1773, with others organized very soon thereafter in Virginia at Petersburg and Richmond. The first black denomination was organized by Richard

Allen in 1816 and received the name African Methodist Episcopal Church. In 1821 the African Methodist Episcopal Zion Church was organized by James Varick. These two bodies flourished primarily in the North, even though the bulk of black Christians was in the South. Blacks continued to hold membership in the Methodist Episcopal Church, South, after the separation of Methodists into two bodies. Similarly, black Baptists in the South continued to worship with the Southern Baptists for some time after the 1844 split of Baptists, but some independent congregations began forming throughout the South prior to the Civil War, requiring the identification of suitable clerical leadership.

Black clergy received their education in pre-Civil War days much the same way white Methodists and Baptists received theirs. Some of the Northern clergy were well educated, and the same may have been the case with black ministers in the South. Training under experienced ministers or in groups of trainees under a skilled educator no doubt provided the bulk of the preparation for black clergy, just as it did for whites. Suspicion of white clergy who were too well educated had its counterpart in black congregations.

The Civil War brought such devastation to the South that most of its theological schools were closed. Virginia Theological Seminary in Alexandria became a hospital for Union soldiers, for example, although one faculty member educated a few priests in his home in Staunton. The war over slavery also deepened the hostility between Northern and Southern white Christians and between blacks and whites in the South. Southern Christianity has still not recovered from this terrible toll.

The postwar years saw a flurry of activity on behalf of education for black people. Northern Christian bodies, with the help of many institutions and individuals, brought into existence a host of black colleges with departments for the education of the clergy: Talladega in Alabama,

Hampton Institute in Virginia, Tougaloo in Mississippi, Fisk in Tennessee, Howard in Washington, Atlanta University in Georgia, and many others. Methodists assisted in the founding of six colleges between 1856 and 1870. The Presbyterian and Reformed Churches established Biddle University (now Johnson C. Smith) in 1867 in Charlotte and Knoxville College in 1875. Baptists worked to create no fewer than 10 colleges during the early decades after the end of the war. Roger Williams University, the oldest, was founded in 1863 in Nashville and still exists as a part of the heritage of the American Baptist College of the Bible.

Slowly, the theological schools of the prewar years began to recover, and a few additional schools were established in the 19th century. As noted above, the Methodists created Vanderbilt University in 1873 with the support of Commodore Cornelius Vanderbilt. The Presbyterians built up their two seminaries, Union in Richmond and the seminary in Danville that would move in 1901 to Louisville. The School of Theology of the University of the South at Sewanee TN began to thrive, joining with its sister institution in Alexandria VA in providing Episcopal clergy for the South. The Southern Baptist Theological Seminary moved to Louisville in 1877 and flourished in the new location. Not until 1901 would the theological school of Baylor University in Waco TX, now the Southwestern Baptist Theological Seminary in Fort Worth, offer competition to Southern Seminary. Methodist seminary education was still concentrated in the North—at Boston, Drew (founded in 1867 in New Jersey), and Garrett (founded in 1854 in Evanston IL), although Westminster (now Wesley Theological Seminary in Washington) Seminary in Maryland was to be established in 1882. Trinity and Randolph-Macon Colleges did prepare Methodist clergy for the South, but it would not be until well in the 20th century that Duke, Southern Methodist, and Emory Universities would develop their strong Methodist theological schools.

Roman Catholic theological education in the South continued strong—in Maryland and the District of Columbia, in St. Louis, and (somewhat later) in New Orleans. The Lutherans continued their program in Virginia and South Carolina, while Missouri Synod Lutherans opened up seminary training in St. Louis.

During the 20th century, theological education in the South has made great advances. There are now no fewer than 57 accredited or associate schools of theology in the South listed in the Bulletin of the Association of Theological Schools. In addition, the Bible school movement is enjoying great growth: there are 54 Southern accredited or associate members of the American Association of Bible Colleges listed in its current bulletin. These 111 institutions are not the only theological schools in the South: some schools, as a matter of principle, are not associated with either of these accrediting bodies. Dallas Theological Seminary and Bob Jones University are two such unrelated institutions. A number of small theological colleges or training centers could also be added to the list.

There are no Jewish schools of theology in the South, although it is the case that a small number of Jewish students enroll in Southern theological schools and graduate programs. Many Christian students of theology study in the nearest Jewish theological center to the South: Hebrew Union College-Jewish Institute of Religion, Cincinnati OH.

A major question facing theological schools in the South today is how the old Evangelicalism of the South is to relate to the new, militant, and sometimes intolerant Evangelicalism that is widespread in the South today. The theological schools can no longer count upon an enrollment of students who are in reasonable agreement on the nature of the religious heritage of their respective theological communities. The bulk of the institutions has an orientation to critical biblical and theological scholarship. They are committed to find a way to prepare men and women for theological leadership in the modern world that will take account of the findings of the natural and social sciences and the Gospel's demand for public justice in institutional, social, and personal life. But there are likely to be many supporters of these theological schools who have lost sympathy with some of these commitments. Some among them will belong to the MORAL MAJORITY, will support Creation Science, will be in favor of prayer in the public schools, and will in general be supporters of causes and understandings long rejected by moderate, critical Protestant and Catholic Christianity in America.

The number and character of the theological schools in the South appear to be fairly stable. Theological education of clergy has undergone great change during the past two decades. The creation of the Interdenominational Theological Center and the strengthening and reorganization of Howard University Divinity School are noteworthy accomplishments. Black institutions are offering excellent critical and constructive leadership for the black churches, both in these black institutions and in others, and in a number of primarily white schools of theology. There are fewer small and struggling black schools of theology today than there were only two decades ago, partly because of the mergers that created the Interdenominational Theological Center. Several black institutions continue to do fine work, though having rather small enrollments and a small number of faculty members.

Women are entering the theological schools of the South in ever-larger numbers, have become equal partners in many of these schools, and are contributing to the renewal of seminary and church life in remarkably fine ways. The problem of their finding suitable pastoral assignments has not been solved, but improvements are notable in several of the denominations.

Roman Catholic enrollment in primarily Protestant theological schools has been a great boon to the quality of the latter. It also has made it unnecessary for

Roman Catholic theological institutions in the South to increase in number or enrollment as the Catholic population has increased in the South. Roman Catholic professors and students are to be found in most of the Southern theological schools of some size and strength.

The teaching of courses in Jewish religious thought and theology has also increased in the theological schools of the South. The education of future Protestant and Catholic clergy in an environment that is hospitable to the Jewish religious heritage, rather than hostile to it, is a most important development. It has come about in part through the initiatives of Jewish national groups, but the decisive factor has been the appointment of scholars trained in Judaica to the theological school faculties and their introduction of appropriate courses and seminars.

The growth of strong programs in religious studies at the universities and colleges of the South has meant that the theological schools often receive entering students who are well schooled in the scholarly study of religion, including non-Western and non-Christian religions. While some tensions still are to be found between a "theological" and a "religious studies" approach to the study of religion, the gain in this tension, for theology and the church, is very great indeed. One clear safeguard that the tension will continue to be healthy is the strength of graduate study in religion at several of these theological schools with a "theological" orientation. The Ph.D. in religion and theology offered by some of the Southern universities and theological schools bears comparison with the best in North America.

See also articles on EDUCATION, CHRISTIAN HIGHER; THEOLOGY.

Bibliography. Sydney E. Ahlstrom, *A Religious History of the American People*; Hugh George Anderson, *Lutheranism in the Southeastern States, 1860-1886. A Social History*; H. George Anderson and Robert M. Calhoon, eds., *"A Truly Efficient School of Theology": The Lutheran Theological Southern Seminary in Historical Context, 1830-1980*; Donald Smith Armentrout, *The Quest for the Informed Priest: A History of the School of Theology*; Boone M. Bowen, *The Candler School of Theology—Sixty*

Years of Service; William Adams Brown, "Theological Education," *Monroe's Cyclopedia of Education* 5: 582-606; W. A. Daniel, *The Education of Negro Ministers*; John O. Gross, ed., *A Survey of Theological Education in the Methodist Church*; E. Brooks Holifield, *The Gentlemen Theologians: American Theology in Southern Culture, 1795-1860*; Charles D. Johnson, *Higher Education of Southern Baptists: An Institutional History, 1826-1954*; Robert L. Kelly, *Theological Education in America*; Lloyd Paul McDonald, *The Seminary Movement in the United States; Projects, Foundations and Early Development (1784-1833)*; Donald G. Mathews, *Religion in the Old South*; Edwin Mims, *History of Vanderbilt University*; John Mostert, ed., *Directory, American Association of Bible Colleges*; Robert Stuart Sanders, *History of Louisville Presbyterian Theological Seminary, 1853-1953*; Horace Greeley Smith, *Methodism's Obsession with Higher Education*; Dwight E. Stevenson, *Lexington Theological Seminary, 1865-1965*; Bard Thompson, *Vanderbilt Divinity School: A History*; Charlotte M. Thompson, ed., *Bulletin, 4: Directory*, Association of Theological Schools (1982).

WALTER HARRELSON
VANDERBILT UNIVERSITY

THEOLOGY (SOUTHERN). The development of religion as the basis for theology in southern North America was manifold: the English established colonies in Virginia, the Carolinas, and Georgia; the Spanish in Florida; and the French in Louisiana. Each colonization brought its own religious heritage. In the early life of the region there was some theological reflection, as exemplified by THOMAS JEFFERSON; but, on the whole, significant theology awaited the more settled society of the 19th century. By this time, the South had become predominantly Protestant and the corresponding theology, through a variety of expressions, has remained representative of the region.

"Southern theology" is North American theology with distinctive social and cultural characteristics. Hence, Southern religious thought, sharing general Protestant convictions, was evangelistic and revivalistic in foundation and construction. Convinced of the reasonable structure of the world, the finality of biblical revelation, and the Christian interpretation of reality, theologians in the region adhered to 19th-century rational orthodoxy. And these commitments were more tenaciously held than was typical of the rest of the nation.

For nearly a hundred years, from the middle of the 19th century, what was received from others was refracted through Southern theologians' regional experience and brought to earth in their setting. The chief factors distinguishing theology as "Southern" were race and slavery. Conscious regional separation and self-aware differentiation became explicit with the denominational divisions prior to the Civil War. The most notable characteristics were a persisting theological conservatism and a primary commitment to biblical authority.

Although many basic theological persuasions were held in common in the South, there were differences, and it is easiest to gain an impression of the overall development through denominational expressions. We shall, therefore, look at theologians within three communions especially, the Southern Presbyterian, the Southern Baptist, and the Methodist Episcopal, South, who helped direct the major trends.

Southern Presbyterians produced the major constructive theologies in the 19th century and were represented by several significant thinkers: JAMES HENLEY THORNWELL (1812-1862) of Columbia Theological Seminary in South Carolina, whose *Collected Writings* in three volumes was compiled in 1871; ROBERT J. BRECKINRIDGE (1800-1871) of the Presbyterian Theological School in Danville KY whose major book, *The Knowledge of God Objectively Considered*, was published in 1855; and ROBERT LEWIS DABNEY (1820-1898) of Union Theological Seminary in Richmond VA whose *Syllabus and Notes of the Course of Systematic and Polemic Theology* was published in 1878. All of these men were greatly indebted to the Scottish common sense philosophy regnant at Princeton, all had great confidence in the rationality of the world, all stood in the tradition of CALVINISM, particularly as transmitted by Scottish covenantal Presbyterianism, and all wrote systematic theologies. Yet there was disagreement over emphases, especially between Dabney and Breckinridge.

Some basic assumptions were held in common: the world is rational, God provides revelational knowledge, and there is a coherence between natural and revealed knowledge. All of these men defended the Christian faith by use of natural evidence and biblical revelation. Upon these bases they developed a comprehensive interpretation of God, the world, and human life. In discussions among American Calvinists, they sided with the "Old School" or more traditional Calvinists, perhaps because of political as well as theological affinity.

Southern Baptists were also theologically productive during the second half of the 19th century. The first theological leader was JOHN LEADLEY DAGG (1794-1884) of Mercer University. Dagg, like many others in the era, was dependent upon Scottish common sense philosophy and used this philosophical system to indicate the truth of theological assertions. Dagg's distinctive emphasis, as found in *The Evidences of Christianity* (1869), was the personal capability of individuals to judge the gospel. JAMES P. BOYCE (1827-1888), the founder of Southern Baptist Theological Seminary in Greenville SC, since moved to Louisville, was also a formative theologian in his tradition. A student of Charles Hodge, the conservative Calvinist of Princeton, Boyce followed his mentor and set the conservative direction of Southern Baptist thought. His work, *The Abstract of Systematic Theology* (1887), was a short, practical textbook that stressed God's sovereignty and the primacy of personal trust in Christ as savior. A contemporary of these two, and perhaps the single most influential man in the Southern Baptist Convention, was JAMES R. GRAVES (1820-1893). It was Graves who insisted upon "Baptist Church Succession" from John the Baptist to the present, who strongly differentiated Baptists from Methodists, and who reinforced evangelical orthodoxy as the Southern Baptist theological position.

A critical moment in Southern Baptist history and theological development occurred in the late 1890s when W. H. WHITSITT (1841-1911) published a book that claimed contemporary Baptist churches had their origin in 1641 when believer's baptism by immersion was recovered in England. Whitsitt was forced, in 1899, to resign the presidency of the Baptist Seminary in Louisville. With this move Southern Baptist theological education was reinforced in a cautious approach.

Methodist Episcopal, South, theologians were also significant. Thomas Ralston (1805-1885), a native of Kentucky, produced in his *Elements of Theology* (1847) the first Methodist systematic theology in North America. He was also persuaded of rational orthodoxy and developed a type of natural theology built upon the continuing light of God in human life. He also insisted that biblical revelation, although central, required reason for its explication. Henry Bidleman Bascom (1796-1850) of Tennessee also developed a similar statement. Thomas O. Summers (1812-1882), a transplanted Englishman, was a prolific writer and editor. Summers produced a two-volume *Systematic Theology* (1888) that was an adaptation of the British Methodist Richard Watson's *Theological Institutes* and remained close to the originating impulse of John Wesley. Albert T. Bledsoe (1809-1877) came to the Southern church late in his career, but he was considered a chief spokesman for the 19th-century Wesleyan emphasis on the freedom of the human will and developed an interpretation of human ability that stressed autonomous human freedom and weakened the emphasis upon gracious foundations. He also wrote an influential study of *Theodicy* in 1854.

For all of these 19th-century theologians—Presbyterian, Baptist, and Methodist—the world is rational, the human mind is capable of apprehending God's presence in the world, and divine revelation is required to correct and fulfill human understanding. These are traditionalists who understood the theological task to be that of making clear what was dimly known through natural reason and given normative expression in Scripture.

The 20th century has witnessed continuity and change. Among Southern Presbyterians there have been no voices that have chartered new directions, although there is a suggestive essay by Kenneth J. Foreman (1891-), *Identification: Human and Divine* (1963), which explores fresh ways of speaking of relations within the life of God and between God and persons. For the most part, however, Presbyterians have continued with their received theology. The most significant contribution of Southern Presbyterians in this century has been in biblical scholarship and there they have excelled.

Southern Baptists have continued a personalistic evangelistic theology and have moved into ecumenically informed biblical study. EDGAR Y. MULLINS (1860-1928) taught at Southern Baptist Theological Seminary and became president after Whitsitt. Mullins was a philosophical personalist and constructed his theology on this base. He also contributed to *Fundamentals: A Testimony to The Truth* (1912). Warm in spirit, he introduced a gentleness into Southern Baptist theology. His books, *Baptist Beliefs* (1925), *The Christian Religion in its Doctrinal Expression* (1928), and *Axioms of Religion* (1978) stress human freedom and personal knowledge of Jesus Christ. With Mullins, this theological tradition continued to be evangelical and biblically based. WALTER THOMAS CONNER (1877-1952) a professor of theology at Southwestern Baptist Theological Seminary and especially influential in the Southwest, was noted for his pithy sayings, "Connerisms." He also stressed in *Christian Doctrine* (1937) personal relation with Jesus Christ as savior and the biblical foundation of doctrine.

By mid-twentieth century there were evident changes in Southern Baptist positions and much of this was found among teachers at the theological seminary in Louisville. WILLIAM OWEN CARVER

(1868-1954) was a professor of missions and among the most provocative thinkers in the convention. His books, *Missions in the Plan of the Ages* (1909) and *The Glory of God and the Christian Calling* (1949), were studies that reached toward a more ecumenical statement of Christian faith. Eric C. Rust (1910-), a transplanted Englishman, was an able historian of thought who interpreted Christian belief in an impressive and engaging manner. His books, *The Christian Understanding of History* (1947) and *Positive Religion in A Revolutionary Time* (1970), represent his central motifs.

The publication of the Broadman Commentary series in the 1960s is most significant in indicating the move of biblical scholars into what might be called "biblical ecumenism." Although the first volume on Genesis was withdrawn, all of the commentaries utilize contemporary biblical critical work and represent a conservative and responsible participation in the general work of scriptural interpretation. The most representative theologian of the present stage of Southern Baptist thought is Dale Moody (1915-) who, in keeping with his tradition, emphasizes personal awareness of sin, new birth, and biblical foundations. But in addition, Moody is in conversation with the wider Christian community from Roman Catholicism to representative Protestant theology. His major works are *Spirit of The Living God* (1968) and *The Word of Truth*, 2 vols. (1980-1981).

The greatest change in Southern theology has been evident among the Methodists. In 1902 Wilbur Fisk Tillett (1865-1936), a professor of systematic theology at Vanderbilt University and dean of the theological faculty, published *Personal Salvation*, which maintained emphases consistent with previous Methodist theologians. In 1924, however, he published *Paths That Lead to God* and with this book moved directly into the mainstream of liberal Evangelicalism. Convinced that modernity has eroded the certitude of Christian faith, he undertook

a defense of faith built upon belief in the immanence or indwelling of God in all of life. Releasing earlier theological categories, Tillett affirmed belief in evolutionary development of human understanding of God and in the gradual realization of God's Kingdom on earth. Gilbert T. Rowe (1875-1960) of Duke University in the period between the wars presented a liberal evangelical theology with primary emphasis upon adaptation to modern culture, Christian experience, God's immanental presence, and the possibility of conformity to the "spirit of Jesus Christ." Liberality, Rowe argued, is a birthright of Methodists, and this means a freedom to interpret Christian faith on a scientific ground. His two books, *Reality In Religion* (1927) and *The Meaning of Methodism* (1930), express these convictions. With the emergence of these two theologians, there is identification of Southern theology with larger contemporary patterns of North American theology.

Two other dimensions of Southern Christianity need to be mentioned because of their importance: the Holiness movement and black theology. The Holiness movement in Protestant Christianity took distinctive form in the 19th century. Derived from many denominational backgrounds, it was especially influential in Methodism. By the 1880s new denominations were being formed and a number of these were started in the South and have remained in that region. A Holiness interpretation of theology was developed in several groups, such as the Pentecostal Holiness Church and the United Holy Church in America, and at such institutions as Asbury Theological Seminary in Kentucky and Oral Roberts University in Oklahoma. This is not a distinctively Southern movement, but it is a growing reality with roots in the South.

Black theologians have made contributions since the middle of the 19th century, beginning with African Methodist Episcopal leaders DANIEL A. PAYNE (1811-1893) and HENRY MCNEAL TURNER (1834-1915). These men were

Methodist in their thought; both stressed the issue of theodicy and began interpretations from a distinctively black perspective. James H. Cone (1938-), an AME theologian from Arkansas, has developed a thoroughgoing interpretation especially in *Black Theology and Black Power* (1969) and in *God of the Oppressed* (1976). Major J. Jones (1919-), a United Methodist theologian at Gammon Theological Seminary, Atlanta, has pursued this theme in his two books, *Black Awareness: A Theology of Hope* (1971) and *Christian Ethics for Black Theology* (1974). Both Cone and Jones begin with black experience; Cone demands an exploration and utilization of this experience in order to bring liberation to the oppressed blacks; Jones utilizes this experience to call for an inclusive affirmation of all humanity in realizing the Kingdom of God.

Current theology in the South continues interest in specific traditions, but there are altering emphases. ALBERT C. OUTLER (1908-) of Southern Methodist University has made significant contributions to the study of the early church and John Wesley in his concern for interpreting the Christian tradition. Robert E. Cushman (1913-) of Duke has set new directions as he has also written on the Wesleyan tradition, but his major contribution has been a reemphasis on human sinfulness and Christology. His study of Plato, *Therapeia* (1958), and his theological construction, *Faith Seeking Understanding* (1981), represent a new initiative in theory of knowledge and in reemphasizing the historical dimensions of the confession, "Jesus is Lord."

Other theological interests have come to central attention among Southern theologians. At Vanderbilt there is a strong interest in the philosophical position of phenomenology and its possibilities for theology, as is evident in the work of Edward T. Farley (1929-). Schubert M. Ogden (1928-) of Southern Methodist University has utilized the work of process thinkers, A. N. Whitehead and Charles

Hartshorne, to develop a theology that is attentive to present culture and the intellectual mood of the time. Continuing the Protestant liberal tradition, *The Reality of God* (1966) and *Faith and Freedom* (1979) express his effort to speak to "post-modern" culture.

Liberation theology has also become a matter of primary interest for some. Frederick Herzog (1925-) of Duke is perhaps the leading liberation theologian of North America. A United Church of Christ minister, Herzog holds together theology and ethics in *Liberation Theology* (1972) and *Justice Church* (1980). Exploring biblical foundations for the assertion of God's liberating intent, Herzog has critically assessed contemporary society for practical implementation of social justice. Theodore H. Runyon (1930-) of Emory University has pursued this theme in relation to his own WESLEYAN TRADITION in *Sanctification and Liberation* (1980).

Especially at university-related theological schools, there has been a clear move toward ecumenical theology (the makeup of the faculties of these institutions illustrates this fact) and a notable effort to assess contemporary values and commitments and to speak from a Christian perspective to present issues. The attention of many of the theologians associated with denominational seminaries has been more fixed upon their own communions and upon the attempt to reinterpret their inherited tradition.

Southern society continues to be a "church society," that is, organized religion remains a reigning cultural reality and theological interpretation is carried on within the awareness of this context. For many theologians this means that their task is a priestly one, ministering to the needs of those within an accepted Christian frame of reference. For some on the current scene, a more prophetic stance is accepted as they attempt to challenge established religious-cultural convictions and move from individualistic and nominal commitment to a more engaged challenge of American secular and religious values.

Southern theology for the last century and a half has been dominantly a conservative force. It has sought rational interpretation of inherited theological traditions and the application of these traditions to personal faith and activity. Only recently have there been signs of change in inherited modes of thought and cultural frames. Southern theology seems to be moving into awareness of more inclusive American society and more extended ecumenical community. Denominational ties remain strong, but there is evidence that even the understanding of biblical foundations may be changing. The challenging task that continues for Southern theology is to relate the richness of its heritage to contemporary life.

See also articles on BLACK RELIGION; ETHICS, CHRISTIAN; ECUMENISM; EVANGELICALISM; HOLINESS MOVEMENT; OLD SCHOOL/NEW SCHOOL; REVIVALISM; THEOLOGICAL EDUCATION.

Bibliography. E. Brooks Holifield, *The Gentlemen Theologians: American Theology in Southern Culture, 1795-1860;* also volumes cited in this essay.

THOMAS A. LANGFORD
DUKE UNIVERSITY

THOMISM. This is a tradition in Catholic theology rooted in the thought of St. Thomas Aquinas (d. 1274) that gave prominence to the natural world and natural human reason in Christian thought. Medieval theology in Thomas's time encountered a rigorous challenge from fresh translations of Aristotle's physics and metaphysics. This newly discovered philosophy appeared to contradict established Christian teaching by proposing the world's coeternity with God and the death of the soul with the death of the body.

Thomas's contribution was to incorporate Aristotle's understanding of God and the world into Catholic teaching so that the integrity of both was preserved. He proposed that Aristotle's conclusions were the fullest and most accurate available to ordinary human reason. By the help of grace, however, these views could be perfected and expanded into the full truth of Christian revelation. For example, in an examination of cause and effect in nature, the necessary existence of God as first cause of all things can be demonstrated. That this first cause is, in addition, the covenanting, triune God of the Scriptures is revealed only to faith.

Thomas thus modified the thought of his great mentor of 800 years earlier, St. Augustine of Hippo (d. 430), for whom faith was the necessary presupposition of any genuine theological reflection. Thomas gave natural reason and natural theology (as distinct from faith and revealed theology) a contributing, if limited, place in the scope of the theological discipline. By so doing, he allowed for a certain knowledge of the divine to be opened to any rational observer of natural existence. Augustine himself had been much drawn to reflection on creation, but apart from at least an implicit faith, saw the virtue of such reflection overwhelmed by human idolatry—the tendency to render nature itself divine.

The position known as Thomism derived from Thomas's achievement in establishing a continuity between the natural and the supernatural in matters of theological knowledge, moral virtue, and salvation. The continuity was, of course, rendered by grace, but not so radically as to obliterate the moderation, rationality, and wholeness of Thomas's outlook. Ordinary, reasonable existence can rise to supernatural fruition through the special teaching of the church as guardian and guide.

Early Thomism was, in effect, brought to a close by the Protestant Reformation, which challenged Thomistic sources into renewal and fresh resurgency, especially in France, Italy, and Spain. Reformation leadership denounced Thomist continuity and graduated increase in salvation, the notion of the believer's justification as a process of growth in righteousness before God. For Protestants, such a process gave the church too extensive an intermediary role in Christ's saving work. Indeed, the grace of Christ's death caused a sharp discontinuity in the individual's claim to righteousness, throwing the Protestant worshiper radically upon the resources of grace in a direct personal relation with Christ (though not without the church).

Thomism countered through the work of the Catholic Council of Trent (1545-1563) and the movement of Ignatius Loyola and the Jesuits, until the French Revolution and Napoleon brought it to the end of its second phase. In the 20th century Thomism has once again come forward in the work of the philosopher Jacques Maritain (1882-1973). Acknowledging the modern world's preoccupation with self-awareness, Maritain has proposed with Thomas that individual existence find a level of continuity with creation as a whole and with the being and love of God.

See also article on ROMAN CATHOLICISM.

Bibliography. F. Copleston, *A History of Philosophy*, vol. 2; E. H. Gilson, *The Christian Philosophy of St. Thomas Aquinas*; M. Grabmann, *Thomas Aquinas, His Personality and Thought*.

WILLIAM MALLARD
EMORY UNIVERSITY

THORNWELL, JAMES HENLEY (1812-1862), Presbyterian theologian and regional champion, was born in the Marlborough District of South Carolina. It is generally believed that the influence of his mother and early teachers inflamed Thornwell's intense interest in the Christian church, although his choice of a ministerial career did not occur until several years after he completed his degree at South Carolina College, Columbia, in 1831.

After teaching school in South Carolina for a few years, Thornwell entered the Presbyterian Theological Seminary at Columbia and in 1834 received his license to preach. In 1835 he became pastor of the Presbyterian Church in Lancaster SC. Thornwell and his family returned to Columbia in 1837 upon his appointment as professor of logic and belles lettres in South Carolina College.

Though periodically suffering bouts of ill health, Thornwell established himself as one of the foremost supporters of Old School Presbyterianism. Noted for his keen intellect and the logical rigor of his thought, Thornwell effectively argued for conservatism in church administration and church-state relationships, maintaining that the church should asssume no administrative responsibilities not assigned to it in the New Testament.

In 1847, Thornwell was elected moderator of the Old School General Assembly (PCUSA). Subsequently (1852) he became president of South Carolina College and later (1855) occupied the chair of theology in the Presbyterian seminary at Columbia.

As a staunch supporter of the South, Thornwell was a significant force behind the organization of the Presbyterian Church in the Confederate States of America in 1861, although illness prevented his active service in its development. During his relatively brief career, Thornwell wrote and lectured extensively; he also served as editor of the *Southern Quarterly Review* and was the founding editor of the *Southern Presbyterian Review*.

See also articles on OLD SCHOOL/NEW SCHOOL; SLAVERY; SPIRITUALITY OF THE CHURCH.

Bibliography. B. M. Palmer, *The Life and Letters of James Henley Thornwell*; H. Shelton Smith, "The Church and the Social Order in the Old South as Interpreted by James Henley Thornwell," *Church History* 7 (June 1938): 45-124.

DORALYN J. HICKEY
NORTH TEXAS STATE UNIVERSITY

THURMAN, HOWARD (1899-1981), black preacher and educator, was born in Daytona Beach FL and reared by his ex-slave grandmother. He is said to have read the Bible aloud repeatedly as a child and to have learned not only of the vicissitudes of slaves but also of their deep religious faith. After attending the Florida Baptist

Academy (later Normal Institute) in Jacksonville (1915-1919), Thurman attended Morehouse College where he reportedly read every book in its library, edited the yearbook, debated, and was class valedictorian.

In 1922 he attended classes with white students for the first time in his life at the Columbia University Summer School. After graduating from Morehouse with an A.B. in economics in 1923, he was ordained a Baptist minister (1925) and pursued a B.D. degree from Colgate-Rochester Theological Seminary. In 1929 a Kent Fellowship enabled him to study mysticism at Haverford College under the Quaker Rufus Jones, thereby fulfilling a request Thurman had initiated upon reading Jones's *Finding the Trail* (1924).

After serving as pastor of Mt. Zion Baptist Church in Oberlin OH (1926-1928), Thurman returned to Morehouse and Spelman Colleges as professor of religion and director of religious life. In 1932 he moved to Howard University to teach religion and become dean of Rankin Chapel, a position he held until 1944 when he took leave to become copastor of San Francisco's multiracial Church for the Fellowship of All Peoples (formed in 1943).

Perhaps one of the most pivotal experiences in Thurman's career was meeting Mohandas K. Gandhi during a 1935 "Pilgrimage of Friendship" tour of India, Burma, and Ceylon sponsored by the World Student Christian Federation. Gandhi's criticism of Christianity for "fostering segregation" triggered Thurman's study of the teachings of Jesus about the disinherited. A 1953 appointment as dean of the Daniel L. Marsh Chapel and professor of spiritual resources and discipline at Boston University made Thurman the first full-time black faculty member at that university.

The recipient of innumerable awards and honorary degrees, he was a prolific writer. A 1972 bibliography of his publications lists 19 books or pamphlets; 14 chapters in books; 21 sermons, addresses, and articles; and four book reviews. His autobiography, *With Head and Heart*, was published in 1979. Thurman's rich baritone voice and expressive hands equipped him well to become what *Life* termed one of 12 "great preachers" of the 20th century.

ROBERT L. HALL
UNIVERSITY OF MARYLAND
BALTIMORE COUNTY

TICHENOR, ISAAC TAYLOR (1825-1902), Baptist denominational leader, was born in 1825 in Spencer County KY. He displayed such oratorical abilities as a youth that he became known as the "boy orator of Kentucky." After ordination in 1848 and some itineration, he settled down in 1852 to serve for 16 years as pastor of the First Baptist Church in Montgomery AL.

From 1872 to 1882 he was president of the State Agricultural and Mechanical College at Auburn AL. During his tenure of office he was a prophet of the later industrial development of the state and laid the foundation for the college's contribution to this future development.

The final phase of his career commenced in 1882 as he became secretary of the Home Mission Board of the Southern Baptist Convention. In this office he made important contributions to the development of denominational consciousness among Southern Baptists. Tichenor urged Southern Baptists to "possess the land." He inaugurated new work west of the Mississippi, started educational projects in the mountain regions, and grappled with mission projects in the emerging urban centers. He also urged the Convention to publish all its own Sunday school literature instead of depending on any outside agencies.

By the time of Tichenor's retirement, a new century had dawned. An era of remarkable denominational expansion had been introduced by his tireless leadership. He had combined missions, evangelism, education, and publishing in a constellation of interests that would mark the Southern Baptist Convention throughout the 20th century.

Bibliography. W. W. Barnes, *The Southern Baptist Convention;* J. S. Dill, *Isaac Taylor Tichenor: The Home Mission Statesman.*

GEORGE SHRIVER
GEORGIA SOUTHERN COLLEGE

TILLY, DOROTHY ROGERS (1883-1970), a prominent Methodist and civil rights advocate, was born in Hampton GA. Daughter of a minister, she was taught as a child to be sensitive to the problems of others. In 1903, two years after her graduation from Wesleyan College, she married Milton Tilly, an Atlanta chemical salesman. From 1918 to 1930 she served as superintendent of children's work for the Woman's Missionary Society of the North Georgia Conference of the Methodist Episcopal Church, South.

After she and her husband witnessed hungry black youths raiding hotel garbage cans for food, she increasingly turned her attention to civil rights. In 1929 she associated herself with leadership conferences taught at Paine College in Augusta to prepare black women to serve as community leaders. In 1931 Mrs. Tilly was one of the first women to affiliate herself with the ASSOCIATION OF SOUTHERN WOMEN FOR THE PREVENTION OF LYNCHING (ASWPL). Named secretary of the ASWPL chapter for Georgia, she helped to investigate lynchings in that state. In the 1930s she also worked in behalf of the Committee on the Cause and Cure of War and called for the United States to join the League of Nations. In 1945 President Truman appointed her to his Committee on Civil Rights. She was the only white woman and one of two Southerners to serve on this commission, which drew up the important civil rights document, "To Secure These Rights." A charter member of the Southern Regional Council, which was formed in 1944, she served as a field worker and director of women's work for this organization. In 1949, with SRC financial backing, she established the Fellowship of the Concerned (F of C) to replace the ASWPL, which had dissolved in 1942. The F of C, an interracial group, worked to combat lynching and to insure that blacks were fairly treated in the courts. Eventually the F of C championed school integration and desegregation of public accommodation facilities. Fellowship of the Concerned members occasionally faced harassment from extremist groups, and the KU KLUX KLAN once threatened to bomb Dorothy Tilly's house.

Bibliography. John P. McDowell, *The Social Gospel in the South.*

ARNOLD SHANKMAN

TOMLINSON, AMBROSE JESSUP (1865-1943), an early leader of the PENTECOSTAL MOVEMENT and first general overseer of the CHURCH OF GOD (CLEVELAND TN), was born in Indiana of Quaker background and heritage. He manifested a deeply religious nature early in life, and later studied briefly at God's Bible School in Cincinnati OH.

In 1899 he migrated to Culbertson NC and traveled in western North Carolina as a Bible colporteur and itinerant preacher. Upon arriving in the region, he became acquainted with the Pentecostal revival that occurred in the mountains in the mid-1890s, and on 3 June 1903 joined the small group that later adopted the name "Church of God." This church was made up of persons who had received the BAPTISM OF THE SPIRIT, with the phenomenon of SPEAKING IN TONGUES, as early as the summer of 1896.

Although Tomlinson did not personally receive the baptism of the Holy Spirit until 12 January 1908, he quickly emerged as leader of the Church of God and became its most prominent spokesman. By that time Cleveland TN had become the center of the church's activities and the site of its general assemblies. At the assembly of 1909, Tomlinson was elected to the newly created office of general overseer, a post he would fill for 14 years.

A man of prodigious energy and labors, Tomlinson assisted in spreading the Pentecostal message throughout the Southeastern USA and beyond. During the period of his overseership (1909-1923), the Church of God grew to more than 20,000 members in 20 states. Numerous church ministries (a publishing house, a Bible school, an orphanage, and missions to several Caribbean islands) were initiated by the growing denomination during that fruitful period.

In June 1923 a growing dissatisfaction with Tomlinson's autocratic style of leadership led to his removal from the office of general overseer. He thereupon withdrew from the Church of God and with several of his followers organized a second group in Cleveland TN. This separatist group was called the Tomlinson Church of God until 1953, at which time it adopted the name CHURCH OF GOD OF PROPHECY. For 20 years (1923-1943) Tomlinson gave the church that bore his name the same energetic leadership he had given the Church of God. By the time of his death, he saw the new church established in many sections of the USA and several countries of the world.

Prolific in his writings, Tomlinson wrote regularly for the *Church of God Evangel* from 1910 to 1923, and for the *White Wing Messenger* from 1923 to 1943. He produced numerous pamphlets on the Pentecostal experience *(Answering the Call of God*, et al.), but is best known for his voluminous diary, *Journal of Happenings*, which dated from 1899 to near the time of his death.

See also article on PENTECOSTALISM.

Bibliography. Charles W. Conn, *Cradle of Pentecost*; A. J. Tomlinson, *Journal of Happenings.*

CHARLES W. CONN
ROANOKE, VIRGINIA

TONGUES, SPEAKING IN: *See* CHARISMATIC MOVEMENTS; GLOSSOLALIA; PENTECOSTALISM.

TOY, CRAWFORD HOWELL (1836-1919), Baptist scholar and controversial educator, was born in Norfolk VA. After earning his degree with distinction from the University of Virginia, he served in the Civil War as a private in the artillery and then as a chaplain. Following the war he taught Greek for one year at the University of Virginia and then spent two years of study at the University of Berlin.

In 1869 he was appointed professor of Old Testament Interpretation at the Southern Baptist Theological Seminary, being considered the "pearl" of the faculty in those early years. By 1875, however, his studies led him to interpret the Bible in the light of its own times and not in the literal manner as with most Southern Baptists. He earnestly believed that this approach solved more biblical problems than it caused, convinced that the Bible was used more seriously if not taken literally. When the seminary moved from Greenville SC to Louisville KY in 1877, it lacked a sound financial footing. Toy continued to teach as he had been teaching, yet for the first time serious outside criticism surfaced. In the midst of a fundraising campaign, seemingly threatened by the controversy surrounding him, Toy submitted his resignation to the seminary's Board of Trustees. The resignation was accepted owing to the "divergence in his views of inspiration from those held by our brethren in general."

In 1880 Toy was appointed as the Hancock Professor of Hebrew and Other Oriental Languages at Harvard University where he remained until his retirement in 1909. By the time of his death he was regarded as an eminent professor emeritus with numerous publications to his credit. He had paid a great price for academic freedom, but the future would attest to his foresight.

See also articles on BIBLICAL INTERPRETATION; THEOLOGICAL EDUCATION.

Bibliography. George H. Shriver, ed., *American Religious Heretics*; C. H. Toy, *History of the Religion of Israel*; *Introduction to the History of Religion.*

GEORGE SHRIVER
GEORGIA SOUTHERN COLLEGE

TRIENNIAL CONVENTION. The General Missionary Convention of the Baptist Denomination in the United States for Foreign Missions, established

on 18 May 1814, was usually called the Triennial Convention because it held plenary sessions every third year.

When Congregational missionaries Adoniram and Ann Judson and LUTHER RICE became Baptist in 1812, Rice returned to America on a fund-raising tour that resulted in the formation of the Triennial Convention. Under his leadership this, the earliest nationwide organization among Baptists in America, attracted support from men such as RICHARD FURMAN, Thomas Baldwin, FRANCIS WAYLAND, and WILLIAM B. JOHNSON. At various times it sponsored a theological institute in Philadelphia, assisted home missionaries in the Midwest, and initiated and controlled Columbian College, Washington DC. However, its long-term function was to furnish aid to missionaries in Asia, Africa, and Europe, and among some American Indians. Its final full year was its most successful: in 1845 about $82,000 was raised to sustain 109 American missionaries, 123 native workers, 79 churches with more than 5,000 members, and 56 schools with 1,350 students. From 1814 through 1846 it had an income of $874,028 and appointed 257 foreign and 16 home missionaries from the United States.

As the Triennial Convention increasingly focused on foreign missions, its leaders began other societies promoting objectives considered worthwhile: the Baptist General Tract Society (1824; became American Baptist Publication Society, 1845), American Baptist Home Mission Society (1832), and American and Foreign Bible Society (1837). The theological institute in Philadelphia merged with Columbian College, which became virtually independent of the convention in 1826.

Two issues ultimately destroyed the Triennial Convention: centralization and SLAVERY. Many in the South favored a unified denominational structure that would supervise all missionary, educational, and publishing activities. Most in the North were content to foster separate societies. On a much more emotional level, the reality of slavery gradually polarized the membership. Ordered by the 1844 convention to maintain neutrality, the North-dominated executive board opposed the appointment of slaveholding missionaries on 17 December 1844.

An amicable agreement ended the life of the Triennial Convention. The SOUTHERN BAPTIST CONVENTION was founded in 1845 and included a foreign mission board that exists to the present. In 1846 the Triennial Convention was formally dissolved, but most of its activities were assumed by the newly constituted American Baptist Missionary Union, which continues after several alterations within the American Baptist Churches.

Bibliography. R. A. Baker, *The Southern Baptist Convention and Its People, 1607-1972*; R. G. Torbet, *A History of the Baptists*; Triennial Convention, *Proceedings*, 1814-1846.

ROBERT G. GARDNER
SHORTER COLLEGE

TRUETT, GEORGE WASHINGTON (1867-1944), prominent Baptist preacher and pastor, was born in Hayesville NC, attending Hayesville Academy and graduating in 1886. He founded Hiawassee Academy in adjoining Towns County GA, and served as its principal from 1887 to 1889. At the age of 19 he was converted and joined a Baptist church. When the family moved to Whitewright TX in 1889, Truett accompanied them and enrolled in nearby Grayson Junior College. He was ordained by the Whitewright Baptist Church in 1890.

Accepting a position as financial secretary at Baylor University, Truett worked for two years in a successful effort at abolishing the school's debt. He then attended Baylor, graduating in 1897.

While a student, Truett was pastor of East Waco Baptist Church. From there, largely due to his gifts as a preacher, he assumed the pastorate of the First Baptist Church, Dallas, a position he held for 47 years until his death. During that time membership in the church increased from 715 to 7,804.

Internationally recognized for his oratorical skills, Truett was an impressive figure, six feet tall, 200 pounds, with a forcefulness, dignity, and grace in the pulpit. During World War I he traveled extensively in Europe preaching to troops at the request of President Wilson. He was president of the SOUTHERN BAPTIST CONVENTION from 1927 to 1929 and president of the Baptist World Alliance, 1934-1939. For 37 summers he was also preacher for the west Texas "cowboy campmeeting."

His sermons and addresses were published in numerous volumes. A supporter of Baptist causes, he frequently raised funds for hospitals, schools, and other institutions. Truett's preaching style, personality, and tenure in Dallas helped make him one of the most famous pulpit orators of his day.

See also article on PREACHING.

Bibliography. John S. Ezell, "Truett, G. W." in *Dictionary of American Biography,* supplement three; Powhatan W. James, *George W. Truett, A Biography*; J. L. Rosser, "George W. Truett, Preacher," *Review and Expositor* 35 (January 1938): 3-23.

BILL J. LEONARD
SOUTHERN BAPTIST SEMINARY

TRUMAN, HARRY S (1884-1972), president of the United States from 1945 to 1953, was born near Lamar MO, and was reared in Jackson County and Independence. When he was 18 years old, he joined and was baptized into the church of his parents, Grandview Baptist. He retained his membership in that congregation for the remainder of his life, even though his wife and daughter were active Episcopalians. He did not like ceremonial religious forms, preferring a simple and informal church liturgy. In his adult years Truman did not attend church regularly, and during his years in the White House he justified this inaction because his attendance at a church service too often detracted from the worship service itself.

Like many other Southern and border-state Protestants, Truman believed the Bible was the inspired word of God and was to be used as a daily guide for Christian living. He often quoted the Bible in his public statements and speeches. His most frequent quotations were from the Sermon on the Mount, and he stated that all the world's problems would be solved if people would follow the Beatitudes. Many of Truman's statements indicated his simplistic approach to religious thought with little concern for complex theological issues.

In addition to a reverence for the Holy Scriptures, Truman manifested a large degree of religious toleration. While he was president, he issued an executive order to end racial and religious discrimination in the armed forces, and he challenged Senator Joseph McCarthy by asserting that "real Americanism" meant belief in the Bill of Rights and freedom of religion. In 1960 when Roman Catholic John F. Kennedy was a presidential candidate, Truman publicly objected to the injection of religious prejudice into that campaign. Finally, Truman aided the ecumenical movement when he appointed a Committee on Religion and Welfare in the armed forces to guarantee that men in the military service be given opportunity to practice and deepen their religious faiths. Although the efforts failed, Truman supported a movement to bring religious leaders of the world together "in a common affirmation of faith and a common supplication to the one God that all profess."

Truman's background, which emphasized a personal religion, did not keep him from espousing SOCIAL GOSPEL concepts, with emphasis upon a better society. While he was president, he saw the implications of the social gospel in many of his political programs: national health insurance, low-cost housing projects, a national education program, and extended Social Security benefits. Above all, he saw the social gospel as an effective answer to the possible spread of communism in the United States and Europe. While many factors influenced President

Truman's political decisions, his religious values and his early religious environment made significant impact.

See also article on CIVIL RIGHTS MOVEMENT.

MONROE BILLINGTON
NEW MEXICO STATE UNIVERSITY

TUCKER, HENRY ST. GEORGE (1874-1959), Episcopal Church leader and presiding bishop, was born in 1874 in the rectory of St. John's Episcopal Church, Warsaw VA. He graduated from the Norfolk Academy, the University of Virginia (B.A.), and the Virginia Theological Seminary (B.D.). After ordination to the Episcopal deaconate and priesthood, he accepted the call as a missionary to Japan. He was soon appointed president of St. Paul's College, Tokyo, and in 1912 was consecrated bishop of Kyoto. During World War I, he accompanied the American Expeditionary Force for a government mission to administer relief in Siberia. In 1923 he resigned as bishop of Kyoto to make possible the incumbency of a native Japanese bishop. After serving as a professor at the Virginia Theological Seminary, he was elected bishop of the Diocese of Virginia in 1927.

In 1936, the General Convention of the Episcopal Church meeting in Cincinnati elected him presiding bishop of that national church. He continued as bishop of Virginia until 1943, when he resigned that position to become the first full-time presiding bishop. His special concerns as presiding bishop included promotion of the missionary work of the Church and ecumenical relations, serving as president of the Federal Council of Churches (the predecessor of the National Council of Churches).

After retiring in 1946, he returned to his home in Richmond where he assisted the bishop of Virginia and served in many other capacities until ill health prevented it.

BEVERLEY D. TUCKER, JR.
VIRGINIA BEACH, VIRGINIA

TULSA, OKLAHOMA. A pleasant, livable city of 350,000 residents, with an economy undergirded by the petroleum, mining, and aerospace industries, Tulsa is also, for reasons not entirely clear, a major center of independent fundamentalist and Pentecostal ministries. Foremost among these, of course, is the Oral Roberts Evangelistic Association, headed by the most famous Pentecostal preacher in the world, himself a member of the prestigious Boston Avenue Methodist Church. ORAL ROBERTS receives more mail than any other citizen of Tulsa and the university that bears the evangelist's name is the city's chief shrine and tourist attraction, a distinction that has led to its informal designation as "Disneyheaven" and "Six Flags Over Jesus." Key structures on the campus include the Prayer Tower, believed by many to hold a license to a clear channel to heaven, and the City of Faith Medical and Research Center, fronted by the world's largest bronze replica of Oral Roberts's hands.

BILLY JAMES HARGIS, stalwart soldier of the Old Right, operates his Christian Crusade against communism from an office building a few blocks north of Oral Roberts University. At one time, Hargis also ran American Christian College, but charges of versatile sexual misconduct led to his resignation and the eventual closing of that institution. In 1981, however, Hargis obtained a license to erect and operate a UHF television station in Tulsa and announced plans to make it a strong electronic weapon in the service of conservative, anticommunist Christianity.

Tulsa is also the site of the home office of the Osborn Foundation, overseen by T. L. and Daisy Osborn. After an indifferent career as a domestic evangelist during the Pentecostal healing revival after World War II, T. L. Osborn began to concentrate on foreign missions and on equipping native preachers with various audiovisual aids to assist them in carrying the gospel to their people. The World Museum Art Centre, just off Interstate 44, not only features displays showing how this equipment is used, but treats visitors to a collection of spiritual treasures that includes shrunken heads, paintings and statuary, primitive and jungle artifacts, and a stunning collection of antique Lincoln automobiles, all the fruits of years of Osborn ministry in faraway heathen lands.

The city's newest and increasingly influential religious educational institution is the Rhema Bible Training Center, operated by the respected Pentecostal teacher and radio broadcaster, Kenneth E. Hagin. In 1981, 2,000 students were enrolled in Rhema's two-year program of intensive preparation for various forms of ministry.

Though his ministry is less well known, and deservedly so, evangelist Ronnie Coyne also operates from a Tulsa base. Not a gifted man by ordinary standards, Coyne has gained some attention for his apparent ability to read Scripture, newspapers, and miscellaneous printed matter through an eye socket from which his artificial orb has been prayerfully and ostentatiously plucked out.

Tulsa enjoys the minor distinction of having been the city where healing evangelist Kathryn Kuhlman spent her last days, at the behest of automobile dealer Tink Wilkerson, who had befriended her a few months earlier and whom she named as major beneficiary in her will.

See also articles on FUNDAMENTALISM; PENTECOSTALISM.

WILLIAM C. MARTIN
RICE UNIVERSITY

TURNER, HENRY MCNEAL (1834-1915), Methodist bishop and leading emigrationist, was born to free parents in Newberry, near Abbeville SC. Nevertheless, Turner labored with slaves before becoming a blacksmith. He was not taught to read until age 15; lawyers for whom he worked helped him master writing. In 1851 Turner joined the Methodist Episcopal Church, South; he was licensed to preach in 1853 and itinerated as a successful revivalist through 1857. The next year, he left the ME Church, South, and was admitted to the Missouri Conference of the AFRICAN METHODIST EPISCOPAL CHURCH. By 1862 Turner was an ordained elder and pastor of the influential Israel Church in Washington DC.

President Lincoln appointed Turner the first black army chaplain in 1863. After leaving the chaplaincy, he served two terms as a Georgia state legislator and led the Georgia Conference of the AME Church to being the largest in the Church before 1876. That year he was elected general manager of his denomination's Book Concern, then became bishop in 1880. He presided over the Georgia Conference until 1892. Turner visited Africa, helped introduce Methodism to African peoples, and was the most prominent and outspoken advocate of black emigration between the Civil War and World War I.

Bibliography. M. M. Ponton, *Life and Times of Henry M. Turner;* "Turner, Henry McNeal," *Dictionary of American Biography,* 1946, 10: 64-65.

HERMAN E. THOMAS
UNIVERSITY OF NORTH CAROLINA
AT CHARLOTTE

UNION BAPTISTS. The first Union Baptist Associations were formed in 1867 over the question of loyalty to the Union during the Civil War. The Mountain Union Association was formed on the fourth Saturday in August 1867 at the Silas Creek Church in Ashe County near Lansing NC. Several ministers and members of the Mountain, Senter, and Three Fork Associations were present. There were eight original churches. This association was in correspondence with two other nearby associations that shared their sympathies—the Stoney Fork Association of Watauga and Wilkes counties and the Primitive Baptist Association of Regular Baptists of Wilkes County, adjoining counties in the northwestern North Carolina mountains.

These churches and associations split from their original associations because of their Union sentiments and because the other associations would not allow membership in secret societies, especially the Union League. Thus these people called themselves Union Baptist in opposition to the other Baptist associations (for example, Primitive, Southern, and Regular) who supported the Southern states in the Civil War. The Mountain Union Association's sentiments and sympathies toward ex-slaves were given concrete expression when in 1868 they helped ex-slaves organize the New Covenant Association of Wilkes County. The Union Baptists taught these ex-slaves their doctrine and ordained four of them into the ministry.

Today there are Union Baptists in North Carolina, Tennessee, Virginia, Maryland, Kentucky, West Virginia, and Pennsylvania. Some of the associations still in existence are: the Mountain Union, the Original Mountain Union, the Union, the Little River, the Mitchell River Union Baptist, and the Primitive Baptist Association of Regular Baptists. Some of these associations consider themselves REGULAR BAPTISTS while others view Union Baptist beliefs and practices as unique. They are Calvinist and have three ordinances: baptism, communion, and FOOT WASHING.

See also article on APPALACHIAN RELIGION.

RICHARD ALAN HUMPHREY
JOHNSON CITY, TENNESSEE

UNITARIANISM. Liberal religion has seldom found the South very receptive to its presence and message. Although THOMAS JEFFERSON predicted that Unitarianism would rapidly become the predominant religion of the new nation, his prophecy was refuted most emphatically in his own region. Early liberal spokesmen like Jefferson and THOMAS COOPER shied away from explicit religious affiliation and had little lasting institutional impact. Although a handful of Unitarian and Universalist churches were established in the Southern and border states during the antebellum period, what success they enjoyed was exceptional and the opprobrium that resulted from their theological and social heterodoxy doomed them to a long period of virtual invisibility.

A few Unitarian churches in urban areas did manage to attract enough followers to succeed, although their fortunes were usually tied to the charisma of individual ministers. Notable examples were Jared Sparks in Baltimore; William Greenleaf Eliot in St. Louis; James Freeman Clarke in Louisville; THEODORE CLAPP in New Orleans; and SAMUEL GILMAN in Charleston. Men like these became deeply and positively involved in community affairs and charitable work, thus counteracting some orthodox hostility, and often, as in the cases of Clarke (the editor of the *Western Messenger*) and Gilman (author of "Fair Harvard"), achieved considerable literary reputations. Still, their success depended either on an audience of transplanted New Englanders (usually in the border states) or, as in Charleston and New Orleans, on a rare indigenous base of liberal theological sentiment.

Antislavery Unitarians managed to sustain themselves only in the border states. Those in the deep South survived only through active or passive support for the "peculiar institution," as in the respective cases of Clapp and Gilman, but thereby set themselves at odds with their Northern contemporaries. Since the denomination was structurally so loosely knit, however, and since so few Southern churches were involved, the struggle over slavery had few direct consequences for denominational identity.

The rural counterpart to urban religious liberalism was Universalism, the history of which ran parallel to that of the Unitarians until the merger of the two denominations in 1961. Southern Universalists drew on several sources: English Baptist splinter groups in 18th-century Virginia and the Carolinas; Dunkards and other German sectarians in the region; Northern Universalists who came South; and a tradition of indigenous Universalism. Universalists engaged in a version of circuit-riding to spread and maintain their faith during the 19th century, but the efforts of such dedicated men as John C. Burruss were never to bear more than scattered fruit. In 1858 a General Southern Convention was organized over sectional differences, but this had little long-range impact. Still, a few churches, generally small, rural, and based on the continued support of one or a handful of families, managed to survive until the time of the merger and beyond (such as the Harmony Universalist Church in Senoia GA).

The years between the Civil War and World War II saw liberal religion expand primarily in those states that were themselves experiencing rapid growth, especially Florida, Oklahoma, and Texas. Unitarian congregations were established in Dallas in 1899 and in Tulsa in 1921; each was eventually to become among the largest in the region. This period also saw the ordination and active ministries of a number of women in both denominations. Eleanor Elizabeth Gordon and Mary Augusta Safford, for example, helped to establish a successful Unitarian church in Orlando FL and Lizzie Crozier French was an active Unitarian feminist in the Knoxville TN area. Other Universalist women preachers also have made their presence known throughout the South, and in 1980 women are serving as ministers at a number of places.

It was not until 1950 that liberalism began to expand rapidly throughout the South. This was due in part to the influx of Northerners attracted by opportunities for employment in urban and academic centers and at such technological meccas as Cape Canaveral and Oak Ridge. In addition, in 1948 Unitarians began to actively promote the Fellowship movement, which provided opportunities for groups of like-minded religious liberals to band together without benefit of formal clergy. Many now-thriving groups began during the 1950s through advertisements placed in local newspapers that invited those who sought liberal fellowship to a meeting at a hotel or other public place. Of the approximately 200 Unitarian-Universalist groups extant in the South in 1980, only half enjoy the services of full- or part-time ministers, while the others depend primarily on lay leadership and ministry.

Unitarian-Universalists have traditionally been known for their social concern and involvement and the Civil Rights era was no exception. Alfred Hobart led the struggle for racial equality in New Orleans, Birmingham, and Jackson, as did his counterparts in many of the urban centers of the South. James Reeb, at the time an assistant minister at All Souls Church in Washington DC, became an authentic martyr when he was murdered during the Selma march in 1965. Although Unitarian-Universalist churches were among the first in the South to welcome black people, few of the latter are represented in their ranks. A major exception is David H. Eaton, senior minister at All Souls, who has been a force in the life of the nation's capital.

Today, Unitarian-Universalists are still not a major presence in the South numerically, although they continue to exert an influence somewhat beyond their numbers in the lives of their communities. They tend to be urban, professional or academic, white, and socially and politically liberal, and are frequently neither Southern nor Unitarian-Universalist by birth or nurture. Many are found in the retirement communities of Florida, the metropolises of Texas, Virginia, and Maryland, and university communities such as Athens, Chapel Hill, and Clemson (home of the Unitarian James C. Calhoun.) (One fellowship even has grown out of a "Walden II" communitarian experiment.) In the words of one Floridian, "The prevailing atmosphere [here] is typical of the fellowship movement in the South: casually organized, heavily Yankee, and compulsively antiauthoritarian." There are few signs that it is likely to be otherwise in the foreseeable future.

Bibliography. Arthur S. Bolster, Jr., *James Freeman Clarke: Disciples to Advancing Truth*; Arthur A. Brooks, *The History of Unitarianism in the Southern Churches*; John Duffy, ed., *Parson Clapp of the Strangers' Church of New Orleans*; George H. Gibson, "Unitarian Congregations in Ante-Bellum Georgia," *Georgia Historical Quarterly* 54 (Summer 1970): 147-68; "Unitarian Congregations in the Ante-Bellum South," *Unitarian Historical Society, Proceedings*, 12, part 2 (1959): 53-78; Clarence Gohdes, "Some Notes on the Unitarian Church in the Ante-Bellum South," *American Studies in Honor of William Kenneth Boyd*, ed. David Kelly Jackson; Catherine F. Hitchings, *Universalist and Unitarian Women Ministers*; Russell E. Miller, *The Larger Hope: The First Century of the Universalist Church in America, 1770-1870*; Douglas C. Stange, "Abolitionism as Maleficence: Southern Unitarians Versus Puritan Fanaticism—1831-1860," *Harvard Library Bulletin* 26 (April 1978): 146-71; Laurence C. Staples, *Washington Unitarianism: A Rich Heritage*.

PETER W. WILLIAMS
MIAMI UNIVERSITY

UNITED CHURCH OF CHRIST. The presence of this denomination in the South is an apparently insignificant one numerically and sociologically. Only 630 churches were reported at the end of 1979 in the church's Southern region comprising the states of the old Confederacy from Virginia to Texas. Furthermore, these churches, with their 123,551 members, are concentrated in a few areas: Tidewater Virginia, Piedmont North Carolina, the coastal retirement areas of Florida, and the hill country of Texas, with only thin scatterings elsewhere. Areas of the church's greatest strength are the Northeast, especially New England, the Midwest, and the Pacific coast.

As a denomination named "The United Church of Christ," the church was only a quarter-of-a-century old in 1982, having been formed in 1957 from a merger of the Evangelical and Reformed and the Congregational Christian churches. These denominations were themselves the products of mergers in 1931 (Congregational Christian) and 1934 (Evangelical and Reformed). The church nationally has been described as a "heady, exasperating mix." What is true of the larger body is an especially accurate description of the Southern portion. Its predecessor bodies were the products of the work of schismatic Methodists (the "Christians"), German frontier settlements (the "Reformed"), Yankee settlement and missionary work among the freedmen following the Civil War (the "Congregationalists"), and German immigration to the Texas hill country in the mid-nineteenth century (the "Evangelicals").

JAMES O'KELLY, an itinerant Virginia Methodist preacher, was the leader of a group that opposed the hierarchical structure adopted by American Methodists following the Revolution. In 1793, he and other Methodists formed a body known for a year as "Republican Methodists"; then their name changed to the simpler term, "Christian," which was regarded as a "sufficient" name for the church. Including the matter of their name, there were six principles that came to express their sense of uniqueness: (1) the Lord Jesus Christ is the only head of the church (in opposition to all hierarchical arrangements); (2) the name "Christian"; (3) the Bible as a sufficient rule of faith and practice (in opposition to all creeds and the Methodist discipline); (4) Christian character as a sufficient test of fellowship, and church membership (as opposed to all sacramental tests); (5) the right of private judgment and liberty of conscience (also an anticredal affirmation); and (6) unity of all believers in Christ. This movement, joined loosely with similar groups in New England and on the then western frontier in Kentucky and Ohio, affiliated with the Congregational churches in 1931.

The German people came into Piedmont North Carolina from Pennsylvania, having traveled down the Shenandoah Valley with other German settlers of Lutheran persuasion. Commonly these groups would establish union houses of worship. Their settlements began in the early 1740s with the organization of churches as a normal part of their establishment. The 17 German Reformed churches were organized into the Classis of North Carolina at the Brick (Klapp's) Church in Guilford County on 21 May 1831, with an official attendance of four elders and four ministers, the Reformed polity being Presbyterian. These people retained contact through the years with fellow believers in Pennsylvania, and their clergy were educated there until the establishment in the mid-nineteenth century of Catawba College.

Congregationalists came to the South as missionaries of the American Board of Commissioners for Foreign Missions and established work at Missionary Ridge (Chattanooga), New Echota (near modern Calhoun GA), and on the Coosa River in what is now Floyd County GA. They assisted the Cherokee in establishing a representative democracy with a bicameral legislature, patterned after that of the United States, in establishing schools, churches, and other institutions. All of this was destroyed when the Cherokee were moved west because their land was ceded to the white men by a treaty that was signed when their chiefs were intoxicated. Following the Civil War, Congregationalists came South in significant numbers, under sponsorship of the AMERICAN MISSIONARY ASSOCIATION, to establish schools and churches for the freedmen. The establishment of public education made these schools obsolete, but black Congregational churches survived, though not in large numbers. Six AMA colleges still continue their work: Dillard (New Orleans), Fisk (Nashville),

Huston-Tillotson (Austin), LeMoyne-Owen (Memphis), Talledega (Talledega AL), and Tougaloo (Tougaloo MS). Black Congregational churches united with Afro-Christian churches in 1931 to form the Convention of the South, including black congregations all across the region. With the formation of the United Church of Christ, black congregations became affiliated with the appropriate regional conferences (Southern, Southeastern, Florida, and South Central). A few congregations were established by white Congregationalists for their own needs in places where they were sufficiently numerous because of retirement (Southern Pines NC) or occupational relocation (Atlanta GA).

The German Evangelicals who came to Texas were part of a significant migration from their land when they arrived on these shores in the second quarter of the 19th century. From 1830 to 1845 there was an average annual migration to this country of 40,000 people. Those coming from Prussia were from a church that had been formed by royal proclamation in 1817, uniting the Lutheran and Reformed bodies. King Frederick III left it to the churches to work out their doctrinal and ecclesiastical differences themselves; but as a state church, they were one. Evangelicals were greatly influenced by the German Pietism that was a response to the rationalism of the Enlightenment. They have been noteworthy for the establishment of homes for children and the aging (the Eden Home in New Braunfels TX) and hospitals. Leon Jaworski, the Watergate prosecutor, was the son of a Texas German Evangelical pastor.

In a region often characterized by religious strife, antecedents of the United Church of Christ and the United Church of Christ itself have been witnesses to a more tolerant attitude. They have elevated Christian character as a touchstone of the faith, although understandings of this have been affected by historically conditioned cultural attitudes. They have been missioners to minority groups: blacks, native Americans, and immigrants. They have championed religious liberty for the individual and for the congregation within the context of an ecumenical vision. They have known themselves to be effective when they have surrendered separate identities to a larger vision. Maybe they are some of the salt-of-the-earth, accomplishing their task silently as they help to preserve and flavor the region where they live and work as Christians.

See also articles on CHRISTIAN CHURCH; CONGREGATIONALISM; O'KELLY, JAMES.

Bibliography. Louis H. Gunneman, *The Shaping of the United Church of Christ*; Kenneth Scott Latourette, *The Great Century in Europe and the United States of America (A.D. 1800-A.D.1914)*; Banks J. Peeler, *A Story of the Southern Synod of the Evangelical and Reformed Church*; J. Taylor Stanley, *A History of Black Congregational Christian Churches of the South*; Durward T. Stokes and William T. Scott, *A History of the Christian Church in the South*.

WILLIAM C. SMITH, JR.
GREENSBORO, NORTH CAROLINA

UNITED METHODIST CHURCH: *See* METHODIST CHURCH, THE; METHODIST EPISCOPAL CHURCH, SOUTH.

UNITED PENTECOSTAL CHURCH (INTERNATIONAL, INC.). This is the largest Pentecostal denomination in that portion of the movement that emphasizes what is sometimes called "Jesus name" or "Jesus only" or "oneness" beliefs. These include, first, the necessity of water baptism in the name of Jesus, for this is thought to be in accordance with Acts 2:38 and Jn. 3:5 and, second, belief in Jesus as the one Person of the Godhead. Both are maintained in contrast to more traditional Trinitarian practice and views. Because of this the church is sometimes referred to as "unitarian."

The church has grown rapidly in its present form, which resulted from a merger in 1945 of two denominations with 34,000 members in 900 congregations. Today it reports a total adult membership of 1,171,724 in 91 nations (in the US, 450,000, of which 9,852 are clergy).

There are 8,413 churches or major preaching points (in the US, 3,225) and 250 American missionaries overseas in 65 nations. It operates eight Bible colleges with over 2,500 enrolled. The international radio broadcast "Harvestime" is broadcast regularly over 300 stations. Recent growth has been notable in the Philippines, Ethiopia, India, and Latin America. Trends indicate that the decade of the 1980s may well witness a doubling of membership. Headquartered in St. Louis (Hazelwood) MO, the general superintendent since 1978 has been Nathaniel A. Urshan. The highest governing body is the General Board, which responds to the Annual Conference vote of the ministerial constituency.

The distinctive beliefs of this church began to emerge at a widely attended 1913 Pentecostal camp meeting in Los Angeles organized by the followers of the prominent leader William H. Durham, who had died suddenly the previous year. At the meeting John G. Scheppe believed that he had received a divine revelation of the power of Jesus' name. He and others advocated rebaptism "in the name of Jesus" as a means of fulfilling the scriptural command in Mt. 28:19 to baptize "in the name of the Father and of the Son and of the Holy Spirit." This approach developed into a denial of the customary doctrine of the Trinity in favor of belief in Jesus as the one Person of the Godhead.

From 1913 to 1916 this "new issue" received widespread discussion and some acceptance among a significant portion of the Durham followers. Since the ASSEMBLIES OF GOD were being organized in the same era, the "new issue" finally brought division. At the decisive 1916 St. Louis meeting, the Assemblies' majority adopted a Trinitarian creedal statement that excluded about one-fourth of their number who could not then accept it because of their belief in the use of Jesus' name. Among those doctrinally excluded were virtually all the black members, along with most of the white leaders who were from the South. These people had for years accepted ordination and ministerial credentials from the hands of the black leader from Memphis, CHARLES HARRISON MASON, and his CHURCH OF GOD IN CHRIST denomination.

By 1918 the overwhelming majority of both black and white members who advocated emphasis upon the name of Jesus had merged into the Pentecostal Assemblies of the World, a heretofore small denomination incorporated in 1914 with headquarters in Portland OR. This step found wide acceptance partly because of the urgency of establishing immediate clergy status with an incorporated body as the nation moved into World War I. In 1919 headquarters were moved to Indianapolis with the white leader E. W. Doak as general chairman and the influential black clergyman, Garfield T. Haywood, as secretary-treasurer. As its membership divided evenly between black and white, this reconstituted denomination became the most thoroughly integrated of any in American church history, with most of its white members located in the South. Surprisingly, this inclusiveness lasted from 1918 to 1924, a period often considered to have been the most violently racist period in American history.

By 1924 racial tensions and pressures led to the separation of most (but not all) of the white members into their own racially distinct organizations such as the Pentecostal Ministerial Alliance, the Emanuel's Church in Jesus Christ, and the Apostolic Churches of Jesus Christ. These gradually developed and merged into two denominations, the Pentecostal Assemblies of Jesus Christ, and the Pentecostal Church, Inc., which represented almost all of the white adherents to belief in "Jesus name." In St. Louis, in 1945, these two united to form the United Pentecostal Church International, Inc.

See also article on PENTECOSTALISM.

Bibliography. Fred J. Foster, *Think It Not Strange: A History of the Oneness Movement*; Morris E. Golder, *History of the Pentecostal Assemblies of the World*; David Arthur Reed, "Origins and Development of the Theology of Oneness Pentecostalism in the United

States," unpublished Ph.D. dissertation, Boston University, 1978; James C. Richardson, Jr., *With Water and Spirit: A History of Black Apostolic Denominations in the United States.*

DOUGLAS J. NELSON
ARLINGTON, VIRGINIA

UNITED PRESBYTERIAN CHURCH.

This branch of American Presbyterianism came into existence as a result of the union of the United Presbyterian Church of North America with the Presbyterian Church of the United States of America (PCUSA) in 1957. The Presbyterian Church of the USA had its origin in 1870 in a union of the Old School and the New School General Assemblies on the basis of the WESTMINSTER CONFESSION OF FAITH. The Old School Church lost most of its border-state communicants because the General Assembly forbade the readmission of Southern Presbyterians unless they were examined and repented of the sins believed to have been committed as a result of secession. Most of the border-state Presbyterians joined the PRESBYTERIAN CHURCH IN THE UNITED STATES (Southern). The New School Church brought to the Northern union three presbyteries in Missouri and the Presbytery of Holston in east Tennessee.

Since the PCUSA did not have many communicants in the South, the Church's energy in the South was largely devoted to three types of missions: the establishment of schools to evangelize the Negroes, mission work and settlement schools in the Southern Appalachians, and Sunday school missions.

In 1870, when the two Northern General Assemblies were united, a unified body called the Presbyterian Committee on Missions for Freedmen was organized with 29 ministers, 27 catechists, and 101 teachers to take over the work of the two former committees that had existed before the union. The work of the Committee on Missions for Freedmen was an effective instrument for bringing Southern blacks into the Northern Church.

Blacks also used another route to come into the PCUSA. After the Civil War, the majority of blacks no longer desired to remain a part of the white congregations of Southern churches with seats in the galleries or at separate services. Negroes left the Southern Presbyterian Church in great numbers. Some of the black churches that were organized were given financial aid by the Board of National Missions of the Northern church and became a part of that body. Separate judicatories for the black churches were set up in the South by the Northern church from the beginning, with the Synod of Atlantic established in 1868 and three others established at later dates.

The most important link to black Presbyterians in the formative period was the educational work carried out by the schools. At the time of the reorganization of the boards in 1923, the Board of Missions for Freedmen conducted 137 schools for blacks that ranged from elementary schools to colleges with theological departments. At first the work of the Presbyterian Church among the Negroes had a paternalistic tinge, but as Negroes secured advanced education they began to replace whites as pastors. By 1880, 40 of the 53 ordained ministers employed by the Presbyterian Board of Missions for Freedmen were blacks and nearly all the pastors serving Negro churches were blacks.

By 1942 the Presbyterian Church still remained the only church that was extensively involved in the Community Sunday School Movement. The National Board of Missions sent leaders into the rural sections of 10 Southern states to organize Negro Sunday schools with missionaries that annually reached more than 125,000 children and adults. From these Sunday schools many were recruited to the boarding schools from which they went on to Presbyterian colleges and later returned to the community as leaders.

As the denominational colleges for blacks began to graduate a large number of young, well-trained Negroes, these young professionals began to demand places on the board of trustees and the faculty of these colleges. When the struggle for black power in these institutions erupted in the 1890s, the Presbyterian Board of Missions For Freedmen moved to answer the complaints.

The PCUSA took the lead in establishing missions in southern Appalachia. The Church operated missions in the Southern Highlands as early as 1879 when a mission school was opened near Concord NC. From this small start mission work gradually spread over the mountain regions of Kentucky, Tennessee, North Carolina, and West Virginia. By the end of the century the Home Missions Board was sponsoring 31 churches and 37 mission schools in that region. The Board of Missions concentrated on settlement schools for the young people in the mountains where public education hardly existed.

The objective of the mountain missions was to make each academy and boarding school a center of influence in all the country or region from which students gathered. The goal of the program was to train envoys of intelligence and moral leadership and send them out into many neighborhoods to pass the truth and training on to the people of the region.

The Woman's Board of Missions was the most active unit of the church in promoting schools. It began educational work in 1875 and eventually specialized in educational work in southern Appalachia. After World War II the Board of National Missions merged its Appalachian Missions with its rural church work in the country at large.

The third area to which the Church devoted much attention in the South was the Sunday school missions. The Sunday school missionaries were the advanced guard of the Church in the un-Christian parts of the South. They worked with children in the formative years and trained children who otherwise would have been neglected because they lived in obscure and deprived areas.

After the Civil War many Northern people moved to the South. Some of these people were Northern Presbyterians and the growth of the Northern Church in the South came as a result of the church following its communicants. The union of the CUMBERLAND PRESBYTERIAN CHURCH with the Northern Presbyterian Church in 1906 gave the PCUSA its greatest increase in the South. This union, as well as the continuing migration from the North, made it necessary in 1942 to organize the Mid-South Synod to accommodate the increased growth of the UPCUSA. More significant, however, was the fact that 13 union presbyteries belonged to both the UPCUSA and PCUS. In 1983, the two bodies merged to create the Presbyterian Church, USA.

See also articles on APPALACHIAN RELIGION; BLACK RELIGION; OLD SCHOOL/NEW SCHOOL.

Bibliography. Clifford M. Drury, *Presbyterian Panorama*; Minutes of the General Assembly of the Presbyterian Church in the USA; Ernest T. Thompson, *Presbyterians in the South*, 3 vols.; Samuel T. Wilson, The Southern Mountaineers.

VICTOR B. HOWARD
MOREHEAD STATE UNIVERSITY

UNIVERSITY OF THE SOUTH. An Episcopal institution in Sewanee TN, it was founded in 1857 when the first Board of Trustees was created by 10 dioceses of the Southern church. The leaders of the enterprise were Bishops JAMES OTEY of Tennessee, LEONIDAS POLK of Louisiana, and STEPHEN ELLIOTT of Georgia. In design, the institution was to be the great Southern University, and over $500,000 was contributed to its endowment and 10,000 acres to its domain. Bishop Polk laid the cornerstone on 10 October 1860. The Civil War swept away the grandiose dreams of the founders, however, when the uncompleted buildings and endowment were destroyed in that conflagration.

When the university finally opened its doors in 1868, it did so largely with funds raised in England. Two future prime ministers, William E. Gladstone and Lord Salisbury, served on its subscription committee. Bishop CHARLES QUINTARD of

Tennessee and George R. Fairbanks of Florida were instrumental in the "refounding" of the university. The early faculty included three former Confederate generals: Josiah Gorgas, Francis A. Shoup, and Edmund Kirby-Smith, while WILLIAM PORCHER DUBOSE, the eminent theologian, served as university chaplain.

In 1909 the departments of medicine, law, engineering, and dentistry were closed, so that the efforts of the university could be concentrated in the College of Arts and Sciences and in the School of Theology. Until 1981 the university maintained a preparatory school that has now merged with St. Andrew's School.

A high proportion of the university's graduates go on to graduate school, and many alumni of the School of Theology become leaders of the Episcopal Church. The buildings on the campus are neo-gothic in style. The most notable, All Saints' Chapel, designed by Ralph A. Cram, was begun in 1905 and completed on the centennial of the university in 1957. The university publishes the prestigious literary quarterly, the *Sewanee Review*.

See also articles on EDUCATION, CHRISTIAN HIGHER; THEOLOGICAL EDUCATION.

Bibliography. Arthur B. Chitty, Jr., *Reconstruction at Sewanee, 1857-1872*; George R. Fairbanks, *A History of The University of the South*; William M. Polk, *Leonidas Polk, Bishop and General*, 2 vols.

JOSEPH D. CUSHMAN
UNIVERSITY OF THE SOUTH

UTOPIAN COMMUNITIES.

The number and strength of utopian communities in the South has rarely equaled utopian activity in the other sections of the United States. The first great surge of American utopian activity, which crested between 1830 and the Civil War, had only minor impact upon the South. The parallel growth of sectional animosity and the evangelical consensus among Southerners limited the prospects for the success of such ventures in the slave states.

The furor stirred by Frances Wright's audacious experiment at Neshoba in Tennessee, where manumitted slaves lived in supposed equality with the gentry, is typical of the sort of reception that might have been expected by other utopias in the antebellum South. The only notable exceptions occurred in the border states. There was a strong Shaker community at Pleasant Hill KY that lasted over a century, and William Keil's Bethel Community in Missouri lasted from 1844 to 1880. Less permanent efforts, such as Cheltenham in Missouri (1858-1864) and the Brotherhood of New Life in Virginia (1851-1853), serve to support the generalization that the antebellum South was unreceptive to communitarian experiments.

Around the last decade of the 19th century, however, utopian efforts began in earnest at a number of places around the South. The SHAKERS attempted without success to colonize both in Florida (1894) and Georgia (1898). In Tennessee, there was a short-lived transplant of Victorian England at Rugby (1880) and a socialistic experiment at Ruskin (1894) that was later moved to Georgia. In Florida, Cyrus Teed established KORESHANITY in their earthly paradise near Fort Myers in 1894; and in 1896 a group of SOCIAL GOSPEL advocates formed the Christian Commonwealth just outside Columbus GA. Perhaps the most notable characteristic shared by all of these latter-nineteenth-century experiments was that the organizers were from outside the South and many of their ideals were inimical to the prevailing Southern ethos.

In the most recent period of American utopian activity, which began at the time of World War II, there seems to have been a greater measure of Southern involvement. Just before the war, a group of conscientious objectors, mostly from the South, organized the Macedonia Community in the mountains of north Georgia. In 1942, CLARENCE JORDAN and his colleagues founded KOINONIA FARM near Americus GA, which survived a time of testing during the Civil Rights era, and has become a significant model for other Christian communitarian activity in the South and beyond.

The late 1960s and early 1970s also witnessed the establishment of a number of other communities in the South, many having their roots in the turbulence of the times. Although some of these more recent utopias, such as Agahpay in West Virginia and Open House in Louisiana, are representative of traditional Christianity, many others, such as The Farm in Tennessee and New Vrindaban in West Virginia, testify to the recent impact of Eastern religions upon American culture. There are also a number of avowedly secular utopian experiments in the present-day South, perhaps the most famous of which is Twin Oaks in Virginia.

JOHN W. KUYKENDALL
AUBURN UNIVERSITY

VEROT, AUGUSTIN (1805-1876), major Southern Roman Catholic bishop and outspoken critic of the excesses of slavery in the South, was born in Le Puy, France. Ordained a priest in Paris, he came to this country in 1830. In 1858, consecrated a bishop, he became vicar apostolic of Florida. Three years later, while retaining authority over the church in Florida, he was appointed to the See of Savannah.

On 4 January 1861 Verot preached a sermon at St. Augustine that would propel him to the forefront of Christian commentators on Southern slavery. Published as "A Tract for the Times: Slavery and Abolitionism," the sermon was used during the course of the Civil War both by those who wanted to vindicate slavery and by those who wanted to ameliorate its worst features. For his biblically based defense of slavery, Verot earned the sobriquet "rebel bishop"; for his call to purge slavery of its potent abuses he was acclaimed as the prophet of a "servile code" that would reform and humanize the institution.

Verot took an active part in ministering to soldiers of both sides in the war. He and three of his priests were the only ministers of any denomination to attend the unfortunate federal prisoners at Andersonville GA. At war's end he championed the cause of the freedmen, particularly in the field of education, with a vigor unmatched by any other Southern Catholic prelate. In Savannah he secured an arrangement whereby the two Catholic schools of the city were supported wholly as public schools. The so-called Savannah Plan, begun in 1870, lasted until 1916. In 1870, while attending the First Vatican Council, where his frequent pro-United States interventions earned him another sobriquet, that of *enfant terrible*, he was named first bishop of the newly erected Diocese of St. Augustine.

See also articles on ROMAN CATHOLIC CHURCH; SLAVERY.

Bibliography. Henry Peter Clavreul, *Notes on the Catholic Church in Florida*; Michael V. Gannon, *Rebel Bishop: The Life and Era of Augustin Verot*.

MICHAEL V. GANNON
UNIVERSITY OF FLORIDA

VESEY, DENMARK (1767-1822), black militant, was born in Africa or the Caribbean. In 1781 at St. Thomas, Virgin Islands, he attracted the attention of slave ship captain Joseph Vesey by his striking appearance and intelligence. Sold in Santo

Domingo, he had to be taken back due to epilepsy, and became a resident of Charleston SC when his master settled there in 1783. In 1800 Denmark Vesey purchased his freedom through lottery winnings, and became a successful carpenter. A literate, able, proud, domineering man, he was influential among free blacks and slaves. Resentful that his wives and children remained in bondage, encouraged by the Haitian revolution and by antislavery writings that appeared during Missouri Compromise debates, especially those of Senator Rufus King, he dreamed of liberty for his people. A member of an African Methodist congregation, he cited biblical passages in planning a slave insurrection.

While full details will never be known, probably hundreds of slaves in a wide area around Charleston were to strike at midnight, 16 June 1822, seize arsenals and guardhouses, kill the whites, and take over the city. But leakage of information by a "house slave" had alerted the authorities, and the plan had to be abandoned at the last minute. Waves of intense fear and excitement swept through Charleston's white population and far beyond. Vesey's name became a symbol of dread. The leaders of the plot were arrested and tried. A special court served as judge and jury, condemned 35 blacks to death by hanging, and ordered the exile of a larger number. One aftermath of the conspiracy was stricter legislation controlling slaves and free blacks. Later leaders of liberation movements praised Vesey's militancy in view of the brutality and violence of the slave system.

See also articles on CARIBBEAN IMMIGRATION; SLAVERY.

Bibliography. John Lofton, *Insurrection in South Carolina: The Turbulent World of Denmark Vesey*; Robert S. Starobin, ed., *Denmark Vesey: The Slave Conspiracy of 1822.*

ROBERT T. HANDY
UNION THEOLOGICAL SEMINARY

VIRGINIA. From the founding of the colony at JAMESTOWN in 1607 until the closing decades of the 18th century the ANGLICAN CHURCH was the established church in Virginia. Throughout the colonial period it occupied a privileged status in Virginia society; there were statutes requiring attendance at its services, the public provided its clergymen with parsonages and farms, and the salaries of its ministers were paid from tax assessments.

At the time of the American Revolution there were more than 90 Anglican parishes in Virginia and the church operated the only college in the colony (COLLEGE OF WILLIAM AND MARY). Authority in the established church resided in the lay vestry of each parish; this self-perpetuating body conducted all parish affairs, selected the clergyman for the congregation, and determined the type of tenure he received. There was never a resident bishop in Virginia and the authority of the commissary was minimal.

Although the Anglican Church was the established church throughout the colonial era, it was not the only denomination in the colony. Virginia authorities and English laws of religious toleration helped to provide an environment that made religious dissent acceptable. From the late seventeenth century Quakers, Roman Catholics, and Presbyterians were in the area. Thomas Story, a Quaker itinerant, moved freely through the countryside and won converts for the Society of Friends; George Brent, a Roman Catholic planter, was elected to the legislature, and FRANCIS MAKEMIE was engaged in promoting the Presbyterian church from the 1690s.

In the 18th century the religious composition of Virginia became highly diversified. The migration of Scotch-Irish and Germans into the colony together with the GREAT AWAKENING had a profound effect on the religious structure of Virginia, and by the time of the American Revolution the dissenters outnumbered the Anglicans. The Presbyterians were scattered from the Tidewater throughout the Piedmont area and into the Blue Ridge Mountains and valley regions. They were the new side or evangelical faction of this church and their chief spokesman was SAMUEL DAVIES. The Germans, who settled mainly in the valley, were predominantly Lutheran or members of the German Reformed Church; however, some were Mennonites, Dunkers, and Moravians. All were welcomed to the colonial frontier and were permitted to worship according to their pleasure.

The Great Awakening, that came to Virginia in the 1740s, 1750s, and 1760s, witnessed the growth of Presbyterianism in the area, the emergence of the Baptists as a significant religious and political force, and the weakening of the established church. Although Baptists had been in the colony since the 1690s they were a small and passive group until the decades immediately preceding the American Revolution. In the 1750s "new light" or SEPARATE BAPTISTS from New England came to Virginia and stimulated the growth of this denomination. Their religious fervor and missionary zeal together with their criticism of the Establishment struck a responsive chord with the inhabitants and resulted in the rapid growth of Baptist churches.

John Wesley's Methodist movement came to Virginia in the 1760s when he sent his first preachers to America. Although this was a movement within the Anglican Church few Anglican clergymen in the colony affiliated with it. Nonchurchmen, however, were more sympathetic and by the close of the 18th century the Methodist movement had become an independent organization, had established "societies" in all regions of the state, and claimed a membership in excess of 13,000.

The Great Awakening in Virginia not only resulted in greater religious diversity in the area, it also stimulated religious activism, promoted political awareness, and prompted increased criticism of the Anglican Church. The attention of some churchmen was directed to the need for additional educational facilities. The College of William and Mary, established under Anglican auspices in 1693, was the only institution of higher learning in the colony. However, in 1749 Presbyterians founded Augusta Academy (Washington and Lee) and in 1774 Prince Edward Academy (Hampden-Sydney).

Another interest of churchmen that received attention at the time of the Great Awakening was the spiritual care of the Negroes. Africans had been in the colony since 1619 and by 1750 they constituted approximately 45 percent of the population, but meager efforts had been made to convert them to Christianity. In the 1750s Samuel Davies preached to the blacks and instructed the Presbyterians of their responsibilities to minister to the spiritual needs of these people and to bring them into the church. Baptist and Methodist ministers also sought to convert the Negroes, and by 1800 these two denominations embraced most of the Negroes who had professed Christianity.

During the American Revolution most church members in Virginia, whether Anglicans or dissenters, were ardent supporters of the colonial cause. The political independence that was achieved by the Revolution also ended the religious Establishment in Virginia. The Anglican Church was reorganized as the Protestant Episcopal Church and Establishment was replaced by the separation of church and state. The privileged status that one denomination had held since 1607 was ended; from now on the response of the people to the concepts of religious voluntarism and religious pluralism would determine the religious structure of Virginia. Although these concepts had been championed by Presbyterian and Baptist spokesmen they were a part of the intellectual climate of the Enlightenment and received the support of many Virginia Anglicans.

From the closing decades of the 18th century the popular churches—the Baptist, Methodist, and Presbyterian—experienced a steady growth and development. By the 1780s the Hanover Presbytery was sending missionaries to settlers in the trans-Allegheny region of the state, and in this same decade FRANCIS ASBURY outlined circuits for Methodist itinerants that reached to the Ohio River. The various Baptist groups in the commonwealth were united in 1801 and 10 years later local associations were formed that embraced all regions of the state. The Protestant Episcopal Church experienced a decline of influence following the American Revolution but began a phase of recovery and revival under the leadership of Bishop RICHARD CHANNING MOORE (1812-1841).

All of the principal Protestant groups in the state were evangelical. Their approach to religion was pietistic and emphasized revivalism and a personal religious experience that the individual could relate to others. Although the service of worship in the Protestant Episcopal Church was more formal than that found in Baptist, Methodist, and Presbyterian churches, the message "of salvation" was essentially the same in all of them and a period of annual revivals was common to churches of all denominations. The High Church movement that emerged in the Protestant Episcopal Church in the early nineteenth century found few adherents in Virginia. On one occasion Bishop Moore declared that the movement was an attempt to revive the worst evils of the Roman Catholic system.

The opening decades of the 19th century witnessed a considerable degree of cooperation between Virginia churches and churches of other states in a number of national agencies. Baptists, Episcopalians, Methodists, Presbyterians, and other denominational spokesmen espoused and urged their fellow members to support such agencies as the American Bible Society and they were active in forming an auxiliary of this Society in the state. Denominational leaders also encouraged support of the American Tract Society, the American Sunday School Union, and the creation of temperance organizations.

Although the different denominations in Virginia were active in a variety of interdenominational enterprises, they were also engaged in developing more effective and sophisticated denominational machinery. In 1823 the Baptists formed a statewide General Association, and by the 1830s each of the major denominations in the state, in cooperation with their co-religionists throughout the nation, had established domestic missionary organizations and foreign missionary societies. Among the Baptist churches there was some antimission sentiment. This feeling was strongest in the trans-Allegheny regions of the state and its leading spokesman to 1830 was ALEXANDER CAMPBELL. In 1840 there were 35 local Baptist associations in Virginia and in 12 there was significant opposition to missions; all of the latter were located in the western portion of the commonwealth.

From 1804 to 1860 church leaders or denominational organizations in Virginia initiated more than 60 publishing ventures, mainly weekly newspapers. Less than 20 percent of these experienced a life of 10 years. Although the casualty rate was high for religious newspapers and journals, all of the major denominations succeeded in establishing weekly newspapers. The first one established on a permanent basis was the *Religious Herald*, a Baptist weekly that appeared in 1828. This paper was followed by the *Richmond Christian Advocate* (Methodist), *The Southern Churchman* (Episcopal), the *Central Presbyterian*, the *Millennial Harbinger* (Disciples of Christ) and others. These publications contained information about the denomination and its various agencies, a digest of the minutes of ecclesiastical organizations, several columns of secular news including excerpts from foreign newspapers, assorted advertisements including those for runaway slaves, devotionals, theological essays, and editorials on subjects and issues of current interest.

Prior to 1819 the only institutions of higher learning in Virginia were founded by churchmen. The College of William and Mary would be closely associated with the Protestant Episcopal Church until the early twentieth century when it became a state institution. The Episcopalians founded no additional colleges in the antebellum era; however, Virginia churchmen were influential in establishing a theological seminary at Alexandria in 1823. Although the Presbyterians established no additional colleges during the antebellum period, in 1824 they created a theological seminary at Hampden-Sydney, and a few years later (1837) added a medical school. Both of these institutions were later moved to Richmond and became known as the Union Theological Seminary in Virginia and as the Medical College of Virginia.

The Baptists and Methodists, which were the numerically dominant and more aggressive denominations, began, in the Jacksonian era, to establish institutions of higher learning. In 1830 the Methodists founded Randolph-Macon College in Mecklenburg County and the Baptists established the Virginia Baptist Seminary, an institution that in 1840 was chartered by the state legislature as Richmond College. Nine years later (1839) the Methodists opened another school, Emory and Henry College, at Emory in the southwestern portion of the Valley. The first institution of higher learning in the trans-Allegheny region of the state, Rector College, was established under Baptist auspices in 1839 at Pruntytown in Harrison County. This school was destroyed by fire in 1855 and not rebuilt. The only college in that area of the state to be a permanent one was Bethany College, founded by Alexander Campbell in 1840.

The church colleges in Virginia were strikingly similar; all featured a curriculum centered on a study of the classics, mathematics, natural science, and philosophy. All were solely for males and the faculty and trustees were mainly clergymen. These institutions were small, having three to five faculty members and a student body of 60 to 125. A principal purpose of these institutions was to pre-pare young men for the ministry, although by 1850 more "practical" courses such as bookkeeping and modern foreign languages were being introduced into the curriculum.

Numerous participants in all denominations were active in another sphere of education: the establishment and operation of academies and seminaries. Academy was the usual designation for a boys' school; seminary often referred to a girls' school. Occasionally an institution such as the West Liberty Academy, which was conducted by a Presbyterian clergyman, was coeducational. In an era when there was no tax-supported public school system, private academies and seminaries afforded the principal means of providing primary and secondary education for many Virginians.

In the colonial era many Anglican and Presbyterian clergymen conducted schools along with their ministerial duties and in the closing decade of the 18th century there were 24 academies in the state. After the American Revolution churchmen of all persuasions operated academies; by 1825 there were more than 300 in Virginia and in 1860 the number had increased to nearly 400; approximately 35 of these were located in the trans-Allegheny region of the commonwealth. Although not all of these institutions were affiliated with churches or denominational agencies, one student of Virginia academies claims that it would be difficult to overemphasize the importance of the part played by religious denominations in their founding and support.

Presbyterian clergymen established academies in all areas of the state, from the tidewater section to the Ohio River. From the early decades of the 19th century Methodist and Baptist leaders were also active in promoting education. Methodist schools were established from Brunswick County to Morgantown, and academies founded by Baptist spokesmen were scattered from Caroline County to the mountainous regions in the western portion of the commonwealth. Among the institutions founded by the Protestant Episcopal Church were an academy for boys at Alexandria and a female institute at Staunton. In the closing decades of the antebellum era (1840-1860) the followers of Alexander Campbell operated academies in a variety of places, including the counties of Orange, Albemarle, and Nelson.

In the valley of Virginia, where most of the Lutheran, German Reformed and other German groups were located, local pastors often taught in schools attached to the church. During the antebellum period Lutheran schools were found in such places as Winchester, Strasburg, and Wytheville. In 1823 a clergyman conducted a theological course in his home at New Market, and three years later Virginia Lutherans were instrumental in helping to found a theological seminary at Gettysburg PA. In 1853 the Lutheran school at Salem was chartered by the general assembly as a four-year college (Roanoke College). The Dunkers (who adopted the name Church of the Brethren in 1908) were affiliated with the Rockingham Academy and Cedar Grove Academy. Prior to 1860 a few schools were established under Roman Catholic auspices, among them were St. Joseph's Academy in Richmond (1834), St. Mary's Academy in Norfolk (1848), and Mount de Chantal, a school for girls in Wheeling (1848). Jewish congregations operated schools in Richmond (1848) and in Norfolk (1853). Although Jews had been in Virginia since the colonial period and had established their first congregation in Richmond in 1791, they were located primarily in the eastern region of the state; their first congregation in the west was formed at Wheeling in 1849.

Although numerous religious leaders and spokesmen were engaged in founding and operating a variety of educational institutions throughout the state in the first half of the 19th century, these activities did not indicate the limits of their interest in education. During the three decades before the Civil War the most articulate advocates of public education in

the commonwealth were clergymen. Two of the principal spokesmen for tax-supported schools were the founder of the Disciples of Christ, Alexander Campbell, and the Presbyterian clergyman from Lexington, HENRY RUFFNER. Although these men were joined by others, their efforts to persuade the politicians of the state to establish a system of schools available to all of its citizens did not receive a favorable response from the general assembly and a system of public education was not established until after the Civil War.

Although the opening decades of the 19th century witnessed considerable interdenominational cooperation in various enterprises, these were also years of emerging tension and factions within American Christianity, and these forces were reflected in the religious structure of the state. During the 1830s and 1840s the Baptist churches in Virginia were wracked by the Campbellite movement. Alexander Campbell was affiliated with the Baptists from approximately 1813 to 1830, when he and his followers embarked upon a reform movement to restore primitive Christianity. He was also opposed to participation in all cooperative societies such as Bible, tract, and mission organizations as being unscriptural. When he left the Baptist fold and established the Disciples of Christ or Christian churches, a number of Baptist congregations followed his lead and others were split. Some "Campbellite" churches were found in all regions of the state but perhaps the area of greatest controversy was in the Meherrin Association in southside Virginia. Within a decade of Campbell's departure from Baptist ranks this association ceased to exist as most of its churches became aligned with Campbell's reformation. Although most of Campbell's following was in Kentucky, Tennessee, and the Ohio valley region, he lived in Bethany VA, where he operated Bethany College and published the *Millennial Harbinger*. At the time of the Civil War some of his followers were divided in their sentiments; however, unlike the older denominations, the Disciples of Christ did not split into sectional factions.

During the years the Baptists were agitated by the Campbellite movement, the Methodists experienced a schism that resulted in the emergence of the Methodist Protestant Church. This schism traces its origin to the JAMES O'KELLY defection from the Methodist Church in the 1790s. From that date certain elements within the Methodist Episcopal Church were unhappy with the authority exercised by the bishop and the prohibition of laymen from participating in conference affairs and in governing the church. Sentiment for ecclesiastical reform that would implement these two concepts centered in the Maryland and Virginia conferences of the church but was also present in other areas. In 1828 and 1829 meetings were held in Lynchburg and in Baltimore by church leaders who wished to institute these practices in Methodism. Their efforts culminated in an organizational conference, that was held in Baltimore in 1830. At this conference the Methodist Protestant Church was organized; its constitution eliminated the office of bishop and provided for lay representation in conference meetings. At this time the Virginia Conference of the Methodist Protestant Church reported 1,000 members; by 1860 it had increased to 5,000. Principal churches were in Lynchburg and Norfolk but other centers of activity were in Amelia County, on the Northern Neck, and in the Monongahela Valley. In 1855 Lynchburg College was founded under the auspices of this church; it was forced to close during the Civil War and did not reopen after 1865.

The Baptists and Methodists were not alone in experiencing schisms in the Age of Jackson. After several years of increasing tension resulting from growing dissatisfaction on behalf of some Presbyterians with the Plan of Union, the influence of the theology of Nathaniel Taylor within the church, and the emergence of an activist abolitionist element in Presbyterian

ranks, this church split into new-school and old-school factions at the General Assembly in 1837. The old-school faction was the dominant one and most Presbyterians in Virginia were affiliated with it; however, there were some congregations that aligned themselves with the new-school faction. In 1850 the Synod of Virginia (old school) consisted of six presbyteries that reported a membership of 13,000. The Synod of Virginia (new school) at mid-century included three presbyteries and a membership of 4,100. From the beginning fraternal relations between these factions in Virginia were cordial and during the Civil War (1864) they merged to form part of what became the Presbyterian Church in the United States.

In the 1830s and 1840s Virginia Christians often manifested attitudes that reflected national trends or movements. The antimasonic sentiment that emerged in the 1830s was noted when the annual conference of the Methodist Episcopal Church in Virginia admonished members for joining a masonic fraternity or the Independent Order of Odd Fellows. Nativist sentiment that flourished in the nation in the 1840s and 1850s was reflected in the annual meetings of the old-school Presbyterian Synod of Virginia. It was customary at these meetings for the delegates to hear a sermon "on popery," which expounded the errors, superstitions, and evils of the Roman Catholic Church. These years also witnessed occasional editorials in the Baptist press and other denominational weeklies of anti-Mormon diatribes, although there were no congregations of the Church of Jesus Christ of Latter-day Saints in the commonwealth.

The issue that caused the greatest concern for Virginia churches in the antebellum era was the one that polarized the nation and resulted in Civil War—slavery. African slavery was introduced into Virginia in the 17th century and by 1840 slaves constituted approximately 35 percent of the state's population. From the era of the Great Awakening all of the popular churches sought to minister to the spiritual needs of the Negro. Although some black communicants were found in all denominations, most of them were members of Baptist and Methodist churches. Slaves were accepted into church membership in the same manner as whites, upon profession of faith and relating of their religious experience. Once on the membership roll they were subject to the same rules of discipline as other members. Most black and white Christians in Virginia worshiped together although the blacks were segregated to a specific seating area in the sanctuary.

From 1840 in Richmond, Lynchburg, Fredericksburg, and other cities separate black churches were formed, but all of these were "branch" churches of white organizations. Their trustees and clergymen were white and usually their deacons were selected by whites. For a few years near the close of the 18th and the opening of the 19th centuries a few independent black churches had been formed but by 1830 state legislation and white fears had eliminated the independent Negro church in the commonwealth.

The type of gospel preached to the blacks was designed not only to convert and keep them firm in the faith but also to make them more obedient and compliant slaves. Spokesmen of all the major denominations in Virginia prepared catechisms or instructional manuals for the teaching of slaves. The type of Christianity expounded in such publications emphasized the virtues of docility, obedience, honesty, and hard work. A bishop of the Protestant Episcopal diocese of Virginia once told a congregation of slaves that their master was God's overseer and that they were to obey him as they would God. Slaves were taught that in this world of sorrow, sickness, and toil it was their duty to work and be humble and patient. They were told that God expected them to work hard in this life so that they would better appreciate their life beyond the grave. Other teachings threatened the slaves with the fires of hell for swearing, drinking, and cheating.

Many Virginia clergymen owned slaves and some local churches accepted gifts of slaves as part of their endowment. Two of the most articulate defenders of slavery were Virginia churchmen: the Baptist Thornton Stringfellow, and William A. Smith of the Virginia Conference of the Methodist Episcopal Church, South. Both of these men wrote books expounding the "biblical" argument justifying slavery. Their writings were circulated in essay and book form throughout the nation during the last 20 years of the antebellum era.

Although most clergymen and denominational leaders in Virginia defended the institution of slavery there were exceptions. The Church of the Brethren did not countenance slavery among its members. Since the American Revolution the Quakers in Virginia had renounced slaveholding and some Quakers continued to agitate for the abolition of slavery in the commonwealth throughout the antebellum period. The Mennonite congregations in the state also forbade slaveholding among their membership, and among the major denominations an outspoken foe of slavery was William Sparrow, a professor at the Episcopal Theological Seminary in Alexandria.

Until the 1840s there were no sectional denominations; all of the major churches were affiliated together in national organizations. The Virginia Conference of the Methodist Episcopal Church sent delegates to the General Conference of this church that met once every four years and consisted of churchmen from all of the conferences in the nation. Presbyterian commissioners from Virginia met annually with their co-religionists from synods throughout the nation to form the General Assembly of the Presbyterian Church. After the old school-new school schism in 1837 there were formed general assemblies of each group but these gatherings represented a national rather than a sectional constituency. Among the Baptist churches the

TRIENNIAL CONVENTION had existed since 1814. This was an affiliation of Baptist churches throughout the United States and was the agency for promoting Baptist foreign missions, conducting the home mission program, and sustaining a publication enterprise. Most Virginia Baptists were active in all of these programs.

Tensions associated with slavery precipitated the destruction of national ties in the two largest denominations in the 1840s and resulted in the formation of sectional ecclesiastical organizations by the Methodist and Baptist denominations. At the General Conference of the Methodist Episcopal Church in 1844, a Southern bishop was admonished for being a slaveholder. This action resulted in splitting the denomination and creating the Methodist Episcopal Church, South. Clergymen, churches, and conferences were free to affiliate with either the Northern church (Methodist Episcopal Church) or the Southern church (Methodist Episcopal Church, South). Following the schism most of the Methodist congregations in Virginia became affiliated with the Virginia Conference of the Methodist Episcopal Church, South. However, portions of the commonwealth, including most of the trans-Allegheny region, a few areas in the Valley and in the northern portion of Virginia, and some congregations on the eastern shore affiliated with the Methodist Episcopal Church. In some places controversy emerged between congregational factions concerning the control of church property and resulted in civil suits and court action. It is estimated that in 1860 there were approximately 47,000 communicants in the Methodist Episcopal Church, South, in Virginia and approximately 22,000 members of the Methodist Episcopal Church. The two Methodist factions were reunited in 1939.

The same year that the Methodist Episcopal Church split along sectional lines the Baptist Triennial Convention met in Philadelphia. The convention discussed slavery but adopted neither antislavery nor proslavery resolutions.

However, when Baptists in Georgia and Alabama failed to receive approval for mission candidates who were slave owners, many Baptists in the South were ready to sever connections with the convention. Baptist leaders of the Virginia Foreign Mission Society called for a convention of Southern churchmen to meet in Augusta GA in May 1845 to form a Southern Baptist missionary organization. This suggestion received a favorable response and in the spring of 1845 the Southern Baptist Convention was formed. The Virginia Baptist leadership, which was instrumental in creating this convention, represented a constituency of 84,000 members.

The mid-1840s also witnessed the formation of the Southern Christian Association. Until 1844 the Virginia Christian Conference, which represented approximately 2,500 communicants, maintained formal relations with various Christian conferences in the North. In this year the New England Conference of Christian Churches adopted an antislavery resolution that prompted the Virginia Conference to sever relations with their Northern brethren. Virginia churchmen then invited their coreligionists in North Carolina and elsewhere in the South to form an organization of Christian churches in the slave states. The Southern Christian Convention would reunite with their Northern brethren in 1922, and in 1931 the Christian Churches would merge with the National Council of Congregational Churches to form the Congregational Christian Church.

Twenty years after the old school-new school schism in the Presbyterian Church (1857), the new school General Assembly repudiated slavery and slave owning. This action prompted the New School Presbyterian churches in the South to form a separate organization, the United Synod of the Presbyterian Church. New School presbyteries in Virginia affiliated with the United Synod until this synod merged with the Old School church in the South in 1864.

After secession and the beginning of the Civil War the Old School Presbyterians in the South formed the Presbyterian Church in the Confederate States of America; the board of publication of this denomination was located in Richmond. In early 1861 leaders of the Protestant Episcopal diocese of Virginia and other dioceses of this church in the South organized a national church under the appellation of the Protestant Episcopal Church in the Confederate States of America. At this time leadership of the Lutheran synods in the South also formed sectional ecclesiastical bonds and the Lutheran churches in Virginia became affiliated with the Lutheran Church in the Confederate States of America. At the close of the Civil War the Southern dioceses of the Protestant Episcopal Church were reunited with their coreligionists in the nation, and in 1917 the Lutheran schism was healed; the Presbyterians in the nation (as the Baptists) still constitute two major factions or sectional organizations.

During the secession crisis of 1860-1861 most Virginia Christians counseled moderation and decried the spirit of "fanaticism" that was present in some areas of the South. ROBERT L. DABNEY, a prominent Presbyterian and moderator of the Synod of Virginia, expressed the sentiments of most when he declared that the election of Abraham Lincoln was not sufficient cause for secession. He also denounced the hasty action of South Carolina in adopting an ordinance of secession. Dabney as well as the *Religious Herald* (Baptist) and the *Richmond Christian Advocate* (Methodist) urged compromise measures to preserve the Union until after the Fort Sumter incident.

Once fighting erupted in South Carolina, churches in Virginia supported public opinion and the action of the state's politicians. Secession was justified on constitutional and economic grounds and blame for the disruption of the nation and the war was placed on zealous and fanatical Northerners. Only a few clergymen opposed the course of their state and migrated to other regions; in Halifax County an Episcopal rector retired from the ministry because his unionist sympathies were unpopular with his congregation.

During the Civil War most church leaders declared that the struggle was a just and righteous one. Virginia clergymen, in patriotic sermons and orations, urged young men to join the army and some assisted recruiting agents in enrolling men for service. Clergymen often set the example for others by abandoning their profession for military action. In the spring of 1861 the Rev. J. M. P. Atkinson, president of Hampden-Sydney College, was elected captain of a military company and the Rev. William N. Pendleton, rector of Grace Church (Episcopal) in Lexington, joined the Rockbridge Artillery with the rank of captain.

During the war denominational leaders directed their attention and resources to the spiritual needs of the soldiers. Numerous ministers served as chaplains and others visited the army as evangelists and missionaries. The activities of these clergymen sparked a series of revivals in the Army of northern Virginia; they were also active in forming army churches and Christian associations among the soldiers.

Throughout the war Virginia church members of all denominations made valiant efforts to provide Bibles, tracts, and religious newspapers for the men in military service as well as for their constituency at home. Some of these efforts were by denominations acting alone, but most were cooperative undertakings with other churches. The Virginia Baptist Publication and Sunday School Board printed more than 100 different tracts and distributed over 50 million pages to soldiers and civilians during the war. The Virginia Conference of the Methodist Episcopal Church, South, organized the Soldier's Tract Society; it published tracts and the *Soldier's Paper*, a religious newspaper for distribution in the army. The society also distributed hymnbooks and Bibles to soldiers.

Virginia Baptists, Methodists, Presbyterians, Episcopalians, and others supported a number of interdenominational agencies that were formed during the war to minister to the religious needs of the men in military service. Among these were the Bible Society of the Confederate States, the Evangelical Tract Society of Petersburg, and the General Tract Agency of Raleigh. Virginia churchmen also sponsored a project to provide education for soldiers' orphans, and in Richmond they formed a society to furnish artificial limbs for maimed soldiers.

Most of the programs of the churches were interrupted by the war. Foreign missionaries were stranded and educational institutions were impoverished as their trustees invested endowment funds in Confederate securities. Scores of church buildings in eastern Virginia and in the Valley were destroyed by the contending armies and others were used for hospitals and stables. Many congregations were scattered and ecclesiastical bonds were weakened. Methodist Bishop John Early was unable to supervise and visit the congregations in his area, and some local Baptist associations did not meet during the war. After Appomattox churchmen urged the citizens of Virginia to accept the result of the war as "part of the workings of Providence," to prove themselves loyal citizens of the United States, and begin the task of rebuilding.

The emancipation of the slaves had a pronounced effect upon the religious structure of the state. In 1860 churches of all denominations contained slave members, but the largest number of black Christians were members of Baptist churches. After the war practically all of these members left their former churches and formed separate and independent congregations. The formation of black churches began prior to 1865 at such places as Norfolk and Alexandria and was encouraged by missionaries from Northern churches. After Appomattox Baptist,

Congregational, Methodist, Presbyterian, and other missionaries and teachers from the North entered the state to care for the spiritual and educational welfare of the freedmen, and by the close of 1866 Negro Baptist and Methodist congregations had been formed in most of the towns and cities in the commonwealth.

Agents of the American Baptist Home Missionary Society assisted freedmen in forming the first black Baptist association in the state (1865). This organization, the Shiloh Association, consisted of churches in the Richmond, Manchester, and Petersburg area. In 1868 the Virginia Baptist State Convention was created; it consisted of associations that embraced all regions of the state. This convention was the principal organization of black Baptists in the commonwealth. American Baptist Home Mission personnel were also responsible for founding a school in Richmond that later developed into Virginia Union University. In 1883 black Baptists established the Virginia Theological Seminary and College in Lynchburg, and by 1900 the membership of black Baptist churches in Virginia was approximately 200,000.

After the Civil War the black membership of the Methodist Episcopal Church, South, left that denomination and entered one of several branches of Methodism. Some affiliated with the Methodist Episcopal Church but most of them became members of either the African Methodist Episcopal Church or the African Methodist Episcopal Zion Church. Both of these were autonomous black organizations that had been formed in the early nineteenth century and had their headquarters in Philadelphia and New York. Agents of these denominations came into Virginia in the wake of Federal forces and found a responsive following among Methodist freedmen. Another body was formed in 1870, the Colored Methodist Episcopal Church, consisting mainly of freedmen who wished to maintain a close relationship with the Methodist Episcopal Church, South. The various black Methodist churches in the state reported a combined membership of approximately 30,000 at the close of the 19th century.

Although the black membership of the Presbyterian and Protestant Episcopal churches in Virginia was small in the post-Appomattox decades, these members were organized into separate congregations. In 1878 leadership in the Episcopal diocese of Virginia was instrumental in founding the Bishop Payne Divinity School, a theological seminary for blacks at Petersburg, and 12 years later the diocese helped to establish a vocational school for blacks at Lawrenceville (St. Paul's College). In the closing decades of the 19th century other industrial high schools for Negroes were founded at Christiansburg, Lynchburg, Manassas, and elsewhere under the auspices of the Society of Friends, the Methodist Episcopal Church, and the United Presbyterian Church.

The formation of separate black congregations in the state was not entirely because of the influence of missionaries from the North. The attitude of white church members in the state toward their black coreligionists reflected a paternalistic and white supremacist approach to race relations and stimulated the formation of independent congregations by freedmen. In the scattered congregations that permitted blacks to worship with whites—mainly rural Protestant and urban Catholic ones—the few blacks who attended services were seated in areas of the sanctuary "reserved" for them as in antebellum days.

Although the white-controlled churches in Virginia lost nearly all of their black members after the Civil War, relations between black and white Christians were not hostile. A number of white Baptists served as trustees of the black school at Richmond and the *Religious Herald* urged its constituency to contribute to the school's support. Black and white ecclesiastical organizations frequently welcomed each others' "fraternal delegates" at their annual meetings and invited them to attend the proceedings. The white religious press deplored the lynchings of blacks and urged that whites treat black citizens with respect and pay them fair wages for their labor. The white denominational press was sympathetic to the establishment of public schools for blacks but demanded that they be segregated. White churchmen were not supportive of black suffrage and they applauded the actions of the state constitutional convention of 1901-1902 that virtually abolished black voting in the state.

Although some church leaders had advocated the establishment of a state system of tax-supported schools prior to the Civil War, such schools were not established until 1870. From the public school system's inception, denominational leaders were some of its firmest and most articulate supporters. The *Religious Herald*, which represented the largest group of church members in the state, applauded the establishment of public schools and frequently urged the general assembly to appropriate increased funds to extend the school year and to establish a normal school for the training of teachers. Church leaders, however, were not unanimous in their support of public education. The Presbyterian Robert L. Dabney and the Baptist spokesman Bennett Puryear disapproved of public schools. They viewed them as extravagant and a misuse of tax funds, as tending to weaken family bonds, and as promoting "godless" education. These men, nevertheless, represented a small faction of the citizens and church members in the commonwealth.

Since most of the public schools in Virginia prior to World War I were limited to the elementary grades, the churches remained active in operating institutes, academies, and seminaries to provide secondary education for young men and women. Throughout the closing decades of the 19th century and the early years of the 20th century all churches sponsored secondary educational institutions for boys and girls. In the 1890s Baptists in Virginia were operating 15 schools for boys and 18 for girls. Secondary schools were also established by Lutherans, Methodists, Presbyterians, Episcopalians, Roman Catholics, and others. Some of these denominational schools were privately owned and operated but others were governed by a board of trustees responsible to a local association, synod, presbytery, or conference. All of the schools solicited funds from churches and individuals within their area. Church-oriented schools flourished until the second decade of the 20th century, when the commonwealth began to devote attention and resources to the establishment of public high schools.

Denominational colleges in the postbellum years faced an enormous task of rebuilding destroyed or damaged property, replenishing their endowments, and reviving interest in higher education. All of the principal colleges had suspended classes during the war but by 1866 most had resumed operations. Within the next 50 years a number of new church colleges were founded in the state. Three of these represented small groups that had been in Virginia since colonial days. In 1875 the United Brethren established Shenandoah College at Winchester and six years later the Dunkers (Church of the Brethren) founded Bridgewater College, and in 1917 Eastern Mennonite College at Harrisonburg was chartered by the state legislature as a four-year institution. Lynchburg College, a Disciples of Christ school, began operations in 1903.

Virginia church leaders were in the forefront of the movement to provide higher education for women. For decades the churches had been active in the operation of institutes and seminaries for young women but it was not until the closing years of the 19th century that women were given the opportunity to receive a college education. By the 1880s some denominational leaders in the Baptist, Methodist, Presbyterian, and other churches were keenly aware of the need to

provide higher education for women and they were urging that the church colleges become coed or else separate ones be established for women. Despite the opinion of a few that educating women would "take them out of their sphere" and make them independent of their husbands and contribute to family dissension, the advocates of higher education for women received a favorable hearing in the state. In some instances a female seminary was transformed into a college; the Augusta Female Seminary at Staunton, a Presbyterian school since 1842, became a junior college for women and later obtained a charter as a four-year college (Mary Baldwin). Hollins Institute, founded under Baptist auspices in the antebellum era, was also transformed into a four-year institution—Hollins College.

In 1898 the board of trustees of Richmond College approved the admission of young women to that institution, but in 1914 the board established Westhampton College, a four-year liberal arts resident college for women on the campus of the University of Richmond. However, the Methodists were the first group in the state to found a high quality four-year liberal arts college for women. In 1893 the Virginia Conference of the Methodist Episcopal Church, South, sponsored the founding of Randolph-Macon Woman's College in Lynchburg. All of the principal denominations also operated junior colleges for women; these institutions were located in Blackstone, Danville, Bristol, Marion, Abingdon, and elsewhere in the state.

The denominations made valiant efforts to provide higher education for women but church leaders were not supportive of the movement to extend the franchise to women. Prominent spokesmen in all churches opposed women's suffrage, claiming that political activities would degrade women and deprive them of their modesty and charm. Not only were women denied political rights until 1920, they were also denied full church-member status. Until the 1890s congregational business meetings and programs were conducted by the male members, and the church's representatives to meetings of the synod, conference, or association were males. Although males dominated ecclesiastical affairs, women were assuming an increasingly important position in the life of the church during the years 1880-1920. Prior to the close of the 19th century a few Baptist churches were permitting women to attend and participate in the monthly business meeting of the congregation. In a number of churches women served on a variety of committees including music, visitation, or hospitality, Sunday school, finance, and communion. From the 1880s leadership in the women's missionary organization in all of the denominations became more active and aggressive and they achieved the right of their representatives to have time on the program of the annual ecclesiastical meetings of the different denominations. It would be another 50 years, however, before the widespread prejudice against the ordination of women would begin to wane; this prejudice was less prevalent in the Methodist Church than in other denominations.

Throughout most of the 19th century the churches' concern for youth was manifested in the formation of Sunday schools. However, from the 1880s on church leaders were active in promoting a distinctive ministry to their youth. Organizations such as the Baptist Young Peoples Union, the Luther League, Christian Endeavor, and the Epworth League were created to minister to youth. The purpose of these societies was to encourage and train young people to participate in the life and programs of the church, to promote their spiritual development, and to detect potential leadership for the church. These organizations were popular and by 1902 BYPUs were organized in 202 churches in the state, and they had a membership of 10,700. Within a few years these youth organizations would sponsor retreats, summer encampments, and a variety of training programs. In 1921 the

Synod of Virginia purchased Massanetta Springs for use as an assembly site and retreat for Presbyterian youth groups. For many years the Synod permitted its facilities also to be used by other denominational organizations within the state. An important aspect of the ministry to youth was the establishment of campus ministry programs for students attending state colleges and universities. Although all of the denominations formed such programs, the first one in Virginia was established in 1901 at Blacksburg by the Presbyterians.

Among the various benevolent activities that occupied denominational leaders in the decades from 1880 to 1920 were the establishment of orphanages and homes for the aged. During these years all of the principal churches established such institutions at Richmond, Lynchburg, Salem, Covington, and elsewhere. In 1919 the Baptists received a charter for the Virginia Baptist Hospital and began the construction of this facility at Lynchburg. The Baptists and the Roman Catholics are the only two denominations to establish hospitals in the commonwealth.

The decades following Appomattox were ones characterized by intellectual, economic, social, and political ferment. Many of the concerns, problems, fears, and aspirations of American society were shared by Virginians. Although Virginia was not a major industrial state the tensions and violence characteristic of labor-management relations during these years were not unnoticed by Virginia church people. Throughout the 1870s and 1880s church spokesmen espoused laissez-faire paternalism as the ideal relationship for harmony between employer and employees. Baptist, Presbyterian, and other church people maintained that all attempts on the part of trade unions to regulate the price of labor were unsound and injurious. It was claimed that labor unions created ill feelings between employees and employers. Labor sympathizers were labeled foreign-born anarchists, socialists, and communists. However, by the close of the century some church leaders were advocating the eight-hour day for industrial workers and were expressing concern about the type of occupation and the hours of employment required of women and children. When the Federal Council of Churches was formed in 1906, all of the major denominations in the state except the Baptists became affiliated with this organization and church leaders expressed sympathy with many of the social and economic reforms proposed by the FCC. Although the Baptists never joined the Council, spokesmen for this denomination in Virginia were sympathetic to many of its aims. Prior to 1914 the *Religious Herald* and prominent Baptist spokesmen advocated effective child labor laws, mine safety legislation, and supported the direct election of United States senators.

Between 1880 and 1920 the nation received a large influx of immigrants from southern and eastern Europe. In Virginia this immigration was responsible for the marked increase in membership of two groups that had been present in the area since colonial times: Jews and Roman Catholics. During these years the Jewish population of the state increased from approximately 2,500 to 25,000, and Roman Catholic communicants increased from an estimated 12,000 to 38,000. Also during these years Greek immigrants established the first Eastern or Orthodox congregation in the state.

The increase of immigrants from southern and eastern Europe into the United States stimulated a revival of nativist sentiment throughout the nation. Although nativist feeling and activities were not as prominent in Virginia as elsewhere in the country, such attitudes were reflected in the religious press and in the statements of some church leaders concerning foreigners, labor sympathizers, and Roman Catholics. On one occasion the *Religious Herald* referred to the immigrants who were "flooding" into the United States as the "dregs of society" who should be excluded from the country. Labor disputes, urban crime and violence, and political corruption were blamed on foreigners.

Since most of the immigrants to America were affiliated with the Roman Catholic Church, the anti-foreign sentiments of Virginia churchmen often manifested a hostility to this church. Although anti-Catholic bias was prevalent among all Protestant groups it was most aggressive in Baptist churches. The Catholic Church was often referred to as "the mother of harlots" and as a tyrannical institution that kept its people in ignorance. The dogma of papal infallibility was described as an incredible and monstrous assumption. Baptist spokesmen maintained that their denomination had existed as a separate group since the time of Jesus Christ and that they had never been affiliated with the church at Rome. Apprehension that Catholic immigrants would overrun the country and the belief that foreigners were responsible for a variety of social and economic problems in American society prompted churchmen to espouse federal legislation that would restrict immigration into the United States.

In the half century following the Civil War and Reconstruction a variety of intellectual forces helped to produce an era of controversy and tension in American religious life and thought. Among these forces were the evolutionary concept of the development of life and the theories of geologists concerning the formation and age of the earth, the critical study of the Bible in universities and seminaries, and the emergence of theological liberalism. Virginia churches were keenly aware of these intellectual forces and spokesmen in all denominations, at one time or another, denounced the evolutionary theory as atheistic and "utterly worthless." However, in 1900 the Baptist weekly published an article that declared that the evolutionary hypothesis enabled man to interpret God as a vital and abiding force. Evolution, it maintained, made possible a noble review of society and confirmed the teaching that man was the acme of creation. In the 20th century denominational leaders in Virginia became more tolerant of the evolutionary theory and Virginia was the only Southern state in the 1920s that did not adopt a law to prohibit the teaching of evolution in the public schools. Virginius Dabney claims that the reason Virginia followed this course was because of the influence of church spokesmen, especially Baptist leaders, who opposed the passage of a law prohibiting the teaching of evolution.

The critical study of the Bible and church history, and the concepts of theological liberalism received a mixed reception in the state. Generally, church leaders maintained that Almighty God was the author of the Scriptures and that people should read and accept the Bible rather than question it. An exception was the Baptist scholar CRAWFORD TOY of Norfolk. Toy had studied at the University of Berlin and was professor of Old Testament at the Southern Baptist Theological Seminary. He was dismissed from the faculty because he denied that Moses wrote the Pentateuch and claimed that one should not use the Scriptures to affirm or oppose the facts of history or the knowledge of modern science. A few years after the dismissal of Toy, who was subsequently a faculty member at Harvard University, a professor of church history at the same seminary was forced to resign because he claimed, in a published article, that Roger Williams had probably been sprinkled rather than immersed, that the Baptist denomination originated in the 17th century, and that the earliest Baptists did not practice immersion. Although this professor, WILLIAM WHITSITT, was dismissed, his opinions were not offensive to Baptist leaders in Virginia and he was immediately employed by Richmond College as professor of philosophy.

Neither Baptist nor Presbyterian churchmen manifested any sympathy for the doctrines of theological liberalism or the New Theology. Proponents of liberalism were accused of being indifferent to the truth and to the Christian doctrines of the Trinity, the atonement, revelation, and the incarnation. The late Hunter D. Farish maintained that Methodists were friendlier to liberal thought and concepts than others. More alumni of Randolph-Macon College and other Methodist schools in the South studied in German universities during these decades and the exposure to different ideas and approaches to learning made them more tolerant of ideological changes than some of their colleagues in other denominations. Unlike some in other areas, no Virginia clergyman was the subject of a doctrinal or heresy proceeding by his peers during these years (c.1880-1920).

The one sociomoral issue upon which church people in all denominations were united was the issue of temperance. The most aggressive and forceful leadership in the fight against "the liquor trade" was provided by the Methodists. Leadership in this church and in the state centered in the Rev. JAMES CANNON, JR., president of Blackstone Female Institute and later a bishop in the Methodist Episcopal Church, South. Cannon, the WOMAN'S CHRISTIAN TEMPERANCE UNION, and the Anti-Saloon League became a national force for prohibition and were instrumental in promoting the Eighteenth Amendment to the Constitution of the United States.

Throughout the period 1880 to 1920 the church in Virginia presented a united front against what was termed a "secular" Sabbath. Baptists, Methodists, Presbyterians, and others were opposed to business establishments remaining open on Sunday. Church members favored legislation to prohibit railroads from operating on Sunday, to prevent athletic contests such as football and baseball from being played on the Sabbath, and to forbid theaters and fairs to open on Sunday. Not until the 1930s would opposition to a secular Sabbath begin to subside, and then mainly in the urban areas of the state.

The influence of the institutional church program, associated with the Social Gospel movement, was reflected in a few metropolitan churches in Virginia by the end of the 19th century. Perhaps the Broad Street Methodist Church in Richmond developed the most extensive program of activities of any congregation in the commonwealth. It sponsored a recreation program of games for the youths and adults, conducted adult education classes, and maintained a visitation ministry to the city jail, home for incurables, and homes for the elderly. This church operated an employment bureau to assist the unemployed to find work, and inaugurated a program to care for unwed mothers. The congregation also sponsored mission work among the city's black population, conducted summer camps for children, and maintained a day care center for children of working mothers. By the close of the 1920s other urban churches had developed institutional-type church programs similar to the one at the Broad Street Church.

During the 20th century the churches in Virginia have maintained their commitment to education and the number of denominational schools has increased, one of the most recent being the first Roman Catholic college in the state, Marymount College (1950), located in Arlington. Since 1945 some denominational junior colleges, in Bristol, Bluefield, Ferrum, and Danville have been transformed into four-year institutions. Church leaders have manifested an increasing interest in the home and foreign mission programs of their denominations and in trying to minister effectively to the religious needs of the church's total constituency: those of all ages, of both sexes, and from diverse ethnic backgrounds.

The Pentecostal churches, which emerged as distinct entities in American Protestantism in the early twentieth century, were organized in Virginia by 1916. The membership of the different Pentecostal groups in 1936 was reported as being less than 4,000, and although these churches have experienced a steady growth since the Second World War the oldest and largest representative of these churches in the commonwealth claimed only 6,000 members in 1973.

The churches in Virginia, as those throughout the country, generally have reflected the prevailing national sentiment on national issues. At the time of World War I prominent clergymen and the denominational press declared that the war was justifiable because it was defensive in nature and was a contest between the forces of righteousness and barbarism. Ecclesiastical organizations endorsed America's entry into the war and the peace aims of President Woodrow Wilson. Most of the churches placed the flag beside the pulpit and many clergymen aided government officials and civic leaders in the sale of war bonds. Denominational leaders urged clergymen to enter the chaplaincy and churches cooperated in programs to minister to the needs of the men in military service.

In the presidential election of 1928 church spokesmen in Virginia were active in the campaign to elect Herbert Hoover and save the country from the pope and the saloon keeper. Although Methodist leaders in the state were more active politically than others, prominent church members in all denominations supported the Republican candidate and advised their constituencies to vote for Hoover. During the Great Depression of the 1930s Christians generally expressed sympathy for the reforms of the New Deal that were designed to aid unemployment, guarantee savings accounts, aid home owners in retaining their property, stimulate the economy, care for the needy and provide old-age assistance and security.

At the time of World War II church leaders were more restrained in their support of the conflict than they had been in 1917-1918. Although many churches again placed the flag in the sanctuary and some congregations invested in war bonds, vocal support for the war was muted and respect and toleration for the convictions of conscientious objectors was much greater than a quarter century earlier. During the conflict churchmen in all denominations expressed sympathy for the idea of creating a United Nations organization to preserve peace, justice, and order in the world once the war ended. Clerical criticism of war was more pronounced during the Vietnam conflict. By the late 1960s a number of Virginia clergymen were critics of this war. One of the most widely publicized of them was the rector of Bruton Parish Church in Williamsburg, who denounced the war in a sermon when President Lyndon Johnson was in the congregation.

The civil rights movement, which entered its most activist phase in the 1950s, attracted the attention of all churches in Virginia. Although the leadership of this movement in the state was provided by black clergymen in Farmville, Hopewell, Richmond and other cities, a number of white church members and ecclesiastical organizations were not unsympathetic to the goals of the civil rights leader Martin Luther King, Jr. Indications of increasing awareness by white Christians of racial concerns antedated the 1954 Supreme Court decision in *Brown v. Board of Education.* In the 1930s the diocesan council of the Protestant Episcopal Church in Virginia voted to give the Negro membership of the church representation on the council. In 1940 the Baptist General Association of Virginia assisted a group of black Baptists in building an orphanage at Fredericksburg, and also entered into cooperation with the black Baptists of the state in home mission activities. In the early 1950s Negro students were admitted to the Presbyterian's Union Theological Seminary in Richmond and the library facilities of that institution were made available to the students of Virginia Union University—a black Baptist school nearby.

When the Supreme Court's decision on school segregation was announced in 1954, it received favorable comment from the Presbyterian Synod of Virginia, the Baptist General Association of Virginia,

and various white church leaders in the commonwealth. The reaction of the state's political leaders to the court's decision, however, was a policy of "massive resistance" to compliance with the court's order. By 1959 this policy was repudiated by the courts. Although there were some exceptions, by the mid-1960s blacks were welcomed at worship services in formerly all-white congregations and black students were enrolled for the first time in such institutions as Hampden-Sydney College, the University of Richmond, Lynchburg College, Randolph-Macon College, and other church-affiliated educational institutions. Sympathy for Negro rights was also expressed by the students at Union Theological Seminary when they joined blacks in picketing department stores in Richmond to protest segregated eating facilities in those stores.

One religious phenomenon of the post-World War Two era in which Virginia churchmen have assumed leadership is the "electronic church." Two men of national prominence in this area are Jerry L. Falwell and M. G. "Pat" Robertson. Falwell in Lynchburg and Robertson in Virginia Beach direct religious organizations that have an international clientele, and each are alleged to receive contributions in excess of one million dollars a week. The religious operations of both of these men are non-denominational or independent. Although Falwell's church and college are Baptist in name neither is affiliated with the Baptist General Association of Virginia. Both of these electronic evangelists expound a theology that appeals mainly to the Fundamentalists or Pentecostals, both are active in the political arena and each preaches a political philosophy that attracts those on the right wing of the political spectrum.

The history of religion in Virginia has reflected the problems and issues of American society throughout its history and only incidentally indicated any distinctive Virginia concern or trait. And as the nation enters the closing decades of the 20th century the concerns and problems of the church in the commonwealth are not unlike those of the church generally. Virginia Christians are concerned about the ultimate effect of the Electronic Church on the traditional churches and their programs and ministry, the emergence and acceptability of the charismatic movement in some of the main-line denominations, the influence of the various liberation movements upon the structure and composition of the churches, and how the church can cope with or direct the ideological and behavioral changes that accompany a revolution in morals.

See also articles on CHURCH AND STATE; ELECTRONIC CHURCH; ESTABLISHED RELIGION.

Bibliography. Reuben E. Alley, *A History of Baptists in Virginia*; Charles H. Ambler and F. P. Summers, *West Virginia: Mountain State*; James H. Bailey, *A History of the Diocese of Richmond, The Formative Years*; Kenneth K. Bailey, *Southern White Protestantism in the Twentieth Century*; Sadie Bell, *The Church, the State, and Education in Virginia*; Myron Berman, *Richmond's Jewry, 1769-1976, Shabbat in Shockoe*; Katherine L. Brown, *Hills of the Lord: Background of the Episcopal Church in Southwestern Virginia, 1738-1938*; George M. Brydon, *Virginia's Mother Church*, 2 vols; Israel L. Butt, *History of African Methodism in Virginia*; Dick Dabney, "God's Own Network, The TV Kingdom of Pat Robertson," *Harpers* 261 (August 1980); Virginius Dabney, *Liberalism in the South*; H. Jackson Darst, *Ante-Bellum Virginia Disciples*; John L. Eighmy, *Churches in Cultural Captivity, A History of the Social Attitudes of Southern Baptists*; William E. Eisenberg, *The Lutheran Church in Virginia, 1717-1962*; Hunter D. Farish, *The Circuit Rider Dismounts, A Social History of Southern Methodism, 1865-1900*; John O. Fish, "Southern Methodism in the Progressive Era: A Social History," unpublished Ph.D. dissertation, University of Georgia, 1969; Louis Ginsberg, *Chapters on Jews of Virginia, 1658-1900*; Cornelius J. Heatwole, *A History of Education in Virginia*; Robert R. Howison, *A History of Virginia From Its Discovery and Settlement by Europeans to the Present Time*, 2 vols.; *The Negro in Virginia*, compiled by Writers' Program of the Works Progress Administration in the State of Virginia; Otis K. Rice, *The Allegheny Frontier, West Virginia, 1730-1830*; Dale Robinson, *Academies of Virginia*; Roger E. Sappington, *The Brethren in Virginia: A History of the Church of the Brethren in Virginia*; Rufus B. Spain, *At Ease in Zion, Social History of Southern Baptists, 1865-1900*; Durward T. Stokes and William T. Scott, *A History of the Christian Church in the South*; Herbert S. Stroupe, *The Religious Press in the South Atlantic States*; William W. Sweet, *Virginia Methodism, A History*; Vinson Synan, *The Holiness-Pentecostal Movement in the United States*; Ernest T. Thompson, *Presbyterians in the South*, 3 vols; *West Virginia, A Guide to the Mountain State*, compiled by Workers of the Writers' Program of the Work Projects Administration in the State of West Virginia; Sister Mary A. Yeakel, *The Nineteenth Century Educational Contributions of the Sisters of Charity of Saint Vincent de Paul in Virginia*.

W. HARRISON DANIEL
UNIVERSITY OF RICHMOND

VOODOO: *See* CARIBBEAN IMMIGRATION; LOUISIANA.

WADDEL, MOSES (1770-1840), Presbyterian minister and pioneer educator, was born to Scotch-Irish parents in Rowan County NC. Educated at James Hall's "Clio's Nursery," he taught school in North Carolina and Georgia. In 1789 he experienced conversion. He graduated from Hampden-Sydney College in 1791 and, after probationary preaching in South Carolina and Georgia, was ordained a minister in 1794. During his initial pastorate he founded his first school, in Appling GA. In the late 1790s he preached to dispersed congregations in his area.

Waddel made his primary impact as an educator. In 1801 he founded a school at Vienna SC, and in 1804 he opened Willington Academy on his nearby estate. In 15 years the academy educated more than 1,000 boarding students, many of whom later achieved academic and civil prominence. Waddel's students mastered the classical curriculum at an exacting pace, interspersing long study periods with recitations. The strict disciplinary system included student courts and monitors.

From 1819 to 1829 Waddel was president of the University of Georgia. Continuing his classical and disciplinary emphases, he revived the university from a moribund condition. He instilled religious influence into the institution and incurred accusations of Presbyterian favoritism. After retiring, Waddel preached and superintended a school in Willington until a stroke incapacitated him in 1836. His *Memoirs of the Life of Miss Caroline Elizabeth Smelt* (1818) enjoyed a popularity that has puzzled subsequent readers.

Bibliography. John N. Waddel, *Memorials of Academic Life*; William B. Sprague, ed., *Annals of the American Pulpit*, vol. 4.

JACK P. MADDEX, JR.
UNIVERSITY OF OREGON

WALLACE FAMILY. The Texas progeny of Wallaces began with Thomas Knox Wallace, immigrant from Alabama, continued through his son Foy Edwin Wallace (1871-1950) and gained increasing prominence through two sons of Foy Edwin: Cled Eugene Wallace (1892-1962) and Foy Esco Wallace (1896-1979) and two nephews: Gervais Knox Wallace (1903-) and Glenn L. Wallace (1907-1982).

These five preachers enjoyed ministries of more than 50 years each and influenced CHURCHES OF CHRIST most extensively from 1930. All were successful evangelists and writers—thoroughgoing controversialists—and were seldom misunderstood. Glenn L. ministered locally for some of the strongest churches in the West.

Foy E., Jr., by 1930 enjoyed prominence as editor (1930-1934) of the *Gospel Advocate*. His leadership was felt particularly in heated discussions of issues. His works on MILLENNIALISM include *The Book of Revelation* (1966), an extreme preterist interpretation. Premillennialists were offered fellowship (unsuccessfully) contingent upon their theories being held as private opinions only. A breach dating from 1915 was solidified by periodicals issued (1935-1949) with Foy, Jr., as editor and Cled as featured writer.

Extrachurch and intrachurch arrangements and organizations in missions and benevolence became a quite divisive area of dispute by the 1950s. Foy Wallace, Jr.'s role was pivotal. His early statements and influence were used by a "new radical party" that "forced issues for lines of cleavage" instead of the moderation intended, according to him.

Wallace spent the last 15 years of his life actively "exposing . . . multiple new translations." In *A Review of the New Versions* (1973), he demonstrated little knowledge of original texts—in essence it placed the "Authorized Version" above the Greek New Testament text. Although rejected by a large majority of academically trained members in the Churches of Christ, this view found acceptance among a considerable number of members and some ministers owing primarily to Wallace's efforts.

R. L. ROBERTS
ABILENE CHRISTIAN UNIVERSITY

WAR BETWEEN THE STATES: *See* CIVIL WAR.

WAYLAND, FRANCIS (1796-1865), Baptist minister, educator, and moral philosopher, was born in New York City, son of an immigrant currier turned Baptist preacher. After graduating from Union

College (1813), he studied medicine, but a conversion experience led him to decide on the ministry. Following a year at Andover Seminary, he returned to Union as tutor (1817-1821), and was then ordained as pastor of Boston's First Baptist Church. In 1826 he was again recalled to Union as professor, but within months was chosen as president of Brown University, the principal Baptist educational institution, which he served with distinction from 1827 to 1855. He restored discipline, improved the recitation method of instruction, reorganized the university, led it to serve community needs more fully, and initiated a limited elective system. A man of great presence and dignity, a prolific writer and speaker, he became well known in education and religion. He was influential in guiding Baptists away from centralized organizational patterns.

Among his many books was *The Elements of Moral Science* (1835), a famous, oft-reprinted ethical handbook that was widely used as a moral guide by Southern clerical moralists. Though they disliked its moderate antislavery views, his combination of rationalist concerns with sentimentalist language gave them an alternative to "relativistic" utilitarianism. In 1844 Wayland was elected president of the Baptist TRIENNIAL CONVENTION, but felt that Southerners were within their rights in organizing separately the next year. He later became a more outspoken opponent of slavery, excoriating it as a sinful practice.

Bibliography. Theodore R. Crane, *Francis Wayland: Political Economist as Educator*; James O. Murray, *Francis Wayland.*

ROBERT T. HANDY
UNION THEOLOGICAL SEMINARY

WEATHERFORD, WILLIS DUKE (1875-1970), churchman, YMCA executive, race-relations pioneer, author and educator, was born in Weatherford TX. After earning a Ph.D. in literature from Vanderbilt in 1902, he joined the YMCA as International Student Secretary for the South and Southwest and worked to develop needed Christian leadership for the South, especially in the area of race relations. He was cofounder of the COMMISSION ON INTERRACIAL COOPERATION (later the Southern Regional Council). He founded and directed both the impressive Blue Ridge YMCA Assembly in North Carolina and the YMCA Graduate School in Nashville. He also taught religion and philosophy at Fisk University.

Weatherford became a member of the Berea College Board of Trustees in 1916 and 30 years later he joined the Berea staff to raise money and to recruit needy but able Appalachian students. When he was 82, he embarked on one of his largest projects, the Southern Appalachian Studies, with a quarter-million-dollar grant he secured from the Ford Foundation, with commitments from the region's universities to contribute their best scholars as researchers, and with the support of the major church denominations. The finished product, under the editorship of Thomas R. Ford, *The Southern Appalachian Region: A Survey*, is the most comprehensive study ever done of the region.

Weatherford was author, coauthor, or editor of 19 books, including: *Negro Life in the South, The Negro from Africa to America* (with Charles S. Johnson), *American Churches and the Negro, Studies in Christian Experience*, and *Life and Religion in Southern Appalachia* (with Earl D. C. Brewer). His epitaph reads: "Man of God and Servant of Men, Life Long Student, Lover of Youth and Friend of all Races, Man of Social Passion and Faith in God Who taught the Sacredness of Persons and Dignity of Creative Labor."

See also article on APPALACHIAN RELIGION.

Bibliography. Wilma Dykeman, *Prophet of Plenty: The First Ninety Years of W. D. Weatherford.*

LOYAL JONES
BEREA COLLEGE

WEAVER, RUFUS WASHINGTON

(1870-1947), Baptist leader and advocate of religious liberty, was born in Greens-

boro NC. He was educated at Wake Forest College and the Southern Baptist Theological Seminary and pursued graduate studies at the University of Cincinnati and The Johns Hopkins University. In 1918, after serving Baptist pastorates in several states, he became president of Mercer University, a position he held for nine years until he was elected secretary of the Education Board of the Southern Baptist Convention. Subsequently he served for two years as pastor of the First Baptist Church in Washington DC, resigning to become executive secretary of the District of Columbia Baptist Convention.

Increasingly Weaver turned his scholarly gifts and tireless energies to the arena of public affairs. He sought to awaken Baptists to their heritage and rally their support for the cause of religious liberty. He was convinced that "religious liberty is the ultimate ground of democratic institutions" and that wherever this liberty is imperiled, "all other human rights are imperiled." In 1938 he helped establish the Joint Conference Committee on Public Relations, now the Baptist Joint Committee on Public Affairs, which represents the major Baptist bodies in the United States in its witness to the principles of religious liberty and separation of CHURCH AND STATE and its efforts to preserve these principles in contemporary church-state relations. Weaver's published works include *The Christian Faith at the Nation's Capital* and *Champions of Religious Liberty*.

Bibliography. C. Emanuel Carlson, "Baptist Joint Committee on Public Affairs," in Davis Collier Woolley, ed., *Baptist Advance; The Achievements of the Baptists of North America for a Century and a Half;* Edward Hughes Pruden, "Weaver, Rufus Washington," *Encyclopedia of Southern Baptists,* 2: 1481; Rufus W. Weaver, ed., *The Road to the Freedom of Religion.*

DANIEL HOLCOMB
NEW ORLEANS BAPTIST SEMINARY

WEIL, GERTRUDE (1879-1971), Jewish leader in social welfare causes, was born in Goldsboro NC. Her father was an emigrant from Germany and a prominent merchant in Goldsboro. After Gertrude graduated from the local public schools in

1895, her family sent her to the Horace
Mann School in New York, then to Smith
College, graduating in 1901 as the first
North Carolinian to earn a degree at
Smith.

Social welfare was Gertrude Weil's
chief interest and upon her return to
Goldsboro she began teaching courses for
mill workers. She also agitated for better
health and educational facilities for the
children of these workers. She served as
secretary of the North Carolina Conference for Social Service and was on the
board of directors of Dobbs Training
School for delinquent girls.

Weil was a prominent suffragette and
some credit her as being the leading proponent for women's rights in North Carolina during the first decades of the 20th
century. She was the first president of the
North Carolina League of Women Voters
and served as secretary of the North
Carolina State Federation of Women's
Clubs.

Proud of her Jewish background, she
was also active in synagogue and state
Jewish agencies. After her parents visited
Palestine in 1909, she became interested
in the Zionist movement and was a vocal
proponent of establishing a haven for
Jews in the Holy Land. She considered the
creation of Israel in 1948 the most exciting event of contemporary Jewish history.

Impressed by Jewish teachings on
social justice and charity, Weil used her
wealth to promote a better life for her
fellow citizens. She donated land for a
Negro park in Goldsboro, paid the salaries of nurses at the Wayne County Health
Department for nearly a year until public
funds became available, and financed the
college education of scores of deserving
youngsters.

Increasingly Gertrude Weil became
interested in civil liberties and civil rights.
Although eligible for membership in the
United Daughters of the Confederacy, she
refused to join the group and claimed it
would be best if the South forgot about the
Civil War. She was one of the few defend-

ers of Frank Graham, a liberal North
Carolinian who served on President Truman's Committee on Civil Rights.

Gertrude Weil was frequently
honored for her various activities. In 1964
she was one of the first five women to win
the Smith College medal for a lifetime of
service to others. Awards also came from
B'nai B'rith, Chi Omega Sorority, and various black organizations.

ARNOLD SHANKMAN

WELD, THEODORE (1803-1895),
evangelist in behalf of ABOLITIONISM, was
born in Hampton CT, but grew up in
western New York. Descended from a
long line of New England Congregationalists, he was one of Charles G. Finney's
evangelists.

Early pledged to temperance, his
effective itinerant lecturing impressed the
philanthropic Tappan brothers, Arthur
and Lewis. They shared his sentiments
and solicited his talents in behalf of slaves,
a cause that became the enduring commitment of his life. Seeking an appropriate
site to combine ministerial education and
antislavery activity, he came to Lane
Seminary, newly founded in Ohio, bringing other abolitionist students with him.
There he organized the "Lane Debates"—
a series of sessions given to exhaustive
study of slavery—and successfully converted most of the community to the cause
of abolition. Departing Lane he concentrated on the program of the abolitionists,
in whose company he met and married
the South Carolina Quaker, Angelina
Grimké.

Though a phenomenally successful
speaker, writer, and lobbyist, he is little
known, because he refused to publish
under his own name, and rejected honor
and office in reform societies. Disenchanted with institutional corruption, he
increasingly distrusted reform movements and organizations—including the
church—and focused on personal piety.
See also article on GRIMKÉ SISTERS.

Bibliography. Robert H. Abzug, *Passionate Liberator:
Theodore Weld and the Dilemma of Reform*; Gilbert H.

Drumond and Dwight L. Drumond, *Letters of Theodore Weld, Angelina Grimké Weld and Sarah Grimké, 1822-1844.*

STUART C. HENRY
DUKE UNIVERSITY

WELSH INFLUENCE. The contribution of the Welsh to a Southern religious tradition is quite unlike that of any other migrant people to America. They differed from the 16th-century New Englanders and those of the Middle Colonies in that the majority who came to Virginia were not seeking freedom for religious worship, did not settle in colonies, and were assimilationist. Their exodus from Great Britain was largely a consequence of political disturbance. The Welsh, along with other Celts of western Britain, had been loyal supporters of King Charles and had been defeated by the Parliamentary forces led by Cromwell.

Several tens of thousands of Loyalists sought refuge in Virginia during the middle half of the 17th century and it is estimated that at least 10 percent of these were of Welsh origin, drawn from all social classes. Their affiliation with the Anglican church was subordinate to personal and political loyalties. The lack of a strong religious commitment can be traced to the situation in Wales. The Established Church there had long suffered from a variety of factors: gross neglect of church organization; the lack of preparation for a qualified clergy; a language barrier that separated a clergy who ministered in English and monoglot Welsh communicants; and a corrupt and commercialized fiscal system. Moreover, festival occasions were embedded in a secular, indigenous, bardic tradition; while the existing tight family and neighbor bonds gave cohesion against internal crisis or external danger.

The 17th-century Welsh migrants arrived in Virginia prior to a fusion between religion and nationality. Their identity as Anglicans was much more a fortuitous consequence of loyalty to the ruling Tudors than to any religious fervor. This indifference to religion stretches from their original conversion to Christianity and was not altered until the arrival of nonconformism. They never experienced any externally imposed religious persecution or internally generated strife and hence were left free from a martyrdom that often accompanies commitment. For example, the Welsh were unconnected to the Irish quarrel with the Papacy over the legitimacy of Celtic or Roman practices. The Reformation touched them lightly and Calvinism found little support until after the arrival of industrialism. Even counting the Welsh Quakers who reached Pennsylvania in 1692 and some Baptists who followed soon afterwards, the nonconformists' numbers were so few that the Welsh census of 1676 recorded that just over three percent were either Roman Catholics or other dissenters. Thus religious nonconformity was insignificant among the early Welsh migrants.

Welsh tradition may be accounted as the source of two major contributions to the American heritage: first, the ritualization in Southern Evangelicalism of many bardic practices and second, what may be a surprise to many, irreligiosity. This latter manifested itself in anticlericalism and antidoctrinalism and the legal separation of church and state as well as the right of a people to be free of organized religion.

The great summer Welsh fairs that combined juridical, economic, and cultural functions seem to constitute a legitimate source for evangelical ritualism. Except for outbreaks of religious exuberance in the camp meetings and religious revivals of the South, these gatherings resemble the bardic aspect of the great Welsh summer fairs. Social cohesion and individual talent were expressed in instrumental and choral music; by oratory (preaching); and by displays of original literary compositions and knowledge. Competitive games and proof of physical prowess were a feature of each.

Parallels (but with no intention to imply a culturally genetic connection) are apparent in the congregational structure of 19th-century Welsh nonconformist chapels and Southern country churches, especially among the Baptists. Congregations were small, composed of neighbors and kinsmen; the local population could be divided into the churched and the unchurched. Internal tensions often led to bifurcation. Both had a circuit-riding ministry, and Baptist preachers were often those who had been blessed with the Spirit. The connection between the family burial site and the location of the chapel is an issue that has not yet been satisfactorily resolved although there are known instances in which the chapel was sited at a family plot.

Religious influences from a transformed Wales of the early nineteenth century never reached the South. In Wales this period saw the beginning of industrialism and the intrusion of CALVINISM plus a surge of Welsh nationalism. Migrants in the decades before the Civil War sought the mines and smelters of Pennsylvania and the rich farmlands of the Midwest where a generation later their children were still aware of their ancestry. In contrast, only two percent of America's foreign-born Welsh were resident in the South.

What conclusion should we reach about the concurrent transformation of Southern folk society from a predominantly subsistence economy to a commercial one and the spread of evangelical Christianity during the first half of the 19th century? Both patterns were associated with the growth of towns outside the plantation area. As folk Southerners became more commercially minded, they also increased their formal religious affiliations.

The success of the evangelical movement among those of Celtic ancestry seems to be directly related to the incorporation of secular practices from the bardic tradition. It is, however, difficult to reconcile the doctrinal insistence of the preeminence of the Kingdom of God and absolute submission to Christ, with Celtic egalitarianism and an attitude of irreligiosity. Where there is no resolution for this apparent contradiction, then community and personal tensions result. It is reasonable to speculate that evangelical Christianity and capitalistic commercialization were linked in the transformation of an agrarian life system.

See also article on HOMECOMINGS.

Bibliography. Alan Conway, *The Welsh in America;* John Monahan, *The Cavalier Remounted: A Study of the Origins of Virginia's Population 1602-1700,* unpublished Ph.D. dissertation, University of Virginia, 1946; John Morris, *The Age of Arthur: A History of the British Isles from 350 to 650;* David Williams, *A History of Modern Wales.*

SOLON T. KIMBALL

WESLEYAN CHURCH, THE. The Wesleyan Church grew out of a merger in 1968 of two denominations—the Wesleyan Methodist Church and the Pilgrim Holiness Church. The merged body subscribes to the interpretation of theology emphasized by John Wesley, including the teaching that Christians may and should witness to a conversion experience and also go on to be entirely sanctified in a second definite work of grace. The church affirms evangelical Protestant theology but officially rejects the validity of speaking in tongues. The Wesleyan Church is affiliated with the National Association of Evangelicals and the Christian Holiness Association.

Headquarters for The Wesleyan Church are located in Marion IN where all denominational officials maintain their offices. The church is led by four general superintendents who are elected at each quadrennial general conference. The church polity is Presbyterian in form. Equal representation by laymen and ordained ministers is required at district and denominational levels.

The church in North America is divided into 43 districts, with 10 of those in the Southeast. One-quarter of the North American membership is located in those 10 districts with the two districts in North Carolina the largest in the South. South Carolina and Virginia are also areas of strength. North American membership grew by over 25 percent from 1968 to 1980; growth in the South was comparable. Evangelism and church growth efforts are emphasized. One effort is the radio program "The Wesleyan Hour" heard weekly over many stations nationwide. The Wesleyan Church carries on an extensive missionary effort worldwide. Membership outside the USA and Canada is approximately one-third that of the homeland. Four liberal arts colleges and two Bible colleges are controlled by the church. Central Wesleyan College, Central SC, is the only college (liberal arts) serving the Southern area of the church.

Both of the previously independent denominations provided traditions that enrich the heritage of the merged church. The Wesleyan Methodist connection was founded in 1843 after a schism from the Methodist Episcopal Church over slavery and the arbitrary rule of bishops. The abolitionist Orange Scott was the most important original leader. From the beginning the Wesleyan Methodist movement maintained a doctrinal emphasis on a second definite work of grace, but gradually the radical social emphasis of the early years was moderated. Nevertheless, women's rights were affirmed and opposition to secret societies, to alcoholic beverages, and to use of tobacco became part of the standing rules. By the end of its first century the Wesleyan Methodist "Church" had emerged, and in the next 25 years powers shifted to the centralized, denominational level.

The Pilgrim Holiness Church originated in the 1890s under the leadership of two evangelists, Seth C. Rees and Martin W. Knapp. These men began an emphasis on holiness evangelism and worldwide missions that was modified but never lost. The original organization was a "prayer league" and not a church. By 1925 there had been a series of mergers by several groups with similar backgrounds, and the church concept emerged along with the denominational name. The missionary effort of the Pilgrim Holiness Church remained very strong. Indigenization was a stated mission goal that met with considerable success. The polity of the Pilgrim Holiness Church also became quite centralized before merger.

Merger talks began in earnest in the 1950s and culminated in 1968 with the formation of the Wesleyan Church.

See also articles on HOLINESS; HOLINESS MOVEMENT; SANCTIFICATION.

Bibliography. Lee Haines and P. William Thomas, *An Outline History of The Wesleyan Church*; R. S. Nicholson and I. F. McLeister, *Conscience and Commitment*; P. William Thomas and P. Westphal Thomas, *The Days of Our Pilgrimage.*

JAMES B. BROSS
CENTRAL WESLEYAN COLLEGE

WESLEYAN METHODIST CHURCH: *See* WESLEYAN CHURCH, THE.

WESLEYAN TRADITION. To portray adequately the Wesleyan tradition is first to speak of its formation in the personal history of the Wesley brothers, John and Charles; second, of the biographies of the earlier Wesleyans; third, of certain doctrinal emphases collectively affirmed; and, only at last, of the Methodist churches that came to organized expression as outcomes of the 18th-century Evangelical Revival and that have in the course of time more or less remained vehicles of the tradition. Here, reference only to items one and three is feasible.

The Wesleyan tradition is rooted deeply in the spiritual pilgrimage of Charles and John Wesley, especially the latter, in whose biography of mind and spirit the tradition is worked through and strikingly enacted with masterful clarity of decisive thought and corresponding organizing power. It is with John that "Scriptural Christianity" was unmistakably defined, preached, written, and tirelessly enjoined upon all humanity—in and out of the churches—as the suitable response of all men and women to the revealed purpose and work of God in Christ for the redemption of humanity, that all might receive their inheritance as the children of God. The Wesleyan tradition promulgates a "Scriptural Christianity" that looks to the restoration of the broken image of God in man fractured in Adam's disobedience. "I refuse," said Wesley, "to be distinguished from other men by any but the common principles of Christianity—the plain, old Christianity that I teach. And whoever *is* what I preach (let him be called what he will, for names change not the nature of things), he is a Christian; not in name only, but in heart and life. He is inwardly and outwardly conformed to the will of God, as revealed in the written Word. He thinks, speaks, and lives, according to the method laid down in the revelation of Jesus Christ. His soul is renewed after the image of God, in righteousness and in all true holiness. And having the mind that was in Christ, he so walks as Christ also walked." Early in his life Wesley was moved by Thomas-a-Kempis's *Imitatio Christi*.

John Wesley had a profound disquiet toward nominal Christianity insofar as it possessed the "form" but not "the power of godliness." The matter at issue is not merely what a nominal Christian believes but whether Christian beliefs are a guide to life, that is, control and find embodiment in believers. Not only is Phil. 2:5, "the mind of Christ," normative, but so also is the "measure of the stature of the fullness of Christ" or "the mature manhood" (Eph. 4:13). If Wesley looked for "Christian perfection" in believers, as mandated by the definition of "Scriptural Christianity," the contrast with the 16th-century Reformers is that they called the Church back to the Pauline way of salvation by grace alone, through faith alone. Wesley, conceding this, calls for acknowledgement of its proper outcome in holiness of life—not for justification by grace through faith only, but for sanctification of life by grace only through faith. If Wesley is Arminian rather than Calvinistic, it is because, with the earlier Augustine, he cannot concede that the revealed universal availability of God's grace for human salvation can go unmatched by an individual's consent to it. As for "Christian perfection," repeatedly Wesley made clear that it fulfills the two Great Commandments: devout love of God and, in consequence and as so enabled, unfeigned love of the neighbor. He is unyielding on the point, therefore, that such is by the express teaching of Christ the true and full vocation of the Christian man and so goes beyond Luther.

Wesley wrote, according to Jonathan Crowther: "In 1729, my brother and I reading the Bible, saw inward and outward holiness therein. In 1737, we saw that this holiness comes by faith, and men are justified before they are sanctified. But still holiness was our point, *inward* and *outward* holiness." While the writer has not located in Wesley's published works the identical statement and while it may be a conflation of matter deriving from two or more sources, its purport is sound, whether one attends to Wesley's *Plain Account of the Methodists, The Character of a Methodist*, or *A Plain Account of Christian Perfection*, namely, that truly Scriptural Christianity "is nothing of or different from" the mind that was in Christ; the image of God stamped upon the heart, inward righteousness, attended by the peace of God, and joy in the Holy Ghost; that the only way to this faith is to "repent and believe the gospel"; and "that by this faith, 'he that worketh not, but believeth on him that justifieth the ungodly is justified freely by his grace,' through redemption that is in Christ Jesus."

But "inward" holiness is to be matched by "outward" holiness: "He loveth his neighbor, every man, 'as himself'; as Christ loved us; them in particular that despitefully use him and persecute him. . . . " That this is at the heart of the Wesleyan tradition is further suggested by the preface to the earliest editions of *The Doctrines and Discipline of the Methodist Episcopal Church in America* after 1784. It is signed by THOMAS COKE and FRANCIS ASBURY: "In 1729 two young men in England, reading the Bible, saw that they could not be saved without holiness, followed after it and incited others to do so. In 1737, they saw likewise, that men are justified before they are sanctified. But still holiness was their object.... And we humbly believe that God's design in raising up the preachers called Methodists in America was to reform the continent and spread scriptural holiness over these lands."

What Wesley was proposing within the Church of England for that church, and by way of reform, is in these words transferred to the American context as an extension of the mandate of Scriptural Christianity as Wesley taught it—no longer in the precinct of a national church but in that of complete voluntaryism in religion.

See also articles on HOLINESS; METHODIST CHURCH.

Bibliography. W. R. Cannon, *Theology of John Wesley*; *Collection of Tracts On Important Points of Scripture Doctrine*; *Doctrines and Discipline of the Methodist Episcopal Church*; R. N. Flew, *The Idea of Perfection in Christian Theology*; F. Holmes, *The Methodist Preacher: Twenty-eight Sermons On Doctrinal Subjects*; T. S. Langford, *Practical Divinity: Theology In the Wesleyan Tradition*; George Peck, *The Scripture Doctrine of Perfection*; J. E. Rattenbury, *Wesley's Legacy to the World*; John Wesley, *A Plain Account of Christian Perfection, Works*, XI.

ROBERT E. CUSHMAN
DUKE UNIVERSITY

WEST VIRGINIA. When West Virginia became a state on 20 June 1863, more than a century of Christian religious history had already elapsed within its borders; and previous to that, centuries of native American religious history had already transpired. The famous West Virginia Indian burial mounds at South Charleston and Moundsville are witness to those centuries of history.

FRANCIS ASBURY had already made his way into many corners of what was then western Virginia in the late eighteenth century, inveighing against drinking and the violence that accompanied it. He organized the Rehoboth Church in Monroe County in 1786. He also visited Morgantown and the Tygart Valley. At Clarksburg Asbury became acquainted with and ministered to Stonewall Jackson's grandmother and great uncle. The energetic missionary work of the well-known first American Methodist bishop had a notable effect on the history of religion in western Virginia where the Methodists, among all the organized Christian Protestant denominations, became preeminent. Until this day there are more Methodist churches in West Virginia than any other kind, and Methodist clergy and laity have supplied a steady stream of political, social, and educational leaders for the state.

West Virginia was early predisposed toward Protestantism, there being virtually no Roman Catholic immigrations or missionary activity until well into the 19th century. East of the Alleghenies, except in Maryland, an overwhelmingly Protestant world prevailed. Second only to the Methodists in West Virginia were the Baptists, organizing their first church west of the Alleghenies in 1773 at Bridgeport in Harrison County. Soon to follow were their churches at Stewartstown in Monongalia County and at Alderson in Monroe County. A bit later Presbyterian churches also were founded west of the Alleghenies. Episcopal missionaries too came to western Virginia at an early time.

By the time of statehood, the work of Thomas and ALEXANDER CAMPBELL had been all but finished. A new denomination, the DISCIPLES OF CHRIST, had been inaugurated by them in nearby Washington County PA. The Disciples founded churches in the northern part of western Virginia, also Bethany College, that continues until this day at BETHANY, at first the headquarters of the new denomination.

It should be added that Presbyterian, Episcopal, Baptist, and Lutheran churches had been planted even earlier in the three counties of western Virginia that lie east of the Allegheny Mountains, namely, Morgan, Berkeley, and Jefferson.

Civil War and Statehood, 1860-1864. A principle formulated by Paul Tillich that "religion is the substance of culture and culture is the form of religion," fits the history of religion in West Virginia from its origins as a state amidst the furor of the Civil War. There is little doubt that Protestant churches were a major contributing force in the abolitionist movement that preceded that conflict. This force also operated in the lands of western Virginia that were to become West Virginia. The abolitionist struggle in America had been prefigured by the emancipation of slaves in England. There, the prominent evangelical Christian William Wilberforce, had agitated for emancipation. Likewise in western Virginia, there was much sentiment for emancipation among Evangelicals. The Methodists, in particular, were in solid majority against slavery. Consequently, two-thirds of all residents of western Virginia opposed secession.

Not all leaders in the churches were explicitly for the abolition of slavery as an institution; but almost all of them were for the humane treatment of slaves. Alexander Campbell, for example, saw nothing wrong with the master-slave relationship. He respected the United States Constitution that allowed slavery; and he disdained the prospects of war over slavery. Though his own sentiments were against slavery, he tried to ameliorate the growing national crisis by suggesting that the South be allowed to practice the ownership of slaves. He also felt that the nation should abide by the Compromise of 1850 that allowed new territories to decide the question of slavery for themselves, and concluded that he had to accept the Fugitive Slave Act. With this complicated dialectical position, Campbell's great influence prevented the Disciples from splitting into Northern and Southern churches as a result of the slavery issue. It is of interest to note that Alexander Campbell's nephew, Archibald Campbell, editor of the *Wheeling Intelligencer*, used this influential medium to herald abolitionist views in the years just before the Civil War.

A number of religious factors contributed to the ultimate emancipation of slaves. As a result of slaveholder's encouragement to their slaves to be Christians, the intimate relationship of Christian to Christian prevailed between owners and slaves, at least in moments of soul searching and self-reflection. There was a consequent undercurrent of guilt about slave ownership. Also, the slaves had been encouraged to form their own independent churches. Allowance of this one dimension of independence generated in the slaves both a special love for their churches and a vision of greater liberties for themselves.

Thus the church (mainly Protestant in those days) introduced several important ingredients that moved the nation toward emancipation. Love of God and fellow human beings—the keystone of Christian theology—helped to form cultural results, though, as is always the case in human affairs, that love was broken and imperfect. This general picture applies directly to western Virginia in the pre-Civil War scene.

Religion combined with other cultural forces to move the nation to the emancipation of slaves. Nonreligious egalitarian thought springing from the Enlightenment and the French Revolution played a big role. The belief that slave ownership was no longer a viable enterprise was a postition held by still others.

Unfortunately, violence and emotion kept the rational resolution to the issue from coming to full term. Among other events, John Brown's raid at Harper's Ferry (in West Virginia) and the attack on Fort Sumter moved the nation toward the devastating Civil War. In an effort to avert bloody conflict, most church people in the pre-Civil War days were willing to stop short of demanding the obliteration of slavery as an institution. However, when war came, such restraint was useless. Consequently, views were expressed more candidly thereafter.

All of the friction that results from candor was experienced in the territory that was shortly to become West Virginia. It must be remembered that the line dividing the North and the South went right through western Virginia; therefore, the drama of the times was amplified in this territory. While all the denominations of West Virginia provided chaplains for the Civil War, some of those supplied the South while others served the North. The churches rendered services of mercy to the sick and wounded on both sides.

Laymen were expelled from the Methodist Church in Mannington for being rebels. Father Malone was driven out of the Roman Catholic Church in Grafton because he was thought to be a rebel. Father Becker in Martinsburg would not pray for Union soldiers. One Protestant church simply closed for seven years until the political climate became less volatile. Other churches invested no great stake in the political and ideological struggle of this time. A few churches ministered to unionists on one Sunday and rebels on the next. No doubt, many laymen had little ideological investment in the war. They only regretted that they had been forced to become involved in the struggle.

Even before the Civil War, the Protestant denominations had divided themselves on a national basis into Northern and Southern churches respectively. Many churches in western Virginia sided with the North or with the South primarily on the basis of the loyalty of the constituency or out of loyalty to synodical affiliations. Thus the Lutheran churches in western Virginia, that had been originally organized by Virginians and that consequently belonged to the Virginia Synod, showed loyalty to the South. Episcopalians, all of whom were closely attached to the Episcopal Church of Virginia, usually showed loyalty to the South. Roman Catholics were aligned with both sides. Residents along the Baltimore and Ohio Railroad so tenaciously held by the North were usually Unionists (whether Christians or

not). Residents of southern West Virginia were often rebels mainly for geographical reasons, the church playing no significant role. Often enough in western Virginia, it was true as elsewhere that culture shaped religion more than religion gave substance to culture.

Western Virginia produced the great Civil War hero, Thomas Jonathan "Stonewall" Jackson. General Jackson did not join the cause of the South merely as the result of geographic or social gravity. A devout Presbyterian, he spent much time in prayer deliberating whether he should fight with the Confederacy or the Union.

In general, once the Civil War began, churches tended to be loyal to their territories and the majority convictions of their constituencies. The church was more influential in molding public opinion before the Civil War than it was destined to be afterwards. In the 1850s, some church people had managed to seed the idea of abolition in the ground of Christian belief in such a way as to provide major influence on the American culture. Of course this implies also that the church was one important cause of the Civil War, though usually not intentionally so. Perforce, the church is a major cause of the formation of West Virginia as a state since the immediate cause of the formation of the state was the Civil War.

From the outset, the sentiment of western Virginians leaned in the direction of the Union. The secular reasons for such a stand include the following: (1) Western Virginians in trans-Allegheny country had long been resentful of the government of Virginia in Richmond. They felt that they had not received their share of benefits in proportion to taxes collected. (2) Western Virginians had few slaves by comparison with Virginians living east of the mountains. (3) The mountains endowed western Virginians with a social and political insularity that made them want to go their own way.

The details of how West Virginia became a state during the period 1861-1863 need not be recounted in this religious history. It should be noted that, in the pre-statehood conventions, representatives were frequently clergymen. One such representative was Gordon Batelle, a Methodist minister, who strove to have the new constitution of West Virginia provide for the gradual emancipation of slaves. He with others succeeded in having the constitution provide for the prohibition of any movement of slaves into West Virginia. Once statehood was achieved, the leadership of the new state was Methodist. Arthur I. Boreman, the first governor of the state, belonged to that denomination, as did the first two senators sent to Congress from West Virginia. Waitman T. Willey, one of those two senators, was also a temperance crusader.

Spirituality ran very high during the Civil War years. It was characterized by biblical literalism, fundamentalistic morality, revivalism, and the preeminence of Protestantism. The ministry was the most respected of the professions, as reflected in the commonly held fond hope of families that their sons would become ministers.

Reconstruction, 1865-1872. Many religious conflicts and lawsuits followed the Civil War in West Virginia as those who had been rebels sought equality for themselves in the church and as lawsuits over ecclesiastical property held by split congregations were settled. Those who fought with the South were even disfranchised for a time; in other words, considerable bitterness existed.

In the early years of statehood the churches influenced culture in several significant ways. Many clergy continued to hold elective office. In so doing the Protestant values of the time made their way into the formation of state laws, especially at the outset when the first constitution was written. This influence can be felt in West Virginia until this day though laws have gradually been modified. The second

constitution, adopted in 1872, was actually written in a Methodist church building in Charleston.

In education the church influenced culture in most significant ways during Reconstruction. The fledgling state had to initiate policy for public education. Virginia, of which it had been a part, had no free, public schools. In the new state public education was to take a radical turn in large measure because of ecclesiastical influence. The churches had long engaged in establishing academies throughout western Virginia. By the time of the Civil War, there were three in Morgantown, for example, two for girls and one for boys, all established by Methodist leaders. Lutheran ministers, as well as those of other denominations, had often served as school teachers in pre-Civil War days when the church buildings had also served as schoolhouses.

In the new state, the ministers joined the cry for free schools. Alexander Campbell had advocated free education for all to be supported by state revenues. The movement to create free public education succeeded. The state's very first constitution provided for public schools. A Methodist clergyman, William R. White, became the first superintendent of schools in West Virginia. He also played a major role in the establishment of normal schools in the young state.

West Virginia also had to establish a state university. At the time of statehood the only public institution that Virginia had bequeathed to West Virginia was an insane asylum in Weston. Morgantown was finally selected to be the site of the state land grant university established under the Morrill Act. That town had acquired the reputation of being a quiet place with good educational facilities because of the three academies already established there by the Methodists. Once the decision was made to establish the university in Morgantown, the three academies were sold to the state. One of them, the Woodburn Female Academy, became the site of the new university, founded in 1867. The first two presidents of the university, Alexander Martin and John Ray Thompson, were Methodist ministers. In this and other ways, the educational dimension of early West Virginia culture was very much the result of the influence of the churches. The interconnection between the Methodist Church and higher education was so great that, when Alexander Martin was fired as first president by Democrats who were at the time carrying out a purge of Republicans at the university, Methodists boycotted the university for a time.

Industrialization and Unionization, 1872-1914. The period of industrialization saw the transformation of West Virginia from an agricultural economy to an industrial one. In the northwest, centering around Wheeling, manufacturing flourished. In the rest of the state industry was based primarily on lumbering and the extraction of coal, salt, oil, and gas. The railway system was greatly expanded during these years.

Labor was needed to staff all these enterprises. Immigrants filled this need, and with their coming the demography of the state changed noticeably. Besides those moving in from Europe, many Negroes came into the state from the South to help fill this need. It was during this period that the most famous of these, Booker T. Washington, grew up in West Virginia. This resident of Malden was to become both a devout man and a prominent public figure.

A large percentage of the immigrants were Roman Catholic. At the beginning of the Civil War there was a fledgling Roman Catholic diocese in western Virginia, having been founded in 1850 with Wheeling as the seat. In that same year Roman Catholics opened in Wheeling the first hospital in what was to become West Virginia. A Jesuit accompanying a French expedition probably offered the first Mass on West Virginia soil somewhere along the Ohio River in 1749. The small company of some 5,000 Roman Catholics in western Virginia in 1850 had swelled to

50,000 by 1914. Under Bishop Donahue (1894-1922) many Catholic mission churches were founded to accommodate the enlarging constituency.

The Jewish population also was increasing slowly. No Jews had lived in western Virginia until the 1840s, the first Jewish community being established in Wheeling in 1849. Records reveal that seven Jewish men from West Virginia served in the Civil War with Union forces. In 1873, in Charleston, the first Jewish congregation was organized and by 1903 there were about 1,500 Jews in West Virginia. From 1910 until 1915 the Industrial Removal Office, which was a part of the Jewish Agricultural and Industrial Aid Society headquartered in New York City, functioned to help settle a few of the many Jewish immigrants in the state, to prevent further overcrowding in New York City and other eastern metropolises.

The Protestant churches also grew in numbers. Many white clapboard churches still found across the hillsides of West Virginia were built during this time. The more urban Episcopal Church organized its first West Virginia Diocese in 1878 and elected George W. Peterkin its first bishop.

The Protestant churches contrived to maintain considerable social and political influence during this period. It has been observed that as late as 1904 Daniel B. Purinton, president of West Virginia University from 1901 to 1911, inaugurated a program within the university for the preparation of Sunday School teachers. This course of study met with much approval and general success. This is likely the only time in American history when such a program has been sustained at a state land grant university. Purinton himself was a devout Baptist often traveling to attend international conclaves of the Baptist denomination. He also authored several theological publications.

The Baptists and Methodists and other Protestant groups as well promoted the temperance movement during this period. They stood behind the Anti-

Saloon League and the WOMAN'S CHRISTIAN TEMPERANCE UNION. The influence of the church on this issue was keenly felt in the cultural life of the state. These crusades also contributed to the ratification of the Prohibition Amendment. It should be remembered that the temperance movement was closely associated (albeit tacitly) with the question of women's rights. Remedying the injustices done to women when drinking husbands beat them or abandoned them to care for the children was a primary goal of the temperance movement. On these issues especially the churches were much involved in social causes.

In 1892 one of the state's most famous citizens was born in Hillsboro. Pearl Buck's Presbyterian parents—her father was extremely pietistic—soon left for China where they were missionaries for many years giving their daughter the rich experience of a Chinese upbringing and creating the soil from which her novels were to arise.

The Sunday School Movement in the Protestant churches wielded great influence in the state. Sarah J. Jones of Putnam County was famous far and wide for her Sunday school stories. Best known were her *Words and Ways, Rest and Unrest,* and *None Other Name,* all published between 1885 and 1893. Songbooks for Sunday schools prepared by M. Homer Cummings were broadly used. The Bible was the object of intense study by adults and children alike. Moral values were fashioned by the Sunday schools. The result was a prevailing morality and view of life that served to hold society together. The family was held in high esteem; neighborliness was considered a cardinal virtue; individuals were regarded as extremely important. Such virtues as these were taught throughout the Protestant churches from the Baptists on the left to the Lutherans on the right.

Modesty, presumably a virtue of much value in heaven, would seem to have less worth in the kingdoms of the earth. Had West Virginians been more cautious in dealing with the timber, coal, and steel interests that bought their land, they would have been better off financially in the long run and the state would have had more capital with which to work. Individualism may have been prized to the extent that the owners of small strips of timberland and of mineral lands could not cooperate in resisting the pressures of big business to buy them out at low prices.

Neither the Protestant nor Roman Catholic churches did much to resist the exploitation of West Virginia resources by outside interests. The social concern of the churches was oriented toward upholding basic individual morality. The churches wanted to do what they could to make the world safe for Christians to live in; and they wanted also to make the world less destructive and less tempting for non-Christians in the hopes that such people might finally find their salvation in the church. It was for this reason that the Wheeling Committee of One Hundred, an antivice committee, was founded. (Incidentally, the labor union movement regarded the work of the Committee of One Hundred as unimportant.) The churches did not think of morality as having to do with political and economic dynamics. Relying on the New Testament promise that the meek are the blessed ones, the churches spent little time fretting over the injustices perpetrated by the very rich. They trusted that in this transitory life the humble sawyer or miner had the potential of reaping as much happiness as the industrialist. As for eternal life, they were certain that the meek would be blessed.

Nor did the churches devote much attention during this period to the labor movement. Atheistic, pre-Bolshevik socialists played the major role here. The labor movement was therefore in the main a secular movement. There were some eccentric exceptions, however. The Irish-born Mother Jones, who played so prominent a role in organizing miners at the site of the violent Paint Creek and Cabin Creek confrontations between laborers and owners, was an itinerant preacher of socialist persuasion. She had worked and taught at Roman Catholic convent schools earlier in her life, but she was not an active communicant of the Church during her activistic years in labor organization. (Later in her life, she resumed being an active communicant of the Roman Catholic Church.) At all events, Mother Jones could not be counted a representative West Virginia religious spirit; for her influence consisted of crusading appearances to the state from another cultural world.

From the archives of the Diocese of Wheeling we know that Bishop Donahue served on a committee of three appointed by Governor Glasscock in 1912 to investigate the violence at Paint Creek, and we have his personal conclusions. Diplomatically, he criticized the miners and the owners in equal proportion. On the side of the owners, he allowed that they had a right to protect their property. He criticized labor for not wanting to work for more than four days a week and noted that the wages of these still nonunion miners were as good as union wages. He was critical of the miners for being careless with regard to their health. On the other hand, he was censorious of the guard system of the owners and noted that the company stores overcharged. He made a number of other observations on both sides, including the judgment that the United Mine Workers of America were the main source of the trouble at Paint Creek.

World War I—World War II, 1914-1945. West Virginia flew its patriotic colors by contributing nearly 50,000 men to the armed forces during World War II and oversubscribed the war bond drives of that era. Such patriotism and willingness to sacrifice for the cause of the nation was to be seen again in each of the wars later to be fought by the United States in the 20th century. This love of country, that extended even to the Vietnam War, sprang in part from that Civil War tradition of loyalty to the Union out of which statehood originated.

By and large West Virginia followed the national trend of less ecclesiastical influence on secular society during this period. Not surprisingly, the churches did make special impact on the presidential election of 1928 in which prohibition was a major issue.

Rural West Virginia and urban West Virginia became ever more distinct during this period. The urban sector followed the trends of the nation in almost all regards including religious ones. Mountainous, rural West Virginia stood back from these developments to form, along with contiguous areas in other states, a special cultural entity known to the nation as "Appalachia." During the next three decades the phenomenon of "Appalachia" became the state's distinctive and most famous sub-culture.

Between 1914 and 1945, many sectarian movements sprang up in the rural sections. This meant a turning away from mainline religions. Private chapels, led and sometimes even owned by charismatic figures in the community, rose up. To them and this subject, we shall return.

During this period the number of churches increased to 4,968 in 1926. As in all periods of West Virginia history, the number of Methodists was the greatest. One newcomer tradition appeared. There had been no Orthodox Churches in West Virginia at the turn of the century, but seven Greek and Russian Orthodox churches had been founded in the state by 1926. Jewish congregations increased from three to 23 in the same period. Black churches too were increasing, doubling in number during these years.

The Roman Catholic Church grew tremendously from approximately 50,000 to about 80,000. Bishop Swint, who served the diocese from 1922 to 1962, is especially remembered as a builder and as a promoter of Catholic education. Considerable mission work in the state resulted from his vision and leadership.

Perhaps because of the increasing number of Roman Catholics residing in the state, noticeable anti-Catholic feelings surfaced during this period. Fear of papist intrusion into American affairs was widely expressed. There are reliable reports that qualified Roman Catholic lay people encountered obstacles in seeking teaching positions in public schools. The anti-Catholic KU KLUX KLAN was quite active in the state in the 1920s, its national meeting was convened in 1925 on the campus of West Virginia University. The burning of crosses on the hill overlooking Morgantown was no uncommon occurrence during those troubled years.

The Great Depression had a devastating effect on West Virginia, economic conditions there being worse than in many other parts of the nation. As a result, the state became a prime recipient of New Deal welfare and was, it is said by some, to become addicted to it. Even the infusion of massive public welfare was not enough to meet the needs of the economically devastated state, however. The private sector worked to bring in food and clothing, an effort in which the churches joined.

Pat Withrow's Union Mission in Charleston was one of these Christian commissaries of charity. Founded in 1911, the Mission had come to full maturity by the time of the Depression. The homeless and hopeless were physically sustained while they were spiritually fed by revivalistic religion. The achievements of Withrow's mission exemplify the growing urban dimension of West Virginia from 1911 on; for it is similar to other missions that had been founded everywhere in larger American cities. The Union Mission continues in a variety of ways to serve Charleston, a city of 60,000 population today. Withrow's motto was "soap, soup, and salvation." A licensed Methodist minister, his work was independent of the Methodist Church.

The Great Depression and the new presence of the federal government in West Virginia provided grounds for a renaissance of the labor unions in West Virginia. In this climate, the United Mine Workers of America under the direction of John L. Lewis built the base for its all-pervasive influence in West Virginia. Although everywhere, the churches had little to do with this important transforming development of its state's history, for better, for worse, or both.

Appalachia as a Problem Area, 1945-1970. World War II saw another record of gallant, patriotic service on the part of West Virginia. However, the unprecedented economic expansion that was to shower great wealth upon the nation for 30 years after the war was not so generous to West Virginia, especially in the rural areas. At least three major reasons can be given for this economic misfortune. (1) The market for coal diminished somewhat between 1945 and 1970. (2) As the result of the further mechanization of the coal mines during this period, many jobs in the mines were abolished. (3) The mountainous terrain of West Virginia makes the interior of the state unpromising as an area for heavy industrial transportation. As a result, while the river valleys remained fairly prosperous during this period, the mountainous regions languished economically.

It was in these ways that the much publicized territory of "Appalachia" came about as an economically identifiable phenomenon. The rural, mountainous areas of West Virginia became more isolated in spite of the modern age of rapid communication and they became distinctly poor. In the 1950s more people were out of work in West Virginia than in any other state. Thousands of welfare checks were distributed to citizens of the state. Many residents moved away to the river valleys or to other states to find employment. (Others were not psychologically bold enough to leave.) As a result of this process the population of the state dropped by several hundred thousand.

The rural folk of Appalachia showed little discontent about their poverty—to the frustration of social activists. Their lives seemed to transcend a "dollar culture." On the one hand, much of the

Christian ideal could be discerned in their life-style; on the other, the question arose for many whether these people had been so benumbed by circumstances as no longer to have earthly ambitions. The real situation of these people was to remain a conundrum much analyzed by assorted writers and by the news media, especially in the activist decade of the 1960s.

The religion of Appalachia is made up of variations on Protestantism ranging from the mainline churches to myriad sectarian churches. Some groups are no larger than a cluster of local people in a single valley or "holler" revolving about a charismatic lay preacher. Much of the religion of Appalachia is extra-institutional. That is, many who are involved in such religious expressions are not counted in state and national membership statistics. A number of groups are too small and amorphous to be codified as separate denominations. Consequently, the current data that indicate that 51 percent of West Virginians are unchurched are deceptive. That enumeration has missed much of the busy religious activity back in the mountains of the state.

Assorted aberrations of Christian orthodoxy can be found among these sectarian Protestants. Most sensational are the SNAKE HANDLERS and the fire handlers, with both standing as examples of Christian holiness groups. The snake handlers base their beliefs on two verses in the New Testament book of Mark. (Biblical scholars think that the verses in question are a later addition to Mark's Gospel.) The relevant text reads:

> And these signs will accompany those who believe: in my name they will cast out demons; they will speak in new tongues; they will pick up serpents, and if they drink any deadly thing, it will not hurt them; they will lay their hands on the sick; and they will recover (16:17-18, RSV).

For this tiny but intense band of Christ's followers, the serpents serve as verifiers of the faith that Jesus Christ has overcome death in victory. The faithful can symbolically handle the poisonous serpents (usually rattlesnakes or copperheads) without dying. It is true that snake handlers are bitten from time to time and usually recover. When recovery happens, this miracle is seen as another symbol of the power of Jesus Christ to overcome death. The Holy Ghost is believed to infuse the practitioner with such holiness as to prevent any harm resulting from the venom of the serpents.

Similarly, fire handlers verify their faith by handling fire without physical injury. Being biblical literalists like the serpent handlers, their practices are based on passages that suggest trial by fire, such as Is. 43:2, Dan. 3:20-27, and Heb. 11:34. To be able to handle fire without physical injury is viewed as a mark of holiness.

The holiness sects also take note of the phrase in Mk. 16:17, " ... and if they drink any deadly thing, it will not hurt them ... " Poisonous mixtures are concocted for purposes of testing faith and experiencing the exalting protection of the Holy Ghost. Often the same Holiness people who have submitted to one kind of these ordeals have submitted to others.

In general, Holiness groups hope to channel to their members the power of the Holy Ghost and a sense of holiness. A part of the strategy is to keep apart from the secular world. They are anti-intellectual, depending rather on the spontaneity of the Holy Ghost to exalt them in this transitory life. This exaltation is manifest in such phenomena as glossolalia, healing power, and ecstatic dancing. More extreme results are sometimes seen: elements of witchcraft; many superstitious acts and practices that must be described as magic.

To obtain a further overview of Appalachian religion, the reader might well refer to James M. Kerr's fine essay, "A Pastor's View of Religion in Appalachia," found in *Religion in Appalachia*, edited by John D. Photiades. Appalachian religion is distinctly Protestant and of the stripe stemming from Puritanism. In church polity the Baptist form is the chief organizational heritage of the mountain religion of West Virginia. This is a heritage of dissent. It has gone hand in hand with the proclivity of isolated populations the world over to be separatistic. Many of the original settlers of West Virginia were Scotch-Irish, it is instructive to recall. These people had come to America in the first place in quest of individual freedom. Continuous with those beginnings is the Appalachian churches' tendency to be individualistic, often having no connection with big denominational groups. Furthermore, they concern themselves very little with social and political issues, with public matters of any sort.

This individualism can be observed, by way of illustration, in the congregations of American Baptist churches in West Virginia. These local churches even today remain affiliated only with that Northern denomination, spurning the covenantal membership that body has with the National Council of Churches and the World Council of Churches.

In general, Appalachian churches lean heavily in the direction of puritanical ethics. The separatistic element of the Puritan heritage makes it easier for Appalachian residents to keep their distance from national trends in ethics. Ministers usually have not been to seminaries and have no peers to criticize their views or their performance as ministers. In the manner of the Baptist tradition's opposition to centralized control, most Appalachian churches are accustomed to having unsupervised clergy. The spontaneous open-air revival remains a principal mode of worship. It was the kind of religion that nurtured frontier people as far back as Daniel Boone, for example, and that dominated 19th-century developments.

Since the educational level of Appalachian society has been low, the historical critical method of study of the Bible has not been applied, though the Bible is read or heard a great deal. The Bible is taken exactly at face value. Consequently, biblical literalism—in many different forms— is common among all the Appalachian church people.

On the subject of eschatology, a dim view is taken of the worsening world. Salvation is finally beyond the world. The Kingdom of God will be fulfilled transcendentally, not on earth. Social action and social programs cannot better the world, fallen as it is. The Devil, who is taken seriously in this religious understanding, has control of the secular world.

The Holy Ghost pervades all aspects of Appalachian religion. Baptism by the Holy Ghost is the rite of passage into mature Christian belief. Glossolalia is considered a desirable gift of the Spirit. So is unabashed willingness to testify freely to one's faith and to witness to the wonderworks of God that the believer has experienced both in his own life and in that of others. Preaching is fervent and under the influence of the Holy Ghost. The nature of this kind of preaching has been portrayed dramatically by Aaron Copeland in the frenetic dancing of the preacher in his *Appalachian Spring* (1944).

The phenomenon of baptistry paintings, that have come into use in Appalachian churches only during the last half century, is most revealing. While Protestant baptistries are not typically adorned with paintings in other sections of the United States, in Appalachian West Virginia they frequently are. Usually the paintings are landscapes with a river or lake central to it. Sometimes the rivers are painted so as to portray the River Jordan in Israel; more often, the landscapes are inspired by Appalachian scenery. Most of the time no human beings are depicted in the paintings. When they are, John the Baptist and Jesus are usually the figures. Often a luminescence in the background of the scenery suggests the transcendent. While it is difficult to account for this phenomenon in West Virginia, it is likely that the paintings emerged to recall the days more than 50 years ago when baptisms were regularly done outdoors. The impression persists that baptisms are more valid when done in natural surroundings with flowing water.

Politicians and the news media declared Appalachia a problem area in the 1960s, suddenly plunging this forgotten world into the limelight. Residents were astonished at the rising tide of newsmen, sociologists, social workers, Vista workers, and OEO agents, who came to observe them and work with them. This focusing of national interest on Appalachia seems to have been triggered by the presidential primary campaign of 1960 when John F. Kennedy, a Roman Catholic, ran against Hubert Humphrey. The question before the nation was whether a Roman Catholic candidate could be successful in a presidential election since none ever had been before. National commentators saw West Virginia's decision in the democratic primary as an accurate indicator of whether a Roman Catholic could now be elected president of the United States. The reason for this calculation was that West Virginia as late as the 1920s and 1930s had shown considerable prejudice toward Roman Catholics. West Virginians were still, in large majority, of Protestant persuasion; and the geography of West Virginia was believed to insulate the still predominantly rural residents of the state from the new ecumenizing tolerance that was sweeping the rest of the nation.

Appalachia became a showpiece of the media; many ugly scenes met the eyes of affluent Americans. Paradoxically, however, the newly disclosed backwardness of West Virginia was offset by the apparent up-to-date ecumenicity it showed in preferring Kennedy. Campaign promises in the area of economics and the lavish campaign expenditures of the charming candidate, however, might have been the real reason for Kennedy's victory in the primary. It should also be remembered that Alfred E. Smith in his bid for the presidency in 1928 won the Democratic primary in West Virginia even though he was a Roman Catholic. He did not carry the state in the national presidential election mainly because West Virginia at that time was controlled by Republicans and because strong prohibitionist sentiments in the state could not tolerate Smith's stand on the abolition of prohibition.

While there was social friction between Roman Catholics and Protestants in the 1920s, deep political envy between the two religious groups in West Virginia never did materialize. Roman Catholics have always been a minority group. The traditional abrasive issues of parochial school support and birth control were never important in West Virginia. Only in recent years has abortion been a public issue in West Virginia. (During the period 1945-1970 Roman Catholics continued to grow in numbers until there were about 105,000 communicants in 1970. Anti-Catholic prejudice had all but vanished.)

Whatever the significance of the results, subsequent democratic presidential administrations rewarded West Virginia with a vast outpouring of aid that ranged from the construction of beautiful new roads to myriad programs for making mountaineers more up-to-date. Activists, who hoped to revolutionize life in Appalachia, as they were partly to succeed in doing in the nation's great cities, were disappointed. Appalachian religion was too individualistic and unconcerned politically for that. Roots for revolutionary social activism were not embedded in the religious soil, nor in the culture at large, at least not enough deep roots.

The civil rights revolution also occurred during this time. In 1950 Negroes comprised about six percent of the population of West Virginia. Integration was achieved quite easily in the years 1956-1957, with only a few incidents of friction. It is unclear whether there were special characteristics of West Virginia religion that contributed toward this easy social transition. It should be noted that Negroes were more willing to leave West Virginia for a better economic climate than were whites. By 1970 only four percent of the population was black.

New Awareness and New Opportunities, 1970—. The growing revival of the coal industry marks the beginning of a new era in West Virginia history. This was correlated with the energy crisis that brought a new prosperity to the state. Just as West Virginia had been economically out of tune with the nation from 1945 to 1970, energy-rich West Virginia now hoped that the fortunes of the state would surpass those of the rest of the nation. This hope has not been altogether justified because a concurrent development, the sagging national economy, has also struck West Virginia. Furthermore, the chronic and prolonged labor strife in the West Virginia coalfields may yet bring the greatest economic benefits of the energy crisis to the nonunion open-pit mines of the western states. Nonetheless, the economy of West Virginia has become less negatively out of phase with that of the whole country than it was between 1945 and 1970.

Church life continues to thrive along established Appalachian patterns in the mountains. The experience of urban churches of the state approaches that of urban churches in the rest of the nation. The mainline churches have all enlarged their vistas of social concern in the last decade. Predictably, this pattern has not had much effect on the churches in the mountainous districts. Bishop Joseph H. Hodges of the Roman Catholic diocese of Wheeling has joined other Appalachian bishops in issuing a joint pastoral letter entitled "This Land Is Home To Me." The letter speaks to the problems of current Appalachia, but ironically has taken shallow root, at most, among the mountain peoples.

Almost every current denomination and movement within Christianity is now represented in West Virginia in either the urban or rural scenes. Once isolated and peculiar, it is not so any longer. The more urbane Fundamentalism now flourishing in America can be found in West Virginia

towns and cities. For example, the Christian and Missionary Alliance Church is thriving in West Virginia towns. Also, the charismatic movement can be found in the ranks of all mainline denominations in the state.

The Church of Jesus Christ of Latter-day Saints has enjoyed considerable growth in West Virginia during recent decades. Now 7,000 members strong, the Mormon church made its first impact on the state by baptizing 40 converts in Cabell County in 1832 long before statehood days. Joseph Smith, the founder, had visited Wheeling in 1832 to buy the paper on which was later printed the *Book of Doctrines and Covenants* that contained many of his revelations. Most 19th-century converts were persecuted, however, subsequently moving to the West.

The most sensational incident involving religious life in West Virginia during the last decade was the Charleston book controversy of 1974-1975. In this encounter, West Virginia's urban religion clashed with its rural religion. The controversy touched on such issues as whether sex should be taught in the schools and whether textbooks that termed Bible stories as myths (a term left undefined) should continue to be used in the schools. By and large the sometimes violent controversy ended with the conservatives gaining more spoils. Just the same a lack of confidence in the educational philosophy of the public schools resulted within the conservative ranks. As a consequence, since the book controversy Christian day schools have cropped up in the Charleston area.

During the last decade, West Virginia has experienced some cosmopolitan religious growth. The Korea-originated Unification Church now carries on work in West Virginia with headquarters in Huntington. The Krishna Consciousness movement earlier established a commune near Moundsville where it has recently built a formidable national temple that has attracted much attention and brought many visitors to the area. International students have brought together a number of adherents of assorted world religions to the university and college towns of the state. In particular, there has been a Muslim presence. Since West Virginia continues to suffer a shortage of physicians in rural areas and in its mental health institutions, a number of foreign physicians have come to practice in the state. With them has come a variety of religious practices and beliefs. Until recently West Virginians have shown little interest in world religions. Perhaps, this pattern will now gradually change.

Religion is an inextricable dimension of human existence and West Virginia culture is no exception. Though religion has always been institutionally weak in West Virginia, its spiritual influence has been very deep and pervasive in the cultural life of the state. This influence may be manifest in part by the relatively low crime rate that the state enjoys. The amiability of its people is another sign of this spiritual influence. Tillich's dictum does hold true in West Virginia as elsewhere: "Religion is the substance of culture and culture is the form of religion." Even as religion has greatly influenced the substance of West Virginia culture, West Virginia in turn has given a unique form to its religion.

Because generalities are always dangerous, one must be particularly cautious when discussing the religion of West Virginia. There must always be at least two parts to the discussion, namely, religion in the towns and the cities and religion in the Appalachian areas. Even as the heretical Albigensians who lived in the Pyrenees during the high Middle Ages were deemed eccentric by the Christian orthodoxy of their time, the mountain folks of West Virginia have maintained expressions of Christian faith aberrant to American urban ideas about normative Christian belief. Even so, as we have seen, the gap has narrowed within the past two decades.

See also articles on APPALACHIAN RELIGION; NATIVISM; SOCIAL GOSPEL.

Bibliography. Charles Henry Ambler, *A History of West Virginia;* Louise Bing, "Soup, Soap, and Salvation," *Goldenseal* 6 (July-September 1980); Phil Conley and William Thomas Doherty, *West Virginia History;* Harry W. Ernst, *The Primary That Made a President: West Virginia 1960;* John D. Photiadis, ed., *Religion in Appalachia;* Abraham I. Shinedling, *West Virginia Jewry: Origins and History,* vol. 1; Paul Tillich, *Systematic Theology,* vol. 3; Jack Welch, "A Heritage of Regional Landscapes: Appalachian Baptistry Paintings," *Goldenseal* 6 (April-June 1980); John Alexander Williams, *West Virginia: a Bicentennial History.*

MANFRED O. MEITZEN
WEST VIRGINIA UNIVERSITY

WESTMINSTER CONFESSION OF FAITH. This Calvinist creed was written by the Assembly, called by the English Parliament, that met in the Jerusalem chamber at Westminster Abbey 1643-1647. The Puritan Parliament intended for the Assembly to further "a more perfect Reformation" of the Church of England. The work of the Assembly never won acceptance in the Church of England, but the Confession and Catechisms became the theological standards of English-speaking Presbyterians and with modifications of the Congregationalists and of many Baptists.

The membership of the Assembly was representative of the range of Puritan opinion. In addition to the members of the Assembly appointed by the English Parliament, a delegation came from Scotland that had been united with the Puritan cause by the Solemn League and Covenant. The Scottish commissioners—led by such able men as Henderson, Rutherford, Gillespie, Baillie, and Johnston—sat in the Assembly not as members but as representatives of one of the parties to the Solemn League and Covenant, which gave them a larger influence.

The Confession is a characteristic 17th-century Reformed theological statement, and it has behind it a broad Reformed theological consensus. This theology had been hammered out in controversies between the Protestants and the Roman Catholics, between the Lutherans and the Reformed, and among the Reformed themselves. The Confession is notable for its high technical quality.

Words are carefully defined. Doctrines are stated precisely. Statements are rendered with logic and coherence. These qualities are purchased at the price of an abstractness, which for those without the necessary theological imagination becomes remote from human experience. In this way the Confession differs from such 16th-century Reformed Confessions as the Scots Confession of 1560 or the Second Helvetic Confession (1561, 1566), which have an experiential warmth and a generosity of spirit but which lack the technical excellence of the Westminster Confession.

The theological background of the Confession is at least threefold. It is rooted first in the native Augustinianism that had developed in Britian through Anselm (1033-1109), Bradwardine (1290-1349), and John Wycliffe (1320-1384). An immediate source of this tradition was the Irish Articles of 1615 and the theology of Archbishop Ussher. A second source was the Reformed theologies of the continent, which were rooted in the work of Bullinger in Zurich and Calvin in Geneva, each of whom had been influential in Britain. The third source was the Puritan movement, with its emphasis upon the Bible, discipline, the covenants, and the Christian life.

The Confession puts together the various elements of Christian faith with remarkable consistency and logic. Yet it has no one central theological characteristic. At least four themes are prominent. The first is the authority of the Bible. The Confession begins with a chapter on the Bible that is one of the best-written statements in the Confession or in any confessional literature. It introduces the theology of the Confession by laying out the sources. A second pervasive theme is the Lordship and sovereignty of God, which finds expression in characteristic emphases on providence, predestination, and effectual calling. A third motif is the covenants that God makes with his people, which modify the teachings on the decrees of God by emphasizing the working out of the decrees in history and the rationality of God's relationship with man. A fourth emphasis is the Christian life, which is analyzed in Puritan fashion and which embodies two-thirds of the Confession.

One of the finest statements in the Confession has to do with Christian freedom. "God alone is Lord of the conscience, and hath left it free from the doctrines and commandments of men, which are, in anything, contrary to His Word; or beside it, if matters of faith, or practice. So that, to believe such doctrines, or to obey such commands, out of conscience, is to betray true liberty of conscience; and the requiring of an implicit faith, and an absolute and blind obedience, is to destroy liberty of conscience, and reason also" (xx 2).

See also articles on CALVINISM; PRESBYTERIANISM.

Bibliography. S. W. Carruthers, *The Everyday Work of the Westminster Assembly*; John H. Leith, *Assembly at Westminster: Reformed Theology in the Making*; Alexander F. Mitchell, *The Westminster Assembly: Its History and Its Standards*.

JOHN H. LEITH
UNION SEMINARY IN VIRGINIA

WHITAKER, ALEXANDER (1585-1616/17), colonial Anglican clergyman, was born in Cambridge, England, the son of William Whitaker, noted Puritan minister, master of St. John's College, and Regius Professor of Divinity at Cambridge. He received his B.A. in 1604/05 and M.A. in 1608 from Cambridge and was ordained to the Church of England ministry. He volunteered for service in Virginia and arrived in 1611.

The early colonists to Virginia, ministers, and leaders of the London Company were generally of the Puritan wing of the Church of England. Whitaker was of this view as were Sir Edwin Sandys and the Rev. Richard Bucks of Jamestown. Such views were prevalent in Virginia until the latter part of the reign of King Charles I. The Puritan influence undoubtedly helped establish Virginia's Low Church tradition.

Whitaker served two new settlements, Henricopolis and Bermuda Hundreds, about 50 miles up the James River. The "Laws Divine, Moral and Martial" recently arrived with Sir Thomas Dale required ministers to preach twice on Sunday and once on Wednesday, with daily morning prayer and evening prayer. Whitaker's most-noted pastoral service was instructing and baptizing Pocahontas in the Christian faith before her marriage to John Rolfe.

In 1613, Whitaker preached a sermon, *Good News from Virginia*, based on Eccles. 2.2. Published in England, the author countered the charges against the colony, encouraged those in the enterprise, and promoted the conversion of the Indians. This sermon plus letters to the Rev. William Crashaw, Sir Thomas Smith, and the Rev. William Gouge are the extent of his known writings.

Bibliography. Philip A. Bruce, *Institutional History of Virginia in the Seventeenth Century*, vol. 1; George M. Brydon, *Virginia's Mother Church and the Conditions under Which It Grew*, vol. 1; Richard L. Morton, *Colonial Virginia*, vol. 1.

FREDERICK V. MILLS, SR.
LA GRANGE COLLEGE

WHITEFIELD, GEORGE (1714-1770), Great Awakening leader who visited the South, was born in Gloucester, England. He attended Pembroke College, Oxford, where he was signally influenced by the Methodism of the brothers Charles and John Wesley. He decided for the ministry, was ordained a deacon (1736), and pursued a program of preaching and prison work. Then he offered himself as a missionary to the colony of Georgia and sailed to America where he first began public ministry in Savannah in May 1738.

Already popular in England, he was enthusiastically received in America where his dramatic style and lively sermons attracted a near-fanatic following. After ordination as a priest in the Church of England back in London, he found himself shut out from many churches by reason of his caustic criticism of the clergy. He then instigated the field preaching that was thereafter to be his distinctive idiom. He made six more visits to the colonies; and in addition to continued activity in the Savannah area where he founded Bethesda, an orphan house, he extended his itineracy and charitable works throughout the Atlantic Seaboard, becoming as popular in New England as he was in the South.

A confessed Calvinist, he expounded a theology that was often understood by his hearers as assurance that they could exercise free will in favor of the Gospel. Ever a controversial figure, he preached more than 18,000 times, typifying the essence, strength, and weakness of the GREAT AWAKENING in America and representing the astringent corrective of moribund religion in England. He was satirized in literature and on the stage. His last sermon was preached in Newburyport MA where he died the following day.

See also article on REVIVALISM.

Bibliography. Stuart C. Henry, *George Whitefield: Wayfaring Witness*; *The Works of . . . Whitefield*, London, 1771-1773, 6 vols.; *Whitefield's Journals*, London, 1960.

STUART C. HENRY
DUKE UNIVERSITY

WHITSITT, WILLIAM HETH (1841-1911), seminary educator and central figure in a major Southern Baptist controversy, was born near Nashville TN. A graduate of Union University in Jackson TN, Whitsitt served in the Confederate army during the Civil War, thereafter continuing his studies at the University of Virginia, the Southern Baptist Theological Seminary, and the universities of Berlin and Leipzig. In 1872 he was appointed assistant professor of ecclesiastical history at Southern Seminary and in 1895 became the seminary's third president.

The "Whitsitt Controversy" was precipitated by an article Whitsitt published in *Johnson's Universal Cyclopaedia* (1893) claiming that according to historical evidence, the immersionist mode of believer's baptism was not restored until 1641 by English Baptists. This statement disturbed many Baptists who assumed the apostolic origins and unbroken historical continuity of Baptist churches and believer's immersion. Faced with mounting and relentless opposition fueled by a number of Southern Baptist newspaper editors and correspondents, Whitsitt, in order to restore harmony and preserve the convention's support of the seminary, offered his resignation on 13 July 1898. He became professor of philosophy at Richmond College, where he taught until his death. Among Whitsitt's published works are *Position of the Baptists in the History of American Culture*; *The History of the Rise of Infant Baptism* (1878); *The History of Communion Among Baptists* (1880); *A Question in Baptist History* (1896).

See also article on Toy, Crawford H.

Bibliography. Gaines S. Dobbins, "Whitsitt, William Heth," *Encyclopedia of Southern Baptists*, 2: 1496; Thomas Meigs, "The Whitsitt Controversy," *Quarterly Review* 31 (January-March 1971): 41-61; William A. Mueller, *A History of Southern Baptist Theological Seminary* (1959).

DANIEL HOLCOMB
NEW ORLEANS BAPTIST SEMINARY

WILMER, RICHARD HOOKER

(1816-1900), second Episcopal bishop of Alabama, was born in Alexandria VA. His father died while he was still young and he helped support his mother by farming. He graduated from Yale in 1836 and from the Episcopal Seminary in Virginia three years later.

He engaged in a rural ministry for many years, being especially successful in attracting men to the church. Later he began a ministry among poor and unchurched people at Brook Hill, near Richmond. During the three years Wilmer labored there he established a church for black people in Richmond as well.

In 1861 Wilmer was elected bishop of Alabama to succeed his close friend, Nicholas Hamner Cobbs. The measures taken to secure permission for his consecration were the source of controversy. There had as yet been no organization of a Protestant Episcopal Church in the Confederate States and only those dioceses and bishops within the Confederate states were asked for permission for his consecration. He was consecrated bishop in Richmond, thus becoming the only bishop consecrated in the Confederate church. He immediately moved to Alabama and labored there throughout the war.

At the end of the war, Wilmer was ordered by the Federal occupation forces to close all Episcopal churches in which the "Prayer for the President" was not read. An impasse ensued until President Andrew Johnson rescinded the order. Bishop Wilmer's consecration was declared valid by the General Convention in 1865.

Bibliography. Joseph B. Cheshire, *The Church in the Confederate States*; Edgar L. Pennington, "The Organization of the Protestant Episcopal Church in the Confederate States of America," *Historical Magazine of the Protestant Episcopal Church* 17 (December 1948): 308-38; Walter C. Whitaker, *Richard Hooker Wilmer, Second Bishop of Alabama*.

LAWRENCE L. BROWN
EPISCOPAL SEMINARY OF THE SOUTHWEST

WILSON, (THOMAS) WOODROW

(1856-1924), 28th president of the United States (1913-1921) was, according to his prime biographer, "a Presbyterian Christian of the Calvinistic persuasion" who "grew up on family worship, Bible reading, study of the *Shorter Catechism*, and stories of Scottish Covenanters." His mother's Scottish and his father's Scotch-Irish lineages were ministerial, and the young Wilson admiringly aided his domineering father, the Rev. Dr. Joseph Ruggles Wilson, with administrative affairs of the Presbyterian Church in the United States (PCUS). The future president grew up in the Presbyterian world of private grammar schools, Davidson, and Princeton, and was a church member while teaching at Bryn Mawr and Wesleyan. At Princeton he belonged to the Second and then the First Presbyterian Churches, was ordained a ruling elder in 1897, and was an eloquent chapel speaker. As president of the United States, he attended the Central Presbyterian Church in Washington.

Arthur Link maintains that Wilson's public actions were shaped by belief in a universal moral law under which "men and nations" were "moral agents accountable to God." Critics agree that his religion was nonspeculative and never-doubting, and they find a theme of Presbyterian legalism in his drafting of student constitutions at Princeton, Virginia, Johns Hopkins, and Wesleyan, and in the League of Nations Covenant at Versailles.

Link believes that Wilson moved to a broadened ethics, based on a loving Christ, while retaining an essential motivating belief in the sovereignty and divine presence of God. Sigmund Freud and William Bullitt accused Wilson of working out his oedipal problems with literal deification of his father and himself. The political scientist James Barber and the neurologist Edwin Weinstein have used ego analysis and medical factors to understand Wilson's public performance, but historians agree in identifying his Presbyterian Christian faith with the moral eloquence of his presidential leadership and the political rigidity that led the Senate to reject the Versailles Treaty.

See also article on CALVINISM.

Bibliography. Frank Bell, "The Man of Faith," *The Greatness of Woodrow Wilson*, ed. E. M. Bowles Alsop; Arthur S. Link, *The Higher Realism of Woodrow Wilson*.

DAVID CHALMERS
UNIVERSITY OF FLORIDA

WINANS, WILLIAM (1788-1857), Methodist planter and preacher, was born at Chestnut Ridge PA. After his father's death in 1790, the family moved farther west and finally to Ohio. Taught to read by family members, Winans was licensed to preach and admitted on trial in the Western Conference in 1808, serving in Kentucky and Indiana. In 1810 Winans was sent to Mississippi and became one of the original members and secretary of the Mississsippi Conference in 1813.

Winans married Martha DuBose in 1815, and gave up preaching in order to work on her family's plantation and on the farm given him by his mother-in-law. He started preaching again in 1820, receiving appointments that allowed him to live on his plantation, which was worked by 35 slaves in 1850.

Elected to nine Methodist General Conferences, Winans early advocated the election of a slaveholding bishop, and expected to be chosen one of the first two bishops of the Methodist Episcopal Church, South, in 1846, but ran a poor fifth. This was a crushing defeat and, while he continued to preach and to go to General Conferences, his heart was no longer in church politics. (He was a Whig candidate for Congress in 1849, but lost that race, too.) Nevertheless, he was one of the slaveholding planter-preachers who dominated antebellum Southern Methodism.

Bibliography. Ray Holder, *William Winans, Methodist Leader in Antebellum Mississippi.*

JOSEPH MITCHELL
TROY STATE UNIVERSITY

WINCHELL, ALEXANDER (1824-1891), Methodist geologist and teacher, was born in Dutchess County NY. Graduating from Wesleyan University in 1847, he taught at the Pennington Male Seminary in New Jersey and Amenia Seminary in his home county.

He and his bride moved to Alabama in 1850, where Winchell taught at three schools and did a geological survey of the state. In 1854 he went to the University of Michigan to teach geology, and 20 years later became the first chancellor of Syracuse University (Methodist), but soon shifted his energies to establishing the university's school of geology.

In 1876, Winchell became a member of the original faculty at Vanderbilt University (Methodist). Two years later presented a series of lectures, published under the title of *Preadamites or a Demonstration of the Existence of Men Before Adam*, which raised the ire of T. O. Summers, head of Vanderbilt's School of Theology and editor of the *Nashville Christian Advocate.* Summers charged that Winchell's position was sympathetic to Darwinism and therefore unbiblical and un-Christian. Under pressure from Summers and other Methodists, Bishop HOLLAND N. MCTYEIRE abolished Winchell's position and dismissed him. This dismissal was cited by leading scientists and some Northern Methodists as an expression of the narrow-mindedness of Southern Methodism and of ecclesiastical interference in academic freedom. Ever an active Methodist, Winchell returned to the University of Michigan and continued his teaching and writing until his death.

See also article on SCIENCE AND RELIGION.

Bibliography. Richard Hofstadter and Walter P. Metzger, *The Development of Academic Freedom in the United States*; Edwin Mims, *The History of Vanderbilt University*; Andrew Dickson White, *A History of the Warfare of Science with Theology in Christendom.*

JOSEPH MITCHELL
TROY STATE UNIVERSITY

WOMAN'S CHRISTIAN TEMPERANCE UNION.

This national social reform movement was founded in 1874. Through it thousands of women banded together to prevent the sale, use, and abuse of alcohol by using direct action against sellers and users.

Women had been involved with temperance from the beginnings of the movement in the late eighteenth century, and in their accepted role as guardians of the home had contributed to the pre-Civil War movement. However, in the postwar period, women became the leaders of the temperance cause. They found temperance the most congenial avenue through which to participate in public life, and used the WCTU as a base for their involvement in a variety of reformist causes, of which temperance was only one, and as a vehicle for supporting a wide range of charitable activities.

However, the WCTU was not organized in most of the South until 1881. It is true that the Maryland Union dated from 1874 and that the national convention of 1878 was held in Baltimore in the hope that proximity would spur on the cause;

also Eliza Stewart, a crusade leader, had attempted to organize in Kentucky, Tennessee, and Georgia in 1879. Still, it was not until Frances Willard (national president of the WCTU from 1879 until her death in 1898) began her work in the region that the organization took hold there. She spent 14 weeks in 1881 visiting every Southern state and the Indian Territory, speaking in over 50 cities and organizing state and local unions as she went. Willard's visit was given the status of an official goodwill tour. President Garfield himself sent her on her way with good wishes for her success. Her tour was widely reported in the Northern press and she was received in the South with generous hospitality and sympathy. Her visit was seen as a healing mission designed to ameliorate sectional strife and bitterness, Reconstruction having just ended. Willard herself made several subsequent Southern trips, and a number of other WCTU leaders and organizers also worked in the South in the 1880s. The result was a strong network of local and state unions below the Mason-Dixon line. By 1882 there were dues-paying unions in nine Southern states, six of them from the former Confederacy. By 1890 all Southern states were organized.

Although Southern women participated in this organizing effort from the beginning, by the 1890s Southern work was taken over almost completely by Southern women and the "foreign missionary" syndrome was replaced by indigenous leadership, including Sallie Chapin, Belle Kearney, Caroline Merrick, Julia Tutweiler, and Rebecca Felton.

Southern women in the WCTU were engaged in an innovative effort. Never before had they participated in a national movement. The denominational missionary societies had introduced Southern women to organization in the 1870s, but these were purely Southern groups, and Southern women had had no experience with nondenominational reform organizations. These women had never spoken in public before mixed audiences; they had never attended a convention and worked as part of a nationwide body; they had never petitioned a legislature. The WCTU brought the region's women onto the national stage and into public life. Through the WCTU they participated, for example, in the prison reform movement and attempted to abolish the convict lease system; they lobbied their legislatures to provide for temperance instruction in the public schools and to authorize local option as a way of controlling the liquor traffic. It is true that Southern unions remained a conservative element within the parent group for decades. They were reluctant to endorse the franchise for women and fearful of allying themselves with the broad social aims of the Prohibition party, but nonetheless the WCTU had much to do with putting Southern women into the mainstream of American life.

Not only did the WCTU assist in reintegrating the South into the larger American society in the late nineteenth century, the WCTU through its work in the South integrated black women into its work. Frances Willard spoke to and organized blacks as well as whites on her first Southern tour. In fact, the WCTU in the South was never an exclusively white organization, even in the Gulf states, although it was by and large a segregated one. Local unions were segregated from the beginning. Most state unions in the South were integrated through the 1880s, but in the next decade eight Southern states arranged for separate black unions on the state level. However, black women did sit as delegates at the national conventions that Southern white women attended.

The WCTU in the South, in cooperation with the Anti-Saloon League, played a large role in the passage of the EIGHTEENTH AMENDMENT. Although the WCTU has lost strength and prestige in the United States since the repeal of prohibition, it is still a relatively strong women's organization in many Southern small towns.

See also articles on PROHIBITION; TEMPERANCE; WOMEN IN RELIGION.

Bibliography. Ruth Bordin, *Woman and Temperance: The Quest for Power and Liberty, 1873-1900*; Mary Earhart, *Frances Willard: From Prayers to Politics*; Anne Firor Scott, *The Southern Lady: From Pedestal to Politics, 1830-1930*; Frances Willard, *Glimpses of Fifty Years.*

RUTH BORDIN
ANN ARBOR, MICHIGAN

WOMEN IN RELIGION. No field in American religious history is whiter for scholarly harvest than the interaction between women and religion in the South. For 200 years women have been the majority in the Christian churches of the region. Their ubiquitous and significant presence and contributions, richly evident in records from the 18th through the 20th centuries, have led Donald G. Mathews to declare that "women made Southern EVANGELICALISM possible." Yet amidst the last decade's outpouring of articles and books on women in American life, one has to scavenge to find more than a handful that treat the relationships between women and religion in the South extensively, reliably, or creatively. Southern religious scholarship still awaits a history of women and religion that will be inherently significant and widely useful in testing scholarly interpretations of the whole Southern religious experience.

Even in the 1980s when the subject of women and religion in the South can be opened up, though hardly wrapped up, one can expect from what has already been learned about the history of women that Southern female religious experience will prove to have been significantly different from Southern male religious experience. It follows that the scholarly perception of everyone's religious experience in the South may be altered, perhaps even transformed, by insights gained from a study of women and religion.

The least productive field of Southern religious experience for scholarly work lies in the 17th and 18th centuries prior to the (First) GREAT AWAKENING. Impressed by the contrast between the effectiveness of the Puritan churches in

New England and the ineffectiveness of the Anglican establishment in the Southern colonies, some historians of colonial religion have concluded that religion was not important in Southern colonial life until the Great Awakening of the 1740s. Others, more impressed by the religious diversity of the pre-Awakening South and the zealous piety of groups like the Lutherans and the Quakers, have estimated that perhaps one-third of colonial Southerners were active nonconformists, DISSENTERS with firm convictions. Even these scholars have concluded, however, that in the early eighteenth century a small percentage of the Southern population claimed church membership.

For the historian of women and religion in the South, such a general picture of religion before the Great Awakening seems to offer barren ground from which to reap a rich harvest. At the same time, the failure to discover highly visible and articulate female characters in Southern religion comparable to Anne Hutchinson and the many women involved in the Salem MA witchcraft episode in 17th-century New England seems to indicate that religion was not a major force for very many outstanding Southern women.

Yet recent demographic studies of women in the colonial South during the 17th century have begun to shed light on that hitherto largely invisible white population which left almost no literary sources for the historian's use. These studies reveal the profound hardships faced by women. It does seem reasonable to suppose that such a beleaguered, largely immigrant female population from the religious-conscious culture of 17th-century England would have been heavily influenced by religious norms and images and habituated to religious practices even when they were not affiliated with or effectively ministered to by any church. Indeed, recent statistical research on church adherence in the British American colonies has begun to alter the older picture of religious apathy in the pre-Awakening South. Thus current trends in both colonial women's history and colonial religious history suggest the probability that the greater and more imaginative use of probate, legal, tax, and church records by scholars of women's religious experiences may make further contributions to a revised understanding of the values and religious practices of the pre-Awakening South.

A similar type of opportunity exists in black women's religious history. It is generally agreed that Afro-Americans did not embrace the Christian religion in large numbers until at least the time of the Great Awakening in the 1740s or the GREAT REVIVAL (Second Great Awakening) beginning about 1780. For this reason, little attention has been given to the role of pre-Christian, African religious faiths in sustaining male and female slaves during the 17th and most of the 18th centuries while they were making the difficult transition from African to Afro-American cultures and while the percentage of women in the black population was growing significantly. As Peter Wood and others have begun to uncover the hitherto hidden and ignored early economic and social history of blacks in the colonial South, historians of black women's religious history could initiate a new understanding of the pre-Christian religious experiences of all blacks in the South. By pursuing the elusive but important task of understanding the religious experiences of unchurched white and black women before the Great Awakening, historians of women and religion in the South might begin a harvest in a particularly neglected field of American religious history.

A more readily attainable approach to the pre-Awakening religious history of women in the South would place a new emphasis on the history of the women among the active nonconformists of firm convictions. One such German-speaking group, the community of MORAVIANS in North Carolina, offers especially ample documentation of women's lively religious participation during the 18th century, independent of the influence of the Great Awakening. Fittingly, this splendid documentation has been made available in English primarily through the translating, editing, and writing of that community's female archivist, the late Adelaide L. Fries.

Another nonconformist group in the South meriting attention is the QUAKERS. A consensus exists among historians of women that Quakers were notable for the degree of sexual equality that they practiced. Yet studies of women and Quakerism have focused on the Northern experience, implying but not proving that the Southern experience was the same. Studies of women's history within Quakerism in North Carolina, Virginia, and Maryland would not only illuminate that tradition in the Southern setting but would offer a basis for significant comparison with the experience of unchurched colonial women as well as with those in the Anglican and other non-Anglican traditions.

To make possible such comparative work an exploration is necessary of what Anglicanism meant in the lives of the wealthiest women in the South as they encountered the great crises of life including illness, death, the Revolution, and entanglement in the growing system of African slavery. Moreover, a new understanding of what Richard Beale Davis has called "the puritan strain"—the moral and antiritualistic force—in colonial Anglicanism might be achieved by approaching its history from the perspective of women.

These and other paths of questioning and research may make the pre-Awakening religious history of Southern women more productive for scholars of Southern religion than ever before. Exploration of this territory could not only produce a substantial scholarly contribution in itself but also a rich introduction to further research and writing in the history of women's interactions with the First and Second Great Awakenings in the South.

When students of women's religious history in the South turn to a study of the Great Awakening (1740-1780) and of the Second, the Great Revival (1780-1830), they find a much more accessible field of research and writing. As Mathews has said, women's participation in these national, democratizing religious movements is evident from memoirs, diaries, and letters and "from almost every surviving local church record as well as from the daily journals, personal letters, and sometimes sentimental memoirs of 'tired and worn out' clergymen." These records have only begun to be explored by scholars. And the meaning for women, both white and black, of the evangelical counterculture that developed under Presbyterian, Baptist, and Methodist leadership in Virginia and other areas before and after the Revolution has only been implied. It is evident from scholarly work already done that the profound sense of community, the comparative equality, and the disciplined protest against frivolous and prideful styles of life and dress that characterized this counterculture had attractions and implications for thousands of previously unchurched or underchurched women.

But what these attractions and implications meant in practice during the 1760s-1780s is a subject we have barely begun to tackle.

One question of significance would be the extent to which the Baptists' sexual leveling with its subversive implications for domestic order helped to provoke the vigorous, often violent, response from the Anglican patriarchy in Virginia. Another line of investigation would compare the experiences of Southern women who were Quakers or perhaps Moravians with those of women in the Presbyterian, Baptist, and Methodist Great Awakening counterculture. A third approach would compare the attractions and implications of the evangelical counterculture for white women with those it held for black women and black men.

In the study of Southern women during both of the Awakenings, attention should be given to what Mathews judges a universal phenomenon in religion, the disproportionate presence and importance of women in religious life. His call for "a convincing analytical paradigm of how religious concerns about sin, salvation, personal responsibility, and human destiny affected or expressed social and cultural realities of sexual differentiation" offers students of Southern religion a fundamental analytical challenge. In his understanding of women's conversions as a chief road to psychological and social space paved by "compassionate, impassioned, even passionate men, such as the clergy seemed to be," he offers a provocative thesis that should be tested in the records of numerous Southern women, families, and congregations.

The participation of women in congregational life across the South promises to be another especially important focus of research in the age of the second Awakening. Again, as Mathews has suggested, it may not be REVIVALISM that was the "quintessence" of the movement, for "that phenomenon had appeared before in the First Great Awakening." Rather, the unique achievement of the second may have been the organizing process by which thousands of people were combined voluntarily in small groups, autonomous and democratic yet sharing a unity of feeling, thought, and purpose with similar small groups across the nation. Within these groups women were such a majority that Mathews believes that event may be "the greatest organization and mobilization of women in American history." As study proceeds of women's participation in the benevolent works of the thousands of small Presbyterian, Baptist, and Methodist congregations across the South, scholars will document and test Linda Kerber's thesis that in the age of the new Republic "patriotism required translation into charity and service before it could be made plausible to the millions of women whose lives

were defined by their domestic responsibilities. . . . Before women could join John Adams's political republic, many of them had first to enlist in the ranks of Hannah Adams's spiritual army."

From this massive and intensive religious mobilization of women came what Barbara Welter has called "the feminization of American religion" in the 19th century. Thousands of women converted and churched in the First and Second Great Awakenings began to engage in benevolent work and societies usually closely affiliated with their local churches and in close cooperation with the male clergy. The leadership of these churches was firmly in the hands of white men, lay and clergy, whose doctrines expressed limited roles for women. But participation in the churches was a complex and paradoxical experience for many women, at once constricting and liberating. In the evangelical Southern churches women found not only a bastion of white male power but also a community, predominantly female, of spiritual and psychological nurture and work that developed autonomy and solidarity. Further, they found considerable male support for women's education as religious leaders and institutions endorsed the movement for female seminaries and women's colleges. The role of the Protestant minister's wife, tireless, self-denying, and unremunerated, offered a few Southern churchwomen a distinctive blend of imitation and opportunity and gave to many others a model of Southern female piety. The resonance of this model is evidenced by the 19th-century religious bestseller, *St. Elmo*, in which the heroine gives up her writing career to help her husband in his pastoral work.

Partly through their complex interactions with Southern evangelical churches and religion some women began to experience and privately to express discontent with the control of the white patriarchy over their lives and those of blacks. Although only the Grimké sisters, Angelina and Sarah, exiles from their native

South Carolina, are known to have dared publicly to protest patriarchal control, Anne Firor Scott's path-breaking studies of Southern women have revealed that "many women of the planter class had strong doubts about either the morality or the expediency of slavery."

Thus what Mathews has called "the Evangelical Woman" and Scott has called "the Southern Lady" often blended in an antebellum "Southern Evangelical Lady" notable for submitting to, benefiting from, and resisting white Southern patriarchy. In the further study of antebellum Southern women's experience Anne C. Loveland's thesis that "southern evangelicalism—and southern evangelicals—were more complicated than has generally been recognized" will find extensive documentation and elaboration.

While the work of Mathews and Scott has initiated the serious study of the personality, concerns, and activities of the white Southern evangelical lady, black women's antebellum religious experiences as distinct from those of black men in the South have received less attention. Nevertheless, Mechal Sobel's study of blacks' adoption of the Baptist version of the Christian faith has shown that black women, though not equal with men in church life, "found much room for involvement, expression, and leadership . . . in keeping with both the Southern Separatist tradition and earlier African traditions." Further study of black women, slave and free alike, in churches both black and racially mixed may reveal that they, like white women, were experiencing a paradoxical interaction with Christianity, at once constricting and liberating.

During the Civil War many white and black women in the South were strong in spirit and somewhat skilled in organization partly because of the experiences they had had in the evangelical churches. For many such women, especially white women in all classes, the Civil War became a revolutionary event because for the first time in their lives no men were available to make decisions for them. As defeat in war and postwar conditions undermined the Southern patriarchy, women learned new lessons of self-confidence and leadership. Moreover, the freeing of the slaves left many white women without the administrative and familial burdens they had traditionally borne on the farm or plantation, freeing them for organization and tasks of compassion beyond the home as never before. The ending of the war and of slavery also brought Northern white women south to serve the needs of blacks, providing examples of women's leadership beyond the home and church to Southern white women. Simultaneously, the plight of the freedmen and freedwomen stirred the activism of Southern white and black women for home mission work at the same time that their interest in missions in Africa and China was aroused by the "new imperialism" in which the United States engaged.

These postwar conditions and the continued male domination of denominational structures led to the movement to establish separate women's denominational home and foreign mission organizations in the various Southern evangelical churches. No event in the history of the interaction between women and religion in the South has been more significant. Between the 1870s and World War I the denomination-wide missionary societies along with the Southern chapters of the national WOMAN'S CHRISTIAN TEMPERANCE UNION, the first large women's ecumenical organization, became the focal point for thousands of Southern women's religious lives. Through these two types of organizations Southern churchwomen almost inadvertently discovered a way to be both religiously respectable in a separate "woman's sphere" and to make of that separate sphere an effective "church within the church." In the missionary societies and the WCTU Southern churchwomen developed their theological ideas, their networks of sisterhood and communication, their skills in raising and administering money, their abilities in planning and carrying out programs, and their understandings of the relationships between the Christian Gospel and the realities of the world. These organizations did for white women what the growing autonomous black denominations and churches were doing simultaneously for Afro-Americans of both sexes: raising their self-esteem, giving them a wide range of experiences relatively free from the domination of white men, lay and clergy, and preparing them not only to coexist with but also to confront the patriarchal and racist assumptions so marked in Southern white male Evangelicalism.

The fruits of these mission and temperance organizations, although still inadequately studied, have been many and continue to the present time. The central concern of the religious devotion of many women shifted from "What must I do to be saved?" to "What must the saved do?" Accordingly, the hungry have been fed, the orphaned and widowed have been cared for, the sick have been healed, the ignorant have been taught, the dying have been comforted, the unconverted have heard the Gospel and seen it incarnated. That many of these good deeds of women's organizations originated in racist, classist, and nationalist assumptions of superiority does not negate their significance in giving people, particularly women and children, both in the United States and around the earth, a more abundant life.

While much of Southern women's home and foreign mission work has expressed the individualistic, evangelistic, ethnocentric approach to the Christian gospel characteristic of the male leadership of Southern denominations, experience in mission work deepened and broadened the Christian understanding of many churchwomen. Current scholarship indicates that this has been and continues to be especially true among white and black Southern women in Methodism.

Women's mission work in this denomination, long before the Methodist Episcopal Church, South, merged with the Methodist Episcopal Church and the Methodist Protestant Church in 1939, emphasized a social gospel informed by the imperative of redeeming social structures as well as individuals. For Methodist women in mission organizations, probably more than for the Southern women in any other major Protestant church, the issues of economic, racial, political, and social justice have been identified as the arena of the Gospel's redemptive implications.

This emphasis on the SOCIAL GOSPEL in some women's mission organizations has produced a divergence from the mainstream of socially conservative Southern Protestantism and has nurtured a willingness to question white male understandings of Southern religion. One of the most important results of this divergence has been that at least from the 1920s to the present a significant number of Southern churchwomen moved far ahead of the Southern white majority in rejecting racism and in embracing the goal of a racially pluralistic and just society. Such women have worked for racial justice through their mission organizations, through ecumenical groups such as the ASSOCIATION OF SOUTHERN WOMEN TO PREVENT LYNCHING, the Young Women's Christian Association, and Church Women United, and through secular organizations such as the COMMISSION ON INTERRACIAL COOPERATION and the Southern Regional Council. In addition, some Southern religious women have individually demonstrated exceptional courage in opposing Southern racial prejudice and violence.

Another result of the social gospel emphasis in Southern churchwomen's organizations has been that a high percentage of women involved in political life and in social reform movements of all kinds in the South, including the CIVIL RIGHTS MOVEMENT and the labor movement during the 19th and 20th centuries, got their start in public life through church organizations, especially within Southern Methodism.

As Southern churchwomen have effectively organized themselves over the last hundred years to help others experience the redemptive power of the Gospel, many of them, almost unwittingly, were themselves liberated from traditionally limited ways of understanding their own roles in church and society. During the past decade scholars have begun to identify the connections among women's mission work, the development of demands for full laity and clergy rights for women within Southern churches, and the pursuit of equality for women in society through the campaigns for women's suffrage and passage of the Equal Rights Amendment to the U. S. Constitution. While there is no doubt that the dominant Southern Protestant evangelical religion has been and still is one of the most powerful forces inhibiting Southern women's desire for and pursuit of equality with men in church and society, it is also true that some of the strongest ideological and practical support for women's equality in Southern churches and society has come from women's denominational and ecumenical mission organizations.

In the late twentieth century, as in the 19th century, it is clear that the dominant Southern evangelical Protestantism continues to be a vital source of both limitation and liberation for Southern women. Southern women's religion still produces both dependable servants and prophetic subverters of the dominant white male version of Southern Christianity. The further scholarly exploration of the paradoxical interactions between women and religion in the South promises not only to give women a new visibility in Southern religion but also to reveal ways in which Southern evangelical religion has been and continues to be a complex and dynamic movement. Such revelation promises to yield a rich harvest for American religious studies.

Bibliography. Adelaide L. Fries, *The Road to Salem*; Adelaide L. Fries and Douglas LeTell Rights, eds., *Records of the Moravians in North Carolina*, 8 vols.; Helen Griffith, *Dauntless in Mississippi: The Life of Sarah A. Dickey, 1838-1904*; Jacquelyn Dowd Hall, *Revolt Against Chivalry: Jessie Daniel Ames and the Women's Campaign Against Lynching*; Samuel S. Hill, *Religion and the Solid South*; *Southern Churches in Crisis*; Rhys Issac, "Evangelical Revolt: the Nature of the Baptists' Challenge to the Traditional Order in Virginia, 1765-1775," *William and Mary Quarterly*, 3rd ser., 31 (July 1974): 345; "Preachers and Patriots: Popular Culture and the Revolution in Virginia," *The American Revolution: Explorations in the History of American Radicalism*, ed. Alfred F. Young; Janet Wilson James, ed., *Women In American Religion*; John Patrick McDowell III, *The Social Gospel in the South: The Woman's Home Mission Movement in the Methodist Episcopal Church, South, 1886-1939*, unpublished Ph.D. dissertation, Duke University, 1979; Florence Mars, *Witness in Philadelphia*; Donald G. Mathews, *Religion in the Old South*, "The Second Great Awakening as an Organizing Process, 1780-1830: An Hypothesis," 23-43; *American Quarterly* 21 (Spring 1969); *Notable American Women: A Biographical Dictionary*, 4 vols., ed. Edward T. James et al.; Anne Firor Scott, *The Southern Lady: from Pedestal to Politics, 1830-1930*, "Women's Perspective on the Patriarchy in the 1850s," 52-64; *Journal of American History* 61 (June 1974); Thelma Stevens, *Legacy for the Future: The History of Christian Social Relations in the Women's Division of Christian Service, 1940-1968*; Noreen Dunn Tatum, *Crown of Service: A Study of Woman's Work in the Methodist Episcopal Church, South, from 1878-1940*; Hilah F. Thomas and Rosemary Skinner Keller, eds., *Women in New Worlds: Historical Perspectives on the Wesleyan Tradition; To a Higher Glory: The Growth and Development of Black Women Organizing for Mission in The Methodist Church, 1940-1968*; Robert Manson Myers, ed., *The Children of Pride: A True Story of Georgia and the Civil War*.

NORMA TAYLOR MITCHELL
TROY STATE UNIVERSITY

WOODMASON, CHARLES (1720-1776),

pioneer backcountry Anglican leader, was born in England and served as an itinerant Anglican minister in South Carolina, Virginia, and Maryland. For a decade after his arrival in South Carolina from England in 1752, Woodmason was a planter and merchant in Prince Frederick Winyah Parish. From 1763 to 1765 he was a popular local official in Charleston, but his popularity plummeted when he attempted to secure the job of provincial stamp distributor under the detested Stamp Act.

Woodmason's unpleasant experience over the Stamp Act, his dedication to the Anglican church, and his strong desire to dislodge the SEPARATE BAPTISTS and other dissenters from the South Carolina backcountry prompted him late in 1765 to seek the position of itinerant Anglican minister for the upper part of St. Mark's Parish. His successful quest for the job necessitated a trip to England for ordination to the ministry, after which he returned to South Carolina in 1766 and took up his duties in St. Mark's.

For six years Woodmason waged a determined battle against immorality, irreligion, and dissenters in South Carolina before moving on in 1772 to Virginia and then Maryland. His main contribution lay not in his vigorous efforts on behalf of the Anglican church and English civilization, but in the revealing descriptions (highly partisan though they were) he wrote in his journal concerning religious conditions in the Carolina backcountry on the eve of the Revolution. Woodmason's strongly Loyalist views made it necessary for him to leave Maryland for England in 1774. Sick and in financial straits, he appealed to the bishop of London for help as a Loyalist refugee in 1776.

Bibliography. Richard J. Hooker, ed., *The Carolina Backcountry on the Eve of the Revolution: The Journal and Other Writings of Charles Woodmason, Anglican Itinerant* (1953).

DAVID T. MORGAN
UNIVERSITY OF MONTEVALLO

WOODROW, JAMES (1828-1907), Presbyterian theologian, is best known for his efforts to reconcile science and religion. He accompanied his parents as they moved from England to the United States in 1837, settling in Ohio. He studied at Jefferson College and taught at Oglethorpe University in Georgia before undertaking graduate work at Harvard under Louis Agassiz and at Heidelberg University, where he received a Ph.D. in 1856. He returned to the faculty at Oglethorpe and was ordained to the Presbyterian ministry in 1860. During the Civil War, he served as a chemist for the Confederates. He accepted the call to teach at Columbia Theological Seminary in 1861, being appointed to a new chair in "Natural Science in Connexion with Revelation." In 1884, when he published *Evolution*, opponents charged him in church courts with undercutting the authority of the Bible. After five years of trials and turmoil in the denomination over his positions, Woodrow was removed from the seminary faculty. He remained in good standing in the Presbyterian Church in the United States, however, and in 1901 served as moderator of the Synod of South Carolina. Woodrow for several years was the president of the University of South Carolina. He published a weekly *Southern Presbyterian* (1865-1893) and edited the quarterly *Southern Presbyterian Review* (1861-1885). He likewise received recognition posthumously as the uncle of America's 28th president, WOODROW WILSON.

See also article on SCIENCE AND RELIGION.

LOUIS WEEKS
LOUISVILLE PRESBYTERIAN SEMINARY

YOUNG, JOHN FREEMAN (1820-1885), was the second BISHOP of the Protestant Episcopal Church in Florida. His predecessor, the Rt. Rev. Francis Huger Rutledge (1851-1866), labored under the handicaps of ill health, paltry diocesan financial resources, extremely inadequate transportation facilities in a huge diocese, and the Civil War. So it was left for Bishop Young to develop an adequate diocesan organization, and to get it operating on a nearly statewide basis. His diocese increased during his episcopate from seven clergymen to 36, and from 13 churches to 45.

Young was born in Pittston ME, and he received his college education at Wesleyan University and the Virginia Theological Seminary. He began his ministry in 1845 in Jacksonville FL, then served successively in Texas, Mississippi, and Louisiana, and as assistant minister at Trinity Parish, New York City, before being called to Florida in 1867.

In Key West Bishop Young organized both the first parish in Florida exclusively for blacks, and a Spanish-language parish for Cuban immigrants. He visited Cuba twice, in response to a petition that the Church be established there. As a result Cuba became an important foreign missionary field for the Episcopal Church in the United States.

Young had special interest in church architecture and music. He scattered churches built in Richard Upjohn's Carpenter Gothic style over the face of Florida. He collected and translated great hymns of various Christian traditions, and these were published posthumously under the title *Great Hymns of the Church.*

See also articles on ARCHITECTURE; CARIBBEAN IMMIGRATION.

Bibliography. Joseph D. Cushman, Jr., *A Goodly Heritage, The Episcopal Church in Florida, 1821-1892*; Edgar Legare Pennington, *Soldier and Servant, John Freeman Young, Second Bishop of Florida*; Byron Edward Underwood, "Bishop John Freeman Young, Translator of 'Stille Nacht,' " *The Hymn* 8 (October 1957): 123-30.

GEORGE R. BENTLEY
UNIVERSITY OF FLORIDA

appendix

COLONIAL PERIOD. Southern religion only gradually developed a regional pattern. During the 17th century, a variety of denominations and religious forms existed in the South, all of them overshadowed by a worldly concern for economic gain. After the Glorious Revolution of 1688, Maryland and the Carolinas emulated Virginia by establishing the Church of England. Southern ANGLICANISM, an American version of the English national faith, became a unifying influence although it was never unchallenged. The South entered a third phase around 1750 when the GREAT AWAKENING and a migration into the backcountry strengthened dissent to the point that the Anglican hegemony could be successfully toppled during the American Revolution.

Southern Anglicanism originated in Virginia. During the post-Elizabethan era, religion was an important concern of Englishmen, Anglicans as well as Puritans. The colonizers of Virginia were interested in spreading the Gospel, and in the colony itself Dale's Law required that settlers attend church and subject themselves to Christian discipline. Early Virginia clergymen like Robert Hunt and Nathaniel Whitaker were godly and

learned men. Piety, however, motivated the settlers less than did economic opportunity. The ready market for tobacco and the availability of land placed a premium on labor that led to the exploitation of servants and paved the way for slavery. The largely male society of early Virginia concentrated on getting rich and returning to England. Only gradually did Virginia become a permanent society, and worldliness remained one of its dominant characteristics.

Despite the secular quality of Virginia, Anglicanism was the official religion of the colony from the beginning. Christian charity was not conspicuous, but Virginia laws required attendance at church and provided penalties for sexual license. The colony was divided into parishes, and a vestry system was set up to administer the church at the local level. Vestrymen exercised a variety of functions, including the administration of relief for the poor; and they departed from the English tradition by asserting authority over the hiring and firing of clergymen. Service on the vestry was an important form of local leadership. Anglican clergymen in the 17th century were sometimes worldly, but usually capable, and they did an effective job of serving parishes that were extremely large by English standards. By the end of the century, Anglicanism was the major cultural as well as religious force in the Old Dominion.

While Virginia modeled itself on the mother country in matters of religion, Maryland struck out in another direction. Cecil Calvert, the Lord Baltimore who received a charter from Charles I to found a colony on the Chesapeake, was a Catholic and he hoped to create a place of refuge for members of his own faith. Catholics did come to Maryland, and with them Jesuit priests, but so also did Puritans, Quakers, and Anglicans. Faced with the economic and political discontents that frustrated every proprietor, Baltimore attempted to neutralize religious rivalry. With proprietary support, the Maryland Assembly in 1649 passed an act concerning religion that granted religious liberty to all those who believed in Jesus Christ and the Trinity. This measure has an important place in American religious history, but it did not prevent "Protestant Associators" from overthrowing Baltimore's government when the Glorious Revolution gave them an opportunity. Politics rather than religion was probably the motive behind the revolution in Maryland, but it did lead to the creation of a second Anglican establishment in the Southern colonies.

The Church of England in the colonial South benefited from an Anglican resurgence in England that followed the Glorious Revolution. Sir Francis Nicholson, the governor whom William and Mary sent to Maryland, was a zealous Anglican who promoted the establishment of the Church of England in that colony. High Church members of the Carolina propriety supported the Anglicans in South Carolina who passed an establishment act in 1704 against the wishes of the majority of colonists who were dissenters. Most important to the colonial church was THOMAS BRAY, an energetic English cleric who served as the COMMISSARY, or bishop's assistant, of Maryland for a time

and who tirelessly promoted the cause of the Church of England abroad. The Society for the Promotion of Christian Knowledge and the SOCIETY FOR THE PROPAGATION OF THE GOSPEL IN FOREIGN PARTS (S.P.G.), the first devoted to sending religious books abroad and the second concerned with finding and supporting clergymen for the colonies, were both founded at the turn of the century through Bray's efforts. The S.P.G. provided most of the clergymen who served in South Carolina down to 1750 and sent missionaries to North Carolina and Georgia as well.

The Church of England was eventually established throughout the South, but its legal structure and its strength varied from colony to colony. The state church of South Carolina was similar to that of Virginia, its dominant feature a strong element of lay control exercised by the lower house of assembly and the parish vestries. Colonial laymen were more powerful than their English counterparts because there was no American BISHOP to govern the churches. The bishop of London exercised a supervisory jurisdiction, often through a commissary, but the Anglican gentry of Virginia and South Carolina held most of the economic and political power in their respective establishments. In Maryland the situation was different because the charter gave control of the church to the proprietor. After an Anglican Lord Baltimore was restored to full power in 1715, successive proprietors treated the clerical positions in the colony as part of their political patronage. North Carolina passed a series of laws providing official status for the Church of England beginning in 1701, but Quakers, Presbyterians, and other non-Anglicans in the colony frustrated their successful operation. Georgia passed an establishment act in 1758, but the youthfulness of the colony limited its effectiveness.

Despite its weaknesses, Anglicanism did give the Southern colonies a cultural uniformity. Anglican clergymen transmitted Christian theology and moral teachings and they provided religious services. They also operated schools that were the most important institutions of secular education in the colonial South. Following the injunction of the bishop of London and of the S.P.G., many Church of England ministers attempted to spread Christianity among the Indians and slaves. These programs met with little success, in part because they were opposed by most of the planters. In their teaching and in their lives, most Anglican ministers manifested a reverence for social and political authority; they were in league with the gentry class and came to share their values. To a great extent the Church of England complemented the worldliness of the South: Sunday worship was a religious event, but it was also a social occasion for conversation and the display of clothing and equipage.

Southern Anglican ministers have been unjustly maligned by writers who have claimed they were immoral and ineffective. Recent studies suggest that only about 10 percent of Church of England clergymen were guilty of drunkenness or loose morals, a figure that is not extreme even by modern standards. Most of the rest performed competently under difficult conditions and a few were outstanding in the best sense.

Commissary JAMES BLAIR of Virginia was an excellent politician whose greatest achievement was the founding of the COLLEGE OF WILLIAM AND MARY. A diligent parish priest, he was also a writer whose learned and reasonable, albeit ponderous, sermons on the Sermon on the Mount were published in England. Commissary ALEXANDER GARDEN of South Carolina was largely responsible for making the establishment there an effective institution. Garden too was a model clergymen whose three decades of service in ST. PHILIP'S CHURCH, Charles Town, won him the love and respect of his parishioners. The Reverend Thomas Cradock of Maryland was a pious and literate man who publicly attacked the immorality of some of his fellow ministers. Cradock was only one of a number of Anglican clerics who treated the moral teachings of their church with extreme seriousness.

The hegemony of the Church of England provided other Christians with much to resent. Virginia was the most intolerant colony, forcing nonconformists to go elsewhere until well into the 18th century. Anglicans in South Carolina in 1704 passed laws that established the Church of England and also excluded dissenters from serving in the assembly. They were aided by the French HUGUENOTS, most of whom eventually joined the Church of England, apparently grateful for aid they had received from Bishop of London Henry Compton and unwilling to be again a religious minority. Presbyterians, Baptists, and Quakers, who outnumbered the Anglicans, carried the issue to England where both measures were repealed. A new establishment was created in 1706, but the dissenters eventually won freedom of worship, political liberty, and the elimination of direct taxes for religious purposes. Outside of Virginia, the major burden the state churches placed on non-Anglican Protestants was economic support for clergymen and church buildings. Maryland Anglicans also enacted severely repressive anti-Catholic legislation. Between 1704 and 1718, Catholic priests who celebrated the Mass in Maryland were subject to a fine of fifty pounds sterling; after 1718 they were free to conduct religious services in private homes. Catholic laymen were prohibited from voting or holding public office, and in 1756 their lands were subjected to a double tax.

The rise of dissent in the middle of the 18th century resulted from a combination of circumstances. An important development was the Great Awakening, during which GEORGE WHITEFIELD came into the South and attacked the validity of Anglican sacramentalism and good works, offering as an alternative the "new birth," an emotional and instantaneous conversion that usually occurred as a result of powerful preaching. Whitefield clashed openly with Commissary Alexander Garden of South Carolina and their pamphlet warfare publicized the issues and provided a platform for the dissenters. Isaac Chanler, a Baptist clergymen in Charles Town, published a notable defense of Whitefield's Calvinism. Despite his attraction to dissenters and many Anglicans, Whitefield's visits to South Carolina wrought little permanent change in the religious situation of the colony. In Virginia, however, the Great Awakening stirred a latent religious interest in the common folk. Evangelical Presbyterians from the North visited the colony, and eventually SAMUEL DAVIES settled in Virginia, challenged a licensing law that restricted proselytizing, and led a movement away from the Church of England.

The Great Awakening appealed to some Southerners, but migration (1700-1820) into the Southern backcountry was more important in altering the structure of Southern religion. In the quarter of a century before the American Revolution, Scotch-Irish Presbyterians, SEPARATE BAPTISTS from the North, and recently arrived settlers from Germany entered the southern piedmont, encouraged by the promise of inexpensive land and favorable treatment from colonial governments anxious for white settlers who would provide protection against slaves and Indians. The religious complexion of the South underwent a startling change. In Maryland, Virginia, and South Carolina, the colonies where the Church of England was strongest, there was a total of 159 Anglican churches in 1750, 44 Presbyterian churches, and 13 Baptist churches. During the next quarter of a century, the Anglican churches increased markedly to 258, but the Presbyterian congregations grew to 167 and the Baptist congregations to 184. By the time of the Revolution, the Anglicans were outnumbered by the combined forces of their two nearest rivals. Quakers, Lutherans, German Reformed, Methodists, and pietistic sects made the imbalance even greater.

The Anglican establishments were on the defensive after 1750 and the American Revolution brought about their collapse. In Virginia, long-standing political disputes between clergy and laity were exacerbated by the growing fear of both parties that the Church of England was losing ground. The Parson's Cause, a dispute over clerical incomes, was only the best known in a series of struggles that illustrated the internal weakness of the established church. In Maryland the Anglican laity, reacting to the Reverend Bennet Allen, an imperious and rapacious proprietary placeman, attacked the established church that they were unable to control. In South Carolina the Church of England functioned effectively in the low country, but the majority of citizens were dissenters living in the backcountry. As the South became involved in a revolution designed to win liberty from the mother country, Southern patriots found it difficult to justify a system that granted religious privilege to the Church of England. Anglicans also understood that a successful military outcome in the American Revolution would require the full cooperation of all denominations. Disestablishment was a small price and a necessary one.

The Anglican establishments of the South toppled in the Revolution, but the concept of the state church was not easily discarded. Maryland and South Carolina made provisions for establishing the Christian religion and Virginia engaged in a prolonged debate over the relationship between government and religion. Many Anglicans and even some Presbyterians believed that Christianity was too important to be left to voluntary support. Church and state were separated because Baptists who believed that the state would corrupt religion allied with spokesmen for the Enlightenment who were convinced that religion would corrupt the state. By the end of the Confederation Period, denominationalism was the new order.

The achievement of religious freedom was only one way in which colonial religious development affected the later pattern of Southern institutions and belief. The Anglican church fell on hard times after disestablishment, and the Protestant Episcopal Church was always low in membership, yet upper-class Southerners continued to aspire to the kind of gentility that had attracted their ancestors. The Anglican social model that involved a recognition of class differences and responsibility for service and benevolence on the part of the upper class remained an important part of the Southern ethic. The fundamentalist, evangelical tone that dominated later Southern religion developed early in the 19th century, but its roots were in the Great Awakening and in the settlement patterns of the 18th century. Pioneers from the Southern backcountry moved west after the American Revolution and the Second Great Awakening flourished among people who were familiar with the doctrines of the first.

See also articles on CHURCH AND STATE; DISESTABLISHMENT; ESTABLISHED RELIGION; HIGH CHURCH/LOW CHURCH; MIGRATION, SOUTHWARD (1700-1830).

Bibliography. Sydney E. Ahlstrom, *A Religious History of the American People*; S. Charles Bolton, *Southern Anglicanism: The Church of England in Colonial South Carolina*; Carl Bridenbaugh, *Myths and Realities: Societies of the Colonial South*; George M. Brydon, *Virginia's Mother Church and the Political Conditions Under Which It Grew*; Lawrence A. Cremin, *American Education: The Colonial Experience*; Elizabeth Davidson, *The Establishment of the English Church in Continental American Colonies*; Richard Beale Davis, *Intellectual Life in the Colonial South*, 3 vols.; John Tracy Ellis, *Catholics in Colonial America*; Edwin Scott Gaustad, *Historical Atlas of American Religion*; Wesley M. Gewehr, *The Great Awakening in Virginia, 1740-1790*; Alan E. Heimert, *Religion and the American Mind from the Great Awakening to the Revolution*; Arthur H. Hirsch, *The Huguenots of Colonial South Carolina*; Rhys Isaac, "The Nature of the Baptists' Challenge to the Traditional Order in Virginia, 1765-1775," *William and Mary Quarterly*, 3rd ser., 31 (1974): 345-68; "Religion and Authority: Problems of the Anglican Establishment in Virginia in the Era of the Great Awakening and the Parsons' Cause," *William and Mary Quarterly* 30 (1973): 3-36; Rufus M. Jones, *The Quakers in the American Colonies*; Henry L. May, *The Enlightenment in America*; Perry Miller, *Errand into the Wilderness*; Edmund Morgan, *American Slavery American Freedom: The Ordeal of Colonial Virginia*; George William Pilcher, *Samuel Davies, Apostle of Dissent in Colonial Virginia*; Leonard J. Trinterud, *The Forming of an American Tradition: A Re-examination of Colonial Presbyterianism.*

S. CHARLES BOLTON
UNIVERSITY OF ARKANSAS,
LITTLE ROCK

RECENT SOUTH. The difficulty of writing recent history is obvious; how can we identify, describe, and evaluate events and movements as yet incomplete? Yet, despite the dangers, it is necessary to proceed.

Southerners are, as they have been for more than three centuries, Americans; most of them are, moreover, Christian Americans; and they are heirs, along with other Americans and other Christians, of Western civilization's rich and identifiable traditions. Yet there has always been and continues to be a distinct "Southern accent" to the South's religion. It is, in Kenneth Bailey's words, "in the sphere of religion that the Southern identity is best delineated."

The currents of world and American events during the period 1940-1980 have deeply affected the South, and of course its distinctive faith. Yet what stands out starkly against the shifting background is the degree to which Southern religion has remained so close to its previously established patterns. The urban-industrial order that has bulldozed its way through the South during the past 40 years, largely heedless of cherished traditions, has not succeeded in uprooting the religious faith and life of the region at all; and the superficial alterations that appear at various places serve to highlight the overwhelming continuity.

World War II, for example, had as great an effect upon the South as upon any other region. It was perhaps during the period 1941-1945 that the South truly rejoined, in mind and soul, the rest of the union. Southern men crossed oceans to fight America's enemies; Southern women and Southern blacks began to realize some release from their previous special status; and racism, at least in Nazi clothing, was exposed and acknowledged across the region.

The postwar rapid growth in population, related to the baby boom and Northern migration to the "sun belt" that gave the Southern states one-fourth of the electorate, led to dramatic social changes. The simultaneous flight to cities, urbanization and its inevitable secularization, further affected and altered human relations and moral attitudes and practices.

The CIVIL RIGHTS MOVEMENT, black Southerners' quest for equality, led to social modifications an earlier generation of Southerners, white and black, would never have dreamed possible. Before the Supreme Court's 1954 order to desegregate public institutions, Southerners (and their churches) had largely avoided the issue of racial justice. For a time after 1954 most major denominational leaders and progressive clergymen encouraged compliance as being both American and Christian. A period of rebellion followed as rank-and-file members rejected the changes confronting them. Finally, they uneasily acquiesced to the reality of integration if not to the logic of it.

Politics responded and reacted to the turmoil of the times. The one-party system that had prevailed since the end of Reconstruction—made up of "yellow dog Democrats"—slowly died to be replaced by an ascendant Republicanism. The two American parties, drawing virtually even in much of the South, in many cases swapped racial constituencies. Blacks, once disenfranchised but favorable to the party of their liberator, Lincoln, were attracted to the Democratic party's pro-civil rights stance under Kennedy, Johnson, and Carter. Whites, who once voted solidly for anyone who called himself a Democrat, found the modern Republican party's neoconservative social and economic programs increasingly attractive. Native Southerner JIMMY CARTER seemed in the 1976 presidential election to have arrested this trend, but 1980 saw him lose even his own home region to Ronald Rea-gan, demonstrating conclusively that the South's national (if not local) voting patterns had been permanently altered.

Yet despite the great surface changes in the South, the South and Southerners remained Southern, and the region's religion retained its distinct accent. As the Southern mountain ballad says, "The more things change, the more they stay the same."

For example, denominations, for the most part the traditional ones, remained strong and rather dominant of their memberships and the society around them. Throughout the region, Baptists, Methodists, and Presbyterians remained one-two-three in membership. Only in Louisiana (though edging closer in Texas and Florida) did Catholics hold third place. Only in Virginia did Methodists outnumber Baptists. With Baptists, as before, holding nearly 50 percent of the church-affiliated population, Methodists 25 percent, and Presbyterians 10 percent, the South remained the most thoroughly Low-Church Protestant region of the United States—and the most thoroughly unified in religious thought and practice. It is true that between 1940 and 1980 the denominations slipped somewhat in the percent of the population they controlled and that secularization prevented as tight a hold upon public morals as before; but denominationalism remained the dominant fact of Southern life as it had been before World War II.

So, too, did the revivalistic character of the denominations. The central theme of Southern theology remained the salvation of the individual. Religious leaders might argue over the fundamentalist-pietistic divisions in their ranks, but they were all at heart "Wesleyan" in their preference for experiential faith. Men like Billy Graham and Oral Roberts, both essentially Southern revivalists, gained tremendous regional and national audiences with this message. The Sunday worship service in most churches bore the unmistakable earmarks of the 19th-century revival meeting. Their message of personal salvation continued to keep the denominations numerically strong. It also permitted them to avoid in large part the difficult decisions demanded by an age calling for social justice. Sin could conveniently be identified not as unjust behavior but merely as a violation of the will of God for the individual. Attention to social injustice could be postponed until lost souls were won to Christ or it would result from that conversion. Southern religion was time and again unprepared for its society's "future-shock." Yet the revivalist message seemed to preserve the traditional faith. History and religion had conspired to teach Southerners more than other Americans, in Bailey's words, "the enormity of the human predicament and the inadequacies of their efforts to improve it." Religion helped make Dixie what it is and what it is not.

Since the denominations and their dominant message are so integral to Southern religious life, it would be helpful to observe their passage through this most recent historical period. Some American churches, strong in various other parts of the United States, are relatively small in the South, though this is hardly to say that they are insignificant. Catholics and Episcopalians, for example, have in the past 40 years added quite a lot of flavor. Catholics have increased in numbers during this time, mainly through migration from the North, from Cuba, and from Mexico. While they have tended to be "Southernized" as earlier they were "Americanized," they have had a continuing effect upon education, civil rights, and social issues such as the debate over abortion. Episcopalians, as the most "cultured" of Protestants, have represented and provided for many Southerners a sophisticated and aesthetic faith, a home for men and women traveling the "Jefferson Davis" path to social, intellectual, or economic respectability. Like the president of the Confederacy, many Baptist-born farmers' sons have culminated lives

of hard-won success with membership in the Episcopal Church. But numerically the past four decades have not seen dramatic changes in such smaller churches. Churches that were small have tended to remain, except through migration, small. Churches that were growing in 1940 have continued to grow.

First among the growing churches is, of course, the SOUTHERN BAPTIST CONVENTION, which by 1980 claimed nearly 14 million members, mostly in its home area. Through a series of professional promotion campaigns and by presenting a simple conservative orthodoxy, the Southern Baptists have remained the largest Protestant church in America and virtually the "folk religion" of the South. There is now a decided westward tilt to the Southern Baptist landscape, both in numbers and in influence, with a resultant growing "frontier" mentality, a trend away from piety and toward a hardening fundamentalism; but the Southern Baptists remain, whatever the orientation, the dominant Southern religious fact of life.

Their success has not been without cost. Being a virtual majority of the South's churched population, the Baptists have had little reason to seek the kind of ecumenical experiences that broaden theological perspective and widen influence. They have taken no serious steps, as have other regional branches of divided Protestant denominations, to reunite with their separated Northern brethren, the relatively small American Baptist denomination. Being so closely allied with Southern social power structures, an inevitable fact for a church so large, they have at times been so culturally captive as to fail in prophetic missions of social criticism. Their numerical success has created a new type of church and ministry, both far removed from the early patterns that gave them success. Their one-time "town meeting" structure of government has given way to a "corporation" model, while their once-charismatic leadership has evolved into a form of executive management.

The twin influences of urbanization and secularization have affected a number of areas of the denomination's life, particularly its institutions of higher learning, causing severe social and theological strains within the fellowship. As educational levels have risen with affluence and interregional exchange, resulting in more sophisticated ideas and techniques, radical conservatives have led crusades to restore purity of doctrine, particularly the theory of biblical inerrancy. Recent national conventions of the Southern Baptists have broken with Southern Baptist tradition to establish creeds for the enforcement of orthodoxy and to violate traditional support for the separation of church and state by supporting movements to make school prayer constitutional.

The Southern Baptist Convention is, as one of its own historians has said, a burgoo of widely divergent personalities, classes, and viewpoints; yet it has always been held together by its common sense of mission, by its dedication to the Great Commission of Christ to convert the world. Efforts were being made by 1980 to divert attention from insoluble controversies to a new Bold Mission crusade to win the world for Christ. Whether this or any other action will succeed in holding this unwieldy denomination in line remains to be seen.

The second- and third-largest Southern denominations have also continued to grow though perhaps not as spectacularly as the Southern Baptists. Southern Methodists rejoined their Northern coreligionists, from whom they had been separated since 1844, in 1939. When in 1968 the united church was joined by the Evangelical United Brethren, Southern Methodists became approximately one-fourth of the United Methodist Church, which was for a brief time, until the Southern Baptists recovered the title, the largest Protestant church in the United States. Even now the United Methodist Church is the most evenly distributed church in America.

Southern Methodists are, like their brothers elsewhere, but perhaps even more so, Wesley's children: experiential, pietistic, realistic. Recent self-criticism says they are a great machine that is slowly running out of steam; but their influence is still strong and it shows few signs of diminishing.

Southern Presbyterians, called the Presbyterian Church in the United States, are also roughly one-fourth the number of Presbyterians in America. By 1980 there were strong indications they were ready to reunite with their Northern brothers and sisters; they voted to do so in 1983. But at the same time radical conservatives were still leaving the P.C.U.S., as they had done for a decade, because of its liberalism; some broke off to form the PRESBYTERIAN CHURCH IN AMERICA in 1973. Presbyterians, a weak third among regional denominations, have for a century exercised more influence than their members seem to command. Generally a well-educated and prosperous people, they have been strongly represented in the professions and have had much to say about social and political affairs throughout the South.

Less numerically significant than the three large denominations but in their own way a potent religious influence in recent times were the charismatic denominations collectively called Pentecostals. In 1940, generally held in contempt by the more established churches, by 1980 Pentecostalism's message and practice had become almost fashionable—though it must be added that it was more fashionable outside than within the South, where it was still identified as a lower-class form of religion. It had itself, in the form of charismatic denominations, "crossed the tracks" to build attractive sanctuaries, moderate its social and racial views, join ecumenical missions, and in general join the Protestant mainstream. It had, as a religious expression separate from the denominations, appeared as charismatic cells in most of the major denominations, both inside and outside the South.

Perhaps the most significant development in Pentecostalism, a development that did little to increase the size of the denominations but did bring the movement to a wide public, was the Healing Revival of 1947-1958. Led by charismatic evangelists such as ORAL ROBERTS, the Revival spilled out of cinder-block churches into tents across the country, where it was eventually transformed into a broad charismatic movement that offered more promise of personal emotional fulfillment than the earlier magic healings. The Pentecostal churches gained a new legitimacy from the Revival's success and used it to climb toward social acceptance.

Another large group to show signs of continuing vitality were the descendants of antidenominationalism's evangelist ALEXANDER CAMPBELL, apostle of "the Reformation of the 19th Century." While the Disciples of Christ, the branch of Campbell's movement that emphasized his doctrine of church unity, declined slightly through the South, the CHURCHES OF CHRIST, the branch that emphasized his doctrine of the restoration of the true New Testament church, gained new membership. There developed, in fact, what can be called a Bible Belt of Churches of Christ from Tennessee through Arkansas to the western part of Texas, with over 20,000 congregations.

The Churches of Christ continued to emphasize, perhaps more than any other Southern church, a careful study of the Bible. They proved the most tough-minded of Protestants, the most convinced of their own doctrines and practices, the best debaters. They exhibited much of the "scholastic" fervor and style of medieval theological exercise. They continued to discourage formal theological education for their ministers, and they were the least ecumenical of denominations. Yet they, too, like the Pentecostals, were by 1980 "crossing the tracks" socially and threatening to edge toward the mainstream and denominationalism. This inevitably caused some strains, and by 1980 roughly one-fourth of

their congregations threatened schism if these trends toward moderation continued.

Too little study has been made of the several black churches of the South. Since they tend not to develop central bureaucracies and therefore have little statistical evidence to provide, they are quite difficult to study. They generally follow the numerical divisions of their white counterparts, however, with Baptists and Methodists predominating. Pentecostalism, in style if not in name, has always been and continues to be strong among them. They have been pivotal to the Civil Rights Movement. While it did not originate in the black churches, they did supply its Southern leadership and the facilities that gave it success. Their full support for the movement helps explain how they have held their constituencies rather well despite the ravages of urbanization, secularization, and the encroachments of new ideologies. There is also the fact of their willingness to provide fellowship, recreation, social services, and a message of hope to disadvantaged people. Black theology, the modern emphasis among some black theologians upon black awareness as a prerequisite to religious consciousness, has been for some years a subtle and growing phenomenon in black religion of the region.

Several predictions based upon recent trends may be made about Southern religion as it nears the end of the century. The South will doubtless continue, like the rest of the United States, to become more secular, less churchgoing, less denominationally secure. Yet it will also continue on its own distinctive path. Left-wing Protestantism will continue to dominate the religious scene, perhaps with diminished powers, and Southern religion will continue to be evangelistic, revivalistic, pietistic, fundamentalistic, and individualistic. While Southerners grow more liberal morally and more conservative politically, they will continue to devote themselves to the same type of religious faith.

Yet questions about the future arise. Southern religion will continue to face controversies, particularly between pietists and fundamentalists. Who will win? Urbanization, secularization, and education will have more effect in the future than in the past. How will such new forces be accommodated? The new electronic evangelism will demand more attention and win more converts. Will the traditional denominations retain their memberships and financial bases? There will likely be interchurch and interregional dialogue. When, how, to what extent, under what circumstances will the Southern churches merge fully with the national mainstream and lead or accompany the South into social, political, and religious ecumenism?

Such questions merely make the future of Southern religion more intriguing. It is a subject that will continue to merit careful attention.

See also articles on CHARISMATIC MOVEMENTS; ELECTRONIC CHURCH; HOLINESS MOVEMENT; METHODIST CHURCH; PENTECOSTALISM; SECULARIZATION.

Bibliography. Kenneth K. Bailey, *Southern White Protestantism in the Twentieth Century*; Jackson Carroll, et al., *Religion in America: 1950 to the Present*; Jimmy Carter, *A Government as Good as Its People*; C. Dwight Dorough, *The Bible Belt Mystique*; Edwin S. Gaustad, *Dissent in American Religion, Historical Atlas of Religion in America*; W. Clark Gilpin, "Common Roots, Divergent Paths: The Disciples and the Churches of Christ," *The Christian Century*, 20 December 1978; David Edwin Harrell, Jr., *All Things Are Possible: The Healing and Charismatic Revivals in Modern America, White Sects and Black Men in the Recent South*; Brooks Hays, *Politics Is My Parish, This World: A Christian's Workshop*; Samuel S. Hill, *Religion and the Solid South; Southern Churches in Crisis*; E. Glenn Hinson, "Southern Baptists: A Concern for Experiential Conversion," *The Christian Century*, 7-14 June 1978; Jameson Jones, "United Methodism: A Cautious Mood," *The Christian Century*, 20 September 1978; Lawrence Jones, "The Black Churches: A New Agenda?" *The Christian Century*, 18 April 1979; Jack Temple Kirby, *Media-Made Dixie*; Charles P. Roland, *The Improbable Era: The South Since World War II*; Kirkpatrick Sale, *Power Shift*; Walter B. Shurden, *Not a Silent People: Controversies That Have Shaped Southern Baptists*.

JAMES T. BAKER
WESTERN KENTUCKY UNIVERSITY

index